Arts from the Scholar's Studio

Catalogue of an exhibition presented by
The Oriental Ceramic Society of Hong Kong
and the Fung Ping Shan Museum, University of Hong Kong
24 October to 13 December 1986

文玩萃珍

香港東方陶瓷學會文
馮平山博物館聯合主辦

一九八六年十月廿四日
至十二月十三日

No. 1054

of an edition limited to

1,500 copies

Contents

Editor: Susan Ribeiro
Art Director: Rosanne Chan
Designer: Esther Poon
Produced by Communication Art Design & Printing Ltd.

2nd Edition 2011

Lenders to the Exhibition

Mr. & Mrs. Selwyn Alleyne
Art Gallery, Chinese University of Hong Kong
Malcolm Barnett
Bei Shan Tang collection
Grace Bruce
Chih-jou chai collection
Harris Chiu
J. da Costa
Robert H. Ellsworth
Fan Chai collection
Flagstaff House Museum of Teaware, K.S. Lo collection
Fung Ping Shan Library, in the University of Hong Kong Library
Fung Ping Shan Museum
Mr. & Mrs. Gerald Godfrey
Brian Harkins
Gerard Hawthorn
H.L. Hei
Hong Kong Museum of Art
Hong Kong Museum of History
Huo Pao-tsai
Ip Chee
Jade Studio
Simon Kwan
Dr. S.Y. Kwan
C.P. Kwok
B.Y. Lam Foundation
Lam Dawei
Brian S. McElney
Mengdiexuan collection
Mr. & Mrs. Edwin L. Miller
Mr. & Mrs. R.P. Piccus
Mr. & Mrs. Wayne G. Quasha
Shuisongshi Shanfang collection
Prof. Tong Kin-woon
Dr. & Mrs. Albert Tsai
C.C. Wang Family collection
Harold Wong
Yingtai Guan collection

Arts from the Scholar's Studio

Over the twenty-five years since the publication of *Arts from the Scholar's Studio*, there have been a number of notable publications and exhibitions that have furthered knowledge of this unique and broad field of study. Yet demand for this ambitious landmark publication, formed around the collections of members of the Oriental Ceramic Society of Hong Kong and Hong Kong's museums has long outstripped its availability. Benefitting from the scholarship and enthusiasm of Mr. Gerard Tsang and Mr. Hugh Moss, its findings remain as relevant today as they were when they first appeared.

The book has long been out-of-print. The Society has therefore decided to publish a new edition of this book in the hope of stimulating further interest and scholarship in the field. The Society is fortunate to have the generous support of the book's original publisher, Ms. Rosanne Chan, and the assistance of its original editor, Mrs. Susan Ribeiro, who I am pleased has since rejoined the OCS Committee. I would also like to thank the Committee's Treasurer, Mr. Joseph S. L. Wu, who first proposed the idea of bringing this publication to light again.

The Oriental Ceramic Society of Hong Kong is dedicated to making scholarship of the arts of Asia accessible to as broad a group of enthusiasts, scholars and collectors as possible. This it achieves through its lectures, appreciation evenings and cultural tours, as well as its exhibitions and associated publications. I am delighted that the fruits of my predecessors' labours continue to be as appreciated today as they were in their day, and would like to acknowledge their great contributions to the Society on this occasion.

The exhibition of *Arts of the Scholar's Studio* was the Society's sixth exhibition and marked its twelfth year. In common with previous exhibitions, its success depended entirely on the dedicated commitment of its members in planning and organisation. Begun under the Presidency of Mr. Angus Forsyth, it was brought to fruition under that of Dr. K. S. Lo (1910–1995), who also loaned to the exhibition through his donation to the Hong Kong Museum of Art, which formed the basis for the Flagstaff House Museum of Teaware. This formula of drawing on private and public collections and resources has fostered an environment in which members of the Society can share and further knowledge of Asian art.

I pay special tribute here to Dr. K. S. Lo, and to Dr. Ip Yee (1921–1984), both important members and former Presidents of the Society, who helped establish the character of the Society in its early years, as well as the spirit of scholarly exchange that the Society continues to aspire to today.

Chris Hall
President
The Oriental Ceramic Society of Hong Kong
October 2011.

The Committee of the Oriental Ceramic Society of Hong Kong
wishes to express its gratitude to

Ms. Teresa Liu and Arts & Education Circle

for their very generous donation to the Society for contribution to
the production of the 1st Edition of this catalogue.

Foreword

The exhibition that this volume is the catalogue to is the sixth held by the Oriental Ceramic Society of Hong Kong and the third that we have organized in conjunction with the Fung Ping Shan Museum at the University of Hong Kong. Very happily, and also most appropriately, this exhibition also coincides with the seventy-fifth Anniversary celebrations of the University.

Although there has long been keen appreciation of the objects that the Chinese scholar favoured and used in his work, the study of this important aspect of Oriental Art has hitherto remained somewhat unco-ordinated. Our aim in this exhibition therefore is to illustrate the life of the Chinese scholar as seen through his arts, and, through the medium of certain objects, to demonstrate his attitude to life and connoisseurship. Little work has been done in this field previously, but we hope that this exhibition will stimulate further research.

Many people have contributed to the assembly of this exhibition, but the inspirational genius behind the planning throughout has been Mr. Hugh Moss. His enthusiasm and driving force have been instrumental in deciding the course the exhibition should take, and it is clear to all of us who have been involved in the planning that the success is very largely due to his efforts. We also wish to express our thanks to Mr. Gerard Tsang who has teamed up with Mr. Hugh Moss in the research on the life and arts of the Chinese scholar. Their joint contribution is reflected in the introductory essays and extensive captions to all the exhibits.

The Society is indebted to Arts and Education Circle for their extremely generous donation of HK$50,000 towards the organization of the exhibition. Our most sincere thanks also go to Mrs. Susan Ribeiro and Miss Rosanne Chan who, at very short notice, very kindly agreed respectively to edit this catalogue and to oversee its production. There is no doubt that without their timely assistance the Society would have experienced insuperable problems in producing a catalogue worthy of the exhibition.

We also wish to thank the Vice-Chancellor of the University of Hong Kong for his permission to hold the exhibition in the Fung Ping Shan Museum, and the Museum Curator, Dr. Michael Lau, and his staff, in particular Mr. C.T. Yeung, for their hard work in mounting the exhibition. For the photography, we are grateful to Mr. Y.K. Chan for his skill and meticulousness, and for his time so generously given. Special thanks are also due to Professor T.I. Jao for contributing the calligraphy.

As I took over the stewardship of the Society only in April 1986, the major burden of organizing this exhibition fell to the previous Committee to whom the credit must go. Finally, I would like to thank all those who have kindly lent items from their collections and also all those, too numerous to mention here, who have contributed in one way or another to the success of this exhibition.

K.S. Lo
President
The Oriental Ceramic Society of Hong Kong
September 1986.

Dedicated to the memory of

Dr. Ip Yee

in whom were found the finest virtues
of collecting and connoisseurship.

Text and Captions
by Gerard Tsang and Hugh Moss

Acknowledgements

In the preparation of this work we have enjoyed the generous advice of a number of experts on a wide variety of subjects. We wish to thank Grace Bruce, Robert H. Ellsworth, Hung Lu-hei, Ma Kwok-kuen, Lee Yun-wun, Wang Tin, Prof. Tong Kin-woon, C.C. Wang, Christer von der Berg, John Lust and Tsang Wing-kwang.

We have also been assisted in various capacities by Robert P. Piccus, Sydney Fung, B.K. Wong, Kerry Roland, Esther Chandran, Blossom Lee Moss, Leung Yin Ling, Janet Nathanail, Pete Suart, David Price and Peter Lam.

Research assistance and the checking of the *pinyin* romanization was undertaken by Lam Hon-kin; line drawings throughout are by Pete Suart, most of the rubbings by Lui Wing-fong, and the bulk of the photography by Y.K. Chan.

We also wish to thank Carl Nagin, whose understanding and creative editing of the text (as opposed to the captions) made a difficult message more manageable.

We have used the *pinyin* system of transliteration throughout, even taking the liberty of standardizing transliteration in quoted passages to avoid confusion, although published titles in other systems have been maintained in the original. We have also followed the usage preferred by living individuals for their own names. All dates given are A.D. unless otherwise stated.

Scholar, Sage and Monk in Chinese Art: In Pursuit of the Absolute

Introduction

The twentieth century has witnessed a profound transformation in the West, an evolution of consciousness so rapid and fundamental as to take on the features of a revolution. The new spirit of the age has created a world view much closer to the traditional wisdom of the East.

In this collective awakening, the arts are in the forefront, expanding the frontiers of consciousness. As they do so, striking parallels have emerged between Modernism in the West and traditional Oriental art. In the past decades, renewed interest in Eastern aesthetics has led to serious studies of the more profound expressions of Chinese art. Though difficult to grasp, something of immense value has been perceived in them. It is elusive, appearing briefly in illuminating moments, only to fade into confusion again — a grail of wisdom beckoning at the limits of our comprehension. In search of this grail, we are engulfed in a sea of scholarly minutiae, only to find ourselves too often before a reputed masterpiece unable to comprehend it.

Nor is this dilemma confined to arts of an alien culture. Much modern Western art poses the same problem. As consciousness evolves, it becomes more sophisticated, exploring subtler levels of meaning which the intellect seems unable to grasp. Aesthetic exploration of expanding consciousness leads us into a realm where the intellect must relinquish absolute authority. It stands confused before this new terrain.

To follow the arts into this new realm, we must reconsider our entire approach to aesthetic experience. The tendency, still prevalent in the West, to approach art as an objective, detached observer precludes the sort of revelation to which the new consciousness aspires. The lesson of both Modernism and traditional Chinese aesthetics dictates a more holistic view, one that emphasizes the process and not simply the products of artistic expression.

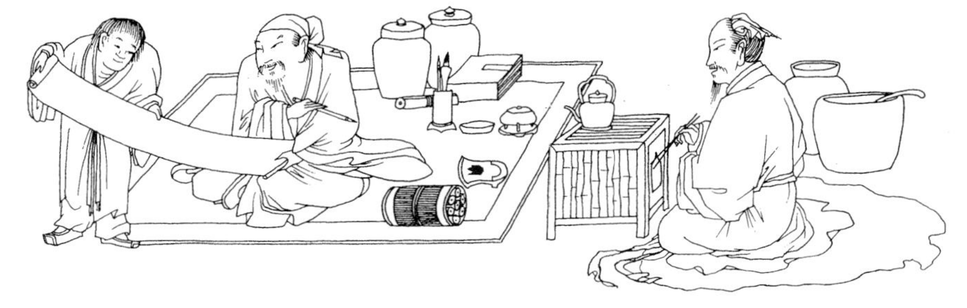

Fig. 1

The traditional Western view focuses on technique and style, systematically categorized through the formal analysis of art historical methodology. It has fostered a belief that technique is what an artist uses to create an end product, the work of art, to which the passive observer then says, in effect: "Entertain me!" But this approach misses the most vital function of art, the very purpose of the entertainment, which is ultimately the expansion and therefore the evolution of human consciousness. Without recognition of this highest goal, the transcendent joys of art peter out at the point where their greatest excitement begins. In China, the holistic view of art was implicit. It is recorded specifically in relation to music theory by the sixth century BC. Subsequently governing all aesthetic practice, it viewed the artistic process, involving artist, medium and audience, as a means to self-realization. The end product was expanded consciousness, enlightenment rather than the physical work of art.

Art plays a vital role in the evolution of human consciousness. However pleasant and diverting the means, it is ultimately concerned with meaning. The arts, in their broadest sense, offer our most powerful means of considering and sharing experience, of expanding human awareness. The mind takes the sensual gestures of art and transforms them in an aesthetic experience which, at the highest level, transcends the intellect. Contemporary aesthetic thought, if it is to move beyond conventional formulations, must take this into account and construct a theory of art *and* consciousness. To that end, we will outline such a theory and explore it in the context of Chinese art, aiming to convey the consciousness which underlies it.

Our approach reflects as much a dialogue with the objects as a statement of theory about them. We have avoided as much as possible the counter-productive impulse to categorize and restructure them according to Western preconceptions. There is no claim here to any comprehensive or definitive synopsis. Indeed, such an approach in selection, arrangement or definition of the materials would contradict the essence of our understanding of them. We have chosen those works we find informative and exciting, concentrating on areas previously neglected in Western publications.

The format and style of this catalogue is intended as a statement about its nature. For us, the various creative activities of mankind have only superficial differences; they are all in their way art, understood in a context where life itself is the ultimate art form. This catalogue is our contribution to that more holistic vision of Chinese art.

For us, the search for the Absolute lies at the heart of Chinese art. We propose that awareness of the Absolute as something real and attainable is a prerequisite for understanding its deeper meaning. Exploring this consciousness and its relation to Chinese aesthetics is the burden of the introductory text. The body of the work is then the illustrations of, and captions for, individual exhibits. The catalogue can be read sequentially or casually, and the apparent disorder of its presentation is deliberate. We have avoided the kind of analytical grouping that characterizes more traditional catalogues — a statement of the need to overcome such objectification in pursuit of the deeper meaning of Chinese art — separating exhibits only broadly into four basic categories depending on whether we are dealing primarily with questions of aesthetics, patronage, connoisseurship or function. For those who require a more explicit map of the territory an index is appended listing exhibits under materials, types, principle subject-matter and artists.

Chapter One

Art and Consciousness

For the Chinese, the intellect was never the sole arbiter of human consciousness. For them, the human intellect danced only on the surface of phenomena; ultimate authority was vested in a state of consciousness achieved by stilling the mind in order to transcend it. For our purposes we will apply the terms "relative" and "Absolute" to consciousness governed by the intellect and the transcendent state respectively. Human consciousness may be broadly divided into two groups according to these perspectives of ultimate authority. This distinction is essential for understanding Chinese consciousness and aesthetics.

The gulf between these two, seen from the point of view of relative consciousness, is immense because the intellect cannot conceive of a state of understanding that transcends it. The gulf is all the more difficult to cross because the solid foundations of reason required by the intellect must first be dismantled in building a bridge to the Absolute. This is the crux of the problem many encounter in approaching both Chinese and modern Western art.

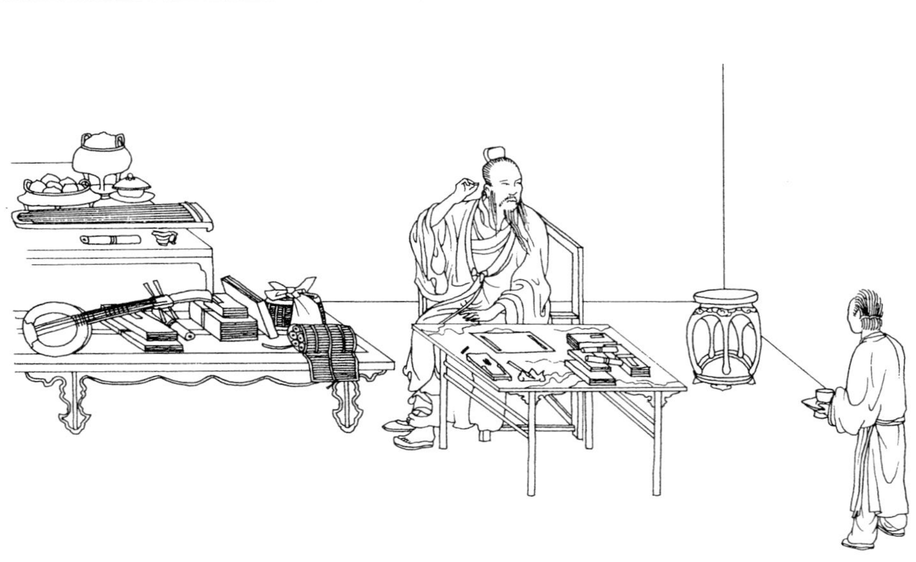

Fig. 2

Art and consciousness both exist in twin realms: one which is finite, temporal and objective, and the other which is infinite and universal, the realm of the Absolute, beyond the confines of reason. We see this clearly with music. Reason can analyse its harmonies and rhythms and reduce their movement and sensual textures with mathematical precision. But the laws of counterpoint are not the music of Bach; they merely serve to design and reveal its workings. At its most profound level, musical experience lies in a more subjective realm, one that engages artist, medium and audience at a level that transcends the intellectual process. Ultimately, all art is the inarticulate speech of the heart.

Western aesthetics, governed for several centuries by relative consciousness, has approached art as objectively as possible. In the relative realm, the products of art are viewed apart from their process and ultimate purpose. Indeed, these can only be understood by more refined, subjective means; they cannot be quantified or analysed independently. Western art historians, critics and theorists have largely avoided these ineffable aesthetic realms. The objectification of art restricts it to the intellectual realm, leaving its untidy, transcendent features to a diminished, subjective one. In articulating the inarticulate speech of the heart, it obscures the very nature of art.

Not so in China, where the search for the Absolute has informed not only its philosophical and religious traditions but its aesthetics as well. To many in the West, Chinese aesthetics seem like mere subjective theorizing; its master/disciple tradition seems a poor substitute for the highly developed methodology of academic analytical scholarship. Only recently have the limitations and authority of the Western approach, grounded in relative consciousness, been questioned.

Hence, the need arises for a new aesthetic theory relating art to its role in the evolution of consciousness. What follows is a schematic attempt to outline the main features of such a theory. They, in turn, provide the basis for our approach to the exhibits.

1. Art cannot be profoundly understood if it is separated from its role in the evolution of consciousness.
2. This evolution is the most important endeavour of the human race. All other aims serve this higher quest.
3. The final goal of this quest is to bring human consciousness into an awakened state of Absolute harmony with the universe.
4. Absolute harmony, by definition, cannot be attained in any relative realm of understanding.
5. The intellect (in the modern sense of the logical, analytical and reasoning faculty of the mind) serves the relative realm of understanding and must therefore be transcended if the goal of Absolute harmony is to be attained.
6. All creative activities stem from an autonomous, persuasive minority, whose role is to uncover the nature of the Absolute through a series of analogical languages capable of communicating at relative levels of understanding.

7. These analogies, whether expressed in terms of religion, science, philosophy, the arts, or any other creative activity, are constructed within the relative realm in pursuit of Absolute meaning. They are channels of communication between the known and the unknown, the finite and the infinite, the mundane and the transcendent.
8. Although the Absolute can be experienced directly by any individual, it can only be communicated by analogy. This subjective dimension characterizes the most profound understanding in any field and is most efficiently conveyed through a disciplic tradition of teaching. The master/disciple relationship is one in which ultimate meaning is taken on faith as a guide to the path along which it may be directly experienced.

As we shall see, Chinese art represents the creative activities of a culture governed by Absolute consciousness, disciplic traditions, and a profound understanding of the transmission of such knowledge. The distinction between the Absolute and its analogies, between the transcendent realm and the relative realm of the intellect, is a prerequisite for understanding Chinese aesthetics. Without it, the intellect responds to Chinese art only as a reflection of its preconceptions. It grasps only what it is predisposed to accept, largely negating the purpose of art in revealing the Absolute.

Chapter Two

The Intellect and the Absolute

At a relatively recent stage in evolution, mankind became possessed of the intellect. With it, intuitive harmony with nature was shattered, for the intellect alone is capable of conceptualizing, and disharmony stems from concepts. That harmony, so precious to the individual and a unifying characteristic of all other aspects of nature, had to be re-acquired, knowingly, through the intellect. Consciousness had evolved to a position of extraordinary potential: if the intellect could repossess absolute harmony, it would do so knowingly and be capable of delighting in it, and therein lies the immense potential absent from pre-intellectual harmony.

However, while the intellect offered us new possibilities for understanding experience, its sphere of activity was relative and incompatible with realization of the Absolute: it had to be transcended to achieve absolute harmony, and the intellect, alone in the universe in its capacity for ambition, would settle for nothing less. An intriguing paradox: an ambitious power had been created whose only important role was to transcend itself. Given a taste of power, the intellect became drunk with it, and was unwilling to relinquish it without a struggle.

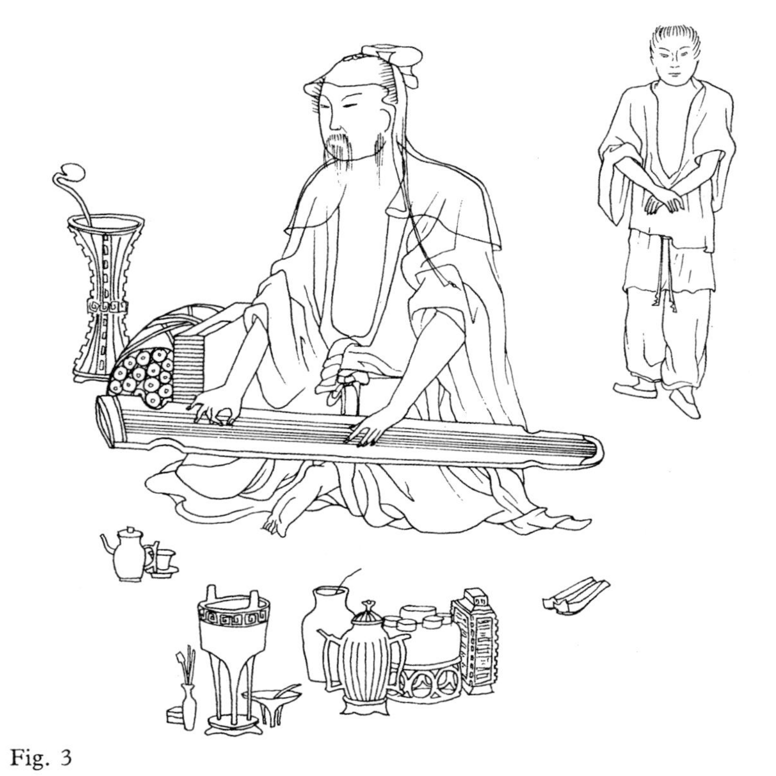

Fig. 3

In the major Eastern civilizations of India and China, the Faustian ambition of the intellect seems always to have been restrained by recognition of its relative role within the broader sphere of Absolute consciousness. Whether in the Hindu or Buddhist traditions of India, or the Daoist and *Chan* (*Zen*) transformation of Buddhism in China, the authority of the Absolute has never been seriously shaken by dominantly intellectual traditions. Even Confucius, a teacher involved in transmitting the ancient wisdom of his culture, was ultimately concerned with ways of bringing man into harmony with the Absolute (*Tian* — 'heaven'). However it is known — as *Brahma, Dao, Wu* ('Nothingness'), *Tian, Taiji* ('the Ultimate'), *Taihe* ('Great Harmony') — knowing acceptance of the Absolute as the perspective of ultimate authority is the unifying characteristic of the major analogical systems of India and China.[1] This unifying characteristic allows these separate traditions to blend freely. A Confucian scholar can be a Buddhist and follow the Dao without contradiction, in the same way that one might read a book, look at a painting and go to a concert without contradiction because all serve the same essential purpose. Only the languages of analogy differ.

Belief in the authority of the Absolute is by no means an exclusively Oriental perspective. Allowing for local cultural differences in the approach to the Absolute, testimonies of its existence are common to all cultures at all times. Whereas sectarian disputes over the nature of the Absolute characterize exoteric spritual traditions, what is remarkable about esoteric teaching is its

1. In a culture where all creative activities are recognized as analogies of the Absolute and comfortably blend into each other, to describe Hinduism, Daoism, Buddhism and Confucianism as religions or philosophies needlessly limits them. They are both, and a great deal more besides. Since their overriding aim is to bring about harmony between the self and the Absolute, they are more sensibly described as psychology than philosophy or theology. The point is that they transcend any such relative distinctions.

homogeneity, regardless of historical or cultural context. It forms an impressively consistent body of experiences as recorded in the fragments of Heraclitus, the writings of Plato, Plotinus, Eckhart, and the Sufism of Ibn Arabi. It informs the mystical and metaphysical branches of all the major spiritual traditions, East and West.[2]

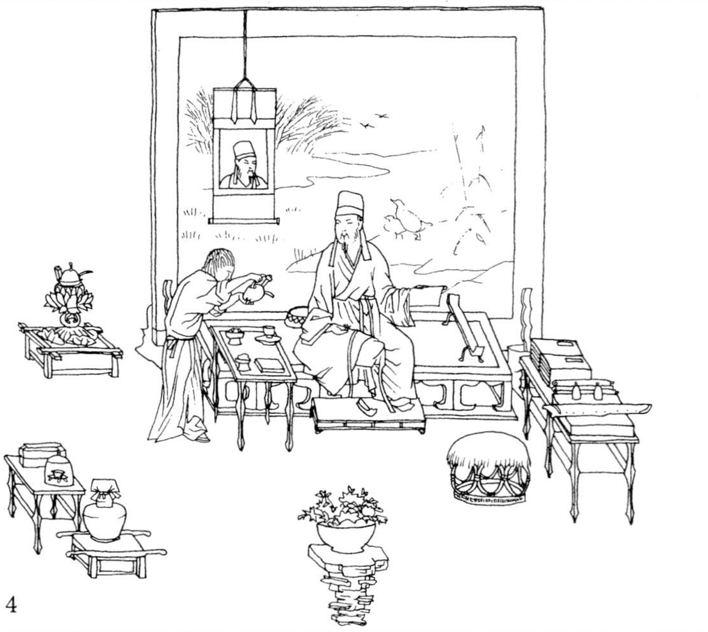

Fig. 4

From the esoteric tradition it is clear that the Absolute cannot be fully understood or explained through intellectual concepts. Paradoxically, all mystics throughout history have devoted their time to explaining the inexplicable. But real understanding of it can only be attained by direct, personal experience that transcends analytical, reasoned analysis: it may only be grasped by the stilled mind, the mind beyond thought.

The relationship of the intellect to the self and the self to the Absolute can be explained as follows. From the point of view of relative consciousness, the self inhabits a large sphere without any real delineation, but appearing to the intellect to have form and, therefore, a confining structure. Within that is another much smaller sphere, which is the intellect, which again appears to be a distinctly separate part of the self, and therefore to have autonomy. The whole is contained within the Absolute. The intellect sees consciousness as being made up of its own small area and the rest of the self (which it tries to cover intellectually by such terms as the subconscious, intuition, soul, etc.). It then sees this broader self, including the intellect, as existing quite separately from all other phenomena.[3] In the context of Absolute consciousness, no real distinction exists between the self and the Absolute. Again, the musical analogy is the most accessible. Intellectual activity stops, however briefly, when we become wholly absorbed in music. No sense of time or place, self or music, or any other intellectual concept interferes: all is subsumed in a unifying experience. It is a glimpse of the Absolute. In these moments, no distinction exists between us and the music.

Once we have crossed the line of demarcation between the self and the Absolute, once the imaginary structure of confinement imposed by the intellect is transcended, self-realization becomes the same as realization of the Absolute. Indeed, the whole process becomes easier to comprehend, for the intellect finds self-realization a much more digestible concept than the search for unification with some mystical Absolute.

Through all the means available to us we are in the process of evolving consciousness. The intellect, which is the dominant sphere of activity on a daily basis, learns to transcend itself and reach into the broader sphere of consciousness. If we recognize this need, we are in a position to do it knowingly and therefore much more efficiently; if we do not it carries on regardless, for it is an intuitive need: the fully awakened mind sets about stilling the intellect directly, the unknowing through prayer, repetitive chant or rhythm, music, dance and other arts, long-distance running, mountain climbing, watching the sunset, or any other meditative pursuit. Or they may reach it through the lengthy process of thinking their way through a succession of paradoxes, to come face to face with the ultimate paradox, which is the nature of paradox itself. There, finally, the intellect is forced to concede that it is incompetent beyond a certain point. Its controlling impulses and magical powers of making analogies reach their limit. The intellect must be transcended if further progress is to be made.

The quest brings one deep into the reservoirs of the self. Although the intellect still acts as master in control of a great chain of knowledge which it lets out and winds in, proclaiming its authority and creating its confusion and disharmony (the price we must pay for the infinite potential it offers us), suddenly, quite at random, impossible to predict or order, the chain bursts asunder. Consciousness is freed of the last vestiges of intellectual domination. It soars in a moment of glorious freedom, possessed instantly of the Absolute. Self and Absolute become one, and the intellect, released from its previously dominant position at the core of all experience, scatters in all directions, unified with all phenomena. No differentiation between intellect, self, or all phenomena remains — only an emancipated consciousness which thereafter informs every aspect of life, immeasurably enriching it.

2. The existence of the Absolute realm is impressively argued by Alan Watts in *The Supreme Identity: An Essay on Oriental Metaphysic and the Christian Religion.* It is also covered in the early chapters of the inspiring work by Fritjof Capra *(The Tao of Physics)*, a physicist who has personally experienced it and has shown some remarkable parallels in modern physics. It is also the subject of *Mysticism — The Ultimate Experience*, by Cecil A. Poole. These three works give an impressive range of historical evidence for the existence and accessibility of the Absolute. Four thousand contemporary individual experiences of it are the subject of an eight-year study at Oxford University, resulting in the book *The Spritual Nature of Man*, by Alistair Hardy, Clarendon Press, Oxford, 1979.

3. It is interesting to note that prior to quantum mechanics, the prevailing Western world view since the Age of Reason was that mankind existed as a separate entity from all other phenomena and that it was possible, therefore, to have an entirely objective view of nature. With quantum mechanics came the realization that consciousness itself had to be considered in observing phenomena. This is now widely recognized in physics, which as a science, like all evolutionary processes, is constantly involved in transcending itself.

This experience and the astonishing powers it brings with it form, as we have pointed out, the basis for the most consistent body of experience known to man. From one of the Hasidic mystics of Judaism comes the following: "There are those who serve God with their human intellects and others whose gaze is fixed on Nothing [the Absolute]. He who is granted the supreme experience loses the reality of his intellect, but when he returns from such contemplation to the intellect, he finds it full of divine and inflowing splendor."[4]

Plotinus, the most philosophical of all Western mystics, wrote: "You ask how can we know the infinite? I answer, not by reason. It is the office of reason to distinguish and define. The infinite therefore cannot be ranked among its objects. You can only apprehend the infinite by entering into a state in which you are finite self no longer, this is the liberation of your mind from finite consciousness. When you thus cease to be finite you become one with the infinite. You realize this union, this identity."[5]

In the Upanishads, the fourth state of consciousness (Absolute) is described thus: "Beyond the senses, beyond the understanding, beyond all expression, is the fourth. It is pure unitary consciousness wherein awareness of the world and of the multiplicity is completely obliterated. It is ineffable peace. It is the supreme good. It is the one without a second. It is the self."[6]

Zhang Zai (1020-1077), an important Song thinker, expounded his doctrine of man's unity with all things. It extends to both the cosmic and social realms, and Zhang spoke of the ability of man, through complete self-realization, to give a heart to the Universe.[7] Tu Wei-ming wrote of Mencius (a Confucian disciple of the fourth and early third century BC): "Mencius claims that within the structure of the human body and the human heart, there is the real potential and great possibility of enlarging the self to become one with heaven and earth. Humanity so conceived is not an unrealizable ideal, but an inexhaustibly abdundant power of moral and spiritual transformation."[8]

When a culture understands the nature of the Absolute and its authority, and where its direct realization becomes the most respected state of consciousness, it nurtures a clarity of understanding and thought which enhances even the relative realm of the intellect. Analogies of the Absolute in such a culture thus bring a high degree of understanding and harmony to other members of society.

Where such experiences occur in a culture dominated by the intellect, they are not broadly understood. Distorted by intellectual analogies, they are viewed as miracles or revelations, and fitted as comfortably as possible back into an analogical structure, normally of a specific religion. Usually they are dismissed as aberrational, and the highest understanding to which mankind may aspire is stigmatized as eccentric or insane.

While the East has traditionally revered its mystic or sages, the West has frequently placed them in a sort of intellectual ghetto. There they are viewed with suspicion, treated as outcasts, to be locked up, beheaded, burned or crucified. Religions then have the posthumous task of validating their vision within an acceptable analogical framework and declaring them saints and prophets.

Chapter Three

The Principal Analogical Systems of the Absolute in China

Recognition of the Absolute in China and self-cultivation as a pre-eminent goal certainly predated written accounts of it. The three most influential analogical systems which evolved from the sixth century BC onwards were Confucianism, Daoism, and Buddhism. As analogical frameworks, they represent the same truth and recognize the Absolute as the source of all phenomena, the perspective of final authority, whose direct realization is life's ultimate goal. The essential unity of these three major traditions, expressed albeit from a Daoist point of view, is summed up in an inscription on a rock, dated to the spring of 1556:

"Vast indeed is the Ultimate *Dao*, spontaneously itself, apparently without acting, end of all ages and beginning of all ages, existing before Earth and existing before Heaven, silently embracing the whole of time, continuing uninterrupted through all eons, in the East it taught Father Confucius, in the West it converted the 'Golden Man' [Buddha], taken as pattern by a hundred kings, transmitted by generations of sages. It is the ancestor of all doctrines, the mystery beyond all mysteries."[9]

These three traditions are confusing if one tries to deal with them as intellectual ideas because essentially none of them are. They are all practical analogies of the Absolute, constructed in the relative realm as guides to enlightened living.

Confucianism

Confucius was not the founder of a faith, or even of a philosophy: he was a teacher who gathered

4. *Mysticism — The Ultimate Experience*, by Cecil A. Poole, p.78.
5. Ibid. p.79.
6. Ibid. p.73.
7. See *To Acquire Wisdom: The Way of Wang Yang-ming*, by Julia Ching, p.9, where the second section is expressed as follows: "He also spoke of the ability of man, by the enlargement of the human mind-and-heart until it embraces everything, to give a 'heart' *(xin)* to Heaven-and-earth."
8. *The Idea of the Human in Mencian Thought: An Approach to Chinese Aesthetics* by Tu Wei-ming, in *Theories of the Arts in China*, ed. by Susan Bush and Christian Murck, p.68.
9. *Tao: The Chinese Philosophy of Time and Change* by Philip Rawson and Laszlo Legeza, p.8.

and interpreted the wisdom of antiquity. The teachings of antiquity as he transmitted them stemmed from the Absolute. From cosmic harmony came the moral and ethical systems which dictated the right way of ordering the material world. Later, Confucianism evolved various systems, depending upon their interpreters, of harmonizing man with the Absolute. These analogical structures created precise systems of ancestor worship, righteous behaviour, ritual and so forth, but at their heart was always the sagely concern for creating perfect harmony between man and heaven, between the individual and the Absolute. However the ideology of Confucianism sometimes obscured the original truth of his teaching.

"The historical process by which truth becomes instituationalized can first be discerned in the case of Confucianism around the first century BC during the Han dynasty. It was later repeated in the Tang and Song dynasties, which witnessed another attempt by the state to reconstruct a Confucian ideology. In this case, however, the new ideology failed to take hold of men's minds, largely because of the challenges posed by Daoist and Buddhist philosophies which had not been sufficiently answered."[10] Subsequently, more independent thinkers went beyond the ideology to discover the lost truth and established a synthesis which became state doctrine under the Yuan dynasty. Julia Ching suggests that challenges from the different systems of Daoism and Buddhism forced these changes. However, these systems were only different analogies of the same truth, so Confucianism could not be successfully divorced from them. The Chinese hunger for wisdom rather than knowledge or information constantly forced the fusion of the various different analogies of profound truth back into a broadly based synthesis.

The authority of Wang Yangming (1472-1529), a thinker whose influence on China, Korea and Japan was considerable, stemmed from his perception that there was little essential difference between the various major systems of belief. He summed it up for Confucian, Buddhist and Daoist alike when at an early age he was told by his preceptor that the greatest attainment in life was to study and pass exams; to which he offered his own alternative that it was, rather, to learn how to become a sage.[11]

Daoism

The *Dao* was one of the names given to the Absolute in China. It was not something new at the time of the writing of the *Yijing* ('Book of Changes'), or the *Laozi*, nor when the sage Zhuang Zi expressed his gentle wisdom and understanding of it. It was simply another name for a timeless, undifferentiated reality from which all things stemmed, including its names and analogies. One of these became known as Daoism and evolved as a psychology, religion, philosophy and, most importantly, as a way of life. Daoism is any one of these or all of them. It manifests itself as an esoteric religion, deeply mysterious and full of charms and magic incantations. It also appears as alchemical practice in an analogical search for the trasmutation of matter to represent the transformation of consciousness. It occurs as well as an analogical search for the elixir of immortality, representing the timelessness of consciousness attained in its perfect union with the Absolute.

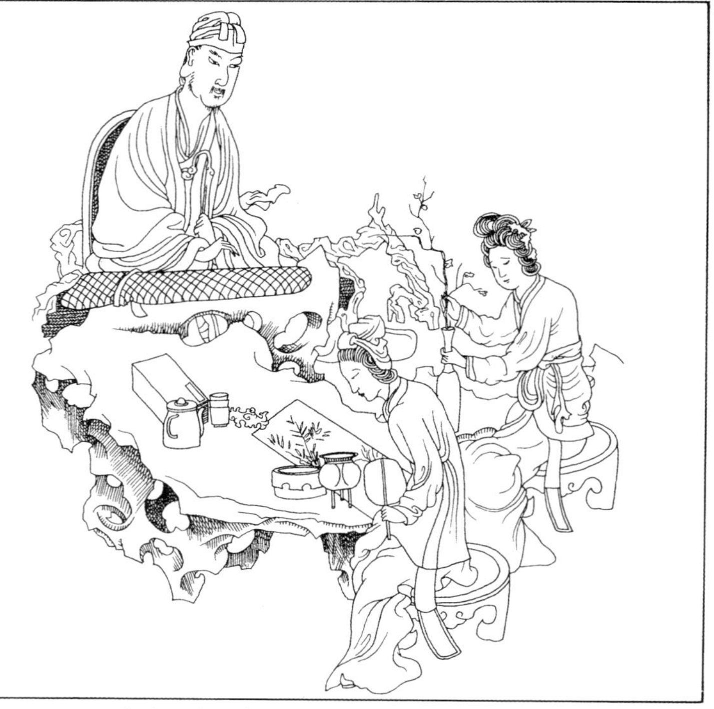

Fig. 5

Daoism manifests itself in every corner of Chinese life. Individuals did not have to be a Daoist in any particular sense to be Daoist in a general sense. Thus the wandering sage in gentle harmony with nature, wanting for nothing, is a Daoist; but so is the Confucian scholar, deep set in his ritual and orthodoxy, and the *Chan* Buddhist. Daoism, in a general sense, is simply a description of a typically Oriental approach to life.

It is, of course, possible to make all sorts of distinctions at the level of the analogical details of Daoism, of this or that religious development that sprang out of it. That is a perfectly sensible study, and will reveal major differences between Daoism, Confucianism and Buddhism at the relative level. It may well throw considerable light on individual works of art with specific Daoist meaning. A grasp of their essential similarity, however, and of the Absolute that informs all three, casts a more revealing light on the nature of Chinese art as a whole.

Buddhism

Buddha, too, was a teacher. Having realized the Absolute, he tried to transmit his experience of it. Buddhism is a disciplic tradition of teaching, whose different branches offer alternative routes to the same Absolute perception. Buddha himself taught essentially one truth: that the union of

10. *To Acquire Wisdom: The Way of Wang Yang-ming*, by Julia Ching, p.2.
11. Ibid. p.27. In the Chinese concept, the sage achieves unity of consciousness with the Absolute, the ultimate state of health: "The Sages attained harmony with Heaven and Earth and followed closely the laws of the eight winds... Their bodies could never be harmed, nor their faculties be dispersed". Quoted from *Internal Medicine*, by Vieth, in *The Human Body as a Microcosmic Source of Macrocosmic Values in Calligraphy*, by John Hay, in *Theories of the Arts in China*, ed. by Susan Bush and Christian Murck.

consciousness and the Absolute can only be directly realized through the self. All other aspects of his teaching were aimed at helping his followers attain that union. The Buddha's Absolute was identical with the *Dao* which made it instantly accessible to the Chinese. The Indian tradition of creating elaborate analogical structures for the Absolute was superimposed on the Buddha's experience of Enlightenment, and Indian Buddhism evolved into a complex philosophico-religious system, which was consolidated in China in the immediately post-Han period. However, the Chinese mind with its refined sense of the Absolute also transformed the imported system along Daoist lines, developing *Chan* Buddhism. *Chan* Buddhism, later adopted by the Japanese, became known as *Zen* and evolved into one of the more direct methods of attaining union with the Absolute.

The Absolute has governed the evolution of consciousness in China throughout its recorded history. It brings to those who attain it what Arthur Waley describes as a "a power over the outside world undreamt of by those who pit themselves against matter while still in its thralls".[12]

Chapter Four

Aspects of Absolute Conciousness

The authority of the Absolute in China helps clarify four important concepts that emerge in its artistic expressions: the intellectual primitive, the authority of the past, achieved syncretism, and immortality.

The Intellectual Primitive

One seemingly paradoxical analogy for mankind's highest goal is the perennial quest for intellectual primitivism. It permeates Chinese art. Since the evolution of the intellect deprived us of primordial harmony we have tried to recapture that original unity, but knowingly. Thus in China, where all creative activities were vehicles for self-realization, the artist cultivated a highly intellectual primitivism.

The primary purpose of the arts of the persuasive minority was to make analogies which expressed a search for the Absolute. These arts tend to express their highest levels of meaning through a simple surface structure. A highly refined intellect that has transcended its own limitations is reflected through the intuitive, direct and simple means of the primitive — the surface of art is pared down to basic essentials. In music, refinement of means reflects the choice of simple instruments like the *qin,* the flute, and even whistling (which requires no instrument at all).

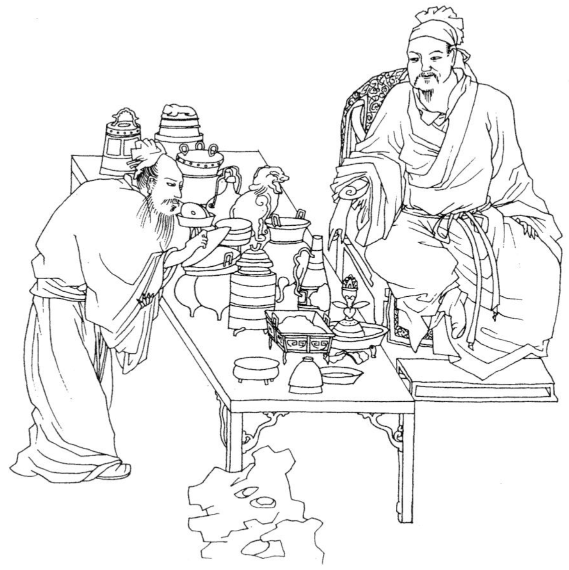

Fig. 6

With these simple instruments, meaning was expressed not so much through what was played as through how it was played. The *qin,* the quintessential instrument of the sage, with its simple pentatonic scale, allows for immense range in such subtle embellishments as vibrato, brushing, strumming and touching techniques, harmonics, variations in attack and decay, glissando etc. In poetry, this simplicity of means is best seen in the *Zen haiku* of Japan which, while not Chinese, illustrates, in its extreme development of a Chinese ideal, its essence. In *haiku,* poetry is reduced to the barest of means to achieve the height of meaning. In calligraphy and painting, intellectual primitivism is found in the re-acquired naivety which qualifies as the highest order of brushwork. There, immense skill with the brush hides within the apparently childish, simple and awkward strokes, which in painting can also often depict seemingly primitive imagery. It is the spontanaeity of a child or primitive but under the total control of the enlightened mind.

These art forms provide a feast of delights for the connoisseur. They all reflect the Chinese concept of recovering one's original nature. Mankind's profound need to reach back to this primitive state of innocence (frequently represented by a return to the idyll of childhood) suggests a desire to recreate the state of mental harmony that existed before the intellect assumed a dominant role. Mencius believed that the whole of education consisted of recapturing intuitive faculties that in the stress of life had been allowed to go astray.[13] He also believed that "The great man does not lose his child-like heart" and that the 'great body' (another term for the Absolute) is, in the last analysis, our original nature.[14]

The Authority of the Past

In all the creative traditions of China, the defining criteria for quality and value are vested in the past. It may seem paradoxical that a culture whose highest aspirations aim for the individual's

12. *The Way and its Power,* by Arthur Waley, p.46.
13. *The Way and its Power,* by Arthur Waley, p.58.
14. See *The Idea of the Human in Mencian Thought: An Approach to Chinese Aesthetics,* by Tu Wei-ming, in *Theories of the Arts in China,* ed. by Susan Bush and Christian Murch, p.66.

enlightenment in the present should, at the same time, place complete faith in the past as a guide for all its activities. Although the union of consciousness with the Absolute can only be directly experienced in the present, all communication either of it, or towards attaining it must by definition be based upon past experience. The moment we translate experience into an analogical language for transmission, we are relying solely upon the past: its very recognition as an analogical language depends upon past experience of it. Thus, in all Chinese art, refinement of existing analogies, manifested as a reverence for the past, is the cornerstone of expression.

There is another consequence of this attitude. In Absolute consciousness there is no higher authority than the self in its union with the Absolute. While this is a perfect basis for harmony in the Absolute realm, it is a tenuous one for order in its relative counterpart. To sustain order in the social matrix of the mundane world, authority could only be vested in the past.

This reverence for the past has been much misunderstood in the West which, in the absence of a broad perspective from which to comprehend Modernism's revolutionary aesthetics, still places considerable emphasis on surface innovation. Modernism has begun to break free from the restraints of relative consciousness. The arts reach a point of maturity where they begin to act as direct analogies of the Absolute and vehicles for self-realization. Sudden emancipation from the restrictions of relative consciousness and the resulting orgy of experimentation give the impression that radical new discoveries are the stuff of art, whereas in fact they are only the stuff of revolution in art. The revolution was over (with the exception of a little mopping up here and there in far-flung corners of the newly conquered realm of perception and expression) by the early 1960s, but critical understanding, as always, lags behind. Hosts of trendy, lesser artists pander to the uncomprehending clamour for newness and clever innovation, and the profundity of art gives way to surface pyrotechnics and banality.

Once the purpose and process of art are seen in the broader context of the evolution of consciousness, it becomes clear that newness only exists in the relative realm of analogies, and is therefore only "relatively" new. All art is essentially an age-old quest to make the most meaningful analogy of the Absolute: when the relative revolution is over, profundity resides in the refinement of existing analogies rather than in the invention of new ones.

Achieved Syncretism

Achieved syncretism is another characteristic paradox of Chinese aesthetics. In the rationally dominated Western tradition, syncretism is defined as the *attempted* reconciliation of opposite tenets or beliefs. But what appear as irreconcilable dualities in the relative realm are perfectly compatible to Absolute consciousness.

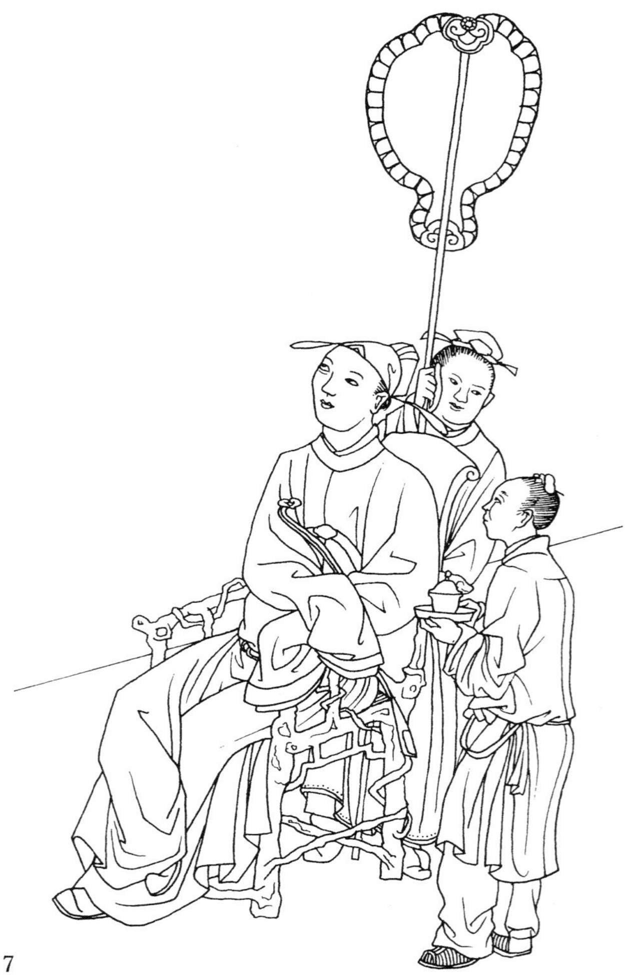

Fig. 7

Chinese syncretism explains much that is puzzling in the Chinese way of life and art. The Chinese were great synthesizers of seemingly opposite beliefs and practices. They understood all phenomena as both *yin* and *yang*, i.e., they perceived opposites as complementary polarities rather than dualities contending for final victory.

Aesthetics finally mature only when art is recognized as a direct vehicle for self-realization, above all other aims. Modernism liberated Western aesthetics from the confines of relative perception and expression, finally fostering maturity in the arts.

By these standards Chinese art has been modern for a long time. Chinese consciousness never allowed the intellect to dominate to the point where a major aesthetic revolution was necessary. Change was more of a gradual evolutionary process. In painting, it became distinctly discernible from the fourth or fifth century onwards. By the eleventh century, it was critically understood and manifested itself during the Yuan dynasty as a fully mature art.

Chinese art appears tradition-bound to Western eyes which perceive only surface values of abstraction, a consequence of its predisposition to objectify art. Chinese artists have been painting wholly abstract and abstract expressionist paintings for many centuries; however their syncretic outlook has allowed them to do so without abandoning representational subject-matter. It is part of the immense subtlety of the Chinese painting tradition that it has been able to express itself in the various langaugues of painting without the need to isolate them. Chinese paintings are multi-dimensional works of creative communication incorporating abstraction, representation, expressionism, cubism, realism, etc. in individual works of art. This is the genius of the syncretic mind at work in the aesthetic realm.

Immortality

The concept of immortality in the Orient illuminates their vision of Absolute consciousness. Whereas the intellectual concept of immortality suggests a notion of eternity seen as endless, linear time, in the Absolute realm one steps completely outside of time, thus achieving immortality in the blinking of an eye.

This also allows for a spiritual community of sages who exist outside of time and place, linking all who have delved into the realm of the Absolute. Writing about creativity and self-realization in poetry Xie Zhen noted: "Once you manage to do these three essential things, your creative powers will attain an undifferentiated whole, no longer will you need to make statues of the 'Banished Immortal' [Li Bo] or paint portraits of Shaoling [Du Fu], and the myriad things of existence will form one self with you, and men who lived throughout countless ages will form one mind with you."[15]

To relative consciousness, the Absolute and its powers are fanciful, imaginary. It seems impossible for understanding to exist outside of the intellect; for an abstract painting to consist entirely of figurative elements; for immortality to last for the blinking of an eye and for sages of today to commune with those of long past ages or even the future. However, for Absolute consciousness these things and many more wonders are palpably real and are directly experienced.

Chapter Five

The Persuasive Minority in the Evolution of Chinese Consciousness

The persuasive minority consists of those in any field of creative endeavour who are most effective in the evolution of consciousness. To understand the role of the persuasive minority in any culture, we must first distinguish between its activities in creating analogies of the Absolute, where it is totally autonomous, and its activities in the relative realm, where such autonomy tends to be constrained by elite groups.

The capacity for creative activity is theoretically the only prerequisite for membership in the persuasive minority. It is a capacity wholly dependent upon learning. Learning is essential to the creative process: first to recognize the need for creative consideration; next, to recognize the analogies; then, to recognize their refinements; and finally, to recognize their inevitable dissolution into the direct experience of what they were constructed to represent.

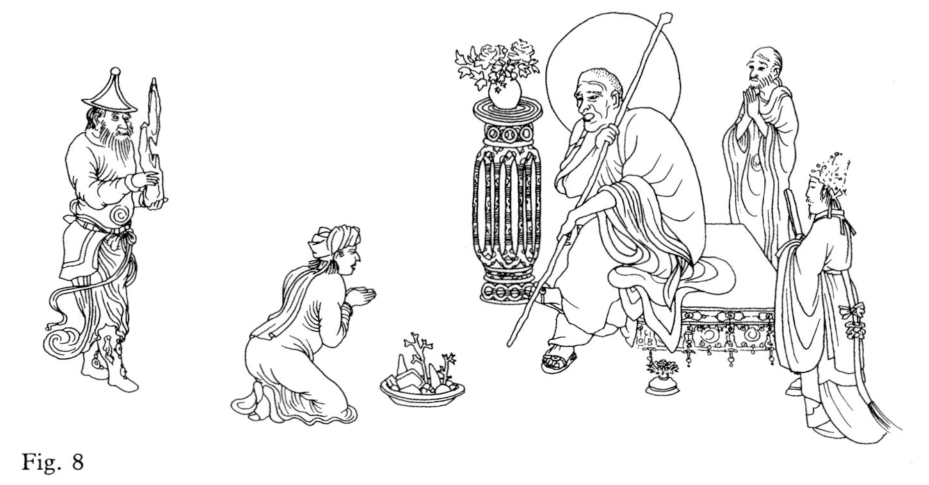

Fig. 8

In the relative realm, however, there is a tendency for the persuasive minority to be concentrated in those systems which promote education. In China, the main systems were not as distinctly specialized as in Western cultures: religion, philosophy and politics coexisted comfortably and were inextricably interlinked. However, two main systems may be identified as convenient focal points for the activities of the persuasive minority: the teachings of Daoism and Buddhism and the evolving meritocracy of the State bureaucracy.

Daoist and Buddhist Educational Systems

Daoism and Buddhism, although they also broadly influenced mainstream Chinese education, may be seen as an alternative, independent source of the persuasive minority. As a distinct system, Daoism probably emerged during the Warring States period; usually, it is back-dated to the rather mysterious, probably composite personage called Lao Dan (Lao Zi), thought to be an older contemporary of Confucius in the late sixth century BC.

Daoism was later consolidated by Zhuang Zi in the fourth century BC. At the time, however, the two were no doubt seen with greater distinction. What they shared was a common perception, apparently part of ancient Chinese wisdom, of the illusory nature of the dichotomy between self and other, subject and object. They shared as well the ability to reach into the inner layers of the self and become one with the Absolute. All of their teachings stem from this one source, as do most major Oriental philosophies of life. Daoism, with its esoteric religion, its abstract philosophy, and the ineffable source it calls the *Dao* or 'Way' seems dauntingly confusing if we try to grasp it by solely intellectual means.

The *Yijing*, a philosophical compilation probably of the Warring States period but thought to have represented much earlier wisdom, together with the thoughts of Lao Zi and Zhuang Zi were, broadly considered, compatible analogies of the Absolute. By the Han dynasty, Lao Zi and Zhuang

15. Quoted from *Siming shihua* (*Xu lidai shihua* edition), by Xie Zhen, in *Alternate Routes to Self-Realization in Ming Theories of Poetry*, by Richard John Lynn, in *Theories of the Arts in China*, ed. by Susan Bush and Christian Murck.

Zi were retrospectively appointed patriarchs of the Daoist school of thought from which an esoteric religion was born. A third group, the Quietists, was later subsumed in Daoism and Buddhism. The name is derived from their practice of quieting the mind in meditation.

It is explained by Arthur Waley: "The process of Quietism, then, consisted in travelling back through the successive layers of consciousness to the point where one arrived at Pure Consciousness [the union of consciousness with the Absolute], where one no longer saw 'things perceived', but 'that whereby we perceive' ... The adept who has reached this point has learnt, as the Quietists expressed it in their own secret language, 'to get into the bird-cage without setting the birds off singing'".[16] The bird-cage is the area of consciousness beyond the intellect, and the singing birds are thoughts; one must creep past them without arousing them to intellectual activity.

What distinguished the so-called Daoist view of the Absolute from its Confucian counterpart was mainly its activity in the relative realm. In the Daoist view, direct realization of the Absolute was man's only concern, even in the relative realm. From sagehood, order and harmony would automatically flow. The Confucian view was that order and harmony were the most likely means of *achieving* direct realization of the Absolute. The goal was the same, but in the relative realm means and ends were reversed.

Daoism and Buddhism differed far less about means in the relative realm, and the teachings of the two may be seen as an educational alternative to the State bureaucracy.

Frequently, in both Daoism and Buddhism, disciples gathered around particular masters in institutions, temples and monastaries, and access was generally unrestricted for the serious and not-so-serious student alike. Both Daoism and *Chan* Buddhism see such distinctions as unimportant. For Daoist or *Chan* institutions to have cared about seriousness would have been like the head of a major Western corporation hiring his top executives based upon the content of their dreams. Reaching the Absolute was the central concern of the system, and no other subject was taught — although often the disciple might think he was being taught any number of other subjects.

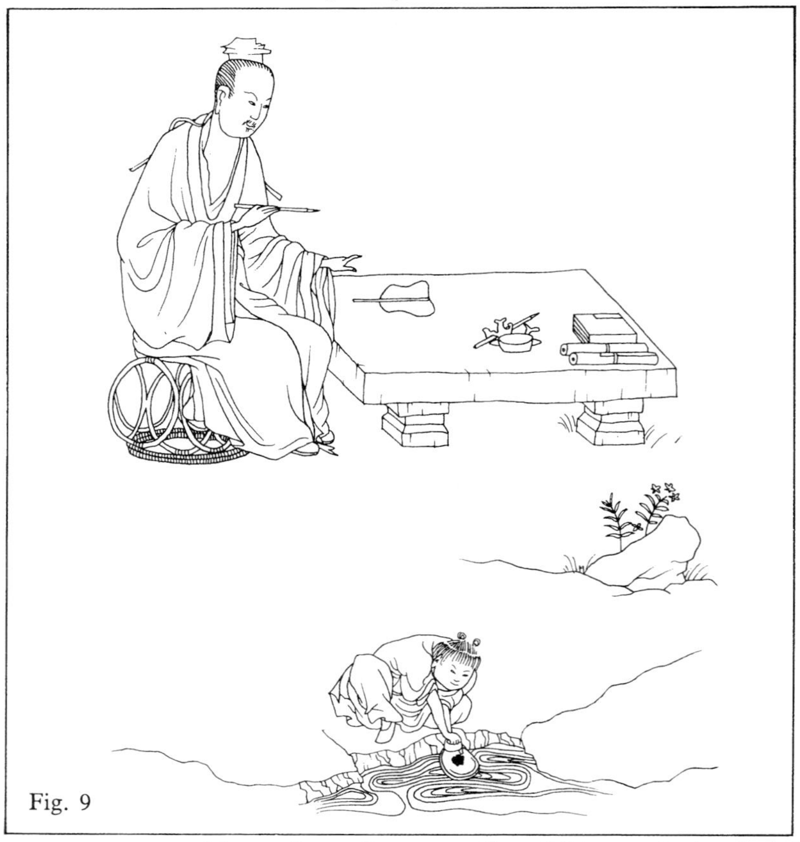

Fig. 9

Meditational techniques were a principal means of this education: through yoga, breathing, chanting, contemplation, etc., the conceptual baggage of the intellect was left behind in preparation for the moment of Absolute realization. The esoteric nature of their teachings necessitated a disciplic tradition removed from the mundane ordering of human affairs in the dusty world. Many became hermits, far from the centres of power, although it was perfectly possible to be an urban hermit, living in the dusty world, though not a part of it.

It was a simple way of life — well suited to the pursuit of the Absolute. As such, it fostered many of the persuasive minority, often in their old age from diverse walks of life; or during brief retreats in the midst of wordly pursuits. As an ideal, it was highly respected, and those who followed it could do so in relative peace.

The State Educational System

The other main system of education arose out of the needs of government. Long before Confucius, rulers required the educated to help them order and sanctify their reigns. The needs of the family-based feudal system of the day encouraged the education of administrators with specialized functions. It also encouraged the teaching of ritual and the maintenance of harmony between heaven, earth and man. Increasingly, the educated elite also assumed a role as advisers. From the complex administrative needs arose the system of scholar-officials who became the backbone of China's social and political structure.

There is a general misconception that prior to the time of Confucius, scholarship was rare in China. As Creel writes: "Books in this period were extremely common. The production of documents of some length was a matter of daily, not monthly occurrence. The ability to write was not, to be sure, diffused among the common people ... But on the other hand it is quite certain that those people (and they were not few) who were able to write used that ability with a freedom and casualness which is denied to a vast number of those who, in Western countries at the present day, figure among the 'literate' in our census estimates."[17] Confucius, however, stands as a convenient watershed in the evolution of the scholar class, or literati *(wenren)* as they came to be called, that arose out of this tradition of scholarship.

Born in the mid-sixth century BC, a time of growing confusion and political unrest in the disintegrating Zhou dynasty, Confucius served in a number of official posts as had thousands of

16. *The Way and its Power*, by Arthur Waley, p.45.
17. *Studies in Early Chinese Culture*, by H.G. Creel, p.21.

other administrative officials before him. He served as an official in his native state of Lu (modern-day Shandong province). After various vicissitudes and despite achieving high office, he despaired of reforming the incumbent Duke of Lu and set out in disgust, at the age of 57, as a wandering teacher. He travelled from state to state seeking a ruler enlightened enough to listen to him. After 12 years he had gathered around him an apparently large number of disciples but had failed to make much of an impression in the field of politics. He returned to Lu to edit the Classics of previous ages and to write the *Spring and Autumn Annals*, his only original work — a record of the state of Lu containing his arguments for a strong, centralized government.

He appears to have differed from previous officials in one respect. Their advice on righteous rule, the achievement of harmony, correct ritual and behaviour, etc., had all been offered in deference to the absolute power of the ruler. They construed their role as advisory, not governing. Confucius, however, elevated the power of the mind above that of the state and acted upon his belief. The evidence he observed from the decaying Zhou Dynasty convinced him that the old system was failing; it prompted him to formulate and teach a system that in the final analysis governed rulers rather than advised them.

This shift of emphasis was an important one, as it placed ultimate authority in the mind — a key feature of the emerging system and an inevitable outcome of the belief in Absolute consciousness. Later Confucian disciples were, whatever the exigencies of their day, to remember this vital new emphasis. The influential Song Confucian Zhu Xi, whose attitude to his sovereign was that of a moral judge and teacher rather than of a servant, epitomizes the broader Confucian attitude. He pursued the new outlook to such an extent that he was impeached by the Imperial Censor, his teachings proscribed as a perverse and heretical doctrine.[18]

One could argue that this single act of vesting ultimate authority in the Absolute while bowing to relative authority in the mundane realm is largely responsible for the considerable longevity of the Chinese civilization. As has been demonstrated again and again, the ruling house could be conquered, even the land could be conquered, but never the Chinese mind; its power was so seductive that conqueror after conqueror, whether indigenous upstart bandit or foreign 'barbarian', was eventually civilized. It was a stroke of immense subtlety and importance to Chinese culture, for while making the Absolute the final authority, it allowed for the vaunting ambition of the intellect to run its human course in seeking relative power. Rulers in the relative realm could be controlled in a general, if not a specific sense, and the cancer of power surgically removed from time to time without endangering the body of the culture or its ideals. Out of this arose a meritocracy which governed the rulers of China increasingly from the Han dynasty onwards. Nor do events in the present century bring the process to an end: the scholar class itself was not the ideal, it merely evolved to serve it — the mirror of Chinese history reflects an intriguing prognosis for the future of the Chinese mind, which exerts its subtle charms still, but now on a global basis.

Basically, what Confucius taught was ancient wisdom, a system based on respect: of child for parent, parent for ancestor, of vassel for lord, lord for King, and King for Heaven — an analogical structure of the Absolute cemented together by correct behaviour in all things, the key to which was ritual. Because it emphasized correct ritual and behaviour as essential to realization of the Absolute, the Confucian system needed to be formally taught, and thus education remained central to its traditions. Its final aim was harmony with the Absolute, but its structure fostered stability in the relative realm through education and correct behaviour. These features and its remarkable flexibility in adapting other analogical systems made it immensely attractive to later rulers.

Confucius was an inevitable outcome of Chinese consciousness, certainly not its source, nor even, in the final analysis, the source of the meritocracy he was so instrumental in promoting. But his was the vision, fostered by the faltering conventional wisdom of his age, that served as the foundations for later thinkers. It provided the bond that would hold together the relative and Absolute realms.

It is not clear to what extent Confucius influenced the establishment of the nascent meritocracy prior to the Han dynasty. One of its key features was the examination system where, in theory although not always in fact, entrants were tested on their qualifications to hold office. These civil service exams can be traced back to the fourth century BC and were documented beginning in 156 BC.[19] During the Han dynasty, although the examinations were not completely open (all candidates had to be recommended by existing officials), those recommended had then to pass the examination on their own merits; although it was not an ideal meritocratic system, it incorporated a number of people of humble origin.[20] Under the Han dynasty the great strength and stability offered by the Confucian way had been officially recognized. Thereafter, it became state orthodoxy inextricably linking

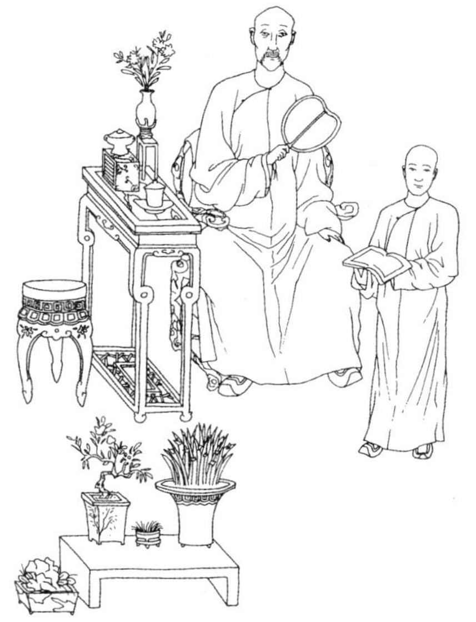

Fig. 10

18. See *To Acquire Wisdom: The Way of Wang Yang-ming*, by Julia Ching, p.17.
19. See *The 'Fa-chia': Legalists or Administrators?* by H.G. Creel, in *Studies Presented to Tung Tso-pin on His Sixty-fifth Birthday*, Taipei, 1961.
20. See *The Beginnings of Bureaucracy in China: The Origin of the 'Hsien'* by H.G. Creel, *The Journal of Asian Studies*, Vol. XXIII, Number 2, February 1964, p.156.

Confucius with the whole system of the scholar- official and making him the archetypal literatus.

From the Han dynasty to the Sui/Tang dynasties although power was firmly vested in powerful hereditary aristocracies, the burgeoning meritocracy always stood at hand. During the Sui and Tang dynasties the examination system, albeit still restricted, was instituted finally as the principle means of access to the administrative hierarchy; and by the ninth century, examination bureaucrats emerged finally as the predominant elite, to remain so into the twentieth century.

The state hierarchy and the examination system served as the power base of the literati. Their activities and influence spread out like invisible filaments into every corner of Chinese life. And from the Han dynasty onwards, the state educational system served as the springboard for the bulk of the persuasive minority in China.

Chapter Six

The Persuasive Minority in Chinese Art

In the broader perspective, once we begin to view art as an aesthetic exploration and expression of higher consciousness, the distinctions which preoccupy us in the relative realm disappear. For the persuasive minority, all the arts are paths to the Absolute. Their products may be seen as the work of a scholar, monk, uneducated artisan, shaman or sage, but their highest function remains the same.

This broader perspective is informative in approaching both the art of the persuasive minority and its audience. In terms of the evolution of consciousness, that art is most profound which brings its audience closest to awareness of the Absolute. Since union with the Absolute is experientially purely subjective, it follows that at this level all art is purely subjective. We can be objective about art history and about means, but the deeper we delve into meaning, the more profound our aesthetic involvement, the more subjective it becomes, and the greater the emphasis placed upon the audience. For what we consider great art is no more than that which a large number of people over a period of time have individually construed as meaningful. In the final analysis the whole process and evolution of art emphasizes the importance of the role played by the audience, for it is they who sanctify art.

Theoretically, there is no hierarchy in the arts in terms of absolute profoundity. Music, the least intellectually hampered medium of expression, may bring the most immediate glimpse of the Absolute, but eventually the intellect must be transcended in more than glimpses; and for this, the more intellectual and verbal arts are no less effective. To believe that ballet is, *a priori,* more profound than the latest street dance or that Bach is necessarily more meaningful than Balinese gamelan or David Bowie is to grasp art only at a local level. There, the relative level of a particular culture at a particular time dictates categories of aesthetic profoundity according to the rules and values of a given socio-cultural context. But from the broader perspective, profoundity is governed by the stage in the evolution of consciousness at which the local values are assigned, thus providing greater and lesser criteria of meaning.

As we explore what constitutes profundity in the arts of the persuasive minority in China, shifting from the greater to the lesser perspective, judgement, with its relative concepts, is required. Art is communication, and therefore involves both the perception and expression of an artist as well as those of the audience; one without the other negates the artistic process, and the most profound analogy of the Absolute becomes meaningless.[21]

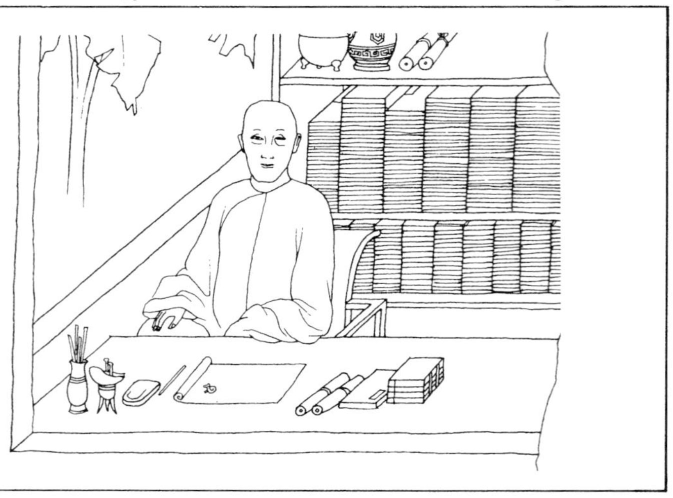

Fig. 11

At the relative level, education was, as we have seen, a major determinant of the persuasive minority in Chinese art. Aesthetic values, therefore, largely emanated from educated groups, the most influential of which was the scholar class. Increasingly from the Han dynasty until the present century, this class dominated the arts. As artists themselves, and arbiters of taste, their influence was widespread. Nor was it necessary to pass an exam or hold office to be a creative member of this class. The education system so permeated the upper classes of Chinese society that the literati ideal of the refined gentleman, educated, elegant and meaningful in everything undertaken, also influenced even those who did not sit for exams.

The consciousness evolved by this group, directly or indirectly in response to its ideals, established the single most important focal point of the profound arts in China. Local, and in artistic as opposed to art-historical terms, relatively unimportant arguments about whether *qin* music should follow the literati or professional trends; whether one school of painting was more profound than another; whether one form of poetry was loftier than its counterpart, etc., tend to obscure the fact that all of the artists involved were educated to some extent. The very fact of learning to play a *qin,*

21. An artist may, of course, act in the capacity of his own audience. Every work of art begins as an act of communication with the self, using the medium as a vehicle, but ultimately mankind has a need to communicate with others. Such is the nature of the quest for the Absolute, for once realized, there is a natural urge to bring its harmony to others in some form.

or paint, or write sufficiently well to raise even the question of relative meaning (which all such dialogues were about) denotes a high degree of education, and one leaning towards, if not wholly of, the literati system.

The literati tradition also influenced the arts of the other major educational system. Many of the Daoist or Buddhist monks and sages were educated literati who had retired, for whatever reason, from official duties. Even those who were not tended to work broadly within the existing framework of artistic languages established by the scholar class.

The Fine Arts in China

Music was the first of the fine arts in China to mature to the point where it was recognized as a direct vehicle for self-realization. The six arts of the Zhou period were ritual, music, archery, charioteering, writing and arithmetic, mastery of which made for a well-rounded person. Confucius labelled as indispensable the singing of the *Odes*, knowlege of ritual music, and the discipline of the *qin* in the regimen of self-cultivation.[22] There can be little doubt that he was expressing traditional wisdom at that time. Zhuang Zi also considered music as a bridge from the known into the unknown, and that in his time it was considered to have been so for millenia is demonstrated by an account he recorded of the legendary Yellow Emperor. After a performance, the Emperor was approached by a subject who said he was at first afraid, then wearied, then confused by the music: "Overwhelmed, speechless, I couldn't get hold of myself." The Emperor replied, "It's not surprising you felt that way, I performed it through man, tuned it to heaven, went forward with ritual principle and established it in Great Purity".[23]

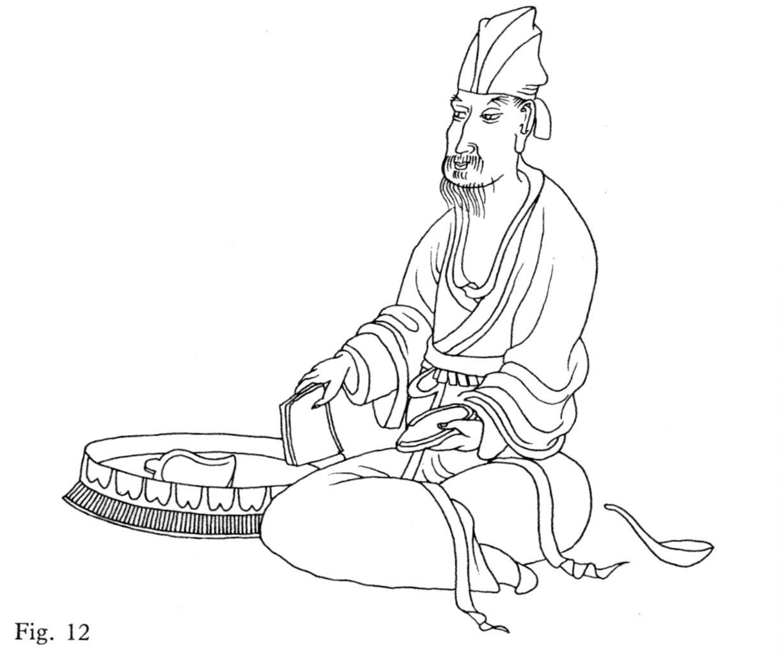

Fig. 12

Zhuang Zi and Confucius differed radically in their opinions as to which was the highest type of music, but both agreed on its significance and association with the Absolute. In their works, from more than two thousand years ago, comes a clear recognition of the role of art.[24] This concept of the arts as a direct path to the Abolute permeates Chinese aesthetics and remains unchanged down to the present century. The arts, accepted within the holistic culture of the persuasive minority, may be seen as essentially no different from religion or philosophy. The sacred function of art in so-called primitive societies has been well established both by anthropologists and historians of religion, and, apart from relative detail, art is no different from religion.[25]

Literature was the next major art form to reach maturity. The earliest use of writing, as opposed to isolated magic pictures, was as a mnemonic aid. It was a record of what people already knew and did not want to forget. As the culture advanced, writing was used to teach people what they did not already know. During the early transitional period, the Classics, philosophical writings, odes and poetry (originally chanted or sung and thus linked with music) were all considered suitable areas for profound expression, and were therefore fine arts.

Writing was one of the six arts of antiquity. At that time the semantic meaning of the written characters would have been pre-eminent in the art of writing. We are not yet dealing with calligraphy as an art form. Apart from the Classics, the highest forms were considered to be poetry/songs and prose of a philosophical or poetic nature; in the Han dynasty lyric poetry began to emerge as a major art form. Thus, Chinese literature as fine art consisted principally of ritual libretti, poetry, and *belle lettres* until the ninth century introduction of the short story, the advent of drama in the thirteenth century, and of the novel in the fifteenth century.

Next came calligraphy. Used originally purely for communication, the potential for self-expression and therefore self-realization first developed in the Han dynasty with the emergence of grass script, which offered a highly personalized mode of expression. Calligraphy was then well established as a fine art by the fourth century AD.

Painting, closely related to calligraphy in its use of materials and line, soon followed suit, and in a gradual progression from the Han through the Song dynasty it matured,[26] laying the foundations

22. *Early Chinese Music and the Origins of Aesthetic Terminology*, by Kenneth De Woskin, in *Theories of the Arts in China*, ed. by Susan Bush and Christian Murck, p.189.
23. Quoted from the Watson translation of Zhuang Zi, pp.156-157, in De Woskin, op. cit. p.191.
24. See De Woskin, op. cit.
25. The museum, as has been noted, is the cathedral of modern man; a point which will not be lost on its habitual visitors, whose devotees are encountered, their tones hushed, standing in awe in front of one icon of higher consciousness after another. The great museums of the world fulfil much the same function for modern humans as did the Gothic cathedrals of the past. Indeed, the great number of visitors to Chartres and Notre Dame approach them more as works of art than as places of worship.
26. The Tang is usually given as the beginning of the emergence of painting as a fine art because Dong Qichang, the immensely influential late Ming artist and theorist, traced the so-called 'literati' school of painting back to Wang Wei of Tang. However scholars painted from the Han dynasty onwards (see *The Chinese Literati on Painting: Su Shih (1037-1101) to Tung Ch'i-ch'ang (1555-1636)*, by Susan Bush, p.3) and there can be little doubt that what Dong Qichang perceived in Wang Wei was the manifestation of a gradual evolution that predated him.

for the so-called Yuan 'revolution' in painting of the fourteenth century.

Even by the Song dynasty this evolution of the various art forms makes it clear that anything to which the persuasive minority turned its hands acquired the potential for profound art. Knowingly or intuitively, the educated began to incorporate an ever wider range of possible art forms into the sphere of fine art. In the Ming dynasty, seal carving became accepted, and as scholars turned their hands to carving, so other forms of sculpture were explored. By the end of the Ming dynasty, a wide range of possibilities in form, expression and materials existed. It led to the gradual realization that the fine arts were as limitless as the mind itself, rather than a fixed concept and set of categories.

Connoisseurship, too, acquired potential as art: collecting, tea drinking, entertaining friends, incense burning, drinking, etc.; were all expressions of the fine art of living. In the same way that the lineage of literati painting had been back-dated in its origins once it was critically understood, so the origins of the arts of connoisseurship and so forth could all equally be back-dated to show that they had in fact been burgeoning or *de facto* fine arts for centuries. The critical understanding of them as arts merely led, as in the Yuan period in painting, to the fullest exploration of their potential. In short, in the post-Song period, every aspect of life acquired the potential for art and life itself became recognized as the ultimate art form.

Patronage of the Arts

In the West, a system evolved which made a sharp distinction between artist and patron and gave an independent role to the critic. In China, the educated tended to be patron, audience, artist and critic all rolled into one. Nor was any one of these pursuits put outside the pale of fine art in its own right: patronage, connoisseurship and criticism could all aspire to profundity of communication, leaving broad possibilities of artistic expression for the persuasive minority. In a culture where the persuasive minority was often artist, audience and critic of their own fine art, the concept of patronage was far-reaching. Frequently, a member of the persuasive minority might team up with a craftsman in the production of works of art where he would dictate materials, form, decoration and style. Such collaborations might then educate the craftsmen involved in the aesthetic of the persuasive minority, resulting in other, independent works, whose lofty nature the elite might then sanctify with their skills as audience. Such patronage incorporated seemingly eccentric artistic forms, but which in their local context were nonetheless vehicles for expanding consciousness. Strangely shaped stones, root and bamboo carvings, bronzes and other works of art thus had the potential to enter the realm of fine art.

We cannot trace here the history and development of patronage as an art form. It is sufficient to note the element of art in the very act of patronage, however disassociated the patron might otherwise be from artistic endeavour. At the other end of the scale, a patron may truly be the artist, simply using the craftsman physically in charge of carving or whatever as a part of his technique. Certainly, patronage as an art form becomes a noticeable trend from the Song dynasty onwards, to be highly developed in the Ming and Qing dynasties.

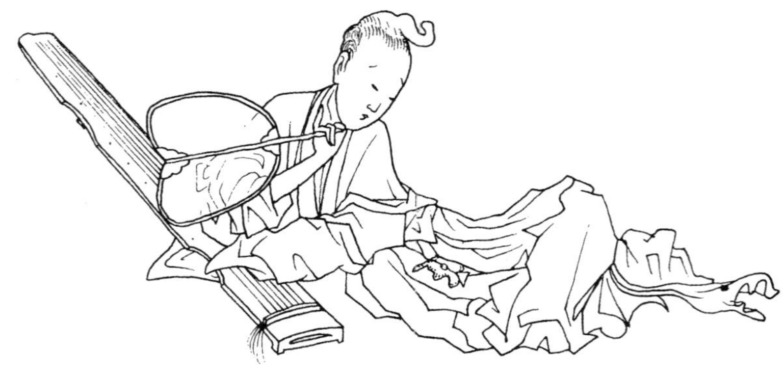

Fig. 13

Collecting and Connoisseurship

Collecting and connoisseurship also evolved the same profundity aspired to in the other fine arts. Connoisseurship can be traced back at least to the time of Confucius, for even the Master himself quoted a historical source for the authentification of an inscribed arrow.[27] By Tang and Song times, both collecting and connoisseurship were widespread, encouraged not a little by the convenience of authentic works of art in influencing official careers. To offer direct bribes in the form of money was hardly conducive to the elegance of Chinese life; but the gift of a fine painting or calligraphy, an ancient bronze or stone rubbing, was a refined gesture and one where great value could easily be concealed from the unknowing mind. Thus collecting and connoisseurship (for to give a poor work or a forgery would be counter-productive) became common social gestures. Scarcely a scholar was trained without some interest developing in that direction. It was also true that many important gatherings were centred around cultural pursuits, and those who were not involved in some way were cut off from an important centre of influence.

The Disciplic Tradition in Connoisseurship

One of the most intriguing aspects of Absolute consciousness applied to collecting is that of the disciplic tradition in connoisseurship. It was a most practical means of transmission in a culture that placed the highest faith in a purely subjective level of understanding. It is a charming system, full of a gentle wisdom and refined understanding of art's role in the evolution of consciousness. It is, however, not wholly compatible with the objective systems preferred by relative consciousness.

The disciplic tradition in connoisseurship dominates most areas of art in China, but it is

27. See *Zhongguo lishi wenwu jiadingshi kaishu* (An Outline History of Chinese Connoisseurship) by Liu Dongrui, in *Treatises on Museology (1)*, Beijing, 1983.

particularly visible in the identification of Chinese woods. Although indigenous equivalents to imported hardwoods must have existed in earlier times, contemporary terminology is based predominantly upon imported wood in log form. These were originally identified in China by characteristics of hardness, fragrance, colour, etc., rather than by species — indeed, detailed identification was not possible in logged form, even had there been any interest in establishing it, which is doubtful. They were named according to their characteristics, or more probably by their resemblance to indigenous woods long exhausted, originally named by the same criteria, such as *huanghuali* ('yellow rosewood'), *zitan* ('purple sandalwood'), *jiqimu* ('chicken-wing wood'), etc. In researching his book on Chinese furniture[28] Ellsworth had a number of pieces of material tested, all of which were considered to be *huanghuali*, and found among them as many as seven different species of wood.

From then on, any piece of cut wood which corresponded to the same visual, aromatic or tactile characteristics was called by the same name. As certain woods gained specific value, and *zitan* is a good example, connoisseurship was necessary to distinguish 'real' *zitan* from other woods that merely resembled it. The only real test of whether something was *zitan* in an objective sense was lost with the initial lack of interest in genus and species.

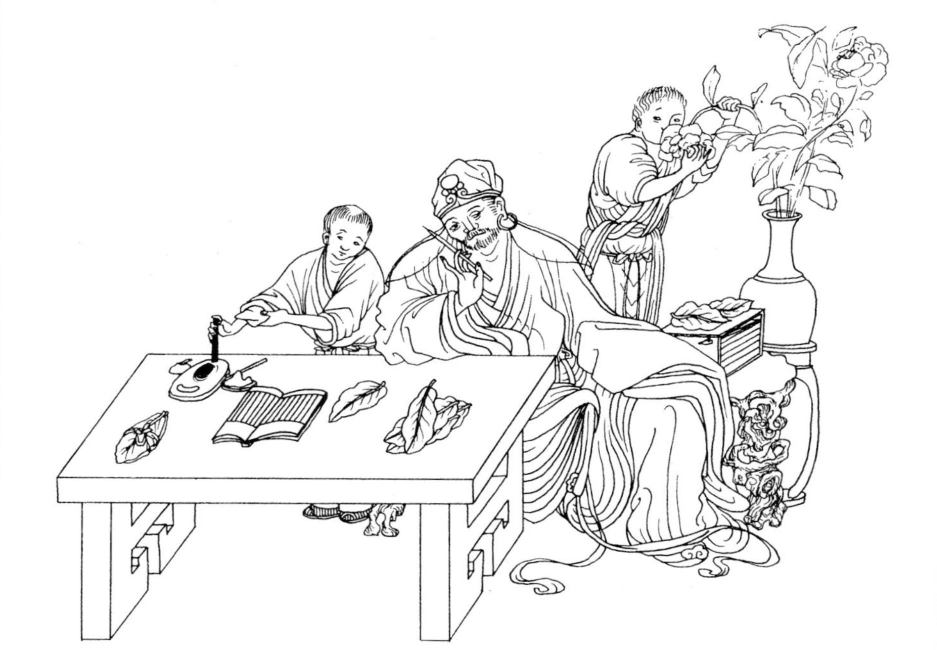
Fig. 14

The criteria for judging 'real' *zitan* was always subjective. Even assuming that all its importers called the same species by the same name and applied a single name only to one species (which in itself is highly unlikely), and that all taught their patrons how to distinguish it from other woods by the same criteria (equally unlikely, considering the size and diversity of markets within China), we are still dealing with a disciplic tradition.

Someone becomes an expert by perceiving the truth of the matter from his own point of view (based undoubtedly on traditional wisdom on the subject as a prerequisite for recognition as an expert). He then transmits his knowledge to anyone with whom he cares to discuss matters of identification; if impressed, the conversant then becomes a disciple, passing on the same criteria, no doubt with minor embellishments. Over the centuries, a general consensus of opinion is formed which may agree unequivocally on certain woods (*huangyangmu* or boxwood is one which rarely seems to provoke confusion or debate among experts), generally on others, and not at all on some. The most valued will tend to provoke the most contention for the simple reason that expert disciples may have commercial reasons for including, by deception or self-delusion, other similar-looking woods in the most valued categories.

Zitan is particularly confusing as it has always been so highly valued. Different disciplic traditions have promoted conflicting criteria for judging it. When these are applied, a core of what we might call archetypical *zitan* emerges, undisputed; but surrounding this core is a group of woods for which it becomes progressively more difficult to get agreement.[29]

The same is broadly true of connoisseurship of the wide range of soapstones, 'inkstones', and other stones so highly valued by the Chinese. A certain source of the material provides a particular visual structural pattern and colour or colour combination. A name is then given based on visual characteristics or source. Thereafter, connoisseurship focuses on visual characteristics and becomes subjective. With many Chinese stones the potential exists for greater objectivity, as many quarries are still worked or sufficiently well recorded for accurate identification. Even so, the tendency to favour the subjective, disciplic tradition continues. *Tianhuang*, the highly valued soapstone of orange-yellow colour, for instance, refers to a stone with particular colour and surface characteristics — without these it cannot be *tianhuang*. This means that it is possible for a single specimen to be genuine

28. *Chinese Furniture: Hardwood Examples of the Ming and Early Ch'ing Dynasties*, by Robert Hatfield Ellsworth.
29. In the case of *zitan*, in Hong Kong alone there are at least two distinct traditions: one includes in this classification a range of material the other would call types of *hongmu*. The visual criteria of each are clear enough, and they are consistent; they simply don't agree. The situation is further complicated by the fact that in the north it was the tradition to fill the surface of the wood with clear lacquer before waxing it, providing a much smoother appearance. In the south, however, this was not done; thus, two pieces of *zitan* could look quite different, while a piece of *hongmu* and a piece of *zitan*, both of which have been lacquered, may appear to be very similar. Names for woods also vary in different parts of China.

So while we may be able to identify most Chinese hardwoods as belonging to the Leguminosae family and their probable genus *Pterocarpus* or *Dalbergia*, we can go no further in superimposing a Linnaean classification upon the subjective tradition of Chinese identification. For a discussion on Chinese woods and their northern names see *Chinese Furniture: Hardwood Examples of the Ming and Early Ch'ing Dynasties*, by Robert Hatfield Ellsworth, Chapter Three. In identifying woods here we have followed Ellsworth, not because we consider him to be 'right' and the local connoisseurs 'wrong' — in the disciplic tradition there is no question of right or wrong, only of differences — but because his book provides the clearest published criteria for identification.

tianhuang in parts and something else entirely in others, a state of affairs that clearly favours the disciplic tradition in connoisseurship.

As long as we understand the system and accept that the identification of stones, wood and other materials are judged by disciplic traditions, there is no confusion: you simply pick the most impressive criteria and follow it until it proves inadequate, at which point you refine it based upon whatever fresh criteria seem more convincing. Aesthetically, the labelling of materials is relatively unimportant. The materials are highly valued in the first place because of their suitability and beauty; such judgment scarcely needs the authority of a sanctifying label. To try to reconcile the objective, critical tradition with the subjective, disciplic tradition tends to be confusing, in the same way that nothing but confusion arises out of applying relative reasoning to the Absolute realm. Throughout this work, the identification of wood, soapstone, strange stones and fantastic rock forms, certain 'inkstones' and other problem areas is based entirely on a knowing acceptance of the disciplic tradition with all its delights and shortcomings. We have taken the best advice available to us, which is reflected in our acknowledgments, but in the final analysis we do not consider it very important whether a work of art is made of *zitan* or a piece of *hongmu* which has similar characteristics and is equally striking. We lean in the direction of judging the visual arts primarily by eye rather than by ear.

The disciplic tradition represents a most sophisticated attitude to art and connoisseurship. In art's primary role, it recognizes the relative insignificance of precise classification and favours instead the delights of subtle interpretation. It also encourages the view that meaning is what ultimately matters in art, not means.

The Concept of Relative Authenticity

The holistic view of art, where artist, medium and audience are seen as means to enlightenment, allows for the intriguing possibilities of relative authenticity. In relative consciousness, art works are either genuine or forgeries; they cannot be both, for the two are mutually exclusive. In Absolute consciousness, authenticity does not rest predominantly in the physical work of art but in its meaning, and therefore also in the audience, raising the potential for an intriguing class of relatively authentic works of art.

In the tradition of painting and calligraphy, for instance, for reasons already stated, early works were frequently copied — sometimes stroke by stroke, sometimes more loosely. Depending upon how closely the copying artist achieved the spirit of the original, even if he superimposed a spirit of his own, the work was regarded as relatively authentic in so far as it transmitted the same meaning. The most famous piece of calligraphy in Chinese history is the Lanting Preface of Wan Xizhi (see no. 28). Later, many copies were made by famous calligraphers, until in the Tang dynasty, what was then thought to be the original was copied by the finest calligraphers of the day and then reputedly buried with the Emperor. Those copies were highly valued and later carved into stone from which rubbings were taken. Each carries some of the original meaning and is relatively authentic, and certainly highly valued.

Chapter Seven

Functions of Art Among the Persuasive Minority

When Ji Kang (third century AD), one of the Seven Sages of the Bamboo Grove, was sentenced to death for his courage in standing by a politically doomed friend, he met his fate with fortitude, calmly watching the shadows thrown by the sun and playing his *qin*. It was a final flourish, the last act in a life lived knowingly as art. It became a glowing example of mankind's highest aspirations, an example which will continue to communicate long after many of the works of art inspired by it have been lost.

This concept of life as art has brought a consistent elegance to every aspect of the lifestyle of the persuasive minority since before the time of Confucius. In his time, the wearing of jade amulets hanging in series from garments was designed less for decoration than as a regulator of orderly, elegant movement — ungentlemanly haste producing a dissonant clanging. Court robes in later times were similarly designed to encourage smooth elegance in all movements.

The recognition of life as the ultimate art form has prompted the Chinese to take the simplest act and turn it into a complex, often ritualized, art form. The most natural act of drawing breath was transformed, through different methods of meditative breath control, into a core of esoteric teaching practised throughout the Orient. The prosaic act of preparing and drinking tea became a highly ritualized art form. Its culmination occurs in the Japanese tea ceremony, borrowed and developed with obsessional refinement from Tang dynasty customs of tea drinking. Worshipping ancestors, entertaining friends, burning incense, playing *weiqi*, and every aspect of more conventionally recognized arts — all might be approached as art and afforded the total creative recognition of the artist and audience.

The persuasive minority in traditions governed by relative consciousness do the same, but less consciously. The grand, all-encompassing notion of life as art is fragmented into relative concepts of style, trend, flair and character. The cohesive vision unifying them is not taught, nor is it widely understood or respected. It surfaces randomly, if at all, and is often doubted when it appears.

The scope of activities the persuasive minority designates as suitable for the refined gentleman underscores a major difference between relative and Absolute consciousness. In the former, such activities are externally and intellectually orientated: mind and body contend with the phenomena of

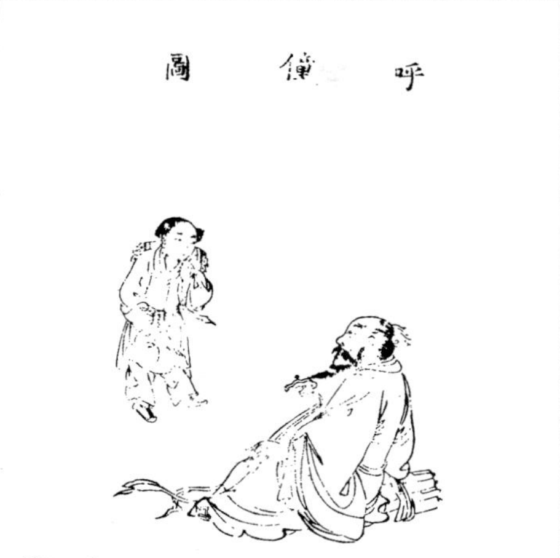

Fig. 1

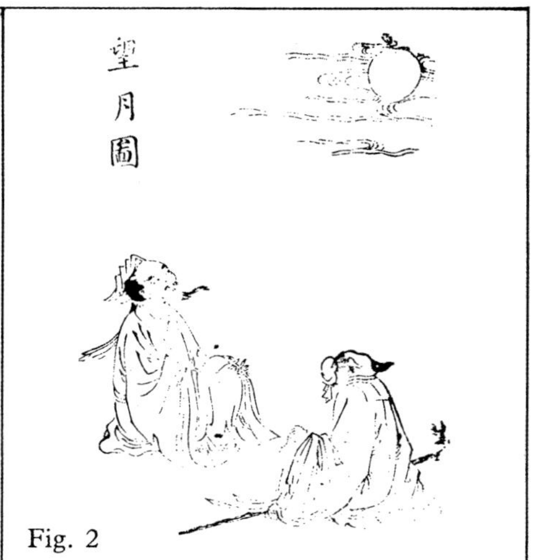

Fig. 2

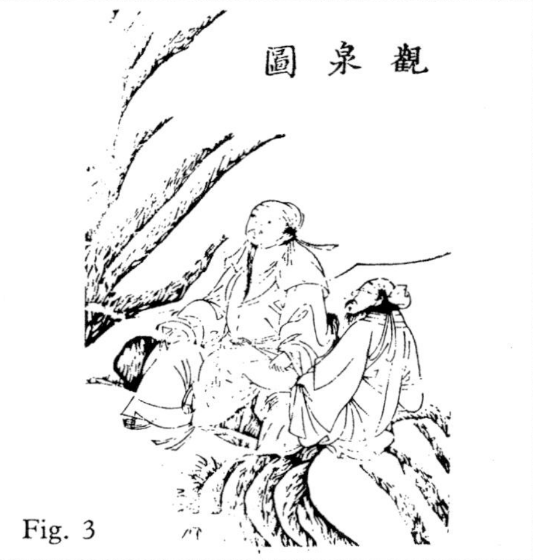

Fig. 3

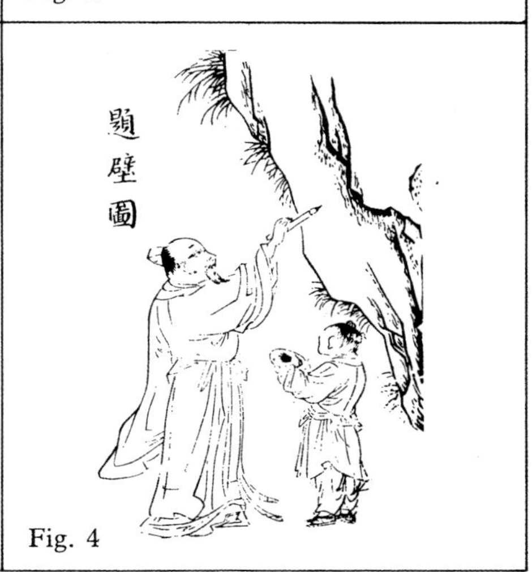

Fig. 4

the external, objective world. The sphere of activities in the latter are nowhere more charmingly demonstrated than in the *Sancai tuhui*, an encyclopaedia of 1607, where in a section on what people do, the leisure activities of the persuasive minority are illustrated.

A series of delightful woodblock illustrations cover such activities as: 'Discussing metaphysics', in which two scholars sit deep in conversation; 'Calling one's attendant' (fig. 1), in which an old scholar leans on a book in the form of a number of scrolls: he holds a *ruyi* sceptre while he summons his servant to bring him a further volume of scrolls and a handwarmer (here the activity is not calling for the servant as such, but having him at hand with fresh books, together with all the other equipment necessary for the scholar to continue his meditational reading and pondering).

In 'Gazing at the Moon' (fig. 2), we see two old scholars enjoying the moon emerging from clouds and sharing the experience silently. Later, they might write a poem inspired by it, or discuss its meaning, but in the illustration they are silently engrossed in the direct experience. 'Watching the waterfall' (fig. 3) depicts two sages enjoying the same sort of experience but with a waterfall. 'Writing on a rock face' (fig. 4) shows a sage about to inscribe an overhanging cliff, while an attendant at his side holds an inkstone with freshly ground ink. This form of elegant grafitti considerably enhanced the Chinese countryside whose endless succession of rocks and cliff faces have been inscribed in beautifully written calligraphy with poetic thoughts, place names, or lofty philosophical musings. Most that have survived were carved into the rock based upon an original calligraphic outline, but doubtless thousands of impetuous inscriptions have, over the centuries, added a poignant record of experience to many a quiet corner of the landscape before fading away like mist.

'Carrying the *qin*' (fig. 5) shows a scholar strolling while his attendant follows, carrying the instrument, its angled disposition a significant part of the art of carrying a *qin*, and therefore of the scholar's life. 'Passing the wine-cup' (fig. 6) depicts two seated scholars, one of whom offers the other a wine-cup on a cup stand. Alcohol consumption in China was never so disdained as in cultures governed by relative consciousness. The intellect is befuddled by alcohol, temporarily losing control, which it finds alarming and dangerous; thus, the more intellectually oriented a culture, the more it is likely to disapprove of drinking. Anyone who gets drunk at a party on a couple of occasions is suspected of having a drinking problem. In a culture governed by Absolute consciousness, confusing the intellect was a means of transcending it (whether one befuddled it with alcohol, art or logic). Wine was used for this purpose by poets, musicians, painters, calligraphers and philosophers alike in search of those regions where inspiration flies freely, for the intellect has a remarkable capacity for inhibiting inspiration.

In the Chinese tradition, the attitude is amusingly illustrated by the most beloved of all Chinese poets, Su Shi, who had a drinking problem as seen through Chinese eyes: he was unable to drink without falling asleep. He wrote, "There is no-one in the world with less capacity for wine than myself. But I like to see people drink. When I see my friends lift the cup and slowly sip the liquor, I feel uplifted in my spirit, and my joy is greater than even that of my friends. I never pass a day without visitors, and never have visitors without wine. Consequently there is also no greater lover of drink in the world than myself."[30]

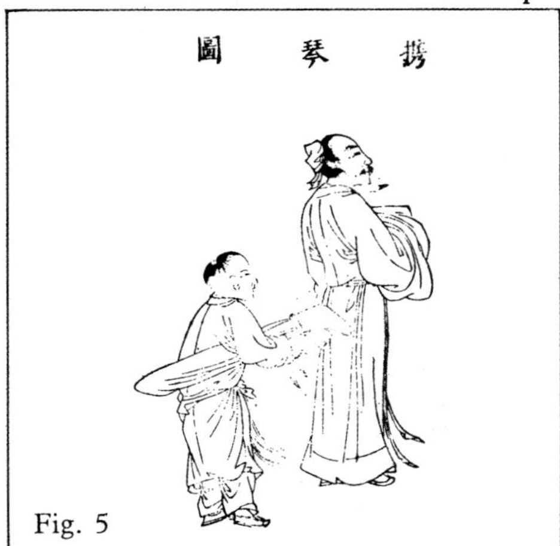

Fig. 5

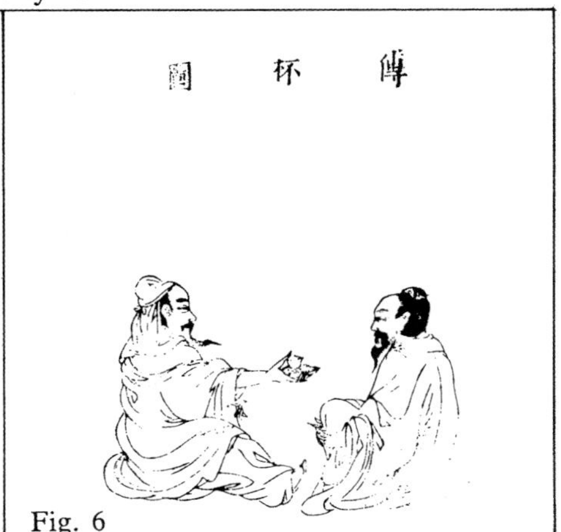

Fig. 6

A related subject is found in 'Reciting while drunk' (fig. 7), although the word 'drunk' is somewhat misleading because of its pejorative overtones in the English

30. Lin Yutang translation, in *The Importance of Understanding*, p.201.

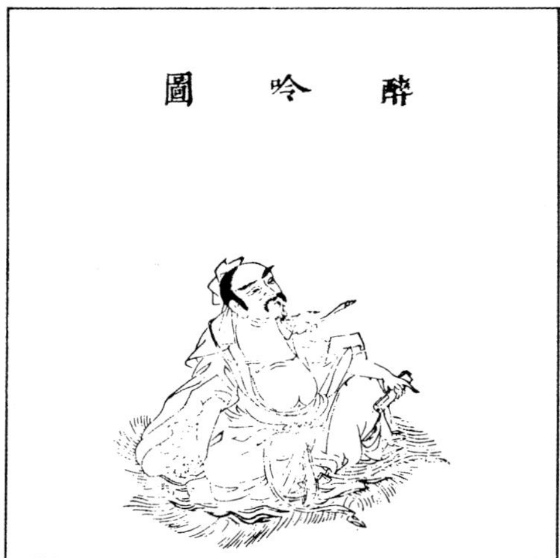

Fig. 7

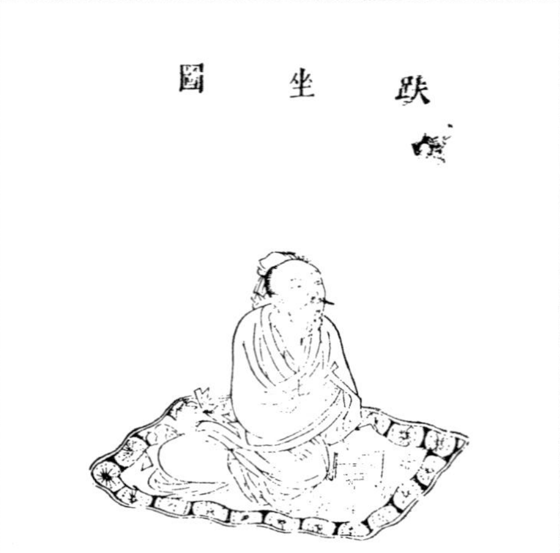

Fig. 8

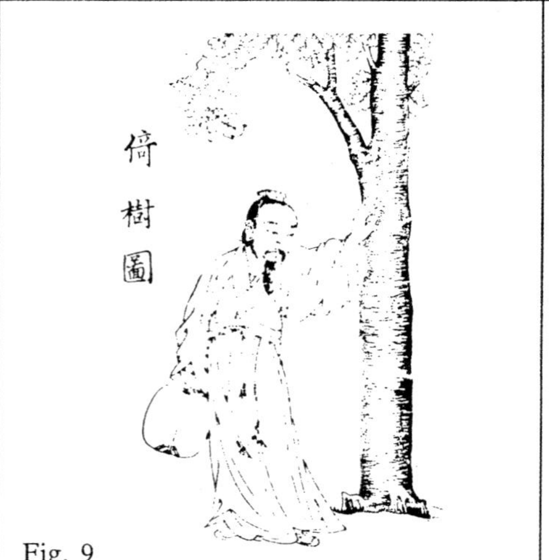

Fig. 9

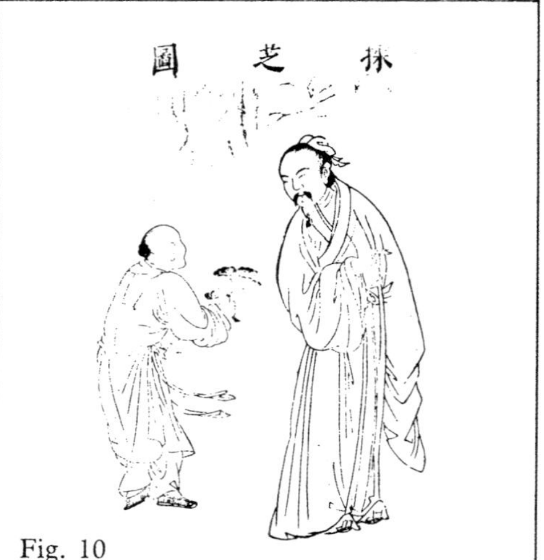

Fig. 10

language. Here, a lone uninhibited scholar sits on a grass mat, holding a single scroll in one hand while he recites poetry aloud. Similarly, 'Getting tipsy' shows a gesticulating scholar being served by his attendant; and 'Drunk' depicts a well-inebriated old man helped to his feet by a servant, his delightful smile showing how successfully he has cut the bonds of inhibition.

Another charming pastime is simply called 'Sitting' (fig. 8), in which an old scholar sits on a mat. The activity is, of course, not simply sitting, for such quiet repose can lead, as do all these pastimes, to the selfless self, hidden like a jewel beneath the shallow surface of the intellect. In the same vein, but perhaps the most delightful (because to the reasoning mind it is so apparently useless as an activity), is 'Leaning against a tree' (fig. 9). Another is 'Picking *lingzhi* (fungus)' (fig. 10) — an almost alarmingly practical pursuit in relation to the other activities. Apart from the pleasant stroll through the countryside depicted here, the image of collecting fungi has another purpose: for these were used to make medicines, and supposed elixirs of longevity or consciousness-expanding drugs. The Chinese were fond of such potions because of their startling ability to alter one's state of consciousness. In popular use they became confused with immortality in the literal sense of living forever. There are, of course, more normal activities like writing poetry, playing the *qin*, writing calligraphy on leaves, etc., but the general trend could not be clearer: they are all directly aimed at self-realization and are inwardly rather than externally orientated.

The difference is perhaps summed up by the attitude to mountain climbing in the Chinese culture. Mallory's famous answer to why he felt he had to climb Mount Everest ("Because it is there") typifies the external approach governed by relative consciousness.[31] The direct goal is the literal conquest of the mountain. In China, mountain climbing for conquest has never been of any interest. The Chinese climb *in* the mountains; they do so to experience nature and to gain a new perspective on it. It is a meditative pursuit. The conquest is not of the mountain but of the self.

Because of the Chinese capacity for seeing every aspect of life as an art form, all of the accoutrements in the pursuit of this aesthetic dimension become knowingly multi-functional. A malachite brush rest in the form of a mountain might equally serve as a paper weight; it was also a miniature mountain capable of conjuring up visions of the grandeur of nature and transporting the scholar in his studio to the mysterious Kunlun mountains, there to join the immortals; it was also a work of art, set on a stand and meaningful in its form, colour and texture. With the casual precision of the truly syncretic mind, it made a statement of the owner's taste and style through its placement and use in his studio. It also provided Daoist symbolism in material and form. Finally, it moved beyond all such explainable functions to join with the consciousness of the scholar in the swirling incense smoke of transcendence where consciousness, the Absolute, and all phenomena including the work of art become one.

Realization of the Absolute enlivens these works of art for those who make and enjoy them, enhancing their powers of communication. The personality of such works is summed up by Chang Chao (died after 1698) in a volume of reflections entitled 'Quiet Dream Shadows': "When a good mirror meets an ugly owner, a good inkstone meets a vulgar person, and a good sword finds itself in the hands of a common general, there is nothing these things can do about it."[32] The delight the persuasive minority took in their arts and their leisure, in pursuit of the all-encompassing art of life, may be seen in the many genre paintings existing from the Han dynasty onwards. We have prepared a number of drawings taken from these to illustrate the usage, at a more mundane level, of works of art and other accoutrements. Some have been interspersed in the captions where they seem appropriate to the works described, others are used decoratively in the text. Those that appear in the text are explained in captions below.

31. Actually, it is thought that Mallory's reply came in exasperation at being asked the same question over and again. It is a significant answer nonetheless.
32. Quoted from *Yumengying* ('Quiet Dream Shadows') in *The Importance of Understanding*, by Lin Yutang, p.70. One might add "...or an act of creative communication meets an uncomprehending audience."

Captions to Text Illustrations

Fig. 1, is taken from a Ming painting by Wang Wen entitled 'Boiling tea'. Two scholars are shown sitting on a rug and an animal skin, with an attendant, surrounded by various objects. One prepares tea on a brazier, a large vat of water behind him with a ladle resting in it; while his friend is considering, with the help of the attendant, a piece of calligraphy he is in the middle of writing. Behind him are two large covered jars, which might contain a number of things, a volume of books, a rolled scroll, a brush pot with two brushes, a small shallow dish, probably a water vessel for painting, and a covered tripod vessel, probably an incense burner. In front of these sits an inkstone with ink prepared on it, and a volume of books in the form of a set of handscrolls tied in a brocade binder — an early form of book in China common between the invention of paper and the first use of woodblock printing.

Fig. 2, from an anonymous Song painting shows a scholar at ease, picking his ear, seated at a marble-topped table piled high with books and scrolls, a piece of finished calligraphy in front of him. On the table are set an inkcake, an inkstone, and a brush resting in a *ruyi*-shaped three-point brush rest; while behind him on another two tables are a variety of books, instruments including a *qin* and a *yuan* (another literati instruments), another volume of books in scroll form, a pouring vessel, and a bronze incense burner and other vessels. It is interesting to note that what would independently be viewed as a typical bronze tripod incense burner of *li* form is here used to hold fruit — a clear lesson of genre paintings is that many of the scholar's accoutrements were multi-functional. In the foreground a servant brings his master a cup of tea, the cup set in a typical cup stand of the shape popular from the Tang to the early Ming dynasty.

Fig. 3, taken from a painting by the Ming artist Tang Yin shows a scholar playing the *qin* while his attendant stands silently behind him. It has been said that the *qin* is unplayable nestling in the lap, a position in which it is frequently seen in genre paintings. It may be awkward to play in certain positions in the lap but the traditional method was in fact to play it seated cross-legged, with the instrument resting at an angle between the lap and the ground. However it was also frequently used as a symbol of the elegant gentleman by people who could not even play it, so it is possible for it to be in a completely unplayable position without losing meaning. The concept of the ultimate form of music being silent was already established at the time of Confucius. Here the scholar is surrounded by various vessels for wine and other requirements; an incense burner, powder box and set of incense tools in a vase are in front of him, as are a wine cup and wine pot, and behind him is an archaic or archaistic *gu* beaker, in which is a *ruyi* sceptre. Beside it are two volumes of books, one in scroll form, the other in the later form of a series of books in a brocaded cardboard case.

Fig. 4, is after an anonymous Song portrait of the famous calligrapher Wang Xizhi. He sits on a low couch, in front of a large painting screen, from which hangs a portrait of him, surrounded by tables laden with the trappings of a pleasant day. There is a *qin* laid across a *weiqi* board (a strategic board-game of great subtlety often misleadingly called chess); various books; a number of containers of different kinds, including what appears to be an elaborate brazier for boiling water for tea and a net covering protecting a cup on a cup stand. There is also a decorative vessel of flowers set on an elaborate rockwork stand.

Fig. 5, is taken from a painting by the late Ming artist Chen Hongshou entitled 'First lessons in art'. In a delightful setting, seated on a spectacular root chair and at an elaborately convoluted rock table, a scholar, his wrapped *gin* in front of him, is giving lessons to two ladies. One sits painting on a piece of paper which is held down by a strangely shaped paper weight, while the other sets flowers in a tall vase. On the table are cups, a wine vessel, volumes of books, an incense burner and a covered box, probably for the necessary incense trappings.

Fig. 6, illustrates the joys of collecting, by the 15th century artist Du Jin. In the section reproduced a scholar sits at a table laden with antiques, while a friend examines a covered bronze. The whole setting includes a garden terrace with a large screen, attendants and other trappings. These garden scenes of enjoying the delights of collecting are not uncommon and demonstrate the dedication with which such pursuits were approached in the art of life. All the furniture and all the pieces on display must be transported to the garden and represent the constant willingness of the influential minority to go to extraordinary lengths (albeit the actual work was done by servants) to enjoy the greatest possible aesthetic delights. Here the subject is not just looking at antiques, it is looking at antiques in an ideal setting — a quite different pastime which is itself a work of art.

Fig. 7, is from a painting by the Qing artist Leng Mei entitled 'Appreciating the moon'. This delight in the perfect setting, complemented by the perfect trappings in the art of life, is seen time and time again in Chinese art. Here a young scholar is seated on a wonderfully constructed root chair, flanked by attendants with liquid refreshments and a fan, while he gazes intently at the moon. In his hand is a *ruyi* sceptre, which one might think adds little to the pastime of gazing at the moon, but it is a touch of elegance, a gesture that completes the delight. The artist in the work of art of life is not just enjoying himself, he is communicating to all those around him through his lifestyle and the tiniest gesture, the smallest detail of dress or deportment. Seen in this light, the *ruyi* is as important a detail as the brushwork in a painting or the surface finish of a carving or piece of furniture.

Fig. 8, after a painting attributed to Lu Lengjia (active 8th century) in the form of six remaining album leaves out of 18, we see the eighth *luohan* seated on an elborate low dais, a tall stand beside him holding a vase of flowers, attendants to either side, one of whom holds a *hu* ceremonial mnemonic device. Bringing him tribute are two foreigners, one holding a convoluted rock formation, the other kneeling and presenting a dish in which a miniature landscape is constructed of what appears to be coral trees and various shaped stones. The aesthetic trappings appreciated by the scholar class were equally enjoyed by sages and monks.

Fig. 9, is after a painting entitled 'Inscribing the Fan' by the Qing artist Yu Zhiding. In it a scholar sits in a landscape setting by a river. On a stone table are a fan, a brush, a coral brush rest, a water vessel and a volume of books and two scrolls. He is about to inscribe the fan, but while he waits his servant washes his inkstone in the nearby stream.

Fig. 10, is after a Qing dynasty portrait of Hong Zhicun by Xu Ji. Again in a garden setting, he sits on a root chair beside a stand on which are a vase of flowers, an incense burner, cup of tea, and a volume of books. In front of him is a low stand and a group of miniature trees, gardens and plants in various vessels. Miniature gardens, both indoors and out, were valued by the persuasive minority as microcosms of nature, as were strangely shaped rocks.

Fig. 11, in this self portrait of Wang Yenshan of the late Qing dynasty, we see the old scholar in his study, books, precious archaic bronzes and two scrolls on shelves behind him, and on his desk more books and scrolls, a piece of paper held down by an animal paper weight, an inkstone, a *jue* (archaic bronze vessel) used as a water vessel, and another archaic bronze vessel used as a brush pot. Here again we see the multi-functional nature of so many of the scholar's objects. The *jue* might be used as an object of purely aesthetic appreciation, a drinking vessel (its original use), a water vessel, a flower vase, or for various other purposes. The bronze vessel, were it not shown here in use as a brush pot, would never be called one, and frequently brush pots are shown holding just about everything but brushes!

Fig. 12, is taken from an album of 16 paintings by Chen Hongshou entitled 'Living in seclusion' and shows a scholar washing his inkstones in a large, strangely shaped pan, a water ladle at his side. Such a large vessel would not normally be particularly associated with the scholar were it not shown in this context. Many is the genre painting which shows a scholar drinking from a vessel we would call a brush washer; using as a water vessel something we would normally assume was for another function; or using teapots as flower vases.

Fig. 13, after a painting by the 18th century Yangzhou Eccentric, Huang Shen, shows a young lady leaning pensively against a *qin*, holding a fan of the fixed-frame variety, in this case of a popular type made of diaphanous material.

Fig. 14, taken from a painting by the 18th century artist Leng Mei, shows an old scholar, seated composing himself in preparation for writing on a leaf. One attendant grinds his ink, while another is enjoying the fragrance of the peony plant from which the leaves have apparently been picked. He sits on an elaborate root couch, a folio of books at his side, from which one has been taken and is open in front of him, perhaps at a passage he will write on the leaf (if the main object of the exercise is calligraphy) or as inspiration for a poem (if it is poetry). A small water-vessel with a ladle, and a group of leaves, already inscribed, are tied in a bundle on the artist's table.

中國藝術的絕對境界

引言

現代科技的進步，已踏入第五代電腦的試驗階段，但人類神經系統的龐大訊息處理能力，至今只有百份之十被利用。雖然電腦的操作速度，是遠遠超越了人類，但對人類智慧的模擬，電腦科技仍然是處於幼稚的階段。

中國人很早就了解到人類對自己智能運用的局限性，語言就是腦子理性運用的產物，無論一種語言是何等先進，它都是局限於人爲的邏輯和有限的經驗。所有的語言文字，都是以比喻的方式去說明某些事物或意念，而不是事物或意念的本身眞像。即如老子在道德經裡就說所有用語言可以表達的「道」，都不是「常道」，所有可以命名的名字，都不是事物本身的「常名」，天地初開的時候是無名的，但是爲了解說的方便，我們就將天下萬物冠以名字。設另一個譬喻來說，人類可以聽音樂，直接受到音樂的感染而引起共鳴，但無論樂譜是傳寫得如何準確，樂譜仍是無聲的，並不等於音樂。

人類都有一個要尋求眞理、尋求生存意義、尋求了解宇宙秘奧的意向。對於那不能用理智充份了解和不能用人造語言所能表達的「眞理」，人們稱之爲「道」、爲「一」、爲「太極」、爲「神」……。但囿於理智的局限性和人類語言的比喻性，以及用有限的經歷去解釋無限的眞像，在人的心目中，神必然是會創奇蹟的超人；在鯉魚心目中，神必然是跳過龍門後的化身龍；在小鳥心目中，神必然是一飛沖天的大鵬。這都是井底之蛙所見的圓圓的小天窗，夏蟲所傳述的冬天冰雪的景象。

中國人雖然一向都是「道」「器」並重的，對形而上的「道」的追求，和形而下的「器」的研究，並無偏廢。但中國人一向並不以爲單靠理智的科技研究，便是人類幸福生活的保證。有時在外族侵凌統治下，更是遺「器」而重「道」；一群少數而又具影響力的人士，更由「師造化」轉到「不求形似」、「聊寫胸中逸氣」的純主觀的絕對境界。這種態度，對中國藝術的表現，有重大的影響。

藝術的功用

藝術的最重要功用，是拓展人類感覺的領域。中國人對藝術的看法，是全面的；中國人的藝術，是包羅了生活的每一個小節的。即如中國人看天地萬物，一花一葉都包含着一個世界，一草一木都流露着一份感情。莊子就在「齊物論」裡說：「天地與我並生，而萬物與我爲一。」要了解天地的秘奧，中國人採取一種溶和的態度而不是一種與天抗衡的對立的。所有偉大的藝術，都觸及人與天地宇宙的關係。從音樂的舉例，可知道樂譜語言是理智的、客觀的紀錄，不能代替樂曲的主觀感受和直接體驗。在人與「道」的體驗來說，同樣地是人爲語言所不能充份表達的。但無論如何，許多過往的賢人志士，他們都以過來人的身份，盡量利用語言來形容他們的經驗，希望藉此比喻的橋樑，助人邁向這個境界，了解人生的眞理。唐代大文學家柳宗元，在「始得西山宴游記」裡，記述登臨西山之絕頂，四望山下風景與天際白雲，覺得「悠悠乎與顥氣俱而莫得其涯，洋洋乎與造物者遊而不知其所窮。引觴滿酌，頹然就醉，不知日之入。蒼然暮色，自遠而至，至無所見而猶不欲歸。心凝形釋，與萬化冥合。」這是柳宗元於唐元和四年（公元809）九月，偶然登上西山，在酒醉之下，擺脫了理智的束縛，在高山絕頂，目覩日落的景像，突然像得到了啓示，覺得放下了心中的疑慮，心像找到了歸屬，擺脫了形體的枷鎖，溶和在大自然之中，與「萬化冥合」，這是親身體驗絕對境界的歷程，其感覺是不能用筆墨來形容的。但這種體驗，是令人心弦震動的，在那一刹那之間，人像與宇宙有直接交通，像億萬的訊息以一刹那之速度直接貫輸到心中，在電光石火之際，人就像踏出了時間的空間，踏入了一刹那的永恒。感覺的領域，得到無限的拓展。

這種絕對的境界，有人是偶然而得之，有人是刻意地依一特定的步驟去尋求。有人會苦修、念經、坐禪，有人會彈琴、燒香，有人會長跑、攀山，有人會作畫、練字，都是將理智思想集中於一點，做一些單調重覆的動作，進一步進入無思想、無概念、超脫理智控制的絕對境界。

明末清初的文學家張岱，他的所學甚雜，故此爲文，「奇情壯采，議論風生，筆墨横恣，幾令讀者心目俱眩」，這是清人對他所作「陶庵夢憶」的讚譽。張岱却替自己寫了一篇墓誌銘，說自己是：「紈袴子弟，極愛繁華。好精舍、好美婢、好孌童、好鮮衣、好美食、好駿馬、好華燈、好烟火、好梨園、好鼓吹、好古董、好花鳥；兼以茶淫桔虐，書蠹詩魔……。學書不成、學劍不成、學節義不成、學文章不成、學仙、學佛、學農、學圃俱不成。任世人呼爲敗子、爲廢物、爲頑民、爲鈍秀才、爲渴睡想、爲死老魅也已矣！」張岱生於官宦之家，深受明末晏安酖毒，驕奢淫佚的社會風氣所影響，過的是中國士人的浪漫生活的極端。但他晚年處於清代康熙年間，「國破家亡，無所歸止，披髮入山，駴駴爲野人。……因想余生平，繁華靡麗，過眼皆空，五十年來總成一夢……遥思往事，憶即書之，持向佛前，一一懺悔……。」在張岱晚年懺悔之間，他又曾經親歷一些怎樣的啓示呢？他的「披髮入山」，是否有助他看破世情呢？他所好、所學、幾乎包羅了中國人所有演藝術，這是否有助他拓展他的感覺領域，而終於使他達到最終的醒悟呢？

新藝術論

了解到理智的局限，如要拓展人類的感覺，領會藝術的絶對境界，便一定要超脱理智的限制，以下的一套藝術理論，是作者認爲可以幫助讀者以另一層面去了解中國藝術的特性的：

(一)如果離開了感覺領域的拓展，藝術便不能全面地領會。

(二)感覺領域的拓展，是人類的最重要使命，其他的一切努力，都是以此使命爲依歸。

(三)這個使命的最終目的，是將人類感覺帶到與宇宙合一的絶對境界。

(四)這種醒悟的絶對和諧境界，是理智控制的客觀相對境界所不能包含達致的。

(五)如要達到絶對和諧境界，便一定要超越理智，拋棄邏輯、科學分析和理解方法的局限。

(六)所有的創作潮流，都源於少數具影響力的人，他們揭開絶對境界的本來面目，試圖在我們理智可了解的範圍内，用不同的比喻語言和方法，去闡述他們的絶對體驗。

(七)這些比喻的語言，不論是用於宗教、科學、哲學、藝術或其他的創作活動，都是建基於相對的境界，以追求絶對的意義的。

(八)雖然任何人都可以直接體會到絶對的境界，但這種體驗，只能以設比喻的語言來形容。無論是那一種學術，最高的層次，最終的了解，永遠是主觀的。這種特點，使師徒式的傳授，成爲最有效的溝通方法。這種師徒的關係，維繫着一種信念，藉此以達到絶對境界的親身體驗。所以，中國人對求學問的態度，是重人多於重術的，所謂「學莫便乎近其人」，就是這個意思。

本書編排

有許多展覽，都是以某類器物、某窰、某代爲主題，但對這些器物所發生關係的人，却沒有充份的探討。加以西方人習慣以理性分析器物的表面狀況，對意境和思想等等研究，每多忽畧。故此，這個展覽是以藝術境界的探討爲主，展品是利用來延續不同角度的討論，而不是以器物歸類才加以說明。但喜歡傳統分類的讀者，還是可以用書後的索引來重組閱讀的次序的。

The Catalogue

1

'Red Bird' Qin

Lu Gongjin

Lacquer on wood; a Ziqi style *qin* lacquered in dark, blackish-brown colour, with seven tuning pegs of buffalo horn, two wood feet, and inlaid mother-of-pearl studs; the back with a rounded 'dragon's pond' and a rounded rectangular 'phoenix-pool'; the surface well worn and patinated with large 'snake-belly' crackle on the upper surface and small 'snake-belly' crackle on the back. Inscribed above the 'dragon's pond' with the title *Zhuque* ('Red bird') in official script, followed by 'Made by Lu Gongjin of Baixia (Nanjing) in mid-spring of the third year of the Zhizheng period (1343)' in regular script.
Nanjing, 1343.
Length: 120 cm. Width: 21.5 cm. (For the anatomy of a *qin* see no. 151.)

With various additional inscriptions and seals: Inside the *qin*, partly visible through the 'dragons's pond': one illegible line of inscription; one stating that the instrument was ordered to be repaired in Zhejiang province in 1523 (the name of the repairer is illegible, but we know it to be a Mr. Wu — see below); the other that it was "opened and repaired at West Lake (Hangzhou), Goushan district, in the spring of the *jiawu* year (1924) by Xu Yuanbai (a famous player and *qin* maker whose son still lives in Hangzhou)".
In the centre of the back, in cursive script: "This *qin* was made in the *guiwei* year of the Shundi Emperor of the Yuan dynasty. During the reign of the Emperor Shizong, of Ming (Jiajing period), Mr. Wu from Zhejiang province opened it and repaired it. Five hundred and thirty-one years have passed (since it was made) and although its tail has been broken, the sound-holes and other parts are in good condition. I acquired it in the autumn of the *renshen* year of the Tongzhi period (1872) at Daliang (in Guangdong province). I have myself restored it. This *qin,* with fine crackle and dark colour, with its comfortable and ancient tone, is very precious. Inscribed by Zhang Mengze of Lanling (Jiangsu province)."
To the right side of the 'dragon's pond': "This *qin* from the Zhizheng period until the present *guiwei* year (1943) is exactly six hundred years old. It was in the collection of my late grandfather, Kezhai (Wu Dazheng 1835-1902 — famous collector, calligrapher and painter). It experienced several difficult periods, but luckily escaped intact. In the spring of the *wuyin* year (1938) I took it from (my home at) Suzhou, and my happiness is boundless, so I record this in my studio (in Shanghai) 'The Pavilion of Luck and Knowledge' *(Shuangxiu Ge)*" followed by two seals in positive seal script *Wu Hufan* and *Wu Pan Jingshu.* A further large seal above the 'dragon's pond' reads *Wu Hufan, Pan Jingshu chenzang yin* ('From the precious collection of Wu Hufan and Pan Jingshu'). Wu Hufan (1894-1970) was a leading collector, connoisseur and painter; Pan Jingshu was his wife.
A further seal above the 'phoenix-pool' reads *Si Ou Tang yin* (a name based on four albums of rubbings of calligraphy by the Tang calligrapher Ouyang Xun), in negative seal script, the hall name of Wu Hufan.

子期式朱雀琴·呂公瑾製
元至正三年(1343), 長120厘米, 寛21.5厘米

Of all our languages of creative communication music is the most universally accessible as a vehicle for transcending the intellect and reaching into the quiet reservoirs of the self. It is extraordinarily effective as a medium of communication regardless of intellectual capacity or training, and, most readily transcending the intellect, it is least easily inhibited or dominated by it.

In China music has been recognized by the influential minority as a direct vehicle of self-realization for thousands of years. According to De Woskin,[1] "In many traditions, the perception of music as a human artifact, operating in a social or social-ritual context, is eclipsed by the perception of it as a medium of communication between man and God, heaven, or nature. In this latter context, which arises in sources as diverse as Aristotle, Plato, Horace, the Hindu Puranas, Bharata, Saringadeva, Confucius, Mo Zi and Zhuang Zi, the gist of music's communicative power is seen as the primary means of bringing to man, in apprehensible form, the ideals, norms, or perfected processes of realms beyond him". In the same source[2] we are told that Confucius labelled as indispensable the singing of the *Odes,* knowledge of ritual music, and the discipline of the *qin* in the regimen of self-cultivation; and that Zhuang Zi considered music as providing a bridge from man's mind to nature, in a mystical rather than intelligible communication.[3] We may also be sure that these were no more than the earliest records of an evolution that was centuries older.

Of all musical instruments, the *qin* or *guqin* as it is sometimes called, was the pre-eminent instrument of the influential minority. It was, by the time of Confucius, equated with the refined mind and its search for self-realization and has remained so to the present day. A number of *qin* masters are mentioned in *Chuang Zi* and *Lie Zi*[4] all of whom are also recognized as Daoist masters. Even as early as this, musical mastery symbolized by the *qin* was synonymous with enlightenment.[5] The association between the *qin* and the influential minority was such that by the Six Dynasties period it had become an emblem of the sage or superior man, and by the Song dynasty possession of a *qin* had become widespread, even among those who could not play it.[6] This latter, symbolic enjoyment of the *qin* became a well-established practice. The late Ming scholar Wen Zhenheng in his book on connoisseurship suggested that "even though one cannot play it, a *qin* should be hung upon the wall".[7] This affectation was, in effect, a symbolic gesture directly related to the concept of soundless music.

The concept of music being in a perfect or ultimate state without sound is a natural one for a culture whose consciousness is governed by the Absolute realm, and was well established by the Han dynasty.[8] Experience of the Absolute has been the ultimate goal of creative communication in China since at least the Warring States period. Once achieved, the sage, in perfect harmony with all phenomena, needs no further vehicle (other than in communicating his understanding) and is capable of hearing music in all things, including silence.

The style (based on form) of *qin* here is known as 'Ziqi' after the famous legend of Bo Ya and Zhong Ziqi, traditionally placed in the 6th century BC.

"When Bo Ya played the *qin* and Zhong Ziqi listened, Ziqi's thoughts were transported to towering mountains. He exclaimed to Bo Ya, 'How marvellous, with majesty akin to Mount Tai!' But in a moment his thoughts were carried to flowing waterways. 'How marvellous,' he said, 'bubbling and flowing like our mightiest rivers.' Ziqi died, and thereupon Bo Ya smashed his *qin* and broke its strings. Never again did he play the *qin,* for he felt no one in the world was adequate to appreciate its voice."[9]

In playing the *qin,* even when as a highly trained musician (which many of the influential minority were not) notation is followed precisely, there is immense scope for personal nuance. No time is indicated, there is no set rhythm or length of pauses between sections; the musician will treat his playing as meditation, timing the music to his heartbeat, allowing for perhaps lengthy pauses as a positive part of the music, and finding infinite personal expression in potential variations of tonal qualities and timbre. "Within its simple pentatonic scale organization, the *qin* provides for a great variety in stopping, half-stopping, brushing, touching, and strumming techniques rendering infinite variability in attack and decay, harmonic content, vibrato, glissando, and other embellishments".[10] This provided a rich communicative feast for the connoisseur, while keeping the structural framework simple — a necessary requirement of elegance in the arts of the persuasive minority generally.

Opposed to the orthodox tradition of *qin* playing arose another, the natural culmination of which was the symbolic *qin* hanging on the wall of a scholar who could not play it well, or sometimes at all. Thus, the scholars, sages and monks familiar with the Absolute realm could laugh in the face of convention, 'tune' their *qin* to the wind, and humming or whistling along create a direct, intuitive and wholly personal channel of comunication to the Absolute, which depended less and less on the orthodox rules of *qin* playing. Controversy between the two approaches raged for centuries, although with the demise of the traditional lifestyle of the literati, the present century has seen the temporary dominance of the orthodox school of thought.

1. 'Early Chinese Music and the Origins of Aesthetic Terminology', by Kenneth De Woskin, in *Theories of the Arts in China,* p.188.
2. Ibid. p.189.
3. Ibid. p.191.
4. Daoist compilations of uncertain date, the first after the Daoist master of the late 4th and early 3rd century BC Zhuang Zhou (Zhuang Zi), and the second perhaps of the 3rd or 4th century AD, but sometimes held to be 3rd century BC.
5. De Woskin, op. cit. p.192.
6. Op. cit. p.192.
7. *Notes on Superfluous Objects,* by Wen Zhenheng, *juan* 7, section 48.
8. De Woskin, op. cit. p.293.
9. Ibid. p.196.
10. Ibid. p.205.

1

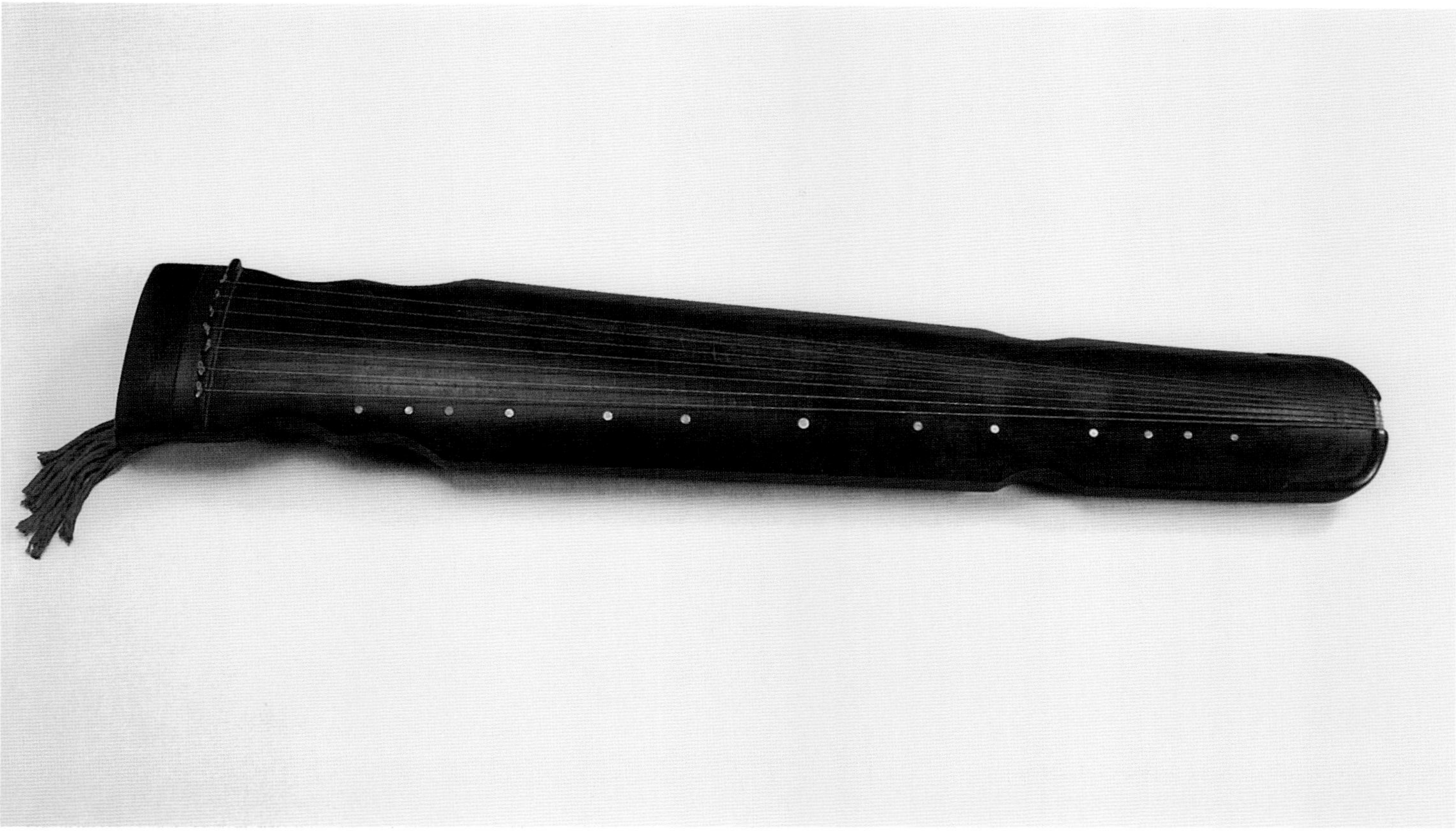

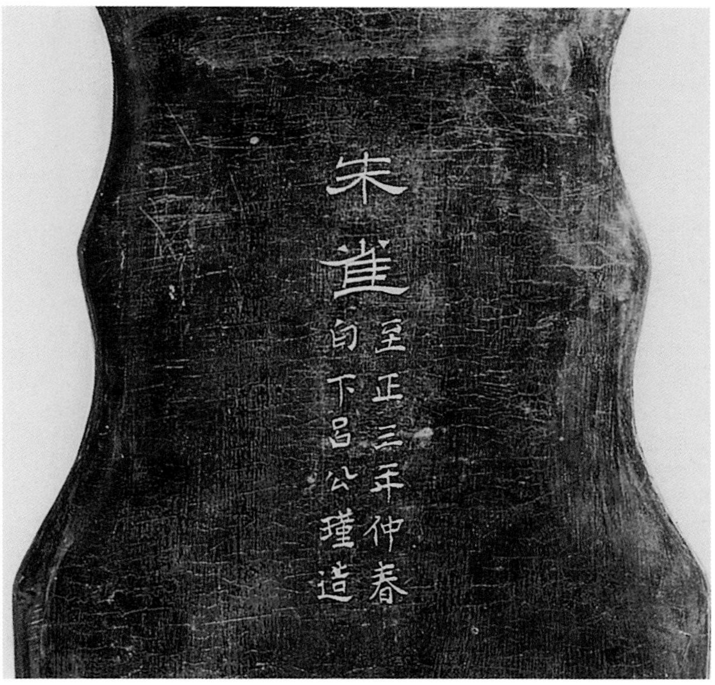

2

Flute

Zheng Zhishan

Bamboo, of golden brown colour; a *'qin* flute' (*qinxiao*), elegantly formed of a single length of bamboo, inscribed with a lengthy discussion on the history of the single pipe flute, tracing it back to the Tang dynasty, and concluding that although it is not an instrument of high antiquity, it is archaic and elegant enough; with a further inscription: "In the second month of the *gengxu* year of the Xuantong reign (1910), (this flute) was completed at the Governor's residence in Zhijiang (Hunan province) by the craftsman Zheng Zhishan of Yuping at the request of Shouyun."
Zhijiang, Hunan province, 1910.
Length: 65.2 cm. Diameter at lower end: 1.4 cm.

竹管刻銘琴簫•鄭芝山製
清宣統庚戌(1910), 長65.2厘米,
尾直徑1.4厘米

The single pipe flute (called *di* prior to the Tang dynasty, and *xiao* thereafter) was an instrument beloved of the literati. It was effortlessly transportable, simple, rustic and yet elegant, extremely expressive as a solo instrument capable of a range from the chirping trill of bird-song to the melancholic moan of the wind through the pines, and therefore capable of accompanying the *qin*, the other quintessential scholar's instrument. It also carried with it the implications of *qi*, the life-breath so important to many Oriental traditions of meditation and esoteric understanding. Ancient Shamanistic practice included blowing or humming into small tubes as a means of harmonizing mystical forces and divining, and such practices and beliefs were gradually subsumed into later beliefs.[1] A scholar seated in the mountains playing a flute would have been consciously setting out not just to entertain himself but, by harmonizing his breath and the sounds of the flute with his surroundings, to bring himself directly into harmony with nature.

This type of flute is known as a *qinxiao* because of its softer sound and resulting suitability for accompanying the *qin*, which is a relatively quiet instrument. The meditative connotations of music in the Chinese tradition are demonstrated by the approach of a modern Chinese master to the instrument: because it is very narrow and extremely difficult to play, he recommends a preparatory 20 minutes of meditation to prepare the breath and spirit. As the artist has long felt that he must grind his ink laboriously before commencing, so the flute player needs to prepare himself; to separate himself from the affairs of the mundane world.

It is worth mentioning here the art of whistling, since no exhibit seemed possible to demonstrate it. Needing no instrument, and unlike singing being free of any encumbering meaning in words, whistling was a perfect musical channel of communication to the Absolute. The lore of whistling is delightfully encapsulated in a story recounted by De Woskin:[2] "A popular story tells of Ruan Ji's visit to the sage Sun Deng in the Sumen Mountains. Ruan goes to interview the sage, but utterly fails to get his attention until he demonstrates his whistling technique, which was highly revered among his friends at home. Sun Deng responds to Ruan Ji's whistling with a laugh and requests an encore. With this done, Ruan starts down the mountain on his way home. He was halfway down the ridge when ... he heard above him a shrillness like an orchestra of many instruments, while forests and valleys re-echoed with the sound. Turning back to look, he discovered it was the whistling of the man he had just visited." De Woskin continues: "The whistling of the sage was the very breath of nature, according to the Tang author of the *Xiao zhi* ('Whistling Pointers'), who considered whistling a method of achieving immortality and communicating with the spirits.[3]

The maker of this instrument, Zheng Zhishan, was from Yuping in Guizhou province, a place famous for the production of flutes where flutemakers of great skill were centered, owing to the availability of suitable bamboo. The local tradition of flutemaking and the traditional family guarding of secret skills is demonstrated by the Han family of that area. Flutemakers for generations, they transmitted their skills exclusively within the family, allowing outsiders no access to their secret methods.

The preference for bamboo flutes over more exotic types is voiced by the late Ming scholar Tu Long (1542-1605). He mentions flutes of various shapes (such as a crane's leg, and a walking cane) and materials (copper, iron and jade) but goes on to say that none are as good as "purple bamboo consisting of nine segments, which when blown give a fantastic sound". The scholar class generally preferred rustic, natural materials to more precious equivalents.

1. See *Science and Civilization in China*, by Joseph Needham, Vol. IV:1, p.135 for a discussion on humming tubes.
2. Kenneth De Woskin, op. cit. in *Theories of the Arts in* China, p.209; the latter part of the quote taken from Mather, *New Account*, p.331.
3. Ibid. p.209, from Holzman, *Poetry and Politics*, pp.151-152.

3

Orchids

Yang Wencong

Ink on paper, hanging scroll; orchids growing from a rocky bank overhanging a stream or pool, with two flower heads floating on the surface of the water; signed in the upper left margin *Wencong*, with seal *Longyou shi* ('Mr. Dragon's friend') in positive seal script.
First half of the 17th century.
64 cm × 32 cm.

The painting with one collector's seal in the lower right corner reading *Miaojin Zhai zhencang yin* ('seal of the precious collection of the Studio of Flourishing Dignity').
Published: *Anthology of Chinese Art: Min Chiu Society Silver Jubilee Exhibition*, pp.166-167, no. 48.

墨蘭圖立軸•楊文驄作
明末十七世紀上半葉, 64×32厘米

Yang Wencong (*zi:* Longyou, Zishan; 1597-1646) was a native of Guizhou and a resident of Jinling (present-day Nanjing, Jiangsu province) who died a martyr to the Ming cause. He was a *zhuren* of 1619. His biography is outlined by Hummel[1] and hints at a life of considerable excitement. He filled various official posts under the ailing Ming dynasty, the most important of which were military. He fled south with the Court, and having convincingly demonstrated his unwillingness to change his allegiance to the Manchu cause by murdering the messenger sent to invite him, he continued to serve the Ming. Finally captured in Fujian, having failed to hold a defensive position in Hangzhou, he was executed after yet again refusing to renounce the Ming dynasty.

However, his lasting contribution lies more in his art than in his personal loyalty to the Ming, although of course the latter would have carried great weight in demonstrating his integrity to a cause highly respected by the Chinese, who had little love for invading 'barbarians'. Integrity is a very important quality in an artist (although it may be interpreted in many apparently contradictory ways). If we cannot believe in the integrity of our artists in expressing their understanding, they are of very little use to us.

Early in his career Yang Wencong was sent on official duties to Huating (Songjian, or Yunjian) in the central area of literati artistic activity in late Ming times. There he studied with Dong Qichang, the quintessential late Ming literatus, artist and theorist. By his early thirties Yang was already famous in the Yangzi valley for his painting, and was immortalized by Wu Weiye's poem 'The song of the nine friends of painting' where he was linked along with others to Dong Qichang, Wang Jian and Wang Shimin (see no. 5), and in Kong Shangren's dramatic masterpiece, *The Peach Blossom Fan*, where he figures prominently as the artist who painted the fan by converting bloodstains into peach blossoms. Before the onslaught of the Manchu invasion, Yang probably spent a convivial sort of life in common with his circle of literati.

In this painting the subject matter serves as a perfect analogy of Yang's plight as a Ming loyalist in the face of the Manchu invasion. The orchid, associated with the high principles of the gentleman since the poetry of Chu Yuan (4th-3rd century BC) here cut off from its nourishing plant, homeless and drifting, may be seen as the artist himself. If this was indeed intended, it would date the painting to the last years of Yang's life when it became clear that the Manchus had conquered large areas of China. The maturity of the brush work would accord with this theory.

The entire painting appears to be the work of a single moment of elan, a flowing, inspired energy permeating the picture as if the artist has hardly paused to take breath between starting and finishing the work. This continuous energy meant that dark ink was laid over still wet paler washes, creating some delightful effects where they blend together. However, for all its obvious immediacy of execution, it is a masterful work where not a single stroke is less than satisfying and where the abstract balance of light and dark ink, long pale wispy lines and short, dark, stabbing strokes, dry and wet brush work is maintained superbly.

1. *Eminent Chinese of the Ch'ing Period*, pp.895-896 — although he is said there to be a *jinshi* of 1601 and a *zhuren* of 1618, which would be unlikely since the *jinshi* is the higher degree.

2

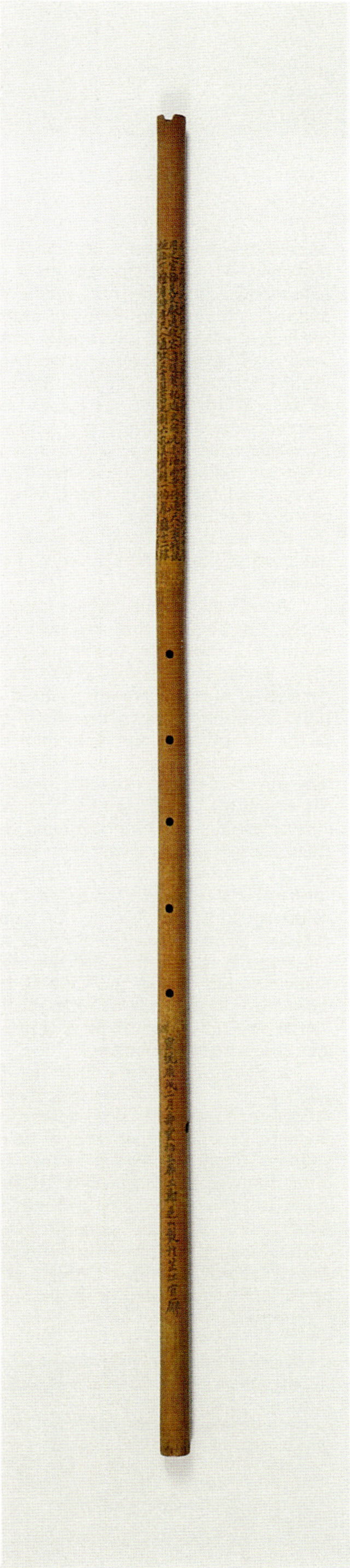

3

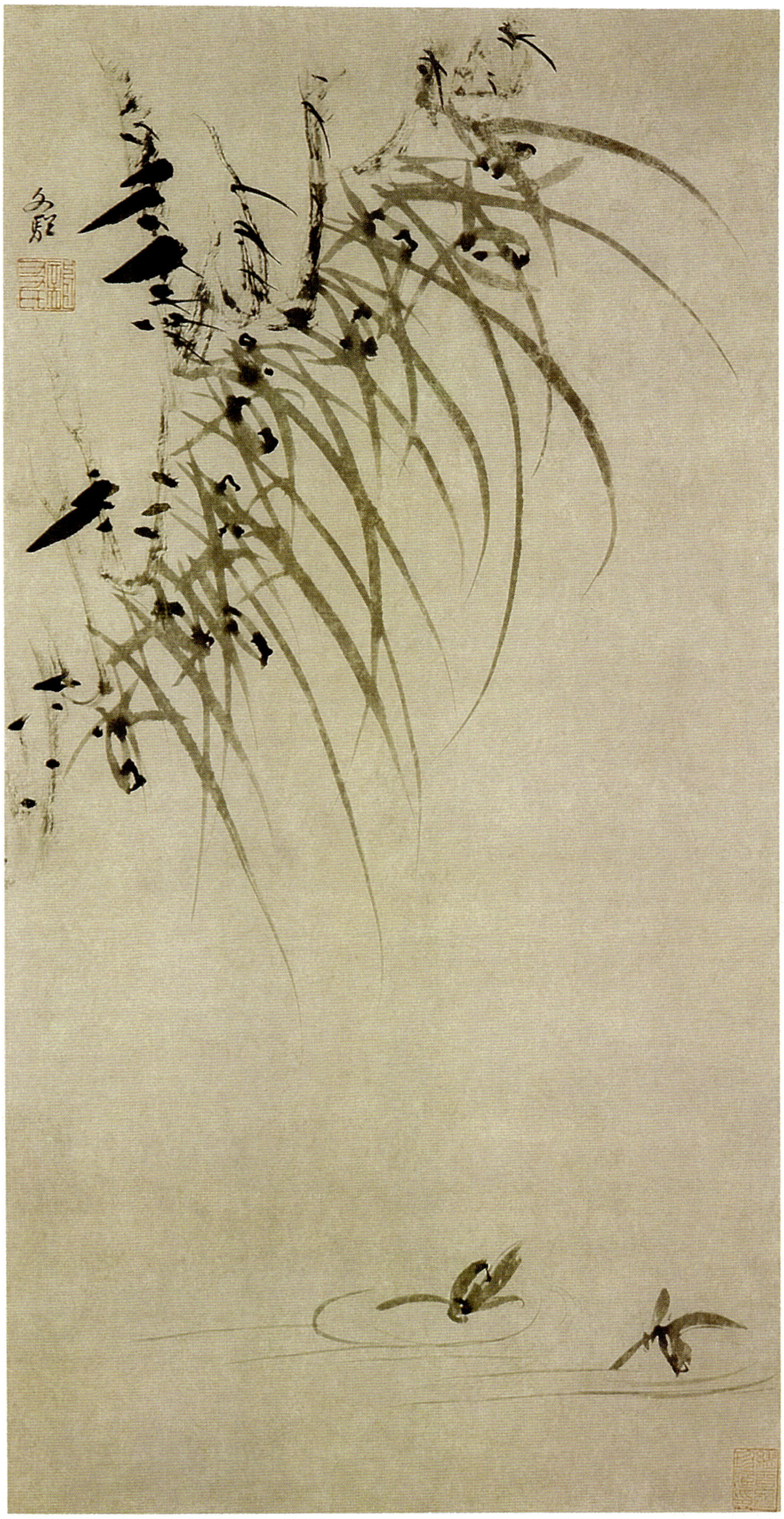

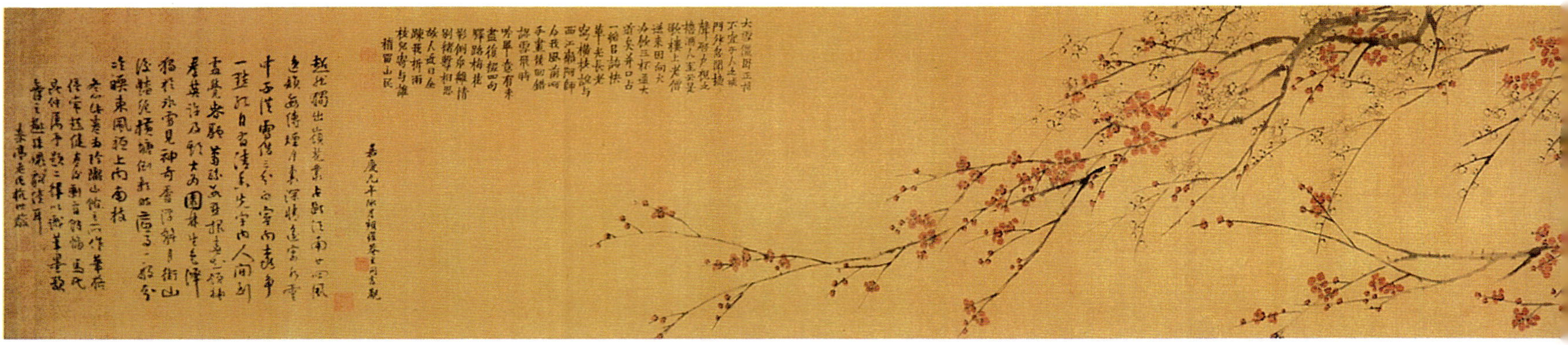

4

Prunus Blossom

Jin Nong

Ink and colour on silk, handscroll; two blossoming prunus trees, one with white blooms, the other with red, growing side by side, their branches harmoniously entwined; with an inscription concerning prunus blossom, signed by the artist, *Jiliu Shanmin,* with two seals *Jin Jijin yin* and *Dongxin xiansheng.*
Circa 1740-1764.
38.7 cm × 349 cm.

Followed by a short colophon on the original silk by Liang Tongshu of Hangzhou (1723-1815 — see no. 227) stating merely that he has inspected the painting, and dated to the first year of the Jiaqing period (1796); followed by his *hao, Shanzhou* impressed as a seal.
Three further seals follow: *Gong; Jun;* and one collector's seal of a Mr. Chen.
Another longer colophon also appears on the original silk, written by Hang Shijun, also of Hangzhou (1696-1773 — see *Eminent Chinese of the Ch'ing Period,* p.276) consisting of two poems, followed by a commentary stating that the painting was done for the Master of the (Xiao) Linglong Shanguan, mentioning that Jin Nong's brushwork is stronger than usual, and that the artist having left space at the end of the silk, the Ma brothers (owners of the Xiaolinglong Shanguan — see below) had asked him to write two poems to record the dance and song of brush and ink, adding a customarily self-effacing comment that he was ashamed to do so, fearing that he might be adding a dog's tail to a mink. It is signed *Qinting Laomin Hang Shijun,* followed by two of his seals *Jinpu* and *Hang Shijun yin* and two further seals, one unread, the other *Menglu xieguan* ('Inspected by Menglu').

The painting is preceded by a title panel, ink on paper, dated *Guangxu gengyin* (1890) reading: "A long scroll of red and white prunus blossom by Jin Shoumen (Jin Nong)", signed *"Written by Fan Zengxiang",* with seal *Fan Zengxiang zhang.*
38.6 cm × 87 cm.

Followed by three colophons written on a separate sheet of paper. The first a short one by Yuan Zhu, dated 1890, correcting a misquote in Jin Nong's original inscription; with the writer's seal *Chongli Fu.* The second, by the same writer in the same year, commenting on the painting and stating that it was done for Qiuyu (Ma Yueguan, one of the Ma brothers mentioned previously), and that the painting was then owned by Yunmen Taishi (*hao* of Fan Zengxiang, 1846-1931); with seal *Hu mo ping zhi* (meaning unclear). The third, dated 1891, by Li Ciming, also for Fan Zengxiang, bears four of Li's seals: *Yueman Laoren; Li Xibo; Hutanglinguan Shanmin,* and *Baihua Jianfu Ge qingke.*

紅白梅花卷·金農作
清代(約1740-1764),38.7×349厘米

The Ma brothers, Ma Yueguan (1686/8-1755/6?) and Ma Yuelu (1697-after 1766) built the Xiaolinglong Shanguan in which to entertain their literati friends. They were wealthy merchants involved in the salt trade who lived in Yangzhou, and were renowned for their lavish hospitality to scholars and artists of all kinds, for their poetry and for their elegant lifestyle. Many scholars were drawn to them and they were associated as patrons with many Yangzhou artists of note. No. 20 also bears their collectors' seal. Li Ciming (1829-1894) was a native of Zhejiang, a *jinshi* of 1880 and a poet, calligrapher and painter.

Jin Nong (1687-1764), a native of Hangzhou but a resident of Yangzhou, was a scholar particularly noted for his connoisseurship in the field of ancient bronzes and stone inscriptions (a field collectively known as *jinshi* — bronzes and stones). He was renowned for his distinctive calligraphy called 'lacquer script' which evolved from the inscriptions of lacquer craftsmen using a brush with its tip cut away. His style in painting epitomizes the sophisticated re-acquired naivety which is the artistic manifestation of the concept of the intellectual primitive (discussed on p. 17, and further explored in the caption to no. 32.) Like his calligraphy it is archaic and appears to be childishly awkward, but has immense hidden strength, cutting straight to the heart of his subject. His self portrait[1] is an excellent example of this style, where all the languages of painting are reduced to their bare essentials.

This handscroll is an example of a subject he especially favoured. Although on the surface it is prunus, with its symbolism of blossoming under the most extreme conditions, there are other layers of subject-matter which are revealing. Having selected the surface level of subject-matter, the artist is dealing with form, line, colour and texture and each is capable of becoming the main subject of the painting. In Chinese painting, for instance, line is frequently the main subject, particularly in the literati tradition, concentrated on by artist and audience alike as being the principle vehicle of expression. In this particular work abstract form is also a 'main' subject — as it is in so many works by major calligraphers — where colour, texture and line are all used to create a language of form which exists, at one level, entirely independent of the prunus they combine to depict.

As we move through the painting from right to left we are first introduced to a light, airy grouping of white blossoms, punctuated by dark, energized dots and connected by a growing and constantly fascinating network of lines. As the lines become more complex in their pattern, heavier ink tones are introduced to add weight, and the stabilizing element of the main trunk of the white blossoming tree is brought into play, giving the previously free-floating forms a solid foundation from which the eye may move through the painting. From the trunk, the branches begin to fan out in the direction in which the eye has been moving, leading it off again, back into the air, where it immediately encounters the first of the red blossoms. A second, stronger main trunk both consolidates the point from which one is now moving as a base and leads the urgent movement along the scroll, now emphasized by a series of jagged, pointing branches drawing the eye inexorably to the left. As the main trunk of the red blossoming tree comes into its own, assuming the role of guide, a canopy of red blossoms forces the eye downwards to it. The artist has now fully caught the attention of the viewer, and the painting becomes a balance of abstract elements made up of the blank space of the silk, the symphony of lines and the forms made up of them, and the red and white blossoms.

As the main trunk moves out of the picture at the top, disappearing into pale ink, our attention is caught by smaller, sharply moving lines, which carry us forward to the finale. This consists of a mixed grouping of red and white blossoming branches coming down from the top of the picture, with the main branch re-emerging, transformed. As white gradually give way to red blossoms (a balancing element for the beginning of the scroll where we first encountered only white blossoms) and a perfect final flourish points onwards to blank silk, Jin Nong's inscription takes over, the solid angular forms of his characters acting as a perfect counterpoint to the floating blossoms, his two red seals giving a final echo of the last blossoms. It is a perfectly orchestrated demonstration of how the Chinese artist quite consciously transcends his immediate subject-matter to deal in languages of pure abstraction and abstract expressionism.

It also shows quite clearly the enormous potential of the handscroll format, where the viewer is encouraged, almost forced, to become involved at a far deeper level as he takes part in adding a temporal element to the usual spacial dimensions of a painting. The handscroll comes closer to the arts of dance and music where the artist is able to dictate sequence in his communication, which ability was also to a large degree extended to other Chinese pictorial forms by the artistic rejection of single point perspective.[2]

1. Illustrated in *Paintings by Yangzhou Artists of the Qing Dynasty from the Palace Museum,* p.191, no. 57.
2. For a discussion of the handscroll format and the languages of art see *The Four Seasons Handscroll* by Hugh Moss, Supplement to *The Experience of Art: Twentieth Century Chinese Paintings from the Shuisongshi Shanfang Collection.*

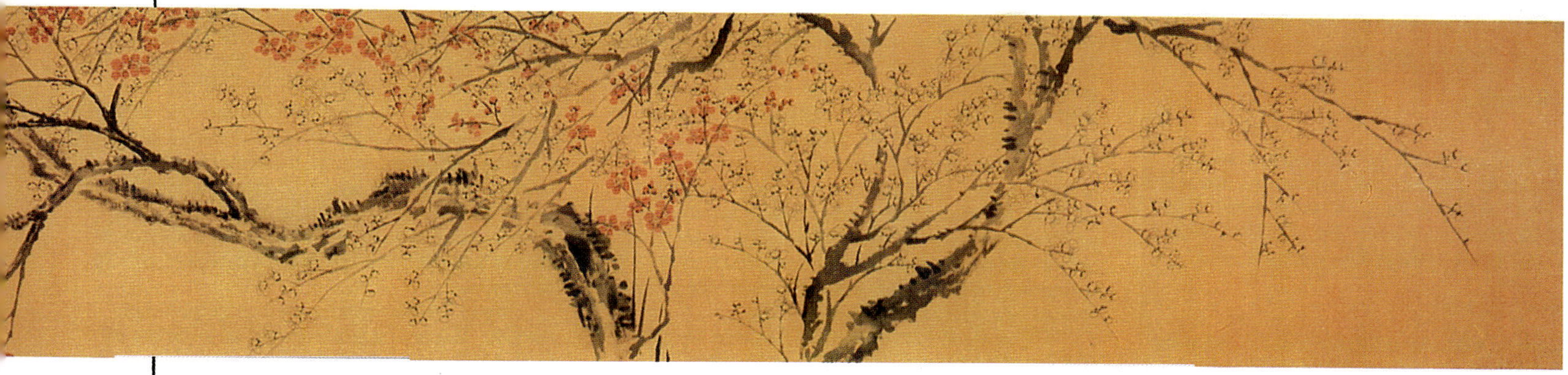

4

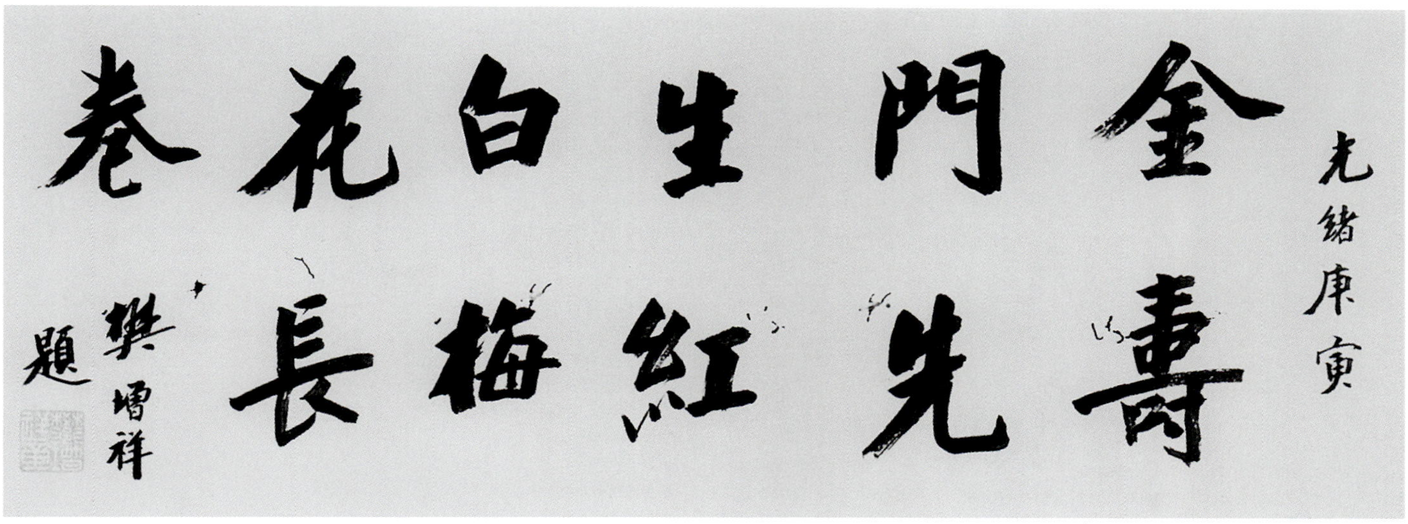

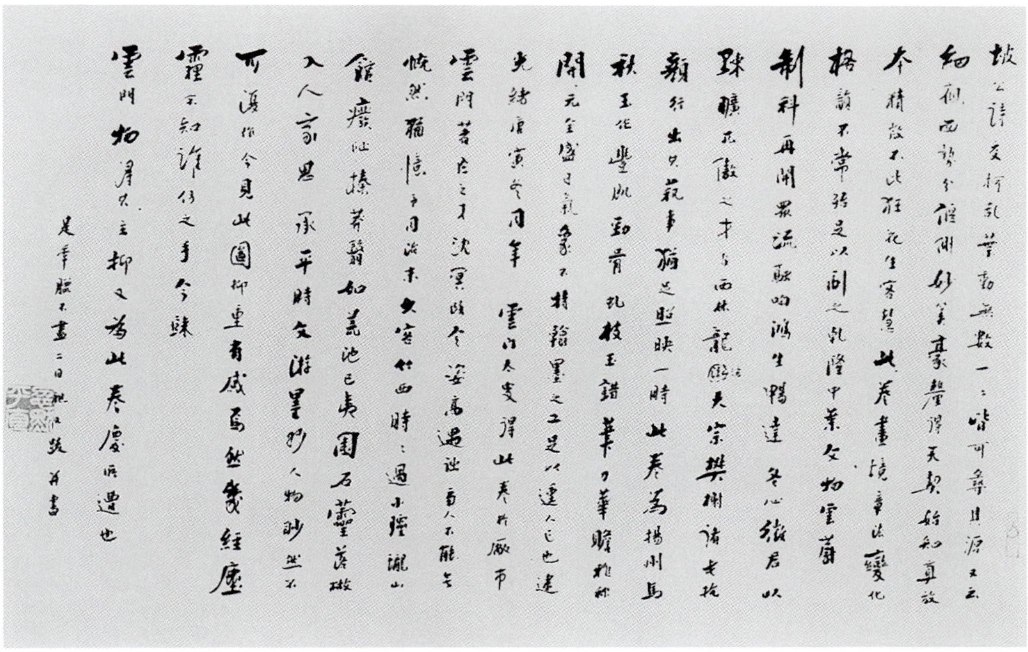

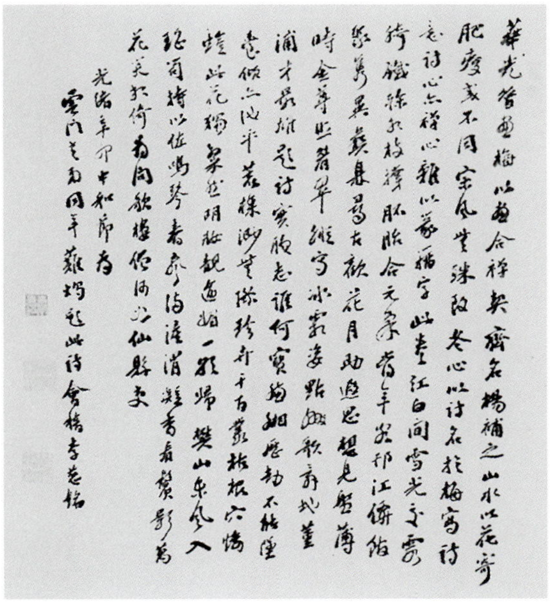

5

Autumn Colours in the Fuchun Mountains

Wang Shimin

Ink on paper, mounted as a hanging scroll; a rustic retreat in a mountain landscape; inscribed in the upper right corner: "A small work after the style of *Dachi,* a winter day of 1649, Wang Shimin" with one seal of the artist, *Yanke.*
Winter, 1649.
46.2 cm × 24.5 cm.

The painting with six collector's seals: *Shouhan Lu* (the studio name of an unidentified collector); *Dongting Zhang shi Yushi zhencang* ('Precious Collection of Mr. Zhang Yushi of Dongting' — an unidentified collector); *Ou Hanbo cang* ('Collection of Ou Hanbo') — also unidentified; *Dong Zhuang* (*hao* of Wang Yu, of Taicang, Jiangsu province, a well-known painter active in the first half of the 18th century who was a cousin and disciple of Wang Yuanqi, Wang Shimin's grandson, suggesting that the painting may have stayed in the family during its early history); *Wu Rongguang yin* ('Seal of Wu Rongguang', 1773-1843, prominent collector and scholar whose opinion on paintings and calligraphy was highly regarded — see *Eminent Chinese of the Ch'ing Period*, p.873); and *Sun Xinzhi* (an unidentified collector). The mount with one further collector's seal *Zhengxin Chengyi Zhai yin* (the studio name of Zhang Xiangning, a contemporary collector).
A colophon, ink on silk, mounted alongside the painting reads: "In 1649, when Yanke (Wang Shimin) was 58 years of age, during his most powerful middle years, he followed the style of Huang Gongwang. It is so ethereal and subtle that it already reaches the utmost state — an incomparable treasure of past and future. Authenticated by Wu Hufan in the third month of 1943" with two seals of the writer, *Wu Hufan* and *Chouyi cijing.*
The mount with an outer label written by Zhang Xiangning, dated 1958, with one seal of the writer.

富春秋色圖立軸•王時敏作
清順治六年(1649), 46.2×24.5厘米

Wang Shimin (*zi:* Xunzhi; *hao*: Nuozhai, Yanke, Xilu laoren, Xitian zhuren, Xitianyi Lao, Guicun Laonong, Ouxie Daoren, 1592-1680) a native of Taicang, Jiangsu province, came from a distinguished family of scholar-officials and himself served in various official capacities under the Ming. Declining to similarly serve under the Qing, he led (despite certain vicissitudes) a life of peaceful retirement, entertaining fellow scholars and artists, teaching and devoting himself to collecting, writing poetry, and painting. He was a quintessential literatus in that he was a scholar, an amateur painter who painted for self-realization and fulfilment rather than for material gain, a thinker and a theorist. He was also a follower of, and of considerable importance to, the line of development that Dong Qichang, under whom he studied, had laid down with such authority as being the mainstream of the literati movement in painting (see no. 16).

Because of his important position in this mainstream, as student of Dong Qichang, teacher and mentor of Wang Hui and grandfather of Wang Yuanqi, quite apart from his own considerable strength as an artist and theorist, references to him in Chinese sources are reasonably plentiful. Several of these are quoted by Siren[1] and a picture emerges of an exemplary scholar governed by a detachment from mundane matters, a wise and lofty character with a Daoist spontenaity and lack of inhibition, wholly immersed in his art.

We are told: "He was (from early years) a collector and a connoisseur; when he acquired a precious picture he used to shut himself up in his study, and there he remained in deep contemplation before the picture without uttering a word. But when he had understood some particular secret he would get up, run round the couch, jumping, shouting and clapping his hands". In the tradition led by the influential minority of scholars, sages and monks, the goal was very clear: perfect clarity of understanding. To this end all communication was creative and all communicators were regarded as prophets, in whose creative works were to be found clues to the ultimate mystery of life. A painting by a past master, highly respected for his grasp of these mysteries, was like the sermon of a religious prophet or the work of a great philosopher — through which the understanding disciple, grasping inner meaning, might achieve a quantum leap in comprehension, perhaps complete enlightenment. This was at the heart of the great reverence for past masters in the Chinese artistic tradition, so frequently misunderstood by many in the West.

Dachi, who Wang Shimin follows here, means 'Great fool' and was the self-deprecating sobriquet of Huang Gongwang, one of the Four Yuan Masters and a crucial figure in the development of literati painting. Wang Shimin admired him above all other artists and spent a lifetime devoted to discovering his secrets.

In this small but impeccable work the artist says, literally, that he is "following the brush method" of Huang Gongwang. In the literati tradition brushwork stands for much more than a mere surface emulation of technique. An artist's brushwork represented character and his level of understanding of the mysteries of life. It is always meaning rather than means that dominates, and the spirit of an artist's painting rather than its surface detail that are sought. This is the meaning of Wu Hufan's statement that in his opinion this painting represents the 'utmost state'.

Some writers have called into question whether Wang Shimin's status as an artist in the Chinese critical tradition is not derived as much from his lofty character and integrity as a scholar as from his ability with a brush. In the literati artistic tradition, the two are inextricably interlinked and both play a vital role in communication.

In the traditional Western objective approach to art, where technique is seen as what the artist employs to create the end product the work of art itself, it is possible to see it as quite independent of the artist and his character. In the holistic approach of the Chinese tradition, where technique is the whole process of artist, medium and audience employed to achieve the end product of enlightenment, the character of the artist assumes a far more important role in artistic communication.

1. *Chinese Painting: Leading Masters and Principles,* by Osvald Siren, Vol. V, pp.95-104

5

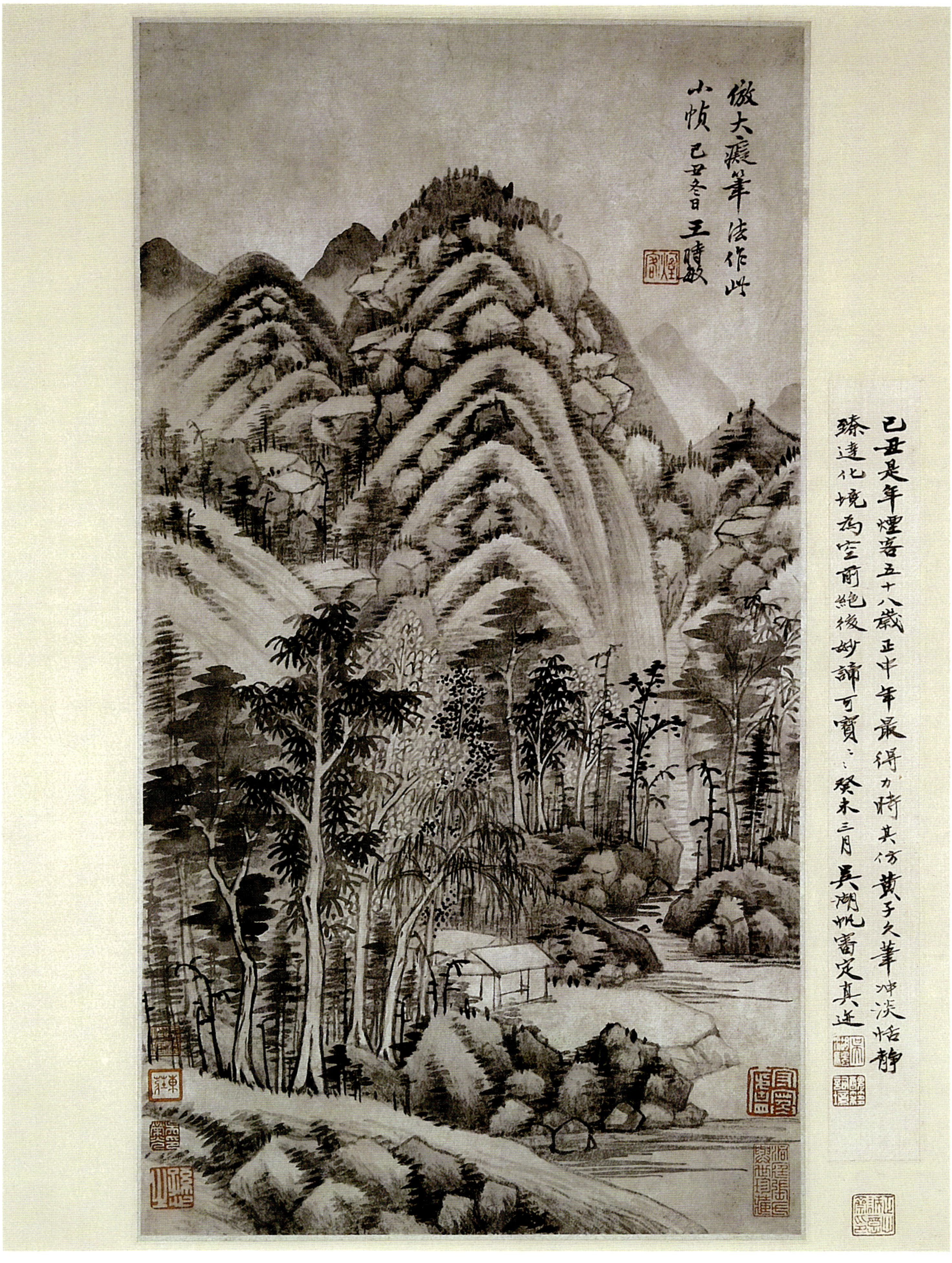

6

Ruyi Sceptre

Wood, *huangyangmu* (boxwood), of yellowish colour; carved as a *ruyi* sceptre in imitation of a natural *lingzhi*, the head of the *ruyi* made up of a large fungus, with several smaller fungi growing from the extended, gnarled stalk; a small fungus at the end of the stalk forming a loop for the attachment of a cord.
Probably first half of the Qing dynasty.
Length: 33.6 cm.

黄楊木雕靈芝如意
可能清早期，長33.6厘米

This *ruyi*, elegantly carved of boxwood, is a masterpiece of naturalism, closely imitating symbolic *lingzhi* fungus. It represents longevity thus being an ideal auspicious gift, to which capacity most *ruyi* owe their existence. Seated in the studio the scholar might play with such a piece and be transported to where Daoist immortals roam.

For a discussion on the origins and purpose of the *ruyi* see no. 270. For a discussion on the artistic qualities of this *ruyi* by comparison with a similar piece, see no. 7.

7

Ruyi Sceptre

Wood, *huangyangmu* (boxwood), of yellowish-brown colour; carved as a *ruyi* sceptre imitating a natural *lingzhi* fungus, the gnarled, partly hollow stalk surmounted by five 'heads' of different sizes; the lower stalk with a hole for a cord in the form of a pierced, knotty section; the lower front stalk incised with a four-character mark *Yongzheng nianzhi* ('made in the Yongzheng period') in regular script.
Possibly Beijing palace workshops, 1723-1735.
Length: 39.2 cm.

黄楊木雕靈芝如意•雍正年製銘
清雍正(1723-1735)，長39.2厘米

At one level this *ruyi* is a masterpiece of naturalism, equal in technical quality to no. 6, but a comparison between the artistic qualities of the two is interesting. Both are technically impeccable. Each *ruyi* is of the same subject-matter and material, and of similar colour and finish, but what of form and line?

In formal terms the artist has disposed the same essential features, a long, gnarled stalk or stem covered with knot-holes, and various *lingzhi* heads of different sizes. In no. 6 he has chosen to do so in the usual manner, with the curving and re-curving stalk supporting one main head, and several smaller heads branching out from the stem and main head at different points. The effect is of a continuous line of motion, punctuated fairly evenly by knot holes and small *lingzhi* heads culminating in the final statement of the main head; charming, but perhaps a little predictable and sweet. This example has greater tension in the layout of the form, and in the line; it is less predictable. It has the same basic four segments of curve in the stalk, but the sweetness has been taken out of them by joining the lower two as a continuous 'S'-shaped curve, broken at the point where it meets the third by a group of diagonally disposed knot-holes (balancing that at the base of the stalk) and accentuating the direction of the thrusting upward movement which continues in the third curve. The fourth is then started with a similar, but still more complex diagonal thrust in the opposite direction. Already the line is far more dynamic. The various *lingzhi* heads are then concentrated as a series of planes following the same diagonal thrust as the series of knot-holes just below it. They are of varying sizes, but each carries weight in its own right. By making them a single group, each smaller than that of the single head in no. 6, they form a satisfactory finale to the upward movement of the stalk. The grouping of the heads in this example gives them the weight necessary to turn the stem's thrust, but each has been left small enough to give the stalk much greater strength by comparison, adding to the dynamism of the piece. Both are superb examples of wood *ruyi* but it could be argued that the artist who made this one was more concerned with abstract formal values, more conscious of the power of line and form and thus added an extra dimension to his work of art.

The incised mark on this *ruyi* is convincing for various reasons. The piece itself is of commensurate quality and taste for the period and has an appropriate degree of natural wear and patination. The mark is correctly written in formal and elegant regular script and in the four-character form typical of pieces made for the Emperor or his court, particularly within the palace workshops. A study of the known wares of the Beijing palace workshops demonstrates that imperial marks tend to be of four characters more often than six (it is also true of pieces made elsewhere — for instance ceramics at Jingdezhen — specifically for the court, where there appears to be some direct imperial interest in the wares as opposed to being made simply as court furnishings).

It is also fair to say that a mark carver of the Yongzheng period might be expected to have had plenty of practice at writing these four characters, thus making his calligraphy fluent, precise and confident, as well as correct in form for the period; a later carver faking such a mark would be less familiar with the nuances of correct form and style. It is also a little unlikely that a later faker would think of putting a Yongzheng mark on such a piece as this, as rustic *ruyi* practically never bear imperial reign marks — indeed, assuming this to be genuinely marked, it is the only such example of which we know.

In recent years, marks, particularly Qianlong marks, have been added to a variety of works, especially in jade, but high-powered magnification clearly demonstrates that the mark here has been on the piece for a considerable period of time, the wear and patination of the mark equalling that of the piece itself. (Particularly telling in considering additional marks is whether the mark cuts through the minute scratches which make up wear and surface patination, or whether such wear runs into the lip and upper depressions of the incised mark. Magnification of 40-80x will reveal whether a mark has been added to an already patinated surface, or whether patina is superimposed on an already marked surface. This may not tell you if the mark is contemporary with the piece, but it will indicate whether or not it has been there for a long period of time.)

An enthusiastic patron of the arts, the Kangxi Emperor conceived of setting up within the palace at Beijing a series of workshops for the production of a large range of arts and crafts. By 1680 27 (some authorities say 30) workshops existed. They included those for the production of metalwork, clocks and watches, glass, cloisonné enamel, jade, gold filigree, lacquer, ivory, moveable type for printing, maps and workshops for joinery and carpentry. The complete list is given by Bushell[1] but among them is a workshop for the production of wood carvings. The palace would have had a considerable demand for wood stands, frames, furniture and so on quite apart from works of art. The art of moulding gourds set up within the palace by the Kangxi emperor also required the production of finely carved primary wood moulds (see no. 91), while some of the stands made for pieces in the imperial collection are of the highest quality and works of art in their own right. The skills certainly existed within the palace workshops to produce a *ruyi* such as this.

1. *Chinese Art,* Vol. I, by S.W. Bushell, p.108.

6

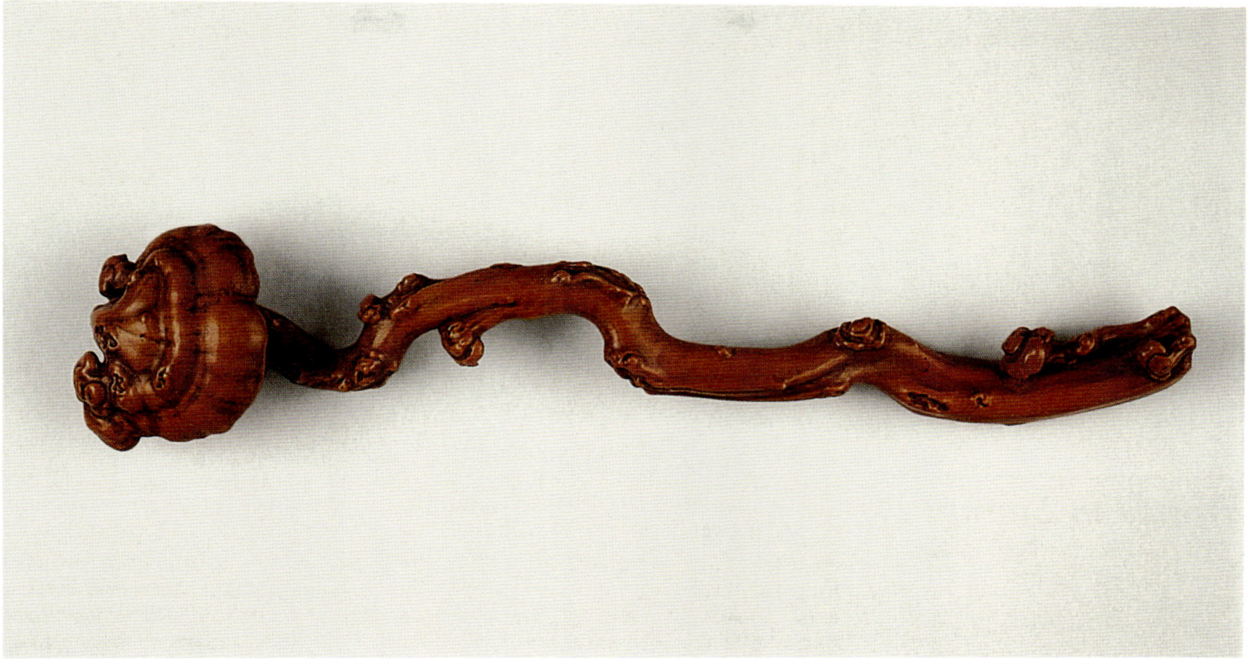

7

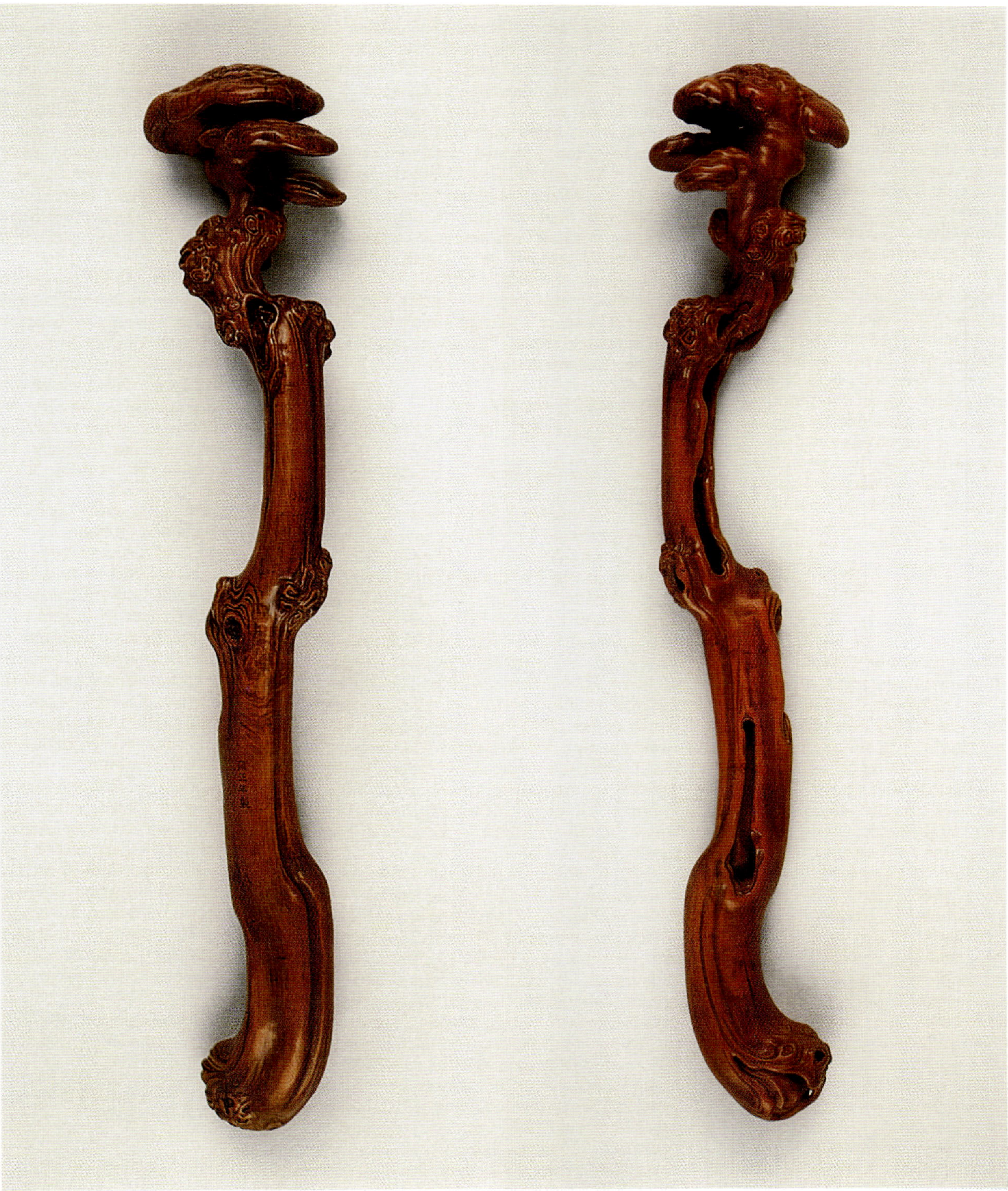

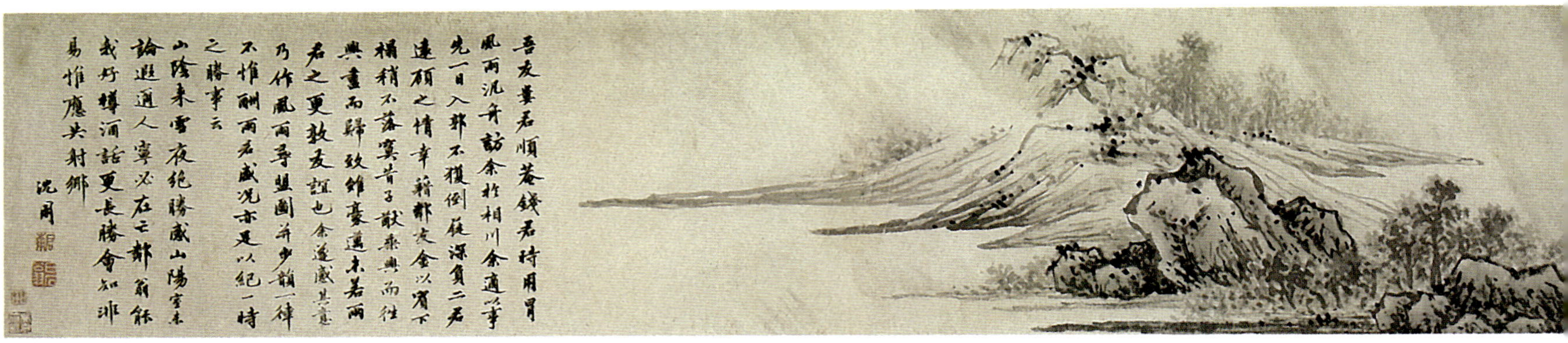

8

Visiting Friends in Stormy Weather

Shen Zhou

Ink on paper, handscroll; a group of visitors in a boat being rowed towards a waterside home in a storm; followed by a long inscription by the artist explaining the circumstances of the painting. Two friends had come to visit him at his home by the water's edge in a storm, but regretfully he had been away and unable to receive them and give them hospitality. Fortunately his neighbour received them for the night, entertained them with wine, and everyone was happy. He then compares the occasion to a legendary occasion in the past when unrestrained expressions of friendship arose out of visiting merrymakers, but feels that his own visitors were no less an expression of their depth of friendship. He continues that, moved by their intentions he painted this painting, which he entitled *Visiting Friends in Stormy Weather* and wrote a poem for them to inscribe thereupon, stating that even though these could not repay the deep affection of his two friends, it would serve as a record of the happy event. There follows the poem about snow falling on the dark side of the mountain at night, and wine being provided by his neighbour to make the conversation flow, although limitless matters for discussion are saved for later, when the host will arrive. It ends with an expression of the difficulties encountered and how they should all make the most of being together. Followed by two seals of the artist, *Qinan* in positive seal script, and *Baishiweng*, in negative seal script.
Shen Zhou, 1485.
28.3 cm × 267 cm.

The painting has two collector's seals (for the various seals on this painting, and Chinese transcription of the colophons, see *Anthology of Chinese Art: Min Chiu Society Silver Jubilee Exhibition*, pp.88-89, no. 12), followed by a colophon by one of the visiting friends, Lou Shunan (Lou Xu), stating that on the tenth day of the fourth month of the *yisi* year of the Chenghua period (1485) he and Qian Shiyong went to visit Shen Zhou only to find he was absent. The same story is recounted, but from Lou's point of view, including details of the terrible weather and how the boatman felt uneasy about continuing. In the wine all their troubles were forgotten, and tales of old friendships were retold, but none to equal the nature of theirs with Shen Zhou. A further poem is appended covering the same ground, and ending with all worries forgotten in a drunken land. The inscription ends with the statement that it was written in Shen Zhou's house, enabling the painting to be dated. It is unsigned but bears three seals of the writer. Another colophon follows this by Wu Kuan (1435-1504), a good friend of Shen Zhou's and a native of the same place. The two lived separated by about fifty miles of navigable water course, allowing for easy access within the day. Wu Kuan was known for his poetry and calligraphy and was also vice-president of the Board of Civil Office, and a teacher of the Emperor Xiaozong.
A third colophon is by Qi Zhijia who departs from the facts of the occasion to discuss connoisseurship. He writes as follows: "Since the four Yuan masters, in our Ming dynasty Shen Zhou with his brush work is definitely the only one who inherits their mantel. However, recently in Jiangsu, there are people who are profiteering by making lots of forgeries, which if one must examine them all would make one nauseous. When I passed the studio of Meng Huisheng, a capable connoisseur, he showed me this scroll and praised it, assuring me of its authenticity." This colophon is signed, with two seals. A fourth colophon by Shen Xiang is dated to the *gengzi* year of the Guangxu period (1900). It includes an intricate and mundane little tale of how the painting was stolen by someone's servant and sold for far below its proper value. It is signed, and with one seal.
At several places on the painting and colophons different seals of a certain Lu family appear, one of which reads, "To be treasured eternally by the descendants of the Lu family".

風雨尋盟圖卷•沈周作
明成化乙巳(1485),28.3×267厘米

Shen Zhou (*zi:* Qinan; *hao:* Shitian, Baishiweng, Yutianweng; 1427-1509) was a native of Suzhou, in Jiangsu province. Painter, calligrapher and poet, more than any other artist he established Suzhou as a centre of painting in the Ming and Qing dynasties. From a wealthy family, Shen managed to avoid official service (as did his grandfather and father who devoted their time and great wealth instead to collecting and the good life). On one occasion Shen Zhou consulted the *Yijing* to discover whether he should take up official duties or not, finding, one suspects conveniently, that its advice was against the idea.[1] After the death of his father, he again decided against taking a post on the filial grounds that he must care for his mother — which he did with great devotion until she passed away at the age of 92.[2]

He lived, apparently in considerable comfort, in the Abode among the Bamboos (Youzhu Zhu), in Xiangcheng, to the north-east of Suzhou, where he seems to have led an extremely pleasant life which by all accounts encouraged his naturally generous and pleasant nature. Apart from his filial piety, apparently demonstrated in a very real and caring concern for his widowed mother (quite independent of its capacity to keep him clear of official duties), he had a reputation for great generosity, giving away his paintings quite freely to scholar and commoner alike, and frequently signing paintings he had not done if he was so asked. His attitude was that people would not have asked him for such favours had they not been needy, and in any case a true connoisseur would be able to judge his genuine works quite easily.

Such a viewpoint might be disparaged by the layman, but scholars such as Shen Zhou felt that any work of art was relatively profound depending upon the understanding of the audience. Thus a forgery was theoretically as capable of moving the uninitiated to a state of grace as was the finest masterpiece of inspiring the initiated. Shen Zhou is reputed to have been equally munificent with money and caring of complete strangers, sending, we are told,[3] money to houses where in cold weather he saw no smoke rising from the chimneys.

Indeed, his good nature may well have been the reason he was away from his home when Lou Xu and Qian Shiyong visited him. Somewhat beset by people calling at his house on a regular basis to avail themselves of his generosity, he was in the habit of absenting himself once a month to various temples and other retreats around Suzhou, where he could enjoy a little contemplative peace for a few days.

Shen Zhou was an important figure in the progression of the literati school of painting which played a vital part in taking painting to the same heights as a vehicle of self-expression that music, poetry and calligraphy had already achieved. Wealthy and in a life of retirement, he could obviously devote his life to collecting, connoisseurship, poetry, calligraphy, painting and convivial company. He had studied and grasped the meaning of the literati development in painting in the Yuan dynasty, and was particularly influenced by Huang Gongwang and Wang Meng.

The Chinese understanding of the work of art as a direct vehicle for self-realization, both for artist and audience, led to complete involvement in it, and to the evolution of certain formats and practices which encouraged such involvement. The handscroll is perhaps the most effective of all Chinese painting formats. To view it one is forced to prepare both oneself and a suitable space so that by the time the work of art is encountered one is already committed.

The additions of comments, poetry and collector's seals, either on the work or on additional sheets of paper mounted with it, are also a reflection of the Chinese understanding of art. The work of art is a living, changing act of communication where the audience is of vital importance. It seems entirely natural to the Chinese mind to add to it records of encounters, whether of brush or seal, and complementary poetry.

1. Quoted from the *Mingshi Shishi* in *Chinese Painting: Leading Masters and Principles*, by Osvald Siren, Vol. IV, p.148.
2. *Dictionary of Ming Biography*, p.1175.
3. Quoted from the *Wusheng Shishi* in Siren, op. cit. Vol. IV, p.149.

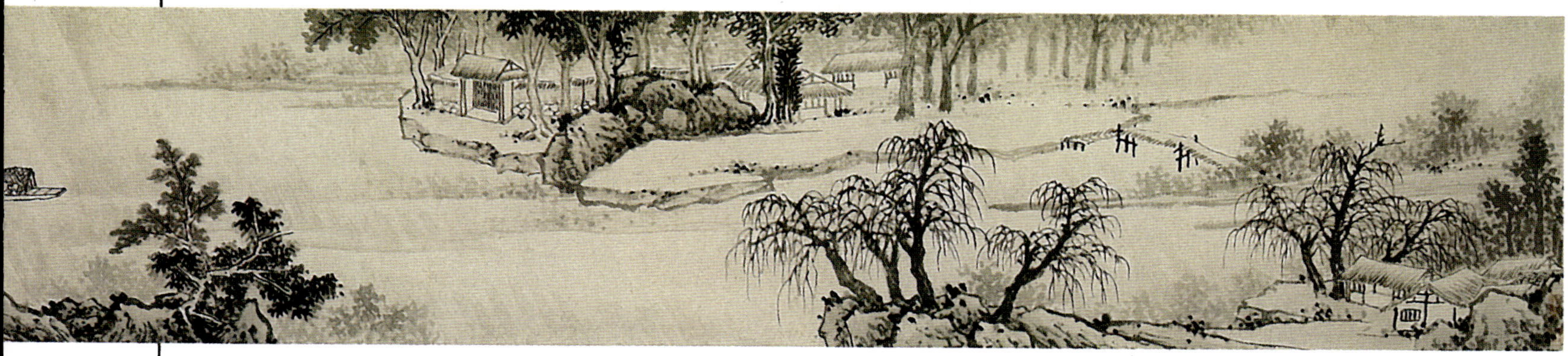

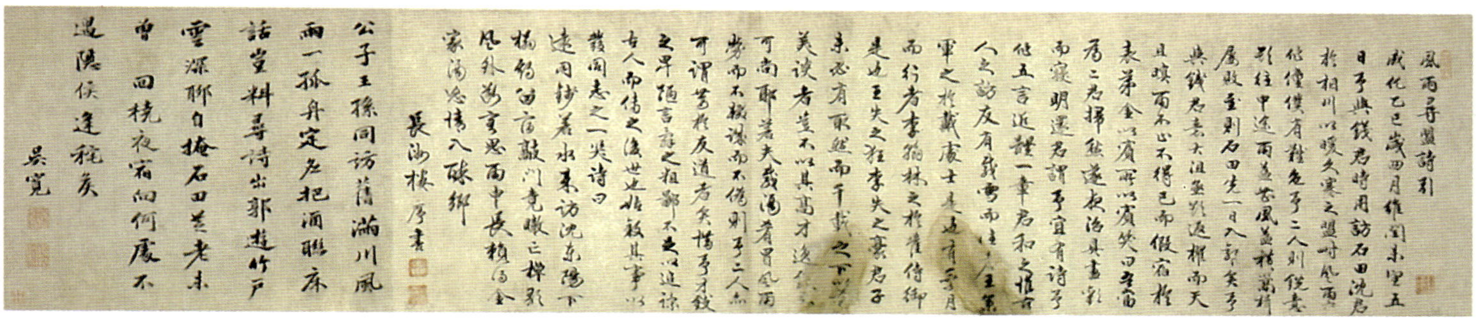

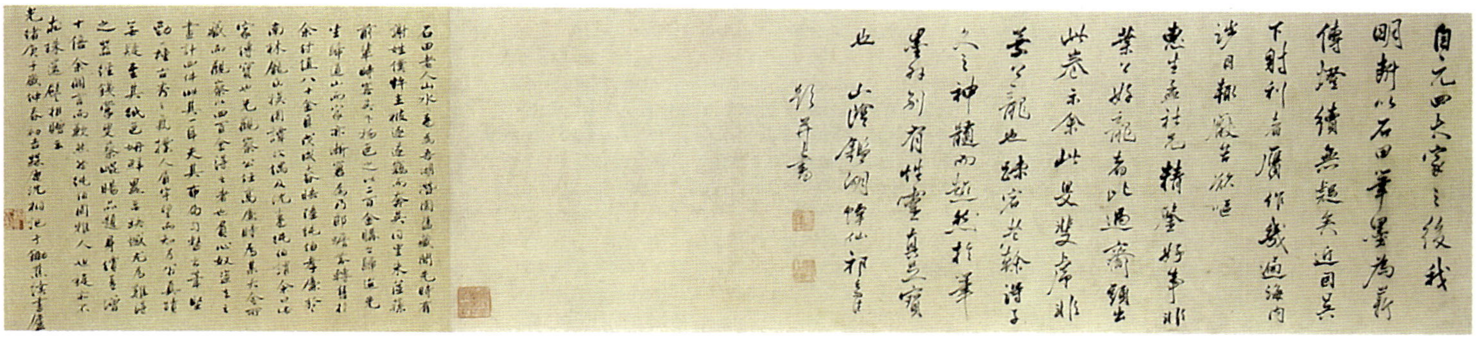

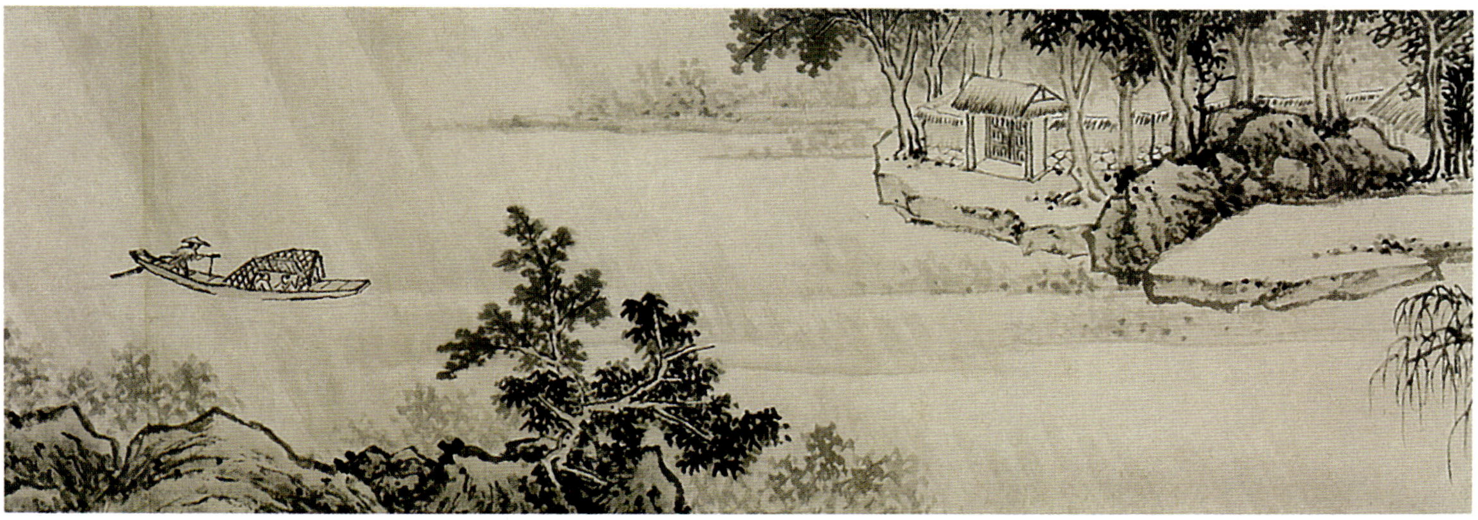

8

9

'Stone Bridge' Rock Sculpture

Stone, in the form of a bridge; mounted on an irregular, wood *(zitan)* stand.
Song to Qing dynasty.
Height including stand: 7.1 cm.
Length of wood stand: 12.7 cm.

岩橋
宋至清，高連座7.1厘米，座長12.7厘米

One of the standard works in Chinese on stones is the 17th century *Suyuan Shipu* of Lin Youlin. It contains woodblock illustrations of 65 stones purporting to be those of the Xuanhe collection of the Song Emperor Huizong, although how they might have been accurately reproduced some five centuries later remains a mystery. One of these somewhat resembles this stone, although it is without a stand as are many of those illustrated. It must have been difficult for whoever made the present stand to decide just how to mount the stone. It is visually evocative from any angle, which is unusual, as stones as art normally have only one, or rarely two, orientations which suggest themselves strongly as being the most suitable.

The Chinese have for many centuries valued naturally strangely shaped stones as objects of aesthetic appreciation. As with the closely related art form involving various kinds of gnarled wood, the hand and eye of man were also involved in selecting and isolating purely natural rock or stone formations, in minor 'editing', and varying degrees of re-working existing material. Collectively such stones are known as *guaishi* ('strange stones'). The earliest work on the subject of stones is the *Wuzang Shanjing* of the 5th century BC, which contained 81 stones and minerals classified according to their usage (such as for polishing, or for making into musical chimes, etc.), nature (such as magnetic stones, sounding stones etc.) and their colour. The earliest reference to *guaishi* appears at about the same time in the *Yu Gong* and the *Shanhai Jing,* but Schafer believes these to be references to ornamental semi-precious stones rather than to strangely shaped rocks as sculpture.[1]

The term seems gradually to have been transferred to stones as microcosmic landscapes or forms of sculpture at some time between the 3rd and 6th centuries AD. Schafer writes: "The origin of the love of stones for their own sake, or more precisely for their microcosmic mimicry of mountain landscapes, must be looked for in the ancient interest in stones shaped naturally like living creatures: a tortoise, a horse, a man, or the Buddha, and in fossiliferous rocks containing 'stone swallows' and other monsters. Such aberrations of the vital fluids of Nature are frequently mentioned in pre-Tang literature. Reinforcing the fascination such objects always had for the Chinese was a mass of folklore about haunted stones in wild rugged places, curiously shaped rocks associated with dragons, devils, saints and gods. It was only necessary to transfer a strangely formed stone, or a stone with an attached legend, to an urban garden, to accomplish the innovation in taste. Add to this a sophisticated intuition of the structure of the world and the operations of 'Heaven' subtly suggested by the contours of a picturesque rock, and we have the attitude of the Tang or Song connoisseur full fledged.[2]

By the 11th century the emphasis in the Chinese interest in stones had shifted to *guaishi* as sculpture and microcosmic landscapes. In the *Yuyangong Shipu,* although only six stones are recorded, they are named according to their shapes for appreciation. This tradition was continued in the *Xuanhe Shipu* of Zu Kao, of the early 12th century, where 63 stones are named according to their shapes. Emperor Huizong built a new palace in 1114 with artificial lakes and fantastic rocks and stones, designed to evoke a fairy landscape. In 1117 he commanded thousands of labourers to build an auspicious hill of such stones collected as tribute from all over the empire. He was not above marshalling the considerable resources of his empire, including his warships, in pursuit of his petromania, which he carried to such an extreme as to enfoeff a particularly large and impressive specimen as Marklord of Pangu.

The *Yunlin Shipu* by Tu Wan (see above for the Schafer translation) was a comprehensive work of about 1126, covering 116 stones from 83 districts of 19 provinces, classified under 12 different headings. In a commentary on the *Yunlin Shipu* Kong Quan wrote, "Stones are well worth study, since they purify the imagination: did not the Master himself (Confucius) say 'The humane person finds happiness in the mountains,' and is not the love of rocks an instance of this, and a suitable devotion for a Confucian gentleman".[3]

By the Song dynasty strangely shaped rocks were among the most highly valued objects in China. The famous calligrapher, painter, connoisseur and theorist Mi Fu was a renowned lover of stones and is frequently depicted in paintings with a *hu* (see no. 245) in his hands, bowing low and paying homage to a strange rock, as if he were bowing to the Emperor. Su Shi placed so high a value on two *Chouchi* rocks in his collection that he made it known that he would part with them for nothing less than a pair of horse paintings by the Tang master Han Kan. Schafer, mentioning this in connection with his series of poems and their prefaces on the subject, also states that there was "...a considerable controversy among Su and his friends about a jocular proposal of Wang Jingqing to steal the stones. The eccentric Jiang Yingshu thought that the best solution was to burn the paintings and smash the stones." Action, according to Schafer, which the atmosphere of the narrative suggests would be comparable to burning the Mona Lisa and smashing the Venus de Milo.[4]

The taste for strange stones and rocks remained a mainstay of the aesthetic of the persuasive minority in the post-Song period. They are a main subject in Chinese paintings into the present century and are still highly valued.

1. *Tu Wan's Stone Catalogue of Cloudy Forest,* by Edward Schafer.
2. Ibid.
3. Ibid. p.13.
4. Ibid.

10

Wrist Rest

Porcelain; formed as a segment of bamboo, with a leafy twig emerging from a node of the lower culm; covered overall with a pale celadon glaze, the upper culm enamelled in black with the poetic inscription: "The skin of the green bamboo is not stained with the tears of Xiang E" followed by two seals in red enamel, *han* and *mo.*
Jingdezhen, Qianlong period.
Length: 16.7 cm.

青瓷竹段形書銘臂擱
清乾隆(1736–1795)，長16.7厘米

Communication among the literati was carried out in a sort of poetic shorthand based upon an elite scholarly conceit that anyone worth communicating with was well educated in the classics and would understand the subtlest of allusions to all aspects of Chinese culture. This meant that the barest allusion to a well-known poem or legend could carry with it a wealth of meaning.

Here the green bamboo acts as a reference to a precious variety of bamboo the skin of which has spotted markings, as if tear drops had fallen onto the surface and stained it. The Emperor Yao, one of the three legendary Emperors of the third millenium BC had two daughters, who were bestowed on the Emperor Shun (another of the three) as wives. At his death their sorrow knew no bounds and it is said that their tears stained the skin of the bamboo which grew over his grave, near the river Xiang (a large tributary of the Yangzi river which flows through Hunan province).

The two seals *han* and *mo* are intended to be read together as 'brush and ink', the first character being that of the *Hanlin* Academy, the prestigious academy to which only successful *jinshi* candidates might be appointed upon passing a further palace examination called *dianshi.*

From the Qianlong period there is a group of ceramic wares of extremely fine quality which are enamelled and frequently inscribed with scholarly inscriptions and seals. Many of these bear reign marks and were clearly made at the imperial kilns at Jingdezhen to be sent to the court. They frequently combine the use of coloured grounds, fine enamelling and calligraphic inscriptions and seals of a scholarly leaning. A few are known, however, which have no imperial marks and were apparently made for private use. One of these bears the signature, following a poetic inscription, of Tang Yin, Director of the Imperial Factory at Jingdezhen from 1728 to 1749.[1] They employ all the skills and presumably facilities developed in perfecting imperial ceramics.

In its use of enamelling to imitate ink calligraphy and seals, the celadon ground, and the exquisite quality, this wrist rest is related to the group.

1. See Soame Jenyns, *Later Porcelain,* 1971, pl. A, and pl. XLIX, B.

9

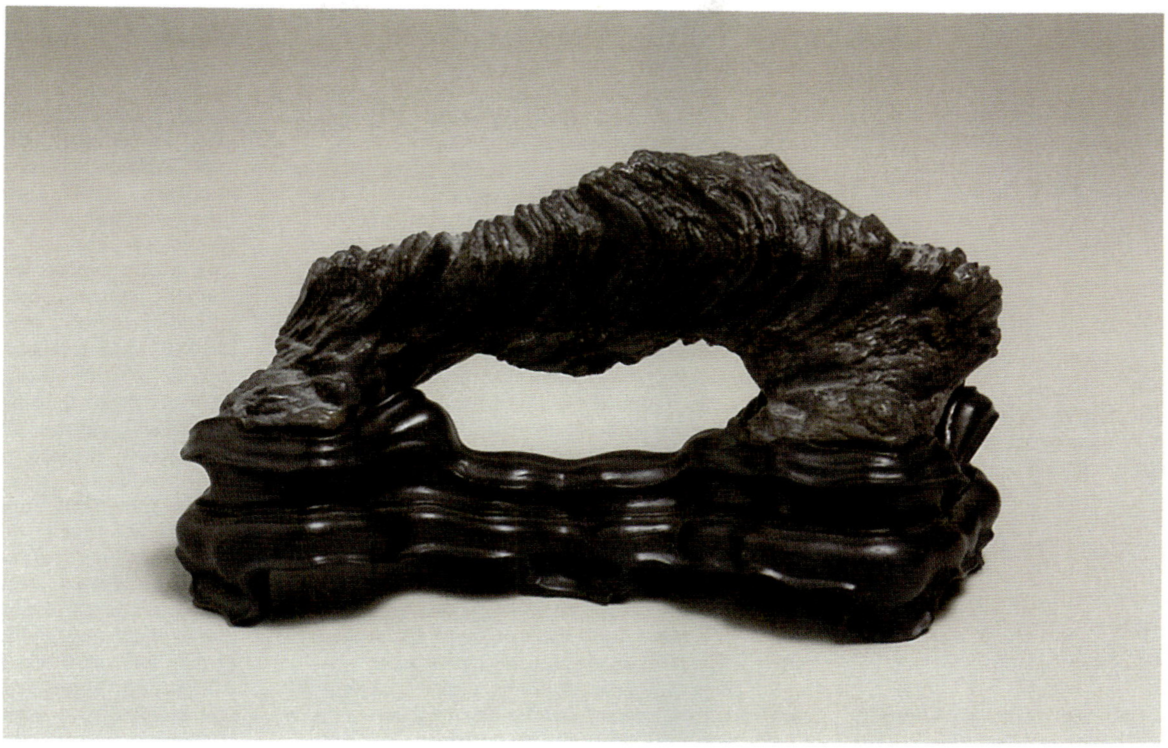

10

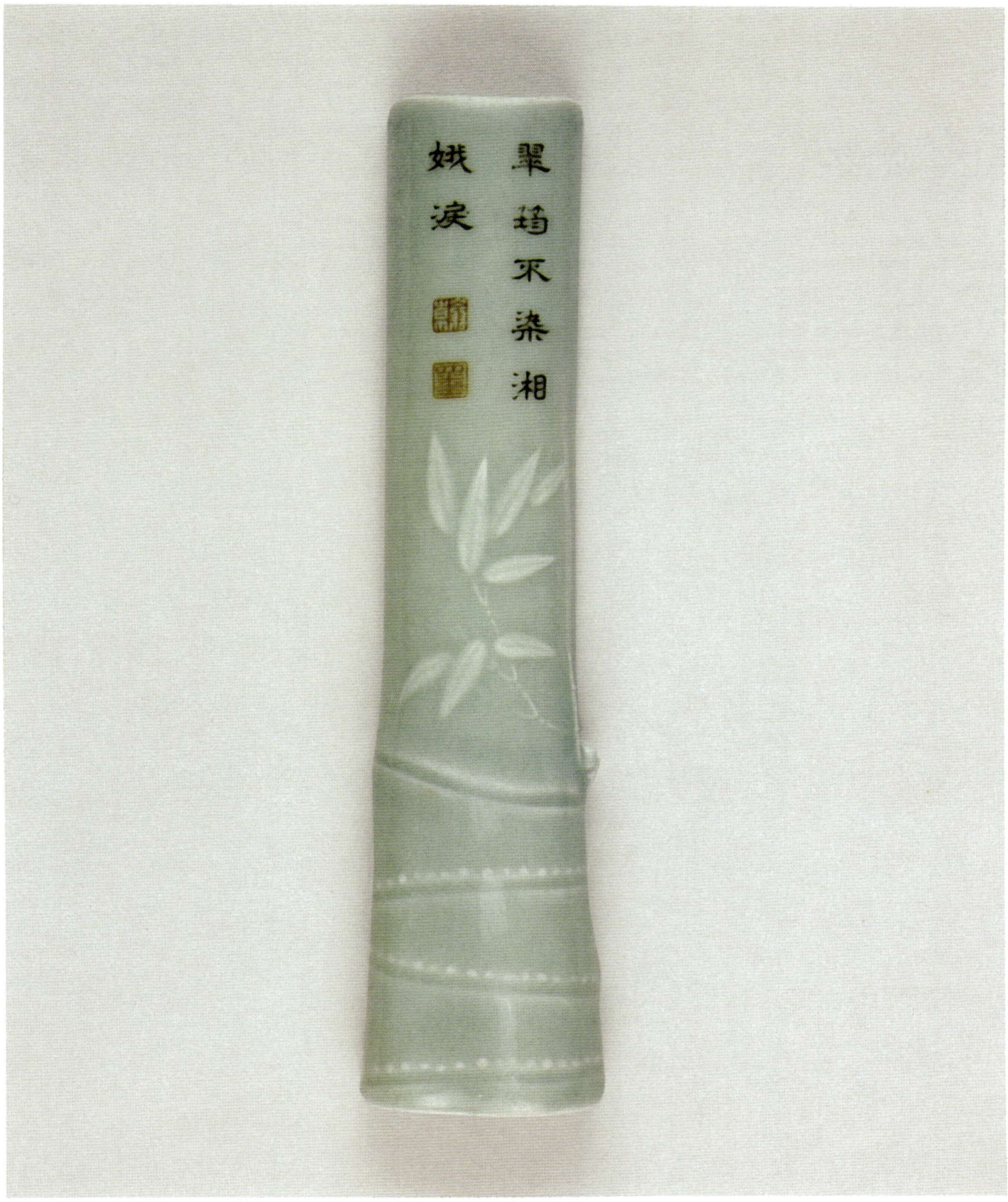

11

Portrait of Yuan Mei

Fei Danxu

Ink on paper, mounted as a hanging scroll; a portrait of Yuan Mei after an original by Zhou Dian, inscribed in the upper right margin: "Portrait of Suiyuan; by Zhou Dian of Liuan and inscribed by Sun Xingyan, copied by Fei Danxu of Wuxing" with seals *Zitiao* and *Fei Danxu.*
Circa 1820-1850.
89.4 cm × 42 cm.

The painting with one collector's seal *Jiangxing Cao Tang Jin Shousheng Suocang* ('collected by Jin Shousheng of the River-song Thatched Hut'). An early 18th century scholar called Jin Zhizhang is recorded as the owner of the River-song Thatched Hut; it is likely that the family maintained the hall name for several generations and that Jin Shousheng is a late Qing or 20th century descendant.

袁枚像立軸•費丹旭作
清代(約1820-1850), 89.4×42厘米

Fei Danxu (*zi:* Zitiao; *hao:* Xiaolou, Ouweng, Huanzhusheng, Xiaolou waishi; 1801-1850) was a native of Wuxing in Zhejiang province and a leading 19th century figure painter. However, our main interest here is in the subject of the portrait.

Yuan Mei (*hao:* Suiyuan; 1716-1798) was a native of Hangzhou. He was a renowned poet, a calligrapher known for his elegant style, a literary critic, essayist and noted gourmet. A *jinshi* of 1739 he filled various official posts for a decade before retiring, in 1749, to his newly acquired 'Garden of Contentment' (Sui Yuan, from which his *hao* was taken) at Nanjing. He served officially again between 1752 and 1755 before retiring to a life of poetry, writing and living the good life in his aptly named garden.

He seems to have been an extremely unusual and self-possessed character. His theories of poetry were controversial in his time, as was much else that he did. He believed in the virtues in poetry of a lack of pretence, naturalness and genuineness. He stated: "Poetry that can touch people deeply is good poetry and does not require the training of an experienced poet. That there is a realm of the poet is beyond dispute, but there are scholars who read lots of books but cannot grasp the art of poetry until their old age, while commoners lacking in education, both men and women, might occasionally come out with sentences to which, were they alive, Li Bo and Du Fu would bow in reverence. This is the greatness of poetry. One learning poetry should understand these two aspects: one can search for poetic inspiration in books, but it is also to be found outside of books."

He was also known for an attitude to women which was, to say the least, unorthodox in his day. Contrary to the prevailing trend he encouraged women to develop their natural talents and intelligence. Despite often harsh criticism and the epithet 'libertine' hurled at him by reactionary scholars and stern moralists, he received women as pupils, and both encouraged them to write poetry and published it for them.[1] The impression gained from this and other sources is that Yuan Mei followed his own way regardless, and whatever his attackers might think of it, he was always at ease.

He was able to do as he pleased, lavishly entertain and patronize the arts because of the high value placed upon his writing. (His will records that he was once paid 1,000 taels of silver for composing a funerary inscription). Through his earnings as a writer he was able to establish a reputation for generous hospitality and patronage, and elevated many other literary figures to public attention by editing or commenting upon their works. He maintained a large household, and was noted for his love of food, about which he wrote in a charming and bantering style — a work since translated into several Western languages.

Scholarship and professionalism are frequently seen as polar opposites in our modern approach to China's past. One or two prominent literati artists make disapproving statements about those who sell their works and there is a tendency to believe they speak for all literati at all times. For every literati comment on the evils of professionalism there were dozens of scholars listed in the various biographical dictionaries as living wholly or in part off their literati skills who nonetheless were highly respected in their fields. Standards that might have existed under the influence of a particularly powerful figure, such as Dong Qichang in the late Ming dynasty, would probably have had little effect on, for example, Qing Yangzhou literati society.

The distinction between professionals and amateurs marked a general tendency among the literati, certainly from the Song period onwards, to associate high art with high ideals, which in turn meant separating them from the mundane concerns of the marketplace. But this was more an indication of a general, theoretical preference. A lofty scholar-painter was permitted to be a full-time professional as long as he went about it in an acceptable fashion. The critic He Liangjun (1506-1573), for example, managed by a masterpiece of syncretic sleight of mind to classify the arch-professional Tang Yin among the scholar-amateurs in painting.[2]

We are unable to trace the artist Zhou Dian, who painted the original picture from which Fei Danxu worked, but Sun Xingyan, who was asked to inscribe it, is listed in *Eminent Chinese of the Ch'ing Period,* pp.675-677. Sun was a scholar, bibliophile and calligrapher who lived from 1753 to 1818; he was married to a leading lady poet and scholar, perhaps suggesting the suitability of his choice as the original inscriber of Yuan Mei's portrait. He entered the Zhongshan Academy in Nanjing where he associated with, amongst others, Yuan Mei himself.

1. See *Eminent Chinese of the Ch'ing Period,* pp.955-956.
2. Quoted from *Siyouzhai Hualun* ('Theories of Painting from the Studio of the Four Friends') in 'The "Wild and Heterodox School" of Ming Painting' by Richard Barnhart, in *Theories of the Arts in China,* p.380.

11

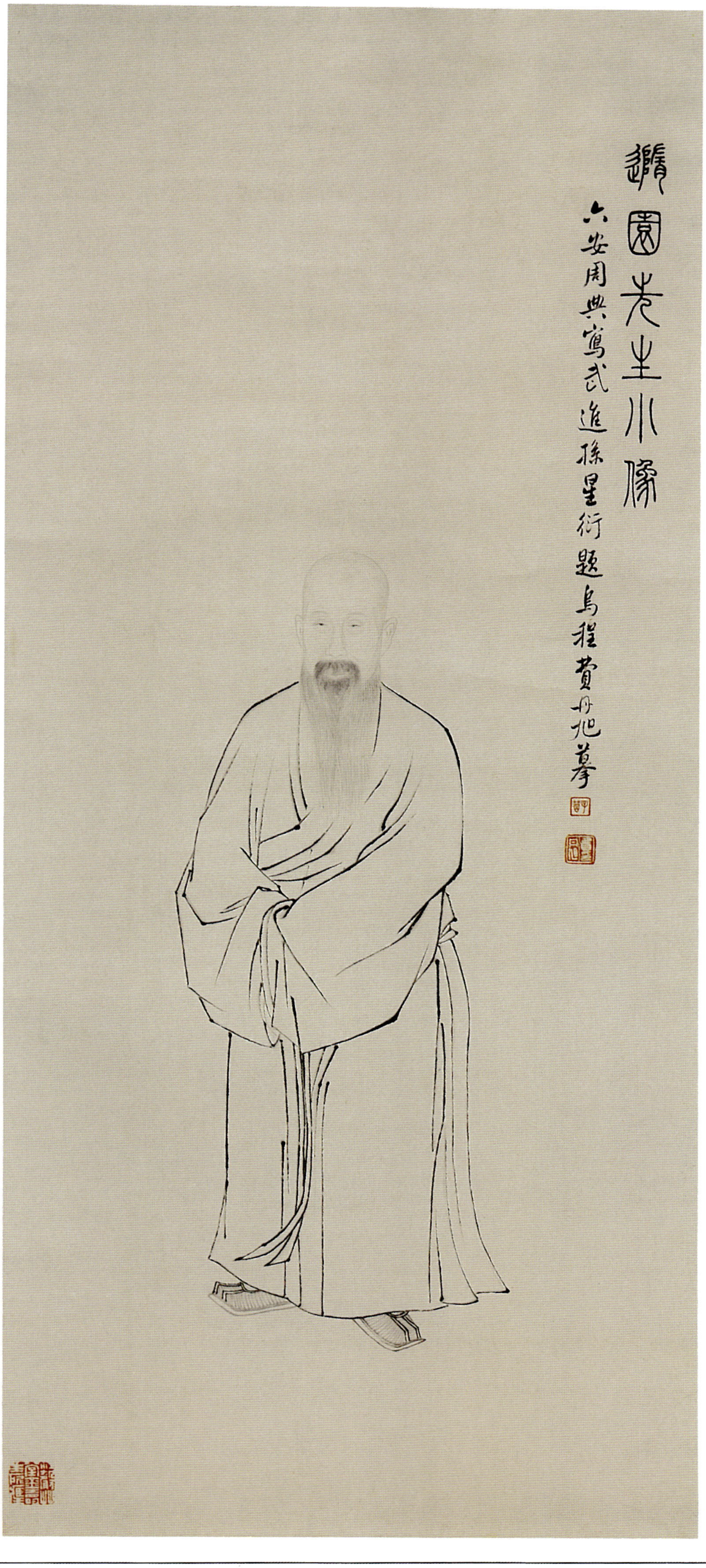

12

Drinking Cup

Rhinoceros horn, of variegated golden brown colour growing darker towards the point; carved as a cup in the form of a water buffalo, its nostrils pierced through to allow for a suspension cord.
Southern Song or later.
Width of cup at broadest point: 7.92 cm.

犀角雕水牛杯
南宋或元，最寬7.92厘米

Rhinoceros horn cups were made predominantly as drinking vessels (see no. 258). With its size, simplicity of form, presence as a work of art and ability to be suspended from the belt this example is an ideal cup for the scholar given to roaming the countryside.

As a work of art it is quite extraordinary, a closely observed piece of realism, superbly sculpted, brilliantly blending form and decoration. But what is most outstanding is the enormous sense of personality in the buffalo. There is an uncanny sense of humanity about it, as if we are looking at an aloof and self-contained scholar rather than the cup he might be drinking from.

The dating of this piece is a matter of educated guesswork. James Watt states: "Although the use of drinking horns goes back to at least the beginning of the Han period...the animal-headed rhyton probably began in China as a result of Sassanian influence in about the 7th century."[1] A superb ram-headed rhyton was found in a hoard of treasures in Xi'an, in a Tang context, and Watt illustrates a bovine-headed rhyton which he ascribes to the Tang dynasty.[2] A drawing of another bovine-headed rhyton appears in the *Guyu Tupu*[3] and a very similar jade carving (described by Watt as bearing 'an almost uncomfortable resemblance') is in the Brundage collection.[4] A drawing of another buffalo-headed drinking horn appears in the *Sancai Tuhui* of 1607, in the section on vessels. It too is pierced through the nose for suspension. Despite the questionable authenticity of some of the sources, and the problems of dating certain objects, there is sufficient indication to suggest that the animal- (particularly bovine-) headed rhyton or drinking cup was a reasonably standard vessel from the Tang dynasty onwards. As far as we know, however, it seems to have faded out of popularity in later times. Subject-matter alone would, therefore, suggest that this cup is likely to be of an early date. The closely observed realism also suggests the possiblity of a Southern Song date, and its functional nature as demonstrated by the pierced nostrils and inability to stand independently would also lend weight to the opinion that it was early (the standard Ming and Qing rhinoceros horn small cup stands independently and seems to have evolved as much into a collector's curio as a practical drinking vessel). The condition of the horn is also commensurate with an early date. Being an organic substance, rhinocerous horn tends to decompose at its surface over the centuries. Close examination of the surface of old rhinoceros horn carvings shows how the fibres begin to separate, creating a texture into which dirt begins to seep. This is apparent here, and to a much greater degree than on the other rhinoceros horn pieces in this exhibition including that with the Xuande reign mark (see no. 158) which is generally accepted to be of the period. Although it is only a tentative attribution, there seems to be some evidence in favour of an early dating, perhaps to the Southern Song period.

1. *Chinese Jades from Han to Ch'ing*, p.55.
2. Ibid., no. 29.
3. *Juan* 90, 1a. This is a work of doubtful lineage, based reputedly on the collection of the Song Emperor Gaozong (1127-1162) which allegedly stayed in manuscript form for 600 years until its publication in 1779.
4. *Avery Brundage Collection: Chinese Jades*, by René-Yvon Lefebvre d'Argencé, plate XXXIV.

13

Bi Symbol

Nephrite of pale, slightly yellowish green colour, with rich dark brown and black markings (the natural pigmentation enhanced by artificial colouring); a *bi* disc, its thickness tapering towards the edge; carved with an identical design on both sides of an outer band of four *taotie*, their curvilinear bodies extending symmetrically out from either side of their heads, and an inner band, flanked by two plain raised concentric circles, of raised and incised spirals.
Probably Song dynasty.
Diameter: 10.7 cm.
Diameter of central hole: 4.1 cm.
Formerly in the Allan Bier collection, San Francisco.
Exhibited and illustrated: *Eskenazi Twenty-Five Years*, no. 21.

玉雕饕餮紋璧
可能宋代，直徑10.7厘米，中孔直徑4.1厘米

The dating of this piece, as in the case of most archaistic works of art, remains questionable. There is no doubt that it is archaistic rather than archaic and therefore highly unlikely to predate the Song, which appears to be the first period in which archaism as a highly sophisticated art form developed. Nor do style, the exquisite quality of the carving and of the archaism, and the level of natural wear and patination suggest the probability of a Qing date. In the light of our present level of knowledge of archaism the Song dynasty is the most likely period for this *bi*, but we simply do not know enough about archaistic style in hardstone carving from the Yuan and Ming dynasties to yet rule out the possibility of it being later.

Archaism is one of the great untouched treasure-houses of collecting and connoisseurship in the Chinese field. In the past, archaic pieces have been too much confused with copies by an unsophisticated collecting public to allow their true nature as art to surface. Archaistic works have been too often relegated to the indignity of being 'the fakes that are easy to dismiss because they aren't like the originals'. We seem hardly to have paused, as yet, to consider why they do not resemble the originals. In the light of the nature of the Chinese consciousness, its long-standing, full and knowing use of the nature of artistic communication, and the maturity and sophistication of its arts, it is worth reconsidering archaism.

Archaism at its best is the creative reinterpretation of antiquity. What happens in archaism is that the past is taken as subject-matter, as it is with literati painting where the style of brushwork, composition, or even subject-matter of an earlier painter is the departure point for the work of art. This subject-matter carries with it a wealth of meaning related to a respect for the past and its weight of wisdom, allowing it to be absorbed at an abstract level without having to be analysed, but in archaism there is no attempt to copy the past as the final statement. The art rests in subtly reordering the elements and languages of the past in a way which relates very much to contemporaneous understanding.

The constraints of the influential minority required that their arts be simple on the surface. Communication aimed at reaching a level of understanding, both for artist and audience, beyond the objective world; to concentrate attention on the physical surface of the work of art with radical change in subject-matter or style, tended to lead in quite the wrong direction. In the context of music, De Woskin wrote, "The richness must not be an obvious intrusion into an ostensibly reiterative act. It may be inaccessible to the non-initiate, but must provide a rich feast for the connoisseur."[1] Inaccessibility was not a prerequisite of such highly refined art, of course, but a result of it.

It is in this light that the finest of archaism may best be understood, once it is separated from the confusing mass of later fakes and lesser works of archaism. Archaism is not better than the archaic, as one great art form is not better than another; they are simply different. But in its own merits, some of which are absent from the archaic, are to be found levels of expression which represent the same aesthetic as a painting by a Yuan master reinterpreting a Tang style. Whether in painting, calligraphy, poetry or jade carving, archaism deals with subtle, multi-layered form of communication.

It is not a coincidence that in nearly all the mature arts of the influential minority, there are to be found elements of archaism. This *bi*, which is one of the finest examples of archaism in jade of which we know, may not be as old as a prototype of the kind that inspired it (see no. 170) but it is a far more sophisticated work of art.

1. Kenneth De Woskin, op. cit. p.204.

12

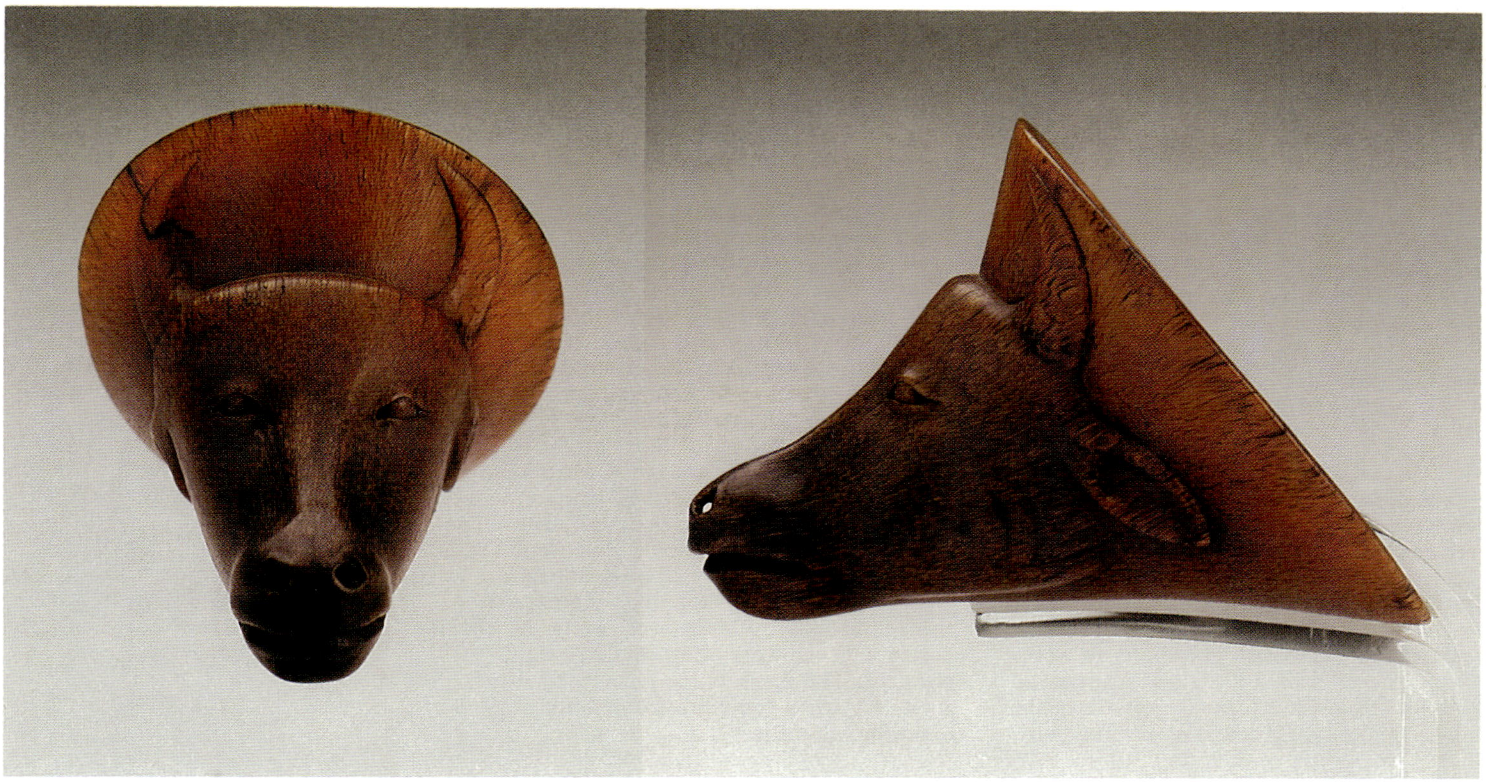

13

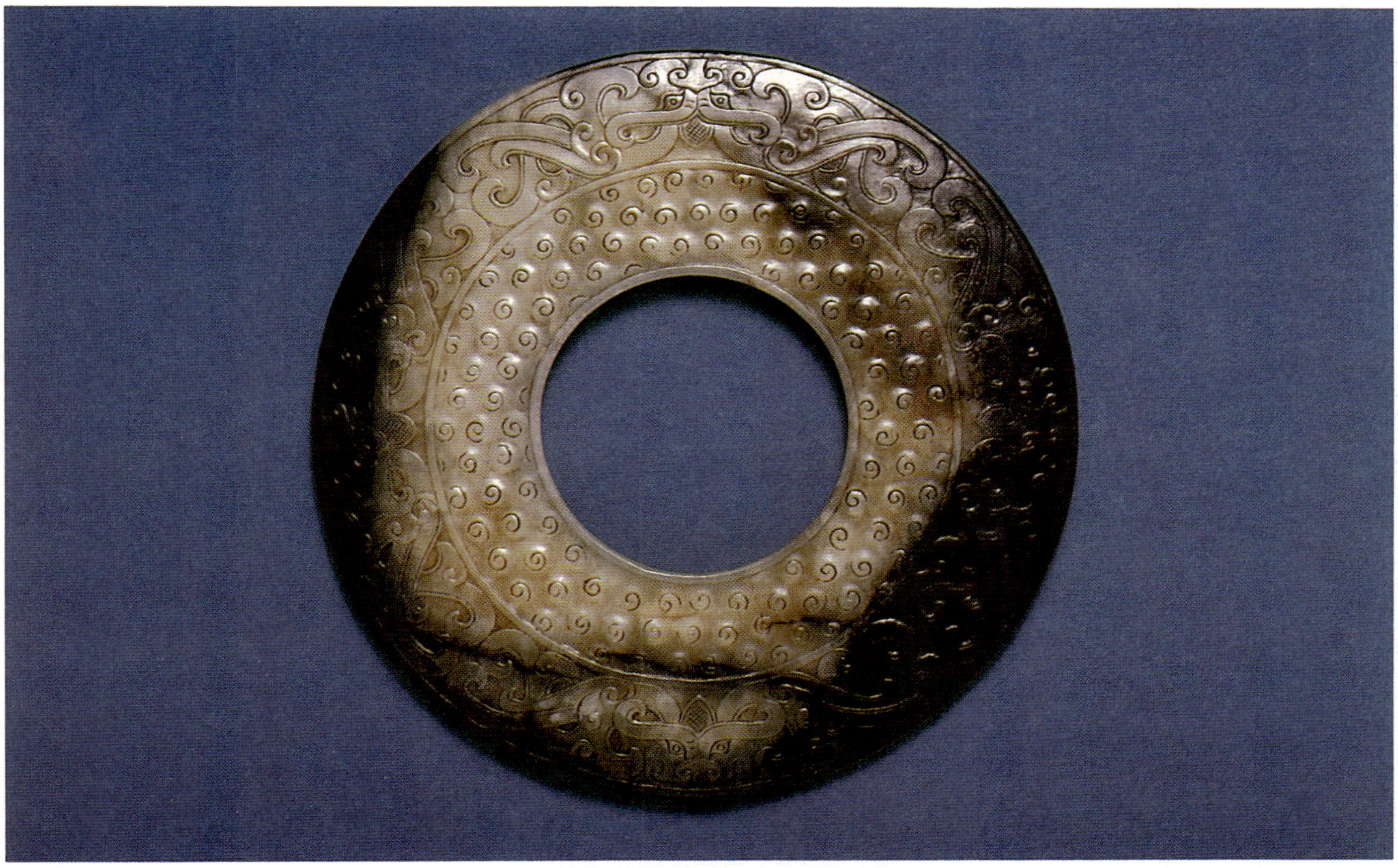

14

Pair of Seals

Soapstone, of mottled grey-beige and russet-red colour, of the type known as 'pumpkin-seed red' *(guarang hong)*, of the 'high mountain stone' *(gaoshan shi)* from Shoushan; each rectangular base surmounted by a crouching mythical beast; one with leonine features, winged jowls and shoulders (partly scaled), eagle-like claws emerging from paws, a bifurcated tail and flames curling around limbs and flanks; the other with a single horn, rudimentary wings, flaming haunches and an extremely fancy tail; both achieved with a gentle lack of menace.
Late Ming dynasty.
5.6 cm × 4.7 cm × 4.6 cm; and 5.55 cm × 4.6 cm × 4.6 cm.

壽山高山石雕異獸印一對
晚明，5.6×4.7×4.6厘米及5.55×4.6×4.6厘米

The various stones of the soapstone group, all very soft and easily worked directly with a knife or chisel, were a favourite material of the literati from the Ming period onwards. Refined taste spurned such substances as gold, silver and precious stones in favour of simpler, less ostentatious materials. The ability to work soapstone directly with a blade also made it suitable for the direct artistic expressions of the influential minority. Of course in valuing these humble soft stones above precious materials, they invested them with enormous value in the marketplace — far higher in many cases than gold.

No other stone in the history of Chinese sculpture has encouraged such refinement of technique and sculptural detail as soapstone. It is fair to say that technically and artistically some of the finest sculpture produced by the Chinese was made in this material. This is wholly due to its adoption by, and close association with, the scholar class and their aesthetic. Soapstone carvings, and other works in softer materials which attracted the direct attention of the influential minority may be said to represent in China the equivalent of the Western concept of sculpture as fine art. This is not to decry the long tradition of religious sculpture in China, which carries, at its best, great spiritual and sculptural strength, but to the Chinese connoisseur, the best sculpture was that done in these humble materials by or directly for the influential minority.

The seal text, the characters which once added a wholly separate level of meaning in a quite different art form to these exquisite little sculptures, has been removed. Seals were frequently the equivalent of a signature in China and it was quite common practice for them to be defaced or removed before the owner parted with the work of art into which they were cut. The depth of the rectangular base allows for an on-going process of adding and removing seal texts.

Although these carvings are not signed, in quality and style they are typical of the late Ming and early Qing period which represents the height of the soapstone carver's art. (Excellent pieces have also been produced since the late 1950s, but it is difficult to avoid the conclusion that while they are technically astonishing in many cases, real substance has, as in so much modern Chinese art, given way to surface virtuosity.)

Shoushan is a place in Fujian province where the village of that name is surrounded by peaks from which large quantities of soapstone of a variety of colours are mined. As a rule soapstone is classified by its general area, then by a specific location and then by colour and other visual characteristics. Gaoshan is one of the taller peaks to the east of the village, while the famous *tianhuang* is mined in fields in a bend in the river running through the village. For further information about types of soapstone see nos. 44, 45 and 164.

15

Seal

Zhu Mian

Bamboo, of finely marked yellowish-brown colour; a section of the 'root' carved to resemble both a mythical beast and a bizarre rock formation, the root riddled with holes as if eaten by insects, inscribed low on one side: "made by Laopao ('Old gourd'), Zhu Mian" with seal *Zhu;* a similar position on the other side inscribed: "appreciated by Huang Yi in the *dingsi* year of Jiaqing (1797)" with seal *Xiaosong* ('Little pine'); the seal text carved in positive seal script with the poetic seal "Seated in one's study enjoying the clear wind on the river and the bright moon".
Mid-18th century.
Height: 5.05 cm.

竹根異獸奇石印・朱冕製
清十八世紀中葉，高5.05厘米

Zhu Mian (*zi:* Laopao) was a native of Yangzhou, Jiangsu province, a poet, painter and calligrapher. Together with Cai Jia (extant works dated 1739 and 1782); Gao Xiang (extant works dated 1724 and 1748); Wang Shishen (d. 1759) and Gao Fenghan (1683-1748) they were known as the Five Gentlemen. He died in poverty in his old age. His inclusion in the Five Gentlemen grouping, and the fact that he exchanged letters with Cai Jia, suggest a mid-18th century period of activity for him.

Huang Yi (1744-1802, *zi:* Dayi; *hao:* Xiaosong; Qiuan) was a native of Hangzhou. He was a calligrapher, renowned for his official script, a painter of landscapes and flowers, and a famous seal carver (a disciple of Ding Jing).

This seal is at many levels a record of the literati response to the arts. It is at once a piece of worm-eaten bamboo root; a bizarre rock formation with its convoluted form and interconnecting holes; and a charming, muppet-like mythical beast, its mouth open as if aghast, bemused eyes staring upwards and long curving body blending into the natural form of the root. The seal text is a typical fanciful artist's seal. The characters carry meaning in the choice of archaic seal script, in the way they are laid out and carved (the abstract form and line so important to the art of seal carving), and in the text itself.

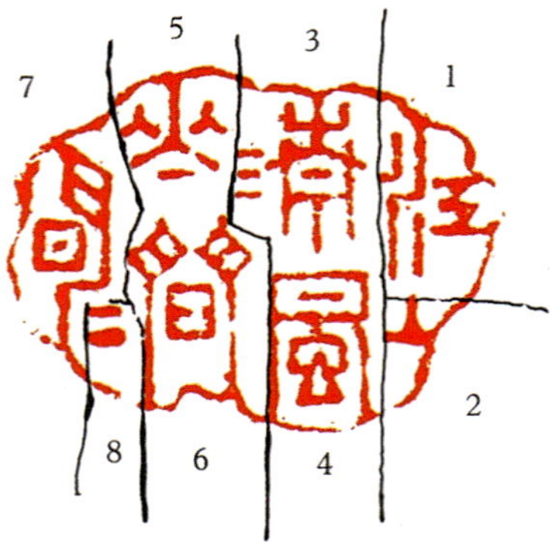

Fig. 1

The layout here is worth considering for the light it throws on the art of seal carving. Fig. 1 shows the seal impression divided into its eight different characters. Character two has been simplified by the exclusion of one stroke to allow for character one to dominate the visual space of the first line, and to blend more comfortably with the irregular shape into which it fits, where the outside profile of the seal must be taken into account. The water-radical on character three (carved as three horizontal dashes) has been extended into the space of character five to break up the vertical regularity. This makes of the central four characters a square unit, flanked on either side by two more characters. The central vertical line of character five has also been shifted to the left to avoid lining up with the central axis of character six, thus creating a more dynamic balance. In character six the upper rectangular element has been slanted diagonally, to match the diagonal in character seven for the same reason. The final touch is to reduce the last character 'moon' to two horizontal strokes, meaning ditto, indicating the repetition of the right-hand element of the character preceding it. The characters are deliberately angular throughout, instead of the usual curving seal script. It is a careful and thoughtful work of art in its own right, and one which carries, as a rule, far more weight with its Chinese audience than would the seal knob.

The immediate meaning of the seal text is not necessarily that the artist is literally sitting in a studio looking out upon a river scene at night. It invokes that mood, and is as likely to imply that the scholar who used it is capable of looking at a painting, reading a piece of calligraphy or listening to or playing music and transporting himself metaphorically to such a setting.

Another layer of meaning is added by Huang Yi, who in seeing and appreciating the seal, decided to add a record of his appreciation by simply saying that he had seen it and liked it at a particular time. He would, as a seal carver, have been referring primarily to the cutting of the seal text and his opinion carries considerable weight. This form of addition, like colophons and collectors' seals on paintings and calligraphy, is, although one open to abuse, a most satisfying level of art. It confirms the understanding that communication in art represents a complex web interlinking artist, audience and culture. Such additions, when tasteful, add considerable levels of meaning (quite apart from documentation) and connect the present viewer with the past.

14

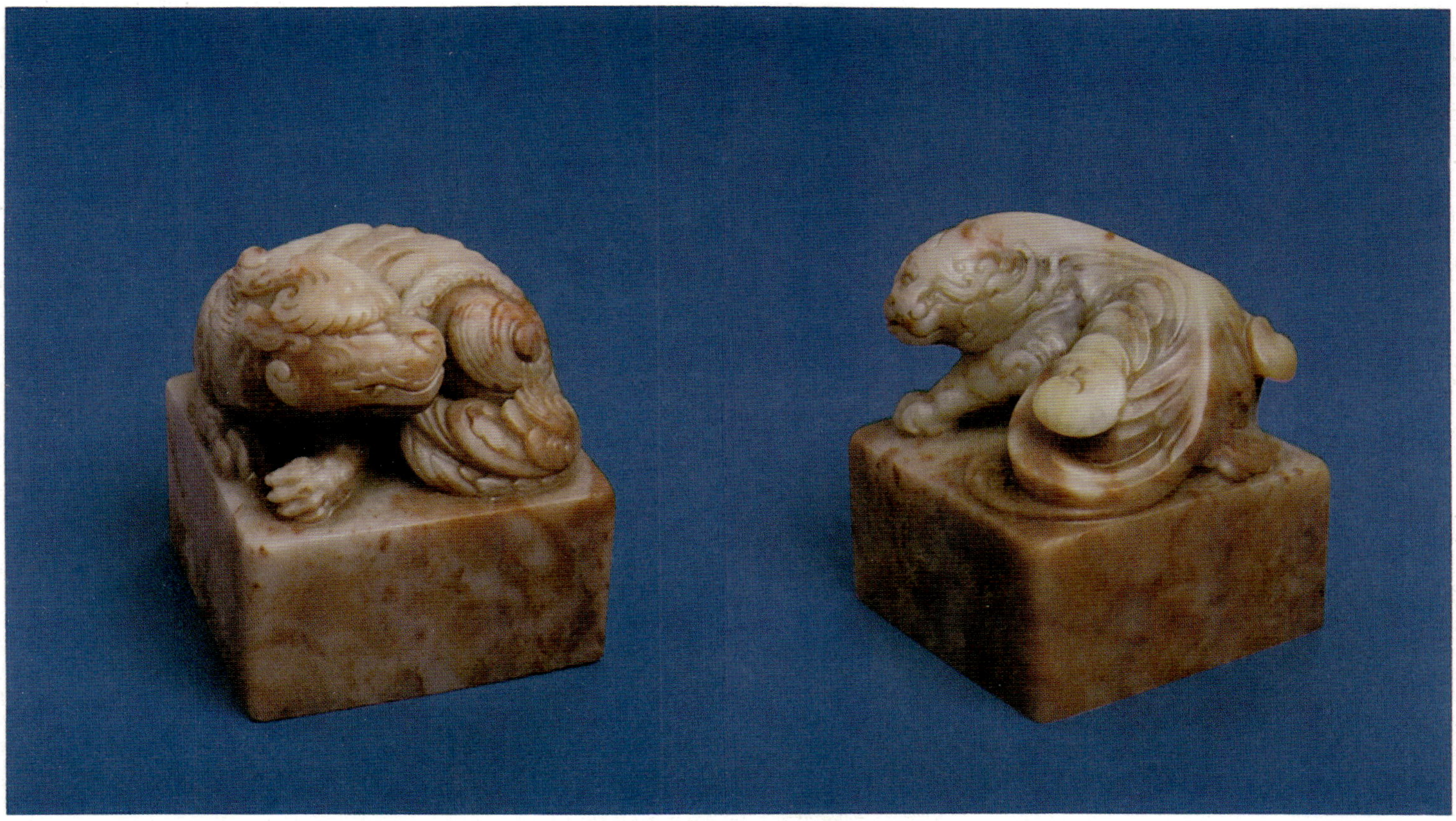

15

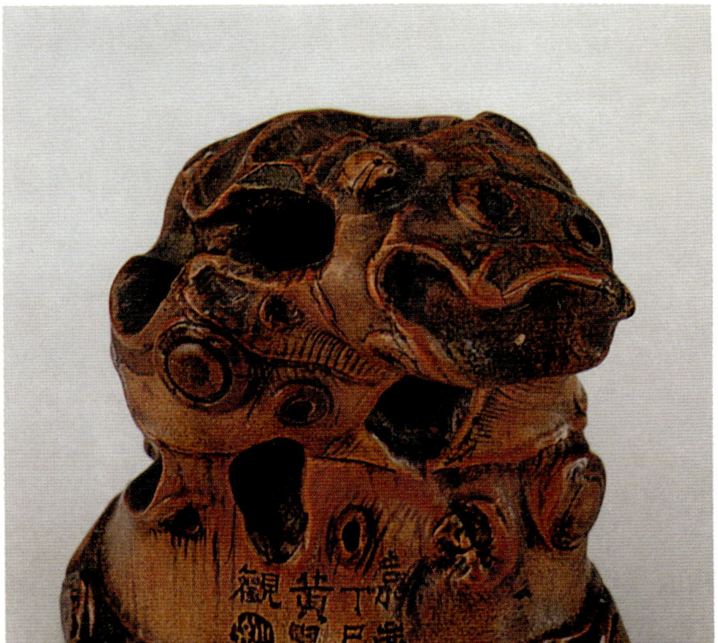

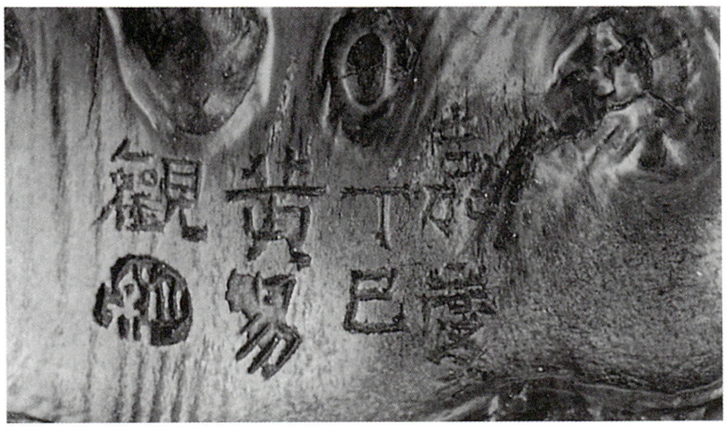

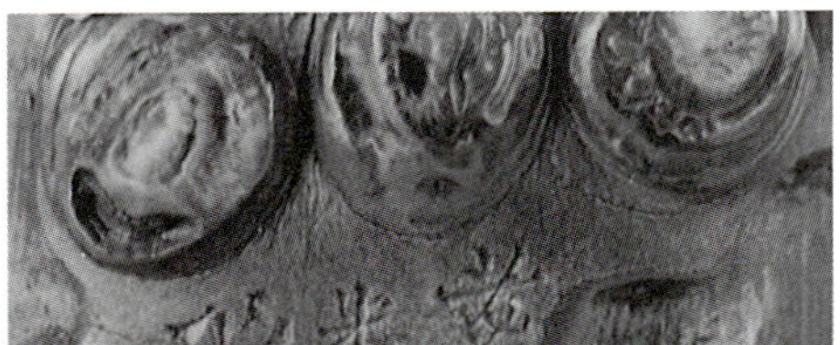

16

Houshan Scenery

Wang Yuanqi

Ink and colours on paper, hanging scroll; mountain scenery of Houshan, the foreground with a small lake-side pavilion, the water leading the eye back into the mountainous landscape set with various waterside houses; inscribed in the upper left area with the date, "Autumn 1694" followed by information about the painting: "Younger brother Diwen after touring Huiqi, told me all about the scenery of Houshan. I have never been there, but I use Shanqiao's brushwork to depict it" and the signature *Lutai, qi;* with three seals of the artist, *Xing yu yanxia hui, Yuanqi zhiyin,* and *Lutai;* a further seal of the artist in the lower right margin, *Shishi Daoren.*
1694.
93 cm × 49 cm.
The painting with one collector's seal of C.C. Wang.

吼山勝概圖立軸・王原祈作
清康熙三十三年(1694), 93×49厘米

'Younger brother' *(di),* in the case of Diwen may not literally mean that he was Wang Yuanqi's younger brother; the character *di* is also used for the purpose of social ranking. As a form of self-address it is used in communications with one's superiors, and in addressing others, in the sense of 'young' so-and-so. Shanqiao is the *hao* of Wang Meng, one of the 'Four Yuan Masters', but the reference to working in his brush-style denotes a spiritual rather than specifically technical influence.

Wang Yuanqi (*zi:* Maojing; *hao:* Lutai; 1642-1715) from Taicang, Jiangsu province, was the grandson of Wang Shimin (see no. 5) and with him, Wang Hui and Wang Jian was one of the group that became known as the Four Wangs of early Qing painting. He was a *jinshi* of 1670 and pursued a distinguished official career culminating in his appointments as Chancellor of the Hanlin Academy and vice-president of the Board of Finance. However, his greatest influence was derived from his activities as an artist and theorist and from the Emperor's appreciation of his paintings. According to his biography[1] the Emperor went often to the South Library, where Wang worked, and ordering him to paint landscapes, would watch fascinated, leaning on the painting table, oblivious to the passing of time. The Emperor bestowed a poem on the artist which contained the line, 'Your pictures should be shown to the people': six characters which Wang had carved on a seal as a record of imperial favour.[2]

In the same source is recorded his grandfather's great approval of Yuanqi as an artist in two separate anecdotes. The first notes that Yuanqi once painted a small landscape and pasted it to the wall of his study. Wang Shimin, passing by, was greatly surprised, asking, "When did I paint this?," assuming it was his own work. When he realized that Yuanqi had painted it, he remarked that the boy was certain to surpass him. Later when Wang Jian and Wang Shimin were discussing Yuanqi, they agreed that they were both a 'head shorter' than him in artistic stature. Wang Shimin is reputed to have said (in one of those delightful verbatim reports which pepper Chinese sources on celebrities even when written years, or even centuries after the event), "Among the four great masters of the Yuan dynasty Huang Gongwang was the foremost. The one who grasped his spirit was Dong Qichang, and I venture to say that I grasped something of his form, but my grandson seems to have grasped both the spirit and the form."

This anecdote is telling, both in the lineage of Wang Yuanqi in the orthodox tradition of scholar painting, and in his role in transcending it. It was Dong Qichang as the most influential of late Ming theorists, critics and artists who finally and for three centuries irrevocably defined the acceptable lineage of literati artists, in his so-called 'Southern School' (based not on geography but on a school of Buddhism which believed in sudden enlightenment rather than a laboured and steady path to enlightenment along a well-trodden and prescribed route — representing the dichotomy between the lofty scholar painting directly from the heart and the professional laboriously relying on technique).

In the 11th century, among Su Shi's coterie of friends, there evolved a new critical grasp of the nature of painting and its role in the evolution of consciousness, which allowed it to join music, poetry and calligraphy as a direct vehicle for self-realization. This paved the way for the Yuan revolution in painting which was centred around a group of scholar-artists who, refusing to serve the Mongol invaders, enjoyed the luxury of lifetimes devoted mainly to the arts. Objective reality had never really dominated the Chinese artistic tradition to the same extent as it did later in the West, but the Yuan artists were free to capitalize on a trend that had been evolving slowly since perhaps as early as the Han dynasty, but noticeably from the Tang. A subtle shift in emphasis from one of brushwork and form being a means of depicting subject-matter to one of subject-matter being a means of expressing abstract form and brushwork gradually emerged. This shift took place without the radical surface changes seen in the modern Western revolution in pictorial art to which it is parallel, but it was nonetheless one of major importance. Although this shift had been explored much earlier, and had been critically understood in the Song, various circumstances gave to the Yuan painters the task of fully exploring its potential and creating from it the new mainstream of art.

With the Yuan, painting finally rose above the remnants of whatever mundane concerns still dominated it to join the arts of poetry and calligraphy in a single sublime art form capable of reaching the most profound depths of perception and expression. This was the formidable contribution of what became known as literati painting — a contribution that so far transcends the details of literati life-style, attitudes and history that it remains today an invaluable legacy.

With clear recognition of this trend in painting it was inevitable that it be traced back along the route of its evolution — a process finally fixed by Dong Qichang. The lineage established was traced back to the 8th century painter Wang Wei and to Dong Yuan and the monk Zhuran of the 10th century, then through Su Shi and his coterie of Song, to the Four Yuan Masters (Huang Gongwang, Ni Zan, Wang Meng and Wu Zhen), Zhao Mengfu (one of the notable exceptions who did serve the Mongols) and others. From the 14th century onwards the mantle of this school of painters passed to Shen Zhou (see no. 8) of early Ming, through Wen Zhengming of mid-Ming to Dong Qichang of the late Ming, gathering more and more adherents as it evolved.

It was Dong Qichang who was largely responsible for taking an artistic trend and laying the foundations for its transformation into an orthodoxy. In a culture where the practice and theory of art were so often in the same hands and where the authority of the past carried so great a weight, it was inevitable that standards from time to time became restrictions. Dong's theoretical dogmatism from a position of immense authority encouraged an exciting and vital evolution in Chinese painting to become an orthodoxy, with all its attendant dangers. As an artist, Dong Qichang was one of the most exciting exponents of the literati evolution in painting and one of China's finest calligraphers; as a theorist his bias consigned whole areas of Chinese painting and classes of artists to an aesthetic wilderness measured in centuries.

Dong passed on his Master's mantle to his student, Wang Shimin. From there the literati tradition became the orthodox tradition with the Four Wangs, Yun Shouping and Wu Li as the leading early Qing exponents. This first generation after Dong Qichang was sufficiently close to the theoretical master to be able to interpret his will creatively, maintaining the best literati ideals without losing a sense of inner vitality. Their works, at best, carry subtle levels of communication of spirit in form and brushwork; they are all orthodox in subject-matter and style, but still vital, still with that mysterious inner strength that illuminates all great art. It was in the generations that followed in the orthodox tradition that the fire was almost extinguished. They followed the outer forms, slaves to Dong Qichang's rules, but few could rise above them, and in the following centuries the essence of what they had developed passed into the hands of other artists for its creative development.

In Dong Qichang's defence it should be said that what he prized in the artists of his tradition was the ability to weave the threads of tradition into a magic fabric of personal expression. This was understood by Wang Yuanqi but was sadly missed by many of the later orthodox painters. In this painting the literati tradition is clearly represented in the subject-matter, form and brushwork with its attribution to the style of Wang Meng, but the spirit that makes the work vital is Wang Yuanqi's alone.

Wang's works were highly valued in his day, and it is related that many who sought them had to be satisfied with the works of his students and assistants, to which he added his own signature. This raises intriguing possibilities for the Chinese concept of relative authenticity (see p.26). Questions are also raised by another version of this painting[3] which we have not had a chance to examine. The two works are remarkably similar, and according to C.C. Wang the other is a later copy of this work.

1. In the *Guochao Huazheng Lu* (see *Chinese Painting: Leading Masters and Principles,* Vol. V, p.201).
2. See *Seals of Chinese Painters and Collectors,* p.42, no. 59.
3. *Chinese Painting: Leading Masters and Principles,* Vol. VI, pl. 423.

16

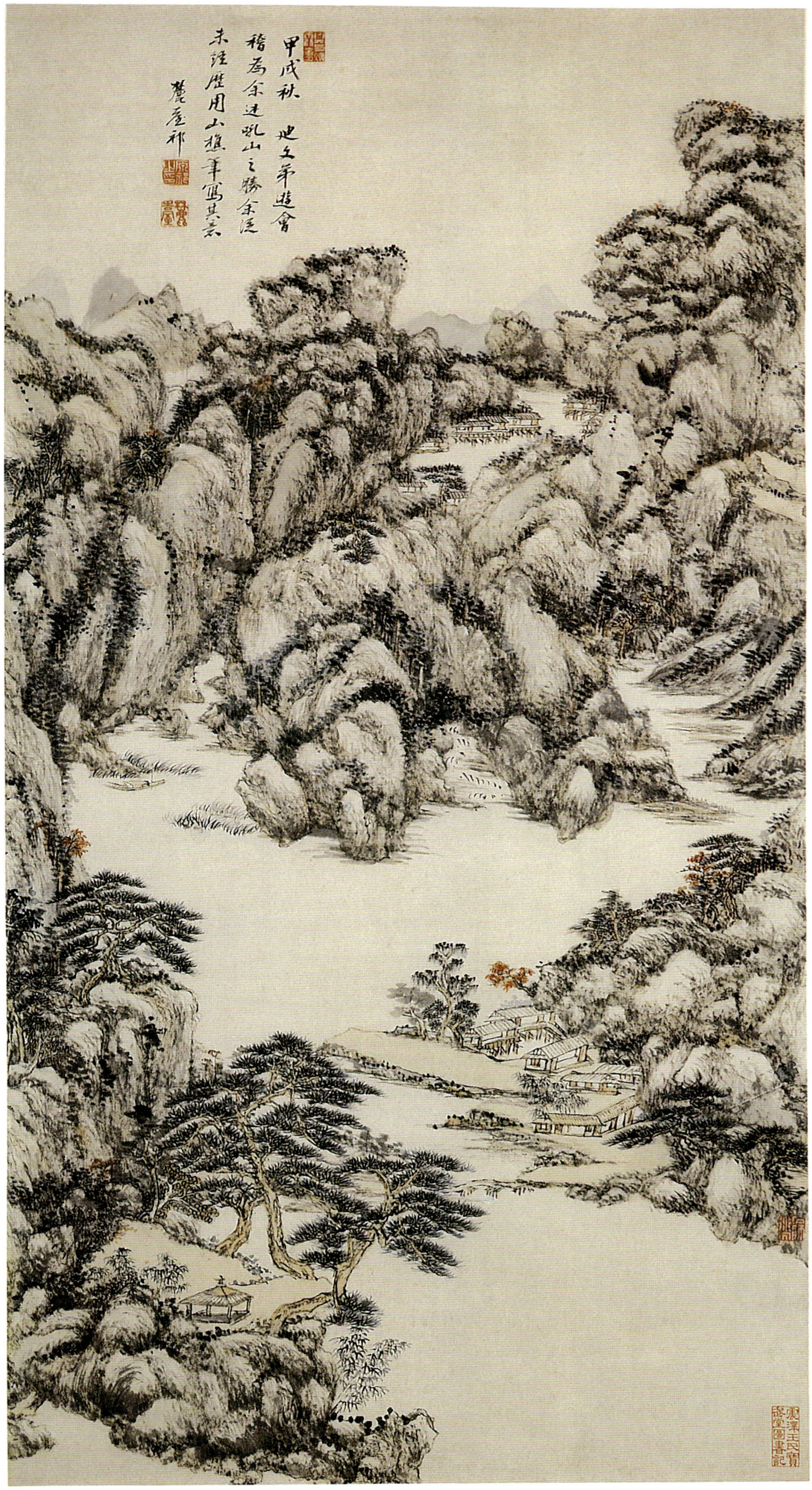

17

Goose

Wood, probably *nanmu* (cedar) root; the natural gnarled configuration of three main and several smaller sections joined together and partially enhanced by carving to create a model of a goose, standing with its head turned across its back.
Probably Qing dynasty.
57.6 cm × 58.5 cm.

楠木鹅
可能清代, 57.6×58.5厘米

From the Neolithic period onwards sculpted works were produced in China as ornaments, for symbolic or ritual use, or as religious images. Originally these were produced by craftsmen in response to varying patronage while the highest expressions of artistic communication tended to be concentrated in initially music, then poetry and later in calligraphy and painting.

As the influential minority began to dominate the arts and culture of China, so whatever they turned their hands to began to be invested with a more profound form of communication. As they began to carve seals and become involved in the production of other small sculptures, whether functional or purely aesthetic, these items were lifted onto a similar plane as the established fine arts. Although the early funerary and religious sculpture of China is immensely powerful, it is better related to the Western tradition of anonymous religious sculpture than to that of Praxiteles and Michelangelo, Rodin and Giacometti. In so far as an equivalent of the Western concept of the fine art of sculpture exists it is to be found in those pieces which come from the scholar's hand or respond most directly to his aesthetic. The Chinese equivalent of a Michelangelo is more likely to be a late Ming soapstone carving; the equivalent of a Rodin or Giacometti, such a gnarled wood carving as this. Nor is it surprising, considering the 'modernism' of the Chinese approach to art over so many centuries, that this goose, which although probably Qing represents a taste and style which could be much earlier, relates so closely to the modern Western aesthetic in sculpture.

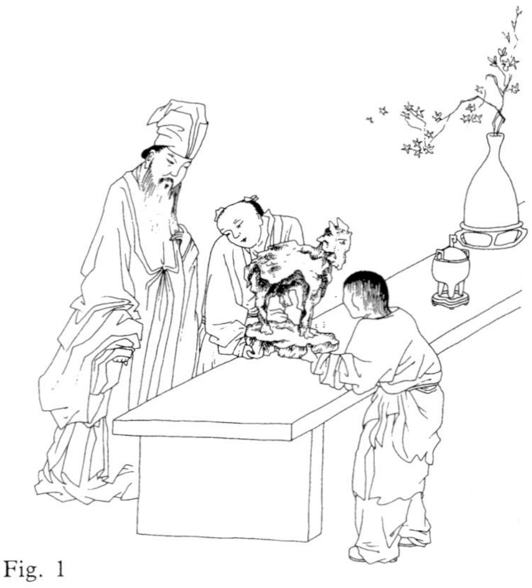

Fig. 1

There is a painting by Liu Han (17th century)[1] which shows an old scholar having a large 'natural' sculpture placed by two attendants on a large table for his enjoyment (see Fig. 1). The sculpture is clearly of a goat set on a stand, but whether it is a stone or root sculpture is not certain. What is clear is that such things were appreciated sufficiently in the 17th century to make the work the central theme of a painting.

The goose as a subject has become in the Chinese consciousness inextricably linked with the most influential of all calligraphers, Wang Xizhi. From the 4th century onwards he dominated style in calligraphy, a grip on the art which only began to loosen quite recently when his mainstream was joined by tributaries of styles and scripts which existed before his time. Wang obviously enjoyed geese, admiring the suppleness of line of their necks and likening it to good brushwork in calligraphy. His biography[2] records: "He liked geese. In Huiji there was a lone spinster who had a goose that was good at shouting [part of the psychological wisdom of the influential minority involved the practice of shouting — see no. 75 — to release pent-up tension, and the goose was perhaps valued in association with that]. She wanted to sell it, but was not successful. Wang Xizhi went to see it with his friends and relatives. The spinster, hearing that he was coming, cooked the goose to entertain him. Wang Xizhi regretted this very much. At another time, in Shanyin, there was a Daoist who liked to raise geese. Wang Xizhi went to see his flock and was delighted, wishing to purchase it. The Daoist said 'Write the *Daode Jing* for me and I shall give you the whole flock'. Wang Xizhi was pleased and after finishing the writing, he took them all back with him and was very happy with the exchange." Thus the goose became a symbol of Wang Xizhi, with all the connotations involved relating to calligraphy, brushwork and the artistic process in general.

1. *L'Eunuque aux Trois Joyaux: Collectionneurs et Esthetes Chinois,* by Michel Beurdeley and M.-Th. Lambert-Brouillet, pl. 76, p.117.
2. In the *Official History of the Jin Dynasty, juan* 80.

18

Monkey and Young

Wood; the natural gnarled form subtly enhanced by carving to give the effect of an entirely natural formation of a monkey, holding a peach in one hand, while its young climbs onto its other shoulder; the eyes of the larger monkey inlaid in what is probably jet.
Perhaps late Ming, but probably Qing dynasty.
Height: 7.2 cm.

木雕母子猴
可能晚明或清代, 高7.2厘米

The resemblance between certain traditional Chinese sculptural modes and modern Western sculpture has been noted in no. 17. It is particularly noticeable from the Song dynasty onwards with the appreciation of the persuasive minority for abstract rock formations and in the later tradition of root carvings (although these are not made exclusively from roots). The Chinese artist, never having been wholly bound by the confines of depiction of physical reality, has tended to emphasise the spirit of his subject. Enquiries into new realms of reality in the West are being reflected in the arts, so that at last the modes of perception and expression in Western and Oriental art are coming into consonance.

Giacometti or Moore reach into the self to discover the essence of their subject rather than its physical reality and bring forth what they find there. The same is true of an anonymous Chinese root carver, and the results are remarkably similar. There is a tendency to approach a Henry Moore with a deep respect, to treat it as high art, whereas the Western viewer will tend to approach a Chinese root carving as a pleasant, if bizarre, little nick-nack turned out by an anonymous craftsman of no importance. But if we approach the finest of root carvings with the same respect we accord a Henry Moore, we will find reflected there the same aesthetic, the same profound understanding of nature and the human condition.

19

Scholar's Object

Bamboo, of yellowish colour, a section of branch twisted around on itself in growth to form a delightful, gnarled scholar's object.
Qing dynasty.
Height: 7.15 cm.

盤竹龍形文玩
清代, 高7.15厘米

To make this object a branch of bamboo has obviously been constrained during growth so that a bizarre shape matures. A similar but larger example, carved with the head of a dragon, is illustrated in *Chinese Bamboo Carving*[1] where no function is ascribed to it. This piece might have served as a paper weight (it stands evenly on a flattened base), a brush rest, or simply as a delightful piece of bamboo, suggesting the form of a dragon in a suitably abstract way. Its charm is largely due to its abstract form and lovely surface texture and colour.

1. Part I, p.540, no. 200.

17

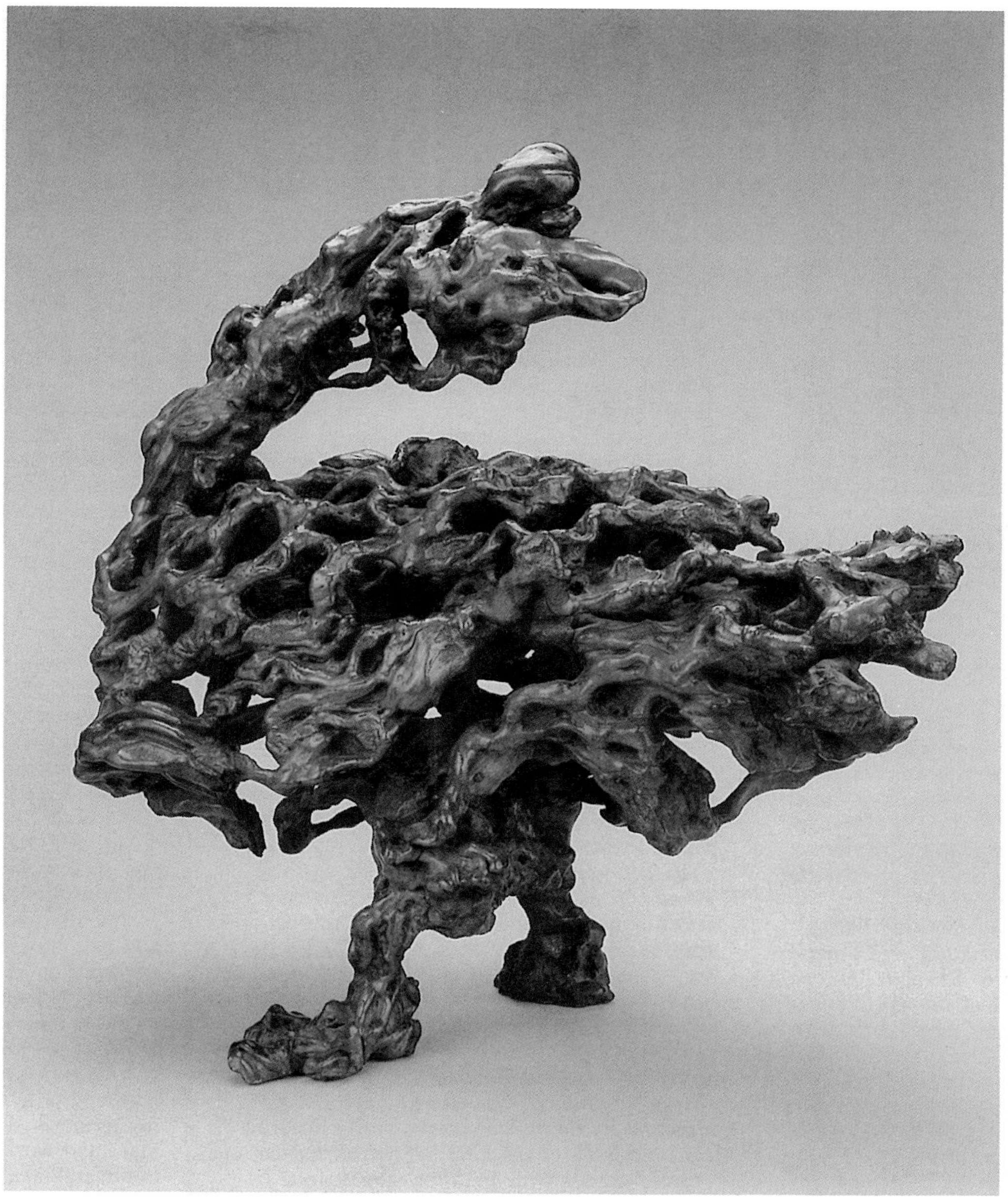

18

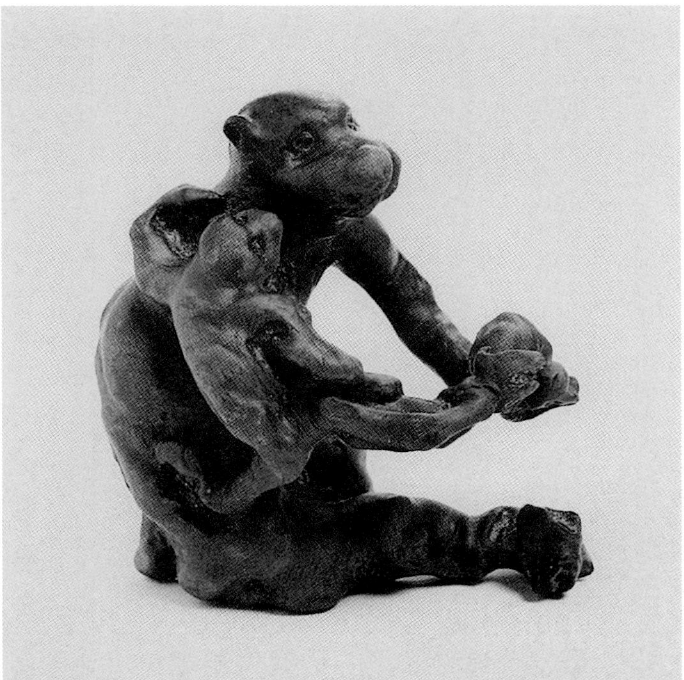

19

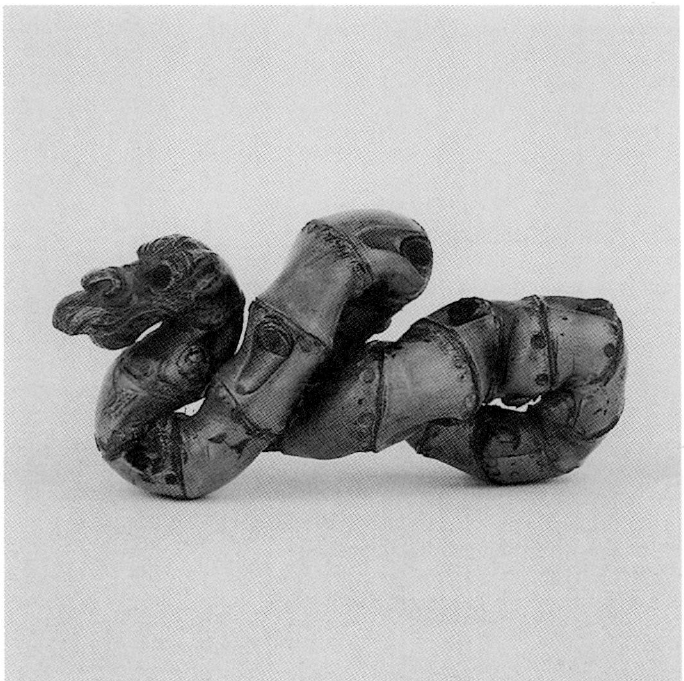

20

Landscape

Kun Can

Ink and colours on paper, hanging scroll; an old scholar fishing from a boat in the foreground, by a waterside house beneath pine trees, leading the eye upwards by way of a small stepped path, past a small mountain village, and a covered wooden path and bridge across a tumbling stream, pouring down from the high mountains above, in which further buildings nestle amid mist-enshrouded valleys and peaks; the upper section with a long poetic inscription about the subject in a vigorous cursive script, concluding that nothing much changes from year to year; followed by: "composed in the mid-Autumn of the *gengzi* year (1660) in the Hall of Prolonged Rest, by Tianrang Shiqi Can daoren" with seal *Shiqi;* the lower right corner with three collectors seals *Xiaolinglong Shanguan, Ma shi Huashan* ('Mr. Ma Huashan'), and *Li Shangming yin* ('seal of Li Shangming').
1660.
256.2 cm × 39.3 cm.

深山漁隱圖立軸•髡殘作
清順治庚子(1660), 256.2×39.3厘米

The Xiaolinglong Shanguan was a mountain establishment built by the Ma brothers of Yangzhou, famous merchant patrons of the arts in the 18th century (see no. 4); Ma Huashan was Ma Yu, son of Ma Yuelu, one of the brothers. We have been unable to identify the other collector, Li Shangming.

Kun Can (*zi:* Shiqi, Jieqiu; *hao:* Baitu, Tianrang, Shitaoren, Can Daoren and others; 1612-1697?) was a native of Changde, Hunan province. Prior to the end of the Ming dynasty he became a Buddhist monk, apparently led more by spiritual fervour than by the need for a safe haven or a symbolic withdrawal, which had driven fellow artists such as Shitao and Zhu Da into monasteries in the wake of the Manchu conquest. He spent the rest of his life in various monasteries, ending up as the Abbot of the Oxhead Temple near Nanjing. He was a recluse who had little taste for his fellow man. A poetic inscription on one of his works sums up his attitude to social intercourse: "I want nothing to do with receptions; the 36 mountain peaks mean more to me. The firs and bamboos waft over to me the hundredfold flower-scent of spring and summer. I read a volume of the Sutras and listen to them mocking me."[1]

Another indication of his reclusive, rustic life and his flight from the mundane is found in a further poetic inscription on a painting, also dating to 1660: "Once more I hope to encounter nobility of mind. Meanwhile I merely meet the coming spring and make a fresh appointment with the plum blossom."[2] He appears to have been a strange, sometimes rather tragic figure, driven by a restless need to fill his days with meaningful activity and yet also possessed of a profound understanding of nature and life. His many inscriptions and the colophons of others give the impression of a paradox of a man driven by some inner force to achieve that harmony with nature which is perhaps incompatible with driving forces.

His health was, by all accounts, dreadful, although this seems not to have interfered too much with his longevity. His disregard for the affairs of the mundane world, including sustenance of the body (he sometimes existed, we are told, on a few grains of rice a day) would not have helped matters, nor his habit of wandering off into the wilderness for periods of time, sleeping wherever a rock or grassy bank supplied a bed. He was also known for shutting himself in his hut away from the rest of the monks for long periods of time. In one of his paintings[3] which appears to be a metaphorical if not literal self-portrait, a monk is depicted in a nest in the branches of a tree, with the inscription: "The question is how to find peace in a world of suffering. You ask why I came hither; I cannot tell the reason. I am living high up in a tree and looking down. Here I can rest free from all trouble like a bird in its nest. People call me a dangerous man, but I answer: 'You are like devils. According to my understanding, all that exists is emptiness. There are plenty of Buddhist books, but listen now to my proclamation: 'The numberless beings and the three boundless continents are all in Amida Buddha'."

One feels that if he could have lived in a tree, far from his fellow man, he would have done so in his apparently restless search for harmony with nature. And yet his suffering brought him harmony in his art, which seems to have been a pastime rather than a driving urge. Siren suggests that no other painter of his epoch could, to the same extent, 'lay bare the heart of Nature and make us feel the very pulse beat of universal life in her shifting phenomena'. Certainly in landscapes such as this, the struggling genius finds a form of harmony with his beloved nature, depicting a scene in which fairies must surely dwell, and where distant unknown peaks soar above the mist and the echoes of roaring tigers. In all his carefully textured and reasoned landscapes, built up with meditative devotion, the viewer may find the very essence of harmony with the universe.

This extraordinary painting is unusually long and thin for a hanging scroll, although such extended formats were more favoured after the Yuan revolution in painting. It encourages a feature of Chinese multi-viewpoint painting which is similar to one of the most endearing characteristics of the long handscroll format — a journey through the painting similar to a journey through the real landscape.

At the bottom of the painting is a tranquil scene of an old man seated in the prow of his boat, fishing in a delightful setting, with a nearby waterside house, presumably his, where he will cook his catch. There is a charming insight to be had from the fact that he has gone fishing so close to his home when he might more easily have cast a line from the house. It is not the catching of fish which is the object of the exercise, although a pleasant bonus, it is the meditative pastime of fishing — setting out in a boat, mooring, allowing the water to gently lull the mind into a meditative trance. As in the tea ceremony of Japan (derived and refined from Chinese practice) tea could more easily be made, but the immediate function is transcended in the ritual. This intimate scene is a picture in itself, and one that might quite easily keep our attention for a long while. However, the narrowing river eventually leads the eye through the overhanging foliage to a path, and to follow it is irresistible.

Once on the path the upward journey is marked out for us, sometimes with steps, sometimes along a covered path and across a bridge, but at others along avenues of mist and the path of a cascading waterfall, leading the eye up towards distant and foreboding peaks — the mind's eye is not limited to the ground, as is the physical body in the real landscape. Finally, upon reaching the heights, we are taken still further by Kun Can's poetic inscription describing the scene, his flying draft script an exciting finale to the dry, textured lines up through which we have just climbed. Or is it a finale? The lines of the calligraphy suggest another aspect of the painting we may have missed in our concentration on the landscape as landscape. Running through it are a number of different languages of line as well. The single brushstrokes that make up the form of rocks and trees, houses and waterfalls; the lines of mountainous forms, that set up a dynamic pattern of interlocking diagonals textured with patches of dark splashes of ink and clumps of trees; the negative lines of white space of waterfalls and mist and, in the foreground, tree trunks and water. Suddenly the painting takes on quite different aspects as we move back through it. By the time we have finished this and many other possible journeys through the painting we have begun to see it as the Chinese artist and his audience saw it, and suddenly we may realise that for a moment all sense of time and place were left behind.

Kun Can himself hints at this mystical aspect of art in an inscription on one of his works: "Now, with the tip of the brush dipped in the ink, I penetrate into that which is not visible to us".[4] Nor is this an isolated view. It is standard to Chinese aesthetics that the distinctions between self and the physical world are illusory and therefore transformable. In Cong Bing's *Landscape Essay*[5] the Chinese view of the potential of art is clearly stated: "I make my place secluded, regulate my vital force, clean the wine cup and strum my lute. [After preparation of mind] I shall open the painting and face it quietly. Then, while sitting, I can reach the limits of the four remote corners of the world, without failing to face a host of supernatural forces, and alone respond to the wilderness where no human forms can be seen. There, with peaks of various shapes towering high and with the cloud-covered forest mysteriously stretching afar, I will sense the sages and worthies shining through the innumerable ages and their divine thoughts clearly showing through the myriad spiritual effects [of the great nature]. Then what have I to do? I will just let my soul be exalted. When one's soul is exalted, there is nothing more left to do."

1. *Chinese Masters of the 17th Century,* by Victoria Contag, p.26.
2. Op.cit. p.27.
3. Mentioned in Siren's *Chinese Painting: Leading Masters and Principles,* Vol. V, p.147.
4. *Chinese Masters of the 17th Century,* p.28.
5. Quoted in 'Concepts of "Lei" and "Kan-lei" in Early Chinese Art Theory', Kiyohiko Munakata, in *Theories of the Arts in China,* p.121.

20

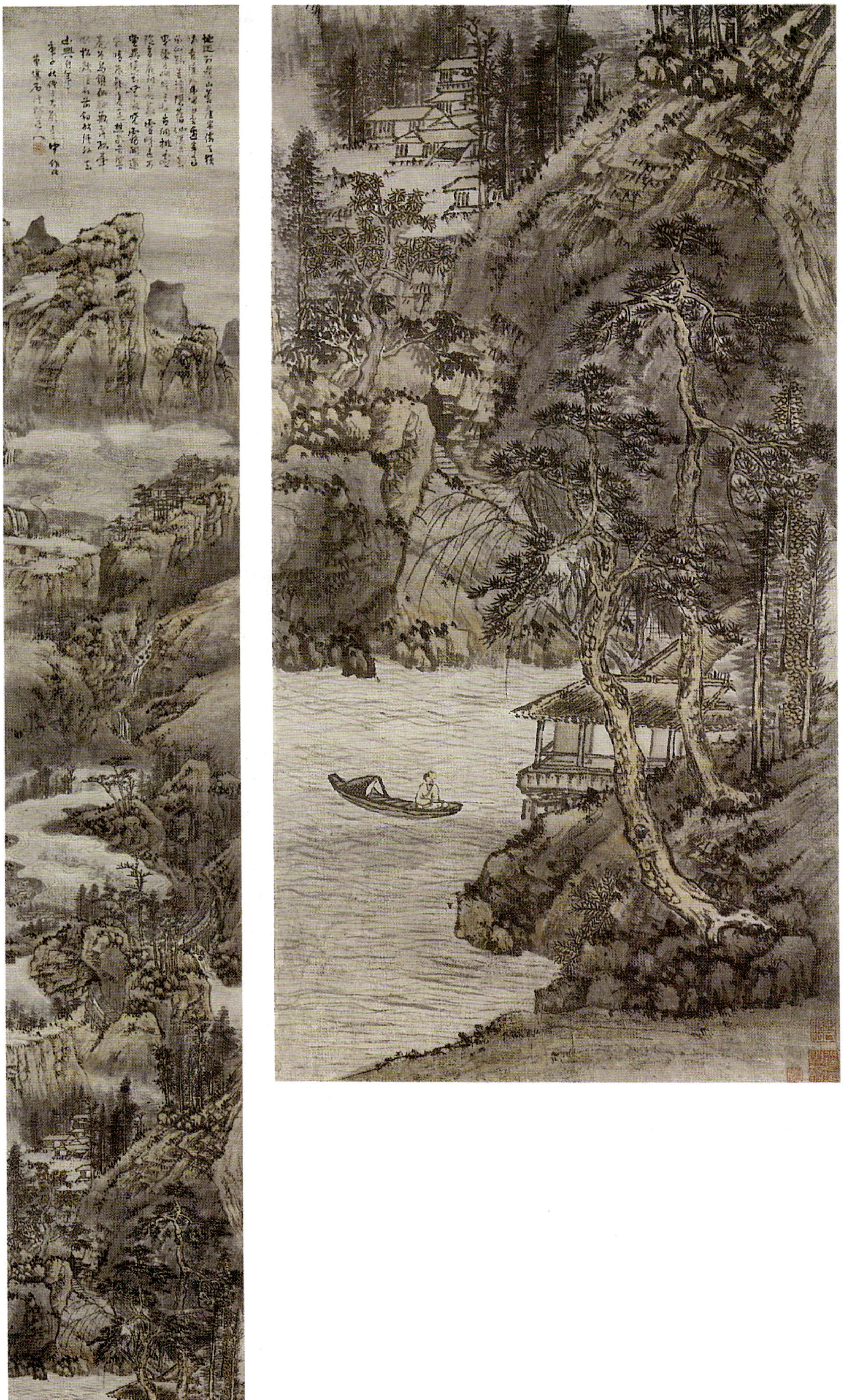

21

'One Thousand Years by the Rocks' Water Vessel

Wood, of golden-blond colour with inlaid pebbles; a hollow vessel in the form of an irregular peach, growing from a branch with leaves and a smaller peach, the larger fruit containing seven pebbles of different materials and shapes, naturally or artificially inlaid in the wood, one of which is inscribed with the title 'One Thousand Years by the Rocks' in clerical script.
Probably Ming or Qing dynasty.
Height: 8.6 cm. Length: 15.9 cm.

嵌石木雕桃杯
可能明或清代, 高8.6厘米, 長15.9厘米

The term for rocks here is 'cloud root'. The mountains of China are so constantly swathed in mists and clouds that a popular belief arose that clouds were born of the rocks, or were rooted in the rocks.

This strange vessel may have served as an artist's water container, in which capacity it would function perfectly adequately, or it may have been intended to exist mainly as an independent work of art. When acquired by the present owner it was filthy, with a very dark blackish brown stain hiding the lovely blond grain of the original wood. In this state it was not possible to see the small inserts and additions which had allowed the stones to be inlaid, and the impression was given of a root which had naturally grown around a group of pebbles. Cleaned up it became clear that most of the pebbles were artificially inlaid, but three appear to be natural insets — all similar stone. A root or burl might naturally grow around a pebble in a rare quirk of nature, but equally it was not beyond the Chinese vision and patience to implant one in a growing tree and induce the wood to enclose it in a natural manner.

Such an occurrence, whether entirely natural or helped a little by the hand of man, was a matter for great wonder, of course, combining as it did the joys of gnarled wood, old stones and the mystical quirks of nature. There was a strangeness, a 'resonance', to such a piece beyond description, but which carried enormous weight with the Chinese connoisseur.

The naming of mysteriously shaped rocks, roots, or other vessels and objects is typical of the Chinese tradition. To the Chinese audience, they would assume a distinct and very real personality, and to give these personalities names was therefore quite natural.

22

'Huangshan' Table Screen

Limestone, of the variety known as Dali marble; an inkscreen made of a circular panel of white marble with natural green and greenish-black markings resembling a tree on a rocky promontory in a misty landscape; the reverse plain white with very pale beige markings; set in a *zitan* wood mount and separate stand, the wood undecorated apart from simple shaped panels and edge details.
Probably Qing dynasty.
Diameter of visible panel: 16.1 cm.
Overall height: 33.2 cm.

大理石黄山圖紫檀座插屏
可能清代, 石直徑16.1厘米, 總高33.2厘米

Dali, in Yunnan province, is the source of marble for marble inlaid furniture and stone 'pictures' such as these, mounted as screens or as hanging panels (see no. 120), or often in groups of smaller ones. The varied and delightful figuring of the marble, often in thin layers as in this case, allows for the exposure of natural pictures by careful slicing and minor adjustments to the surface, which is frequently not flat but slightly undulating, like this example, where the artist has used his skills to accentuate the natural design.

In their combination of natural materials and the hand of man in isolating and enhancing them, they are similar to the strangely shaped rocks so beloved of the literati (see no. 9). Many have a dreamlike quality to them in being neither a definite landscape nor wholly abstract, which prompted Jean-Michel Beurdeley to coin the name (for an exhibition in Paris some years ago) 'pierre des reves' or 'dreamstones' — a name which has stuck in the West. Here the abstract markings of the stone are clearly intended to represent a known landscape, that of Huangshan, in Anhui province. Even if no such association was deliberate, no one familiar with it could look at a lone pine tree on a rocky crag, the mist encircling the peaks and forming a blank white ground, without seeing Huangshan.

This is very fine example of this type of screen, combining a superbly effective image with a discreetly elegant stand. So often these panels are mounted in a heavily ornate manner which seems out of harmony with the aesthetic of the natural stones.

23

Wrist Rest

Bamboo, of rich, reddish-brown colour; a section of culm carved as a narrow wrist rest to simulate a growing section of bamboo, flattened out, and with a bowed profile, the upper surface carved in low relief at both ends with foliated branches.
Probably mid-Qing dynasty.
Length: 22.5 cm. Maximum width: 2.3 cm.

竹刻竹枝葉紋臂擱
可能清中葉, 長22.5厘米, 闊2.3厘米

This elegant wrist rest is of unusually narrow form, although of usual length. The carving is restrained but powerful — the sort of work that does not impose itself upon the viewer, but is rewarding once revealed. The simple, repeated elements of the culm segments counterpoint the superbly carved branches and leaves at top and bottom. Perhaps the masterstroke of the conception is the contrast of the static lower leaves with the windswept upper leaves. As the eye moves from one end to the other, and the wind catches the upper branches, the piece appears to take on a life of its own. It also reaffirms the similarities between wrist rests and paintings in the artist's approach to pictorial arrangement of an essentially flat, elongated rectangular format.

24

Brush Pot

Wood, *nanmu* (cedar), of richly varied brown and purplish-brown colours; a section of tree trunk including the bark, simply hollowed out and polished to create a brush pot of irregular form; the base inscribed in running script: "On this frosted old tree trunk a distinction is to be made between purple trunk and green leaves, it has a heart to withstand the wind and the rain. Bringing my *qin* I like to sweep clean the mossy rock at its roots. I want to evoke the autumn sounds, but find myself just staring at the clouds. This poem is for the Daoist Airuo, written by Huang Zhen" with seal *Zichen;* the base of the interior lined with a thickness of hard but still pliable material which bears the impressions of many brush ends and other shapes.
Qing dynasty.
Height: 18.8 cm.

楠木刻銘筆筒·黄鎮銘
清代, 高18.8厘米

The first part of the poem probably refers to the noble nature of the withered old trunk, representing wisdom in old age (as opposed to the fresh green shoots of youth) which brings with it the 'heart' (the level of understanding necessary) to withstand all hardships. The second part shifts attention to the poet who takes his *qin* to sit metaphorically on an old rock at the base of the tree to compose poetry or otherwise express the feel of autumn, but finds himself lost in the wonder of it all and staring at the rolling clouds. Even the Daoist's name is in harmony with the whole feeling, as it may be translated as 'The Daoist like cloud-filled skies'.

Both Huang Zhen, who gave the piece to the Daoist and may even have made it (although this is less likely as the poem says only that he wrote it), and the Daoist himself are unrecorded.

The base lining inside the pot is unusual. Its main function was presumably to add weight and therefore stability, which it does admirably, but presumably the same effect would have been achieved had a thicker base of wood been left, since the substance does not appear to be heavier than the wood. It might have been intended as a cushion for things deposited in the brush pot to avoid chipping the ends of wrist rests, *ruyi,* etc. Even today, although it has apparently hardened considerably over the years, it still performs this function.

21

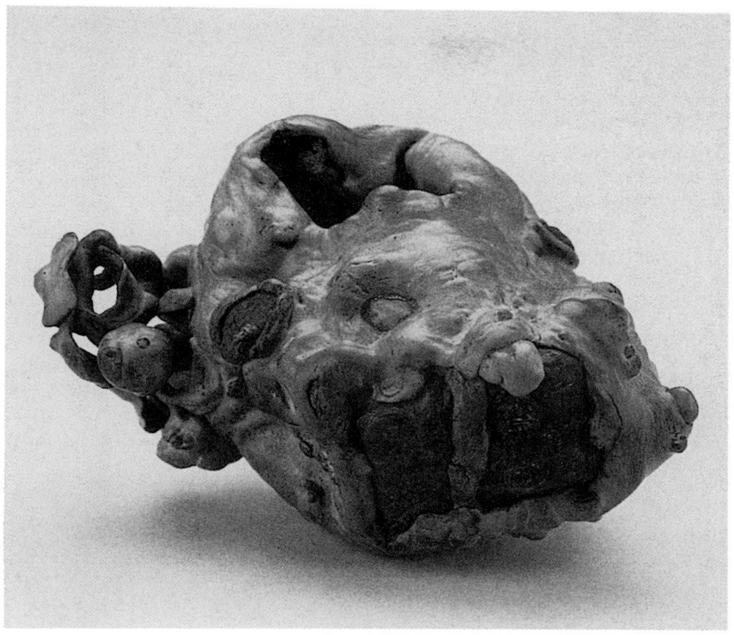

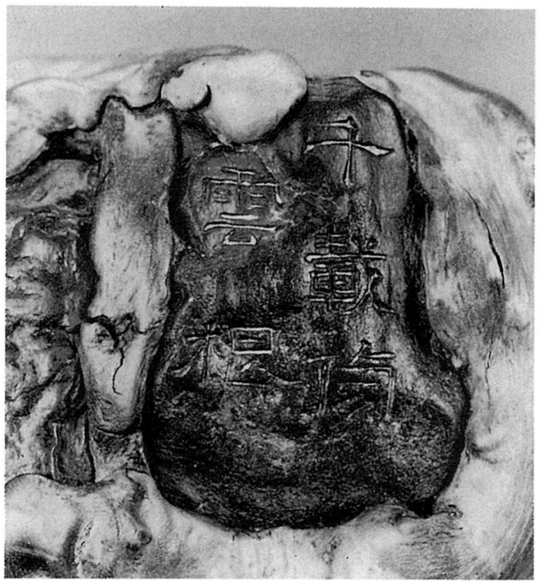

23

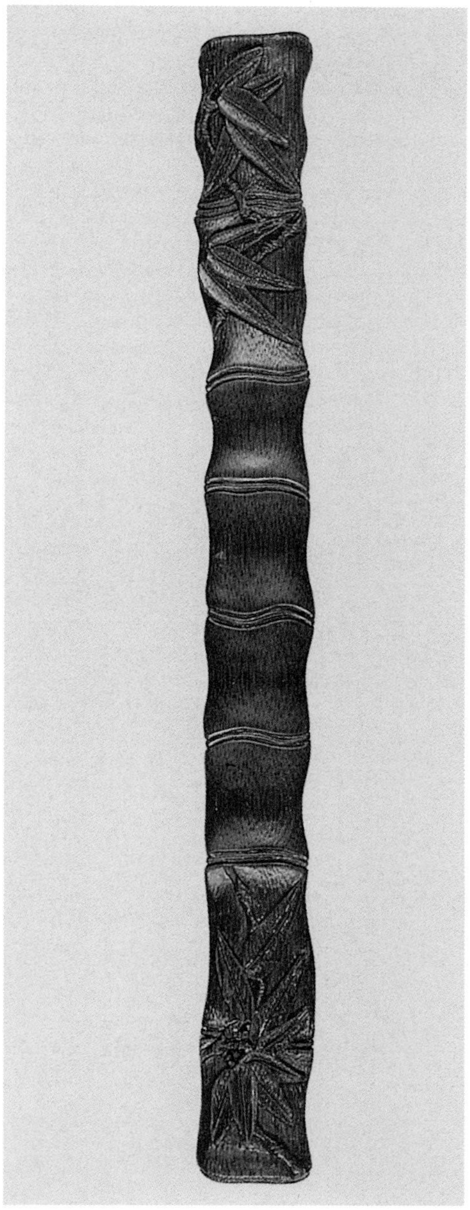

22

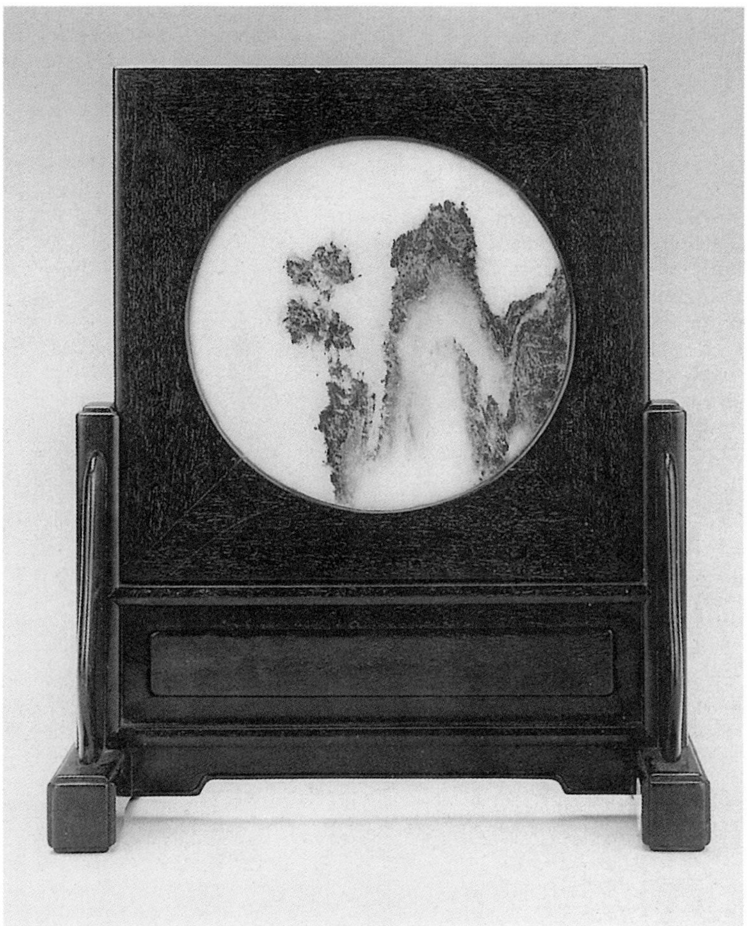

24

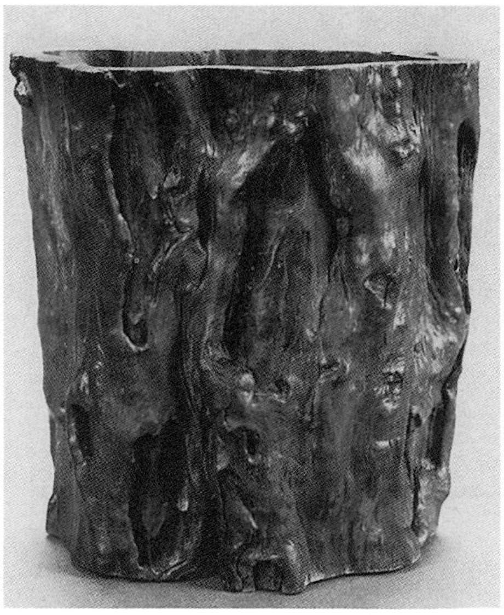

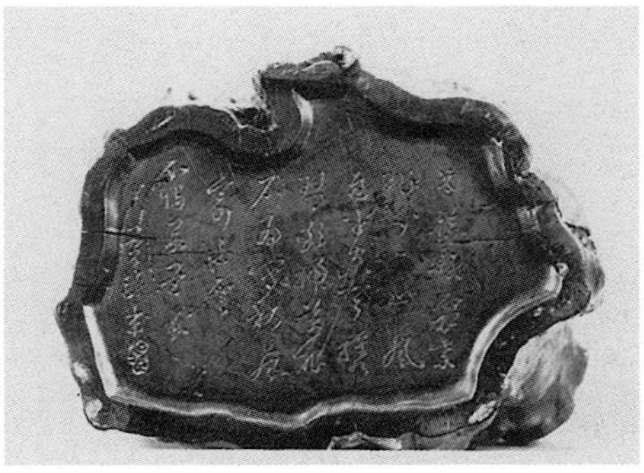

25

Fan Frame

Zhou Yi

Wood, *huangyangmu* (boxwood), of brown colour; fan frame carved on one side as a section of flowering tree, the naturalistically carved root and trunk sections giving way (in an unusual inverted format) to a smoothed and stylized handle; the other side carved in a similar fashion, but as an uprooted bamboo, with leaves growing from a sprig close to the roots, one leaf realistically worm-eaten; the ribs are made of *zitan*, which has also been used to line the inside edge of the two ends. Attributed to Zhou Yi of Changsha.
Late Qing dynasty.
Length: 32.2 cm.

黄楊木刻花木扇骨·周義製
晚清, 長32.2厘米

The similarities between this frame and the ivory example signed by Zhou Yi (no. 58) are obvious. Both are carefully observed examples of naturalism giving way to a stylized handle, with superbly carved details and use of openwork. They appear to be of similar age and are stylistically and technically very close. Zhou is reputed to have left many of his best works unsigned while his copyists apparently signed their works, further confusing the issue. Another problem is that Zhou worked at times from other people's drawings and we have no idea how accurately he would have copied them, and to what extent he would have overlaid his own stylistic habits.

We return here to the concept of relative authenticity (see p.26). Although we cannot be certain that even the ivory fan is genuine, with these two works we are dealing with the spirit of Zhou Yi, which is the pre-eminent concern. Should further research demonstrate that neither is anything like the style of the master (despite his fame as a carver we have seen no other pieces by him to establish a standard style), then they will become fine works of art by an anonymous artist. In the meantime they are reasonably associated with Zhou Yi, and assume all the meaning which is inevitably added to a work of art when we are afforded knowledge of the artist.

The bamboo side of this example is a particularly well-executed work of naturalism and a beautifully conceived abstract design. The nature of this has been accentuated in a sketch in Fig. 1, with three basic elements of the main stem, the branch growing out of it and crossing it twice, and the two textured leaves laid out for maximum dynamic effect.

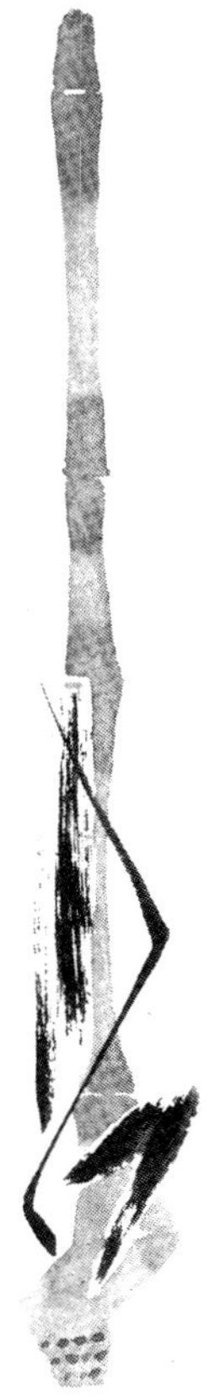

Fig. 1

26

Fan Ends

Ivory; a pair of fan ends, the simply shaped handles supporting an upper section carved in deep relief, leaving certain areas in the round, with 18 monkeys (nine on each end) picking peaches in a mountainous landscape with peach trees, pines and various shrubs and vines growing among rocky grottoes, with drifting clouds above; the monkeys' eyes all inlaid with a dark brown material.
Probably mid-Qing dynasty.
Length: 31.7 cm each.

象牙刻山水猴群扇骨
可能清中葉, 長31.7厘米

There is an arcadian feeling to this subject, with its happy band of monkeys playing in an idealized setting. The monkeys are obviously having a wonderful time as each follows his own pursuit unaware of mundane problems, but, in the story it illustrates, these delights were brought to an abrupt end. Here we see the realm of the Monkey King, the Waterfall Cave, on Flower and Fruit Mountain. The Monkey King was the central character of the classic Ming novel *Xiyou Ji* ('Journey to the West'). Tired of his ideal surroundings where food and water were in unlimited supply, he departed in search of adventure. He eventually found himself wandering in the Heavenly Palace at the time of the Heavenly Queen's birthday, with immortals and fairies coming from far and wide to celebrate. Enraged at not having been invited, he caused chaos in the Palace and ate the peaches of longevity, gifts for the Queen. Since the trees from which these were taken took 3,000 years to flower, and a further 3,000 years to bear fruit, the Queen was rather cross. She punished him by imprisoning him under a rock. The Monkey King was finally freed from his imprisonment by the Tang monk Xuanzhuang, on the condition that he accompany him on a journey to the West to obtain Buddhist sutras, the journey being the main subject of the novel.

The detailed carving is exceptionally good, combining a fine sculptural sense with marvellous detail. The layout of the subject is particularly clever. Each fan end, and it is worth remembering that they were made to be viewed independently of each other, is carefully planned so that a single monkey at the base captures the attention, and through a series of lines of trees, gorges between rocks, creepers etc. leads the eye upwards, keeping it interested on the way with groupings of other monkeys, to the centre of attention which is in the upper section. This is the natural focal point of the fan end, whether the fan is opened or closed; at each end a group of monkeys, playfully interacting with each other, holds the centre stage. Above, in each case, is a single monkey placed to keep the eye moving upwards until it is returned to the main subject by an enclosing band of clouds.

We have attributed this carving to the mid-Qing period based on little more than the degree of wear. Stylistically it might have been made at any time during the late Ming and Qing dynasties, but the ivory, although smoothed through handling, is not much discoloured, as one would expect a much used fan to become. It certainly seems more worn, however, than the late Qing example signed by Zhou Yi (see no. 58).

28

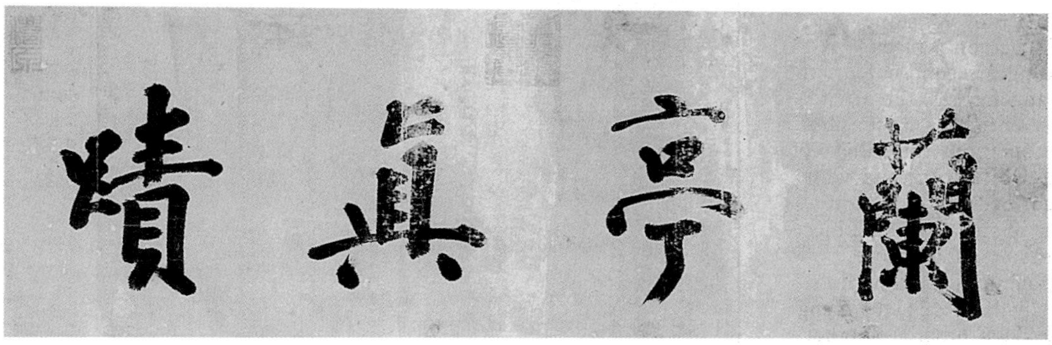
蘭亭真蹟

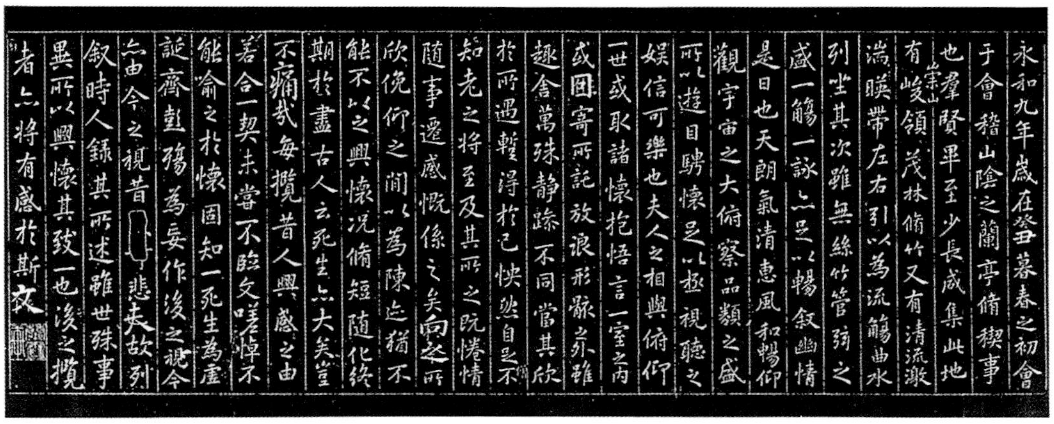

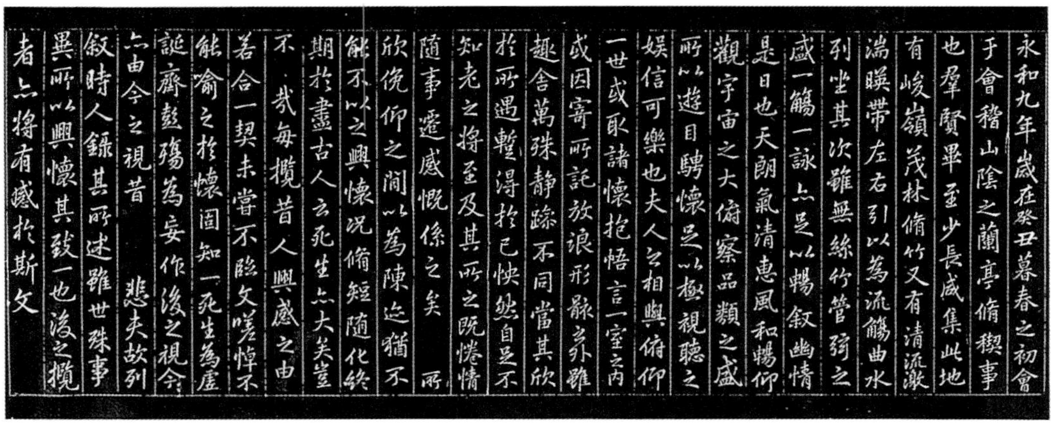

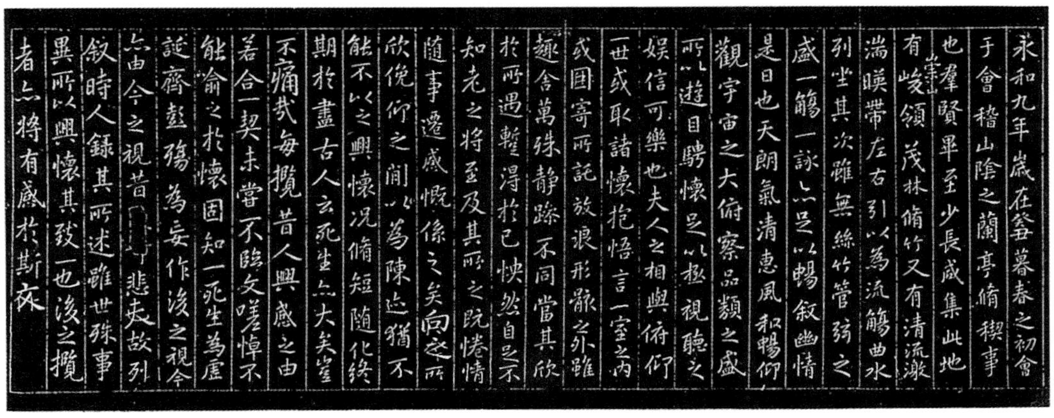

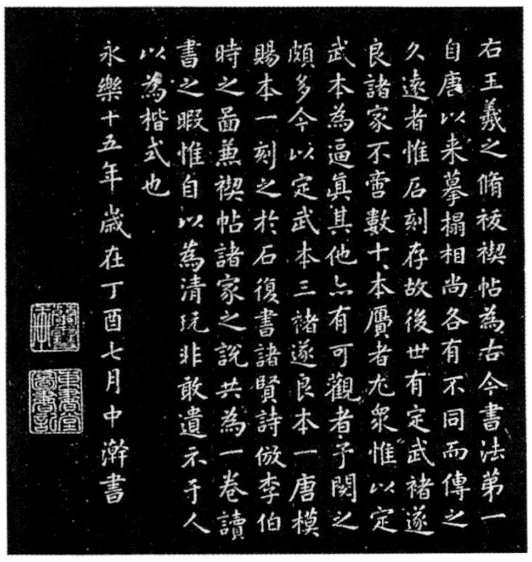
右王羲之脩禊帖為古今書法第一
自唐以來摹搨相尚各有不同而傳之
久遠者惟石刻存故後世有定武褚遂
良諸家不啻數十本麿者尤衆惟以定
武本為逼真其他亦有可觀者予閱之
頗多今以定武本三褚遂良本一唐模
賜本一刻之於石復書諸賢詩倣李伯
時之畫兼禊帖諸家之說共為一卷讀
書之暇惟自以為清玩非敢遺示于人
以為楷式也
永樂十五年歲在丁酉七月中澣書

original work. This is particularly apparent in the way in which blocks of tone are used throughout the work. As a rule the stone engraver is using white space on a black ground, but here by adding a second colour, the pale beige of the water and figures, the artist has added an enormously enriching dimension. By playing with the combinations this allows of black space, beige space, white space and white line the artist has created levels of communication quite independent of the original subject-matter and peculiar to the art of rubbing.

The first stone engraving of Li Gonglin's painting was apparently made in 1241 by Zeng Hongfu. In 1417 Prince Zhou ordered another engraved.[3] This version is taken from the 1417 Prince Zhou version, and was obviously made to be an exact copy of it, differing only in very minor details. A foreshortened version which appears to be taken from this, or the 1417 version, is illustrated by Goepper[4], where it is dated as probably 18th century.

Paul Moss has devoted a great deal of attention to this particular rubbing, identifying all its elements and translating the inscriptions and seals in *Emperor, Scholar, Artisan, Monk: The Creative Personality in Chinese Art.* He also refers the reader to a number of related sources for further information. Editions of the *Lanting Preface* are also discussed at length, together with various stories attached to their history, in the *Gegu Yaolun* (pp.38-68 in Sir Percival David's translation).

1. Translated as *Chinese Connoisseurship,* by Sir Percival David.
2. *Chinese Art,* Vol. 3, pp.247-272.
3. See *Shodo Zenshu,* Vol. 4, p.5, for two details of this version, and for a lengthy discussion on the various editions of the *Preface.*
4. Op. cit., p.254, no. 119 a, b.

28

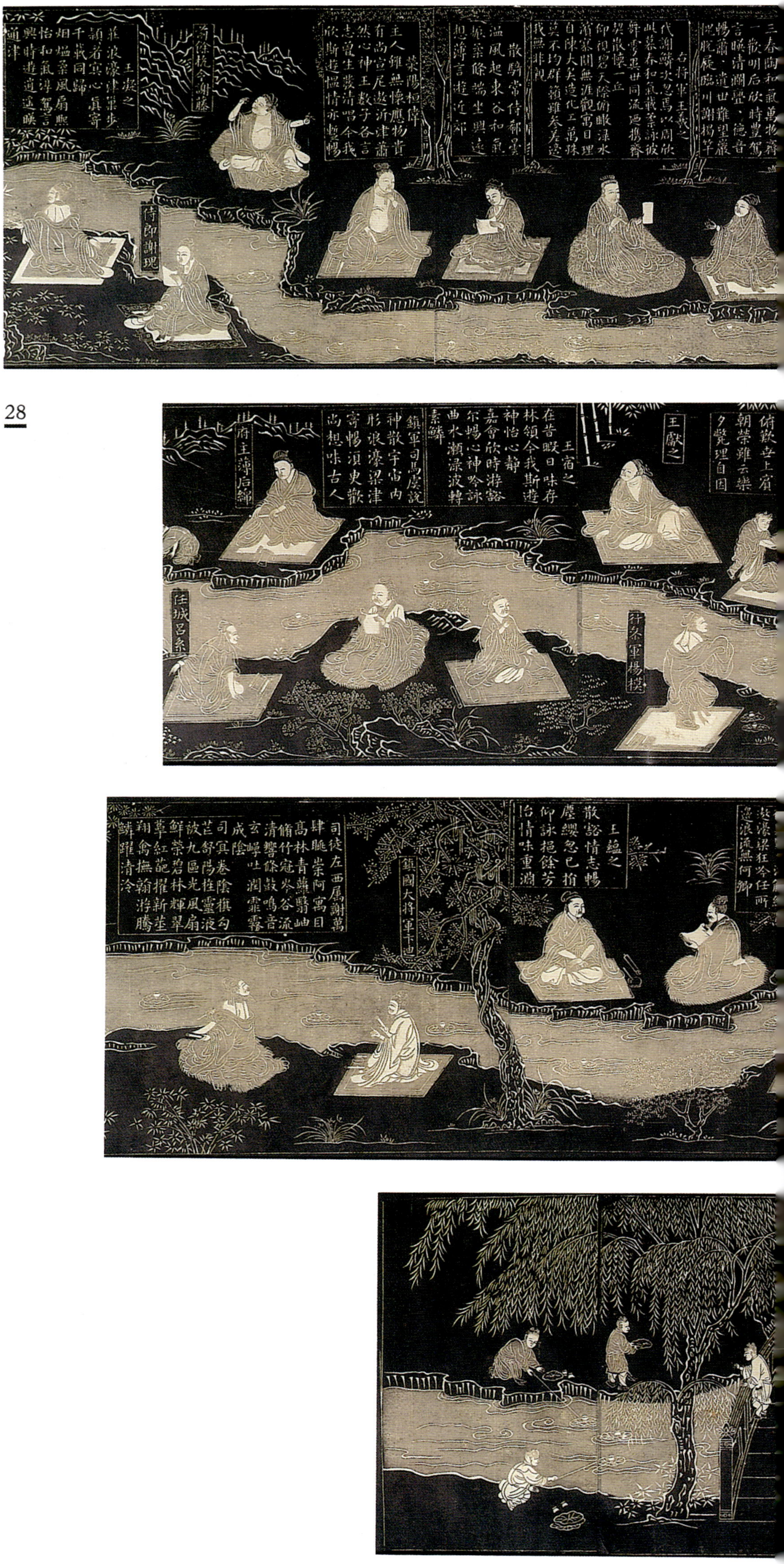

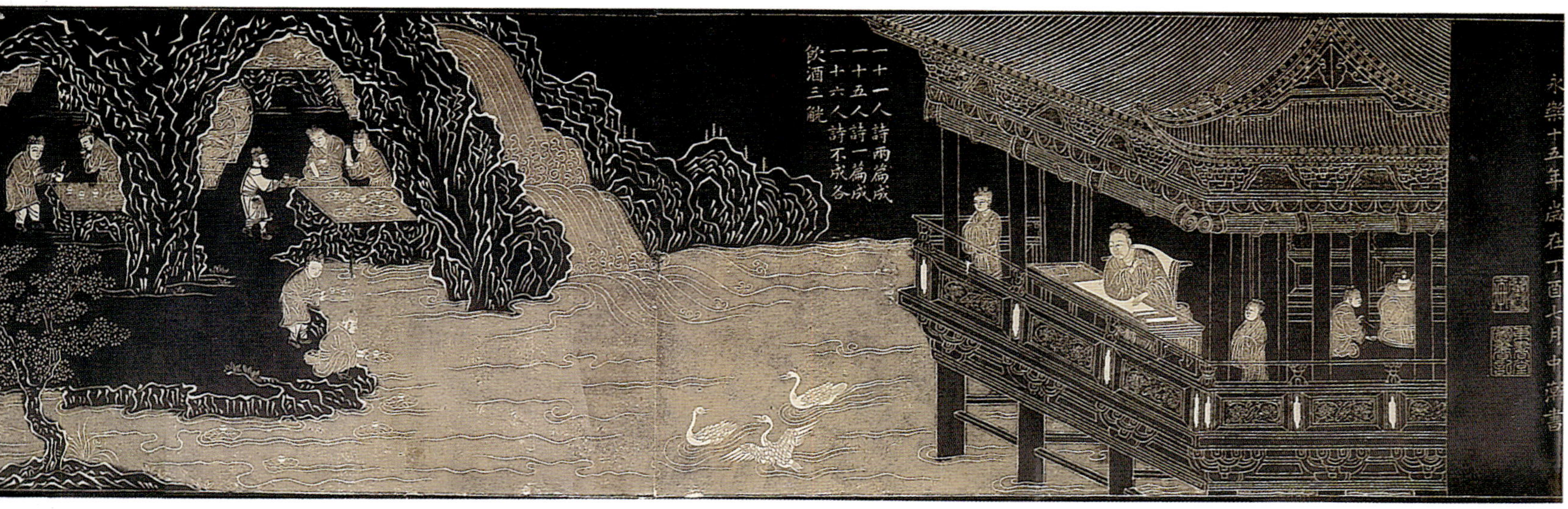
一十一人詩兩篇成
一十五人詩一篇成
一十六人詩不成各
飲酒三觥

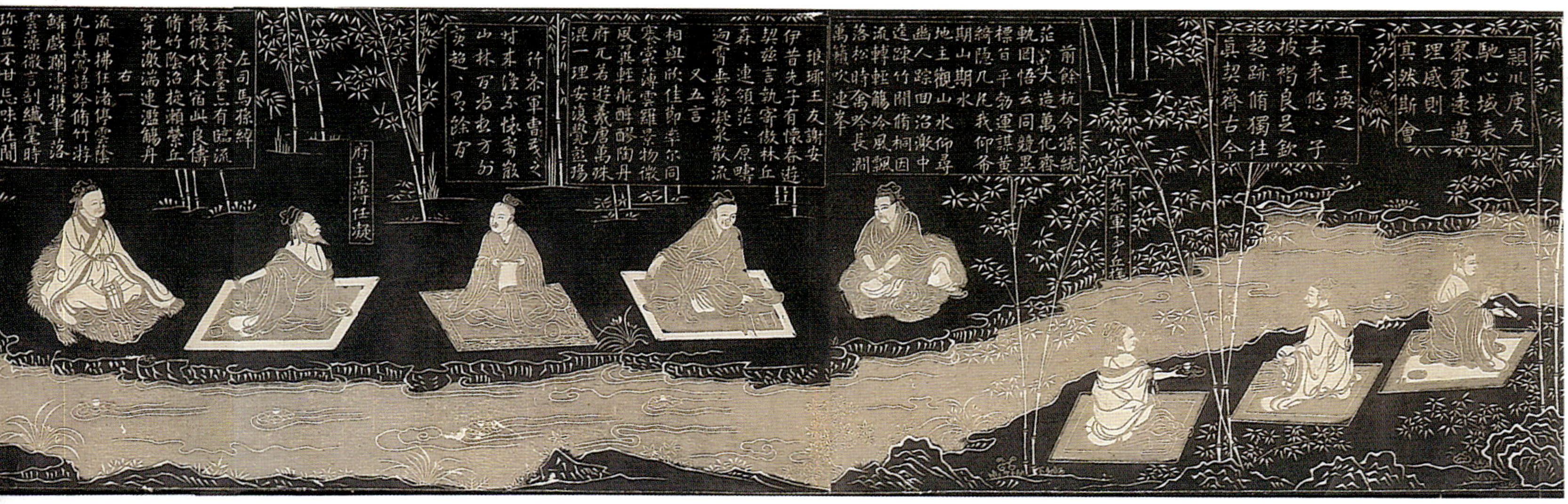

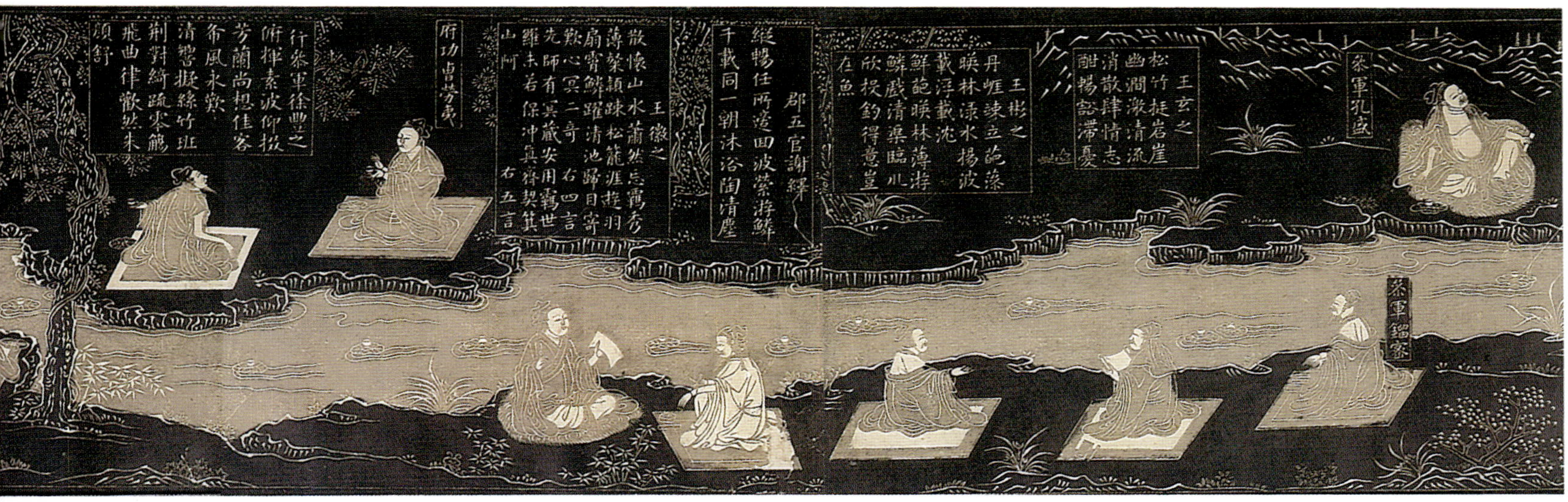

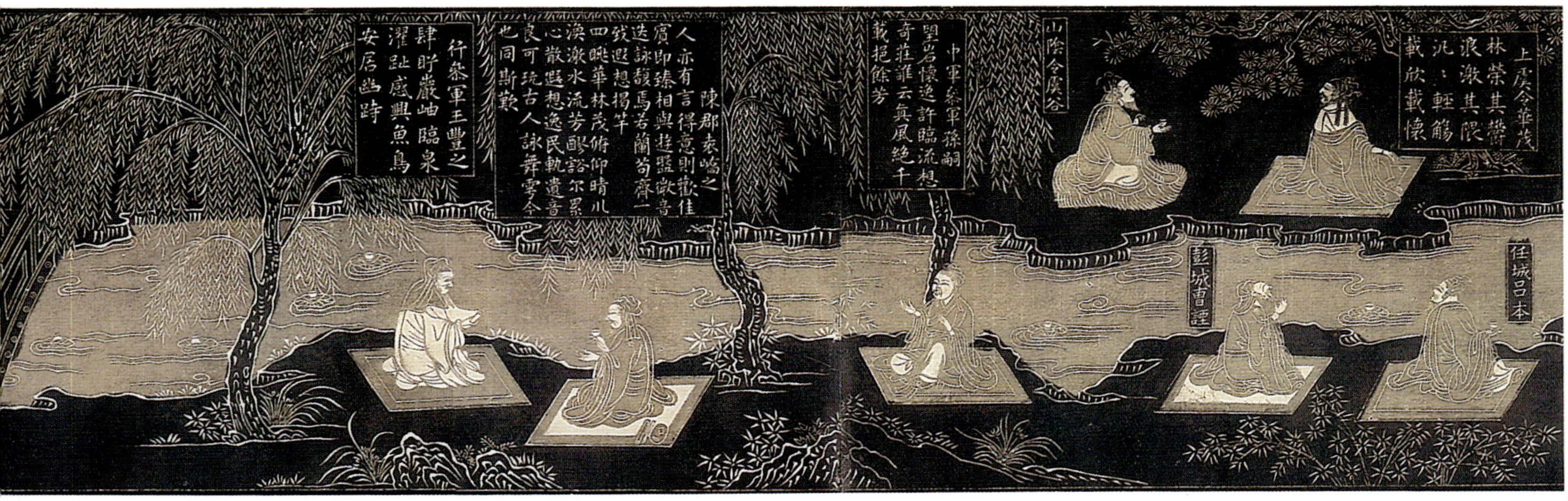

29

Mountain Retreat Title

Yi Bingshou

Ink on gold paper, hanging scroll; the title *Gongyu Shanfang* (see below for translation) in clerical script, inscribed thereafter: "Written by Yi Bingshou in the tenth month of the sixteenth year of Jiaqing (1811)," with two seals of the artist, *Yi Bingshou yin* ('seal of Yi Bingshou') in positive seal script, and *Xihu Chang* ('Old man of West Lake') in negative seal script.

With one collector's seal, *Tuohu* (Hui Jun, 1902-1974).
1811.
37 cm × 113 cm.
Published: *Anthology of Chinese Art: Min Chiu Society Silver Jubilee Exhibition,* p.260, no. 89.

隸書橫額•伊秉綬書
清嘉慶十六年(1811), 37×113厘米

In the use of studio, retreat, pavilion and hall names the Chinese language is used as allusively as in poetry. The literal meaning of this mountain retreat name is 'Attacking Jade Mountain Retreat'. But the sense is one of revealing the beauty of the jade in the rough boulder of stone, so it also means jade carving. Another popular saying implies that jade not worked upon is not art, and therefore a person who has not gone through the hardships of life is not a real person. Superficially this means self-cultivation; however, beneath this meaning is a reference to a well-known saying that the boulders on one person's hill may be of great value to others — that what is a rough boulder to one, may be fine jade to another. But beyond that, boulders and jade are also analogies for experience, and what is really meant is that if one listens carefully to others, their experience may be of immense value to one's own quest. There is a humility implied here and one might, not unreasonably, end up translating the name as the 'Mountain Retreat of the Humble Listener' — a seemingly far cry from the literal meaning, and a quite wrong translation on the face of it.

The subject-matter of Chinese calligraphy presents complexities; the subject is, at one level, the meaning of the characters. But the fact that calligraphers over the centuries have written and re-written the same poems and phrases, the same quotations from famous philosophers or sages, demonstrates that this is only one tier of subject-matter. Beyond its role of transmitting meaning in the written language, calligraphy transmits abstract meaning, as does painting. Critical theory in calligraphy recognized this at an early stage; in the 9th century Zhang Huaiguan wrote: "In literature several words are necessary to express a meaning; in calligraphy one character is sufficient to show the writer's mind."[1] In this role the meaning of the characters is not the subject but their form.

Certain forms for each character, depending upon the chosen script, dictate the range of variations within which it may be written. This range, although quite rigidly proscribed, is extremely varied, allowing for great personal choice and inflection. It suits ideally the mind of the influential minority as it allows for infinite personal variation of expression within a structured framework, the latter being essential in providing the artist with an audience capable of following his high refinements of the analogical language. In effect, however, the practised calligrapher will have the details of this framework so deeply embedded in his being from endless practice that it will hinder him not at all. When the moment of elan comes, and the loaded brush makes contact with blank paper the exercise is an abstract one. The meaning of the character is irrelevant at this point; what matters is line and form, colour (the Chinese consider tones of ink to be colour) and texture. Any difference between the carefully considered and balanced strokes here and a Mondrian or a Motherwell, are more the concern of means than of meaning.

Yi Bingshou (*zi* Zushi; *hao* Moqing; 1754-1815) was a native of Ninghua in Fujian province. He was a *jinshi* of 1789 and served as an official in various posts. He was well-known as a calligrapher, particularly for his seal, clerical and regular scripts.

1. Quoted from *Wenzi Lun* in *Fashu Yaolu* 4 *(Wangshi Shuyuan)* 53a, in *The Chinese Literati on Painting: Su Shih (1037-1101) to Tung Ch'i-ch'ang (1555-1636),* by Susan Bush, p.21.

30

Poem

Li Jian

Ink on paper, hanging scroll; a poem in cursive script, followed by the date and signature "1794, Erqiao, Jian"; with three seals of the artist, *Changwu Xiangji* in positive seal script; *Jianmin* in negative seal script, and *Erqiao shanren* in negative seal script.
1794.
135 cm × 39 cm.

With two collector's seals, *Li Weiluo Jiancang yin* ('seal of the authenticated collection of Li Weiluo') and *Lantang Shuwu* ('Blue Pool Studio') both of the contemporary collector Li Guorong and in positive seal script.
Published: *Anthology of Chinese Art: Min Chiu Society Silver Jubilee Exhibition,* pp.254-255, no. 86.

草書七言詩立軸•黎簡書
清乾隆甲寅(1794), 135×39厘米

Li Jian (*zi* Jianmin; *hao* Erqiao, Erqiao Shanren; 1747-1799) was a native of Shunde, in Guangdong province. He was a scholar and poet skilled in seal carving, painting and calligraphy. As an artist he was impressed by the Yuan masters Ni Zan and Wu Zhen.

The abstract nature of calligraphy has been discussed in no. 29. It is seen here in its exciting cursive mode where, within a structured framework of the form of each character, the artist is free to express himself in an abstract expressive manner. Following the lines, regardless of the meaning of the characters, one begins to grasp the art of calligraphy as an invigorating language of movement. There is a continuous energy that can be followed from the first stroke to the last. This line of energy, materializing through the brush into the ink trace, is considered by John Hay to be the fundamental characterization of calligraphy.[1] Zhang Huaiguan in the 9th century wrote: "The body and force-form of a character is complete with a single stroke. There may happen [a passage] where [the brush line] is not continuous but the blood-artery is uninterrupted. Where there is continuity, then the energy communicates through from one line to the next. Only Wang [Xianzhi] understood this profound principle, thus the character at the top of a line in his calligraphy often continues [the energy] from the character at the bottom of the preceding line."[2] This is based upon the belief (fundamental to Chinese medical theory and manifest throughout the fine arts) that "patterns of energy deep in the body's interior are palpable at its surface".[3] In calligraphy (as in all the fine arts, but it is perhaps more easily recognized in calligraphy than in painting, for instance) what we are dealing with is the visible trace of these patterns of energy.

The language of line is fundamental to Chinese pictorial expression, which includes calligraphy once the meaning of the characters is transcended. Literacy in China required mastery, at least to some extent, of brush and ink and therefore of line, and led inevitably to an immense respect for this language in art, and a great sensitivity to it. To the knowing audience the manner in which a particular form is delineated (whether in calligraphy or painting), the strength and energy of the brush work, and the amount of restraint exercised in concealing obvious skill while expressing elegance and refinement speak volumes for the character of the heart behind the brush. It can also convey a wealth of meaning, specifically and generally, about the past, by subtle allusions in the form or style of a character to past masters of the art. This language is exploited for its potential for creative communication in China as in no other culture.

This piece of calligraphy has been chosen for the relative ease with which the beginner might become enchanted with this powerful language, so essential to understanding the more profound aspects of Chinese painting and calligraphy and, therefore, so much else in Chinese art. A simple, playful exercise will soon reveal the language.

To start the process we simply follow the lines with our heart (with the aid of the eyes, and if necessary an imaginary brush) and follow the dance. (It is, incidentally, extremely difficult to keep still while involved in this process, and watching an initiated audience look at calligraphy can be as much fun as looking at the calligraphy itself.) It begins in the upper right-hand corner with the solid oblique upward stroke of the first element of the first character, which then pauses and sweeps downwards in a deep curve, to turn in on itself, and with a flourish, leaps out of its own confines to touch the 'floor' again for the first stroke of the next character. Throughout the work the direction of the brush is fairly obvious, so the beginner may enjoy the dance independent of any knowledge of stroke order. Soon one becomes familiar with the movements and begins to get caught up in them, being swept along on the energy, pausing here for a deep sweep, or sliding in a graceful, snakelike twist to pirouette and begin again in another direction. With a series of continuous movements the viewer is carried along to the end. That is the language of line. It is simple to follow once we recognize its existence, and with a little fluency in its use direct experience of the heart of the calligrapher or painter becomes second nature.

1. 'The Human Body as a Microcosmic Source of Macrocosmic Values in Calligraphy', by John Hay, in *Theories of the Arts in China,* p.88.
2. Ibid., p.87.
3. Ibid., p.89.

29

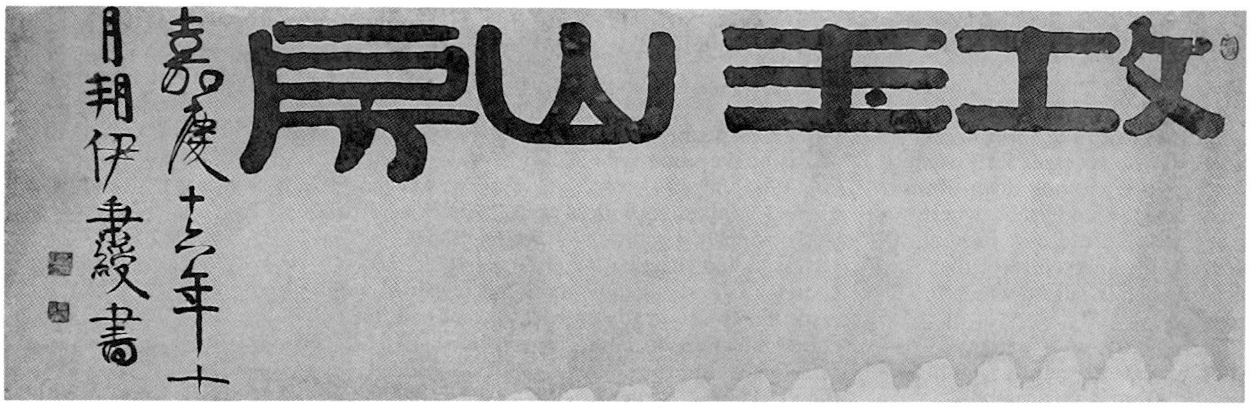

30

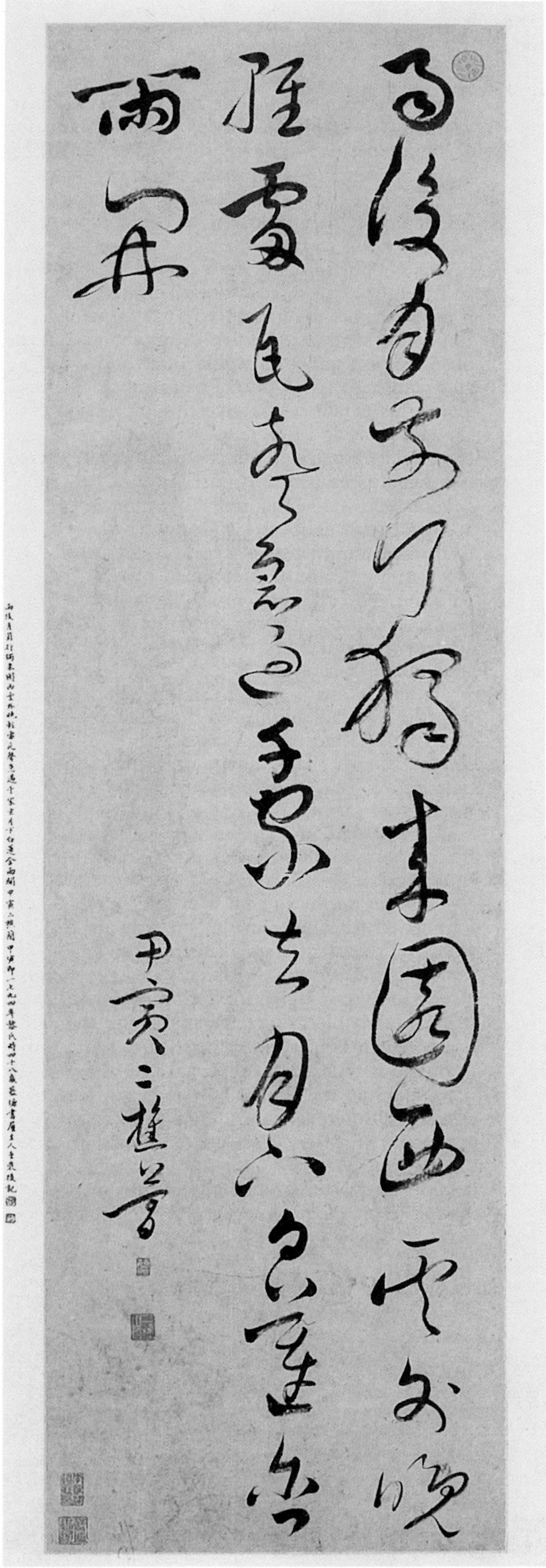

31

Water Vessel

Bamboo, of yellowish-brown colour, the surface well worn and patinated; a water vessel and cover, imaginatively carved in the form of a chrysanthemum flower, the severed, leafy stem from which it has been cut curving down from one side of the vessel to the underside, where the bloom itself begins to spread out, forming the vessel, the cover being the centre of the bloom from which the petals fall outwards to curl back underneath.
Probably early Qing dynasty.
Set on a dark wood, openwork stand, carved as a branch of blooming peonies intricately interwoven.
Height including stand: 6.35 cm.
Maximum width: 7.4 cm.

竹雕菊花形蓋盒
可能清初，高連座6.35厘米，寬7.4厘米

This exquisitely conceived and carved vessel is of the same type as the covered gourd (no. 196) and was probably a water vessel for use in conjunction with a small ladle. The artist was obviously a sculptor of considerable technical and imaginative ability, but he has chosen to allow a simple subject, conceived with restraint, to say it all. As with the most refined communication in literati arts, it is what is not said that becomes the most eloquent. Indeed, the vessel itself strikes such a perfect chord that the stand, which is quite well carved, becomes a trifle vulgar by comparison, suggesting it is a later addition.

With an unsigned object of this type it is impossible to know whether it is the work of a scholar-artist turning his hand to carving, or an artist-craftsman responding to the aesthetic of the literati they served — the distinction is, in any case, a rather shallow one on which we place perhaps too much emphasis.

32

Landscape in the Style of Ni Zan

Zhu Da

Ink and colours on paper, hanging scroll; landscape in the style of Ni Zan, with the houses of a fishing village on a rocky shore; signed in the upper left corner "Painted by Bada Shanren" followed by two seals *Bada Shanren* and *Heyuan,* with a third seal of the artist, *Luwu Renwu* in the lower left corner.
17th century.
177 cm × 93 cm.
Published: *Chinese Masters of the 17th Century,* pl. 19.

仿倪瓚山水圖立軸•朱耷作
明末清初（約1626-1705），177×93厘米

Zhu Da (*hao:* Bada Shanren, Heyuan, Xuege, Renwu, Wulu, Luwulu, Geshanlu, Shunian and others — *circa* 1626-*circa* 1705) was a scion of the Ming imperial house who remains one of the most intriguing eccentrics in the entire history of Chinese painting. From any normal point of view he appears to have been a deeply disturbed man, given to fits of ecstatic elation and deep depression. His father was born dumb, and after his death Zhu Da seems to have been similarly stricken: retiring one day, he attached the character 'dumb' to his door and never spoke again. Accounts of his life are confusing and often contradictory, but he was one of those who retired into monastic life in the face of the turmoils of the Qing conquest, bitterly regretting the loss of Chinese soil to the Manchus, to which two of his inscriptions attest:[1] "My tears stream when I look at the mountains and rivers, which are still as of old, (but) the ink-drops have no soul. Only stones piled up in the stream and the naked trees in the twilight remain and can be rendered with the brush." "The brush may paint the mountains and stones, but the actual ground is lost."

One account of his life has him in his early years as a Buddhist teacher in the mountains for a 20-year period, while another has him married with children at the same time (not necessarily incompatible pursuits). Whatever the details of his early life, he appears to have ended up as a recluse, given to fits of madness and wild behaviour but released from his mental burdens sufficiently often to enjoy company (particularly if a few drinks were involved) and to paint. Reputedly he painted when drunk, accepting the hospitality of any who would offer him wine and painting in wild fits of exuberance. At first glance his extant works give the impression of the looseness and spontaneity that might result from such intoxicated abandon. However, there is a remarkable control underlying the spontaneity; his genius for abstraction is achieved with deliberate and powerfully controlled movements of the brush. Part of his great strength, and that of much of Chinese painting and calligraphy at its best, lies in the syncretic capacity for the outer limits of expressive spontaneity to be explored under such singular control.

Zhu Da is a supreme example, both in his painting and calligraphy, of that highly sophisticated and much valued quality of re-acquired naivety in Chinese art — the artistic manifestation of the Chinese quest for intellectual primitivism (see p.17). This is manifested time and time again in the arts of the persuasive minority, but to deal with it in brushwork is a sufficient guide to its nature.

In calligraphy (which is the essential foundation for brushwork in the fine art of painting) the artist starts with no skill or knowledge; both must be acquired. This entails a very long training in mastering the brush so that it is capable of directly expressing the heart, which is in turn trained to be worthy of expression. First comes material skill, how to hold and load the brush, how to get different effects on different papers, how to form the characters of different scripts, and with practice comes ever greater fluency until the artist completely masters the details of brushwork. Then all of that skill, all of the flashy, technical cleverness must be pared away from brushwork and heart until all that remains is essence. It is a process that cannot be forced — it must come naturally from within. The result is the spontaneity of a child or primitive, but under highly sophisticated control.

Here, despite being expressed within a stylistic reference to the Yuan master Ni Zan, Zhu Da demonstrates the aesthetic with his simple depiction of rocks, houses and trees, capturing the essence while paring away all unnecessary detail, with restrained yet strong brushwork. The 'awkwardness' of this sort of brushwork is perhaps most clearly seen in the small, scraggy tree in the middle distance to the right of the painting. It is equally apparent in the Wang Shimin (no. 5) and Jin Nong (no. 4) paintings.

A large hanging scroll illustrated by Cahill,[2] is one of the most exciting paintings by Zhu Da known to us. It is also an example of the Chinese artist's capacity for painting stunningly abstract and expressive works made up entirely of figurative elements (see p.18). That work, showing how abstract form and expressive brush marks can so easily transcend landscape elements without discarding them, is useful in leading the eye unaccustomed to Chinese painting beyond mere scenery to the level of Zhu Da's most powerful expression.

1. *Chinese Painting: Leading Masters and Principles,* Vol. 5, p.155.
2. *Chinese Painting,* p.179.

31

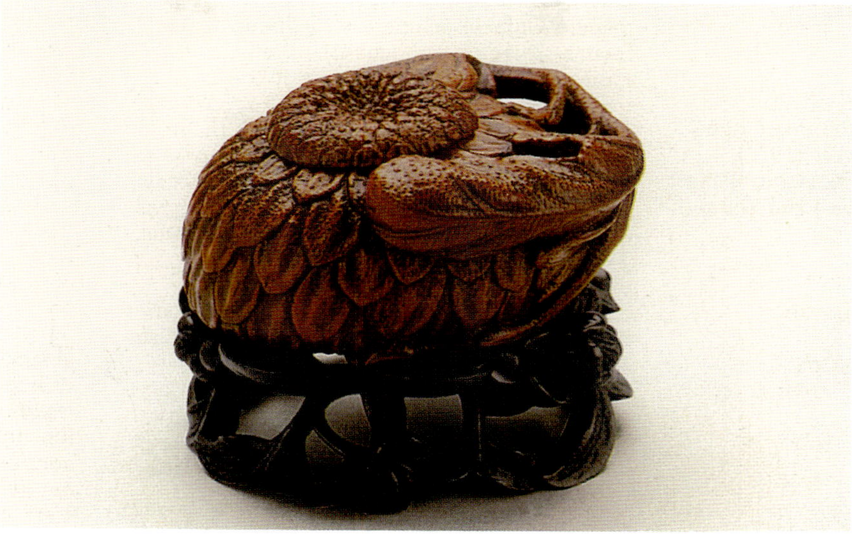

32

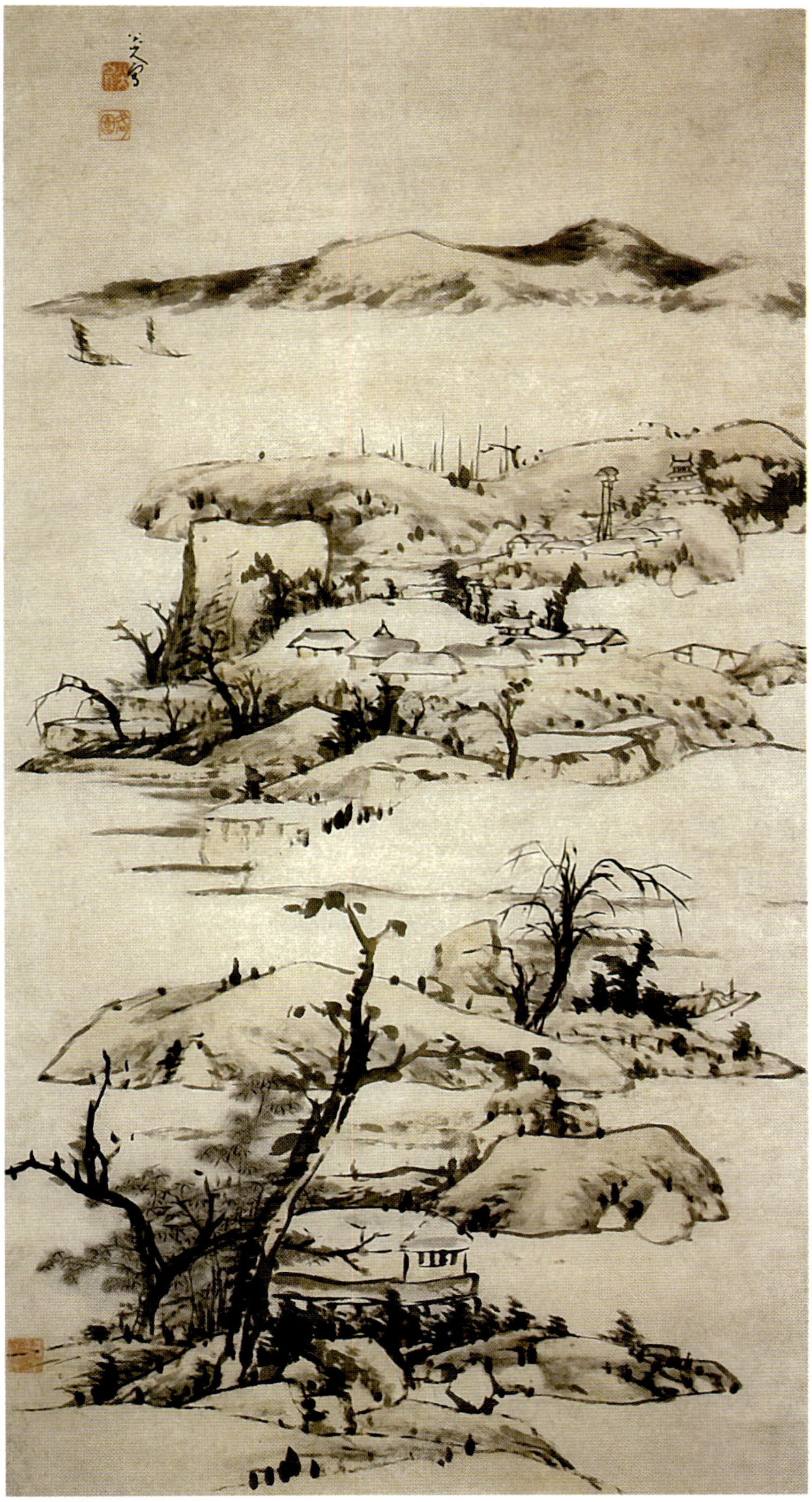

33

Landscape Number 173

C.C. Wang

Ink and colour on paper, hanging scroll; autumn landscape; inscribed in the lower right margin '7th month of the *renzi* year (1972), Wang Jiqian' with two seals of the artist, *Wang Jiqian xi* ('the seal of Wang Jiqian') and *Ouran shide* ('Picked up by chance').
New York, 1972.
60.2 cm × 75.5 cm.
Exhibited: Fogg Art Museum, Harvard University, 1973.
Published: *Mountains of the Mind: the Landscapes of C.C. Wang,* no. 27, front cover and end papers.

山水173・王季遷作
1972年，60.2×75.5厘米

C.C. Wang (Wang Jiqian — b. 1907) was originally from Suzhou, but moved to America in 1949 and has been based in New York ever since. He is today one of the leading collectors, connoisseurs and artists in the Chinese tradition, and his main work in the field of scholarship, undertaken with Victoria Contag *(Seals of Chinese Painters and Collectors)* remains a standard and indispensible reference work.

It was essential that we include a modern work of art in this exhibition to demonstrate the fact that the evolution of Chinese consciousness continues and that the details of the various groups that have over the centuries made up the influential minority are incidental. Here C.C. Wang's painting and the level of understanding it represents stands for a broad spectrum of continuing activity.

There is a general misunderstanding about modern Chinese painting. In so far as modern Chinese painting is traditional, it is thought to be unexciting without any real meaning for a modern world; if it is not traditional, it owes its modernism to the West. Nothing could be further from the truth. In the West we view pictorial art as modern in so far as it reaches beyond the bonds of patronage, physical reality and any other relative concerns and becomes a direct vehicle for self-realization. This is a stage Chinese painting art went through from some time before the 8th century, being fully and critically understood by the 11th and having become the mainstream of pictorial expression by the 14th.

The contribution of C.C. Wang and a host of other modern Chinese artists has been to help break out of the confines of a dominating orthodoxy (the very minor revolution that has concerned the Chinese in this century, although this has been misunderstood by the Chinese themselves).[1] When these artists approach Western art they may admire the individual creativity of a Picasso or a Cezanne, but they find nothing fundamentally new there. When Lui Shoukwan's later 'abstracts' (which never were, in the modern Western sense, pure abstraction since they followed the time-honoured Chinese concern of reducing expression to its essentials — subject-matter, usually a lotus, was always there) began to look remarkably like modern Western works by Gotlieb, Kline or Motherwell, it was not because he was copying them, but because both traditions had finally arrived at the same point. It is difficult to defend the position that an artist, heir to a thousand-year-old tradition of abstraction and abstract expressionism, was copying another whose culture had discovered only within the century the same realms of perception and expression, and even in its means had borrowed much of that from glimpses of Oriental art through calligraphy, Japanese prints and so forth.

Although this painting may have been a direct result of C.C. Wang's move to New York, the main result of that was more a personal nudge in the direction of greater freedom of creativity. It is more clearly understood as being a modern and exciting manifestation of the same realms of perception and expression as that represented by the great masters of his own tradition. It has the monumentality of Northern Song painting, the abstraction of the Yuan masters, the naturalness of line of the highest levels of the calligraphic traditions, although not achieved with a brush (but that is a minor detail, as C.C. himself amusingly pointed out to a recent symposium on 20th century Chinese painting: "Oh, brush work doesn't have to be done with a brush!".)

1. The material and technological wonders that were the fruits of Western civilization so overwhelmed China during the past century that it lost sight of the fact that what was superior technologically might not be superior in the spiritual realm of the arts. Chinese art has, itself, been in some confusion as a result of this.

34

Brush Pot

Wood, *huangyangmu* (boxwood), of well-patinated dark brown colour; brush pot carved as a segment of bamboo set on three small feet, the base recessed to imitate a nodal diaphragm; decorated with a branch of blossoming prunus and three couplets praising the virtues of bamboo, one followed by a seal, *Woyun* ('Reclining in the clouds') in positive seal script and with a signature *Ezhu, Banshan* ('Banshan of Ezhu') followed by the seal *Banshan* ('Halfway up the mountain') in a raised square cartouche in negative seal script, all in low relief.
Probably late Ming or early Qing dynasty.
Height: 13.7 cm.

黃楊木竹段形刻銘筆筒・半山製
可能明末清初，高13.7厘米

All we know about the artist of this marvellous little brush pot is that his art names were Woyun and Banshan and that he came from Ezhu, which is in the Wuchang district of Hubei province. Both are art names which might have been used by a number of people, but of several artists that are listed bearing them, none comes from Ezhu. Banshan was a particularly popular *hao* as it could be associated with the popular Chinese philosophical concept of the middle way.

A bamboo wrist rest in the National Palace Museum, Taipei, decorated with bamboo and a relief inscription is also signed Banshan, but despite similar quality and superb elegance, any relationship between the two is made purely aesthetic by the inclusion of a different place name for the artist (Zhongyin).[1]

With its superbly carved relief, delightful form (imitating the distinctive type of bamboo from which no. 82 is made) and fine calligraphy expressing poetic sentiments related to the qualities of the bamboo so beloved of the scholar, this is a masterpiece of wood carving. It carries those two qualities of elegance and restraint which are so important to the literati aesthetic.

1. See *Masterpieces of Chinese Writing Materials in the National Palace Museum,* no. 45.

33

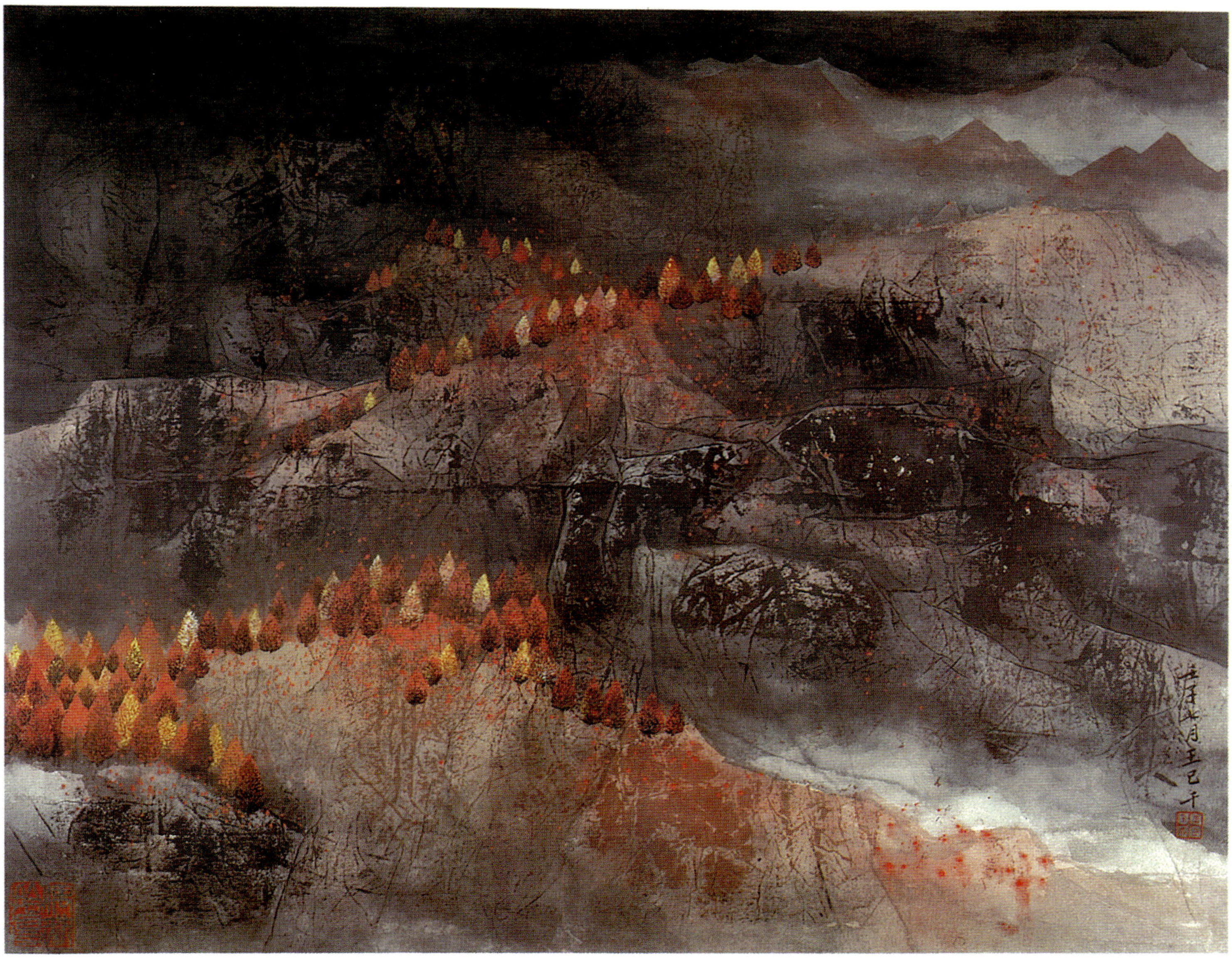

34

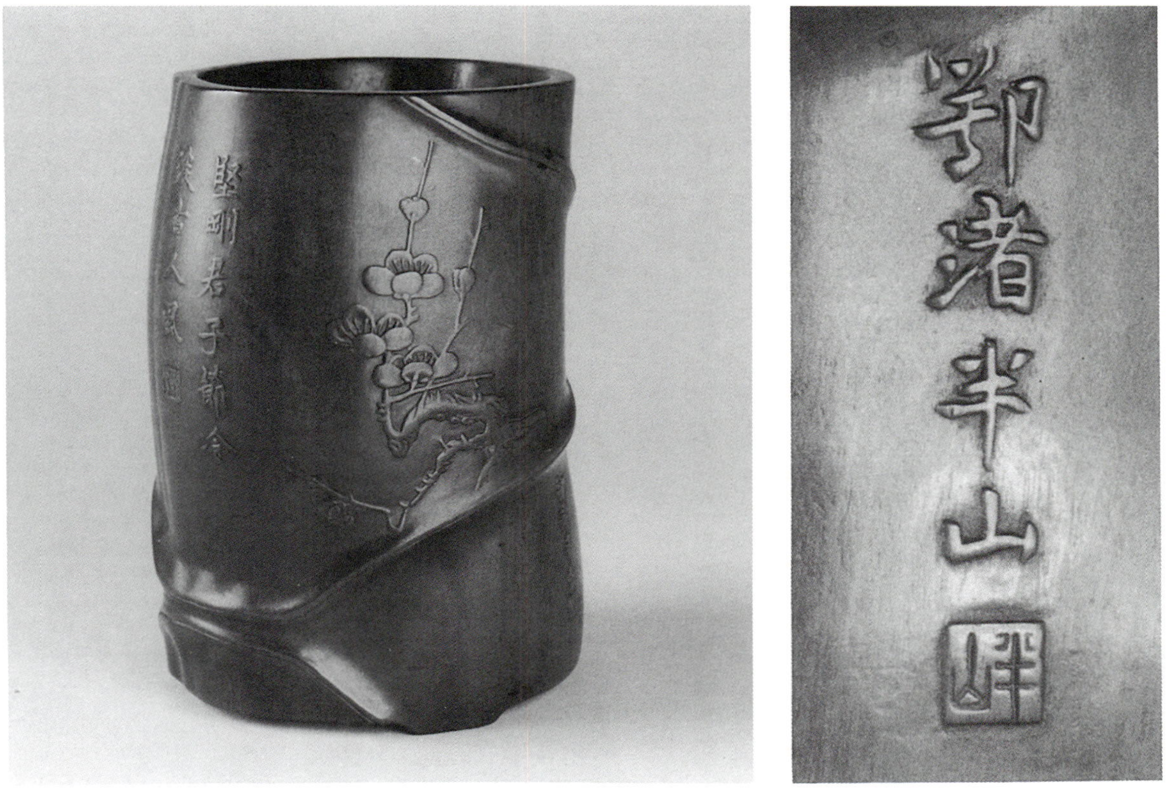

35

Brush Pot
Wu Zhifan

Bamboo, patinated to a rich, dark brown colour; a brush pot made from a section of culm, a section of diaphragm acting as its base, carved on the outside with a continuous design of a bearded archer, clad in loose robes with his hair tied inside a cloth hat, shooting at a goose flying overhead, the arrow half-way from longbow to target; two more arrows are tucked into the archer's belt, but the first seems to have the job well in hand; nearby the archer's horse stands idly, its reins loosely looped over its saddle, its tail knotted; a clump of three pine trees grows nearby, through the branches of which the archer has fired; signed *Wu Zhifan zhi* ('made by Wu Zhifan').
Late 17th century.
Height: 15.95 cm.
Outer diameter of mouth: 10.05 cm.

竹雕丁山射雁筆筒·吳之璠製
十七世紀晚期，高15.95厘米，直徑10.05厘米

Wu Zhifan was considered one of the great bamboo and wood carvers of all time, and his fame was such, even in his own day, that copies would certainly have been made. Of the reasonably large number of pieces which have come down to us bearing his signature, we must assume that many are not from his hand. Later, when studies of individual artists who have so far only been briefly mentioned in Chinese sources are undertaken and a large group of pieces bearing their signatures can be studied, a clearer picture of authenticity will emerge. In the meantime attributions must be tentative. We may assume that a boxwood brush pot with the Qianlong Emperor's inscription and still in the imperial collection (see below) is genuine as, quite apart from its excellent provenance, it is of such extraordinary quality that anyone capable of making it would be unlikely to be wasting his time enhancing another man's reputation.

The brush pot shown here is one of a group of bamboo pieces with low relief carving, for which Wu was famous; it seems as fine as any of them. The superb control of both detail and movement suggest the hand of a master, and therefore the master himself. The integrity and crispness of the carving of the pine needles, where a host of repetitive detail is magnificently handled is a good sign, as copyists who are following someone else's style often give themselves away in their lack of dedication to detail in such areas. Here the simple, repeated pattern is such that it is a part of the strength of the work of art with a rhythm of its own, which creates a textural counterpoint to the gnarled, thrusting forms of the trunks and branches of the pines. It is the mark of a great artist that whatever he choses to do is done with the same dedication, given the same weight in the overall work of art. The same is equally true of the audience, whose full involvement in the art of appreciation (see no. 1 where the importance of a truly creative listener in music is discussed) is vital to the whole process of art.

Wu Zhifan (*zi:* Luzhen; *hao:* Donghai Daoren — 'Daoist of the Eastern Sea') was a native of Jiading, near Shanghai, who lived initially at Nanxiang but later moved to Tianjin.[1] He was known as a figure and bird-and-flower painter and was capable of elegant and powerful calligraphy in the cursive and running scripts, as well as being renowned for his skills as a bamboo and wood carver. Much of his best work was considered to be in low relief, but there are several equally superb examples with high relief carving extant. A certain Ma Ling of Tianjin became his patron and kept him as a honoured guest in his home; but when Ma retired from official duties, Wu accompanied him and nothing further is recorded about him. Apparently one of his carvings was presented at a later date as tribute to the Qianlong Emperor (in 1775) prompting him to ask the identity of the carver. Court officials looked into the matter, and discovered details of him in *Nanchuan Suipi* ('Miscellaneous Writings of Nanchuan') and Wu's later fame was assured.[2] Wu is reputed to have been the first to carve subjects on plain grounds, for which he is constantly mentioned, although only a part of his accepted output is of this category.[3]

Two pieces with cyclical dates are in the George Ye collection in the Kansas City Art Museum. Assuming their authenticity, and if Wu was indeed a carver of the early Kangxi period, they establish a period of activity for him of between 1668 and 1700.

1. Some examples of his work give Chaxi as his native place, which we have been unable to trace. It was perhaps the name of a small village unrecorded in the standard dictionaries of place names.
2. Information from *Zhongguo meishujia zhenglue,* p.277, and *Zhongguo jindai shougongyeshi ziliao* by Peng Zeyt, Beijing 1984, *juan* 1, p.63.
3. Other pieces are to be found illustrated in *Bamboo Carving of China* where the artist is discussed on pp.27-29, and as fig. 13 on p.28, where a bamboo brush pot is carved with the subject of an old sage seated beneath a pine greeting a flying goose; fig. 14, on p.29, another bamboo brush pot with a boy on a buffalo, losing his hat in the wind; p.80, no. 20, a bamboo cylinder referred to as a perfume holder (see no. 233 for discussion on this form) where a doubtful signature is discussed; p.82, no. 22, bamboo brush pot with a seated figure; p.84, figs. 51 and 51a, a superb boxwood brush pot inscribed by the Qianlong Emperor (illustrated in colour in *Selected Handicrafts from the Collections of the Palace Museum,* no. 88) and no. 23, a bamboo brush pot with a similar subject. Another bamboo brush pot, with a similar subject to this example but differently arranged, is illustrated in *Chinese Bamboo Carving* Part I, p.219, no. 43, and another with a man seated on a buffalo is on p.221, no. 44.

36

Ruyi Sceptre

Wood, *huangyangmu* (boxwood), of richly patinated reddish-brown colour, carved as a *ruyi* sceptre, the elegantly tapering and curved handle of bowed section, terminating in a simple, formalized *lingzhi* head, the handle with a *chi* dragon coiled around it, the upper body pulling itself powerfully to the front of the *ruyi* to look towards its tail, below which is incised a poem in seal script: "What swims in clear water and eats in clear water is a dragon. What swims in muddy water and eats in muddy water is a fish. What swims in clear water but eats in muddy water is a *chi* dragon. Being a *chi* dragon, is this the reason I can be as free as I wish?" followed by the signature "Old man Xinfeng".
Late Ming or early Qing dynasty.
Length: 37 cm.

黃楊木刻銘靈芝如意·辛峯老民製
明末或清初，長37厘米

The poem compares the most elegant of minds, the ascetic sage of the scholarly ideal, the dragon, with the unrefined consciousness of the dweller in the mundane world, the fish. The writer likens himself to the *chi* dragon half way between the two, suggesting that since he has access to both realms he may have whatever he wishes — thus making a pun on the *ruyi.*

The elegant simplicity of the *ruyi* combined with the powerful sculpture of the *chi* dragon which plays on its handle and the delightful poem in its ancient script make this an ideal work of art for the scholar, capable of communicating on many different levels. Zhou Yi's comment about polishing (i.e. finishing) being 60 per cent of the carver's art and carving only 40 per cent (see no. 58) is well demonstrated here. The carving is finished as well as can be imagined, demonstrating complete control of the medium, and the carver has managed almost perfect separation between the relief dragon and the object around which it climbs so that it is possible to imagine peeling off the dragon and being left with a perfectly finished plain *ruyi* — a sign of technical mastery in such works.

Although a date in the early Qing dynasty cannot be ruled out, the style and degree of natural wear and patination suggest that a later Ming date is more likely, and perhaps even a mid-Ming date.

37

Display Stand

Wood; display stand carved to imitate a natural root, its flat upper surface lacquered in a variety of hues of red, beige and green with painted red lines to create a speckled and textured pattern.
Qing dynasty.
Height: 18 cm.

木雕仿樹根器座
清代，高18厘米

This stand appears to be entirely contrived, made of wood to look like a natural root formation. Root furniture, whether natural or contrived, was much favoured by the literati. It appears frequently in genre paintings mostly in the form of chairs or other low, couch-like seats, tables or stands for incense and other objects, although collectors' cabinets are also found. A similar idea is expressed in the use of natural or natural-looking stone tables and seats. The symbolism is clear: the sage at his final level of understanding has no need of worldly, material things and can turn to nature for his furniture (although of course to make such natural-looking objects requires considerable technical skill).

Fig. 1 is taken from a painting by Luo Pin (see no. 52), the 18th century Yangzhou artist, in which an elaborate low table is constructed out of root (the strange-shaped object in the upper branches is an incense burner). The old man leaning thoughtfully against the table also holds a root sceptre. Fig. 2, from a painting by the late Ming artist Chen Hongshou, shows an old scholar seated on a root and holding a tall root staff beloved of the literati in their wanderings. In Fig. 3, after a painting by Cui Zizhong dated 1640, a scholar is seen seated against the base of a tree, a splendid table at his back made of a slab of stone with a root stand. He is surrounded by various precious objects and scholarly trappings in a typical outdoor scene, while his attendant holds what is either a natural root or stone sculpture.

35

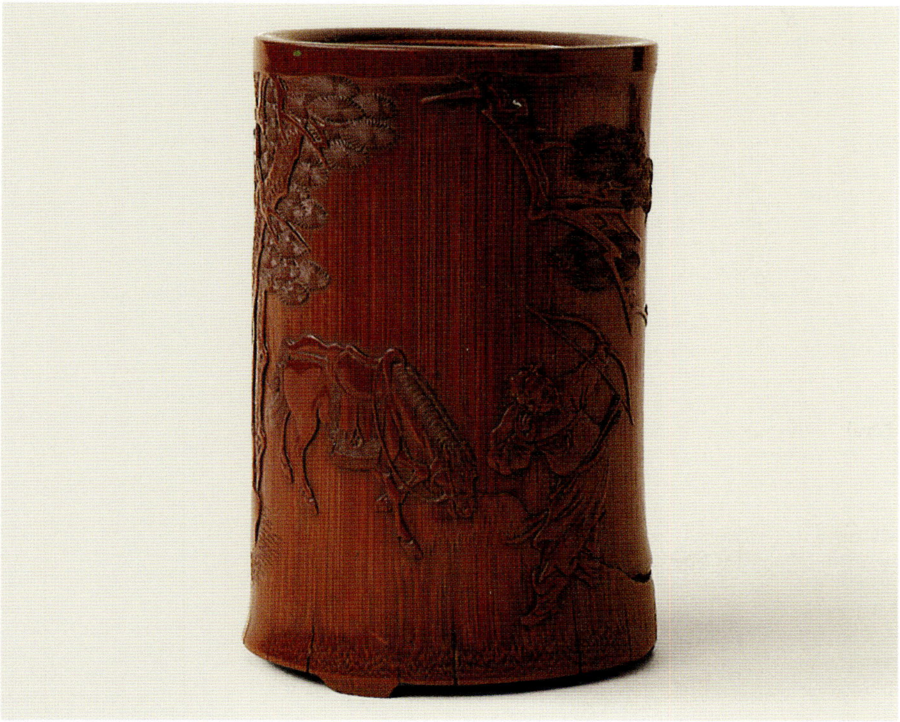

36

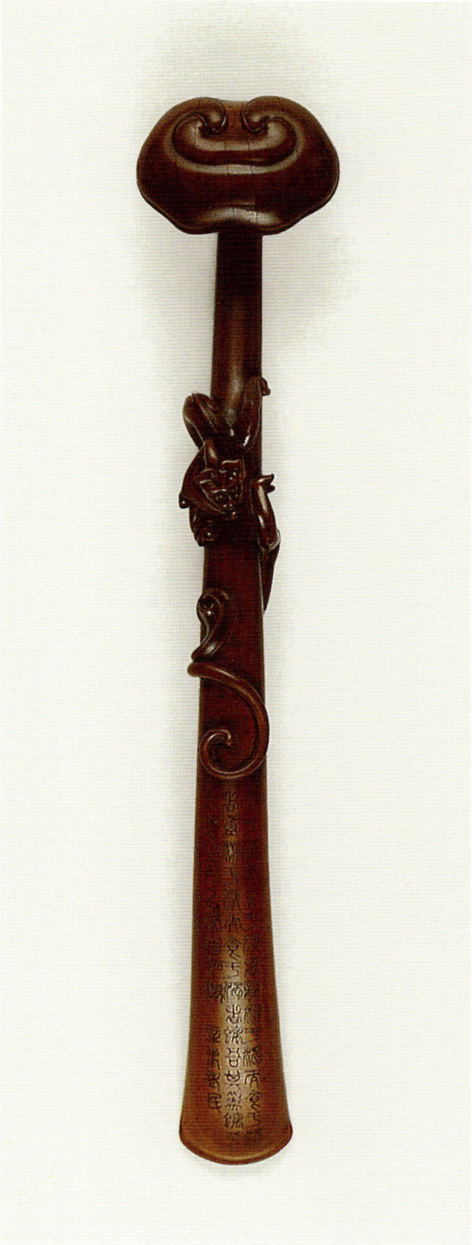

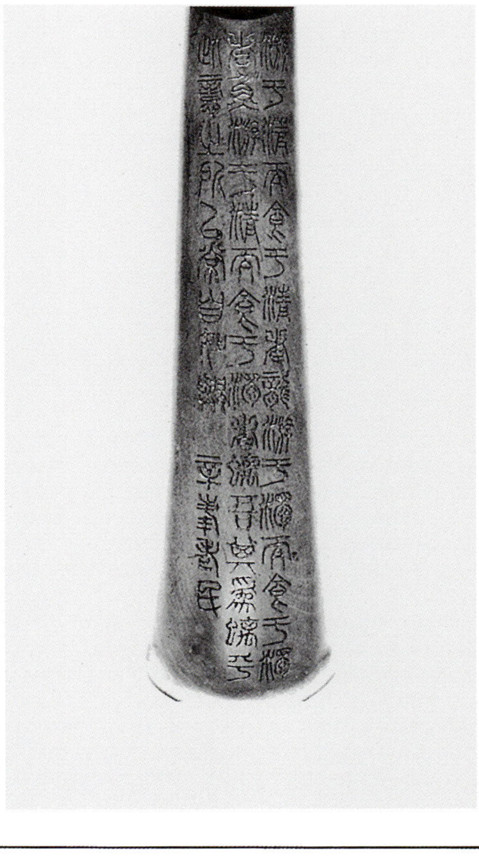

37

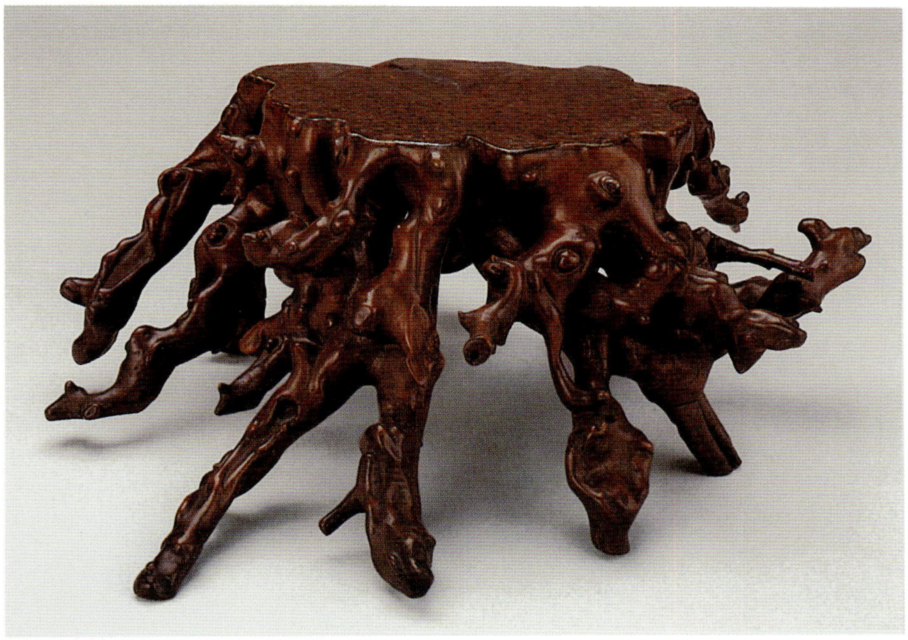

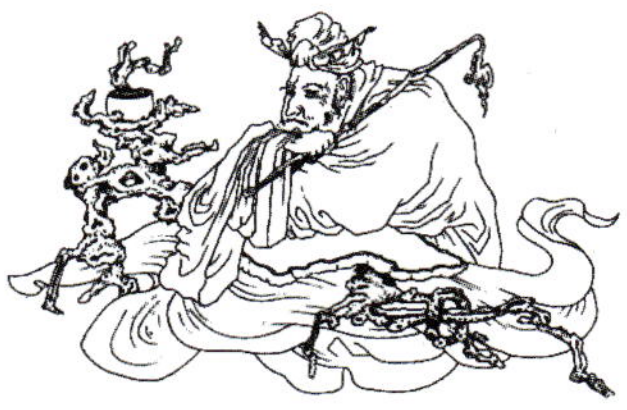

Fig. 1

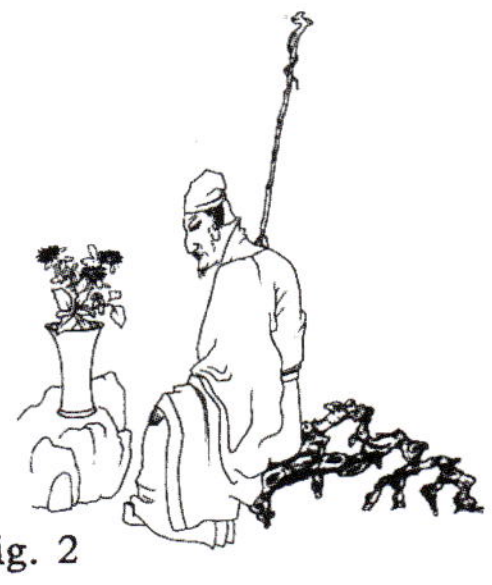

Fig. 2

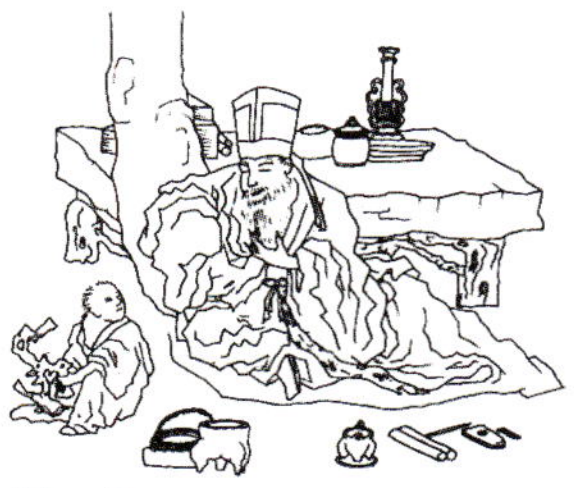

Fig. 3

38

'One Hundred Boys' Ink

Cheng Junfang

Ink, black with gilt details, of flattened circular form, moulded on each side with one hundred boys (fifty on each side) at various pursuits in a garden setting, one side with the impressed gilt title in clerical script 'Picture of one hundred boys'; the rim inscribed on one side *Wanli jiachen nianzao* ('made in the *jiachen* year of the Wanli period [1604]') and on the other *Cheng Junfang fanggumo* ('Cheng Junfang copying an old ink').
Mould by Cheng Junfang, 1604; ink probably an early impression.
Diameter: 12.8 cm

仿古百子墨•程君房製
明萬曆甲辰(1604), 直徑12.8厘米

The exact dates of Cheng Junfang (*zi*: Shifang) are questionable. The *Zhonguo Anhui Wenfang Sibao* by Mu Hiaotian and Li Minghui give his date of birth as the first year of Jiajing (1522), which is unlikely. The same work gives his date of death as 1566, however, and then quotes an extant dated example of 1594, calling into question its reliability. The *Dictionary of Ming Biography* gives his date of birth as 1541, and of death (based upon extant dated inks) as 1616, but this too seems unreliable, as it confuses Cheng Junfang with his father, Cheng Dayue, giving them as one person — a common mistake found in a number of sources, but corrected in the *To-boku Wa-boku Zusetsu* (*Book on Chinese and Japanese Inksticks*). We may assume that he was born at some time in the mid-16th century and if extant examples cited here are any indication, that he died after 1624. He was a native of Huizhou, south of Nanjing, an area well known for its attainments in the fields of painting, woodblock engraving, paper and ink manufacturing.

Cheng Junfang led a colourful life. He was the imposing-looking son of a wealthy merchant, Cheng Dayue. He aspired to scholarship but failed his exams and eventually purchased a minor official post which he filled for a short time, before retiring to the commercial world to follow one of his earlier passions for ink. As a youth Cheng had collected old ink. Claiming that his particular recipe for making ink had come to him in a dream, he set up his own manufactory and became one of the two most celebrated inkmakers of the late Ming.

His aspirations to scholarship and his activities with ink gave him a circle of literati friends and acquaintances. He knew Matteo Ricci, the famed Jesuit scholar. One-time friend and partner of the other great late Ming inkmaker, Fang Yulu, Cheng fell out with him claiming that he had befriended Fang and taught him the art of inkmaking only to have him leave and set up his own rival concern. Their acrimonious feud was a celebrated scandal in late Ming literati circles and was exacerbated by Fang's reputed affair with Cheng's favourite concubine, for which Fang was brought to trial. Another story has it that while Fang was still working for Cheng he sent some of Cheng's inks as tribute to the Court, using his own name.

Fang Yulu published in about 1588 the *Fang Shi Mopu* (see no. 175), which led his rival to publish his own work, the *Cheng Shi Moyuan* in 1606. Each is a compendium of inks, with various essays and comments by noted literati of the day (including in Cheng's case three essays by Ricci) and by the authors; they are beautifully illustrated by the finest woodblock carvers.[1] The feud between the two was further fuelled by the fact that Fang included a number of Cheng's designs in his book as if they were his own. Cheng then published them in his own later work to establish their true ownership. Cheng also used the fable of the wolf bent on devouring the man who had saved its life by protecting it from a hunter — a clear reference to Fang and his lack of gratitude.

Cheng seems to have had a penchant for rows, as he is recorded as having fallen out bitterly with others for the same offence of abuse of friendship. He was also imprisoned for seven years, being exonerated and released in 1600, on a charge of murder, and according to one source ended his days in prison by starving himself to death after being convicted yet again for murder. A particularly unpleasant legend is attached to this, and again Fang figures as the suspected informer who landed Cheng in court. It is said that Cheng built a snake pond in his native village to raise snakes for their bladders and fat (it was common knowledge that certain animal bladders add lustre to ink). It was rumoured that he fed the reptiles on little boys, and he was arrested, leading to his second imprisonment and death.

Ink was as much a part of the lifestyle of the influential minority as brush and paper (which together with the inkstone make up the 'Four Treasures of the Studio'). It is difficult to imagine the magic aura that great ink might carry for the literatus, poet, painter and calligrapher (not for its decoration but for its content) without grasping the immense importance the influential minority placed on the arts. Many scholars made their own ink, and great ink by a master inkmaker would be treated with reverence.

Although a number of processes were involved in inkmaking, which meant a certain level of industrialization, the ink recipe, design, carved wood blocks, and the processes of moulding and colouring the surface was under the control of one man. A contemporary account of the value placed on Cheng's inks is found in a comment by the noted late Ming literatus Dong Qichang: "In a hundred years' time, there will be no Junfang, but his inks will remain; in a thousand years' time there will be none of Junfang's inks left, but his name will remain."[2] The characteristics of Cheng's ink were summed up by another writer: "Compact and with lustre; dark and moist; not sticking to the brush, nor diffusing on the paper."[3]

The *Dictionary of Ming Biography* states that Cheng was still active in 1616 based on an ink of his dated to that year. Jenyns mentions two dated to 1621 also with his signature[4] and we have a record of one in the British Museum dated to 1624, which would seem to extend the period of his known activity. What is considerably more puzzling is an excellent ink bearing his name which was sold at Christies in London,[5] on the rim of which is inscribed that it was made in the thirteenth year of Hongwu (1380). Possibly Cheng was copying an earlier design and included the date of the original; it is also possible that it was a later forgery by a maker who was unclear of Cheng's actual period, although it is difficult to imagine a later inkmaker capable of such a fine ink not knowing the period of one of the two most famous Ming inkmakers, whose book he must surely have known.

The design of one hundred boys was an auspicious one, and popular with inkmakers. Cheng did more than one version of the subject[6] and it was also used by other inkmakers.[7] Another by Cheng is in the collection of the Anhui Provincial Museum.[8]

The original mould for this ink seems acceptable for Cheng, and both ink and condition seem to suggest that it is an impression of some age, taken from an undamaged mould.

1. See *Chinese Rare Books in American Collections*, pp.104-105 for a discussion of Cheng's work and no. 175 for Fang's.
2. *Cheng Shi Moyuan.*
3. Ibid., written by Xing Taipo.
4. *Chinese Art*, Vol. 4, p.313.
5. Lot 74, on 9 July 1979.
6. For another, see *To-boku Wa-boku Zusetsu*, pp.20-21.
7. See, for instance, ibid. pp.104-105.
8. For other works by Cheng see *Masterpieces of Chinese Writing Materials in the National Palace Museum*, no. 8; *The Arts of the Ming Dynasty, T.O.C.S.* Vol. 30, 1955-1957, pl. 25, no. 71 (where a page of the *Cheng Shi Moyuan* is also illustrated as no. 64), and most other works on ink. A particularly useful if laborious source of inks is the *Gugong Zhoukan*, a series published in the 1930s in Beijing, which illustrates, mostly as rubbings, a large number of them. Cheng Junfang's are illustrated (always on the fourth page), of issues 490, 491, 493, 495 and 498. Others are in the Shanghai Museum and the Beijing Palace Museum.

39

Roosting Bird

Wood, probably *hongmu* ('red wood') of well-figured dark brown colour; the natural gnarled configuration enhanced by carving to create a sculpture of a roosting bird, its head bent down to rest against its right wing while it rests on one leg.
Probably Qing dynasty.
24.6 cm, excluding modern stand × 30.6 cm.

紅木雕睡鳥
可能清代, 24.6(不連座)×30.6厘米

The dating of gnarled wood sculptures and related furniture is extremely difficult. Style was so frequently dictated by the exigencies of the material that stylistic analysis is of minimal value. Where pieces appear in illustrations to printed books or in paintings the style seems not to change significantly over the centuries. A few pieces are inscribed, and fewer still are dated (mostly to the mid- or late Qing period) and where the identity of an owner or inscriber can be established, it gives only a terminal date (again, mostly in the late Qing period). As on paintings, scholars might inscribe these sculptures at any time after they were made as a record of their appreciation or ownership.

It is also often difficult to judge to what extent a natural form has been worked. Every single sculpture, piece of furniture or vessel of this group has been manipulated in some manner, even if only in the minimal sense of having been isolated and presented as a work of art. This act of isolating a natural form as a work of art represents one extreme of the art form, while the other is represented by wood which is wholly worked to give the impression of natural, gnarled wood (see no. 37). Between these two lies an enormous variety of combinations of the forms of nature and the hand of man, the mysterious subtleties of which appealed enormously to the Chinese mind. In this example although certain features of the bird's head and wings are obviously contrived, it is otherwise impossible to decide where natural form is enhanced by the human hand.

38

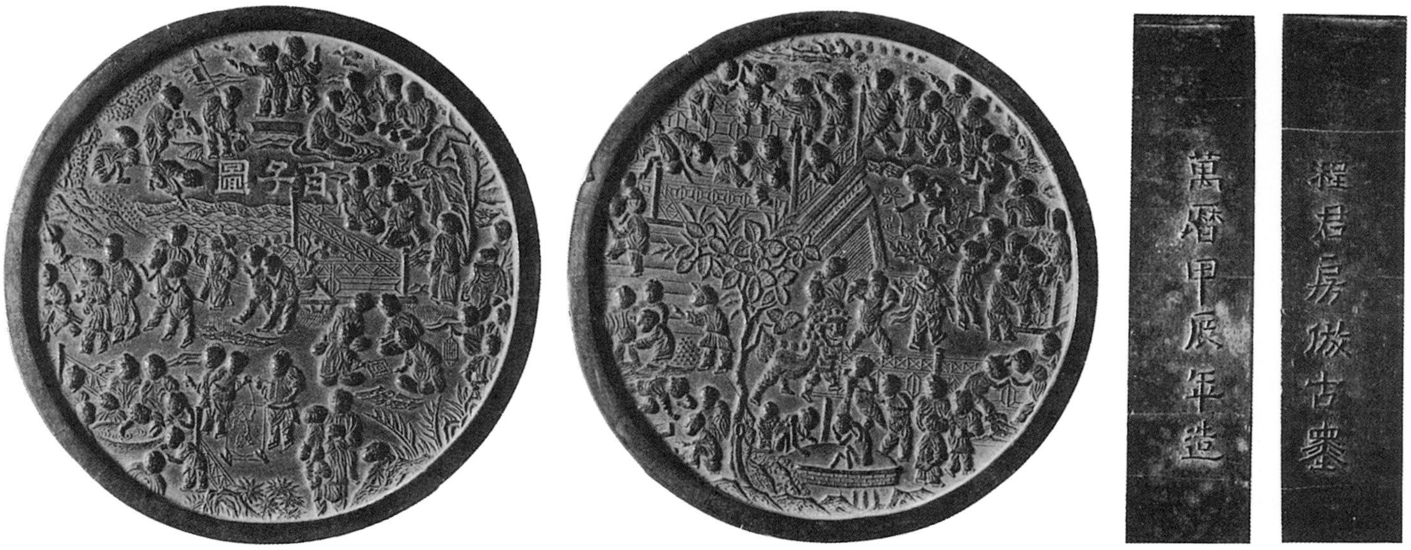

39

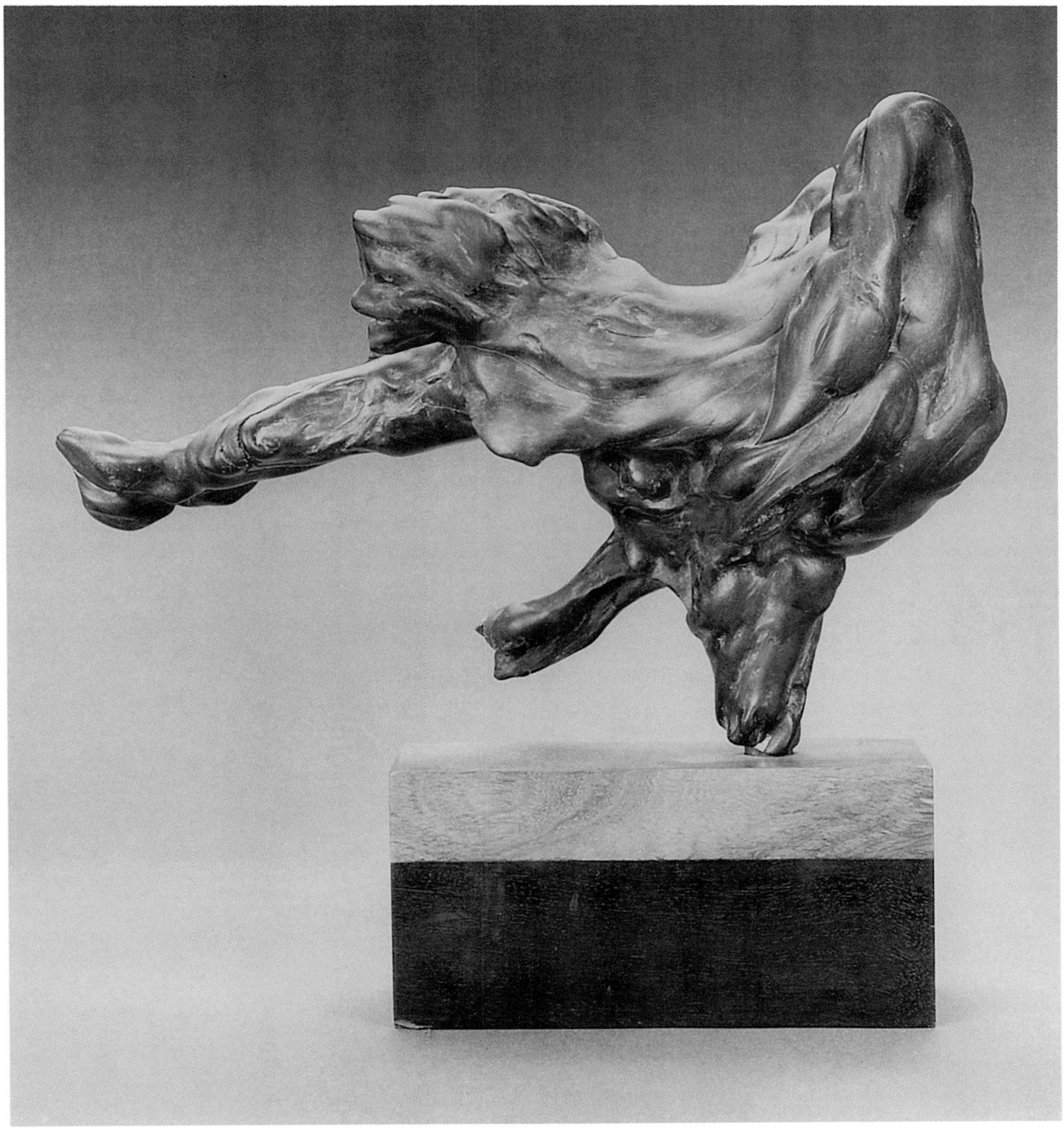

40

Bowl

Glass; a shallow bowl, with gently curving sides and a shallow recessed foot; the interior plain ochre-coloured, the exterior mottled red and ochre with a green streak running through it and a cloud design achieved in the surface of the glass.
Probably 18th century.
Height: 3.7 cm. Diameter: 11.2 cm.

仿雄黃料碗
可能清十八世紀，高3.7厘米，直徑11.2厘米

This little bowl may seem somewhat uninspiring at first glance, with its well-worn and dull-coloured interior, but to the scholarly mind, particularly that well versed in Daoism, it would be seen as a wonderfully mysterious and magical object. What is extraordinary about this bowl is the manner in which the design has been controlled. Such vessels were made by blowing the glass into a mould, and although the vast majority show random patterns of swirling glass (as in no. 94) or carefully contrived designs where a surface of one colour is cut away to reveal a different colour beneath, occasionally the colours were manipulated to remarkable effect.

The mixture of red and yellow glass was obviously highly sensitive to temperature changes. The average vessel, whether free-blown or the far more common mould-blown, displays a concentration of red near the outer surface, where temperatures cooled fastest. This is apparent on no. 94 where the lines representing the mould joins have created a wonderful pattern of markings, due presumably to temperature differences at this point. The glass makers found a way to control these random surface designs in a manner allowing them to reach into the same sort of realms of expression enjoyed by the literati in their enjoyment of rocks, marble panels, roots, etc. where natural phenomena were enhanced to create a mysterious 'joint work' of man and nature. That such an art form with 'realgar' glass was difficult to control is demonstrated by the rarity of attempts, and the relatively high number of vessels where the end result was hardly worth the effort. However, when they work there is a sense of magic in them ideally suited to the mysterious realms of Daoist alchemical practice from which they were born (see no. 94).

Here the clear pattern of swirling clouds is suddenly broken by a dynamic scar of green, as if a lightning-fast dragon had crossed the sky so quickly that only a negative image is left as the viewer stands transfixed. No other example of induced 'realgar' glass design known to us is as effective as this one.

41

'Seated Sage Stone' Rock Sculpture

Stone, of dark blackish-brown colour; the more eccentrically shaped side resembling a bearded sage, seated in a rocky outcrop, the voluminous sleeves of his loosely fitting robe falling to blend with the rocks below; mounted on an elaborate wood stand, the upper part of which is carved to represent gnarled wood which gradually gives way to a more formal stand on long curved legs.
Ming or Qing dynasty.
Height including stand: 20.6 cm.

石雕隱士岩
明或清代，高連座20.6厘米

The image of the sage, which has suggested the name for this stone, may be seen when standing in front of, and preferably slightly above the rock — see Fig. 1. This figure seated in its rocky outcrop seems to be almost a touchstone for the aesthetic represented in these gnarled wood and rock forms. It is the experience of its present owner that either people are quite unable to see it or, when it is pointed out, look sceptical and put the whole thing down to an over-active imagination; or they see it quite easily and find in it a very strong personality which breathes a whole new life into an already interesting stone.

The dating of rocks poses several problems. The rocks themselves measure their age, of course, in eons, but they become datable when they are isolated and mounted in some way. This mounting may take the form of a wood stand, as in this case, or in the case of larger rocks, stone pedestals; or it may simply be a matter of being placed in position, such as on the ground in a garden setting, or in a vessel of earth, water or pebbles, either in or out of doors. At that point they begin to represent the aesthetic of their day and take on an independent identity as works of art.

Our understanding of wood stands has not yet advanced to the point where we can date them at all accurately, and we are rarely afforded the luxury of inscriptions on either stone or stand to help us. This stone is dated, albeit somewhat broadly, on the appearance of the stand. However, it is possible that the stand is a replacement for an earlier one.

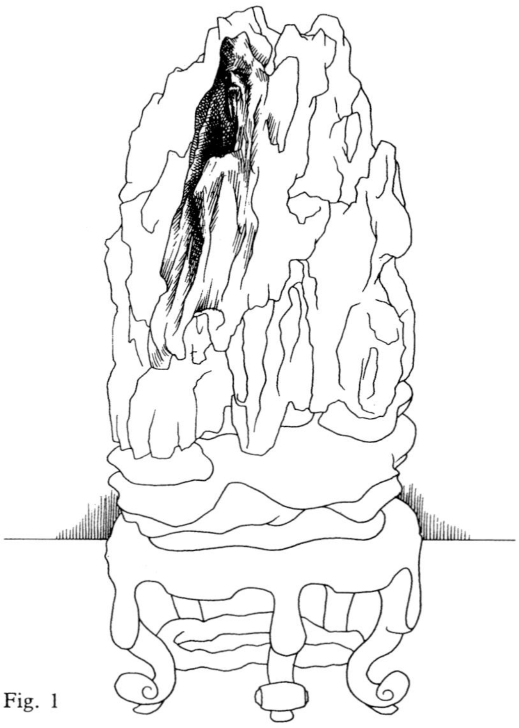

Fig. 1

40

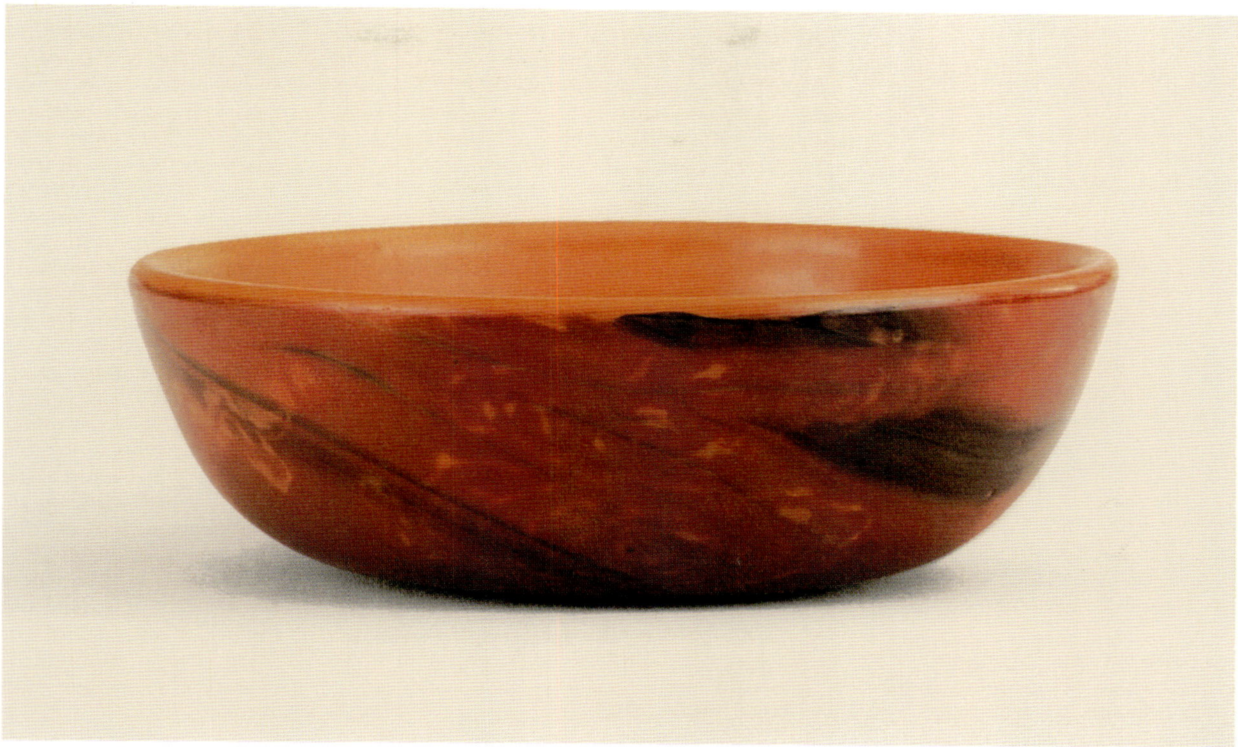

41

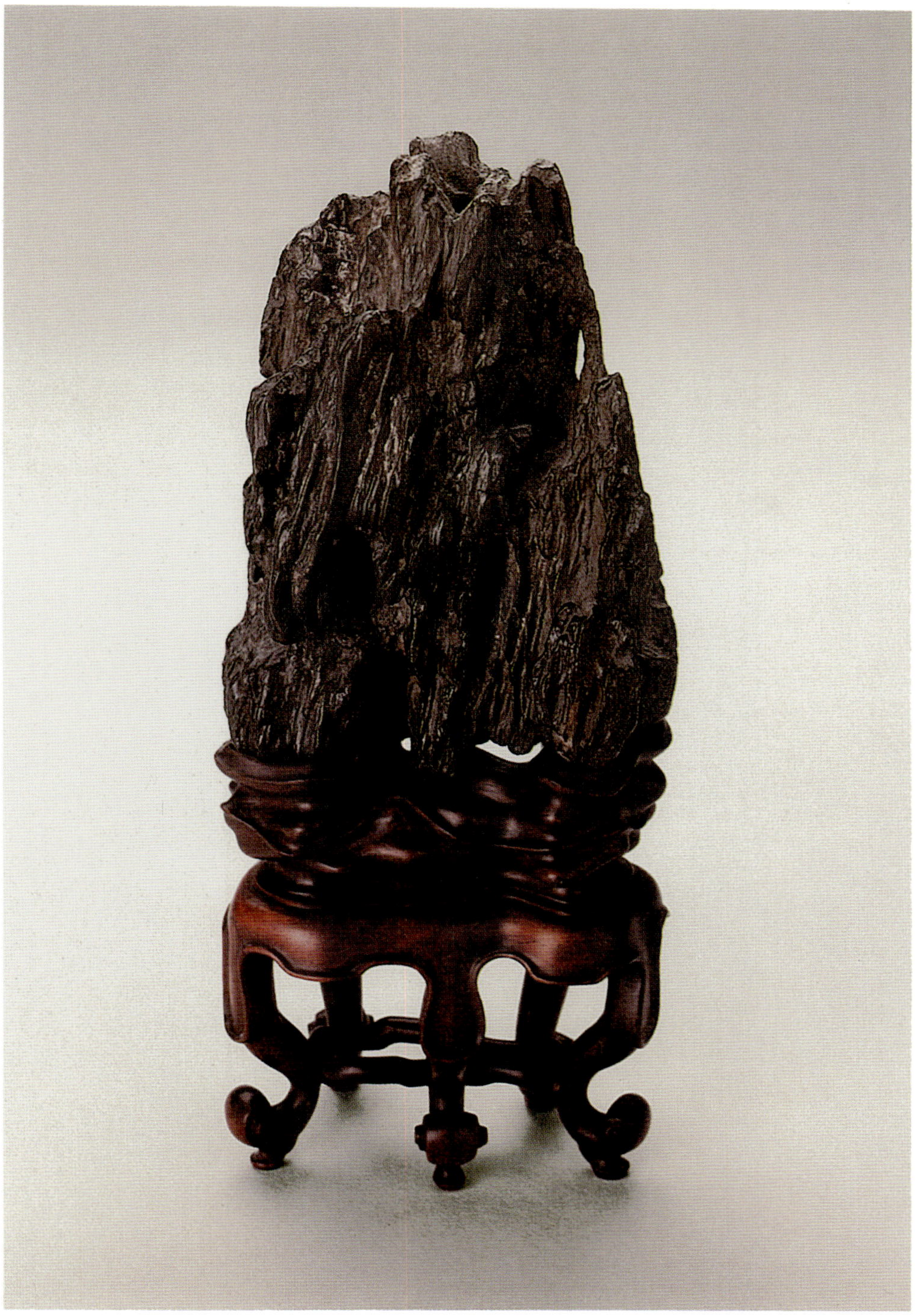

42

Brush Pot

Porcelain, the white biscuit unglazed; a brush pot based upon the shape of a bamboo segment, standing on three short feet, the exterior carved in low relief with two ladies, one seated on a stool and holding a book, leaning towards the other who is reclining on a low couch and holding a fan; the two appear to be discussing the book; set on the couch are also an archaistic *gu* beaker holding a spray of peonies, two volumes of books, and a group of three tied scrolls; the scene is set against a plain background; the recessed base with a positive seal in seal script: *Huyin Daoren* ('the Daoist hidden in a pot') set in a recessed square cartouche with an enclosing incised line.
Jingdezhen, probably second half of the Qing dynasty.
Height: 15 cm. Diameter at top: 9.7 cm.

白瓷素雕仕女圖筆筒•壺隱道人製
可能清代下半期, 高15厘米, 頂直徑9.7厘米

This brush pot represents two late Qing trends. The first, which began earlier in the dynasty but flourished in the late 18th and particularly the 19th century, was for ceramic copies of other materials. This can be traced back to Yongzheng imperial copies made at Jingdezhen of wooden tubs, and Qianlong copies of turquoise, puddingstone and marble objects. The second took place in the 19th century whereby individual potters emerged from the traditionally anonymous mass production of ceramic wares at Jingdezhen.

Among the most famous were Chen Guozhi of Qimen, of the Daoguang and Xianfeng periods, who was still active in 1858, and Wang Bingrong, of the Tongzhi and Guangxu periods. The former was renowned for his capacity to create 'paintings' in ceramics. Several other artists are also recorded. They specialized in fine carving of the biscuit porcelain, which was then sometimes covered with thin enamels in a variety of often pastel colours, sometimes imitating the colour of other materials. Since these artists were all involved in the production of works of art for the persuasive minority, their output was mainly scholarly trappings: brush pots, seal-paste boxes, table screens and other desk utensils, snuff bottles, etc. Their brush pots were frequently of bamboo form and sometimes enamelled to imitate the original material (they are usually referred to as being glazed, as colours are predominantly monochrome, but the normal covering was enamel low fired directly onto the biscuit.)

The *hao* 'the Daoist hidden in a pot' refers to the popular legend of Daoist sages/immortals who were capable of disappearing into a gourd (representing an alternative world, which might equally be found in other vessels) and entering different realms. It was the *hao* of Wu Wei (also known as Wu Shijiu), a native of Jingdezhen and a known poet and calligrapher as well as a potter of the Wanli period of late Ming. He was famous for his extremely fine wares, known simply as 'Hu ceramic wares', and is recorded as having made egg-membrane cups as thin as the name suggests and covered with a bright, white glaze. Wu also did relief carving of dragons that were considered to be very fine, and made wares resembling those of the Yongle and Xuande periods of early Ming.[1] A table screen bearing the same signature, with relief decoration of a cockerel and flowering plant enamelled in yellow, is recorded.[2] Stylistically neither piece could be considered as of the late Ming period, while both are entirely consistent with 19th century production at Jingdezhen. It is likely that a later potter was aware of Wu's fame and adopted his name, but it is also possible that the name was merely adopted for its Daoist associations without any reference to the earlier man or intent to mislead.

It is indicative of how far the barriers between artist and craftsman, and between those who could reasonably aspire to the persuasive minority and those who could not, had broken down by the Qing period that out of the ceramic industry at Jingdezhen — traditionally one of the least conducive to individual artistic creativity — should arise a group of individual potters who signed and dated their works and produced mainly for the scholar class. It had been a gradual process since the Sui and Tang, when the examination system was firmly established, to create a governing class based on merit (in theory at least). Merchants and other classes, through a variety of avenues, might seek office through scholarship. Craftsmen mixed more and more with the literati as the roles of patron and artist blended into each other in the Song and post-Song periods. By the late Ming and Qing dynasties artists such as Hu Wenming (see no. 73) and Lu Dong (see no. 63), the Yixing potters and a host of others shared the aesthetic, and sometimes even the lifestyle, of the literati as a variety of arts provided access to the highest levels of cultural influence. On this brush pot a consummate technique has superimposed a low relief design with complete confidence of line and form onto a ground plane that is miraculously even. There is not a tool mark visible on the whole surface and the finish is perfect — it is the quintessential example of Zhou Yi's maxim that the most important part of carving is found not in the cutting, but in the polishing or finishing (see no. 58).

1. *Zhongguo Meishujia Renming Cidian,* p.521.
2. The *National Palace Museum Monthly of Chinese Art,* February 1986, no. 35, p.120, pl. 15.

42

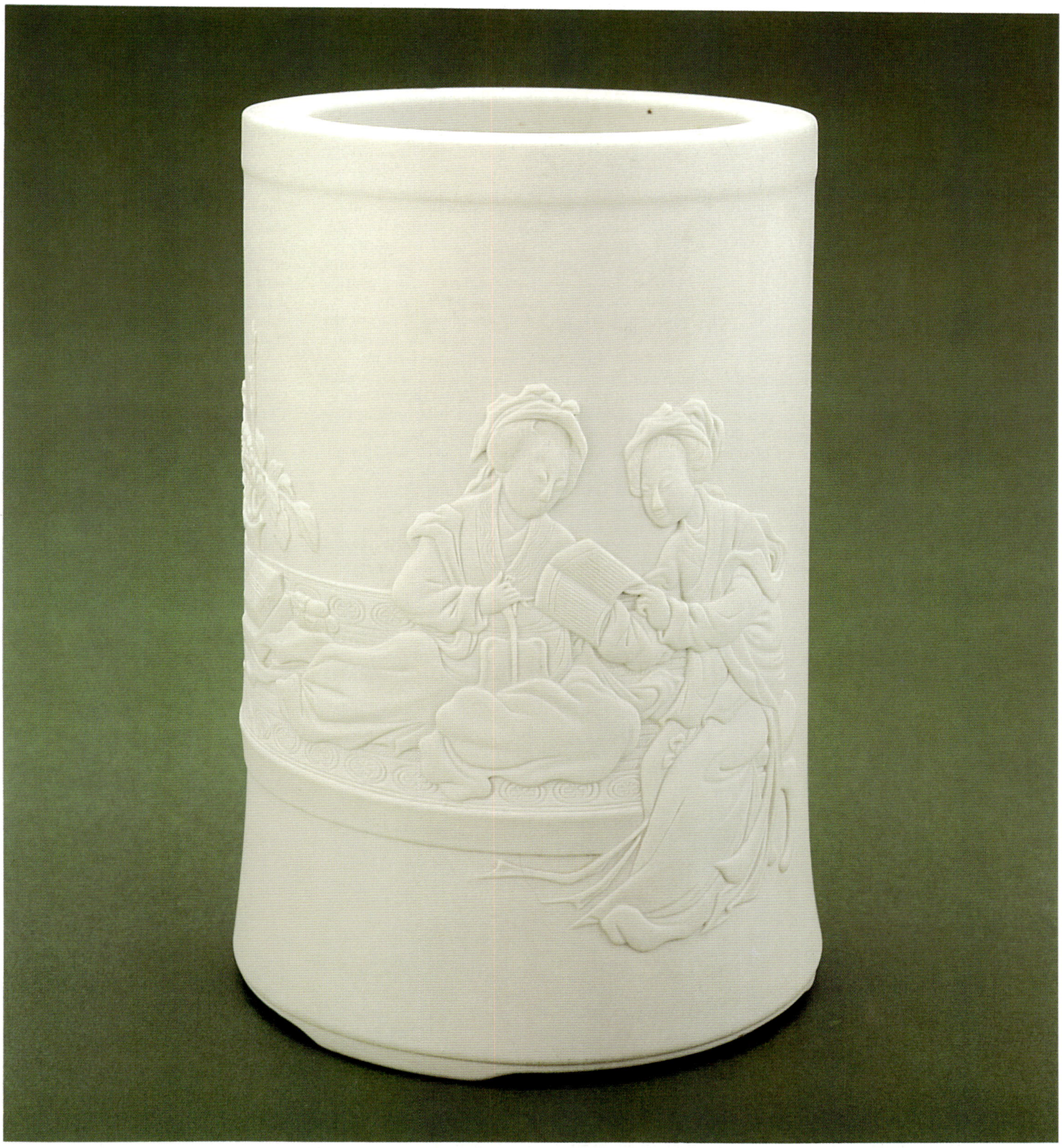

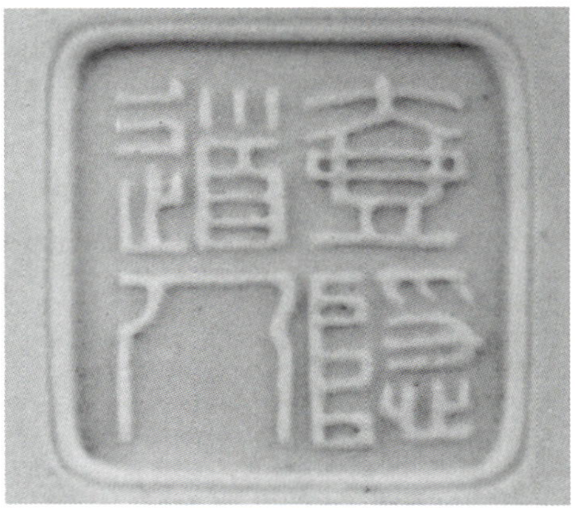

43

Pair of Seals

Zhou Bin

Soapstone, of the translucent beige-white colour known as *baifurong*; a pair of uncut seals, each of tall rectangular form carved on the upper surface with two formalized *chi* dragons back to back in low relief against a ground of incised *leiwen;* the upper end of the seal pedestals with a continuous freize of four stylized *chi* dragons set against a recessed, incised ground of *leiwen* enclosed within line borders; each with a minutely incised signature seal, *Shangjun,* in seal script, set in relief in a recessed cartouche in the border between the upper freize and the top of the seal pedestal.
Fujian, mid- to late 17th century.
5.2 cm × 2.1 cm × 2.1 cm.

壽山白芙蓉石刻螭印一對•周彬製
清初十七世紀, 5.2×2.1×2.1厘米

Zhou Bin (*zi:* Shangjun) was a native of Zhangzhou, in Fujian. He was a renowned carver of seal knobs (see last paragraph for the anatomy of a seal). He was also one of a small group of carvers who represent the zenith of the Chinese tradition of sculpture arising out of the influence of the scholar class (see no. 14 for a discussion on the nature of sculpture and the fine arts in China). He and Yang Yuxuan (see no. 45) were considered to be the finest of these sculptors working in the soft soapstone range of materials, and their works are exceptional, both technically and artistically.

There is some doubt as to the exact dates of Zhou Bin. A seated Buddha in the collection of Mr. & Mrs. Wayne Quasha is inscribed with a 1627 date, in the Tianqi period, while Chinese sources traditionally list him as Kangxi period. There is also a suggestion that he was a student of Yang Yuxuan and was enlisted as an imperial craftsman to work in the palace workshops of the Kangxi Emperor, but research in China has failed to uncover any records of this.[1] While powerful sculpture, the Quasha figure seems to be less sophisticated in its finish and detail than characteristic pieces by the artist, and it is possible that it represents his early work, in which case perhaps Zhou worked from the 1620s into the Kangxi period (a hypothesis borne out by the working period of Yang Yuxuan, who was apparently active in the mid 17th century (see no. 45), but called into question by no. 84 where the matter is considered further).

Whatever his dates, and his relationship with Yang Yuxuan, he was clearly an artist whose works were highly valued by the influential minority, and who expressed himself entirely within their aesthetic. Literati appreciation of his works is recorded. Zheng Jie, a Qing painter, wrote: "I have an addiction for seals [literally 'stones']. For over thirty years I have collected over five hundred pieces, large and small. They are all the works of past masters of our province and the knobs were mostly the work of Yang Yuxuan and Zhou Shangjun".[2] The famous late Qing painter, calligrapher and seal carver Wu Changshuo inscribed in seal script the side of a stone carved by Shangjun: "This stone was carved by Zhou Shangjun, we should especially treasure it".[3]

Fang Zonggui tells us that Zhou's works were always treasured in artists' circles and became known by the name 'Shangjun knobs'; and that he employed the Chinese painting *xieyi* method in carving deeply to create landscapes, flowers, pine and bamboo as decorative motifs on his seals. Fang also claims for Zhou Bin the origin of the thin, low-relief, painterly style of carving seals.[4] *Xieyi* means literally 'idea painting'. Although it became associated with a certain free, expressionistic style, it actually stands for the literati ideal of painting as an analogy of the Absolute rather than as a representation of the objective realm. From the Ming dynasty, when the influential minority began discovering the delights of soapstone as a medium for their artistic expression, sculpture in this medium assumed the potential for profundity (regardless of the physical size of the objects produced) associated with the fine arts.

Zhou Bin's works are characterized by extraordinary technical skill combined with great sculptural power, more obviously apparent in no. 44 perhaps, but equally present here in the restrained use of low relief carving and the confidence of the formalized, paired dragons on the upper surface. The concept allows the highly valued stone, with its subtle texturing and colour, to speak for itself while overlaying a level of sculptural expression of great elegance. The tiny signature in positive seal script tucked away in an upper border is typical of Shangjun (see also no. 164).

It is interesting to note that the exhibition of a level of technical skill which would have been considered 'flashy' by the scholarly class in their painting and calligraphy was frequently highly valued in various sculptures, whether executed by the literati themselves, or by the artists who responded to their aesthetic demands and, indeed, joined them in influencing the artistic evolution of the culture. Fang Zonggui describes a work by Shangjun as being in a carving style which was simple and rustic.[5] These are terms reserved for the highest levels of literati painting and calligraphy and are highly complimentary, and yet on the surface nothing could be further from the aesthetic of literati painting than the astonishingly crafted carvings of Shangjun. The answer is, as always, that one cannot possibly comprehend Chinese art by its surface, only through what lies beyond the surface. It was not the skill itself that mattered, in the final analysis it was how the skill was used, to what end it was put. Shangjun was perceived, along with his fellow soapstone masters, as expressing something profound with his skills, and his rusticity and simplicity were seen in his meaning, not his means.

Furong stone is characterized by its resemblance to jade. It is a product of the Shoushan area (see no. 14) and of the highest peak of the Jialiang hills to the east. It is a pure and clear version of *yela* stone (pyrophyllite), which is soft, fine, slightly translucent, smooth and moist. It is distinctly different from other Shoushan stones, and has a white speckling within the translucent surface. When it was first mined in the Ming dynasty it did not attract great attention. The Kangxi scholar Wang Shizhen noted in 1705 that "*Furong* stone did not cost as much as one fifth of the price of other Shoushan stones."[6] In the Qianlong period the cave from which the finest material was excavated was owned by a general and became known as 'General's Cave *furong*' (*Jiangjundong furong*), and more widely appreciated and valued. By the late Qing period it had become extremely rare and highly valued, and was listed, along with *tianhuang* (also from Shoushan — see no. 54), and Changhua stone (from Zhejiang province) as the 'Three Treasures' of seal stones. The *furong* stone from the 'General's Cave' was considered the best. This cave collapsed at some time during the Qing period, and extant examples are all considered to be over one hundred years old, although in January 1972 another quarry shaft was dug aimed at the bottom of the General's Cave area. These seals are particularly fine examples of the material.

The anatomy of a seal is as follows: the overall seal is called either *yin* ('seal') or *shi* ('stone'). The uppermost part is called *niu* ('knob'), and the platform upon which it sits at the top of the pedestal, the knob platform, is called *pingtai* ('flat platform'). The sides of the pedestal are called *bian* ('side') and any inscription upon them (usually added by the person who cuts the seal text, but see below) is called *bianhuan* ('side inscription'). The text on the base of the seal is called *tuzhang* (literally 'pictorial impression' but not intended to mean specific pictorial seals) or *yinzhang* ('seal impression'), while the content of the text is called *yinwen* ('seal text'). These may be in a variety of scripts and either *yinke* ('negative cutting') or *yangke* ('positive cutting'), the former leaving the final impression with white lines on a red ground, the latter with red lines on a white ground — which may alternatively be referred to as *baiwen* ('white writing') or *zhuwen* ('red writing') respectively. The carving of the seal and the seal text are independent skills and are usually not carried out by the same person.

1. See an article on Zhou Bin in *Shoushanshi Zhi (Records of Shoushan Stone)* by Fang Zonggui.
2. Ibid., quoted from *Mingzhong Lu* ('Fujian Records') by Zheng Jie.
3. Ibid., from 'Selected Seal Carvings of Wu Changshi', p.23.
4. Ibid.
5. Ibid.
6. *Xiangzu Biji,* by Wang Shizhen, 1705.

43

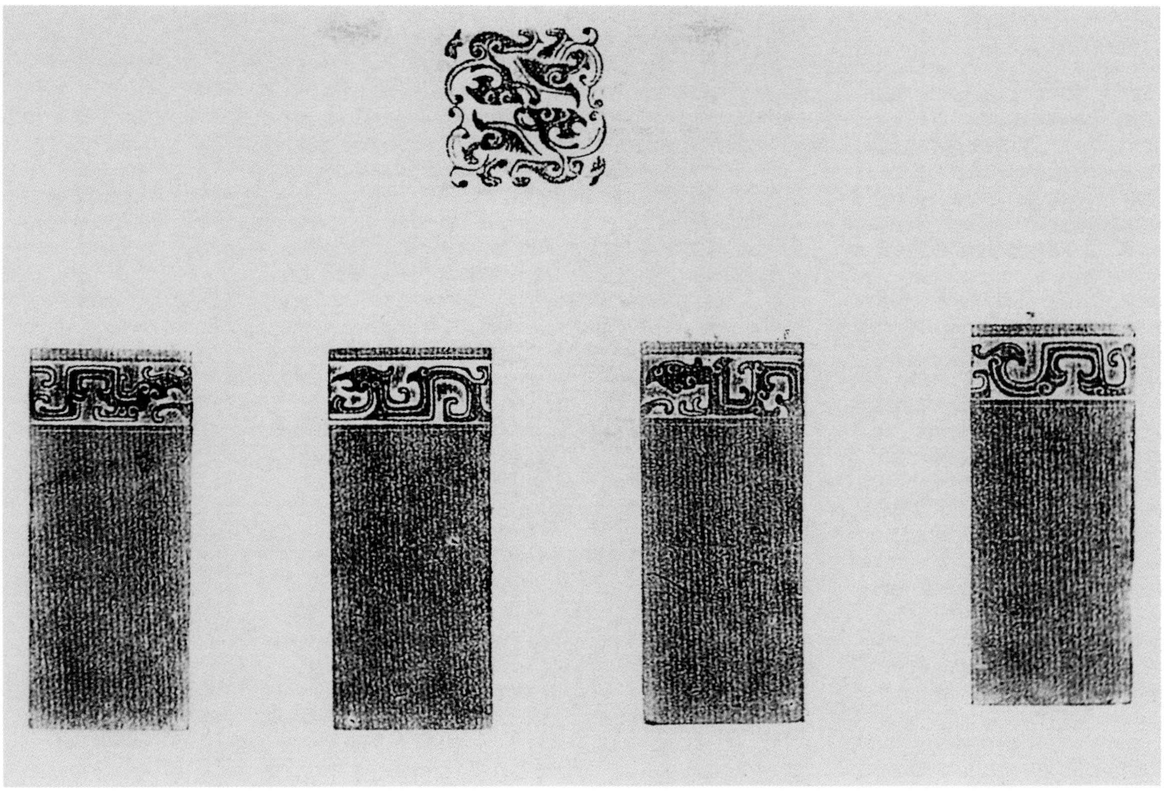

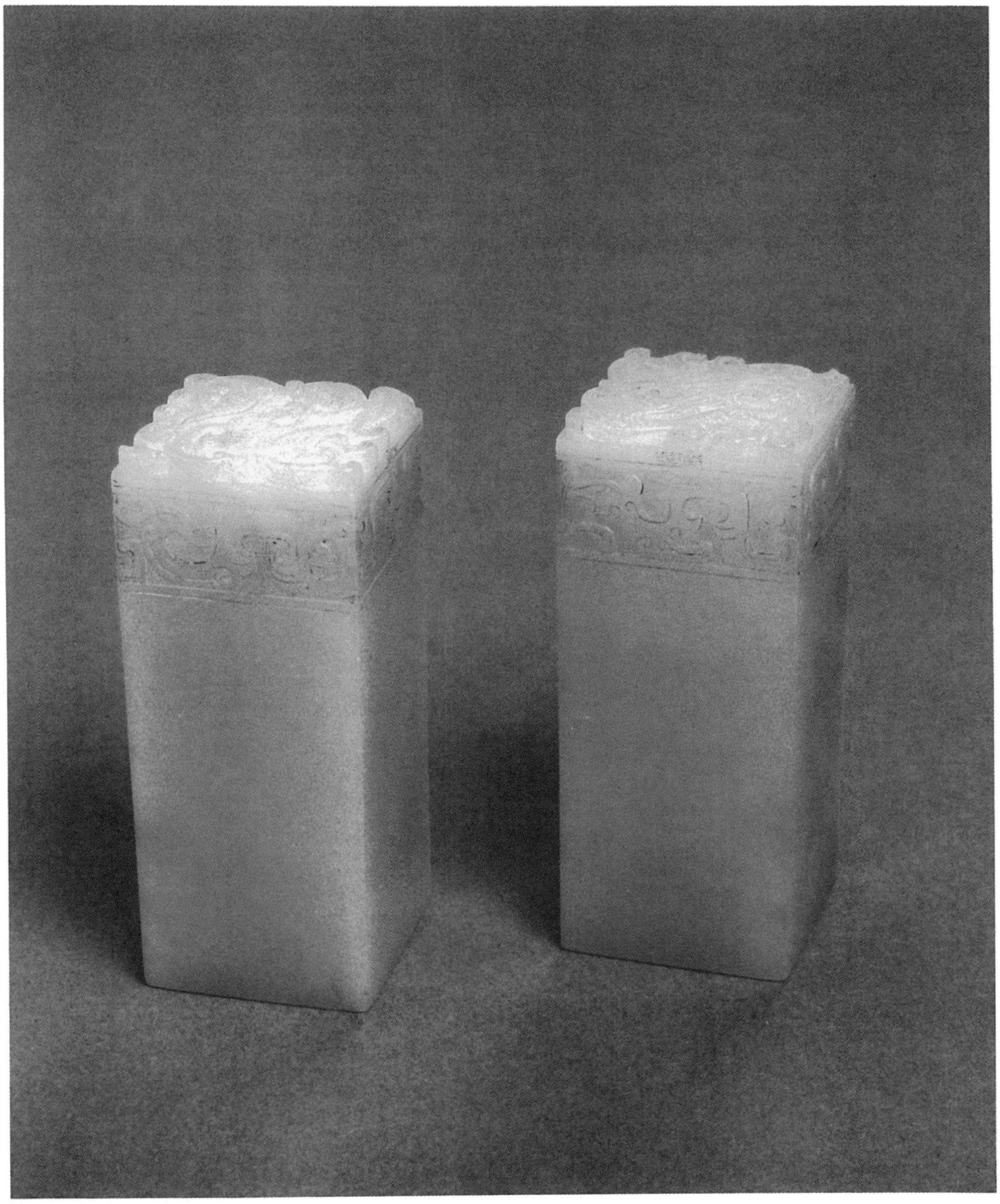

Larger than life size

44

Luohan

Zhou Bin

Soapstone, of mottled grey colour of the Shoushan variety known as *niujiao dong* ('ox-horn ice'); carved as a seated *luohan* staring intently at his open hand, his loosely fitting robes partially covered by a cloak, gathered around the neck and clasped at the throat, decorated with three phoenix medallions, with edging incised with scrolling Indian lotus on a formalized wave ground, repeated on the collar and cuffs of the inner garment; incised detail, eyes and stubble on head and chin gilt, the lips originally coloured red; set on an original elaborately decorated cushion of mottled red Shoushan soapstone, its top incised with lotus on a formalized wave ground, surrounded by a thin cloud band and a broad band of foliate medallions of alternating *chi* dragons and Indian lotus, set against a ground of Indian lotus on waves; the edge with a narrow band of formalized, wavy lines with rudimentary floral flourishes, the curved and shaped lower lip of the cushion with a band of Indian lotus on a formalized wave ground, the incising all gilt; the base inscribed *Gumin Zhou Bin Shangjun shi zhi* ('made by Mr Zhou Bin, Shangjun of Gumin [Fujian]') in clerical script, the characters gilt.
Fujian, 17th century.
Height: 11.1 cm.

壽山牛角凍石雕羅漢像•周彬製
清初十七世紀, 高11.1厘米

The figures of the early soapstone masters have certain features in common. Apart from the obvious ones of types of material used, fine quality of carving, incised garment edges and designs, choice of subject-matter, fixed bases made separately in the form of fancy padded cushions, root or rockwork, and the gilding of details, there is one key feature that sets them apart from those that followed. Every one is conceived as an individual work of art. Although certain decorative traits are apparent over and over again, the model itself, the characterization of the person depicted, the posture and mood of the figure is newly worked out every time. Some of the early group of artists are better technically than others, but all display more than adequate and frequently total control of the medium.

Too often with the later works of this tradition there is the impression that the carver has simply been turning out another Shou Lao or another Guanyin. The technical control is there, but the spirit and the individuality are, by comparison with the early group, absent.

This dedication is clearly exhibited here. Sculpturally the figure is flawless (although a little recut at the lower knee where damage has occurred), the lines of the robe falling down the back giving a good idea of the mastery of the artist in dealing with the fall of a heavy material, but the attention to detail is perhaps best seen in the incising. Zhou's incising of robe edges, decorative medallions and cushion details is second to none. When he incises a robe pattern it is independently fascinating in design and execution. His ability to draw with the 'iron brush', also seen on his seals (see the frieze designs in nos. 43 and 164) is remarkable. Although Yang Yuxuan, Zixiu and others are sculpturally in a class with Zhou Bin, they rarely maintain their concentration and devotion to detail right down to the last incision quite as effectively as he does. Their borders tend to be decorative filling, support for the main sculpture without independent fascination.

There is another figure in the Quasha collection of a *luohan* seated holding a small beast in his hand, also of grey soapstone seated on a red cushion, but of a different shape. It is of similar quality to this example, and is also similarly signed on the cushion. An exciting possibility is that a set of 18 existed originally and others may come to light.

Both stones used here are Shoushan stones. The base is carved from a piece of stone that is otherwise unremarkable (as the bases often were) and therefore the Chinese have not bothered to give it further classification. The figure itself, however, is of a material classified by its visual appearance as 'frozen' or 'ice' stone *(dongshi)* where the surface is translucent and has the appearance of ice, regardless of its colour. This is then further classified as being a particular type of *dongshi* which, because of its resemblence to oxhorn is called 'oxhorn ice' About 1.5 km to the southeast of Shoushan there is a peak called Kengtou Shan, at the foot of which is a quarry coinciding with an underground spring. According to the Chinese belief the presence of water has moistened the stones and made them transparent and glassy. These are known as 'water quarry stones' *(shuikeng shi)* and much of the Shoushan 'ice' stone is found there. It is also the source of the *chang shi* or 'crystal stone' variety of soapstone.

45

Luohan

Yang Yuxuan

Soapstone, of variegated creamy-beige and yellow-beige colours of the variety known as Changhua stone, carved as a *luohan* seated with an alms bowl, his loosely fitting robes partially covered by a cloak, caught at the neck by a clasp inset with a tiny green gem, the edges of which are incised with bands of Indian lotus scroll on a ground of formalized waves; the back inscribed *Yu Xuan*.
17th century.
Height: 5.9 cm.
Formerly in the Spencer Churchill collection, Northwick Park.

昌化石雕羅漢像•楊玉璿製
清初十七世紀, 高5.9厘米

Yang Xuan (*zi*: Yuxuan, using a different second character; Yang Ji) was a native of Zhangpu in Fujian province, but resided in the provincial capital, Fuzhou. Like Zhou Bin, he is considered to be a carver of the Kangxi period, but we have recently established that he worked during the mid-17th century. Zhou Lianggong in his *Min Xiaoji* ('Notes on Fujian Province') wrote of Yang Yuxuan: "The excellence of his knife work is the equivalent of that done by supernatural beings."[1] Zhou's book contains a preface dated to the fifth year of Kangxi (1667) and he was writing of his years as a local offical in Fujian to which he was posted in 1647 and where he served for eight years. Thus by 1655 at the latest, Yang was sufficiently well established as a soapstone carver to have been recorded by Zhou, suggesting that he began working in the mid-17th century.

That he did work into the Kangxi period is suggested by a description found in the district gazette of the Jianpu area of the Kangxi period (no more precise date available): "Yang Yuxuan is a capable carver of Shoushan stone (soapstone). All his figures, birds and animals and his vessels are exquisite in the extreme. Collectors compete to engage him."[2] He also features in a poem by the Kangxi scholar Zhu Yizun entitled "Song of *Shoshan* Stone". In a respectful reference to an old man ('old Yang') the subject-matter of some of his seal knobs is described.[3] The fact that Yang was a respected old man at the time of Zhu's poem, the date of which we are unable to establish, suggests that he began work at some time in the late Ming dynasty and worked into the Kangxi period.

The extent to which carvers such as Yang and Zhou became part of the influential minority (their main source of patronage) is demonstrated by some effusive statements about Yang's art. Apart from the opinion of Zhou Lianggong mentioned above, we have that of Gao Xiao, in his *Gunshi Lu* ('Record of Inspection of Seals') who is even more complimentary, praising Yang's seal knobs as the equivalent of horses by Han Gan, buffalo by Dai Hao and tigers by Bao Ding. "Once taken from their containers", he continues, "his works were aggressive (presumably referring to the animals depicted) and full of power — excellent paintings".[4] This likening of the creative powers of communication of a small sculpted seal to that of paintings, and comparison of Yang's works with some of the great painters of antiquity, is informative. It represents the extent to which a number of media previously excluded had become part of the range of arts through which the influential minority expressed itself.

Yang is also credited with inventing (although it is more likely that he merely popularized an existing trend) the use of the natural colours in the stone to enhance the subject-matter. Soapstone is frequently of variegated colour, and these different colours can be used to great effect in the carving.

Yang and Zhou Bin (see no. 43) were undoubtedly two of the most influential masters of soapstone carving of their day and the majority of signed pieces confirm their technical and sculptural skills. This little carving is a masterpiece, displaying subtle and well-observed characterization and an excellent grasp of formal qualities. This is demonstrated by the balance of horizontal and vertical elements in the arrangement of the legs and the fall of the draped robe, with dynamic tension introduced by the diagonal line made up of the bowl and the drawn-back, carefully poised left hand, a diagonal which is cleverly accentuated by the tilt of the head.

It is conventional Chinese wisdom on the subject of soapstone carvings that relief signatures are to be relied upon while incised ones are to be suspected on the grounds that anyone can add a signature to the soft material without difficulty. A useful caution, but a shallow piece of connoisseurship. While it is true that an incised signature is easily added, and no doubt often was, it is equally certain that some artists incised their signatures, while others sometimes signed in relief. It is equally probable that later copyists might also have used a spurious relief signature.

We have never seen a Yang Yuxuan signature in relief , whereas two of the most convincing Zhou Bin pieces (one of which is no. 44) have incised signatures. If we include the artists who cut the seal text into the existing seal and subsequently signed the sides, we are dealing predominantly with incised signatures, the removal from consideration of which would leave us very little evidence. The situation is further confused by the fact that original works unsigned by the artist might have been either correctly or incorrectly attributed by a later owner and a signature added accordingly.

1. Quoted in *Shoushanshi zhi.*
2. Ibid.
3. Ibid.
4. Ibid.

44

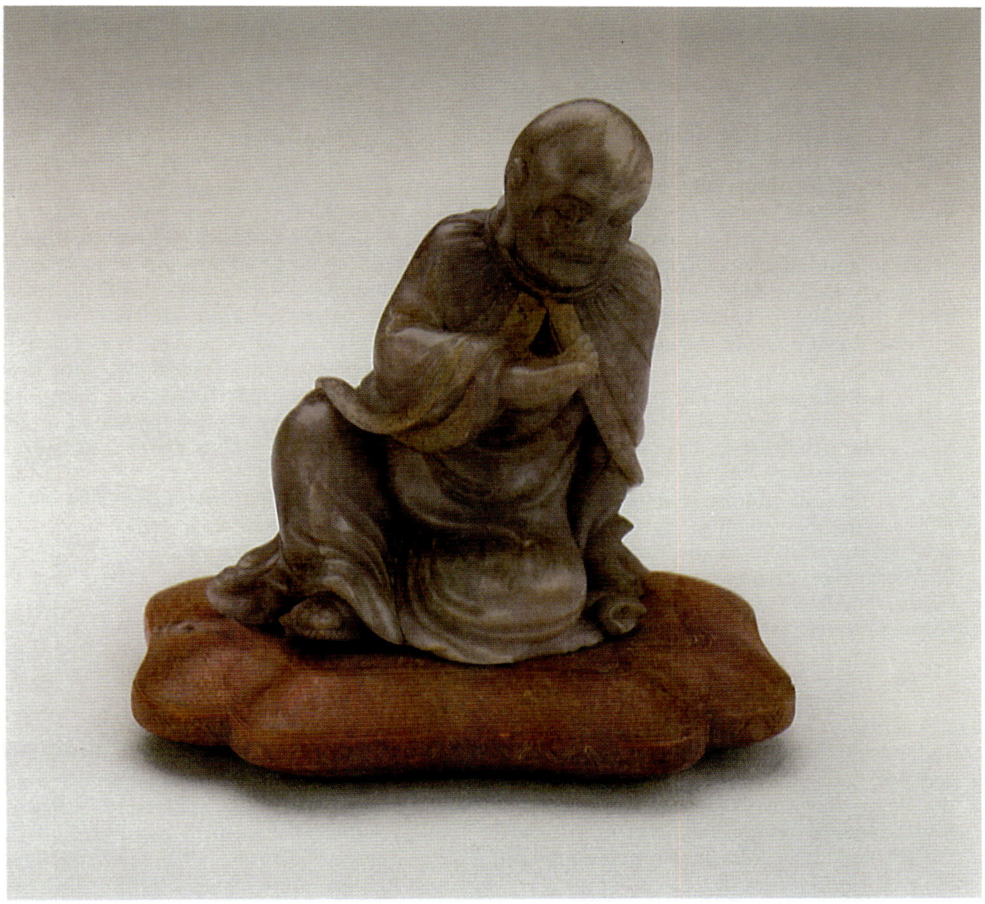

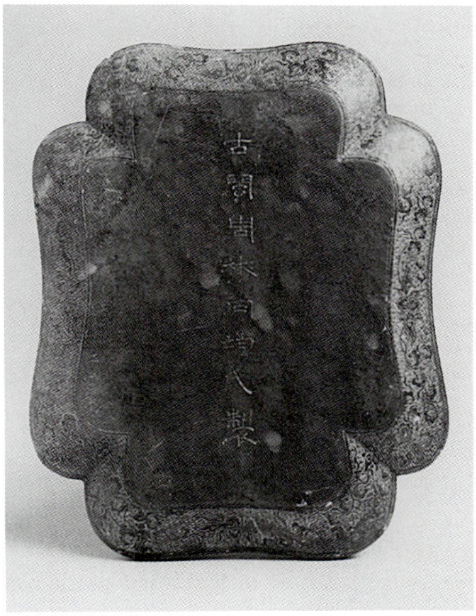

45

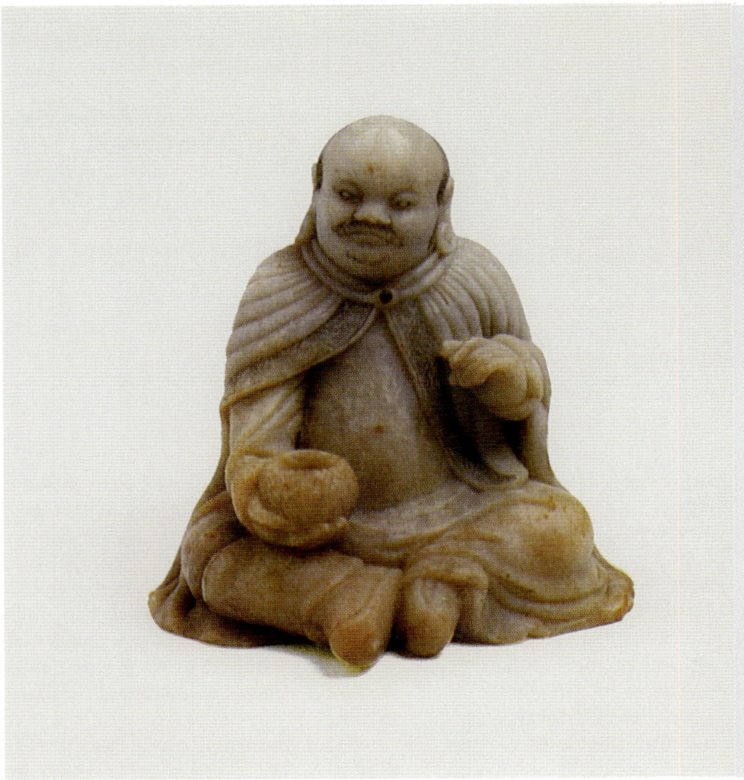

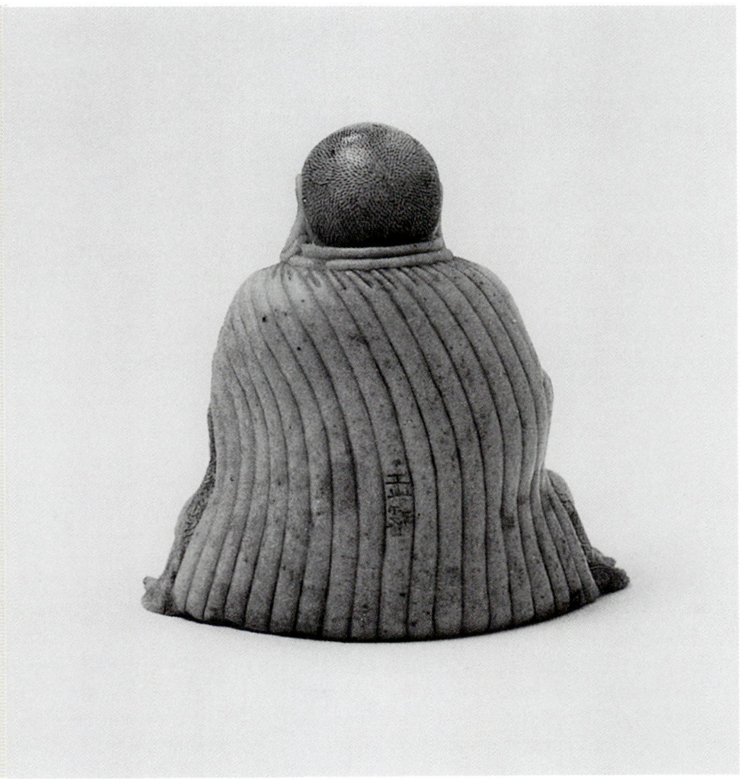

46

Studio Name

Zhao Zhiqian

Ink on paper, hanging scroll; the studio name *Bulele Shi* (see below for translation) in seal script, followed by an inscription stating that Cheng Liujie adopted the studio name *Bulele Shi* in order to complete unfinished business and asked the artist to write it for him; the inscription is dated to the sixth month of 1872, and signed by Zhao Zhiqian, with one seal of the artist *Zhao Zhiqian.*
1872.
32.7 cm × 79.1 cm.

篆書橫額·趙之謙書
清同治壬申(1872),32.7×79.1厘米

The meaning of this studio name is another enjoyable round of puns and allusions. There is a popular saying (*bulele zhi*) which implies that what is unfinished will probably remain unfinished. It implies that the details of the material world are endless in their complexity and that one can waste too much effort tracking them down only to find that they have got you nowhere. However, the inscription makes it clear that in making a pun on the similar sounding *Bulele Shi* for a studio name the last *le* has been used as a verb, thus making it positive, in the sense of 'The studio where what is unfinished will be finished'.

However, nothing is as it seems, for the only person who would need to have a studio name that encourages him to complete unfinished business is one who is hopeless at doing so. Thus we are left with the impression that in this studio Cheng Liujie, the owner, will use his time in loftier pursuits rather than settling his unfinished business.

The popular scholarly habit of naming studios, pavilions, country retreats, and so on gave rise to a demand for titles, often written by famous calligraphers and, for outdoor use, frequently carved in wood or stone. This is a study title, which would probably have been mounted either inside the studio, or above the door to it.

Zhao Zhiqian (*zi:* Yifu, Huishu; *hao:* Beian, Meian, Wumen, Hanliao; Lengjun and Sibeiweng; 1829-1884), was a native of Kuaiji, Zhejiang province. He was a noted scholar, bibliophile, calligrapher, painter and seal carver. From a merchant family, his fondness for scholarship led to a *juren* degree in 1859. Although five attempts at the metropolitan exams failed to secure his *jinshi* degree, he secured several government posts, but was best known for his artistic and literary activities. He was one of the foremost calligraphers, painters and seal carvers of his day. He also published a work on the subject of snuff bottles, one of the few serious studies undertaken by the Chinese on the subject and useful for its record of late 19th century attitudes to certain types of bottles. It is a typical Chinese work of scholarship where hearsay is mixed in with fact and no sources are given to differentiate between the two.

Cheng Liujie was a friend of Zhao Zhizian's. Three paintings are known to have been painted by Zhao for Cheng. One, which is undated, celebrates Cheng's mother's birthday, and is of chrysanthemums, peaches and archaic bronzes. Another was executed before Zhao left for Jiangxi in 1872, and is of three archaic bronze *jue* with flowers. It is dated 1872 and it is recorded that Cheng asked for it to be painted as a gift for a third party. The third, of prunus and rocks, is also dated to 1872 and is a farewell gift before Zhao's departure.[1]

1. All three are in *Beian Shengmo* ('Ink traces of Beian').

47

Kang Tao's Snuff Bottle

Jet; a snuff bottle of flattened form with rounded edges, carved in low relief on one side with a long-tailed bird on the branches of a blossoming tree; the reverse also carved in low relief with a 14-character inscription in seal script which discusses the charm of dew on the red stamens of the flower, and the beauty of the multicoloured bird and its sweet voice; the poem followed by two seals *Yi* and *zhai,* which together form the signature of the writer of the poem, and presumably the owner of the bottle, Yizhai; the surface well worn and patinated.
Probably first half of the 18th century.
Height excluding stopper: 5.45 cm.

黑褐炭刻花鳥題詩鼻煙壺·康濤銘
可能十八世紀上半葉,高(不連蓋)5.45厘米

Yizhai is the *zi* of Kang Tao (a native of Qiantang, modern day Hangzhou, whose other *zi* was Kangshan and whose *hao* were Shizhou and Tiandu Laoren), a scholar renowned for his filial piety. He excelled at figure painting, but was also recorded as a landscape artist and calligrapher who even at the age of 70 could still write small regular script very well. Paintings by him are recorded from 1726 to as late as 1755, and he is elsewhere listed as a Kangxi period scholar, so he was presumably born in the Kangxi period and continued painting into the mid-18th century.

It is not clear whether Kang Tao made this bottle himself (which if he was a seal carver would have presented no problems for him as jet is a soft material, easily carved directly with a blade), or whether it was made for him. The

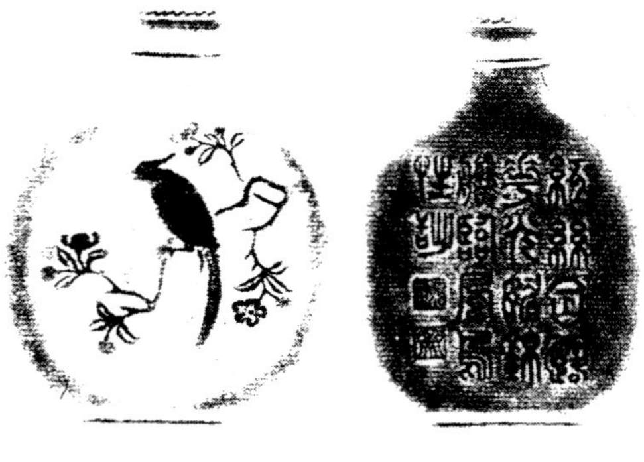

form of signature and the fact that Kang Tao was not known as a poet would make it unlikely that a later patron would choose to have his poem inscribed. If Kang Tao did not make it, it is very likely that he wrote the original calligraphy to be copied onto the bottle.

Snuff was introduced from Europe at some time during the late Ming period, and seems to have taken two routes: directly to the southern ports trading at the time with Europe, and via Japan, Korea and Manchuria. The Manchus established its popularity in the north of China after the conquest of 1644. It remained an imperial habit, centred around the Court at Beijing for a century before it began to spread south, and become a nationwide habit during the late 18th and 19th centuries. Snuff bottles, being highly valued by the ruling minority and having enourmous potential for innovation in materials and their usage, became popular collectors items among the elite. They served also as a convenient currency for buying favour at Court, leading to the amassing of some very large collections as early as the 18th century.[1]

The influential minority was involved in a number of cults from time to time. Each involved the production of a wide range of works of art, such as tea wares associated with the tea cult (see no. 104) and wares for the incense cult (see 229). They also became involved with singing birds, requiring cages and a host of fittings; and crickets for singing and fighting, involving cages, fighting pens and other paraphernalia.

1. For details of snuff and snuff bottles, see *Snuff Bottles of the Ch'ing Dynasty.*

48

Lingzhi Gatherer

Wang Zhu

Soapstone, of even dark brown colour, of the variety known as *taohua dong* ('peach blossom ice') from Shoushan; carved as a gatherer of *lingzhi* fungus reclining against a rock, gazing up into the sky, his loosely fitting robes revealing a well-fed figure covered by his lengthy beard; what remains of his hair tied in a knot on top of his head; at his knee is a basket full of fungi and a hoe; his hat hangs over a rocky outcrop behind him, and a large clump of *lingzhi* grows by his shoulder; a smoothed section of rock at the back of the figure inscribed with the title "Picture of gathering *lingzhi*" and the seal of the artist *Wang Zhu.*
Probably late Ming dynasty.
Height: 5.5 cm. Length: 10.3 cm.

壽山桃花凍石雕採芝老人像·汪洙製
可能晚明,高5.5厘米,長10.3厘米

Wang Zhu is perhaps an assumed name of an artist whose true identity remains unknown. Three pieces are known bearing his signature (see no. 267 for one, the other is of a scholar reclining on a pillow of books on a rock. It is signed in a seal and is in a private collection in Canada). All are convincingly early, outside the mainstream of other early soapstone carvings, and of a distinctly literati flavour. Here we have an old Daoist, resting after wandering the hills in search of *lingzhi* — a delightful and very well carved little figure that almost seems to grow out of the rockwork, and a similar carving to the other figure subject known. The third piece is a typical literati landscape painting translated into a three-dimensional sculpture. It would not be unreasonable, therefore, to guess that Wang Zhu is the art name of a late Ming scholar/artist who turned his hand to soapstone carving from time to time.

The Shoushan stone here is of a variety that is known to change its colour over the years, and the deep caramel-coloured surface is revealed in a small chip to conceal a lighter, more distinctly pinkish tone appropriate to its name.

46

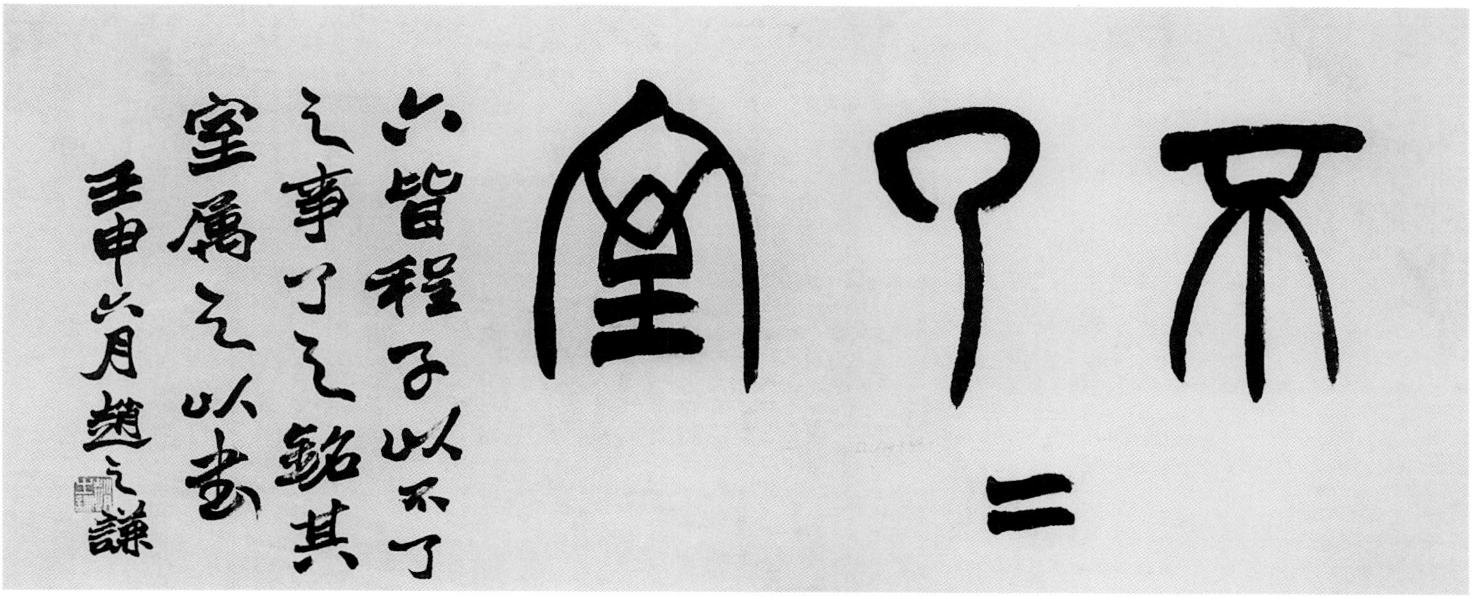

47

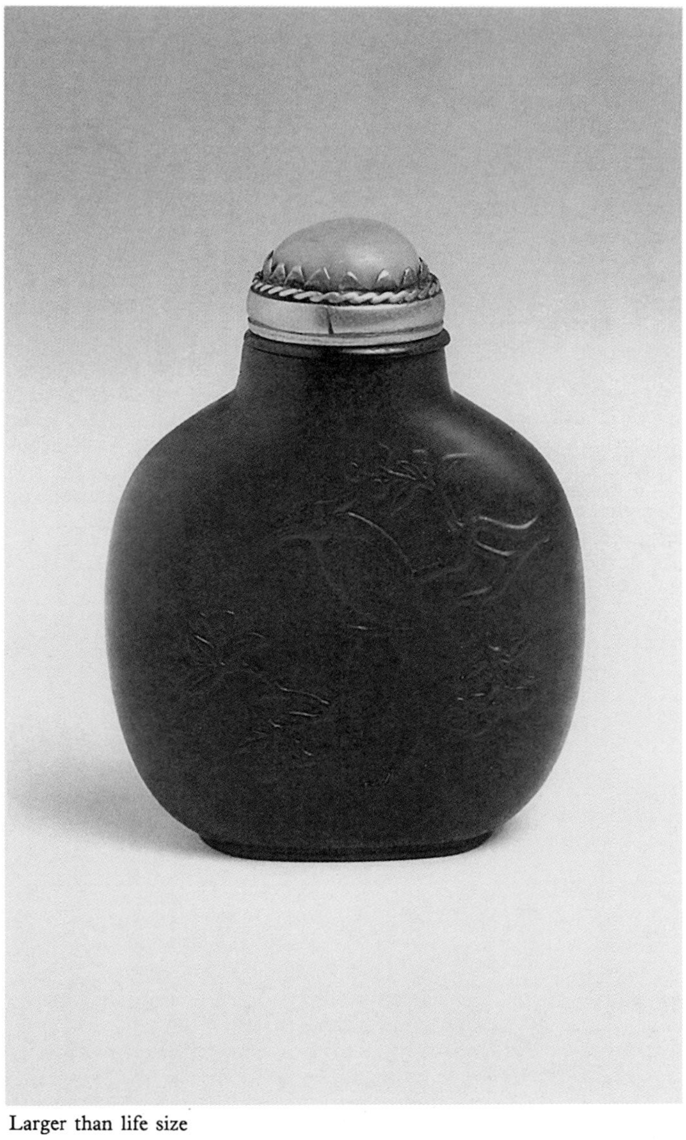

Larger than life size

48

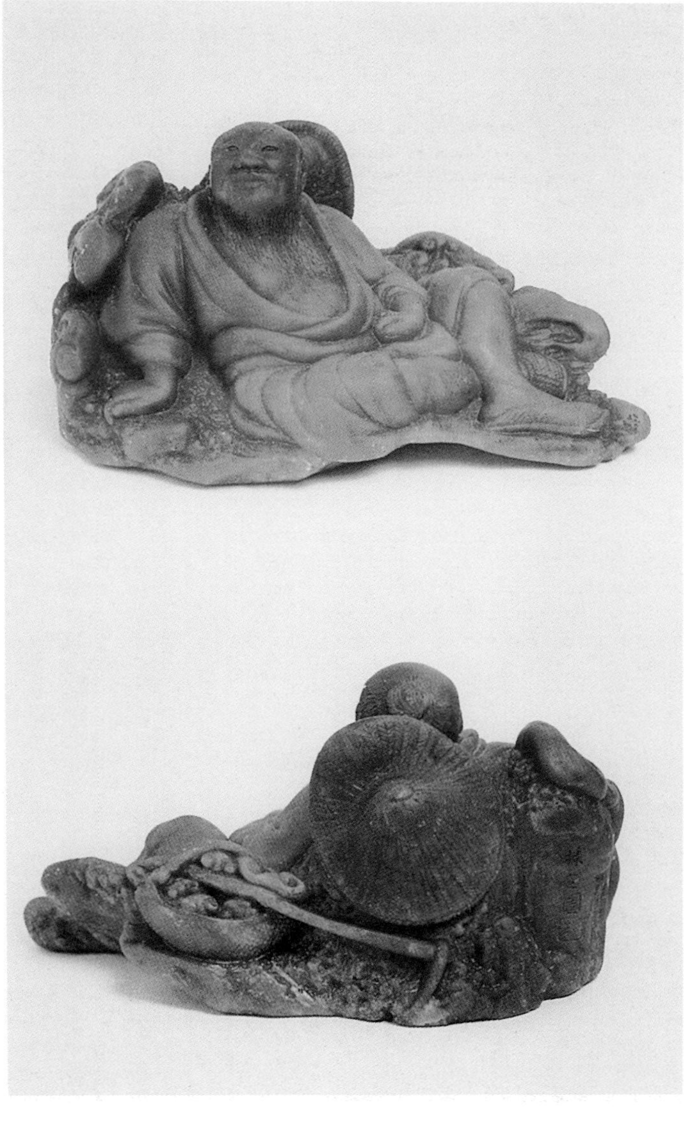

49

Sakyamuni as an Ascetic

Bamboo, of yellowish grey-brown colour; carved as Sakyamuni, his emaciated body reclining against a three-legged, low root table or arm rest, his left hand holding a distinctly non-Indian string of beads.
Set on a bamboo stand, perhaps original, simulating a natural root formation.
Qing dynasty, probably first half.
Height including stand: 10 cm. Length: 10.7 cm.
Formerly in the Dr. Ip Yee collection.
Published: *Bamboo Carving of China* p.109, no. 52, and colour plate 6; *Chinese Bamboo Carving* p.387, Part I no. 126, and pl. 36.

竹雕釋迦苦修像
清代，可能上半期，高連座10厘米，長10.7厘米

In his search for enlightenment, Sakyamuni joined a group of ascetics in order to overcome the desires of the body. He fasted until he could feel his spine through his belly, but close to death from starvation he decided that such bodily deprivation was not a prerequisite for enlightenment. In this exquisitely carved sculpture the exhaustion of Sakyamuni is depicted with great sensitivity; the starkness of his feeble body, its every bone showing through the skin, is contrasted against the flowing and relatively substantial appearance of the material of his trousers. The root stand or arm rest against which he rests is, like the beads he holds, a rather Chinese addition to an originally Indian subject. Such a beautifully crafted little root stand is hardly the furniture of ascetics but more a treasured possession of a Chinese scholar, but it represents a simple root arm rest selected at random in the wilderness.

The high art of sculpture represented by these small figures of the late Ming and early Qing dynasty has been discussed elsewhere, and is again demonstrated here. This is a subject carved many times by later wood and bamboo carvers, to the point where it became a simple formula for depicting a starving figure, executed without integrity and frequently without dexterity. However in this early example we see the full capacity of a great sculptor — albeit anonymous and working on so small a scale — to move us.

50

Dongfang Suo

Wood, *hungyangmu* (boxwood), of golden-brown colour; carved as a figure of Dongfang Suo, in a studied pose, holding a large peach in his hands, his hair tied in a knot on top of his head and contained in a cloth hat, the ribbons hanging down over his shoulders, the hem and cuffs of his robes finely incised with a formalized pattern of scrolling flowers on a wave ground; the figure set on a separate but original base simulating a bizarre rock formation.
Probably Fujian province, 17th century.
Height including original base: 15.4 cm.

黄楊木雕東方朔像
清十七世紀，高連座15.4厘米

Although carved in boxwood, this figure has all of the features of a soapstone figure of the 17th century Fujian group. Size, subject-matter, the placing of a figure on a separate base imitating a convoluted rock formation, hems and cuffs incised with floral patterns over a wave ground, and quality of carving are all precisely what one would expect of a figure of the soapstone group popularized by Zhou Bin (Shangjun) and Yang Yuxuan (see nos. 44 and 45). Whatever its origin it is another example of the superb sculpture of the period.

Dongfang Suo is a legendary figure to whom many myths are attached. He was believed to have had several re-incarnations, and to have been able to change his appearance at will (see no. 271 for a discussion on the metaphorical meaning of such supernatural abilities). He was said to have stolen three of the peaches of longevity from the garden of Xi Wang Mu, consumption of which granted him immortality. In one of his re-incarnations he is said to have served the Han Emperor Wu Di (140-86 BC). A man of ready wit, it is said that when the Emperor was informed that Dongfang Suo had been imbibing copiously from his private jars of wine of immortality, Dong saved himself from the death sentence imposed by pointing out to the Emperor that if the wine worked, he could not be killed by execution, and if it didn't, then the wine was a sham and he had stolen nothing of importance. Amused at this clever reply the Emperor pardoned him.

1. For further details see *A Dictionary of Chinese Mythology*, pp.528-530, and *Pointers and Clues to the Subjects of Chinese and Japanese Art*, p.197.

51

Paper Weight

Bronze, gilt; a paper or book weight in the form of a seated lion (quite clearly a male of the species), shown with an ecstatic expression on his face as he scratches behind his ear with his left rear leg, while using his left foreleg to vigorously scratch his lower back; the body well formed and muscular, the shaggy mane partly hiding a double rope collar from which a small bell dangles; originally gilt overall, but now much worn down to the original bronze.
Ming or earlier.
Height: 6.7 cm.
Formerly in the Robert A. Hall collection.

鎏金青銅坐獅紙鎮
明或較早，高6.7厘米

This strongly sculpted weight is an enigma. Although on the surface it seems to fit into the group of bronze paper weights of the Ming/Qing group, it has certain distinguishing features. It is larger than usual; the style of the lion depicted is closer to the still imposing creatures of the Tang dynasty than to the pussy-cats of Ming; it has prominent genitalia which are usually far more discreet if shown at all in Ming and Qing versions, and the sculpture is far more individual and powerful than is normal for the group. Were it not for certain similarities in size, type of metal and patination to no. 195 (although this example is far more convincingly worn), which is more readily acceptable as of the Ming/Qing group, we would be tempted to date it as pre-Ming. Perhaps this was a prototype for certain features which the later example followed, or it may be simply a later, eccentric piece.

49

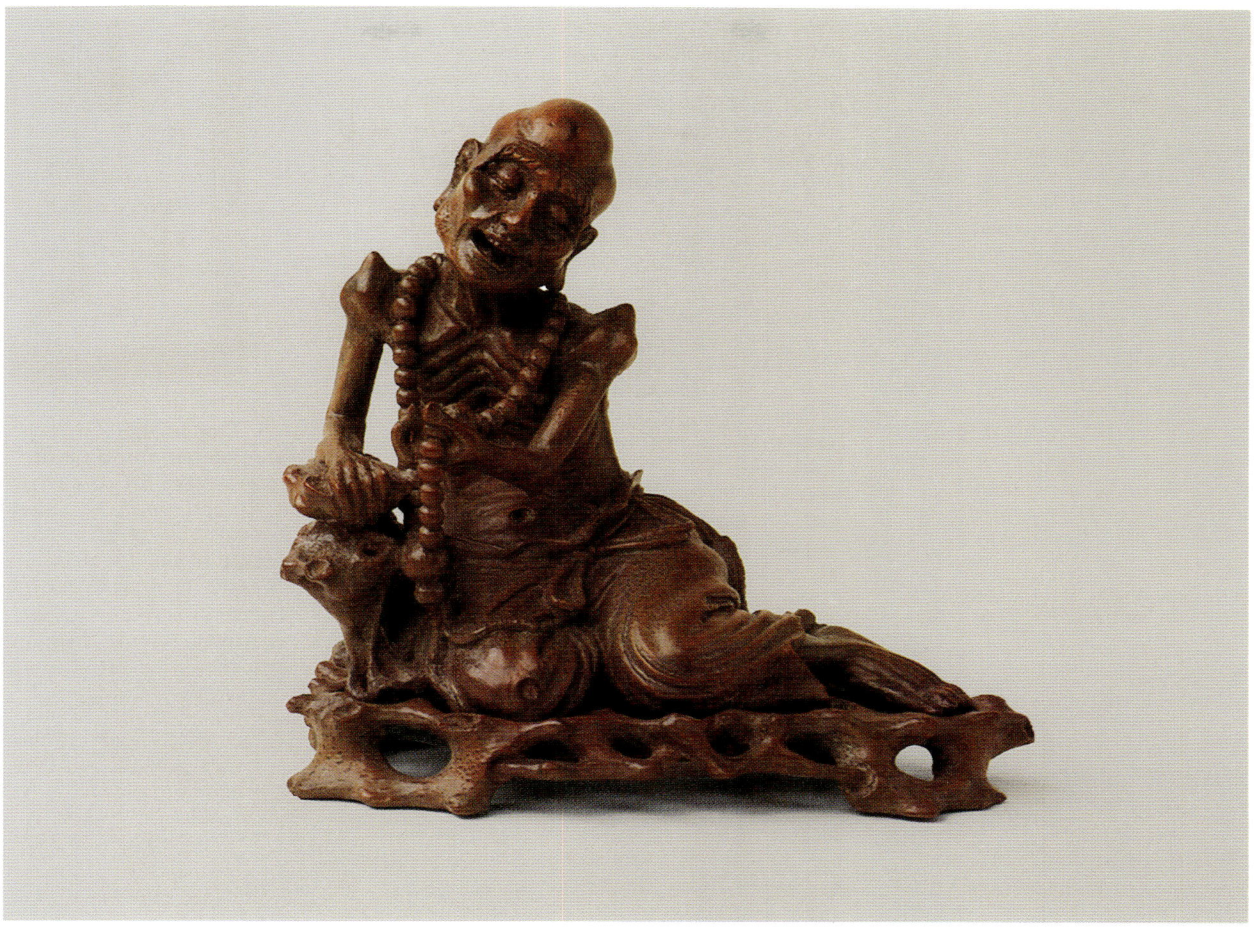

50

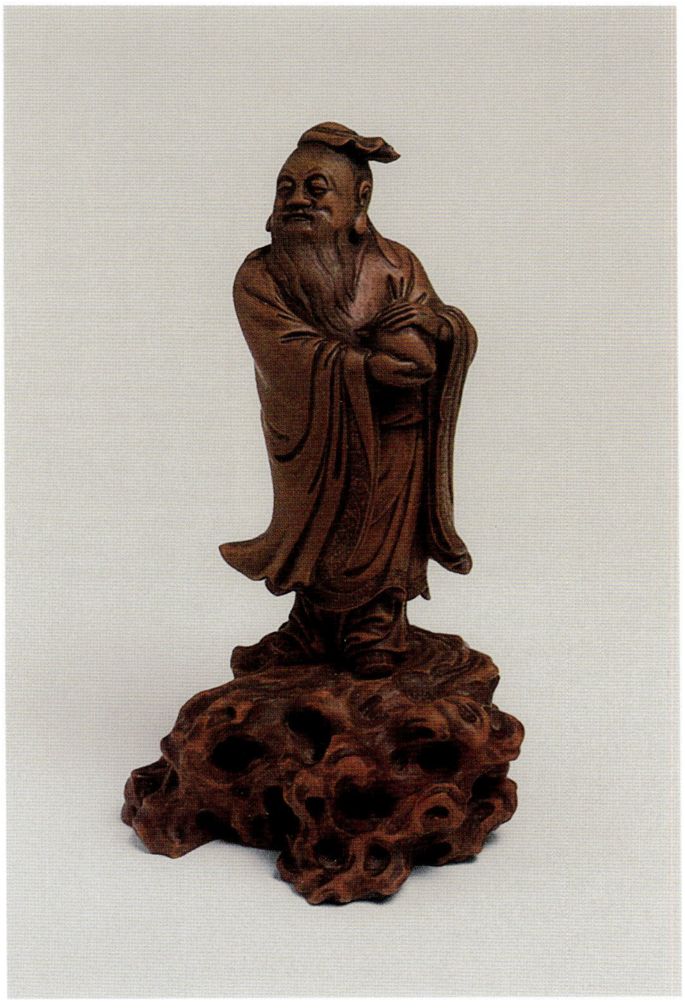

51

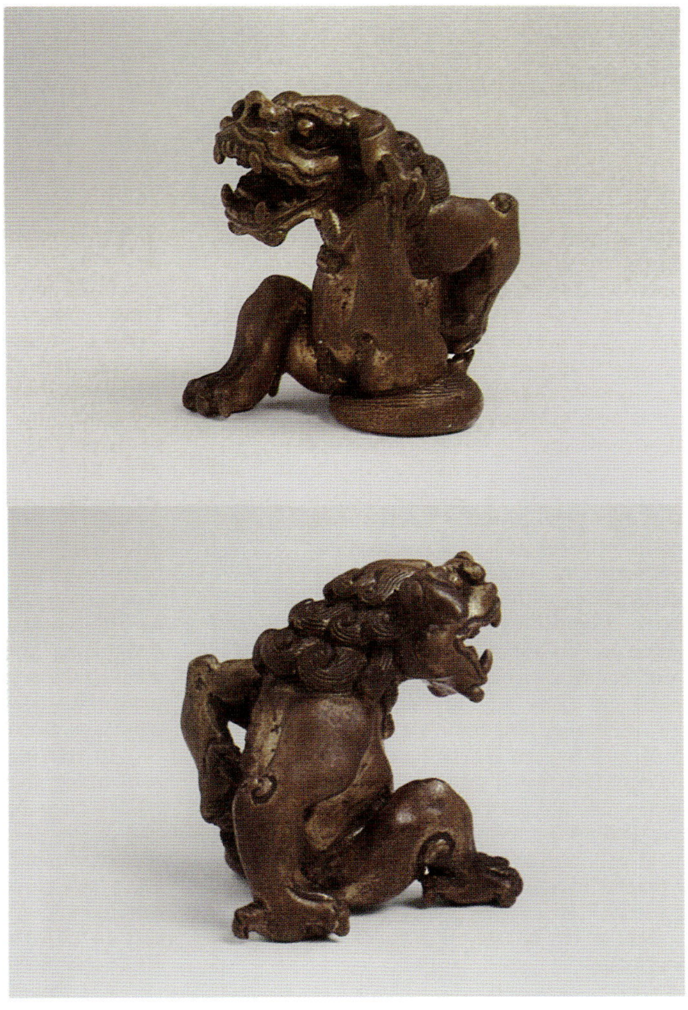

52

Pair of Seals for Wan Chengji

Wang Yingshou

Soapstone, of variegated, translucent pale cream colour of the variety known as *baifurong* stone; the tall, rectangular seals acting as pedestals for miniature sculptures of immortals; one the leader of the Daoist immortals, Shou Lao, seated backwards on a stag, his head turned to meet the backward-looking stag, holding in his hands a rolled scroll or mat, his hat hanging on his back, a bunch of the peaches of immortality tied to his waist-band, the animal set on clouds; the other with Ma Gu, a female immortal, seated side-saddle on a mythical beast, her hat hanging on her back, and holding in her hands a tall covered jar of wine she has specially prepared for the birthday of Xi Wang Mu; one face of this seal signed *Ziruo zuo* ('made by Ziruo').
The bases cut with two seals, *Wan Chengji yin* ('seal of Wan Chengji') and *Lianshan shi* ('Mr. Lianshan').
Probably Jiaqing period.
Heights: 8.5 cm. and 8.45 cm.

壽山白芙蓉石雕麻姑壽老印一對・王應綬製
可能清嘉慶(1796-1820),高8.5厘米
及8.45厘米

Wan Chengji (*zi:* Lianshan; Liansan), a native of Nanchang, was recommended for examination in the Qianlong period and became an official. Through military successes at the beginning of the Jiaqing period he was appointed a local governor and then was promoted to Governor of Haifang and acting Governor of the Yangzhou area. He was an artist whose paintings resembled those of the Northern Song dynasty, and whose calligraphy was like that of Li Yangbing. He was a good friend of the artist Luo Pin (1733-1799) and a seal carver who followed the style of He Zheng and He Tong. Wan collected stone stele of the Han and Wei dynasties, and had their inscriptions copied onto the back of a large number of inkstones he had also collected, calling them the 'one hundred Han stele inkstones' — a tantalizing prospect for collectors of literati objects.

Ziruo was the *zi* of Wang Yingshou (*circa* 1788-1841), seal carver, painter, calligrapher and scholar. He was the fifth generation descendent of Wang Yuanqi (see no. 16). In 1838 he undertook the recarving of the stones for the publication of Gao Fenghan's 'History of Inkstones' *(Yanshi),* but died three years later with the work still uncompleted.[1]

Although we have identified the owner of the seals and the carver of their text, the carver of the seals themselves remains anonymous. It is possible that the seals existed for some time prior to the addition of the seal text, which probably took place at some time during the early 19th century. We can establish this date within a reasonable timeframe because we know that Wan Chengji was a good friend of Luo Pin, who died in 1799. The seal text carver, however, was only seven years old at the beginning of the Jiaqing period and would not have developed his full skills as a seal carver until later in life. A suggested date for the carving of the text might be somewhere late in the Jiaqing period, perhaps in the second decade of the 19th century, by which time we may assume that Wan was reaching his old age.

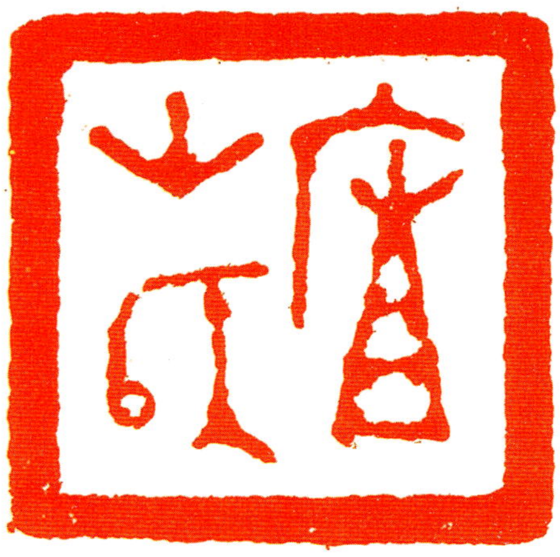

One of the seal texts of this pair of seals is an easy one by which the uninitiated may begin to grasp the art of seal carving (discussed in no. 125). Here we have enlarged one seal text considerably to give some idea of the formal nature of the art of seal carving. On this scale it is easier to understand the importance of the choice of script style, the manner in which it is executed, leaving thick and thin areas, neat lines and rougher areas, and overall layout in the art of seal text carving.

1. See *Wenwu,* 1962, no. 9.

53

Immortal in Landscape

Dai Benxiao

Ink on silk, hanging scroll; a mountainous landscape scene with an 'immortal' and a crane wandering near a rustic retreat; inscribed in the upper right corner with a descriptive poem: "Amidst tall peaks, where the endless snows dwell, deep in the landscape of shrouded rocks, the early spring prunus first appears. Where the clouds nest and the dust of the world cannot reach, a wandering immortal chances to pass, attended by a crane." This is followed by a discussion on the theory of landscape as expressed by Zong Bing (375-443), a recluse and painting enthusiast: "Landscape pleases the *Dao* with its form. From this I know that painting theory is very refined, and not easy to understand. One should strive for a genuine understanding, with which no other pastime can compare. The difference between immortals and common people lies in the landscape touching you and revealing your heart. Those who are merciful and those who are wise are integrated in the landscape, and their activities are never far from it." Signed *Ashan tiangen qiaofu* ('Heavenly root wood cutter of Ashan'), "Benxiao, for old man Feng Taican". Followed by two seals *Ying Ashan qiao* and *Benxiao,* with one seal preceding the inscription, *Shi zhenshan* ('my teacher is real mountains'). A further seal in the lower left corner, *Liyan Hecun Daishi* ('Mr. Dai of He village, at Liyan')
17th century.
192.5 cm × 99.5 cm.

Published: *Shadows of Mt. Huang,* p.117, no.51.

峻嶺古雪圖立軸・戴本孝作
清初(約1660-1693),192.5×99.5厘米

Dai Benxiao (*zi:* Wuzhan — 1621-1693) was a native of Hezhou, and the eldest son of the Ming loyalist Dai Zhong. In 1632 the family moved to Nanjing in the face of late Ming turbulence, and after five years moved several more times to avoid trouble. Dai Benxiao's background and early life certainly influenced his later activities as a *yimin* ('leftover') artist, one of that group of artists who, loyal to the Ming were unable or unwilling to become integrated into the newly established Qing administration and retired instead to a life of private endeavour, often becoming hermits. Dai Benxiao's love of the landscape is clearly demonstrated in his paintings and in his spiritual association with Zong Bing, the early 5th century painter who, when he was too old to travel into the mountains personally, covered his walls with paintings and travelled therein instead.

In relating painting to the *Dao,* Dai is confirming the literati understanding of the self-realizational potential of all creative endeavours, and of the potency of art as a vehicle of enlightenment for both artist and audience. Dai's magnificent abstractions, in the typical dry line technique of the Anhui school, unite him and us with the *Dao* through the vehicle of the art of painting.

His explanation of the difference between immortals and ordinary people is also instructive. Because the highest aspiration of the cultured in China was, over so many centuries, conquest of the self rather than of the physical world, individual immortality was achieved by transcending concepts of life and death, time and space. An endorsement of immortality was then bestowed on those who best demonstrated complete control of self and harmony with environment. The sage, whether considered to be Daoist, Buddhist, or Confucian, becomes immortal not by living forever as he would have to do in Western terms, but by rising above all mortal concerns and limitations.

Dai's painting, with its towering peaks, waters and trees, its wandering sage and unfearing wildlife, is an idealized portrait of a perfect state of understanding — one far removed from the 'dusty' details of mundane concerns, and symbolized so often by the misty peaks of inaccessible mountains.

52

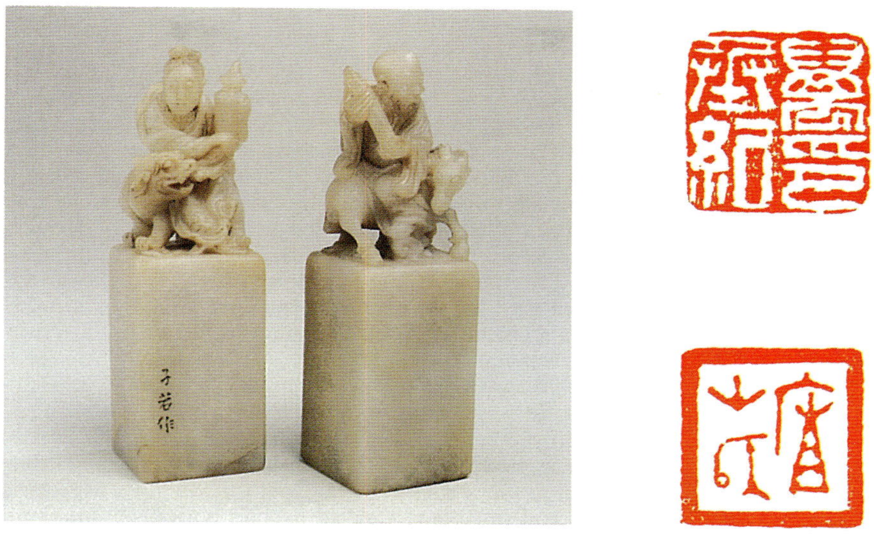

53

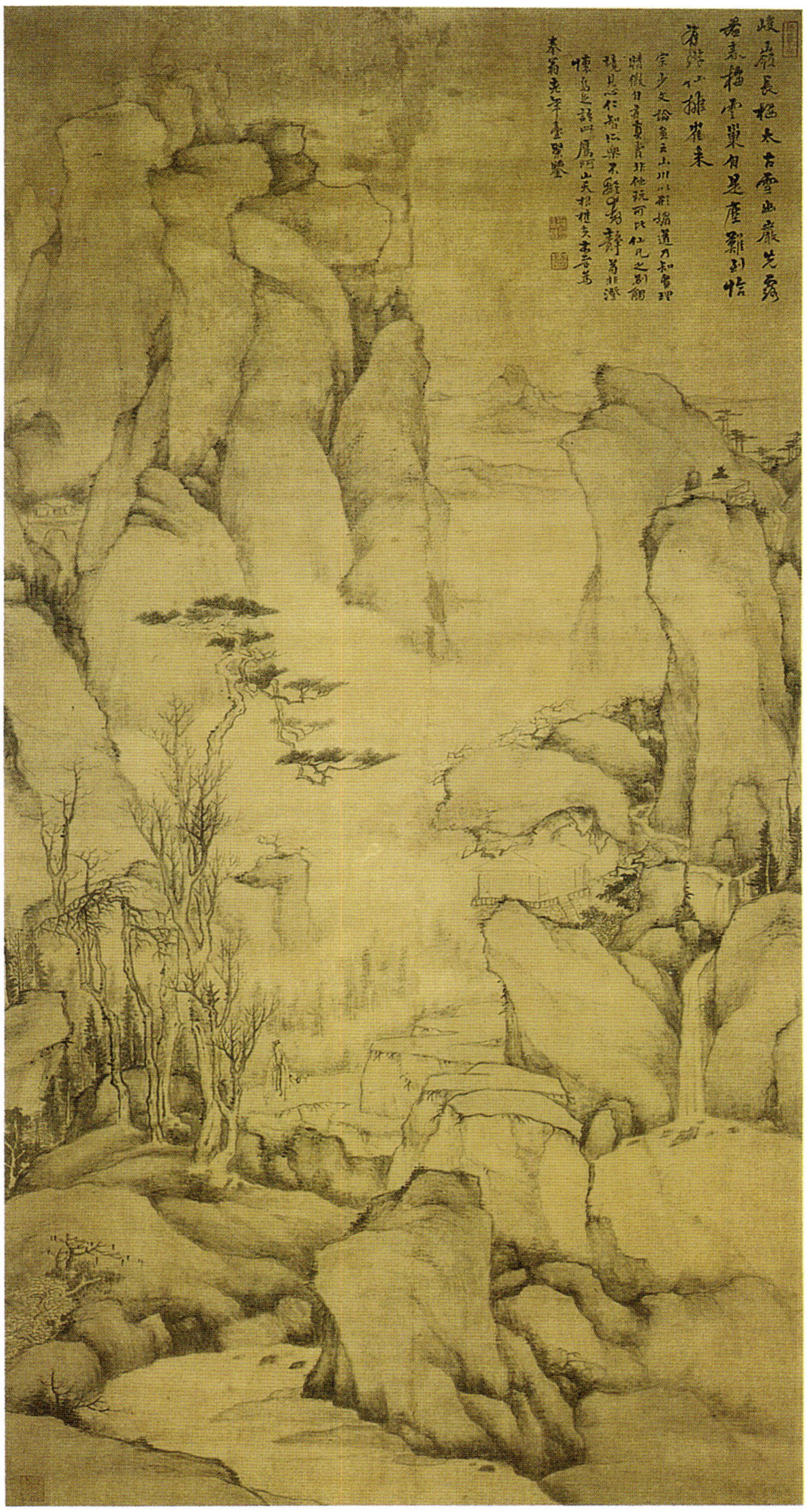

54

Seal
Lin Ji

Soapstone, of translucent deep golden orange-brown colour, with lighter opaque 'skin', of the variety known as *tianhuang;* carved with a continuous design of two three-clawed dragons chasing a flaming pearl amid ribbon-like clouds; inscribed in relief on one face: "Gentle, like jade", followed by the signature *Ji;* another face inscribed, also in relief: "A treasure for the sleeve" followed by the artist's seal *Jiren.*
Fujian province, *circa* 1680-*circa* 1730.
Height: 6.3 cm.
Formerly in the Robert A. Hall collection.

壽山田黃石雕龍戲珠印•林佶製
清(約1680-1730),高6.3厘米

Lin Ji (*zi:* Jiren, *hao:* Luyuan), was a native of Houguan in Fujian province. Born in 1660, he was a *jinshi* of 1712 and was still alive in 1720 at the age of 61. He was a calligrapher known for his clerical, regular and seal scripts and was also a seal carver. He was believed to have died during the Yongzheng reign. It is perhaps significant that this superbly carved seal has obviously never been cut with a seal impression (evidenced by the rounded base into which the design continues slightly and the evenness of surface patination), suggesting that it was valued as an independent treasure without needing to fulfil any other function. The inscription on its side, claiming that it is a treasure for the sleeve (that is a precious object to be carried on the person) endorses this supposition. The other inscription is a line from the *Shijing* (*Book of Songs*), probably noting that the material is so fine that it is to be compared with the gentleness of jade, but also acting as a channel of communication to the Chinese classics.

Tianhuang ('field yellow') is one of the most highly valued of all soapstones in China. It is a Shoushan stone, and these may be classified into three main groups according to their source. The first group is known as *tiankeng* ('field quarry') and consists of isolated pebbles buried in paddy fields flanking the streams of Shoushan. The second, known as *shuikeng* ('water quarry'), consists of stone quarried in veins in the foothills around Shoushan which are below the water table. The third, called *shankeng* ('hill quarry'), consists of quarries in the hills surrounding Shoushan. A meandering stream known as Shoushan Stream runs for several miles through the area; under the paddy fields, in the sediment, can be found occasional isolated pebbles all of which are known by the generic name *tianshi* ('field stones'). There being no veins of material to follow as in quarries, and being buried at random in the fields, stones are hard to find. These 'field stones' may be yellow (the most common colour), white, red or black or variations thereof, and of varying degrees of translucency. *Tianhuang* is considered to be the best of them. Its colour is deepest near the surface and becomes gradually paler into the stone, and a distinguishing feature of all 'field stones' is their skin (which may or may not be used in a carving), which is usually of greyish or yellow tones, and sometimes figured with red net-like markings. 'Field stones' are characterized by a turnip-like texture within the translucent surface of the stone. This example is typical and displays all the classic features of *tianhuang.*

55

Inkstone
Chen Duanyou

Limestone, Duan stone, of finely striated purplish-brown colour of the variety known as *yulinqiang qinghua* ('rain-splashed wall green spots'), with a single 'eye' of pea-green colour, with a russet-brown centre; a rectangular inkstone, the front carved in low relief with an archaistic vase *(hu),* with two *chi* dragon handles, and a band of decoration consisting of two further *chi* dragons, confronting a *taotie* mask against a ground of *leiwen;* the reverse with a standing elephant, its one visible eye using the natural 'eye' in the material to considerable effect; the front signed *Duanyou zhi* ('made by Duanyou'), in positive seal script in a seal below the left hand curve of the vase.
Contained in a *zitan* box and cover with richly figured grain and black lacquered interior.
Circa 1911-1959.
Inkstone: 2.75 cm × 12.55 cm × 19.15 cm.
Box: 5.27 cm × 13.65 cm × 20.4 cm.

雨淋牆青花端石雕太平有象硯•陳端友製
現代(約1911-1959),硯2.75×12.55×19.15厘米

Chen Duanyou (1891-1959) was a native of Changshu, Jiangsu province, who studied inkstone carving under Zhang Daping of Yangzhou. After Zhang died, Chen moved to Shanghai, where he mixed with painters, calligraphers and seal carvers, improving his art. After the establishment of the People's Republic in 1949 he worked at the Huadong Art Institute, and for the last year of his life at the Shanghai Institute of Literature and History. He was known for his simple and elegant personality. He was reputed to have frequently spent years in the making of a single inkstone, sometimes taking decades to complete one (although presumably he was not working on only one stone at a time).[1] Chen also made his own inkstone boxes. Other works by him demonstrating his extraordinary flair for design and technical accomplishments are in the Shanghai Museum, one of which, carved with a bronze bell in relief, is similar in style to this example.[2]

There is a salutory lesson in the problems of dating here. Were this inkstone not signed by a 20th century artist it would generally be considered to be earlier, by a century or more at least. Even the plain *zitan* box, so elegantly made, would quite comfortably pass as equally old.

Chen's name (it is not recorded whether it is his real name or a *zi* or *hao,* but unless his father was also a devotee of Duan stone it is likely to be one of the latter) means 'friend of Duan', an appropriate name for a man who seems to have devoted his life to the carving of Duan stone. In Chen we see the end product of a lengthy evolution; a man who could study a craft of interest to the literati, perfect it, move comfortably among scholars and artists, bridge the gap between the craft workshop and the highest institutions of scholarship and make a nonsense of distinctions made between arts and crafts based upon media of expression.

Duan limestone is found in present-day Zhaoqing, in Guandong province (called Duanzhou prior to the reign of the Song Huizong Emperor, hence the name). Mining first began in the Tang dynasty. *Qinghua* ('green spot') Duan stone originated as a descriptive term from a Tang dynasty book which described small greenish-blue spots, as small as the tip of a chopstick, set against the greenish-black stone, like stars in a dark sky. In this example the green spots are as small as dust specks and arranged in a slanting pattern, like rain on a lime-washed wall, hence the name for this particular variety. The 'eye' used for the elephant's eye here is called *lüdou* ('green pea') because it does not have the layers of other colours surrounding the green area in concentric circles that sometimes accompany these 'eyes' (see no. 192).

The colour in Duan stone is best judged while it is submersed in water, when what appears to be a fairly dull piece of material suddenly comes to life, glowing with colours. As an alternative to complete submersion, the surface may be wiped with a wet cloth. The photograph of this example was taken under water.

The motifs on this inkstone are a pun on the saying *Taiping you xiang* (an omen of peace), homophonous with 'Big vase with elephant'.

1. See *Zhonguo Meishujia Renming Cidian,* p.1035, where a number of his recorded inkstones are also listed.
2. *Bimozhiyan Tulu* (*Brush, Ink, Paper and Inkstone Pictorial*).

54

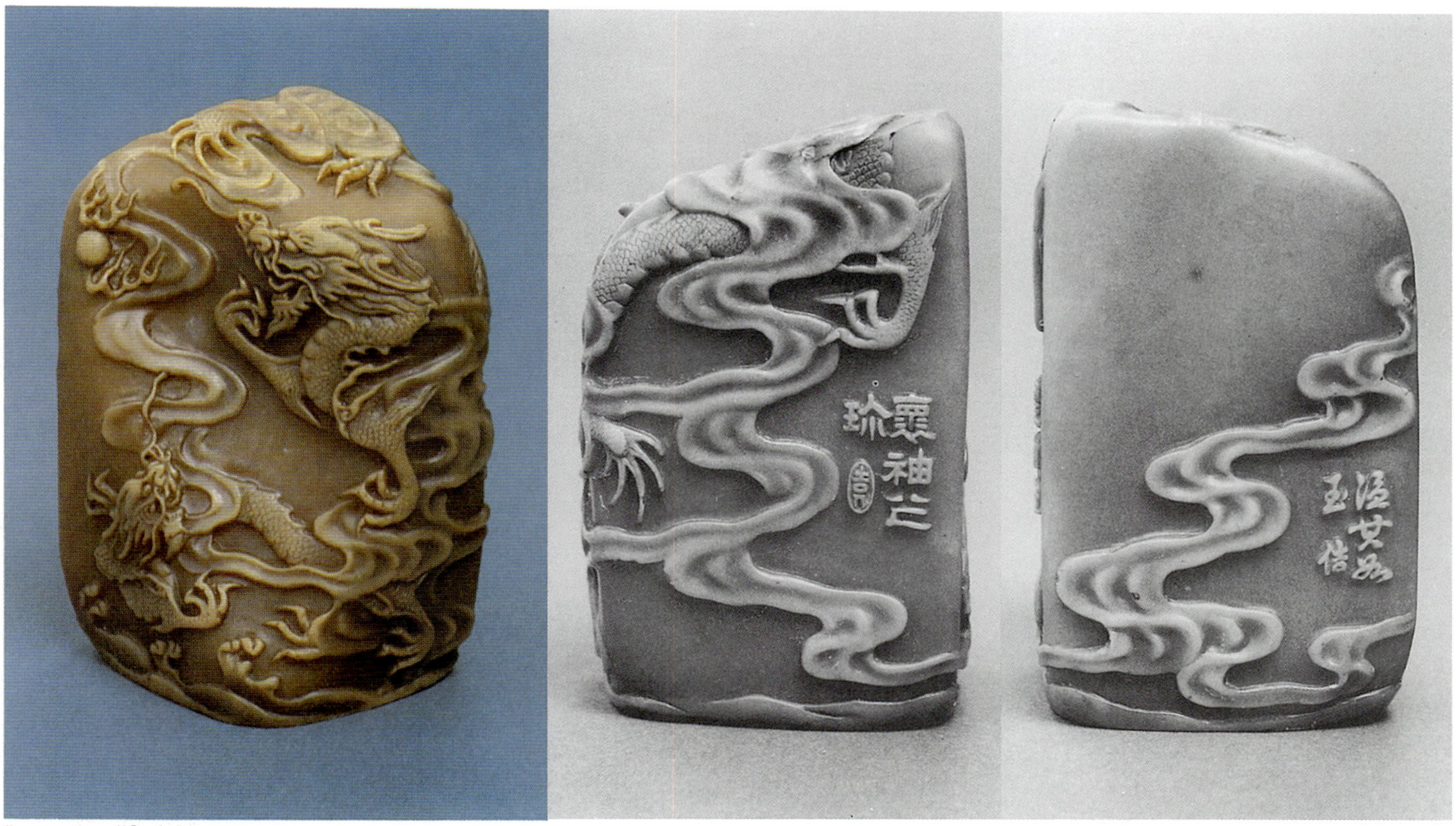

Larger than life size

55

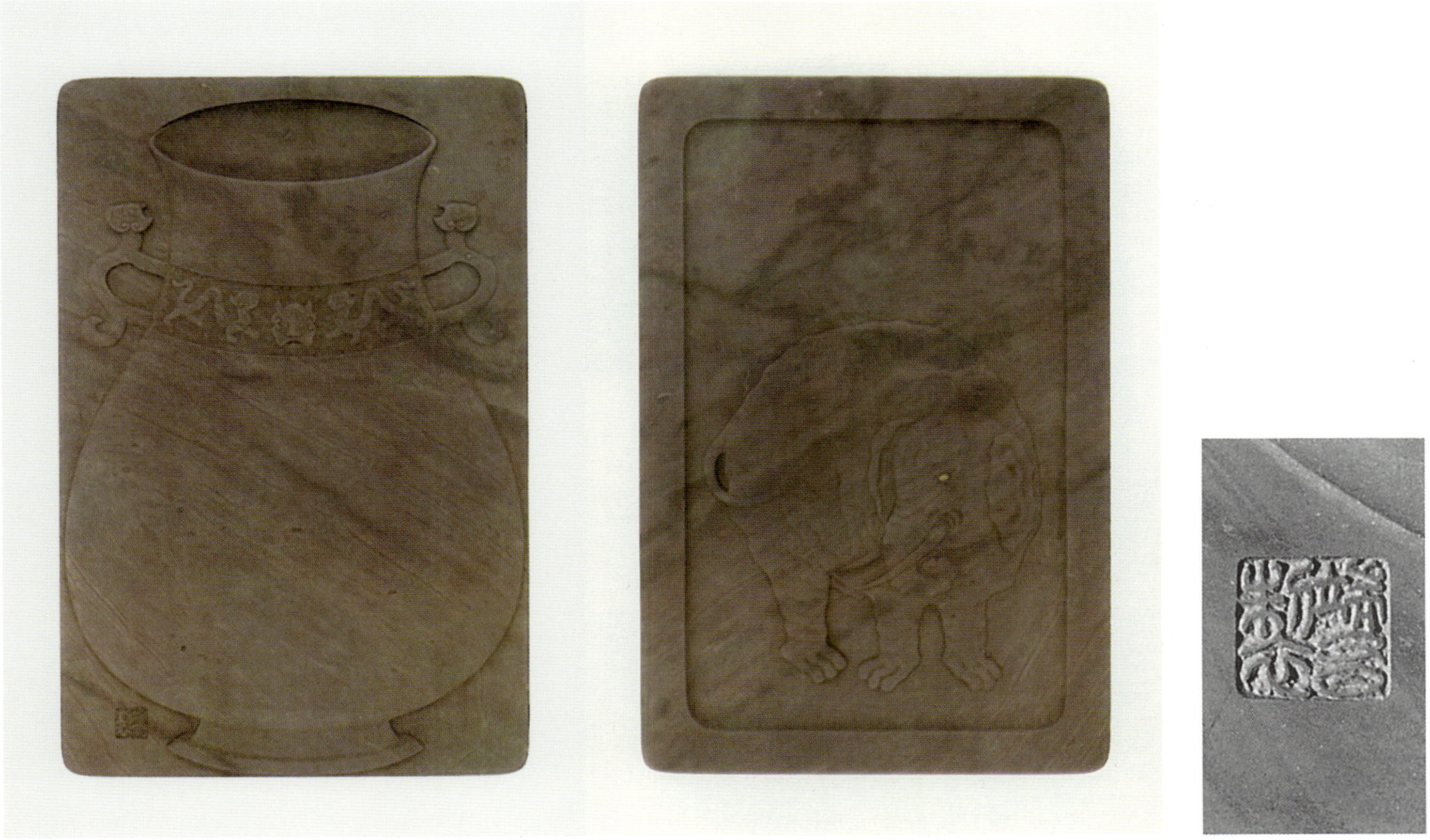

56

Water Vessel
Hu Muyun

Bamboo; a short section of the base of the culm with a narrow space between two diaphragms forming a natural container surrounded by the thick material of the culm stalk (root), carved as a water vessel in the form of a resting goose, the head turned back against the body, the beak tucked under one wing, the plumage and body achieved with broad, roughly hewn strokes in an unusually abstract rendering; the base signed *Hu Muyun zhi* ('made by Hu Muyun'), the smooth exterior surface of the upper diaphragm with an inscription in clerical script stating that the piece of bamboo was already very strangely shaped when it was introduced to the carver, that it is a vessel for the scholar's study, and that if Wang Xizhi were able to see it, he might value it at more than one thousand pieces of gold; followed by *Muyun zhi, Yian ming* ('made by Muyun, [inscription] carved by Yian'); one wing incised with the seal, in ancient bronze script, *Yian baoyong* ('for the treasured use of Yian').
Probably Qing dynasty.
Height: 5.2 cm. Length: 9.9 cm.

Together with a nephrite water ladle, of even, pale greenish-white tone, carved in *ruyi* form, the spoon bowl giving way to a naturalistic *lingzhi* stem and head.
Qing dynasty.
Length: 8.2 cm.

竹根雕鵝形水丞連玉勺·胡牧雲製
可能清代, 高5.2厘米, 長9.9厘米,
玉勺長8.2厘米

This is one of the most convincing early sculptural equivalents of the literati painting aesthetic, where the essential spirit of the subject is revealed through an almost independent exercise in boldly realized abstract form and powerful line, pared of all decorative excesses. Like literati painting it is a visual exercise in asceticism.

Implied here is a relationship between scholar and carver (who may also have been a scholar), the two of them working together to produce the vessel. Unfortunately, the identity of neither can be established with any certainty. Hu Muyun is unlisted either as a bamboo carver or as a scholar. Yian was the *zi* of the famous late Ming painter Xiang Shengmo, from Jiaxing, Zhejiang province (1597-1658), but the degree of patination and wear on this vessel do not seem to be compatible with such an early date. Although the possiblity cannot be entirely ruled out that this was his water pot, it seems somewhat remote. Another possibility is Yi Daan, the Guangdong scholar, seal carver, artist and poet (1874-1941), who apparently sometimes left out his middle name in signing works. However, the attribution is again unlikely for two reasons: the piece would appear to be older than early 20th century and Yi Daan's calligraphic style is well known and does not match the calligraphy (both of the inscription and the seal) on this vessel. Also the form of signature makes it quite clear that whoever Daan was, he actually carved the inscription himself.

The reference to Wang Xizhi in the inscription (under another of his names, Youjun) refers to his love of geese (see no. 17) and the certainty that he would have appreciated such a goose-shaped vessel. It is true that Wang would have enjoyed the subject-matter, but its treatment would have been many centuries ahead of its time in the 4th century.

Water vessels of the type used to supply the inkstone were used in conjunction with small spoons or ladles, nearly always of a different material and if aspiring to art at all, quite independent. Genre paintings show these small spoons in large numbers in association with small water pots (and indeed a range of larger ladles in larger vessels of different forms — see no. 220), but among collectors the spoons have normally become disassociated from the vessels.

The small jade spoon in this vessel was a recent match, but is ideally suited. The carving of the spoon is quite crude, which from the point of view of a jade carving would verge on the unacceptable, but is somehow ideally suited to the rusticity of the vessel. The spoon also fits perfectly, the head and angle of the twisting stem of the *lingzhi* nestling into a double depression on the lip of the vessel as if it was designed for it. It is an interesting caution on the question of fixed standards in judging works of art that a carving which would generally be considered to be a failure as jade, achieves a quite different level of appeal in conjunction with a work of art which reveals merit in its crudeness. Whether the original carver had a naivety, natural or sophisticatedly re-acquired (which is perhaps unlikely), or was simply unable to do any better we shall never know, but it was a fortunate accident which brought the two pieces together.

57

'Three Buddhists' Brush Pot
Liu Xihai

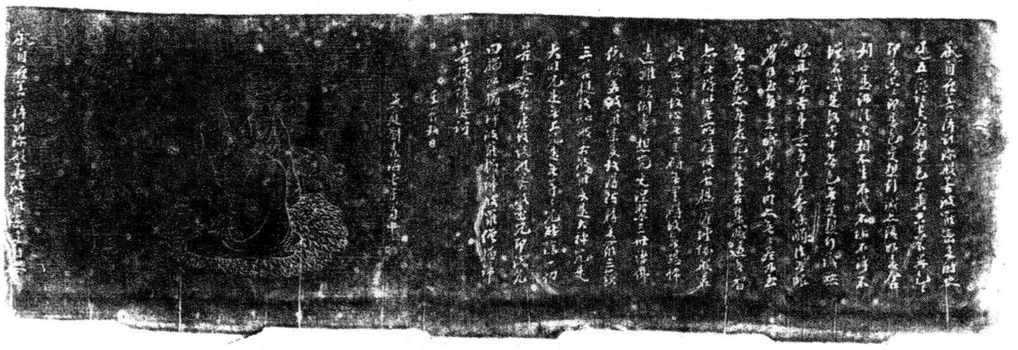

Bamboo, of dark reddish-brown colour; a cross-section of culm, using the diaphragm as a base, acting as a natural brush pot; the outside incised with three *luohan* seated on a leaf mat, while an extraordinary dog with a distinctly human face watches; a globular pot boils on a brazier nearby, and a Buddhist staff lies on the ground beyond them; the *Lotus Sutra* is inscribed around the remaining surface, followed by: "Written in central Shu (Sichuan) on an autumn day of the *renchen* year (1832) by Yanting Liu Xihai" with seal *Xiaoyin* ('Little seal').
Sichuan, 1832.
Height: 13 cm.

竹刻羅漢圖筆筒·劉喜海製
清道光壬辰(1832), 高13厘米

Liu Xihai (*zi:* Yenting), a *zhuren* of 1816, was an official and scholar who died in 1853. He was a native of Zhucheng, in Shandong province. In an official career spanning more than 30 years he filled a number of posts, but was deprived of rank and retired from office in 1849 when it was discovered that the deficit in the provincial treasury of Zhejiang, where he had served as financial commissioner from 1847 to 1849, had increased massively over the preceding 27 years. Possible involvement in this led to Liu losing his rank and retiring from official life. The Governor of Zhejiang reported that Liu had devoted his time to archaeology instead of to his official duties.

Liu is known best as a student of ancient inscriptions on bronze and stone, in which field he produced a number of important works. He also had a considerable collection, part of which was published.[1]

Bamboo, wood, gourd, various soft stones and other easily carved materials were often carved or decorated by the literati, particularly in later times when seal carving became fashionable and large numbers of scholars became familiar with the 'iron brush' (carving tools used by the literati in transferring their brushwork aesthetic to other media). Liu was a scholar devoted to inscriptions on stone, which would have involved taking large numbers of rubbings for his own collection, and doubtless experiments with carving on stone. His facility with the tools is demonstrated here in the lengthy Lotus Sutra;[2] the characters are confidently cut, and there is a flow of energy which runs through the well-balanced inscription suggesting that the artist's 'iron brush' moved as unhesitatingly as his more conventional calligrapher's brush.

1 See *Eminent Chinese of the Ch'ing Period*, p.520.
2 Also known as the *Guanyin Jing*, which discusses the nature of the Buddhist bodhisattva who was transformed over the centuries into the popular Guanyin, Goddess of Mercy.

56

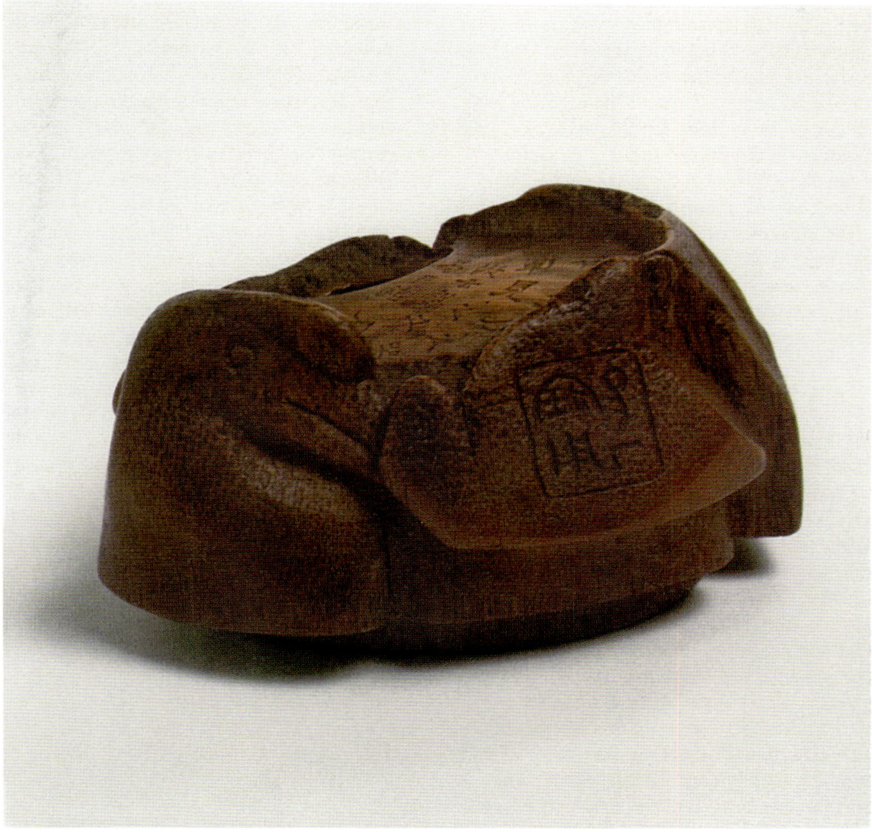

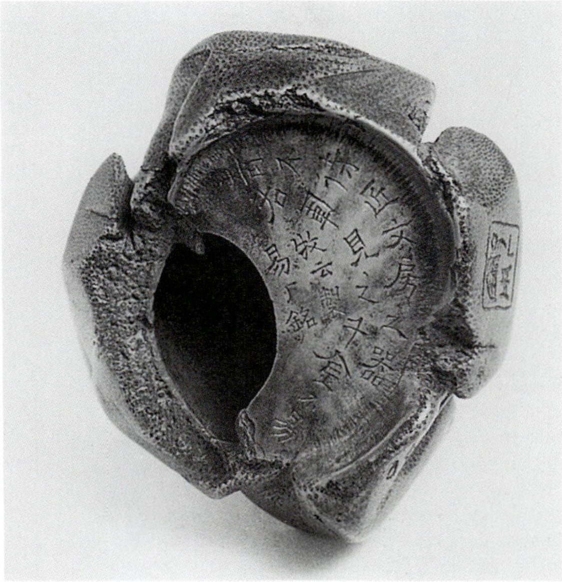

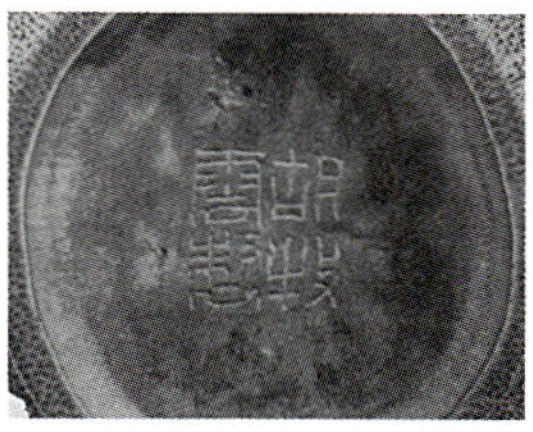

57

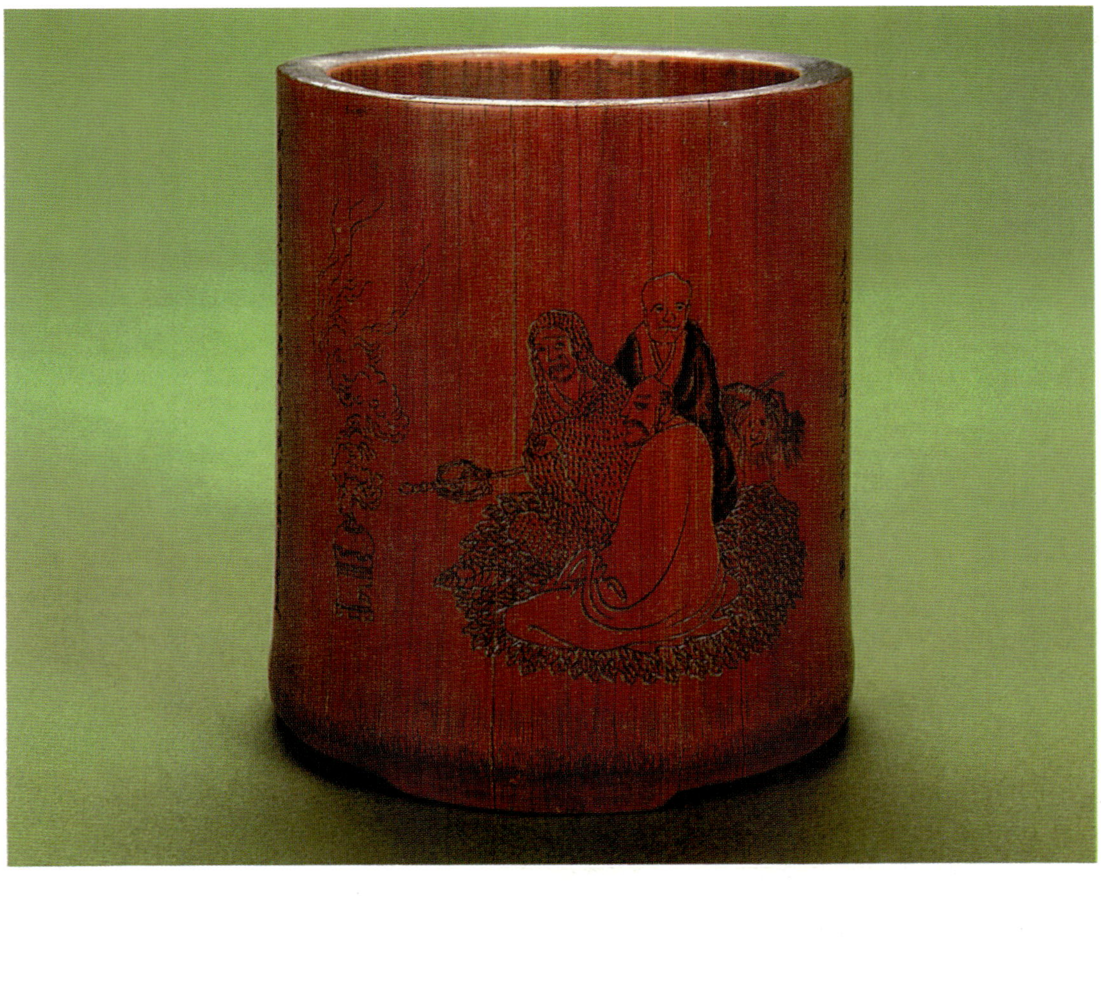

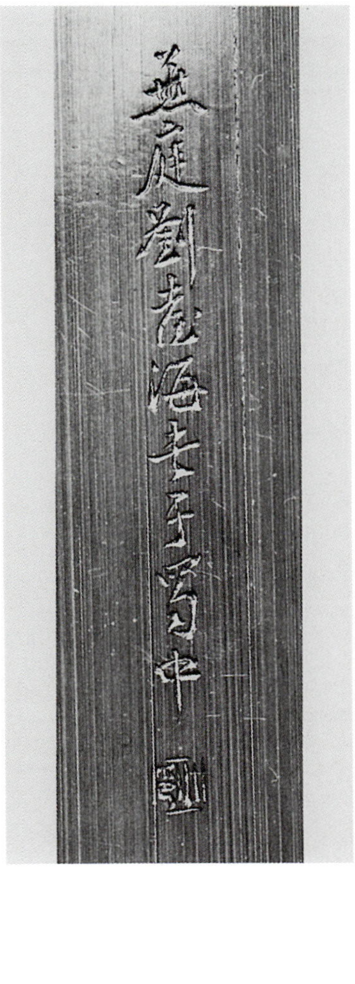

58

Fan Frame

Zhou Yi

Ivory; fan frame carved in the form of blossoming branches, the handle section on each side a plain, slightly curving, stylized branch, giving way to detailed interwoven branches, leaves, buds and blossoms; signed in relief on a lower branch of one side *Zhou Yi zuo* ('made by Zhou Yi').
Changsha, late Qing dynasty.
Length: 31.5 cm.

象牙雕花扇骨•周義製
晚清, 長31.5厘米

The *Zhongguo Yishujia Zhenglue*[1] has a long entry on the carver Zhou Yi which is worth recounting at length for its amusing details, and for the light it throws on the development of an artistic spirit. In China the artistic spirit might be developed very differently depending upon the stratum of society into which it was born. At the well-educated level, it would be cultivated and channelled into poetry, music, painting and calligraphy, with a tendency towards pure expression divorced as much as possible (in theory if not in practice) from the taint of an obvious involvement in the marketplace. At the other end of the scale artistic expression was not automatically fostered; if it developed at all it did so in the face of severe repression. Between these two the spirit would have met with various levels of encouragement. That born into a craft family employed in some aspect of artistic production would be encouraged, but probably at a practical level, with financial gain being the predominant consideration. However, the need to express is inherent in human beings, and has a tendency to be fulfilled in some manner at all levels of society, and the story of Zhou Yi (albeit doubtless idealized and embroidered by a man who claims detailed knowledge of Zhou's life without giving us his dates of birth or death) is illuminating.

When Zhou was young, opposite his school there worked a wood carver who was extremely skilful. Zhou Yi frequently avoided school to spend his time watching this craftsman, fascinated. Returning home he would try to emulate him by carving the door screens and bed legs in his home. His father was frequently angry and beat him, but Zhou was undeterred and eventually mastered the carver's skills. Another local figure was a skilful painter of birds and flowers (a certain Mr. Yang). Zhou took the opportunity to visit him whenever he was painting and bothered him with questions. Yang impatiently replied that since he could not paint he should not bother him with such questions. Zhou retorted that although he was no painter, anything Yang could paint, he could carve in wood. Yang immediately set about painting an old cypress tree, wrapped in a thousand strands of entwining vines reaching to the sky, like dragons and snakes. Once completed he gave it to Zhou telling him that if he could not carve it as convincingly as it was painted, he need not bother to return. Zhou Yi went straight home and taking some hard wood worked without eating and sleeping for three days until the carving was perfected. Yang was astonished by the result and undertook to teach him all he knew of art, taking out of his cupboard all his drafts for paintings and giving them to Zhou. He also taught Zhou calligraphy, particularly seal script and clerical script. He advised him that skill was not sufficient for a great artist — that self-respect was required if the world was to recognize his works; and that he should not work for anyone who did not understand his art, or ever work in other than the best of wood. In possession of Yang's painting drafts Zhou's skills as a carver improved immensely. He usually carved in *zitan, huangyangmu* (boxwood) or ivory. The author goes on to say that all his works are good, but that the best are his fan frames, and that his works are seldom seen.

Also recounted is the tale of Zhou Yi and the courtesan. In return for her favours, he made her a bed of boxwood, with the two main posts of the canopy support carved with an old prunus and a gnarled pine, which met on the cross member, entwining. It took a year to finish making the bed, and another half year to polish it, whereupon he sent it to the lady's house. She was delighted and asked him to stay the night. Shortly thereafter Zhou Yi died (it is not recorded whether there is any connection between the favours for one night of bliss with the lady being, apparently, worth the efforts of 18 months of artistic effort, and Zhou's demise) and the courtesan married someone else. What is euphemistically referred to as the courtesan's 'aunt' refused to let her take the bed with her, and it remained in the house of pleasure. The author saw it with his own eyes, doubtless on a visit prompted by research for his book.

After Zhou's death his younger brother Zhou Yen continued to work in his style and forge his signature. He states that Zhou Yi did not sign all of his works. He draws the rather obvious conclusion that of the forgeries all bear the signature whereas genuine ones are sometimes unsigned. His own opinion as to how to tell the difference is offered: "I have tried to authenticate genuine works by Zhou Yi. Even though flowers and leaves were carved in layers, and branches were entwined, the carving was still as round and moist as pearls and jade, smooth to the touch and not catching the hand in sharp areas. So any piece which is rough to the touch and catches the hand is a forgery. As Zhou Yi has said, 'Carving skill is only 40 per cent of my art; the other 60 per cent is finishing, which is more difficult than carving.'" His brother was, apparently, unable to finish his works as well as Zhou Yi.

The author of the work in question carried out his research in the late Qing and early Republican periods, the final work bearing a date of 1914. The implication is that Zhou Yi was a late Qing carver.

1. By Li Fang, dated 1914.

59

Brush Pot

Tang Zu

Wood, *huangyangmu,* (boxwood), of golden brown colour; a brush pot in the form of a natural section of gnarled and worm-eaten tree trunk, carved with two fat birds on one of three blossoming branches which grow from the trunk; the lower edge of the brush pot with an original dark-stained boxwood lining, the base open, suggesting that it was originally intended to be fixed to a separate stand; signed near the base at the join between the main branch and the trunk *Youji* with seals *Tang* and *Zu.*
Probably Kangxi period.
With separate, but probably not original, dark wood stand carved with five *ruyi*-shaped feet.
Height including stand: 15.5 cm.

黄楊木雕花鳥筆筒•湯組製
可能清康熙(1662-1722), 高連座15.5厘米

Tang Zu (*zi:* Youji) was a scholar, painter, and calligrapher from Taiping in Anhui province. The *Zhongguo Yishujia Zhenglue* says that he was good at carving old wood roots into figures, birds and animals and that when one plays with them they are difficult to put down. The *Zhongguo Meishujia Renming Cidian* repeats this observation but gives the source as the *Linguo Fu Gazette,* while the *Zhongguo Lidai Shuhua Zhuankejia Zihao Suoyin* adds the information that he was of the Kangxi period, which in such works usually means that he worked during that period. The *Zhongguo Renmin Dazidian* also lists him but without adding anything more.

This piece is a considerable rarity among scholars' objects. Although seal texts were frequently carved by scholars and signed, works in bamboo, wood, stone, etc. are much less frequently signed by known scholars. It is also of exceptional quality and is a carefully observed piece of realism, balancing the beautifully carved and finished birds and branches against the rough and raggedly finished worm-eaten bark. It is not difficult to see why his works acquired the reputation of being difficult to put down once in the hand.

The original lack of a base on this piece is an interesting feature. That it was made with no base is suggested by the fact that the lower section of the interior is clearly carved out from the bottom, the strokes going upwards towards the lip. It was a feature of late Ming metalwork to make hollow forms with cylindrical foot sections with separate bases, and this may have some bearing on methods for the early Qing. However, it is more likely that Tang Zu, being a scholar/artist who, we may assume, turned to wood carving primarily as a vehicle of expression, was mainly concerned with the pictorial surface rather than details of inner structure. It probably would have seemed unimportant to him how he made his base, leaving it open to him to do so in the simplest manner.

58

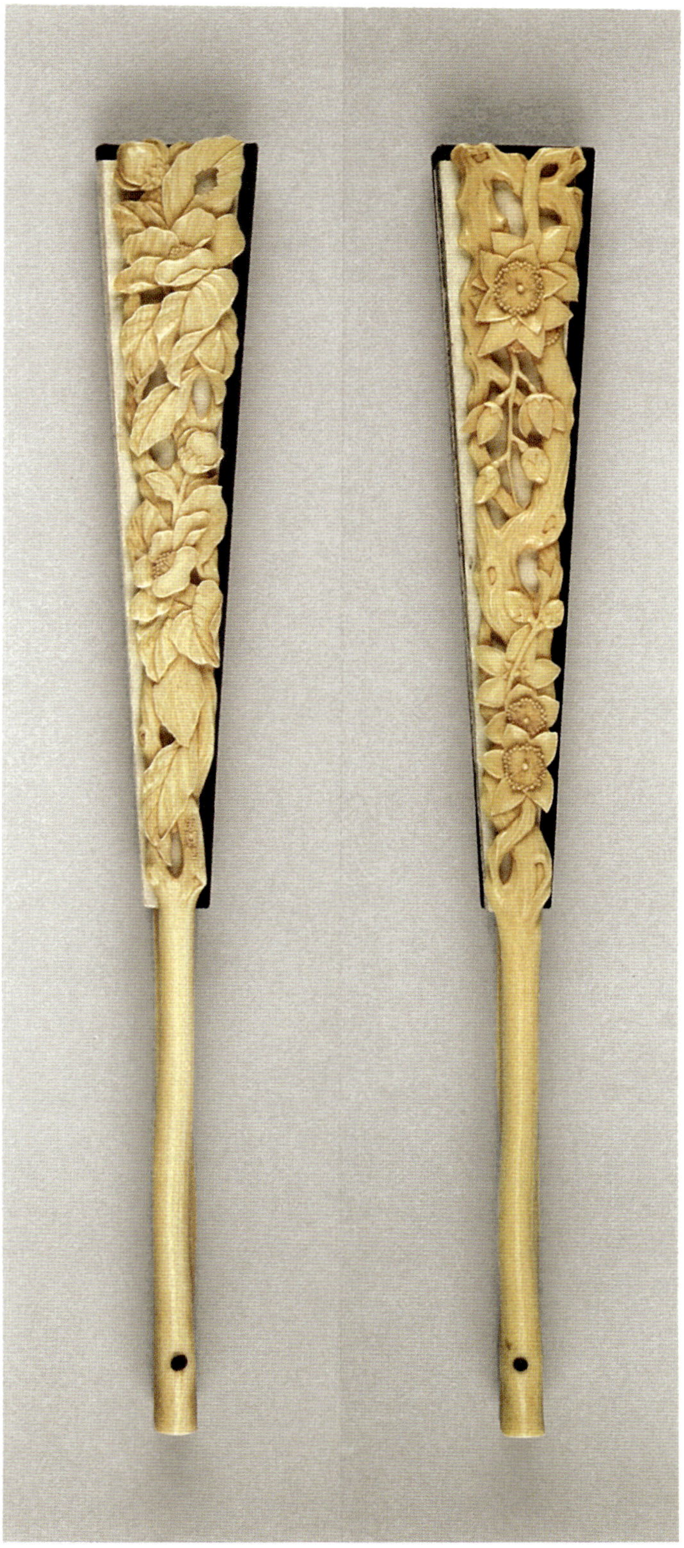

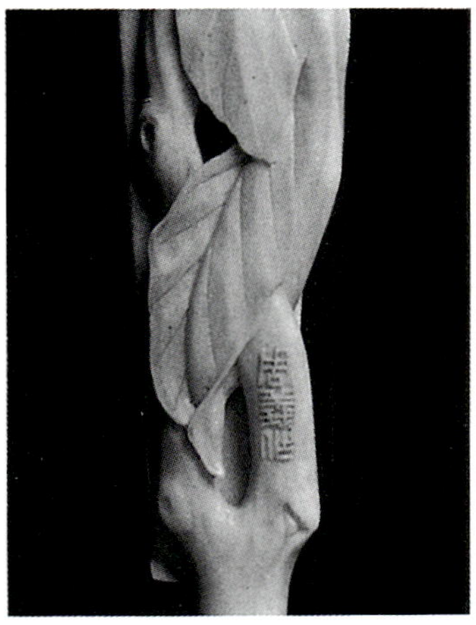

59

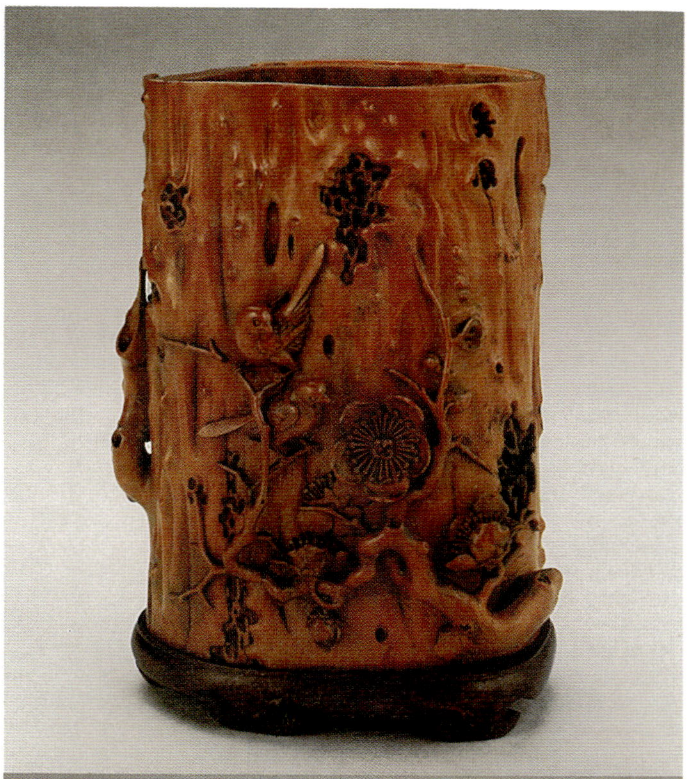

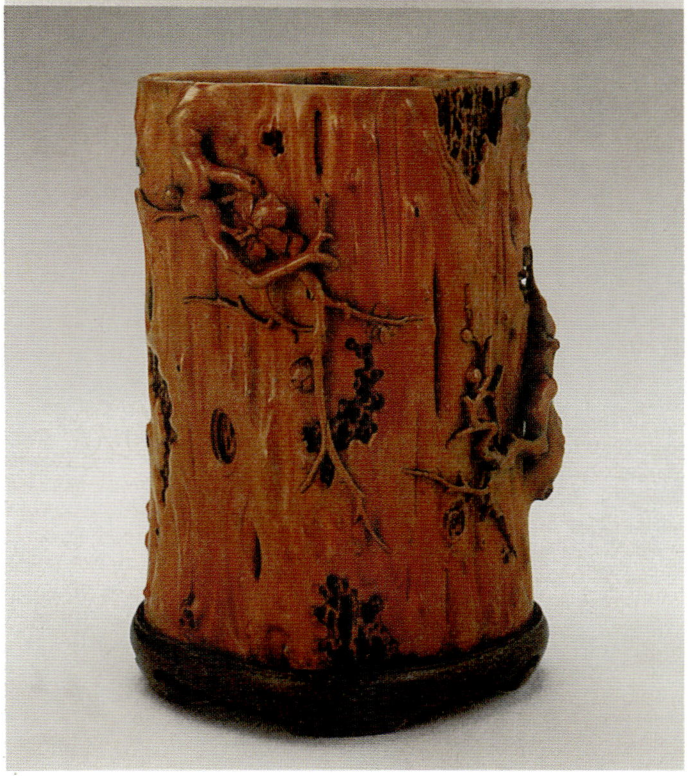

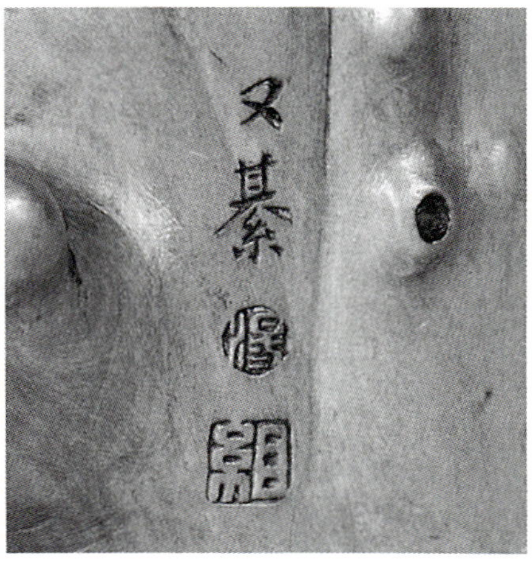

60

Seals

Huang Shiling

Soapstone, of mottled pale green colour; a set of seals of various shapes forming a rectangle.
Late Qing dynasty.
The rectangle: 3.7 cm × 6.7 cm × 6.9 cm.
Contained in a *hongmu* wood box, with domed cover.
Height: 5.8 cm.

Thirteen of the seals carved by Huang Shiling for Sheng Jingxuan in 1903 and 1904. (We have concerned ourselves here only with his works.) There are basically three types of seal: personal seals (4, 5, 7, 8, 13 and 14), studio seals (2 and 6) and poetic seals (1, 3, 9, 11 and 16).

1. *Baocan shouque* ('Clinging to remnants, guarding the incomplete' — a reference to collecting ancient bronzes and rubbings where pieces are frequently incomplete but still highly valued), in negative seal script. Inscribed on the knob platform, and signed *Mufu.*
2. *Miaojixiang Shi* ('Wonderfully Auspicious Studio'), in positive seal script. Inscribed on the knob platform, dated 1904 and signed *Mufu.*
3. *Weimiao* ('Indescribably wonderful'), in negative seal script. Inscribed on the knob platform, dated 1904 and signed *Shiling.*
4. *Jiling Shengjiu,* in negative seal script. Inscribed on the knob platform that 13 seals were presented by Huang Shiling while a guest at Wuchang.
5. *Jiying,* in negative seal script.
6. *Yuxiao Zhai zhu* ('The master of the Remnants of Filial Piety Studio' — implying that filial piety is no longer a common trait, but that the owner of this studio clings to the ancient traditions), in negative seal script.
7. *Fengcheng Chengji* ('Chengji of Fengcheng'), in negative seal script.
8. *Jingxuan yinxin* ('Seal of Jingxuan'), in negative seal script. The knob platform inscribed and dated 1903.
9. *Suiyuan* ('As fate determines'). The side signed Mufu followed by the information that he considers this the most satisfying of the seals.
10. Not by Huang.
11. *Dali* ('Great fortune'), in negative seal script.
12. Not by Huang.
13. *Shengjiu,* in positive seal script.
14. *Jingxuan siyin* ('Personal seal of Jingxuan'), in negative seal script.
15. Not by Huang.
16. *Wuke* ('Nothing is possible') — part of a popular saying that 'nothing is possible and nothing is impossible', depending on one's attitude.

石刻印十三方•黄士陵刻
晚清，總體3.7×6.7×6.9厘米

Huang Shiling (*zi:* Mufu — 1849-1908), was a native of Yixian, Anhui province and a painter, calligrapher and seal carver. As a painter he was known for employing Western perspective in his paintings of ancient bronzes. He was under the patronage of Wu Dazheng, the famous late Qing scholar and artist, assisting him in the selection and rubbing of his archaic bronze seal collection and in the editing of his catalogue of them. He moved to Guangdong in 1882 at the invitation of Wu, who was then the Commissioner of Guangdong province. After Wu left office, Huang stayed on, working at the Guangya Book Company. Huang went north to Beijing between 1885 and 1887 but he returned to Guandong and remained there until 1906.

He was enormously influential in the art of seal carving in Guangdong province, acting as the focus for a school of carving known as *Yuepai* (Guangdong school). Though influenced by the Zhe (Zhejiang province) school, Huang did not fall into the Zhe pitfall of being vulgar and aggressive in the use of deliberately accidental chipping of the cutting stroke ('saw teeth' and 'swallow tail'). His incised lines were clear, sharp and beautiful. He was particularly known for his composition, which is well-balanced and stable but at the same time dynamic in the use of daring counterpoints to the regular rhythmic layout of characters (to provide movement in an otherwise stable design).

Huang carved these seals while staying as a guest in Wuchang, Hubei province. One of the inscriptions states that in the spring of 1903 he was requested by letter to carve seals for Sheng Jiling, but only began to do so in the autumn. Another inscription tells us that in the summer of 1904 he sent the seals to Sheng, while staying at Wuchang. Since Sheng lived in Guangdong we may assume that Huang stayed for some time at Wuchang. The majority of the seals are carved in the *Mouzhuan* style of seal script, a Han dynasty script specially developed for seal carving. Its main characteristics are that the strokes are bent and continue to fully occupy the seal text space, and that diagonal strokes are reduced in favour of vertical or horizontal ones.

Sheng Jingxuan (*zi:* Jiying; *hao:* Jiling; Shengjiu — 1880-1929) was a native of Guangdong. He was a salt merchant, poet, painter, calligrapher, and a collector of archaic bronze inscriptions and stone rubbings and ancient stele.

61

Scholar's Plaything

Gourd; grown into a nine-part sectional primary mould to form a hexagonal scholar's plaything, decorated with various scholarly trappings in relief, each tied in billowing ribbons, recognizable among which are: a *qin* wrapped in brocade, a *ruyi* sceptre, the symbols of the God of Literature, a pair of rolled scrolls, and two portfolios of books.
Probably first half of the Qing dynasty.
Height: 8.5 cm.

葫蘆模製六角文玩
可能清代上半葉，高8.5厘米

A similar object is recorded from the collection of the late Dr. Ip Yee, but inscribed with poetry and with its stem missing.[1]

The gourd, quite apart from its various functional possibilities, was developed into an art form unequalled by any other culture for two main reasons. First, the Chinese have traditionally considered workmanship to be of greater importance than material, allowing the humblest of substances to acquire great importance in art. In Western cultures in the past a greater emphasis was placed upon the inherent value of the materials themselves.

The second reason was closely linked to the symbology of Daoist paradises and fairy lands. The link was made specifically because of the shape of one type of gourd, the 'double-gourd', which grows with upper and lower bulbs separated by a narrow waist (see no. 108) — a shape copied in many art forms. The entrance to paradise, like the entrance to the bulb of the gourd, was thought to be through a narrow gap and the space inside was identified with a secret, arcadian world. This narrow gap, as demonstrated in the story of the 'Peach Blossom Spring' (see no. 132), became a metaphor for enlightenment.

1. See *Chinese Decorated Gourds,* p.55, no. 9.

62

'Dragon Raft'

Du Meigen

Wood, *nanmu* (cedar); in the form of a log boat, inscribed on one side with the title 'Dragon raft' and the studio name of the carver *Jilou* ('Odds and Ends Studio') and on the other side with a lengthy inscription referring to the provenance of this particular gnarled log: "At the Shun Emperor's tomb on Mount Jiuyi (Hunan province), although you cannot find the tomb there is his altar. With such an illustrious person (buried there) the cutting down of trees is forbidden, so it remained in an undisturbed atmosphere. But in our dynasty, in the Guangxu era, the Provincial Governor, using the excuse of a heavy storm which had blown down some of the trees, cut them all down. A regrettable business when wandering and gazing at the clouds, as one can no longer see the trees. Occasionally it is possible to find a small piece left behind and the whole country will treasure it. There is an old gentleman by the name of Liu Zhun who had one log which he gave to me. Its shape, especially the branches (at the back) looked like a wandering dragon, so I have given it an elegant name and today I am thinking of the Emperor Yu and make a permanent testimonial to this revelation. Even though I love this sort of plaything, it will not ruin my ambition, so I have inscribed this piece. Does one cut the tree simply to expose a record of the years that have passed? Does one ride this vehicle for the purpose of achieving unity with heaven? Hey ho! Is Shun also an immortal?" followed by the signature Meigen.
Guangxu period.
Height: 13.5 cm. Length: 31.7 cm.

楠木刻銘龍槎•杜梅根製
清光緒(1875-1908)，高13.5厘米，長31.7厘米

Du Meigen was a late Qing dynasty monk, a native of Hezhou (Hexian, in Anhui province) who lived in the Sanmei An ('Three Mysteries Monastery') in the Wuhu district. He was noted as a calligrapher, painter and seal carver.[1]

This is the only gnarled wood carving we know of where the source of the wood is recorded. Its association with the ancient legendary emperors adds considerable weight to an already evocative natural form. The grain of the wood may be seen in two ways: as the grain of the log raft, or as water flowing around the log as the Emperor steers it through the tumultuous waters of the Yellow River. Seen as the latter, the raft changes from a relatively static form independent of its watery environment to a dynamic piece.

1. Recorded in *Hezhou Ji* (*Hezhou Notes*) in *Zhongguo Meishujia Renming Cidian,* p.904.

60

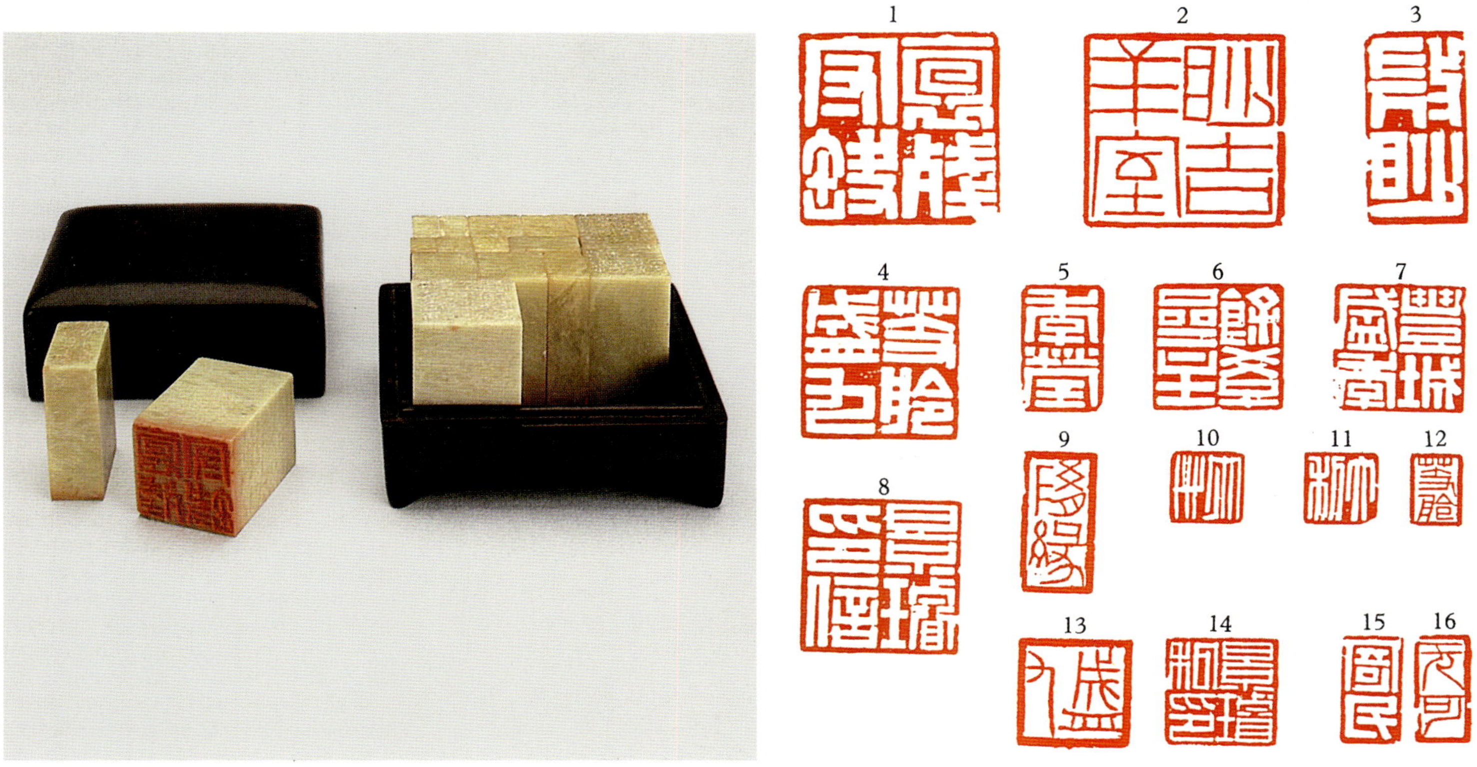

61

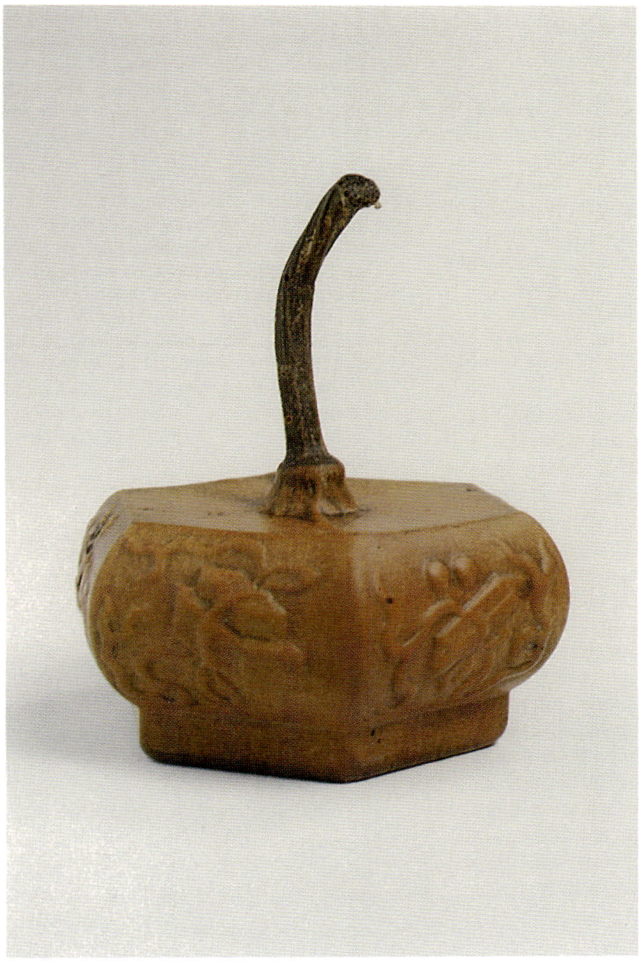

62

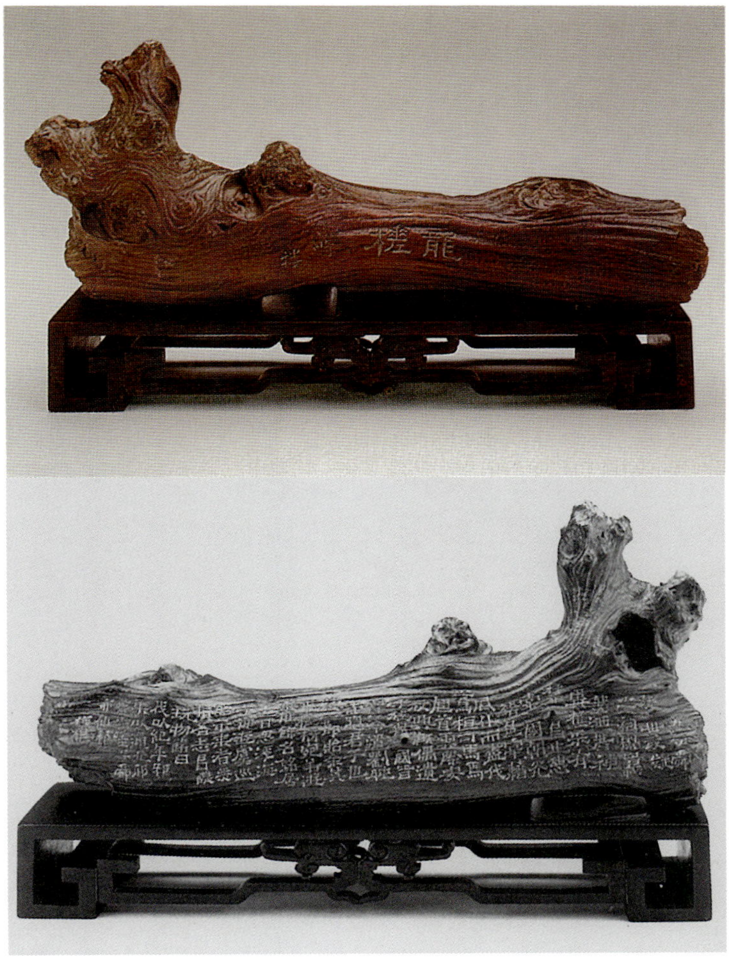

63

Inkstone, Box and Cover

Lu Dong

Lacquer, of jet-black colour; of flattened, ovoid form, the cover carved with a picture of two geese on a reed bank with windswept reeds beyond, inscribed *pingsha xiying* ('resting on the broad sands') in clerical script, with seal *Kuisheng* in seal script; the base with *Kuisheng* in an elaborate seal script painted in red lacquer to imitate a seal impression in vermillion ink. Together with its original plain sand-lacquer inkstone.
First half of the 19th century.
Length: 9.6 cm.
Formerly in the Edward T. Chow collection.
Published: *Emperor, Scholar, Artisan, Monk,* pp.261-262.

漆沙硯連平沙落雁漆硯盒•盧棟製
十九世紀上半葉, 長9.6厘米

A number of pieces by Lu Dong (*zi:* Kuisheng) are included here (see nos. 64, 85, 149, 216 and 217) because he demonstrate the extent to which the scion of a Qing craftsman's family could aspire to and achieve acceptance among the literati through his skills as an artist/craftsman, thus joining the ranks of the influential minority. Although Lu is listed elsewhere, the richest source of information about him was published in *Wenwu,* 1957, no. 7, the work of Wang Shixiang and Yuan Quanyou. Seven pieces are illustrated and discussed together with a lengthy article on the life of the artist.

Lu Dong was born into a lacquer craftsman's family. His grandfather, Lu Yingzhi, had become a renowned lacquerer by the mid-Qianlong period (although active as early as 1717 — see below). Lu Yingzhi was famous for imitating sand-lacquer inkstones (that is, the inkstones themselves rather than the boxes containing them, which are made of lacquer mixed with some hard granular material, presumably fine sand) of the Xuanhe period of the Song dynasty, and was immortalized by the 18th century poet Yuan Mei (for a portrait and discussion of whom see no. 11). Yuan wrote of a lacquer stationery tray made by Lu: "Old Lu was famous for his wares. His lacquer was smooth, on a well-bonded body. He excelled at making utensils of all shapes and his carved decoration is very fine. His colourful works are delicate, with shaded flowers contrasting with bright coral".[1]

Lu Dong inherited not only his grandfather's skills but the Yangzhou tradition of embellished lacquer wares, and further developed them to become even more famous than his grandfather. One source mentions that Lu made the inkstone boxes for the famous female inkstone maker Gu Erniang; those of red lacquer were considered the best, with carvings of flowering branches, birds, animals, insects and fish quite beyond the skills of a common artist. In the same source we are told that he put his full name only on works where others had co-operated. On his independent works he used only a small seal, *Kuisheng.*[2]

Perhaps the most intriguing source of information about Lu Kuisheng is to be found in two pieces of paper, still intact, which were originally attached to one of his inkstones.[3] The first is a warning about imitations, a piece of commercial literature presumably included with his genuine wares to warn of copies already being made. Lu Kuisheng not only made inkstone boxes, but he also made the inkstones themselves, as did his grandfather. These were made of sand-lacquer (one is seen here, and another inscribed 'supervised by Lu Kuisheng' in no. 149). The warning states that Lu Kuisheng's inkstones are all made of sand-lacquer, which if done properly will last in use. He states that it has been a family product for more than 110 years and is like no other. Recently, he continues, the market has been infiltrated by fakes, which are not made properly and will not last. Patrons are advised to check the seals on the wares carefully, and to make sure that the address of the maker is correct. His precise address is then given: the south end of Dashi alley, Gengzi street, Chaoguan Gate, Yangzhou City.

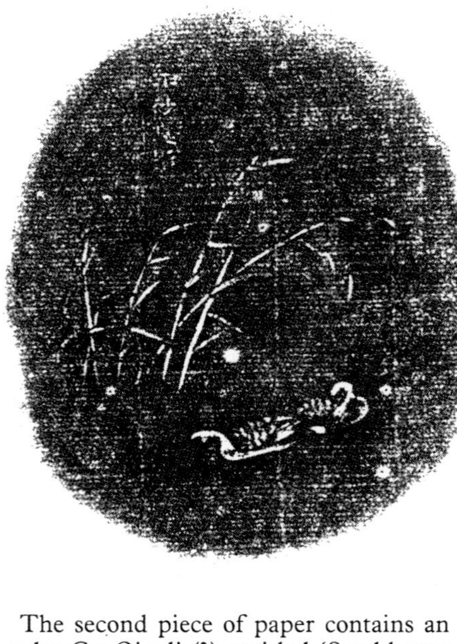

The second piece of paper contains an essay by Gu Qianli (?) entitled 'Sand-lacquer Inkstone Essay' in which he mentions that Lu Kuisheng had presented him with a sand-lacquer inkstone and had recounted the story of how Lu's grandfather (Lu Yingzhi) had found in 1717 a sand-lacquer inkstone in a market which was inscribed with the six-character mark *Song Xuanhe neifu zhi* ('made in the Imperial household, in the Xuenhe period of the Song dynasty'). This inkstone had the quality of fine pottery but was extremely light, being able to float in water, which puzzled people until they discovered it was sand-lacquer. Lu Yingzhi made exhaustive efforts to discover the secret of this material and finally achieved perfection, to the point where those who used his sand-lacquer inkstones said that their quality was quite unprecedented. The famous 18th century Yangzhou artist Jin Nong (see no. 4) composed an essay recording the method so that it would not be lost.

There follows some comments on the best types of inkstone from the Duanxi quarries in Guangdong province (see no. 55), noting that these quarries were now exhausted; and about fine pottery inkstones, regretting that the skills in this direction were now lost, making it hard to find good inkstones. Sand-lacquer, however, if properly made will have the quality of *huamo* (being able to make good, dark ink successfully and easily, but without damaging the hairs of the brush when loading it on the stone — that is, rough enough to cut the ink but not the brush), and Gu compares this material to the two best types from antiquity. He then praises the Xuanhe product, and Lu's grandfather for discovering the same secret six centuries later.

Gu then moves on to some revealing information about Lu Kuisheng himself. Lu is described as having a happy, easy-going personality, near the *Dao;* and as being elegant and well-versed in antiquity and highly esteemed by the Hangzhou scholar Yuan Mei, in whose collected essays his name appears. He is described as a man who can uphold his family tradition and as being a capable painter (in a purely subjective but fairly widely used method of classification where the top class is divine, the second untrammelled and the third capable — below which are two further levels). It is noted that Lu moves in a wide circle of scholars. The opinion is then offered — this seems effusive, but we must remember that it was written by an enthusiastic friend and patron of the lacquerer and used for public relations — that sooner or later Lu's value will be above that of Mi Fu (the Song painter, calligrapher, inkstone connoisseur and quintessential literatus), and that eventually his fame, of which this essay is just a beginning, will be world-wide. The paper is signed by Gu Qianli at the age of 61, in 1826 *(Daoguang, bingwu).* The same essay also appears in *Sishi Zhai Ji*[4] where there is also recorded an inscription on a sand-lacquer inkstone (perhaps the one presented to Gu by Lu Kuisheng) which reads: "Every day ten thousand characters worth of ink may be ground hereon. With such an inkstone another from the Xuanhe period is superfluous".[5]

For other works by Lu Kuisheng see note 6.

The subject of geese and reeds seems to have been popular in the Yangzhou area. The Eight Eccentrics of Yangzhou of the 18th century frequently painted the subject.[7]

1. See Yuan Mei's collected essays, *juan* 24.
2. *Luochuang Xiaoduo.*
3. *Wenwu* 1957, no. 7, illustration 1.
4. *Juan* 5.
5. Ibid., *juan* 17.
6. There is another snuff bottle in reddish-brown lacquer on metal with incised decoration of a flowering branch and a poem in the Shuisongshi Shanfang collection; an inkstone in the form of a fruiting gourd in *Bunku Mandara* (no. 38); a prunus design inkstone box and cover in *Komeigen,* Tokyo, Vol. 5 (no. 102); and another of irregular shape with prunus inlaid in mother-of-pearl in *Bimozhiyan Tulu* ('Brush, Ink, Paper and Inkstone Pictorial') from the Shanghai Museum collection. A lacquered pewter teapot from the collection of the late Sir Percival David is to be found in Jenyns (who misses the point that it is lacquered and that the signature is of the lacquerer not the pewter-maker), *Chinese Art,* Vol. II, p.153, no. 69. (The other side of this teapot is illustrated by Sothebys in their catalogue of 15th October 1968 (Lot 44), where it is correctly described and translated but wrongly dated to the 17th century.) The end of an inkstone, presumably of sand-lacquer, is illustrated in *The National Palace Museum Monthly of Chinese Art* no. 11, 1984, p.11, without comment or caption. It is inscribed "made to copy (an inkstone) of the Xuanhe inner palce" with seal *Kuisheng.*
7. Examples may be found illustrated in *Paintings by Yangzhou Artists of the Qing Dynasty from the Palace Museum,* by Huang Shen (no. 65) and by Bian Shoumin (nos. 85, 87, 88 and 89).

63

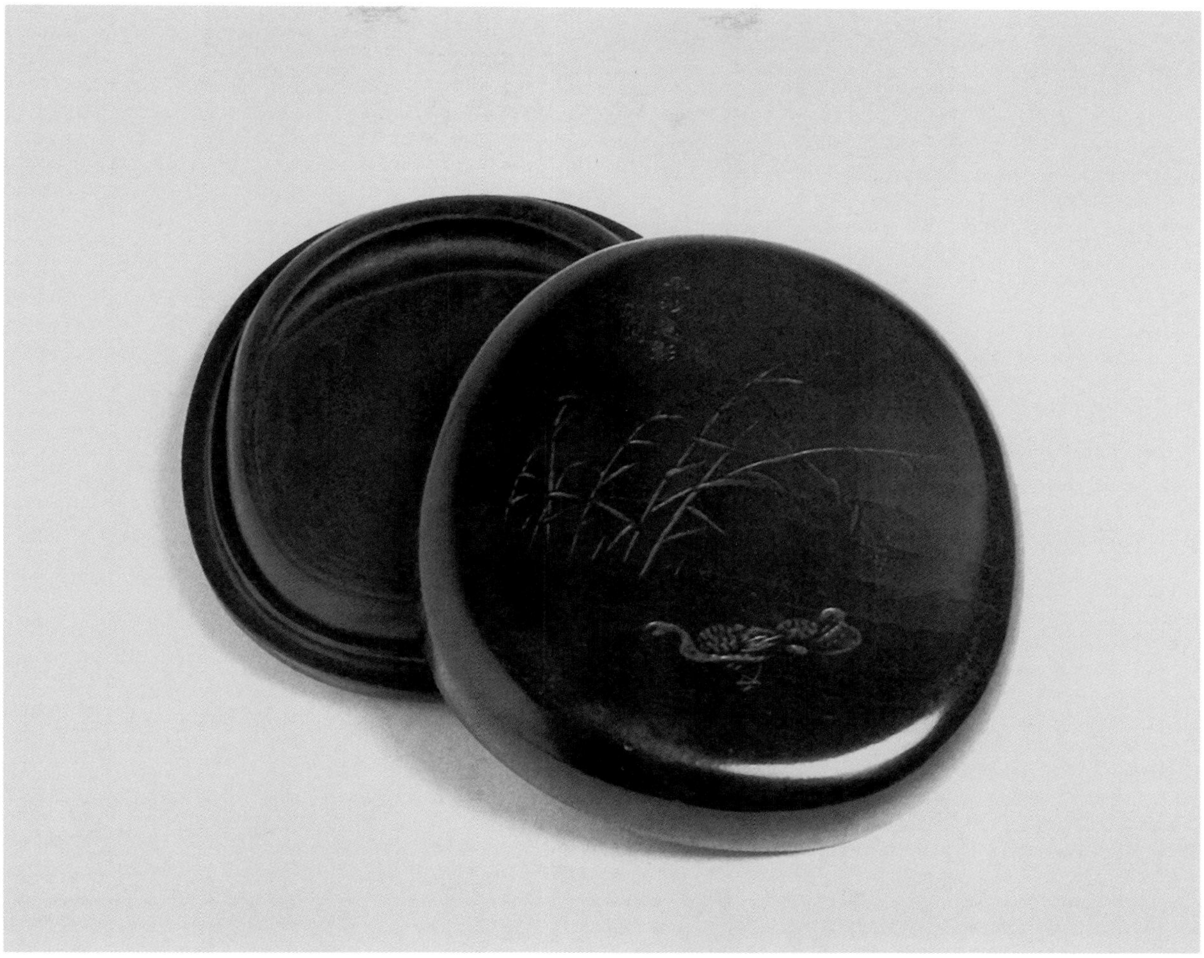

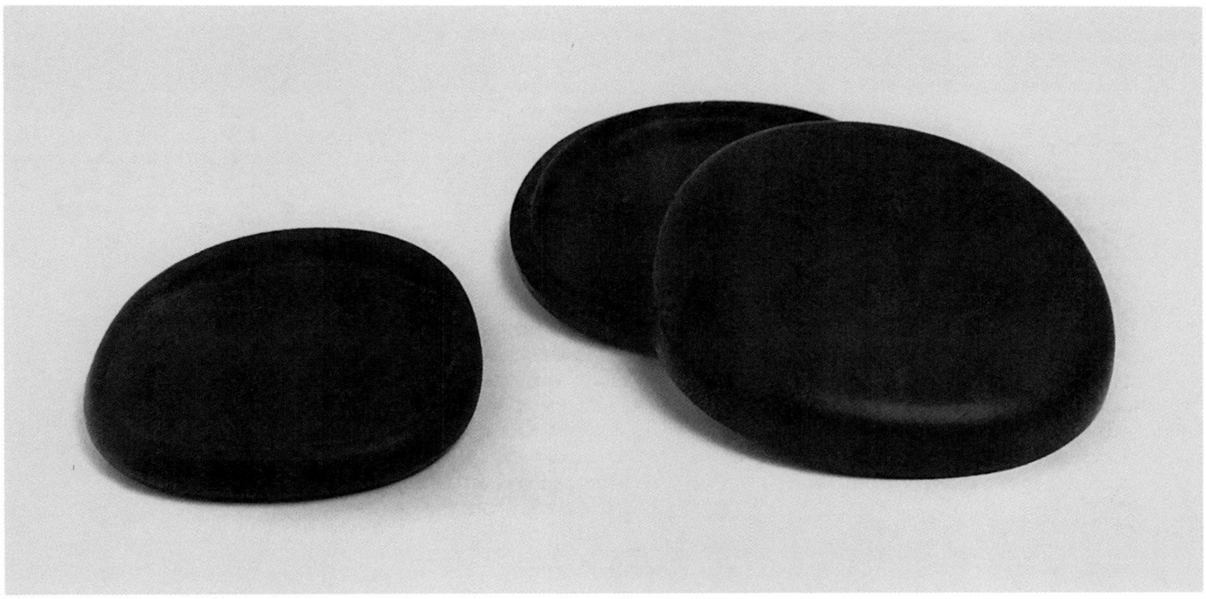

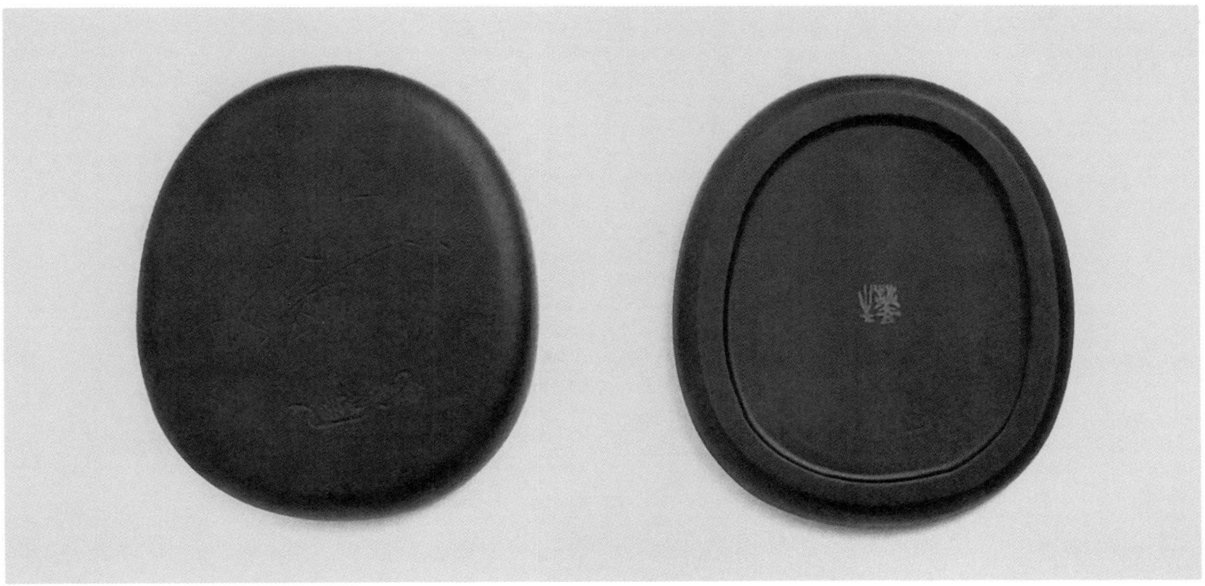

64

Inkstone Box and Cover

Lu Dong

Lacquer, a thin layer at the surface made up of a large number of tiny chips of a variety of different materials in a variegated red and brown lacquer matrix giving the overall impression of a pale speckled purplish-brown material; an inkstone box and cover of compressed globular form, the lid incised with a blossoming prunus branch, with the rectangular seal *Kuisheng* in seal script; the base incised, in seal script, with a circular inscription "(made by) Kuisheng, in imitation of antiquity *(fanggu)*, sixth summer month of the *wuxu* year of the Daoguang period (1838)".
1838.
Diameter: 9.4 cm.

漆沙仿古梅花硯盒•盧棟製
清道光戊戌(1838), 直徑9.4厘米

The speckled, purplish-brown material and the decoration leaving texture and brush-like character in the strokes, reveal a clear association with certain Yixing wares. The teapot shown in no. 107 represents a group of Yixing pieces popular during the 19th century where these same characteristics are displayed. While Yangzhou was in fact north of the Yangzi River, and in late Ming times only on the northern fringe of the key literati area of Jiangnan (literally 'South of the River'), its emergence by the 18th century as a major industrial centre of wealth, based upon the salt trade, had brought it firmly and influentially into this cultural centre. The scholars who patronized the Yixing tea wares would have been well aware of Lu Dong's output from Yangzhou, just as he knew of Yixing wares. (See no. 217 for a lacquered Yixing box and cover by him.) The mixing in of tiny chips of other materials (high-powered magnification reveals what might be chips of other colours of lacquer and perhaps other materials ground up and sprinkled in the surface of the lacquer) may be a reference to the speckled appearance of some Yixing pottery, or be derived from the mixing of other materials into lacquer for the making of inkstones in which Lu and his forebears specialized (see no. 63).

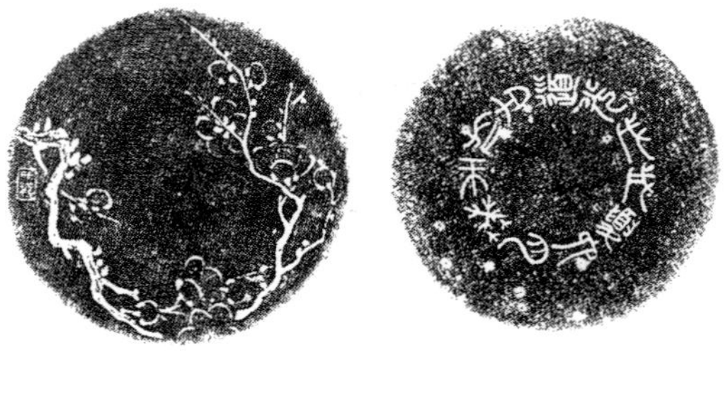

The style of decoration is clearly derived from painting, not only in subject-matter, but more importantly in the emphasis on 'iron-brushwork'. The key characteristic of this whole range of decoration is its conscious extension of the effects of a brush and ink on paper to other materials. The original derivation of this must have been calligraphic inscriptions on stone, but as a trend across a broad range of arts it does not seem to have developed popularly until the Qing dynasty. It seems to have arisen in part out of the much increased use of calligraphy on the sides of seals added by the seal-text carvers from the second half of the Ming and particularly in the Qing dynasty.

The perceived distinction between arts and crafts in China has been discussed elsewhere. The traditional hierarchy may be a convenient general guide, but the situation was more complicated. There was certainly a greater tendency for the influential minority to be musicians, poets, calligraphers and painters, and later seal carvers and carvers of other soft materials, but they also expressed themselves in a very wide range of other media, and frequently indirectly through the hands and technical skills of craftsmen.

By the early 19th century in Yangzhou, with craftsmen such as Lu Dong mixing with scholars, being recognized as personalities 'close to the Dao', and painting to a standard as respectable as the majority of his circle (see no. 63), any serious distinction between artists and craftsmen governed by medium was no longer sensible. The gradual blurring of the distinction between artist and craftsman, art and craft, is clearly seen in a wide range of post-Song Chinese works of art and in the much greater identification of individuals, both by signature and in literature. Lu Kuisheng and many of the other individual artists represented here are the epitome of this trend.

65

Wrist Rest

Ivory, of evenly patinated creamy-yellow colour; carved as a wrist rest after the form of a bamboo section, the upper side carved in low relief with a raised line design of a scholar, seated, on a mat, in a pose of studied concentration, holding a wine cup, while behind him his servant stands beside an enormous wine jar and, taking advantage of his master's inattention to worldly matters, drinks wine directly from a winepot he is holding; all set beneath an adumbrated new moon; the underside carved in deep relief, leaving a good deal of the detail in the round, with various figures in a landscape setting with towering cliffs, water-side pavilions, and a variety of trees.
Probably mid-Qing dynasty.
Length: 26 cm.

象牙雕山水人物臂擱
可能清中葉, 長26厘米

This wrist rest has the same *qin*-like proportions and appearance as no. 86. It is a superbly carved object, its underside representing the literati landscape with its simplified and abstracted elements and delight in the rustic life. There seems to have been a trend in the mid-Qing period for superbly carved ivory wrist rests of this type (see no. 128 for a discussion on the group). What sets this one apart, however, is the extremely effective, and very rare, treatment of the scholar and his attendant.

The importance of line in Chinese art resulted in a good deal of carving where the individual lines take on an importance of their own — inevitable in a culture that expressed itself in and understood so well the language of line. Here the carver has given his lines the same importance in the work of art as the brush-line has in a literati painting, forcing the pictorial content to act in a secondary role. It is difficult to look at the resulting picture without the lines taking over and leading the eye off on a visual romp which carries abstract meaning quite independent of the figures depicted. It is brilliantly conceived, and demonstrates the mastery over line that is almost second nature to the Chinese artist.

66

Seal

Soapstone, of variegated and speckled deep russet red colour in a translucent, smoky matrix, of the variety known as *mayuhong* ('horse-flesh red') with an area of translucent orange-yellow of the variety known as Shoushan *bai* ('white Shoushan' — which turns yellow when handled); the knob carved as a leonine creature, standing with its head turned downwards and to one side.
Probably early Qing dynasty.
Height: 7.4 cm.

壽山馬玉紅石雕異獸印
可能清初, 高7.4厘米

This beast is probably based upon a lion, but might well be a mythical animal. Whether the original beast was real, a composite creature made up of features of various real beasts, or entirely imaginary was unimportant; to the carvers they were all 'fabulous' animals, and a real lion was to most pre-modern Chinese just as wonderous as a flying unicorn. This creature resembles Buddhist lions as depicted in the Tang dynasty.

The Chinese have always appreciated natural markings in materials, frequently above purity, and have developed a high skill in their use. Such markings were not considered to be flaws or impurities, but were simply natural; artists made the best of them, resulting in some imaginative and spectacular uses of natural markings and flaws in a wide variety of materials.

Here the natural yellow markings have been cleverly used to form the mane and tail of the creature. Clearly the positioning of the different colour dictated the placing of the beast to an extent, but such preconditions have been well met to achieve a powerful and fluid sculpture. This trend in soapstone carving has been attributed in Chinese sources to the early Qing master Yang Yuxuan (see no. 45) but it may be that he simply popularized a natural trend for the Chinese carver. The manipulation of strange stones certainly predated the Song dynasty (see no. 9) and was a frequent subject of discussion and appreciation in the 12th century *Yunlin Shipu.* [1]

1. Translated as *Tu Wan's Stone Catalogue of Cloudy Forest,* by Edward H. Schafer.

64

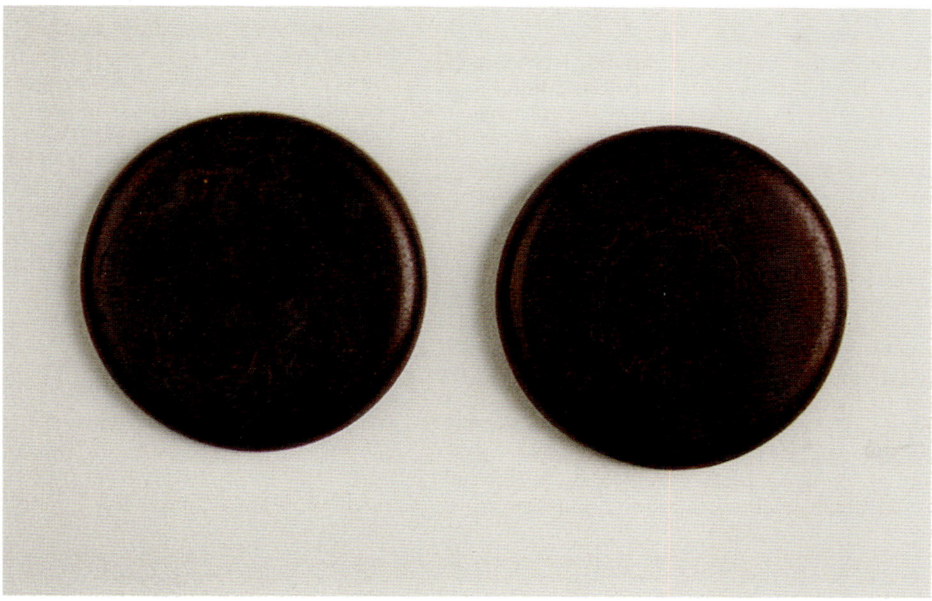

66

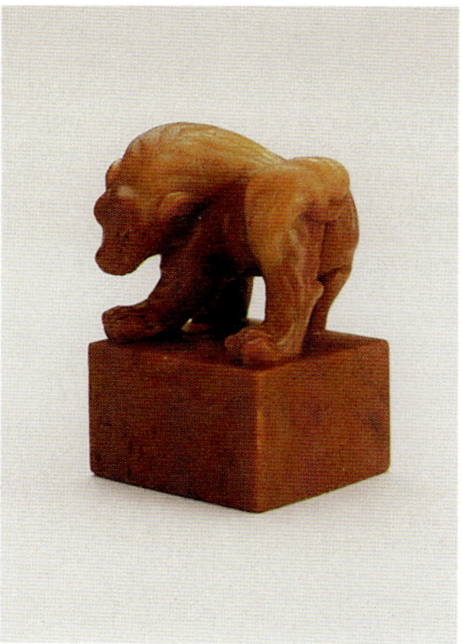

65

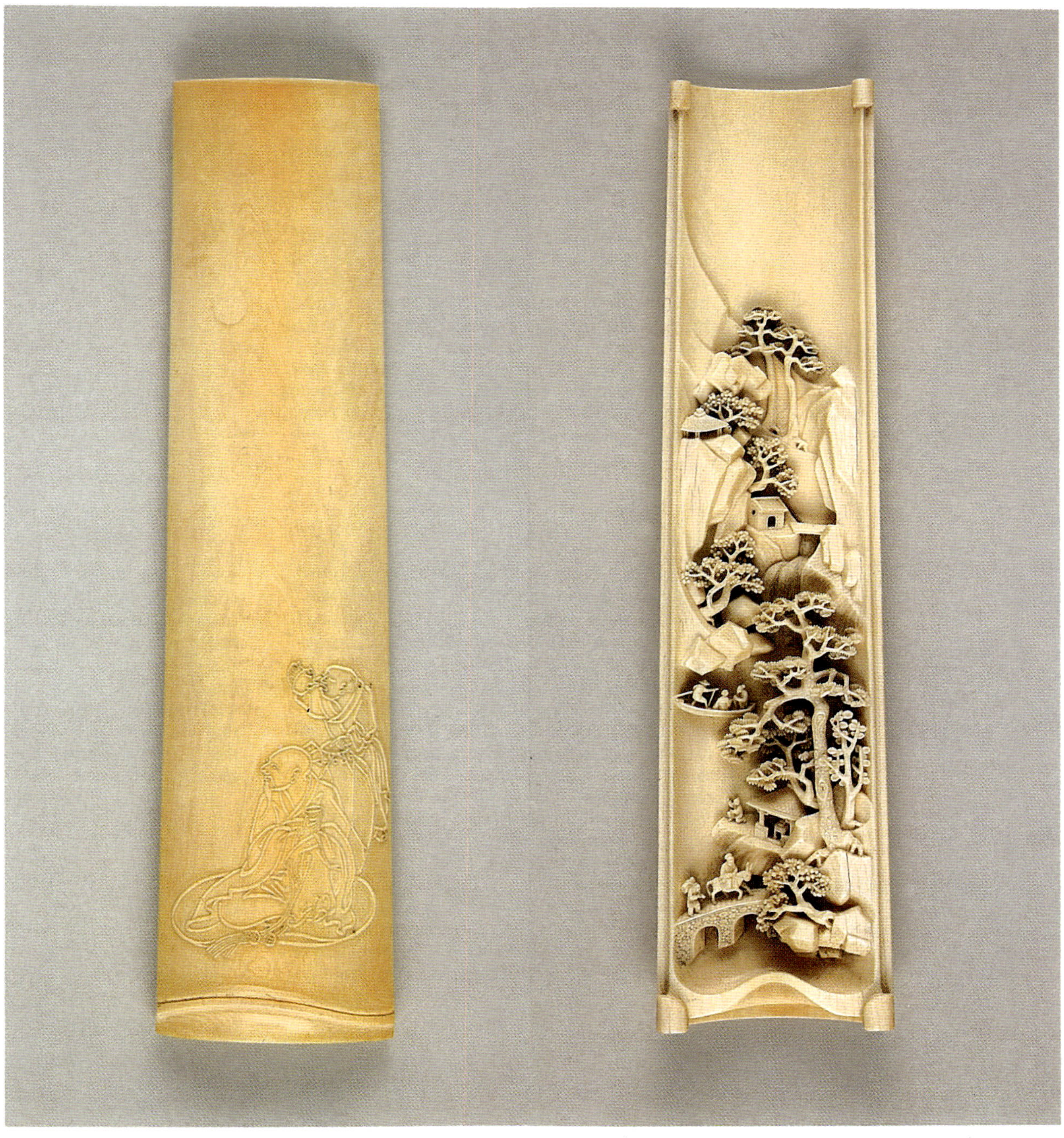

67

'Withered Monk' Ruyi Sceptre

Bamboo, of golden brown colour; a *ruyi* sceptre, the stem made up of a natural section of culm, carved at its edges to simulate gnarled wood with worm-holes, bent over at the top to allow the diaphragm to act as the *lingzhi* head; a small twig cleverly grafted onto the outer culm at the back to simulate a natural growth, which curls through a hole to the front of the lower handle; incised on the front of the handle with a poetic inscription in seal script: "Following his scholarly temperament from the green hills, this withered monk grows among a family of many. Naturally one likes plainness, although the vulgar may prefer elaborate motifs. This piece was obtained from a natural growth, it resembles a flower emerging from the water. Sometimes it rains, sometimes it is sunny. What can I add even with the most earnest wish?"
Probably late Ming or early Qing dynasty.
Length: 41 cm.
With early if not original cord and tassle.
Formerly in the Mrs. Sheila Riddell (Lady David) collection.

竹雕題詩靈芝如意
可能晚明或清初，長41厘米

In the poetic inscription the first line refers to the association between the literati and bamboo, the latter growing straight and true, bending without breaking, and so on, symbolizing the character of the ideal scholar. The association between the scholar and the bamboo is also strengthened by use of the character *jie,* meaning both the node of the bamboo and moral integrity. Bamboo also became, by the Song dynasty, a standard literati subject in painting as it was believed that the strokes used in painting bamboo came close to calligraphic strokes. The understanding that the two arts were essentially the same reached its culmination in the 11th century among Su Shi and his coterie. The gnarled old bamboo growing amongst many others is an analogy of an old monk in the community. The next section refers to natural good taste, which implies a sophisticated love of the humble and restrained, as opposed to the noisy and flamboyant. The last section is a statement that things are such as they are so the most earnest wishes in the world will not change them, a wry comment on the meaning of *ruyi*: '(may things be) as you wish'.

This brilliantly conceived *ruyi* is a faultless artistic statement. Delightful material, imaginatively used by a superb technician (the unusual touch of the added sprig curling through the worm holes lifts an otherwise fine work of art into the inspired class) is combined with the poetry in archaic style, with its various allusions, to bring other levels of meaning to the subject.

68

Scholar at Ease

Wood, *huangyangmu* (boxwood), of even orange-brown colour; a miniature carving of a scholar at ease, reclining against a section of gnarled tree trunk, a duster idly held in one hand, his hair tied up in a cloth hat, the retaining ribbons hanging loosely over his shoulders; at his side on a protruding section of tree trunk a brazier decorated with a crackled pattern burns, its smoke rising in a wafting cloud into the severed branches of the fallen tree; the scholar's eyes picked out in tiny dots of black material.
Late Ming or early Qing dynasty.
Height: 5.1 cm.

黃楊木雕高士像
晚明或清初，高5.1厘米

This exquisite little sculpture represents the ideal of the rustic scholar. Here the old sage sits in his rustic setting, represented by the gnarled log which makes a natural seat, thinking lofty thoughts, while the material world is metaphorically flicked away with his duster (see no. 265 for a discussion on the flywhisk, or duster as it is called in China). The brazier by his side is of a type used for heating water to make tea and is usually seen in genre paintings and other works of art attended by a servant while a scholar or group of scholars entertain themselves with less mundane matters. Here there is no kettle boiling and the proximity of scholar and brazier suggests that he is unattended and that the brazier is perhaps serving to keep him warm. Here is a scholar pursuing one of the pastimes found illustrated with such charm in the *Sancai tuhui* (discussed on p. 27).

In the Chinese view of sculpture, large size had no particular merit. The Chinese understanding of art led to the appreciation of intimate works of art: paintings on scrolls or in album or fan formats; small objects that could be enjoyed on the desk, or kept in boxes and brought out from time to time with a view to total involvement in them for a while. Items had the added advantage of being mobile; they could be carried to elegant gatherings of friends, or on picnics, and longer journeys. Even very long handscrolls, for example, were never intended to be seen all at once, and could be rolled up and carried as easily as a small painting.

The subject-matter and the style are typically late Ming to transitional in period. Even the crackled pattern on the brazier was a design which was a popular development of the period. However, such individual works of art are very difficult to date accurately and if pressed one would have to accept the possibility, although not the probability, of this carving having been made at any time from the 16th to 19th century.

69

Brush Rest

Wood, *huangyangmu* (boxwood), of yellowish tone; carved as a multi-peaked mountain brush rest, the base concave; set on a *zitan* stand.
Probably Qing dynasty.
Height including stand: 5.9 cm.
Length of stand: 16.8 cm.

黃楊木雕筆山
可能清代，高連座5.9厘米，座長16.8厘米

Here is a superb example of the simplicity and elegance to be found in Chinese scholarly art. The artist has created a faultless, abstracted mountain range made up of a pattern of small peaks, just as mountains in paintings are so often built up of smaller hillocks joined in a pleasing abstract pattern. The brush rest has then been perfectly finished and enhanced with a simple wax polish, allowing the beauty of the wood and the abstract form to speak for themselves. The understated, darker wood stand completes the sense of restrained elegance.

The difficulties of dating literati works of art where known makers or a body of similar works is lacking is epitomized by this brush rest. The main clue we have to dating here is taste. Where only one object is known of the type, the patination on the wood is only the vaguest hint to period. We can never be certain that a piece has not been cleaned and re-polished, or that it was not shut up in a box for long periods of time or otherwise not used. Equally the stand might have been added at any time or may be a replacement. Taste, therefore, is our main guide, and one in which little confidence may be placed. It might, for instance, be reasonable to suppose that the brush rest meets the same sort of standard as the *ruyi* sceptre with which it goes so well (no. 6), which might tentatively be associated with the Yongzheng marked example (no. 7) that we may provisionally accept as genuine, but this is evidence so circumstancial as to be almost meaningless.

67

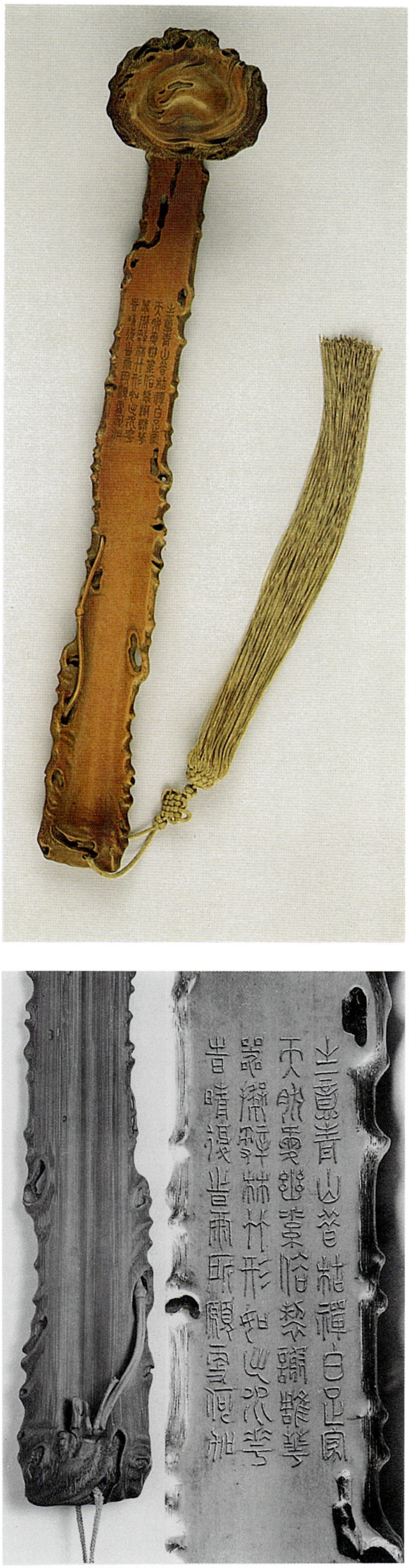

68

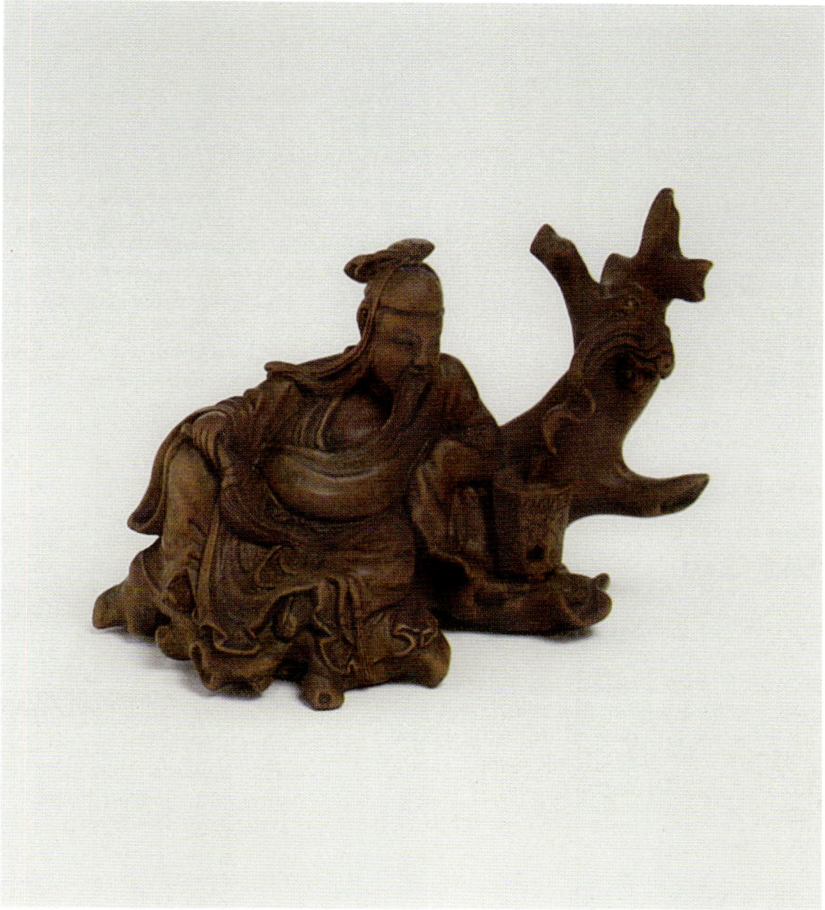

69

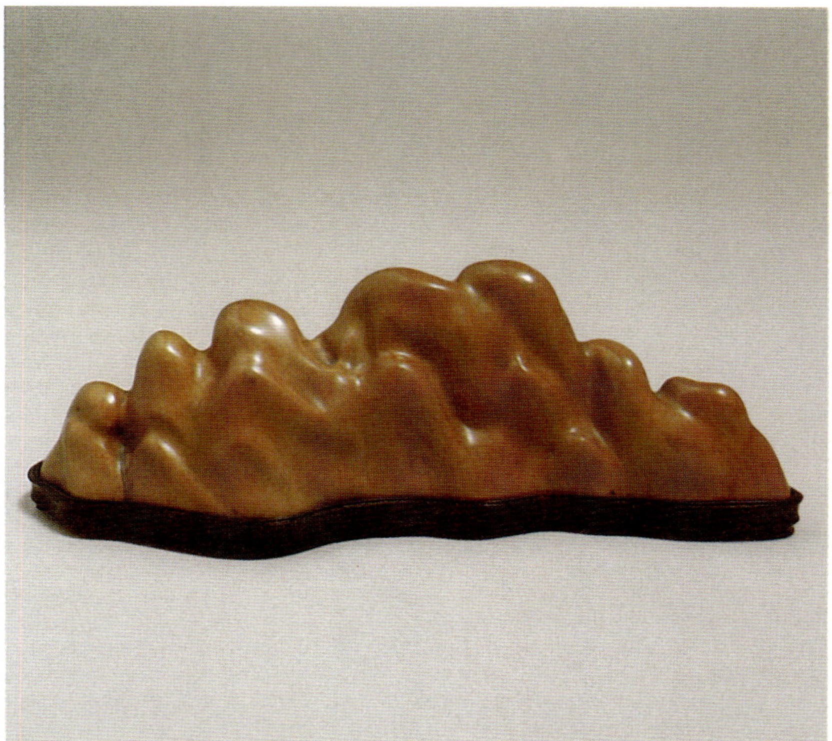

70

Paper Weight

Nephrite, of crystalline greyish-white colour, with dark grey-black markings and a 'skin' of black on two faces of the rather rectangular form; a paper weight carved in the form of a tough-looking cat, seated on a group of acanthus leaves, with a further leafing branch of the same plant held between its tightly closed teeth, the fat tail curled up against the body and ending beneath the jaw; a butterfly behind the cat's head shares the black 'skin' of the pebble on its head and upper wings; the base fully carved. Mid to late Ming dynasty, perhaps 16th century.
Height: 5.3 cm.

白玉雕貓蝶紙鎮
明中至晚期，可能十六世紀，高5.3厘米

James Watt[1] has identified this leaf, which here resembles a banana leaf, as an acanthus, which he says is commonly found as a floral decorative motif on Ming works of art. This sculpture makes full use of the shape of the original pebble and its outer layer of darker colour, and captures the playful but amoral nature of the animal. As it lurks camouflaged in the leaves, its expression gives no clue as to whether it is about to jump out to playfully chase a leaf or to kill a bird. That it is ready to spring out at the slightest provocation, despite the apparent restfulness of the front paws, is indicated by the taught and poised position of one hind leg. In the context of the symbolism the carver would not have conceived of it killing the butterfly, which might otherwise be considered to be dicing with death. The characters for butterfly (*die*) and cat (*mao*) have the same sound as those meaning living into the seventies and eighties, forming a wish for longevity.

The subject of a cat and butterfly is, because of its meaning, one of the most popular in later Chinese jades, but this is an early example and certainly one of the most powerful known. It is also an extremely practical weight, being heavy and very sturdy and yet sufficiently compact to be easily grasped and moved about.

1. *Chinese Jades from Han to Ch'ing*, p.74, no. 55.

71

Brush Pot

Wood, *zitan*, of dark, purplish-brown colour; a brush pot, the straight-sided cylindrical form carved on the outside to simulate the gnarled trunk of a tree; a hole in the centre of the base fitted with a flanged plug of different wood.
Probably first half of the Qing dynasty.
Height: 16.6 cm. Diameter of top: 18.6 cm.
Published: *Wood from the Scholar's Table*, p.42, no. 13.

紫檀雕樹皮紋筆筒
可能清代早期，高16.6厘米，頂直徑18.6厘米

The natural-looking gnarled and knotty appearance of this piece is entirely contrived (compare it, for instance, with no. 24). But within the scholar's aesthetic it was almost certainly not intended to be entirely natural looking. No. 24 was made for a Daoist, for whom the markings of nature were enough; this is one of a group of brush pots made, we may assume, for a different audience. They employ highly stylized, simplified and abstracted naturalism, in which aspect they echo the paintings of the literati. To their patrons such pieces spoke eloquently of the subtle human mind and express the understanding that good art is no slave to nature, but a full partner in man's pursuit of understanding. Dong Qichang, the late Ming artist and literati theorist, wrote: "As for those who meticulously and carefully delineate, they can only be called slaves of nature".[1]

1. Quoted in *The Compelling Image*, p.34, from a Wai-kam Ho translation.

72

Incense Burner

Bronze, inlaid with silver wire; an incense burner of slightly flared, straight-sided form, with scalloped strap handles; the exterior decorated with an inlaid silver design, repeated on each side, of an elaborate archaistic *taotie* mask, the handles with double unit *leiwen*, the base with the relief mark *Jixin Zhai qingwan* ('For elegant appreciation in the Studio of the Reliable Heart') in seal script in a recessed rectangular cartouche.
Ming or early Qing dynasty.
Height: 5.1 cm.

嵌銀線饕餮紋銅香爐·寄心齋銘
明或清初，高5.1厘米

We have been unable to find a record of the Studio of the Reliable Heart. Although it would conventionally be dated to the late Ming dynasty, vessel no. 153 demonstrates that this sort of quality and integrity of archaism was by no means impossible for the early Qing period.

The term *qingwan* represents a variety of such terms used in marks. It might be translated literally as 'elegant plaything' as long as one understands the nature of 'play' to the Chinese scholar, who over many centuries frequently referred to the act of painting the most subtle literati works as 'play'.

The form and decoration of this vessel represent an interesting development in archaism. Archaism is, essentially, an art form where form and decoration are derived from the archaic because of a respect held for the ancient. The highly refined connoisseurship of the scholar class did not develop archaism to fake old bronzes, any more than they copied earlier paintings as an empty exercise in reproduction.

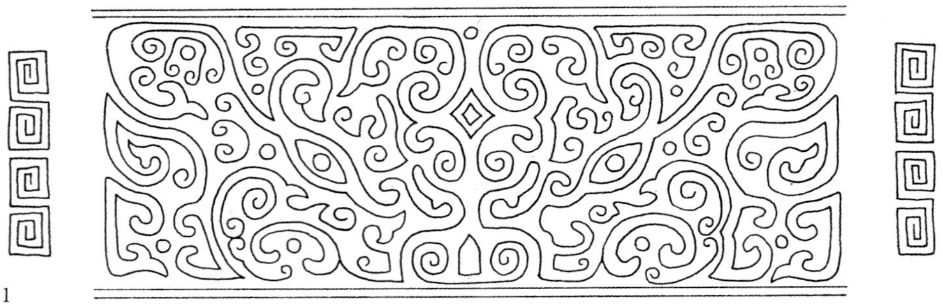

Fig. 1

It was a process of creative re-interpretation of the old, a wholly new artistic form using the ancient as its point of departure. This process did develop further and further away from its ancient origins but this should not be regarded as a simple linear evolution in which Song archaism could be viewed as closest to, and late Qing archaism as most distant from, the source. It would depend entirely upon how individual artists and their patrons interpreted the archaic and archaism. Although later pieces tended to make more subtle references to the archaic with abstract original motifs, these would almost certainly have co-existed, at any particular time, with other productions which would have been more 'faithful' to the originals.

In this vessel the form is not derived from the archaic in any recognizable aspect; if anything it is based very loosely upon archaistic forms in perhaps Song ceramics. The design however (see Fig. 1) is quite clearly based upon an archaic *taotie* mask taken originally from a Shang or Zhou bronze. Although all the elements are recognizable once the rhythm of the line is grasped, they have been almost wholly transformed into a piece of subtle archaism where the features of the *taotie* merge with positive and negative lines to form an independent work of art. The quality of the work is not in question, but it might well have been too advanced in terms of the evolution of archaism to have struck a chord as early as the Song dynasty. To a late Ming or early Qing dynasty audience steeped in centuries of archaism, on the other hand, the merest hint of the ancient was enough to allow a host of associations to add levels of meaning to the work. (For further discussion of archaism see no. 13).

70

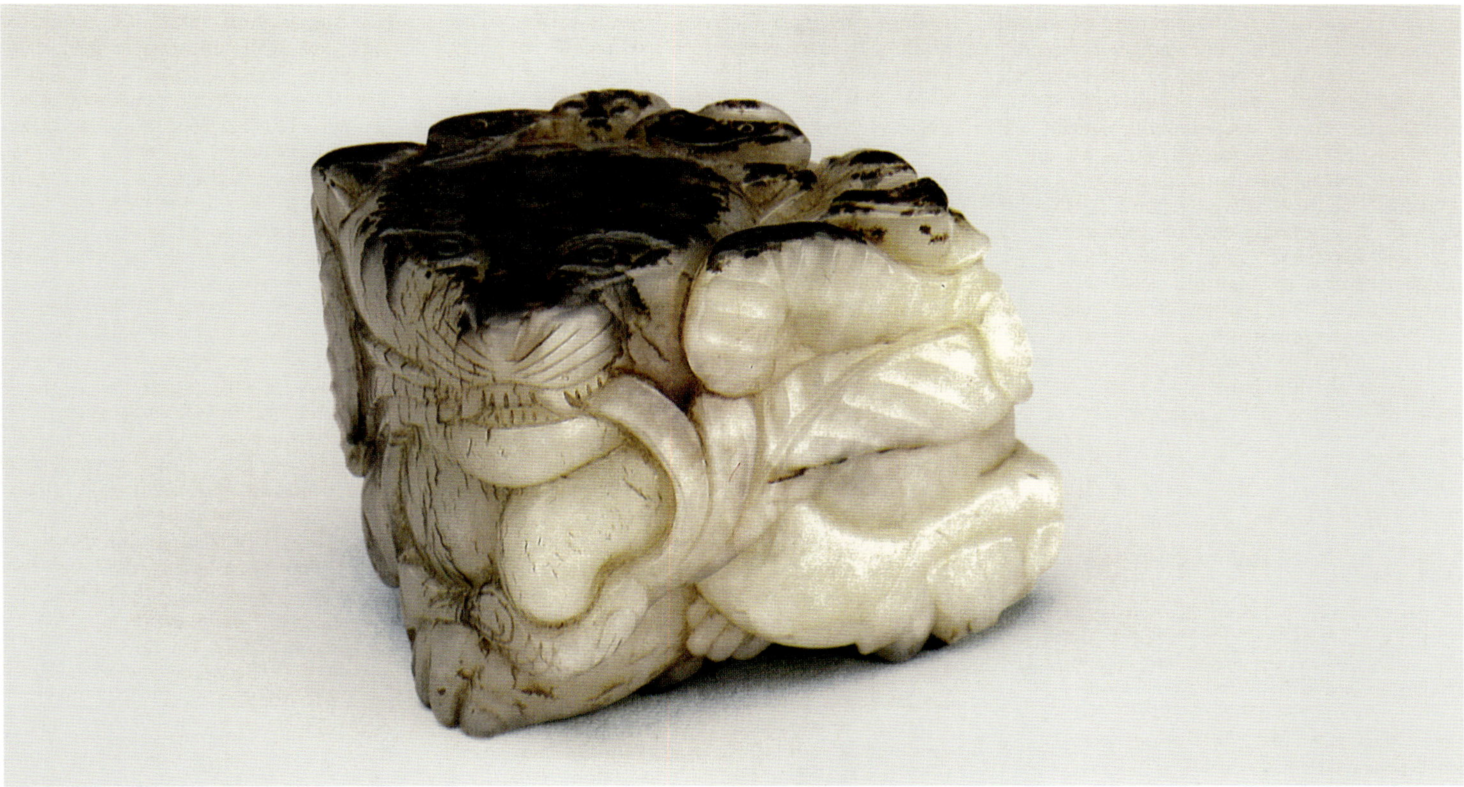

Larger than life size

71

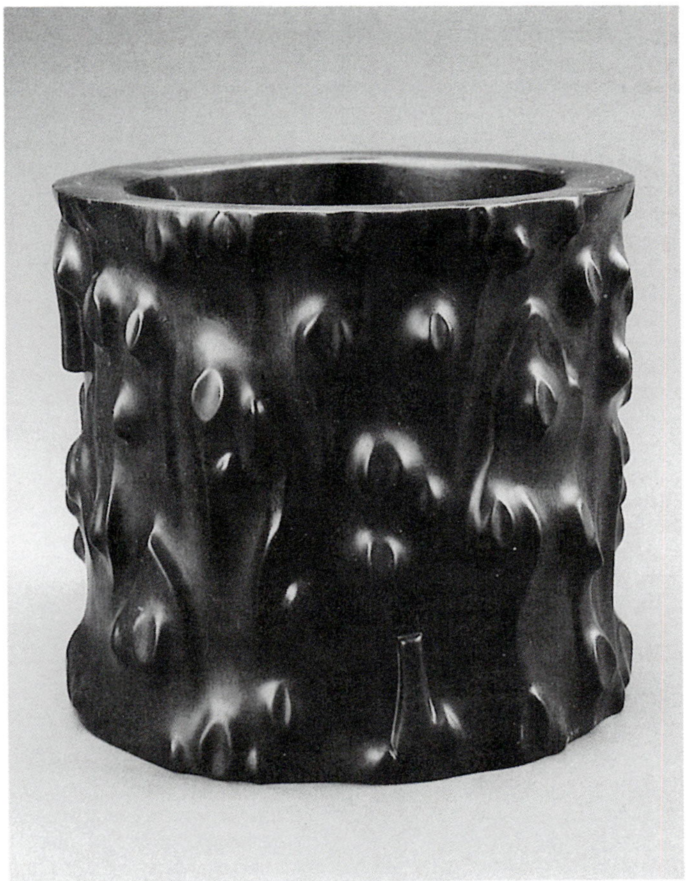

72

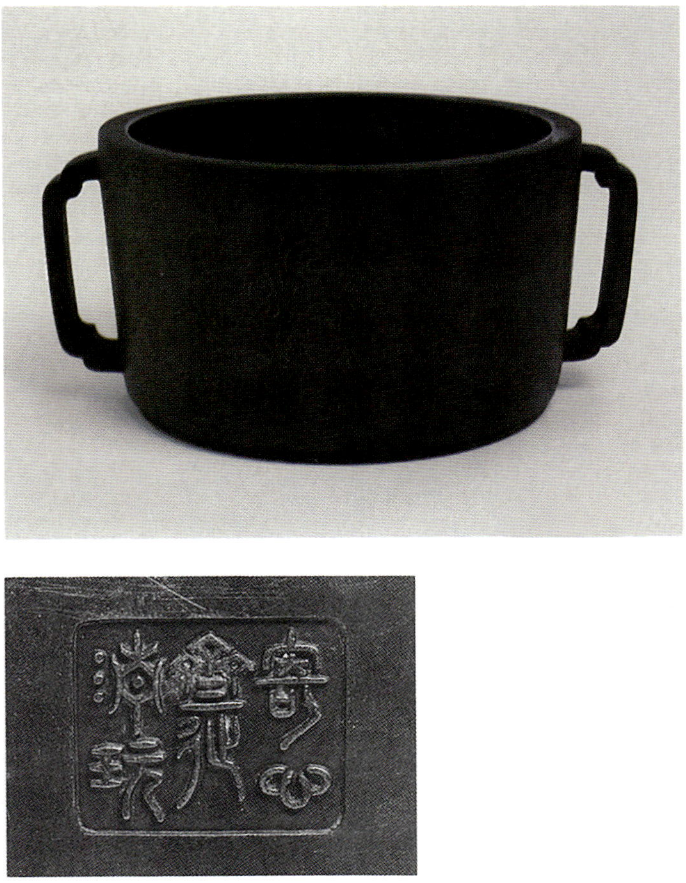

73

Incense Burner

Hu Wenming

Bronze, inlaid with gold and silver; a *gui* incense burner, the central and upper sections decorated with a formalized design, repeated on each side, of a central *taotie* mask flanked by two stylized *kui* dragons, beneath a border of alternating whorl and quatrefoil reliefs, flanking central animal masks; the deep, splayed foot with *kui* dragons confronting the character *wang* (king); all set against an inlaid silver ground of double unit *leiwen;* the integrally cast handles in the form of self-consuming *taotie,* with details extensively inlaid with gold and silver; the interior with the characters *zizisunsun yongbao* ("to be treasured eternally by innumerable descendants"); the base inscribed *Wanli guiwei jinyue Yunjian Hu Wenming zhi* ('made by Hu Wenming of Yunjian in the ninth month of 1583').
Yunjian, 1583.
Height: 10.3 cm.
Width including handles: 21.5 cm.

Formerly in the Betty James Westbrook collection, Connecticut.
Published: *Archives of the Chinese Art Society of America,* XI, 1957; *Dated Chinese Antiquities 600-1650,* p.140; *Chinese Metalwork of the Hu Wenming Group,* no. 1.

嵌金銀線饕餮夔紋青銅香爐·胡文明製
明萬曆癸未(1583), 高10.3厘米,
寬連把手21.5厘米

Hu Wenming was one of the most celebrated late Ming metalworkers. He specialized in wares for the scholar, and specifically in wares for the incense cult. He came from, and presumably worked in Yunjian (the old name for Songjiang, also known as Huating), to the southwest of Shanghai in the key cultural area known as Jiangnan — the same area in which Nanjing, Shanghai, Yixing, Wuxi, Suzhou and Hangzhou were situated.

We have dealt extensively with Hu Wenming and his workshop elsewhere.[1] These wares represent the fascinating relationship between craftsman and scholar that produced in the post-Song period, and particularly from the late Ming onwards, a series of works of art which were the expression of the influential minority, but produced in workshops in an industrialized setting. Out of this arose some outstanding works of art in the late Ming and Qing period, particularly in metalwork (much of which was archaistic).

We know that Hu Wenming had a son, Hu Guangyu; a few incense burners very much in the father's style are signed "made by Guangyu, son of Hu Wenming of Yunjian". Another artist making similar wares in the same style, Zhu Chenming, also of Yunjian, may have been trained by him. In any case it was quite normal in the applied arts in China for male children to be trained in the father's artistic skills and to help with production. A typical workshop might consist of the owner/artist-craftsman, one to three sons and a small group of menial workers. Regardless of the size of the workshop, the wares produced would, if identified by name at all, go under the name of the owner, even if he had not actually had a hand in the production of a particular piece. The genuine wares of the workshop might vary significantly in quality, as they do in the Hu Wenming group, depending upon a variety of factors. To demonstrate his ability, or in response to a particularly valuable commission, Hu might produce his very finest work in which we could see more of, if not the exclusive hand of, the master metalsmith.

This is the case with two pieces in the exhibition, this *gui* and the *pou* in no. 103. It may be no coincidence that these are also the only two dated examples recorded from Hu's workshop. These two, and a preface mentioning his works written by Wen Peng who died in 1573, establish a definite period of activity from sometime prior to 1573 to 1613, and a likely period between the 1560s and the 1620s.[2] However it is very likely that his workshop continued under his son(s)' guidance to produce Hu Wenming wares for some time after his death; for as long, indeed, as there was a demand and the necessary skills existed in the family to fulfil it.[3]

The late Ming dynasty was an exciting time for the arts. Administrative careers, which usually took up so much of the creative energy of the literati, became less and less attractive as the Ming Court became more corrupt. In the late Ming dynasty honour and selfless service no longer promised respect in the administration; on the contrary, they were likely to bring one up sharply against the intriguing factions who vied for power, leading to disgrace, banishment or even death. As in the 14th century, many of the country's finest minds preferred to stay away from Court and spent instead long periods of time in 'retirement'. The Jiangnan region had for long been the favoured retirement place of the gentry, being temperate, bountiful and beautiful, and having via the Grand Canal easy access to the seat of power at Beijing. Out of office the literati were able to set aside their concern for ordering worldly affairs and enjoy more artistic pursuits.

The patronage of the scholarly class extended far and wide, but the growth of workshops to satisfy artistic demand was also fuelled by a social phenomenon of the time. Jiangnan had traditionally been a major crop-raising area, usually producing a surplus and bringing considerable wealth to the people. However, during the Ming dynasty parcels of productive land had been successively subdivided into smaller and smaller units, inhibiting the large-scale improvements necessary to produce surpluses. Despite the enormous accumulated wealth of the landed gentry, farmers frequently lived below subsistence level and many turned from their traditional pursuits in search of supplementary income. Part of this labour force was drawn off into the production of arts and crafts, creating a large workforce to meet the demand for works of art created by the influx of retiring scholars.[4]

Largely due to their association with the literati and the refined aesthetic that grew out of it, the artist-craftsmen of the late Ming began to rise from their traditionally self-effacing status to become known in their own right as artists. The names of many late Ming artist-craftsmen are recorded, and many signed their works. This seems to have been the beginning of a golden age of co-operation between those who governed and evolved aesthetics and those who responded to it, breaking down the barriers that traditionally separated them to a certain extent (see nos. 63 and 55 for its manifestations in the 19th and 20th centuries respectively).

This vessel is based upon a late Shang dynasty *gui,* originally used for ritual offerings of food. The handles represent *taotie* eating their own bodies, a popular form of handle on archaic vessels, particularly of *gui, jue* and *he* forms. The origins of the *taotie* are lost in China's prehistorical period, and like all mythological creatures do not take kindly to precise analysis of form and function. However, there is a popular belief that they were voracious beasts who devoured everything in sight, including their own bodies. Leaving aside the practical difficulties involved in this feat, Shang decoration seems to suggest that this belief was a contemporary part of the mystique of the beast, as the disembodied heads are its most common manifestation, and the reversed, open-mouthed head in the process of eating the rest of its body is a popular form of handle. As early as the 3rd century BC, attempts were made to explain the *taotie* (which by then had enjoyed more than a millenium of evolution) as a moral symbol. "On the Zhou dynasty *ding* tripods was the *taotie* mask motif. Only the head was shown, without the body, because the taotie consumed people, thus hurting its own body."[5]

The inscription on the base of this vessel is not, as stated frequently elsewhere, inlaid in silver, nor ever was. This may be an error arising out of the filling of the mark with chalk for emphasis in photography.

1. *Chinese Metalwork of the Hu Wenming Group.*
2. Ibid. p.47.
3. We suggested (ibid.) that the extant works of the Hu Wenming group seemed to be those of the master metalsmith, his sons, and perhaps his workshop continuing after his death while demand lasted and that later copying seemed not to have taken place. Upon reflection this would seem unlikely, although as yet we have still not seen pieces which seem obviously to be separate and later wares of a different nature. However, the matter deserves further consideration.
4. Ibid. p.36.
5. From *Commentary on the Spring and Autumn Annals* by Lu Buwei of the Qin dynasty, quoted in *Zhongguo Lishi Wenwu Jiandingshi Kaishu* by Liu Dongduan.

74

Contemplating Scholar

Ivory, of well-patinated cream and golden brown colours with a network of age cracks running through it; carved in the form of a scholar seated on the ground, leaning against a rock, his left hand resting upon his knee originally holding a separate object (presumably a duster); the rim and ribbons of his hat and the hem, cuffs and collar of his robes with traces of original darker staining.
Late Ming or possibly early Qing dynasty.
Height: 10.3 cm.

象牙雕高士像
晚明或清初, 高10.3厘米

Ivory figures appear to have been much in vogue in late Ming times and a number of them make dating by style and collective degrees of wear, decomposition and patination a task one may approach with relative confidence. This carving may be dated to the 16th or 17th century, although later expertise is likely to be more precise and perhaps will place it slightly outside that period range.

73

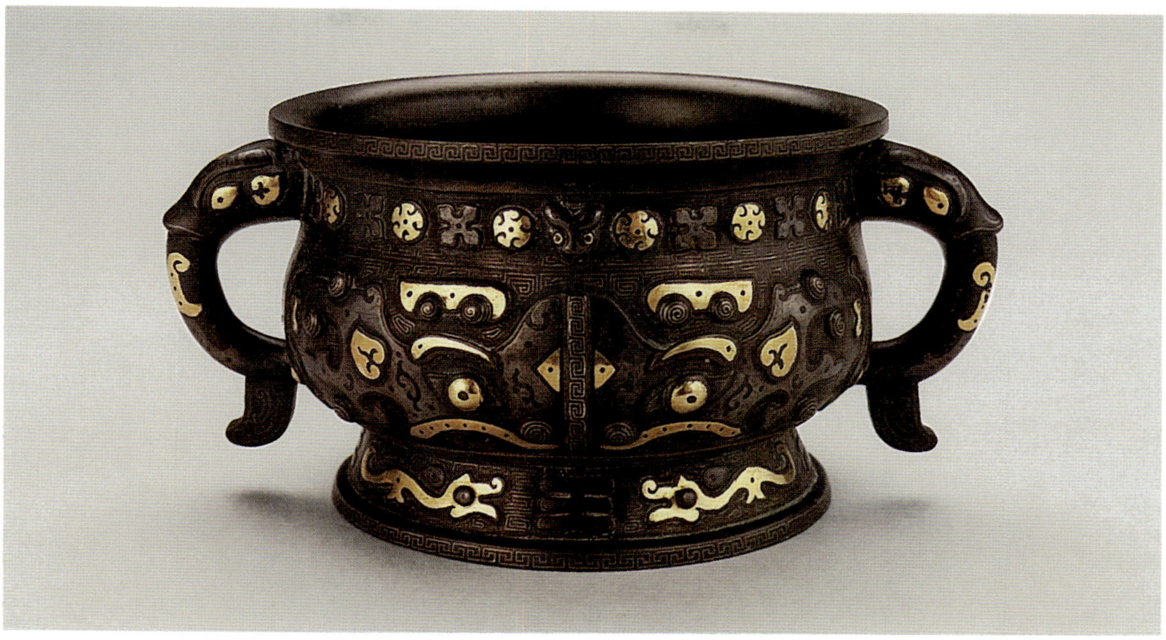

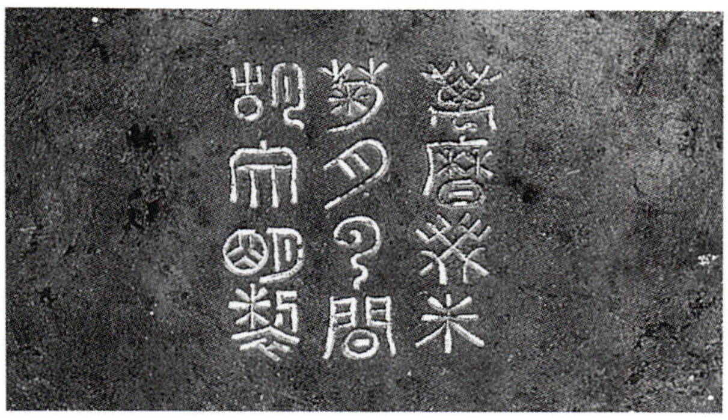

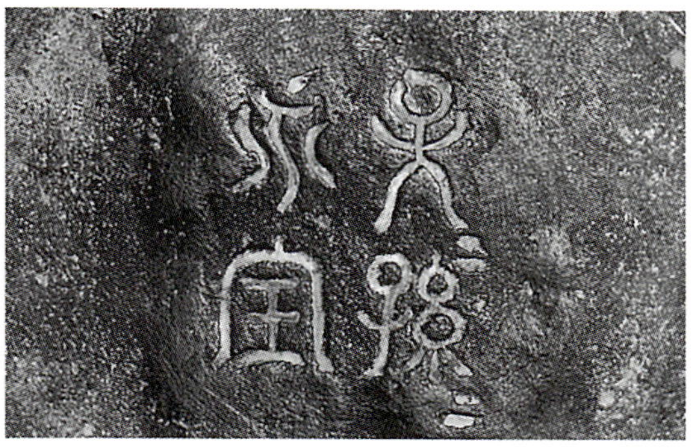

74

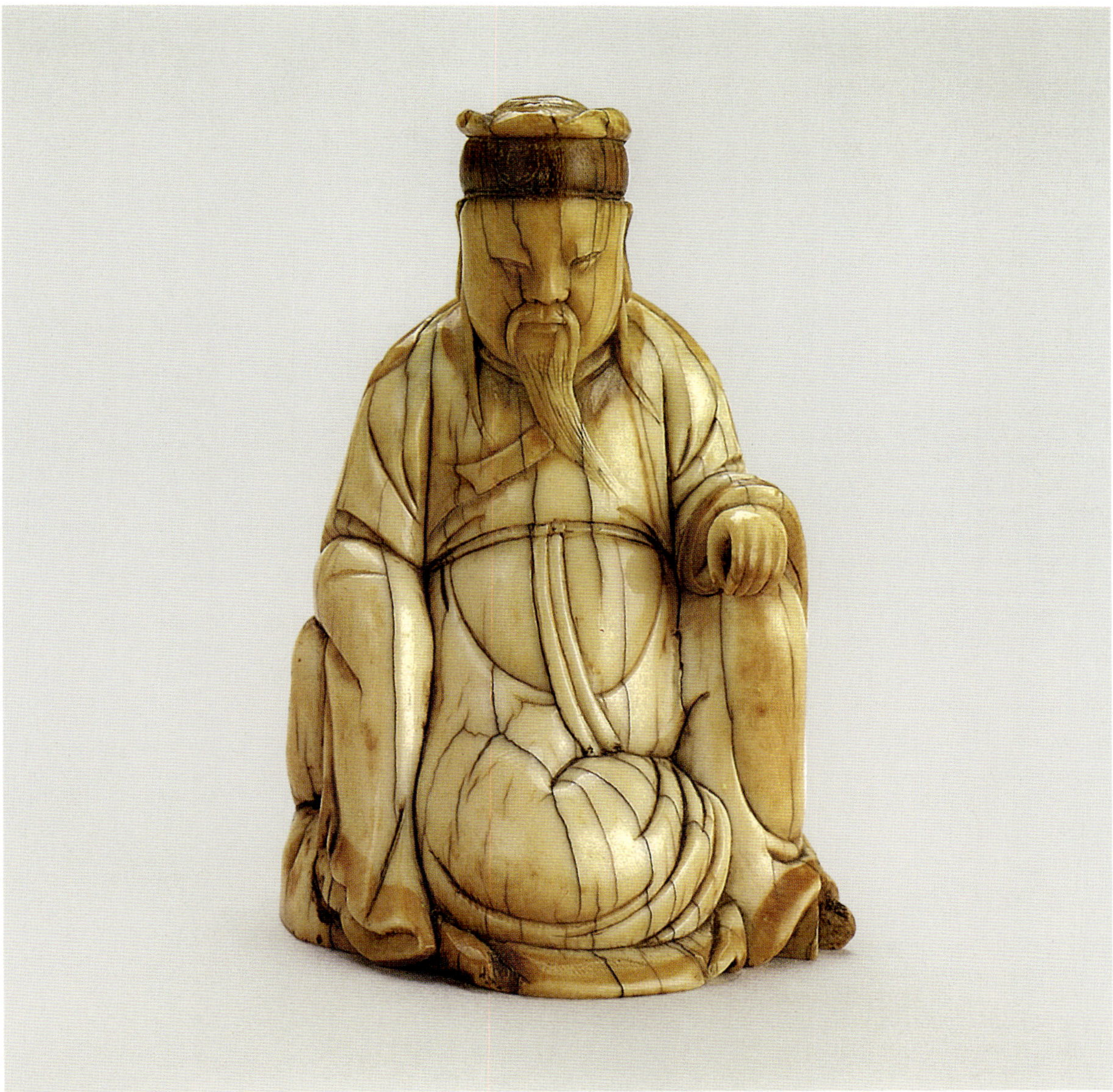

Larger than life size

75

'Drunken Sage' Brush Pot

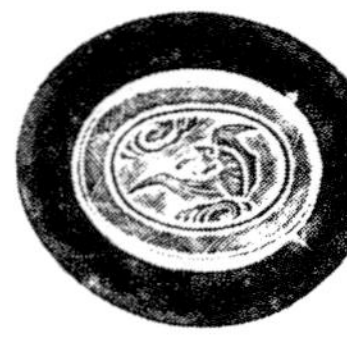

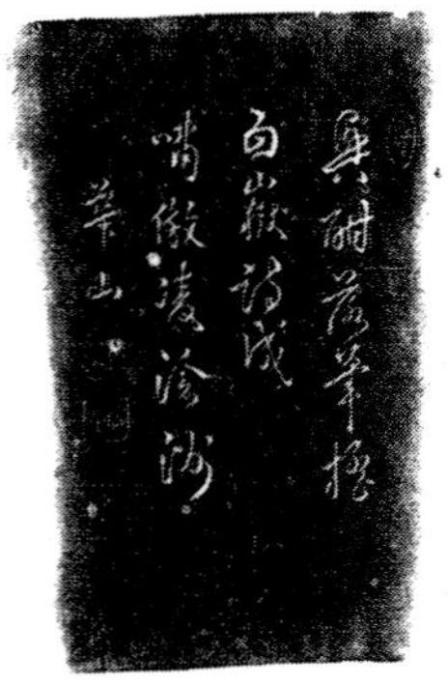

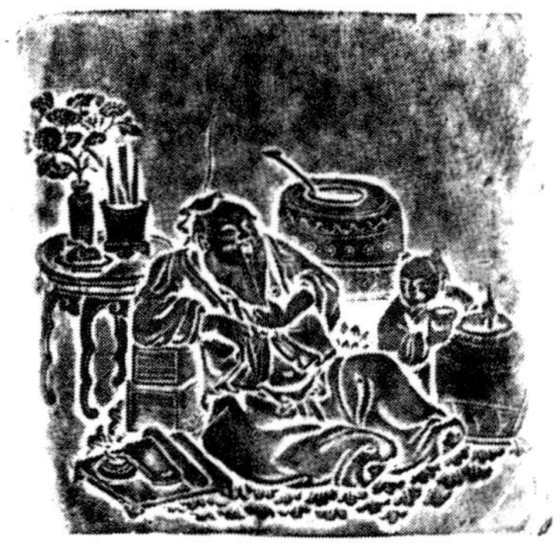

Ivory, of well-patinated creamy colour with a network of age cracks running through it; a brush pot carved in low relief with a scholar reclining against a pile of books and on a leaf mat, surrounded by leisurely trappings, while a nearby serving boy ladles wine into a large cup; the reverse with a poetic inscription in running script, "After drinking sufficient wine the brush begins to move over a hundred hills. After the poem is finished, a scream is released to traverse the oceans."
Preceded by the seal *Mingyue* ('Bright moon') and followed by the signature *Huashan* ('Flower Mountain') and by two seals *Wuhua* (which may refer to a district in Fujian province) and *Shanren* ('Mountain Man'); the base plug carved with a bat and clouds set against a cross-hatched ground within a formalized wave border.
Perhaps Fujian province, late Ming or early Qing dynasty.
Height: 13.3 cm.

象牙雕醉酒高士筆筒·五華山人製
晚明或清初，高13.3厘米

In the poem inscribed here, the brush moving over a hundred hills equates to the flying spirit. The scream (*xiao*) across the oceans is a habit practised by the literati consisting of screaming or shouting as loudly as possible, to purify the spirit and rid the body of unwanted frustrations.

The seal giving a place name in Fujian province (although it could also be an unrelated adopted name) is interesting. The preceding ivory figure is similar in style, size and feeling to a group of Fujian soapstone figures of the late Ming and early Qing dynasty, and it is possible that Fujian was also a centre for ivory carving at the time.

In this delightful scene an aged scholar wears a cloth hat of the type usually associated with Daoists and an expression of total contentment. He has done rather well with the enormous jar of wine from which the servant is refilling a capacious cup, and he reclines against two large volumes of books. His disregard for worldly conventions is demonstrated by his tailor's despair of an outfit, with trousers too large and too long, apparently made of old sacking and tied at the waist with a crude sash, and a jacket which when buttoned strains but fails to cover a well-filled belly. His eyes are closed, he holds a brush in his hand, and he strokes his beard as he ponders, perhaps composing a poem he will shortly write with the materials ready at his elbow. These consist of an inkstone and a water vessel with small ladle, which are on a low table at his side. There is also on the table what might at first glance be mistaken for a sheet of paper at the ready, but upon closer examination it has a brocaded design of formalized waves. These are the outer bindings of groups of scrolls which made up an early form of book, where each volume in a set was on a separate scroll. When the scrolls were in use, the outer binding would be rolled, like this, and set aside, or put in to a brush pot, where they are frequently found in genre paintings. In the famous painting of Fu Sheng teaching, attributed to Wang Wei of the 8th century, but probably later (a copy of which is shown here as Fig. 1), the sage is shown pointing to one open scroll, while the rest of the set lies at his feet, loosely wrapped in such a binder. Others may be seen in the illustrations to the text, Figs. 1, 2 and 3.

The old man sits upon a mat made of leaves. Leaves were commonly associated with wandering Daoists, either as clothing or as matting, beds etc. Beyond the wine jar is a still larger jar, also with a ladle, which we may assume was for water. Behind him on an ornate table are a vase of chrysanthemums, setting the season as autumn, a persimmon and a brush pot on a stand. The brush pot contains a *ruyi* sceptre, what might be a handscroll, and two brushes.

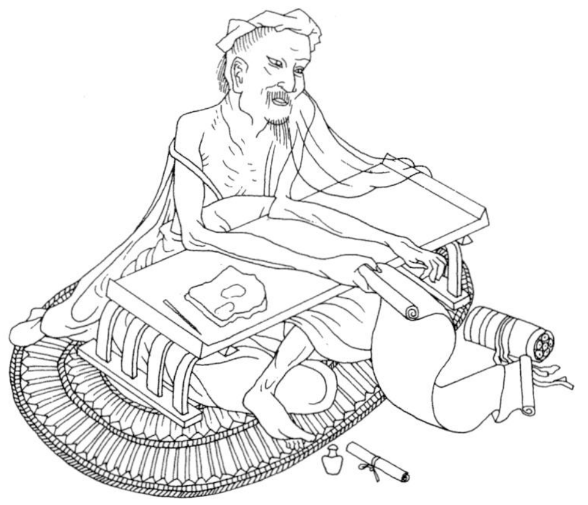

Fig. 1

76

Rock Sculpture

Stone, of pale beige colour; resembling a towering cliff with a series of plateaux, set on a wood stand carved to represent naturally gnarled wood, the base inscribed "On a winter's day of 1710 for my old friend Elou on his 70th birthday. I respectfully use this stone to celebrate his birthday and to wish him many years to come, inscribing these few words to serve as a permanent record. Recorded by Hengyun Shanmin ('Horizontal Clouds Denizen of the Mountains')".
1710.
Height including stand: 16.3 cm.

The stone carved low on one side with a collector's seal *Baiyi Shanfang Zhenzang* ('Precious Collection of the One Hundred and One Mountain Retreat').

石雕懸崖·王鴻緒製
清康熙庚寅(1710)，高連座16.3厘米

Hengyun Shanmin was the *hao* of Wang Hongxu (1645-1723), a native of Huating (also known as Yunjian or Songjian — also the native town of the metalsmith Hu Wenming, see no. 73), a poet and a celebrated calligrapher. He was a *jinshi* of 1673 and became a Hanlin academician. In a characteristically chequered career he served in various posts and was dismissed from them alternately, serving as an editor of the Ming history *(Ming Shi)* and as President of the Board of Works and later the Board of Revenue. During this time and later in his life he acted as a spy for the Kangxi Emperor, submitting secret reports on other officials, frequently with scandalous results.

Three different people are recorded as having a retreat called 'One Hundred and One Mountain Retreat', any of whom might be the collector who later added the collector's seal. One is Ying Shiliang (1784-1856), an artist from Haining in Zhejiang province. The other two are related, suggesting that the retreat remained in the family. Sun Shiyi (1720-1796) is the earliest possibility. A native of Hangzhou and from a poor family, he overcame considerable difficulties to finally become a *juren* in 1759 and a *jinshi* two years later in a special examination taken in Hangzhou while the Emperor was on his third tour of the Yangzi valley. He pursued, despite certain setbacks, a distinguished career in both the military and political arenas. He was granted a dukedom of which he was promptly deprived, and later became a baron of the third class. Posthumously he regained his dukedom and was canonized. Sun was an able and diligent official and a good calligrapher, thought to have been less corrupt than most of his colleagues.

His grandson Sun Zhun was the third possible inscriber of the collector's seal. He is chiefly remembered for an unfortunate incident in 1806 when he requested, on a plea of lameness, that his family's rank should pass instead to a cousin. The Jiaqing Emperor was very annoyed by this request and deprived him of it instead, pointing out that Sun Shiyi had not deserved his rank in the first place (based upon his close association with He Shen, the powerful Prime Minister of the Qianlong Emperor's later years who was disgraced by the Jiaqing Emperor).

The capacity of these strange stones to invoke images of immense grandeur is demonstrated by this example. It is easy to imagine it as a precipitous cliff overhanging a river, sheer sides rising for hundreds of feet above one's tiny boat as it drifts downstream — even the rippled surface of the wood stand comes to the aid of this transformation by resembling reflections in water.

75

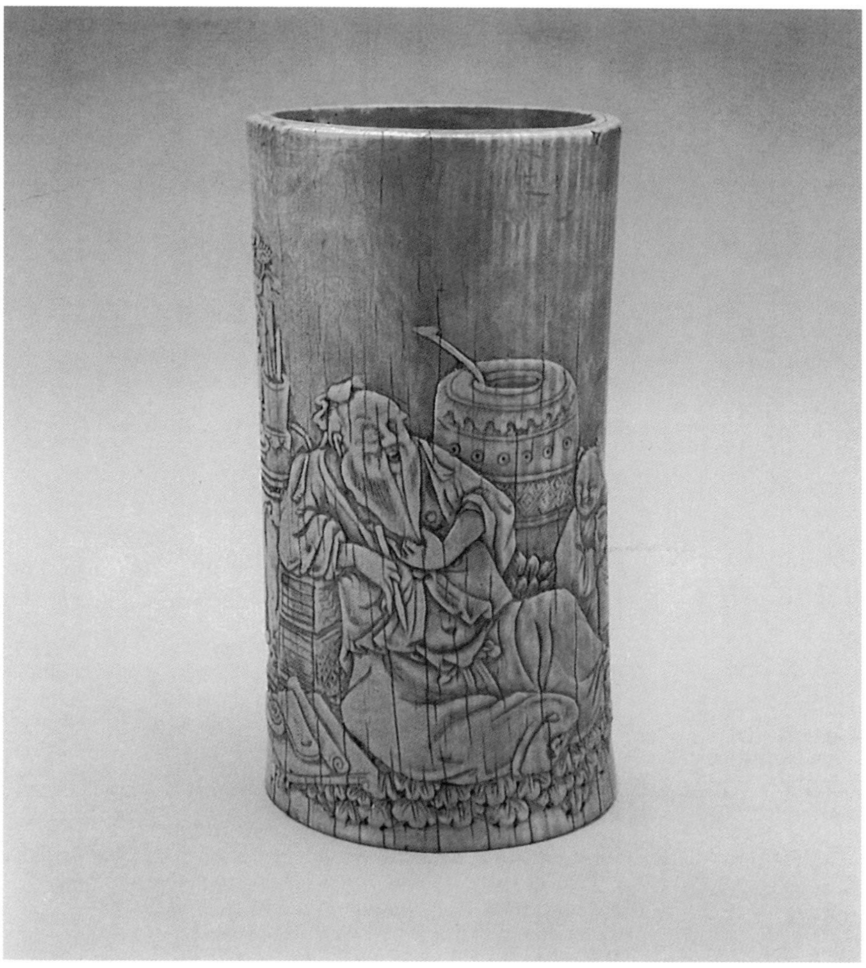

76

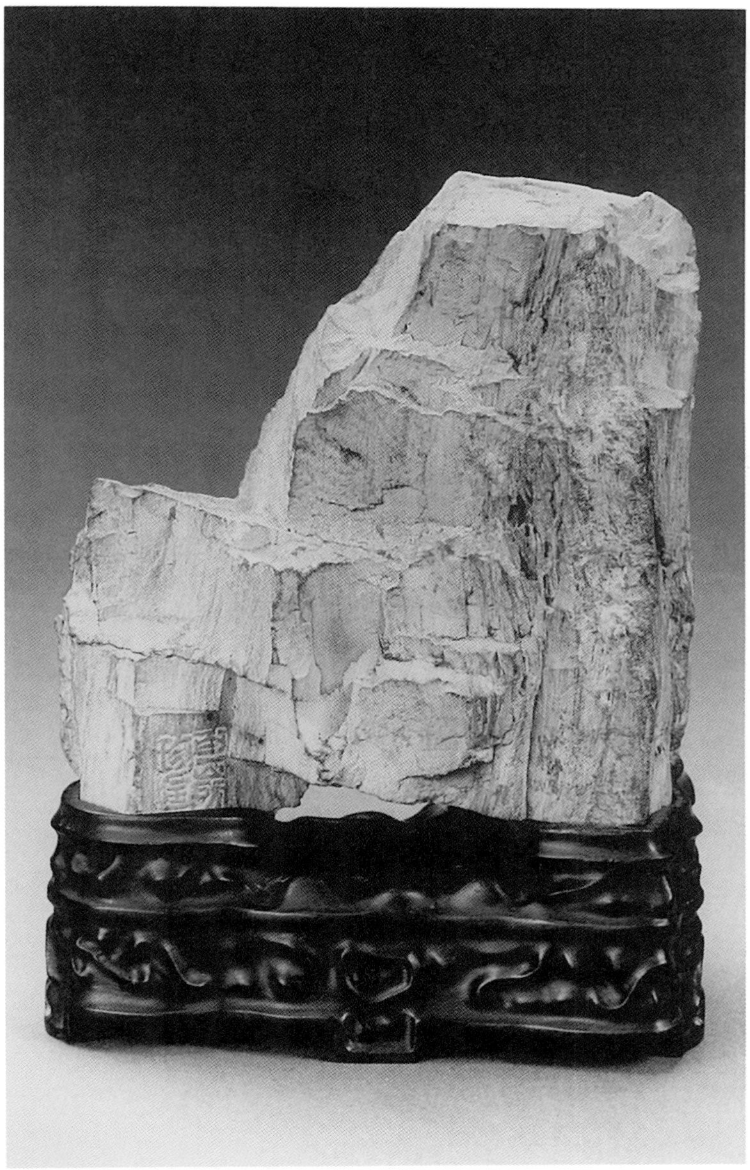

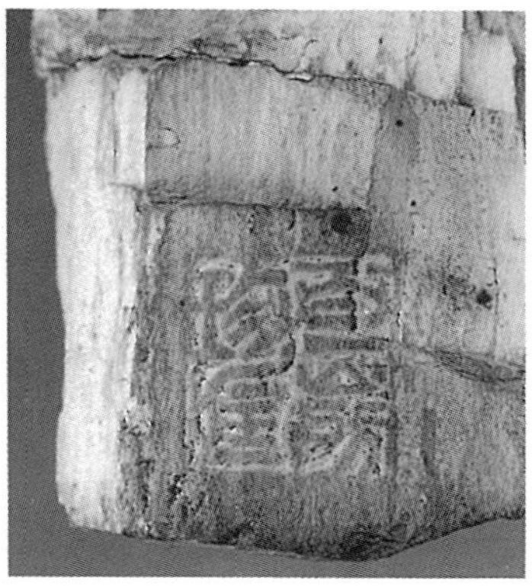

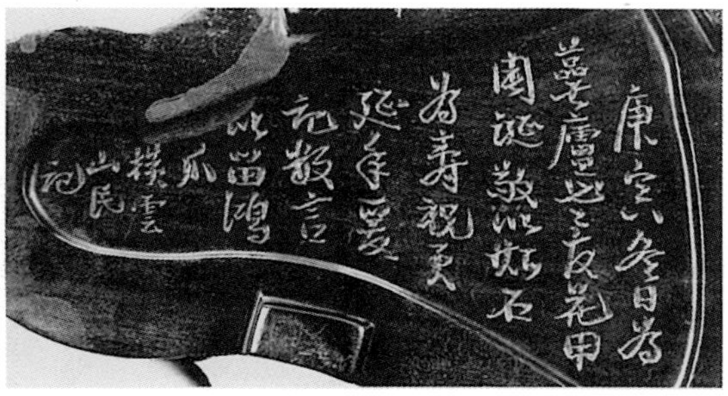

77

Display Stand

Wood, *jichimu* ('chicken-wing wood'), of beautifully figured golden and dark brown colouring; a display stand in the form of a miniature table.
Probably mid-Qing dynasty.
10.8 cm × 28 cm × 15.2 cm.
Published: *Wood From the Scholar's Table,* p.130, no. 81.

鷄翅木束腰附托泥器座
可能清中葉, 10.8×28×15.2厘米

The delights of well-figured wood grain are perhaps more obviously demonstrated here than in any piece in the exhibition. The entire stand seems to be alive with a swirling pattern of movement, as if incense smoke has been somehow locked into a solid form. Part of the joy of such pieces is the intriguing visual tension set up between the swirling movement of the patterned grain and the solid stability of the form.

The function of miniature furniture and stands of various kinds is discussed under no. 248.

The Chinese classify their tables in two broad groups: those where the sides come straight down from the top, and those waisted beneath the top. This stand is after a table of the latter type. The four legs rest on a support known as a *touni* ('mud support') which both strengthens the legs and gives the table broader support for a mud floor. In earlier days when stamped mud floors were common these mud supports served a very practical purpose, preventing the individual legs of heavy furniture from sinking into the floor.

78

'Grandfather and Grandson' Rock Sculpture

Stone, of the variety known as Lingbi, of glossy grey colour; two strangely shaped stones suggesting a grandfather and his grandson; the degree of cutting and shaping uncertain.
Set on a dark wood stand to simulate a natural root formation.
Perhaps Qing dynasty.
Overall height including stand: 26.7 cm.

靈璧石雕祖孫岩
可能清代, 高連座26.7厘米

There is no name carved on these stones; the title has simply been passed down with the piece. Perhaps there was an old tradition of having two stones together to represent this relationship, symbolizing the strong Confucian trait of respect for one's elders.

The sculptural balance between these two figures is delightful: the old man a little bent, his shoulders bowed, standing solidly, moving slowly; the youngster sharp and thrusting, full of energy simply achieved by placing him at a slight angle as if he is on the balls of his feet and about to race off.

Lingbi stones or rocks come from Lingbi county, Suzhou, in north Anhui province. In the 12th century *Yunlin Shipu* we are told that there was more than one variety, and that some were of considerable size and great elegance. They could be found in the shape of natural objects, such as clouds and vapours, sun and moon, or figures of the Buddha.[1] Lingbi stones are also sometimes referred to as *Qingshi* ('Qing stones') as some are found on Qingshan, a peak in the area. They are all excavated, and must be worked and polished: "The stone of Lingbi ... was scraped with iron blades, then brushed with a broom of bamboo or 'yellow bud' *(huangbei)* dipped in magnetite particles."[2] The late Ming connoisseur Wen Zhenheng stated that they were buried in the deep hills and had to be excavated. He particularly admired those with natural and curious shapes, such as cows, coiling *chi* dragons, etc.[3]

1. *Tu Wan's Stone Catalogue of Cloudy Forest,* p.50.
2. Ibid. p.30.
3. *Changwu Ji, juan* 3.

79

Water Vessel

Bamboo, of dark brown colour, carved as a miniature water vessel in the form of a section of pine trunk with twisting branches and clumps of needles emerging from it, the wood intricately patterned with knot-holes and bark, the base and lip carved to simulate weathered cross-sections of the trunk.
Probably 16th or 17th century.
Height: 4.5 cm.
Published: *Chinese Bamboo Carving,* Part I, p.141, no. 7 (where it is dated as late Ming).

竹雕松幹水丞
可能明或清初, 高4.5厘米

This is a water vessel for use in conjunction with a small ladle to deliver water to the inkstone (see no. 209). The period between the late Ming and early Qing dynasty seems to have been a time of great creativity for the bamboo carver. In various centres of production such as Jiading in Jiangsu province, the art flourished to such an extent that the standard was set for the entire Qing dynasty. The arts of this period managed to combine total mastery of medium with a rare artistic vision capable of investing a range of relatively small works of art with a spirit that belies their size.

The style of this piece is very close to a brush pot in the Nanjing Museum,[1] particularly in the treatment of the clusters of pine needles in overlapping groups, the individual needles radiating out from an off-centre smooth area. It is signed by Zhu He, and dated with a cyclical date corresponding to either 1511 or 1571.

1. See 'The Art of Chinese Bamboo Carving' by Wang Shixiang, in *Bamboo Carving of China,* p.19, fig. 5.

77

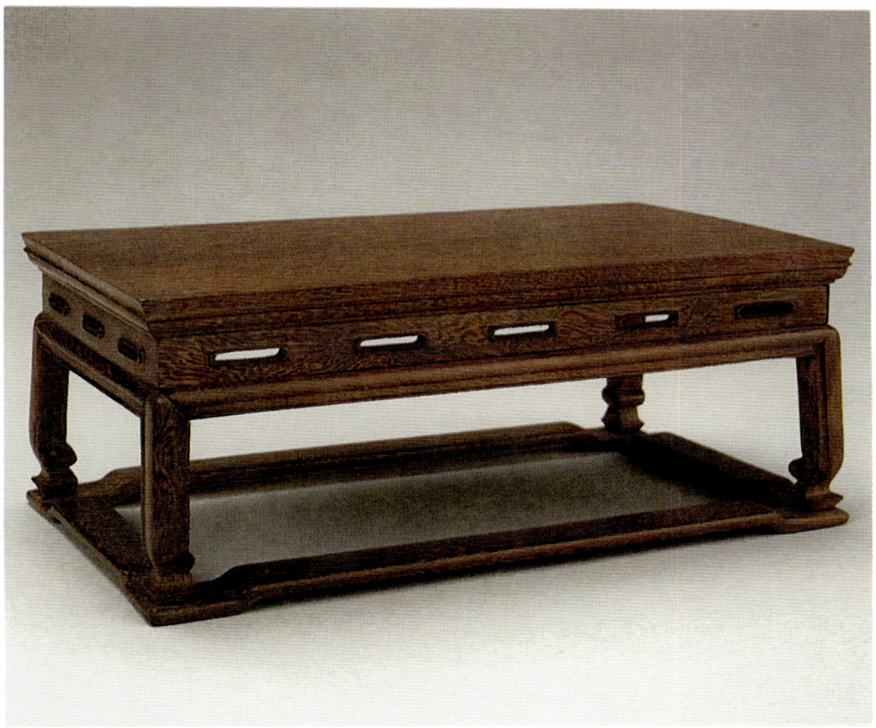

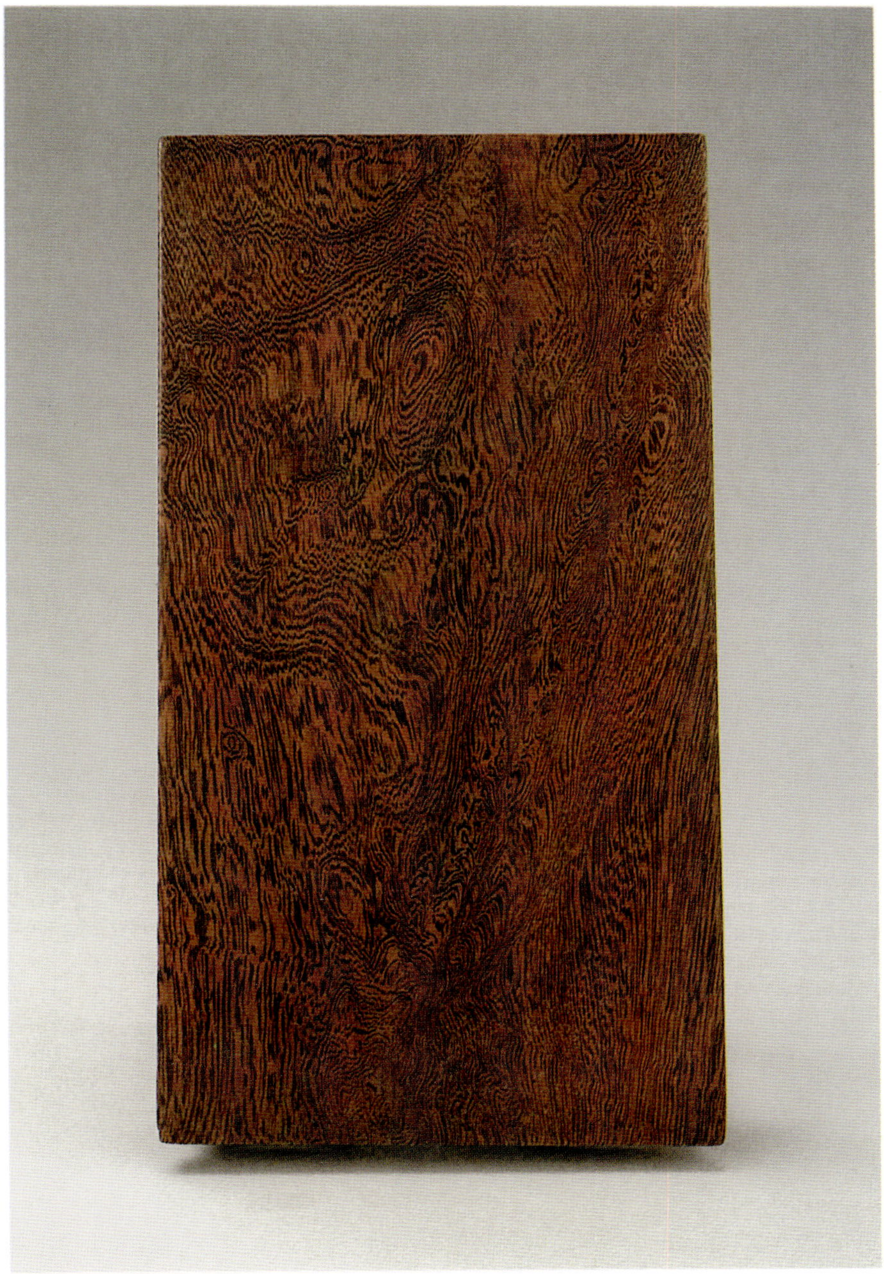

78

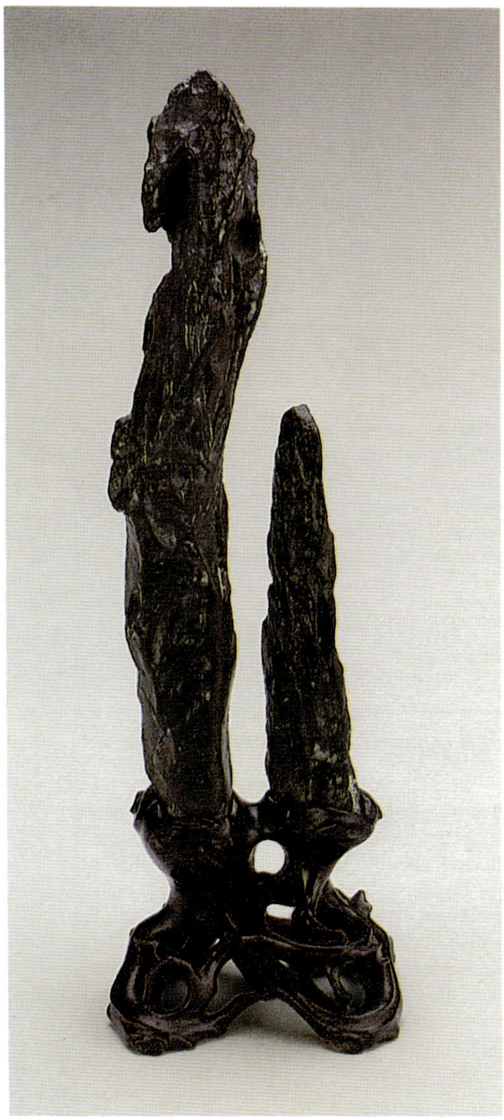

79

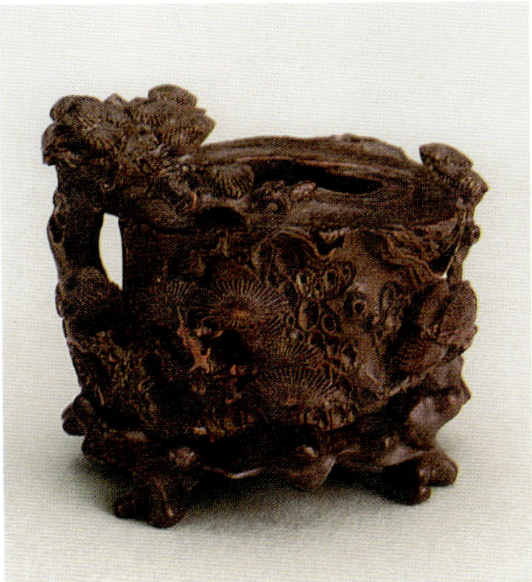

80

Paper Weight

Nephrite, of pale celadon grey-green colour with mottled russet brown markings; the natural form of the pebble carved in low relief and incised lines overall as a stylized phoenix, its plumage formalized, its legs and feet carved on the underside, along with some *ruyi*-shaped cloud-like markings; the bird holding in its beak a long branch of an imaginary plant with formalized peonies and acanthus leaves curling up around its head, over elaborate leaf-shaped head plumage and across its back; the surface well worn and smoothed through use.
Probably 17th century.
Length: 11.4 cm.

青玉雕鳳形紙鎮
可能十七世紀，長11.4厘米

A natural pebble of jade, such as those in the set exhibited as no. 154, makes an excellent paper weight, as do a variety of fully carved pieces of various suitable forms. It was not unnatural, therefore, for the carver to experiment with all stages in between. The wonderful sculpture of the cat in no. 70 shows a stage where material and subject seem to be equal partners, whereas here, the pebble form has been allowed to dominate to a much greater degree. What matters, ultimately, is the harmony of the partnership. This depends upon the artist's ability to completely control his medium and coax forth a wholly 'natural' looking sculpture. This is a piece difficult to put down once grasped, as the smoothness and comfort of the surface in the hand encourage its meditative role.

There is a group of jades (of which this is an excellent example) with very crisp, confident carving, often following pebble forms, and frequently of this range of jade colour, which are generally dated to the 17th century. We have seen other birds of this type; the feeling is that they may be late Ming but would not be unlikely for the Kangxi period as well. The scrolling imaginary peony with acanthus leaves portrayed was a popular Ming feature on jade carvings (see no. 70), which spilled over into the Qing.

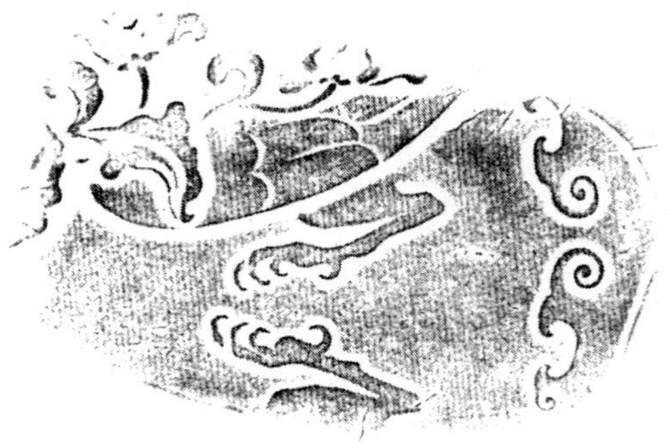

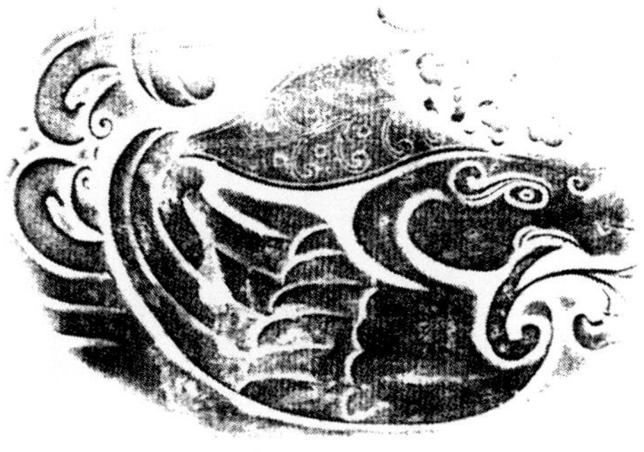

81

'*Yinyang*' Inkstone

Limestone conglomerate, of mottled greenish, grey-brown colour, enclosing at one end a fossilized shell which shows on one side as a white circle with a greenish, grey-brown eye surrounded by mottled brick-red and white crystalline material, and on the other side in the same colours, but excluding the brick-red colour, as a shape resembling a *yinyang* symbol; an inkstone of plain, rectangular form.
Probably Qing dynasty.
Inkstone: 3.7 cm × 22 cm × 11.55 cm.

Contained in a *hongmu* ('redwood') box, the plain, essentially rectangular form with a slightly domed top, and set on four small, pointed feet.
20th century.
Box: 5.8 cm × 23.4 cm × 12.8 cm.
Formerly in the Guo Zhongyi collection.

乾坤化石硯
可能清代，3.7×22×11.55厘米

The title of this inkstone, *Qiankun,* means the same as *yinyang,* the ancient symbol of the negative and positive aspects of nature. *Qian* and *kun* are the names of two of the eight trigrams which represent male and female and therefore stand for *Yinyang.* The title was given to the stone by Guo Zhongyi and is inscribed on a separate piece of paper enclosed in the box.

There is some controversy over how to classify this stone. It has in the past been considered a Duan stone, but various experts have dismissed it as of little interest. One of the determining characteristics of the great inkstone materials is that they grind ink well: they are rough enough to grind ink, while being smooth enough not to damage the brush when it is being loaded; they are hard enough for the job, but soft enough to allow a minute amount of surface material to be mixed into the ink. Once these essential qualities are established, visual characteristics take over to determine the finest stones. This particular type of limestone is smoother than the Duan variety and is not quite as efficient in its primary role, although it has much in common with Duan stone: both are limestones and both are frequently found bearing various fossils. However, it is far more suitable than jade, crystal and some other materials of which inkstones are made, so it is certainly adequate. It is a marvellous and mysterious piece of stone bearing a natural image of perhaps the most potent symbol of the Chinese culture. In the face of this, its classification as a stone within the canons of connoisseurship would seem a somewhat minor concern.

82

Wrist Rest

Bamboo, of brown colour, with a coating on the outside of reddish-brown, translucent lacquer; a wrist rest, the natural diagonally opposed nodes forming the only decoration.
Perhaps late Ming or first half of the Qing dynasty.
Length: 21.9 cm. Maximum width: 7.8 cm.

斜節漆竹臂擱
可能晚明或清初，長21.9厘米，寬7.8厘米

The influential minority had a particular genius for adopting the natural forms of nature as works of art, allowing them to speak for themselves with a minimum of tampering. Here a strangely shaped piece of bamboo, a symbol of integrity and therefore of the scholar (see no. 67), which grows naturally with alternating nodes diagonally opposed has been cut to shape and covered with a thin layer of lacquer. The resulting simple abstraction of the design, combined with the softness of a well-mellowed surface, speaks eloquently of the sophistication of the late Ming scholar. (For a discussion on the wrist rest and its development, see no. 216.)

80

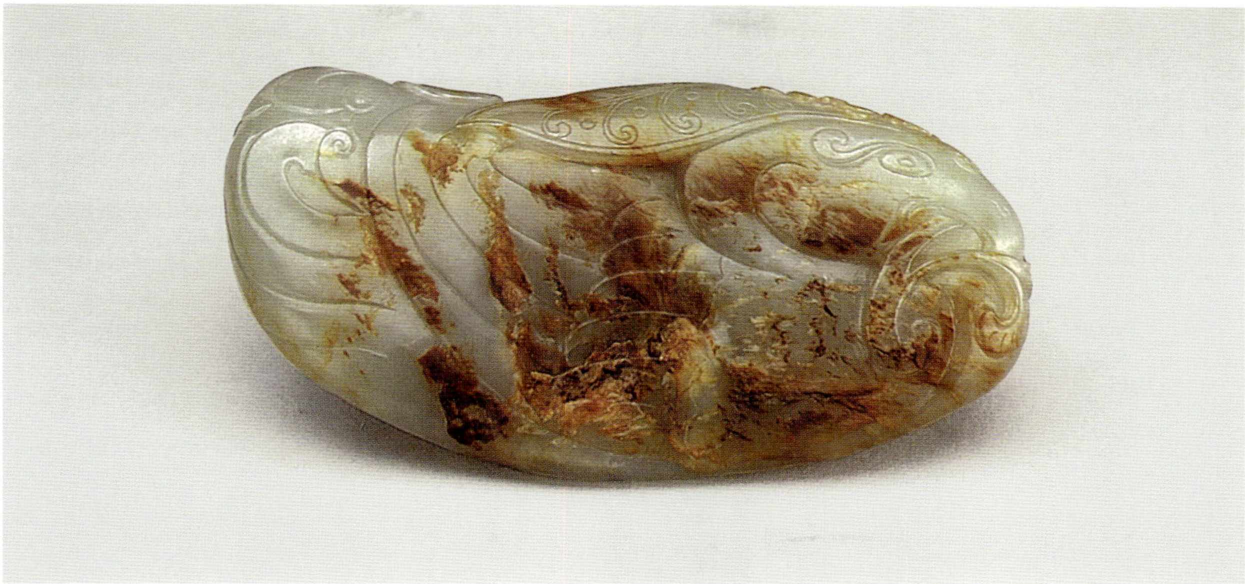

81

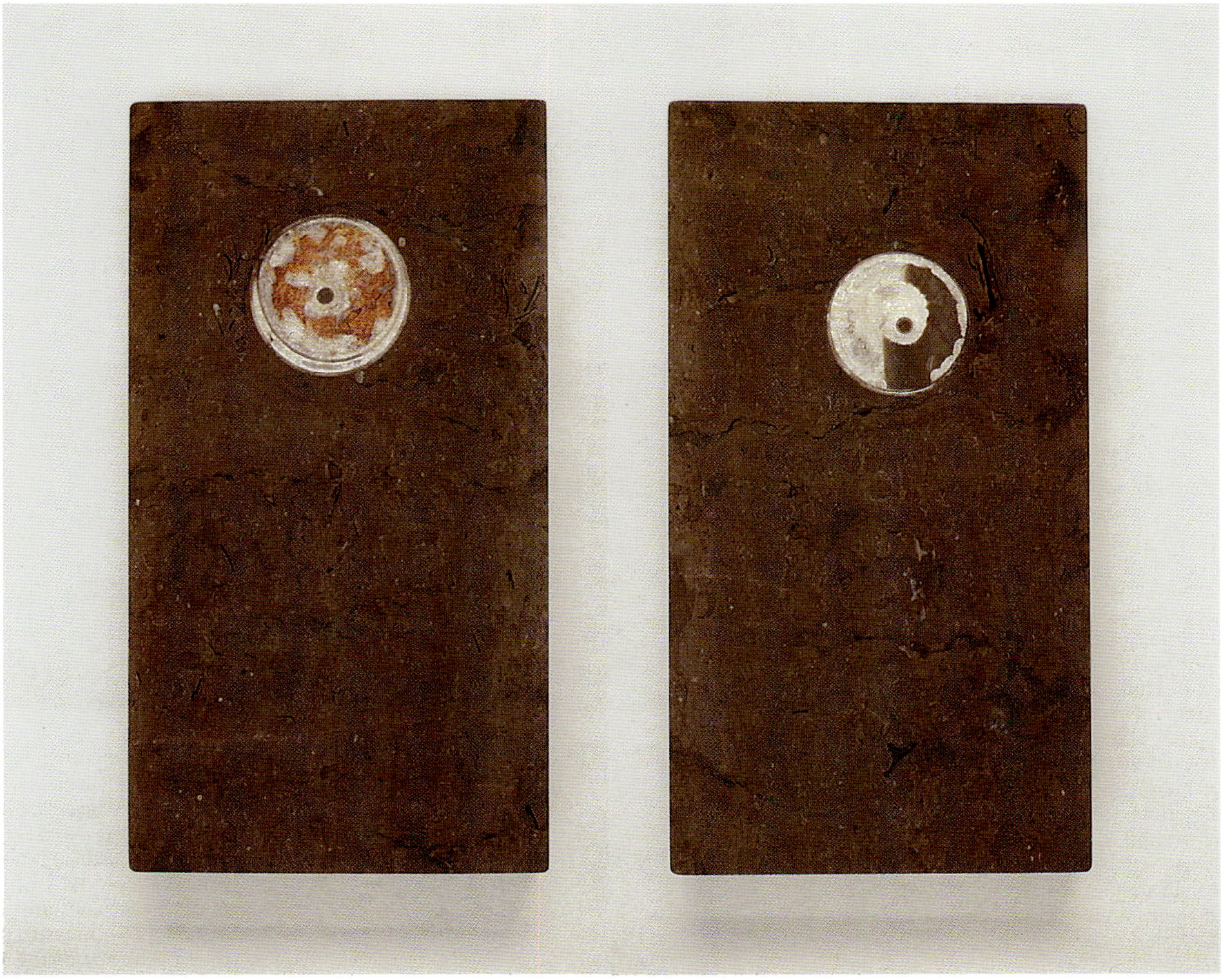

82

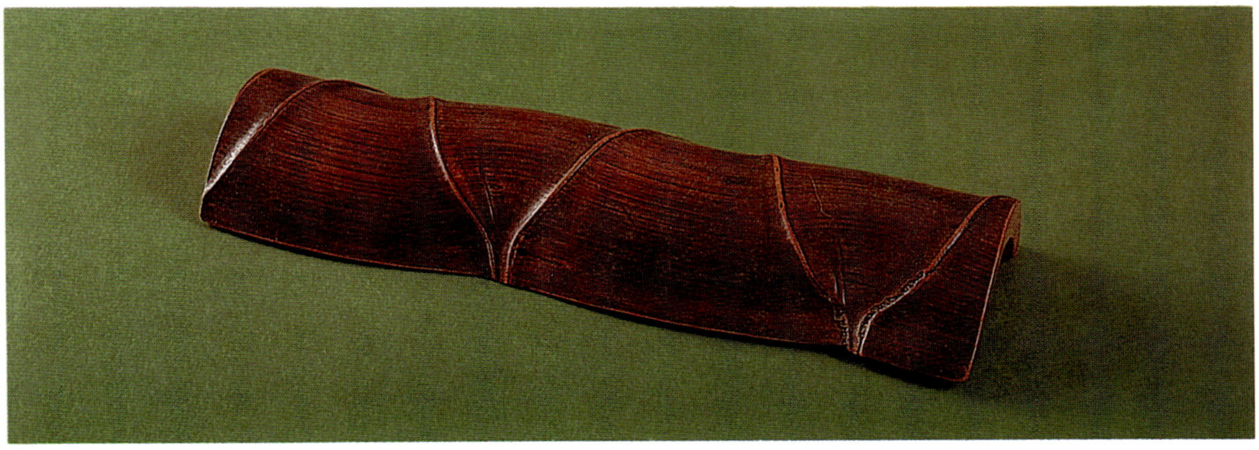

83

Covered Box

Lu Zigang

Jade of even, white colour; compressed globular form carved in low relief with a design of flowering narcissus, starting at the foot and covering the side and top of the box; the slightly recessed foot inscribed in seal script *Jiaqing xinyou Lu Zigang zhi* ('made by Lu Zigang in the *xinyou* year of the Jiaqing period [1561].
1561.
Height: 2.1 cm. Diameter: 4.5 cm.
Published: *Chinese Jade Throughout the Ages,* no. 386; *Chinese Jades from Han to Ch'ing,* no. 114.

白玉雕水仙蓋盒•陸子岡製
明嘉靖辛酉(1561),高2.1厘米,直徑4.5厘米

Lu Zigang was a famous jade carver, a native of Taicang in the Suzhou area in Jiangsu province, active during the latter part of the 16th century. In the *Gubugu Lu* by the Ming scholar Wang Shizhen (1526-1590) his works are mentioned (along with those of the rhinoceros horn carver Bao Tiancheng and the silversmith Zhu Bishan) as having doubled in value, repeating a rumour that their works were being collected inside the palace.[1] The *Taicang Zhi* ('Records of Taicang') notes under local products, jade carving that Lu Zigang worked (or died) 50 years previously, and that since then no others had equalled his skills.[2] Lu was also the subject of a poem by the Ming artist Xu Wei (1521-1593); and the scholar Chen Jiru (1558-1639) in a publication of 1595 mentions seeing a white jade drinking vessel, the cover connected to the handle with an integral chain of thirteen links, that was made by Lu.[3] This evidence, in combination with the date on this box, suggests a period of activity for him of the second half of the 16th century.

Lu was reputed to have finished his works with a diamond knife, which is described in the *Haiwai Shizhou Zhi*[4] while other jade carvers used the traditional methods of abrasives and mechanical tools. His name appears on a very large number of 17th century and later works, but pieces sensibly attributable to his hand are extremely rare. James Watt believes that of the thousands of pieces which bear his signature, this small box is deserving of the most serious consideration as a genuine work.[5] Lu Zigang was also supposed to be a good painter and was particularly well known for his rendering of narcissus in jade carving.[6]

Two cups are known bearing Lu's signature, both of which are archaistic.[7] Even if Lu did not actually carve the second piece it is likely to represent his style more closely than a host of later, Qing works bearing his name. Both of these cups represent the sort of archaism that was typical of the late Ming period, and which was expressed in the works arising out of the close association between the literati and craftsmen of the Jiangnan area (see a discussion of this in relation to the bronzemaker Hu Wenming, no. 73 and no. 103). We believe that both of these cups should also be given serious consideration. The difference in style between this box and cover and the cups is reasonably explained by the fact that the former is a purely late Ming design and style, whereas the latter are archaistic reinterpretations of Han style.

Considering Lu's fame and the relatively small number of works attributable to his hand it is likely that he produced a large number of unsigned works, but the fact that any are signed is an indication of the partnership which had evolved between the influential minority and the craftsmen they patronized. Jade carvers from earlier times are practically never identified either in their works or in literary records.

1. *Gugong Shuangyue Kan, juan* 17, no. 1.
2. Volume 5, quoted in ibid.
3. Ibid.
4. Ibid.
5. *Chinese Jades from Han to Ch'ing,* p.138, no. 114.
6. Ibid.
7. One from the Bull collection, illustrated in *Chinese Jade Throughout the Ages,* no. 385, and the other excavated from a 17th century tomb in Beijing and illustrated in *Wenwu,* 1963, no. 1, p.50, fig. 18.

84

Brush Pot

Zhou Bin

Soapstone, of mottled, opaque honey brown colour, with darker veining; carved as a brush pot of cylindrical form set on three shallow feet; the exterior carved with a continuous design in low relief of a seated scholar/sage, the branches of a tree overhanging him as he sits beside a strange rock formation, a jar of wine and a cup by his side; all set against a patterned ground of formalized floral hexagons; signed in relief *Zhou Bin* in regular script with seal, also in relief, *Shangjun* in negative seal script; the base with a recessed circular central medallion with a low relief *chi* dragon holding in its mouth a spray of fungus, all set against a minutely incised formalized wave ground.
Fujian, probably second half of the 17th century.
Height: 11.5 cm. Diameter of mouth: 8.9 cm.
Formerly in the Spencer Churchill collection, Northwick Park.

石雕陶淵明像筆筒•周彬製
可能十七世紀下半葉,高11.5厘米,
口直徑8.9厘米

The balance of expression between patron and artist is infinitely variable, and local exigencies of geography and chronology — and indeed how a particular medium is viewed at a particular time — are crucial. In Yuan China, in the art of painting, to stand aloof from patronage was a symbol of lofty expression — the act itself was part of the artistic communication. In Tang China, before the influential minority had become significantly involved in personal creative expression outside of music, poetry, calligraphy and, to a degree, painting, other arts were considered crafts, and a clearer distinction existed between patron and craftsman. In late Ming Jiangnan and Fujian (among other places) no such clear distinction could be made.

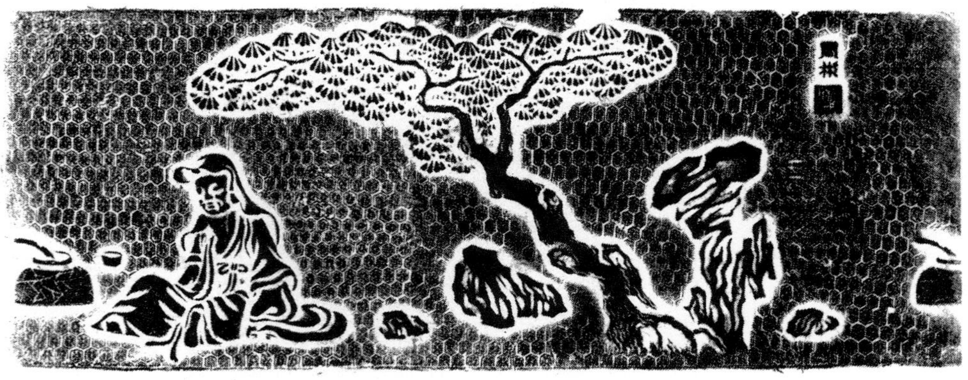

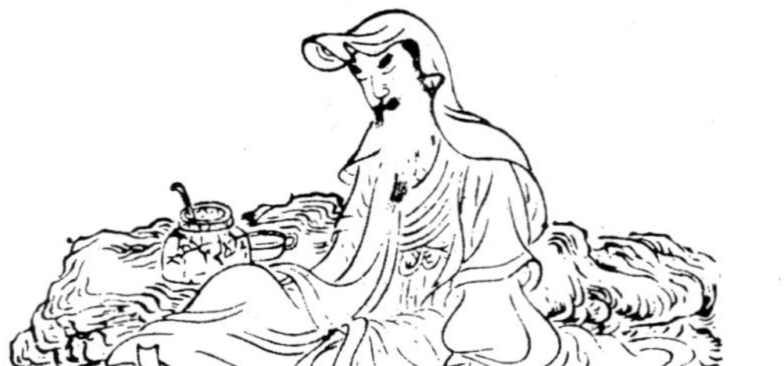

Fig. 1

There can be no question about the source of the design for this brush pot, and it raises some interesting problems. In 1651 the artist Chen Hongshou completed a series of designs for playing cards used in a drinking game, which were printed in 1653 in a woodblock edition. The figure, and the crackled wine jar and cup, are taken directly from one of these (see Fig. 1), although the setting has been changed.[1] Therefore we may be certain that this brush pot does not pre-date 1653. However, if the Quasha figure (see no. 43) which is dated 1627 is genuine, then Zhou had enjoyed more than a quarter of a century of refinement of his skills between the two pieces, and the quality of this brushpot does not match Zhou's mature works as represented by the seated *luohan* of no. 44 and the seals of nos. 43 and 164. It is sculpturally good, but the sheer technical skill in finishing and polishing that we expect of Zhou Bin at his mature best is missing. Nor is the signature, particularly in the seal script writing of the characters *Shangjun,* commensurate with his mature work. Yet it is clearly old: the style is typical of the late Ming or early Qing period, and its surface patination and wear are commensurate with long usage.

In the absence of the Quasha figure it would be reasonable to assume that this is a work of Zhou's early years, showing considerable promise, but without the perfect technical control he was to achieve later. We would then be justified in dating his period of activity to the second half of the 17th century. If, however, the Quasha figure is genuine then the conclusion is that this brushpot is an early work in the style of Zhou Bin. This is quite possible as we know that Lu Dong, the 19th century lacquer artist, was copied in his own time (see no. 63). Chen Hongshou was, by the time of his death, a very famous artist, and the publication of his drinking cards would certainly have led to the instant borrowing into other fields of art. We may be reasonably sure that this brush pot is a late 17th century carving.

For biographical details of Zhou Bin, see no. 43.

1. See *Chinese Rare Books in American Collections,* p.116, no. 36 for the edition, and pl. 36a for the illustration of the figure.

83

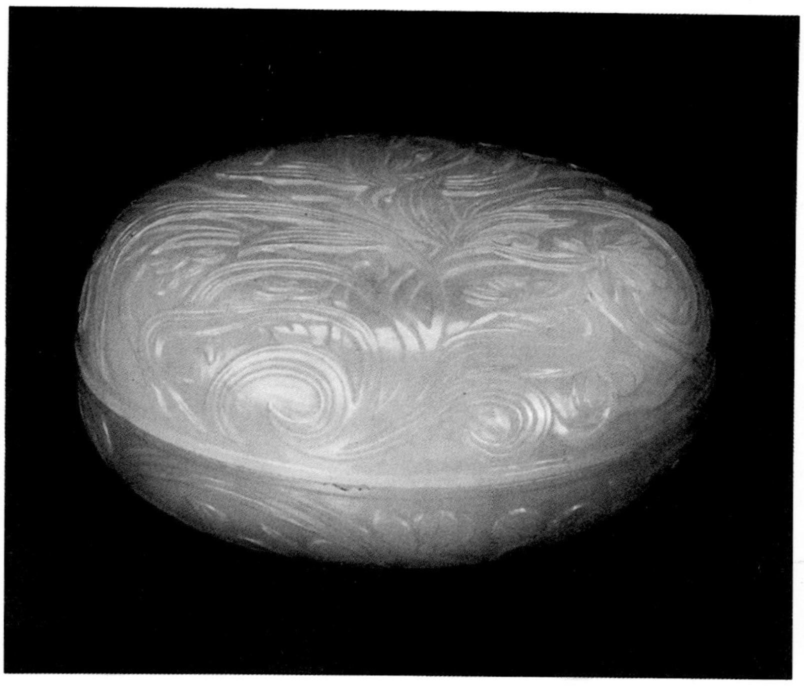

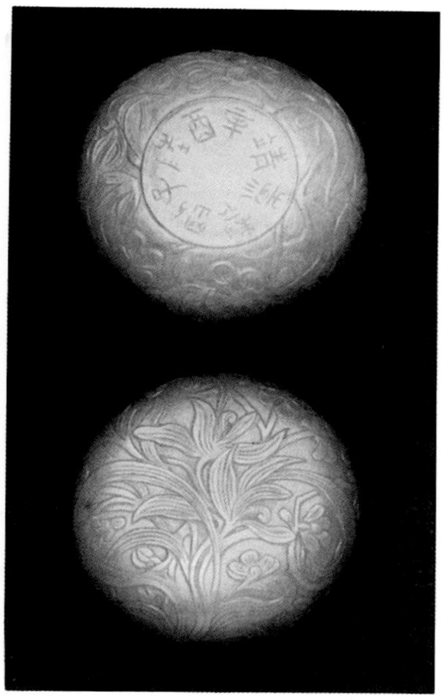

84

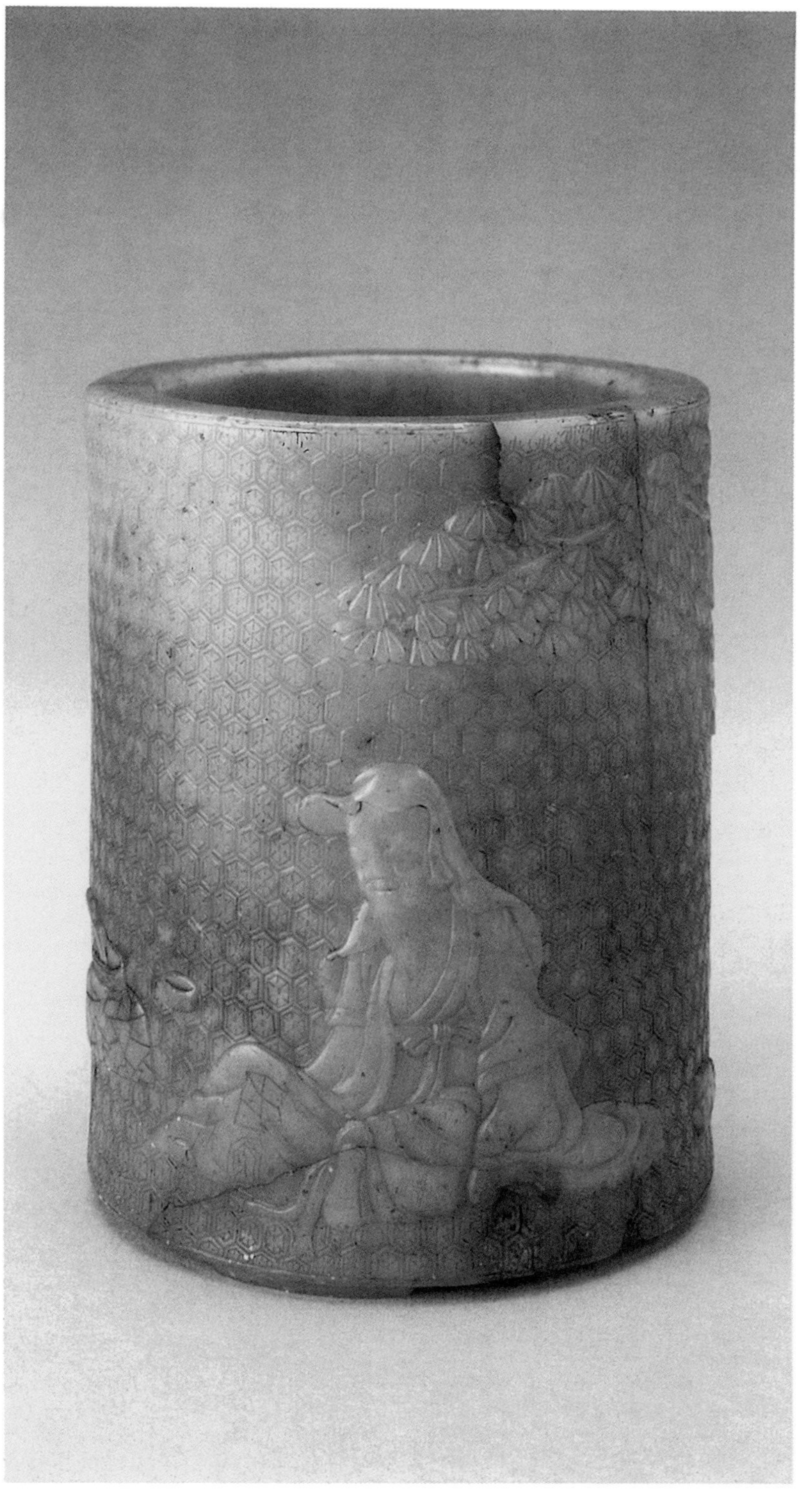

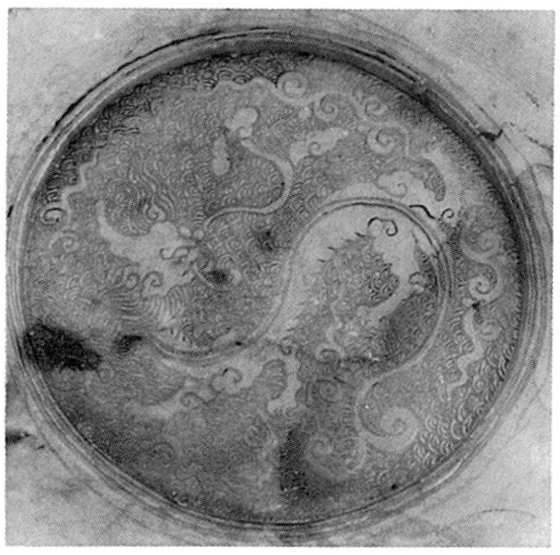

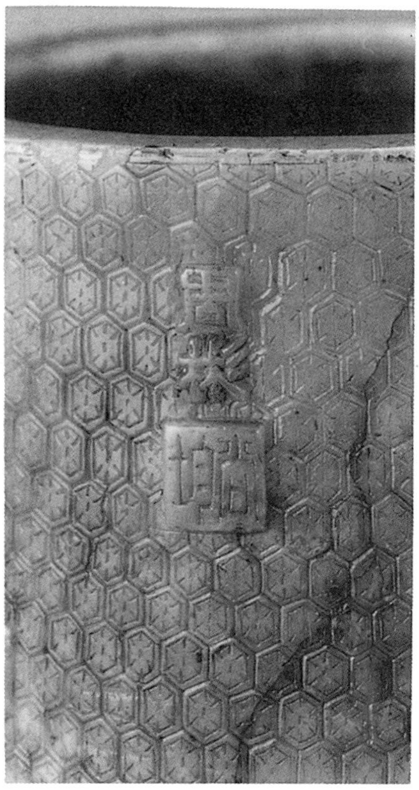

85

Snuff Bottle

Lu Dong

Lacquer, presumably on wood; the lacquer of dark olive-green colour; a snuff bottle of flattened ovoid shape, one side decorated with two fish swimming beneath an overhanging willow; the reverse with a cricket and a spray of grass, with a small seal in the lower left corner *Kuisheng* in positive seal script; the shoulders with *taotie* masks with rings in their mouths in low relief.
Yangzhou, 1800-1850.
Height excluding stopper: 6.85 cm.

木胎髹漆畫蟲魚鼻煙壺•盧棟製
清(1800-1850), 高(不連蓋)6.85厘米

For biographical details of Lu Dong, and a discussion on his relationship with the literati and his standing as an artist, see nos. 63 and 64.

By the first half of the 19th century, when Lu Dong was active, snuff-taking had spread from its earliest phase in China (centred around the Court at Beijing) to become a nationwide habit (see no. 47 for further details of the history of snuff-taking). A small group of snuff bottles is known by Lu Dong, all in restrained taste and decorated with designs specifically suited to the scholars who were clearly his patrons, suggesting that he was frequently commissioned to make snuff bottles, or that he made them speculatively because of the demand. The *taotie* mask handles in this case are clearly an afterthought. They are in low relief only because the original surface of the lacquer has been carved back to accommodate them. It is possible that Lu Dong himself added them, but their relative crudeness suggests that they may have been added by a later carver who decided to 'gild the lily'.

86

Wrist Rest

Wood, *qiu* (catalpa), of pale brown colour with a fine wavy grain, with inlaid ivory; carved as a wrist rest in the form of a *qin,* the studs inlaid in ivory; carved with a poetic couplet in draft script: "Clouds and rocks do not contend; the brook protests its passage past the rocks" followed by the seal *Lanshi* ('Orchid Stone') in negative seal script, the seal filled with the remains of red pigment.
Mid-Qing dynasty
Length: 30.5 cm.

楸木雕古琴式刻銘臂擱•蘭石銘
清中葉, 長30.5厘米

Lanshi was the *hao* of Guo Shangxian (*zi:* Yuankai, other *hao:* Boyi; hall names: Fangjian Guan; Zengmo An — 1785-1833), a native of Putian, Fujian province. He was a *juren* of 1807 and a *jinshi* of 1809; a compiler of the Hanlin Academy, he served officially as an education director and examiner in several provinces. He was known as a painter of orchids and rocks (hence his *hao*), and as a seal carver, but it was as a calligrapher that he was best known, in which field he was regarded by his contemporaries as the equal of Zhao Mengfu of the Yuan dynasty and Dong Qichang of the late Ming. Another *qin*-shaped wrist rest is published by Paul Moss, also inscribed with his calligraphy and the same seal.[1]

It was common practice for the works of famous calligraphers to be inscribed on wrist rests and other objects. The original would be copied faithfully onto the object, and the original signatures or seals would accompany it. Although occasionally a seal carver might inscribe his own calligraphy, it was more usual for a usually anonymous craftsman to do so. This practice was part of the complex association between the influential minority as artists and patrons and the craftsmen and artists who served them and sometimes joined them.

The *qin* form, miniaturized and minus its strings and tuning pegs, makes an ideal wrist rest and several are known in both wood and bamboo. In this case the shape of the *qin* has been quite faithfully copied, although an elegant, very slight 'S'-shaped curve has been applied to its length. While giving the object a subtle intrigue of form, this would have been unsuitable for the flat string-profile of the real instrument. The rest has a number of ink stains on it.

1. *Documentary Chinese Works of Art in Scholars' Taste,* p.162, no. 104.

87

Speckled Toad

Stone, of the variety known as 'puddingstone' with various coloured pebbles of quartz in a grey-beige matrix; carved in the form of a squatting toad, its head turned balefully to one side, the back carved overall with raised lumps.
Qing dynasty.
Height: 4.1 cm. Length: 7 cm.

礫石雕蟾蜍
清代, 高4.1厘米, 長7厘米

The overwhelming majority of works such as this are unsigned, undated, and without any indication of the identity of a patron. We must resort to guesswork based rather tenuously on function, or upon independent literary records, if we are to learn more about the relationship between patron and craftsman/artist. This delightful toad, making excellent use of the natural markings in the material, represents a group of anonymous works made largely, although not at all exclusively, for the scholar class.

The Chinese seemed to have used two distinct forms of so-called 'puddingstone': a soft, limestone conglomerate, often containing the skeletal fossilized remains of coral and other marine creatures, and used since at least the Tang dynasty (see no. 219) and this material, which is much harder, and consists of pebbles of quartz in a siliceous matrix. Also known as 'Hertfordshire' puddingstone, this latter material may well have been imported into China, along with large quantities of other hardstones during the Qing dynasty. In any case, we know of no examples of this material used in China which can definitely be dated to a period prior to the Qing dynasty.

Small sculptures of toads of this type, probably used as paper weights but possibly intended as independent sculptures, are known in jade dating from as early as the Ming dynasty. The toad covered with other creatures (no. 206) is perhaps even earlier. This example, which is fatter than the usual jade version, is most likely to date from the mid- to late Qing period.

85

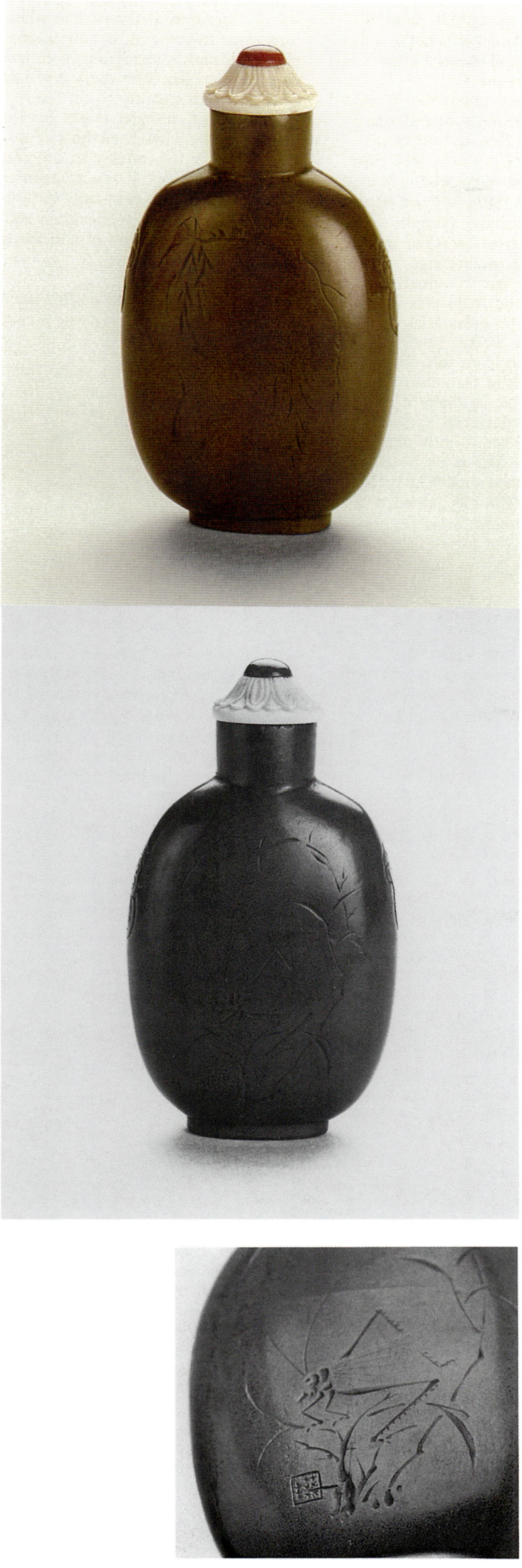

86

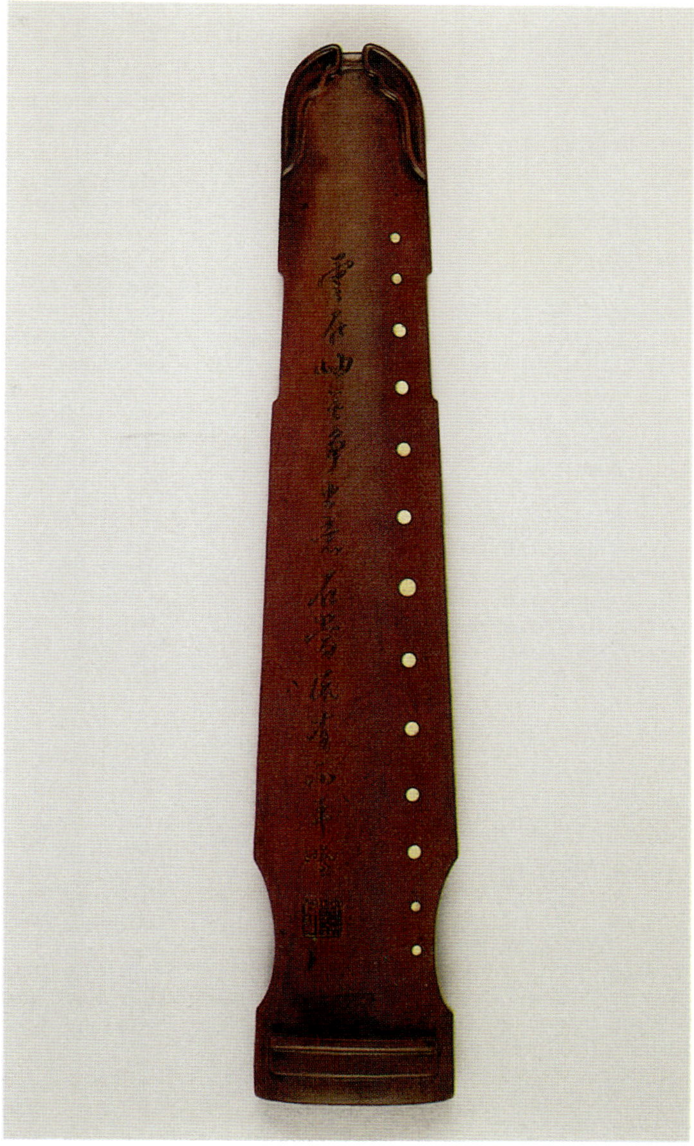

87

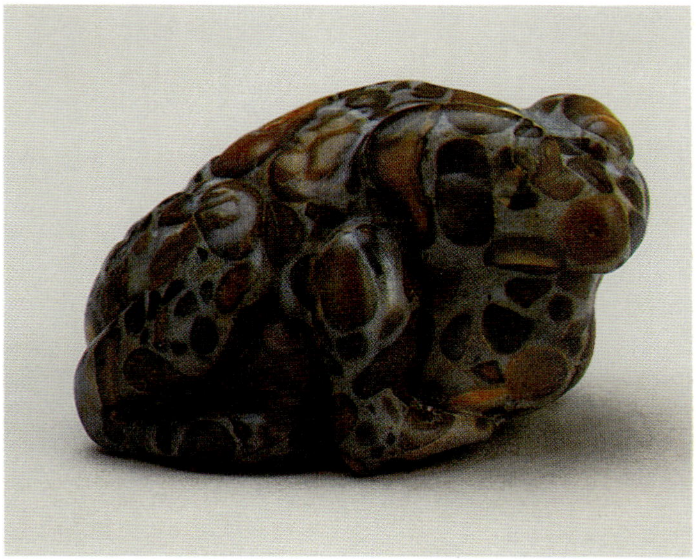

88

'Reclining Sage' Stone

Stone, of soft material made up of layers of alternating beige and dark grey colours; the face of the irregular form with a natural-looking design of an old man seated, reclining against a rocky outcrop, with an incense burner at his feet; the upper surface covered with a lacquer coating.
Perhaps Song dynasty or later.
11.8 cm × 12.2 cm × 2.8 cm.

漆面石雕臥老圖
可能宋或元，11.8×12.2×2.8厘米

The stone here is perhaps Dali marble, from Yunnan province, which was also used for the making of screens and furniture (see no. 22). The 12th century *Yunlin Shipu* mentions in several contexts stones which are valued for their natural designs. Su Shi said of the patterns on his treasured agates, "Even though an artist might aim to delineate and depict them, he would be unable to achieve this".[1] In the same work a stone from Zhuyangxian, Guozhou in western Henan province is discussed as follows: "White enclosures in a dark violet matrix, moon-shaped, tortoise-shaped, or toad-shaped. Local artisans perfect these forms with chemicals and tools... Another variety shows mountain peaks and valleys on a pale yellow background. Small pieces are often shaped into figurines and it is also suitable for palettes [inkstones] and for plaques displayed like paintings on taborets. The natives say the designs are caused by seepage of water."[2] Although this stone does not seem to fit the colour range of Guo stone, the reference demonstrates the value placed on natural designs and mentions the methods used to enhance them.

Strangely marked stones and fantastic rocks frequently involved a particularly interesting relationship between the influential minority and craftsmen. The craftsmen would take their stones and strangely shaped rocks from a variety of sources and either leave them in their natural state if it was considered suitable (simple cleaning and polishing their surfaces) or more often alter them by cutting, patinating, smoothing etc. However, what was finally important in such stones and rocks was that they meant something to the influential minority, the patrons. The worker in charge of production therefore had to learn to understand that aesthetic so that he could respond to it — and eventually was even able to shape it.

That this stone is of considerable age is certain, but otherwise to place it chronologically is pure guesswork. A Song date is proposed here simply because it represents a type which from Tu Wan's catalogue we know was valued at that time, and because of its obvious antiquity. However it could equally have been the product of several centuries later, or indeed earlier. It may well have served as a paper weight, and has obviously been very much handled and not, apparently, given the benefit of a stand. The figure of the old man, although well worn and less distinct now perhaps than when it was first formed or discovered, is nonetheless still powerful, and is mysteriously enhanced by the wear of the ages. The coating of lacquer, which adds a certain nobility to the overall effect with its fine, glossy texture, might have been added to protect the surface of the soft stone from wearing away too quickly in use and thus may be a later addition. It is also distinctly possible that the figure was originally entirely contrived out of a paler layer in the stone and simply appears natural because of considerable wear prior to being lacquered.

1. *Tu Wan's Stone Catalogue of Cloudy Mountain,* p.10.
2. Ibid. pp.69-70.

89

Water Vessel

Nephrite, of pale greyish-green colour, with extensive grey-brown markings and some calcification; a water vessel, of rounded rectangular form, with flared sides, the exterior decorated with three dragons (one five-clawed and two three-clawed) chasing a flaming pearl amid clouds and above swirling waves, which cover the underside with a dynamic pattern of cresting breakers and whirling vortices; the three dragons' heads and the pearl forming a raised knob at each corner so that the vessel can also act as a brush rest.
Early Ming dynasty, probably first half of the 15th century.
Height: 5.5 cm. Length: 15.8 cm.

The interior is carved with incised clouds which partly disguise crack-like flaws in the stone; the style and quality appear to be inconsistent with the rest of the carving raising the possibility that they were added later to give the appearance of the flaws having been used creatively in the original carving.
Published: *Jade of the East,* p.106; *Chinese Jades from Han to Ch'ing,* pp.134-135, no. 111.

玉雕龍戲珠筆洗
明初，可能十五世紀上半葉，高5.5厘米，長15.8厘米

This magnificent vessel was discussed by James Watt in the above-mentioned catalogue, where he dates it for a number of reasons to the 15th century. A feature he did not mention, but which strengthens his opinion on dating, is the use of a combination of three- and five-clawed dragons. Imperial ceramics of the first half of the 15th century and those that copy them in the early 18th century have this combination, which is otherwise rather unusual. This also suggests that the vessel is imperial, which would not be surprising, as it is based upon a massive wine vessel with the same subject of the Yuan dynasty, now in the Round Fort, Beijing and illustrated by Watt[1] — almost certainly the one mentioned by Yuan writers as one of the wonders of the Mongol Court at Beijing. The wine vessel was completed under the reign of Kublai Khan in 1265. It must have been known to the early Ming Court as the piece appears to have been in Beijing ever since[2] and it doubtless inspired a number of later jade carvings.

The Court as patron exerted a major influence on the arts of China over the centuries. But equally the Emperor, in so far as he was interested in the high arts at all, was also heavily swayed by the aesthetic of the persuasive minority. Under the most enlightened rulers the imperial and scholarly aesthetic sometimes became one and the same.

1. *Chinese Jades from Han to Ch'ing,* p.22.
2. See *Chinese Jade Carving,* pp.75-78 for its history, acquisition and inscription by the Qianlong Emperor.

90

Inkstone

Porcelain, decorated in underglaze cobalt blue on a white ground; an inkstone of flattened drum shape, the bulging sides painted with four foliate panels of wonderfully foolish-looking mythical beasts in a setting with formalized waves, reserved in a patterned ground of lozenge-shaped formalized floral motifs; the recessed and concave upper surface left unglazed, with the exception of a foliate water-pool which is glazed; the deeply recessed base inscribed *Da Ming Longqing nianzhi* ('made in the Longqing period of the Great Ming dynasty') in regular script, within a double circle in underglaze blue on a bluish-white ground; the unglazed biscuit at the foot edged with a distinctly salmon-pink colour where the iron in the porcelain has oxidized at the surface.
Imperial kilns, Jingdezhen.
Longqing period.
Height: 4.2 cm. Diameter: 13.6 cm.

青花異獸圖瓷硯•大明隆慶年製銘
明隆慶(1567-1572)，高4.2厘米，直徑13.6厘米

The Court was patron for works produced all over China, and in certain cases established imperial production lines far from the Court. One of the largest of these was maintained throughout the Ming and Qing periods at Jingdezhen, the porcelain metropolis in Jiangxi province, where vast quantities of ceramics were produced ranging from those of specific interest or for the direct use of the emperor and his immediate family, to a wide range of wares for numerous official establishments, temples, palaces and so on. The output of these kilns has been so often discussed elsewhere that we have largely excluded their wares from this exhibition, choosing only one or two examples to represent an immense output.

Imperial inkstones made of porcelain are extremely rare, as are imperially marked Longqing wares. Although the cobalt has diffused considerably into the glaze, making for rather fuzzy decoration, the creatures depicted are charming. The surface is naturally and extensively worn from use, with scratches and flaws in the water-pool stained with ink. It has obviously been put to good service since the 16th century.

88

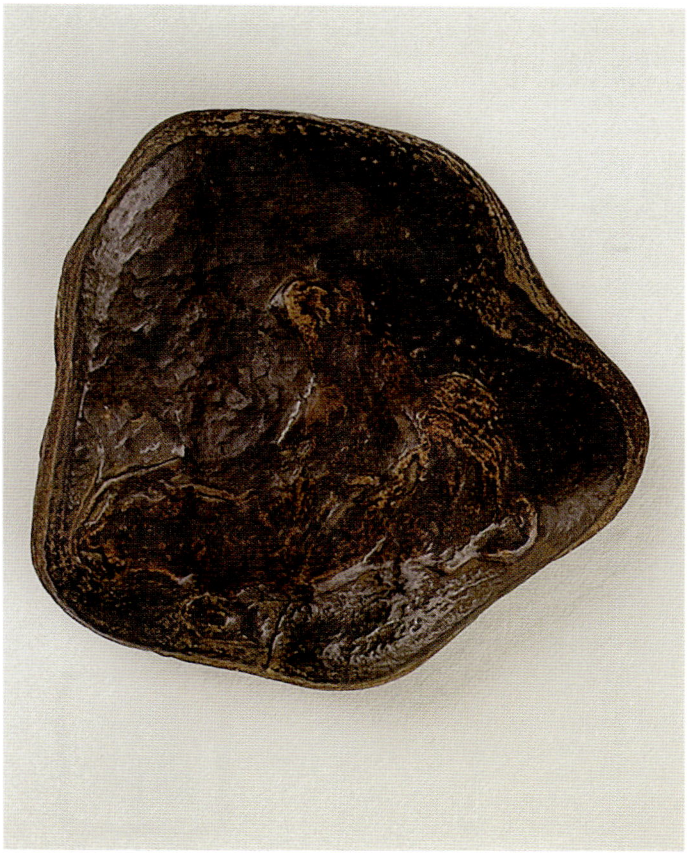

90

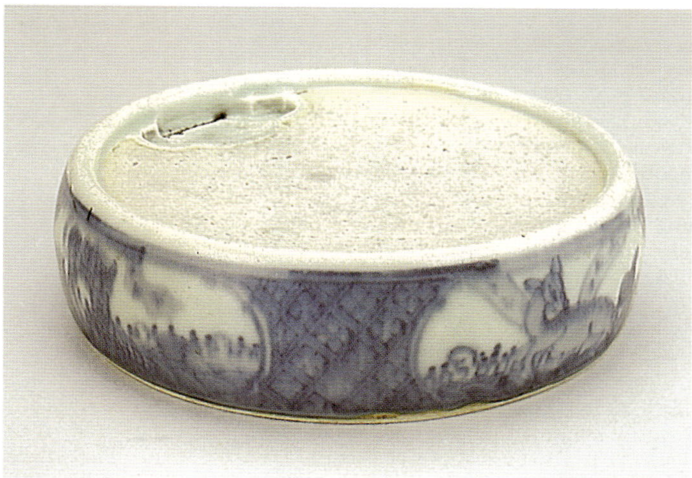

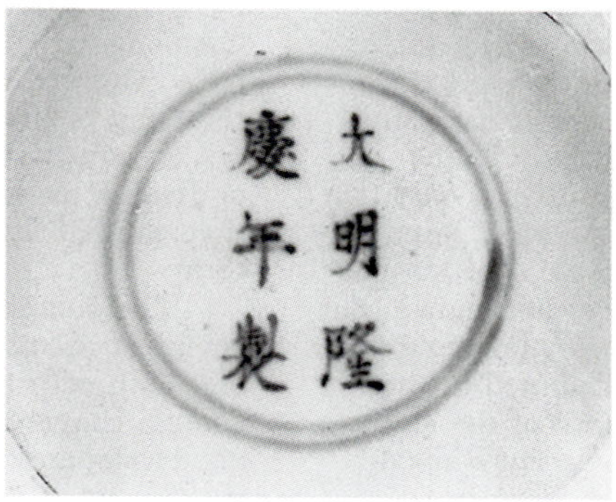

89

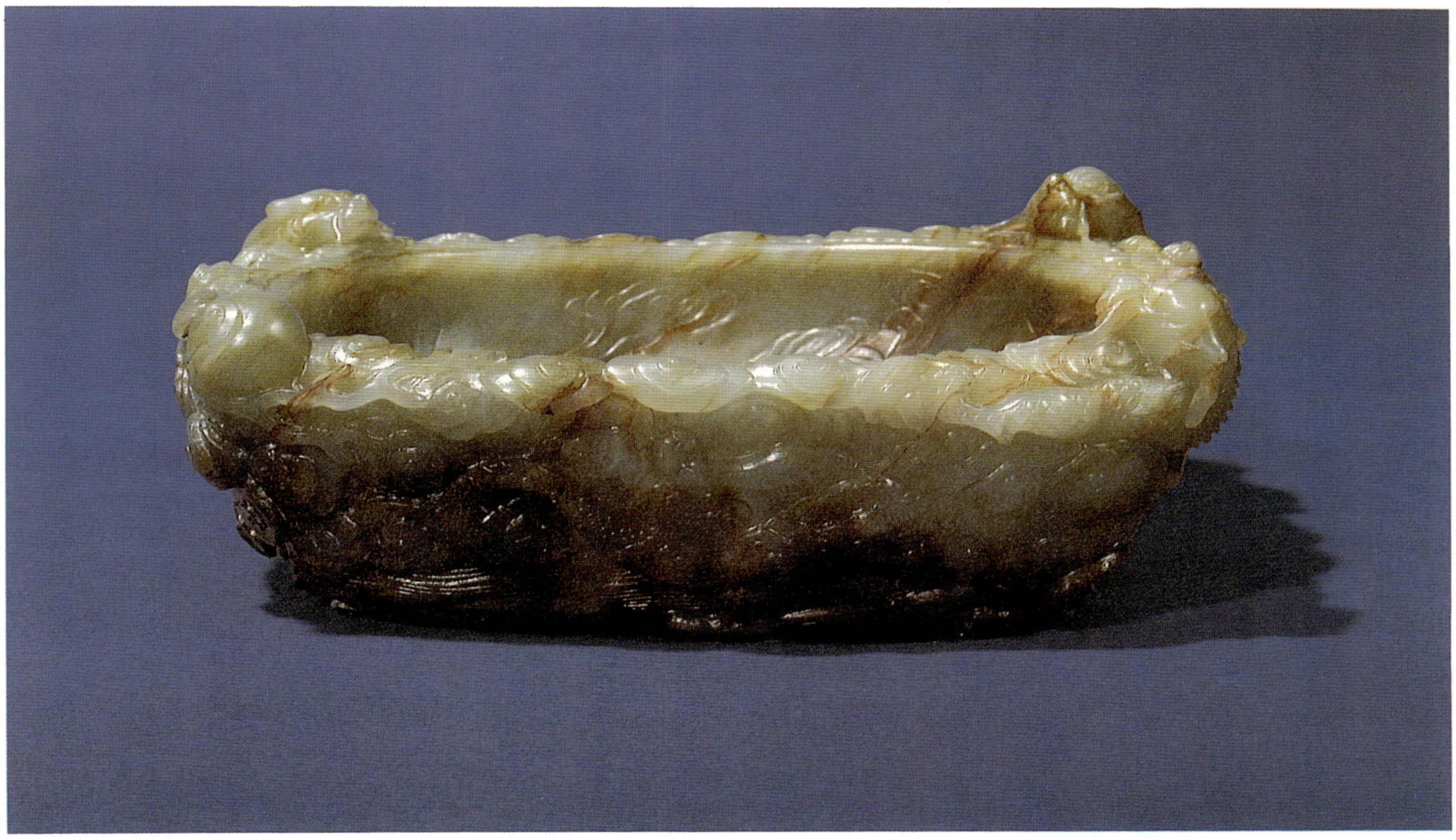

91

Vase

Gourd and ivory; the gourd grown into a seven-part sectional primary mould to assume a rectangular form, its four faces decorated with relief designs of various auspicious trees and plants, including magnolia, plum blossom, bamboo, pine, *lingzhi* fungus, rose and lotus; the base moulded in relief with the mark *Kangxi shangwan* ('appreciated by the Kangxi Emperor') in regular script; the neck mounted with a plain ivory everted lip.
Beijing palace, probably early Kangxi period.
Height: 17.7 cm.
Published: *Chinese Decorated Gourds,* p.49, no. 1.

葫蘆模製花木方瓶·康熙賞玩銘
清康熙(1662–1722), 高17.7厘米

With its combination of man and nature, its rustic connotations and mellow surface, the gourd was a natural focus of literati appreciation. We have dealt at length with its history and functions elsewhere.[1] The rind of the gourd, when cleaned out and dried, makes an ideal container and has been so used since time immemorial wherever it grows naturally. In China its use can be traced back to the Warring States period[2] but we may be sure that it was used long before that. At what point it occurred to the Chinese to develop the various methods of decorating gourds is not known, but it is likely that it was early on. A few gourds are known which might be attributed to the Ming period, but the florescence of the art seems to have taken place under the Kangxi Emperor, in the palace at Beijing.

Having consolidated the conquest of China, the Kangxi Emperor allowed himself the luxury of indulging in the arts. He set up within the palace at Beijing a series of workshops for the production of various arts and crafts (most of which survived him by nearly a century).[3] The practice of moulding gourds was probably established well before his time, but few unquestionable pieces have survived; the Emperor's interest led to a blossoming of the art that resulted in two centuries of its greatest popularity and development. Gourd production was divided into two main groups: the palace production, using mainly the traditional primary mould system, and the non-imperial production which it later inspired, the majority of which utilized the secondary mould system. The primary mould system employs directly carved wood moulds which are tied around the growing gourd. The secondary mould system employs a master mould made of wood, carved as a positive image, which is then used to create large numbers of clay moulds, which are in turn used on the growing gourd. The latter method allows for the same master mould to be used for a long period of time, whereas the former does not, as the wood sectional moulds must weather a season of growth and were probably at their best for only one or two seasons. This particular vase was grown into a seven-part mould (see Fig. 1 for diagram).

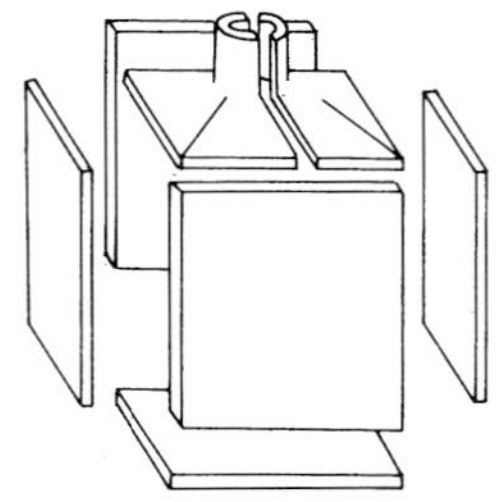

Fig. 1

The palace workshops were responsible for most of the finest moulded gourds known from the primary mould system. The Kangxi, Qianlong and Daoguang Emperors all seem to have exhibited an interest, although those from the reign of the latter consist of only a few cricket gourds. There are no known Yongzheng or Jiaqing marked palace gourds, suggesting that they showed little interest in this particular art form.

The Kangxi and Qianlong periods mark the height of decorated gourds for the good reason that both emperors were keen collectors. The Kangxi Emperor's enthusiasm is vouched for by his development of this humble art form in the palace, and is further endorsed by the demonstration of the Qianlong Emperor's interest, when he wrote a foreword to a poem entitled 'In Praise of a Gourd Vessel' as follows: "The manufacture of gourd vessels started in the Kangxi era when the Emperor ordered that gourds be grown into moulds to produce bowls, jars, dishes and boxes as required. The vessels are admirably natural and yet exquisite, something not possible by man alone."[4]

The simple construction of this vessel, with all the decorated surfaces being flat, suggests that it represents an early phase of palace production. More complex curving and multi-faceted forms are likely to have been developed after the basic art had been mastered.

The form of mark employed here is typical of Kangxi production, and although we have not seen examples, Chinese sources list other possible marks. The Qianlong Emperor mentions the form *Kangxi yuwan* ('Kangxi imperial curio'), and elsewhere are mentioned *Kangxi yushang* ('for the imperial appreciation of the Kangxi Emperor') and *Kangxi yubao* ('imperial treasure of the Kangxi Emperor').[5] Others are possible, as in no 269, marked *Kangxi baowan* ('treasured plaything of the Kangxi Emperor').

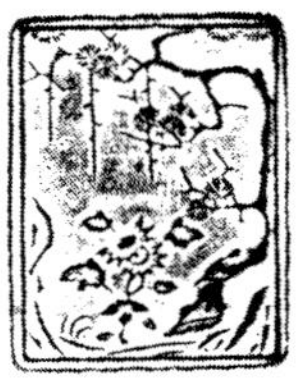

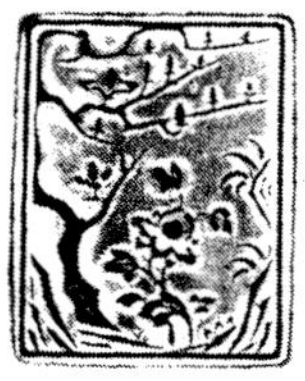

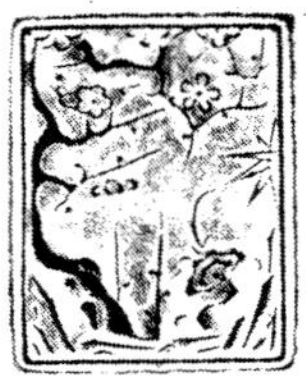

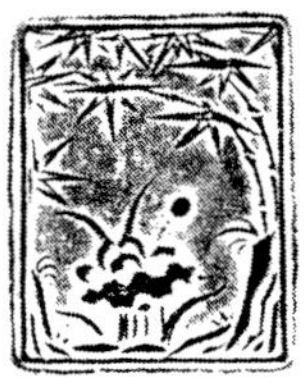

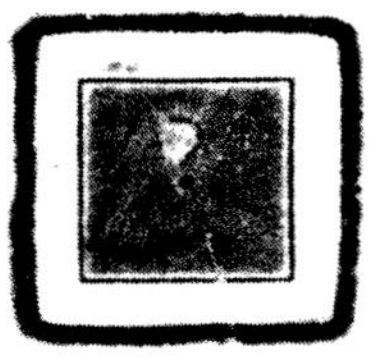

1. See *Chinese Decorated Gourds.*
2. Ibid. p.52.
3. The composition of these workshops by 1680 is discussed by Bushell, in *Chinese Art* I, p.108, and by Lady David, who adds a plan of the Forbidden City and notes on their location and capacity in *Illustrated Catalogue of Ch'ing Enamelled Ware in the Percival David Foundation of Chinese Art.*
4. Wang Shixiang, 'Discussion on Gourd Wares' in *Gugong Bowuyuan Yuankan,* 1979, no. 1, pp. 86-91. An English translation of this work by Craig Clunas has recently been published in *Chinese Translations,* no. 10, by the Oriental Ceramic Society, London. In our own article (see note 1) and here we have worked from our own, unpublished translation.
5. See *Chinese Decorated Gourds.*

92

Brush Pot

Gourd, ivory and lacquer; the gourd grown into an eleven-part sectional primary mould to form an octagonal brush pot, the four major faces decorated in relief with a design of four bats surrounding a *shou* ('longevity') character, the minor faces each decorated with two formalized *chi* dragons; the base with the relief mark *Qianlong shangwan* ('appreciated by the Qianlong Emperor'); the interior and ivory lip lacquered a deep blackish-brown colour.
Beijing palace, Qianlong period.
Height: 14.2 cm.

Boxwood stand, the recessed top carved with four bats surrounding a *shou* character, the apron with sets of twin *chi* dragons, the base with the two character seal *Chen Li* of the maker.
Chen Li, Hong Kong, *circa* 1977.
Formerly in the Mrs. Sedgewick collection, London.
Published: *Chinese Decorated Gourds,* p.51, no. 3.

葫蘆模製八方蝠壽筆筒·乾隆賞玩銘
清乾隆(1736–1795), 高14.2厘米

The Qianlong period was responsible for the largest output and the greatest number of forms in the Beijing palace period of production of gourds. Wang Shixiang advances the opinion that "Qianlong period examples are especially elegant — really the best scholarly objects from the Imperial Household".[1]

The interior of this brush pot has been lined beneath the lacquer with a thickness of some material to add weight to the naturally light gourd — a practical consideration for a vessel expected to take often top-heavy brushes, *ruyi* sceptres, wrist rests or whatever else a scholar might place in it.

1. Wang Shixiang, 'Discussion on Gourd Wares', op. cit., pp.86-91.

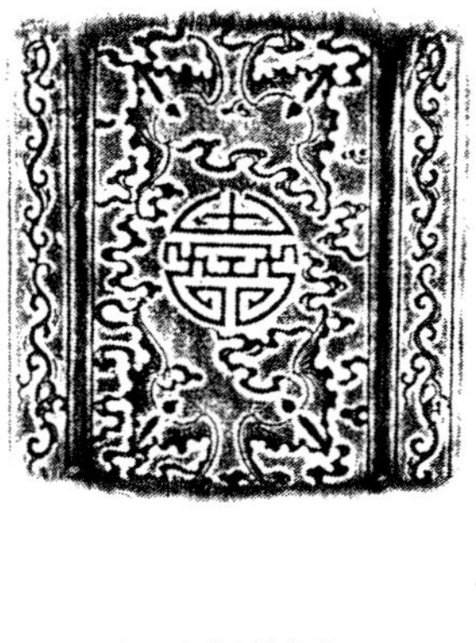

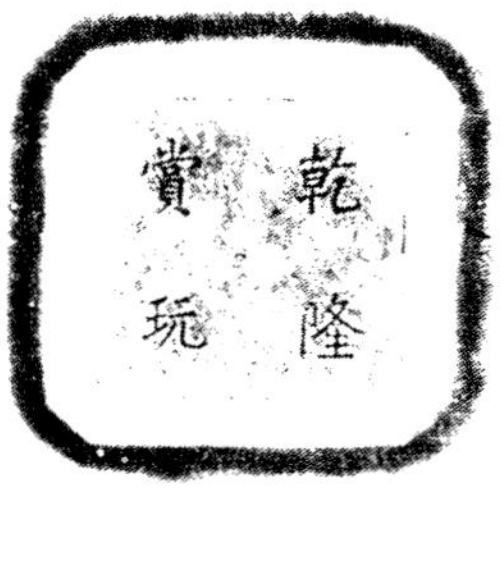

91

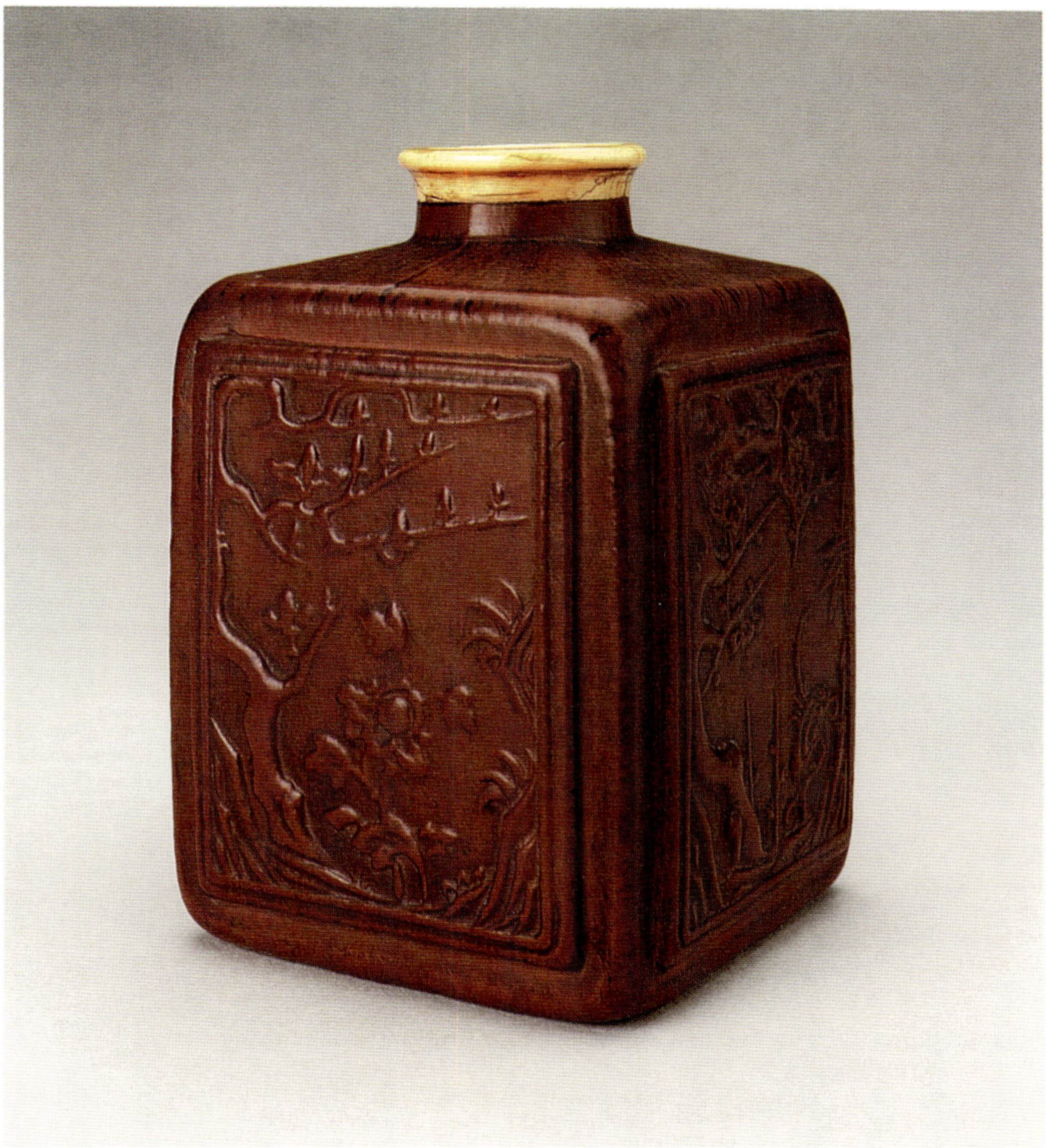

92

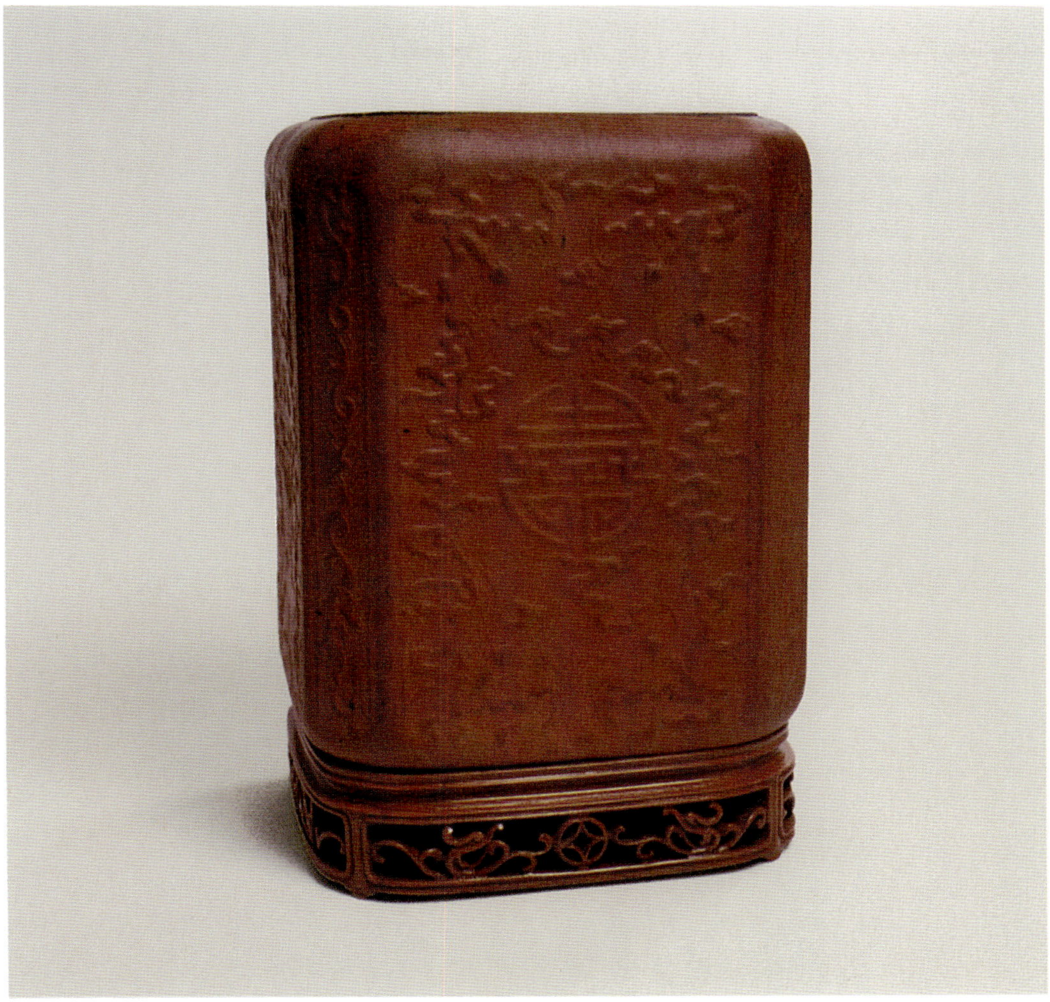

93

Water Vessel

Crystal; the flawless material carved as a small globular artist's water vessel, decorated in low relief with a band of two *kui* dragons, back to back, repeated on each side and separated by two *taotie* mask and ring handle motifs; the base with a wheel-cut inscription *Qianlong nianzhi* ('made in the Qianlong period') in seal script.
Beijing palace workshops, Qianlong period.
Height: 4.35 cm.
Together with an ivory stand (an early example but clearly not the original as the fit is poor) and white jade spoon.

水晶雕夔紋水丞·乾隆年製銘
清乾隆(1736–1795), 高4.35厘米

Together with the crystal vessels nos. 130 and 235, this piece represents the more refined side of the Qianlong Emperor's character. There is a tendency today to view the Qianlong period as one of decorative excess and taste somewhat out of consonance with the classical scholarly, restrained ideal of earlier periods. This is largely due to a very large official production of rather garish ceramics, furniture, lacquer, metalwork, etc. However, the Emperor himself clearly had a quieter side to his aesthetic character as is demonstrated by objects made for his personal use and by a good deal of the more scholarly palace production which reflected the literati style to a greater extent. There was also a continuing non-imperial elegance of taste which was more in line with the classical ideal.

For a discussion on the type of mark found here see no. 130.

94

Flower Vase

Glass, with swirling markings in various hues of brilliant orange, with some areas of pale green showing through on the base; a flower vase, the base inscribed with a wheel-cut mark *Qianlong nianzhi* ('made in the Qianlong period') in regular script within a double square.
Beijing palace workshops, Qianlong period.
Height: 19.6 cm.

仿雄黃料花瓶·乾隆年製銘
清乾隆(1736–1795), 高19.6厘米

This vessel is based on a mallet, the broad base and narrow neck making it exceptionally sturdy and an ideal shape for a single blossoming branch, or other flowers, to decorate the scholar's studio. As a ceramic and glass form it occurs occasionally during the first half of the Qing dynasty.

Variegated orange, or frequently red and orange, glass was extremely popular during the Qing dynasty, particularly in snuff bottles. It imitates realgar (arsenic bisulphide), an important substance in Daoist alchemichal practice. Although some Daoist figures and one snuff bottle are known in realgar itself, the material is soft and prone to disintegrate into powder; and of course it is potentially lethal — hence the glass substitute.

The swirling patterns visible at the surface of this vessel are full of possibilities for the imaginative mind. It may be read as a landscape, drifting incense smoke or a variety of strange living creatures, but it also represents the endlessly changing pattern of energy from which all phenomena emanate in the Chinese view, particularly as expressed by Daoism. To a Daoist scholar it would be a work of art of subtle complexity and endless fascination, to be enjoyed like incense smoke as a meditative aid.

Under the Qianlong Emperor a typical feature of palace glass production was the four character wheel-cut mark (a calligraphically fairly crude-looking mark, since its fluidity was severly handicapped by the characteristically straight lines of a spinning cutting wheel). This was not the only form of mark used, but it was certainly the most popular for the period, and even appears, somewhat uncomfortably, on some of the finest Qianlong palace enamelled wares on glass.[2] As a type of mark it appears to be limited to palace production (or, of course, to copies thereof).

1. The history of this effort is covered in *By Imperial Command: An Introduction to Ch'ing Imperial Painted Enamels* while the palace workshops are discussed in the caption to no. 91.
2. Ibid. pl. 35, for an octagonal brush pot with European decoration of the highest quality and with such a mark.

95

Covered Box

Clear glass, with blue and gold enamel; a covered box, decorated on the outer curve of the box and on the cover with well-foliated branches laden with berries or blossoms; the base carved with the four-character mark *Qianlong nianzhi* ('made in the Qianlong period') in regular script.
Beijing palace workshops, Qianlong period.
Diameter: 6 cm.

清料畫珐瑯花果蓋盒·乾隆年製銘
清乾隆(1736–1795), 直徑6厘米

The form and style of mark used here, combined with the exquisite quality of the glass and the enamelled decoration, make an attribution to the Beijing palace workshops irresistible.

The arts of enamelling on glass and on metal were introduced to the Beijing palace workshops under the Kangxi Emperor, with the aid of Jesuit missionaries. At the same time undecorated porcelains made at Jingdezhen, in the south, were also sent to the Court to be enamelled. This was the origin of the palette of enamels known as 'famille rose' which replaced the traditional and more limited palette in the early 18th century.[1] Enamelled glass, tentatively first tried in the Kangxi period (we know of only a single extant example[2]) and perfected only with a much larger output under the Qianlong Emperor, represents the rarest of the three wares painted with enamels in the palace workshops. A number of previously unpublished examples of enamelled glass from the Beijing palace workshops appear in *The National Palace Museum Monthly of Chinese Art*, 1985, no. 33.

No other example is known from the classic output of the palace workshops which is on clear glass, or which uses only two colours of enamel. There are examples known on clear glass of the *Guyue xuan* group[3] which is thought to be connected with the palace in the late 18th and early 19th century, and perhaps a piece such as this was a model for these.

The aesthetic impact of a large lump of scarlet seal-paste if placed in the clear glass of this box would seem to suggest some other role. It might have been intended as an incense powder box, or perhaps a cosmetic box, if it was seriously intended for use at all.

1. For a study of these wares see *By Imperial Command: An Introduction to Ch'ing Imperial Painted Enamels*.
2. A small cup, illustrated ibid. pl. 33.
3. For a study of this group of enamelled wares see *Enamelled Glass Wares of the Ku Yueh Hsuan Group*, by Hugh Moss, in the *Journal of the International Chinese Snuff Bottle Society*, Vol. X, no. 2, pp.5-25.

93

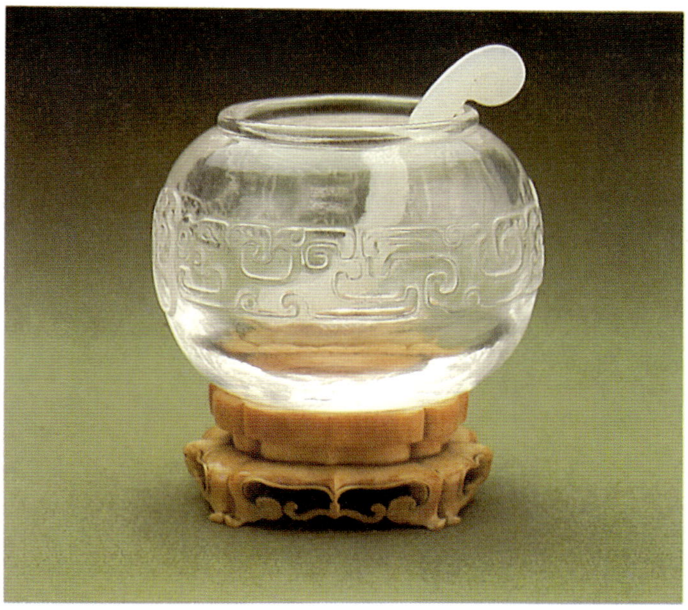

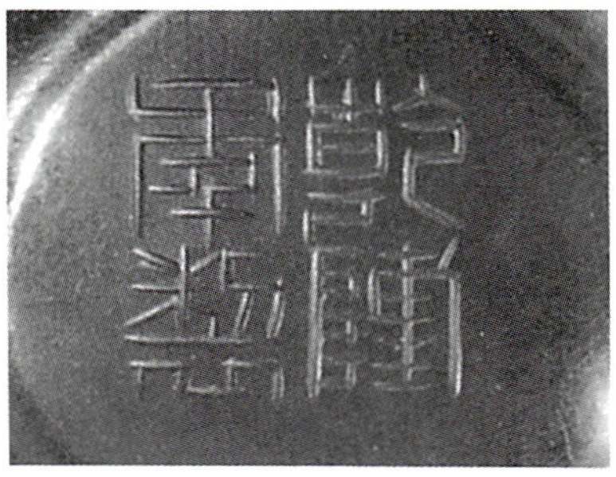

94

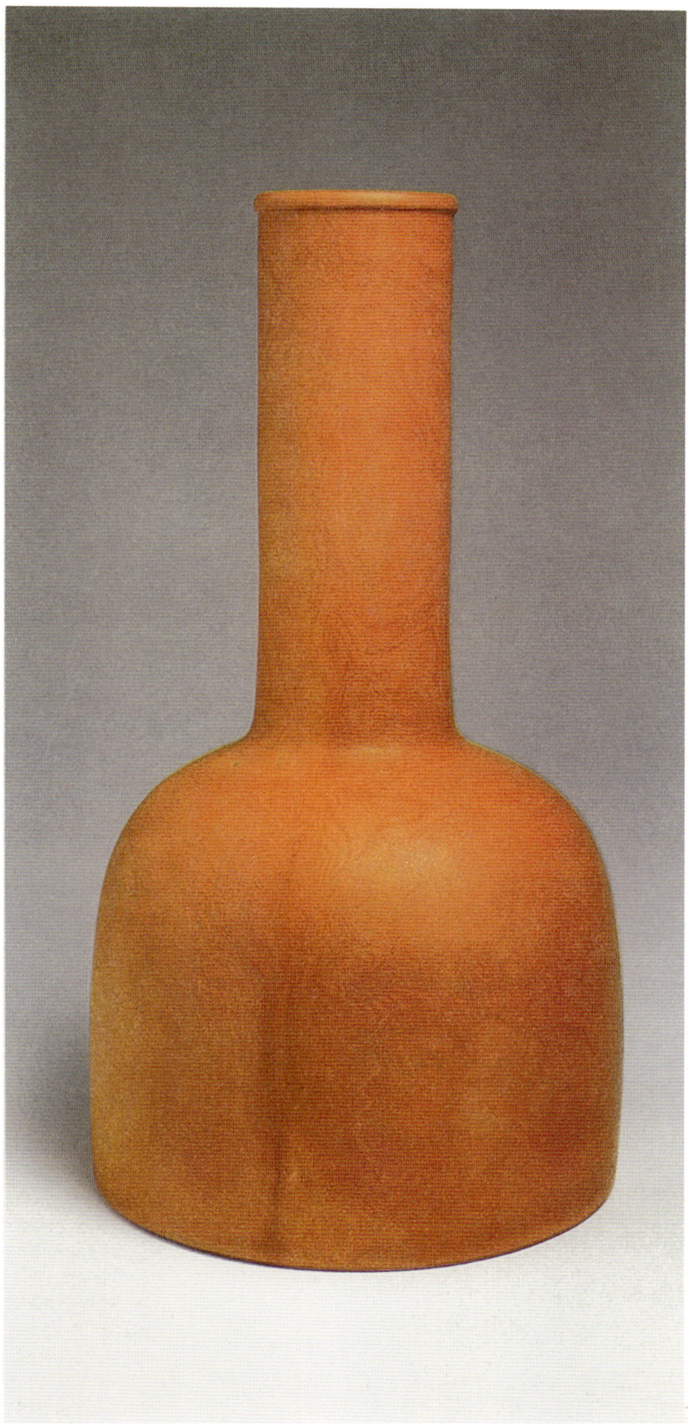

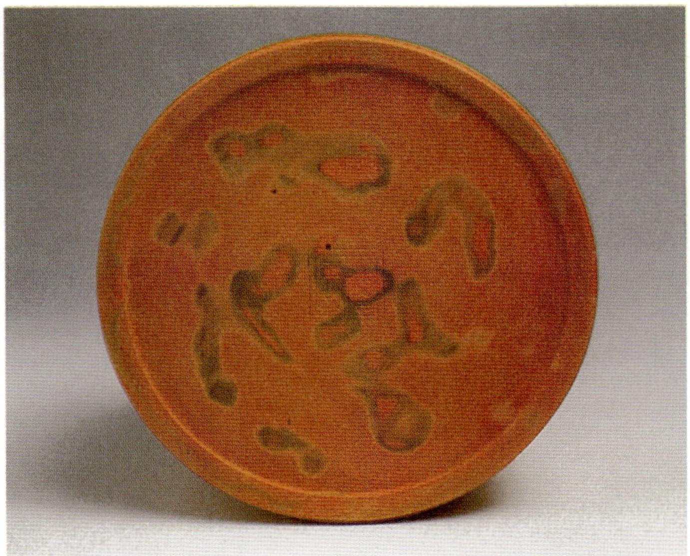

95

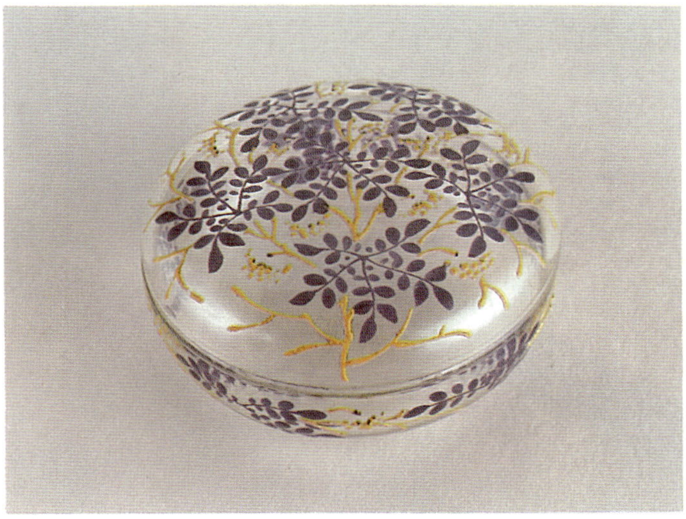

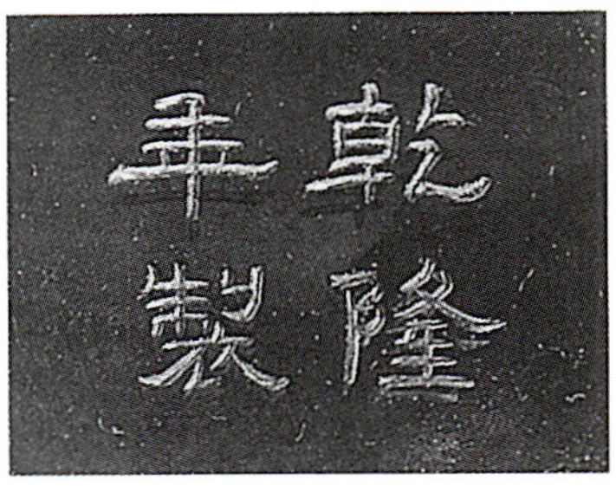

96

Miniature Wrist Rest
Huang Zhao

Ivory, of cream colour, patinated to a yellowish colour on one side; carved as a miniature wrist rest, the exterior curved surface with three men and three children playing with kites (two men are flying one kite, while a child grasps one of their coats in excitement; a child tries to launch another kite by running across the foreground, while another adult with a child on his back watches); the protected underside of the wrist rest carved with technical audacity with the Eighteen *Luohan*, with various familiar animals and attributes, and three demons who support two of them in a blanker on clouds above the others; the rest supported on small feet at each corner, one edge inscribed 'respectfully made by (Your Majesty's) humble servant Huang Zhao in the mid autumn of 1763'.
Beijing palace workshops, 1763.
Length: 9.7 cm.

象牙雕十八羅漢臂擱•黃兆製
清乾隆癸未(1763), 長9.7厘米

The technical virtuosity of this piece is astonishing. Each of the figures and animals depicted is exquisitely carved and invested with individual personality. The carving of whisps of smoke, loose rings dangling from staffs, water pouring from gourds, and the other elements of the intricate tracery that make up the openwork subjects is remarkable. It is narrowly saved from being little more than an absurd display of technical virtuosity by the sheer flair of the miniature sculpture which is more readily apparent in the less busy subject of the kite flyers. This sort of work of art which rests so heavily on its technical virtuosity was a favourite of the Qianlong Emperor's, and the palace collections in both Beijing and Taiwan have many examples of it. At the court such virtuosity was usually accompanied by a total dedication to each work, lifting it into the realms of art. Unfortunately similar displays of technical proficiency made largely for export at Guangzhou and later in Shanghai lacked this individual devotion and quickly degenerated into shallow souvenirs (a good example of this may be found in the ivory series of spheres carved each within the other with intricate tracery, sometimes aptly described as 'Canton balls').

Huang Zhao was an ivory carver from Guangdong province. He was one of 11 ivory carvers sent to the palace workshops from Guangdong during the Yongzheng and Qianlong periods. He was seconded to the Beijing palace workshops (which were under the control of the *Zaoban Chu,* or Bureau of Works) in 1749 and continued to work there until 1790.[1] A remarkably similar little wrist rest signed by another palace artist, Yang Weizhan (also from Guangdong), dated 1738, is still in the imperial collection.[2]

That this piece was made for the Emperor is demonstrated by the use of the characters *xiaochen* immediately preceding the signature. The form *chen* is frequently found preceeding signatures on paintings done for the Emperor; it may be translated as 'your servant'. The addition of the character *xiao* adds a further level of humility and may be translated as 'your humble servant' — suitable for a mere ivory craftsman from the palace workshops when addressing the Son of Heaven. The social gulf that existed between the two goes some way to explaining why Huang Zhao would go to such extraordinary lengths to catch the fleeting attention of the Emperor with this remarkable piece of craftsmanship.

1. A list of recorded Ming and Qing dynasty carvers of jade and other materials is given in *Gugong Bowuyuan Yuankan,* 1983, no. 1.
2. *Masterpieces of Chinese Miniature Crafts in the National Palace Museum,* no. 23.

97

Seal

Ivory, of creamy-yellow colour with some patches of darker patination and age cracking; a seal, the rectangular base with rounded vertical edges surmounted by a strap handle around which two *chi* dragons entwine, each with inlaid eyes of brown horn; the base cut in seal script *Yi shanshui wenji ziyu* ('To enjoy oneself in landscape and books').
Probably Beijing palace workshops, first half of the 18th century.
Height: 5.8 cm.

象牙雕雙螭方印
十八世紀上半葉, 高5.8厘米

The Beijing palace workshops produced some of the finest ivory carvings in the history of the art in China. Known pieces from the workshops of the Qianlong Emperor exhibit an extraordinary technical capacity (see no. 96), combined with a feel for sculpture which lifts what might otherwise be mere technical wizardry into the realm of art. Very little may be definitely attributed to the pre-Qianlong palace ivory workshop, but there is a large seal with a knob carved with dragons in the J & J collection in Brazil which is of the Kangxi period. A series of Qianlong snuff bottles from the palace are the epitome of the combination of high quality and fine sculpture.[1] There is also a group of ivories in the Palace Museums of both Beijing and Taipei which may be confidently attributed to the palace workshops and which also help to establish a sense of style for the workshops.[2] This example exhibits both the taste and quality of this group, and in style might even be an early example, perhaps from the Kangxi or Yongzheng workshops.

This subject of *chi* dragons entwined around a circular form (in the case of seal surmounts normally a semicircular handle) seems to derive from jade *bi* symbolism of the Warring States period where formerly plain discs began to be embellished with dragons on their rims.

The seal is a typical *jianzhang;* a fanciful seal which might be used on a painting or piece of calligraphy in addition to personal name or studio seals. It is a particularly scholarly sentiment.

1. For examples see *The Collectors' Book of Snuff Bottles,* nos. 767 and 786; *Chinese Snuff Bottles* (Magazine), no. 1, front cover, and *Chinese Snuff Bottles* (Magazine), no. 6, nos. 01-05.
2. See *Masterpieces of Chinese Writing Materials in the National Palace Museum,* nos. 38, 39 and 40; and *Masterpieces of Chinese Miniature Crafts in the National Palace Museum,* nos. 23, 24, 25, 26, 27, 30, 32, 33, 34, 35, 36 and 37.

98

Seal

Ivory, patinated to a rich, brownish cream colour; a seal, the rectangular base surmounted by a reclining broad-tailed sheep; the material cracked and well smoothed through handling, particularly on the back.
Probably early Qing dynasty.
3.95 cm × 2.6 cm × 2.6 cm.

象牙雕羊方印
可能清初, 高3.95厘米, 寬深各2.6厘米

This seal appears from the surface texture, pattern of cracking and patination never to have been inscribed with seal text. Its most likely period would seem to be the early Qing, probably the Kangxi period, with which the degree of patination would be commensurate. The seal knob is a work of carefully observed realism and remarkable sculptural quality, suggesting the possibility of the early Beijing palace workshops as a provenance. However, there is so little evidence of the style of ivory carving from the first fifty or more years of production from these workshops that at this point we can only raise the possibility on the most tentative basis.

James Watt discusses the broad-tailed sheep in a caption to a nephrite ewe and lamb in *Chinese Jade from Han to Ch'ing.*[1] Currently common in Xinjiang, it was apparently regarded as a rarity worthy of notice by early travellers to the Western regions. He notes that a Tang book[2] records its existence in Samarkand and identifies it with the 'fat-tailed dumba of Bukhara and the Kirghiz steppe, whose young are the source of the famous Astrakhan fur'.

1. No. 35, pp.58-59.
2. *Youyang zazu* by Duan Chengshi.

96

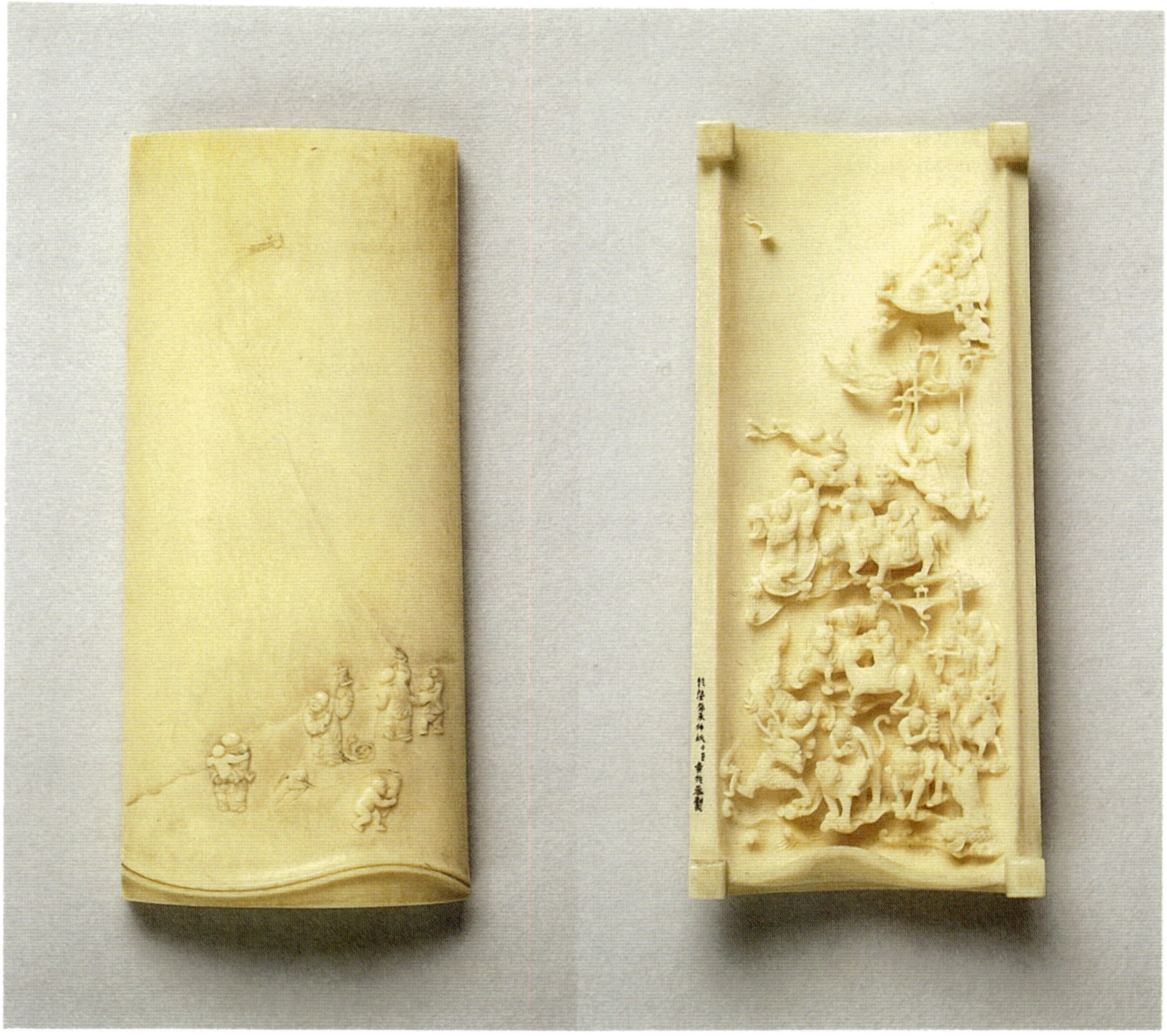

97

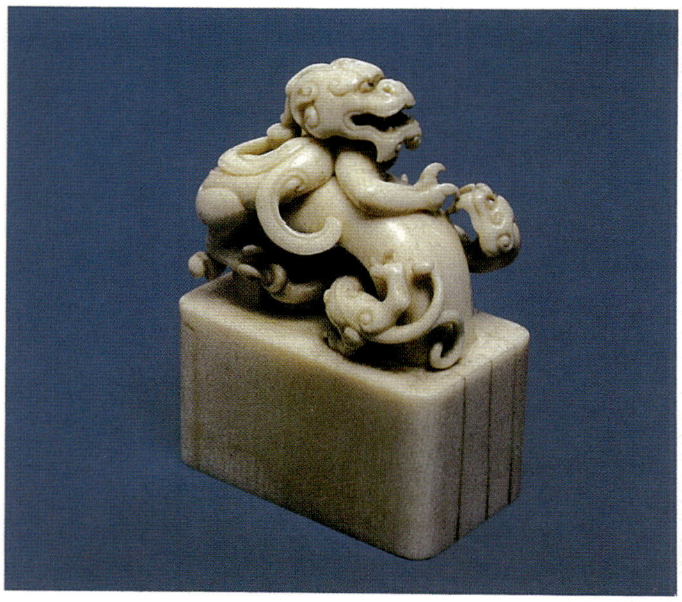

98

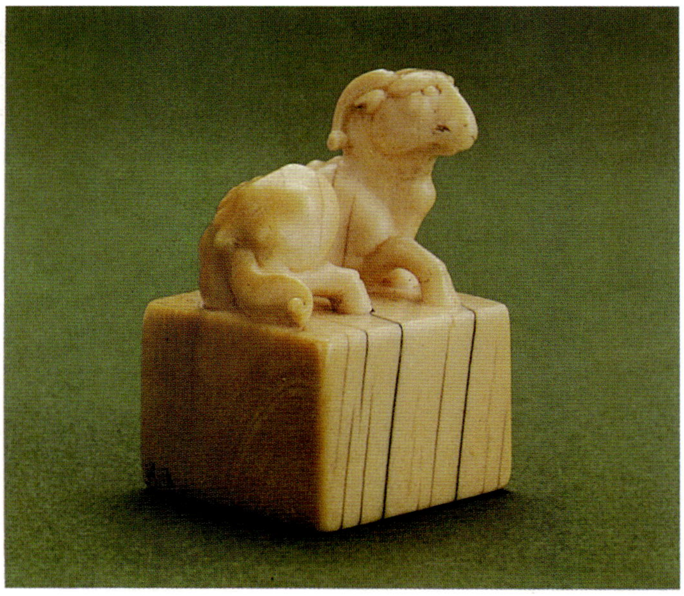

99

Ink

Ink, black with gilt surface decoration; cast in the form of a square seal, with a domed knob, the knob with two gilt five-clawed dragons in clouds; the four sides with low relief decoration of two facing *kui* dragons making up *taotie* masks; the seal text reading *Yunxing yushi wanguo xienning* ('Clouds move, rain falls, and so there is peace on earth') in positive seal script. Attributed to the Beijing palace workshops, mid to late 18th century.
3.2 cm × 8.2 cm × 8.2 cm; weight 241 g.

雲行雨施萬國咸寧御璽墨
十八世紀中至晚期，3.2×8.2×8.2厘米，
重241克

This appears to be in the form of an imperial seal, and exactly this text was used on a circular red ink of the Kangxi period also marked *Yumo* ('Imperial ink') and dated 1691,[1] with a three-clawed dragon on the other side. This suggests that this is an imperial ink made at Beijing. Another from the same mould as this example is in the Anhui Provincial Museum (weight 270 g), attributed to Wang Weigao, although it is also unsigned.

Wang Weigao was the second son of the famous early Qing inkmaker Wang Jinsheng. In the sixth year of Qianlong (1741), the Qing Court was looking for an ink-making instructor from Huizhou, the famous inkmaking centre. The Xixian local governor, Zhao Ben, recommended Wang Weigao who took up the post of instructor at the ink-making workshops of the Imperial Secretariat, Beijing. This appointment was in recognition of his and his father's achievements in ink-making.

The works of the two Wangs were later collected and published as *Jiangu Zhai Mosou* ('Collection of Inks of the Studio for Authenticating Antiques'), but this ink does not appear in that work. It may be that it was supervised by Wang in his position of instructor, but without knowing the reasons for the Anhui Museum attribution we are unable to say. If it is connected with Wang, it would date from sometime after 1741.

In the difficult connoisseurship of ink, where moulds were used time and time again sometimes centuries after they were first carved, and were copied frequently, the question of weight may prove to be of significance. The different ingredients of fine ink would have meant that weight varied with inks taken from the same mould but by different makers at different times. If it were possible to establish what the weight of certain categories of inks was from certain makers, it might be possible to determine original impressions from later ones. It should be noted that the two examples discussed here differ in weight.

1. See *The National Palace Museum Monthly of Chinese Art,* No. 12, p.12, Taiwan, 1984.

100

'Han Tile' Ink
Zheng Rui

Ink, black with gold and silver surface details; moulded in the form of a Han tile inkstone of flattened oval form; the plain back with a poetic inscription in impressed regular script, partly gilt, partly silvered:

"Sea and sky, the new moon rises from the water;
Pure brightness shines beyond compare.
Duke Cuo's tile inkstone had no such ink to grind;
Is it not hard to find a name for such an ink?
Use the brush in solitude, its fineness is surpassing;
Bringing forth thoughts, disclosing mysteries — such is my ink.

An Imperial composition by the Qianlong emperor" followed by two seals *Qian* and *long;* further inscribed in three places around the edge, in relief regular script: "Copying the 'Sea and sky new moon inkstone' made from a tile of the Weiyang Palace of the Han dynasty"; "made in the thirtieth year of the Qianlong period" and "respectfully presented by Zheng Rui".
1765.
Length: 13.6 cm.
Contained in a *hongmu* ('redwood') fitted case, probably of later date.

仿漢瓦硯御題詩墨·徵瑞製
清乾隆三十年(1765)，長13.6厘米

Han dynasty tiles were considered from antiquity to make excellent inkstones (the most common form in which they have been preserved) with the circular end-section of an eave-tile cut and its back either carved to form ink and water pools, or left in its natural state. Duke Cuo was presumably the owner of the Han Weiyang Palace, a tile of which formed the original oval inkstone entitled 'Sea and sky new moon inkstone' which inspired the form of this ink.

For ease of production inscriptions and detail in moulded inks are usually in relief on the final product because of the increased difficulties of leaving fine lines and characters in relief on the original mould (which is always the reverse of the ink itself — see no. 201). Negative inscriptions are usually short, and impressed with a separate die of some kind. Here, however, the entire inscription seems to have been skilfully left in low relief on the original wood mould, maintaining perfect surface integrity.

We have been unable to further identify the inkmaker Zheng Rui. Over the centuries the Court employed its own inkmakers, commissioned inks from outside inkmakers and received ink as tribute from independents (see no. 38). It would seem likely that Zheng Rui in this case was working directly for the Court on a specific commission. The Emperor clearly owned a Han inkstone of this shape, and wrote a poem about the ink that was to be made after its form, suggesting the sort of co-operation most conveniently and usually carried out in the context of a full-time employee of the Beijing palace workshops.

99

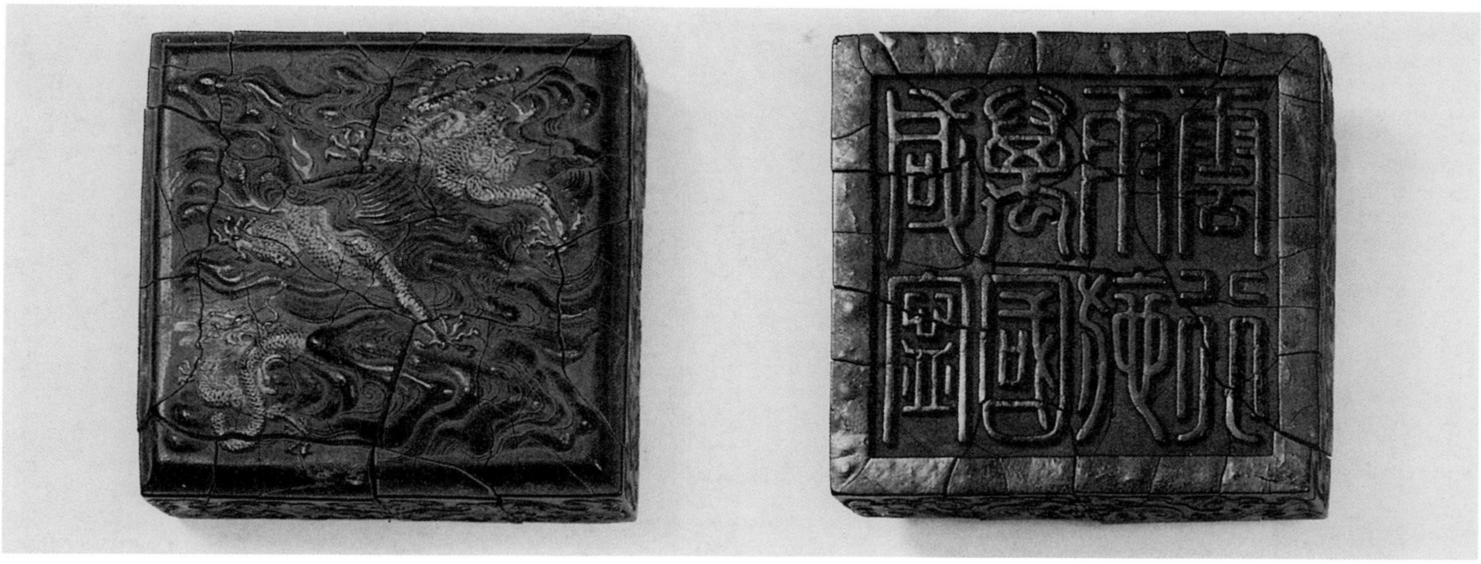

100

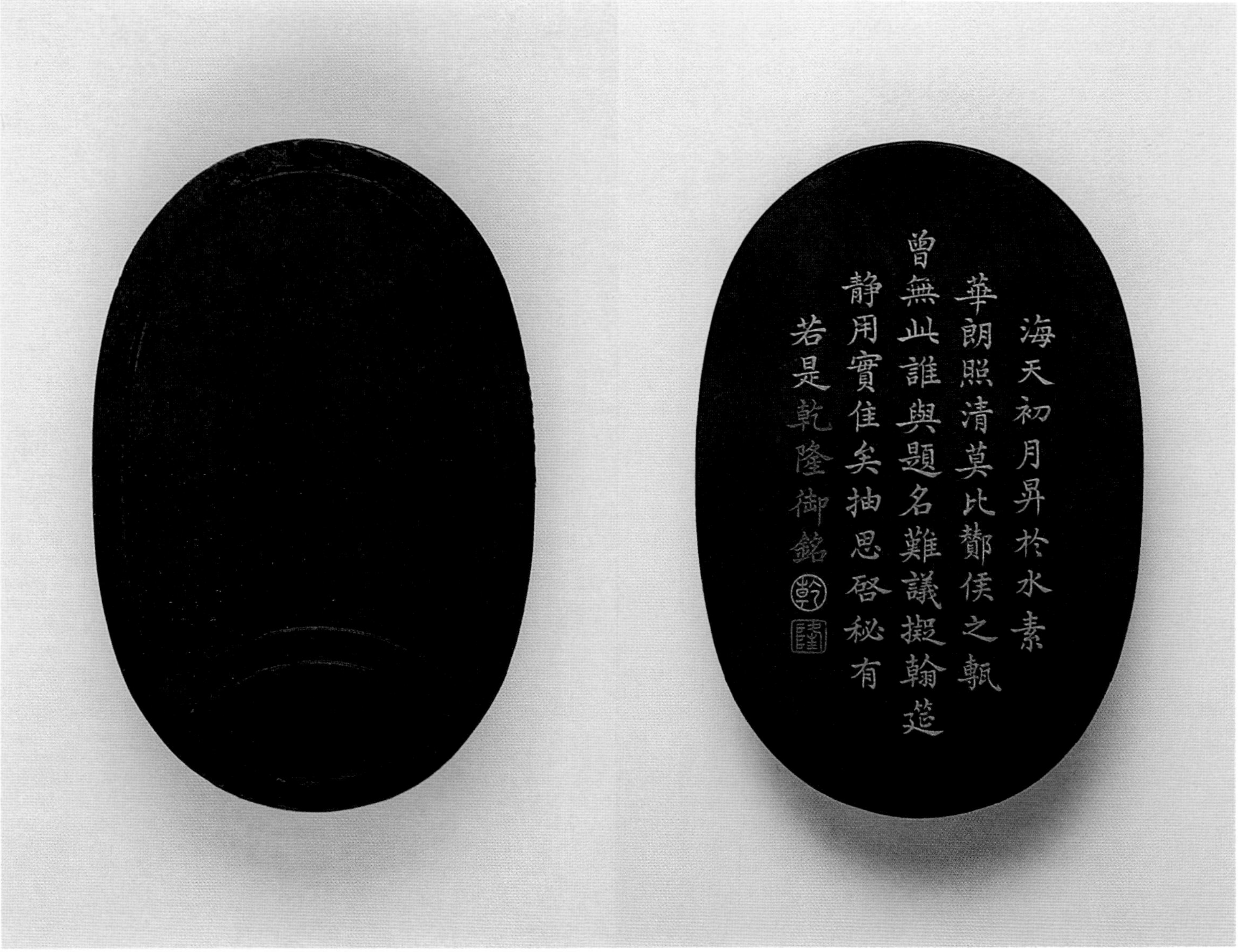

101

'National Treasure' Ink

Zhan Chenggui

Ink, black decorated with gold, silver and blue surface colouring; of rounded rectangular form, one side moulded in relief with two four-clawed dragons amidst flames, encircling the two impressed characters *Guobao* ('National Treasure'); the reverse with the mark *Daming Yongle nianzao* ('made in the Yongle period of the Great Ming dynasty'), surrounded by formalized clouds; a raised signature at lower left reading 'made by Zhan Chenggui' in raised regular script.
Suzhou, probably second quarter of the 18th century.
Length: 17.5 cm.

仿明永樂國寶墨•詹成圭製
清雍正/乾隆年間，長17.5厘米

'National Treasure' inks of this design are reasonably common and bear either Yongle, Xuande or Qianlong imperial marks. All are decorated with four-clawed dragons, however, which are uncharacteristic for imperal objects of any of the three periods; nor is there any clear evidence that any of the existing examples are as early as the Yongle and Xuande periods — indeed, there is a good deal of evidence to suggest that they are not. 'National Treasure' ink was a classification of a type of ink. In the *Fang Shi Mopu* (see no. 175) Fang Yulu, the famous late Ming inkmaker, lists six categories of ink, the first of which is 'National Treasure' ink. Under this heading three dozen designs are listed, and clearly the designation has no particular imperial implications.

This leaves us, however, with the puzzle of why reign marks of such an imperial form should accompany privately made inks. It would seem reasonable to assume that these are not imperial inks as in any of the periods of the marks four-clawed dragons would have been totally out of keeping with all other known imperial wares. However all were periods of imperial strength when private inkmakers would not dare presume the use of a five-clawed dragon. The state of preservation of known late Ming and Qing inks is generally such as to suggest the unlikelihood of a number of early 15th century examples surviving. It would seem reasonable to assume, therefore, that the *Guobao* inks of this design are mostly, if not wholly, later productions, perhaps of the late Ming and Qing periods and inspired by an early imperial design which would have had either three- or five-clawed dragons (standard imperial dragons for the early 15th century).

Several other examples of similar designs are known, although there are clearly many different moulds used of the same pattern. In the *To-boku Wa-boku Zusetsu*, on p.68 is reproduced the surviving upper section of another Yongle marked ink of this type, which is there attributed to the Yongle period. The carver of this mould has obviously copied very accurately the same design (or both are copied from another original), as only minor discrepancies reveal that they are not from the same mould. Another is illustrated by Jenyns[1] which he dates tentatively to the period of its mark. A Xuande example is also shown in the *To-boku Wa-boku*, pp.64-65, and a Qianlong one on pp.132-133.

The signature on this example, discreetly in relief on a blank section from which it could be easily removed without trace, suggests that others might once have borne the marks of private makers. Two other similar inks, also with Zhan Chenggui's signature, are in the imperial collection in the National Palace Museum, Taipei.[2] The writers of the book in which they are published either missed the signatures completely, which would seem unlikely as they are quite clear even in illustration, or were unaware of the period of Zhan Chenggui. However, even here, although the design is identical, the inks are from different moulds, showing that Zhan himself made more than one mould of the design — not an uncommon practice amongst inkmakers with a heavy demand for certain inks.

Zhan Chenggui was active in the second quarter of the 18th century. He is mentioned in his local district gazette:[3] "Zhan Yuansheng, *zi:* Chenggui, a native of Hongguan (of Wuyuan)... He resided in Suzhou and sold inks for a livelihood." He was also described as filial, friendly, honest and philanthropic. He died at the age of 84. A recent publication on Qing dynasty inks by Zhou Shaoliang[4] provides further information on Chenggui. He lists a set of four inks by him, which are rectangular, inscribed with four poems with the signatures of the poets coloured in blue, dated to 1738, signed *Zhan Chenggui jianzhi* ('supervised by Zhan Chengui'); the other side decorated with bamboo and swallows. The *jianzhi* form is frequently found on workshop productions where the master himself has supervised but not actually made the product.

Another of Chenggui's inks is in the Anhui Museum dated to the same year (1740). It is inscribed *Yuying Tang zhencang* ('treasured collection of the Jade Shadow Hall'); and on the edges *Guo Yi zhi* ('made by Guo Yi') and *Gengchen nian Zhan Chenggui zhi* ('made by Zhan Chenggui in the *gengchen* year [1740]'). This also demonstrates a not uncommon practice amongst inkmakers of copying each other's designs, and including thereon both the original maker's name and their own.

In commercial workshops once a master's name had been established it would have continued in use, even after his death. In the case of Zhan Chenggui we may assume that his sons continued to use his name. One son is recorded who would have been the second generation in the workshop, Zhan Ruolu (*hao:* Weiyi shi).

1. *Chinese Art,* Vol. 4, p.313, no. 209.
2. *Masterpieces of Chinese Writing Materials in the National Palace Museum,* no. 6.
3. *Wuyuan Xianzhi* ('District Gazette of Wuyuan').
4. *Qingdai Mingmo Congtan, 'Discussion on Famous Qing Dynasty Inks',* Beijing, 1982, pp.66-71.

102

Inkstone

Limestone, of striated pale sea-green colour of the variety known as Songhua stone; an inkstone of flattened circular form, the central, slightly concave ink-pool surrounded by a circular water-pool enclosed in an irregular, cloud-form lip extending over the edge of the stone and partially down the sides, the concave base inscribed in elegant draft script: "For peaceful use through all eternity", followed by two seals, *Kangxi* in negative seal script, and *Yuming* in positive seal script.
Beijing palace workshops, 1706.
Height: 1.85 cm. Diameter: 11.8 cm.

Contained in its original lacquer box and cover, of slightly domed, circular form set on five small feet; the lacquer of brownish-red colour, with black interior; the top of the cover inscribed in draft script with Dong Qichang's poetic prose on a treasured inkstone, followed by the inscription: "Respectfully recording Huating, Dong Qichang's treasured inkstone (prose) by Imperial order at the Peiwen Zhai, on the eighth day of the eighth month, autumn, of the *bingshu* year of the Qing Kangxi period (1706)," with two seals, *bijing* ('skilful brush') in positive seal script and *momiao* ('excellent ink') in negative seal script.
Height of box and cover: 3.9 cm. Diameter: 13.1 cm.
Formerly in the Mrs. Sedgwick collection, London.

松花石圓硯連漆盒•康熙御銘印
清康熙丙戌(1706)，高1.85厘米，直徑11.8厘米

The inscription on the base of the inkstone composed by the Kangxi Emperor also seems to follow his calligraphic style, an example of which may be found in the 1696 edition of the *Gengzhi Tu* (*Pictures of Tilling and Weaving*). In the same work the Kangxi Emperor's preface is preceded by the seal *Peiwen Zhai,* implying that the Emperor wrote his original preface to be reproduced in the woodblock edition of 1696 in that studio. There is also a book compiled by order of the Kangxi Emperor entitled *Peiwen Zhai Shuhua Pu* ('Collection of calligraphy and paintings in the Peiwen Zhai'). The Peiwen Zhai was clearly an imperial studio, almost certainly in the Forbidden City, in which the above collection was kept and where the Kangxi Emperor enjoyed following the inclinations of his scholarly nature in moments away from administrative duties. The meaning of 'by Imperial order at the Peiwen Zhai' must be that the original order came from the hand of the Emperor at this studio, rather than that the box was inscribed there.

This distinctive type of inkstone is the subject of an article in *Wenwu,* 1980, no. 1, entitled 'Songhua Stone Inkstones'. In a poem by the Qianlong Emperor it is recorded that Songhua 'jade' (as he described it) was a product of Jilin, where the Songhua river joins the Heilong river, in Heilongjiang, modern-day China's northernmost province, north of Korea. Literary records show that it was used in the early Ming period, but Song use is uncertain. Another inkstone of this material (in a Beijing palace, Kangxi-marked, enamel on metal case) is in the collection of T.Y. Chow in Hong Kong, and one similarly cased and of the same period, although not marked, is in a private collection in Reading, England. Each of these latter examples has a water pool inlaid with a section of baroque mother-of-pearl, as does one illustrated in the *Wenwu* article.

It would appear that the stone was used, even if not exclusively, for imperial inkstones during the Qing dynasty, and it is recorded that the source was not mined further after the end of the Qing.

101

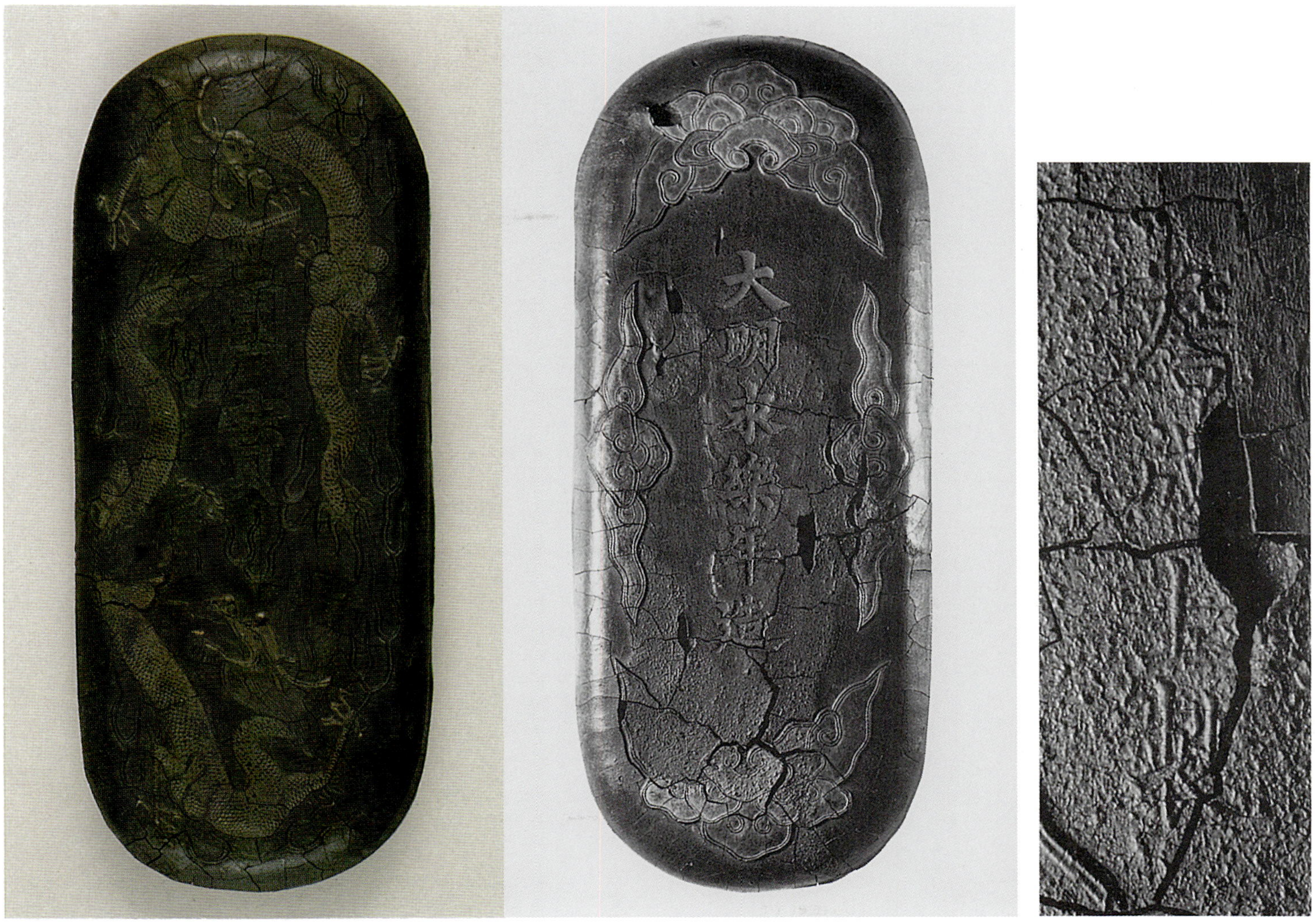

102

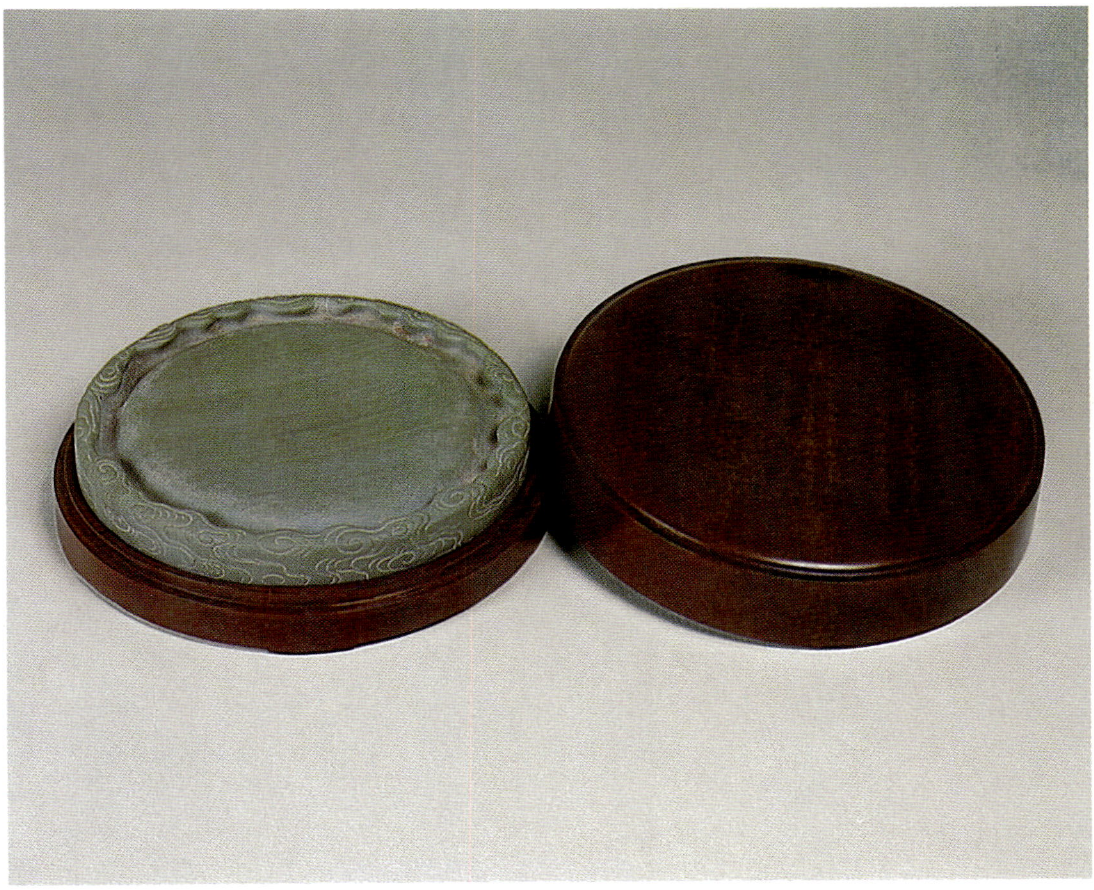

103

Incense Burner

Hu Wenming

Bronze, inlaid with silver and partly gilt; a *pou* incense burner decorated around the body with a broad band of *taotie* masks flanked by stylized bird-like creatures repeated on each side against a ground of continuous *leiwen*, below a continous band of interlocked twin *kui* dragon motifs on a geometric, floral diaper ground; the foot with a band of continuous inlaid silver *leiwen;* relief detail, plain separating bands, neck and foot rims all gilt; the base inscribed *Ming Wanli guichou qiuzhong Hu Wenming zhi wei Shiyu Zhai yong* ('made by Hu Wenming in the mid-autumn of 1613 for use in the Studio for Discussing Stones') in a square, gilt cartouche.
Yunjian, 1613.
Height: 8.38 cm.
Formerly in the Dr. & Mrs. Peter Plesch collection.
Published: *Chinese Metalwork of the Hu Wenming Group,* p.49, no. 16.
Discussed by Jenyns and Watson (although described as a *gui*) in *Chinese Art,* 1963.

鎏金嵌銀線饕餮紋青銅香爐•胡文明製
明萬曆癸丑(1613), 高8.38厘米

The 'Studio for Discussing Stones' is recorded as that of Zou Diguang, a well-known scholar-artist from Wuxi, also in the Jiangnan area not far from Yunjian. He attained his *jinshi* degree in 1574 and served at the court of the Wanli Emperor, rising to the post of Deputy Literary Chancellor for the provinces of Hunan and Hebei. It is likely that he would have retired to his home town by 1613, the date of this vessel.

The relationship between artist and patron is hinted at in this vessel as it was clearly made to specific order. The rare *pou* form is seldom seen in archaic bronzes and is extremely rare in archaism, where more standard forms were usual, suggesting that perhaps Zou Diguang had such a vessel to act as a prototype for Hu's archaistic version. It is not difficult to imagine artist and patron seated over tea discussing the details of the commission, studying the original *pou,* and perhaps taking a rubbing.

The question of what lies behind archaistic decoration is worth considering. There is a view that subsequent editions of illustrated printed books showing collections of archaic bronzes (notably the Song Emperor Huizong's collection published in the *Xuenhe Bogu Tulu),* were responsible for the gradual simplification and corruption of archaic design. While these later, corrupt editions were responsible for some archaistic efforts and later fakes, the simplistic opinion that the less like the original design the later the piece has been properly debunked by Ulrich Hausmann in his work on later bronzes.[1]

From the Song dynasty, when archaism was first popularized, its source of forms and decorative motifs would have relied variously on original vessels and rubbings taken from them, as well as from illustrations in woodblock printed editions, and from memory based upon either of these sources. We know that as early as the Southern Song, archaism on ceramics is extremely formalized and far-fetched by comparison with archaic originals (*guan* wares, for instance). The court, despite the loss of much of the Northern Song imperial collection, cannot have been unaware of true archaic design. We also know from late Ming sources that archaic originals were freely available in the antique shops of the day.[2]

Rubbings taken from original vessels, although never mentioned in discussions on archaism, were probably an important element in the simplification, abstraction and exaggeration which is typical of archaism. A natural tendency of a rubbing is to accentuate relief surfaces. Elements which on an original bronze tend to merge visually with their background are brought out as more individual motifs in a rubbing. This would lead naturally to similar exaggeration in an archaistic piece based on such sources. Exactly this effect is found in the decoration on this vessel, where the gilding of the main elements visually separates them from their ground.

1. 'Later Chinese Bronzes' by Ulrich Hausmann, in *Documentary Chinese Works of Art In Scholars' Taste.*
2. See *Chinese Metalwork of the Hu Wenming Group.*

104

Teabowl and Stand

Porcelain, covered with a whisper-pale blue glaze with some crackling; the cup of wide mouthed form, with an elegant, very slightly 'S'-shaped profile, flaring at the lip and standing on a narrow cylindrical foot; the interior with a small raised bump in the centre, giving the impression of looking into an open flower; the stand with a dissected spherical upper bulge supported on a wide, upward-flaring, lipped saucer, set on a deep, cylindrical, slightly flared ribbed foot.
Qingbai ware; Jingdezhen, Northern Song dynasty.
Height of cup in stand: 8.7 cm.
Height of cup alone: 4.4 cm.
Diameter of cup: 10.2 cm.

青白瓷茶盞連托子
北宋(960-1126), 總高8.7厘米, 盞高4.4厘米
盞直徑10.2厘米

Tea has been popular in China since before the Han dynasty. Originally considered to be a medicinal drink, it developed by the 3rd to 5th centuries into a pleasant drink to be taken with confections, but it seems to have been transformed into a serious cult only by the Tang dynasty. In a Tang book on tea the *Chajing* (*Canon of Tea*), Lu Yu (733-804) noted that in his day drinking tea as a beverage was popular and that it had become a drink in every household in the two capitals (Chang'an and Luoyang).[1] The delights of tea drinking were also recorded by a number of Tang poets,[2] and by many later poets and scholars.

Originally tea was served in powder form which was mixed with hot water in a wide-mouthed bowl, and whipped into a frothy concoction. It was not until the Northern Song period that tea leaves began to be steeped in water in a pot, which became by Ming times the general practice. These wide-mouthed bowls of a variety of shapes were among the commonest of ceramic forms from the Tang and Song dynasties and were made in a number of wares with different opinions placing those from this or that kiln as the most suitable. The cup stand was considered to be a Tang invention (see no. 257).

The evolution of tea drinking to a cult meant that the influential minority required large numbers of finely made wares to suit their taste: initially wide-mouthed teabowls, then teabowls and stands, such as this example and that of no. 257, then teapots and other forms of bowls and cups in ceramics and a variety of other materials.

The form and glaze of this example are quite exquisite. The pale colour and purity of the glaze and the deep-footed form suggest an early date.

1. 'Tea Drinking, Tea Ware and Purple Clay Ware' by Song Boyin, in *K.S. Lo Collection in the Flagstaff House Museum of Tea Ware,* Part 2.
2. Ibid.

103

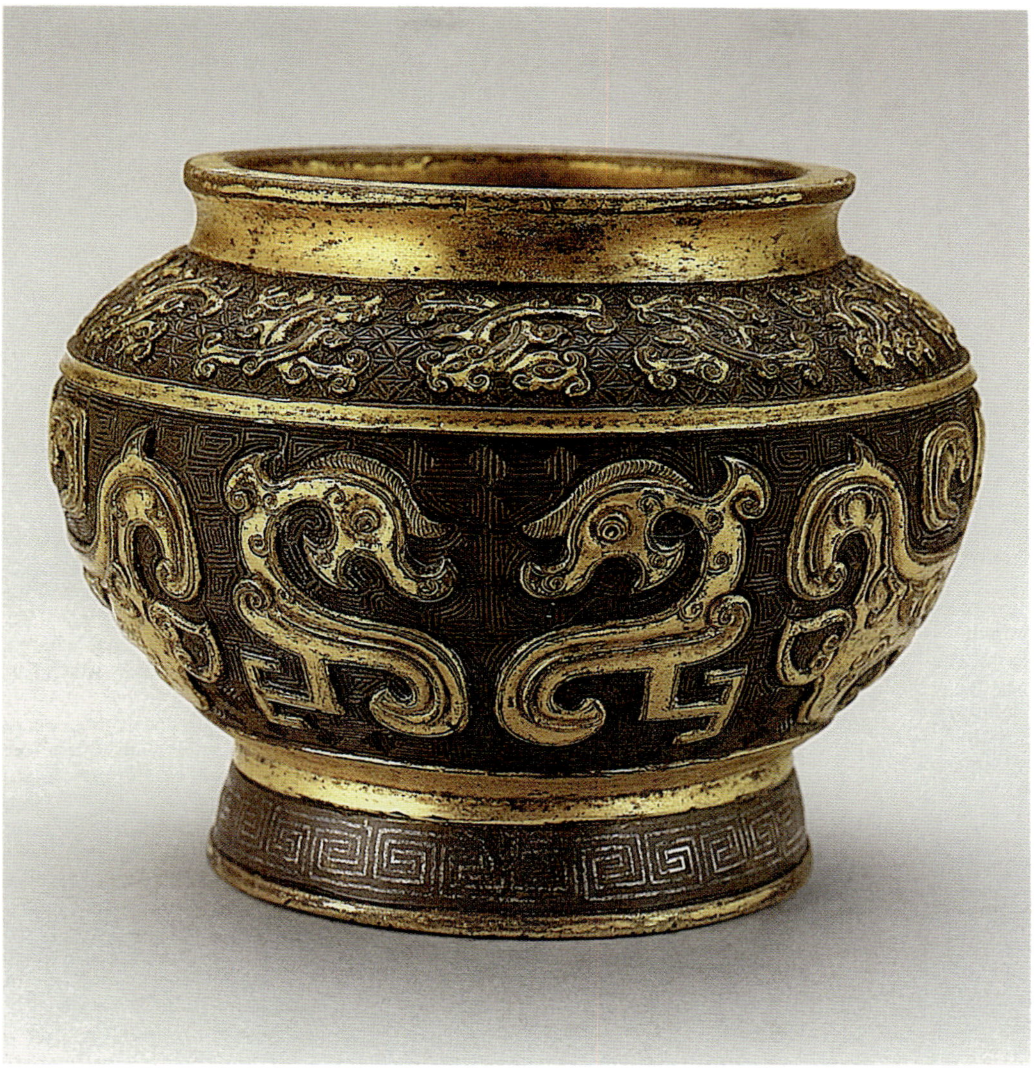

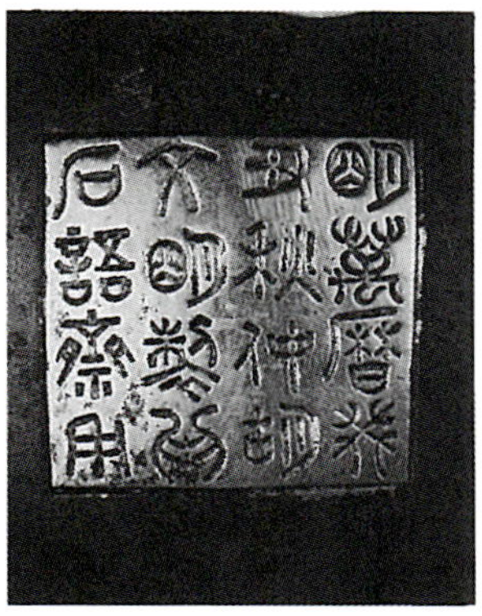

Larger than life size

104

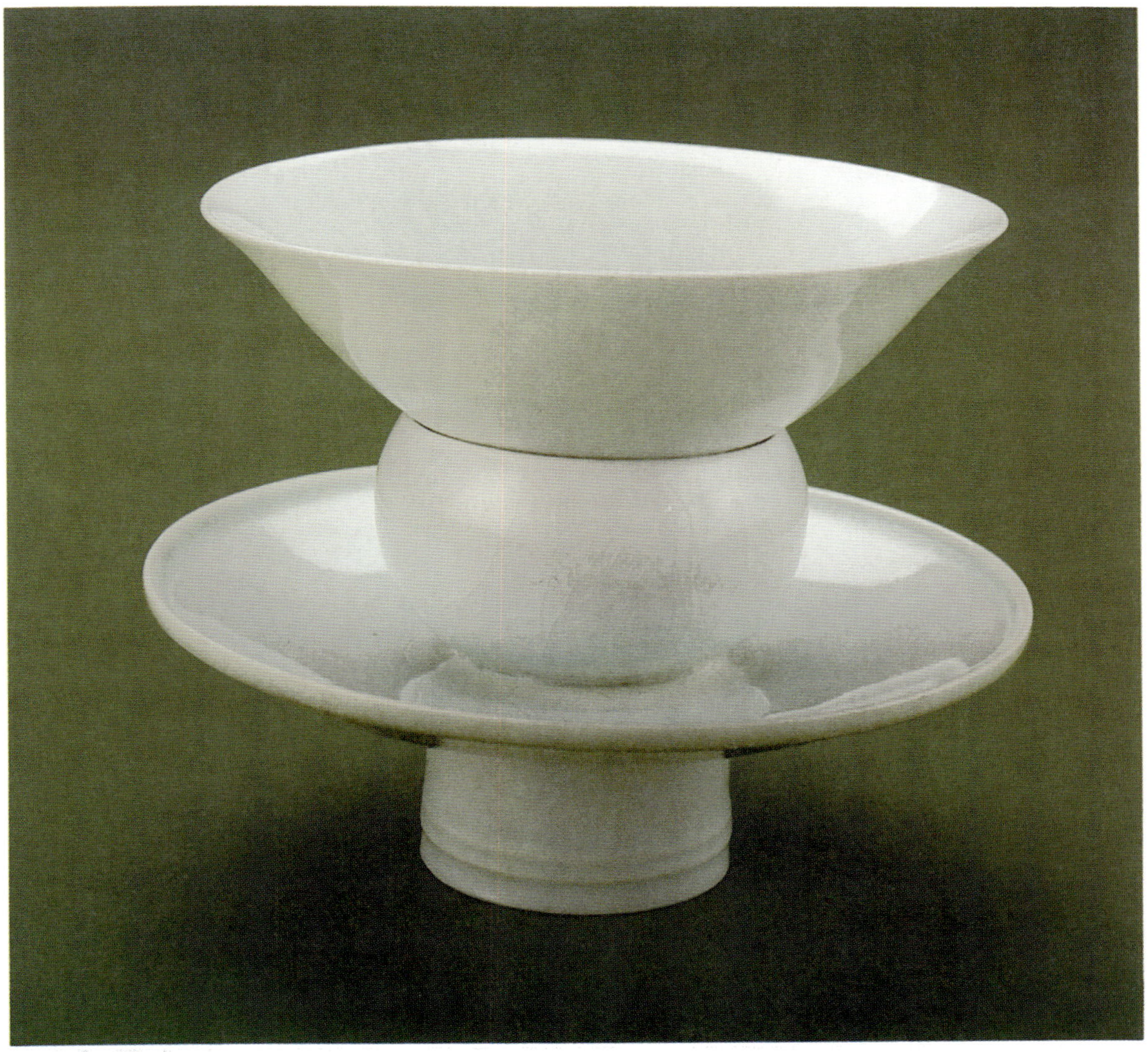

Larger than life size

105

Root Sculpture

Wood, *nanmu* (cedar), of variegated golden and dark brown colours; the partly natural formations and gnarled surface enhanced by cutting to form a strange rock with four monkeys, one holding a peach, set in the various niches of the convoluted stone, which is pierced through in groups of interlinking cavities.
Probably mid-Qing dynasty.
Height: 22 cm.

楠木雕岩中四猴像
可能清中葉, 高22厘米

Tang Zu, the scholar and wood carver who made no. 59, was also known for his ability to carve roots, although no extant pieces are known to be carved by him (or to the best of our knowledge by any other member of the literati). Root carvings were largely anonymous so we are at a loss to know which were made by members of the influential minority and which by craftsmen responding to their demands.

Incense was sometimes burnt in association with pierced and gnarled rocks, so that the smoke would swirl in and out of the holes and give the appearance of mist around a peak. This root, although there is no evidence of it having been used as such, would have been ideal for this. The hole in the centre of the base reaches upwards, to divide and emerge at several locations in the boulder. Incense fixed somehow in the main base hole would swirl delightfully from these apertures.

106

Brush Pot

Bamboo, a section of culm of reddish-brown colour; carved as a brush pot, using the natural form of the culm with the diaphragm as the base; the exterior cut away to leave in relief a boating party enroute to the Red Cliff, with three scholars seated at a table set with food and wine, while two boatmen steer and two attendents heat wine over a brazier in a somewhat cramped boat, which flows in a fast moving river, beneath an overhanging pine tree and clouds, partly hiding the moon; giving way to a rocky cliff, upon which is incised the title 'Night Outing to the Red Cliff' followed by the information that it was made for the elegant enjoyment of the Master of the Yunxiang Guan in the mid autumn of the *yisi* year (1665/1725) by Zhihe.
Probably 1665 or 1725.
Height: 14.8 cm. Diameter of top: 12 cm.
Formerly in the Dr. Ip Yee collection.
Published: *Chinese Bamboo Carving,* Part I, p.281, no. 73.

竹雕夜遊赤壁筆筒•稚鶴製
清乙巳(1665或1725), 高14.8厘米,
頂直徑12厘米

This brush pot was dated to the 18th century in the above publication, leaving open the question of whether the cyclical date should therefore be read as 1725 or 1785. Although the style is 17th century, the authors felt that the modelling did not reach the standards of the 17th century pieces of this group. While it is true that it is not as fine as some examples, qualitative judgements on individual items have their dangers. In the 17th century there must have been artists working in the style of the day to supply various levels of patronage, and poorer quality works are just as likely to come from the 17th century as from a later time. Equally, in an artistic environment such as that of China, where variations on past themes are a staple and where a demand for antiquity in every sphere was constantly supplied by opportunists, the possibilities of later work in 17th century style are plentiful. Until further detailed research into the styles of individual carvers is undertaken, we believe that the most probable readings of the cyclical date would be either 1665 or 1725, although 1785 is not out of the question.

The subject here owes its existence to the two works by Su Shi entitled *Chibi Fu* ('Prose Poem of the Red Cliff'). Su Shi records in the first that in 1082 he took some guests on an excursion by boat, under the Red Cliff. They drank wine and became merry, chanted poetry, and drifted with the currents as if on a mysterious journey into the unknown. One of their number accompanied the sung poetry on a flute, and as they discussed poets of old, the typically exquisite melancholy of Chinese poets was enjoyed by all. On the second trip, undertaken later in the same year, Su Shi is with two guests on a similar boat ride. This time they step ashore and Su Shi, climbing above the waters ahead of his friends, begins to feel strange energies of enchantment in the air, a disquiet he cannot shake loose. He unleashes a cry into the night air: "I gave a long, shrill whoop. Trees and grass shook and swayed, the mountains rang, the valley echoed. A wind came up, roiling the water, and I felt a chill of sadness, a shrinking fear. I knew with a shudder that I couldn't stay there any longer."[1] He returns to the boat and there, reunited with his guests, they let the boat drift again. A crane flies overhead in the moonlight, and lets out a single cry in passing, a long, dragging wail. The guests depart and Su Shi sleeps, but is visited in his dreams by a Daoist monk, swaggering in a feathered robe. He asks if Su Shi enjoyed his trip to the Red Cliff. Su Shi realises that the Daoist immortal was the crane that flew overhead, answering his shout into the wilderness. He awakes with a start, to find no sign of the Daoist. (Su Shi's shout in this case is the same kind of scream to release pent-up emotions that was frequently practiced by the Chinese, and which is referred to quite often in Chinese sources, see no. 75). The imagery is typical of the literati, where the real world mingles with other, mysterious realms and with art.

On this brush pot, we probably see Su Shi with his guests, although the fact that one guest plays a pair of clappers (a rhythmic instrument made up of two pieces of wood, like castinets) and not a flute might suggest the second boat trip, except that no crane is shown, and it is such a central part of the story that it would seem strange to leave it out. Another possibility is that it does not actually depict Su Shi and his party of guests. The *Chibi Fu* immediately entered the Chinese literati consciousness, becoming familiar to all educated Chinese; it also made a popular tourist spot of the Red Cliff, to which countless night boating trips have since been taken. The subject here might be a non-specific reference to Su Shi and his excursion.

For another bamboo brush pot with this subject, dated to the Kangxi period, see *Chinese Bamboo Carving,* Part I, p.236, no. 52.

1. Quoted from 'Su Shih's Reading of the "Chung yung"', by Christian Murck, in *Theories of the Arts in China.*

105

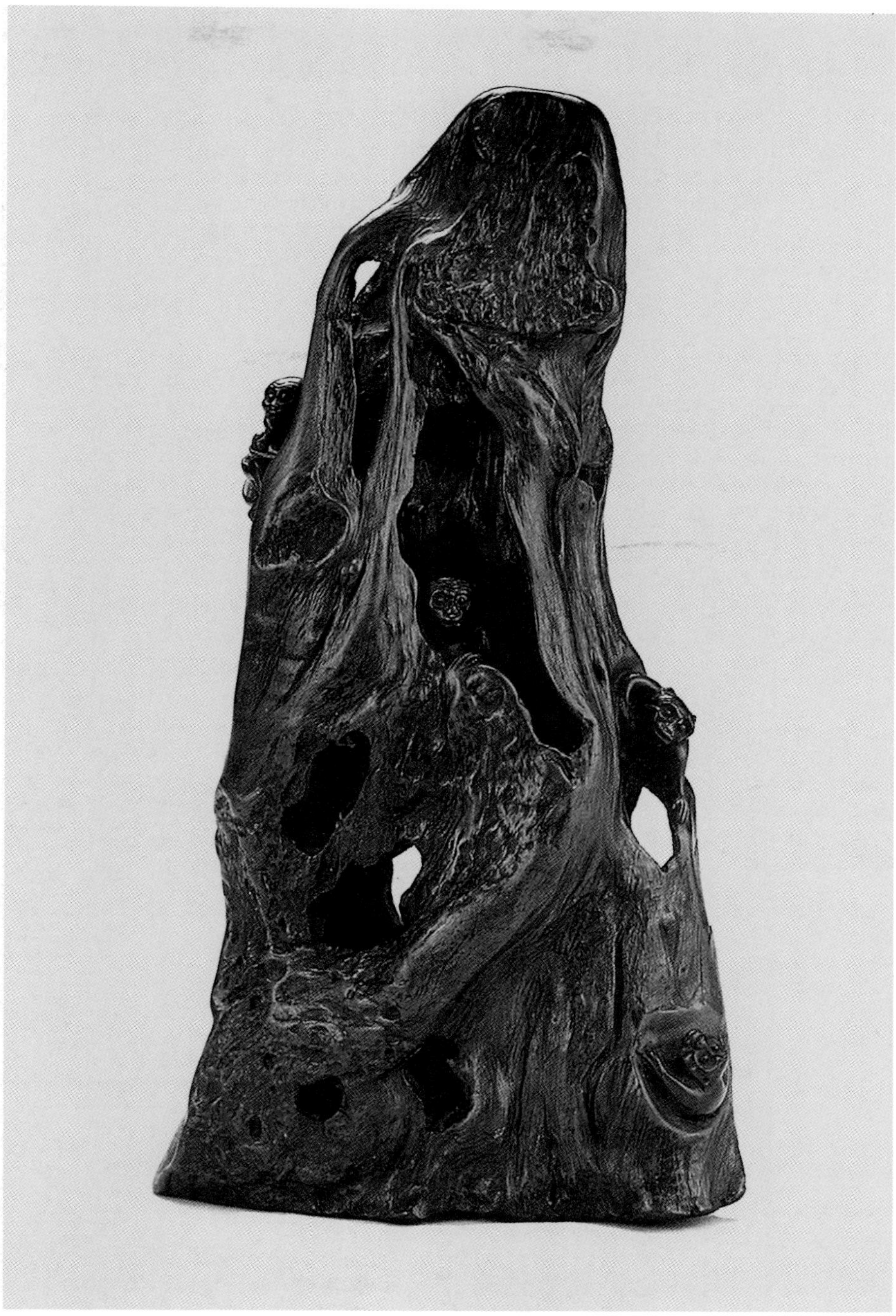

106

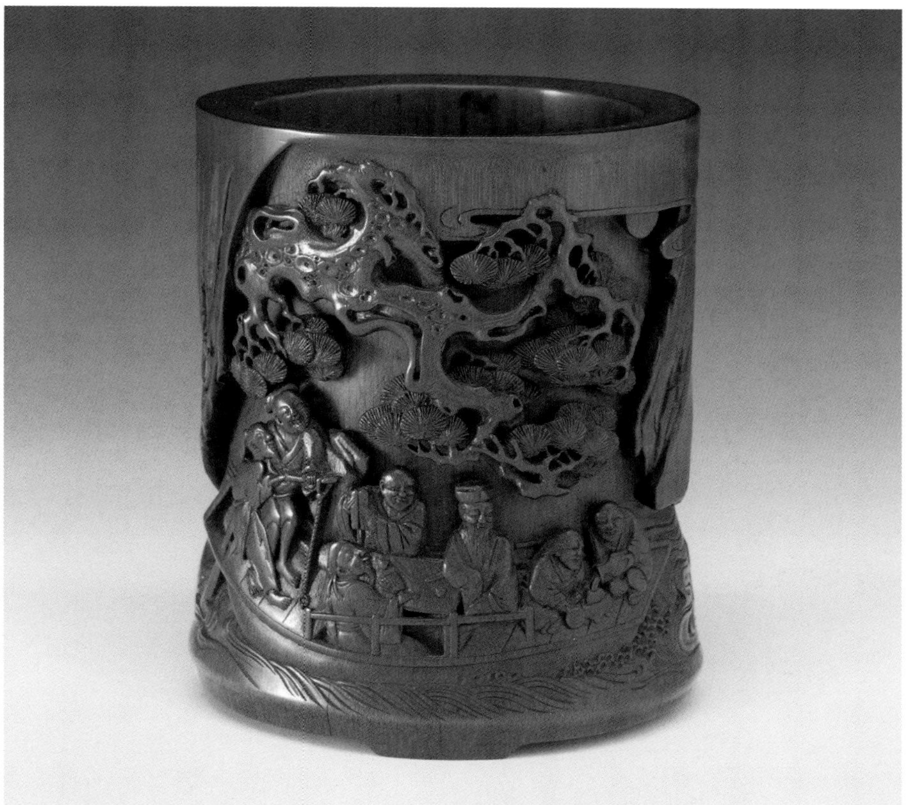

107

Teapot

Qu Yingshao, Deng Kui and Jian

Stoneware, of brown colour with beige, textured speckling; a teapot in the form of a stone weight resting on three button feet, the centre of the base impressed with one seal of Qu Yingshao *Hugongyefu* in postitive seal script, a second seal *Jian* impressed at the base of the handle in positive seal script.
After firing the surface of this teapot has been carved with a design of flowering plum blossoms extending from the base of the handle to both sides and the lid, with the title 'Transmitting Spring's Message' (a reference to the plum blossom), followed by the inscription: "In the style of Qian Shumei, (by Deng) Fusheng".
Perhaps Shanghai, *circa* 1815-1845.
Height: 6.8 cm. Greatest width: 15 cm.
Exhibited and illustrated: *Yixing Pottery*, Hong Kong Museum of Art, 1981, no. 62 (under the potter's *hao*, Qu Ziye, which is misprinted as Qu Zhiye; it is also wrongly described as decorated by Qian Shumei).

宜興紫砂刻梅枝茶壺•瞿應紹,鄧奎及吉安製
十九世紀(1815-1845),高6.8厘米,最寬15厘米

Qu Yingshao (*zi:* Ziye, *hao:* Yuehu, Qufu, Laoye; active 1795-1850) was a native of Shanghai, a scholar, poet, painter, calligrapher and seal-carver who became famous during the first half of the 19th century. He was an avid collector, particularly fond of ancient bronzes and stone inscriptions, who enjoyed a reputation as a connoisseur with a keen eye. He was also well-known for the care with which he placed his works of art wherever he lived, adding to them a fresh dimension for the visitor. Another of his hobbies was the production of teapots. He sent his friend Deng Kui (Deng Fusheng) to Yixing to supervise the manufacture of the teapots he commissioned, and was reputed to have decorated the finest of these himself while getting Deng Kui to decorate the others.

Deng Kui (*zi:* Fusheng), from Wuxing in Jiangsu province, was known in his own right as a calligrapher and seal carver. Here he is copying the style of Qian Du (*zi:* Shumei — 1763/4-1844/5), a scholar, painter and calligrapher in the circle of Qu Yingshao. Jian is probably the *hao* of an otherwise unknown potter who was commissioned to make the piece by Qu Yingshao through Deng Kui (see no. 109 for another piece made for the fifth Prince Ding, which also bears the seal Jian.)

This little teapot represents the cult of tea connoisseurship which developed over the centuries in China. It expresses the refinement of mind that tends to make a complex form of communication out of the consumption of a simple beverage. Tea wares made in response to this cult of highly refined connoisseurship take on a new depth of meaning, particularly those which carry the direct expression of the scholars involved. The simple, functional elegance of material and form, with their rustic sophistication; the subject-matter derived from the twin traditions of painting and calligraphy; the poetic inscription; even the manner of decoration, where the hard material is incised with a blade (the 'iron brush' of the scholar/seal carver); all speak of ineffable refinement.

The source of much of the information on Qu's activities is the *Yangxien Shahu Tukao* by Li Jingkang and Zhang Hong where it says that he tried to make pots himself and sent his friend Deng Kui to supervise their production at Yixing. It is more likely that Qu designed the pots and commissioned them, adding his name to them, but did not make them himself. This is also the source of the statement that if the pieces were good he decorated them himself, and if not he would get Deng Kui to do so. Such bold statements in Chinese sources must be taken with a pinch of salt as they too frequently originate in the most insignificant passing comment which, repeated time and again, becomes accepted fact.

Several pots are known of this form, each with different decoration. Bartholomew illustrates one[1] which Qu himself incised with bamboo and calligraphy. Paul Moss illustrates another[2] also decorated by Qu with bamboo and calligraphy in the confident cutting strokes of an accomplished seal carver. Two more are in the K.S. Lo collection in the Flagstaff House Museum of Tea Ware, Hong Kong. The first[3] bears the same seal as this example, but is wrongly catalogued as being by the well-known potter Yang Pengnian. It is inscribed and decorated, also with bamboo, by another carver going by the name of Xiaogu. The second (no. 48) bears two seals: one, presumably of the potter, Shenxi and the other the same seal as on our example of the patron and inscriber, but again with the *hao* misprinted as *Zhi*.

Another teapot which we believe was wrongly attributed to him is also in the K.S. Lo collection (no. 152). It appears as no. 109 in this catalogue where the question of its attribution is discussed.

1. *I-Hsing Wares*, no. 19 (from The Art Institute of Chicago).
2. *Documentary Chinese Works of Art in Scholars' Taste*, no. 91.
3. *K.S. Lo Collection in the Flagstaff House Museum of Tea Ware*, Part 2, no. 42.

108

Scholar's Plaything

Gourd, of rich dark, reddish-brown colour; the natural form carved with a phoenix standing on a rocky outcrop, from behind which grow flowering peonies, the sun above set in a formalized 'frame' of clouds, the reverse of the upper bulb inscribed: "made for the Hall of Constancy on the sixteenth day of the second day of spring of 1801, the sixth year of Jiaqing" in clerical script, followed by the seal *Xingyouheng Tang* in seal script within a square cartouche with rounded corners.
1801.
Height: 24.5 cm.
Formerly in the Dr. Ip Yee collection.
Published: *Chinese Decorated Gourds*, p.68, no. 27.

葫蘆刻丹鳳朝陽圖文玩•行有恒堂銘
清嘉慶六年(1801),高24.5厘米

The *Xingyouheng Tang* (usually translated as the 'Hall of Constancy' although adequate translations of hall marks are particularly difficult as they frequently had more than one layer of meaning) belonged to the fifth Prince Ding, Zaichuan, who died in 1854. He was a great-great-grandson of the Qianlong Emperor, and inherited the princedom upon the death of his father in 1836. A brief biography is given in *Eminent Chinese of the Ch'ing Period*. Zaichuan was educated in the palace school for princes. In 1816, presumably after an examination held for imperial clansmen, he was appointed a nobleman of the tenth rank, from which position he gradually moved up through the ranks, achieving in 1835 the sixth degree, before inheriting his father's princedom of the second degree together with all the family estates.

During this time he served in various official capacities, including the presidency of the Boards of Ceremonies and of Works, holding other posts concurrently such as general commandant of the Light Division stationed at Xiangshan, west of Beijing. In the last decade of the Daoguang Emperor's reign he held the post of presiding controller of the Imperial Clan Court. Despite one charge of improper behaviour and temporary deprivation of office, he continued to enjoy the favour of the succeeding Xianfeng Emperor.

Zaichuan was a keen collector and connoisseur of works of art ranging from paintings to snuff bottles, which bear his hall mark. Apart from the series of carved gourds made for him,[1] there is a glass overlay globular water vessel, a crystal snuff bottle and a chalcedony snuff bottle,[2] a red glass snuff bottle and a crystal snuff bottle (with recently added decoration),[3] a snuff bottle in green glass,[4] and a crystal snuff bottle (now painted inside by the contemporary aritst Wang Xisan) in the collection of Mr. & Mrs. George Bloch of Hong Kong. Also in the Shuisongshi Shanfang collection are a boxwood fan frame with dragons and relief inscription and a boxwood elaborate *ruyi*, with intricate openwork and interlinking *lingzhi;* and a white nephrite thumb ring with a calligraphic inscription.

1. See *Chinese Decorated Gourds*, nos. 26 and 28 for others.
2. *Documentary Works in Scholars' Taste*, nos. 190, 110 and 111 respectively.
3. *L'Eunuque aux Trois Joyaux*, p.157, no. 113 and pp.158-165, nos. 114-117 respectively.
4. *Chinese Snuff Bottles of the Ch'ing Dynasty*, p.71, no. 74.

107

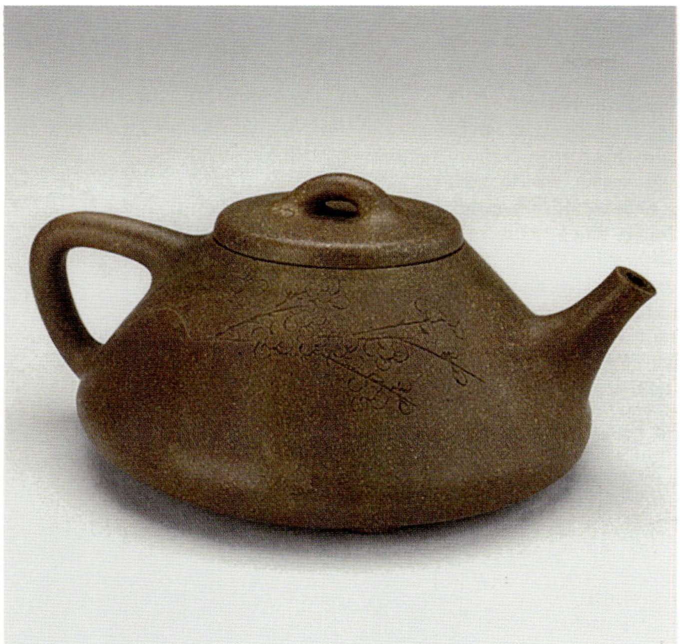

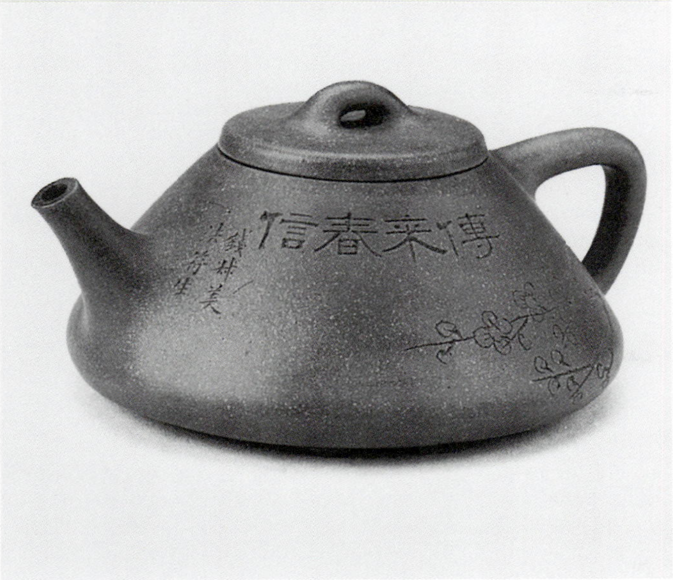

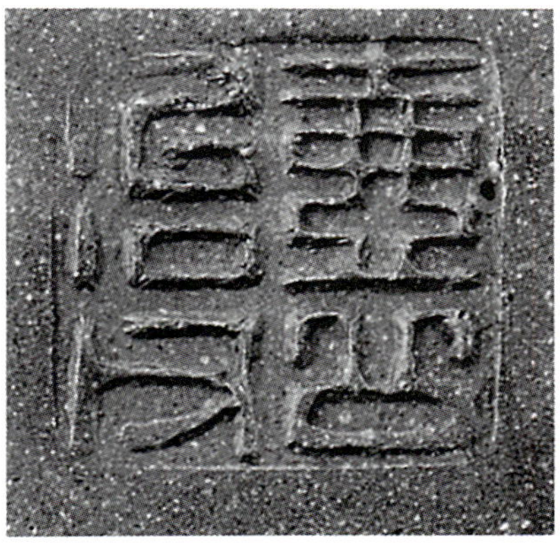

108

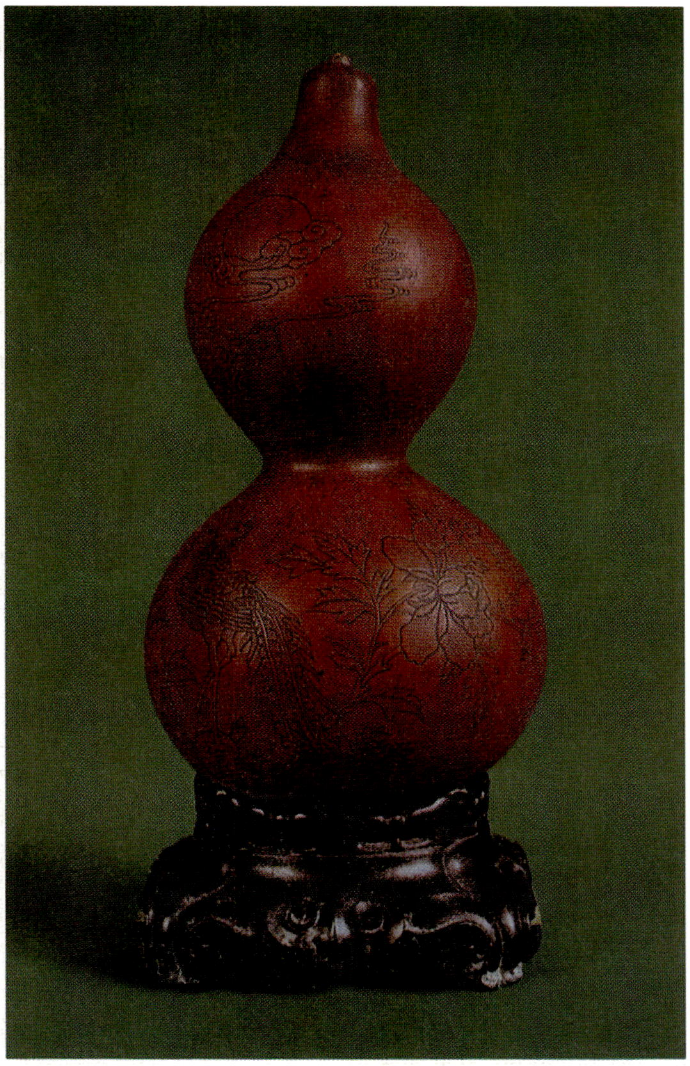

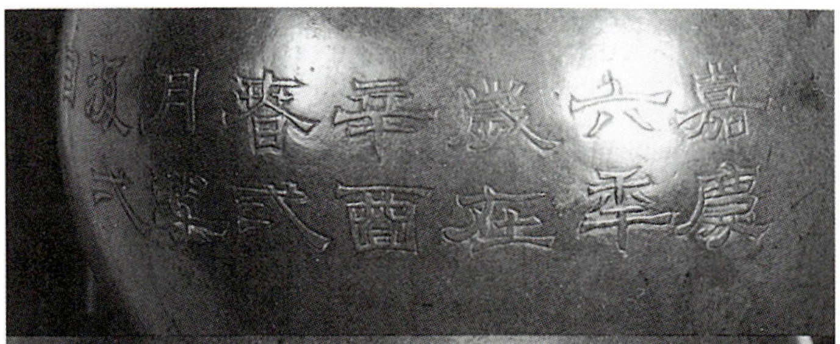

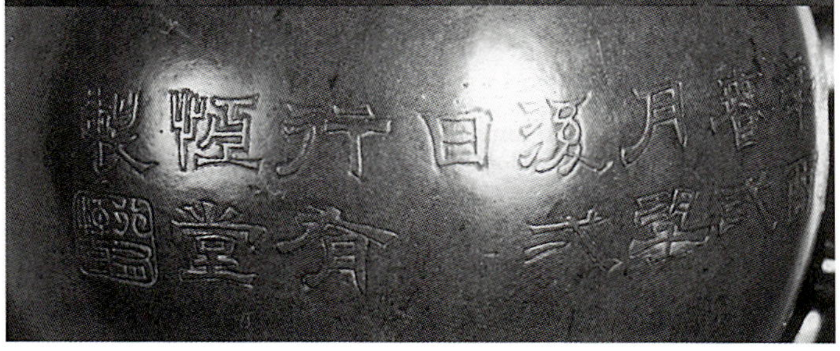

109

Teapot

Jian

Stoneware, of buff colour, with enamelled decoration; a gourd-shaped teapot, decorated on one side with blossoming prunus branches in *famille-rose* enamels; the other side incised with the inscription: "Made for the Master of the Xingyouheng Tang, in the spring of 1849 (*Daoguang jiyou*)", followed by the seal *Dingjun qingshang* ('for elegant appreciation in the Ding domain') in negative seal script; a small impressed seal under the handle with the name Jian in positive seal script.
Yixing, 1849.
Height: 9.1 cm.
Published: *Yixing Pottery*, p.121, no. 61.

宜興陶畫粉彩梅枝茶壺•吉安製
清道光己酉(1849),高9.1厘米

This teapot was catalogued in the above publication as being by Qu Yingshao on the strength of the name Jian impressed under the handle. This name appears on two teapots associated with Qu Yingshao mentioned in the *Yangxian Shahu Tukao* (p.38, nos. 1 and 3) where it is read once as Jian and once as Anji (the seal could be read either way), and on the teapot from the Lam Dawei collection (shown here as no. 107) which also bears Qu Yingshao's seal.

We believe that it is the name of an otherwise unknown Yixing potter commissioned by Qu Yingshao, perhaps through Deng Kui (see no. 107) to make pots for him, and that the same potter is here working on a commission for Prince Ding. We know that Qu Yingshao was in the habit of commissioning pots, and sent his friend Deng Kui to Yixing to supervise them (see no. 107) which implies that he must have supervised a third party, the potter. It is likely that the potter's name would appear quietly somewhere, as it does on all these works discreetly under the handle in the form of an auspicious *hao* or pseudonym, and it would have been rather unnecessary for Qu to add a second seal so discreetly, when his own takes pride of place in the centre of the base. The *hao* Jian is not recorded as belonging to Qu Yingshao in any of the works which list this well-known scholar and his various names. It is also unlikely that Prince Ding would have commissioned a teapot from Qu Yingshao, who himself seems to have acted mainly as patron rather than potter, but in the unlikely event that he had, it is even less probable that Qu would then have signed it with an obscure name by which he was not otherwise known. Had Prince Ding commissioned Qu, it would have been because of Qu's reputation as a scholar interested in Yixing wares, and his association with the work would have been the main purpose of the commission and more obviously noted. All the evidence points to Jian being the name of a separate potter.

We have translated the unusual seal of the Prince which appears here as 'for elegant appreciation in the Ding domain' as the character *jun* means a large area, but it might also be used to mean 'household' in this case.

(For details of the the fifth Prince Ding, see no. 108.)

110

Water Vessel

Nephrite, of pure, flawless pale greenish-white colour; a water vessel, of compressed globular form set on a wide, flared foot; the deeply recessed base inscribed *Xingyouheng Tang* ('Hall of Constancy') in seal script.
Circa 1815-1854.
Height: 4.32 cm. Diameter: 13.9 cm.

白玉水丞•行有恒堂銘
清(約1815-1854),高4.32厘米,直徑13.9厘米

The foot of this vessel is made of a separate section, presumably removed from the inside of the hollow vessel. Flawless stone was difficult to come by, and was appreciated under the influence of the Qianlong Emperor and his successors (much more so than in earlier times where markings in the stone and flaws were both utilized and valued). The material presumably had some flaws, and to maximize size while achieving flawlessness, the carver has obviously used the section removed from the interior of the vessel to form the foot. It is conventional wisdom in the West that a piece of jade is better if it is made of one piece, and that such sectional manufacture indicates a somewhat second-class object, but the simple form here combined with purity of material speak eloquently for its refinement. Under the Qianlong Emperor there seems to have been a shift, apparently reaching down from the Court, towards an emphasis on material itself, whereas previously the emphasis had been on what was done with material.

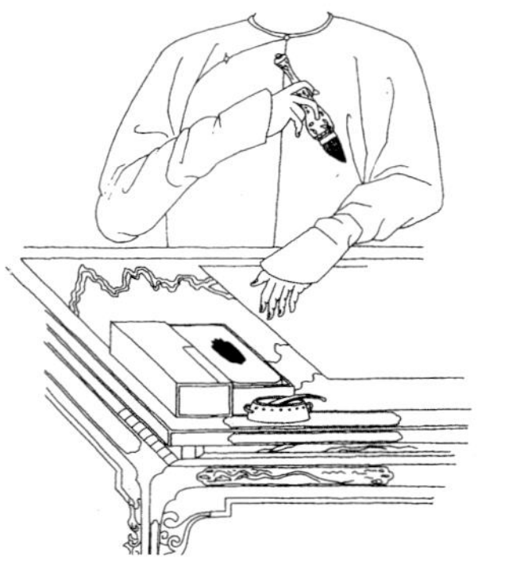

Fig. 1

Broad, shallow forms of this type were often used as brush washers, to clean the brush and to add water to an inked brush for toning (sometimes done on a small palette, but also easily achieved by a practised hand, particularly if varying tones are required in one loading of the brush, in this sort of washer). They usually have a lip suitable for 'pointing' and controlling the amount of water left in the brush. However, broader mouthed vessels such as this might also have been used in conjunction with a ladle to supply the inkstone, as can be seen in a portrait of the Kangxi Emperor at his desk from the Beijing Palace Museum, a line drawing of which is reproduced in Fig. 1, and in the late Ming painting by Chen Hongshou of *The Four Pleasures of Bo Juyi* (see Fig. 2).

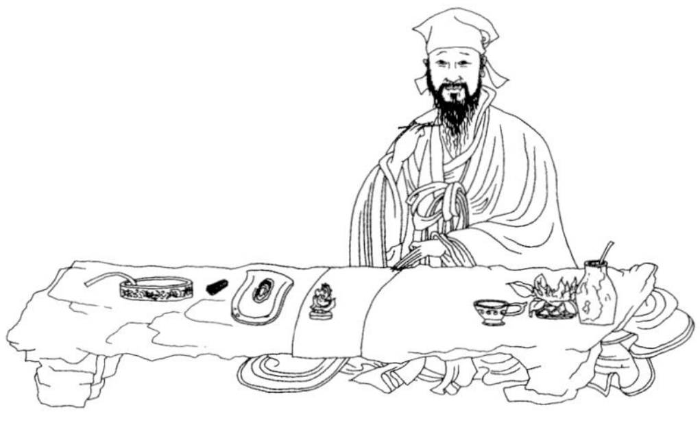

Fig. 2

111

Water Vessel

Soapstone, of variegated creamy beige colours, with some red inclusions; a water vessel, of slightly flared cylindrical form with a concave lip section; the exterior incised with a design of a scholar fishing from a boat in a river scene with rolling hills and rocks, trees and flying birds, the variegated markings in the stone cleverly used to 'colour' the landscape (opaque areas are used as rocks and land, while a more translucent grey-beige forms the water; the small red speckled inclusions are used as tree foliage, etc.); the shallow, recessed base, surrounded by a simple footrim, inscribed *Daoguang jiyou Xingyouheng Tang zhi* ('Made for the Hall of Constancy in 1849'), in clerical script.
1849.
Height: 3.85 cm. Diameter: 5.95 cm.

石雕山水水丞•行有恒堂銘
清道光己酉(1849),高3.85厘米,直徑5.95厘米

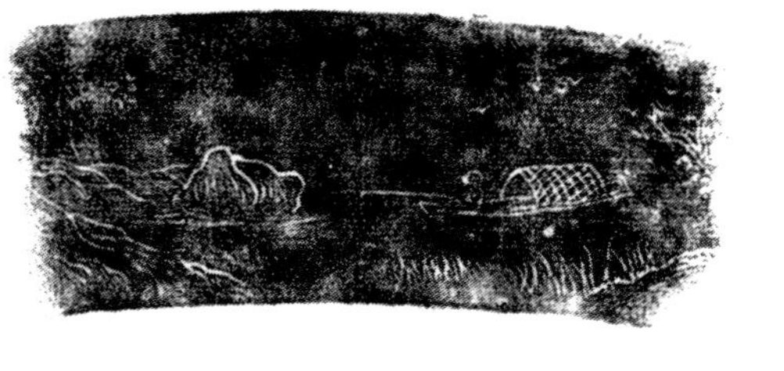

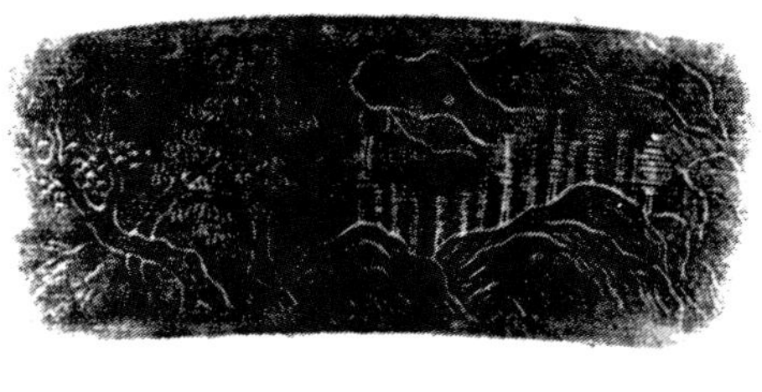

This is a water vessel of the type used in conjunction with a small ladle to provide water for the inkstone. It is made of a material beloved of the literati and is decorated with a subject typical of literati painting, depicting a scholar leading the idealized life of a fisherman (the association often made between the two being that the fisherman comes and goes as he pleases, dictated to only by nature; he represents the ideal rustic existence). It is incised with the 'iron brush' of the seal-carver, and is identified by the hall mark as being for a well-known collector and connoisseur. This is exactly the sort of piece a scholar might carve for himself in an idle moment, picking up his 'iron brush' and 'painting' on the surface of the soft stone, although there is no indication of who made this particular vessel.

109

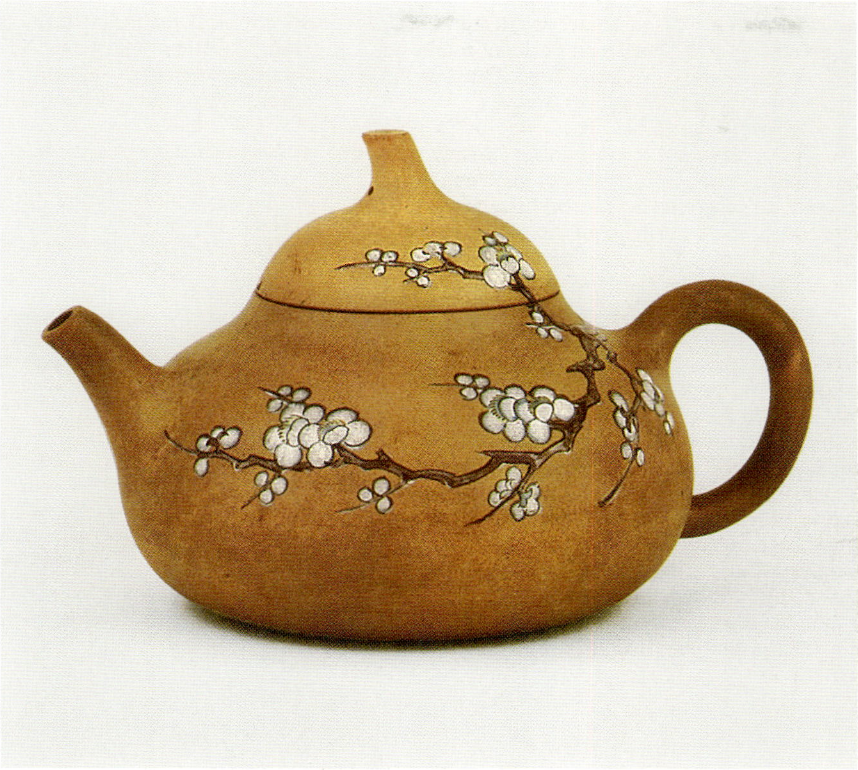

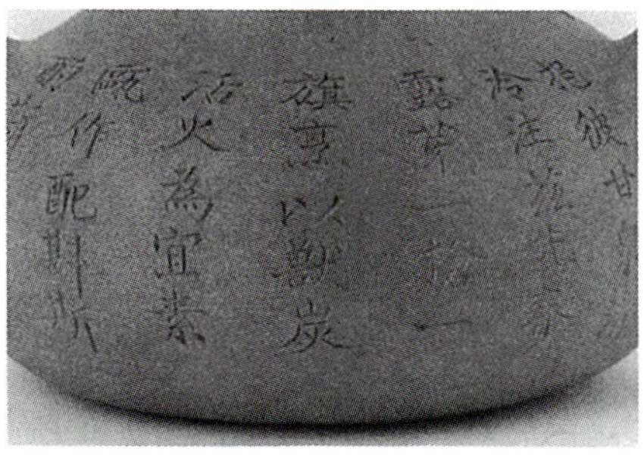

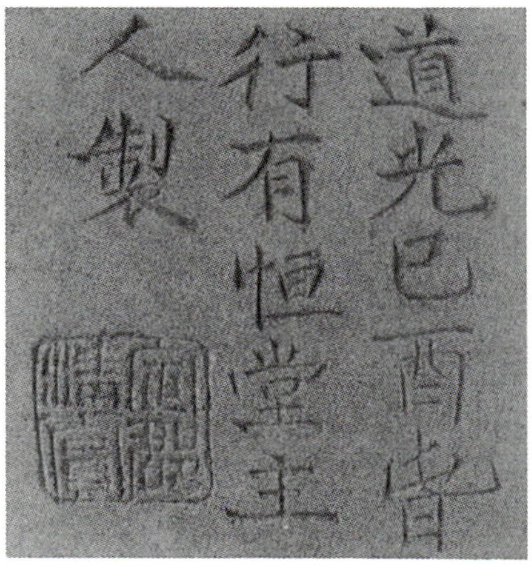

110

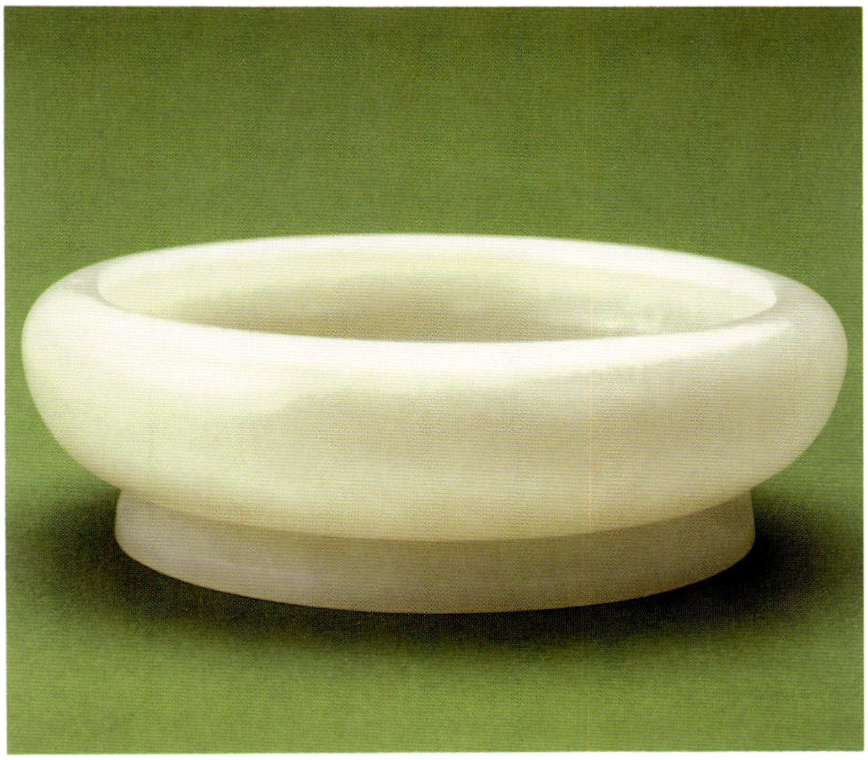

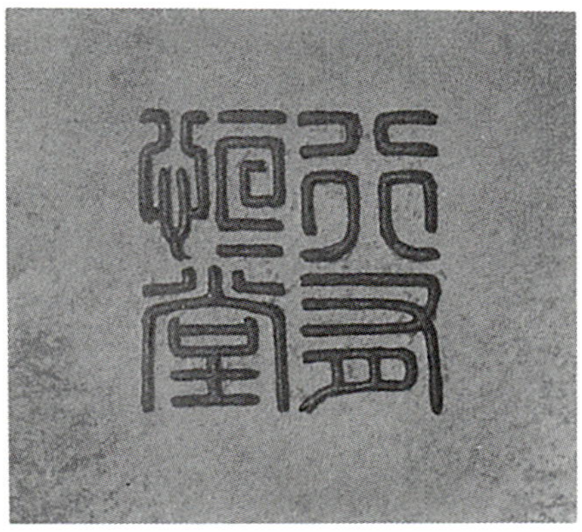

111

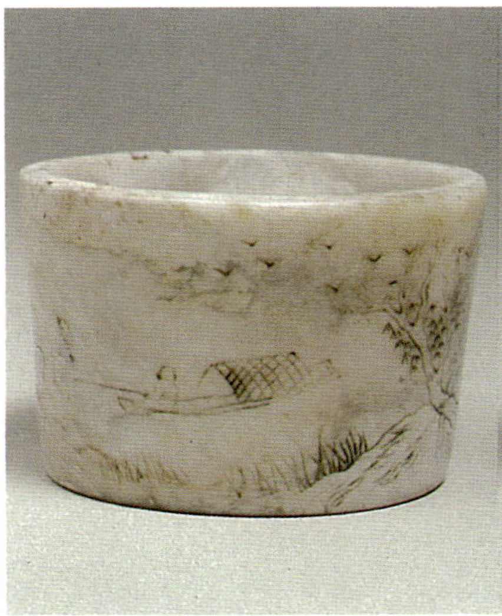

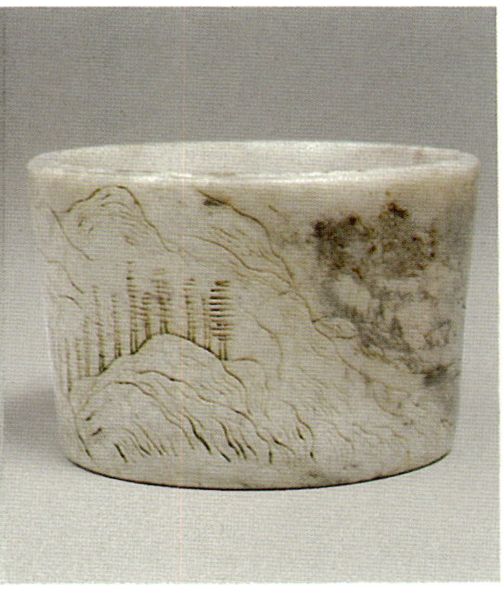

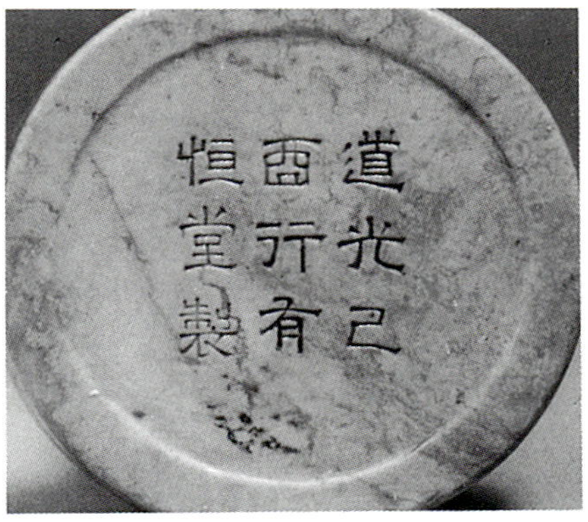

112

Brush Pot

Yang Jichu

Stoneware, of yellowish-beige colour, with various colours of slip; a brush pot, the plain, cylindrical form decorated on the outside with a continuous landscape scene delicately painted in various colours of slip, including an unusual pale pink; two men negotiate a boat towards a lakeside house nestling in the trees; the shallow recessed foot with an impressed seal of the potter *Yang Jichu* in positive seal script.
Yixing, probably first half of the 19th century.
Height: 15.2 cm. Diameter: 15.4 cm.
Published: *Yixing Pottery*, p.133, no. 73.

宜興陶畫山水筆筒•楊季初製
十九世紀上半葉,高15.2厘米,直徑15.4厘米

Yang Jichu is not recorded, but another brush pot bearing the same seal, also decorated with slip landscape, is recorded.[1] Two more, also with slip decorated landscapes but on dark brown pottery grounds, are in the Suzhou Museum and the Yangzhou Museum.[2] No details of signatures are availalable, but it would be reasonable to assume that all are from the same hand. One of these is dated to between the Qianlong and Daoguang periods, while the other is listed only as Qing. The three examples where dimensions are known are all approximately the same size.

The workmanship on all these brush pots is impressive. The various subtly coloured slips are applied with considerable skill and sensitivity, and appear to be the work of an artist well versed in literati painting. There is the possibility that Yang Jichu was a scholar painter who took to decorating Yixing wares (the associations between scholars and the Yixing potteries are well recorded — see 107 for instance, and *In Scholars' Taste.*[3]) However, in that case he must have been a fairly minor figure as he is not recorded in any of the standard works which list large numbers of artists. It is perhaps more likely that he was a Yixing potter who, working for literati patrons, achieved a certain mastery in their style of painting. The subtle use of different slips, some very thinly applied to represent washes of ink, is delightfully executed, and the overall effect is of a continuous handscroll painting: the viewer's eye is led through the landscape in the direction suggested by the boat, from the first glimpses of distant land to the intimacy of the foreground clump of trees that partially hide the rustic dwelling, and then beyond, to a further shore dotted with reeds, before drifting off again.

1. *Yangxian Shaqi Jingpin Tupu,* pl. 40, where it is dated to the Qing dynasty.
2. Illustrated in the Yixing volume (23) of *Zhongguo Taoqi Quanji,* nos. 24 and 70 respectively.
3. Page 144 where Chen Mansheng's association with Yixing is discussed — an association interestingly illuminated in an article in *Wenwu,* 1985, no. 12 concerning a teapot commissioned by him excavated from an early 19th century tomb, predating his supposed first association with the kilns by several years.

113

Buddha

Ivory, stained golden brown, the stain worn through in places and patinated to a rich creamy yellow colour; carved as a seated Buddha, eyes closed in meditation, a swastika in relief on his chest.
Late Ming or early Qing dynasty.
Set on a wood stand carved as a lotus pod, surrounded by formalized leaves.
Height including stand: 8.1 cm.

象牙雕佛祖坐像
晚明或清初,高連座8.1厘米

This figure is part of a broad group of superbly sculpted small figures of deities popular in the late Ming and early Qing dynasty. They appear in soapstone, bronze, wood and bamboo. Although similar small sculptures continued to appear throughout the Qing dynasty there is no doubt that the late Ming and early Qing period represents the height of this vogue for 'table'-sized sculptures of *luohan,* Buddha, and various legendary figures where aesthetic content seems to take precedence over iconographical content. The vogue appears to have lasted into the early Qing period, and similar figures continued to be made throughout the Qing, but their original spark of inspiration dies out other than in rare examples. Artistic inspiration in the later period shifted to other areas.

Religion was in China, as elsewhere in the world, a major patron of the arts. Chinese culture encouraged syncretism and no conflict was seen in subscribing to several religions at once. This meant that any one religion might develop an incredible complexity of deities — major, minor and frequently hardly relevant at all as borrowings were made from other religions. Because of the difficulties for the uninitiated in keeping up with them all, they are constantly evolving through errors of interpretation and convenient combinations. At one extreme, represented by this little sculpture which is very clearly the seated Buddha, they are easily identified; at the other, where they blend with sages and scholars 'dusting' and idling in the wilderness, they are as incense smoke — better enjoyed without analysis.

114

Incense Tool Vase

Ivory, of creamy white colour with some darker markings; a small, fluted incense tool vase, the elongated form with the cross section of a formalized petal, standing on five small feet, a small, lipped mouth giving access to a cylindrically drilled interior of similar size.
Probably early Qing dynasty.
Height: 9.75 cm.

象牙雕葵花形筋瓶
可能清初,高9.75厘米

Of the large quantity of functional objects required by the scholar class many were made by craftsmen to certain basic formulae. They had to be elegant, discreet and tasteful, but otherwise could be produced fairly easily in a workshop on a mass-produced rather than individual basis.

This type of vase, solidly built with only a narrow cylindrical interior of the width of the mouth opening, was probably made to hold incense tools; either just the chopsticks, as would seem the case with this unusually narrow-necked example, or chopsticks and spade. Another possible use is suggested in the caption to no. 234 where the function of these vases is discussed.

Two popular designs seem to have been made during the late Ming and the Qing dynasty to augment the many individual designs produced. This is one, and the other is of similar section but pear-shaped, with an elongated neck. In each case the cross-section is based on a formalized *kui* flower creating a series of verticle flutes on the exterior. It is likely that shops selling scholars' utensils in the Qing dynasty would have had a selection of such wares awaiting customers. These vases are usually found in wood rather than ivory, but others in ivory are known.[1]

1. There is a pear-shaped example in the Hong Kong collection of Awon Golding which appears to be of similar age to this one.

112

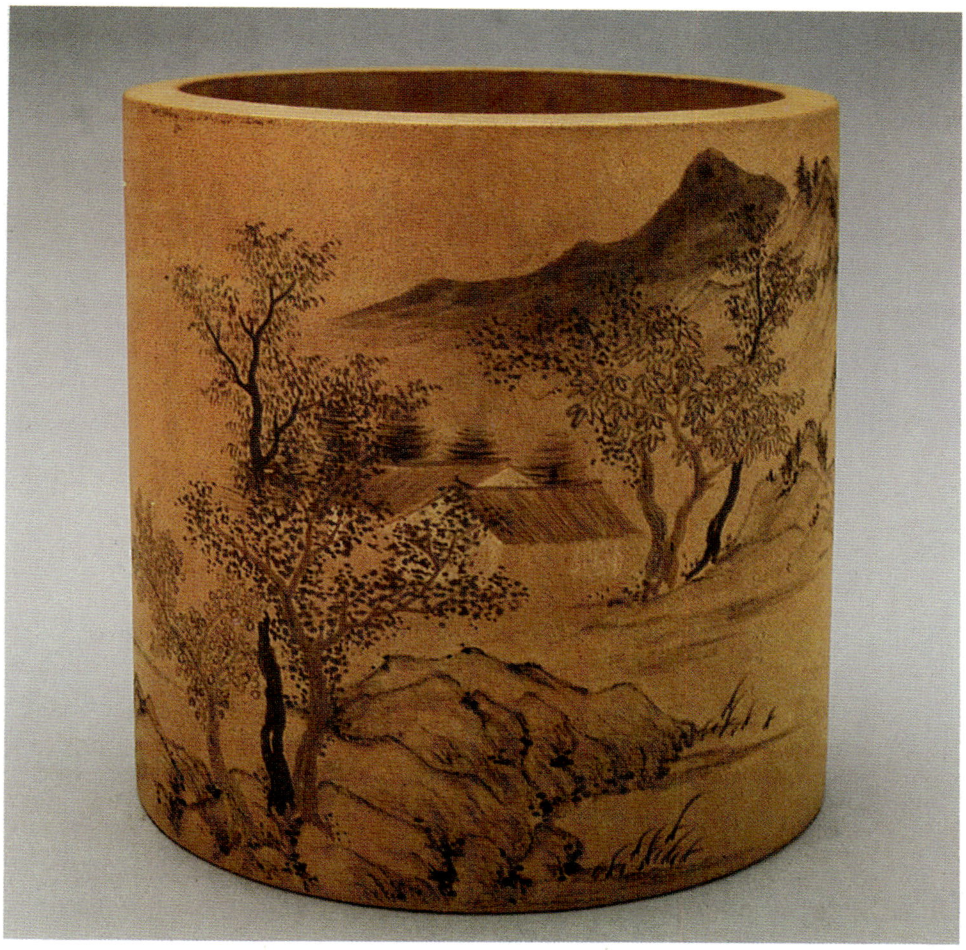

113

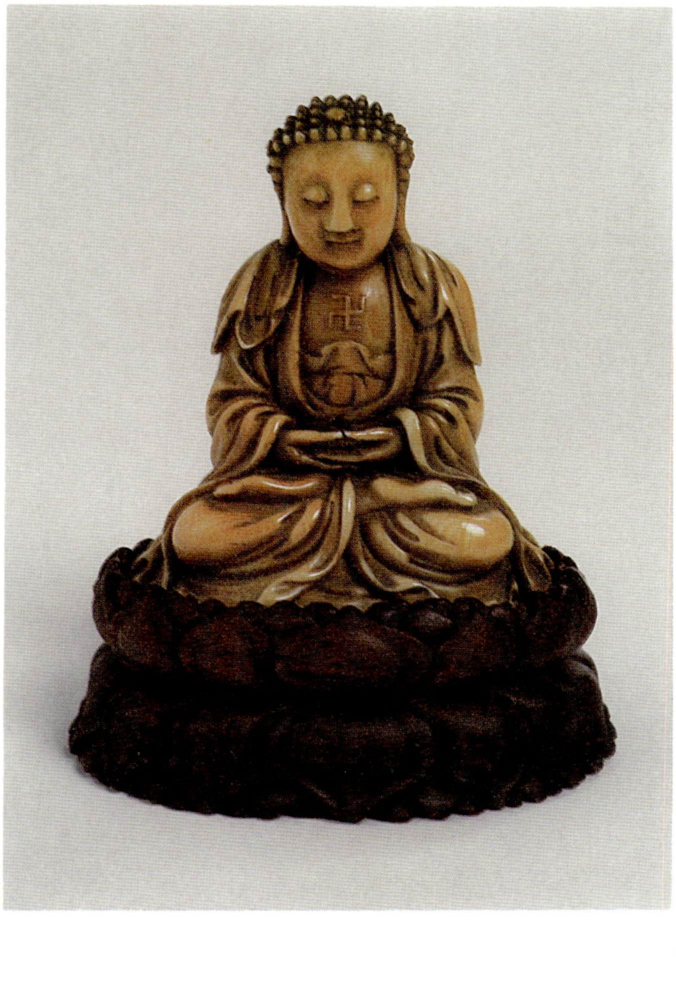

114

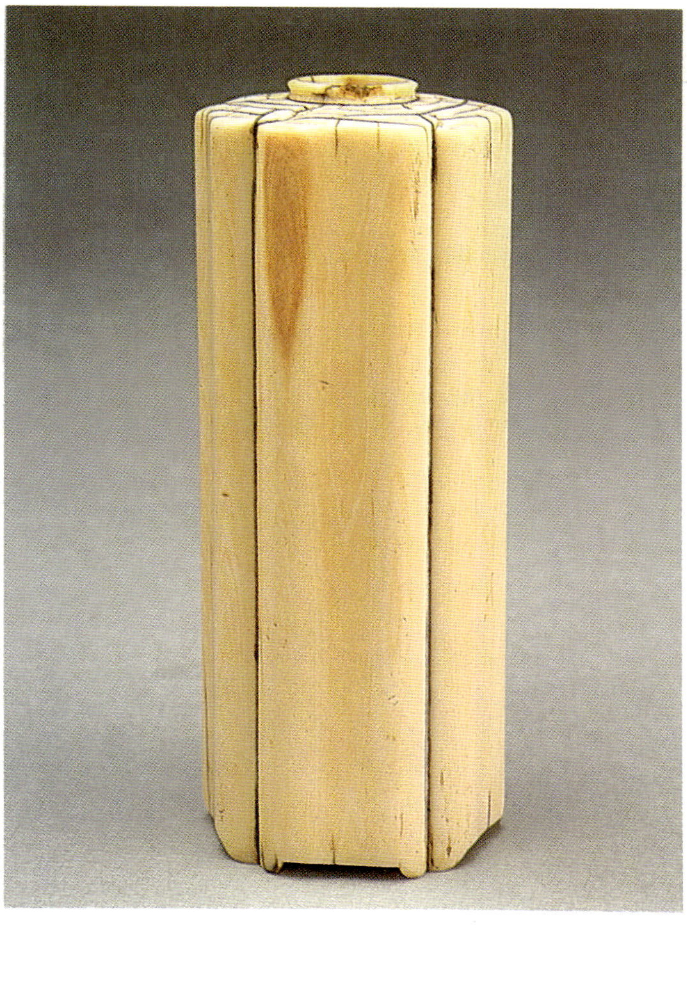

115

Covered Box

Soapstone, of mottled creamy-beige and pinkish-red tones of the Shoushan variety, with added colour and gilding; carved in the form of a box and cover, its form dictated by the shape of two overlapping, open fans; the upper fan with a design of blossoming plum branches growing from behind a convoluted rock formation, set against a background of formalized waves; the lower fan with a landscape design with tree-clad hills and islands rising out of water, also rendered as formalized waves; the overlapping fan frames realistically carved; the sides of the box and cover decorated with panels of inverted 'T' motifs, set against formalized waves, surrounded by various sprays and continuous borders of formalized flowers; the interior of box and cover each with a central formalized floral medallion; decorative incising filled with gold, and with touches of paint added to act as *dian* dots in the simulated paintings; base and interior stained a deep maroon colour.
17th or early 18th century.
Height: 4.4 cm. Length: 14.7 cm.

壽山石雕梅花山水扇形蓋盒
十七世紀或十八世紀初，高4.4厘米，
長14.7厘米

This box may be related in style to a group of soapstone carvings produced in the province of Fujian in the late Ming and early Qing dynasties (see no. 14). The vast majority of this group appears in two major forms, as a rule not closely connected stylistically: artists' seals, and small figure sculptures of *luohan* and other religious and mythological beings. Other wares are less common. The style and quality of carving suggest that this is an early Qing work, and the use of gilding is commensurate with the group of figures discussed in no. 44, which appear to have begun in the 17th century and continued into the 18th. The staining is also found on the more commercial range of figure carvings which seem to have developed out of the Zhou Bin/Yang Yuxuan (see no. 45) group and which seem to have been contemporaneous.

The subject-matter of the fans is based upon literati painting of the late Ming and early Qing dynasties. The landscape, particularly, is a typical orthodox work of a style one might expect from an artist such as Wang Hui (1632-1717), suggesting a likely class of patron.

116

Ruyi Sceptre

Wood, probably *nanmu* (cedar), of creamy brown colour; a striated, gnarled root formation the natural form enhanced by carving to form a *ruyi* sceptre, the back of the head with two small pebbles embedded in the wood.
Probably Qing dynasty.
Length: 42.7 cm.
Published: *Wood from the Scholar's Table*, p.163, no. 109.

嵌石楠木雕如意
可能清代，長42.7厘米

This *ruyi* appears to be largely natural, with carving only at one end of the head where the handle joins the head and at the end of the handle. The stones appear to be naturally embedded as opposed to being inserted in the process of manufacture (cf. no. 21). It is possible that they were placed in the growing root to allow nature to take its course and enclose them.

The possibility of the pebbles having been implanted some time before the making of the *ruyi* to allow the wood to grow around them in a natural manner, and perhaps at the same time manipulation of the growing root to a suitable form, is a demonstration of the Chinese patience in their pursuit of an ideal. This *ruyi* represents the concept of taking a lifetime, perhaps even a generation or two, to produce perfection. Like rocks that were carved and submerged again in Lake Tai (see no. 266) to allow nature to smooth the intruding marks of the carver's chisel, the result might not even be seen by the instigator.

117

Duster

Wood, covered with black lacquer and horsehair; a duster, the horsehair fixed to the handle and decoratively enclosed with an elaborate series of knots.
Probably Qing dynasty.
Maximum length, including hairs: 61 cm.

漆木馬尾拂子
可能清代，總長61厘米

Although these are often referred to as flywhisks, they are usually called 'dusters' in Chinese sources. They were not, of course, used in housework, but by scholars, monks and sages as elegant extensions of the wrist and as symbols of authority. They might also have been used for keeping the occasional fly at bay, but such a mundane function was secondary. For further details see no. 265.

Dusters must have been made in vast quantities, as they occur frequently in paintings, and were clearly a fairly standard accoutrement for scholar, sage and monk alike. It is strange, in fact, that so few have survived intact. No doubt some of these would have been made by individuals for their personal use, but the majority would probably have been made professionally by craftsmen. The principle skill involved in such a 'duster' as this is that of knotting. The Chinese over the centuries developed considerable skill in macrame, the art of intricate knotting of cords, hair, etc. Here the horsehair section of the duster is held to the handle by a complex pattern of knotted tufts enclosed in a decorative fringe.

115

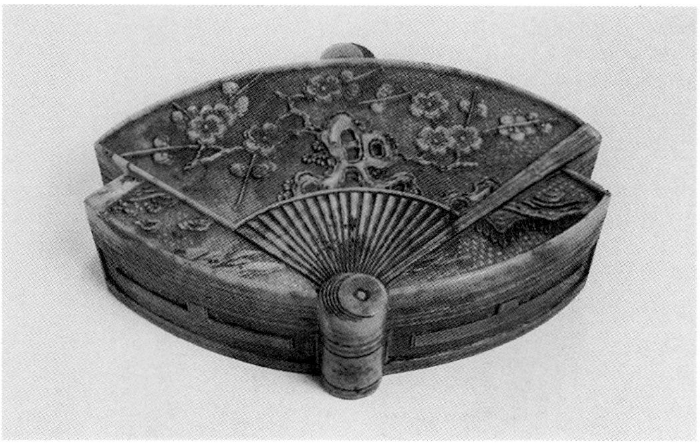

116

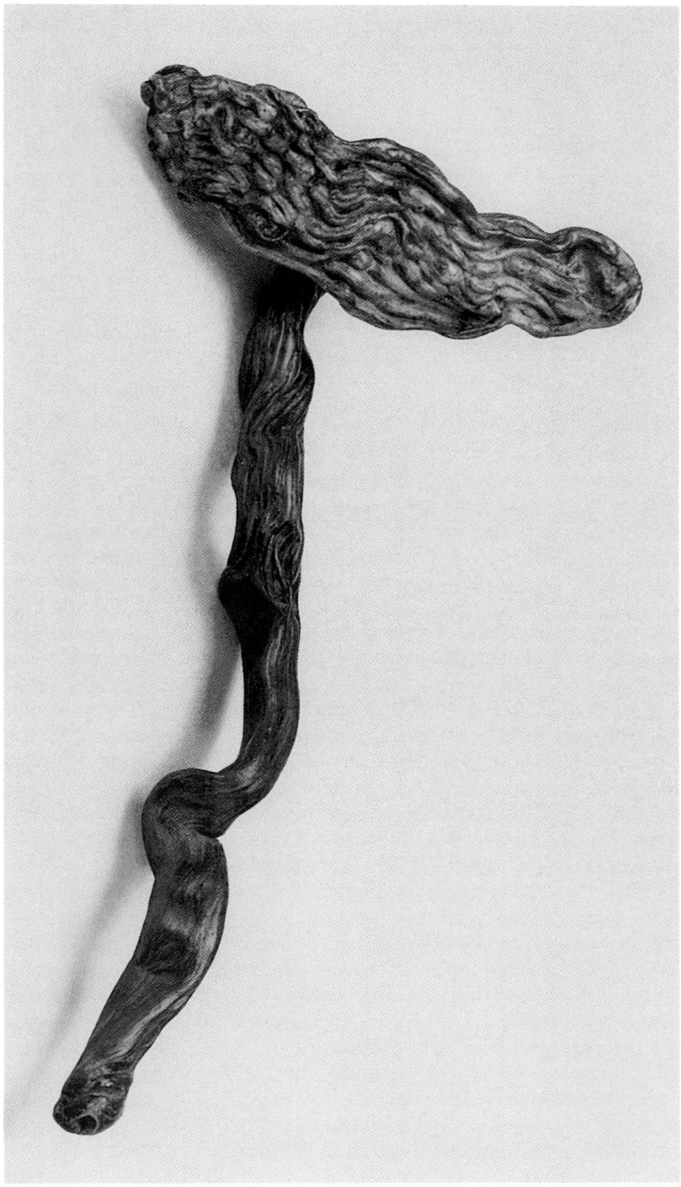

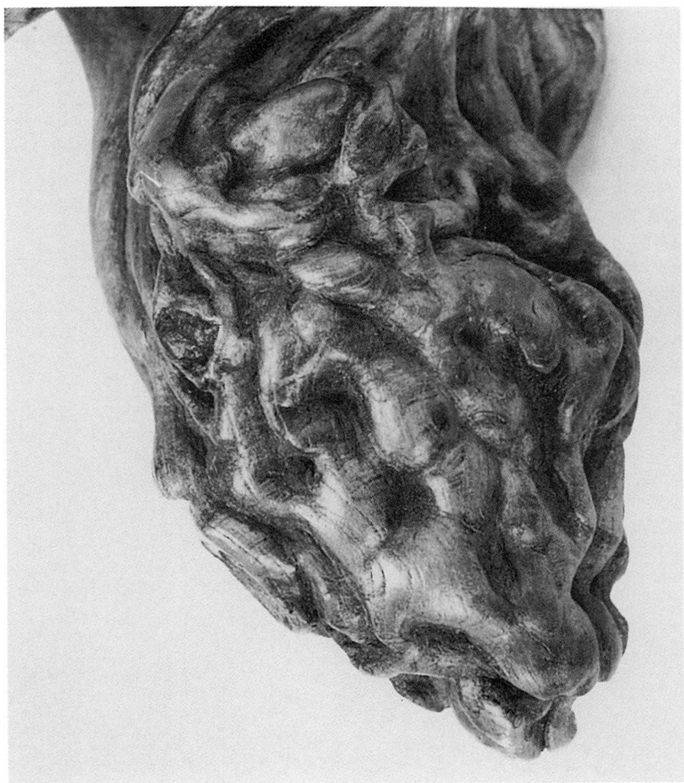

117

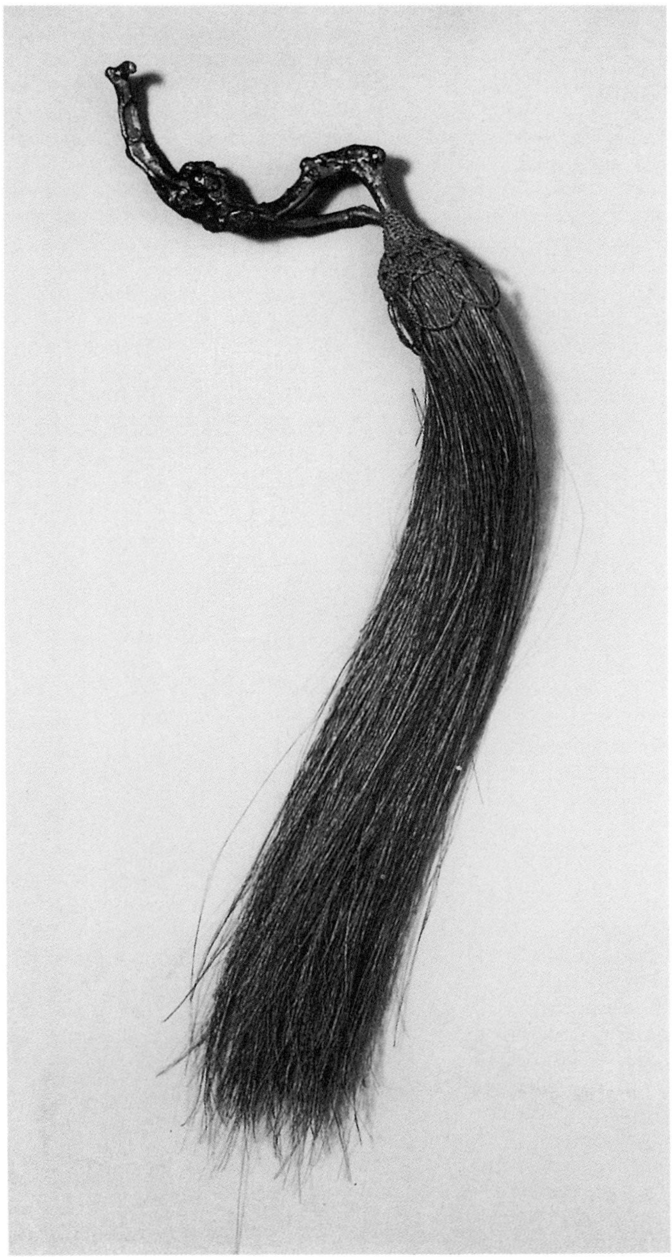

118

Brush Pot

Porcelain, decorated with underglaze cobalt blue in varied tones of rich colour; of very slightly waisted cylindrical form; the exterior decorated with a continuous scene showing the Seven Sages of the Bamboo Grove at various pursuits in a rocky garden setting with bamboo, banana and other plants; the essentially horizontal picture wrapped around the cylindrical form and joined as a continuous image with the help of bands of obscuring mist; set between two incised borders, the upper one with a series of wavy lines between double incised lines, the lower simply with a double incised line, the base unglazed; the interior glazed white, the lip unglazed.
Jingdezhen, transitional, probably second quarter of the 17th century.
Height: 19.4 cm. Diameter: 20.9 cm.

Published: *Anthology of Chinese Art: Min Chiu Society Silver Jubilee Exhibition,* p.373, no. 168.

青花竹林七賢圖瓷筆筒
明末清初, 高19.4厘米, 直徑20.9厘米

During the Ming dynasty the imperial ceramic kilns at Jingdezhen in Jiangxi province required large numbers of potters skilled in various aspects of production. During the 17th century, when the Ming regime was in turmoil from internal decay and rebellion and external conquest, this skilled workforce was left largely unemployed by the Court. Not unnaturally they turned their skills to other ends, creating a range of exciting wares for local use and also for the burgeoning export trade to Europe. These so-called 'Transitional' wares are distinctive in the quality of their manufacture and their style. The quality arose from the high skills of the potters released from imperial duty, and in part from the demands of fresh patrons. The change in style was directly due to freedom from imperial restraints and the different tastes of new patrons.

Out of this group of distinctive wares a number were clearly made for the literati. This brush pot represents this group admirably, not least in its decoration of a popular literati subject. The Seven Sages of the Bamboo Grove were a group of scholars of the late 3rd century AD who gathered together to enjoy music, poetry, elegant conversation, contemplation and the wine that so often inspired them. They were ministers of state, philosophers, poets, calligraphers and musicians and the group has since been used to symbolize the elegant gatherings of creative minds, becoming a popular subject in later Chinese art. They were Xiang Xiu; Ji Kang (223-262); Liu Ling; Shan Tao (died 283), Yuan Xian; Yuan Ji (210-263) and Wang Rong (235-306).[1]

1. For biographies see *Chinese Biographical Dictionary.*

119

Armchair

Wood, *huanghuali* of well-figured, pale golden yellow colour; a chair, the horseshoe-shaped arm made of five sections joined together by a double tongue-and-grooved, half-lapped and pressure-pegged joins; the concave back splat with beaded-edged flanges and a central *ruyi*-shaped medallion carved in low relief with formalized tendril pattern, the whole tongue-and-grooved into the arm and the seat frame; the upright members of the chair mortised and tenoned to the arm, passing through the seat frame to form the legs; the two rounded, 'S'-shaped, tapering side supports set into round sockets in the arm and the seat frame; where the front upright members meet the arm decorated with small cloud-shaped spandrels; the mitred seat frame drilled for soft seat construction and the present recessed hard mat seat with two dovetailed, transverse braces; below the seat frame is a curvilinear, shaped, beaded-edged apron, whose beaded edges are echoed on the side aprons, all of which are tongue-and-grooved into the legs and butt-jointed to the underside of the seat frame; a horizontal footrest between the two front legs with a shallow standard apron below and mortise and tenon horizontal stretchers on either side, with another joining the back legs at a higher level.
16th century.
Height: 98.4 cm. Width: 69.2 cm.
Depth: 66.6 cm. Seat height: 51.4 cm.

黄花梨圈椅
明十六世紀, 總高98.4厘米

Furniture was obviously an important part of the range of scholars trappings: it dominated his studio and home and was a setting for both playthings and functional objects. That it was of a refined nature is certain but as a general rule, as with jade carving and bronze making, it was not a craft in which the influential minority was personally involved as maker. In much the same way as we treat furniture today, suitable pieces were selected from the output of craft workshops. Most furniture, with the exception of some of the more individual pieces, retained standard forms and styles over a fairly long period of time, implying that it was intended less as art than as the setting for art.

It is interesting to note that while the early Ming work *Gegu Yaolun* pays no particular attention to furniture of any sort, the early 17th century work on connoisseurship by Wen Zhenheng[2] covers it in great detail, devoting a whole section to furniture and another to its correct placing. It may be argued that Wen's work is much more comprehensive (covering as it does architecture, gardens, etc.) but that does not explain why. Presumably in the post-Song period the influential minority came to the view that every aspect of their lives was an art form, and so they included in their works on connoisseurship a far wider range of interests. Clearly the art of choosing and using furniture was highly developed by Ming scholars.

1. Translated as *Chinese Connoisseurship* by Sir Percival David.
2. *Changwu Ji* ('Notes on Superfluous Objects').
3. Ibid. *juan* 6, section 13.

120

Pictorial Panel

Limestone of the variety known as Dali marble with brown, orange and grey markings in a mottled grey-white ground; a pictorial panel resembling windswept, foliated peaks rising from mist; mounted in a wood frame; two wooden panels above and below the marble picture inscribed with three excerpts from the writings of Zheng Xie, all carved in the style of his calligraphy; the first followed by his seal *Zheng wei dongdaozhu* ('Zheng as the host'); the second followed by his signature, Zheng Xie, and his seal *Gukou* ('Mouth of the valley'); the third by his signature *Banqiao jushi Zheng Xie,* and his seal *Banqiao.*
Mounted in a *hongmu* ('redwood') and *nanmu* (cedar) frame
Probably mid- to late Qing dynasty.
Marble panel: 26.5 cm × 32.5 cm.
With frame: 56.1 cm × 35.5 cm.

大理石紅木刻書法掛屏
可能清中至晚期, 總大56.1×35.5厘米

Zheng Xie (*zi:* Kerou; *hao:* Banqiao — 1693-1765) was a native of Xinghua, Jiangsu province, a famous painter and calligrapher and one of the group of artists known as the Eight Eccentrics of Yangzhou. His calligraphy has a distinctive style which is reproduced here. It was quite common for scholars, particularly those who enjoyed calligraphy, to jot down notes from time to time, whenever a thought occurred to them. This might be on any subject: on a painting or calligraphy they had just seen, or the thoughts that arose from it, on religion or philosophy. They were random jottings; from time to time they might be gathered together and even published, but on a daily basis they were just written on scraps of paper and put aside. The three here are all literary notes of this kind. They are often difficult to understand without their context, but the middle one here is interesting. It is inspired by an entry in the journal of the famous Song literatus Su Shi and is Zheng's commentary upon it, using much of the same language: "Su Shi became drunk, and after consuming enough is reclining on a couch. White clouds entwine to the left and clear streams join them from the right; doors are open to reveal forests and hills. His expression seems to suggest a thought, but it also appears that he is thinking of nothing at all, sensing instead the unity of all things on earth."[1] This seems to be an ideal sentiment to have chosen to reproduce on such an evocative marble picture.

Late Ming connoisseurship on Dali marble is represented by Wen Zhenheng thus:[2] "Dali marble is produced in Yunnan (province). White as jade, black as ink are precious. The poor quality ones are those where the white is greenish and the black areas greyish. If one can obtain old stone with naturally formed landscapes with clouds and mists like Mi Fu's landscape, these are unsurpassed in excellence. In the past people used it to inlay in screens. Recently people have used it in stands and couches, but this usage is not old." It is interesting to note that in his usual brief and didactic style Wen dismisses those which are not pure black and white, and then goes on to admire the most those that look like Mi Fu's landscapes[3] which relied very considerably for their appeal on shades of ink, without which, clouds and mist would be quite unlike Mi Fu's paintings. It is probable that in the first case he was referring to the best stone, judged independently of what is done with it, but in the second to the artistic content, which would always transcend objective criteria.

The use of marble in furniture, which began (according to Wen) in the late Ming period became extremely popular during the Qing, when Dali marble was widely inlaid in table-tops, desks, chairs and couches, stools, low tables and so on.

1. For a translation of the original entry in Su Shi's journal see *The Importance of Understanding,* pp.197-198.
2. *Changwu Ji, juan* 3 in a special section on Dali marble.
3. Mi Fu was a Song painter, calligrapher and connoisseur who pioneered an impressionistic style of painting using wet dabs of ink to form mountainous ranges enveloped in floating mists.

118

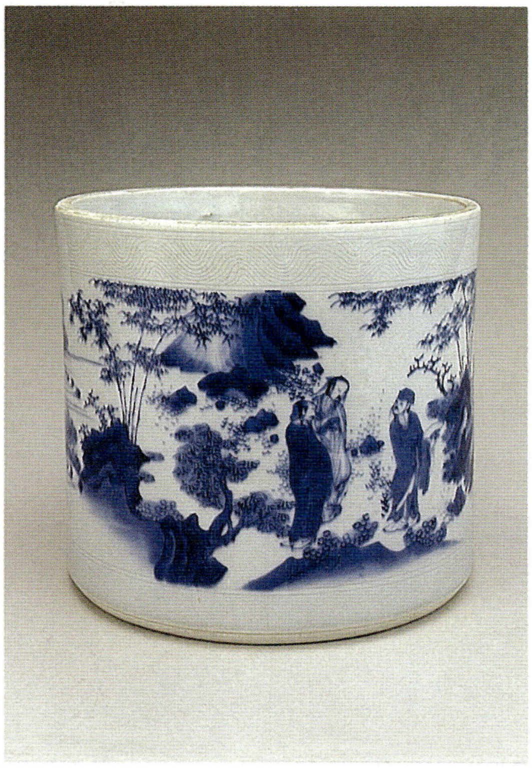

120

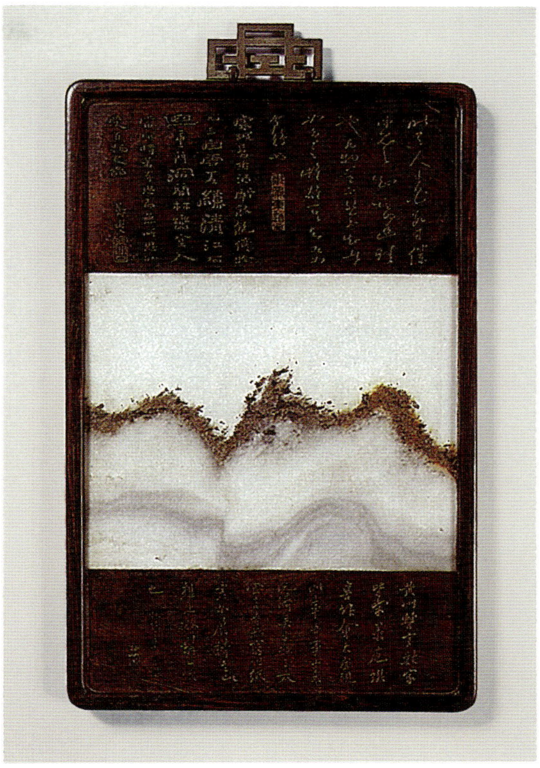

119

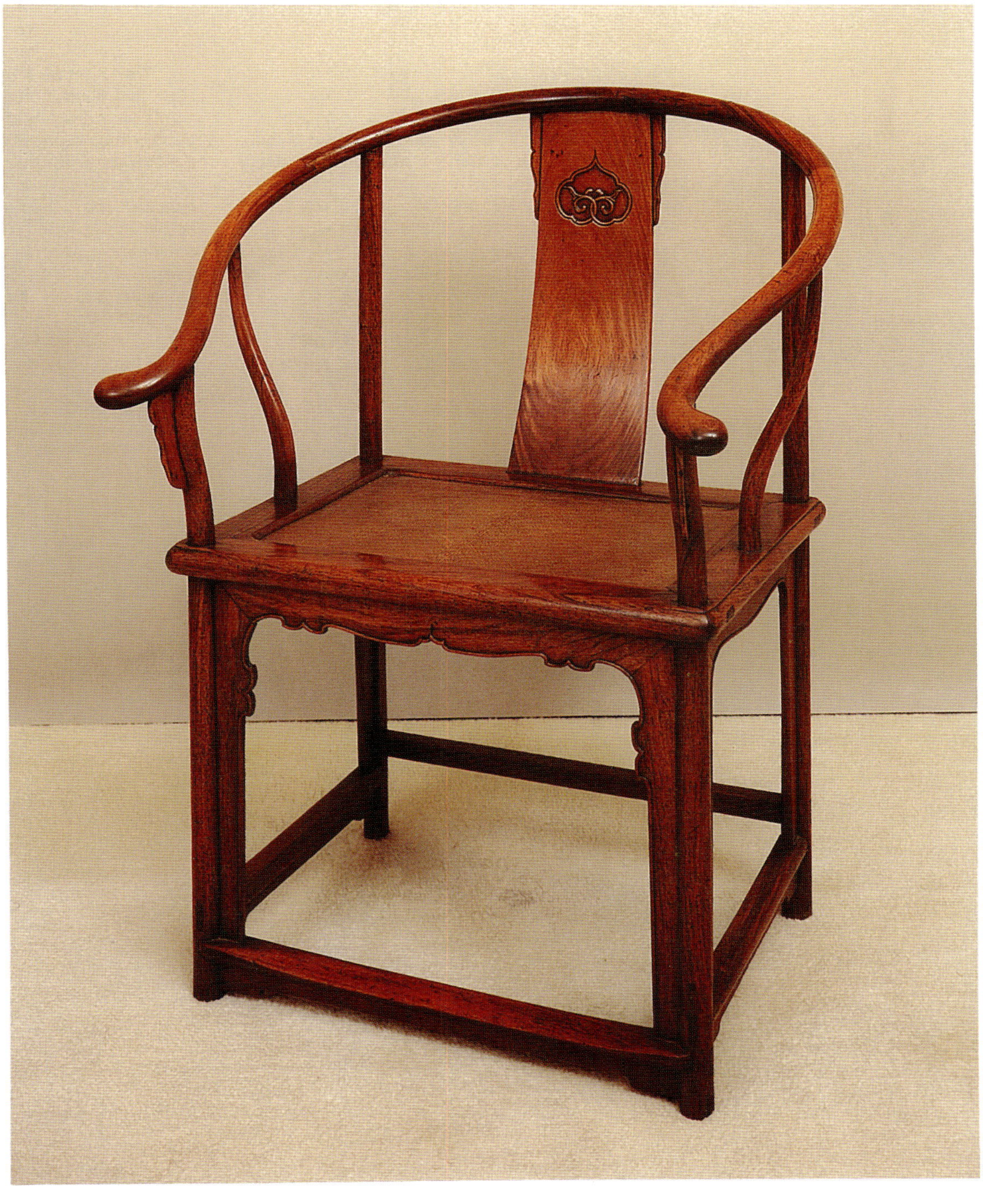

121

Ruyi Sceptre

Bamboo veneer, of golden brown colour; a *ruyi* sceptre, the surface veneered with flattened sections of bamboo culm, carved with incising and very low relief work on three separate planes (using up to three layers of veneer) as a *lingzhi* plant, the stem with various smaller fungi growing from it, curving at the top to split into twin stalks culminating in two overlapping fungus heads; the stem carved to simulate gnarling and knot holes; the lower handle with a cord hole formed by a small *lingzhi* growing out at an angle from the main stem; the back of the head carved with a poetic inscription: "My literary heart appreciates the prose of (Li) Deyu; in *Chan (Zen)* I follow the poems of monk Jiaoran; with natural nodes, and no side branches. Master Luo's magic will eventually prove to be fantasy; monk Shao's gift is genuinely suitable. I am particularly fond of elegant discussions, as when meeting refined gentlemen." Followed by *Qianlong yuti* ('Imperial composition of the Qianlong emperor'), and the seal *Guxiang* ('Ancient fragrance').
Perhaps Beijing palace workshops, probably Qianlong period.
Length: 34.7 cm.

竹雕題詩靈芝如意•乾隆御題銘
清乾隆(1736-1795), 長34.7厘米

The poem alludes to the qualities the Emperor sees in himself, partly by references to figures of antiquity and partly by comparison to the bamboo of which the *ruyi* is made. The node of the bamboo is pronounced *jie* and the same character is part of the term *qijie,* meaning integrity. The metaphor is strengthened by the statement that there are no side branches, which is to say that he is straight or upright in his dealings.

The Qianlong Emperor was in the habit of inscribing works of art in his collection, especially during the last third of his reign when he devoted more time to private pursuits, leaving the running of the Empire more in the hands of his trusted but reputedly corrupt Prime Minister, Heshen (d. 1799). Such inscriptions appear on a large number of early pieces in bronze, jade, porcelain, wood, rhinoceros horn and lacquer (see no. 181), and occasionally on pieces made specifically for him which particularly caught his fancy. The three possible types of pieces so inscribed are early pieces on which he had inscribed either a laudatory inscription, or a poem; newly made pieces similarly inscribed; or pieces made specifically to be inscribed with an already composed poem that was considered suitable.

The context of this inscription and object do not make it clear into which category this falls. However, the art of bamboo veneering seems to have flourished in the mid-Qing period, and it is more likely that this example was not an old object freshly inscribed, and probably dates from the last third of the Qianlong Emperor's reign. The question is further complicated by the fact that the Qianlong Emperor's vast output of tepid poetry may well have been added to pieces after his death and while this inscription states that it is his composition, it says nothing about him ordering its inscription on this piece, nor is a date given. Later forgeries also exist with purported Qianlong inscriptions. However, the quality of this piece, its correctness of form and style of inscription and its unusual nature would seem to rule out this possibility.

122

Luohan

Bamboo, of yellowish-brown colour; carved as a *luohan* in loosely fitting robes, a cloak clasped across his chest with a *ruyi*-shaped hook, seated on a rocky outcrop, writing on the cover of a book he is holding, an inkstone set on the rock beside him. Perhaps by Feng Shiqi.
Probably 18th century.
Height: 7.4 cm.
Formerly in the Dr. Ip Yee collection.
Published: *Chinese Bamboo Carving,* Part II, p.282, no. 93; *Bamboo Carving of China,* p.111, no. 54.

竹雕羅漢像
可能十八世紀, 高7.4厘米

The tentative nature of the dating of literati works of art is again demonstrated in this piece. The two publications cited above attributed it to the 18th century, as we have here. However, the vogue for such small sculptures in a variety of materials certainly began in the late Ming period, and continued well into the 19th century without, apparently, much stylistic evolution. As a general rule it is probable, as with the soapstone equivalents, that as time progressed what was produced as a vital work of art degenerated into a formula for producing small sculptures, and that the difference could be clearly seen by a critical observer. However, while such a general trend is probable it was certainly confounded in detail by the existence of early craftsmen catering to a less critical audience, and later ones fired by an artistic integrity. One example of the latter is illustrated in *Bamboo Carving of China*[1], a comparable figure to this which it would not be unreasonable to attribute to the same hand. It is signed by Feng Shiqi, who was apparently active in the Qianlong and Jiaqing periods. Without the example signed by Feng, this *luohan* might easily have been dated to a century or more earlier than its likely period.

Feng Shiqi (*zi:* Shizhou) to whom this figure is tentatively attributed solely on the strength of the similarities between it and the above mentioned signed example, was a native of Jiading, in Jiangsu province, listed by the Hong Kong Museum of Art[2] as "a proficient professional bamboo carver". The Churen Lu ('Record of Bamboo Carvers')[3] however, is more enthusiastic about his talents, stating that his skills brought his family food and clothing, and that his work was capable and marvellous. The signed work mentioned above — while not of the sheer quality of finish and detail of some — has considerable character as sculpture, as does this example.

While brush pots, perfume holders, wrist rests and other cylindrical or curved profile wares were usually made out of the bamboo culm, often using the diaphragm to good advantage, sculptures in the round were usually carved from what is often referred to as the bamboo 'root', a solid mass of woody material below the ground where the culm stalk grows out of the rhizome and becomes the base of the culm (see no. 148, Fig. 1 for sketch). This rooty substance has a delightful natural texture of markings which is particularly well suited to the carving of rockwork, a frequent 'pedestal' for small figure carvings of this type.

1. P.110, no. 53.
2. In *Chinese Bamboo Carving.*
3. Quoted in *Zhongguo Yishujia Zhenglue.*

121

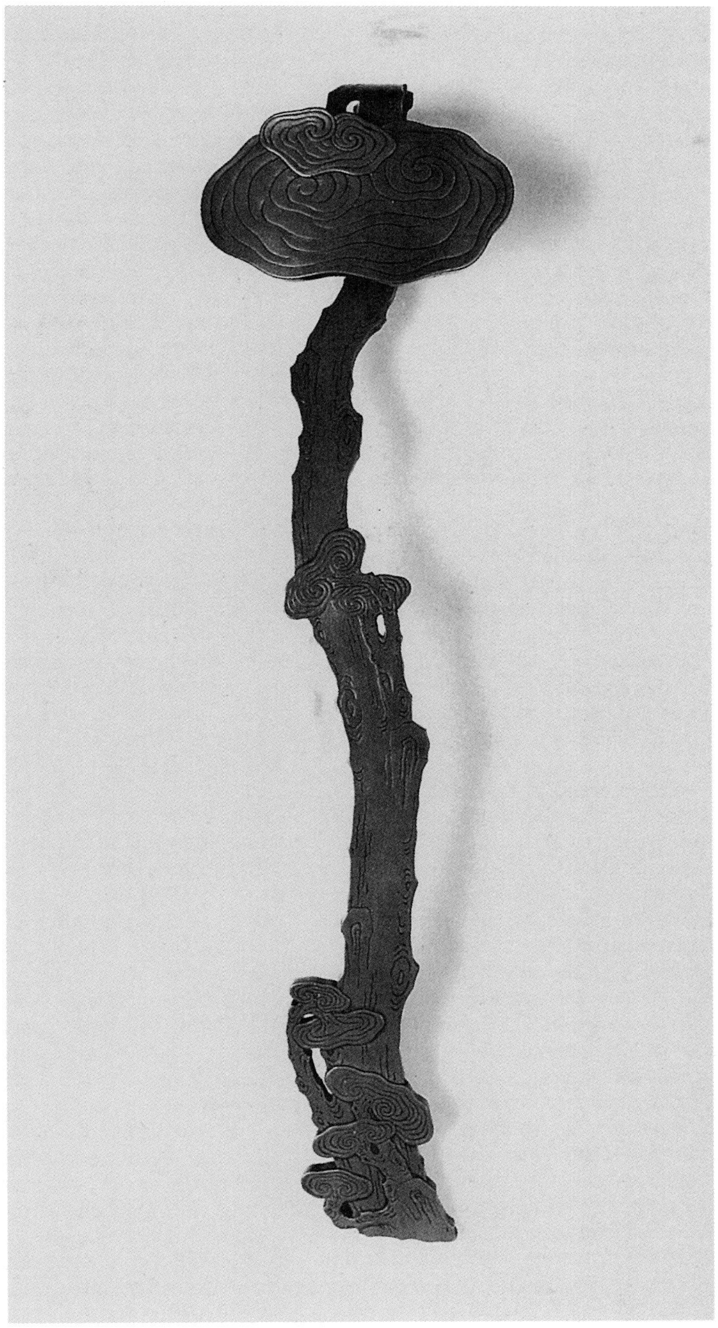

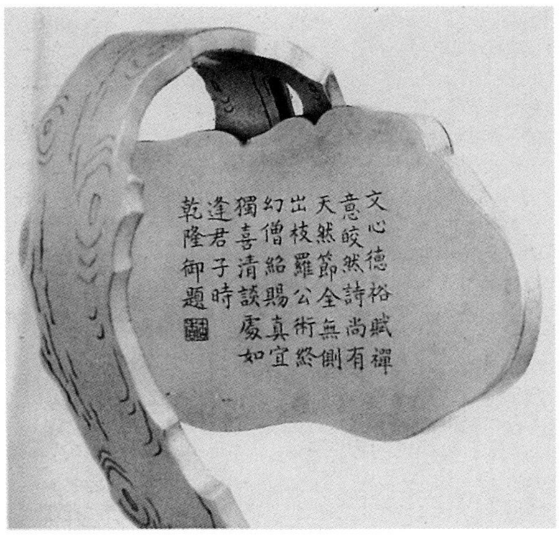

122

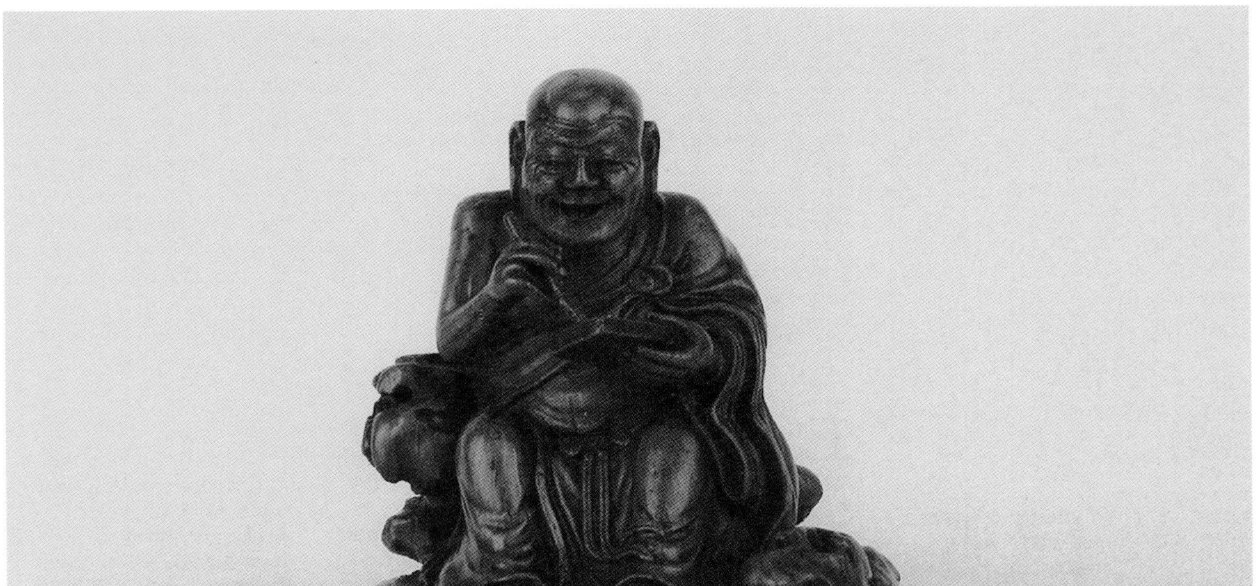

123

Incense Burner

Bronze, of well-patinated, reddish-brown colour with gold splashing; an incense burner of modified *li* tripod form, the base with a rectangular cartouche enclosing the mark *Da Ming Xuande nianzhi* ('made in the Xuande period of the Great Ming dynasty') in regular script; set on an original but separate base in the form of a formalized *kui* flower, the petals terminating in three highly formalized *ruyi* feet; covered overall with irregularly disposed 'splashes' of gold applied to the surface.
Ming dynasty, perhaps Xuande period.
Height including original stand: 13 cm.
Fitted with a pierced wood cover, decorated with a formalized floral scroll enclosing two *shou* characters, and inset with a carnelian knob. Probably late Ming dynasty.

灑金青銅鬲形香爐•大明宣德年製銘
明代, 可能宣德, 高連座13厘米

The question of the Xuande bronzes is one of the most vexing in the history of later Chinese works of art and may now be beyond a definitive answer. The problem revolves around a large group of bronze wares, mostly incense burners, produced during the Xuande period (1426-1435) which introduced, or at least popularized, a series of new forms in bronze making and a variety of new methods of treating their surfaces, and inspired later copies. Apart from the wares themselves (which include examples from the 15th century to the 19th and probably 20th century), there are a number of manuscripts, published at various times, which deal with the question during the Ming and Qing dynasties. We list below those which are central to the problem.

1. The *Xuande Dingyi Pu,* a publication in eight *juan* under the names of the Minister of Works, Wu Zhong, and the Minister of Rites, Lu Zhen. It purports to be based upon an original copy of documents relating to imperial instructions to cast large numbers of bronzes in 1428. The original copies of these documents were presented to the Emperor and no copy was to be kept, but we are led to believe that a eunuch of the Rites Office, one Wu Cheng, kept an illicit copy which passed into the household of Yu Qian, from whose family it was eventually borrowed by the famous Ming seal carver Wen Peng (1498-1573) who copied the text in 1534 and apparently asked craftsmen to make drawings. This remained in manuscript form until it was included in the encyclopaedia *Siku Quanshu.* This encyclopaedia was commissioned by the Qianlong Emperor in 1772, and finished in 1780. It contained 3,470 works on a variety of subjects, and was hand-written in four copies to be placed in four imperial libraries. Later three more copies were made to go to various libraries in cities around China. The original manuscript of the *Xuande Dingyi Pu* apparently bore a preface dated to the third year of Xuande (1428) by Yang Rong, and attached to it in the *Siku Quanshu* was an essay on it entitled *Xuanlu Bolun,* by the famous late Ming collector Xiang Yuanbian, dated 1626. An illustrated version of this first appeared in 1942 — the first version with wood block illustrations, despite Wen Peng's apparent request for illustrations at an earlier date.

2. The *Xuande Yiqi Tupu* in 20 *juan* also purporting to be by Lu Zhen, where a similar story is told of transmission of an illicit manuscript copied by a eunuch, although in this case his name is given as Zhang Bin. It has a postscript under the name of Yu Qian dated 1451, and its supposed provenance states that it was obtained in 1526 by Zhu Yunming (1460-1526).

3. The *Xuande Yiqi Pu* in only three *juan* supposedly by Lu Tang of the Ministry of Works, and again Zhang Bin, a Rites Office eunuch. It purports to be a Ming dynasty hand copy of the original.

4. The *Xuande Yiqi Tupu* in two *juan* and a larger format under the name of Cao Lizhai, with prefaces by Yu Qian and Zhu Yunming, which includes Mao Xiang's *Xuanlu Ge* ('Song of Xuande Burners'). This work does not avoid the use of characters which make up the names of the Ming Emperors, which it would have to do as a matter of protocol if published under the Ming, so presumably it is a Qing hand-copied manuscript.

All these sources claim to represent the original records of a particular event, which was that at some time prior to early 1428[1] the Xuande Emperor received as tribute from the King of Siam (modern-day Thailand) 31,680 catties of a yellowish copper, said to resemble gold. The Emperor considered at that time that the imperial altars, temples and Court ritual vessels were not archaic enough and asked that new ones be cast to replace them, ordering 3,365 pieces in the third month of 1428. After several audits and amendments, the order was agreed in the sixth month and manufacture began. At the beginning of the tenth month the Emperor requested an additional 2,000, which delayed the project another five months. By the middle of the eleventh month the order was completed. The Emperor was content and placed a third, larger order for 15,000 vessels on the first day of the twelfth month, presumably finished in 1429. The models for these new designs were to be taken from the *Xuanhe Bogu Tulu* (dated 1123 and recording the Xuanhe Emperor's collection of archaic bronzes — itself not above suspicion as an authentic work); the *Kaogu Tu* (dated 1092 — also a publication consisting of archaic bronzes reproduced in wood-block illustrations); and from Song ceramic wares in the imperial collection. 88 models were chosen from the bronze catalogues, and 29 from Song ceramics, totalling 117 models for the first order.

The vast production of Xuande bronzes and the vogue they created suggests that the imperial order and casting of the bronzes is fact. By the late Ming dynasty several works (including Wen Zhenheng's *Changwu Ji*) attest to the popularity of these incense burners and the difficulties even then of telling genuine originals from later copies. However, the manuscripts and publications all seem to be questionable, as although they agree on the basic information given above, they differ so much in other details (including the names of people involved such as that of the eunuch who was supposed to have spirited the illicit copy out of the palace) that they cannot be taken seriously.

This doubt is confirmed by two serious mistakes by the original forgers. Lu Zhen (*zi:* Kesheng) was a native of Lintong, who in 1386 passed his district exam at the age of 20. He was serving in the Ministry of Punishments in 1405 and was a teacher of the royal princes in 1425, rising finally to the rank of Minister of Rites. He died in the first year of Xuande, 1426 — two years before the Emperor received his tribute of copper and before the possible writing of the manuscript for which he was supposed to have been responsible. The other person purportedly responsible for the work was Wu Zhong. He was the Minister of Works in 1407. He was imprisoned in 1421 and released again in 1425. In the first year of Xuande he was rehabilitated but after some military excursions to Lean, he was again imprisoned in 1428 for giving government wood and stone to one Yangqing for the building of a private house. Wu died in 1442. Thus it seems that in the very year in which he was supposed to have spent his entire year supervising the manufacture of imperial bronzes he was imprisoned. Although we do not know at what point in 1428 he was imprisoned, the completion of the order in the eleventh month must have preceded any manuscript on the subject, and leaves little time for subsequent wrong-doing, conviction and imprisonment.

Zhang Bin is also recorded as a *jinshi* degree holder, which seems incompatible with his being the eunuch who copied the original manuscript.

It seems that accurate identification of the very large number of extant bronze incense burners and other wares arising out of the tribute of copper and the Xuande Emperor's interest in re-casting the imperial ritual wares must therefore rest largely on the wares themselves. Analysis of bronze content should help in this case, as the original bronzes were presumably made under reasonably controlled circumstances and with a certain type of copper which may prove identifiable in alloy from other copper used later. It is also possible to identify certain characteristic groups by weight, types of mark, colour and type of gold-splashing (where it exists), etc., which will no doubt prove useful. But at present we are faced with a vast body of works, no reliable textual evidence, and a long uphill struggle if we are ever to solve this intriguing puzzle.

This example is obviously of some age, well patinated and substantial, and is excellently cast. It bears a mark which is credible for the Xuande period.

1. The *Xuande Yiqi Tupu* gives the date as 1427.

124

Water Vessel

Glass, of transparent ruby red colour; a water vessel, the flattened pear-shaped body with a wide, slightly flared mouth, and a convex base; the centre of the base inscribed with a wheel-cut mark *Qianlong nianzhi* ('made in the Qianlong period') in regular script within a square cartouche.
Beijing palace workshops, Qianlong period.
Height: 2.72 cm. Diameter of body: 5.6 cm.

紅料水丞•乾隆年製銘
清乾隆(1736-1795), 高2.72厘米,
身直徑5.6厘米

Few more elegant examples of the production of the palace workshops exist than this small water vessel for use in conjunction with a ladle to supply the inkstone. It represents a series of palace glass objects for the scholar's table (water vessels, seal-paste boxes, small vases for flowers, and so forth of which another example is no. 94).

Early technological problems in the palace workshops from the Kangxi and Yongzheng periods resulted in the decomposition of the surface, prompting many pieces to be dated to much earlier than they are. However, once that problem was solved, the 18th century represents a zenith in Chinese glass-making. The palace workshops appear to have been the first to introduce a full glass-making technology, capable of blowing vessels, luting, moulding and carving, overlaying and mixing varieties of glass in different ways. Prior to the establishment of these workshops, these various methods had apparently been used in China only sporadically. Once the technological problems of the early years had been overcome, the Qianlong glassmakers set out to capitalize on their newly perfected skills, creating a wide range of wares of the highest quality. Despite their ability to create the exotic and fanciful, it is a measure of the restraint possible at this most unrestrained of Courts that vessels of this type were still made.

123

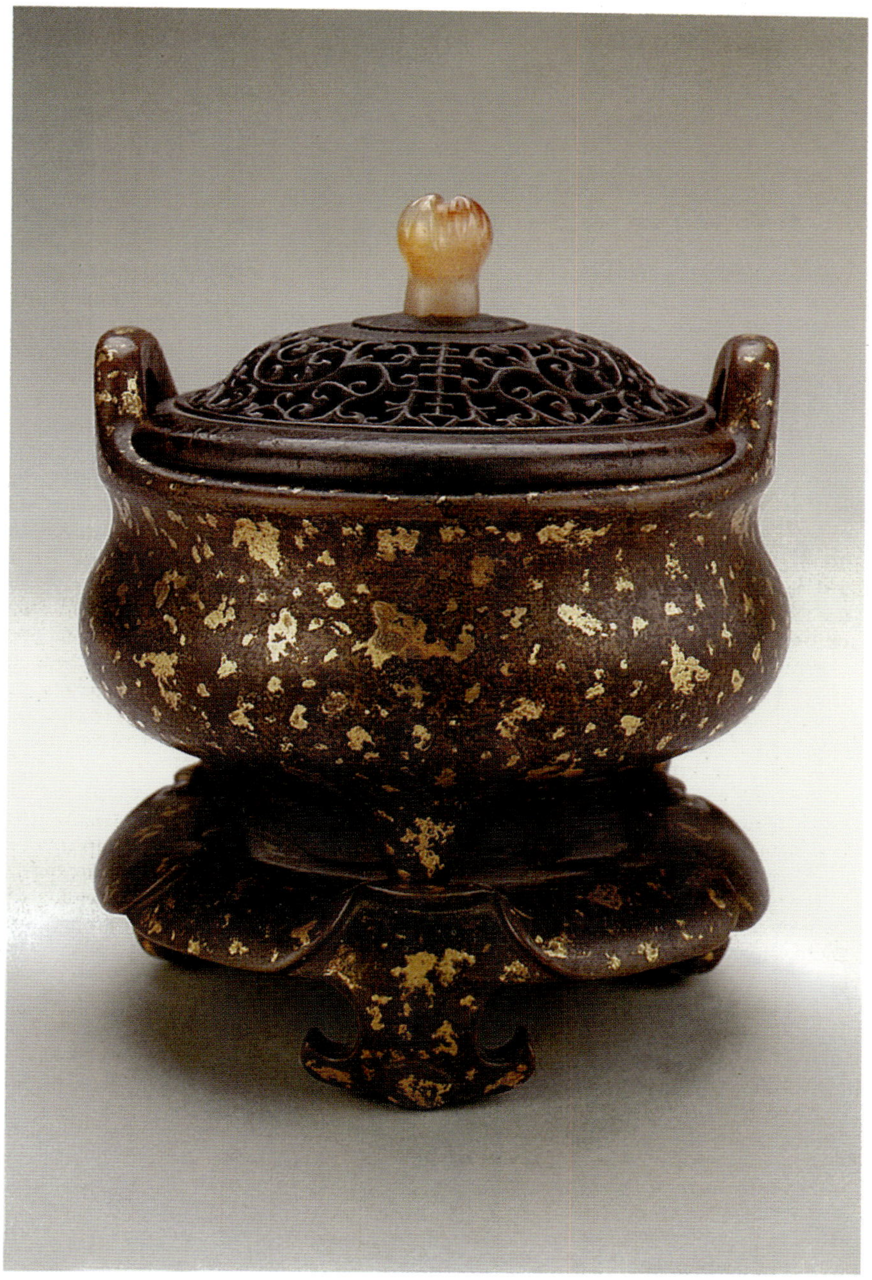

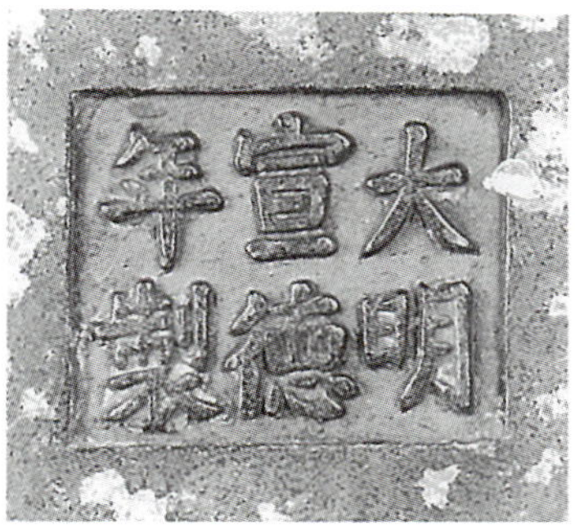

124

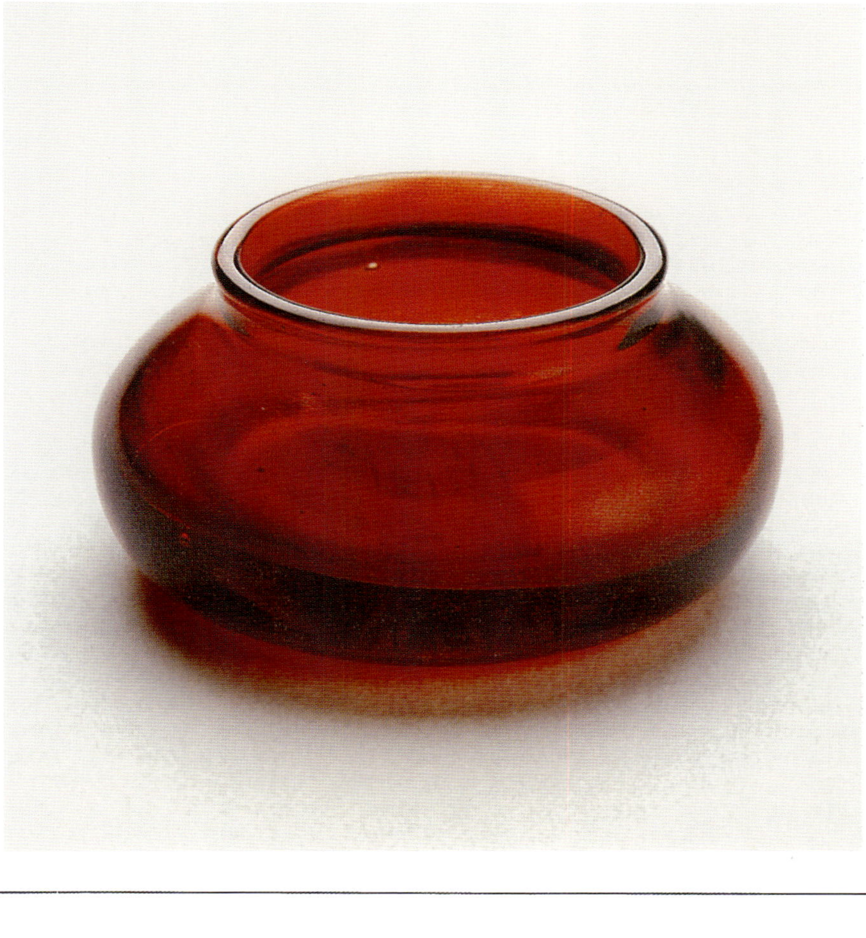

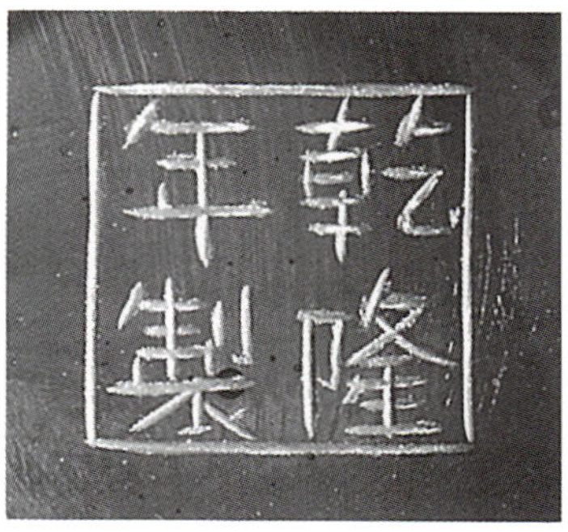

125

Seal

Bronze, partly gilt; a miniature personal seal, the knob in the form of a snarling mythical beast, standing at bay; the animal with wings, two horns, a beard and swirling flourishes at its haunches, probably intended as flames; the knob and knob platform gilt, the sides plain; the seal-text reading *Yang Fang siyin* ('personal seal of Yang Fang') in negative seal script.
Six Dynasties, probably 6th century.
2 cm × 1.25 cm × 1.3 cm.

鎏金青銅異獸印·陽防私印
六朝，可能六世紀，2×1.25×1.3厘米

Early seals were frequently of small size as before the invention of paper, when they were used to stamp clay impressions, they were carried at the belt as symbols of power as well as serving as identification and authentication. The early phase of the use of seals covers the period from their first use to the 14th century. The use of decorative stamps to impress repetitive designs on pottery is evident in Neolithic times, but at what stage these developed into seals bearing characters for official and personal use is not clear. There is some doubt as to whether seals made their appearance as early as the Shang dynasty, despite two examples with undeciphered characters which were said to have been excavated from the late Shang capital at Anyang. However, by the Spring and Autumn period of the Zhou dynasty both private and official seals were already called *xi* ('seals') and in some cases *guxi* ('archaic seals'), suggesting that they were already of some antiquity, so we may assume a beginning perhaps as early as the late Shang, and development in the early Zhou period.

Under the Qin dynasty (221-106 BC) the term *xi* was reserved for official seals and *yin*, the name by which they were all to be known later, was used for other types. These early seals were mostly of bronze, although in Han times official seals were rigidly controlled, with imperial seals made of jade, those of princes of gold, and the rest in bronze.

With the invention of paper and its growing popularity during the 3rd to 5th century AD, clay impressions gave way to vermillion impressions. With this development the previously ubiquitous negative impression (*baiwen* — 'white writing' or *yinke* — 'negative carving') gave way to a more frequent use of a positive impression (*zhuwen* — 'vermillion writing' or *yangke* — 'positive carving').

Also under the Han, the identification of rank by the subject of the seal knob and by the material of its ribbon became formalized. High ranks had tortoise-shaped knobs, while lower ranks had simple looped knobs. Private seals, however, might have any design, and there is a variety of different possible knobs recorded from the period.

With the change from clay to paper impressions another development was towards larger and more decorative seals. With this development came another shift in usage, as they became too heavy to be conveniently carried about as symbols of authority. In being confined to the scholar's desk, the carving of the knobs would have become more important: what was previously a primarily symbolic statement began to evolve into a primarily aesthetic one.

In the Tang and Song dynasties seals evolved from their primarily functional, identifying and authoritative role into objects of art, not only in the carving of the seals and seal knobs but in the use of the seal text. Seals of collectors, studio names and other fanciful names, poetic and enigmatic phrases or passages and so forth were developed and the seal became an indispensible appurtenance of the scholar, so to remain into the modern period.

According to literary sources the Song artist Mi Fu (1051-1107), and the Yuan artists Zhao Mengfu (1272-1311) and Wu Yan (Wu Qiuyang, 1272-1311) were all accomplished seal carvers, although at what stage seal carving became an art fully involving the artist and scholar as craftsman as well as designer is not clear. Ivory, rhinoceros horn, wood and bamboo might all have been carved by the literati themselves, although in the early stages of seal use it is more likely that they simply designed them and had specialist craftsmen do the carving. All these materials could be worked directly with a blade, thus avoiding the social bias against technological crafts, but it was the introduction of soapstone that really allowed the scholar full rein with his 'iron brush'. Tradition ascribes its earliest use to Wang Mian (1287-1359), but there is some question as to whether he was even a seal carver. Another major figure in the development of the use of soapstone was Wen Peng (1488-1573). In his biography, written by Zhou Lianggong (1612-1672), we are told that Wen first used ivory seals, asking someone else to carve them. One day while in Nanjing he is supposed to have seen two men quarelling beside a cart full of soapstone. He bought the cartload of material, and thus began to use soapstone for seals.[1]

In the mid-Ming period it began to be popularly used, creating a watershed in the history of seal carving. From that point onwards the scholar was fully involved, able to carve his own seals directly and easily into an ideal, soft stone which encouraged him to use his carving blade as a brush — hence the term 'iron-brush' used in seal carving — and develop a distinctive style of writing for stone. Following this a number of treatises on seal engraving appeared, further popularizing the art to the point where a very large number of scholar-artists from that time onwards were also seal carvers. Out of this also arose the much wider use of seals on paintings and calligraphy, a key factor in the refinement of the artist's and connoisseur's approach to these media. This development also encouraged the integration of seals into the work of art and its conception, rather than as something added to an already completed work. In calligraphy the seals created a final layer of meaning, a last flourish and emphasis, an exercise in abstract form used to balance the overall picture and to create an independent pattern of their own (in the same way that the *dian* dotting on paintings may be read as foliage, shrubbery etc. but also has an independent abstract level of meaning).

In painting, seals began to serve the same purpose, as a final harmonizing, formal element. After the 11th century critical understanding of painting was consolidated in the 14th century, when calligraphy, painting and poetry became the 'Three Perfections'. The collector's seal, added not by the artist but by the owner of the painting, then became an extension of this, an

As far as the seal text was concerned Chinese connoisseurship has tended in the past to look upon the Han period as being the golden age, and to judge everything else by it. It is probably true that the post-Han period of the Six Dynasties represents a decline, as it was a period of unrest, and one in which the main new developments concerning the introduction of paper and the shift from clay impressions to vermillion impressions apparently did little to encourage any new incentives to equal Han script engraving. The rather lacklustre text on this example is a typical example of this decline. However developments from the Tang to Song period had almost certainly suffered from a rigid reference to Han models as representing perfection. Yet the period from the mid-Ming onwards was an exciting one, and developments continued right into the present century. The 19th century represents the beginning of an interesting new period for seal text carving with such carvers as Deng Shiru (1743-1805), Zhao Zhiqian (1829-1884 — see no. 46) and Wu Changshi (1863-1927) reaching beyond artistic enslavement to ancient seal text styles to create exciting and vital new forms much more in accord with what was going on in calligraphy, and related to ancient scripts revealed by a mid-Qing rennaissance of interest in archaeology. These developments were carried on with immense strength by the modern artist Qi Baishi (1863-1957), poet, seal carver, calligrapher and painter, bringing the art form into the present.

Despite its unexciting seal text this tiny seal has strength in the sculpture of its knob, particularly in relation to its tiny proportions. The winged beast, with its striding stance, upturned toes, snarling mouth and features of mouth, whiskers, eyebrows is remarkably close to a monumental stone animal at the mausoleum of Emperor Wu of the Chen Dynasty (reigned 560-567).[2] On this basis it would be reasonable to assign this seal to the 6th century.

1. This and much of the other information about seals in this caption are taken from two articles by Ma Kwok-kuen which appeared in the South China Morning Post series *Chinese Art: Courses by Newspaper*, 4th January 1985 and 11th January 1985.
2. See *Liuchao Yishu*, Wenwu publishers, 1981, no. 105, and colour plate 14.

126

Brush Handle

Bronze, originally gilt, the surface encrusted with malachite and azurite; a brush handle, the flattened, rectangular bristle holder surmounted by a finial of a rather flattened group of two battling tigers supporting a triumphant dragon, the details largely lost to rich encrustration.
Probably early Western Han dynasty.
Height: 8.5 cm. Width: 6.05 cm.

青銅龍虎筆把
可能西漢，高8.5厘米，寬6.05厘米

A later ivory handle of a similar sort of brush is shown as no. 240, and other examples in ivory of the late Ming or Qing dynasty are known, demonstrating that the same basic form of brush has been in use for at least 2,000 years. The standard type is a small, flattened, broad-ended brush, with bristles extending about five to six centimeters from the handle. Their purpose is a mystery. To have retained the same form for so long suggests some specific use. It has been suggested that they were for dusting the area of the strings and the inaccessible surface below on a *qin*, for which purpose they would be perfect, but in the copious literature on the *qin* there is no mention of such a brush. They may have been simply general brushes for use in the studio, to brush dust off rocks and gnarled wood (difficult to achieve with a cloth) or to brush charcoal dust from painting sketches, and so on. A larger and rarer size is represented by no. 241, perhaps a more likely candidate for a general brush.

This is a particularly interesting example. It was originally gilt, apparently all over, but close examination reveals that the gilding may have been well worn long before it was buried. The subsequent build up of the carbonates of copper as the bronze came into contact with damp in burial, forming a coating of malachite and azurite, has almost completely obscured whatever remains of the gilding. Although it is possible for this encrustration to build up over a gilt surface, gold, as a rule, protects the surface of the bronze from the effects of damp and inhibits such overall patination.

125

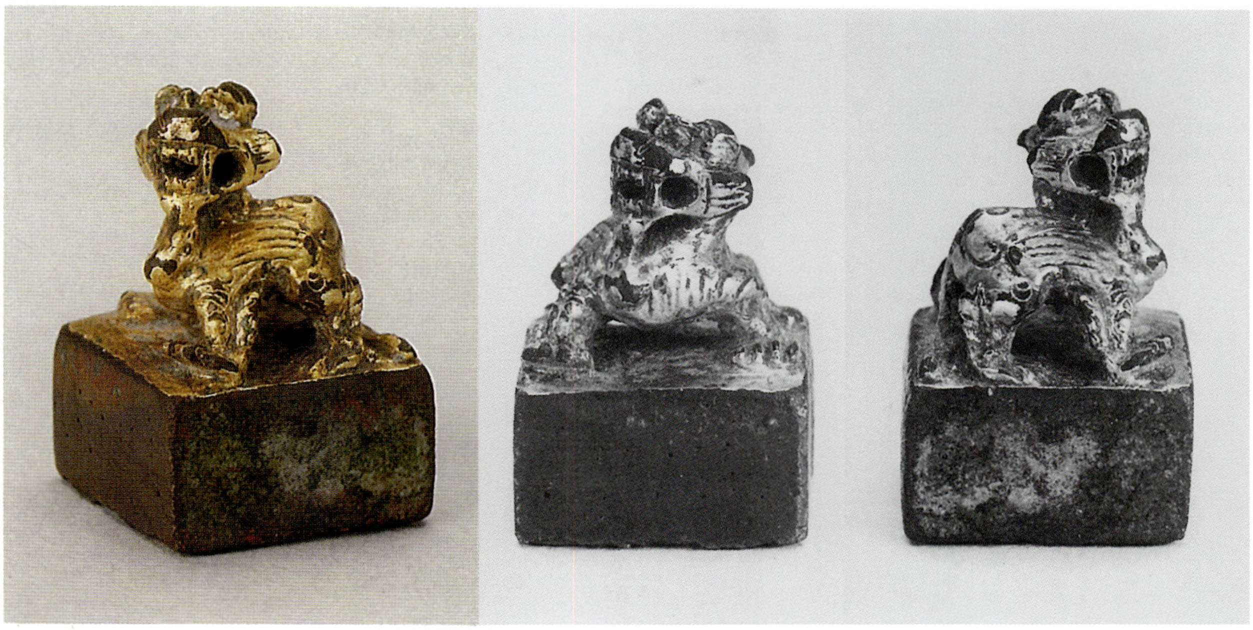

126

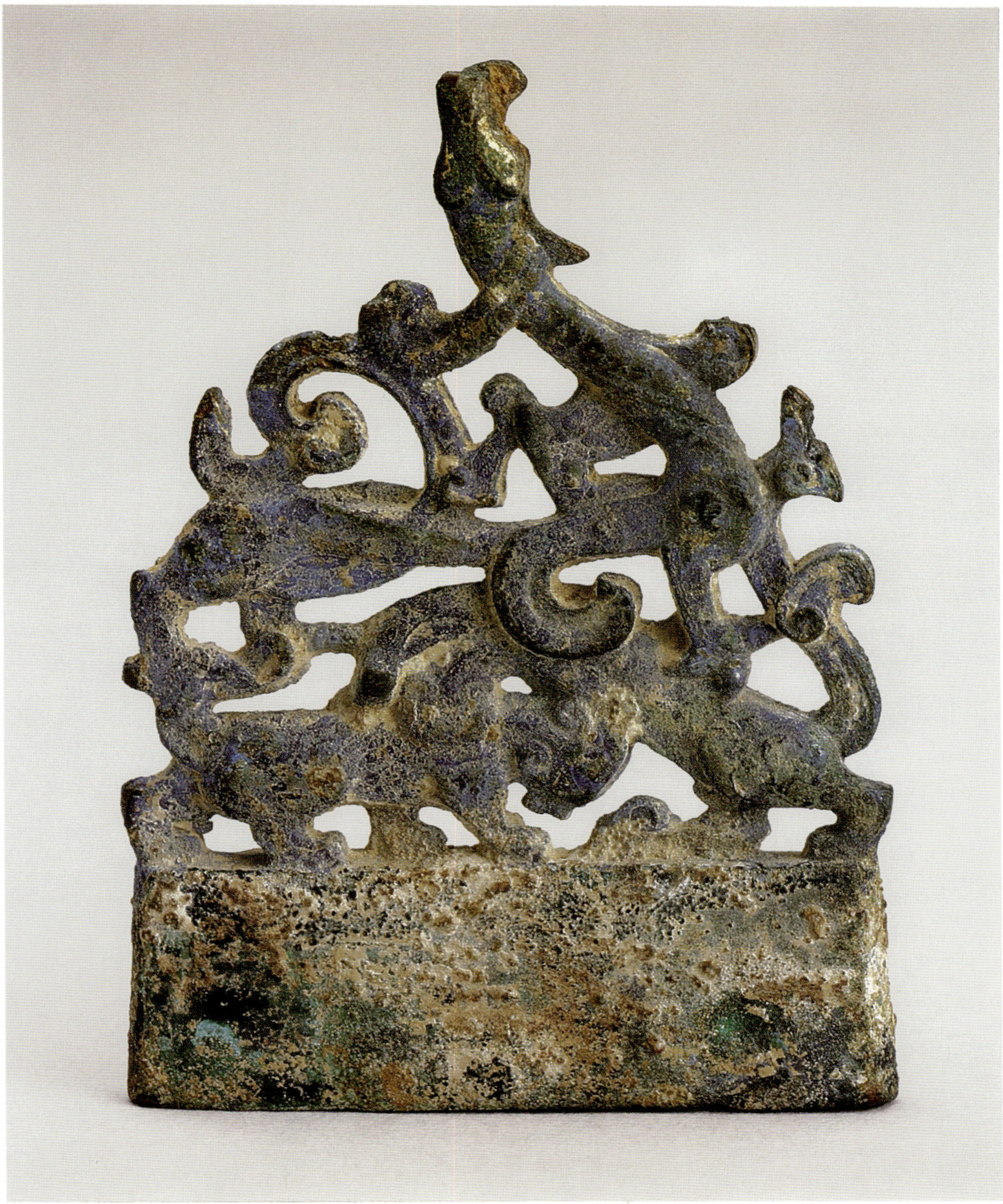

Larger than life size

127

Symbolic Wine Vessel

Bronze, inlaid with gold and silver; an imaginary animal-form miniaturized *zun* wine vessel, the raised harness blending into swirling patterns on either side of the rump, with raised flame-like motifs rising above and behind the forelegs, all extensively inlaid with various linear motifs in silver decorated with occasional small patches of gold inlay; the hinged cover surmounted by a nesting mythical bird; covered overall with random patches of simulated green and red encrustration.
Song to late Ming dynasty.
Height: 12.1 cm. Length: 16.05 cm.

嵌金銀線青銅獸形犧尊
宋至晚明，高12.1厘米，長16.05厘米

The animal-shaped *zun* was originally a wine vessel usually of about twice this size. The integral hinged lid, which is not designed to remain open without being held, limits the later uses of this miniaturized version. It would not have been suitable as an incense burner, nor convenient as a water vessel in conjunction with a ladle (neither is it watertight). It would appear to have been made solely for decoration.

The dating of archaistic bronzes with inlaid designs, usually after Warring States or Han originals, is no less problematical than that encountered with other forms of archaism; but it is further confounded by a traditional belief that the finest examples were made in the Song dynasty and thereafter quality declined. There can be no doubt that late Ming and probably even Qing metalworkers were capable of producing archaism of the highest quality, and would have been well informed as to accuracy by archaeological activities. These had been going on systematically from at least the Song dynasty, and accidentally every time a capital was rebuilt on the foundations of an old site (the Tang rebuilding of Chang'an on the site of the old Han capital, for instance).

This vessel has, to our knowledge, passed as Song dynasty for many years, but we believe it is more sensibly related to the late Ming florescence of archaism, the integrity and quality of which have been demonstrated by the identification of a range of wares by Hu Wenming in the late 16th and early 17th century (see no. 73). An interesting feature is the application of simulated encrustration. On a genuine vessel of this type, encrustration would tend to build up based upon the copper content of the bronze (it being the decomposition of copper in association mainly with moisture and its transformation into another mineral) and would not occur, other than as overlap, on silver and gold inlays. Here, however, the maker has spread his 'encrustration' at random over gold, silver and bronze; a minor anomaly, and in archaism, where no attempt at forgery was intended, one that would not have worried either maker or patron.

These miniaturized animal *zun* were quite popular and were probably made from the Song dynasty onwards. From a sculptural point of view this example has marvellous presence. The way in which the upward thrust of the neck and head is counterbalanced by the pattern of swirling lines is inspired, the raised and inlaid lines forming a dynamic unit moving in a diagonal from the front legs up and back to the rump. The whole movement is brought to an elegant conclusion in the angular, curving tail.

A woodblock impression of the sort of *zun* which would have inspired this example, and is likely to have been known to late Ming metalsmiths, was published in the 1528 edition of the *Bogu Tulu*[1] — see Fig. 1. A drawing of the inlaid design on their vessel appears as Fig. 2.

1. A revised edition of the catalogue of the Song Xuanhe Emperor's collection.

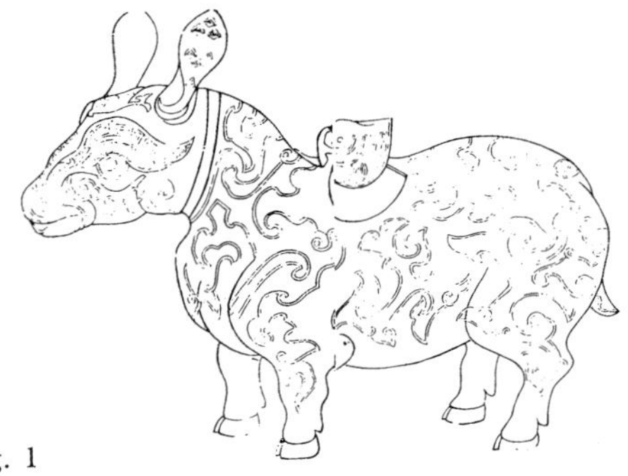

Fig. 1

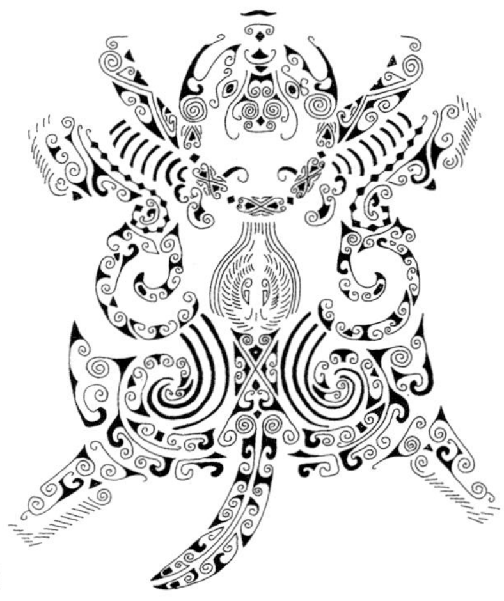

Fig. 2

128

Wrist Rest

Ivory, of creamy colour; a wrist rest in the form of a natural segment of bamboo set on small, scrolling feet; the upper section carved with Bodhidharma, seated enveloped in his robes, a tied bundle of books by his side; the recessed underside carved with a spray of millet, and another flowering plant, around which a group of creatures are shown in various stages of courtship; with a pair of crabs, two kissing frogs, four mating crayfish, another pair of frogs and various snails and clams; all carved in deep relief leaving most of the creatures and details in the round.
Probably late 18th century.
Length: 21.5 cm. Maximum width: 6 cm.

象牙雕達摩及水族臂擱
可能十八世紀後期，長21.5厘米，寬6厘米

A vogue for ivory wrist rests with elaborately carved undersides seems to have been initiated by the Qianlong palace workshops. The wrist rest in this standard form seems to have been a late Ming development popularized in the Qing (see no. 216). Part of that popularization seems to stem from the Qianlong palace workshops where a large number were produced, some of which are signed and dated by known palace artists (see no. 96). They mostly follow the standard format of being shaped like a bamboo segment, using the node, and standing on small feet which seem to owe a good deal to the *qin*, whose profile they seem to simulate, with the node representing the bridge of the instrument and the feet the tuning peg protectors.

There is one ivory wrist rest of this form which bears a collector's seal of the Ming collector Xiang Yuanbian, and an inscription of Wen Peng, a famous early 16th century artist known as a seal carver and to have carved ivory seals.[1] Published twice, it was accepted at face value. Jenyns questioned it in *Chinese Art*[2] and when sold at Sotheby's as Lot 201 on 14th December 1976, it was left discreetly undated. There can be little doubt that it is not genuinely from either Xiang's collection or the Ming dynasty. Indeed it is possible that it is by the same carver as this example. They are remarkably similar, using a bamboo node low on the face, four small scrolling legs, and even being carved with the same crayfish subject (with similar tails spread out like butterfly wings). If they are not from the same hand or workshop, they are certainly related in some manner.

It seems likely that a vogue for such ivory wrist rests was started under the Qianlong Emperor in the palace, and spread during the latter part of the 18th century to become a popular form elsewhere. It is even possible that this group also emanated from the palace workshops, but is simply of a different style from the signed and dated examples mentioned earlier. The type continued throughout the rest of the Qing dynasty, and was revived as a vehicle for works to demonstrate technical virtuosity in the post-1950 period. The wear and patination of this example are consistent with known 18th century examples still in the imperial collection in the National Palace Museum, Taiwan, and a late 18th century date seems reasonable.[3]

1. *The Arts of the Ming Dynasty,* no. 366, pl. 100; *Chinese Exhibition at Burlington House in 1935-1936* (Catalogue no. 1947).
2. Vol. 4, p.197.
3. Further examples of similar format are also illustrated in *Masterpieces of Chinese Writing Materials in the National Palace Museum,* nos. 46 and 47.

127

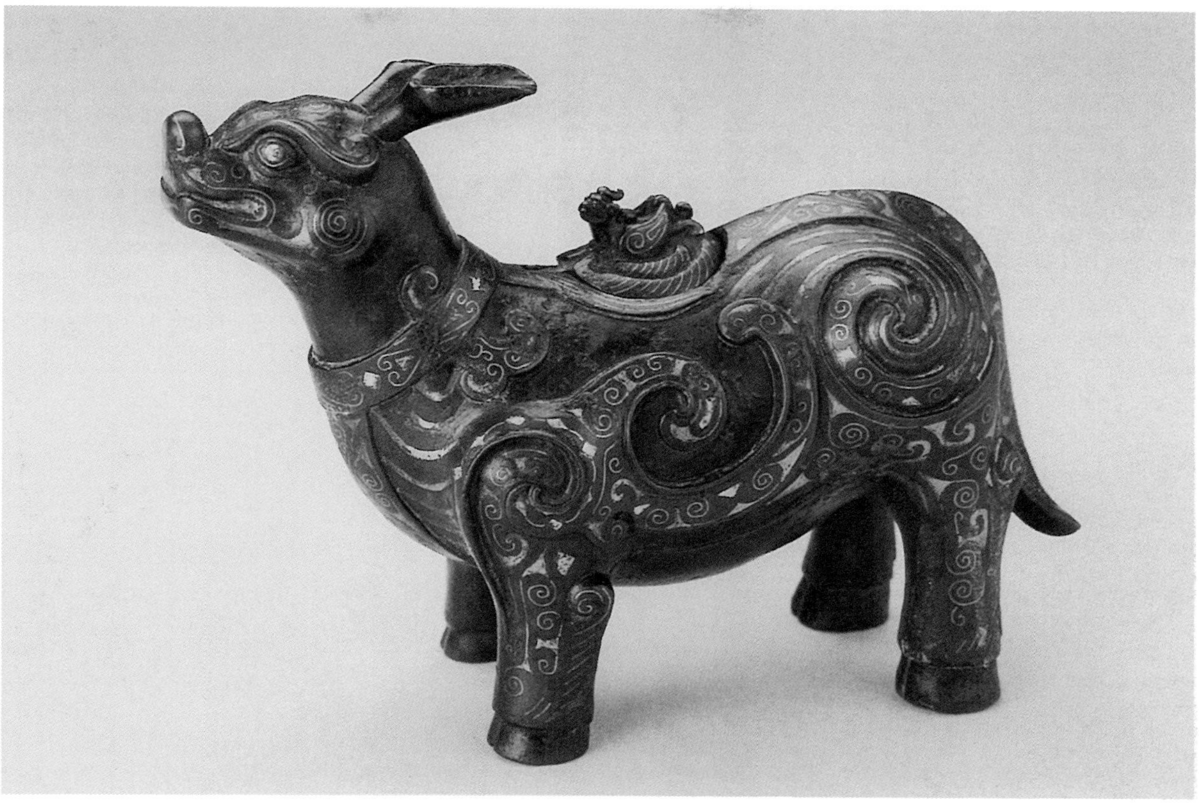

128

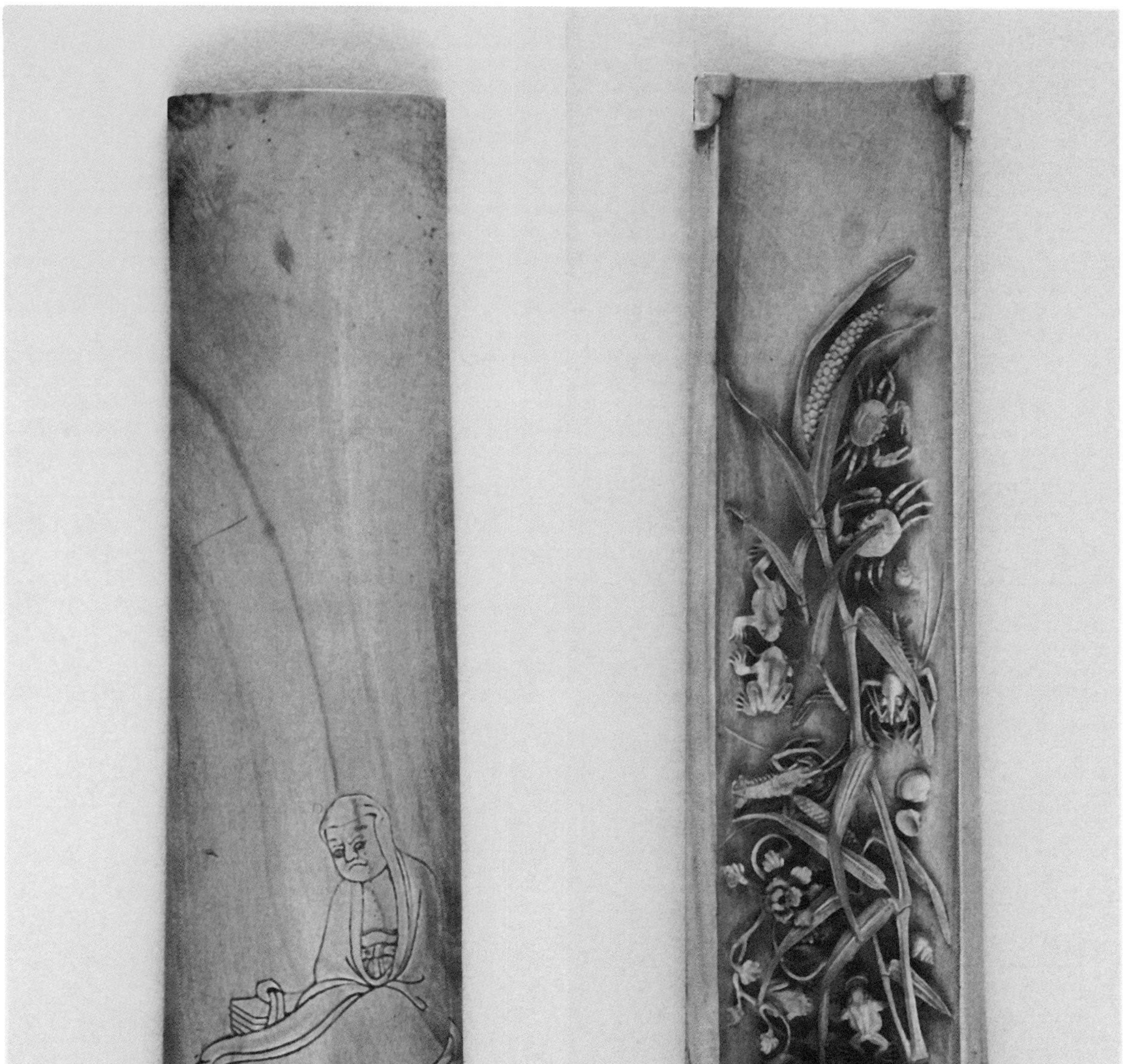

129

Tally

Nephrite, of yellowish-green tone with russet brown markings probably enhanced by staining; carved as one half of a tally in the form of a stylized mythical feline, with formalized flames rising from its haunches, and a shaggy stylized mane and body fur; the reverse with positive and negative circular 'keys' (to lock into its other half) and two seal-script characters carved in relief in a recessed panel: *Pingding* ('To pacify'), surrounded by the outlines of the feline but incised entirely in archaistic, curling lines.
Perhaps Song dynasty.
Length: 10.3 cm.

玉雕平定虎符
可能宋代, 長10.3厘米

The tally originated with the need to authenticate orders. Military commanders or ministers used them as symbols of authority. The earliest kind of which we are aware was in the form of various jade *gui* or *zhang* tablets. Later double tallies were developed with two closely fitting sections so that they would match only their authentic other half. These were a development of either the late Warring States period or the Han, and were made in the form of fish, cranes, tigers, etc. Few authentic ones have survived as they were considered to be inauspicious omens, connected with political intrigue and disasters and were not preserved.[1] Another a popular material for these early double tallies was bronze, usually in the form of a tiger or tiger-like beast, sometimes inlaid in gold or silver, of which many later versions were made.

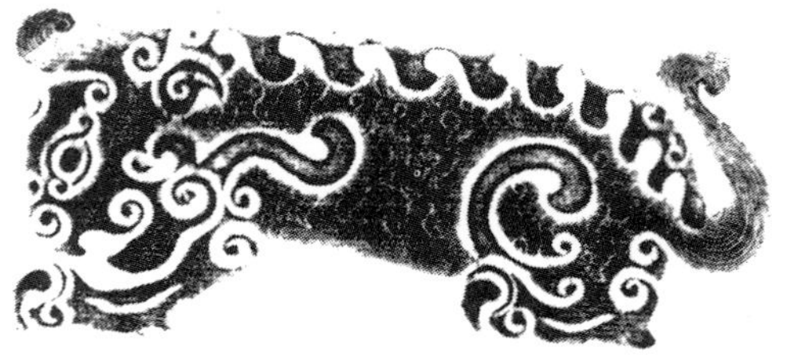

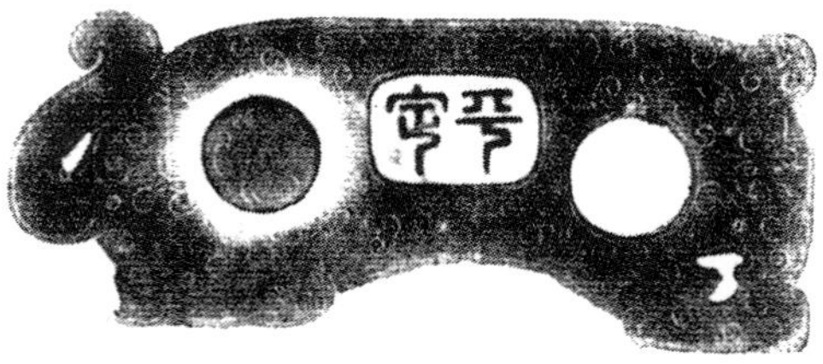

The symbolism of the tally clearly lived on even if they were not used in later centuries. Zhang Zhao (died after 1698), in rhyme-prose about an attempt to revitalize a friend who had given up on life and was ailing, suggests seven possible remedies, one of which involves taking high office. He wrote: "Why don't you take a journey to the capital and perhaps see the Prime Minister! Ah, you will be given an official tally and have your official parasol shining in the sun in some region."[2]

As symbols of antiquity, these tallies were frequently made later as archaistic objects. In Song or later times it might even have been felt unnecessary to make two halves any more, since as an archaistic work of art it no longer needed to be functional.

The tentative dating of this piece to the Song dynasty is on very slim evidence. The archaism is confident and powerful, but with an endearing friendliness that might speak of the Song. James Watt also claims finely incised archaic designs on naturalistic animals as a characteristic of the Song jade carver.[3] This colour of jade was apparently popular at the time, and other than that it has a 'Song feel'. However, there are probably large numbers of pieces as late as the Kangxi period which have a similar 'feel'.

1. *Illustrated Catalogue of Ancient Jade Artifacts in the National Palace Museum,* Foreword (unpaginated).
2. *The Importance of Understanding,* p.93.
3. *Chinese Jades From Han to Ch'ing,* p.78.

130

The Qianlong Emperor's Brush Pot

Crystal; the flawless material carved as a simple, cylindrical brush pot, the base inscribed *Qianlong yuyong* ('made for the imperial use of the Qianlong Emperor') in raised regular script in a recessed square with a roughly stippled ground.
Probably Beijing palace workshops, Qianlong period.
Height: 8.35 cm. Diameter: 6 cm.
20th century wood stand carved with a frieze of two pairs of facing *kui* dragons.

水晶筆筒•乾隆御用銘
清乾隆(1736-1795), 高8.35厘米, 直徑6厘米

This brush pot is probably part of a set including no. 235, with which it is currently contained in an elaborately fitted orange *huamu* box. Although the marks are of different form, they are clearly related in style and in the unusual use of a stippled ground. The vessels are also related in being plain, pure crystal miniature objects for the scholar's table.

In the hierarchy of imperial marks the form *yuyong* ranks highly. As a very general rule, particularly during the Kangxi, Yongzheng and Qianlong periods of the Qing dynasty when the Beijing palace workshops were in full production to complement a wide variety of wares made elsewhere for the Court, the hierarchy is as follows. At the lower end of the scale come the six-character marks which include the name of the dynasty; above these are the four-character marks which exclude it, using the designation *nianzhi* (literally 'made in the year of' but usually translated as 'made in the such and such period'); this form was widely used in the Qing Beijing palace workshops. Then comes a group of marks which use the form *yuzhi,* literally 'imperially made' but usually translated as 'by imperial command of' a particular emperor. These indicate that the pieces were made at the specific command of an emperor, nearly always in Court workshops, be they within the Palace or elsewhere, such as at Jingdezhen. This meant that the emperor had a special interest in their production and monitored it more closely than was the case with other wares, although it did not imply that all the pieces were made solely for his use. Above these comes the series of marks which denote specific interest or use of an individual emperor. These include the marks which appear typically on gourds, denoting in various forms (see no. 91 for a discussion on these) that it was for the emperor's treasured use or his appreciation, etc., and also the form here, where it states specifically that it was for a particular emperor's personal use. As a general rule six-character marks which include the name of the dynasty and the use of the form denoting some specific imperial interest are spurious, put on by later craftsmen who did not understand correct form.

Two other crystal pieces are known which relate to this vessel, both equally plain and pure. One is a narrow cylindrical vessel in the Lam Dawei collection. The other is similar to this (*The Literati Mode,* no. 115). Both are similarly marked.

The stand on this brush pot is certainly a later addition, probably made at the same time as the fitted case.

129

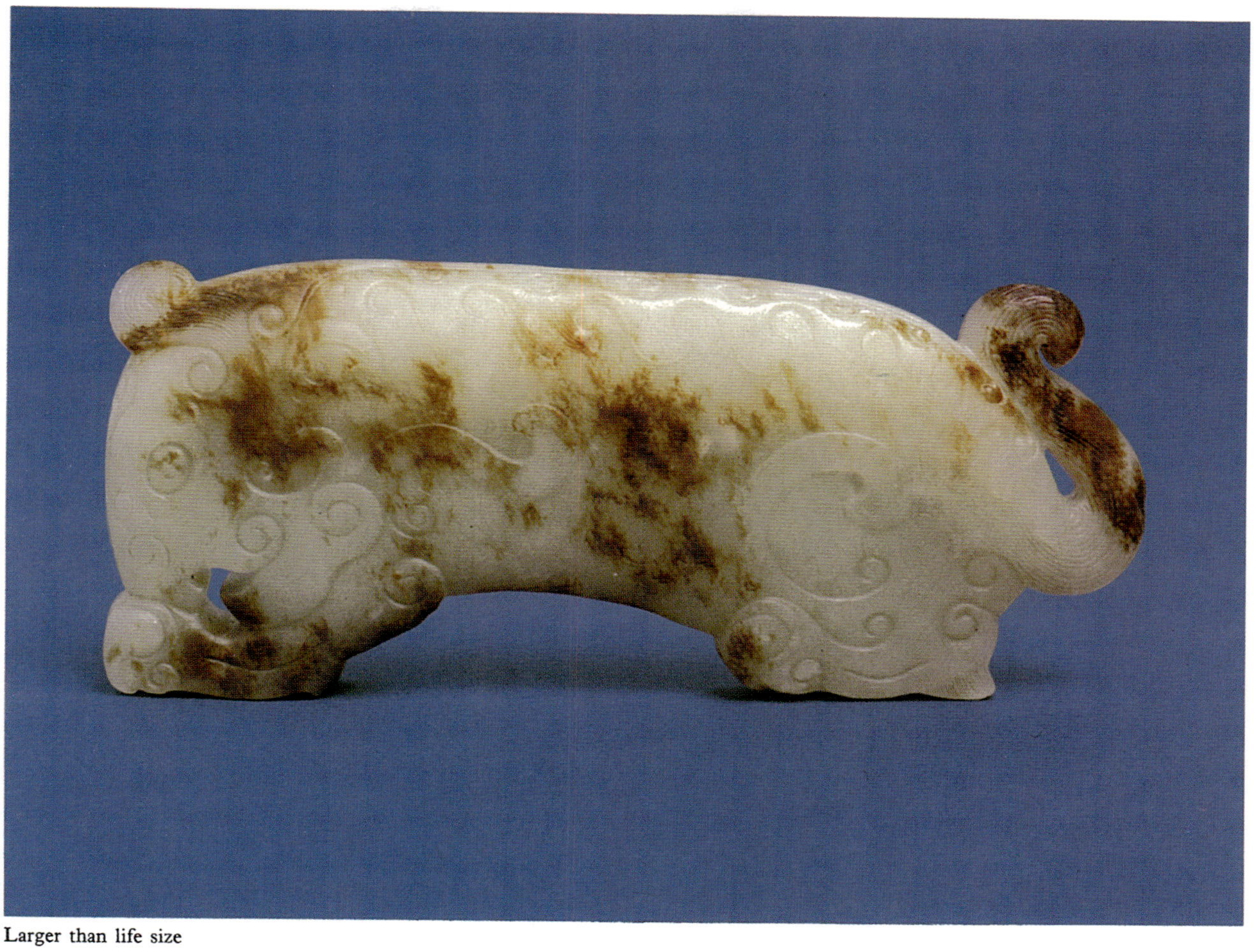

Larger than life size

130

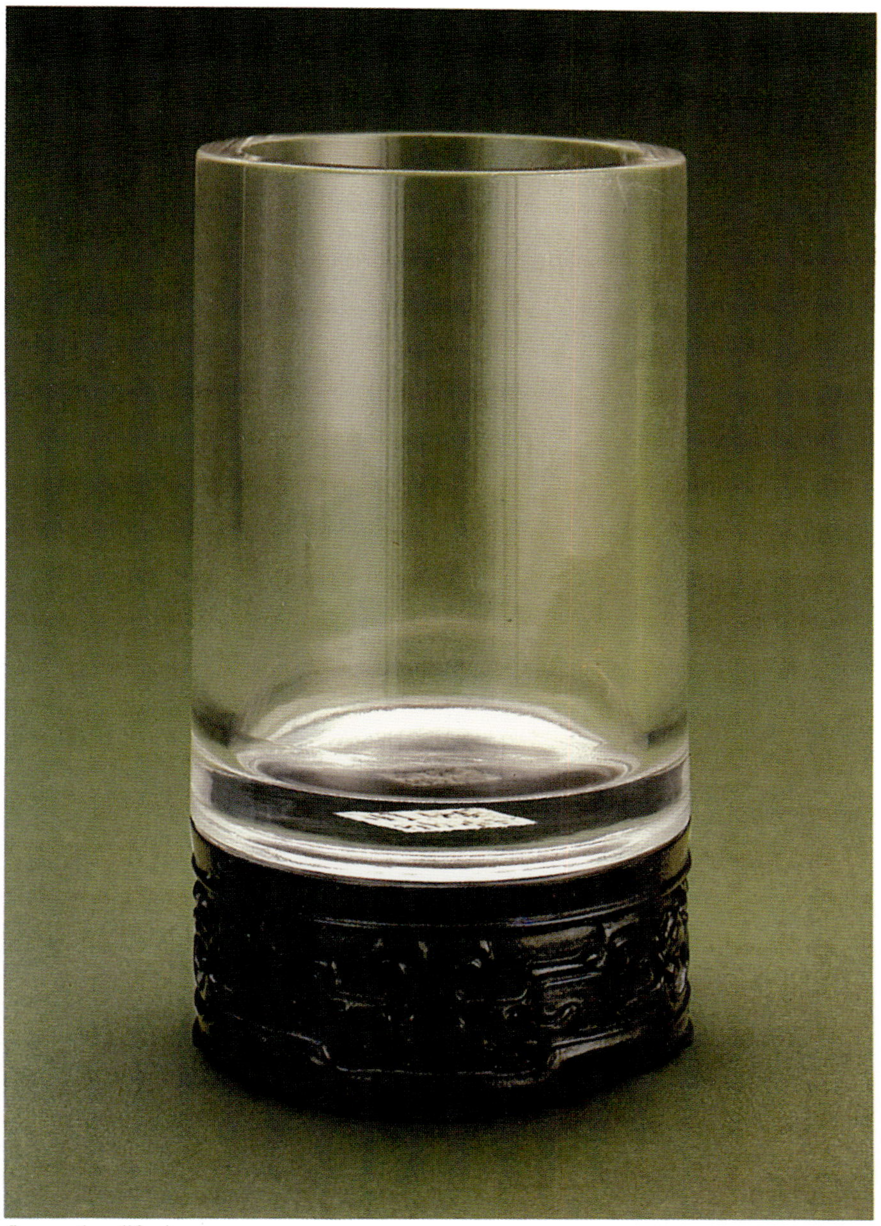

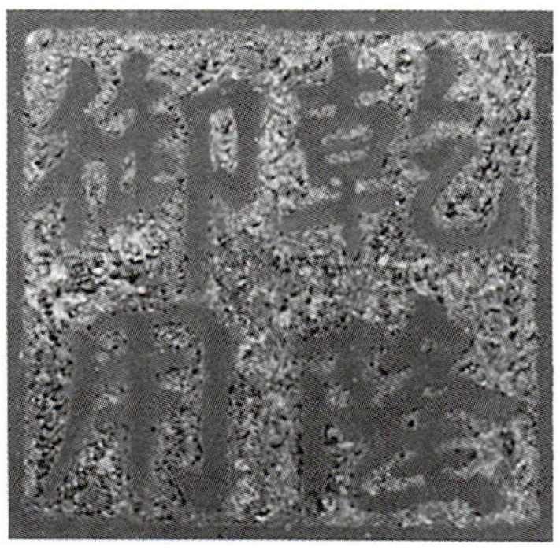

Larger than life size

131

Water Vessel

Nephrite, of pale green colour with brown markings; carved as an artist's water vessel in the form of a *tuolong* (a mythical beast combining the features of a dragon and a tortoise), the dragon-like head with a single central horn, the carapace with a series of hexagonal patterns bordered by a single band of double-unit *leiwen* and with flames, carved in relief, flickering across it, the beast set amid waves which emanate from a single central vortex on the fully carved underside.
Ming dynasty, 16th century or earlier.
Height: 6.35 cm. Length: 15.8 cm.
Published: *Chinese Jades from Han to Ch'ing*, pp.78-79, no. 61.

玉雕鼉龍水丞
明代十六世紀或較早，高6.35厘米，長15.8厘米

In the above publication, James Watt dated this vessel to the 16th century, partly on the evidence of the particular pattern of the whirlpool and waves design which he believes is typical of the mid- to late Ming period. A comparable water vessel, of the same mythical beast, although differently treated in both form and technique, is illustrated by Desmond Gure[1] and dated to the early Song period, which seems rather enthusiastic. However, we believe a date earlier than the 16th century might reasonably be entertained. Watt's dating is based upon the particular pattern of whirlpool, formalized and emanating from a central vortex. The wave-base in jade carving is found as early as the 13th century (see no. 89 where a massive wine jar with dragons and waves, completed in 1265, is discussed). This wine jar was such a famous and influential work that it inspired many later developments of the same theme. However the lack of reliable evidence in the dating of later jades makes the attribution of these stylistic developments to particular periods very tentative.

The carving, the twisting curve of the head and the wind-whipped waves cresting around the flaming beast give it a strong dynamism.

1. 'Selected Examples from the Jade Exhibition at Stockholm, 1963; A Comparative Study', *Museum of Far Eastern Antiquities Bulletin*, Vol. 36, 1964, pl. 28, 4.

132

Rock Sculpture

Malachite; the natural form worked in places to create a series of ridges connecting five peaks of various sizes with a grotto and an opening from one side of the stone to the other; mounted on a simple ridged wood stand with five feet.
Ming or Qing dynasty.
Height including stand: 8.75 cm.
Length of stand: 18.5 cm.

孔雀石雕五嶽筆山
明或清代，高連座8.75厘米，座長18.5厘米

Malachite is one of the stones that is most easily and reliably identifiable in the 12th century *Yunlin Shipu*. Indeed, in Song times stones with blue and green colouring seemed to have been particularly valued. Malachite was also used as a pigment and for medicinal purposes. It is particularly suited to use as fantastic stones because of its naturally convoluted shapes and markings, forming as it does in layers in conjunction with decomposing copper. This characteristic is noted in the *Yunlin Shipu:* "The Stone Green of Qianshan ('Lead Mountain') county in Xinzhou is produced within a deep pit. One species is fused and knotted to make the contours of mountain cliffs, but it is not very hard."[1] In this example the cross-section of areas of polished stone resembles a forest of trees blanketing the slopes of the mountainous form.

Grottoes and caves have been long adopted as shelters for those who wander the landscape and were considered from earliest times to be the homes of immortals, fairies and other strange creatures. A natural opening, such as is found in this stone from one side of the mountain to another, might also have been seen as a metaphor for stepping from one form of reality into another. The classic example of this is found in 'The Peach Blossom Spring', a popular story immortalized by the poet Tao Yuanming (365-427), in which a poor fisherman stumbles through an opening in a rock upon an ageless paradise. Upon returning home, he finds that during his sojourn in this arcadian civilization several generations have passed in the real world; he is, of course, unable to find his way back to Utopia.

This stone probably served as a brush rest, to which function it is well suited. With its five albeit ill-defined peaks it also conforms to a popular form of brush rest, representing the Five Sacred Mountains of China: the eastern, Taishan, in Shandong province; the southern, Hengshan, in Henan; the western, Huashan, in Shaansi; the northern, Hengshan in Zhili, and the central, Zhongshan in Henan. The auspicious nature of this number (or perhaps the five peaks) are also reflected in the five feet of the stand.

1. *Tu Wan's Stone Catalogue of Cloudy Forest*, p.23.

131

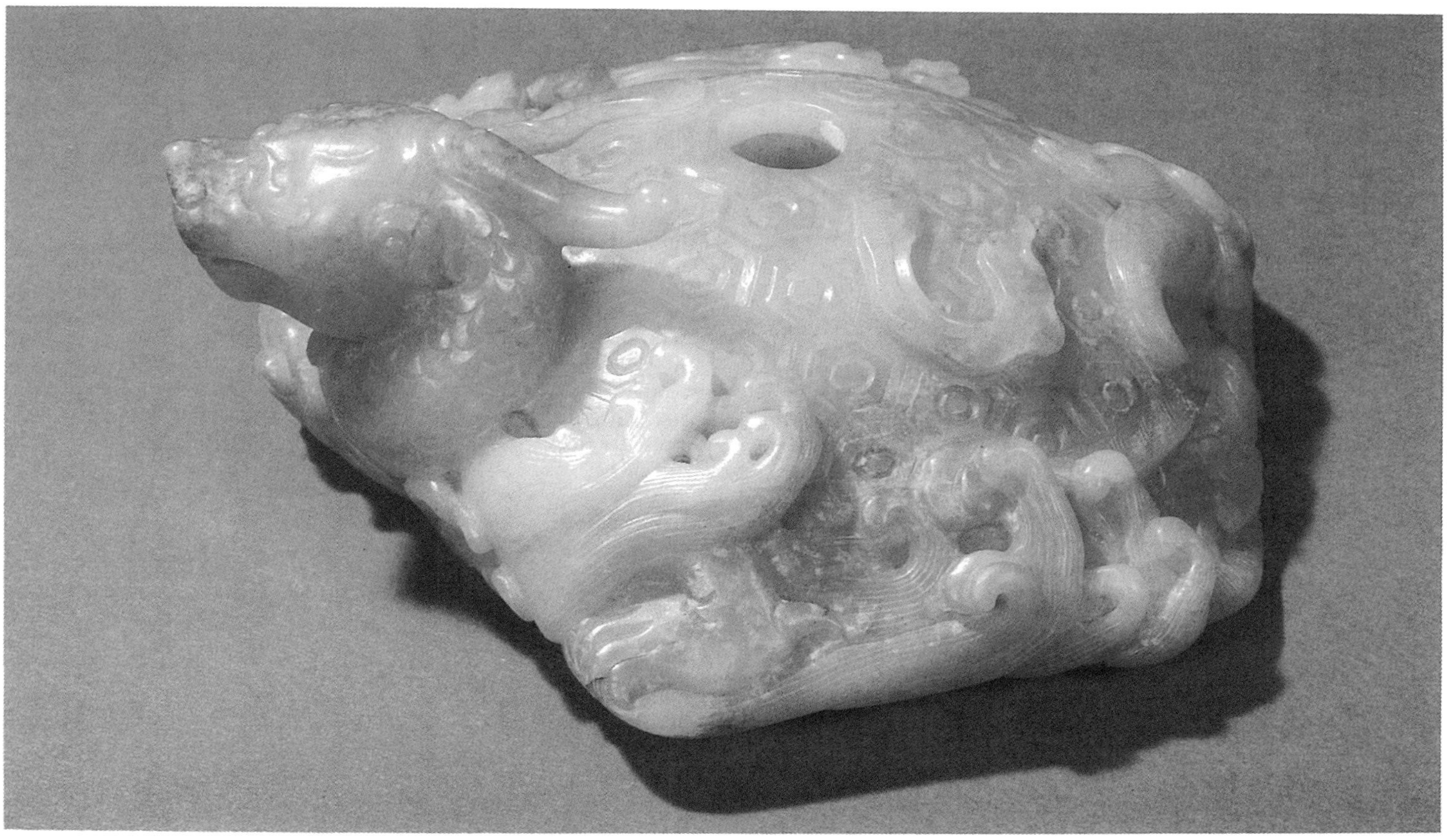

132

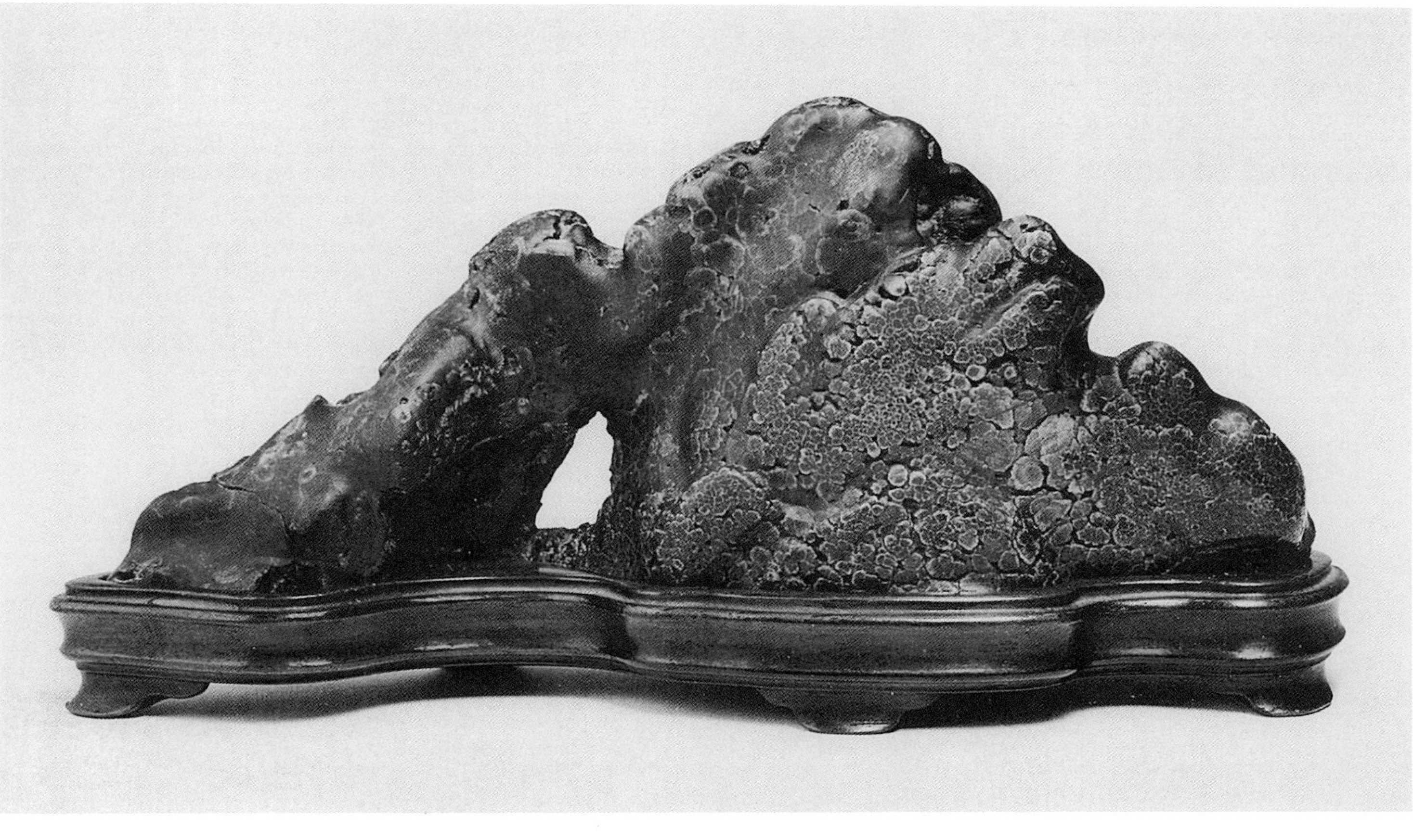

133

Snuff Bottle

Chalcedony, of pale variegated grey-brown colour; natural darker markings in the stone cleverly used to form a silhouette design of a strange rock set in a rectangular vessel, with a butterfly to one side of it, and a three-character title to the other: *Zhenji tu* ('Picture of real likeness').
Mid-Qing dynasty.
Height excluding stopper: 5.1 cm.
Coral and pearl stopper.

棕石髓雕眞集圖鼻煙壺
清中葉, 高(不連蓋)5.1厘米

The snuff bottle represents a wide variety of arts, and was popular among the influential minority in the Qing dynasty. It provided a suitably intimate vehicle for the expression of their aesthetic and was exploited to a remarkable extent. In this example the natural picture in chalcedony of a fantastic stone reflects the scholar's love of natural markings in materials and of natural materials turned into art. The restraint with which the markings are brought out, discreetly set in a simple vessel, with a title alongside, is typical scholarly taste and would have carried considerable weight with the literati. The fact that it is also a snuff bottle adds a convenient function to its various roles, and gives the scholar an excuse to carry it about and play with it, or to share it with friends.

134

Paper Weight

Bronze, patinated to a dark, greenish-grey brown colour inlaid with silver wire; a paper weight in the form of a crouching leonine mythical beast, scratching the back of its left ear with a hind paw; details of mane, beard, tail and backbone all inlaid with silver wire; the base largely unworked and flat, with the exception of some rudimentary delineation of the underside of the paws, and silver inlay on the flattened underside of the tail.
Probably Song dynasty.
Height: 4.1 cm. Length: 6.1 cm.
Set on a plain, dark *zitan* wood stand.

嵌銀線青銅獅形紙鎮
可能宋代, 高4.1厘米, 長6.1厘米

Although this is of a group of bronze, sometimes inlaid, paper weights discussed elsewhere (see no. 225 for example) it has independent features well worth considering. In a field where only the foolhardy venture reasonably precise attributions to period, we are tempted to be uncharacteristically confident here of a probable Song date.

This is a distinctly individual sculpture; clearly it is not one of a group produced to a formula as are so many later examples. It is a powerful and beautifully sculpted beast with considerable character and strength as a work of art. The sculptural style and form of the animal have certain similarities with sculptures in stone, both monumental and miniature, of the Six Dynasties period in the powerful thrust of limbs and tautness of muscle structure, but it is too refined to be so early, and the fiercesome beast of that period has been tamed here towards becoming one of the 'pussycats' of the late Ming (see for instance the beast associated with the soapstone *luohan* in no. 135). The soft, grouped curls of the mane are distinctly reminiscent of Tang bronze sculptures of Buddhist lions. James Watt[1] mentions that the subject of a coiled feline scratching its ear is one of the most common motifs in the sculpture and decorative arts of the 8th century. He illustrates a jade example[2] dated to the Tang period or before, which bears marked similarities to this piece in its powerful style, and particularly in the depiction of the mane and limbs.

The flat, largely unworked base on small sculptures is also an early characteristic found from the Han onwards. Here a distinction must be made between unfinished undersides which were a product of the evolution of paper weights, or book or mat weights, from a still functional to a primarily aesthetic role, and those which were made that way as a matter of easier production. On a piece of this sculptural individuality, however, we may assume that the artist was not simply taking the lazy way out, and that the flat base suggests an earlier stage in this evolution. There is also considerable natural wear on this bronze, particularly noticeable in the exposed area of the mane at the back of the head and down the back and shoulders, where the sharply delineated original curls have become worn to a rich smoothness by centuries of handling. Stylistically, therefore, we have a piece which might reasonably be attributed to the period between the Tang and the end of the Song dynasty — from the 8th to the early 12th century. A date as late as the Yuan or Ming dynasties seems less likely, although it cannot be entirely ruled out.

This leaves us with the silver inlay to consider. Tang exotic decoration in metalwork seems to have been confined mainly to the silversmith and goldsmith, who produced sumptuous wares with these two metals. Other materials were sometimes used as embellishment, but as a rule bronzes were either left with their bronze surfaces (patinated perhaps) or gilt overall. There seems to have been no Tang tradition of inlaying bronzes with gold and silver, using silver wire extensively as there was in the Warring States and Han periods. Nor was the Tang with its innovative lust for life and its cosmopolitan culture archaistically inclined to draw upon the distant past for its repertoire of means of expression. It was not until the Song dynasty that a respect for the past as such rather than its individual details combined with an archaeological interest to prompt the beginnings of archaism in art. From the Song onwards elements of ancient style and methods become standard across a wide range of arts, and the silver inlay on this beast hints at a new-found respect for the inlaid silver wire techniques of the Warring States period. The most likely period to produce a combination of all these qualities would seem, therefore, to be the Song.

The wood stand for this piece, a highly impractical addition for a still functional paper weight, seems to have been made for it a considerable time ago. It is of a fine piece of *zitan*, simply and well carved, worn and patinated and not a little knocked about over the years. While it is impossible to date accurately, it might be attributed to the early Qing or even the late Ming period.

1. *Chinese Jades from Han to Ch'ing.*
2. Ibid. no. 26, p.53.

135

Luohan and Mythical Beast

Zixiu

Soapstone, of cream, beige, grey and deep russet red colour of the variety known simply as Shoushan stone; carved as a *luohan,* seated holding a *ruyi* sceptre in his right hand while his left rests on his left knee, leaning against a clearly besotted mythical beast, whose inlaid eyes stare adoringly up at its master; from what must be an uncomfortable role as armrest, the loosely fitted robes of the *luohan* edged with bands of incised lotus scroll on a formalized wave ground, which are inlaid with beads of pearls and turquoise-coloured glass; the back incised with the signature *Zixiu* in seal script.
Probably Fujian province, 17th century.
Height: 6.05 cm.

壽山石雕服獸羅漢•子秀製
十七世紀, 高6.05厘米

The name Zixiu, always signed in seal script in similar style, appears on a number of superb soapstone figures of the Zhou Bin/Yang Yuxuan group (see no. 45). It seems strange that Zhou and Yang should be recorded and revered, while other artists such as Zixiu are not mentioned when their work is obviously of the same group and class. Possibly Zixiu is an art name for one of several carvers who are recorded in literature but whose signatures do not seem to appear on works of art. It is also possible that Zixiu did not also carve seal texts and therefore did not attract the attention of the literati to the same extent as Zhou and Yang. In China the literati tended to record seal text carvers, while ignoring artists who carved other works. There are records of thousands of seal carvers (even mediochre ones) to attest to this, while records of those who made other works of art for the scholar's studio are rare.

Although the inlaid precious stones and pearls common to this group of soapstone sculptures may often be replacements, Zixiu favoured a combination of pearls and pale turquoise glass beads. They alternate in this example, and in the Quasha piece mentioned below; no. 136 also has a similar combination, although augmented by other, possibly replacement pieces. The origin of this turquoise glass is unclear. Ming *cloisonné* technology produced exactly this colour of opaque turquoise for its enamel inlays (which are also, of course, glass) and there seems to be no reason why small glass beads could not have been made at any time since the 15th century. What is intriguing is that despite the Ming *cloisonné* use of white enamel, crucial to the production of a range of pastel-coloured glass and enamels for working on porcelain, metal or other glass vessels, the full range of enamels possible with white as applied to porcelain had to await the Jesuit introduction of new technology and palettes to the Beijing palace workshops in the Kangxi period, resulting in the so-called *'famille-rose'* palette of enamels on porcelain, metal and glass. Enamels were imported by the Jesuits as lumps of glass, and it is possible that the Fujianese might have had access during the 17th century to direct imports from Europe which would have been independent of any shortcomings in the native Chinese tradition of glass making.[1]

1. Zixiu's signature appears on the large seated *luohan* published in *In Scholars' Taste,* no. 123 (now in the Mr. & Mrs. Wayne G. Quasha collection, New York), and another in *Chinese Decorative Arts,* Bluett and Sons, London, 1974, no 130. In the same publication no. 128 (although no signature is noted) is clearly by Zixiu, and apart from the obvious identity of style in the faces and other details of sculpture (it is a similar seated *luohan* holding a *ruyi* and leaning on a beast) one look at the adoring animal is enough to convince that it is by the same hand as this example. Both the last two cited are also published in *The Arts of the Ch'ing Dynasty, Transactions of the Oriental Ceramic Society* Vol. 35, nos. 427 and 428, where the former is described as having a two-character signature, which we may assume was that of Zixiu. A seated figure of a *luohan* holding a scroll, with a monkey offering him a peach and an incense burner on a rock beside him, is noted in the records of Hugh Moss Ltd., no. 1088; and a figure of Guanyin seated on a mythical beast, and a small figure of a *luohan* are also in the Shuisongshi Shanfang collection.

133

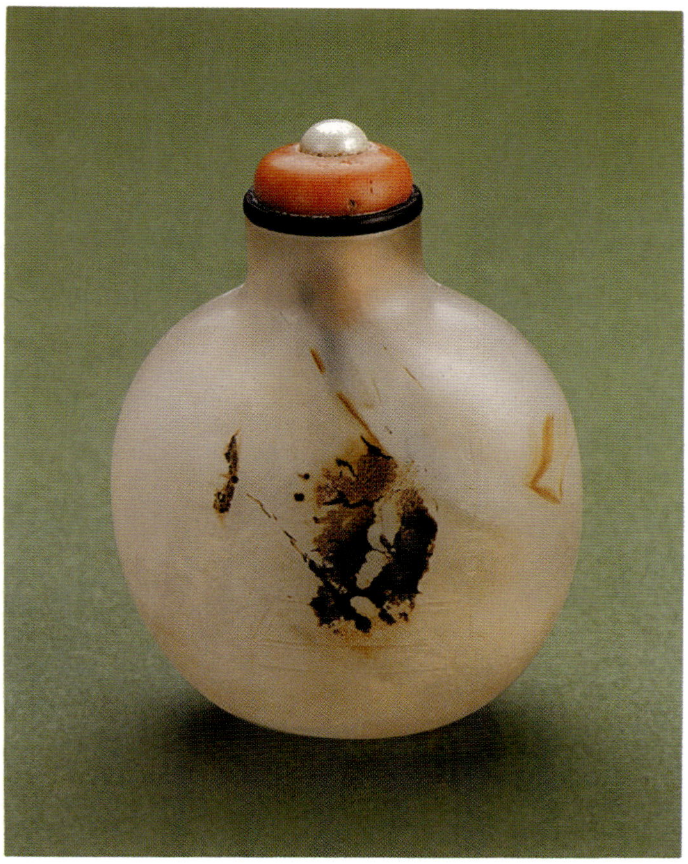

134

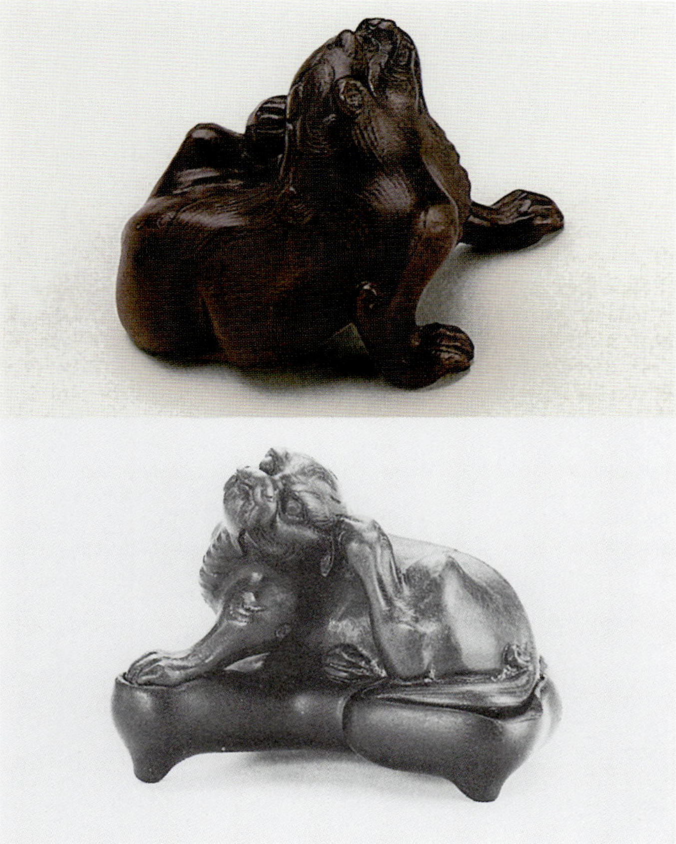

135

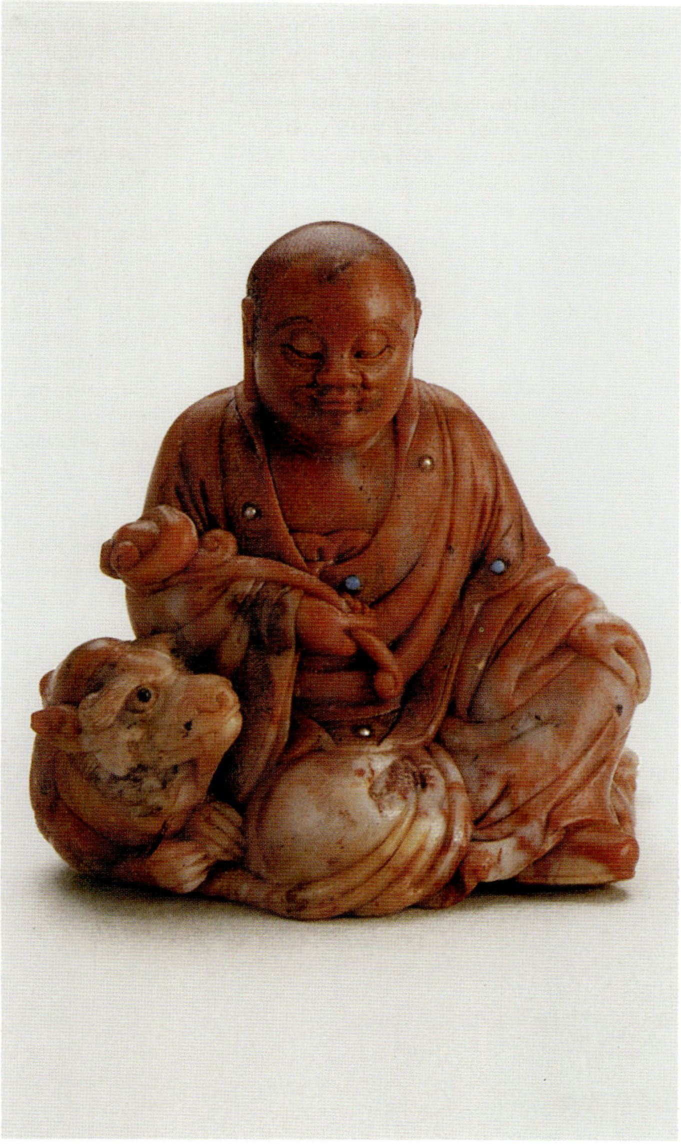

Larger than life size

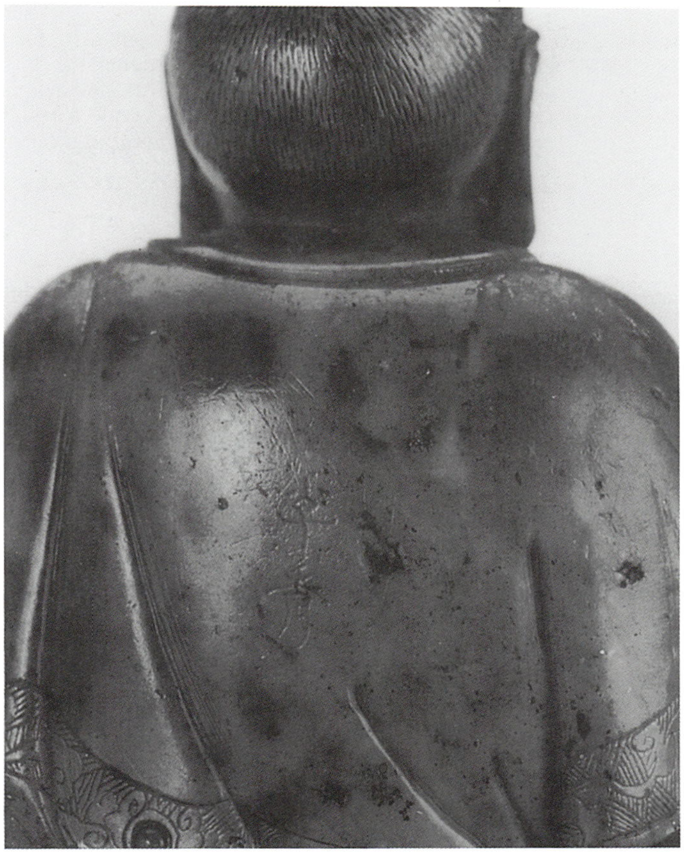

136

Luohan

Zixiu

Soapstone, of mottled greenish-grey colour of the variety known as Shoushan *dong* ('Shoushan-ice'); carved as a seated *luohan* in a meditative pose; the collar, sleeves and hem of his robes incised with a design of scrolling lotus on a formalized wave ground, inlaid with pearl, turquoise glass, coral and turquoise, the latter apparently replacements; signed on the lower back in seal script. Probably Fujian province, 17th century.
Height: 14.65 cm.

壽山牛角凍石雕羅漢坐像•子秀製
十七世紀, 高14.65厘米

The question of dating a range of soapstone carvings of the highest quality has been touched upon elsewhere (see nos. 43 and 45). The two key figures are Zhou Bin and Yang Yuxuan, mainly because they are recorded figures and both dated examples and literary evidence exist as guides to dating. This evidence suggests that Zhou Bin may have been active from as early as 1627 through to the third quarter of the 17th century, or that he began working in the mid-17th century and continued into the second half of the century (see no. 84 for a discussion of these two possibilities). Yang and Zhou are related stylistically, and in one Chinese souce (of questionable accuracy) Zhou is said to have been Yang's student.

Further evidence is offered by a group of soapstone carvings published by Jenyns.[1] These are in the British Museum and were part of the Sloane bequest in 1753. Sloane's records show that he bought a "Chinese idol with a pott" *(sic)* in 1718, which might be either of two pieces illustrated. The larger of these, a seated *luohan* with a begging bowl, is of a small group which are made of an even greyish-green material, well carved but not in the same class as the Zhou/Yang group (although one of these in the Stewart collection is confusingly if unconvincingly signed with Zhou Bin's name). The other is a standing *luohan* with a begging bowl of the Zhou/Yang group. One of these must pre-date 1718, and it is not unlikely that Sloane bought his other soapstone pieces at about the same time, suggesting the possibility that they all predate the early 18th century. If accepted as original the spurious signature on the Stewart figure (and it has certainly been there a long time as the extent of wear indicates) suggests that Zhou Bin predates that group. The overall impression is not only that Zhou and Yang were active in the early to mid-17th century, but that a whole school of carving arose out of their activities to be common enough by the early 18th century for a travelling foreigner to acquire a number of pieces.

It is tempting to assume, simply because of their relative celebrity, that Zhou and Yang were the popularizers of this school of soapstone carving but there is no clear evidence to suggest this. They may simply have caught the local imagination most firmly by being both seal text carvers as well as making the seal knobs themselves. It is possible that Zixiu pre-dated Zhou and Yang, but it is more likely that he was a contemporary, responding to the same patronage and rising to similar levels of inspiration. Were the material of this figure rather more even it would qualify as a *niujiao dong* ('ox-horn ice') stone (see no. 44), but it has too many uncharacteristic markings and inclusions.

For a discussion on Zixiu see no. 135.

1. *Chinese Art*, Vol. IV, p.270.

137

Brush Rest

Bronze; a brush rest in the form of a striding *chi* dragon, a flaming pearl mounted in the centre of its back; the metal well patinated to a blackish-brown colour.
Probably Song or shortly thereafter.
Mounted on an early wood stand in the form of turbulent waves.
Height including stand: 7.9 cm.
Length: 14.5 cm.

青銅螭形筆擱
可能宋或元, 高連座7.9厘米, 長14.5厘米

As with any of the pieces made for the scholar, functional objects also had symbolic and aesthetic roles. With the passing of time what might originally have been mainly functional might take on a primarily aesthetic role. Thus a porcelain flower vase might be placed reverently on a shelf and no longer be used; a ritual bronze wine vessel might become a flower vase, or an object purely for appreciation as an independent work of art. Similarly a brush rest, or paper weight, ink stick or brush might become a collector's item. Here it is possible that the brush rest, if indeed it was a brush rest originally, started life at table level and was later placed on a wave stand. Brush rests, brush pots and such were sometimes originally made and used with stands, but usually low and practical ones. The height of this stand would have rendered the brush rest somewhat unstable in use, suggesting that the owner who had the stand made had already promoted the piece to an aesthetic role.

Apparently such a transformation might have taken place by the late Ming dynasty with this particular piece. Wen Zhenheng mentions something that might be such a brush rest as this.[1] Under the heading of 'Brush rests' he describes a number of types. Among those in antique bronze he describes the following examples: "twin *chi* dragons wrestling with each other; those with twelve peaks; single chi dragons with curved backs" and goes on to remark that "these are just for collection and appreciation, and there is no need to put them on the desk with the inkstone" (ie: use them).

It is a pleasant change to find an object which met with Wen Zhenheng's approval, as so much of his text is devoted to disparaging remarks about how tasteless certain objects are. It is a dispiriting read when time and again interest leaps elatedly to find a mention of something similar to a piece in one's own collection, only to see Wen describe it as "in the worst taste, and quite beyond use", or "even if these are old they should be dispensed with", or worse still as "despicable, and should be abolished".

1. *Changwu Ji* ('Notes on Superfluous Objects'), *juan* 7, section 6.

138

Buddhist Acolyte

Bronze, with inlaid silver and gold; a Buddhist acolyte, standing on a pierced bizarre rock formation, his head turned to one side and shaven except for a forelock, his hands together in a respectful gesture, his loosely fitting robes inlaid in silver at sleeves, hem and collar with a continuous design of floral scroll with *lingzhi* heads, a buckle holding the robes across one shoulder linked to a clasp at the back inlaid in gold with a Sanskrit character; the bronze evenly patinated to a copper, brownish-red tone. Perhaps Fujian province, probably late Ming dynasty.
Height: 21.3 cm.

嵌金銀青銅侍童
可能晚明, 高21.3厘米

This piece represents a small group of bronzes attributed to the late Ming dynasty which are amongst the finest bronze sculptures from the Ming. They relate in style to late Ming or early Qing 'Blanc de Chine' figures from Fujian province in their combination of superbly sculptured inspirational figures with rough rockwork bases. The folds of garments are handled with a particularly well-observed and rounded plasticity, and on stylistic grounds the group would seem to fit comfortably into the Fujian area in the late Ming period.[1]

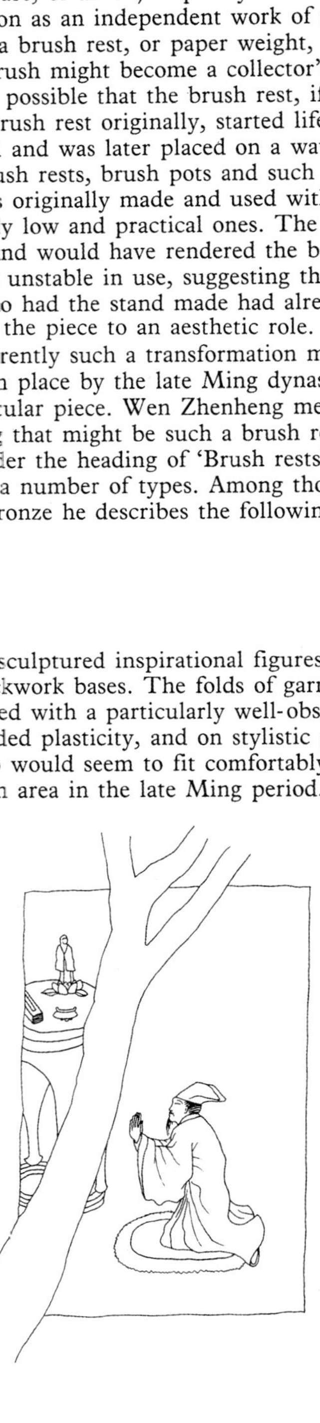

Fig. 1

This figure also fits into the larger group of inspirational sculpture of the late Ming and early Qing dynasties where a lack of formality and a softness and individuality set them apart from the mass of images for temples and public shrines. These pieces would be more suitable for private shrines and for use among the scholar class. In a painting by the 18th century Yangzhou artist Jin Nong (see no. 4) entitled 'Worshipping the Buddha'[2] we see the devotional use of such figures, where a scholar in a small pavilion kneels praying to a standing figure of Buddha. However, at the same time the immense care and attention to detail devoted to the group as a whole demonstrates beyond doubt that these were also works of art to which the scholar addressed his full aesthetic attention.

1. However see no. 169 for the question of dating certain later bronzes including a related piece in the light of some test results from The Research Laboratory for Archaeology, Oxford.
2. Taken from *Paintings by Yangzhou Artists of the Qing Dynasty from the Palace Museum*, no. 60, p.196.

136

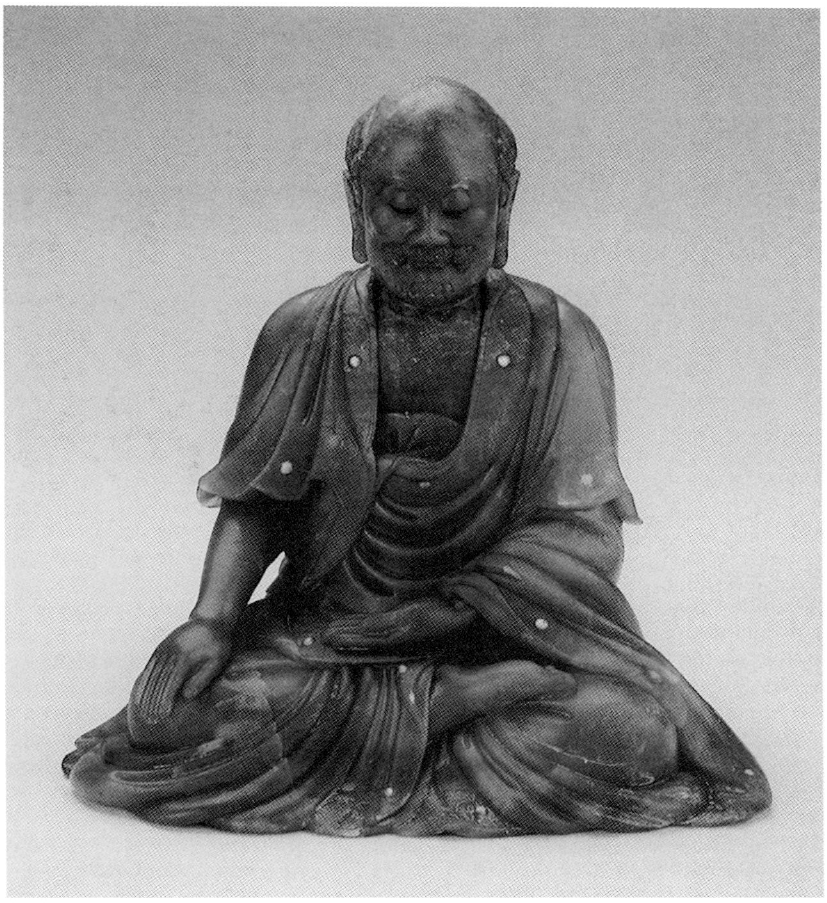

137

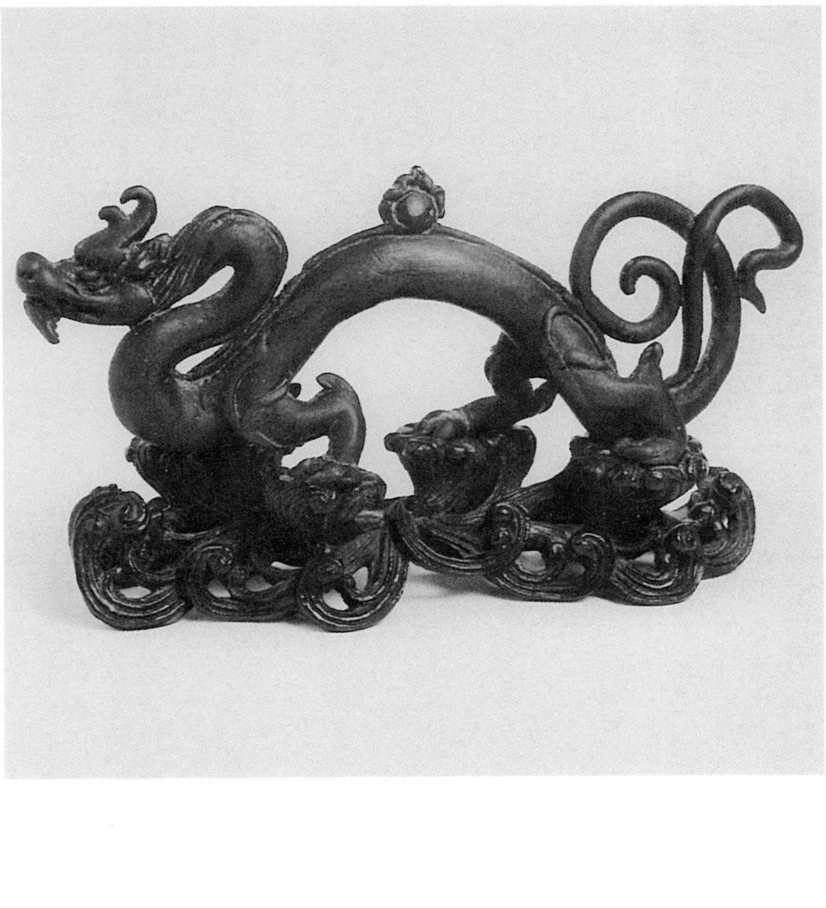

138

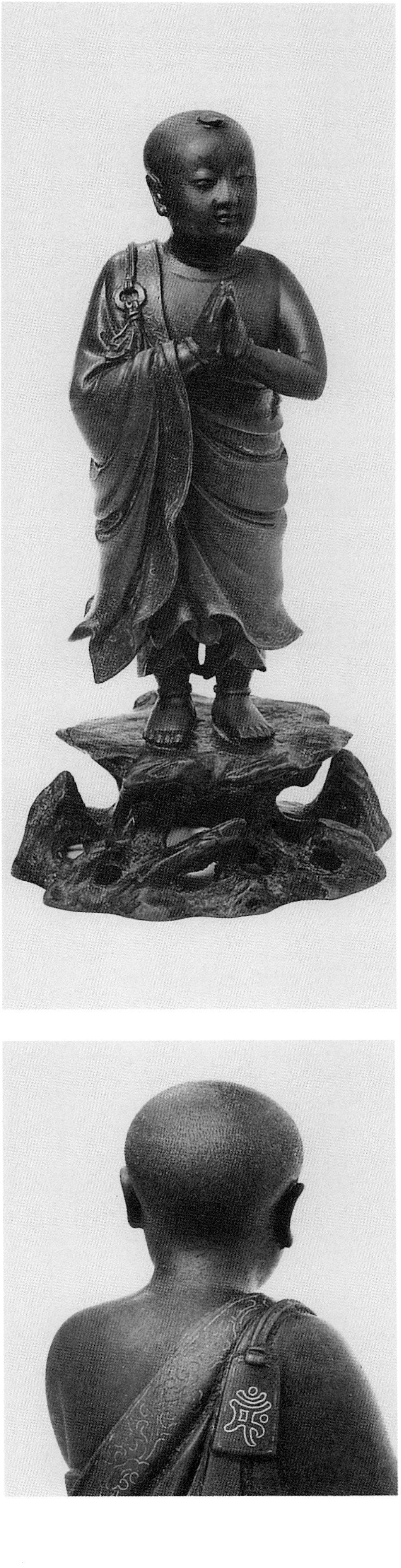

139

Incense Burner

Bronze, partly gilt; an incense burner of *gui* form, decorated with a continuous design of two three-clawed dragons amid clouds; with two protruding handles made up of a *taotie* and elephant composite creature; the dragons' heads and feet, and the handles gilt; the base with the mark *Da Ming Xuande nianzhi* ('made in the Xuande period of the Great Ming dynasty') in raised regular script in a recessed rectangular cartouche.
Probably Xuande period.
Height: 8.5 cm. Diameter of mouth: 14 cm.

鎏金青銅雕雲龍香爐・大明宣德年製銘
可能宣德，高8.5厘米，口直徑14厘米

This powerfully decorated incense burner is an anomaly. It bears an excellent Xuande mark, but has nothing apparently to do with the whole Xuande bronze controversy (see no. 123), and its decoration is so close in style to early 15th century lacquer decoration that the mark is entirely believable. If it is of the Xuande period it is presumably an imperial piece (three-clawed as well as five-clawed dragons were sometimes depicted on imperial wares of the Ming and Qing, and were particularly popular in the 15th century; it is the four-clawed dragon which denotes a lower than imperial rank), and we may expect the mark to accord closely with those on imperial ceramics of the period, which it does. That it is not part of the Xuande bronze controversy, other than in being purportedly a bronze of the period, is demonstrated by its decoration and style. The reason why the Xuande Emperor ordered large numbers of vessels to be cast (mostly incense burners apparently) was because it was felt that those in the imperial palaces and temples did not accord with the correct models, and that new ones should be made imitating archaic originals taken from bronzes and certain Song ceramics.

This burner follows neither archaic bronze nor Song ceramic decoration and would appear to be a quite independent Xuande bronze incense burner. Viewed as such, with its excellent mark and decoration closely related to Xuande lacquer, there seems no reason to question its authenticity.

140

Liu Hai

Feng Sanguan

Bamboo, of dark brown colour; carved as a figure of Liu Hai, reclining against a gnarled rock formation, holding a cash in one hand, while his three-legged toad crouches at his bare feet; the back of the rock inscribed *Sanguan zuo* ('made by Sanguan').
Jiading, probably first half of the Qing dynasty.
Height: 5.5 cm. Length: 11 cm.
Published: *Chinese Bamboo Carving* Part I, p.399, no. 132.

竹雕劉海戲蟾像・封三官製
可能清代早期，高5.5厘米，長11厘米

The *Zhongguo Yishujia Zhenglue* lists Feng Sanguan as a Qing dynasty bamboo carver from Jiading, in Jiangsu province. The same source gives two other members of the Feng family, Feng Yuanguan and Feng Wenguan, as also being bamboo carvers from Jiading, while Jenyns lists several other carvers of this surname associated with the carving of peach-stones, including Feng Wanguan (perhaps a mistake for Wenguan), Feng Benguan and Feng Yuanguan[1]. It was common practice in China for several sons of a single generation to share a common character in their given names, and equally common practice for bamboo carvers to work in other similar materials. It is likely, therefore, that the Fengs were wood and bamboo carvers with one generation of brothers excelling, who worked at some time during the Qing dynasty. This figure may be dated to the first half of the dynasty on its style, patination and the quality and style of the (probably original) *zitan* wood stand upon which it is placed.

Liu Hai was a popular immortal who was believed to have lived in the 10th century AD and who achieved immortality after meeting one of the Eight Immortals (see no. 173) and acquiring from him the secret of making the secretions of gold into pills of immortality. He lived as a while as an ascetic and then joined the ranks of the immortals. Several tales are told of him, one concerning his association with the three-legged toad that he fished from a well.[2]

1. *Chinese Art,* Vol. II, p.421.
2. *A Dictionary of Chinese Mythology,* pp.255-256.

139

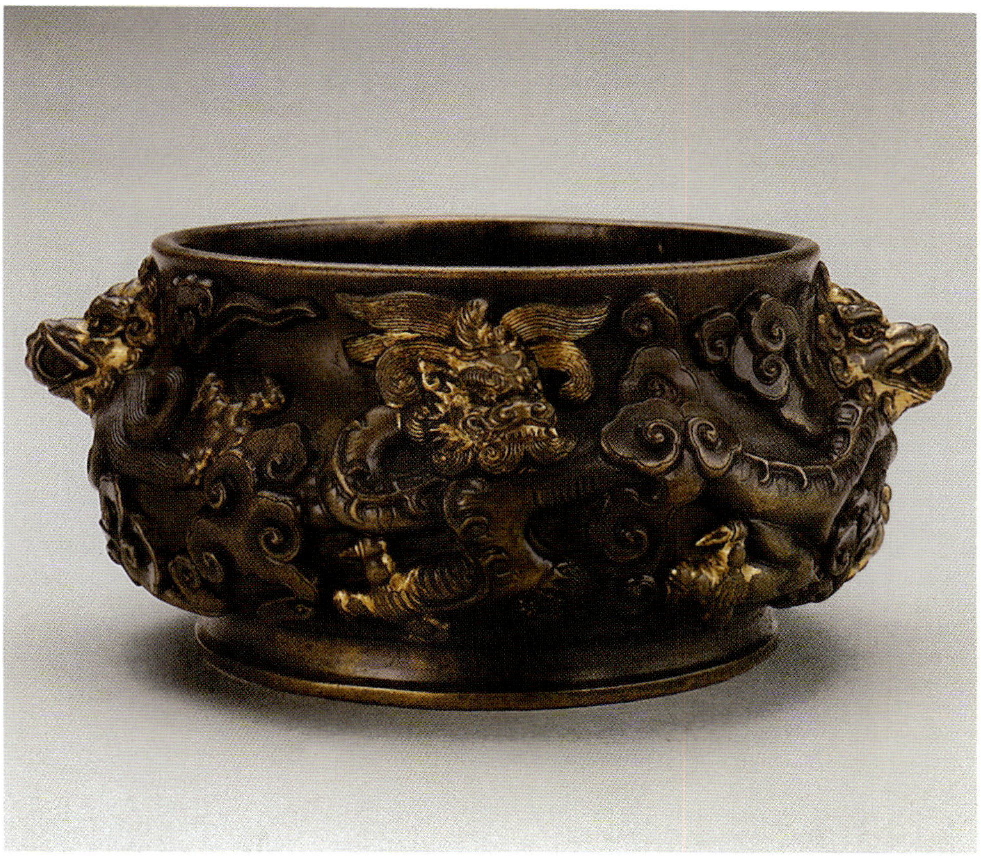

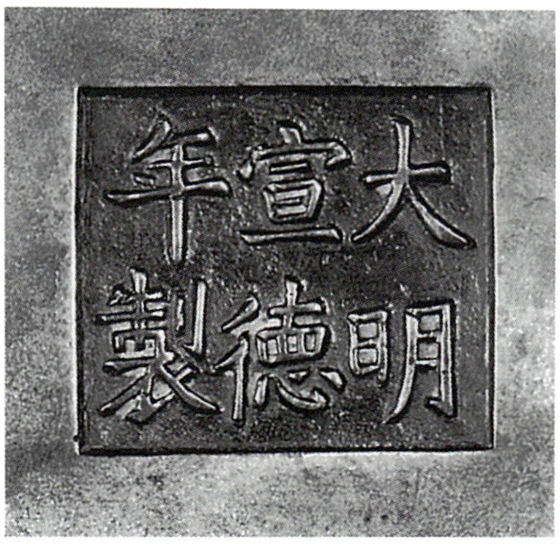

140

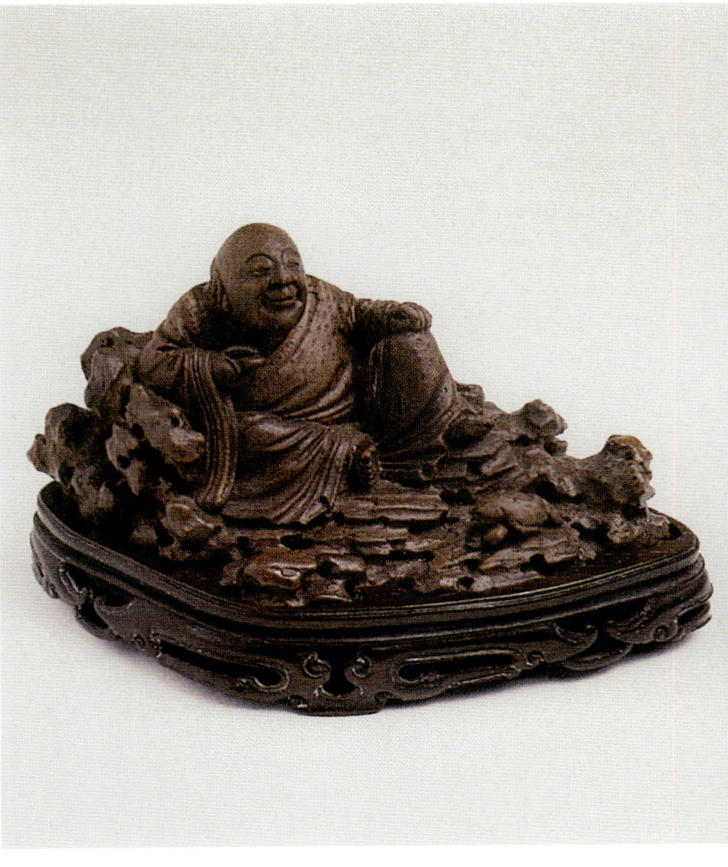

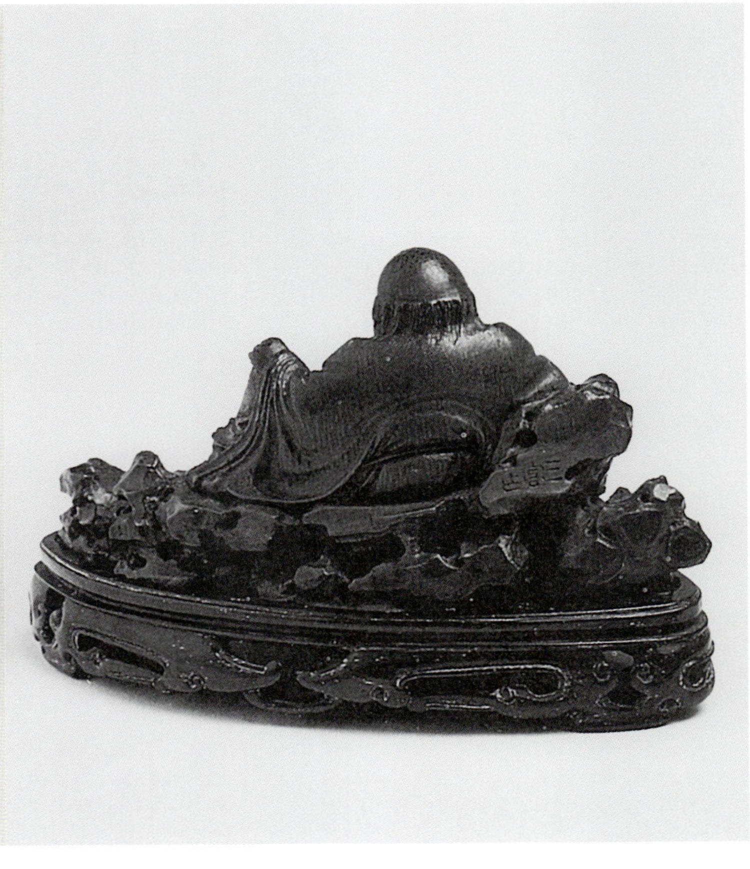

141

Couplet
Fang Yizhi

Hanging scroll, ink on paper; a couplet in cursive script: "Midnight, crossing the Songjiang river beneath the moon/All the way spring lingers in the gardens"; followed by *Xianchun Ji* (presumably the literary anthology from which the couplet was taken).
Signed Yuzhe ('Stupid One'), with two seals of the artist: *taochu* (?), in positive seal script, and *Foushanyuzhe Yizhi,* in negative seal script; and one collector's seal *Bojiao jianding* ('authenticated by [Xu] Bojiao' — a Hong Kong art dealer) in negative seal script.
Mid-17th century.
131.2 cm × 32 cm.

草書七言詩立軸•方以智書
明末清初，131.2×32厘米

The couplet is a unique Chinese form of poetic expression. It is made up of two lines (called the 'head' and 'tail') and the number of characters in each is the same. The form arises out of the satisfying symmetry of antithesis and parallelism in poetic expression, a key feature of Chinese poetry going back to the Classics. In the couplet a balance must be found between head and tail, between each character in the one and its usually contrasting character in the other, in tone, rhyme and meaning. Combined with the capacity for multiple layers of meaning in individual characters and the esoteric allusiveness of Chinese poetic expression, the form provides potential for infinite wit and subtlety of expression — a combination which has always delighted the scholarly Chinese mind.

The history of the couplet is traced briefly by T.C. Lai in *Chinese Couplets.* Its evolution from a poetic trend favouring parallelism and antithesis towards the specific art form it was to become in the post-Tang period was a gradual process, but one which first becomes noticeable in the late 5th and early 6th century. Liu Xie wrote at the time: "Nature, when endowing living things with limbs, does so in pairs. Man's imagination, in its function, never sees things in isolation. In the creation of rhetorical language, the mind shapes and polishes a hundred thoughts that cluster round it, and by balancing the high with the low, produces antithesis and parallelism without apparent effort."

The first known couplet in its fully evolved form dates from the Tang dynasty, when a playful reference to a one-eyed friend was made when the Daoist poet Shi Jianwu wrote: "Twenty-nine persons passed the imperial examination/Fifty-seven eyes were admiring flowers". The earliest record of these couplets being divided into two and used on either side of the entrance to a room, pavilion or other building was in the early 10th century. Whether or not this was the origin of the idea is not known, but such couplets, carved into columns or into panels of wood, bamboo or other materials, became one of the most popular applications of the form, particularly at New Year.

Although this application of the couplet was clearly popular at an early date, the evidence of extant examples suggests that for calligraphy executed on silk or paper such division was a late development. There are divided couplets recorded by mid-Ming artists, but there appears to be some controversy about many of them. It is not until the late Ming period that the trend first seems to have become popular. Indeed, some surviving couplets of this period appear to have been divided later from an integral form, demonstrated by the uncomfortably narrow margins on facing sides of each. In the Qing dynasty it became common practice to write couplets on two separate sheets of paper. This example represents an early form, where the couplet is written on one paper.

The arcane nature of the communication in the couplet form makes it particularly difficult to translate, and some defy translation altogether. The often many levels of meaning are quite untranslatable in any case. This is the nature of Chinese poetry, made more complex by the need in couplets to balance characters for meaning and sometimes for visual impact, and even to play games with the constituent parts of each character — using the same radical in opposed characters, or even in some extreme cases in all the characters of head or tail sections.

Fang Yizhi (*zi:* Mizhi, Wuke; *hao:* Luqi, Foushanyuzhe, Yuzhe, Yaodiheshang, Wulao, Moli, Muli; monastic name, Hongzhi (died 1671?) was a *jinshi* of 1640, from a prominent literati family. His life (as outlined in *Eminent Chinese of the Ch'ing Period)* seems to have been a colourful affair in which a minor official career under the Ming gave way to being a long-time fugitive from the Manchus as they gradually consolidated their 1644 conquest of the north of China in a long, bitter campaign in the south. Fang's adventures included imprisonment and ransoming, and a later escape in the disguise of a drug-peddler from a persecution aimed at members of the politico-literary group Fushe. He eventually retired into monastic life, and spent the remainder of his days travelling, changing his name as he moved from one monastary to another to hide his tracks. He was highly regarded as a scholar.

142

Fish

Wood, of yellowish colour; the natural form enhanced by carving to create a thoroughly disgruntled-looking fish, its broad mouth open, its tail curled back over the lower portion of its body; a small circular inset under the lower jaw sealed with a reddish lacquer.
Probably Qing dynasty.
Length: 10.5 cm.

木雕游魚
可能清代，長10.5厘米

When creating root sculptures it was often necessary to join different sections or to patch small holes. These were sometimes hidden as carefully as possible, or lacquered in red as in this case. The root water vessel, no. 21, has a similar method of construction, but it was covered with black stain to hide the joins. It is possible that this fish was also once stained (it has traces of a darker stain in the grooves of the surface grain) and that these red lacquer joins were merely a form of glue and filling, which were not originally intended to be seen.

143

Brush Rest

Ivory, of well-patinated creamy and golden-yellow tones, with inlaid details; carved as a three-peak mountain brush rest rising from crashing surf that surrounds the back and part of the front of the rock formations; a dragon is entwined through the cave-riddled base of the rocks, emerging at one side of the front, chasing a flaming pearl and startling a flying phoenix, while below a *qilin* and a tiger shelter in two caves; the dragon's passage through the wave-filled caves seemingly ejecting a rather startled mythical tortoise or turtle, which was probably originally intended to have a dragon's body and tortoise's shell (see no. 131 for such a beast), but a small chip has given it the appearance of a bird-headed tortoise; the eyes of the various creatures inlaid in translucent brown material (except the dragon, which has green eyes), perhaps soapstone.
Probably late Ming or early Qing dynasty.
Height: 4.3 cm. Length: 8.4 cm.

象牙雕瑞獸三嶽筆山
可能明末清初，高4.3厘米，長8.4厘米

This small brush rest is of exceptional technical quality perfectly enhanced by the natural wear and patination of use. These obvious signs of graceful old age would suggest that it was made no later than the early Qing dynasty, and the style of carving seems commensurate with a late Ming or very early Qing date. The use of inlays of tiny beads of circular translucent stones and the exquisite combination of technical quality with considerable sculptural flair are features consistent with the 16th and particularly the early 17th century, where both are found on a group of soapstone figures (see no. 45 which has a very similar green stone inlay to the eyes of the dragon in this case).

That it has also been extensively used is borne out by its state of wear and the ink which stains its two valleys. Although small in size, its sturdiness allows it to act as a convenient rest for unexpectedly large brushes.

141

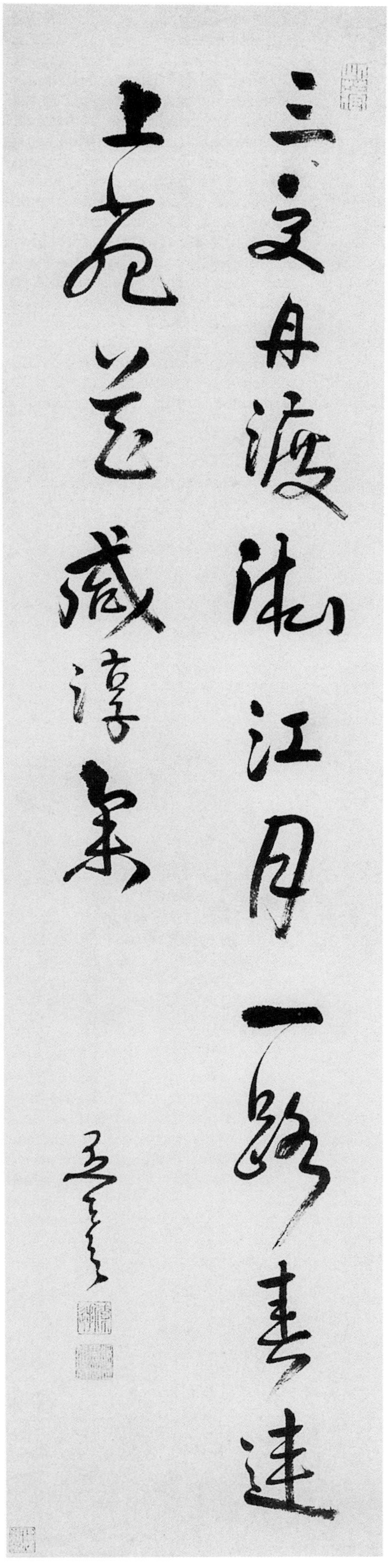

142

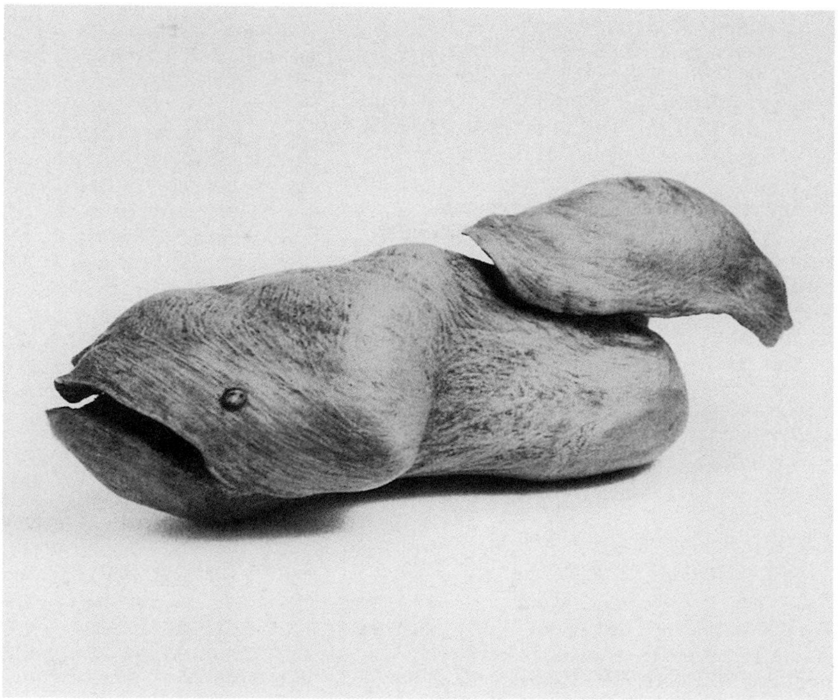

143

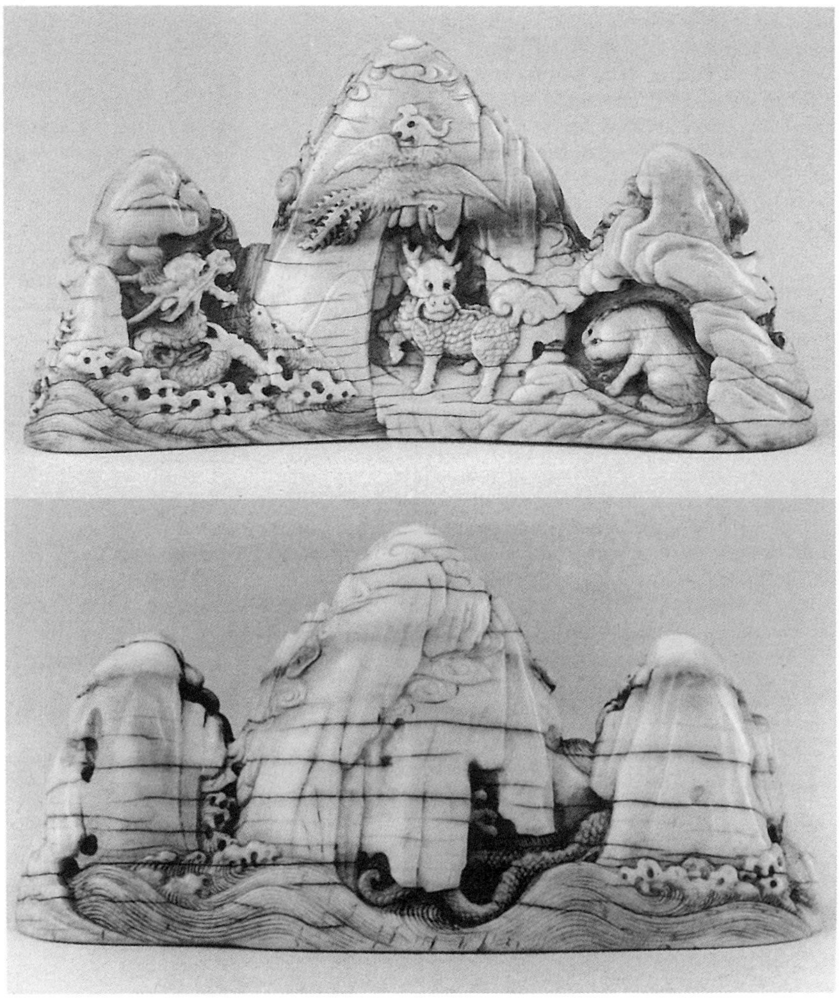

144

Covered Box

Jiang Qianli

Lacquer, of brownish-black colour inlaid with gold and iridescent sections of abalone shell (of the type known as *lac-burgauté*); a fluted box and cover of formalized petal form with form and design radiating out from a central point on the cover, the different segments made up of the formalized petals, and planes of the box inlaid with a variety of different patterned grounds; the lip rims inlaid with a formalized gold design, separating box and cover, the foot rim set with a sheet of gold, the recessed foot with a formalized floral scroll design in abalone shell surrounding the circular, gold-inlaid signature *Qianli* in seal script; the inside of the box and cover plain except for two naturalistic fruiting branches.
Probably late Ming dynasty.
Height: 3.65 cm. Maximum width: 7.15 cm.
Published: *The Minor Arts of China*, p.10, no. 1 (where it is dated as late 17th century).

鑲金嵌貝花瓣形漆蓋盒·江千里製
可能晚明，高3.65厘米，寬7.15厘米

Jiang Qianli is described in traditional Chinese sources as a late Ming dynasty lacquerer, although he has more recently been dated to the Kangxi period. He is listed as being a specialist in inlayed lacquer ware, and has suffered the fate of many artists whose works were so exceptional that their names became associated inextricably with a type of ware they made — the confusion of endless later works bearing his name. It appeared throughout the Qing dynasty, and even into the post-1949 period on a series of snuff bottles made in Shandong province. He and other artists in this field are frequently referred to as experts at inlaying mother-of-pearl, but in fact the main source of the iridescent inlays seems to be abalone shell, which provides brilliantly coloured and variegated material in the blue-green-purple colour range (this, together with gold and silver foil and a lacquer ground, are the ingredients of *lac-burgauté*). In differentiating the genuine Qianli wares from the later works in his style, or simply using his name more as a description of a ware, two factors seem to suggest themselves as paramount: quality and style.

This piece displays the artist in total command of his medium, as demonstrated by the perfectly arranged design of an enormous number of tiny pieces of individual foil or shell (a very approximate calculation suggests that there are in the region of 25,000 individual sections inlaid). What is even more impressive is the remakable artistic control of this technique. The design is simple enough — a very pleasing but formal arrangement which is, in itself, not extraordinary — but where it is lifted to the level of a masterpiece is in the choice of colour for the inlays. Each panel is subtly different, with the four main colours (either gold foil, green, blue or purple shell) providing the dominant theme, and slight variations in border colours or in hints of changing tone making the overall effect quite fascinating. The sheer artistry of this box suggests very strongly that it was by Qianli himself.

Stylistically, the creation of rich surface textures by the use of a number of different patterned grounds is typical of the late Ming period. It occurs either as the sole decoration, or more usually as an extensive background, in lacquer and in metalwork. Although concrete evidence of the period of Qianli is absent we see no reason why Jiang Qianli should not be accepted, as tradition has him, as a late Ming artist, and perhaps even 16th century.

A lengthy discussion on the artist is published in *Emperor, Scholar, Artisan, Monk: The Creative Personality in Chinese Works of Art*, p.258, where a pair of oval boxes and covers is shown, and a number of other pieces by Qianli are discussed. A box similar to this example is in the Suzhou Municipal Museum, illustrated as Fig. 29 on p.187 of *Chugoku no Raden.*

145

Water Vessel

Limestone, of the variety known as Duan stone of purplish-brown colour with slight green veining; a shallow, straight-sided water vessel, the interior carved in very slight, recessed relief with three swimming fan-tailed carp, the water indicated by wavy incised lines; the base incised with the inscription *Xingyouheng Tang zhi* ('made for the Hall of Constancy').
Circa 1815-1854.
Height: 2.1 cm. Diameter: 10 cm.

端石雕三鯉筆洗·行有恒堂銘
清(約1815-1854)，高2.1厘米，
直徑10厘米

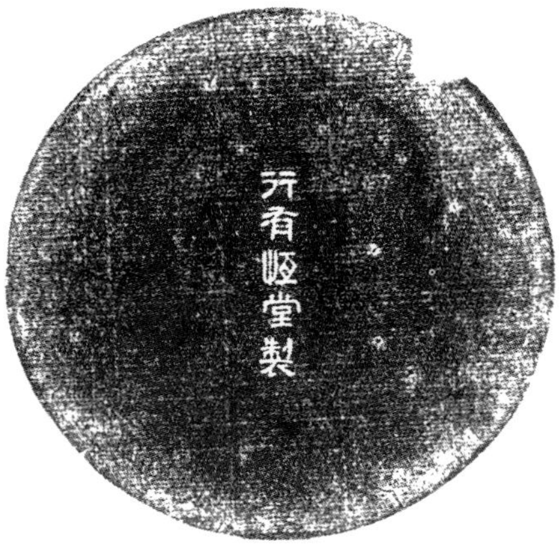

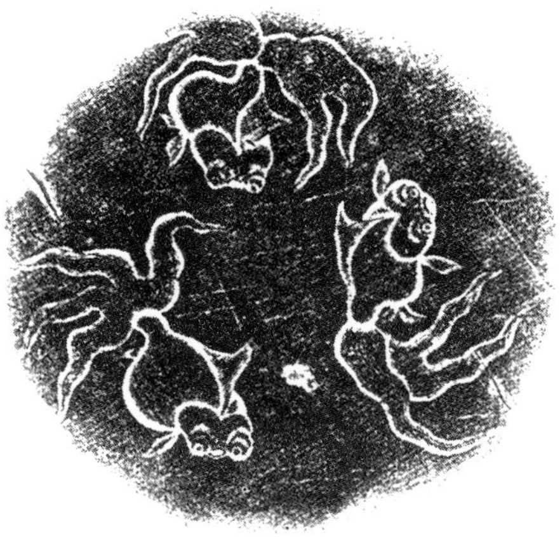

For a discussion on this hall mark and its owner, the Fifth Prince Ding, see no. 108. It is a hall mark which appears on paintings, and works of art made of wood, crystal, glass, jade, gourd, etc. It is probable that pieces were made bearing the mark which never graced Zaichuan's collection, and that the mark was added to existing pieces. Allowing for all the variations of genuine and fake pieces, added marks to earlier, contemporary or later pieces, and different workmen applying both genuine and fake marks with varying degrees of skill, it is unlikely that we shall ever be entirely certain of any individual piece.

The mark on this vessel for example, is not written as neatly as one might expect, although the wide variation in quality of recorded marks does not necessarily suggest that this alone would bring it into question. However, what is strange is that the mark occupies a slight depression in an otherwise flat base, suggesting that another mark may have been erased and this one superimposed. It is of course possible that the original maker carved a *Xingyouheng Tang* mark with which he was dissatisfied, and carving it off, proceeded to do another. The piece itself, however, is of sensible material and style for the period and may be tentatively accepted as from Prince Ding's collection.

144

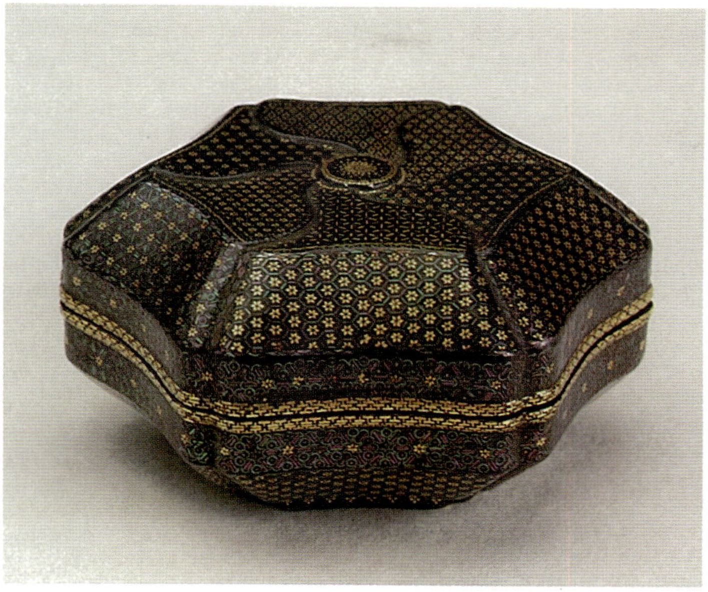

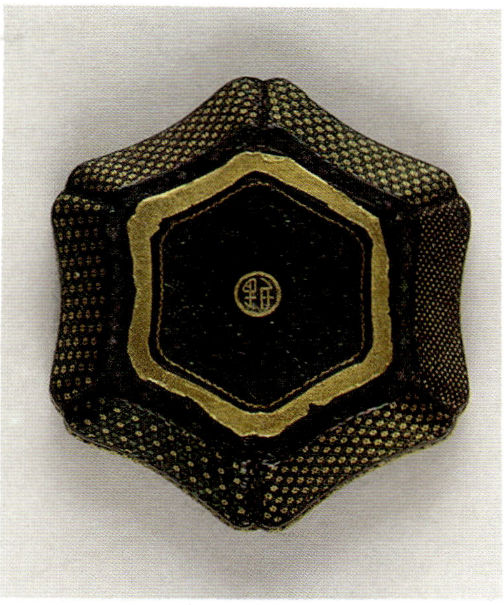

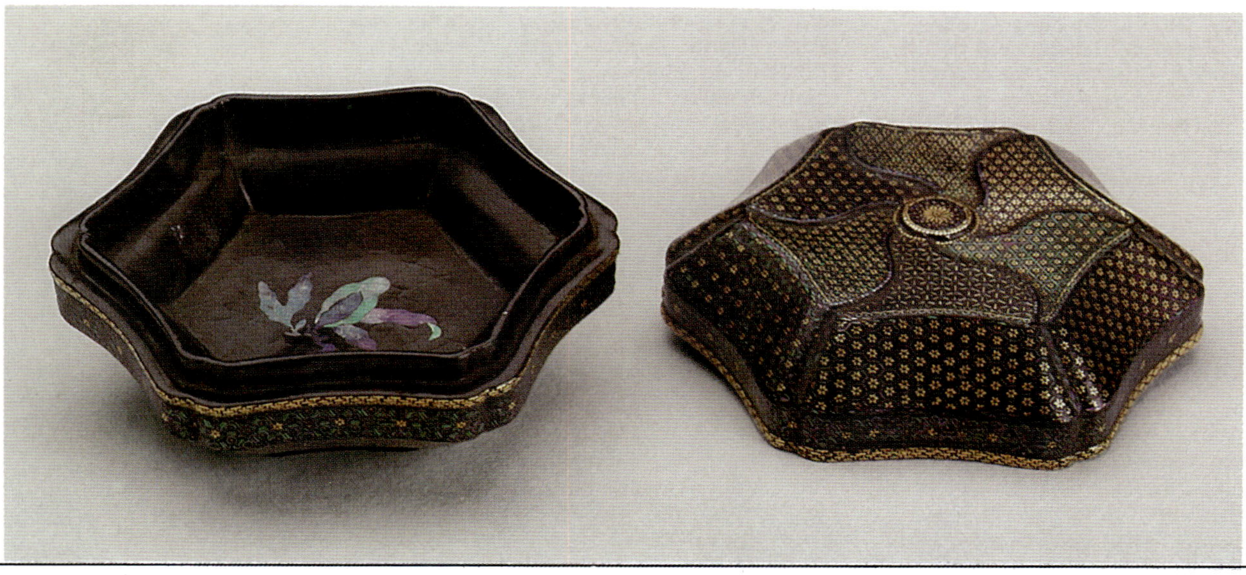

145

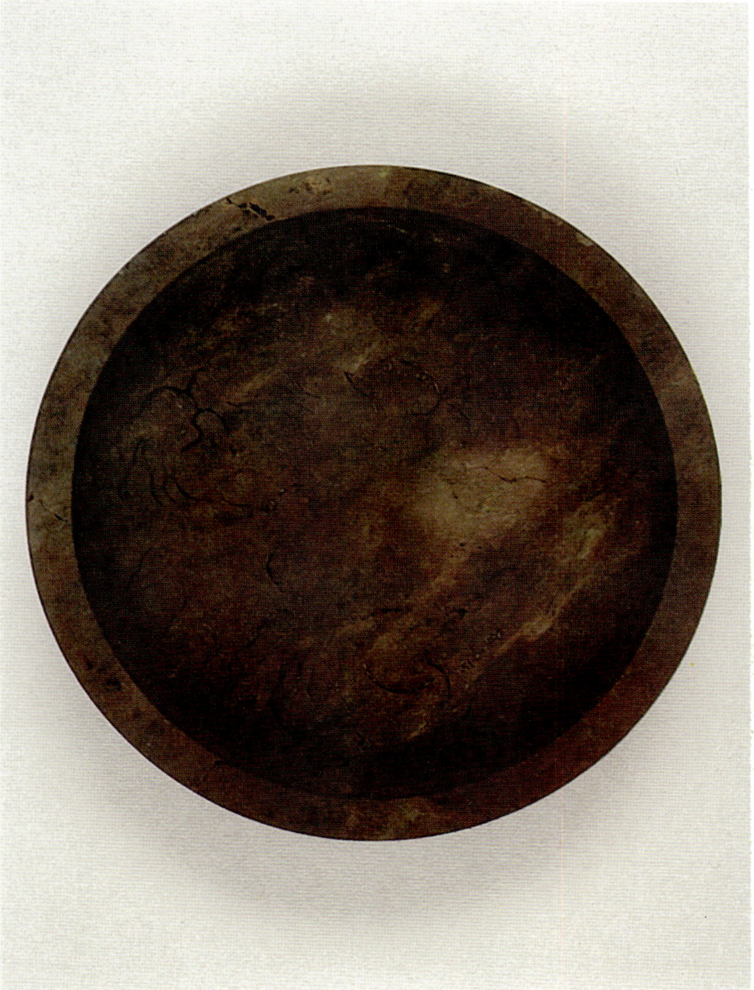

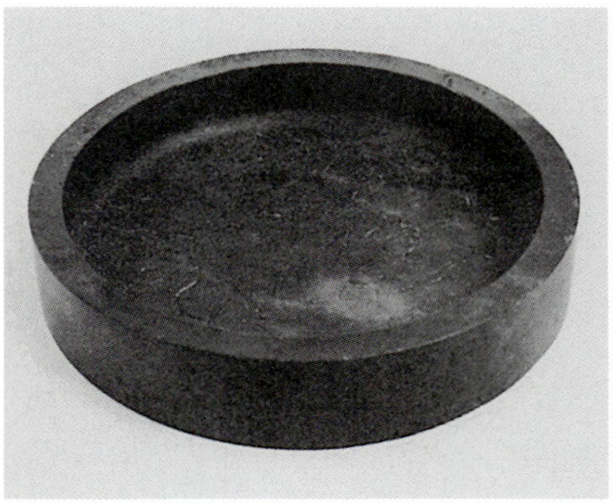

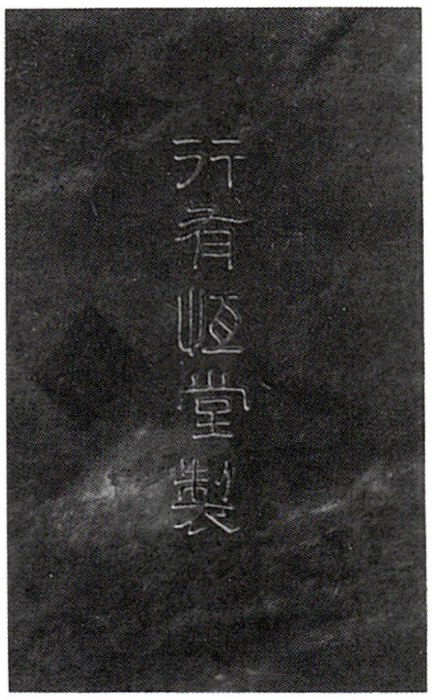

146

Scabbard Clasp

Nephrite, of mottled brownish-beige colour with extensive rich, dark brown markings (the natural colour of the exterior surface of a pebble enhanced by staining) covering most of the upper surface; a scabbard clasp carved in relief with a *chi* dragon and young in swirling interreaction.
Probably Song Dynasty.
Length: 10.9 cm. Width: 2.25 cm.
Depth: 1.5 cm.

玉雕螭龍劍璏
可能宋代, 長10.9厘米, 寬2.25厘米, 深1.5厘米

The scabbard clasp *(zhi* but sometimes also called *wei)* was one of several fittings used in ancient times in conjunction with the fighting sword, many of which have survived in jade from burials. It was bound through the elongated rectangular hole to the sword scabbard, which was then tucked inside the belt, the long curving section of the clasp sitting outside the belt to prevent the scabbard from slipping (vertical being, therefore, the corrrect way to grasp the original dynamics of the design, despite the fact that their usual diassociation from original context has led us to view them more comfortably as horizontal works of art).

This is another example of sophisticated archaism where the original has been subtly altered. Han originals tend to be in higher relief with a greater degree of abstraction and formalization and, consequently, a more powerful sense of sculpture.[1] Here the bodies of the beasts are more lithe and flowing. The movement is now the gentle swirling of incense smoke rather than the martial curl of a war banner. This is a mood better suited to the Southern Song period, which attribution would be reasonable, although our knowledge of the development of archaism from the Song onwards is too shallow to allow much confidence in any such chronological attributions.

The scholar class delighted in archaism and this clasp would have been made purely for aesthetic appreciation, although it might have served as a paper weight quite conveniently. With its subtle variations on an archaic language, its symbolically powerful material and its qualities as sculpture, it would have delighted a Song or post-Song scholar.

Originally, nephrite was obtained in the form of pebbles of various sizes from the beds of rivers in the Kunlun mountain range (Khotan). As this source was depleted over the centuries quarrying began to supplement it, but the material obtained by quarrying (which was not carried out on a large scale until the late Ming dynasty), was considered inferior to pebble jade. Indeed, it was frequently stained to simulate the structural change which over the millennia affect the surface colour of pebbles. This process of staining was also used to enhance the preferred colours of pebble jade in early times. Visual identification of staining is not always possible, but here the colour can be seen to sit on the surface as a stain in areas where the brown meets the paler beige tones. Natural colour is caused by the decomposition of the surface whereas the stains rely upon a chemical reaction. The most difficult problem of identification arises where the one is used to enhance the other.[2]

1. *Illustrated Catalogue of Ancient Jade Artefacts in the National Palace Museum,* pl. 168, nos. 310 and 312.
2. Scabbard clasps of this design from the Han dynasty can be seen in *Chinese Jade Through the Wei Dynasty,* pl. XXX, no. 1; *Ancient Chinese Jade,* p.395, no. 572 and p.397, no. 574, and *Chinese Archaic Jades,* pl. LVIII, nos. 1, 4 and 7, and pl. LIX, no. 3.

147

Water Vessel

Bronze, the entire surface gilt but now worn through in places to the bronze beneath; a small water vessel in the form of a boy standing at the rim of a large basin, the surface of which is decorated with a continuous band of scrolling 'Indian' lotus.
Mid- to late Ming dynasty.
Height: 5.6 cm. Maxium width: 7.5 cm.

鎏金青銅童子大缸水丞
明中至晚期, 高5.6厘米, 寬7.5厘米

This vessel, which was almost certainly designed as a water vessel in conjunction with a ladle, is connected in style to Ming and Qing bronze paper weights — indeed, its size would allow it to double in that capacity. A similar piece in the Hong Kong Museum of Art lacks the gilding, as do most of the wares of this group. The style of the large basin, of a type used to store water at various strategic points (not the least of its possible functions being to aid in fire-fighting), strongly suggests that it is derived from *fahua* wares of the late 15th or early 16th century, indicating a slightly later date of manufacture.

148

Drinking Cup

Bamboo, a section of the underground stem, with an applied section of branch; a drinking cup, the natural pattern of the 'root' formation cut and polished as a decoration of three bands of irregularly arranged rings encircling the cup; an applied handle made of a section of branch; the interior with a silvered copper liner.
Probably late Ming or early Qing dynasty.
Height: 3.6 cm. Maximum width: 8.3 cm.

竹雕酒杯
可能明末清初, 高3.6厘米, 寬8.3厘米

This cup's considerable elegance arises mainly out of its naturalness. It is made of a common material allowed to speak for itself, but with an overlay of good taste applied to selection and execution. The rustic simplicity makes it a perfect vehicle of inspiration for the literati.

Bamboo was an ideal material for a wide variety of uses. The so-called 'root' grows out of underground, creeping rhizomes (see Fig. 1) and is the beginning of the above-ground culm. As this culm grows upwards, still underground, it forms into densely packed miniature versions of the culm, node and internodal hollows of the upper bamboo. Solid at its base, it gradually grows into larger and larger sections, until above ground it becomes the familiar pith-filled, segments of bamboo. Thus from the culm stalk or 'root' may be had both solid sections and foreshortened hollow sections between diaphragms. Both are patterned by the actual roots, which grow outwards in profusion from this underground culm and when cut in cross section appear as concentric circles, seen as bands of decoration on this example. This cup is made from a section of the culm stem of oval shape carefully using the root markings as decoration. These root protruberances exist only within a certain range of the surface of the culm stem and the inside of the cup has no such markings.

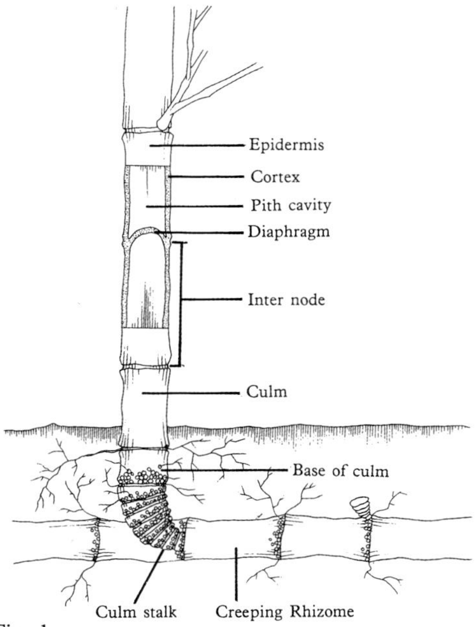

Fig. 1

146

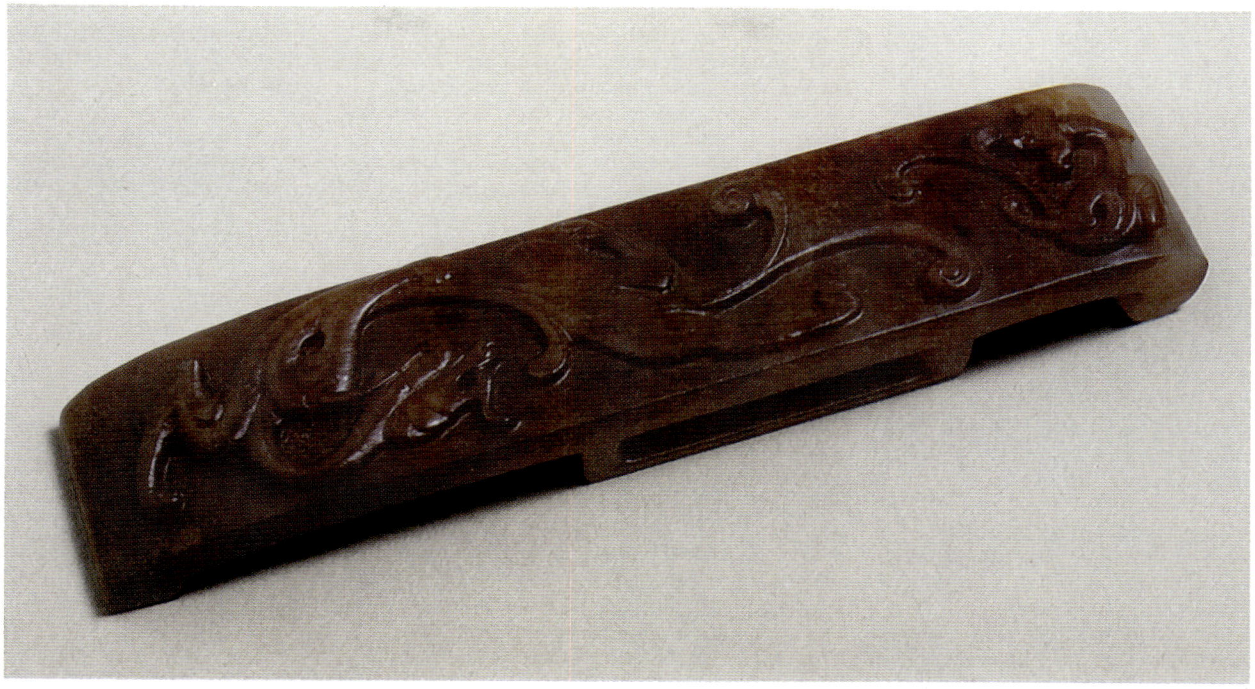

147

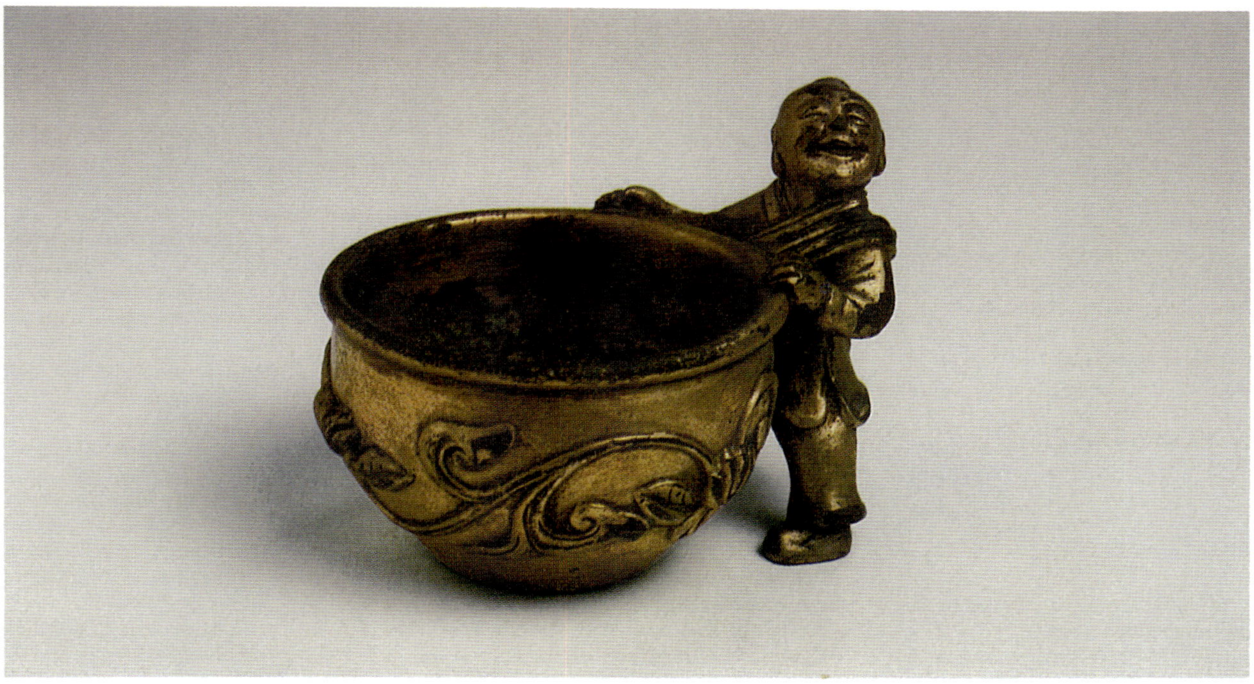

148

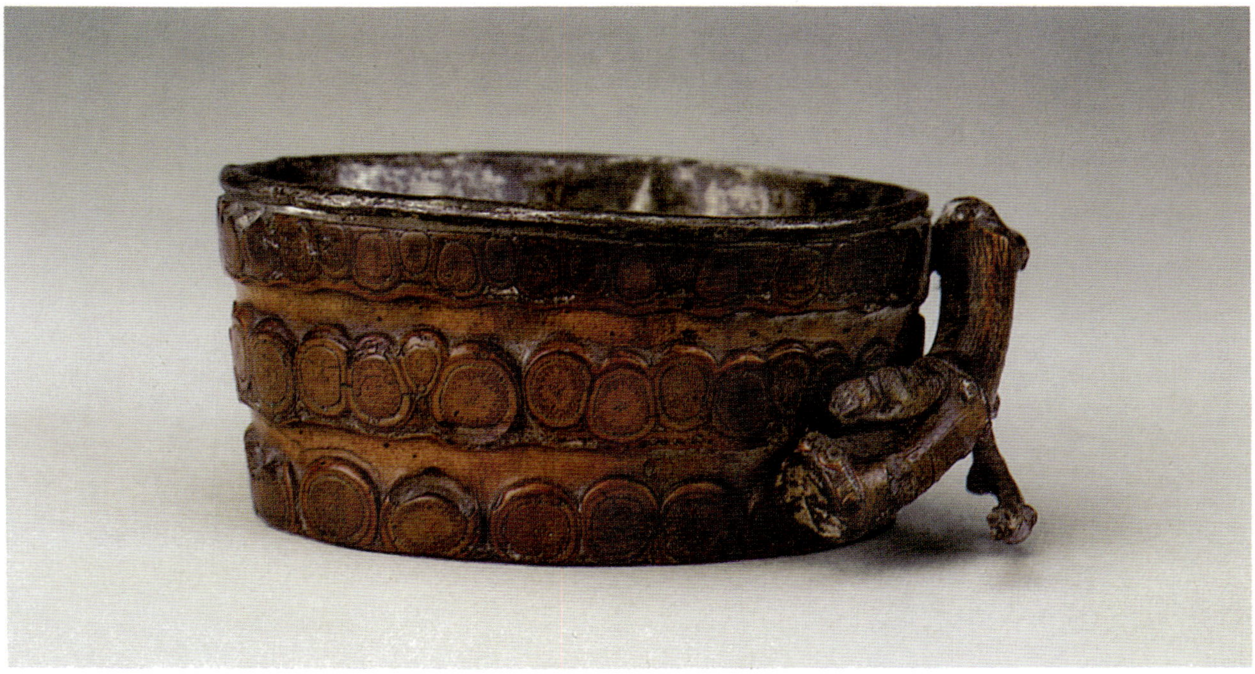

149

Inkstone, Box and Cover
Lu Dong

Lacquer, base material unknown; the exterior of the cover and the outer lip of the base covered with a thin layer of composition consisting of a mass of tiny chips of various materials in a black lacquer matrix, giving a speckled blackish-brown appearance; the interior and base lacquered plain black; an inkstone box and cover of rectangular form, the cover decorated with a branch of blossoming prunus and a spray of orchids inlaid in mother of pearl and sections of pre-carved lacquer, in low relief; the base, set on small L-shaped feet at each corner, with a red lacquer seal simulating a vermillion seal impression: *Lu Kuisheng zhi* ('made by Lu Kuisheng') in seal script within a square cartouche.
Together with its original plain sand-lacquer inkstone, inscribed on one edge *Kuisheng jianzhi* ('supervised by Kuisheng').
Yangzhou, first half of the 19th century.
Box: 2.5 cm × 14.1 cm × 9.85 cm.
Inkstone: 1.1 cm × 12.55 cm × 8.15 cm.

漆沙硯連嵌螺鈿梅蘭漆硯盒•盧棟製
十九世紀上半葉，硯1.1×12.55×8.15厘米，
盒2.5×14.1×9.85厘米

The sand lacquer used by Lu Dong for his inkstones is discussed in the caption to no. 63, where it was not clear whether Lu Dong had also made the inkstone, although from what we know of him it seems likely that he did. Here it states that he supervised it, presumably as a work from his workshop but not actually made by his own hand. There is also a circular lacquer inkstone box and cover recorded, which states that it was supervised by Lu Kuisheng[1] suggesting that he made an unusual distinction for a commercial workshop between those wares from his own hand and those where assistants made them. This might be connected with his obvious claims to being an independent artist and an equal in the eyes of his patrons, rather than a patronized craftsman.

Inlaid works involving other materials were a speciality of Lu Dong's, and their superb quality demonstrate his wide range of skills. Another, similar inkstone box and cover (containing the fascinating documentary evidence discussed in no. 63), is illustrated along with a remarkable *pipa* (a string instrument) in *Wenwu*[2], and an irregularly shaped inkstone cover is in the Shanghai Museum. It is the cover to an inkstone which bears the inscription "Copying an inkstone from the *Tingyun Guan* collection (the *Tingyun Guan* belonged to the Ming artist Wen Zhengming), supervised by Mr. Lu Kuisheng of the *Guyu Shuwu* (Old Yu Tree Studio)" with seal *Kuisheng*[3], Shanghai Museum, 1981. This adds to our already considerable information about Lu Dong the name of the studio in which he worked. (For biographical details on Lu Dong, see no. 63.)

1. Shuisongshi Shanfang collection. It is a circular, flat-topped box and cover with bulging sides and an incised landscape design.
2. 1957, no. 7. p.11.
3. *Bimozhiyan Tulu* ('Brush, Ink, Paper and Inkstone Pictorial').

150

Miniature Rock Sculpture

Stone, of the variety known as Lingbi; the dark grey-black material with a horizontal band of greyish-white dissecting it horizontally, creating the illusion of an eccentrically shaped rock formation rising from the water and reflected in it; mounted on a *zitan* wood stand carved in the form of entwined *lingzhi* fungus.
Ming or Qing.
Height including stand: 5.3 cm.
Length of stand: 6 cm.

靈璧石雕怪石
明或清，高連座5.3厘米，座長6厘米

The capacity of small stones to represent far grander experiences of nature is demonstrated admirably here in what must surely be one of the smallest rock sculptures known. Although closer attention is required, it is no more difficult to project oneself into the landscape with this stone than with a larger one, creating in the mind an immense structure of towering, eccentrically shaped rock. For a discussion of Lingbi stones see no. 78.

The problems of reconciling the traditions of connoisseurship of West and East are as well illustrated by strange stones as by wood. It appears to be impossible to identify accurately existing stones with traditional Chinese names, many of which are derived from places of origin ('Stone of Jiangzhou', 'Stones of the Lo River', 'Stone of Lingbi', 'Stone of the Grand Lake in Pingjiangfu', etc.), or are based on visual qualities ('serried insignia stones', 'stone bamboo shoots', 'pines transformed to stone', etc.), followed frequently by their place of origin, and a description. In the *Yunlin Shipu* for instance, 'Stone of Xiangzhou' (The Pear Garden, north of Xiangzhou in northern Henan province) is described as follows: "Several kinds of glossy stone found in deep water. Some are spotted as with ink. Some are dark yellow, and are called 'ginger pickles' *(jiangshi)* by the natives. They can be worked into utensils or ground into paper weights; these are sold at very reasonable prices."[1]

Even when descriptions are more precise we are certain to be dealing with criteria based upon visual properties and a knowledge of sources and materials based more on hearsay than on scientific investigation. Nor is this surprising; the mind that saw such wonder in old rocks and strangely shaped roots was scarcely compatible with analytical investigation of a nature that would satisfy a Western observer. In many cases connoisseurship is based upon the inadequate description of a long-dead author of the visual properties of a type of stone he believed came from a certain place. Devoted research into these sources, cross-referenced to other art forms which are frequently mentioned (particularly ink-stones), combined with petrological analysis of existing stones would provide clues to a more scientific analysis of materials and sources, but could never hope to make the two traditions of connoisseurship wholly compatible.

Schafer applies what seems to be a reasonably sensible method of classification of stones by dividing them first into two groups: aesthetic and utilitarian (not mutually exclusive). In the second category he places stones used as materials for inkstones, masonry, sculpture, and so on. His first classification relates to the cult of fantastic stones. Prefacing his classification with the comment that a more sophisticated analysis would take into account the fact that aesthetic purposes are inextricably intermingled with moral notions, he divides aesthetic stones as follows:

1. Realistic (resembling actual mountains, divinities, animals, etc.; dendriform markings on agate, etc.; also fossils).
2. Fantastic (bizarre shapes: cavernous, perforated, suggesting no real mountain, yet appealing to the imagination as Daoist fairy grottoes, etc.)
3. Crystalline (composed of a single mineral, showing natural crystal forms).
4. Sensuous (as polished agate pebbles, lustrous to the eye, sleek to the touch).
5. Antiquarian (bearing old inscriptions, or associated with famous men or epochs).
6. Curiosities (having a legend attached).

1. *Tu Wan's Stone Catalogue of Cloudy Forest,* no. 52.

149

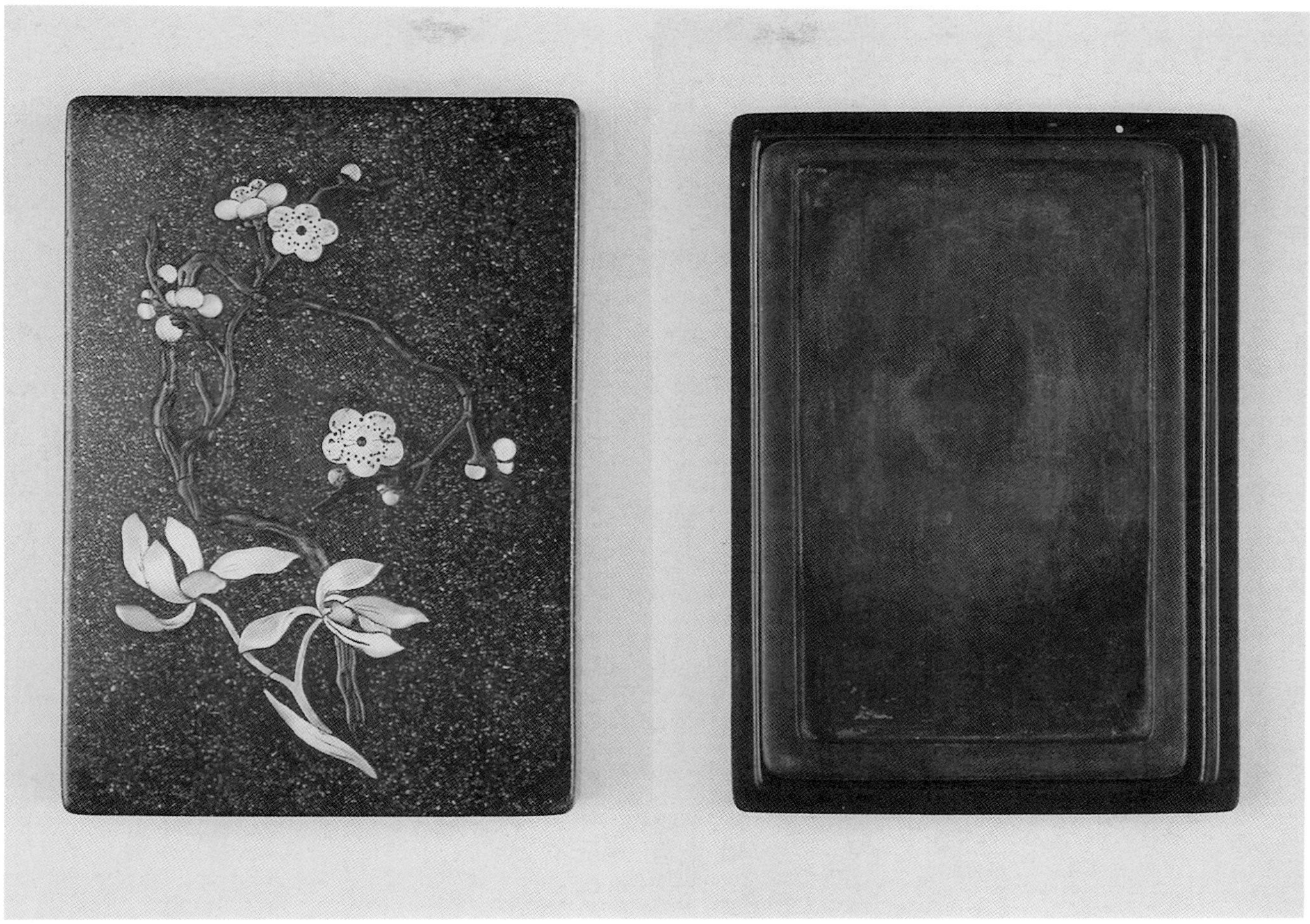

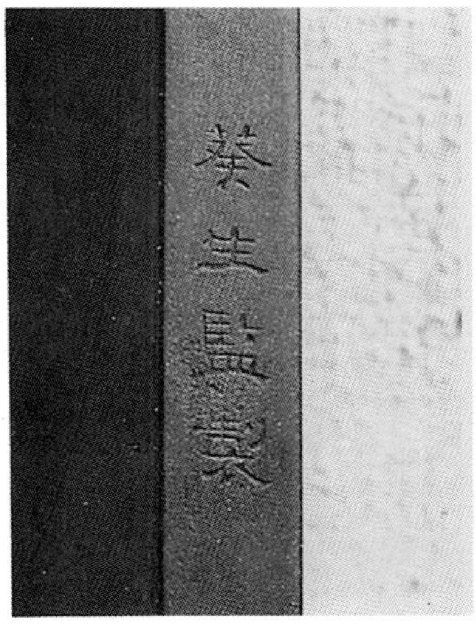

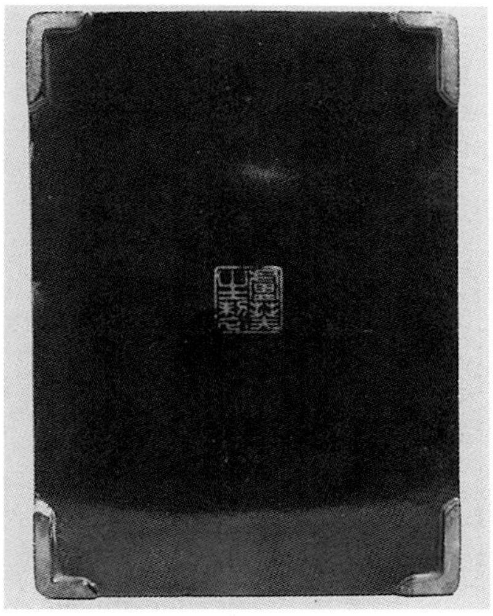

150

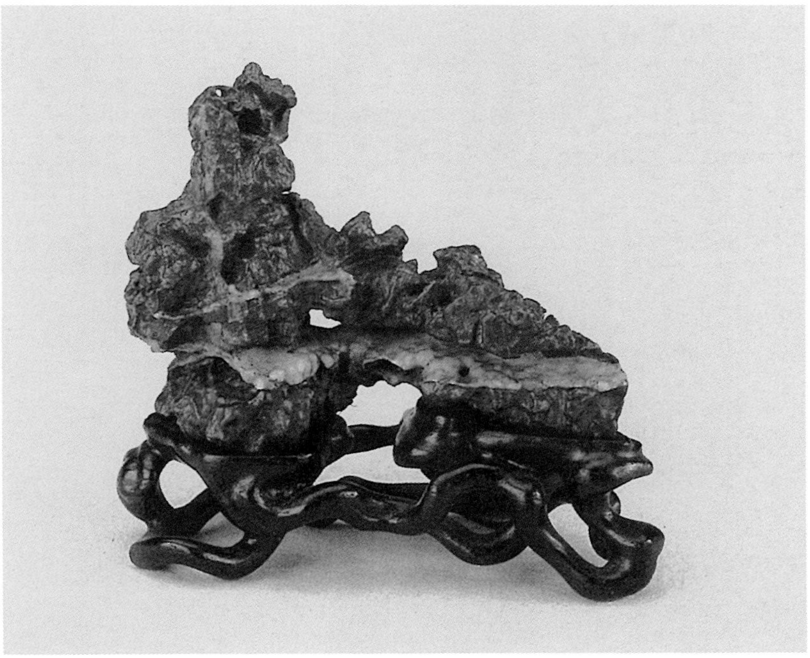

151

'Waterfall' Qin

Lei family

Lacquer on wood, the upper board of *tong* wood; a *haozhong* ('resonant bell') style *qin,* of black colour, with seven nephrite tuning pegs, two nephrite feet, and mother-of-pearl studs; the back with an elongated rounded, rectangular 'dragon's pond' and a similar shaped, but shorter 'phoenix pool'; the surface well-worn and patinated, with a combination of small 'snake-belly' and 'cracked-ice' crackle. Inscribed inside the 'dragon's pond' on one side 'Made by the Lei family in the third year of the Kaiyuan period of the Tang dynasty'; and above the 'dragon's pond' in running script *Feiquan* ('Waterfall').
Tang, 715.
Length: 120.6 cm. Width: 19.1 cm.

Inscribed with various seals and colophons:
Below the title: a seal *Shanshui qingyin* ('Pure music of the landscape') in negative seal script.
To the right of the 'dragon's pond', a poem in cursive script:

"Shouting into the wind, beneath the moon,
Playing the *qin* in circular movements, its tone goes to heaven.
Who was the previous idle owner of this *qin* who never cleaned and polished it?
How fortunate that its antique tone has not disappeared."

followed by: "composed by Lu Shangsi, in the mid spring of the *gengxu* year of the Hongzhi period (1490)."
To the left of the 'dragon's pond', a poem in running script:

"Mountains beneath a white moon, cool sea breeze,
Waterfalls and waves are heard in the strings,
Images of towering rocks and overhanging cliffs
Are seen beneath the fingers"

followed by a partly illegible inscription stating that the poem was composed by the Master of the *Qin* and Sword Pavilion.[The poem means that when playing the *qin* one is able to hear the music of mountains beneath a pale white moon, to feel sea breezes and to conjour up images of the landscape. The *Qin* and Sword Pavilion refers to two traditional skills expected of a scholar: the playing of the *qin* and mastery of martial arts. Confucius himself was skilled in both, and the two represent the 'Renaissance man' concept of a man who could turn his hand to anything and, being pure at heart, succeed.]
Between the 'dragon's pond' and the 'phoenix pool', a poem in clerical script:

"High mountains and running water,
The spring of ancient times.
Ah, such excellence!
Who may aspire to such profound feelings?"

Followed by the seal *Wang Guoshu yin* ('seal of Wang Guoshu') in positive seal script.
Above the 'phoenix pool', a large square seal *Jianhou zhenzang* ('precious collection of Jianhou') in negative seal script. [Wang Jianhou was a *qin* expert of the 20th century, already in his sixties in 1966. His studio name was *Qinqian Huyin Lou* ('Studio of the Hidden *Qin* and Inscribed Teapot'), a reference to this *qin* which he kept hidden in a buried stone case for fear of losing it during the political turmoils of this century, and to a Yixing teapot he treasured.
To the right of the 'phoenix pool', a poem in regular script:

"Impenetrable clouds over high mountains;
Endless waters in vast rivers.
The *qin's* virtuosity of tone is brilliant;
My happiness is endless."

followed by the signature "written by Wang Xishen" and two seals *Xishen* and *Wang Wenzhang yin* ('seal of Wang Wenzhang'). [Wang Wenzhang (*zi*: Xishen) was a novelist of the early 20th century.]
To the left of the 'phoenix pool', "This *qin* was made by the Lei family in the Tang dynasty. Parts of its tail and head were missing when I acquired it, and the lacquer was falling off the worm-eaten wood. Happily, I was able to restore it, and when played it now gives a very deep musical tone resembling that of large bells and stone chimes. Indeed, this is a most precious *qin* that has endured and survived so many dangers. Repaired and inscribed by Wang Jianhou of Haoan, in autumn of the *bingzi* year of the Republic (1936)."
Also to the left of the 'phoenix pool', immediately beside it, an inscription in seal script: "Its body is rustic and simple; its tone is like bronze bells and jade chimes".

號鐘式飛泉琴•雷氏製
唐開元三年(715), 長120.6厘米, 寬19.1厘米

The Lei family was a famous Tang family of *qin* makers, renowned for their ability to make superb instruments that also looked beautiful. There were said to be nine members of the family involved in the art of *qin* making. They lived in Sichuan province, on Emei mountain, where they gathered ancient wood to make instruments. The Lei *qin* was the Chinese equivalent of a Stradivarius violin, and they have been immortalized in the writings of scholars and poets ever since.

The *qin* was originally a five-stringed instrument, each string being a note in the Chinese pentatonic scale. The extra two strings, bringing the number to the standard seven seen on all surviving *qin,* adding two half-tones, were said to have been introduced during the Zhou dynasty[1]. The body of the *qin,* the sounding box, consists of two different kinds of wood; the upper, curved section is made of *tong* wood, while the lower, flat section (which has two sound holes) is made of *zi* wood. The anatomy of a *qin* is described as follows:

A. The bridge is called *yueshan* ('high mountain') and is usually made of the hardwood *zitan.*
B. Markers as guides to fingering are called *hui* ('studs') and are usually inlaid in either mother-of-pearl or metal.
C. The rounded end is known as the *jiaowei* ('burnt tail') from a Han story of a *qin* maker who heard a piece of particularly resonant wood crackling in a fire, and pulling it out made a *qin* from it. Its sound was excellent, but the end had been burned and rounded.
D. An end view of the *qin* resembles a stylized dragon's mouth, from which is derived the name *longyin* ('dragon's gum') for the small section over which the strings are stretched at the 'burnt tail'.
E. The upper, larger sound hole in the back of the *qin* is the *longchi* ('dragon's pond'), a name derived from the analogy of the mythical beast bathing in a pond.
F. The lower, smaller sound hole is the *fengzhao* ('phoenix pool').
G. Two small pegs, around which the strings are bound, and which also act as feet, are called *yanzu* ('wild-geese feet') and may be made of jade, wood, horn etc.
H. The strings are tuned by a series of turning pegs, frequently made of either jade or other hardstones, or horn, which are called *zhen* ('tuning pegs').
I. Two small, curling finials come down from the back of the head of the instrument, which are frequently mistakenly called feet, but they are in fact there to protect the tuning pegs when the instrument is carried. They are fitted so that in the event of an accident they break off, protecting the instrument from more serious damage. They are called *huchen* ('peg protectors').

The lacquered surface of a *qin* is made of lacquer mixed with powdered horn, which creates a particularly hard and smooth surface. Over a long period of time this surface will develop cracks, which may inhibit playing. They are then smoothed down, and filled with further lacquer from time to time, creating a rich surface patination over many centuries. As a rule the first of these patterns of cracks to develop runs across the instrument from side to side, parallel to the 'high mountain' or bridge. This is referred to as 'serpent-' or 'snake-belly' crackle, either large or small. With more time a finer crackle might develop between these snake-belly cracks, connecting them and running in the same direction as the strings. This is called ice crackle. On very old *qin,* a distinctive crackle may appear in a series of little circles, formed where the otherwise rectangular patterns of crackle join up. This is called 'plum blossom' crackle, but is very rarely seen, and only on very early instruments.

1. *The Lore of the Chinese Lute,* p.4.

152

Incense Tool Vase

Copper, partly gilt; an incense tool vase decorated around the main body with a continuous design of the 'three friends of winter' (pine, bamboo and prunus); the neck with a band of *ruyi* heads and another, near the lip, of raised knobs; lip, foot rim, and raised detail all gilt.
Perhaps Jiangnan area, late Ming dynasty.
Height: 10.5 cm.

鎏金刻歲寒三友銅筋瓶
晚明, 高10.5厘米

A small, shallow bowl signed by Li Qiyun (?)[1] offers a possible attribution to a maker for this delightful small vase. It has on it a pine tree with clumps of needles executed in exactly the same method as used here consisting predominantly of overlapping fan shapes. Li is not recorded in any literary sources of which we know, but was clearly either influenced by, or influenced Hu Wenming, the famous late Ming metalsmith (see no. 73).

This vase is apparently worked from a thick sheet of copper, cut and beaten into shape with the final form possibly spun on a lathe to create an even shape before chasing of the surface was undertaken. The foot rim has been made separately and attached. The hand carving of decorative surfaces, if not of the whole vessel, was a feature of the Hu Wenming workshops and even his substantial bronze vessels which we assume were cast (although even they may have been spun from solid lumps of bronze) reveal that the surfaces were finished if not wholly achieved by chasing. It is possible that these methods and materials were common to late Ming metalsmiths, but in any case the similarities between this work and Hu Wenming's are strong evidence for an attribution of Li to the late Ming period and perhaps even to the same general area as Hu.

1. Exhibited in *The Arts of the Ming Dynasty,* Cat. no. 288, where the signature was read as Li Qibao. The script is eccentric and quite unlike any known script or variation, leaving open different interpretations. Either the maker was unfamiliar with correct forms of ancient script, which he seems to be using, or it is a sinicized version of a foreign script. The same piece is illustrated in *The Literati Mode: Chinese Scholar Paintings, Calligraphy and Desk Objects,* no. 148.

151

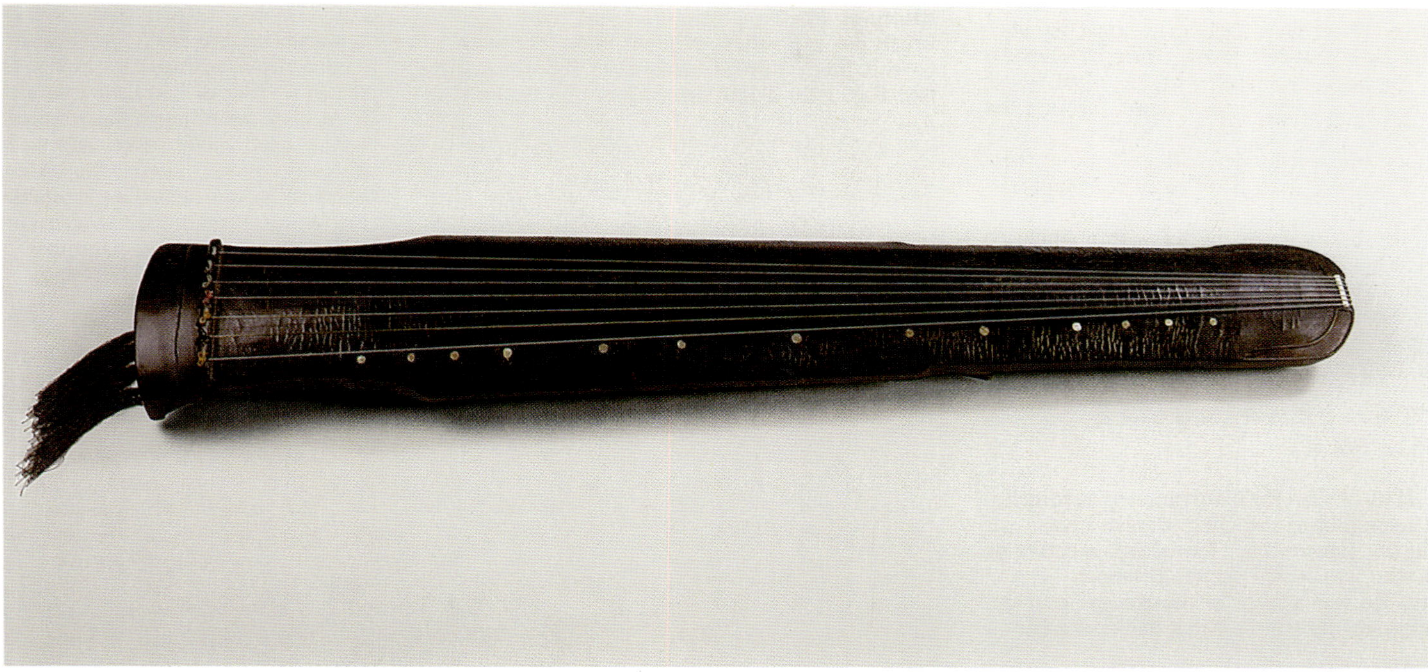

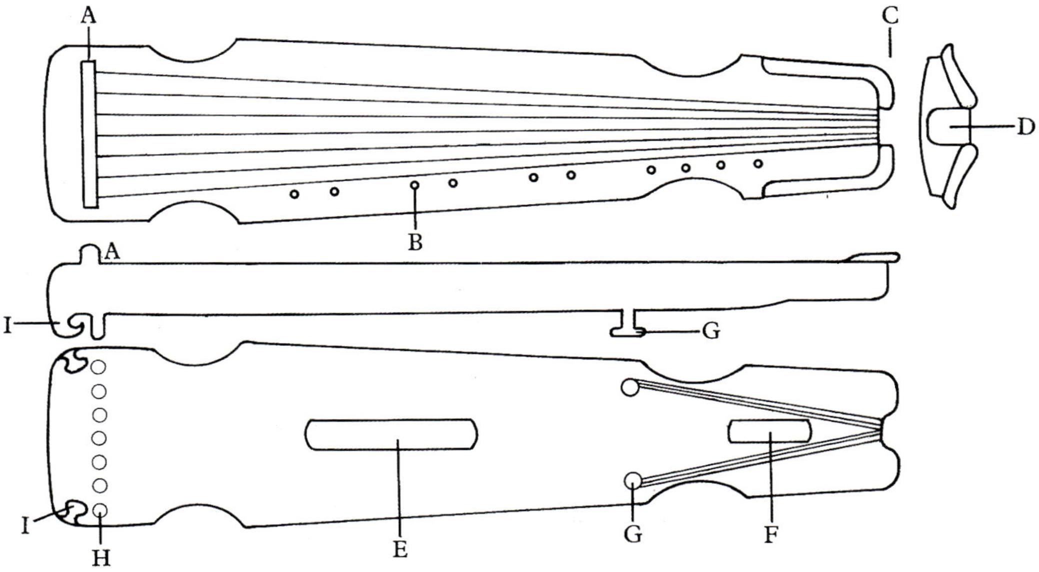

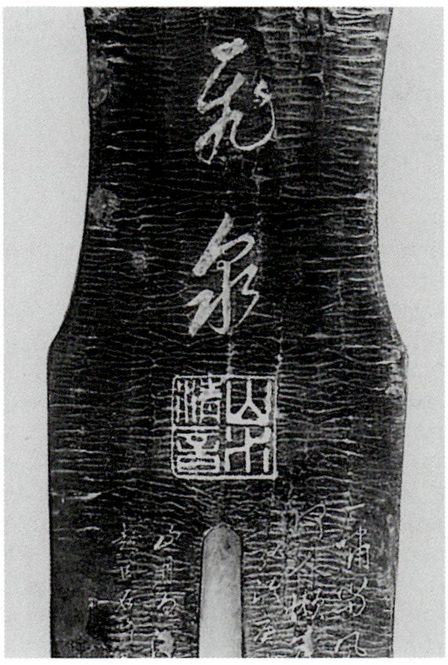

152

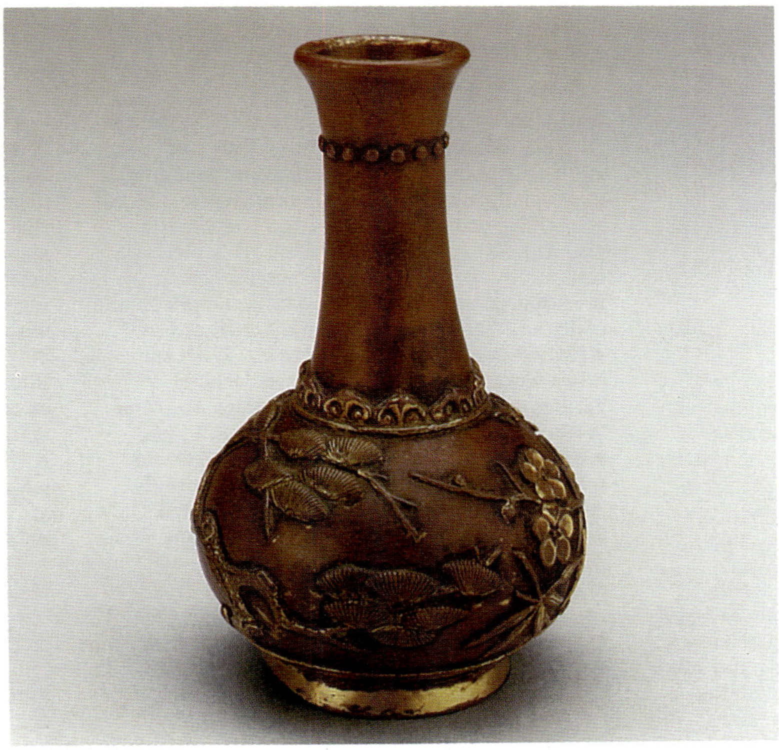

153

Spittoon for Liao Tengkui

Bronze, inlaid with silver; a spittoon, the globular body set on a short cylindrical flared foot, and with a widely flaring trumpet-shaped mouth, the body decorated with an inlaid silver design of four archaistic *taotie* masks around the main bulb of the body, above a band of continuous *leiwen* (thunder pattern) around the foot, and below a neck band of cicada lappets above a band of zig-zag and comma-curl decoration; the inside of the lip with a single band of wavy design beneath a straight line; the base cast with the hall mark *Shenxiu Tang yin* ('seal of the Hall of Careful Cultivation').
Early Qing dynasty.
Height: 12.5 cm.

嵌銀線饕餮紋青銅渣斗•愼修堂印銘
清初, 高12.5厘米

The Hall of Careful Cultivation is recorded as belonging to the Qing scholar Liao Tengkui (*zi:* Jianwu, *hao:* Lienshan), a native of Jianglo who was famed for his personal integrity. He was a *juren* of the Kangxi period.

Although the spittoon may not represent the more aesthetic side of the scholar's activities, some of the vessels made as spittoons were works of art of merit. Indeed, they were also put to other uses as evidenced by genre paintings where we have seen one used as a brush pot and others as plant pots. The inlay on this finely formed vessel is of superb quality (see Fig. 1 for a line drawing of one section).

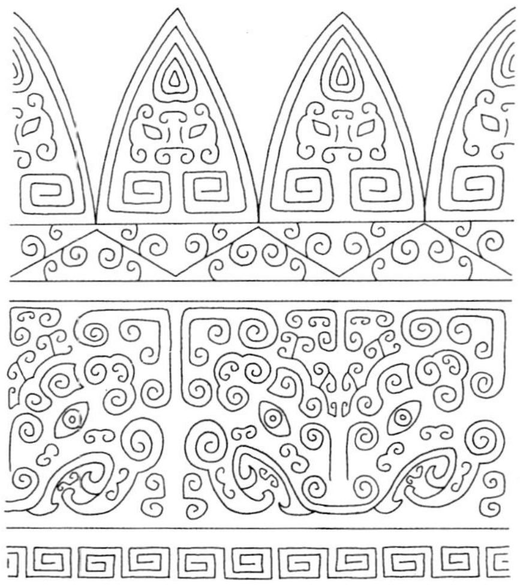

Fig. 1

Inlaid silver work was first popularized in the Warring States period. It was revived as a popular method of decoration in the Song and post-Song vogue for archaism, but usually in combination with gold inlay. Silver inlay on its own soon became fashionable and the late Ming monk Shisou (see no. 157) is believed to have created a fresh demand for this sort of work. From his time onwards large quantities of bronzes with inlaid silver wire designs have appeared, mostly bearing Shisou's name. It is useful to have a dateable object such as this as a clue in the difficult task of assessing the vast and largely anonymous output over at least three centuries.

154

Paper Weights

Nephrite, of greenish-white tone, with varying degrees of russet brown markings; a group of four pebble-shaped paper weights, each inscribed on one side; the first (upper left) inscribed with the title of their place of use *Chunhe Yuan* ('Garden of Peaceful Spring'); the second (upper right) inscribed with a couplet "The peaches of the Mountain of Immortals (Suishan) are beautiful and everlasting/Natural gems of jade have the same longevity"; followed by "recorded by *Chunhe*" (the name of the garden being transferred to its owner), with seal *Chunhe;* the third (lower left) with a poetic description of jade "Unsophisticated [as a virtue] like a pebble from Khotan; embracing the moon, condensing the mist; having the longevity of the pine; with the brilliance of a new year flower" followed by the signature "written by the Master of the *Chunhe Yuan*" with seal *Chunhe;* and the fourth (lower right), also having a poetic description of the stone: "Outstanding jade, naturally produced; not collected from the streams of Khotan; treasure of the waters and mountains; essence of ten thousand years of gathered beauty," followed by the seal *Bao* [?] *Zhai* ('Precious [?] Studio' — part of the middle character has been worn away by handling and is no longer legible).
Probably 18th century.
Greatest single dimension of each: 6.3 cm, 5 cm, 7.4 cm, 8.5 cm respectively.

白玉卵形刻銘紙鎭四件•春和園銘
可能十八世紀, 長6.3厘米, 5厘米,
7.4厘米, 8.5厘米

This set of paper weights demonstrates clearly the esteem in which jade was held, quite apart from the workmanship expended upon it. Here seemingly humble pebbles have been simply polished, their natural beauty allowed to speak for itself and transformed into treasures for the scholar's studio. Although the poems add a level of meaning to them as works of art, it was the simple pebbles that inspired them in the first place.

We have been unable to trace the ownership or location of the Garden of Peaceful Spring, but we may be fairly certain that it included a place where the scholar/artist/poet could sit, enjoy the peace and meditate. Here would have been kept the necessary equipment to write or paint, to play music and drink wine and tea and to engage in elegant conversations. Such objects as these would have been associated with that place, and even if used elsewhere would have carried with them the tranquility of this special garden, as indeed they do to a degree today despite our ignorance of its details. There may well be some connection between this garden and the "Hall of Peaceful Spring" *(Chunhe Tang)* which is recorded as having belonged to the Qing dynasty prince You Li.

155

Horse

Nephrite, of yellowish-green colour with brown veining; a model of a reclining horse.
Probably Yuan or early Ming dynasty.
Height: 3.8 cm. Length: 8 cm.

玉雕臥馬
可能元或明初, 高3.8厘米, 長8厘米

Recent opinion on the dating of post-archaic jades would probably tend to date this example as Song or Yuan. However, the criteria for doing so are still extremely doubtful for a variety of reasons. They are largely based upon comparisons with excavated wares and with known, datable works of art which have remained above ground. The known dateable works upon which stylistic analysis can be based are frequently imperial wares, bearing reliable reign marks, usually in other materials and often responding to a somewhat different aesthetic than that of the literati. The problem with excavated pieces is that, as a rule, the higher up the scale of aesthetic hierarchy a work of art was situated, the less likely it was to be buried with the dead. The incidence of fine paintings and calligraphy found in tombs, for example, is very small indeed, and the more highly something was valued as art the less likely it was to end up in a burial. With paintings and calligraphy we have the advantage of well-recorded artists, signatures, dates, colophons and collectors' seals to help establish a record of stylistic change over the centuries. With the other works of art enjoyed by the scholar at various levels such direct associations are rarer. With wood, gourds, soft stones, even Yixing pottery and other easily worked materials the scholars were more likely to add inscriptions consisting of comments, poems, signatures, dates, seals and other useful information. Spontenaity, that key factor in literati expression, could be maintained as the inscriber could at any time pick up a tool and express himself directly on the material. Although there are exceptions, harder materials, where the addition of inscriptions was more of a technological task involving planning and workshop facilities, inhibited such artistic expression.

In dating many of these problem areas there is a tendency for over-enthusiastic early dating. Ironically this attitude may be viewed as derogatory to the pieces in question, implying that they have little artistic merit and must stand or fall on their period. The literati aesthetic places age low on the list of criteria for judging art. A particular period may carry with it meaning, but not age as such.

In so far as this carving responds to the literati aesthetic, the stylization and exaggeration of certain features for sculptural rather than realistic ends suggests a Yuan or post-Yuan response. It was the Yuan masters in painting who finally and full-bloodedly transformed the art of painting into a fully matured art, where its direct self-realizational role became pre-eminent. To what extent and how quickly the new-found possibilities in pictorial art were reflected in literati-inspired sculpture is not certain, but it is worth bearing in mind that the sculptural qualities of a Yuan or post-Yuan jade horse might be quite different from a Song one, and possibly much more exciting.

153

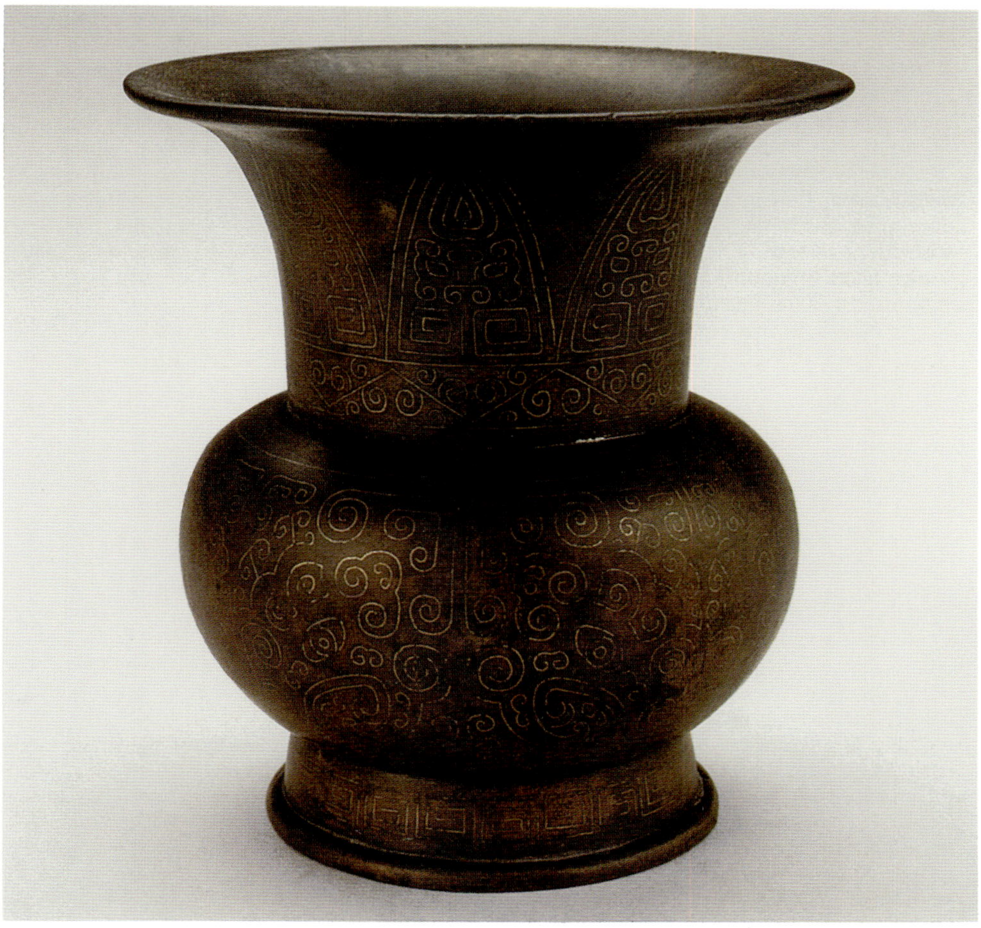

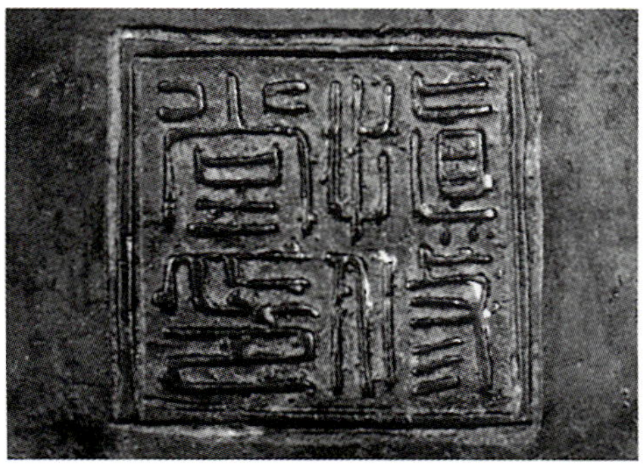

154

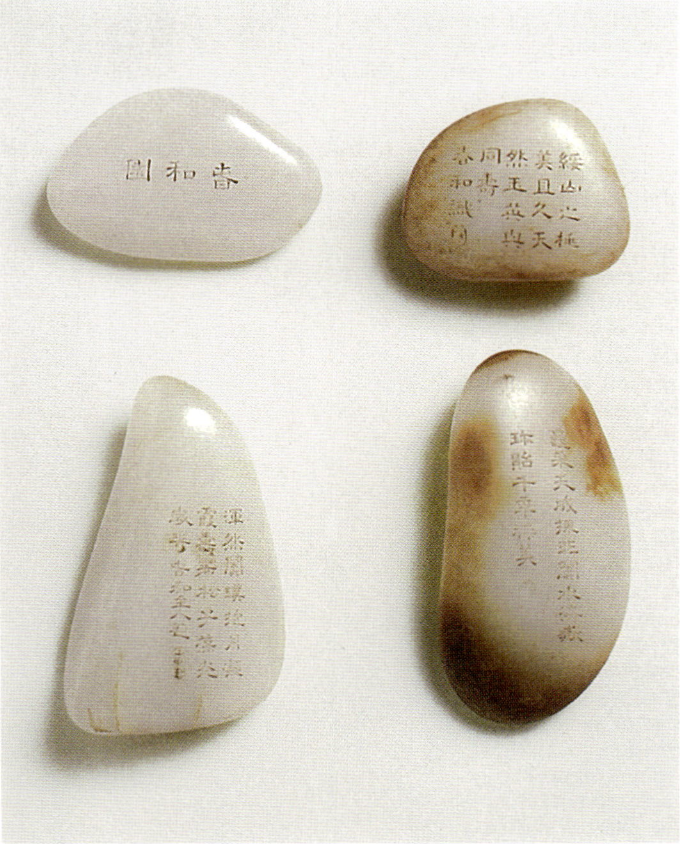

155

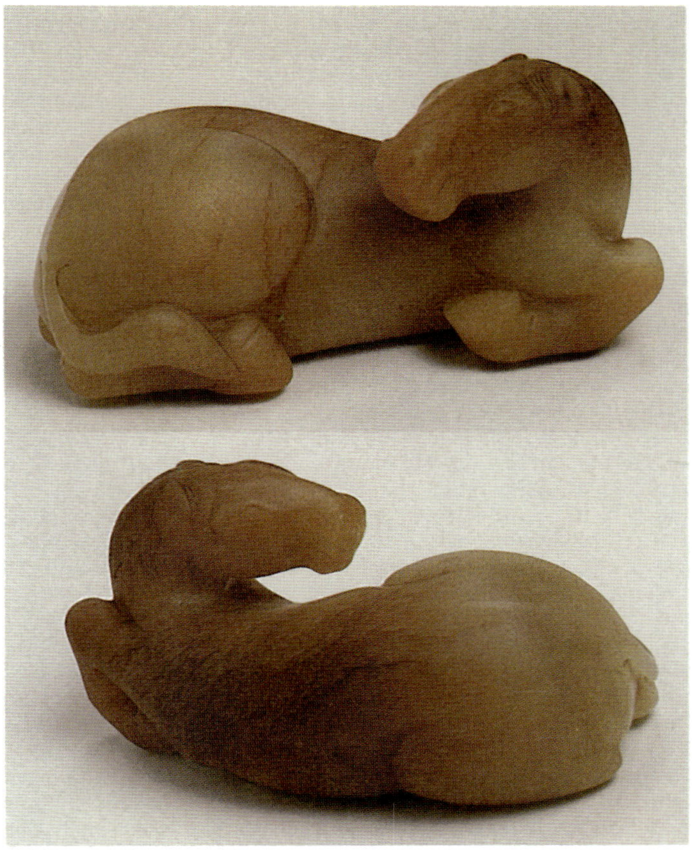

156

Brush Rest

Bronze, with gilding and gold splashing; a brush rest in the form of two frolicking *chi* dragons, the smaller dragon gilt, the larger with gold splashes; the back of the larger dragon inscribed with a small, neat mark *Qianlong nianzhi* ('made during the Qianlong period') in regular script.
Probably Beijing palace workshops, Qianlong period.
Length: 7.3 cm.

鎏金青銅雙螭筆擱·乾隆年製銘
清乾隆(1736–1795)長7.3厘米

Whether or not this small bronze was made in the palace workshops, it seems reasonable to suppose that it was made for the Court. It has a four-character mark consistent with much of palace production, and its small size, exquisite nature and subject-matter all lend it the air of a palace piece. However, in its origins it is a pure literati work of art. The material itself (popularized for scholars' objects by the literati love of ancient bronze vessels), the gold splashing and the ancient subject-matter taken from archaic decoration as developed under the Han are all commensurate with literati usage. The form of this brush rest is also taken from antiquity. The Ming connoisseur Wen Zhenheng describes antique bronze brush rests in the form of "twin *chi* dragons wrestling with each other".[1] When such an object was used at Court, whether by the Emperor or by any of his family or courtiers, it is not difficult to imagine the scholar taking precedence over the ruler or adminstrator.

1. *Changwu ji, juan* 7, section 9.

157

Water Vessel

Shisou

Bronze and copper with inlaid silver and gold; an octagonal water vessel, the main body panels decorated with the eight trigrams, carved into the surface, flanked by various archaistic motifs inlaid in silver; the slightly domed top with a narrow, lipped opening, inlaid with four highly formalized designs based on *taotie* masks, separated by *leiwen,* the lip with decorative 'S' shapes derived from *gui* dragon motifs, all inlaid in gold and silver; the inlaid copper base with a carved twelve-character inscription: "made by Shisou in archaic style at the Festival of the Double-Ninth (ninth day of the ninth month), chrysanthemum month of the *xinchou* year (1541/1601)".
1541 or 1601.
Height: 5.7 cm.

嵌金銀線八卦水丞·石叟製
明辛丑(1541或1601)，高5.7厘米

Shisou is perhaps the most mysterious figure of all the known Ming metalsmiths. He is listed as a monk of the late Ming whose proper name and place of birth or activity are unknown.[1] He specialized in making inlaid bronzes, most of which were scholar's objects. His name usually appears in the form of two characters, *Shisou,* in a style between seal script and clerical script. His works were said to be rustic (that is, to have simple strength) without being vulgar — which was high praise in the terminology of the influential minority.

Very large numbers of inlaid bronzes are known which either bear his two-character signature (sometimes with the addition of the hall name *Jinyu Tang* — 'Hall of Prosperity') or are obviously in the style associated with him. Few of these are convincingly pre-Qing and the vast majority appear to be quite late Qing. One standing figure of Guanyin, an imposing and dignified work in the Jade Studio collection, Hong Kong, is marked with his signature and hall mark in the usual manner, but also has the mark *Da Ming Zhengde yuzhi* ('by imperial command of the Zhengde Emperor'). Although the imperial mark is unconvincing (see no. 130 for a discussion on the forms of imperial marks), the figure is of some age — certainly 19th century, and quite possibly as early as 17th century. What is interesting is that an artist (and presumably his audience of connoisseurs) should have believed, a century or more ago, that Shisou was working during the Zhengde period. A large number of pieces purporting to be by Shisou are religious figures, with Guanyin featuring prominently. Several of these might lay sensible claim to a late Ming or early Qing date (including a large figure seated on rockwork in the Hong Kong Museum of Art; an imposing Guanyin on a lotus throne and now set on a gilded wave base, in a private Hong Kong collection; and a seated Buddha and seated Guanyin published in *Emperor, Scholar, Artisan, Monk: The Creative Personality in Chinese Works of Art,* nos. 131 and 132 respectively).

To our knowledge, this small water vessel is the only known piece bearing a date. Its quality, style, unique mark and the typically late Ming metalworker's habit of inlaying a separate copper base to a bronze vessel make it as credible as any known Shisou piece, although with its cyclical date its exact period is still uncertain. The 'late Ming' designation of the *Zhongguo Yishujia Zhenglue* might include any period within the 16th or 17th centuries — if indeed it is based on anything more than hearsay in the first place. If the opinion that Shisou was in a position to make something for the Zhengde Emperor has any basis, then the earlier date of 1541 would seem more senible for this vessel. If not, 1601 might not be too late, since it coincides with a known vogue for metalwork to which Hu Wenming and others responded.

However, there is a danger of 'overworking' the late 16th and 17th centuries in our attempts to put a chronology to various types of works of art. While there is no doubt that the late Ming period is one of considerable activity in a wide range of arts, it must be remembered that it was also a period of great activity on the part of the connoisseur and collector. Scholars' objects were in demand from the time when there were first scholars, in large quantities and over a very wide range of arts as time progressed. The metal, lacquer, wood, rhinoceros horn, bamboo and other craft industries did not spring up overnight in the late Ming period, although there was apparently a considerable florescence. Spare time on their hands increased the scholars' demand for works of art, but it also increased their capacity to act as connoisseurs, with two obvious effects: the first, that with a closer association between patron and craftsman/artist, the latter began to be considered and to consider himself as more of an individual artist, and responded by identifying his works; the second was that out of connoisseurship arose a greater need to record its esoteric details by writing about taste in works of art, which inevitably included details of these artists. Thus, although we are dealing on the one hand with a greater supply of works of art, we are also dealing with a much greater identification of the supply, which gives an unbalanced picture.

From what little evidence we do have of literary sources and the range of extant objects, it would seem likely that Shisou was a skilled late Ming metalsmith who rarely signed his works. In response to his high reputation a number of pieces bearing his name was then made from perhaps as early as the 17th century to the 20th, with large quantities being made in the late Qing period.

There is one other possibility, which was raised by the 19th century results of three tests on core samples of pieces where the overwhelming stylistic evidence would place them at least two centuries earlier carried out at the Research Laboratory for Archaeology, Oxford (see no. 169). Perhaps we are entirely mistaken about the dating of whole areas of Ming and Qing bronzes generally and that a very large quantity of the standard Ming and early Qing objects by which we stylistically date other wares, should all be re-assigned to the 19th century.

A net drawing of the inlaid design of this vessel is shown as Fig. 1.

Fig. 1

1. *Zhongguo Meishujia Renming Cidian* where the source is given as *Luochuang Xiadu,* which was presumably also the source for the very similar information in the *Zhonguo Yishujia Zhenglue.*

156

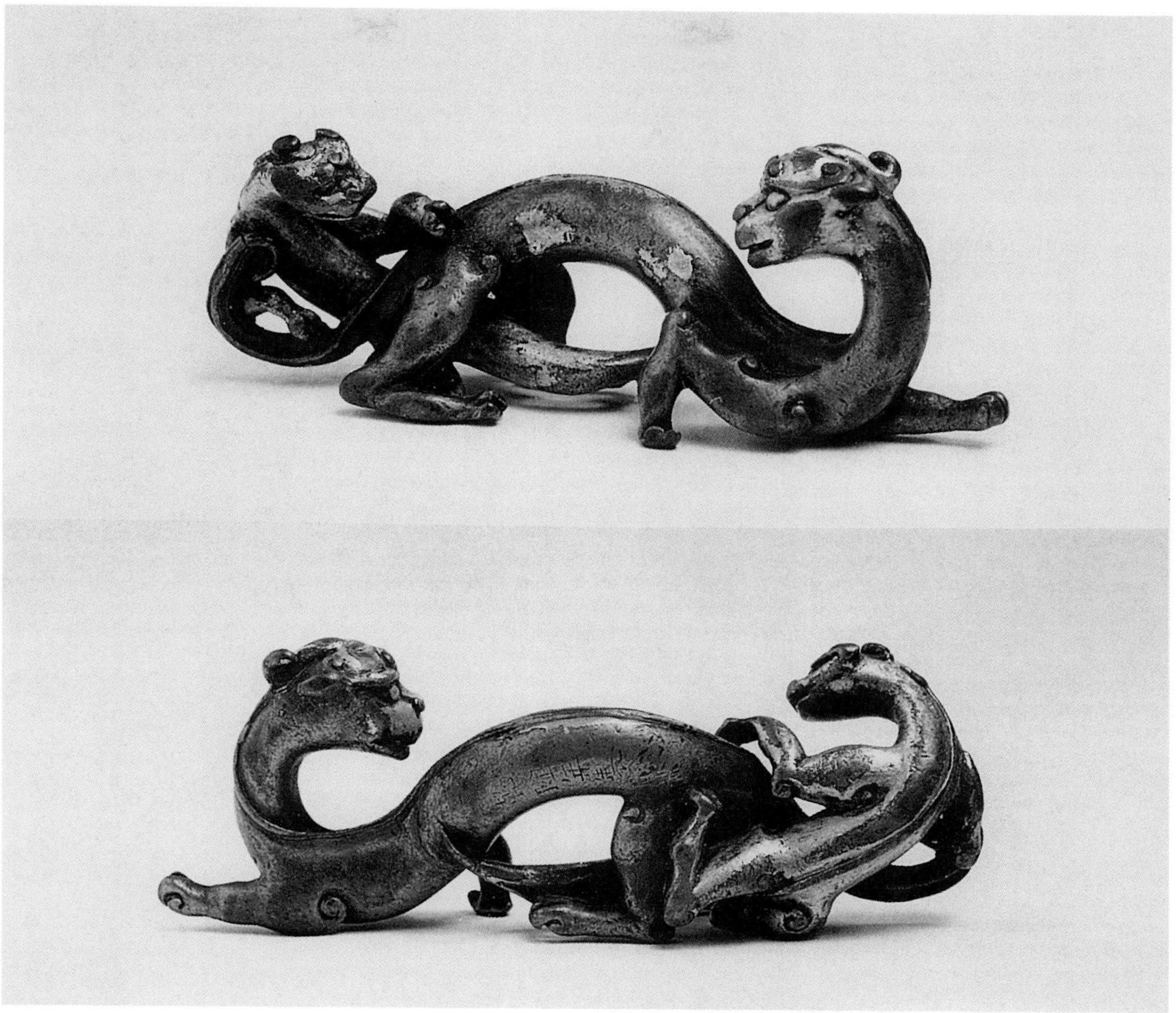

Larger than life size

157

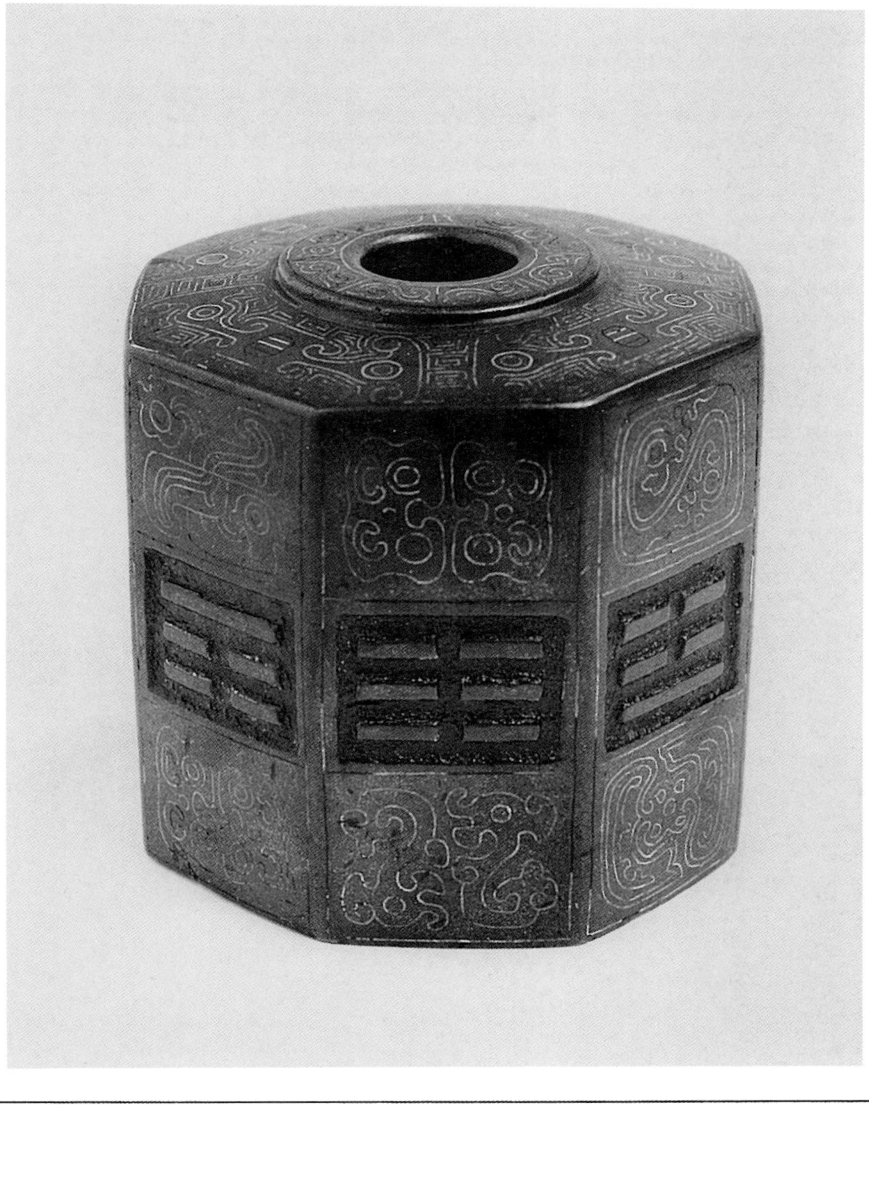

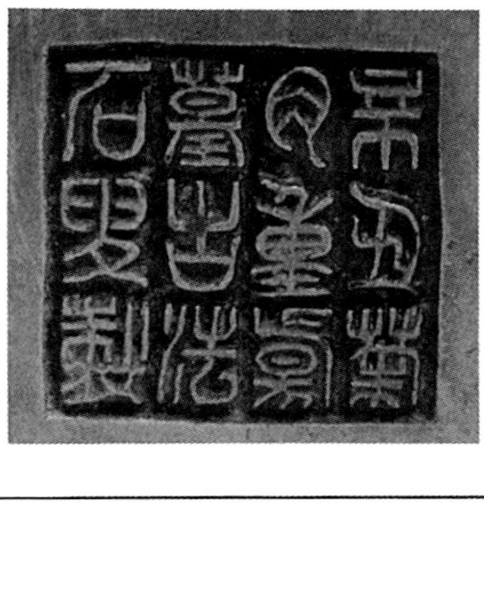

158

Drinking Vessel

Rhinoceros horn, of strikingly variegated golden-brown and deep blackish-brown colour; a stem cup, the boat-shaped bowl set on a pointed oval flared foot with scalloped edge, the darker colour in the horn concentrated in the foot and centre of the bowl, superbly used to enhance the low relief decoration of two *chi* dragons (one of golden colour, one of black) amidst swirling clouds emerging from a rock-strewn raging torrent, the clouds and beasts giving way to a plain upper section of the outer bowl, decorated only with a band of highly formalized but still recognizable *gui* dragons around the lip; the interior plain but so translucent and thinly worked that the exterior scene is clearly visible, creating a mysterious 'hidden' design; the pointed-oval, recessed base incised with the mark *Da Ming Xuande nianzhi* ('made in the Xuande period of the Great Ming dynasty') in regular script within a square cartouche.
1426-1435.
Height: 8.6 cm. Length: 16 cm.
Published: *The Arts of the Ming Dynasty, Transactions of the Oriental Ceramic Society,* Vol. 30, 1955-1957, plate 101, no. 379; *Chinese Art,* Vol. 4, p.206, no. 136; *The George de Menasce Collection,* Part I, Spink & Son Ltd., London, 1971, p.42, no. 158.
Formerly in the collections of Baron George de Menasce and Dr. & Mrs. Peter Plesche.

犀角雕螭龍高足杯•大明宣德年製銘
明宣德(1426-1435), 高8.6厘米, 長16厘米

This extraordinary rhinoceros horn carving stands alone in the range of drinking horns known from the Tang dynasty to the late Qing. The combination of superb technical skill applied to an unusual and imaginative use of the natural colours in the material, and the material itself with its vividly variegated colours is not unknown, but the form and the Xuande mark are each unique in the field. The early Ming book on connoisseurship, *Gegu Yaolun,* mentions in its entry on rhinoceros horn combinations of yellow and black (colours are often used misleadingly in Chinese sources, but since no more extreme example is known of a combination of 'yellow' and 'black' than this, we may assume that this is what was meant) as being one of the most valued types of horn at that time. It also mentions that the best should be translucent and show cloud-like mottling at the top, and raindrop-like spots at the bottom (see no. 159 for relevant passage). This horn satisfies all these criteria, fitting classically into the type of horn most valued in early Ming times.

Although dated horns are known from later in the Ming period, no other imperial or purportedly imperial rhinoceros horn is known from the dynasty, suggesting that it was not an art form dominated by imperial production as were ceramics and *cloisonné* enamels. It seems fitting that if a single piece was to be made for the Xuande Emperor (who was apparently a patron of arts and crafts on a grand scale), it would be of the most valued piece of horn that could be found at the time, combined with the finest workmanship and artistry possible. This horn fulfils those expectations.

Spink's, without discussion, dated it to the late Ming dynasty; Harry M. Garner[1] singles it out as having been attributed to the Xuande period, but it is captioned only as bearing the mark, leaving the question of period unsettled. Jenyns[2] on the other hand writes that it is the only marked Xuande piece which has come to light, and sees no reason to doubt the dating evidence of its mark. Since we find several reasons to accept this vessel as Xuande and none to doubt it, we agree with Jenyns.

The rhinoceros horn as a drinking vessel is of considerable antiquity. They appear in the *Shijing* (*Book of Songs*), compiled by Confucius, where they are called *sigong.* In a later commentary quoted from *Notes of the Han Kingdom* (a Warring States kingdom), the *sigong* are explained as being made from the horn of the rhinoceros and their capacity is given. Rhinoceros horn cups are also discussed in relation to the game *taohu* (throwing arrows into vases) in the *Liji* (*Book of Rites*) — see no. 264.

It is clear that the rhinoceros horn cup has a very long history indeed. Known Tang examples are found in the *Shoso-in.*[3] Other dated examples which should be taken into account are the Xuanhe marked cup in the Chester Beatty collection (although generally considered doubtful)[4], a simple vessel resembling a well-smoothed section of gnarled tree trunk; the possibly Yuan vessel shown in this catalogue (no. 258), and this Xuande example. Then there is a series of later Ming cups which are either dated, signed or can be shown to have been in existence by certain times, many of which are covered by Ip Yee, Jenyns and Chapman.[5] A vast number of cups have been assigned by conventional wisdom to the late Ming or Qing periods, but perhaps a more realistic chronology reflecting the continuing popularity of these vessels from remote antiquity to the Qing dynasty might now be expected. Such reattribution was begun by the late Dr. Ip Yee.[6]

That these cups are perfectly suited to their original function as drinking vessels was amusingly demonstrated by this particular vessel. The late Dr. Ip Yee who, after Chester Beatty, formed the largest known collection of rhinoceros horn vessels over a relatively short period prior his death, had long coveted this cup. Its present owner however was unwilling to part with it for longer than the time it took to serve Ip's postprandial brandy in it.

An intriguing and striking parallel to this vessel was given to the British Museum by Sir Hans Sloane in 1713. The shape of the upper vessel is very similar, but it stands on a low, fluted foot. It is also similarly thinly worked, a most unusual feature of rhinoceros horn cups. However, it is attributed by the British Museum, quite reasonably on the strength of the simple decorative borders, to Mughal India, and is possibly a cup mentioned in literary records which would dated it to *circa* 1525.[7] There may be some connection between the two vessels.

1. See the introduction to the *Arts of the Ming Dynasty.*
2. *Chinese Art,* Vol 4.
3. Ibid. p.204, no. 123, a and b.
4. Ibid. and *The Chester Beatty Collection of Chinese Carved Rhinoceros Horn Cups* in *Arts of Asia,* May-June 1982, pp.73-83.
5. *Notes on a Collection of Chinese Rhinoceros Horn Carvings* by Ip Yee, in the handbook of the International Asian Antiques Fair, Hong Kong, 1982; for Jenyns and Chapman see note 4.
6. Ibid.
7. See *Islam in the Department of Oriental Antiquities,* by J.M. Rogers, in *Arts of Asia,* May-June 1986, p.107, no. 52.

158

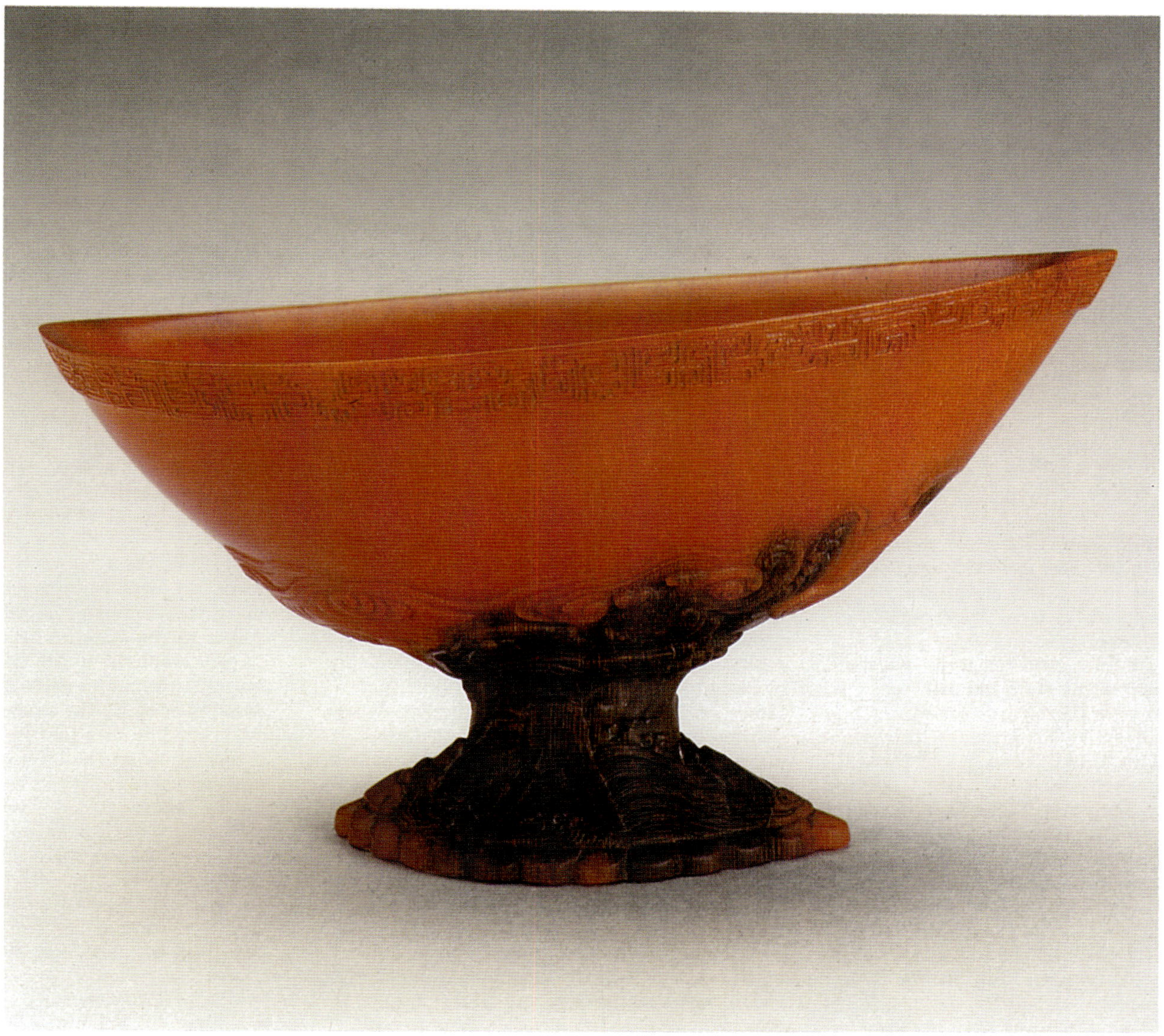

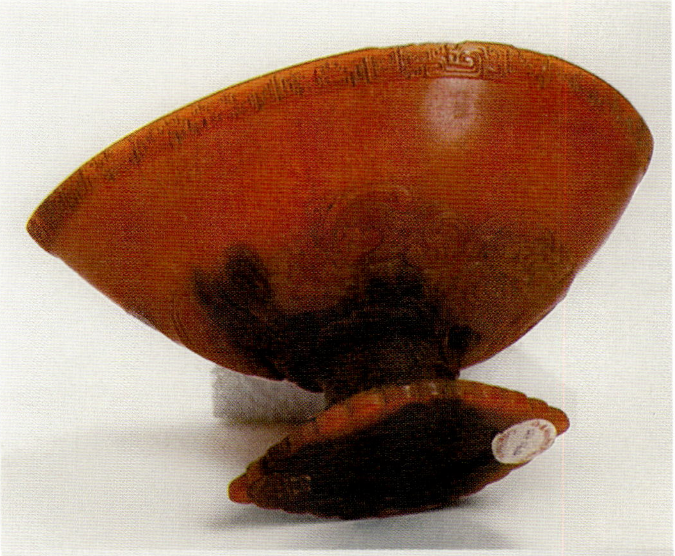

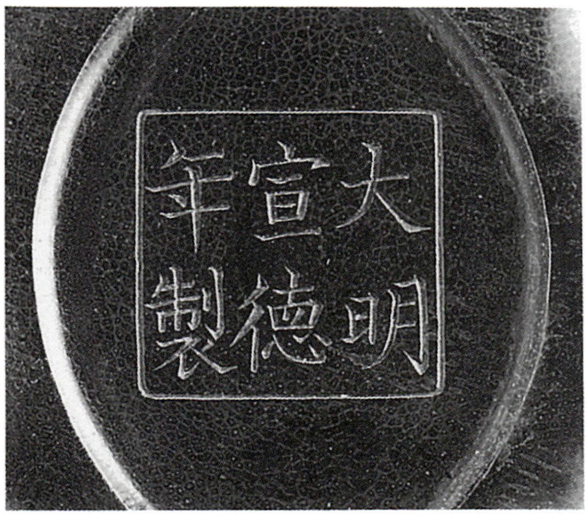

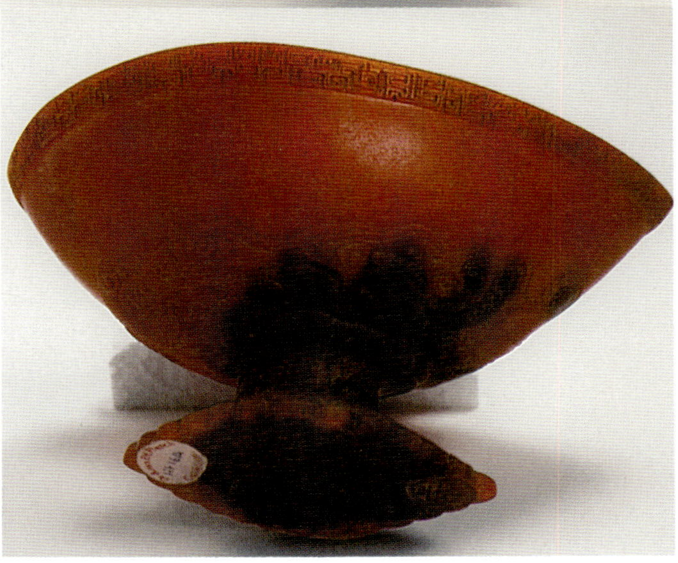

159

Luohan

Rhinoceros horn, of variegated dark and light brown with areas of almost yellow colour; carved in the form of a seated *luohan* holding a duster, his face with an expression of studied concentration.
Inscribed on the base: 'Precious collection of Liu Shian, first month of spring, Qianlong, 1781'.
Probably late Ming dynasty.
Height: 8.6 cm.
Formerly in the collection of Liu Yong (Liu Shian — *circa* 1719-1804).
Published: *Emperor, Scholar, Artisan, Monk: The Creative Personality in Chinese Works of Art*, pp.178-179, no. 56.

犀角雕羅漢坐像•劉石菴銘
可能晚明,高8.6厘米

In the early Ming *Gegu Yaolun* the section on rhinoceros horn includes the following: "Those which are long, thick, transparent, dappled with delightful designs are expensive. But the long, slender, light and unpleasant dappled pieces are only good for medicinal use. [There is a variety with] grain like fish roe, generally known as 'millet spots' (*suwen*), each of which has an eye like a 'millet eye' (*suyan*) and so called. This kind of horn is known as mountain rhinoceros horn.

"Rhinoceros horn pieces should be smooth and mellow: the 'millet spots' or other designs that are in the horn should be pleasing to the eye. Its colour should be either lac black or chestnut kernel yellow; and the horn should be translucent from end to end. It should show clearly 'clouds' (mottles) on the top and 'rain-drops' (spots) at the bottom. Such are the criteria of fine pieces.

"The most valuable horns have in them designs resembling definite objects, extending from the bottom of a piece to the top. Two other varieties are also valuable — the double-dappled (yellow on black and black on yellow) and the plain dappled (yellow on black, anciently called *tongxi*). The inverted dapple (yellow spots barred with black) is a less valuable variety. An even less valuable kind has a darker [yellow] colour dappled with spots like wild pepper seeds *(xanthoxylum piperitum)*. The pure black variety is the cheapest, good enough merely for making chessmen or similar objects."[1]

Apart from the statement that the most precious horns have natural designs resembling objects, we are left with some rather vague terms, as is usual with Chinese sources. The difference between pieces 'dappled with delightful designs' and those 'unpleasantly dappled' must to a very large extent involve personal taste, and it is our experience that most if not all rhinoceros horn exhibits what might be called 'millet spots' with a central 'eye' if cut across the grain. A general idea can be gleaned from the comments about colours and double dappling, although even this is far from being beyond interpretation. There is little doubt that the enthusiastic owner could find in the above a reference to practically any rhinoceros horn carving he happened to have in his possession, unless it was pure black — again, we have never seen a pure black piece, although we may accept this as a reference to the darker and duller tones of brown that are common enough.

Rhinoceros horn figures are rare. There is one in the Fogg Art Museum, Cambridge, Mass.[2] of a Guanyin figure with an acolyte which is dated to 1599 and was made as an offering to the Jingang Dong (a Buddhist shrine) at Jiuhua mountain. There is possibly some connection between these two; both are religious sculptures in rhinoceros horn of the same sort of period and of apparently equal quality. However, there was a vogue in the late Ming dynasty for these small figures in various materials and it was possible for artists and their workshops to produce similar wares in several materials provided they could be worked by existing methods (for instance, soft stones, lacquer, ivory and horn could all be worked directly with the blade, while hard stones required a lapidary method which was quite different). There were probably several workshops capable of carving this and other materials, and the fact that two of similar period are in the same material and quality might indicate a general trend rather than a specific workshop. A *Budai* with children playing around him is also illustrated in the same work[3] and there is another from the Dr. Ip Yee collection, probably by the same hand.[4]

The inscription on the base of this piece was added by the celebrated scholar, poet, connoisseur and statesman Liu Yong (Liu Shian). The history of Liu's administrative career reads like a game of snakes and ladders played in deadly earnest, and for the highest stakes. Alternately promoted and disgraced, brought into imperial favour and exiled, and at one point sentenced to death only to have the sentence commuted by the emperor who was soon to bestow further honours on him, his was nothing if not an exciting life. Nor was his story an unusual one in the history of China's administrative bureaucracy. Although the literati collectively were the dominant force in government, as individuals they were frequently at the mercy of imperial whimsy and the intrigues of imperial favourites, which could hasten exile or death as readily as it could satisfy vaunting ambition or the Confucian moral need to serve.[5]

Quite apart from his official career, Liu was a renowned connoisseur (especially of ink rubbings) and calligrapher. The style and confidence of the inscription on this figure suggest that he carved it himself. Although he is not listed as a seal carver it is highly likely that he was at least conversant with the 'iron brush'. It is, of course, possible that he brushed in the characters and someone else did the cutting, but two strokes where the moving blade has chipped away tiny pieces of horn suggest that the carver was not familiar with working on horn.

While there is much to recommend this work, the back perhaps sums up the high level of artistic expression. The natural striations of colour in the material have been cleverly used to give emphasis to the fall of the cloak, but the abstract, formal qualities of the carving are demonstrated by the single, superbly confident, sweeping line of a fold in the cloak, running diagonally from the level of the raised knee downwards towards the hem. This line breaks up the otherwise static, vertical drop of the robe, and turns the entire back of the sculpture into three distinct main areas: the head and two sections of the robed body, lending it a dynamic abstract quality. (For a soapstone sculpture similarly inscribed by Liu Yong on the base and also from his collection, see no. 165.)

1. *Chinese Connoisseurship.*
2. *Chinese Art*, Vol 4, p.212, no. 144.
3. Ibid. p.212, no. 145, from the Dreyfus collection.
4. Dr. Ip Yee, op.cit., p.37, no.31.
5. Liu Yong's career is outlined in *Eminent Chinese of the Ch'ing Period*, pp.536-537.

159

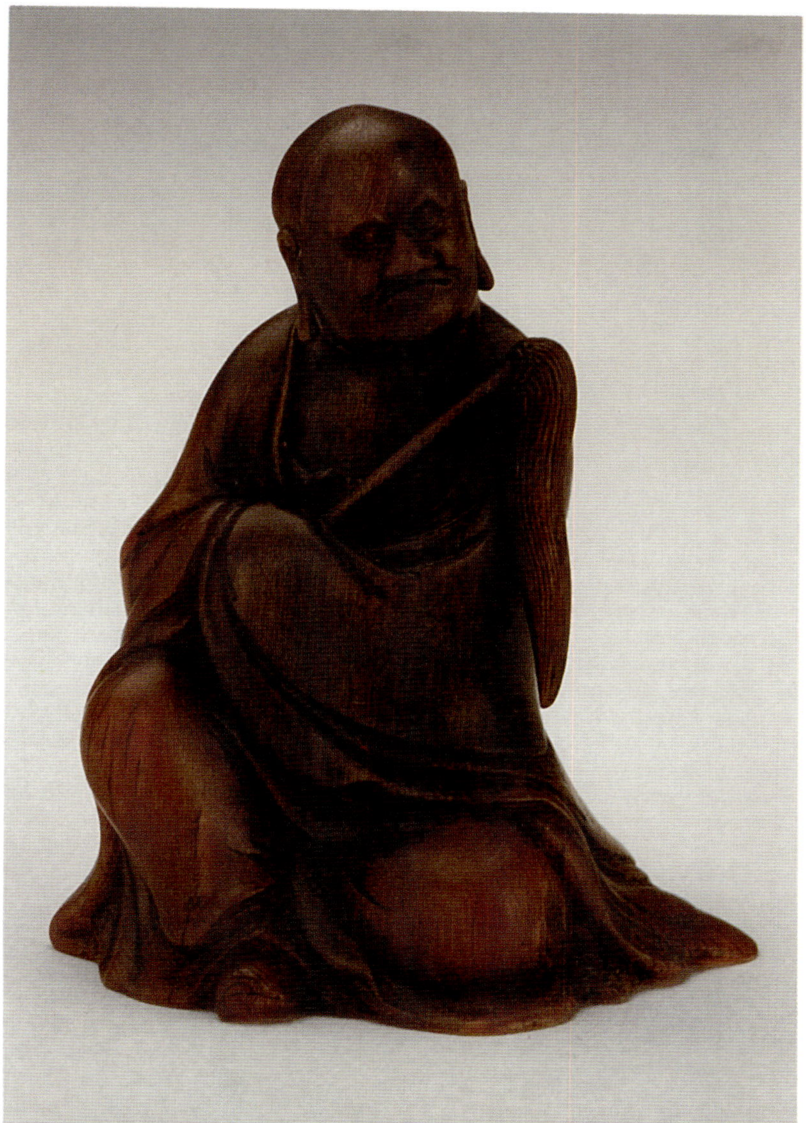

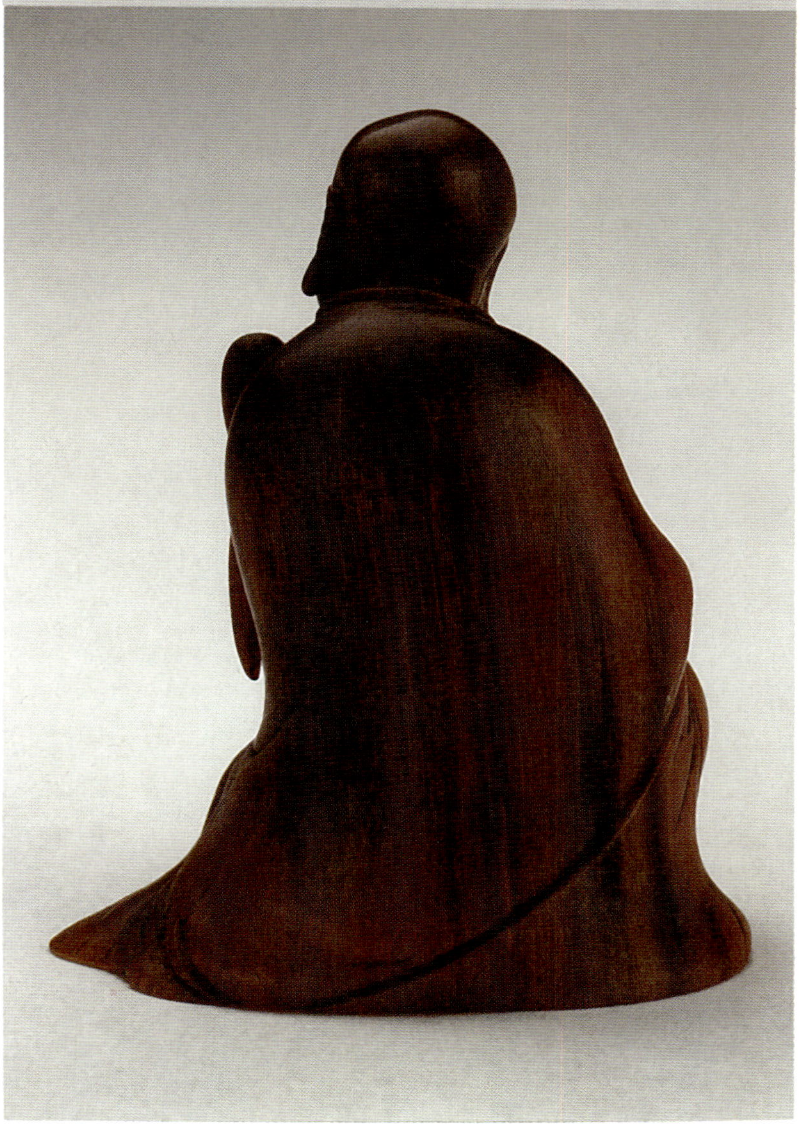

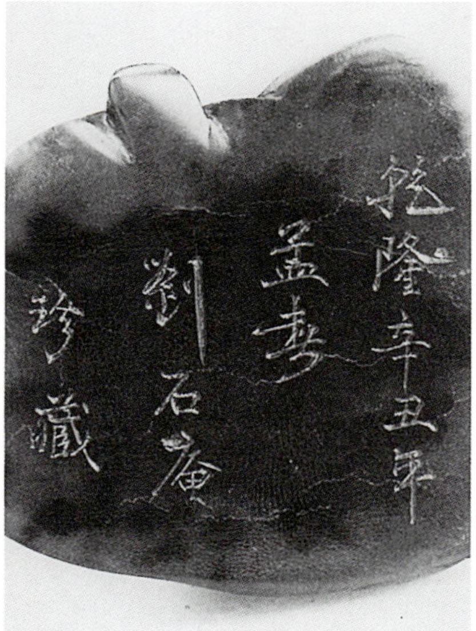

Larger than life size

160

Vase

Bronze, of richly patinated golden brown colour, with gold splashes; vase of *hu* form, the body decorated with three raised horizontal bands (one forming the lip rim), set with two separately cast *taotie* masks acting as lugs for loose ring handles; the base inscribed *Da Ming Xuande nianzhi* ('made in the Xuande period of the Great Ming dynasty') in raised regular script within a recessed rectangular cartouche; the exterior surfaces covered overall with irregularly disposed gold splashes.
Probably late Ming or early Qing dynasty.
Height: 15.3 cm.

灑金饕餮紋青銅壺·大明宣德年製銘
可能晚明或清初, 高15.3厘米

The origins of gold-splashing on bronzes is obscure. Since a very large number of early gold splashed bronzes are related to Xuande ritual vessels (see no. 123), and since the genre seems to have flourished if not in Xuande times then in response to what people thought, at quite an early date, was a Xuande type, we may assume that the enormous popularity of this type of surface decoration was fostered by Xuande originals. What prompted the sudden introduction of this decorative technique in the Ming dynasty remains speculative. It seems likely that it was a direct result of archaism, and that gold splashing on original archaic bronze vessels or even the appearance of gold splashes resulting from uneven patination as viewed by later connoisseurs was its origin. There is a Jin dynasty mirror published which has a surface remarkably similar to Ming gold splashed bronzes.[1]

1. *The National Palace Museum Monthly of Chinese Art*, 1983, no. 6, p.34.

161

Wine Vessel

Bronze, with a rich golden brown patination and gold splashes; a vessel in the form of a *jue* (ritual wine vessel); the body decorated with a *taotie* mask set against a ground of irregularly disposed double *leiwen* repeated on each side and separated by two raised flanges, the centre of one covered by a handle made up of a rather bovine-looking *taotie* consuming its own body; the two raised finials with whorl pattern knobs, the underside of the belly cast with the inscription *Boshen zuo baoyi* ('Boshen made this treasured wine vessel') in bronze script; covered on all exterior surfaces with irregularly disposed splashes of gold.
Probably late Ming dynasty.
Height: 21 cm.

灑金饕餮紋青銅爵·伯申銘
可能晚明, 高21厘米

The enormous quantity of bronze wares associated with the scholar is an indication of the symbolic importance of the material. During the great Bronze Age of China it shared with jade the distinction of carrying the greatest symbolic weight of any material. When in later times the past began to take on increasing significance for the literati these same two materials had survived best, above and below ground. In addition bronzes were, from the late Shang dynasty to the beginning of Han, when the written language was evolving radically, frequently inscribed, giving later scholars an additional epigraphic reason to value them. Ulrich Hausmann sums up the association between the two: "Archaic bronzes and their inscriptions, the subject of centuries of epigraphic and stylistic studies by literary men and artists, became inseparable; so much so that since that time scholars writing characters have seen at the back of their minds the image of ancient bronze vessels whose rubbings they had carefully studied. Generations of painters and calligraphers...spent a lifetime studying these inscriptions. What could be more fitting than to embellish one's studio with subtle allusions to the magnificent past, or to furnish the ancestral altar with vessels expressing the continuation of their inheritance."[1] From the Song dynasty onwards, when reverence for the past began to manifest itself across a wide range of arts, bronze inevitably became a favourite material for the scholar class.

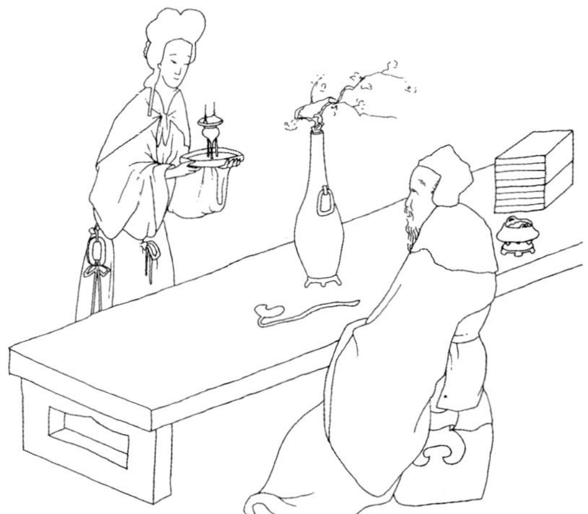

Fig. 1

This example, probably after an early Zhou vessel, includes the inscription which would have appeared on the original.[2] It is a typical late Shang or early Zhou bronze inscription stating the name of the maker, the purpose of the vessel, and the wish that it be treasured. Although the form of this *jue* is a faithful reproduction of an original, the decoration has been somewhat exaggerated, simplifying and stressing certain elements of the *taotie* typical of archaism and, although not exclusively, of the late Ming dynasty. The *jue* was originally used both for warming wine and for drinking it.

The *jue* continued to be used as a drinking vessel in later times and frequently appears in genre paintings. Fig. 1, taken from a mid-Qing painting, shows an old scholar being offered a modified *jue* presumably containing wine. Although it may seem an awkward drinking vessel, the Chinese have traditionally used pouring vessel forms from which to drink, as in the large number of rhinoceros horn cups which are essentially similar to the ancient *yi* vessels. However, they would also have been pressed into service like the *gu* and other vase forms to contain anything from flowers to brushes, or of course would have served a purely aesthetic role.

1. 'In Search of Later Chinese Bronze' by Ulrich Hausmann, in *Documentary Chinese Works of Art In Scholars' Taste.*
2. Unless Boshen is late Ming.

160

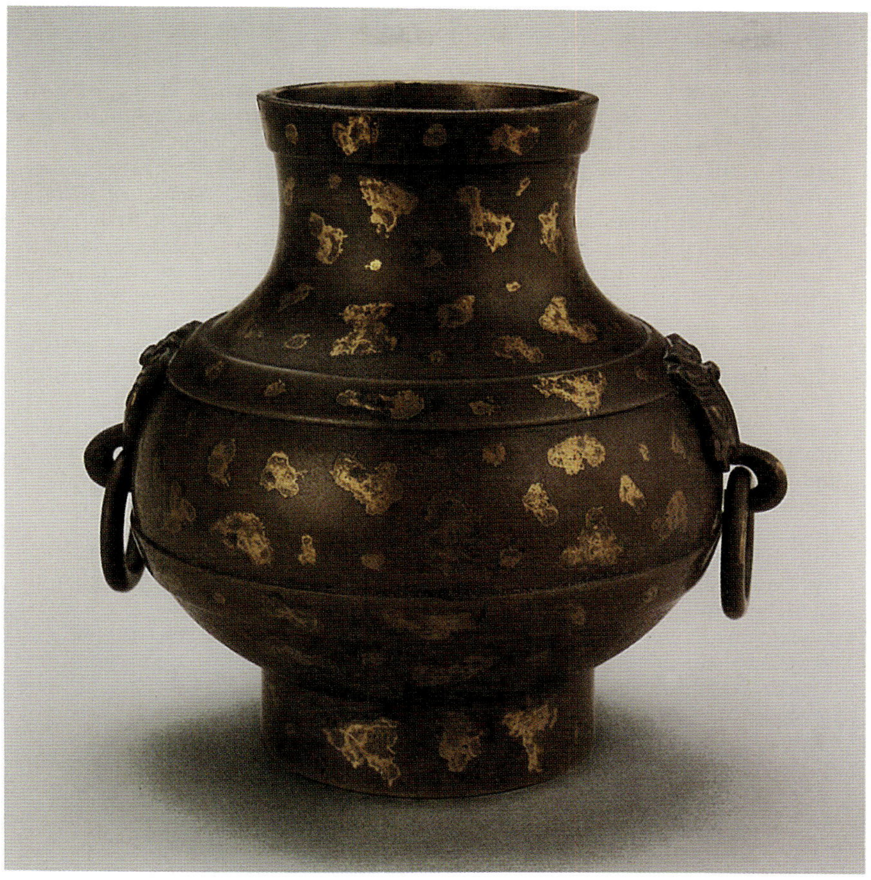

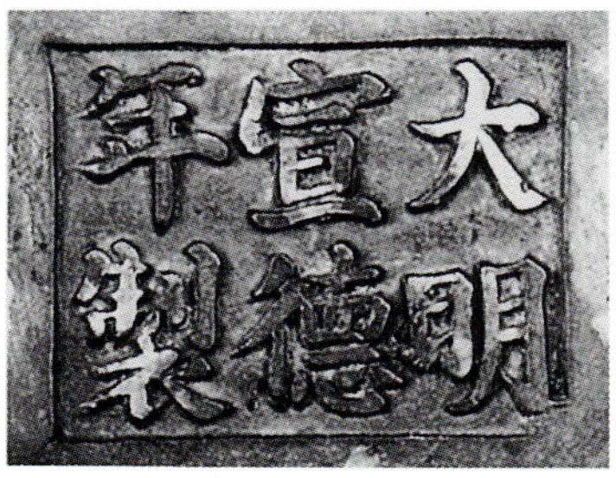

161

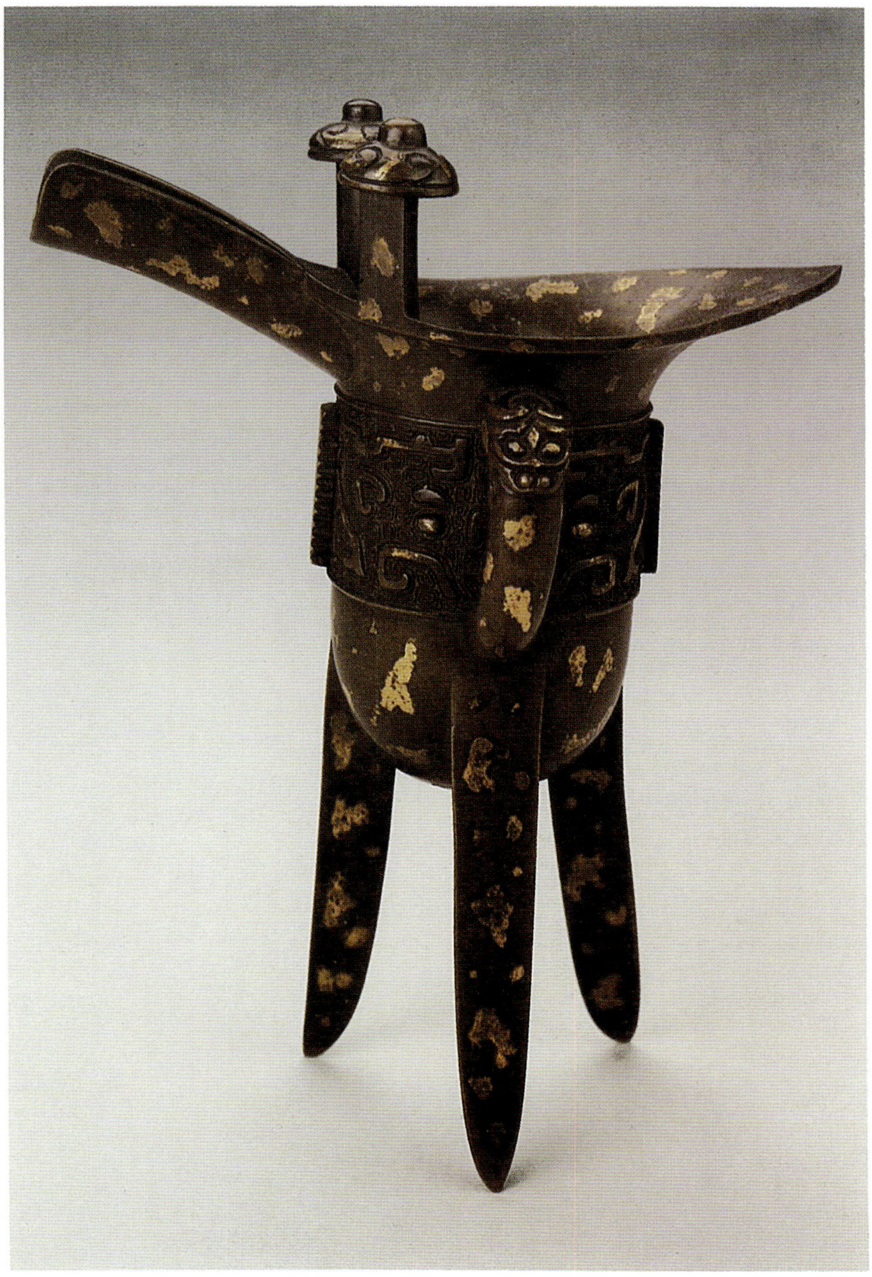

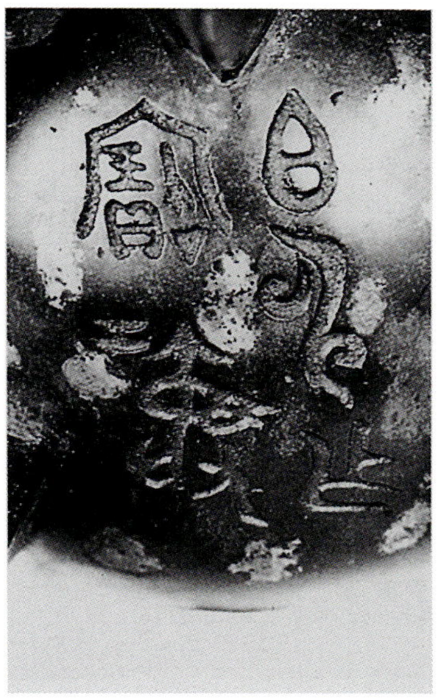

162

'Ink Field' Inkstone

Limestone, of the variety known as Duan stone; the irregular, gnarled form carved in low relief with pines growing from a rocky landscape, the natural shape of the stone indicating rocky cliffs from which some of the pines grow, the face with a recessed, irregularly shaped panel; the reverse inscribed *Xiangquan zhenzang* ('precious collection of Xiangquan').
Length: 13 cm.
Cased in a plain *zitan* box, inscribed on the lid with the title *Motian* ('Ink Field'), and "Respectfully made by Shuzuo for Xinyu"
Length: 14.5 cm.
Qing dynasty or Republic.
Formerly in the Pu Ru collection.

端石刻松硯・香泉銘
清或民國，長13厘米

Pu Ru (*hao:* Xinyu, 1896-1963), painter, calligrapher and poet, was a cousin of the last Emperor of China, Pu Yi. After receiving a traditional education in Beijing, he studied at Berlin University, returning in about 1917 with a doctorate in astronomy and more pride than his mother thought fitting. At her request he retired to a Buddhist temple to the west of Beijing for several years, immersing himself in painting and poetry. During this time he referred to himself as *Xishan yishi* (the retired scholar of the Western hills). In 1926 he exhibited some of his paintings in Beijing and began to establish his reputation as an artist. As a traditionalist he believed that the arts of poetry, calligraphy and painting should be developed equally.

Pu Ru left China in 1949 for Zhousan Island, then in the hands of the nationalists, and in 1950 settled in Taiwan, where he supported himself by teaching at Taiwan Normal University and by selling his paintings and calligraphy. He also became a director of the China Spinning Construction Company. In Taiwan, as on the mainland, he wore the traditional long gown of the Confucian scholar, insisted on proper respect from his students, and smoked cigarettes constantly. He died of cancer of the throat in 1963. He had many students in Taiwan who studied painting under him and was clearly an influential if conservative teacher.

The sequence of events and possible participants in the manufacture, subsequent ownership and presentation of this piece is unclear. Xiangquan is a relatively common *zi* (several are listed in Chinese biographical dictionaries who might have been the collector who treasured this stone, but none with any obvious connection to Shuzuo, whose name appears as the maker of the box). We may assume that Xinyu refers here to Pu Ru as the pine trees are very similar in style to his crisp, academic paintings of the same subject. However, it is not clear whether the inkstone is an earlier one, the coincidentally similar style of which inspired the gift to Pu Xinyu, or one made for him in his style. Xiangquan is not one of Xinyu's recorded names; since he is a very famous figure, had he used the name it would probably have been recorded, so we may assume that if the collector's inscription was not that of an earlier owner, it is that of an owner who acquired the piece subsequent to its gift to Xinyu, ie. quite recently. Since Xinyu died in 1963 and this stone was not acquired by its present owner until a decade later, there was time for it to have passed through the collection of an unidentified Xiangquan.

163

Seal

Soapstone, of the variety known as *tianhuang* of the *dongshi* ('frozen stone') class, of translucent, variegated, brilliant orange-yellow hues, the stone with cloud-like markings beneath the surface; carved as an oval seal, the plain, uncut seal forming a pedestal for two mythical beasts amidst clouds, one with a long, central bifid horn, rudimentary wings, and stylized flames emerging from the shoulders, its exaggeratedly long tail splitting into four formalized, curling sections, the other a phoenix-headed *chi* dragon with a similar tail and flaming haunches, the slight variations in the colour of the stone cleverly used to differentiate between beasts and clouds.
Late Ming or early Qing dynasty.
Height: 4.55 cm. Width: 4.85 cm.

壽山田黃凍石雕異獸印
晚明或清初，高4.55厘米，寬4.85厘米

Soapstone, a very soft material not at all valued as a precious material in the West (it is used there in a finely ground form as talcum powder) became one of the most highly valued of materials in China. To the educated Chinese this seal of *tianhuang* is far more desirable than if it were made of solid gold, aquamarine, amethyst or other precious stone. There are two main reasons for this. The first is that as seal carving developed into a major art form, the qualities of soapstone as an ideal, grainless stone hard enough to survive and make a crisp, clear impression, yet soft enough to carve directly and easily with a blade, became abundantly clear. Thus it attracted the attention of those who governed taste and bestowed 'value'. The second reason is that once attention was attracted, it became clear that the Chinese soil was host to abundant supplies of soapstone in a wide variety of distinctive colours, well marked, and of great beauty — ideal subject for the development of the particular form of connoisseurship so beloved of the Chinese scholar.

Identification of soapstone varieties is based largely upon colour and surface characteristics, which are then often related to a particular quarry, or have their source in a particular area; but it is the visual and tactile characteristics which are predominant in connoisseurship. This is a *tianhuang* ('field yellow') stone (see no. 54), but of a particularly valued kind known as *dongshi* ('frozen stone' or 'ice stone') because of its pattern of pale markings visible at the surface in the translucent golden matrix, like the opaque white markings in ice. The *dongshi* classification is purely visual and may be applied to a number of different stones. *Tianhuang* comes from the Shoushan region of Fujian and is found as random pebbles in the paddy fields along the banks of the streams of Shoushan.

This superbly carved seal has obviously been highly valued since the day it was made. The seal seems to have remained uncut, and the unusually undamaged and relatively unworn state of the carving suggest that it has been kept very carefully in a fitted case for much of its life. The carver was inspired to create an imaginative and powerful miniature sculpture, making brilliant use of slight variations in the colour of the stone and exhibiting a technical control of the medium second to none.

In common with so many scholars' arts the period from the 16th century to the end of the 17th century seems to represent a height for soapstone carving. This can be directly attributed to the wealth of skills that were encouraged and refined by literati deserting the ailing and corrupt Ming dynasty bureaucracy and declining to serve the Manchu Qing dynasty that replaced it. This created an artistic climate which inevitably spilled over into the lives of even those scholars who continued to serve the Court.

162

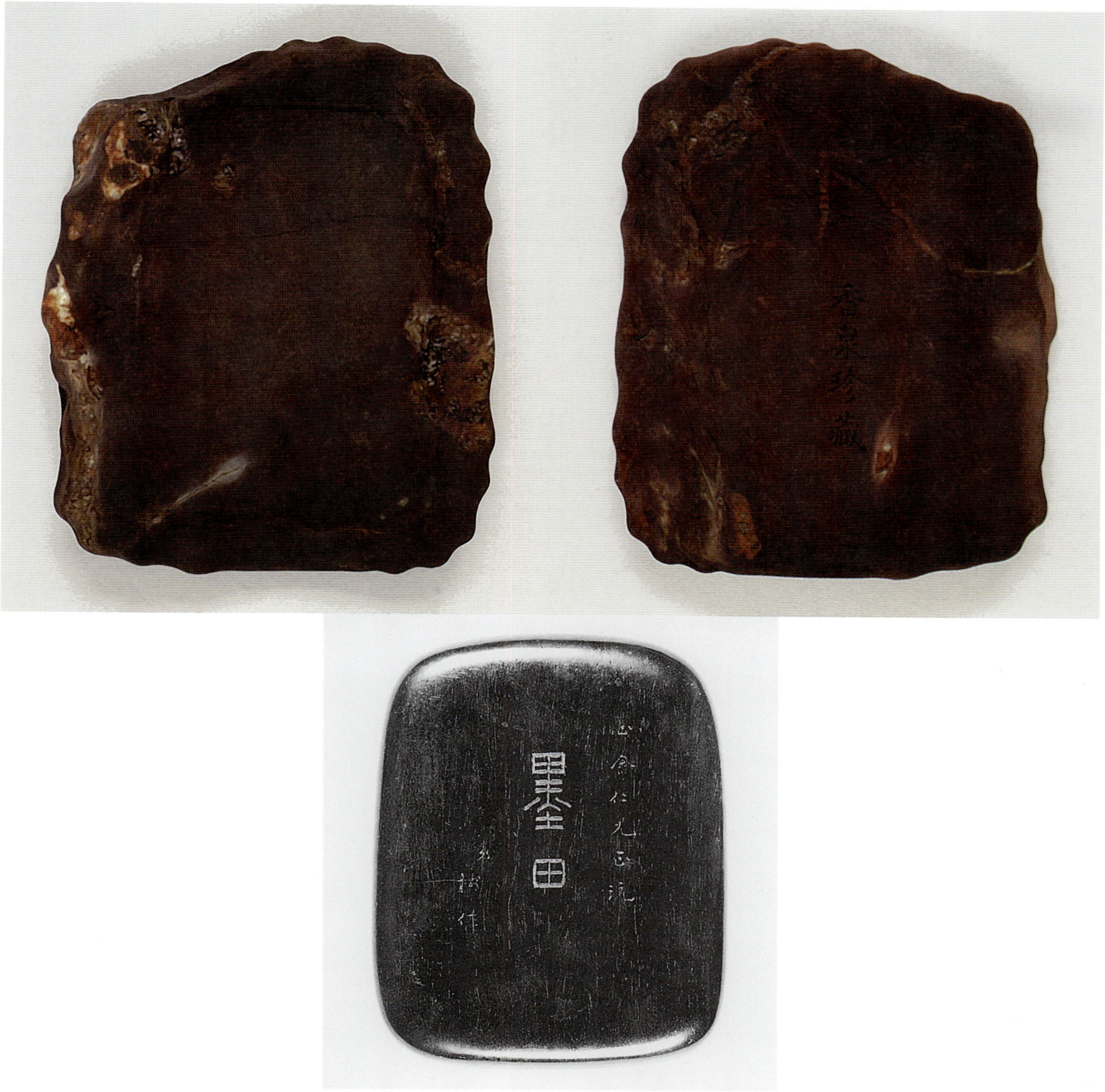

163

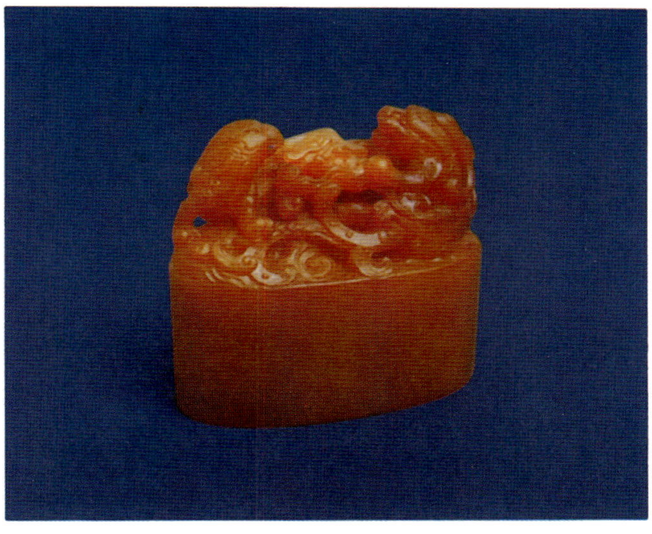

164

Seal

Zhou Bin

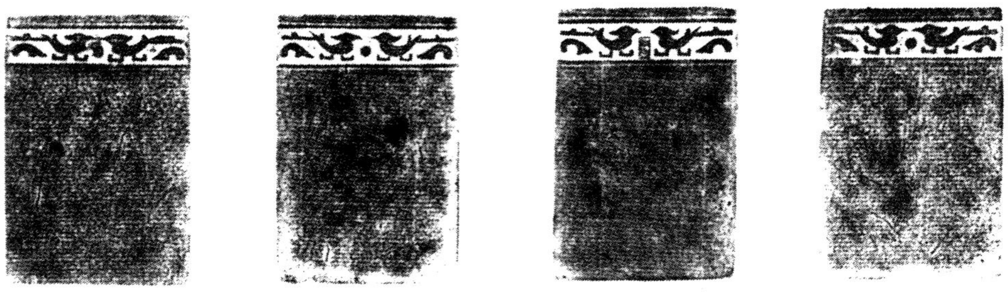

Soapstone, of even, pale, lime-green colour of the variety known as *baiguo* (ginkgo fruit), a Qingtian stone of Zhejiang province; the uncut seal serving as a pedestal for a crouching, stylized mythical beast, its wildly eccentric form decorated with incised patterns derived loosely from archaic bronze decoration, indicating fur and flaming haunches but also becoming purely formal decoration in places (the rear legs, for instance, decorated with *leiwen* which terminate in *ruyi-leiwen* 'boots'); a frieze around the top of the rectangular pedestal incised with a design, repeated four times, of two archaistic bird motifs set on a low relief plane against an incised ground of *leiwen;* the panel below the beast's mouth with a tiny rectangular relief seal bearing the signature *Shangjun* in seal script set between the two facing bird motifs.
Fujian province, mid-17th century.
7.6 cm × 3.35 cm × 3.35 cm.

青田白果青石雕鳥紋印•周彬製
十七世紀中葉,7.6×3.35×3.35厘米

Qingtian country in Zhejiang province is the second major source of soapstone in China, Shoushan being the largest (see no. 14). The materials from there are known as Qingtian stones. Quarrying began in the Song dynasty and originally the stone was only used for carving animals and minor sculptures. In the early Ming, however, the famous painter Wang Mian (1497-1576) is reputed to have started using *huayushi* ('flower-milk stone') from Qingtian to carve seals instead of the traditional materials of jade, rhinoceros horn, ivory, etc. Legend has it that this was the first time Qingtian stone and soapstone generally was used for seal carving (see no. 125). In the Jiajing period the famous seal carver Wen Peng (1498-1573) used Qingtian stone in carving seals and began a fashion for doing so. His disciple, He Zhen (active 1521-1566) continued to use the material. Through these two the popularity of certain translucent or semi-transparent stones from Qingtian was established, and mining increased accordingly. Although Shoushan produced large quantities of stone, Qingtian was reputedly the first to produce soapstones for carving.

As a material it is compact and slightly harder than Shoushan stones. It has a bright, lustrous appearance, and apparently makes a slight resonant sound when being cut, whereas the softer Shoushan stone does not. The Qingtian stones are generally greenish, but can tend to yellow and white, and there are even black, brown and red varieties. Quality varies a great deal. The usual Qingtian stone is somewhat similar in appearance to the *Laoling shi* ('Old Peak stone') of Shoushan.

This superbly carved seal is typical of the quality of Zhou Bin's work, and is characteristically signed in a tiny cartouche just below the knob platform. *Baiguo* stone is of one of the more highly valued Qingtian stones. For details of Zhou Bin (Shangjun) see nos. 43 and 44.

165

Guanyin and Acolyte

Zhou Bin

Soapstone, predominantly of the variety called *tianhuang,* the unusually large piece of material with typical *tianhuang* colour separated by a mottled opaque grey colour from a mottled, golden yellow colour used in the design on the reverse of the piece; the front carved with Guanyin, seated in the position of royal ease on a mythical animal, whose bushy tail curls around behind her; her foot rests on a lotus leaf growing in a wavy stream and she holds a spray in her hand; a sacred book rests on another lotus leaf at her side, while a young acolyte, his hands joined in prayer, bows respectfully to her from his position on another nearby lotus leaf; above the group a parrot flies and a monkey climbs on a branch; the reverse with a low relief design of bamboo and a pine tree growing against a gnarled rock, a relief title *Shiyu ping'an* ('It rains peace', referring to Guanyin's power to bring rain, peace and salvation with the sprinkling of holy water with a willow spray) and the signature *Shangjun,* all in seal script, on the face of the rock below the pine.

Fujian province, mid-17th century.
On the base is an added inscription recording the entry of the piece into the collection of Liu Yong (Liu Shian, 1719-1804) reading "In the *yimao* year (1795) my student Mr. Pan presented this as my birthday gift. Its carving is exquisite and the stone is moist, therefore I shall keep it. Recorded by Shian."
Set on a dark *zitan* wood stand, carved as a gnarled rock formation, which may be the original.
Height including stand: 10.5 cm.
Excluding stand: 8.9 cm × 6.2 cm × 4.1 cm.
Formerly in the Liu Shian collection.
Published: *The Literati Mode: Chinese Scholar Paintings, Calligraphy and Desk Objects,* No. 84.

壽山田黃石雕觀音侍童像•周彬製
十七世紀中葉,8.9×6.2×4.1厘米

For details on Zhou Bin (*zi:* Shangjun) see no. 43. For details on the collector, Liu Yong, see no. 159, also inscribed by him and from his collection. Here Liu Yong is revealed in a somewhat ungrateful light in dealing with a social inferior who has given him this delightful gift, identifying him in an offhand manner only as 'a certain Mr. Pan' and stating condescendingly that he has decided to retain the gift.

The works of Zhou Bin may be very broadly divided into three groups: small devotional and inspirational figure carvings such as, of no. 44, the seals of no. 43 and the mainly *tianhuang* carvings of small groups (of which this is the largest known). The latter, although displaying his quality of workmanship, seem to be in a broader style without the characteristic use of minutely engraved details. An interesting feature here is that the master sculptor, whose total command of his medium is shown in the superb figural group at the front of this piece, has chosen in a literati manner to adopt a cruder approach for the back. This is a clear demonstration of the transfer of the literati painting aesthetic of re-acquired naivety (see no. 32) to a three-dimensional object — the cruder, more awkward workmanship of the back arises out of choice rather than a lack of ability.

166

Seal

Yu Lifu

Bronze; cast as a seal, the knob in the form of a mythical animal with a dog-like head, scaled chest, flaming flanks and bushy tail, seated on a rectangular plinth, one side of which is inscribed "the *bingyin* year of the Tongzhi period (1866)" and the other "made by Yu Lifu"; the seal text reading "A thing of pleasure for the master of the Studio for Planting Bamboo and Flowers" in positive seal script.
1866.
4.6 cm × 3.5 cm × 3.5 cm.

青銅異獸印•余笠夫製
清同治丙寅(1866),4.6×3.5×3.5厘米

We can find no record of the maker, Yu Lifu. Lifu is probably an assumed name and suggests a hermit, but in the adoption of fanciful names, as in so much else, the Chinese did not feel at all bound by physical reality, and it would be perfectly acceptable for an urban bronzemaker to describe himself as a hermit.

What is particularly interesting about this seal is that were it not dated it would be thought to be quite a bit earlier. It is one of many bronze scholars' objects (including a wide range of paper weights, many of which are of figures or animals) which are nearly always called Ming, for no better reason than that some of them are. There can be no doubt that this group of objects was made from the Han period to the present day, and that blanket dating of even certain groups of them is misleading. We have shown here a group of these pieces which are reasonably datable from the Song dynasty onwards, but this example raises the likelihood of a great many of the so-called Ming paper weights being much younger.

It is likely that Yu Lifu made both the seal knob and cast the text, as the two would have been done at the same time.

164

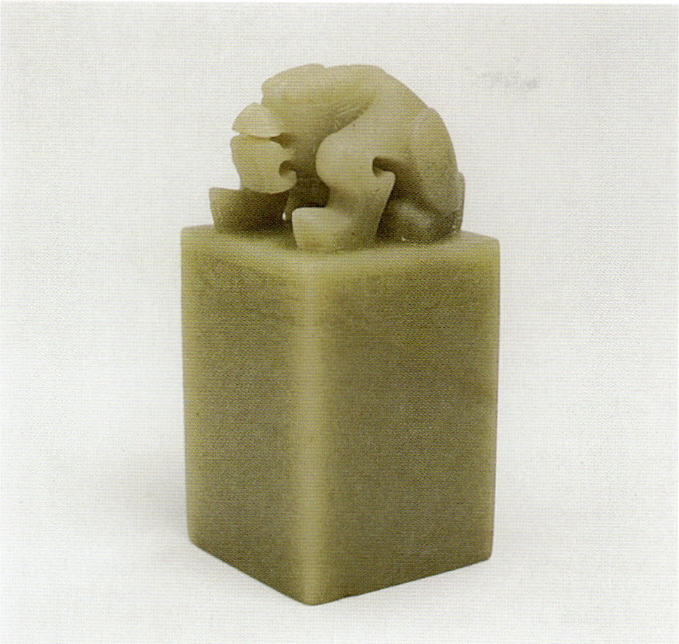

166

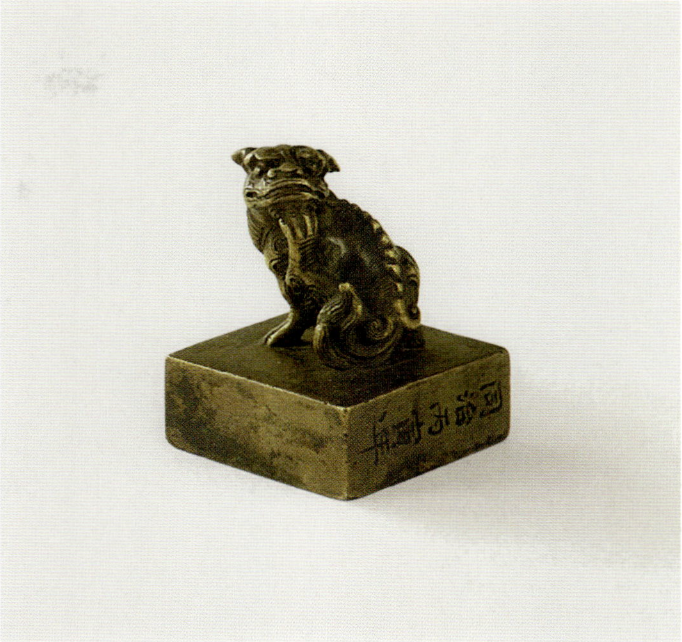

165

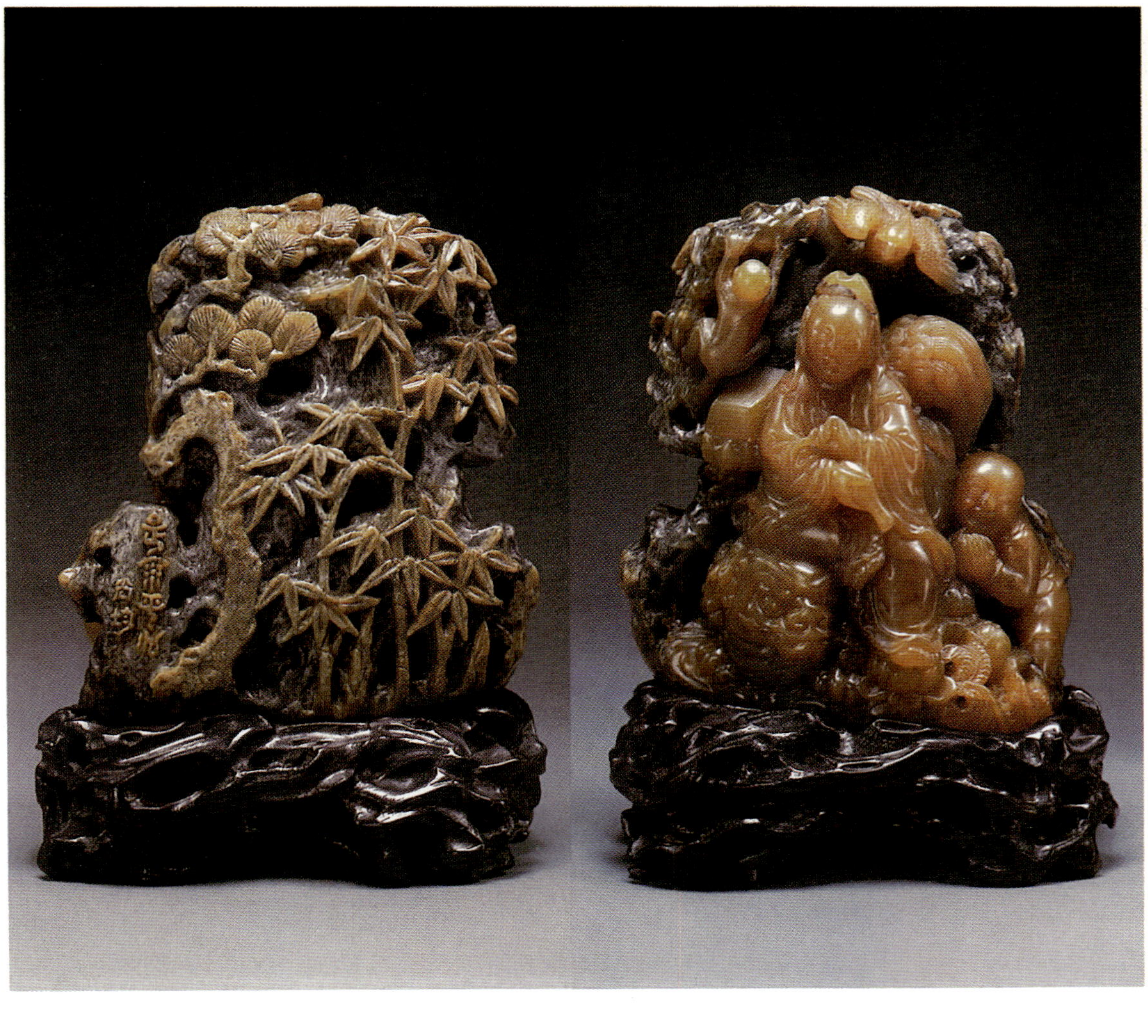

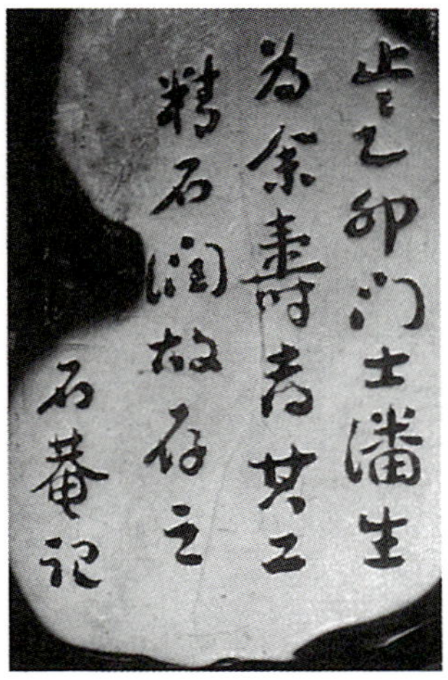

167

Water Vessel

Stoneware, of reddish-brown colour with lighter, textured speckling; a water vessel, one side with an applied *chi* dragon, one foot clutching the rim of the vessel as it pulls itself up to peer inside; the recessed base impressed with the seal *Chen Ziqi.*
Yixing, signature of Chen Ziqi, but probably early 20th century.
Height: 6.3 cm.
Formerly in an anonymous collection dispersed by Sotheby Parke Bernet (Hong Kong) Ltd., 24th May 1978, Lot 349.
Exhibited and illustrated: *Yixing Pottery,* no. 19.

宜興紫砂螭龍水丞•陳子畦銘
可能二十世紀初, 高6.3厘米

The earliest record we have been able to find of the name of Chen Ziqi appears in 1786:[1] "Chen Ziqi is the best at imitating Xu [Youquan — a Wanli potter]; his works are treasured by people nowadays. It was said that he was the father of Chen Mingyuan [a potter of the Kangxi period]." In 1788, the same writer admits that the dates of a group of earlier Yixing potters are not known, and confirms that he is not sure if Chen Ziqi was Chen Mingyuan's father: "Chen Ziqi, Xu Cijing, Mengchen, Zheng Ninghou were all famous craftsmen of Yixing. However, their periods are not known. It was said that (Chen) Ziqi was the father of (Chen Ming)yuan. Chen Ziqi is believed to be the father of the famous early Qing potter Chen Mingyuan."[2] This tentative information was taken by Li Jingkang and Zhang Hong and repeated, with the addition of a probable Ming date: "...judging from the style of his works, Chen Ziqi is of the Ming dynasty."[3] They add, apparently judging from two pieces only, that his works "are mostly done in purple clay with thin body and exquisite workmanship."

Terese Tse Bartholomew, in *I-Hsing Ware,* illustrates a pumpkin-shaped teapot bearing his signature (although the last character of his name is there printed as *hsi xi*). She mentions that he was active during the early 17th century and was famous for both the lightness of his pots and his fine craftsmanship, basing her information on the 1937 work of Li and Zhang. Four pieces with the seal of Chen Ziqi are illustrated in the 1981 Hong Kong Museum of Art exhibition mentioned above (nos. 16-19). They are a crab on a leaf, the same pumpkin-shaped teapot illustrated by Bartholomew, a pomegranate-shaped water dropper, and this vessel. Another brush pot, with applied flowering branches, was published as Lot 348, in the above-mentioned Sotheby's catalogue of Yixing wares. All five pieces bear the same impressed seal, in positive seal script.

Li and Zhang record two works: a small purple clay round teapot, with spout missing and replaced, and a large purple clay teapot in the shape of a flower basket, with thin body and incised three-character signature in regular script on the base. A further piece, a black clay water-chestnut, is illustrated by Pang Yuanji.[4]

This waterpot is faultlessly formed and elegantly proportioned. The *chi* dragon has the life and movement that arises only out of impeccable technique combined with careful observation of life. This piece is by an artist in total control of his medium and represents the height of the Yixing potter's art. However, we question the traditional belief that this summit was reached in the late Ming and early Qing dynasties. We believe that further research into the field of Yixing pottery is likely to reveal that the best Yixing pieces were created in the first half of the 20th century when highly sophisticated works of art were made to superb standards of craftsmanship by a group of potters centred in Shanghai. These potters may well have completely altered subsequent perception of the pattern of Yixing production by using the names of recorded potters of old (such as Chen Mingyuan, Chen Zhongmei, Chen Ziqi, etc.) and producing a whole range of superbly crafted wares bearing their names which bore no relation to their original output.

That such potters were active cannot be doubted; the older generation of living Yixing potters includes Gu Jingzhou who was one of them, and the late Jiang Yenting is known to have made superb pieces bearing the mark of Chen Mingyuan. What remains in doubt is the extent to which they invented several hundred years of Yixing output, and the balance between genuine examples by the famous early potters and their own pieces. What is clear, however, is that whatever the outcome of this further research, the group of exquisitely crafted scholarly objects represented by this example are masterpieces from the height of Yixing production, regardless of when they were made and the motives behind their manufacture.

The elegant confusion of Chinese connoisseurship over the centuries has given rise to the recording of famous artists whose works could no longer be found, even centuries ago. This has resulted in a variety of responses from artists, patrons and connoisseurs and a complex pattern of works of art ranging from commercial forgeries to lofty moments of artistic expression. While it would be convenient if the relationship between motive and expression were constant (i.e. the commercial forgeries worthless craft, and the loftier moments artistic masterpieces) nothing in Chinese connoisseurship is so simple. Many an artistic masterpiece may have been born of the basest motives of patrons and merchants, and lofty motives are no guarantee of fine art. Where patronage and motive are separated from production (so often the case with Chinese arts) it is possible for a group of artists to rise to unsurpassed heights while satisfying the requirements of their patrons for spurious signatures.

In the case of the Yixing potters of the 20th century, we believe it is likely that they were encouraged to create a range of scholarly objects in response to the taste of a connoisseur or group of connoisseurs (regardless of their motives) and that they fulfilled this brief with astonishing success. The fact that they used the names of earlier potters does not alter the relevance of their contribution to the Yixing tradition; it merely confuses it temporarily, and leaves a fresh generation of connoisseurs the intriguing pleasures of sorting out the details. This process was recently begun in earnest.[5]

1. *Yangxian Mingtao Lu* ('Famous Pottery of Yangxian' — Yangxian is Yixing), by Wu Qian, dated 51st year of Qianlong.
2. *Tuxi Keyu* ('Guest Discussions of Tuxi'), by Wu Qian, 1788.
3. *Yangxian Shahu Tukao* ('Illustrated Catalogue of Yixing Pottery') by Li Jingkang and Zhang Hong, published without the illustrations in 1937.
4. *Xuzhai Mingtao Tulu* ('Catalogue of Famous Pottery in the Xuzhai Collection' — his own collection) probably published in the 1930s. It contains rubbings, with marks and inscriptions, of 81 items bearing such famous names as Gong Chun (two pieces), Shi Dabin (four pieces), Chen Mingyuan (35 pieces), Yang Pengnian (10 pieces) and the one piece by Chen Ziqi. Pang sold some of his pieces to the Freer Gallery, Washington in 1939 (see *The World's Great Collections of Oriental Ceramics,* Vol. 9, Kodansha, 1975).
5. See *Milestones in the Identification of Yixing Pottery,* where Gerard Tsang deals with excavated and documented works to re-establish the history of the development of Yixing pottery, in *Antiquary* magazine, July 1986, Hong Kong (in Chinese).

168

Brush Pot

Hu Wenming

Bronze, inlaid with silver and partly gilt; decorated with a continuous design of various dwellings and gardens in a mountainous landscape setting in which three officials exchange greetings or farewells; two scholars sit in conversation by a mountain pavilion, a dog lies guarding a rustic retreat, and a group of dismounted soldiers wait with their horses beyond a distant bank of clouds; the lip with a single band of inlaid silver continuous *leiwen;* the lip and foot rims and certain details gilt; the interior and base undecorated.
Yunjian, *circa* 1560 - *circa* 1620.
Height: 13.1 cm. Diameter: 12.3 cm.
Published: *Chinese Metalwork of the Hu Wenming Group,* p.60, no. 37 (where the dimensions are incorrectly stated).

鎏金嵌銀線雕山水人物青銅筆筒•胡文明製
明末(約1560-1620), 高13.1厘米,
直徑12.3厘米

A number of unsigned pieces may, with varying degrees of confidence, be attributed to Hu Wenming on the basis of style, decorative features and methods of manufacture. After we attributed this piece to Hu Wenming in the above publication, Paul Moss published the only signed brush pot known by the artist[1] and disagreed with our attribution, suggesting instead that this piece was an 18th century work after the style of Hu Wenming. The bowl signed by another maker, probably also of the late Ming dynasty, and the incense tool vase which although unsigned is also probably by him (see no. 152) — both of which might otherwise have passed for Hu's work — show that a definite attribution to Hu Wenming here is not possible. However, we believe it is highly unlikely to be Qing. The style is typical of the late Ming period, as is the thickness of the silver wire inlay and the method of construction, with the base made separately from the cylindrical form; indeed the latter are two features of Hu Wenming's works. It is also interesting to note the unusual bulge around the base of the vessel — a feature which also appears on the signed Hu Wenming brush pot, and on a few wood brush pots which appear to be of considerable age. Acknowledging the tentative nature of the attribution to Hu Wenming, we remain convinced of a late Ming date.

That Hu made so few brush pots is probably due to his fame as a maker of incense wares. His brush pots and other pieces such as spoons, *ruyi* sceptres, bells, etc.[2] were probably made as occasional commissions for scholars. It was not unusual for an artist to specialize in certain wares and rarely branch out from them, as there was little demand for a wide range of matching objects. The consistency of mind requiring a matching set of scholars' objects was at odds with the scholars' aesthetic. Certain materials gained popularity at different times for certain wares, and brush pots were most frequently made out of wood, although they do, of course, exist in many other materials.

Apart from Hu's popular line of archaism, he also made a number of objects with other subjects. Flora and fauna with meaning to the literati were often chosen, and here we seem to have a specific scene or scenes depicted, perhaps from a popular novel, play or legend.

1. *Emperor, Scholar, Artisan, Monk: The Creative Personality in Chinese Works of Art,* no. 127.
2. For a list of all pieces known at the time see *Chinese Metalwork of the Hu Wenming Group.*

167

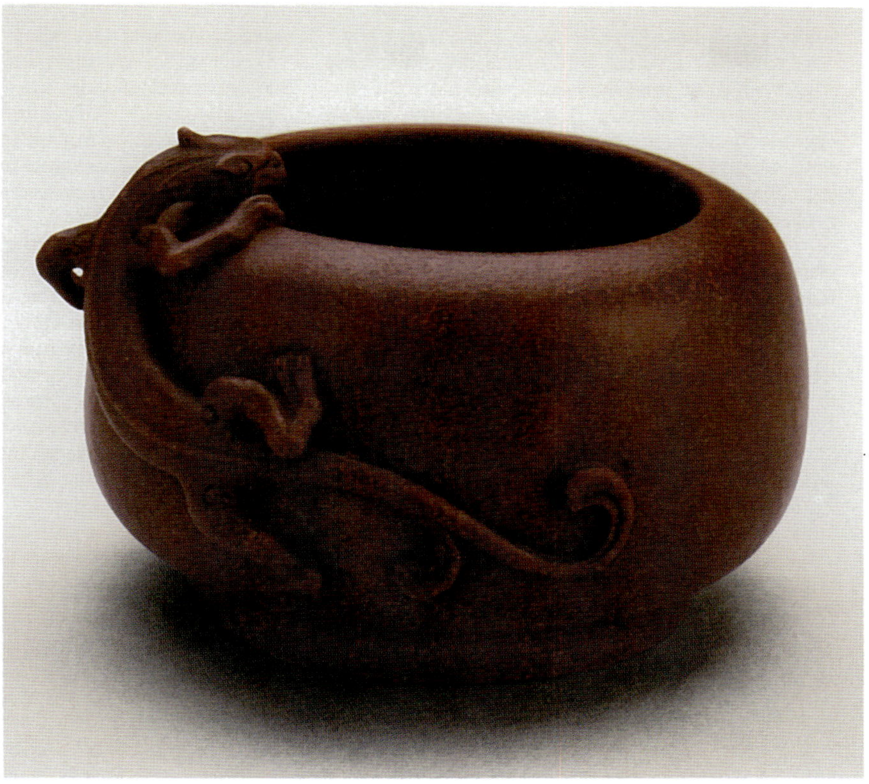

168

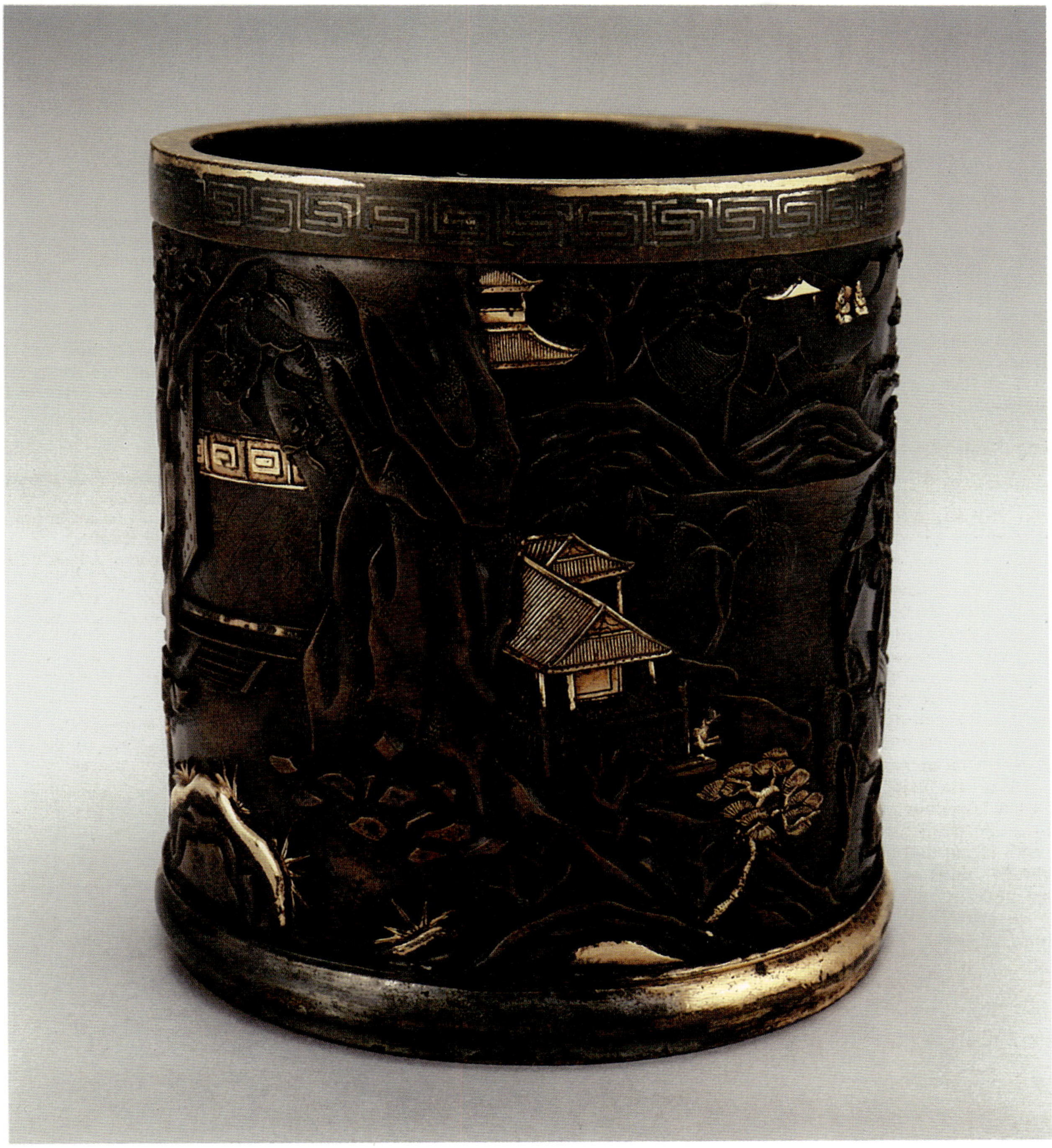

169
Crouching Deer

Bronze; the surface patinated to a deep reddish-brown colour with some black encrustration and with a few gold splashes; a vessel (possibly intended to be used as an incense burner) in the form of an alert, crouching deer; the surface with a few patches of gold splashes painted on; the copper cover (probably not original) with a knob in the form of a rolled scroll.
Late Qing or earlier.
Height: 15.7 cm. Length: 17.1 cm.

灑金青銅鹿
晚清或較早，高15.7厘米，長17.1厘米

Although this would seem to be a somewhat impractical incense burner, we cannot imagine what other function it may have served unless it was intended purely for aesthetic appreciation and the opening in the back was no more than a vague reference to archaic animal *zun* forms (see no. 127). Regardless of its use, it is a delightful work of art in its own right. The deer, apart from its implications of the wilderness and escape from the dusty world, was a familiar companion of the God of Longevity, Shou Lao, making it an auspicious subject.

The dating of this piece is particularly uncertain in the light of the results of a thermoluminescence test at the Oxford Research Laboratory for Archaeology of a sample of its core (a considerable amount of which remains inside the vessel from its original casting). The result suggested a late 19th century date for the piece. Similar results were recorded for two other pieces tested at the same time, also from core samples; a seated figure of a dignitary with inlaid silver decoration which would otherwise be confidently dated to the 16th century, and another standing bronze deer of quite different style to this example for which a late Ming date would also be widely acceptable.[1] The results seem to contradict stylistic features and degrees of wear and patination to such an extent (and on three widely different pieces which have been independently dated by a number of experts to earlier periods) that we feel justified in reserving judgement for the time being despite our respect for the TL test and the excellent record enjoyed by the Research Laboratory for Archaeology.[2]

There are two features of this sculpture which are particularly interesting. The work is unusually realistic in the details of muzzle, antlers, hooves and body shape for Chinese bronze animal sculpture, and we know of no comparable piece. The gold splashing (painted on with gold lacquer rather than gilded in the manner of other gold-splashed bronzes) is remarkably restrained and in larger patches than normal, appearing only on three legs, one rear haunch, the edges of the ears and over one eye. The realism is certainly possible for the 19th century, but it is also typical of the Southern Song period, when hand-in-hand with an intense interest in archaism went a delight in close observation of nature and its representation in art. The restrained and atypical painted gold splashing would seem highly unlikely for the late Qing, when gold splashing had long been fashionable and its even distribution as a decorative surface a set tradition. One would expect a late Qing metalsmith either to leave it undecorated or to splash it overall. The surface patination, which includes a heavy layer of what appears to be encrusted incense smoke, is inconclusive evidence in relation to a single piece; however, it would suggest a greater age than a century.

In the absence of the TL test we would entertain the possibility of a Southern Song date, but in any case be confident in dating it to well before the late 19th century; in the light of it the question of period must remain open. The widely different styles of the three objects tested present us with an interesting prospect: if the tests of the core samples accurately indicate the date of manufacture of the bronzes then we must reconsider the dating of a whole range of later Chinese bronzes.

1. The test certificate numbers and results are as follows. This vessel: 381f78, 19.4.83 — result 70-150 years of age. Standing bronze deer crossing a stream: 381f80, 19.4.83 — result 80-150 years of age. Bronze seated figure with silver inlay: 381f79, 19.4.83 — result 120-200 years of age.)
2. One of the pieces called into question by these tests is no. 138. It was not the subject of a test as there is no remaining core sample, but the seated dignitary on a rockwork base inlaid with silver wire design was, and is stylistically so close to this Buddhist acclyte as to be sensibly attributed to the same hand.

170
Bi Symbol

Nephrite, of mottled and flawed, transclucent grey-green colour; a *bi* symbol carved with an identical design on each side of an outer band of four *taotie*, their curvilinear bodies extending symmetrically out from either side of their heads, separated by a thin border of rope design from a broad inner area of raised hexagonal units.
Western Han dynasty.
Diameter: 23.7 cm.
Diameter of central hole: 2.4 cm.

玉雕饕餮紋璧
西漢(公元前206-公元8)，直徑23.7厘米，
中孔直徑2.4厘米

The influential minority have, over many centuries, collected and treasured relics of their own past and delighted in connoisseurship.

The earliest reference to connoisseurship goes back to Confucius, where the master identified an inscribed arrow by relating it to historical events in the Shang dynasty.[1] As early as the Qin dynasty there is a record of the identification of motifs on archaic bronzes.[2] The earliest extant records of a major collection date back to the Tang dynasty, but long before that collectors acquired and treasured works of art from the past, both recent and distant.

Jade was always valued as a material, and as time passed a subtle overlay of symbolism was invested in the material iteself. In archaic times (generally considered to cover the period from earliest times to the end of Han) jade was used as personal ornament, for various functional tools and fittings, for ritual and symbolic use and as insignia of rank. It was, therefore, little wonder that later collectors treasured jade artifacts. In the view of later connoisseurs when creating a hierarchy of value in those objects which might be collected, calligraphy and paintings came first (seal carving was later included as an extension of calligraphy, and rubbings of calligraphy carved in stone were always so considered) followed by ancient bronzes and jades. Below that came the various other possible fields of collecting.

From the Neolithic period onwards the *bi* was considered to be a symbol of heaven and the afterworld. According to William Watson[3] in the 3rd century BC the compilers of ritual texts, who drew on ancient materials, described the *bi* as a symbol of the sky appropriate for the emperor's use in performing the sacrifice to heaven. In tombs of the Warring States period they are found placed at either side of the head and under each knee of the corpse. They also appear to have been used as symbols of rank. Among the 'six sacrificial utensils' to be held by the lowest of the feudal lords, earls and barons, were *gubi* and *pubi* (*bi* discs with different forms of decoration). That such pieces were highly valued by later collectors is attested to by their appearance in certain books over the centuries (the *Guyu Tu*, an illustrated description of ancient jades, compiled in 1341; the *Guyu Tukao,* an illustrated study of jades in the collection of Wu Dazheng, 1889, and the *Guyu Tupu,* purporting to be the catalogue of the Song Emperor Xiaozong (1163-1189) but probably an 18th century forgery). Their popularity is also seen in the endless commercial fakes made in recent centuries and in the exciting archaistic versions made in response to literati dominated taste over the past milleneum (see no. 13).

The dating of this example is based upon a similar *bi* excavated in 1977 from a Western Han tomb at Hongtushan, in Heze county, Shandong province[4] and upon three more examples of this group excavated in 1968 from the tomb of the princess Dou Wan, datable to the late 2nd century BC, at Mancheng, Hebei province.[5]

1. See *Zhongguo Lishi Wenwu Jiandingshi Kaishu,* by Liu Dongduan.
2. See no. 73 for a Qin text on the identification of the *taotie* motif.
3. *The Genius of China,* p.102.
4. *Kaogu Xuebao* 1983 no. 4. 20, fig. 1.
5. Excavation notes in *Kaogu* p.8, illustrated in *The Genius of China,* p.102, nos. 143-148.

169

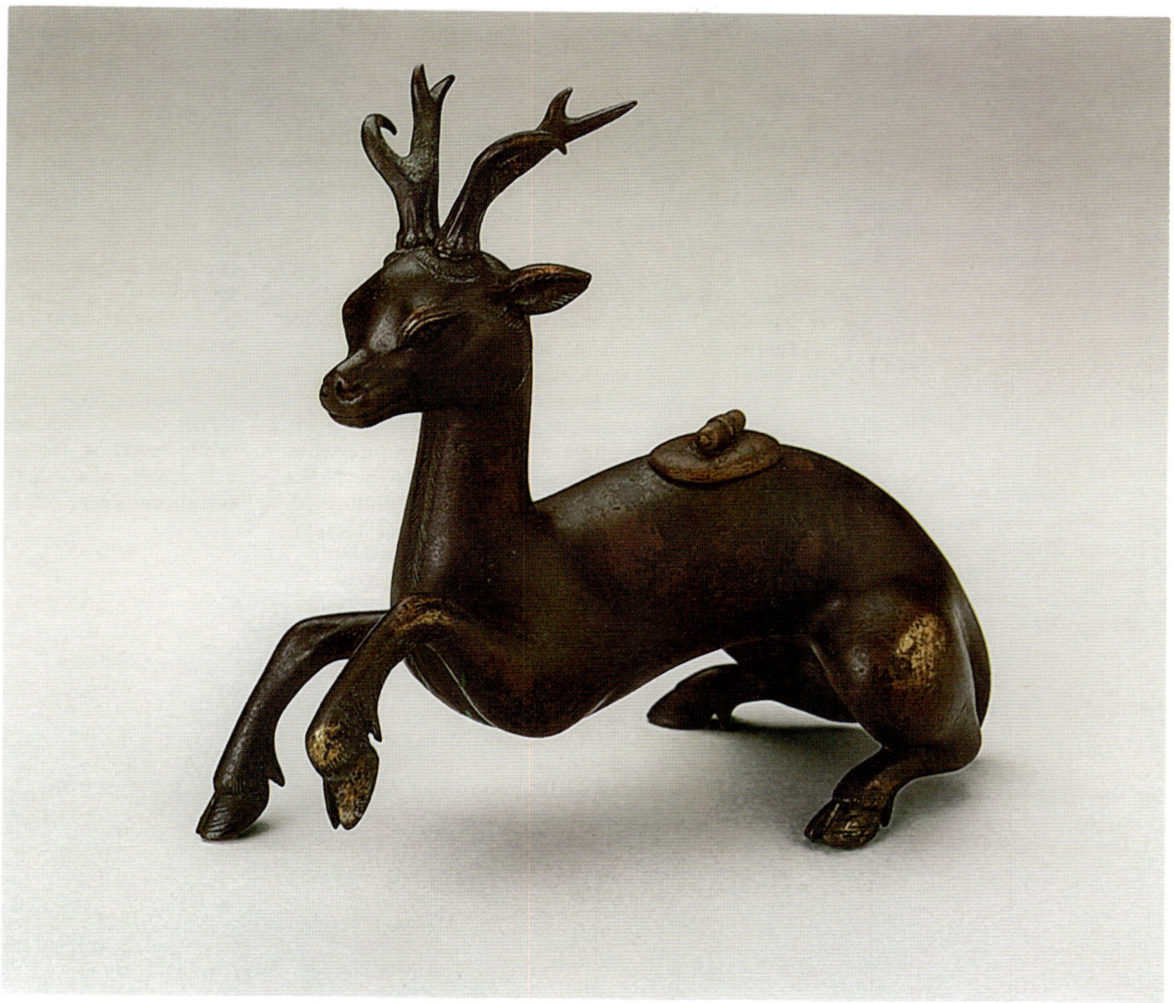

170

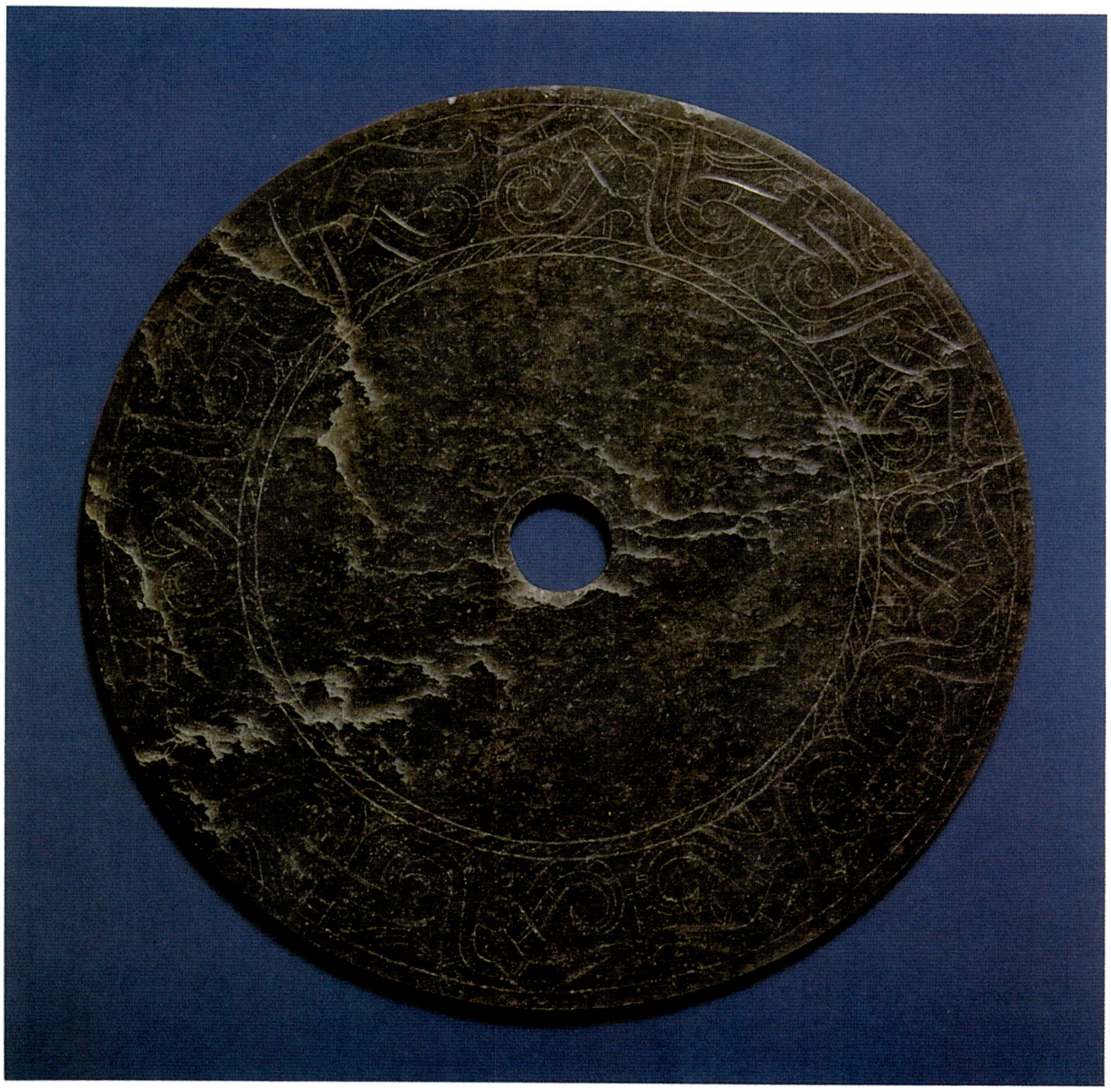

171

Ritual Food Vessel

Bronze, with variegated grey-green and green patina; a *gui* ritual food vessel with two handles in the form of bovine-looking self-consuming *taotie* decorated with abstract scrolling patterns based on *kui* dragons, dividing the body decoration into two symmetrical sides, each with an upper band of a central, raised *taotie* flanked by two raised whorl motifs, all interspersed with highly stylized *kui* dragons above a broad band of highly stylized *taotie* divided by a central raised ridge, which design is echoed in a narrow band around the deep, flared foot; the interior with a single pictogram; all crisply cast.
Shang dynasty, probably 13th century BC.
Height: 14.95 cm.
Width including handles: 27.8 cm.
Published: *Bulletin of the Museum of Far Eastern Antiquities,* Stockholm, 1959, Vol. 31, pl. 9b; *Weltkunst aus Privatbesitz,* Chinese Section, pl. 32, Cat. no. 53; *Bulletin of the Museum of Far Eastern Antiquities,* Stockholm, 1944, Vol. 16; *Some Early Chinese Bronze Masters,* no. 1G.

青銅饕餮紋簋
商代, 可能公元前十三世紀, 高14.95厘米,
寬連把27.8厘米

Over the centuries the Chinese scholar has devoted a great deal of his connoisseurship to ancient bronzes. They combine technical mastery with ritual significance and mysterious symbolism, and provide a vital key in their pictograms and inscriptions to the birth of the written language. As an art form they represent the perceived 'Golden Age' of antiquity to the post-archaic culture. Their dominant role in connoisseurship and in later artistic output may be seen in the very large number of archaistic arts derived from them, and in the ubiquitous motifs which appear on a wide range of Chinese arts and crafts, right down to the humblest of modern-day restaurant crockery.

The ritual bronzes of antiquity would have been treasured from the day they were made, but they began to take on a different signficance for the connoisseur as archaeological evidence of the past. Once archaic forms of written language had become obscure and little understood (a conscious intention of Qin Shihuang in his effort to unify the empire when he instigated the infamous burning of the books in the 3rd century BC) and once the dignity of great age had been added to bronze surfaces, what was always valued became irresistible. Accidental and later systematic archaeology supplied scholars with these treasures of the past, and they were collected almost as a part of the essential refinement of the scholar. No educated, refined gentleman was without a knowledge and appreciation of ancient bronzes, even if he was not a collector. It is probably fair to say that no other single art form has exerted such an all pervading influence over Chinese art.

This *gui* was originally a ritual food vessel, although the form was later popularly adopted for incense burners (see no. 73, for instance, which has similar handles and decoration around the upper body). Its crispness of casting, integrity of design, condition and patination make it a classic example of the height of the Shang bronzemaker's art. Particularly intriguing is the abstraction of the elements of design, where the *taotie* mask of the main body decoration has been all but transformed into a swirling abstract pattern with great independer energy, held to its figurative purpose by little more than the two raised and rounded eyes, their slit pupils staring menacingly at the viewer.

A comparison between this vessel and its archaistic equivalent (no. 73) is interesting in demonstrating the important point that archaism is an independent art form based on the archaic, rather than a poor relation copying it. The two, while based on the same forms and decorations, use subtly, often distinctly different languages of communication, for largely different purposes.

172

Ritual Wine Vessel

Bronze, of smooth, black colour with applied green and brownish-red patination; a *jiao* with its original cover; the cover with a roof-shaped finial decorated with *taotie* masks on each side, the cover with a more elaborate version of the same design on each side of the sloping, curved form, a pictogram cast beneath one sloping side; the main vessel with an upper band of stylized, facing bird motifs above *taotie* masks, repeated on each side; one side with a handle made up of a bovine-looking self-consuming *taotie,* its inverted body also acting as the central ridge or nose around which the main decoration is centred; a pictogram beneath the handle repeating that of the lid.
Shang dynasty (the dating of this piece is consistent with a TL test of a core sample taken from inside the handle by the Research Laboratory for Archaeology, Oxford, Certificate no. 366 K74, dated 4th July 1985).
Height overall: 25.5 cm.
Maximum width: 17.5 cm.
Formerly in the K. Kitazawa collection, Tokyo.

青銅饕餮紋角·亞字父丁銘
商代, 總高25.5厘米, 寬17.5厘米

From the Chinese scholar/collector's point of view this bronze could hardly be more interesting. Apart from its rare form, its state of wear indicates that it has either never been buried, as was customary with ritual bronzes, or has been excavated so long ago that all traces of burial have been worn off. The patination is apparently entirely false, and appears to be very similar to the induced and applied patination of some later archaistic bronzes of the Song or post-Song period.

The wear on this vessel is entirely consistent with centuries of handling. All the places one would naturally tend to hold it are considerably more worn than the less accessible areas, with certain exposed areas of the main body being so worn that the original relief decoration is almost completely missing, blending in with the surface plane. The piece has obviously been handed down from collector to collector and much handled.

At what stage the patination was added is impossible to judge from the visual evidence alone. Chinese bronze makers of the Song and post-Song period were well aware of various means of inducing and applying patination to match that of antiquity, and having so little criteria available for the accurate dating of archaism, dating archaistic patination is impossible. However, the patination on this vessel seems to have some age and is itself worn, so it would not be fanciful to suggest that it might have been put on as early as the Ming period. It has certain similarities in the applied areas of 'malachite' encrustation with the patination on a group of inlaid bronzes probably of the late Ming period (see no. 127). Whether it was put on in response to an earlier disbelief in its period or to enhance its value, we shall never know, but from the point of view of literati works of art it remains one of the most fascinating of early bronzes.

171

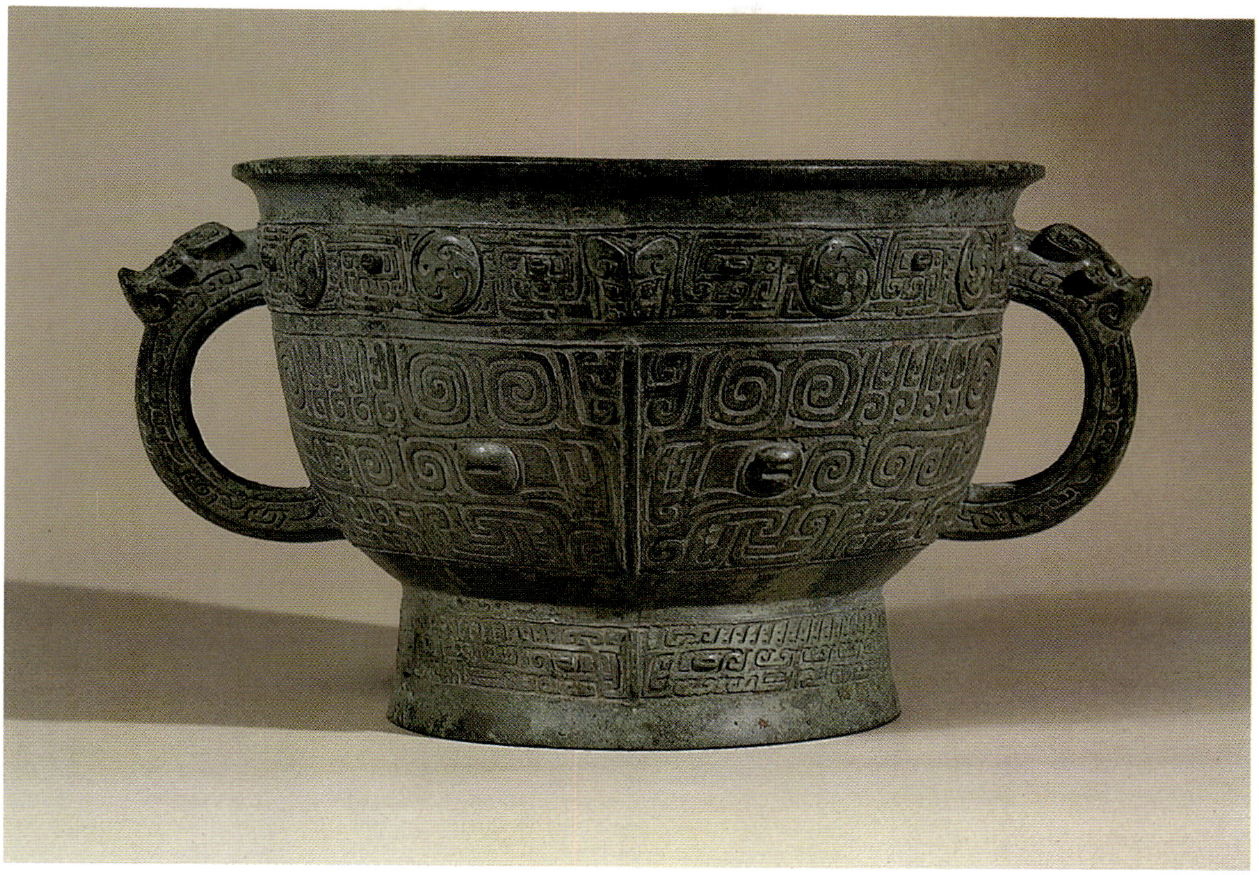

172

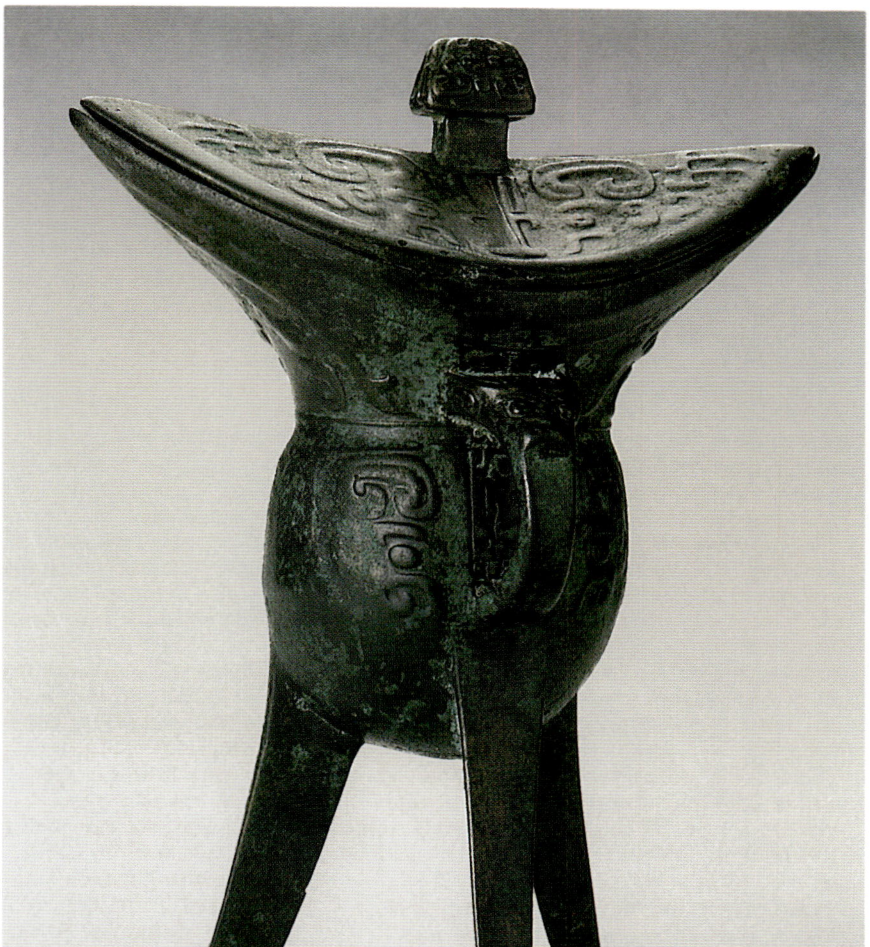

173

Water Vessel

Gourd; grown into an eleven-part sectional primary mould to form an octagonal water vessel, the eight curving faces each decorated with one of the Eight Daoist Immortals; set with an ivory lip.
Probably first half of the Qing dynasty.
Height 5.7 cm.
Published: *Chinese Decorated Gourds,* p.55, no. 8.

葫蘆模製八仙水丞
可能清代早期，高5.7厘米

The ivory neck on this piece appears to be later than the vessel. It is possible that this was a scholar's plaything (see no. 61) the stem of which was damaged, and thereafter it was turned into a water vessel for use in conjunction with a ladle.

In the holistic view of a culture governed by Absolute conciousness physical damage to the art object need not detract from its aesthetic appeal. The impermanence of all material phenomena is recognized and works of art, like people, are appreciated for their personalities regardless of external circumstances.

Here the Daoist symbolism of the gourd (see no. 61) is enhanced by the depiction of the Eight Daoist Immortals, also known as the 'Eight Inebriated Immortals' or the 'Eight Immortals of the Wine-cup'. This is a group of people who, for various reasons and at various times, became Immortals. Their legend as a group is probably a product of the Song or Yuan period. Three of them are historical personages, while the rest come from fables and romances.[1]

1. For further details see *Dictionary of Chinese Mythology,* pp.341-352.

174

Brush Pot

Wood, *huanghuali,* of beautifully figured orange and brown colours; the slightly waisted form carved from a single piece of wood with a small plug in the centre of the base made from a separate piece of *hongmu.*
Late Ming or Qing dynasty, the waisting probably a recent enhancement.
Height 18.9 cm. Diameter at top: 19.1 cm.
Published: *Wood From the Scholar's Table,* p.25, no. 1.

黄花梨筆筒
晚明或清，高18.9厘米，頂直徑19.1厘米

The dating of plain brush pots is largely based on hopeful guesswork. Made from a single section of hollowed-out tree trunk, they were the simplest form to make, and have been produced for several centuries. A vogue for plain wood brush pots of this kind may have sprung up in the Ming dynasty, but it certainly continued well into the late Qing period — as the enormous quantities of examples of all sizes and types, in a wide variety of states of repair and patination, attest. Dating theories exist founded on the fact that certain woods were supposed to have been exhausted by certain times, but this is only a general guideline. Systems of logging and distribution throughout the Orient in late Ming and Qing times might have meant that even if a wood was supposedly exhausted, logs might have remained stored or fresh sources found. All these variables make it impossible to judge accurately whether a plain wood brush pot is more likely to be Ming or Qing. We may be able to judge age by degree of wear and patination (although modern habits of completely cleaning and re-polishing them, sanding away any damage or wear, have confused even this minimal aid), but how many centuries of age are involved is almost impossible to ascertain.

Nor should it matter too much. The great appeal of a plain wood brush pot is in its form, its markings and colouring, and its association with the literati. We believe that the waisted form of this brush pot, which is very unusual, is a recent attempt to gild the lily. However, the piece of wood is so sensational and the resulting form attractive enough to allow it still to speak powerfully regardless of this visual editing. Its delights far exceed the importance of accurately dating it.

175

Fang Shi Mopu

Fang Yulu

Printed book, woodblock; six *juan*/eight volumes, irregular columns and characters; a compendium of essays and prefaces by contemporaries of Fang Yulu followed by some 400 illustrations of ink designs.
Fang Yulu (compiler).
Date of original edition, *circa* 1588/9;
Meiyintang Ji edition (date unknown).
Printed page size: 14 cm × 15.1 cm.
Contained in brocade case inscribed in ink with the title *Fang Shi Mopu.*

方氏墨譜•方于魯著
美蔭堂集版，頁大14×15.1厘米

The *Fang Shi Mopu* bears a preface dated to 1583 and is thought to have been first printed about 1588 or 1589. Its success apparently led to further printings during the late Ming and perhaps even early Qing periods, some of which exhibited discrepancies in the blocks suggesting that its popularity led to the cutting of later sets of blocks. This edition seems to be taken from the original set of blocks, suggesting an early date. Early impressions of the first edition are said to bear the red imprints of Fang's own seal. For the original edition Fang employed two of the leading artists of his time, Ding Yunpeng and Wu Tingyu, and the woodblock carver Huang Shouyen (a member of the Huang clan of Huizhou, famous in its day for woodblock carving).

Fang Yulu (original name Da'ao; *zi*: Jianyuan, fl. 1570-1619) was one of the two most celebrated late Ming inkmakers — due in part to his feud with the other, Cheng Junfang (see no. 38), which was partly responsible for this book and the rival *Cheng Shi Moyuan* published nearly two decades later. According to Cheng, Fang Yulu when impoverished had been taken in by Cheng and taught the art of inkmaking, only to master the skills astonishingly well and set up his own rival concern. This started a feud which involved much of the literary circle of the time in the resulting scandals. Like Cheng, Fang mixed with the scholarly elite and was a member of the most prestigious literary and social club, the exclusive Fenggan Society — a fact that must have been bitterly resented by Cheng, his former benefactor, who denounced him as an ingrate, fraud and sycophant. Fang was also a poet of some note, and was interested in antiquities, travelling widely. His son, Fang Jiashu, followed in the family business and became a celebrated inkmaker in his own right.[1]

The *Fang Shi Mopu* was exhibited and discussed in *Chinese Rare Books in American Collections,* p.102, no. 29, which is also an excellent introduction to the subject of Chinese printed books in general, containing essays by a number of experts. To a culture that placed so much emphasis on scholarship for more than two and a half millenia, the written word in communication was of vital importance in China. Earliest attempts at transmitting and storing information in the written language were, of course, by hand, which severely limited distribution. To overcome this problem various methods of printing were developed. The earliest was in the form of rubbings, where original texts were engraved in stone and rubbings taken from them onto paper, allowing potential for considerable circulation of a single text (see no. 28). This method appears to have been in use by the early 6th century and the earliest extant rubbing has a preface dated to 653.[2]

The other form of printing developed by the Chinese was with carved wood blocks, a natural enough development from the rubbing method of printing from stone blocks, which later evolved into systems using movable type. According to *Chinese Rare Books in American Collections* there exists evidence of simple printing in the 8th century, sophisticated printing in the 9th and a flourishing printing trade by the 10th century. By the beginning of the 11th century printed books were common among educated Chinese. A good deal of this early activity in printing related to the transmission of Buddhist texts. Movable type was first made in earthenware in the mid-11th century, and in wood and metal later. However, the invention of movable type did not replace carved woodblock editions. Much of the activity in printing was, naturally enough, for the well-educated and while the processing of information was important, the manner of its distribution was also a consideration. As in all things the scholar class wanted not just communication but elegance of communication, and movable type could never achieve the balance required of Chinese calligraphy. There was also the problem of typographical errors which arose with the constant resetting of type. — potentially disastrous in a language as complex and elusive as Chinese. Both these factors inhibited the development of movable type and encouraged the far more elegant development of woodblock printing, of which this work is an example.

In one of the essays in *Chinese Rare Books,* Wang Fangyu deals with the history of the illustrated book in China, which evolved out of the need to illustrate religious texts. This form flourished in the late 16th and early 17th century in response to the growing affluence of the merchant class and its developing patronage of the arts. Wang describes this period as the 'Golden Age' of pictorial printing, and certainly books such as this, which took Fang Yulu at least five years to prepare and incorporates the skills of a number of artists and craftsmen of the age, are extraordinarily beautiful examples of the art of printing.

1. See *Dictionary of Ming Biography,* pp. 438-439 for further information.
2. Information from *Chinese Traditional Rubbing Techniques.*

173

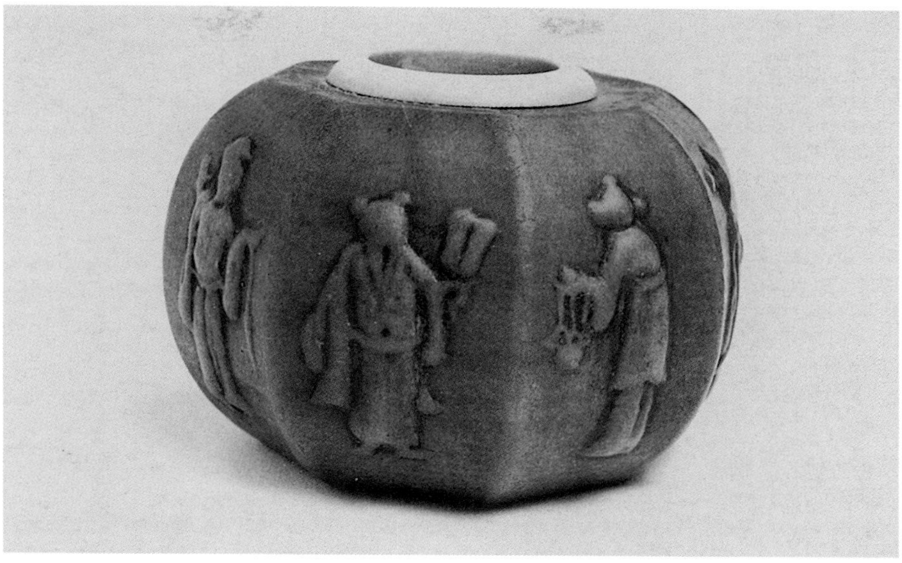

174

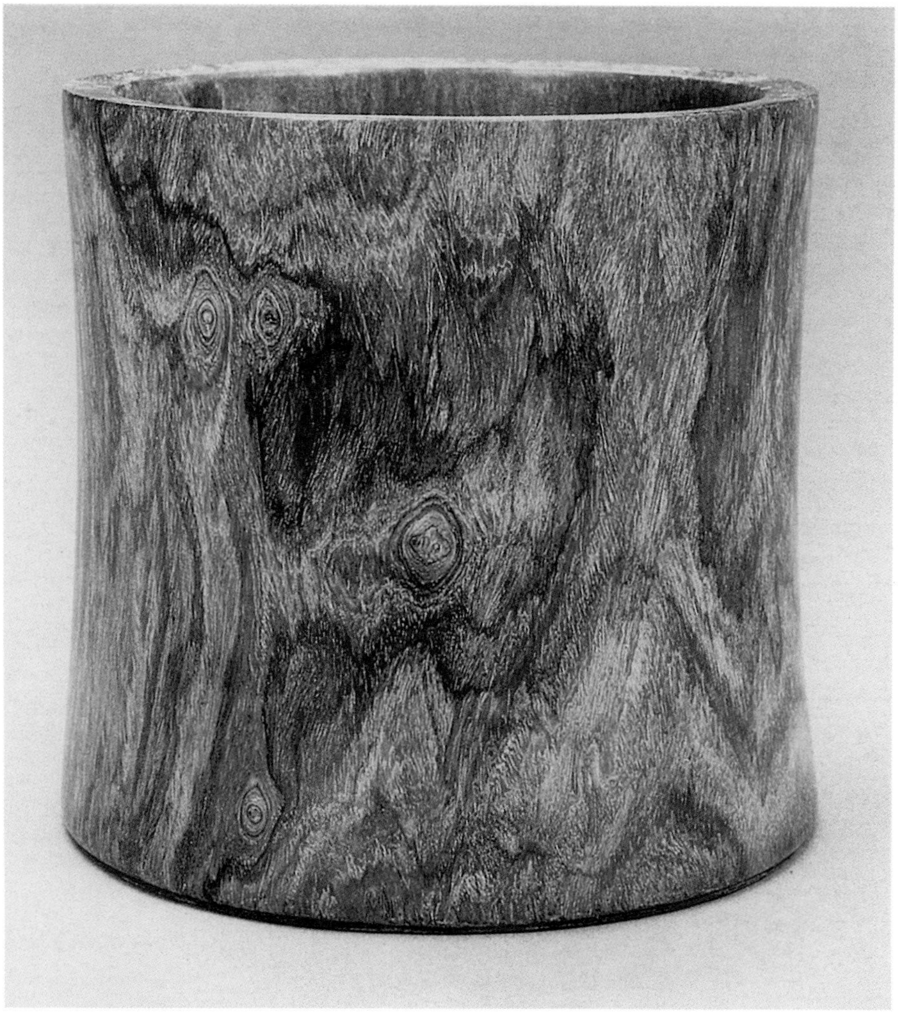

175

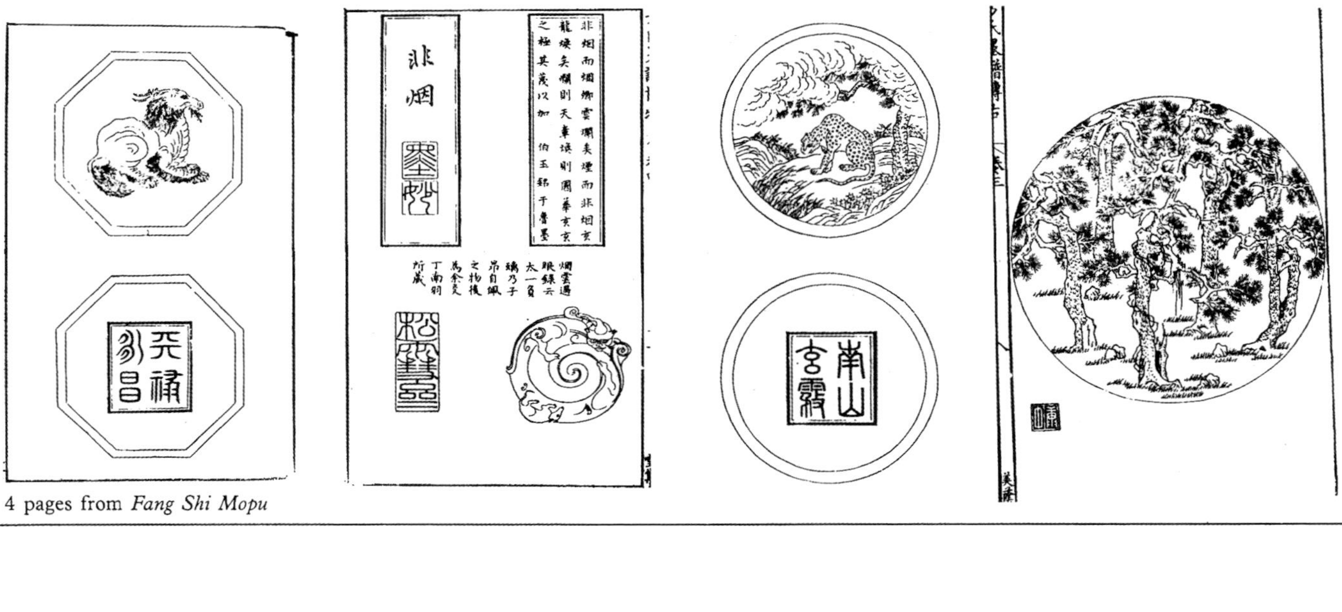

4 pages from *Fang Shi Mopu*

176

Reversible Box and Cover

Wood, *zitan* and *hongmu,* of deep, purplish-brown colour; box and cover, the rectangular domed top echoed by the base; the cover carved on the outside with bats amidst formalized clouds, the top panel with five bats, surrounded by narrow panels each with three, and broader side panels also with three each; the base, with lower exterior panels of formalized clouds, with an interior lip designed so that both base and lid may be inverted, to create an open container on a stand, at which point the lip becomes the foot of the stand, carved as a series of formalized *ruyi* forms; the interior lined with silk brocade.
Probably 18th century.
Height when closed as box and cover: 9.15 cm.
Height when inverted as open container on stand: 10.1 cm.
Width and depth: 22.65 cm and 22.5 cm.

紫檀紅木五蝠祥雲蓋盒
可能十八世紀，高9.15厘米，
寬深22.65×22.5厘米

No other box of this kind seems to have been recorded. That it was intended to be reversible is proven by the inner lip/foot area which acts as a decorative gallery, but only comes into its own as logical decoration when inverted to become the foot. The lining also suggests that the inside was intended to be regularly viewed (whether or not it is original). What it was intended to contain is a mystery, but presumably something could be carried in the box, and when set down, displayed in some manner or made readily available.

When the influential minority went travelling, whether for a day in the hills or on a longer journey, they did not as a rule travel light. Woodblock illustrations constantly show servants toiling along after a scholar and burdened down with a carrying stick from which hang a multitude of accoutrements for the day out. The late Ming scholar Tu Long in his *Youju Jian* ('Notes on Travelling Accoutrements') describes an extraordinary quantity of things that might accompany the scholar and clearly would have required a number of containers (elegance being required of some, no doubt). For touring in the hills his list of objects, too long to cite in full, includes combs, teabowls, dice basins, the 'three friends of incense' (see no. 229), inkstones, ink, brushes, water droppers, books, stationery, paper knife, hole punchers and markers for drinking and poetry games.

Zitan is one of the most valued of all woods used by the Chinese and the presence in this box of what appear to be panels of *zitan* mixed with panels of *hongmu,* which can often resemble it, allows for a brief discussion of this material. In the *Guwan Zhinan* (*Handbook of Chinese Antiquity*) of 1942, Zhao Ruzhen describes *zitan* as a hard and heavy reddish wood, and gives some historical details: "In the Ming dynasty *zitan* used by the Imperial Court was taken from South China. Later the wood was in insufficient supply and the Court sent people in search of fresh supplies to South-East Asian islands, which developed into an annual search...the wood was imported not only for immediate use, but for storage against future use...at Beijing. All *zitan* used in the Qing dynasty was from the Ming stock, and until the end of the Qing, the palace still had Ming *zitan* unused. The stock was exhausted only in the Hongxian period (1916). *Zitan* imported during the Qing dynasty was thin, not exceeding the width that could be grasped in two palms, and the wood twisting and not straight — unsuitable for use. *Zitan* grows very slowly and takes several hundred years to grow to a suitable size for use...it has an extremely fine and dense figured grain and is very hard."

Wang Shixiang, in his recent *Mingshi Jiaj Zhenshang,*[1] wrote: "*Zitan* was first recorded in the 3rd century work *Gujin Zhu* ('Notes on Past and Present') by Cui Bao and was subsequently discussed in a number of works. The location of sources for the wood were different, mostly in the Indo-Chinese peninsula, in Yunnan, Guangdong, and Guangxi provinces." He then goes on to discuss the classification of the wood, concluding that it is of the *Leguminosae pterocarpus* family and that about 15 different species are involved.

It would appear that some kinds of *hongmu,* if cut and polished in a certain manner, resemble some kinds of *zitan.* The general criteria seem to be that *zitan* is of considerable weight and density, of black, purplish, or reddish-brown colour, is of limited trunk size (allowing for diameters or plank widths rarely exceeding about nine inches), and has a compact and twisting grain with tiny grooves (like worm marks) on the surface, the direction of which is twisting and turning. *Hongmu,* on the other hand, is not quite as heavy, is naturally of a purplish or reddish-brown colour — although it is frequently stained a darker colour and sometimes black — and can be of much larger plank size. It generally has a straighter grain, and the grooves on the surface run in a more orderly fashion. Although there seems to be agreement on the general criteria, how it is applied varies, and there is a still a group of woods which is *zitan* to certain experts and *hongmu* (or its southern equivalent *suanzhi*) to others.

1. English edition, *Classic Chinese Furniture.*

177

Brush Rest

Bamboo, of greyish-brown colour; carved as a brush rest in the form of nine *chi* dragons, presumably a parent and eight young, set on swirling waves originating from two points on the underside of the brush rest.
Early Qing dynasty.
Height: 5.3 cm. Length: 11.55 cm.
Set on a plain, dark wood stand.
Formerly in the Dr. Ip Yee collection.
Published: *Bamboo Carvings of China,* p.114, no. 57; *Chinese Bamboo Carving,* p.341, no. 103 and slip-cover.

竹雕九螭筆擱
清初，高5.3厘米，長11.55厘米

This delightful brush rest, with its bad-tempered *chi* dragons doing their best to look thoroughly menacing but somehow failing, was dated as 18th century in both the above publications. While this is a reasonable attribution, we see no reason to rule out the 17th century, and particularly the latter part of it. Here is another case of a functional brush rest being elevated to the level of independent work of art by setting it on a stand. This might have taken place quite soon after its manufacture, as the delights of the piece as a non-functional plaything are obvious. The stand, however, does make the piece rather less practical as a brush rest as it increases the angle at which smaller brushes would rest, allowing them to slip off more easily.

176

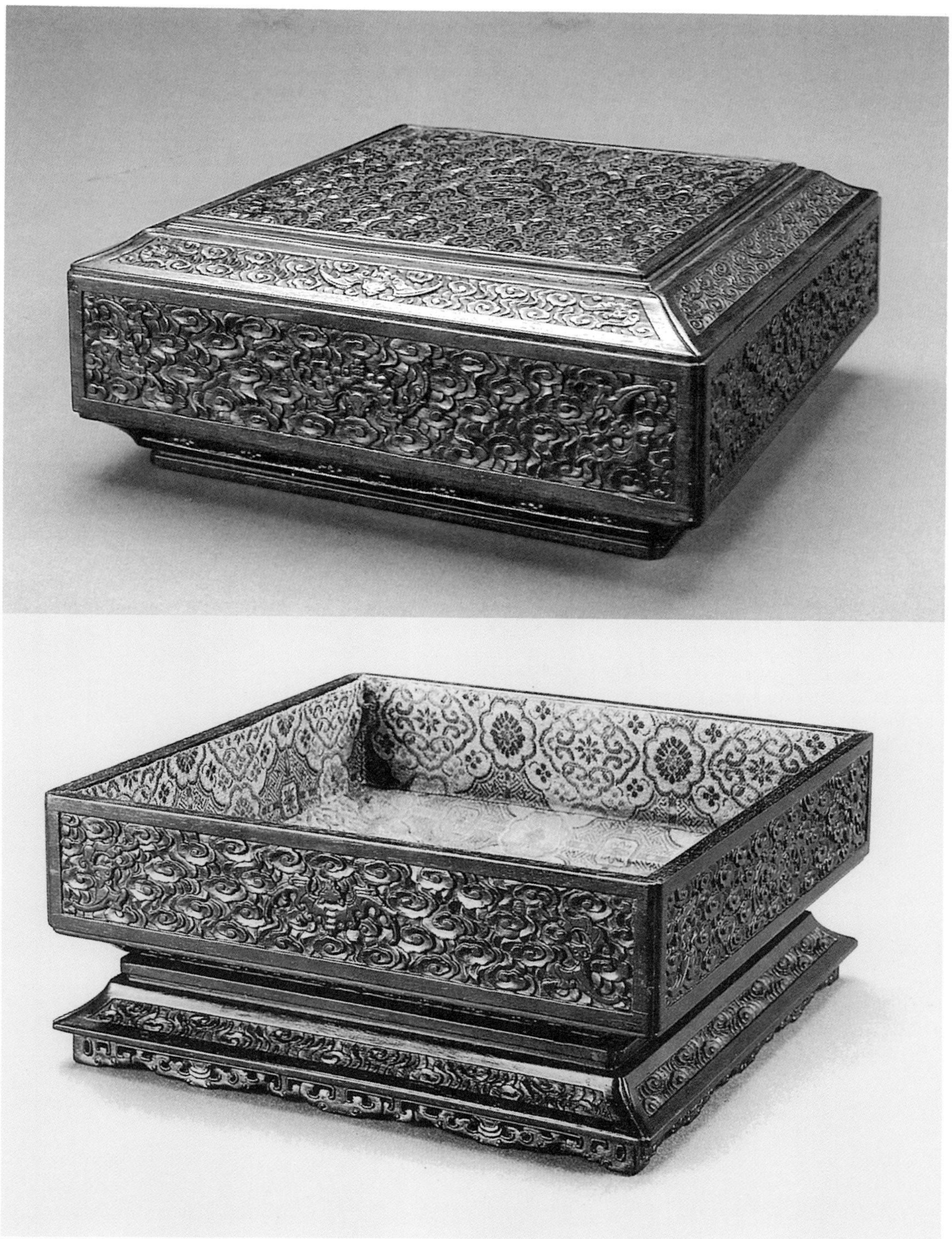

177

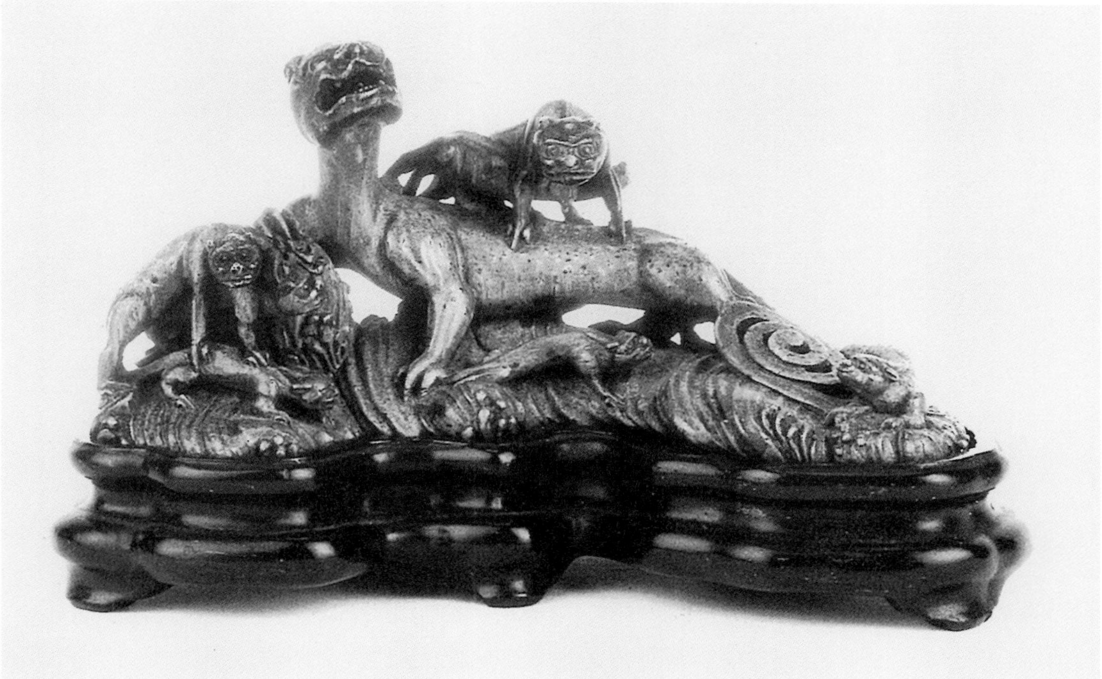

178

Pebble Sculpture

Jasper-agate, of alternating dark brownish-red and off-white colour; in the form of an inverted peach, the surface weathered into irregularly concentric ridges; set on a wood stand carved in the form of formalized waves.
Probably Ming or Qing dynasty.
Height including stand: 8.6 cm.

桃形瑪瑙石卵
可能明或清代，高連座8.6厘米

About two-thirds of the 12th century *Stone Catalogue of Cloudy Mountain* is devoted not to the sort of rocks we have come to associate with the scholar, the strange gnarled and pierced stones, but with small, unusual or strangely marked stones such as agate and carnelian and with stones worked into various objects such as inkstones, belt hooks, paper weights, ornamental plaques, seals, incense burners, *weiqi* pieces, foot rules, and so on. Some are mentioned as being pebbles so small as to be suitable for making beads, and it is clear that stones of all kinds were valued, particularly if beautifully or strangely marked. This curious piece of agate was nothing more than a pebble, its surface weathered and polished by the action of water, until it was discovered and mounted on a suitably watery stand. The peach shape may be significant (the peach is a symbol of longevity), but it may have been appreciated simply for its odd markings.

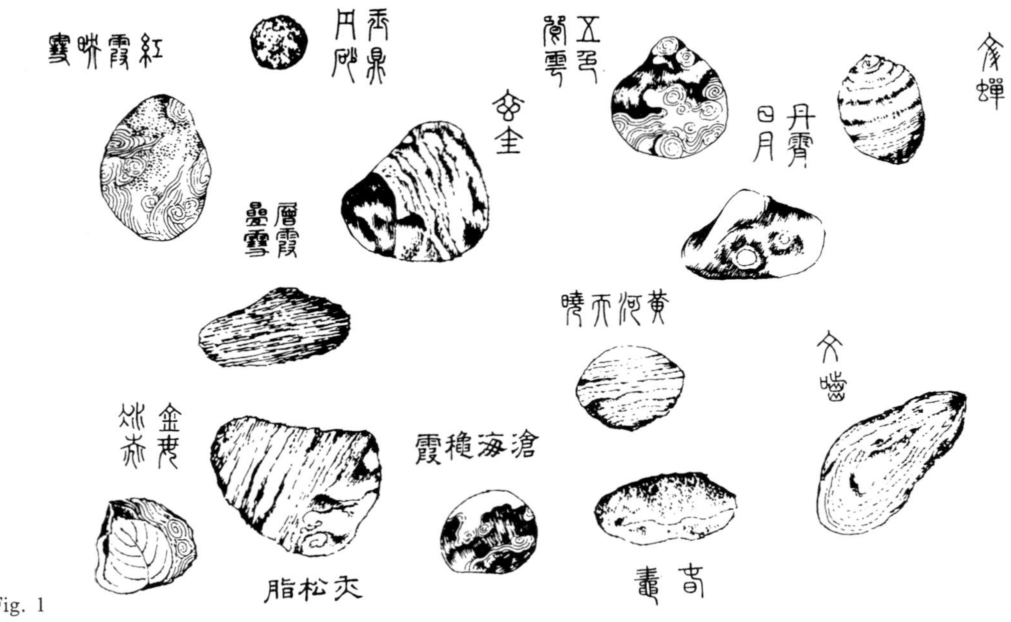

Fig. 1

The type of association made with these pebbles is illustrated by the type known as *Yuhua* ('Rain-flower') stone found at Yuhua Tai, Nanjing. The name derives from a legend of angels throwing flowers from the heavens while a great monk was preaching; the flowers turned to beautiful stones.

In the *Suyuan Shipu*[1] two pages illustrate small pebbles with various markings (see Fig. 1). Unquestionably such pebbles were valued in the 17th century, and presumably although not necessarily of the type illustrated, in the Song and even before. Odd stones were certainly highly regarded as early as the Tang dynasty for their sculptural appeal and their curiosity value.

1. The 17th century illustrated book on strange stones purporting to be of the Xuanhe Emperor's collection.

179

Mythical Animal

Nephrite, of pale greenish-white tone with extensive russet brown markings probably partly enhanced by staining; carved as a model of a crouching mythical leonine snarling beast with a bifurcated tail.
Probably Six Dynasties.
4 cm × 7.5 cm.

Formerly in the collections of J.M.A.J. Dawson and Wilfred Fleisher, Stockholm.
Exhibited at the National Museum, Stockholm, 1963 and published in *Celadon-Jade*, no. 65; 'Selected examples from the Jade Exhibition at Stockholm, 1963: A Comprehensive Study', pl. 13, no. 2.
Exhibited at the Victoria and Albert Museum, and published in *Chinese Jade Throughout the Ages*, London, 1975, no. 186 and in *Chinese Jade Throughout the Ages*, 1976, no. 186.
Exhibited and published: *Chinese Jades from a Private Collection*, Eskenazi, London, 1976, no. 7; *Chinese Works of Art from the Collection of J.M.A.J. Dawson*, no. 44.
Published: *Yu-ch'i Tzu-tien* (Dictionary of Chinese Jade), p.72, no. 0533.
Exhibited and published: *Eskenazi: Twenty-five Years*, Eskenazi, London, pp.50-51, no. 18.

玉雕異獸
可能六朝，4×7.5厘米

One can hardly overemphasize the meaning of jade to the Chinese. That it went far beyond the visual appeal of a pleasant stone is demonstrated by the comments made in the preface to *Illustrated Catalogue of Ancient Jade Artifacts in the National Palace Museum* by Ch'in Hsiao-yi. He wrote: "Jade was not only used to regulate the actions of gentlemen in ancient times, but also as a symbolic image cherished by scholars and used by them to measure their characters. Yet the worldly have generally held gold in higher esteem than jade. Even a porcelain piece made a few decades ago commands a price many times higher than jade of two or three thousand years ago. This is most regrettable. People fail to realize that ancient jades regulated form, distinguished cause from effect, evaluated meanings, established historical truth and separated the pure from the adulterated. How much are the ancients to be envied! They had among them men of such wisdom as to know that nothing else is worthy of being mentioned on the same day as jade."

The identification of the various mythical animals which turn up with such regularity as subject-matter in the various Chinese arts is nigh impossible. In antiquity confusion reigned among the Chinese themselves in the identification of such creatures. In the *Hanshu*, a history of the Han dynasty compiled in the 2nd century, a statement that beyond the borders at Wuge Mountain there existed *taoba* lions raised only tentative identification in a later commentary: "Meng Kang says that *taoba* is another name for *fuba*, an animal like a deer with a long tail. Those with one horn are probably *tianlu*, while those with two horns are probably *bixie*".[1]

Thus two-horned leonine creatures were apparently a type of *taoba* lion called *bixie*, the Chinese name of which means literally 'to ward off evil'; they served as good luck emblems. However, as time progressed other names were given to animals with similar attributes, and the creatures themselves changed. None of this helps much in the identification of this beast — particularly as it is not even clear whether it has two horns or stylized and extended eyebrows of a rather fancy nature.

1. Quoted from the *Xiyu Chuan* in *Illustrated Catalogue of Ancient Jade Artifacts in the National Palace Museum*, section V of the foreword (unpaginated).

178

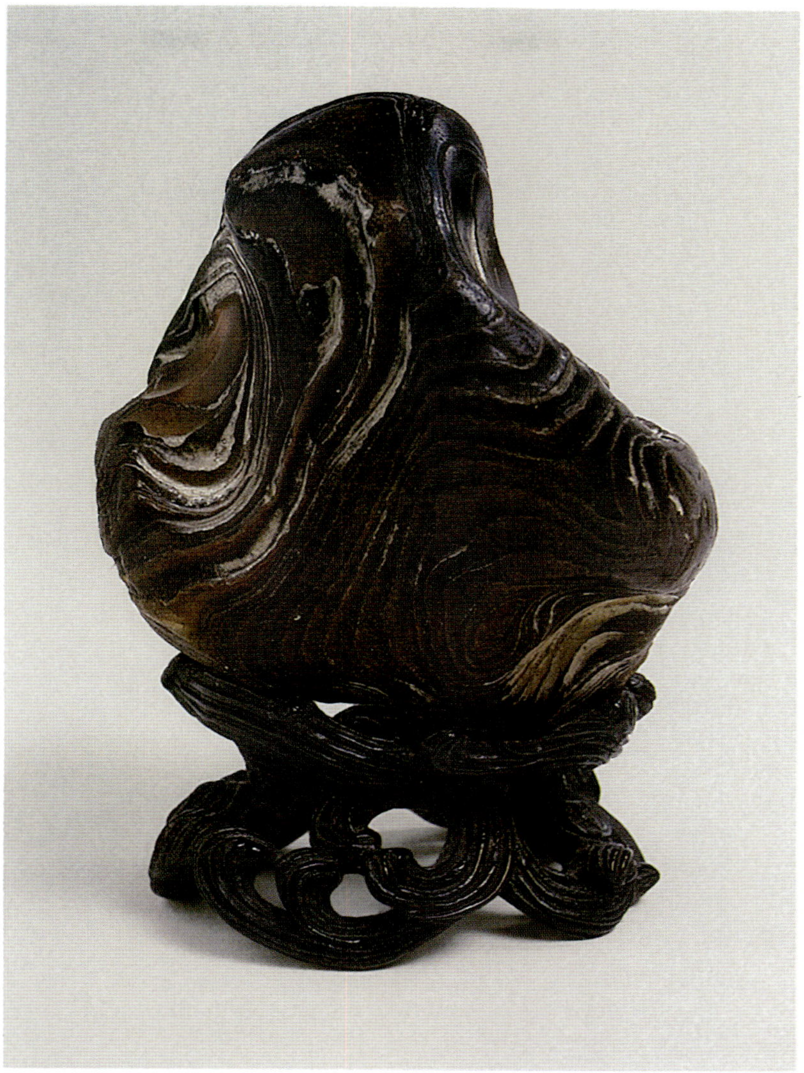

Larger than life size

179

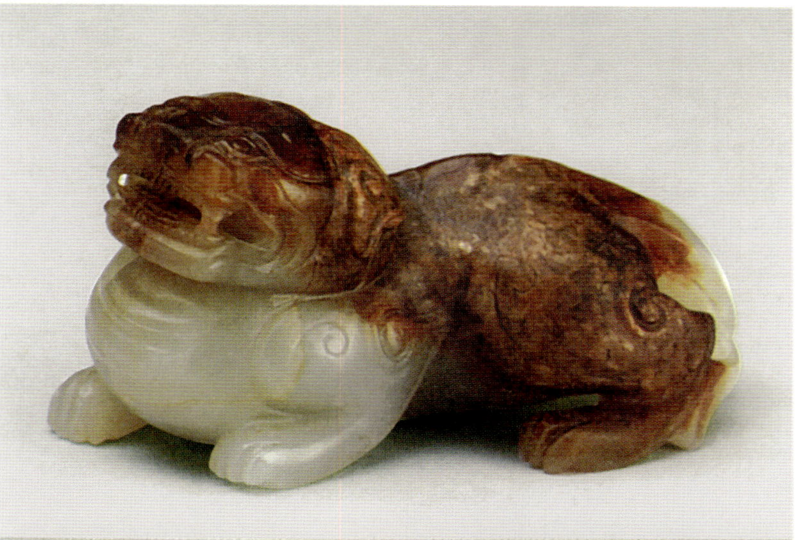

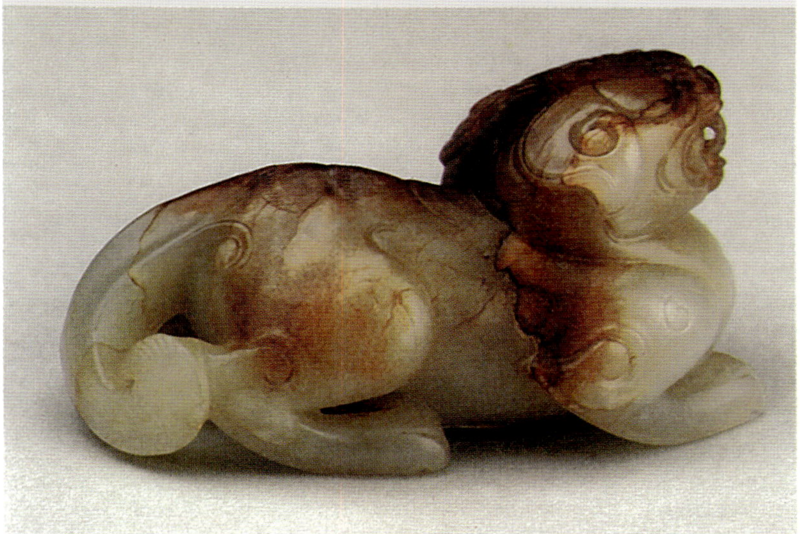

180

Water Vessel

Soapstone, of mottled dark brownish-red colour; a rectangular water vessel set on four small feet; each of the four exterior panels decorated with rustic scenes of scholars gazing out of lakeside houses at passing boats and distant mountains, sitting meditatively in moored boats, or seated watching waterfalls; the flat base incised with the seal *Hewu baowan* ('Hewu's precious plaything') in negative seal script.
Probably first half of the 19th century.
5.5 cm × 9.7 cm × 8.9 cm.
Set on a tall, elegantly proportioned dark wood stand.
Height including stand: 9 cm.

石雕山水高士圖方形水丞•荷屋寶玩銘
可能十九世紀上半葉,5.5×9.7×8.9厘米

Hewu was the *hao* of Wu Rongguang (*zi:* Borong, Tianyuan; *hao:* Hewu, Shiyun shanren, Boyun shanren, Baijing laoren; 1773-1843). He was a *jinshi* of 1799 and joined a group of celebrated scholars of the mid-Qing period, entering the Hanlin Academy and serving in a number of posts. His career was the usual mixture of progress through the bureaucratic ranks checked by occasional dismissals and punishments for infractions; in his old age his devotion to duty forced the Emperor to finally order him to retire. He was a celebrated scholar and collector in the traditional fields of ancient bronzes and stone rubbings, as well as of paintings and calligraphy.[1]

This lovely vessel, which might have functioned in several capacities, is similar in feeling to no. 111. Both are incised with an 'iron brush' technique which might represent the hand of a scholar 'painting on stone' or a soapstone carver versed in the tradition of literati painting. We have called this a water vessel because of the evidence of an 18th century painting by Yu Zhiding (see Fig. 1)[2] in which just such a square vessel is being used as a water pot for the inkstone, complete with a small ladle, by a scholar in a garden setting.

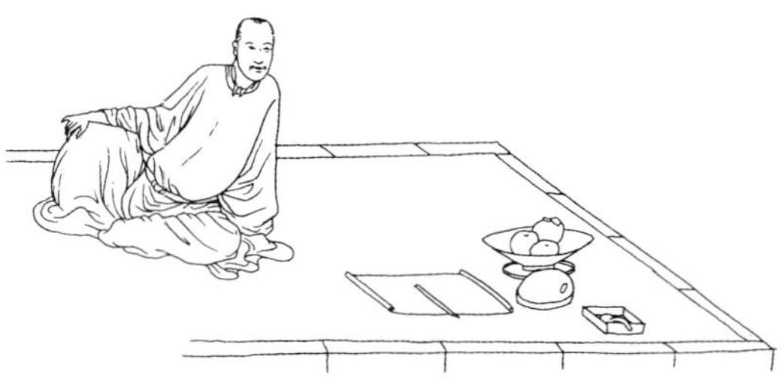
Fig. 1

Wu Rongguang served as a provincial judge in Fujian province in 1821 and 1822, and served again in that province for three years from 1837. Since the main source of soapstone for scholars' items was Fujian it is tempting to associate this vessel with his years of service there. As a local official it is likely that he would have been presented with such a piece as a gift and have had it inscribed as a 'precious plaything', but equally, soapstone objects were freely available to scholars elsewhere in the country, as was the raw material.

1. See *Eminent Chinese of the Ch'ing Period,* pp. 872-874 for further details.
2. *Wenrenhua Cuibian,* Jin Nong, p.68.

181

Bi Symbol Mounted as a Table Screen

Nephrite, of mottled cream and russet tones showing signs of calcification to the more heavily russet areas; a *bi* symbol, the surface undecorated.
Probably Han dynasty.
Diameter: 6.7 cm.
Diameter of central hole: 4.8 cm.

The rim of the *bi* inscribed with an appreciatory poem in seal script composed by, and inscribed to the order of, the Qianlong Emperor: "Though its decoration is plain and simple, this jade disc is more valuable than those decorated with designs of rushes or grain. It has an archaic and circular form, surpassing the works of the Xia and Shang jade carvers. The long-tailed phoenix is placed between the string-plucked instruments of *qin* and *se* (a 25-stringed instrument with long horizontal body) while Gongyu (a Han scholar) places himself among the sumptuous jades. The jade assumes a solemn and reverent style, embodying the breath-resonance; its light is as brilliant and gleaming as a gem; its body translucent. The gentleness of the void is balanced by the strength of the body. Whether the jade is buried or unearthed, hidden or exposed, its qualities will eventually be revealed. If what I have said can be interpreted better than I have managed, then the way of the Ancient King (Wenhuang) will be understandable. Composed by the emperor in mid-spring of the *jiawu* year of Qianlong (1774)." With one seal, *guxiang* ('ancient fragrance').

Mounted in an elaborate *zitan* wood stand in the form of a table screen supported by four five-clawed dragons standing on rocks set on a pedestal base, the screen carved with four *chi* dragons enclosing the circular panel of the enclosed jade on one side and the same inscription that appears on the edge of the jade on the other; with various archaic ornamental elements elsewhere, including a highly formalized *taotie* along the pedestal apron; a central plug which pierces the *bi* and locks into the sliding back-panel, decorated with the trigram, the name of which is the *qian* character of the Qianlong Emperor's reign title, gilt and surrounded by two *chi* dragons and a band of *leiwen;* the inscription in regular script repeats exactly that translated above, except the character for 'mid' before 'spring' is omitted in the date, and two more complex seals appear in place of the *guxian* seal on the jade: *Huxin buyuan* ('Not far away from mutual understanding') and *Deliang lintong* ('Virtue brings brightness to the uninitiated').
Beijing palace workshops, 1774.
Height: 22.8 cm.
Formerly in the collection of the Qianlong Emperor.

漢玉璧題詩紫檀插屏•乾隆御題銘
清乾隆甲午(1774),璧直徑4.8厘米,
中孔直徑6.7厘米

Plain jade discs are referred to as *bi* if the central hole is smaller than the radius of the jade body; *huan* if it is equal, and *yuan* if it is larger. Thus strictly speaking this is a *yuan,* but the term *bi* is often extended to cover them all, and since the Qianlong Emperor went to so much trouble to compose a poem about a *bi* it would seem tactless to contradict him at this stage. Their dating is particularly difficult, plain examples having been made from Neolithic times through to the Han dynasty. This example is dated partly on the strength of the Qianlong Emperor's reference to a Han scholar, suggesting that he believed it was Han and partly because there are several examples in the imperial collection similar in style and feeling to this which are dated to the Han dynasty.[1]

The Qianlong Emperor was the last major collector in a long line of imperial collectors, and certainly one of the most prolific and least self-restrained. Inheriting the imperial collections of his forebears he set about expanding it with a rare devotion to acquisition. A minor poet and calligrapher with major aspirations, he was in the habit of inscribing works of art in his collection. In the case of paintings and calligraphy this meant writing in his flaccid calligraphic style on any blank space to be found on the original work of art. These inscriptions together with large quantities of his prominently placed, far from self-effacing seals do provide valuable documentary evidence of provenance but are not as a rule considered to be in the best tradition of the addition of such colophons.

On other works of art, although similarly inclined to flamboyant self-expression, his inscriptions are less of an obvious defacement. This is largely due to the fact that the inscribing of jade, ceramics, wood and other materials was a technical task beyond the Emperor himself so he employed others to inscribe them for him, often introducing an element of taste into the positioning and relative obtrusiveness of such inscriptions. In the case of works of art which were fancily mounted at his behest, as in the present example, an addition was made to the original piece without unduly spoiling its appeal. Thus while his inscriptions on paintings are generally frowned upon, those on other works of art are considered to enhance their appeal considerably.

The majority of poetic and appreciatory inscriptions by the Qianlong Emperor on the works of art in his collection date from the latter part of his reign. A series of similarly mounted jades may be found in the imperial collection, much of which is still maintained in the National Palace Museum, Taiwan. Most of these pieces are inscribed around the rim of the jade, and all are mounted with the central retaining plug decorated with the *qian* trigram.[2]

1. See *Illustrated Catalogue of Ancient Jade Artifacts in the National Palace Museum,* nos. 184, 197, 206 and 207; and in *Gugong Bao Ji* ('Treasures of the National Palace Museum'), Taipei, 1985, pp.35-36, pl. 18.
2. Several are to be found in the *Illustrated Catalogue of Ancient Jade Artifacts in the National Palace Museum,* amongst which the following are similar jade discs in miniature screen-form mounts: pl. 63 (a *bi* with inscription dated to 1770); plate 68 (a *huan* mounted with dragon supports like this example, with inscription dated to 1764); plate 84 (a *huang* pendant with inscription dated to 1796, also with dragon supports and similar *chi* dragon decorative surround); plate 87 (a *huang* pendant in a simpler mount without dated inscription); and plate 189 (a *bi* also with dragon supports, with an inscription dated to 1778).

180

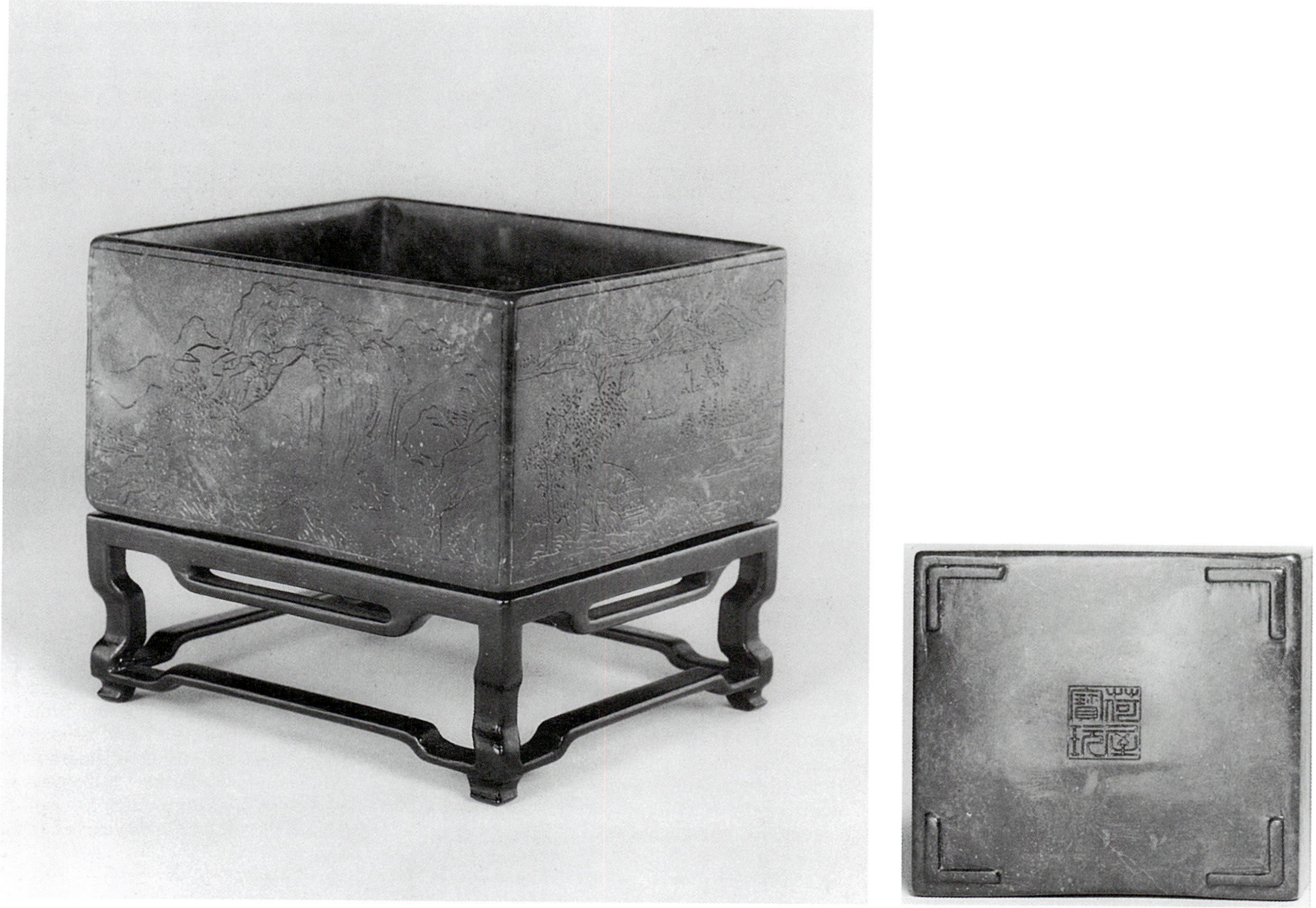

181

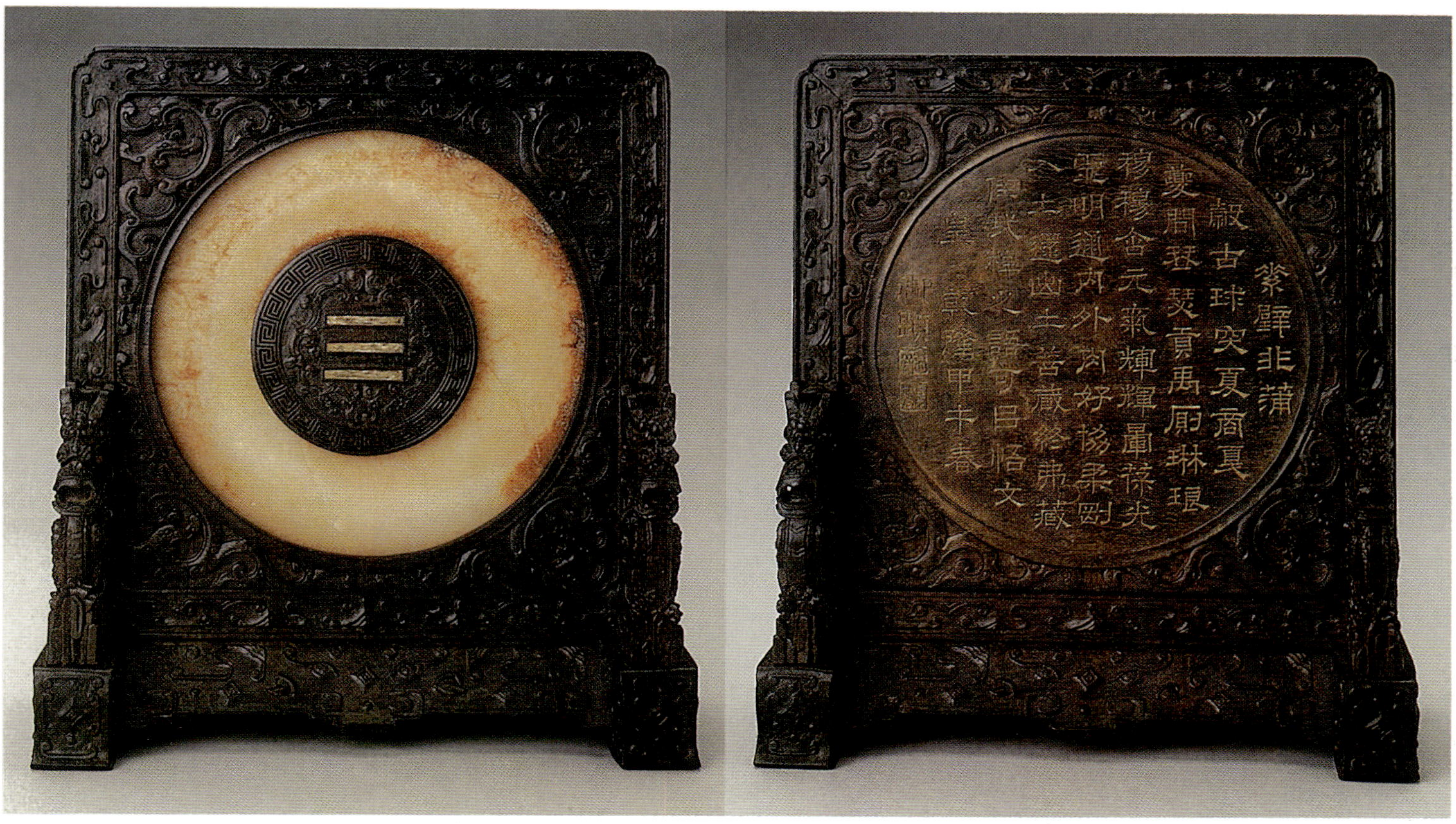

182

Brush Rest

Nephrite, of beige-grey colour with darker brown and almost black markings; carved as a brush rest with two *chi* dragons amidst clouds, the underside also fully carved, with the emerging lower bodies of both beasts.
Probably Yuan or early Ming dynasty.
With an early wood stand, carved as swirling clouds.
Height including wood stand: 5.2 cm.
Length of wood stand: 13.3 cm.
Formerly in the Eisenbach-Erie collection.

玉雕雙螭筆擱
可能元或明初, 高連座5.2厘米, 座長13.3厘米

Although this piece may have doubled as a paper weight, it would appear to have been primarily designed as a brush rest. It has two positions from each side at which a brush might comfortably rest, but we suspect that its main function is indicated by a groove along the length of the piece bounded on each side by the dragon's bodies, where a brush even of good size may rest securely.

The re-acquired naivety of the persuasive minority, so evident in the brushwork of literati paintings (see p.17) was certainly transferred to objects from time to time, particularly from the Yuan dynasty onwards (the bamboo water vessel of no. 56 is a good example). To the neophyte, distinguishing between this naivety (in vision and in execution) and incompetence is one of the more difficult tasks in approaching Chinese painting. With objects it is still harder, as it was not a standard mode, and was to a certain extent reflected at second hand by craftsmen in response to literati sophistication — a remarkably difficult feat to achieve successfully. Thus the difference between what is intentionally crude or awkward and what is simply bad is often difficult to judge. Frequently our only criteria is an entirely subjective response to the general feel of a piece.

A comparison between this carving and that of no. 97 (the palace ivory seal) is informative. The ivory seal is a technical masterpiece; the artist is in total technical control. It is faultless: a superb work but an obvious one, where the skill of the carver sits on the surface. Here the carving is cruder, the two *chi* dragons less fluid, more awkward; they are indicated by strong, crudely cut but confident lines. The clouds are stylized rather than being modelled with elegance. In the former the power is mainly concentrated in the subject of the dragon, realistically portrayed; in the latter it is concentrated in the more subtle languages of how the subject is portrayed.

183

Brush and Cover

Lacquer, of 15 layers of alternating red, ochre and black colours; a brush and cover of elegantly waisted form, the surface cut with 'V'-shaped incisions in a scrolling, curvilinear pattern to reveal the different layers of colour.
Ming dynasty, probably 16th century.
Length of brush shaft: 17.5 cm.
Length of cover: 8.8 cm.

剔犀毛筆連套
明代, 可能十六世紀, 桿長17.5厘米,
套長8.8厘米

Marbled lacquer (*guri* in Japanese) first appears on a suit of lacquer armour found by Sir Aurel Stein in East Turkestan, dating from the Tang dynasty (see *Chinese Lacquer* by Sir Harry Garner, p.69, Fig. 25). It flourished, along with other types of carved lacquer, during the Yuan and Ming dynasties, and continued, though at by no means so popular a level, during the Qing. The standard form of decoration was to cut 'V'-shaped grooves in formalized designs consisting mostly of *ruyi* forms and curvilinear scrolling shapes, thus revealing the layering of different coloured lacquer. An alternative form of marbling, and one much better suited to the name, is found on the top of the root stand, no. 37, where unevenly applied lacquer in different colours are then rubbed flat, leaving a marbled surface.

Lacquer appears to have been a popular material for brushmakers and a reasonable number have survived from the Ming dynasty.

The brush seems to have been invented as long ago as the Neolithic period where painted pottery jars of the Yangshao culture bear the clear evidence of brushstrokes in their zoomorphic and geometric designs painted usually in black or purple pigments. In recent decades a number of brushes have been excavated from tombs dating from the Chu Kingdom of the Warring States period onwards. Some Tang dynasty brushes are to be found in the Shoso-in Repository in Japan; they are made of goat hair with an outer layer of deer hair and have elaborate decorative stems and caps (see also no. 205).

184

Ink

Ink, black with faded gold details; of elongated rectangular form, decorated on one side with Penglai, the mythical Daoist paradisical mountain of the Immortals rising steeply out of tumultuous waves, a plateau near its peak with doors opening into a cave, the sun and moon above, with drifting clouds; the reverse with the impressed title 'Penglai Shan' ('Mount Penglai') above a long inscription in positive regular script describing the Daoist paradise, followed by the signature *Zhutian, Qingsong Yuan zao* ('made by Bamboo Field (of the) Green Pine Garden'), with two seals *He* and *Quan*.
Probably late Ming or early Qing dynasty.
24.5 cm × 5.3 cm × 1.8 cm.

蓬萊山墨·竹田青松園製
可能晚明或清初, 24.5×5.3×1.8厘米

Another example of the same subject, also signed *Zhutian, Qingsong Yuan* but from a different mould, is illustrated as no. 211, p.315, in *Chinese Art*, Vol. 4, where it is attributed to the late Ming or early Qing dynasty. There is also a Japanese copy of a similar inkstick illustrated in *To-boku Wa-boku Zusetsu*, p.181, made in the Tokugawa period (1615-1867). We have been unable to find any record of either Hequan or Zhutian, both of which are obviously fanciful art names, or of the Qingsong Yuan.

The poetic inscription here describes Penglai (also known as Yunlai — or 'Origin of the Clouds'), stating that it is in the middle of the Eastern Sea and is 1,000 miles high and 3,000 square. On its top is built a golden pavilion with jade gates, where the Immortals of the Divine Emperor stroll and take their leisure. Although the sea is without wind and is impenetrably black, the waves rise to the height of 100,000 feet so that no human being can cross them, leaving access only to those who have become Immortals and no longer need human forms of transportation. Only the legendary Emperor Yu is said to have managed the journey (but he is hardly considered mortal).

The earliest traceable form of ink was natural graphite, which was ground together with water to make ink. Ink in solid form appears to have been a development of the Qin or shortly before. A piece of ink with an inkstone and grinding pestle (see also no. 188) were discovered, together with a brush, in a Qin dynasty tomb at Shuihudi, in Yunmeng, Hubei province, in 1975.[1] Solid ink was made from soot gathered from the burning of various materials, with pine being the favourite and later the standard. This was mixed with glue, made from various sources such as boiled ox-hide. Other ingredients were also added by different inkmakers over the centuries. Legend has it that the famous late Tang inkmaker Xi Zhao and his son Xi Tinggui used pine soot with deer glue, and mixed it with twelve precious substances (including musk, pearl, rhinoceros horn, herbs and gold foil). Tinggui's ink was so fine and highly valued that he was granted the usage of the Emperor's own name, changing his name to Li Tinggui.

In the Ming dynasty ink was developed using oil soot, derived from burning resin, wood oil and pork lard. Glue and water were added to this mixture and pounded together with various other substances (fragrant herbs, camphor, gold foil, etc.). The oil soot ink was lustrous and suitable for making certain rubbings, whereas the pine soot ink was less glossy, being more suitable for paintings and calligraphy.[2]

1. Published in *Bimozhiyan Tulu* ('Brush, Ink, Paper and Inkstone Pictorial').
2. Much of the above information is taken from *Chinese Traditional Rubbing Techniques*.

182

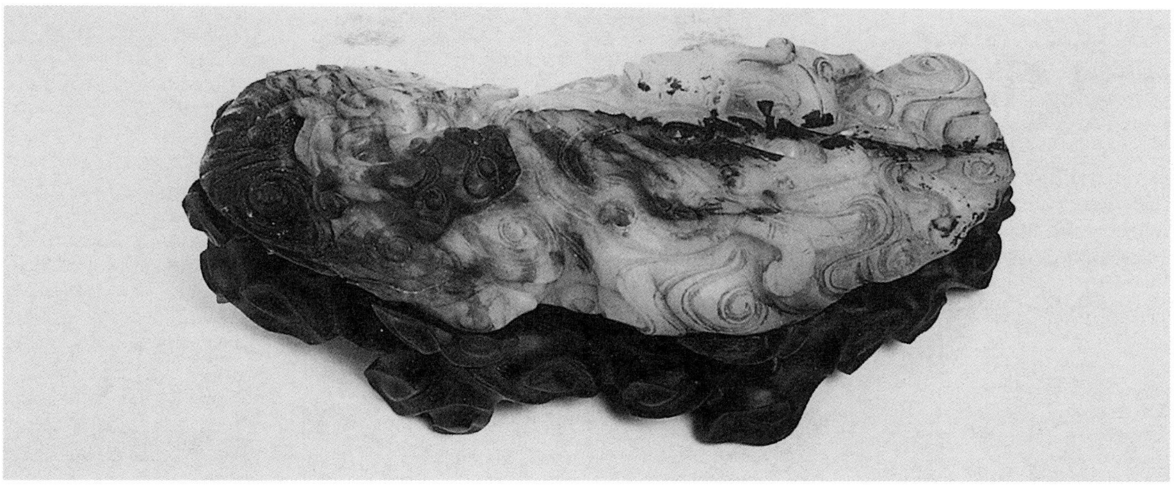

183

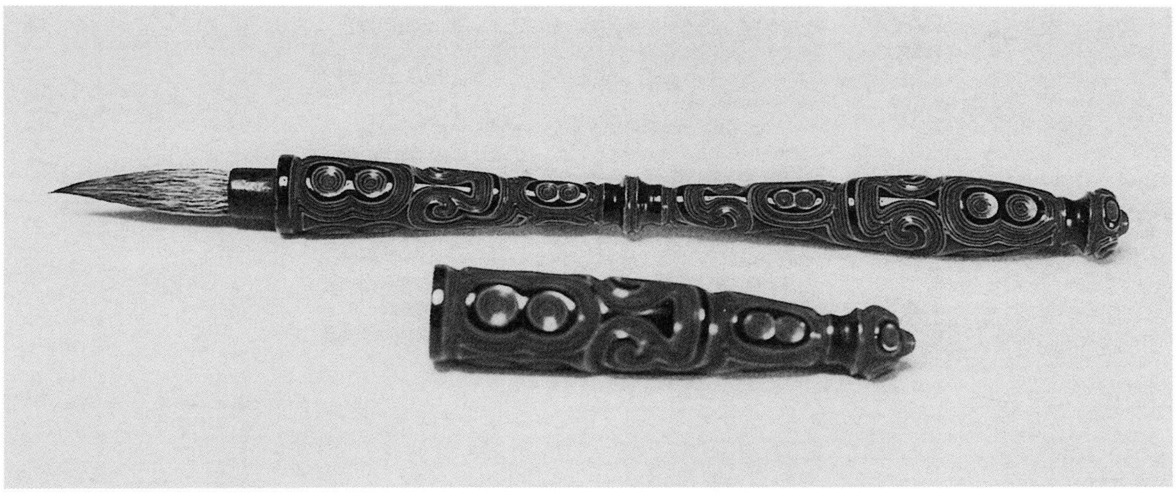

184

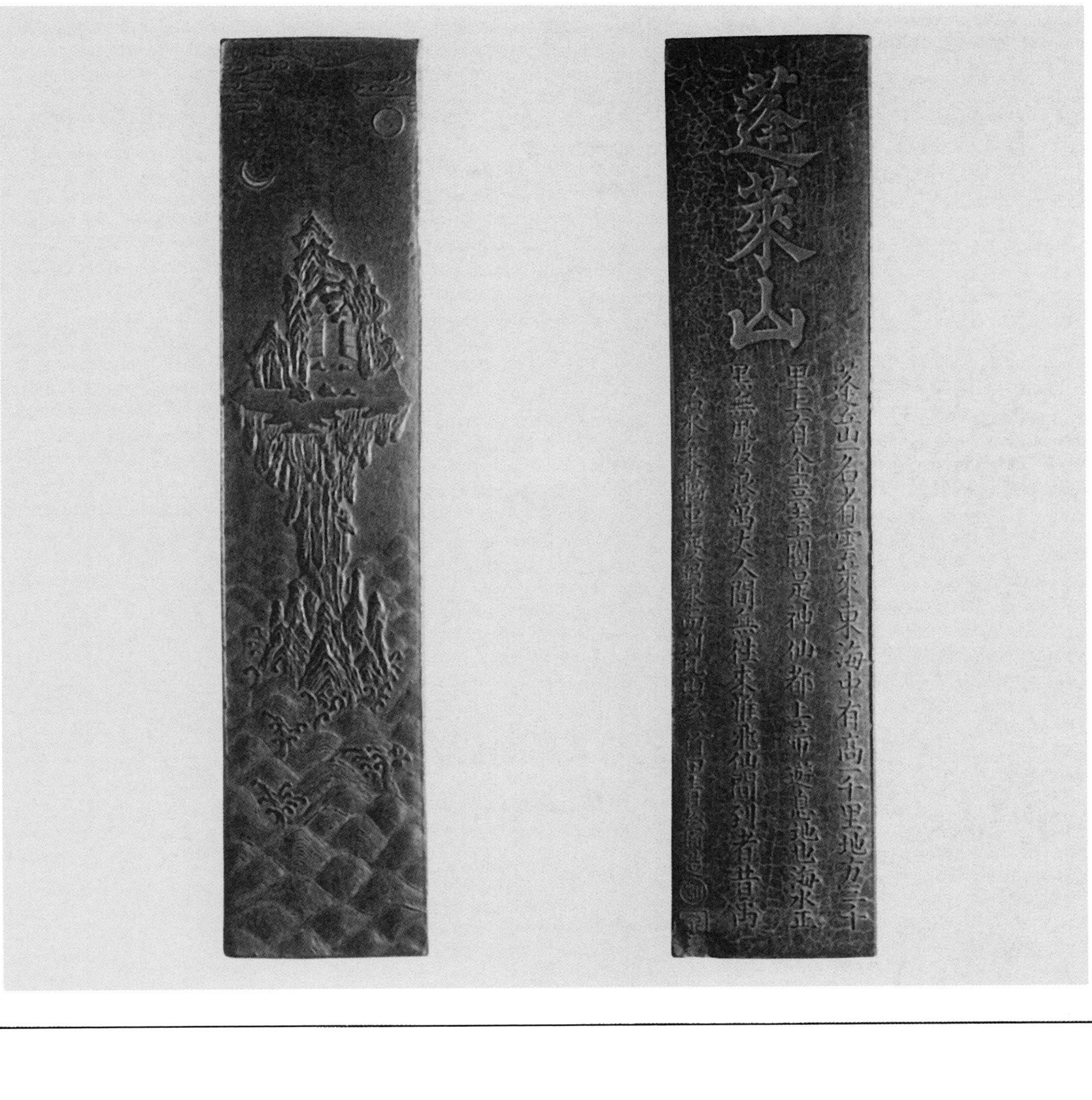

185

Ink

Ink, black with gilt detail; moulded in the form of a seal, the knob with a gilded group of reclining mythical beasts with two young, one side inscribed in regular script: "curious characters from (ancient) bronzes"; the other with a recessed seal *Hezhao Zhai* ('Shining Crane Studio') in positive seal characters; the seal text with four characters in positive fanciful seal-script.
Probably late Ming or early Qing dynasty
5.4 cm × 2.7 cm × 2.6 cm.

鐘鼎奇字獸紐印形墨·鶴照齋銘
可能晚明或清初, 5.4×2.7×2.6厘米

The characters of this seal text are in one of well over a hundred different forms of fanciful seal scripts identified by such names as 'phoenix-tail script', 'bird script', 'metal hook seal script', 'mosquito-feet seal script', 'rainbow seal script', etc. Prior to Qin unification in the 3rd century BC, with its attendant standardization of the written language, there was wide variation in the use of different scripts. Even after standardization, arcane fanciful scripts continued to be used for particular purposes and in certain groups. The Daoists, for instance, employed them in their magical activities. With the growing interest in archaeology of the post-Tang period many early script forms began to come to light and there was a revived scholarly interest in their interpretation and use. Such characters ideally suited literati esotericism in communication and familiarity with them represented a high level of scholarship.

Ink could, of course, be moulded into any number of different forms and there is wide variety. However this seal form is unusual. We have been unable to trace the ownership of the Hezhao Zhai, but stylistic evidence helps in the dating of this ink. The seal form, with its fanciful script, large pedestal and mythical beast knob is of a type which one would not expect prior to Ming dynasty developments in the art of seal carving (see no. 125), and a mid- to late Ming date might be more reasonable for the original form being copied in this ink. The mythical beast of the knob is of a type which one would expect from the mid-Ming through to the Kangxi period, with its well-tamed features, long elegant body and bifurcated single horn. Ink is a delicate material that is particularly susceptible to wear, desiccation and breakage, so early inksticks in fine condition are extremely rare. Bearing all this in mind, plus the dangers of stylistic dating in a field where popular forms were made and remade, and moulds could be used over a long period of time, a date of manufacture perhaps in the 16th or 17th century would not be unreasonable for this example.

Today we might view with horror the destruction of a work of art such as an inkstick in the production of a painting or calligraphy. The oriental attitude was quite different. However fine the ink, the Chinese scholar would generally not hesitate to use it in the greater service of the production of a work of calligraphy or painting, and old ink was traditionally more valued for its quality as ink than for its quality as a work of art. According to the *To-boku Wa-boku Zusetsu* the essential qualities of the glue in ink change after a period of time (given as two centuries, but it must vary for different types of ink) and it becomes no longer usable. For the artist, to use a fine ink stick is a part of the subtle preparation for the production of an inspired work of art rather than an act of vandalism. The artist prepared himself in a number of ways, clearing the mind of mundane concerns by preparing incense or going through the ritual of making and drinking tea, gradually transporting himself to a suitably ethereal level at which the source of great art might be tapped directly. The very purpose of making ink in such delightful forms was so that in the act of their transformation, a commitment was made: one could hardly grind up an ancient ink without taking seriously the resulting work of art. The act of grinding the ink was also meditational and the beauty of the ink-stick was a part of the elegant transformation from the mundane realm to the mystical, from mere mortal to artist.

186

Ink

Ink, black; of flattened circular form, one side moulded with a scene of figures on a terrace listening to a flautist, the reverse with a poem entitled "Love poem, by Li Yi:
Ice in the treasured jar, thoughts wander far away; a promise of marriage arranged over one thousand miles dissolves in a moment. After this I have no heart to seek love; just let the bright moon fall below the West Pavilion."
Late Ming dynasty.
Diameter: 10.6 cm.

李益寫情詩意墨
晚明, 直徑10.6厘米

Li Yi was a famous Tang poet, who excelled at writing songs. (Early poetry was usually sung to music — when poems were written, musicians of the day would compete to obtain them to set them to music). The Xianzong Emperor (806-820) appointed him a scholar of the Jixiang Palace, and he died as Minister of Rites. He was also renowned for his over-suspicious nature, particularly regarding his wife and concubines. The subject depicted here is associated with the verse. In the poem Li Yi is writing on behalf of a lady who after a lengthy arrangement of marriage, finds herself rejected. The reference to ice in a treasured jar is an oblique reference to the heart, although the illustration shows a treasured jar being proffered. The Western Pavilion with the bright moon rising above it is common Tang imagery in love poems, reversed here as the broken-hearted girl cares not if it rises or sets.

Another ink from the same mould, but with added surface decoration in red, green, white and gold, is illustrated in the *To-boku Wa-boku Zusetsu,* pp.74-75, where it is dated to the Ming dynasty. It is incomplete, having been used, but only a small section of the rim and lower foreground is missing. This example has also been used, or perhaps tested, as the rim at one point has been ground. Even quite recently old ink was still valued in certain circles more for its functional qualities than for its qualities as an independent work of art. The story is told of a Japanese calligrapher who valued Chinese ink highly and recently commissioned a dealer to scour the world for old inks, which he would then test by grinding a small section in this manner. If the ink was good he would use it; if not, it would come back on the market in due course slightly ground.

The dating of ink is actually an impossible task on stylistic grounds, although it may be possible to date the moulds in which they were made. Inkmakers' moulds were used to make very considerable numbers of inks, and might have continued in production for a very long period of time. Much later impressions from earlier moulds are apparent in frequent cases where chips in the wooden moulds are faithfully reproduced in the ink. The *Zhongguo Wenfang Sibao Shi* records that in the 17th century the famous scholar/inkmaker Cao Sugong (1615-1689) retired to his native town to take up inkmaking by taking over equipment, including all the moulds, of the Ming inkmaker Wu Shuda. In that case first class ink might have been moulded in the 17th century in a mould bearing an earlier date, and the distinction between it and an original would seem to be somewhat irrelevant today. Early moulds may also have been used in the production of poor ink. With several moulds of the same design being used by one workshop, and the production of fake moulds over a period of many centuries, the potential for confusion is considerable.

There are two separate areas of concern in the connoisseurship of old ink, which usually but not necessarily overlap. One is the quality of the ink. Famous inkmakers were renowned primarily for the fine quality of their ink, rather than for the decorative aspects of their works. The other is the quality of the work of art made from the ink. The modern connoisseur has reversed the priorities of these two concerns, caring more for independent artistic qualities than for the quality of ink. With the secondary issue of the ink itself as an independent work of art, we are in fact dealing with two issues: the artistic quality of the original moulds, and the quality of the impression taken from them. The work of art rests primarily in the moulds. Any good impression from them in fine ink is capable of conveying whatever artistic communication is involved, regardless of whether it was taken a day or a century after the carving of the moulds.

The concept of a 'first edition' is meaningless with ink, and connoisseurship must switch to the ink itself if it is to progress further. If the ink is excellent then we may be reasonably sure that both concerns of the art of inkmaking have been satisfied. If the ink is poor, as it quite obviously is in some cases, then we may assume that we are not dealing with an 'original edition' even if we are dealing with the original block. There is no question that visually a rich, black lacquer-like quality seems to be a characteristic of the best ink, particularly that which has been patinated by time without undue mistreatment, and that this imparts to the impression a richness which adds considerable appeal. It is the same relationship that exists between the quality of the blocks in printing and the use of a fine paper.

185

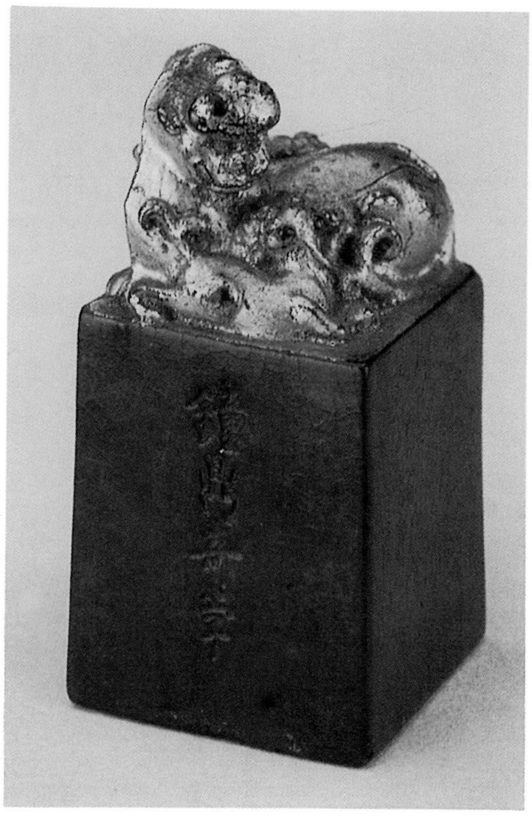

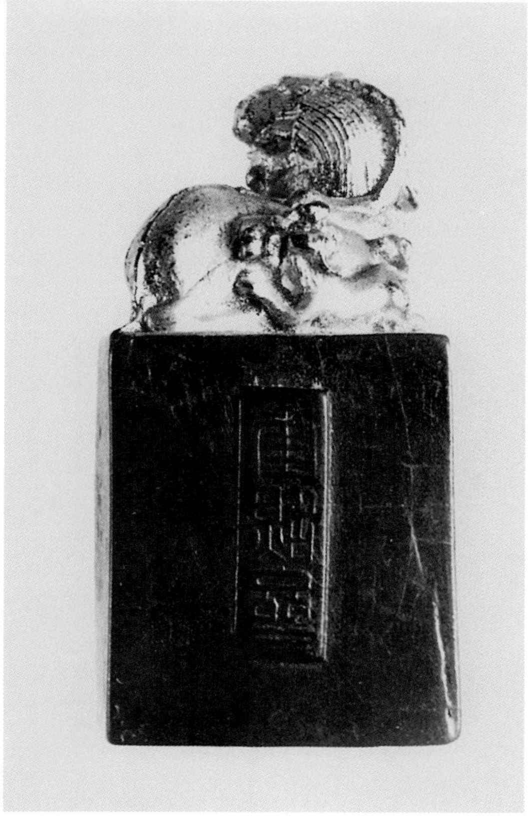

Larger than life size

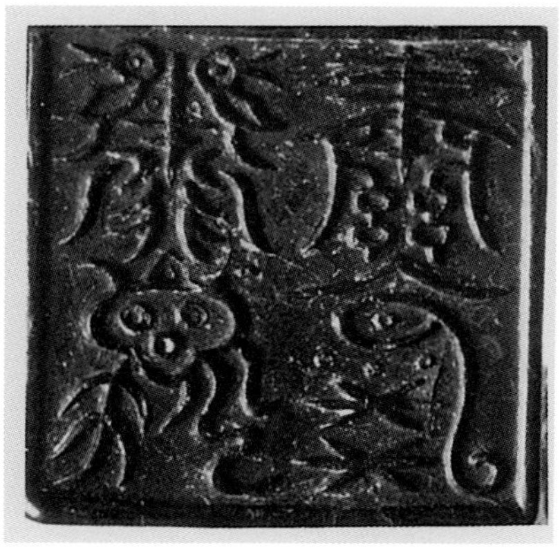

186

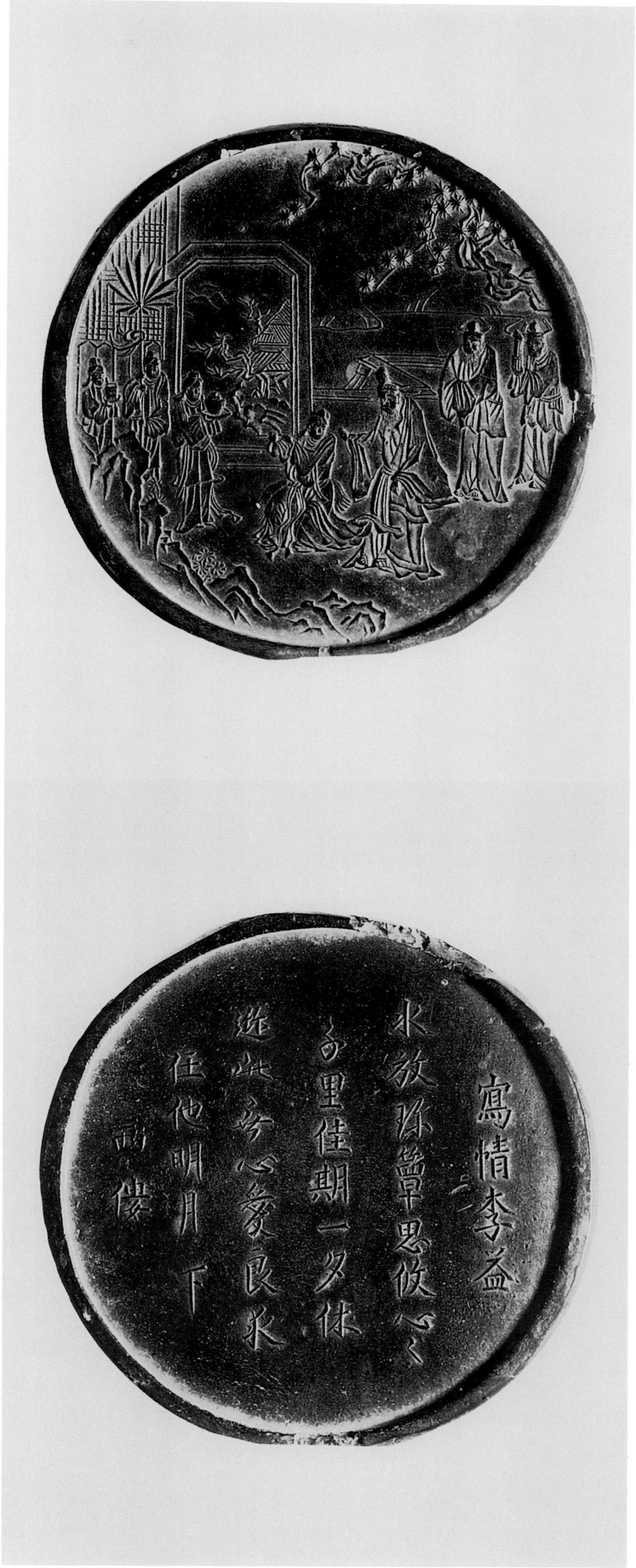

187

Poetry

He Shaoji

Ink on four different colours (pale blue, mauve, and two slightly different shades of creamy white) of gold-splashed paper; four mounted panels of poetry in draft script, followed by the date "Winter day of *dingmao*" (1867), and the signature *Yuansou, He Shaoji* with two seals of the artist *He Shaoji yin* in positive seal script, and *Zizhen* in negative seal script.
1867.
Each panel: 151 cm × 41 cm.
Published: *Anthology of Chinese Art: Min Chiu Society Silver Jubilee Exhibition,* p.270, no. 91.

灑金四色箋詩軸·何紹基書
清同治丁卯(1867),四屏各151×41厘米

He Shaoji (*zi:* Zizhen; *hao:* Dongzhou jushi, Yuansou; 1799-1873) was a native of Daozhou (present-day Daoxian), Hunan province. He was a *jinshi* of 1836 and a minor official. His fame rests in his abilities as a connoisseur, poet and particularly as a calligrapher, in which field he was considered to be unsurpassed in his day.

Our main concern here is with the paper upon which he wrote. Paper, of all the four 'Treasures of the Studio' (see no. 205) transcended least its functional role. Paper was highly valued, but almost exclusively for the way in which it could be transformed into a painting or calligraphy rather than for any independent aesthetic appeal. The finest papers, and particularly old papers which had matured, were much sought after by calligraphers and painters alike. Nor was it uncommon for artists to use papers of often considerable antiquity, and to collect large quantities for future use. Here He Shaoji is using gold-splashed paper typical of the 18th century, possibly predating his calligraphy by a century or more. The origin and meaning of decorative gold-splashing on surfaces remains unclear, but no doubt there was some aesthetic connection between this type of paper and a large group of gold-splashed bronzes of the Ming and post-Ming period (see no. 160); both make use of random patterns of splashed gold.

Paper appears to have been an invention of the Western Han period, at some time during the 1st and 2nd centuries BC, despite its legendary invention by Cai Lun around 195 AD. Its widespread use in painting and calligraphy does not appear to have been developed until the Jin Dynasty (265-420). By the Tang there is evidence of a very wide selection of papers being made, including fancy varieties with gold or other coloured surfaces, decorative motifs, or with gold splashing as in this case. For a detailed history of the introduction of different sorts of paper see *Chinese Traditional Rubbing Techniques* by Lui Wingfong.

188

Inkstone and Cover

Stone, of pale grey colour and very fine grain; carved as an inkstone and cover, with original matching flat-based pestle; the inkstone of plain, flat-topped construction raised slightly above a supporting pedestal, the gently convex base of which is supported on three feet in the form of stylized bears with incised decoration; the outer rim with an incised design of formalized, repetitive pattern, the underside with incised concentric lines forming a central circle and a double outer band; the cover domed and carved in partly free-standing relief with five *chi* dragons entwining with each other and emerging from the surface of the cover to surround a cash (copper coin) in the centre; the dragons with incised decoration, the rim with a formalized repetitive pattern, the outer edge of the cover with a scrolling cloud design, the central coin inscribed *wuzhu* (a standard Han unit of currency); the interior plain; the pestle cut from a dome-shaped central recess inside the lid and of matching dome shape, decorated with a series of incised lines, one running horizontally above the base, and others segmenting the upper hemisphere into eight sections; a single patch of malachite encrustration attached to the leg of one dragon.
Eastern Han dynasty.
Height: 12.15 cm. Diameter: 22.4 cm.
Diameter of pestle: 4.5 cm.

石雕五螭三足圓硯連蓋及磨石·五銖錢銘
東漢,高12.15厘米,直徑22.4厘米

A very similar inkstone of the same construction and dragon decoration surrounding a *wuzhu* cash, but of smaller size and with the addition of an interior water-pool, was excavated from an Eastern Han tomb at Xiyan Village, Yanshi, Henan province[1]. In the same excavation a number of *wuzhu* coins were also found.

The *Bimozhiyan Tulu* ('Brush, Ink, Paper and Inkstone Pictorial') gives a useful brief history of the early phase in the development of the inkstone from which this example comes. In 1975, in a Qin dynasty tomb at Yuman, a brush, ink and an inkstone were discovered. This early inkstone was just a flat, rectangular stone surface with an additional small flat-faced pestle (or grinding stick) used when ink was made from ground natural graphite. In the same year, from a Western Han tomb at Fenghuang Shan, at Jianling county, Hubei province a further set of writing instruments was discovered. The inkstone was a circular one with an additional grinding stone still used.

In these early times the popular form for inkstones seems to have been circular, set on three small feet. During the Han dynasty, and into the period of the succeeding Six Dynasties, another shape began to emerge which was round, and set on high feet (see no. 190). The inkstone raised on feet owes its existence to the fact that scholars in those days worked at floor level, or on raised platforms which still left scholar and inkstone on the same plane, making it useful to raise the inkstone to a comfortable functional height. It was not until the advent of a separate desk and chairs that these legs were no longer required. By the end of the Six Dynasties the manufacture of ink had progressed to such an extent that the separate grinding stone was no longer required. The first inkstones without feet appear to have been made in the Five Dynasties period.

1. See *Kaogu,* 1985, no. 8, pp.721-735.

187

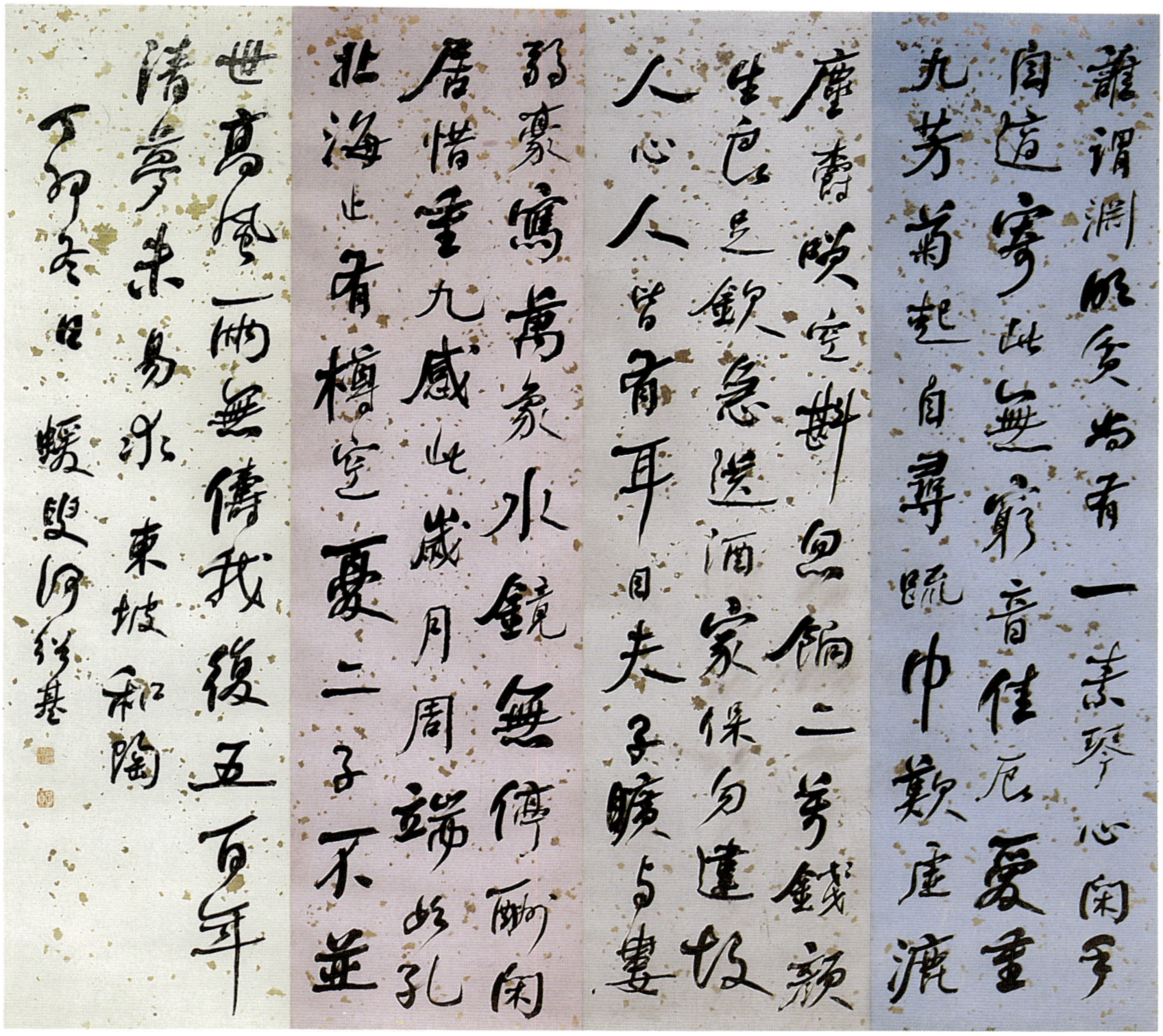

188

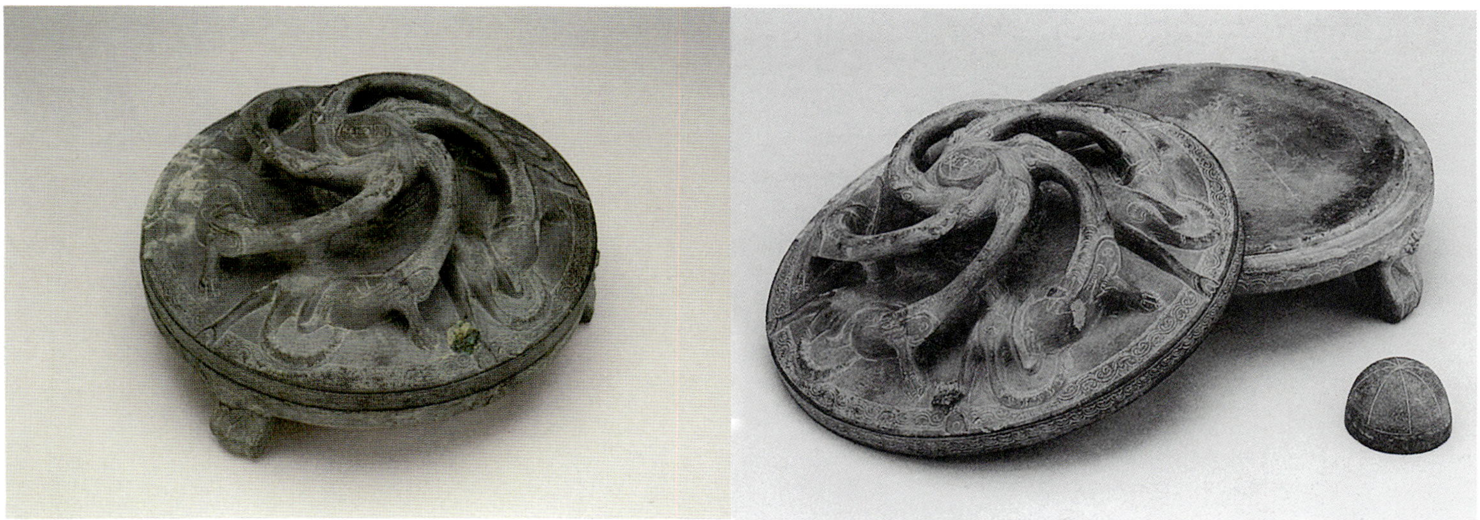

189

'Kunlun' Inkstone

Limestone, of the variety known as Duan stone, of even, dark purplish-brown colour; an inkstone, the irregular form carved in low relief with a pine tree growing up one side, its branches enclosing the upper section and the irregular, gnarled water-pool and smooth, very slightly convex ink-pool; the reverse unworked, apart from the inscription of the title *Kunlun.* Probably early Qing dynasty.
Inkstone: 4.3 cm × 21 cm × 20.5 cm.
Contained in a *zitan* wood box, with an inscription written by Wu Hufan, giving the title *Kunlun,* followed by "Zhongyi has obtained a fine stone from the water quarry of the Great West Cave. It is moist and rustic and in the spiritual class. Noted by Wu Hufan". With a collector's seal of Guo Zhongyi *Guo shi Qinyan Zhai zangyen yin* ('The seal for the collection of inkstones in the *Qin* and Inkstone Studio of the Guo family').
Box: 6.9 cm × 23.3 cm × 23.2 cm.
Formerly in the Guo Zhongyi collection.

端石刻松崑崙硯
可能清初，4.3×21×20.5厘米

Duan stone was first mined in the early Tang dynasty, the stone coming from quarries beside the 'Antelope Gap' outside Shaoxing city (known in the past as Duanzhou or Duanxi). Mining is thought to have begun in the early 7th century, and the material was noted by various Tang and Song poets (Li He of Tang described cutting of Duan stone as "stepping up to the sky, sharpening the knife and cutting the purple clouds"). In Tang times the best stones were reserved for imperial tribute, selected by a specially appointed envoy. There are currently about ten main quarries still producing the stone, each having its own characteristics; while one is famous for producing stones with eyes, another will produce purplish blue stones with green moss spots, and others have reflective gold speckling and purple 'fire blemishes' in the stone. The best stone is considered to come from the *Shuikeng* ('water quarry'), also known as *Huangkeng* ('Emperor's quarry') as it was reserved for imperial tribute. Since the Kangxi period it has been called simply *Laokeng* ('Old quarry'). The quarry branches off into four caves, and that which produces the best stone is the *Daxidong* ('Great West Cave').

In the *Changwu Ji* ('Notes on Superfluous Objects'), Wen Zhenheng wrote in praise of this stone: "...there are natural pebbles, warm and moist as jade; when ink is ground on them, no sound is produced. It has the quality of *famo* [that is, not slippery in grinding, but grinds easily and retains the ink for a long time without drying, creating reflective, lacquer-like ink which is considered to be a quality of the stone as much as of the ink], and will not damage the hairs of the brush. It is indeed a rare treasure of this world."[1]

Guo Zhongyi is the present owner's father. He was born in 1900, and was a good friend of Wu Hufan, sharing a house with him in Shanghai for a time.

1. *Juan 7,* section 50.

190

Inkstone

Stoneware, of grey colour; an inkstone, the small, flat ink-pool surrounded by concentric rings and set in a deep water-pool in the form of a gutter; the outer lip of which is rimmed with concentric ribs above a band of formalized flower heads and a band of formalized lappets, all in stepped progression and supported on 23 densely packed lion feet, each consisting of the lion's head giving way immediately to a large paw, and all supported on a plain circular flanged base; the interior hollow and the central recess with a lip of double concentric rings.
Sui or early Tang dynasty.
Height: 11.9 cm. Diameter: 23.1 cm.

白瓷二十三獅足圓硯
隋或唐初，高11.9厘米，直徑23.1厘米

Stoneware inkstones of this general type were popular in the Sui/Tang period. They are characterized by central ink-pools surrounded by guttered water-pools set on a series of elaborate and often densely packed feet. Another in buff stoneware is shown as no. 202, and there is one illustrated in *Shogakukan* ('Ceramic Art of the World', Vol. 2, no. 107, p.126), also in buff stoneware. As a rule the feet are formalized, but in this example they are very clearly lion heads set on exaggeratedly large paws (all apparently formed in the same mould). The lion is also of typical Sui/Tang style as found in a range of gilt bronzes and other works of art of the period.

189

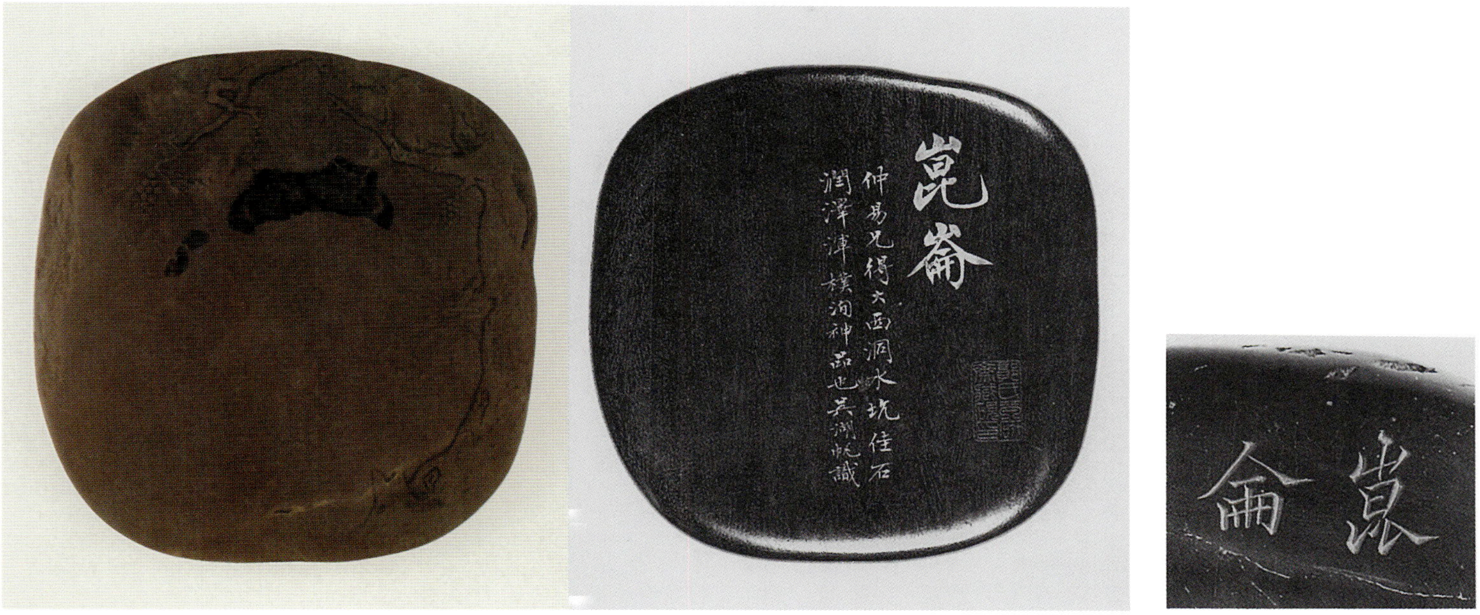

190

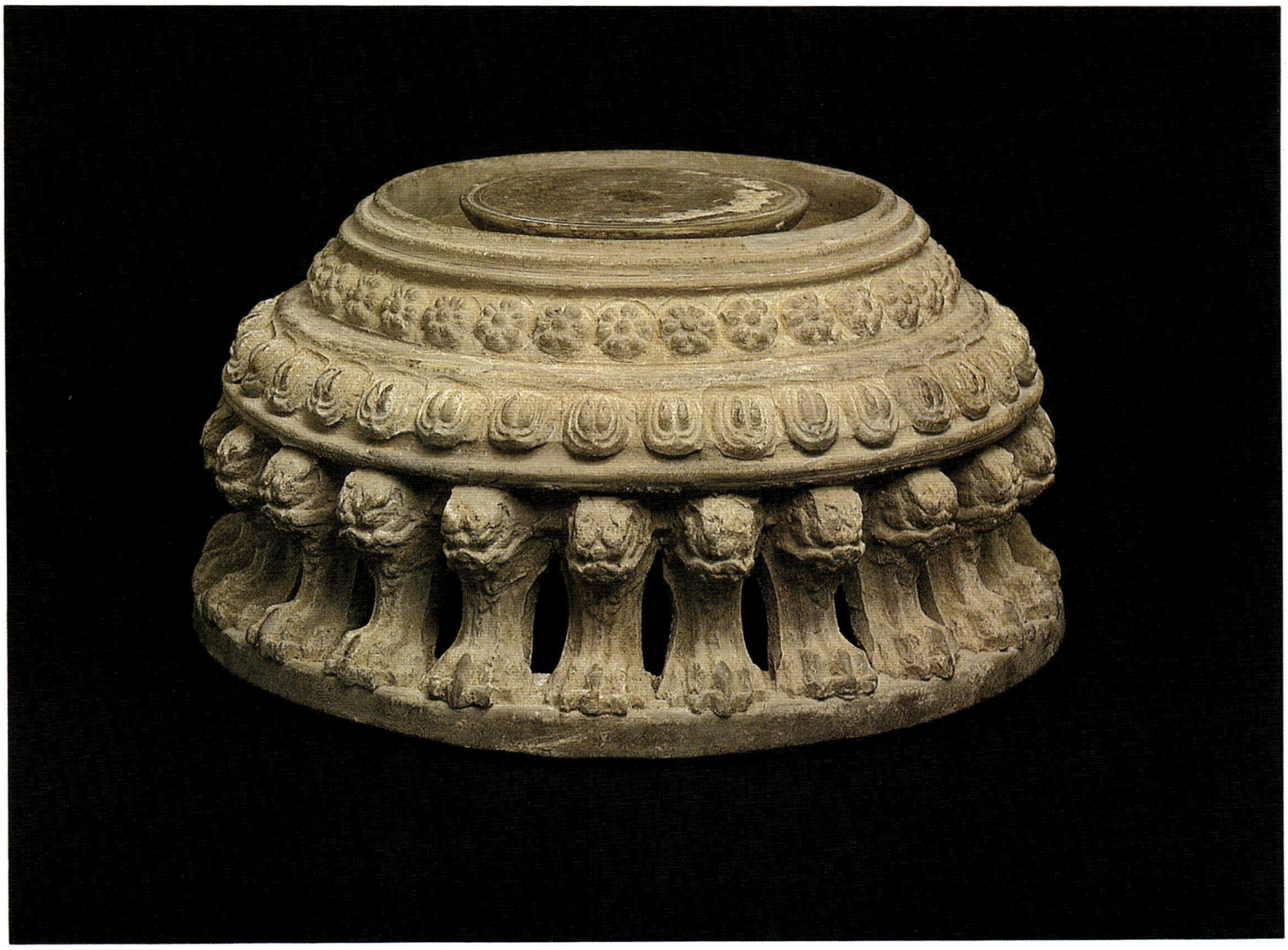

191

'Banana Leaf White' Inkstone

Limestone, of the variety known as Duan stone, of purplish colour, with grey-green and beige-grey markings; a plain, rectangular inkstone, the natural pattern in the stone resembling a banana leaf.
Qing dynasty.
Inkstone: 2.9 cm × 21.8 cm × 14.7 cm.
Contained in a wood box of domed rectangular shape, set on four small feet.
20th century.
Box: 6.1 cm × 24.3 cm × 16.7 cm.

端石蕉葉白素方硯
清代, 2.9×21.8×14.7厘米

The connoisseurship of inkstones, once functional suitability was established, rested on certain visual characteristics, the presence of which could add immensely to the value of a stone. Traditional praise for the type known as *jiaoye bai* ('banana leaf white') was a mixture of admiration and mystery. The banana leaf pattern was described as 'soft and dense, as the autumn clouds, as mist over waves.' It is hardly visible until the stone is submerged in water. (This photograph was taken under water to show the mysterious markings more clearly.) The leaf-shaped pattern resembles a young banana leaf before it turns deep green. In the purplish, dark grey stone surrounding it are traces of *huona* ('fire blemishes'), purple markings characteristic of Duan stone. The stone has been left as a plain rectangle to allow its beauty to speak for itself.

The flat stone without an ink or water-pool does not hold a great deal of ink, but is suitable for the preparation of dense black ink used sparingly in painting, for the writing of small characters in calligraphy, or for writing letters or notes.

192

'Clouds and Moon' Inkstone

Limestone, of the variety known as Duan stone, of purplish-brown colour with some green streaking, with a single 'eye' of varying shades of green, orange and beige of the variety *quyu yan* ('mynah's eye') and areas of rough 'skin' of various colours; an inkstone, the irregularly shaped ink-pool with billowing clouds in low relief at its upper edge, enclosing the single 'eye' which appears like a mysteriously glowing moon; various facets left in their rough state, a flat section of the back inscribed in seal script: "Naturally upright; with a strong and long-lasting texture. Good for calligraphy and painting; it will last a long time." Followed by an inscription in regular script praising the elegant pursuits of Fan Chai (the present owner) and his wife stating that it was his sixtieth birthday in the second month of 1980, and that the inscriber was asked to celebrate the occasion by writing on this inkstone. Signed "Blind old man, Fang Kenghou, at the age of eighty" with seal *Feng* in negative seal script.
Probably late Qing dynasty.
Inkstone: 3.5 cm × 20.3 cm × 14.7 cm.
Contained in a *hongmu* wood box of plain rectangular form with a domed cover.
Probably 20th century.
Box: 5.7 cm × 22.8 cm × 17 cm.

端石水坑鸜鵒眼雲月硯•馮康侯刻銘
可能晚清, 3.5×20.3×14.7厘米

This is a *shuikeng* ('water quarry') Duan stone characterized by its moistness. The eye, with its concentric rings of different colours, is known as *quyu yan* ('mynah's eye'). In the *Duanshi Yanfu* ('Prose-poem on Duan Stone Inkstones') the early Qing scholar Pan Chikeng differentiated between *quyu yan* and *wuya yan* ('crow's eye'), stating that the former was rounded or oval, while the latter was elongated, with pointed ends. These eyes were much valued in Duan stones, and the same prose poem describes those of concentric rings with a pupil in the middle as lovely, and in the *huoyan* ('living eyes') class. This 'real life' quality was highly valued. See no. 55 for another example of a Duan stone eye, used cunningly as the eye of an elephant.

The lively and finely coloured and marked stone has been used brilliantly, with some areas of rough and stained stone left to form a counterpoint to the smoothness of the polished surface. The natural design of the moon is enhanced with low relief carving of clouds in a masterpiece combining the human hand and nature.

Fang Kenghou (1900-1983) was a famous Hong Kong seal carver and artist.

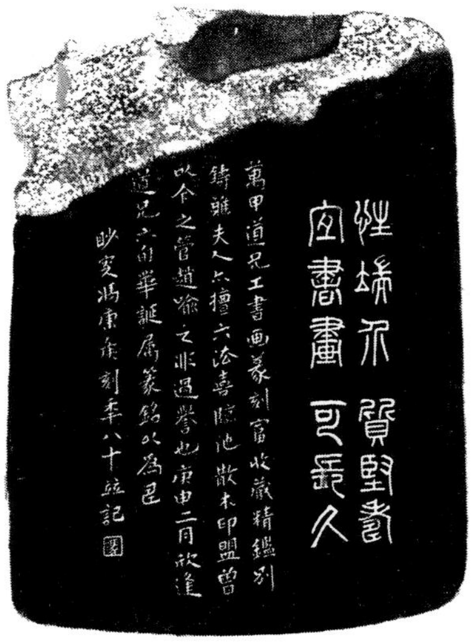

193

Inkstone

Marble, of mottled, yellowish lime-green colour; an inkstone carved in the form of a stylized nightingale, its head, wings and tail enclosing the well-worn ink-pool of its breast, a deeply recessed water-pool with a raised rim set near the tail; the surface extensively eroded where the calceous material has weathered.
Probably Song dynasty.
Height: 7.3 cm. Length: 23.8 cm.

雲石雕夜鶯硯
可能宋代, 高7.3厘米, 長23.8厘米

The famous Song literatus Mi Fu owned a nightingale inkstone of this type, which is illustrated in the *Sancai Tuhui* of 1697 (see Fig. 1) where it is described as half an ancient tile which had been carved into a nightingale. The workmanship is described as excellent, and the material dense and strong. The tail is inscribed

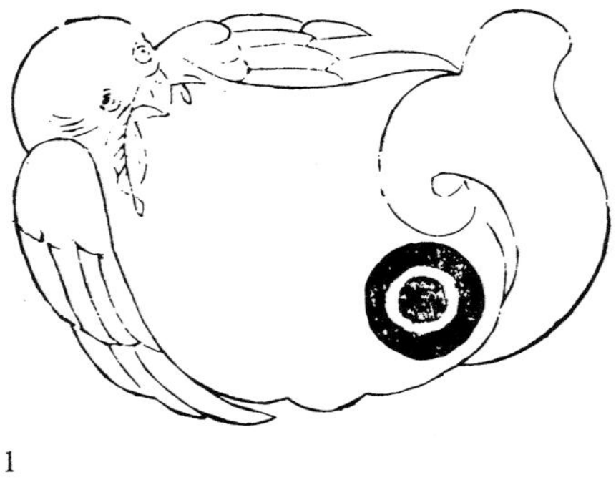

Fig. 1

with Mi's *zi* Yuanzhang, and the seal *Mi*. Another of very similar form but inscribed "parrot inkstone" is in the Tianjin Museum[1] where it is dated to the Song dynasty. It bears the collector's seal of a certain Zhang Xitian and has the same formal concept, including the unusually deep water-pool, and massive structure. The three are unquestionably related in some way.

Presumably these bird-form inkstones were popular in Song China, perhaps partly in response to Mi Fu's example which would have been reasonably well known among the influential literati of his day. The state of surface degredation and wear on this unusual example would suggest considerable age, and it seems reasonable to accept it as probably of the Song dynasty.

The mottled lime-yellow marble used here is a most unusual variety of limestone. The very popular Duan stone is also a type of limestone, as were many of the other stones used for grinding ink.

1. *Tianjin Shi Yishu Bowuguan Zangyan* ('Inkstones in the Collection of the Tianjian City Art Museum'), no. 12.

191

192

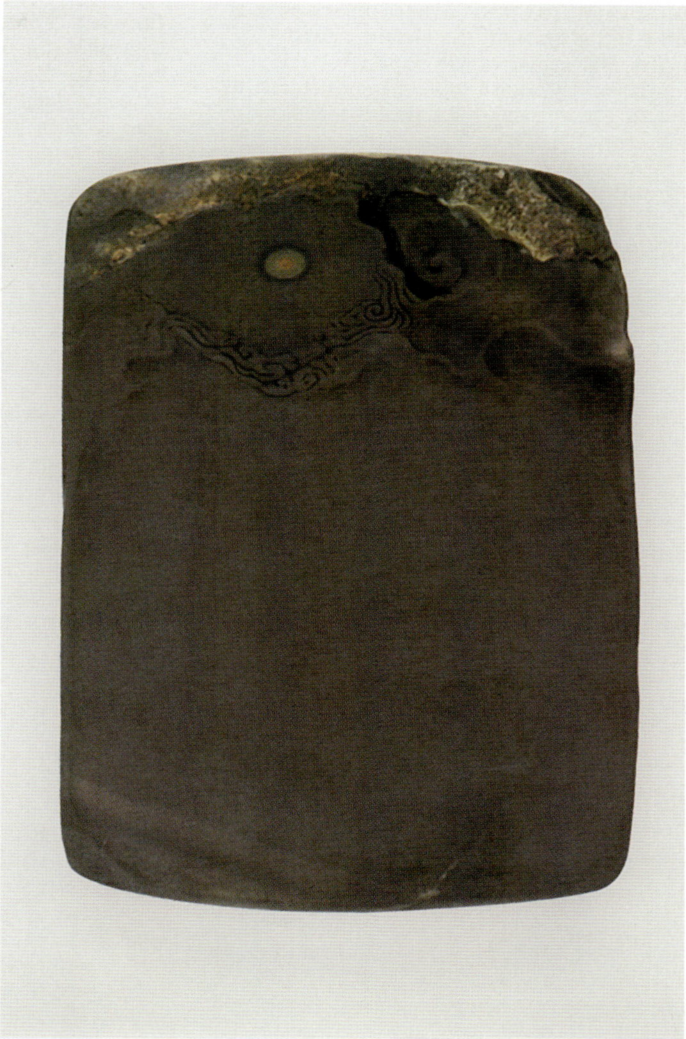

193

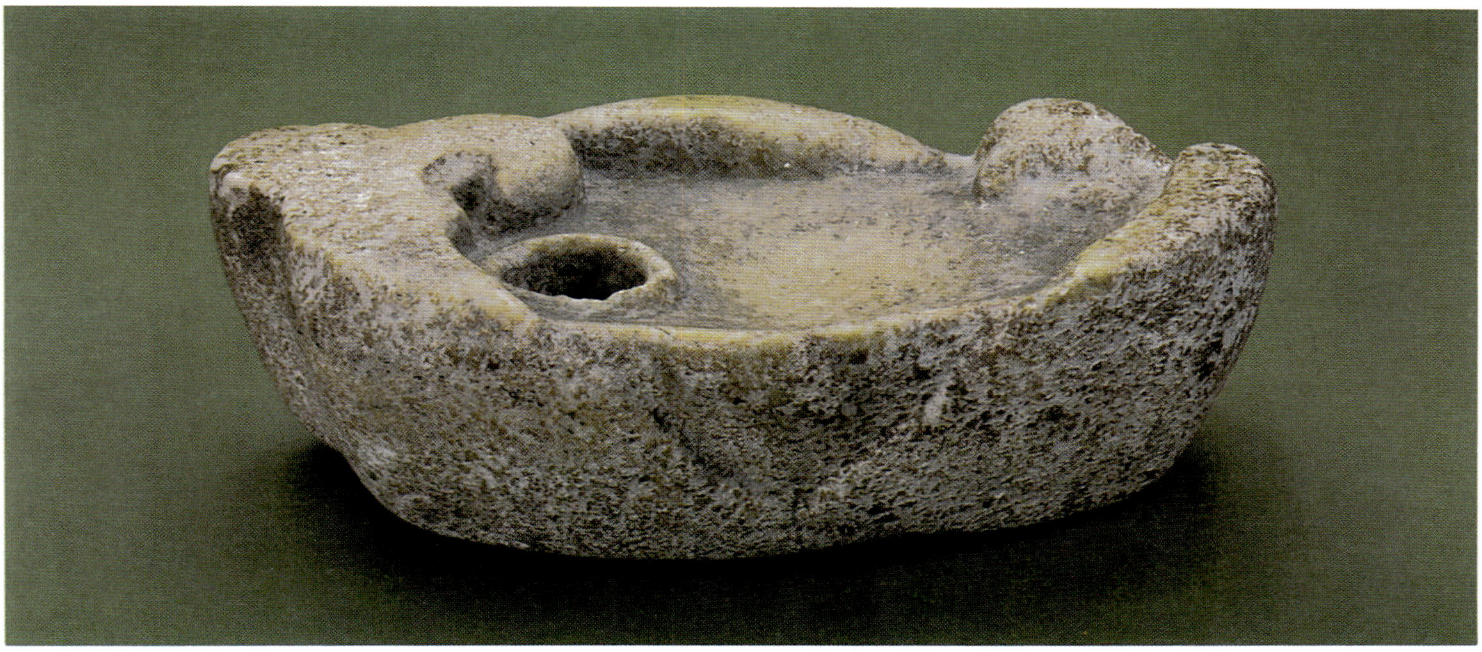

194

Paper Weight

Bronze, with gilding which is worn through in places to reveal well-patinated bronze beneath; a mythical beast, the body covered in scales with flames curling up from the shoulders and haunches, the conventional mane with a mandorla-like extension immediately behind the head acting as a frame for a protrusion of double central horns on the crown; the entire surface covered with gilding, now worn through on all protruding surfaces.
Probably early Ming dynasty.
Height: 6.5 cm. Length 6.6 cm.

鎏金青銅異獸紙鎮
可能明初, 高6.5厘米, 長6.6厘米

This rare paper weight might be as early as the Yuan dynasty or as late as the 16th century, but the early Ming period would seem to be a reasonable attribution. It is an unusual model of which we have seen one other early example. However, recently a series of copies of it have appeared on the market from China which are exactly the same model, but not gilt. Presumably they have been taken from an original such as this.

We have discussed the problems of identifying mythical animals elsewhere. However, this strange creature with its goat-like beard and hooves, its double but central horn and scaled body may be identified with two beasts. One arises out of a legend that is recorded in the *Yunnan Tongzhi* (*'Yunnan Gazette'*). There was, apparently, a shepherd who played a fine flute while grazing his sheep beside the Peach Tree River. One day the dragon's daughter arose out of the waters and greeted him, ushering him to follow her, together with his goats into the river. Upon entering the river the goats were transformed into fish, which in the Chinese view could be transformed again into dragons upon leaping the *Longmen* ('Dragon's Gate') falls (also a metaphor for becoming a scholar). The place was thereafter called the *Yanglong Tan* ('Goat-dragon Pool'). It is, of course, highly unlikely that this piece derives from that legend, but it is worth mentioning as an example of the huge diversity of sources for the invention and evolution of mythical beasts.

It could also be associated with the *zouyu,* a creature which in the eyes of Fang Yulu, the famous late Ming inkmaker, looked like the illustration in Fig. 1. It is taken from his *Fang Shi Mopu* and appears on an ink of the 'National Treasure' class (see no. 175 for this work and no. 101 for a discussion on 'National Treasure' class inks).

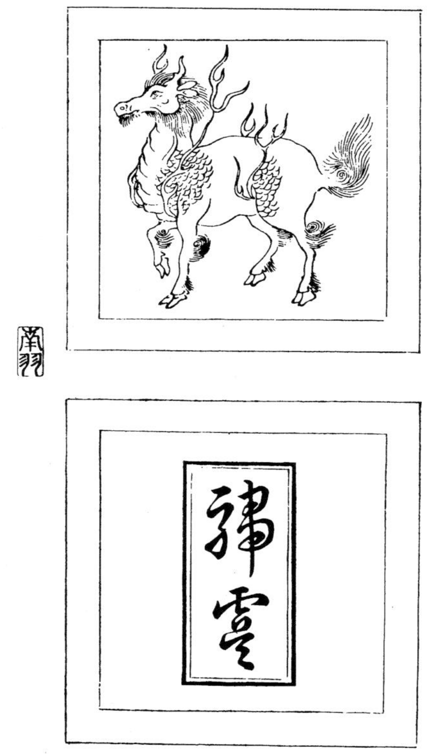

Fig. 1

195

Paper Weight

Bronze; a paper weight in the form of a reclining mythical beast, the leonine features with a ribbed chest and belly, a body completely covered in highly stylized flames, some of *ruyi* form, a bushy tail, and a single, *ruyi*-shaped horn between its floppy ears; the mouth snarling to reveal business-like teeth below a pair of intense and angry eyes; the neck draped with a belled collar with tassles; the base also fully worked.
Probably Ming or early Qing dynasty.
Height: 5.6 cm. Length: 8.1 cm.
Formerly in the Robert A. Hall collection.

青銅異獸紙鎮
可能明或清初, 高5.6厘米, 長8.1厘米

Although this beast is neither gilded nor inlaid, it is set apart from the run of 'Ming' bronze paper weights by its size and forceful modelling. It is probably intended to be a *xiezhai,* a mythical beast found in Chinese works of art from the Han dynasty. It was considered to be able to distinguish between good and evil, and so became the emblem of judges and of the Imperial Censors, whose job it was to deal with any breach of integrity among officials. It is distinguished by its single horn, leonine features, paws and lack of scales. The *ruyi*-shaped horn is a most unusual embellishment for this beast, and might suggest a rather late development of it, perhaps from the early Qing period.

Most of these bronze and jade paper weights also function as brush rests, which cannot have been wholly accidental. It is convenient for the collector to expect a particular piece to perform a specific function — it makes cataloguing so much easier — but when an artist was painting or writing, caught up in the inspiration of the moment, proper function of his scholars' objects would hardly have concerned him. A weight, easily to hand, that could serve also as a brush rest, or a *ruyi* sceptre or small wood carving doubling as a weight or brush rest, were much more convenient than single function objects. The lesson of genre paintings and woodblock illustrations in this direction is clear: however we may describe classes of objects in our catalogues, there was a remarkable degree of flexibility in use. Incense burners were used as water vessels, *ruyi* sceptres as hooks from which to suspend things or as brush rests, vases as brush pots, teapots as flower vases, and so on.

196

Covered Container

Gourd, cut open at the neck and lined with a *zitan* rim, the cover carved from boxwood, the whole in the form of a persimmon growing on a sprig.
Probably mid-Qing dynasty.
Height including cover: 5.8 cm.

葫蘆製柿形盒連木蓋
可能清中葉, 高連蓋5.8厘米

The gourd has served as a natural water container since earliest times and it is possible that this vessel was for water. There are, however, other uses to which a small container of this type might be put in the scholar's studio. With its rustic simplicity and restrained taste, and its combination of a natural form embellished by the human hand, it is a representative 'scholar's object', designed to delight the 'inner eye' as much as the physical eye.

An great amount of Chinese art carries symbolism, the nature of which we have only been able to hint at here in many cases. The persimmon *(shi)* is homophonous with the character for 'affairs'. A popular wish, *shishi ruyi* ('may all your affairs go as you wish') would be brought to mind by the persimmon. But that is only the most obvious level of meaning. The persimmon is also known for its longevity as a tree; for the excellent shade it provides; for the fact that birds do not nest in it and it has no worm or insect problems; for the appearance of its leaves on frosty autumn days and for their good size, which allows them to be used for writing calligraphy on (writing on leaves was a popular habit among the literati), and of course for its fruit. Any or all of these associations might also work their subtle magic of communication in the subject of a persimmon on a scholar's desk.

194

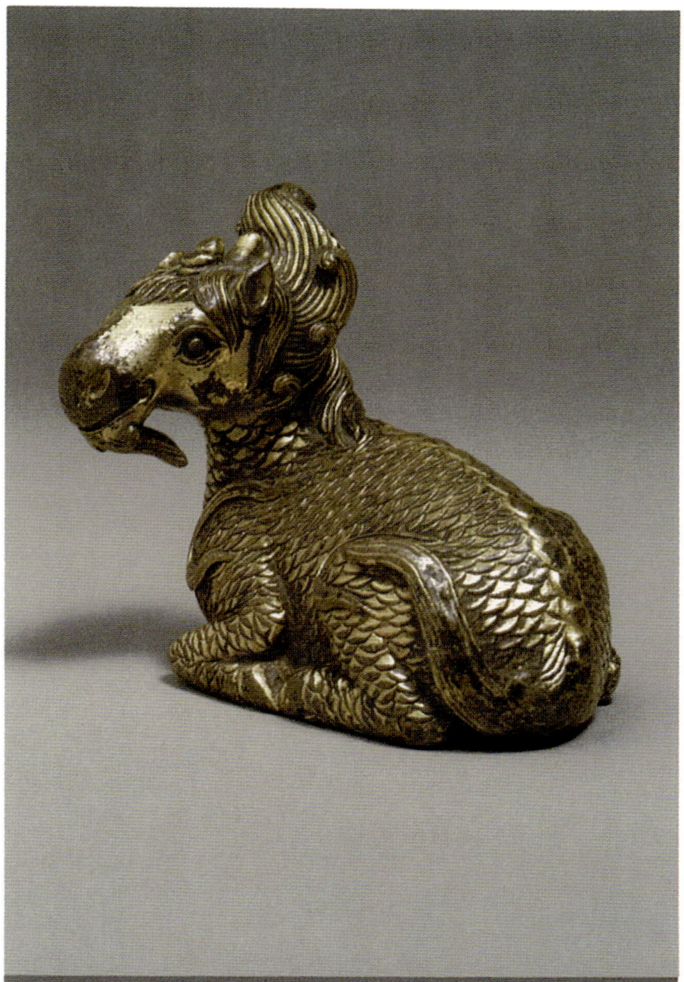

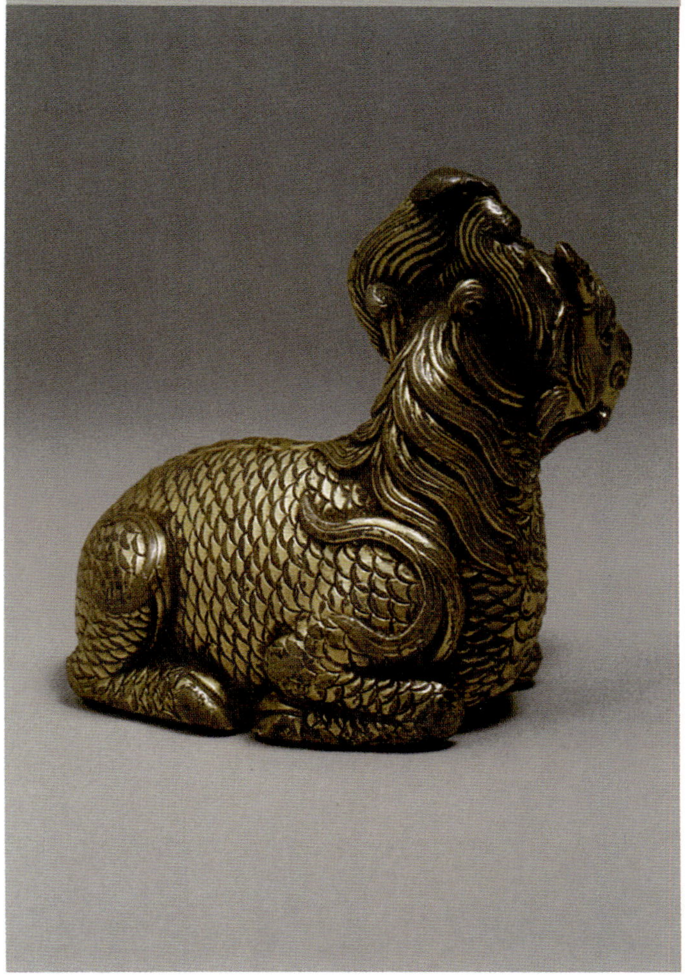

195

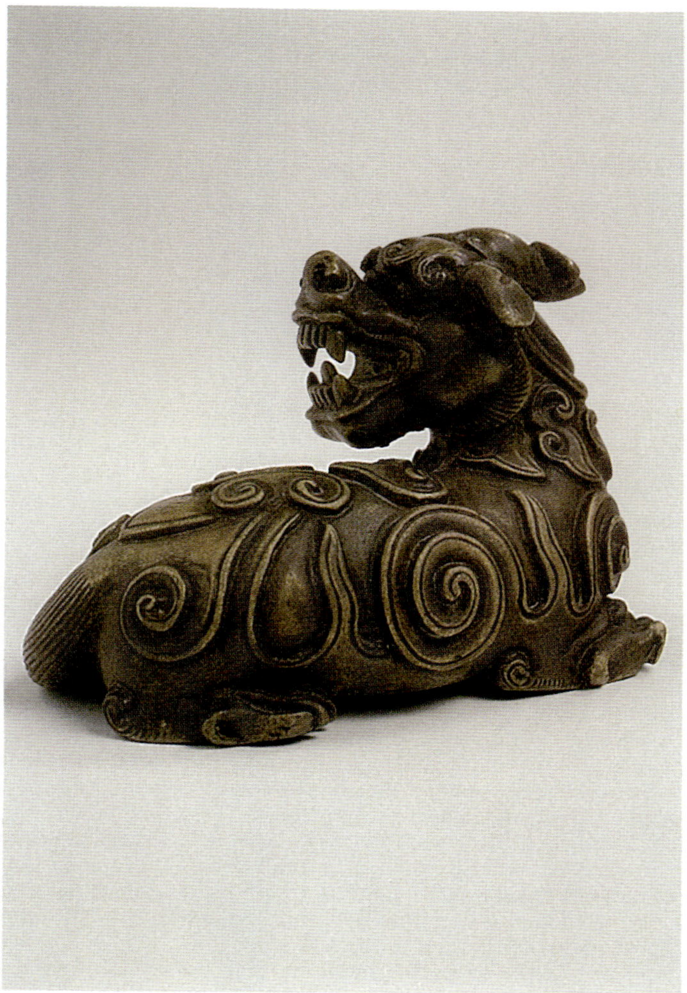

196

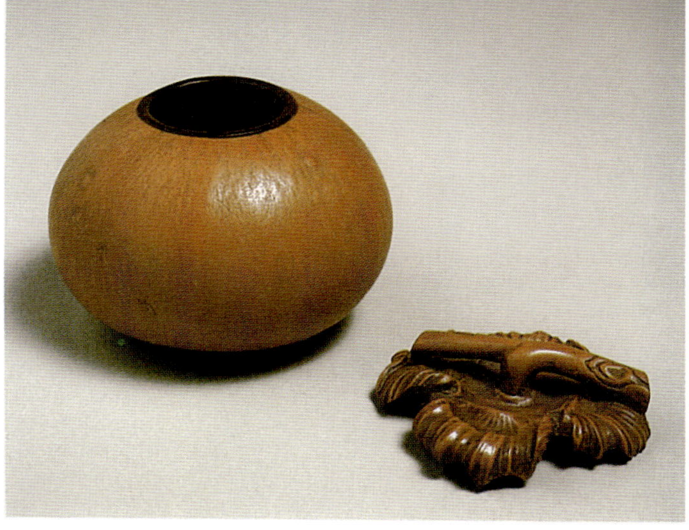

197

Brush Rest

Wood, *zitan,* of dark, blackish-brown colour, with areas of yellow and golden brown; a brush rest carved in the form of a six-peaked mountain range.
Ming or Qing dynasty.
Height: 7.8 cm. Length: 21.5 cm.
Published: *Wood From the Scholar's Table,* p.76, no. 39.

紫檀六嶽筆山
明或清代, 高7.8厘米, 長21.5厘米

The blond markings in this example are apparently characteristic of *zitan* where pieces are cut from the base of the tree; they represent the points at which the roots join the main trunk.

The dating of such a piece as this is almost impossible. Contrived to look natural and simulating a miniature rock formation, it would have found favour from at least the Song dynasty onwards, and although the dating in the above mentioned publication of 'perhaps 17th century' is a reasonable guess, it is no more than this.

This rest has a thin layer of transparent lacquer applied to the surface — a fairly common manner of treating Chinese woods giving them an even and quite high gloss. It does, however, tend to obscure to some extent the colour and beauty of the wood and is sometimes stripped off by modern collectors who prefer to let the grain speak for itself. Similar lacquer coats are found on a good deal of furniture, particularly from the north where extreme changes in temperature encourage a sealing coat of lacquer to make moisture levels remain constant within the wood.

198

Seal

Ivory, of well-worn and patinated golden and creamy yellow tones; carved as a seal, the knob in the form of a *chi* dragon coiling around on itself, set upon a double gourd-shaped plinth; the seal text reading *yiyang* ('the same as').
Ming dynasty, probably 15th century.
Height: 4.1 cm. Maximum width: 3.4 cm.

象牙雕螭龍葫蘆印
明代, 可能十五世紀, 高4.1厘米, 寬3.4厘米

A surface level interpretation of this seal is completed by the double-gourd shape of the seal impression. A double gourd is called a *hulu* and *yiyang hulu* ('the same as the gourd') means to follow in the same manner as something already established. However at a deeper level it may be taken as meaning stupid, in a positive sense. In Yuan dynasty songs there is a term *hulu ti* ('pretending to be stupid'). The stalk of the gourd is also called *ti;* thus the seal shape may also be taken to mean 'pretending to be stupid'. This corrupts to *hutu* meaning stupid, or chaotic of mind, muddled.

Zheng Xie, the 18th century Yangzhou artist, had a plaque inscribed *lande hutu* ('it is not easy to be stupid'), and C.C. Wang once fondly described one of his favourite artists of antiquity as a 'stupid painter'. It implies the sort of mind that has risen above the intellectual grasp of matters, like that of the poet Tao Yuanming, who was fond of reading but refused to go to any lengths to explain or understand in detail the things he came across. The intellectual level was not considered to represent the real truth, but only a relative truth, and a certain degree of 'stupidity' was required to rise above this.

The shape might also carry a hidden Daoist meaning, in so far as the double gourd, with its two bulbs separated by a narrow waist, represented Daoist paradisaical realms. Several stories relate how Daoists were able to disappear inside the gourds so often shown at their belts or hanging from their staffs, and inside would be whole new realms of existence. Thus it might also be taken in a Doaist context to mean that the painting upon which it is affixed is an alternative realm of existence.

A circular plaque in the Metropolitan Museum of Art (illustrated as no. 13 on p.32, and colour plate 1, of *Chinese Ivories from the Shang to the Qing)* relates closely to this seal in the subject-matter, style and wear and patination. The plaque is carved in high relief with a group of *chi* dragons which are remarkably similar to that on this seal, with sinuous, recurving necks, flat, broad-backed heads and flaming muscular flanks. What is even more unusual is that the Metropolitan plaque has one beast with a quite distinctly hairy tail, rather than the usual smooth one, and the *chi* here has that rare feature. Also related, particularly to the larger *chi* dragons on the Metropolitan plaque, are those on the rhinoceros horn cup with the Xuande mark, no. 158, which we confidently date to the early 15th century. The Metropolitan plaque has been variously dated at different times from the Song to the Qing dynasty, but is now tentatively dated to the 14th or 15th century. In the above-mentioned work the *chi* dragon is noted as becoming popular during the Yuan period, and certain features are mentioned as typical features of 14th century *chi* dragons. These include the long narrow necks and the raised line down the backbone and along the branching tail, similar to those on the plaque.

However, the possibility of archaism from a somewhat later date cannot be excluded. The *chi* dragon, a popular motive of Han decoration (especially on sword scabbard buckles) was likely to have been revived under the archaistic fervour of the Song dynasty, although it may have become particularly popular in the 14th century. From that point onwards it remained a favoured motif, retaining its Han form reasonably consistently, although stylistic changes are noticeable; the greater use of bird and other animal heads on *chi* bodies seems to characterize its archaistic evolution. The features of sinuous necks and raised backbones are equally common on snuff bottles of the first half of the Qing dynasty and may not, in themselves, be read as specifically early features. A square plaque which appears to be of the same group (op. cit., p.34, no. 16) is given a broader possible dating range extending to the 17th century on the grounds that it might represent a 17th century resurgence of the earlier Yuan or early Ming style.

Another square plaque of the same group was offered by Christies in London, as Lot 267, on 19th April 1983, also with *chi* dragons. It too was well-worn and patinated. Where a group of related wares of this type are all well-worn and patinated, with considerable age cracking, the evidence becomes more convincing. With a single well-worn example a lifetime of unusual use may be to blame, but this likelihood is all but ruled out with four examples. From the state of known groups of Qing ivories, and that of dated early Ming ivories (see *Dated Chinese Antiquities,* p.239, nos. 189 and 190, dated 1418 and 1427 respectively) the patination on this *chi* dragon group would be consistent with a Ming date, although we believe that a 15th century date would be more likely than one in the 14th century. Whatever their period, we believe it is likely that they were all made at the same time.

199

Brush Rest

Wood, *chenxiangmu* (lignaloes), of rich reddish-brown colour made up of several sections joined together; a brush rest in the form of a mountainous landscape, with a scholar and attendant strolling by a river, with a nearby rustic retreat.
Set on a *zitan* wood stand.
Probably Ming dynasty.
Height including stand: 6.8 cm.
Length: 12.8 cm.

沈香木雕山水高士筆擱
可能明代, 高連座6.8厘米, 長12.8厘米

Chenxiangmu is a fragrant wood identified as lignaloes by Ellsworth[1] and as gharu wood *(aquilaria agallocha,* so called because it sinks in water) by Sheila Riddell[2] — although this example does not sink in water. Apparently this wood was held in high esteem, the best coming from Cambodia according to a renowned 12th century traveller.[3]

A number of small cups exist in this material, not unlike rhinoceros horn cups in appearance. They are characterized by being made of separate sections of wood joined together, suggesting that it was commonly found in small pieces. It was also, along with sandalwood, used as incense (see no. 229) and was probably imported in small chunks for that purpose. Carvers finding it suitable for the manufacture of small objects for the scholar might have used these small pieces either because of the unavailability of larger sections or because the reference to the incense cult carried its own meaning and the use of incense-size pieces added weight to an already scholarly piece.

The range of small cups, and occasionally other pieces such as this brush rest, made of this wood are all closely connected in style and subject-matter. Indeed, they might all be from the same workshop. Three are illustrated by Bo Gyllensvärd.[4] Two are signed by brothers who were renowned 12th century wood carvers, but these signatures are not credible. This whole group echoes certain trends in painting which were firmly established only in the Yuan dynasty. Gyllensvärd also illustrates an enamelled silver cup bearing the signature of Zhu Bishan, the Yuan silversmith; while it is related in style to these cups, it is again not wholly convincing for the period as it is enamelled in a manner which is otherwise unknown for the period. We believe that a Ming date is much more likely for the whole group.

1. *Chinese Furniture: Hardwood Examples of the Ming and Early Ch'ing Dynasties.*
2. *Dated Chinese Antiquities 600-1650.*
3. Ibid., p.228.
4. *'Two Yuan Silver Cups and Their Importance for Dating of Some Carvings in Wood and Rhinoceros Horn',* by Bo Gyllensvärd, in the *Bulletin of the Museum of Far Eastern Antiquities,* Stockholm, no. 43, 1971, pp.223-233.

197

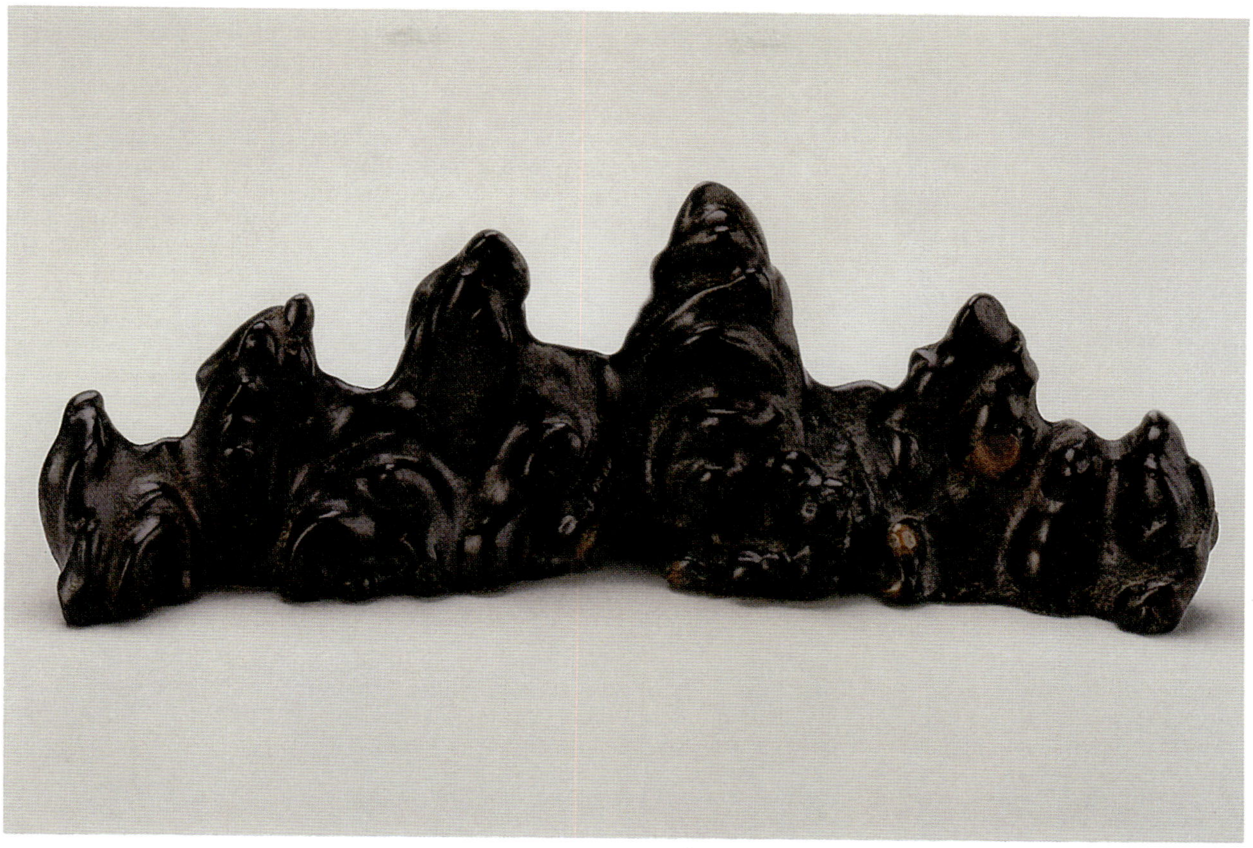

198

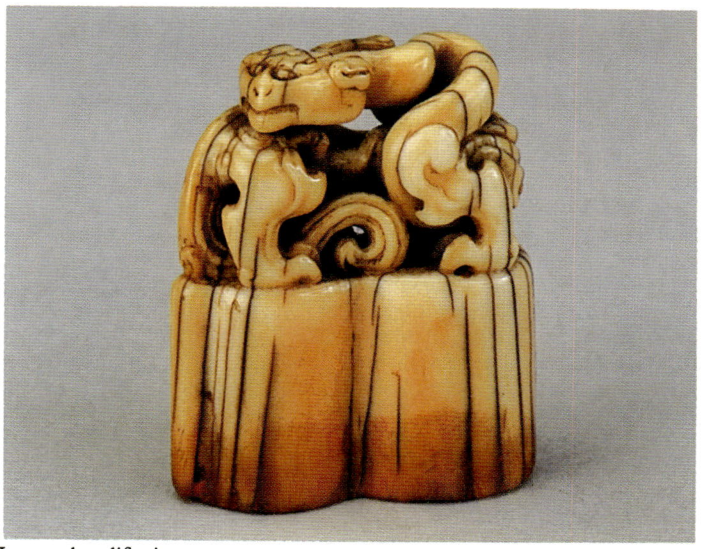

Larger than life size

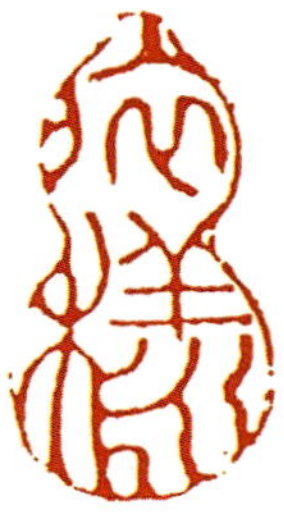

199

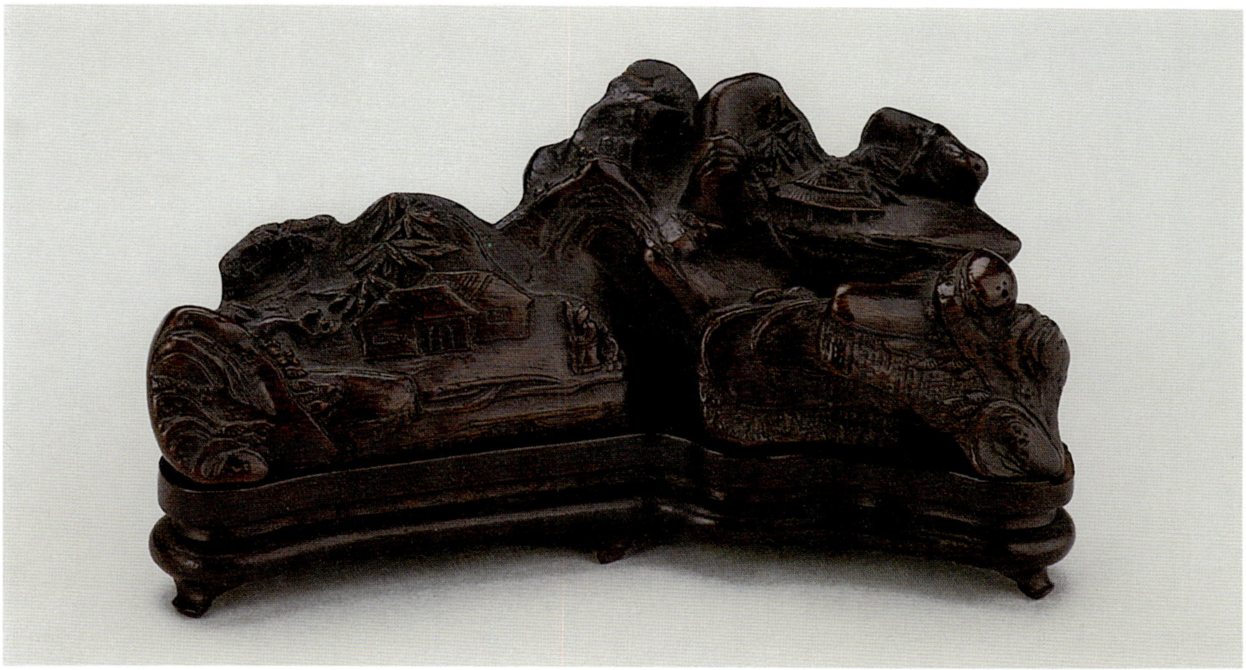

200
Table

Wood, *huanghuali*, of well-figured golden brown colour; a table of high rectangular form, with typical mitred, mortised and tenoned frame top with a tongue-and-grooved, flush floating panel supported by four dovetailed, transverse stretchers; all without exposed tenons; the plain, moulded apron and the section between it and the top of one piece, the upper area thumb-moulded, while the lower is convex; the rounded legs mitred, mortised and tenoned into the apron and double lock tenoned into the top; below the apron is a round 'humpback' stretcher made up of five sections, mitred, half-lapped, mortised and tenoned into each other and the legs.
17th century.
85.7 cm × 163.7 cm × 70.5 cm.

黃花梨畫桌
十七世紀, 85.7×163.7×70.5厘米

It is clear from genre paintings that tables of a wide variety of sizes and shapes could be and were used for painting, writing calligraphy, reading, displaying, and even eating. To call something a 'painting' table or a *'qin'* table is, therefore, a useful general indication of suitability, but no more. Wen Zhenheng comments on the range of uses for individual pieces of furniture: "In the past people made side-tables and couches (*ta,* a sort of low day-bed) of a number of different sizes. When placed within the studio or other rooms they are archaic, elegant and lovely. Whether one sits, lies on, or reclines against them, they are all suitable and comfortable. After a feast, at leisure, one uses them to spread out and read the classics and history, to look at calligraphy and paintings, to display archaic bronzes and ritual vessels, to place food upon, and for placing pillows and mats. They are suitable for all purposes."[1]

A later comment by the same writer on the placing of furniture within the studio is also interesting for the light it throws on the care with which every aspect of the scholar's life was approached. "A side table is placed in a room on its left side (Chinese houses generally face south, suggesting that the left side is the east). It should not be placed near the window so as to avoid wind and sun. On the side table one places an old inkstone, a brush pot, a brush dish (palette for testing and pointing the brush before use), a water vessel and a *yanshan* (this is like a mountain brush rest, where a series of little peaks make up a mountain formation, but is largely for appreciation only). People in the past usually placed their inkstone on the left of the table in order to avoid dazzling the eyes by reflections in the ink. It is also more suitably placed so when using a lamp at night. One also places a book ruler and a paper weight. These should be wiped and rubbed often so as to keep them as bright and shining as a mirror."[2]

Wen continues to write about two other types of table, the reading table (*shuzhuo* — a desk without drawers in Ming times) and the square table. On the subject of the former he wrote: "The reading table should have its largest board as the centre panel, with a narrow rim of slightly more than half an inch framing it on all four sides. The legs should be slightly short and thin and then the style is archaic (and therefore elegant). All the narrow long ones with rounded corners are vulgar and should not be used. Lacquer ones are especially vulgar."[3] About the latter he had this to say: "Square tables should ideally be old lacquered ones. They should be large, square, archaic and rustic, capable of accommodating ten people, for the purpose of spreading out (for appreciation) paintings and calligraphy. As to those made recently of the *Baxian* ('Eight Immortals') type, these are only for feasting and are not elegant items."[4]

1. *Changwu Ji, juan* 6.
2. Ibid. *juan* 10, section 1.
3. Ibid. *juan* 6, section 6.
4. Ibid. *juan* 6, section 6.

201
Ink

Ink, black, of flattened circular form; decorated on one side with the Eight Daoist Immortals, and on the other with different forms of the character *shou* ('longevity') in raised seal script, the centre with the impressed title *Wanshou Tu* ('Picture of Endless Longevity').
Probably late Ming dynasty.
11.5 cm × 8.5 cm.

八仙萬壽圖墨
可能晚明, 11.5×8.5厘米

This ink has been used considerably, leaving only about two-thirds of the original circular form intact. However the user has obviously been sensitive to the design in his use as he has managed to retain all the Eight Immortals, even if only the upper portion of two remain. Probably this ink was never signed. Another, not from the same mould but of the same subject, appears in the *To-boku Wa-boku Zusetsu,* pp.118-119 (also sensitively used to preserve the images of the Immortals, suggesting a pattern of such respect in the use of inks with auspicious subject-matter). The design of *shou* characters was a popular one and appears in combination with other subjects.[1]

In ink designs linework is nearly always in relief for the obvious reason that the wood blocks were carved directly; it is much easier to carve a line into a wood block than to reduce the entire surrounding area and leave a line in relief. It is also common practice for negative characters (as in the case of the title here) to be impressed into the still soft surface of the ink with the use of a separate, seal-like stamp, to avoid the considerable trouble of carving characters in relief in the original wood mould.

1. Op.cit. pp.8-9, for a version coupled with the subject of one hundred boys.

200

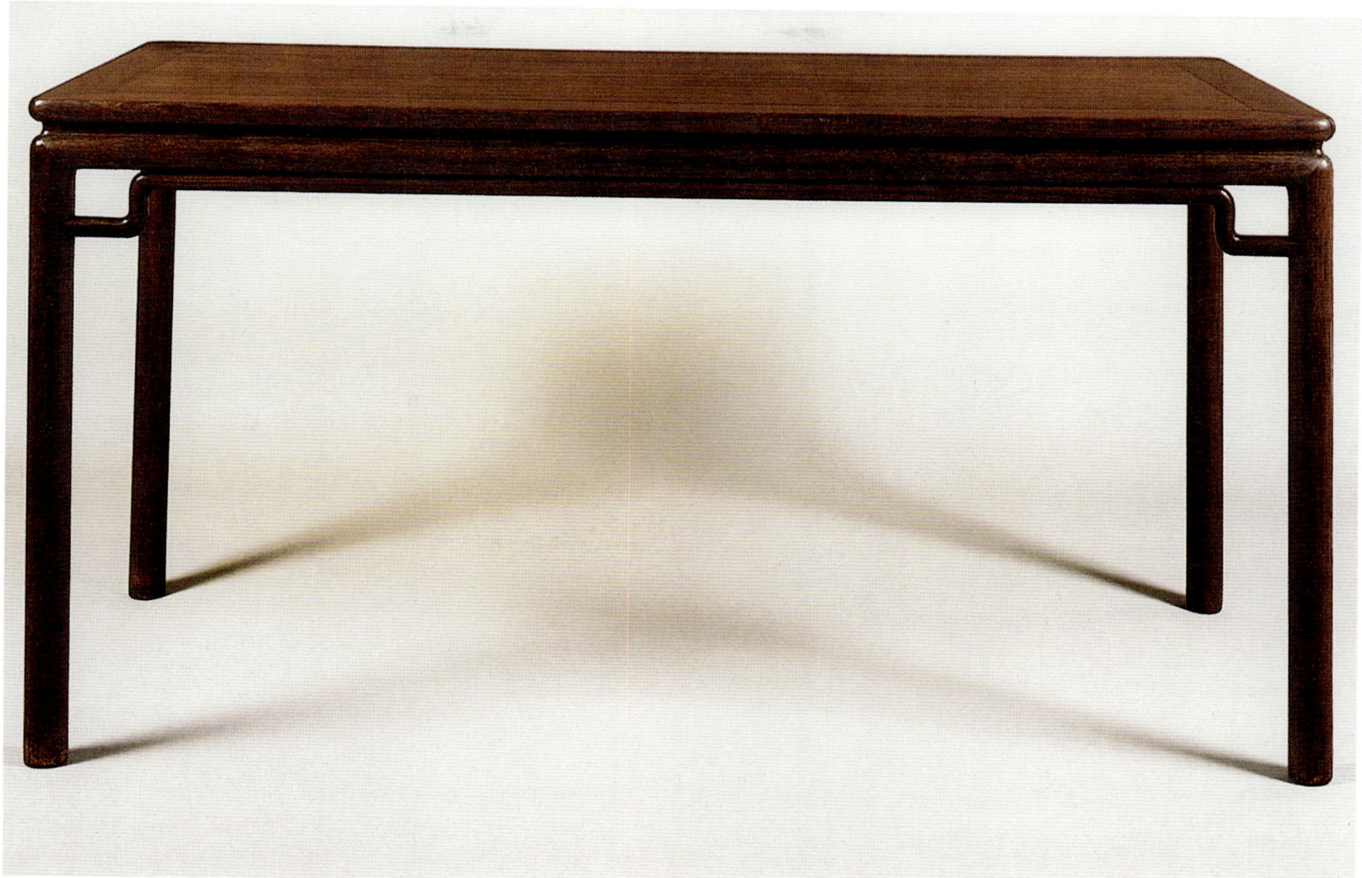

201

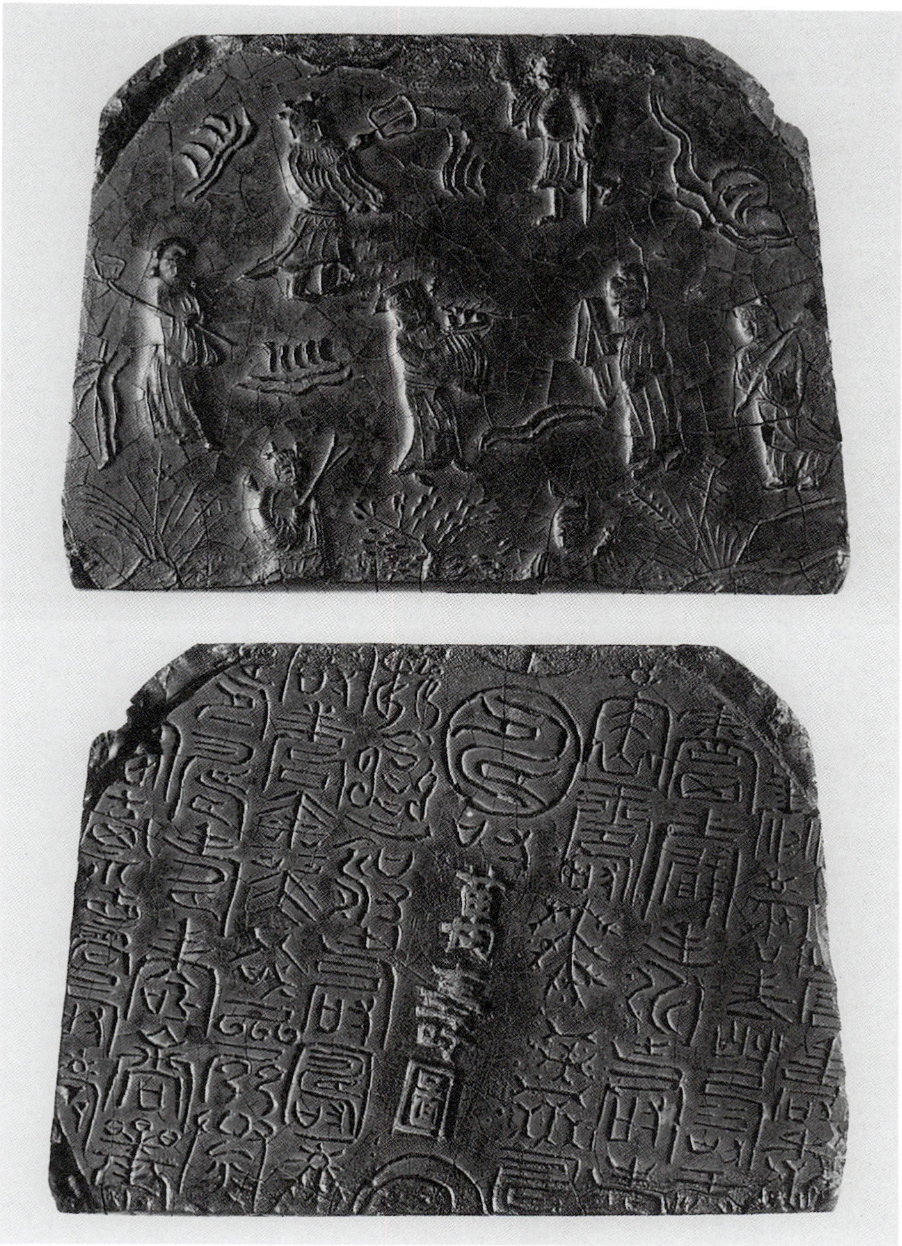

202

Inkstone

Stoneware, of creamy beige colour, partially covered with a transparent very pale green glaze, the current state of fine crackling of which gives the impression of an overall beige colour; the circular domed ink-pool very slightly concave, falling sharply away over two concentric incised lines at its rim to a gutter-shaped water-pool, the straight-sided rim of which rests on a freize of 25 legs each standing on the upper section of a plain disk-like footrim; the ink-pool and the deeply recessed underside unglazed.
Sui or early Tang dynasty.
Height: 7.9 cm. Diameter: 23.5 cm.

白瓷帶釉二十五足圓硯
隋或唐初,高7.9厘米,直徑23.5厘米

The inkstone was an essential utensil for all who used ink in China. Whether in the original form of ground graphite or its later form of solid ink-cakes, a surface was needed upon which to grind the material while adding water to form useable ink. (See no. 184 for the history of ink.) For this function a variety of materials was possible, but over the centuries some proved to be more effective than others and were favoured for the majority of inkstones. Requirements were that the surface be sufficiently abrasive to grind the ink, but without being so rough that it did not grind finely enough, or that it cut the hairs of the brush when applied to the inkstone for loading. In effect this was usually a very fine surface, but not a hard shiny one. A second important function in the finest of inkstones was that it be hard enough to serve its purpose, yet soft enough to allow a tiny proportion of the surface to be added to the mixture of ink, thus giving it a subtle yet distinctive additional quality.

A series of relatively soft stones, mostly limestones, proved excellent in this respect, plus certain types of ceramics, which became standard for the making of inkstones. From time to time other materials, such as the sand-lacquer of the Song copied by Lu Dong's grandfather in the Kangxi period (see no. 63), proved successful. Inkstones were also made of jade, crystal and other less ideal materials, but the glossy hardness of surface made these much less practical, and they were consequently rarer and less treasured by scholars.

In ceramics the grey pottery from which tiles were made in the Han dynasty was ideal for the grinding of ink, particularly in mixing a suitable amount of minutely ground clay with the ink. Consequently very large numbers of the circular tile ends, or finial tiles, stamped on one side with characters, have over the centuries been pressed into service as inkstones and become famous in that role. Clearly, however, other harder fired ceramics such as this stoneware also proved highly effective, and were made in fairly large numbers. This type of inkstone is frequently seen in genre paintings, particularly those depicting early scenes.

The surface of this example seems not to have been much used and it is probably an excavated piece made for use in the afterlife.

203

Inkstone

Stoneware, of grey colour fired brown at the surface, partly covered with a celadon green glaze; an inkstone and cover, the partially glazed base set on four corner feet, joined by a glazed scalloped apron; the recessed pool unglazed, the water reservoir with an unglazed fish in relief against a glazed ground; the cover decorated with a boy holding an uprooted lotus plant, the exterior glazed, the interior unglazed.
Zhejiang province, probably Yuan or early Ming dynasty.
4.9 cm × 12.8 cm × 7.7 cm.
Formerly in the Edward T. Chow collection.
Dispersed by Sotheby's, London, 16th December 1980, Lot 307.

青瓷貴子有魚蓋硯
元或明初,4.9×12.8×7.7厘米

This rare celadon inkstone was catalogued by Sotheby's as late Ming dynasty, but we believe that it is probably earlier. The biscuit fish 'swimming' in a sea of green glaze is a typical feature of Yuan Zhejiang production, and the subject of boys and lotus leaves is also associated with the same period in a group of miniature water vessels of boys playing in a tub. The glaze here is also typical of an earlier period in Zhejiang production.

This inkstone appears not to have been extensively used, as the brown fired surface of the grey stoneware (a result of iron impurities in the material reacting to firing) is only found as a thin layer on the surface and would have been ground away with constant use.

There are various types of inkstone, but basically they fall into three main categories: those where a flat or slightly recessed surface functions alone, those where this surface has an integral recess to act as a water pool, and those where the pool is separate. When grinding ink a quantity is prepared on the surface of the inkstone and used directly from it. However, the water content will gradually evaporate over a period of time and must be added to occasionally in a controlled manner so as not to flood the prepared ink and make it too pale. This can be done, in the case of inkstone without a water pool, by using a water dropper of some kind (see no. 206), or by transferring water from a water vessel with the aid of a small ladle (see no. 209). Or it can be achieved with the brush by transferring water from a recessed pool in the inkstone itself. These pools were often imaginatively contrived, as in this case, so that aquatic creatures would emerge from them or be seen beneath the surface of the water before it became inky; they also provided an edge so that the brush-tip could be trained or shaped before use if necessary, and enabled excess ink or water to be squeezed from the brush.

An octagonal stoneware inkstone with decoration of the eight trigrams *(bagua)* also covered with a celadon glaze and dated 1372 is in the Percival David Foundation, London.[1]

1. Illustrated in *Dated Chinese Antiquities 600-1650*, p.41, no. 10.

204

Ink Rest

Stone, of translucent yellowish-beige colour of the variety known as *lashi* ('wax stone'), one side with a darker 'rind', the surface hard, smooth and undulating; set on a dark wood stand carved in the form of an old, worm-eaten and splitting leaf and a segment of branch from which it grew.
Probably Qing dynasty.
Maximum length of stand: 9.2 cm.
Height including stand: 2.45 cm.

臘石墨床連木雕葉座
可能清代,高連座2.45厘米,座長9.2厘米

Although strange rocks and stones were primarily objects of aesthetic delight, they might also perform other functions as brush rests, paper weights or, as in this case, ink stands. A stick of ink in use has one very messy end and care is required in its handling. It can be placed across the top of an inkstone, or leaned against it with the wet end upwards. However, specially made ink rests were also used in the form of low, flat-topped objects, on which the stick could rest while not actually being used. These were often of porcelain, stone or some other easily washable material. The material and design of this example, with its flat cleanable top and sturdy stand, was well suited for this purpose. Since ideally the wet end of the stick should overlap the ink rest to avoid getting it dirty, it could also accommodate inks well beyond its own length.

The dating of a stone or rock isolated from its natural setting and without the aid of identifying inscriptions is virtually impossible. If we assume that the stand on which it rests today is the original, then we may find a clue to dating the point at which the stone was first considered a work of art, but the dating of wood stands is in itself largely a matter of guesswork at present. It is also clear from this example that, as with many rocks, the wood stand plays an important role in the overall work of art — in fact here it may be said to play the dominant role in transforming a pleasant but hardly inspiring chip of stone into a delightful work of art.

202

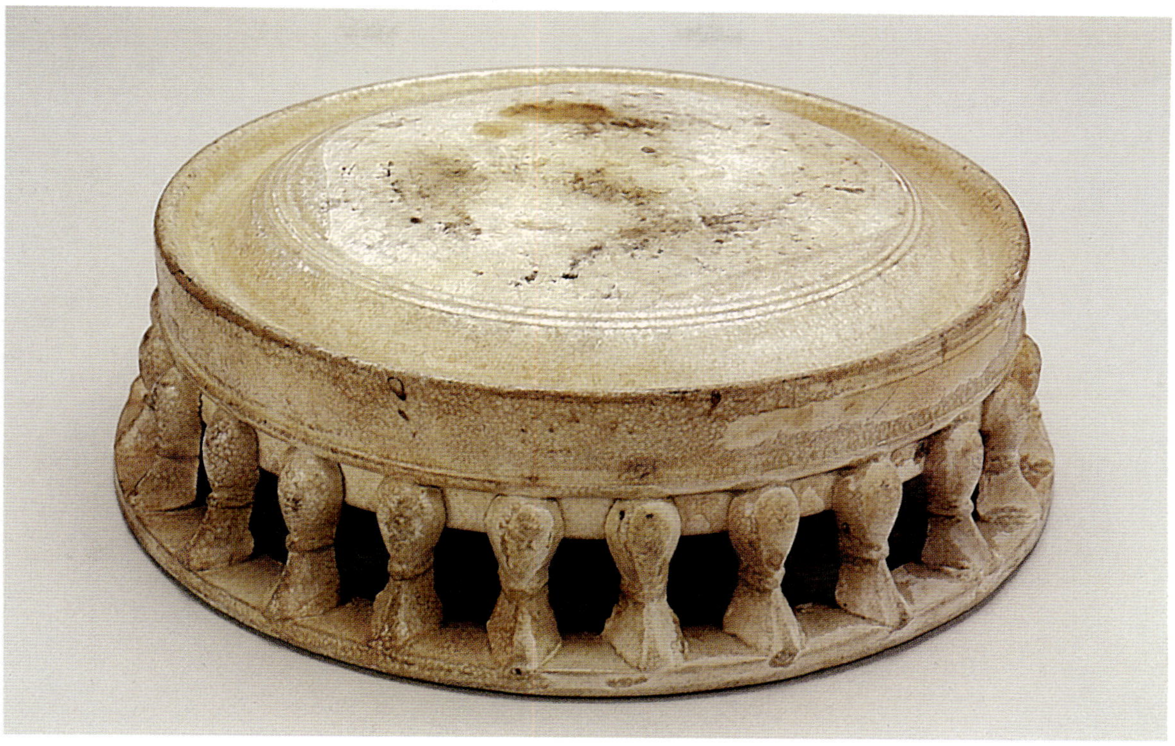

203

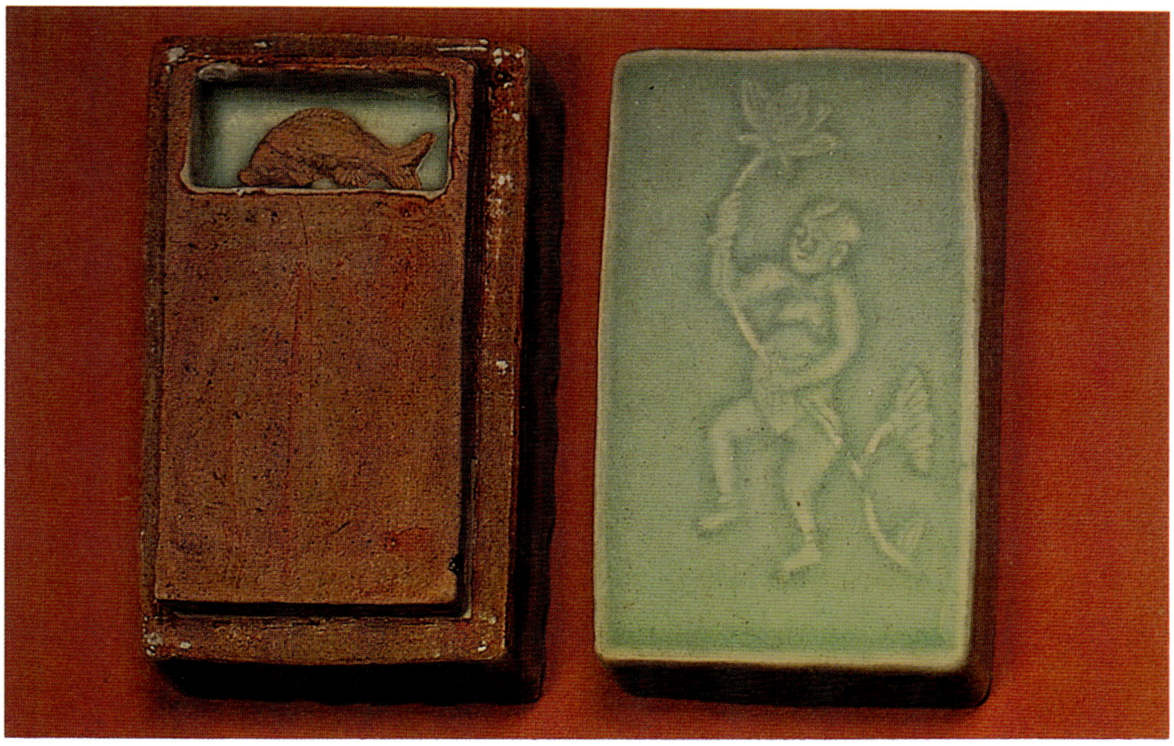

204

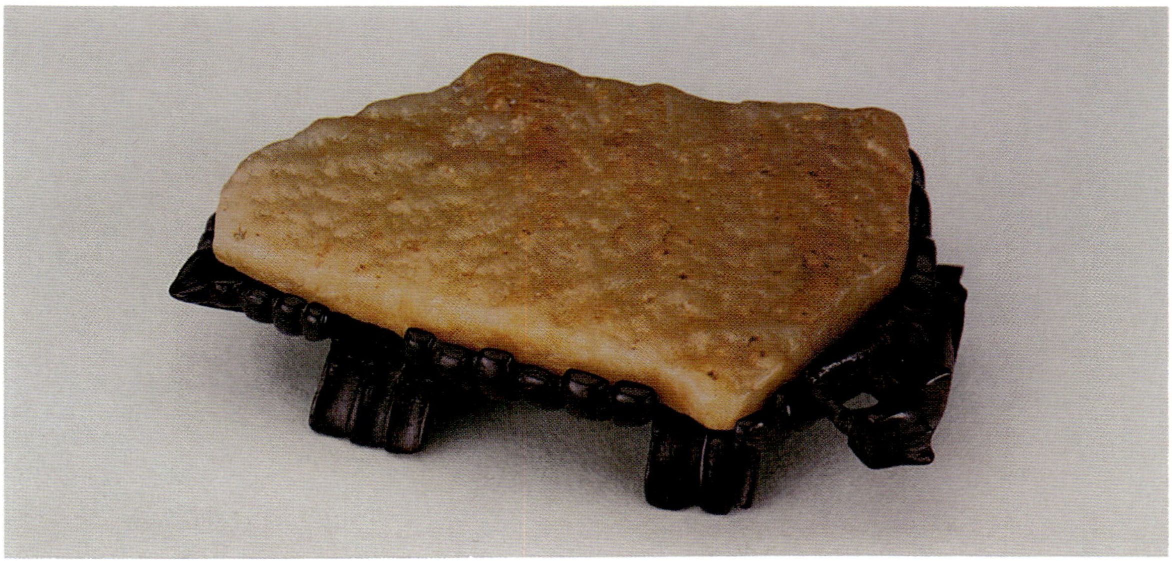

205

Brush

Porcelain, wood, silver wire and goathair; a brush, the hairs contained in a bud-shaped wooden holder, inlaid with a formalized floral design and a band of lappets in silver wire, mounted on a tapering cylindrical handle decorated in underglaze cobalt blue with a five-clawed dragon, chasing a flaming pearl amidst flowers above a ground of rocks rising from formalized waves; a lower band of similar rocks and waves balancing an upper band enclosing the reign mark *Da Ming Wanli nianzhi* ('made in the Great Ming Wanli period'); the top with a circular formalized floral design.
Wanli period.
Overall length: 29 cm.
Length excluding hairs: 20.5 cm.

青花龍戲珠紋瓷筆•大明萬曆年製銘
明萬曆(1573-1620), 總長29厘米
筆桿20.5厘米

The brush was one of the four treasures of the scholar's studio, along with ink, paper and inkstone. However, these were treasures first and foremost because without them one could not write, which was the very basis of scholarship. They were the essentials (or represent them, as silk or other materials could be substituted for paper) needed to record works of art such as poetry, calligraphy and painting, and works of scholarship, criticism and philosophy. In theory they were the basic treasures because all four were transformed in the process of creating other works of art: paper was marked, ink ground up, brushes worn out, and part of the strength of a good inkstone was the tiny amount of surface material incorporated into the ground ink, eventually wearing away the surface. Being tools in the service of other works of art allows for two directions in which they may develop as art. The first is the craft of making something perfectly suited to become a subordinate part of a larger whole, and the second is where the form transcends this to become a work for aesthetic appreciation in its own right. Inkstones and ink both evolved to this independent form, brushes to a lesser extent, and paper hardly at all.

Paper was hardly ever made or considered as an independent aesthetic experience; it was treasured almost solely for its potential in contributing to a future work of art. Even the fancy printed and hand-painted papers used in certain pieces of calligraphy, for various imperial uses, and as title-papers for handscrolls were, whatever their current appeal, not traditionally collected on their own merits. Although brushes aspired to an independent aesthetic level from time to time, leaving us with sometimes excellent examples in lacquer, porcelain and jade, they did not do so on the same scale as ink and inkstones. Brushes were made by artists in a number of fields, but there was a general tendency for these to be simply luxurious statements by rulers and wealthy patrons rather than any great response to the brush as an independent vehicle of artistic expression. The art of brushmaking was in making a brush with good balance, that handled well, had a suitable tip and so forth. They were made to be used, worn out and discarded: like paper they were transformed in their major contribution to the scholar's activities and the traces of a great brush remains in a great work of calligraphy or painting.

Many of the best brushes were generally made of humble materials and have not been treasured or kept once their functional life was over. Many of those that survive have done so either because they are in materials otherwise valued (ceramics, lacquer, jade, etc.) or are in the imperial collection where they have survived from the Qing dynasty in an unused state. Of the former some would probably have been considered vulgar by the literati, and perhaps even unusable; while the latter are a relatively uninspiring lot as independent works of art. (Both types may be seen in *Masterpieces of Chinese Writing Materials in the National Palace Museum,* nos. 1-5.)

206

Water Dropper

Nephrite, of pale grey-green colour with brown markings in the stone enhanced by artificial staining; a water dropper in the form of a toad creeping forward over a fruiting and blossoming branch; his body carved in relief with the other four of the Five Poisonous Creatures, the snake, centipede, lizard, and, on the dropper itself, a spider.
Probably Ming dynasty or earlier.
Height with dropper in place: 4.65 cm.
Length: 8 cm.

玉雕五毒水滴
可能明代或較早, 高4.65厘米, 長8厘米

Water vessels for the writer or painter take various forms depending upon their intended function. The inkstone requires a controlled amount of water, particularly in the case of inkstones without an integral water pool (see no. 191). There are four basic systems, each requiring a different form of water vessel. One is to deliver water from a separate vessel with the aid of a small ladle; another is to pour it from a narrow spouted jug; another is to use a form of jug where the rate of water pouring out can be controlled by the finger or thumb covering a small opening and thus controlling the rate of air flowing in; and the last is this type, where a long cylindrical tube forms a part of the stopper in which a small hole is similarly blocked by the finger or thumb, retaining the water in the tube until air is allowed into the tube, which releases it onto the inkstone.

Although the artificial staining of jade pebbles has been going on for centuries, it is often difficult to tell visually whether a piece has been enhanced by staining and to what degree. Artificial stains closely resemble the natural stains of nature working inwards from the outside of a pebble as its surface decomposes and is physically transformed. However, in this case the brown artificial stain is quite visible on the surface, almost as a paint-like substance in some areas, and a close examination reveals why such a heavy application was necessary. The centipede, which crawls along a flaw on one side of the toad, is mostly made of a separate piece of material which has been stuck on, probably to hide a flaw. This was then blended into the surrounding area (which includes its legs) and the joins lost behind the staining.

Pebbles of nephrite from the rivers of Khotan were much valued in early times[1] and the application of such high skill to a flawed pebble of this type is probably an indication of an early carving, executed before the late Ming introduction of mining for large deposits began to create a taste for purer materials. The sculptural qualities of the creature are excellent, as it crawls forward on powerfully carved limbs, seemingly resigned to being host to such a motley assortment of passengers. The details are all superbly carved.

The dating of this vessel to the Ming dynasty would not be controversial and is probably correct. However, a great deal of jade carving went on in the Song and Yuan periods and we can be fairly sure that a lot more of it has survived than our current attributions suggest. To reflect this, future research will no doubt spread out more evenly the large number of jades that are currently placed in the Ming dynasty category simply because they are clearly earlier than Qing. The sort of realism and quality employed here would not be at all unlikely for the Southern Song period and the possibility of such an early date is worth considering.

1. See *Chinese Jades from Han to Ch'ing.*

207

Water Jug

Porcelain, covered with a pale aquamarine-blue glaze; a jug of ribbed, octagonal form with short cylindrical spout, and a handle in the form of a *chi* dragon.
Qingbai ware, Jingdezhen, Yuan dynasty.
Height: 5.3 cm.
Published: *Anthology of Chinese Ceramics,* no. 54; *Jingdezhen Wares: The Yuan Evolution,* p.105, no. 50 and p.59 (colour plate).

青白瓷螭龍八角水注
元代, 高5.3厘米

This is the type of water vessel used to deliver water to the inkstone where the smallness of the spout allows a measure of control in delivery. The fact that such small water vessels were exported in large quantities at the time to neighbouring Southeast Asian countries suggests many other uses for these small jugs, but this represents a type used by the artist.

The ceramic industry provided vast quantities of incense burners, flower vases, water vessels of various kinds, ewers and wine vessels, teapots and cups, inkstones, paper weights and brush pots from the post-Han period to modern times. Ceramics figured to a much greater extent in the production of wares for the literati than is demonstrated in this exhibition. As stated elsewhere, the reason for our virtual exclusion of this material is that it has been covered so extensively — not least by this Society — during the past decades that it is already both widely and well understood, whereas the many other areas upon which we concentrate are not.

For a small bronze water jug see Fig.1, taken from an early 16th century painting by Qiu Ying in the Cleveland Museum of Art.[1]

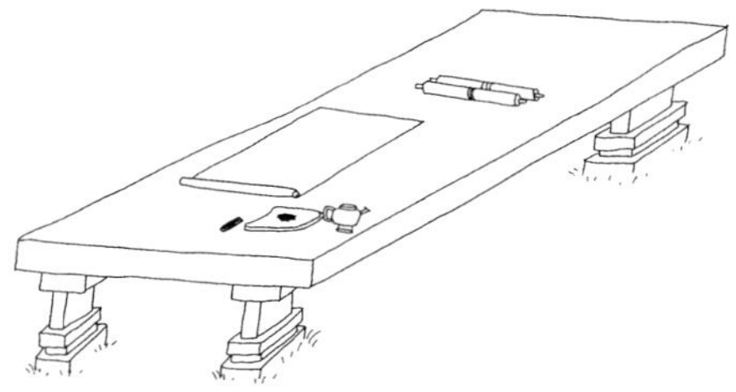

Fig. 1

1. *Art of Dynastic China,* p.144.

205

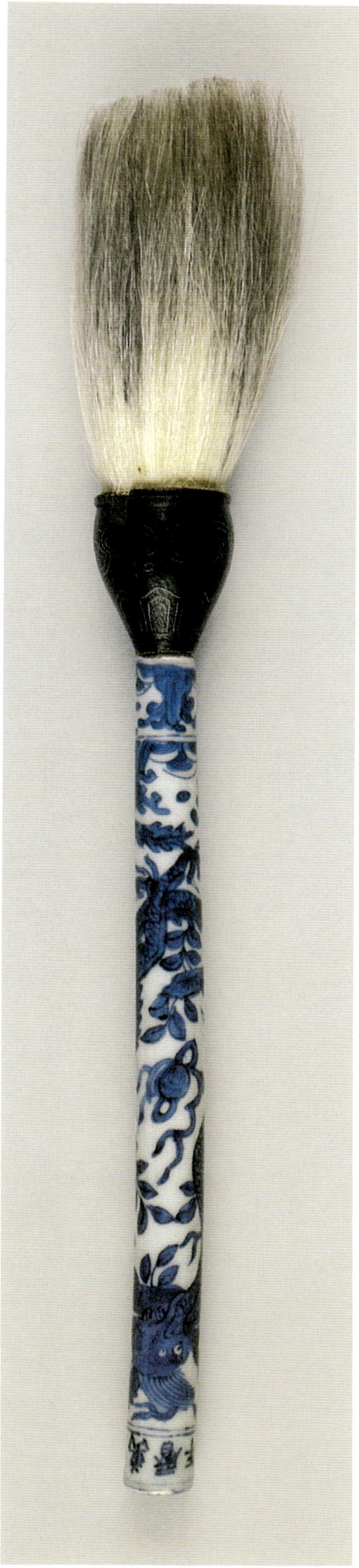

206

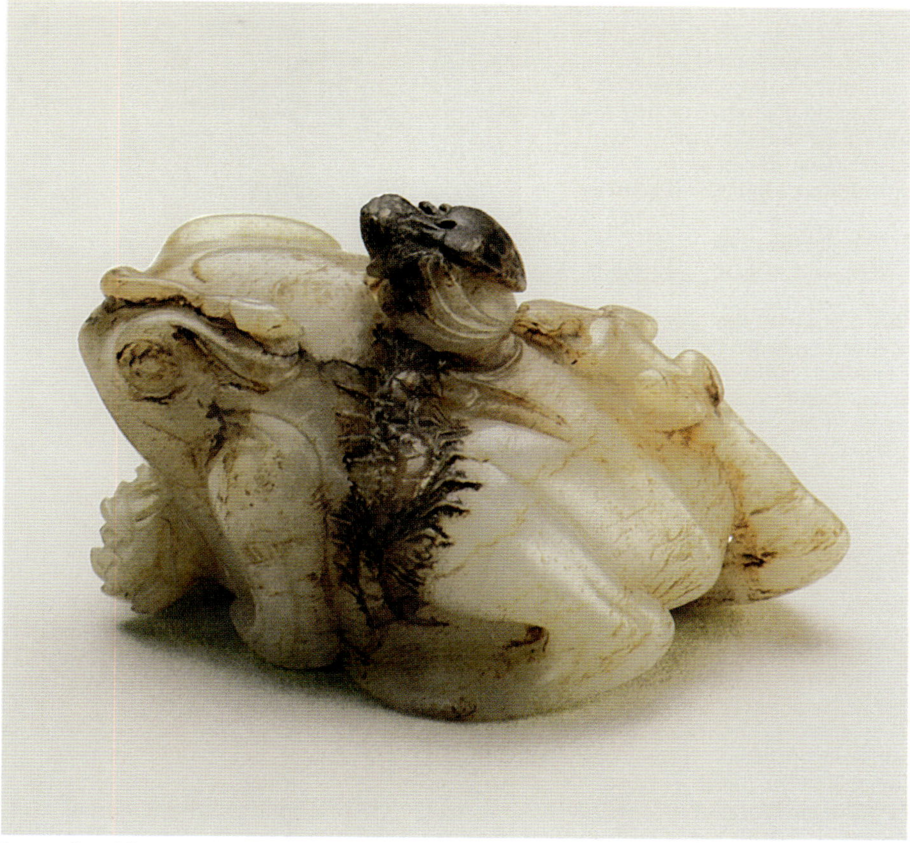

Larger than life size

207

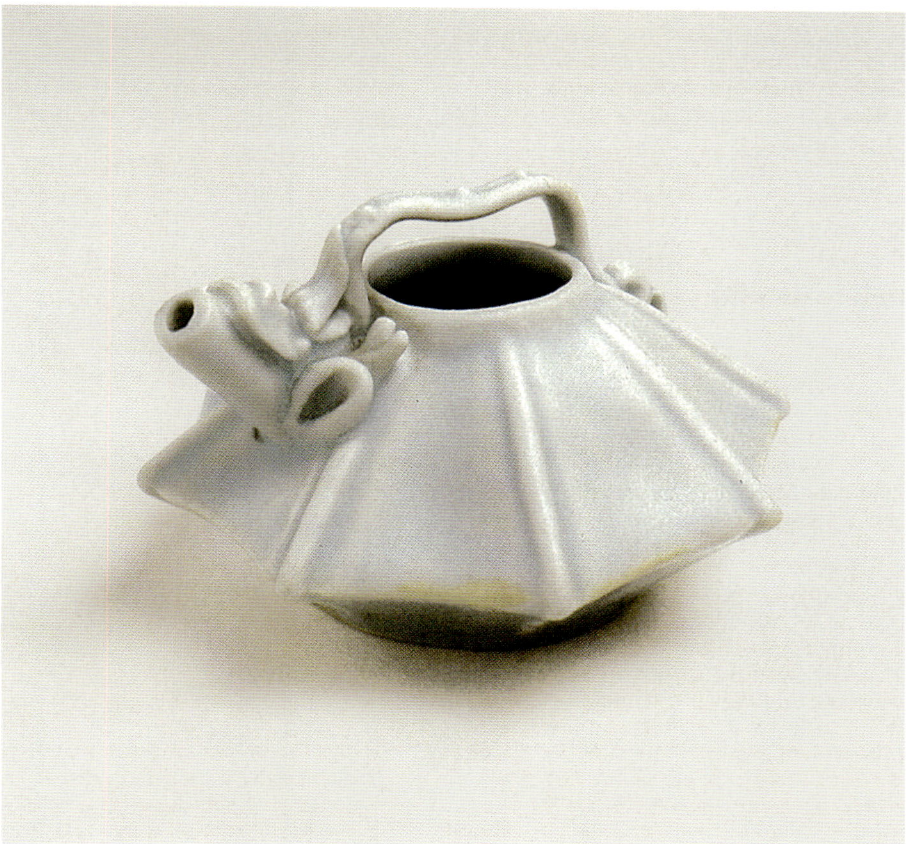

208

Water Dropper

Bronze, inlaid with gold and silver; a water dropper in the form of a mythical animal, the hornless, fat feline with a scaled chest and flaming haunches, the surface inlaid with a series of archaistic motifs in gold and silver; the base unfinished and plugged with a large separate piece of bronze; a tiny hole in the mouth acting as the spout.
Probably Ming dynasty.
Height: 4.9 cm. Length: 6.6 cm.

嵌金銀青銅異獸水滴
可能明代, 高4.9厘米, 長6.6厘米

This represents the type of vessel for delivering water to the inkstone where the flow of water could be controlled by placing a finger or thumb over the air-hole. This vessel allows for a tiny amount of water to be deposited on the inkstone.

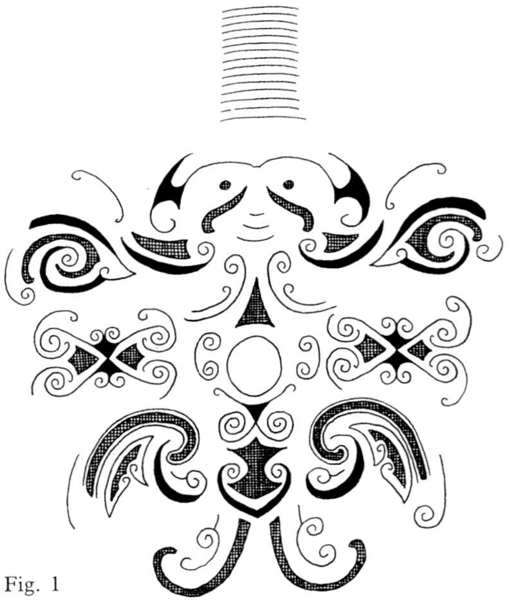

Fig. 1

The problems of dating archaistic works of art has been discussed elsewhere (see no. 127 for instance). Although this vessel may be as early as the Song dynasty, it is probably more likely to be Ming. Inlaid copper sheet is under all the gold although whether this was done to improve the colour of the gold, save on the quantities required of the precious metal, or to serve as a better bond is not certain.

A drawing of the inlaid design is shown in Fig. 1 where the silver portions are represented by solid black and the gold by cross-hatching. We believe that by comparing drawings of this type taken from a wide range of inlaid archaistic wares a sense of style could be acquired which would separate them into useful groups for dating.

209

Water Vessel

Zhitong

Soapstone, of mottled golden orange and beige colour carved in the form of a 'finger-citron' ('Buddha's-hand fruit') water vessel, the leaves and tendrils from which it grows coloured in green and brown, a narrow band of incised wave-pattern around the mouth inlaid with alternate coral and turquoise beads; a two-character signature *Zhitong* incised at the top of the fruit beneath a leaf.
Late Ming or early Qing dynasty.
Height: 3.25 cm. Length: 9.6 cm.

石雕佛手形水丞·治同銘
晚明或清初, 高3.25厘米, 長9.6厘米

The range of shapes in this type of water vessel for use with a small ladle is very wide. Since the ladle controls the supply of water, any size or shape of water vessel will serve. They range in size from those with very small capacity, such as this, to much larger vessels with larger ladles. For writing small characters a tiny amount of ink goes a very long way, and a vessel such as this would suffice. For painting or writing bigger characters larger vessels are required. Such vessels frequently turn up in genre paintings in some rather surprising shapes. Fig. 1, for example, taken from a painting by the early 18th century artist Leng Mei,[1] shows a conventional small vessel on the left next to two inkstones, and on the right a bronze vessel which would normally be called an incense burner being used for water. This painting also has a spittoon used to hold scrolls and even the brush pot is of unconventional shape.

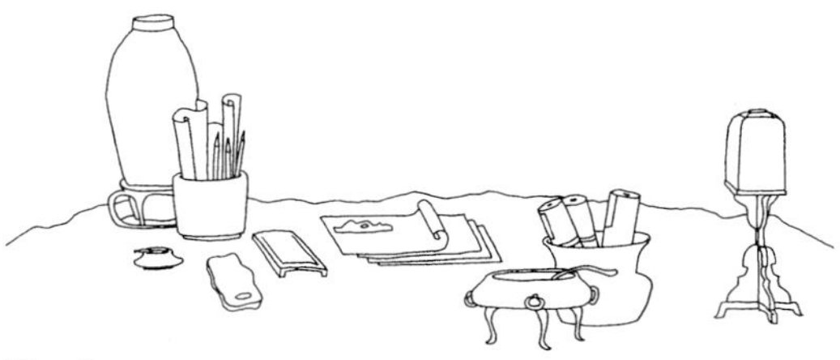

Fig. 1

The simple yet powerful formalization of the leaves on this piece, capturing their essence without any frills is exactly what one might expect of a literati artist, and it is not unreasonable to entertain the possibility of this being from the hand of a scholar. The name signed excludes the family name and is, without further information, impossible to identify. The type of stone here has not been positively identified, but it may be a Qingtian ('Green Field') stone from Zhejiang province rather than a Shoushan stone. As a rule the Zhejiang stones do not appear as compact as those from Shoushan, nor do they have the same oily appearance. We have no particular view on this example, but it has been suggested to us that it is probably from Zhejiang. However, regardless of the source of the stone, the incising and inlaying of semi-precious stones directly connects the piece with the group of soapstone figures made by Yang Yuxuan, Zhou Bin and others (see no. 43) during the late Ming or early Qing period in Fujian province.

1. In the National Palace Museum, Taipei. It shows a gathering of scholars at a spring evening banquet.

210

Water Vessel

Quartz, of speckled yellowish-beige tone with patches of red-speckled grey colour; carved as a water vessel in the form of a lotus leaf, the stem forming the base, the edges of the leaf curled over to form the lip.
Probably late Ming or Qing dynasty.
Height: 5.3 cm. Maximum width: 12.7 cm.

石英雕蓮瓣形洗
可能晚明或清代, 高5.3厘米, 寬12.7厘米

The rather open grain in parts of this material are filled with the residue of ink stains, suggesting that it was used for toning the ink while painting or writing, a process which does not so much involve washing the brush as getting a judicious mixture of ink and water, sometimes unevenly applied for particular effects. The edge of this vessel with its several sharply defined indentations would be perfect for this purpose, which often involves squeezing the brush out against an edge of this sort. However, the artist used a wide range of various other vessels which might also be used for this same purpose. Small dishes for colours or for toning ink appear in genre paintings as do palettes with various divisions. A vessel such as this might equally have been used with a ladle for supplying the inkstone, and it is even possible that it was used as a drinking vessel. Strange as this may seem, there is a painting by Chen Hongshou, the late Ming artist (for a drawing of which see Fig. 1)[1] which shows a scholar seated in a wonderful root chair drinking from an elaborate lotus vessel which were it not being lifted to his lips, would never be considered a drinking vessel.

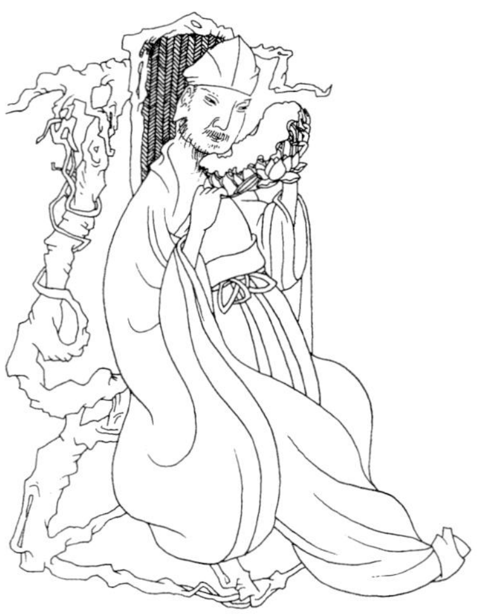

Fig. 1

The dating of this sort of carving is problematic. It is a material rarely used, so dating by material is difficult, and the form would be possible from prior to the Song dynasty to the early 20th century. Being a very hard material, natural wear gives little indication of age, and we are left with the most unscientific approach of a vague guess. The reasonably humble material and the delightful, restrained design are features one might expect of the latter part of the Ming dynasty, but certainly not exclusively.

The subject-matter here also alludes to the scholar. The lotus, which rises from the mud through murky waters to put forth a brilliant flower on a tall, straight stem, has for long been seen as an analogy of the upright scholar, born in the mundane world, and rising through the mire of corruption and intrigue to lofty perfection.

1. Taken from *Style Transformed: A Special Exhibition of Works by Five Late Ming Artists*, no. 099-7.

208

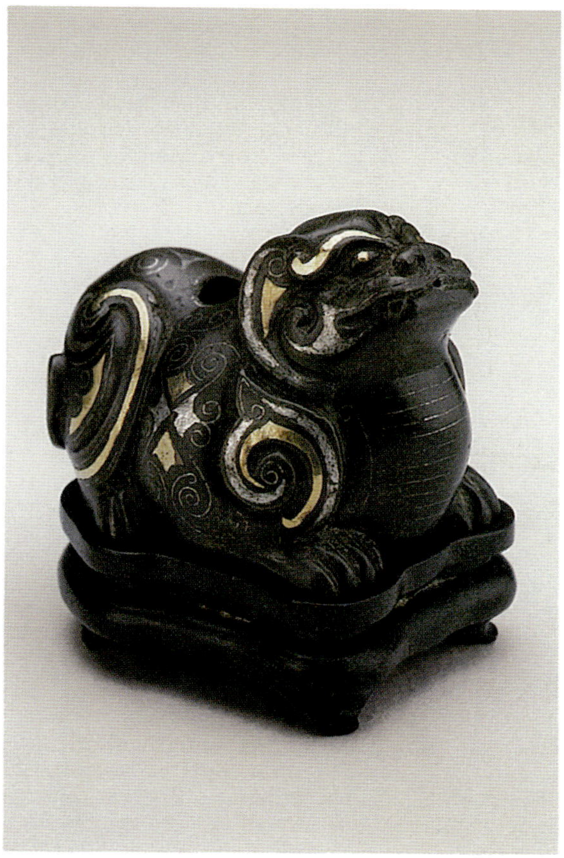

210

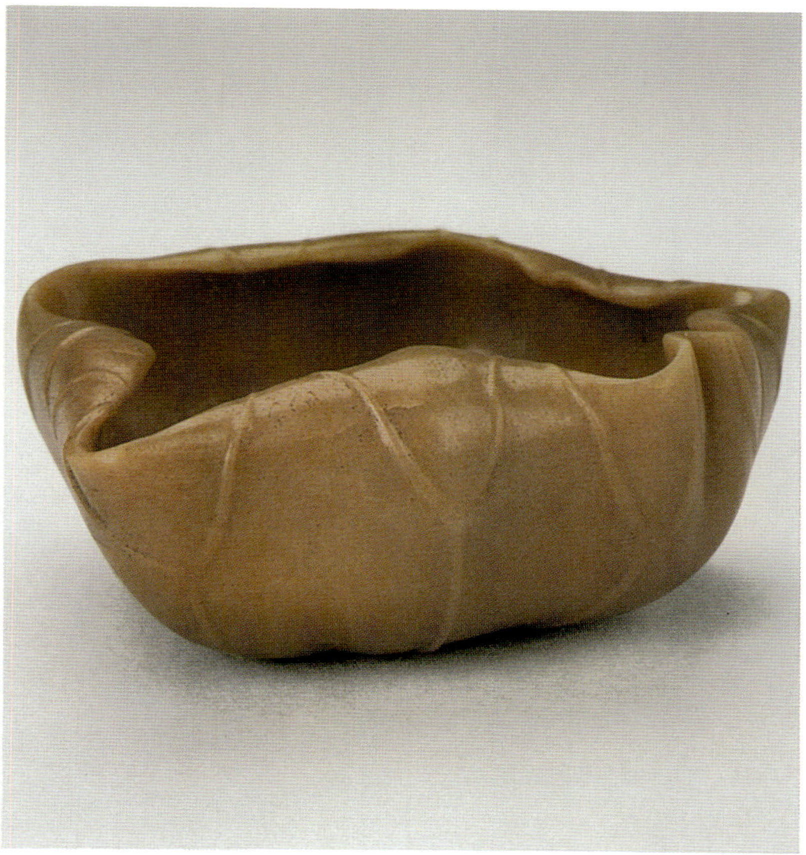

209

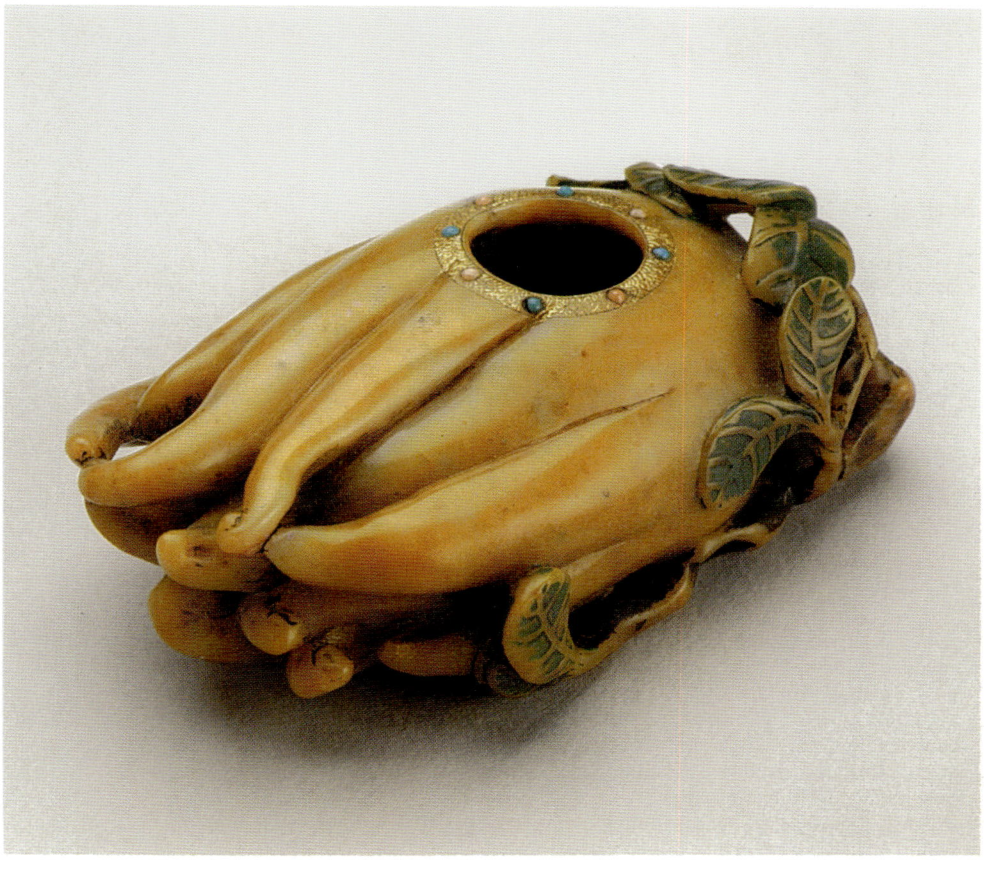

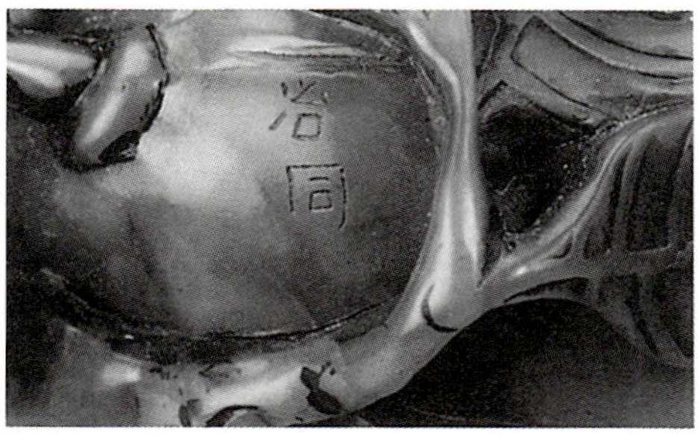

211

Brush Rest

Nephrite, of variegated pale green and pale grey colours, with some dark brown flaws; carved as a highly formalized mountain brush rest, one side flat, the other convex.
Probably late Ming dynasty.
Set on an elegant *zitan* stand of later date.
Height including stand: 11.7 cm.
Width of jade only: 15.25 cm.

玉雕筆山
可能晚明, 高連座11.7厘米, 玉寬15.25厘米

The brush rest in various forms is a standard functional object for the scholar. A brush, loaded with ink or wet from washing, needs to be rested securely somewhere to avoid accident. Genre paintings demonstrate a variety of methods of doing this, but the most popular, certainly in later times, was the brush rest. It might consist of any number of different materials and shapes, its prime requirement being only that it would support a brush clear of the working surface. They were made in a very wide variety of materials and styles, from the most elaborately carved examples to simple pieces of gnarled wood or natural rock formations where hardly any working was required at all.

Since brush rests needed 'valleys' in which to rest the brush, the mountain form naturally became popular. The most popular was the five peaked rest, representing the Five Sacred Mountains of China.

The appearance of this example may be misleading. It is very simple and quite crudely carved, its peaks and valleys being formed by a series of straightforward facets and drilled curves without any great attempt at an elaborate finish. One would be forgiven for assuming that it was a simple and crudely made functional object made without undue care. However, this is to judge it without taking into account the literati aesthetic of intellectual primitivism (see p.17 and no. 32). Unlike painting and calligraphy, in the field of three-dimensional works of art we have no record of the artists to demonstrate their aesthetic, and in a piece of this type the difference between crude workmanship and highly refined awkwardness rests not in the physical object itself, but in what its maker intended, and in what the viewer reads into it. Since we are unable to ascertain the former, the viewer must decide on an individual basis. There is no doubt that, whatever the original intention of its maker, this piece fits comfortably into the literati aesthetic. It is elegant and restrained with great abstract strength (all of which would seem to link it with the literati painting of its day), and of a subdued and subtle material. Whoever made the tasteful *zitan* stand, which seems later than Ming, obviously considered the jade worthy of an elegant stand and presumably saw in it hidden strength.

212

Brush and Ink Stand

Porcelain, decorated in underglaze cobalt blue; a drum-shaped brush and ink stand, the top with three circular and one rectangular openings to the interior; decorated with floral motifs on the top, and a continuous band around the body of two phoenixes in flight against a ground of scrolling, formalized lotus heads set between an upper band of of formalized *ruyi* heads, and a lower one of stylized lappets; the recessed foot and the interior both glazed.
Jingdezhen; Ming, Jiajing period.
Height: 8.7 cm. Diameter: 12.7 cm.
Published: *Chinese Blue and White Porcelain,* 1975, no. 36.

青花瓷雙鳳紋鼓形筆墨插
明嘉靖(1522–1566), 高8.7厘米, 直徑12.7厘米

The use of this vessel is clarified by a painting of the famous philosopher Wang Yangming seated at his writing desk which illustrates a handscroll of his letters and other related material,[1] a drawing from which is reproduced as Fig. 1. The piece is shown on his desk with three brushes placed, tips upwards, in it, together with a small vase of flowers, an inkstone and a water dropper or paper weight. The natural assumption that the rectangular section is to hold an inkstick, although none is shown in this particular illustration, is confirmed by the late Ming scholar Wen Zhenheng, who in *Changwu Ji* ('Notes on Superfluous Objects') under the heading of brush pots wrote: "...there are also drum-shaped ones with holes in them for inserting brushes and ink. These may be old, but they are not elegant to look at."[2]

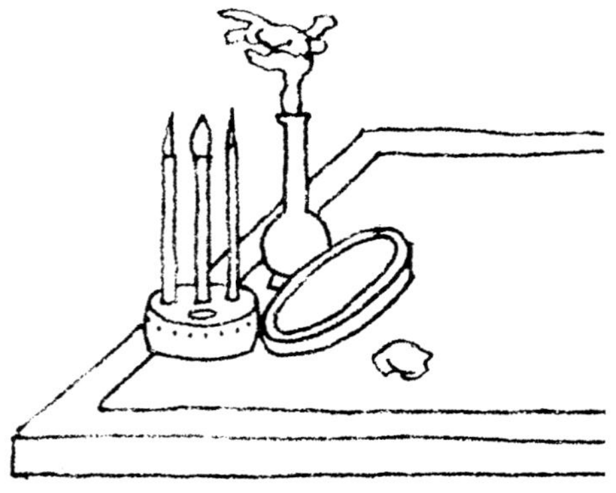

Fig. 1

The only surviving examples of this type of brush holder appear to be in porcelain, and those are few in number. This suggests that it was a form which never achieved widespread popularity, which seems reasonable as (despite Wang Yangming's apparent ability to get his brushes standing straight as arrows in it) it would seem to be rather poorly designed for holding brushes. As an ink receptacle it is suitable only for use with a fairly new ink which has not been much used, as once a stick was less than about 12 cm long it would be messy to negotiate in its receptacle, and below 8 cm would simple fall inside the vessel, wasting about half the length of the average inkstick.

Another porcelain vessel of this type is in the Percival David Foundation, London.[3]

1. *Images of the Mind,* p.351.
2. *Juan* 7, section 12.
3. *Illustrated Catalogue of Porcelains Decorated in Underglaze Blue and Copper Red in the Percival David Foundation of Chinese Art,* section 3, 1963, no. B605.

213

Brush Box

Wood, *hongmu* ('redwood'), of golden-brown colour, with inlaid ivory; a brush box in the form of a *qin,* the studs (see no. 151 for the anatomy of a *qin*) inlaid in ivory; the interior divided into compartments for six brushes.
Mid- to late Qing dynasty.
Length: 29.4 cm.

紅木嵌象牙古琴形筆盒
清中至晚期, 長29.4厘米

Qin-shaped weights and wrist rests for scholarly pursuits are not uncommon (see nos. 224 and 86) but this is the only example we know of that was obviously made to hold brushes. We may also tentatively guess that it was a presentation box. To have used such a box in the ordinary way for the storing of brushes would have been somewhat impractical. Damp brushes would not dry properly and would rot; the inside shows no sign of having been used in such a way. It may be, however, that a fastidious scholar treasured certain brushes, which others always dried and replaced in the box only when ready for use again. It would not be at all unusual for a scholar to decide that in his pursuit of the art of life everything must be just right, and to view assistants, brushes and brush box all as part of his technique in achieving the perfect work of art.

211

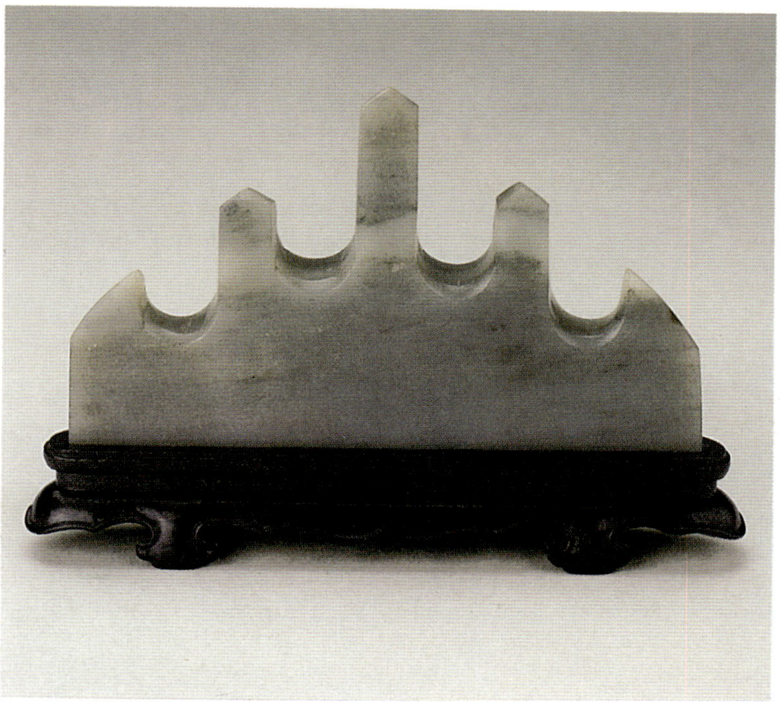

212

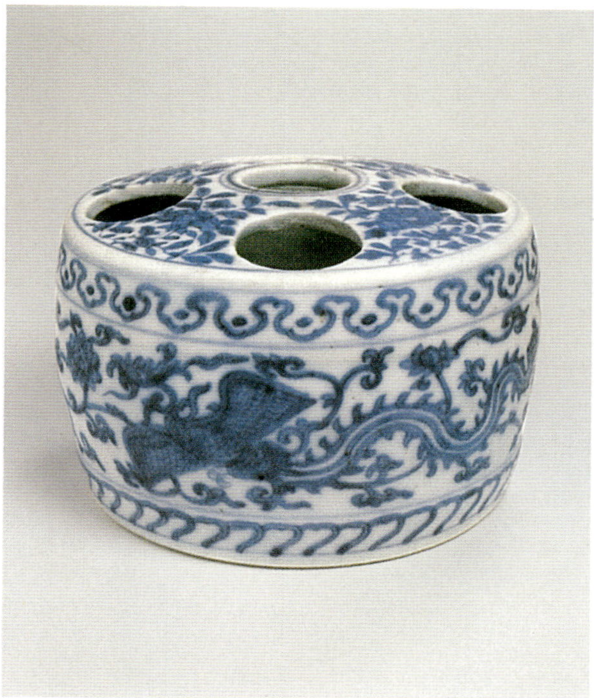

213

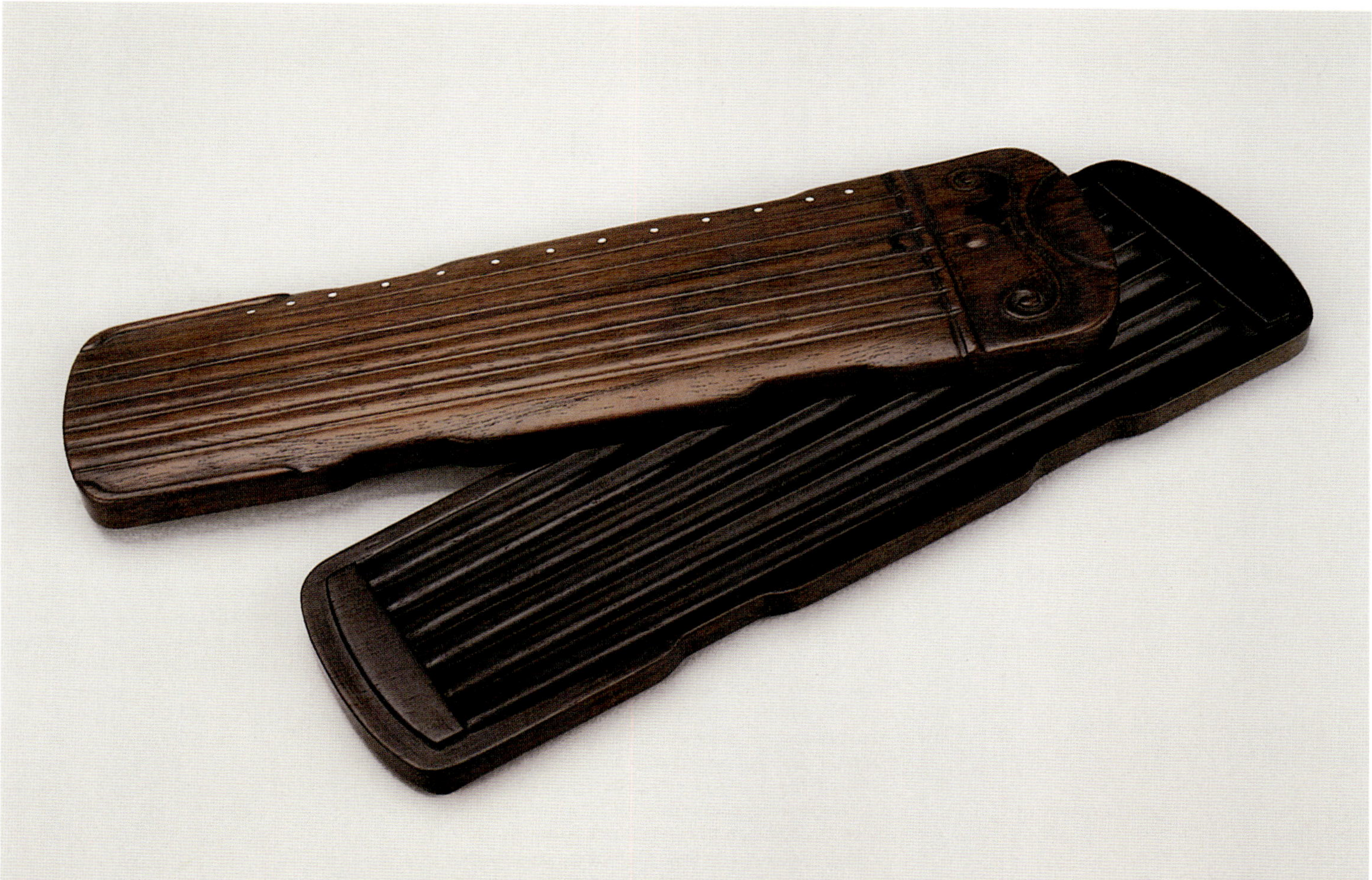

214

Brush Pot

Wood, *huamu* (burl), of richly figured brown colour; carved from a solid piece of wood, the base a separate section of burl.
Late Ming or Qing dynasty.
Height: 19 cm. Diameter of mouth: 21.3 cm.
Published: *Wood From the Scholar's Table,* p.57, no. 25.

樺木筆筒
晚明或清代, 高19厘米, 口直徑21.3厘米

In later times the brush pot seems to have been a standard item for the influential minority. There is a very wide variety of sizes and shapes, and the fact that some are impractically large to hold brushes indicates their main function, which was the equivalent of a Western desk drawer. Although they are called brush pots, any number of things were kept in them and one frequently gets the impression from genre paintings that storage for brushes was almost incidental to their main use. They are shown in a large number of paintings and wood block illustrations containing scrolls, *ruyi* sceptres, branches of coral, rolled portfolios (the binders for the early form of book where a group of handscrolls were bound together in an outer casing which when removed was rolled up and perhaps kept in a brush pot), peacock feathers, and a host of other functional and decorative objects including, of course, brushes.

Brush pots were obviously made in very large quantities of various standard forms in a host of materials, and plain wood examples, mostly from the late Ming and Qing dynasties, abound. Wen Zhenheng mentions in his *Changwu Ji* that one might make occasional use of brush pots of *zitan,* blackwood or *huali* (in his usual rather dismissive fashion) but advises the aspiring aesthete to avoid octagonal, petal-shaped ones. This is a clear reference to fluted brush pots where the cross-section is like that of a formalized *kui* flower (see the incense tool vase in no. 234). It is interesting to see that these existed as early as the late Ming; there has been a recent tendency in Hong Kong to take old brush pots and recarve them into this form, distorting the rarity of genuine early examples and leading the wary to cast a cautious eye over all such brush pots. We have also begun to see some rather impressive modern carved *huanghuali* brush pots of good size with *chi* dragon motifs, and other carved decoration, some on a fluted ground.

Burl brush pots are rare, particularly of this size, presumably because the material went further as thin panels for inlaying into table and display stand tops, and other furniture. The material has a delightful surface pattern, which is often as intriguing as swirling incense smoke or root formations.

Huamu covers a variety of burls from such trees as the birch, camphor, poplar, elm, ash and amboina, as well as those of the harder woods used in Chinese cabinet-making. To distinguish them from each other in finished products is currently not possible.[1]

1. See *Chinese Furniture: Hardwood Examples of the Ming and Early Ch'ing Dynasties,* Chapter 3.

215

Brush Pot

Wood, *huangyangmu* (boxwood), of golden brown colour; a small brush pot carved as a section of the trunk of a pine tree, with an eagle clinging to a branch growing from near the lip and spreading out downwards around the trunk, clumps of pine needles growing from it; with creeping ivy growing up from the base of the trunk to encircle the branches and dangle leafy tendrils; the foot recessed.
Late Ming or early Qing dynasty.
Height: 8.5 cm.

黃楊木雕鷹松筆筒
晚明或清初, 高8.5厘米

Although larger brush pots were used to contain a host of different objects (see no. 214) the smaller ones were more practical for brushes alone. The standard writing brush of the scholar, used in the pursuit of his scholarship, in writing books, notes and letters or in practising calligraphy, was fairly small. It was only in painting or writing large calligraphy that the more impressively proportioned brushes were used. The interior of this vessel shows signs of it having been used as a brush pot for some time.

There seems no reason not to associate this small brush pot with other late Ming or early Qing boxwood pieces of similar quality. In quality of carving, patination and even style it is equal to the seated scholar of no. 68.

216

Wrist Rest

Lu Dong

Bamboo covered with a thin layer of black lacquer; a wrist rest, the lacquer cut through to create a silhouette design of a branch of bamboo, poetically inscribed: "Bamboo with an empty heart is my teacher" followed by the signature *Kuisheng,* with seal *Dongyin* ('seal of [Lu] Dong') in seal script in a rectangular cartouche.
Yangzhou, first half of the 19th century.
Length: 28 cm. Width: 6 cm.
Formerly in the Dr. Ip Yee collection.
Published: *Chinese Bamboo Carving,* Part II, p.237.

竹胎黑漆地刻竹銘臂擱•盧棟製
十九世紀上半葉, 長28厘米, 寬6厘米

The poem here is a play on different meanings of the character *xu,* which can mean empty or open-minded, humble. *Xuxin* is a compound meaning either an empty central core, as in bamboo, or a humble heart. The meaning is that the poet learns humility from the bamboo.

The wrist rest was another staple of the scholar's studio. It was used in writing small calligraphy. Large calligraphy was executed without resting the wrist, allowing the whole body to participate in the exercise, but with smaller and more formal script the wrist was often rested either on the table (or paper) or on a wrist rest.

Wrist rests survive in large numbers, but mostly from the Qing dynasty; surprisingly few are pictured in paintings. 17th century or earlier examples are relatively rare, a reason for which may be found in Wen Zhenheng's *Changwu Ji* ('Notes on Superfluous Objects'). In a section on wrist rests he writes: "Wrist rests made with long archaic jade *zhi* (sword scabbard clasp — see no. 146) are most elegant. Otherwise Japanese-made ones of black lacquer resembling archaic jade *gui* (elongated tablets, usually with pointed tops) as light as paper are best. As for *zitan* with carved motifs, or bamboo with elaborate figures, these are not to be used."[1] It is likely that the vogue for wrist rests in the form which later became the standard shape commenced at some time during the late Ming dynasty, and did not become popular until the Qing. In any case, if Ming scholars preferred archaic jades or Japanese imports (neither of which would today be recognized as Chinese Ming wrist rests) it would explain why so few early wrist rests of the standard form are extant.

It is also likely that the standard form developed to a large extent in response to the new-found arts of the literati who took to carving soft surfaces during the second half of the Ming dynasty. The essentially flat, rectangular format, so like that of the standard hanging scroll, was perfect for this new means of expression, presenting an elongated surface suitable for calligraphy or pictorial illustration while using the 'iron brush' without straying too far from two-dimensional depiction.

1. *Juan* 7, section 22.

214

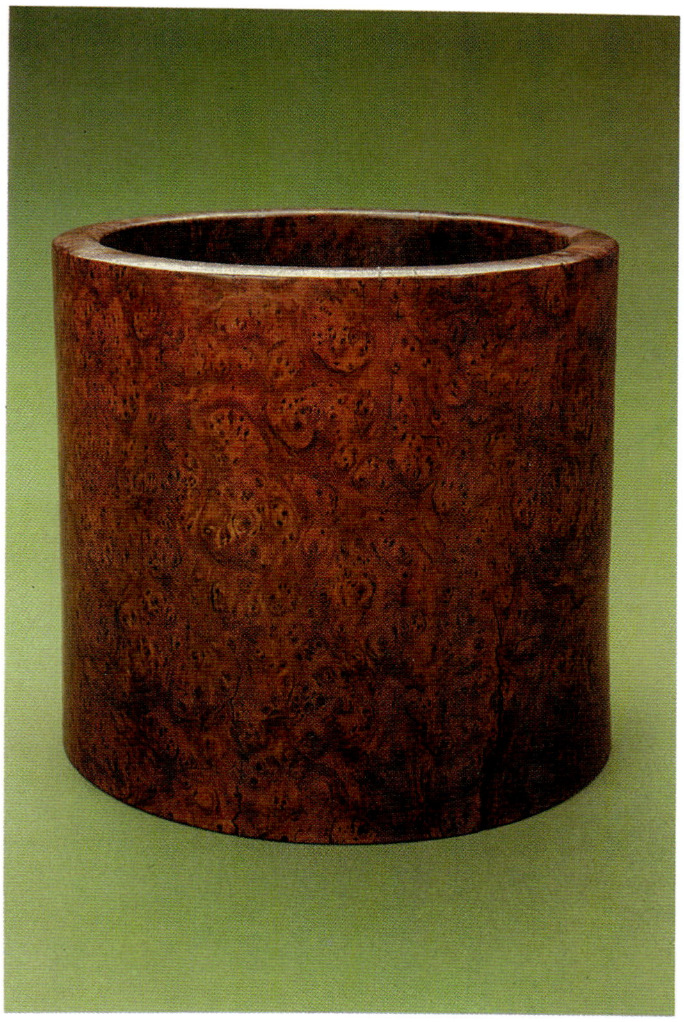

215

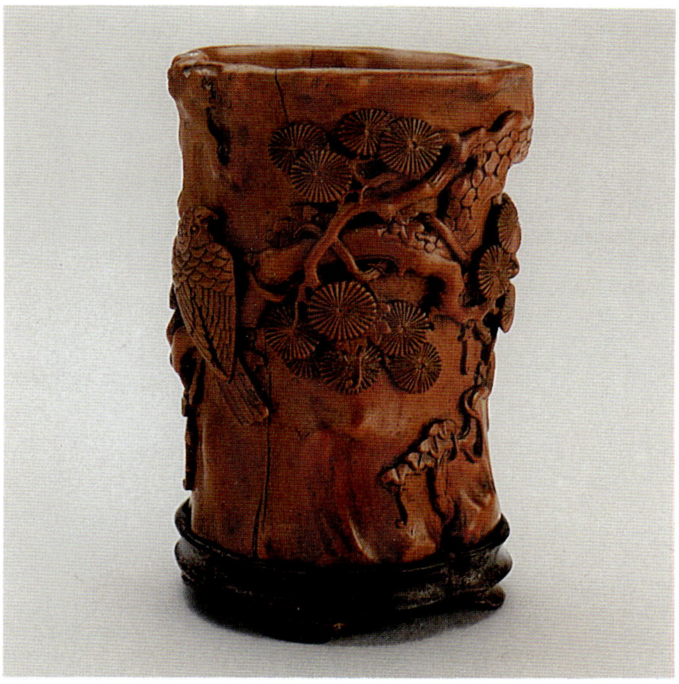

216

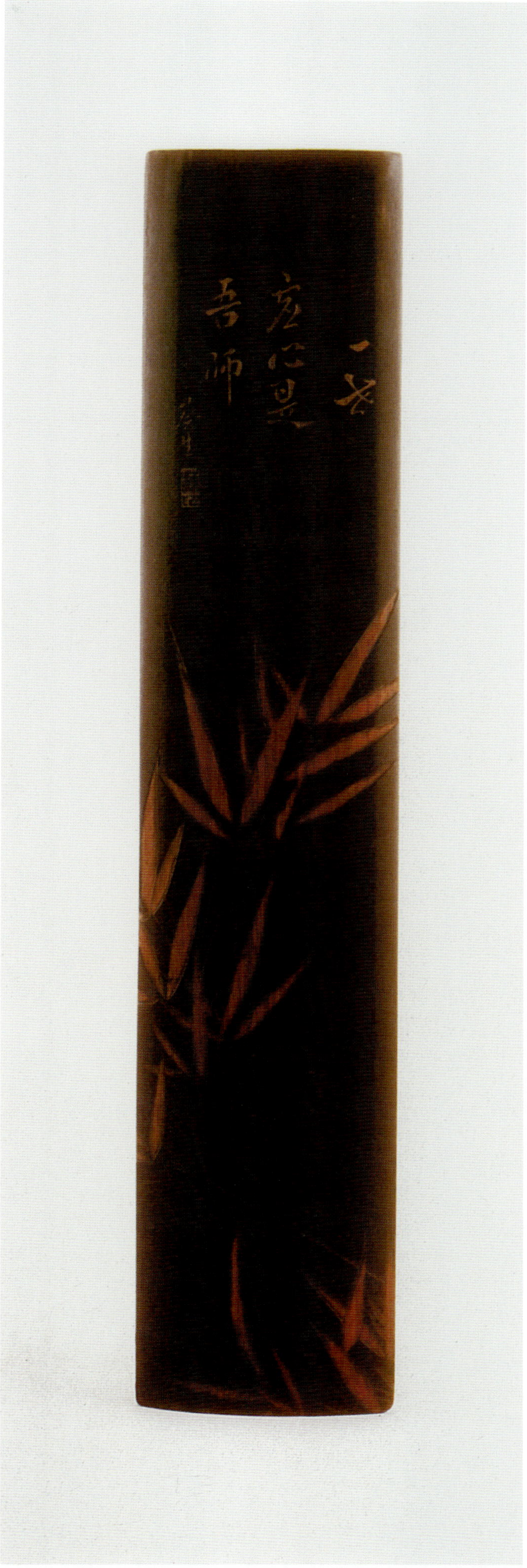

217

Seal Paste Box and Cover

Yixing pottery, the interior and the recessed foot covered with a crackled cream-coloured glaze, the exterior covered with reddish-brown lacquer; a seal-ink box and cover, of bulging, octagonal form set on a broad cylindrical foot, the top panel carved in 'iron brushwork' with a branch of blossoming prunus, and a seal: *Kuisheng* in seal script within a rectangular cartouche.
Lacquer work by Lu Dong of Yangzhou, early 19th century.
Height: 3.2 cm.

宜興胎罩漆刻梅印色蓋盒·盧棟製
十九世紀上半葉，高3.2厘米

Seal paste consists of three essential ingredients: ground cinnabar, mixed with a small amount of caster oil and a very small quantity of moxa punk. On top of the basic ingredients may be added, for various effects, ground gold, coral or pearl. This is the formula of Wen Peng (1498-1573), a famous Ming dynasty literatus influential in the development of seal carving. The earliest red seal pigment was ground like any other mineral pigment and mixed with water; it only later developed into an oil-based material, which necessitated the use of the cotton wool pad containing the seal paste in a covered box. At what point this transition took place is not certain, but popular wisdom has it as an early Ming invention.

Small boxes and covers of this type might have been used for a number of purposes, including holding other ground colours for painting, or for cosmetics. Wen Peng in his *Yinzhang Jishu* ('Discussion of Seals') advises that the best seal paste containers are porcelain or jade, which prevent the paste from turning bad. Metal boxes of gold, silver or copper will adulterate paste after about ten days and are unsuitable. If soapstone is used (Wen uses the term Qingtian stone which was the principle source of soapstone in his day), because of its slightly porous nature he recommends the waxing of the interior so it will not absorb the oil.

The seal acted as an official sign of office, as a personal signature, and in the arts as an additional level of meaning, both lexically and visually. Every scholar would have had a number of seals for his own use, quite apart from those he collected, and artists may have had many hundreds at one time. (Qi Baishi, the famous early 20th century artist, owned several hundred, frequently signing his name as the 'old man wealthy with three hundred seals'.) The demand for handy seal paste was constant. Every scholar would have had a number of these containers, not only for different places around the house where he might use them, but for different qualities and colours of paste suited to different tasks. The standard format that evolved for these boxes, although by no means the only one, was a shallow, domed box of a variety of sizes, or in some case rectangular flat-topped boxes. The size of these boxes depended upon the size of the seals to be used, but as a rule they ranged from about 5 to 12 cm in diameter or width.

For information about Lu Dong, see no. 63. His association with Yixing wares is here demonstrated not only in the material, but also in the decoration and its style.

218

Covered Box

Nephrite, of pale greenish-white colour carved as a cylindrical box and cover; decorated overall in low relief with the branches of a fruiting lychee tree, one fruit rendered realistically, the rest decorated with various diaper patterns.
Probably 16th century.
Height: 2.8 cm. Diameter: 5.8 cm.
Published: *Chinese Jades from Han to Ch'ing*, p.139, no. 115.

玉雕荔枝圓蓋盒
可能十六世紀，高2.8厘米，直徑5.8厘米

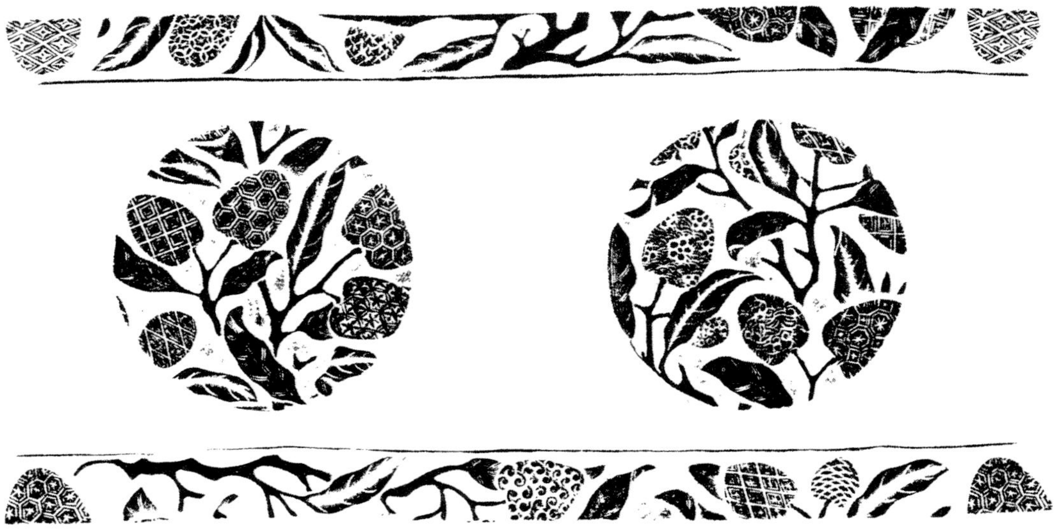

It is likely that this box was used for seal paste or incense powder, but it might have served any number of other functions, including holding colours or ladies' cosmetics. A range of small boxes and covers was certainly made from the Tang dynasty onwards, and probably before. Most of these are described rather indiscriminately as 'seal paste' boxes, but in fact seal paste was not invented until the Ming dynasty (see no. 217). Prior to that vermillion was mixed with water and glue like any other ground pigment for painting, and might well have been kept in such a box, but no more so than other colours. The vast numbers of 8th to 14th century small boxes and covers in porcelain, for example, nearly always referred to as seal paste boxes, were definitely made for other purposes.

Another possible literati function for this example was an incense powder container (see no. 231). Although frequently made of bronze in the Ming dynasty, Chinese paintings show these small boxes in what appear to be a variety of materials as quite common objects. They must have existed in many materials, and this is exactly the right size and shape to be used in that way.

Whatever purpose it served it is a marvellous piece of workmanship, obviously derived from a series of small lacquer boxes made during the mid- to late Ming dynasty (an example of which is to be found from the collection of the late King Gustav VI Adolf of Sweden as no. 125 in *Chinese Art*, by Gyllensvärd and Pope). The use of a variety of diaper grounds, consisting of a wide range of patterns (analysed in astonishing detail in *Zhongguo Gudai Diaoqi Jinde Yishu Zhi Yanjiu* ['A Study of the Art of Diaper Grounds in Carved Lacquer in Ancient China'], by Wu Fengpei) was standard to lacquer ware from the Yuan dynasty to the present day. They served both as formalized grounds, to separate one ground plane from another, and as fillers for elements of decoration, as they are used here.

217

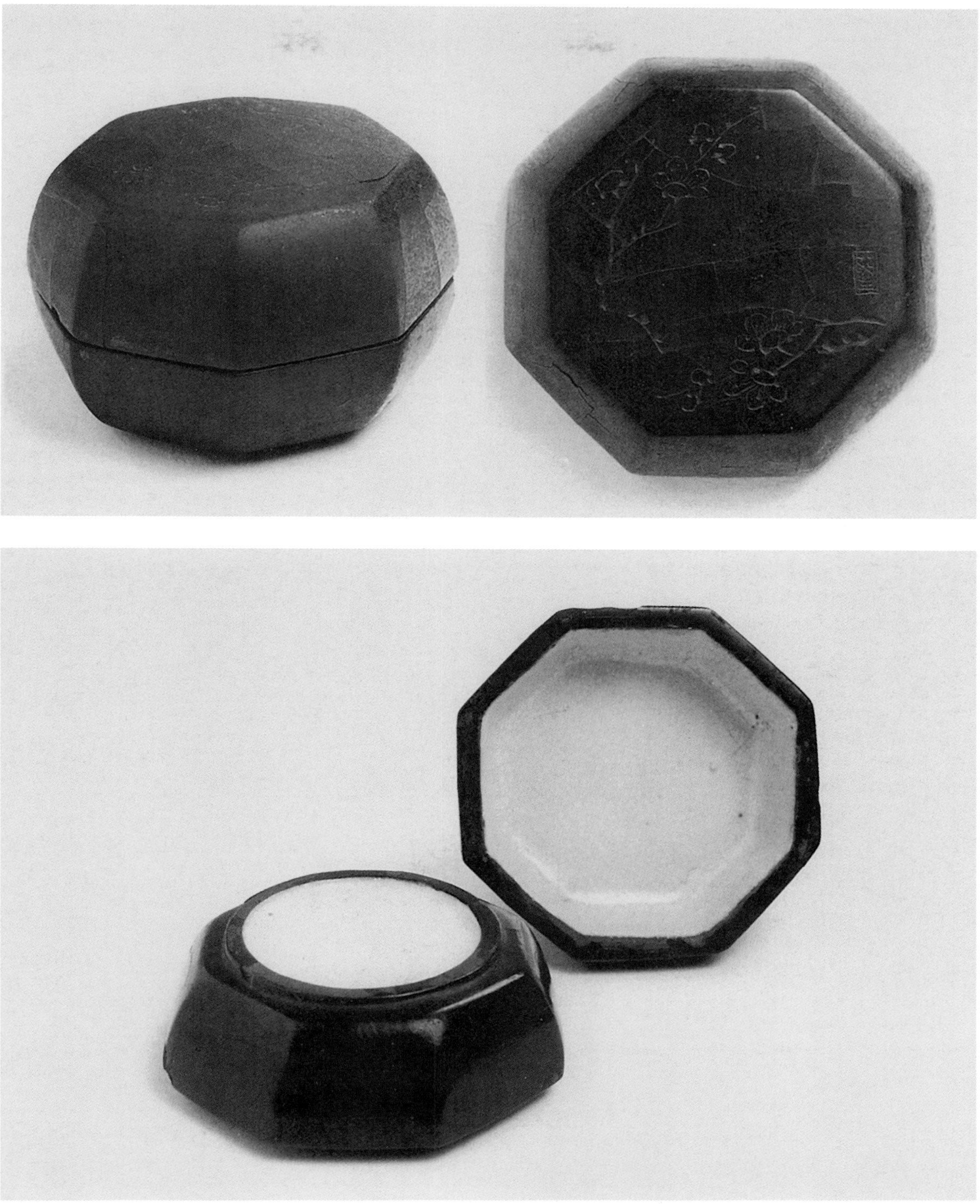

218

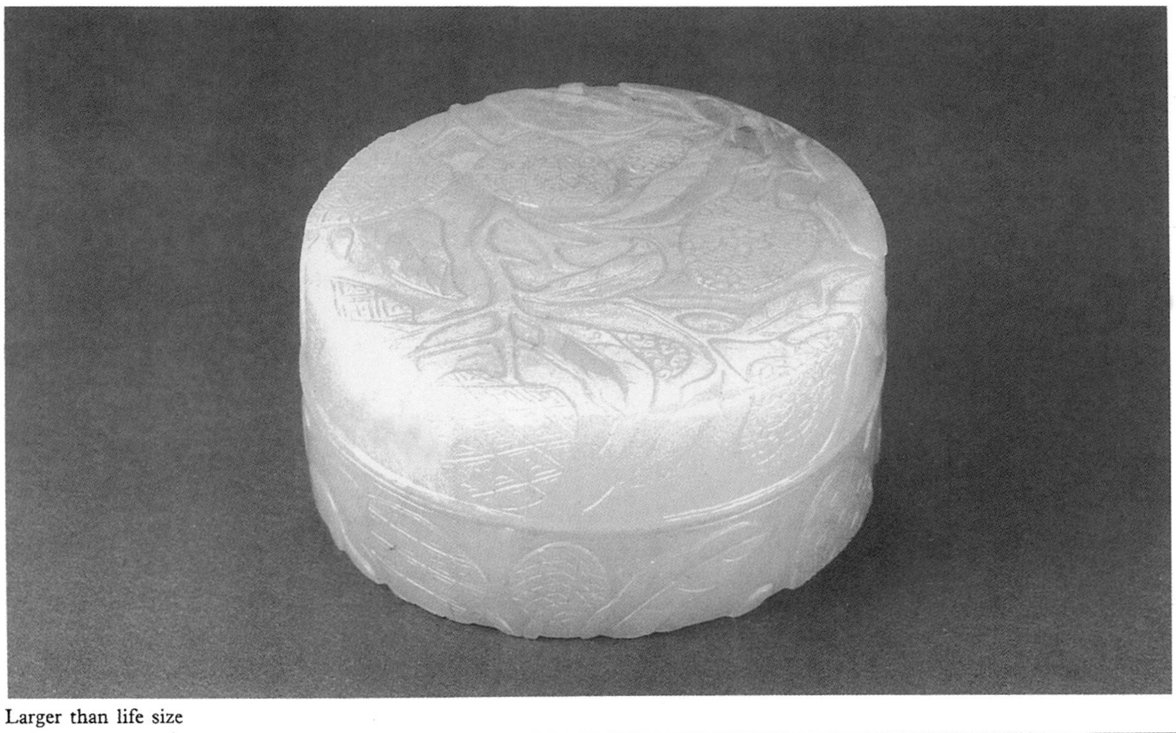

Larger than life size

219
Table Screen

Limestone conglomerate; a plain rectangular panel mounted in a wood stand as a table screen; the stand carved on each side with five bats, one holding a spray of peaches in its mouth, flying around a rock on a continuous ground of formalized clouds.
Mid- to late Qing dynasty.
Height: 29.2 cm.

磔石五蝠插屏
清中至晚期，高29.2厘米

These screens were originally functional items called 'inkstone' screens, and served several purposes. They were placed to protect paintings or paper from ink accidentally splashing from the inkstone while in use. They were also useful if a servant was grinding ink to allow the scholar to continue his musings without having to watch the manual labour of grinding, and to protect him from accidental splashing. They were also used subtly to allow the scholar to maintain his secrets of brush-loading and pointing from other guests if necessary. Certain tricks in loading the brush were vital to some forms of calligraphy (clerical script, for instance, where the oblique forms depend upon careful shaping of the brush) and some people might feel inclined not to reveal them. However, apart from its practical functions it undoubtedly also became a decorative item in later times.

Limestone conglomerates are sometimes also called 'puddingstone'. They are one of two forms of 'puddingstone' used in China (see no. 87 for the other, harder variety) and that which was available to the Chinese, presumably from local sources, from at least the Tang dynasty.[1] The material is a sedimentary rock which frequently contains fascinating patterns of a variety of materials including fossilized shells, coral formations and other organic material. In it can be seen an endlessly changing variety of faces and forms, abstract patterns and colours and textures that serve much the same function as swirling incense or gnarled wood in concentrating the mind.

The wood stand, here an integral part of the work of art rather than simply a base, is obviously meant to be viewed as two separate sides, although the cloud pattern is continuous. The subject of ten bats holds no special significance, while five is a homophonous pun based on *wufu,* meaning both 'five bats' and 'five happinesses' (longevity, wealth, health, virtue and peaceful demise). The rocks (rising presumably from waves, although they are not shown) and the peaches are symbols of the Western Paradise, in which Xi Wangmu (the Goddess of the West) grows the peaches of longevity.

1. A number of seated lion sculptures exist in this material, datable to the Tang dynasty (see for example, *Treasures from The Metropolitan Museum of Art,* China Institute of America, 1979, p.39, no. 28). It is also imitated in porcelains of the Qianlong period.

220
Ladle
Hu Wenming

Copper, inlaid with silver and gilt; a ladle, in the form of a quatrefoil spoon, the exterior inlaid with silver lines in a formalized *lingzhi* fungus design supported by an irregularly shaped bamboo handle, branching into twigs and leaves, which spread out in relief across the base of the spoon, the handle inlaid with silver dots, the larger of which are of gilt copper, to accentuate the bamboo segment joints; the top of the handle, and leaves and tendrils all gilt.
Attributed to Hu Wenming.
Yunjian, *circa* 1560-*circa* 1620.
Length: 16 cm.
Published: *Chinese Metalwork of the Hu Wenming Group,* no. 40.

鎏金嵌銀線竹枝銅勺・胡文明製
明(約1560-1620)，長16厘米

This ladle was almost certainly used as a water ladle in conjunction with a large water vessel of some kind. It has a series of water marks running across the spoon as if the ladle were kept for a long period of time in a vessel after it had been emptied, but with some water remaining in the bowl of the spoon.

It is attributed to Hu Wenming on the strength of its style, materials and method of manufacture, and is the only ladle known which may be confidently attributed to this or any other late Ming metalworker. The elegance of this example attests to the care that would have been taken with such ladles of all sizes (this seems to be an unusually large one) and it is surprising that as a class, like incense tools, they seem not to have survived in quantities related to their obviously extensive manufacture.

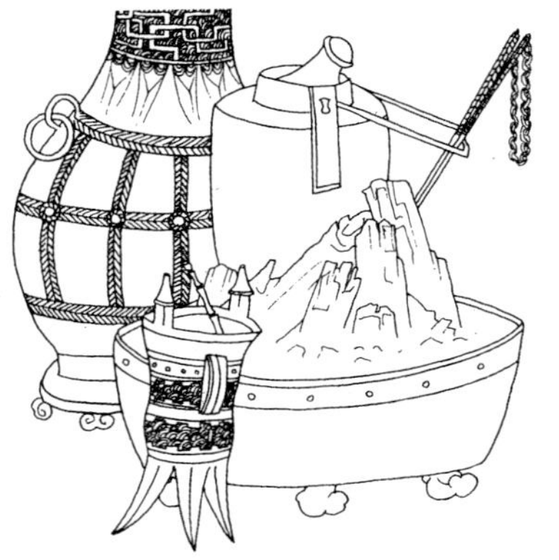
Fig. 1

Ladles of various sizes are a common feature of genre paintings (see Fig. 1, where what could be just such a ladle as this rests in a *jue*) in conjunction with a wide variety of vessels. Another object which figures in the same painting is a brazier, a common feature in genre paintings. They were used for heating wine, and indeed anything else that needed heating, and for warming the hands and feet. It is likely that hand warmers (see no. 246) were also replenished from such braziers from time to time. The linked metal chopsticks resting in the handle of a water vessel (in which a pot of wine is warming) were commonly used in conjunction with these braziers.

221
Seal

Ivory, of extremely well-patinated mottled orange yellow and golden brown tones with considerable age cracking and natural wear; a seal, the knob in the form of a mythical animal *(xiezhai),* the powerfully carved beast crouching tensely, filling the whole of the knob platform; the seal text inscribed in negative seal script *Fengyu guren lai* ('In the midst of the storm old friends arrive').
Probably Ming dynasty.
7.1 cm × 6.1 cm × 6.35 cm.

象牙雕異獸印
可能明代，7.1×6.1×6.35厘米

Early ivory seals are relatively rare, and this is one of the more impressive examples known.[1] The seal text is of a type known as *jianzhang* which carries a message, rather than the name of a person or place. Here the message is that when the weather is foul and one is not inclined to go out, it is pleasant when old friends drop in to while away the time. In the evolution of seal texts (see no. 125) it represents the stage where fanciful seals were applied to paintings and calligraphy as an extra layer of meaning, rather than just as a signature or record of ownership. This stage was reached during the Ming dynasty when a number of seals were customarily added to a work of art; apart from the messages revealed in their texts they also carried meaning as abstract form, balancing with the painting and calligraphy, in some cases on a level approaching equal terms.

The flamboyant size of this seal, and its fanciful text suggest that it is unlikely to predate the Ming, perhaps even the middle Ming, but the patination and wear of the seal text suggests that it is a later addition. The recarving of seal texts on old seals was a common practice and it is possible that an official seal of some kind might have preceded it. The *xiezhai* was an emblem of well-considered judgement and as such was frequently symbolic of the judiciary. It would have been a suitable official seal for a judge, where perhaps flamboyance was more appropriate at an earlier date. If this was the case, in view of the style and the very considerable patination and wear a date earlier than mid-Ming might be considered, perhaps even of the Yuan.[1]

1. Two large, dated ivory seals are illustrated in *Dated Chinese Antiquities 600-1650,* p.239, nos. 189 and 190. One has a *xiezhai,* but of a quite different style, and is dated to 1418; the other has a Buddhist Wheel of the Law and is dated to 1427. Two further large ivory seals, one inscribed with a seal text stating that it was the seal of the Wanli Emperor (which we have not had the opportunity to examine), are illustrated in *The Arts of the Ming Dynasty,* nos. 363 and 364.

219

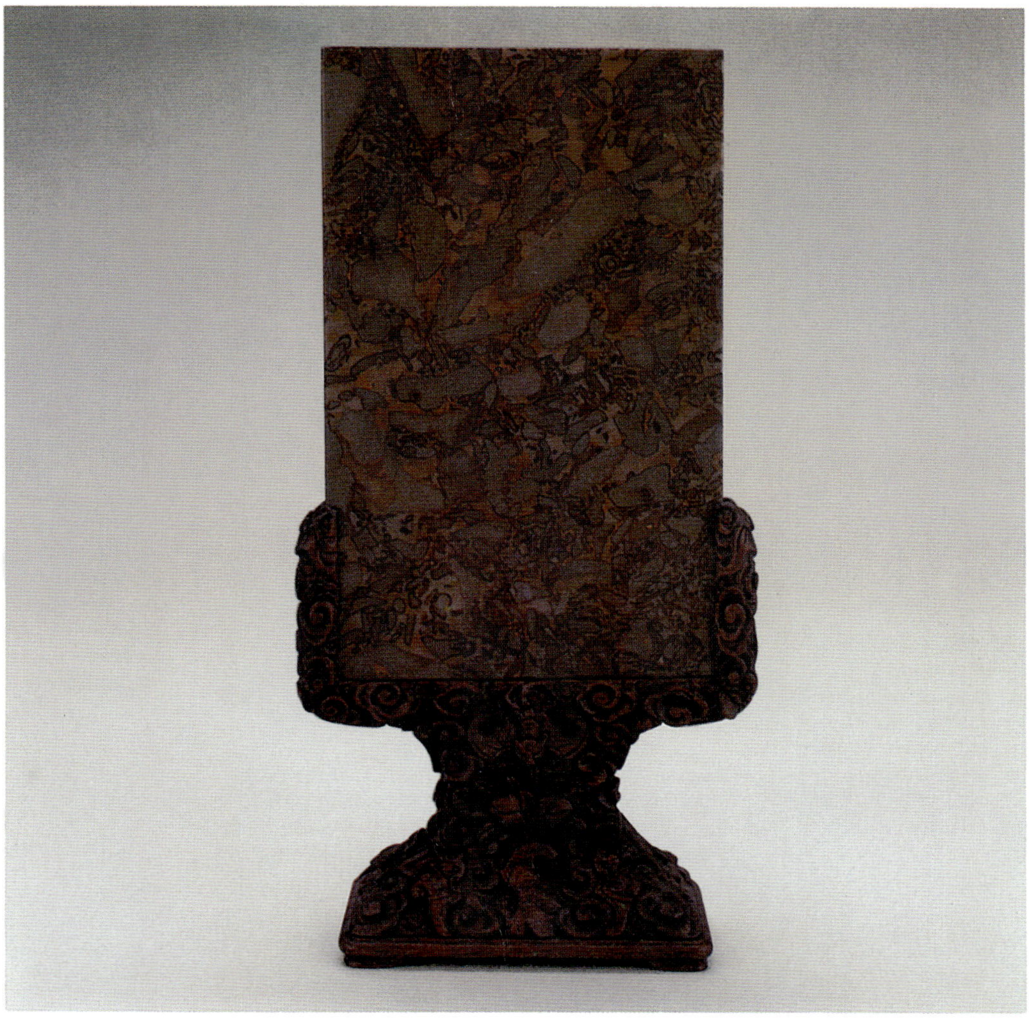

220

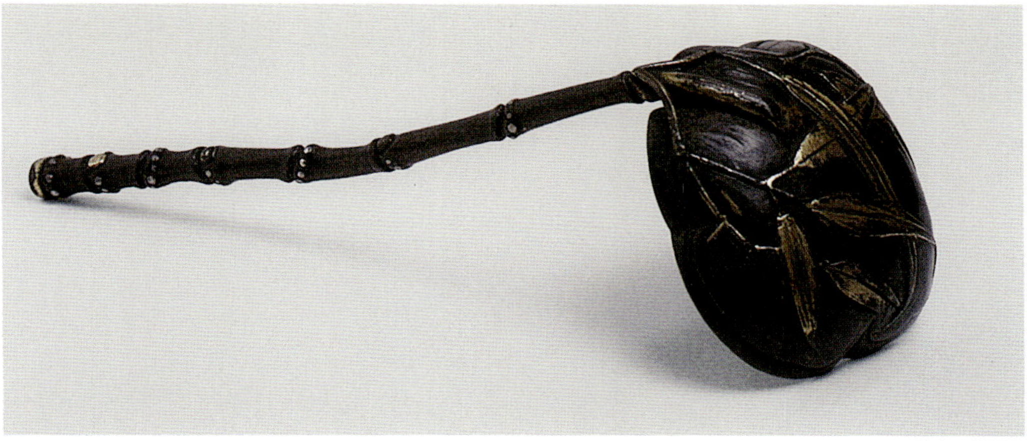

221

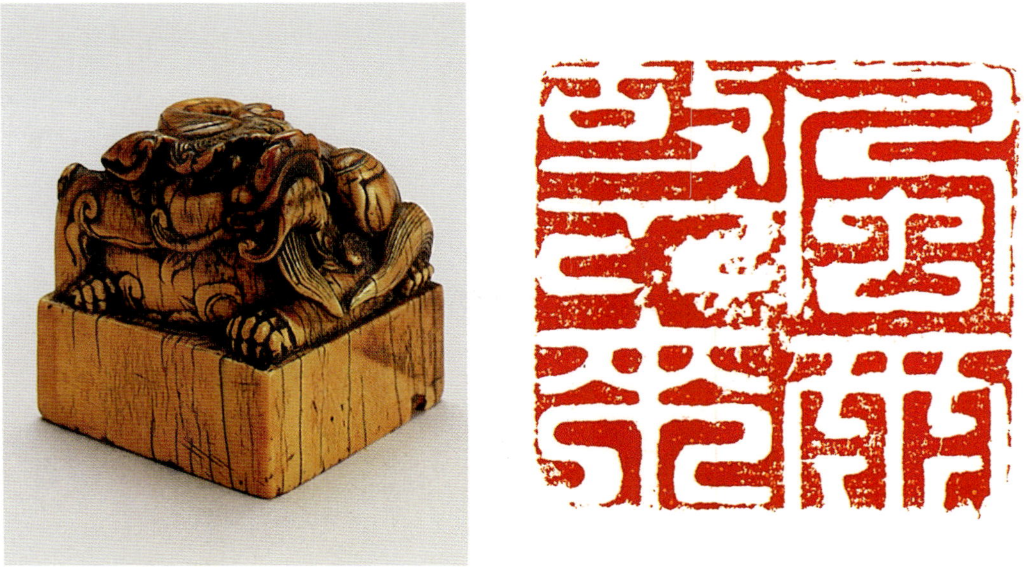

222

Scroll Weights

Wood, *hongmu* ('redwood'); of well-figured golden and dark brown colours; carved as a pair of scroll weights, the plain, rounded rectangular bases surmounted by elaborately carved and pierced grips, each with a fairly crudely carved *chi* dragon, snarling amid a confusion of *lingzhi* fungi, one weight with a triangular original insert in its base, the other with a rectangular section set into the body of the dragon.
Qing dynasty.
Length of each: 37.7 cm.

紅木雕螭龍紙鎮一對
清代，各長37.7厘米

Pairs of weights of this kind, in various sizes, were used to hold back handscrolls while reading or viewing. The handscroll format (see no. 4 for instance) was made to be moved through at the viewer's pace. This was usually accomplished simply by holding the two ends of the scroll apart with the two hands, but a variety of reasons for pausing made scroll weights convenient.

Individually they might also serve as paper weights, in holding down loose paper while painting or writing, although single weights were also made as paper weights. Of similar shape, these single weights often had a decorative finial at the centre, whereas as a rule scroll weights were level along the top to fit better against the loosely rolled ends of a handscroll in use.

These two have obviously been made from an old piece of furniture, the triangular and rectangular inserts replacing original gaps where morticed and mitred joints occurred. It was not uncommon for precious wood to be re-used in the event of a piece of furniture being scrapped, and a reasonable quantity of Chinese furniture is made up of earlier pieces re-worked.

223

Paper Weight

Wood, *zitan,* of well-figured dark purplish-brown colour; a paper weight of plain rectangular form, the upper surface inscribed in draft script: "My friends, please do not flip or disturb my private collection of books, brushes, inkstones, paper and silk. I remain deeply grateful. A cordial appeal."
Perhaps late Ming, or Qing dynasty.
3.3 cm × 32.5 cm × 6 cm.

紫檀刻銘紙鎮
晚明或清代，3.3×32.5×6厘米

Weights for the scholar's studio take various forms: small objects, such as animal sculptures, pebbles of jade, etc. (see nos. 51 and 70); pairs of scroll weights (such as no. 222), single elongated weights of this type, and fancier ones made to contain other implements (such as no. 224). They are interchangeably known as paper weights, scroll weights or book weights in the West, although in China they are usually referred to as book weights. However, this term is slighly misleading and comes from the time when Chinese books were in the form of series of handscrolls, wrapped in a cloth binding. Their function is better described by the general title of paper weights.

224

Paper Weight

Wood, *zitan,* inlaid with ivory; a paper weight in the form of a miniature *qin* with a small drawer set into each end; the strings and studs inlaid in ivory; constructed from several pieces of joined wood.
Late Ming or Qing dynasty.
Length: 25.1 cm.

紫檀琴形紙鎮
晚明或清代，長25.1厘米

Wen Zhenheng supplies the clue to the purpose of this skilfully made and elegant small container as a paper weight. In a section on what he calls book weights, he closes with the comment: "Then there are some which are hollow, in which knives and hole-punchers (*zhui* — sharp pointed instruments for piercing holes in book-binding) are kept. These are vulgar products."

222

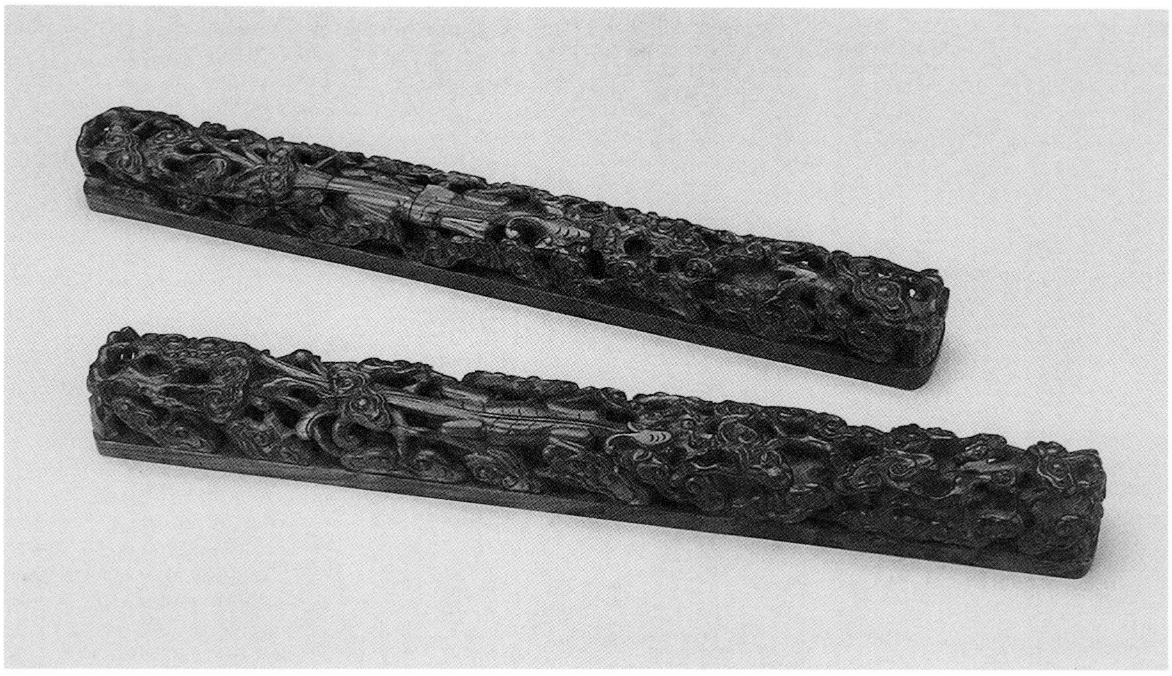

223

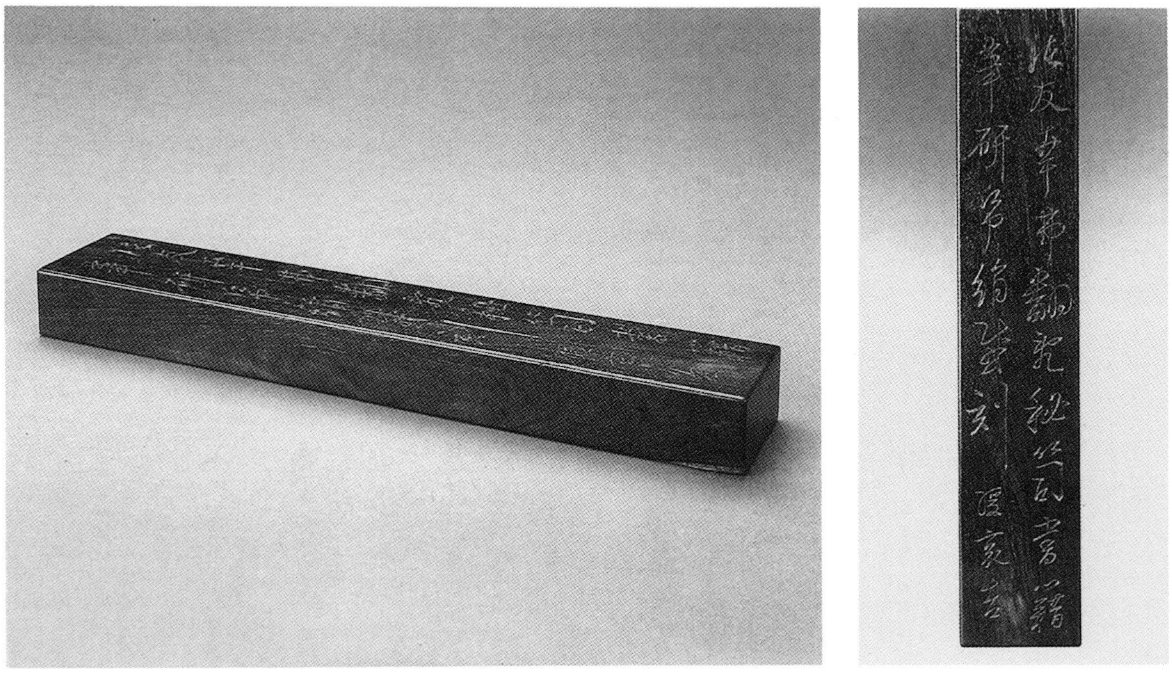

224

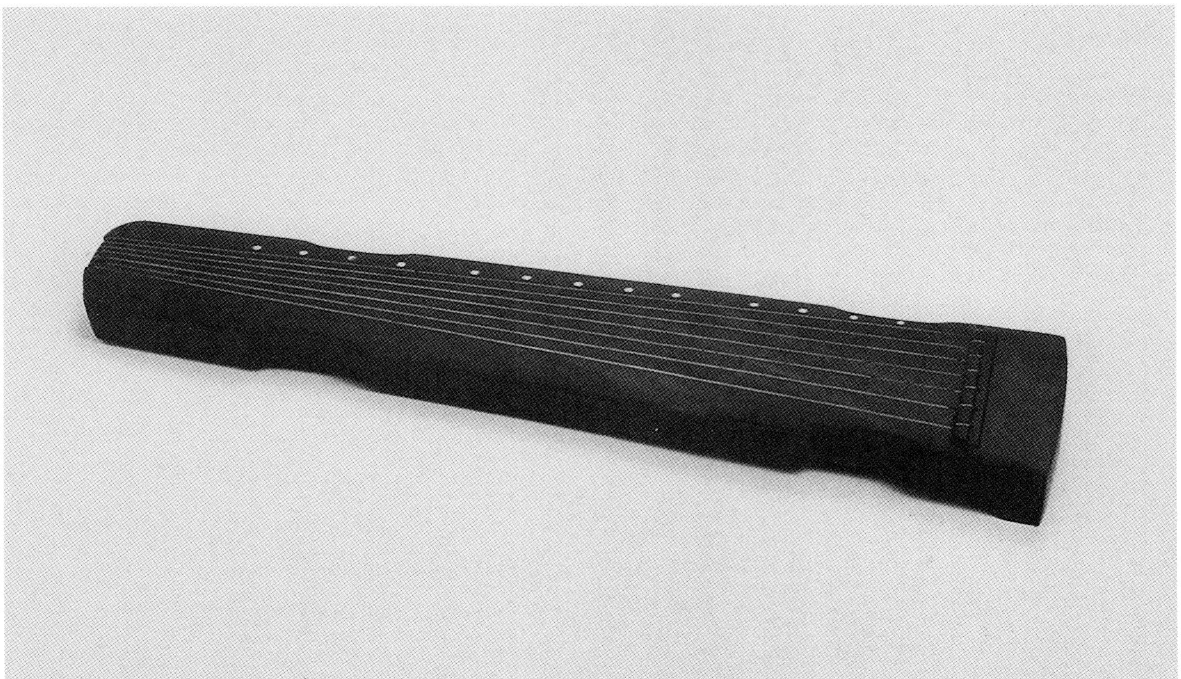

225

Paper Weight

Bronze, inlaid with gold and silver; a paper weight in the form of a crouching mythical beast, the dog-like creature with inlaid silver flames rising from its legs, and various other details inlaid in silver or gold; the base unworked.
Probably Ming dynasty.
Height: 5.1 cm.
Formerly in the Robert A. Hall collection.

嵌金銀青銅異獸紙鎮
可能明代，高5.1厘米

Paper weights are amongst the most common of all literati objects. Every scholar might find a need for half a dozen or more, and since they also functioned as works of art they fell into the category of things of which one could not have too many. Ideal as gifts, it is likely that the average scholar ended up with many of them. Today it is not uncommon for a working artist to have half a dozen or more about his studio (even if they are modern reproductions, of which many have been made in the past decade to fill the demand left by the disappearance into collections of the very large numbers of extant early examples).

The paper weight in the form of animal sculptures or figures seems to have its origins in the mat weight. These came in sets of four and were for weighting down the corners of thin mats upon which people sat at ground level in ancient times. Sets of four such weights have been discovered in various Han tombs, and in one Warring States tomb.[1] These early mat weights were often in bronze or inlaid bronze, but jade examples are also known from the Han dynasty. It is likely that once paper became popularly used by artists and writers, the similarity of requirements for mat and paper weights would have meant a parallel development, until the mat was largely supplanted by raised furniture.

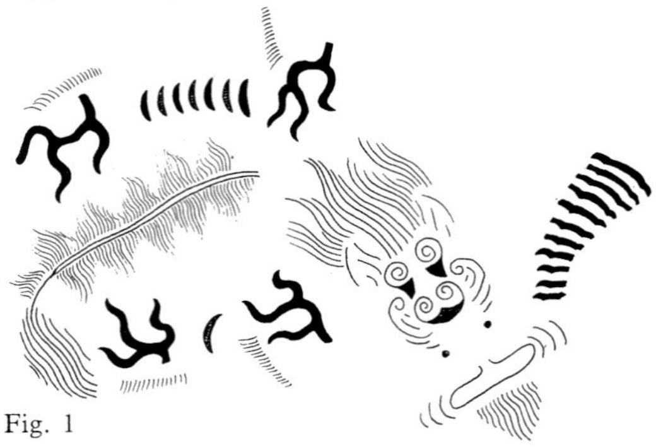

Fig. 1

Regardless of the date at which mat weights became paper weights, there is a clear tradition of small sculptural weights which is continuous from the Warring States period to the present day. Most of these are made either of bronze, sometimes inlaid, or of jade, but other materials were also used. There was also clearly a considerable vogue for small bronze weights from the early Ming period onwards, as a large number of them bear Xuande reign marks (for Wen Zhenheng's remarks about these see no. 226), although most are later than their marks. The surviving numbers of these Ming and Qing examples suggests that they were made in huge quantities over a period of several centuries.

There is a small group, however, which set themselves above the rest by certain features: they are usually larger, better sculpted, often inlaid or gilded, and give a much greater sense of being individual works of art rather than a mass-produced and utilitarian weight of the standard type. This stocky, powerful little creature is one of this superior group, and is a delightful piece of sculpture.

Further research into these later bronzes may reveal more sensible criteria for accurate dating; at present we must rely on little more than an educated guess. Although the Song archaistic revival of inlaid bronze has left that period with a reputation for having produced most of the fine work in this medium, the Hu Wenming wares demonstrate quite clearly that fine inlaid work was not a Song prerogative, nor is the inlay here sufficiently archaic in style to suggest so early a date. It is rather the inlaying of largely realistic, if a little formalized, detail; it is more characteristic, we believe, of the Ming, and perhaps even the late Ming. A net drawing of the inlay is reproduced in Fig. 1 where the gold inlay is cross-hatched and the silver is solid black.

1. See the *National Palace Museum Monthly of Chinese Art,* no. 12, p.4.

226

Paper Weight

Nephrite, of pale greenish-white colour, with some flaws in the stone and a small area of brown staining, carved as a paper weight in the form of a brocade-wrapped *qin* tied together in an enclosing sash with a case of books, two hand scrolls and two hanging scrolls, a folded *weiqi* board and a duster.
Late Ming or early Qing dynasty.
2.3 cm × 13.5 cm × 5.3 cm.

玉雕書畫琴棋紙鎮
晚明或清初，2.3×13.5×5.3厘米

Wen Zhenheng's discussion on paper weights[1] gives a clear impression of the vast variety possible: "In jade from earlier times there may be found rabbits, oxen, horses, deer, rams (*yang,* which might equally mean sheep, goats etc.), toads, squatting tigers, *bixie* (mythical beast), and *chi* dragon and young. These are all archaic and elegant. In bronze there are green frogs, squatting tigers, squatting *chi* dragons, sleeping dogs, gilded *bixie,* reclining horses, toroises, and dragons. These are all useful. As to those made of agate, crystal, or of *guan, ge* or *ding* ware, they are not elegant. Among Xuande bronzes there are horses, oxen, cats, dogs, and *limao* (mythical beasts that like fire and smoke and are therefore associated with incense burners, either as a companion, or a cover knob). Some of these are excellent."

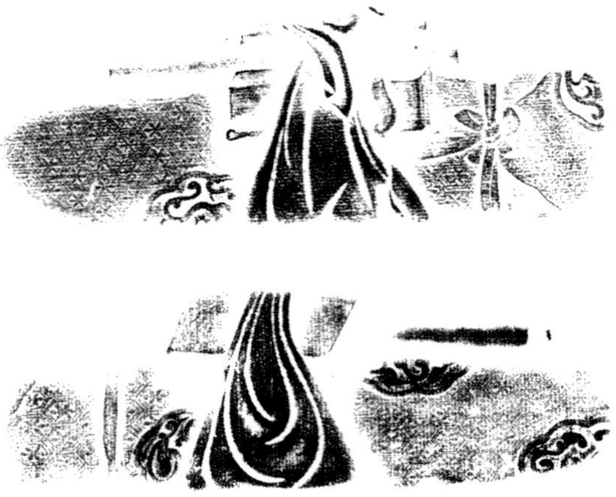

In this example the carver has made a weight with purely literati subject-matter. Wrapped and ready for an excursion are the trappings that a scholar might find useful on a day's outing: a *qin,* scrolls of calligraphy or paintings to enjoy, books of poetry to read, a duster and the game of *weiqi* — indicating that the scholar will not spend the day by himself.

1. *Changwu Ji, juan* 7, section 20.

227

Writing Paper for Liang Tongshu

Xu Xubai

Paper, of varying shades of yellow, beige and pink, with printed designs in pink, blue and pale beige; 50 sheets in all; 25 printed with a design of a dragonfly and a spray of two types of branches, one with blossoms; the picture inscribed: "Written by Xiangquan" and with the seal *Xubai* of the printer; 22 with a design of an open book, its title inscribed in the upper left margin of the book, and *Xubai zhai zhi* ('made in the Xubai Studio') in the lower left margin; three sheets simply lined, inscribed in the lower left margin *Xubai zhuren zuojian* ('stationery made by the master of the Xubai Studio'); contained in a paper folder with a title panel inscribed "Famous paper from the Xubai studio of Mr. Xu of Wulin (Hangzhou)" followed by "Inscribed by 82-year-old Shanzhao, Tongshu, in the fourth month of the *jiazi* year of Jiaqing (1804)" with seal *Shanqiao.*
All contained within two brocade edged cardboard folders, and still with three strips of paper which appear to be the original colour samples for the commission.
Hangzhou, 1804.
Paper sheets: 22.4 cm × 16.8 cm.

虛白齋彩箋·許虛白製
清嘉慶甲子(1804)，22.4×16.8厘米

Printed stationery was commonly used in China with one essential difference from its Western counterpart: the paper was printed with a decorative design, usually pale but distinct, rather than a name and address. The advent of woodblock printing gave the stationery printers considerable scope to develop their skills, and the finest of these printed papers were often designed by famous artists. They also provided a delightful medium for the expressive calligraphy of letter writing and the elegant thoughts so often expressed in short letters. The abstract communication that went on among the educated in China meant that a brief note with a few thoughts was capable of carrying profound communication in a suitably elegant manner. The letter was often not so much a record of events, as the starting point for the consideration of lofty matters. Such sheets of paper as these were ideally suited to these brief notes.

Xu Xubai, with his *Xubai Zhai* ('Xubai's Studio'), was a famous paper maker of Hangzhou in the mid-Qing period. Liang Tongshu (*zi:* Yuanyong; *hao:* Shanqiao — 1723-1815) was a native of Hangzhou. He was a *jinshi* of 1752, and a member of the Hanlin Academy. He served in various official posts until the death of his foster-father in 1758, at which point he retired to private life. Liang was a renowned calligrapher, whose fame spread in his time as far as Japan, and a well-known patron of the arts who employed a number of specialists to make various things for him. His relationship with the papermaker Xu Xubai is demonstrated here, where he commissioned a series of papers and inscribed a title panel for their binding.

225

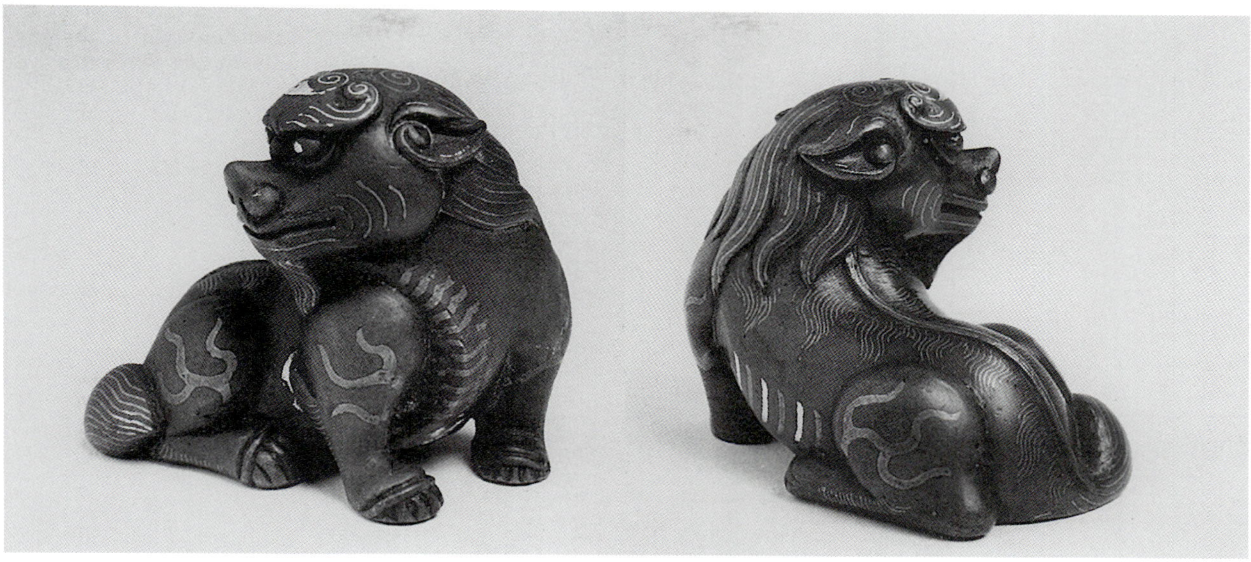

226

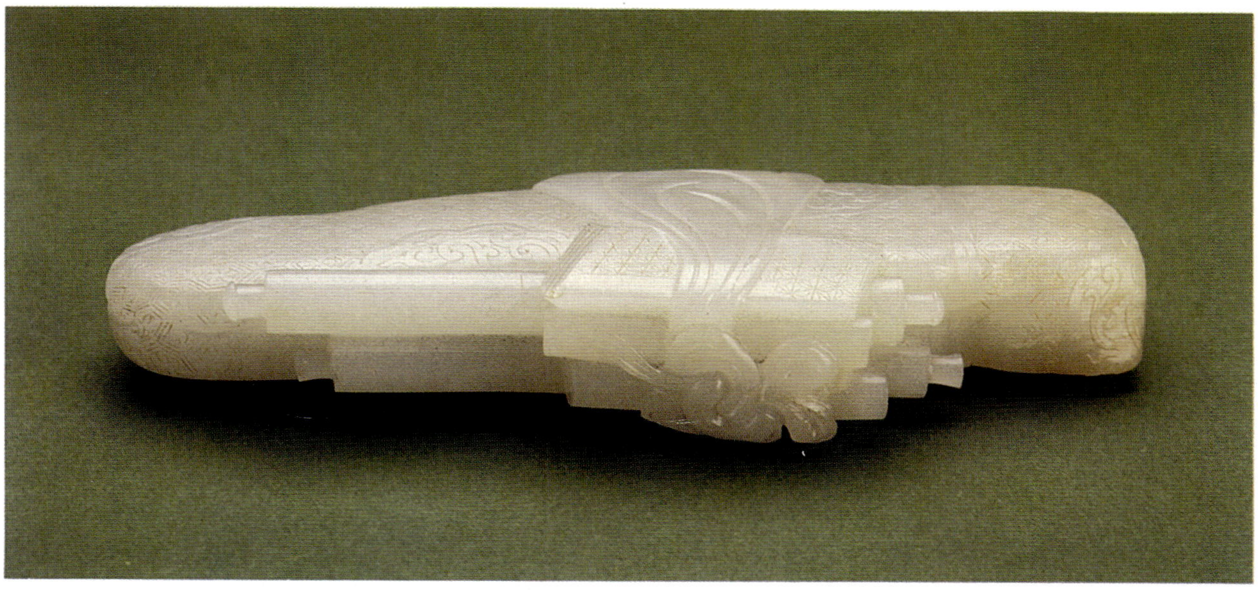

227

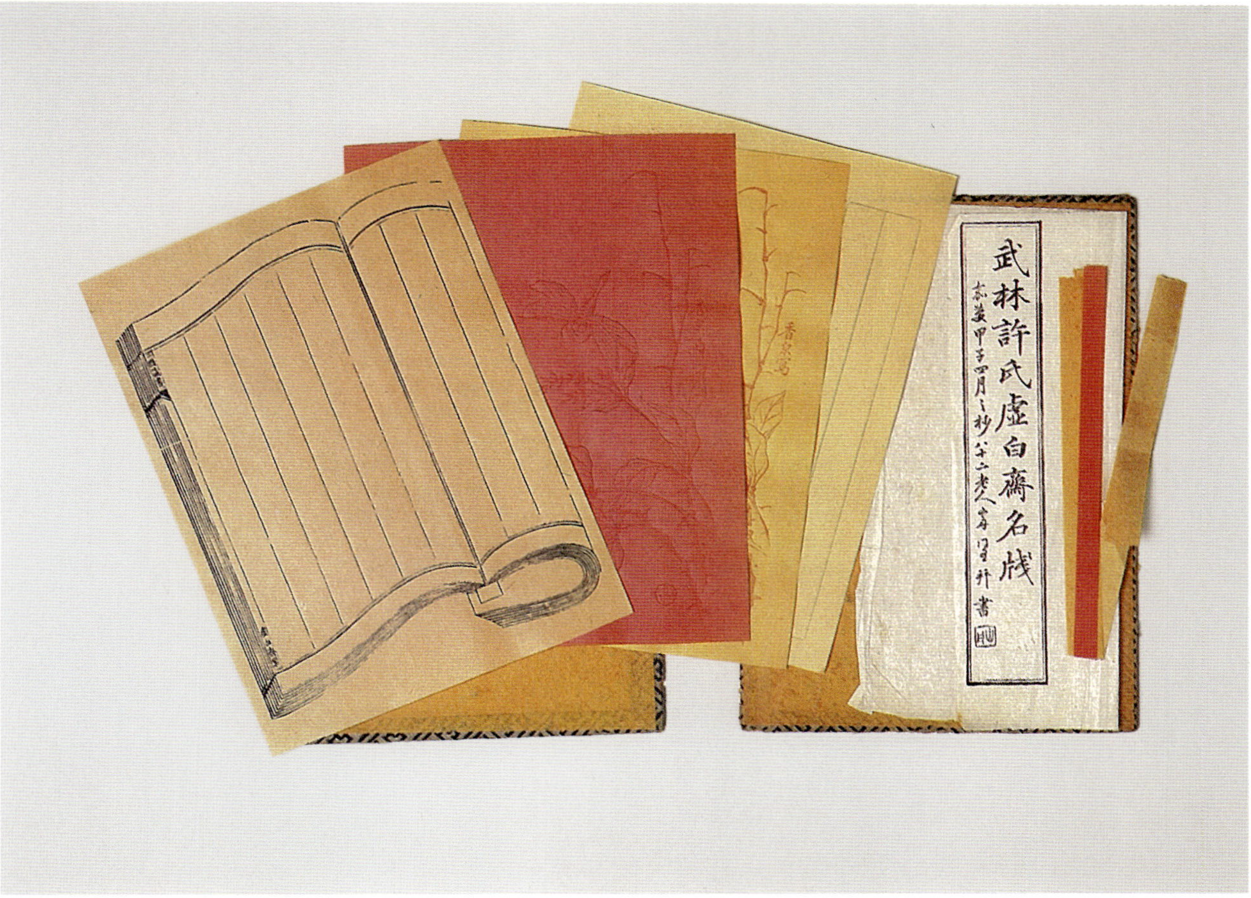

228

Paper Weight

Limestone, Duan stone, of deep, brownish olive-green colour; carved as a paper weight in the form of a section of bamboo using what appears to be natural layers in the material to enhance the subject.
Ming or Qing dynasty.
Length: 7.5 cm.

端石竹形紙鎮
明或清代, 長7.5厘米

This paper weight, while ideally functional, has layers of meaning dependent upon the bamboo symbolism and in the material, which was also widely used for the manufacture of inkstones. It is a most unusual little weight, as a rule Duan stone was reserved for inkstone manufacture, although a series of snuff bottles is known in the material. A water vessel is also recorded (see no. 145) and a large tray for a miniature landscapes of green Duan stone are also in the Shuisongshi Shanfang collection.

229

Incense Burner

Bronze; an incense burner in the form of an alms-bowl; the exterior surface covered with irregularly disposed splashes of gold; the base with the two characters *bao yong* ('for treasured use') applied to the surface by the same method as the splashes.
Ming or early Qing dynasty.
Height: 5 cm. Diameter: 10.55 cm.

灑金缽形青銅香爐•寶用銘
明或清初, 高5厘米, 直徑10.55厘米

Since we may assume that an owner who could afford such an elegant and expensive vessel was not in need of alms, it seems likely that this served as an incense burner. The alms bowl, used by wandering, often Buddhist mendicants, carried with it symbolism of having stepped beyond the dusty world. The idealized wandering mendicant monk was a man who cared not for worldly possessions, concentrating his attention on the Absolute realm, a symbolism with considerable meaning to the Chinese scholar. Similarly the idealized scholar was often portrayed as one who has turned his back on the material world, an eccentric who cared not for convention or material wealth, but lived in rustic retirement engaged in pursuits of the spirit. A vessel like this which combines this symbolism with the archaic meaning of gold splashed bronzes (see no. 160) is a subtle statement of fundamental literati values. The inscription on the base means literally that this vessel should be treasured, but the words *bao yong* are common in ancient bronze inscriptions where a ritual vessel is made for a particular occasion or to honour a particular ancestor and is further inscribed as being for the treasured use of innumerable generations of descendants. Thus the message of the gold splashing is reinforced by this allusion to archaic bronze inscriptions.

Incense burners are the most common objects seen in genre paintings and illustrated books. Usually they appeared in the form of the *gui*, the tripod *ding* or *li*, or a straight-sided, cylindrical vessel, often on three small feet and similar to the *lian* in form, but many other shapes were used. The censers are frequently seen in conjunction with two other vessels, a vase for holding incense tools (see no. 230) and a small covered box for holding incense powder (see no. 231). These three vessels appear so often together that we have taken the liberty of coining for them the term 'the three friends of incense'.

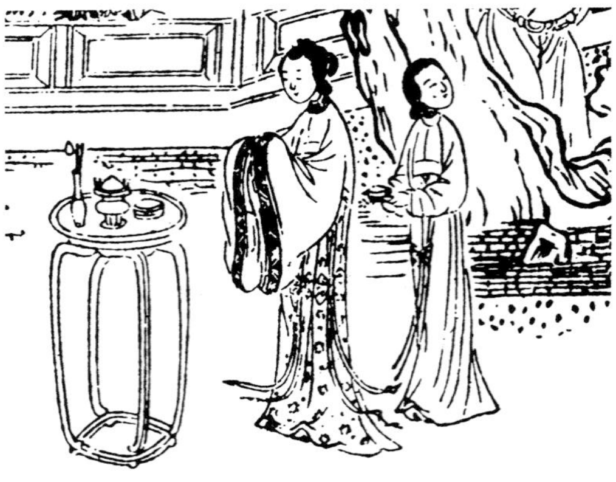

Fig. 1

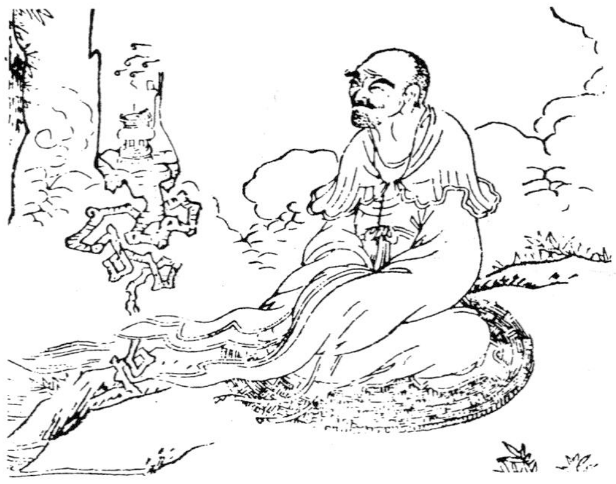

Fig. 2

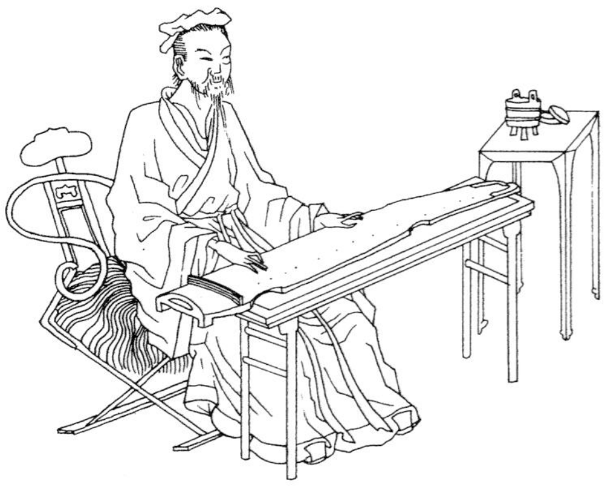

Fig. 3

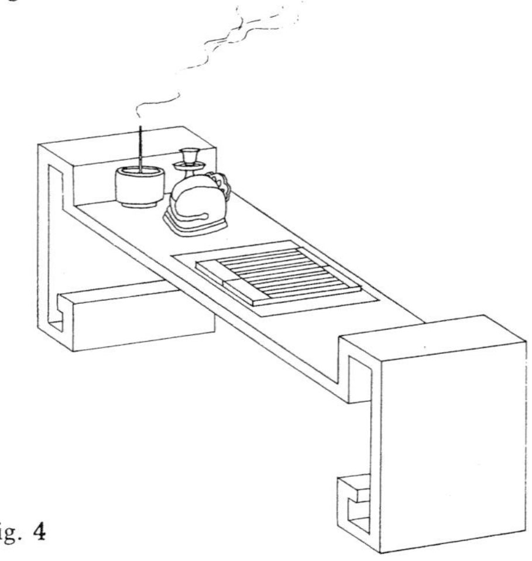

Fig. 4

Incense was commonly burned by scholar, sage and monk alike, indoors and out. It acted as a direct vehicle to the Absolute, both symbolically in the form of the smoke dispersing into the heavens, and meditatively in following it.

The two principal methods of burning incense were in the form of incense sticks and in conjunction with small chips of fragrant wood, such as sandalwood. As a rule the latter was favoured by the scholar, no doubt because it was more complicated and involved a certain meditative ritual in preparation. (Strictly speaking this method does not actually involve the burning of incense but of the sandalwood chips; the incense is only used to light the chip.) The incense burner is filled with ash, usually of the leaves of the *wutong* tree. Using a spade (one of the three tools for incense burning which sit in the vase — see no. 230) the ash is formed into a peak, in the top of which a crater is made. This crater is filled with incense powder from the covered box, and a chip of sandalwood is pressed down into it. The surrounding incense is then lit with pieces broken from an incense stick or burning spill, using the chopsticks which are the other part of the incense tool set. It burns down and lights the bottom of the chip of sandalwood, which then smoulders for a long time, giving off fragrant smoke. The incense burners used by the scholar were designed for this type of incense burning, but from time to time a stick might be placed in the ash as a more convenient method (see Fig. 4). Figs. 1-4 show incense burners in use from various paintings and printed books. In Fig. 3 a burner is shown beside an open powder box, while a scholar plays the *qin*. *Qin* players traditionally play with an incense burner either in front of them, or nearby.

228

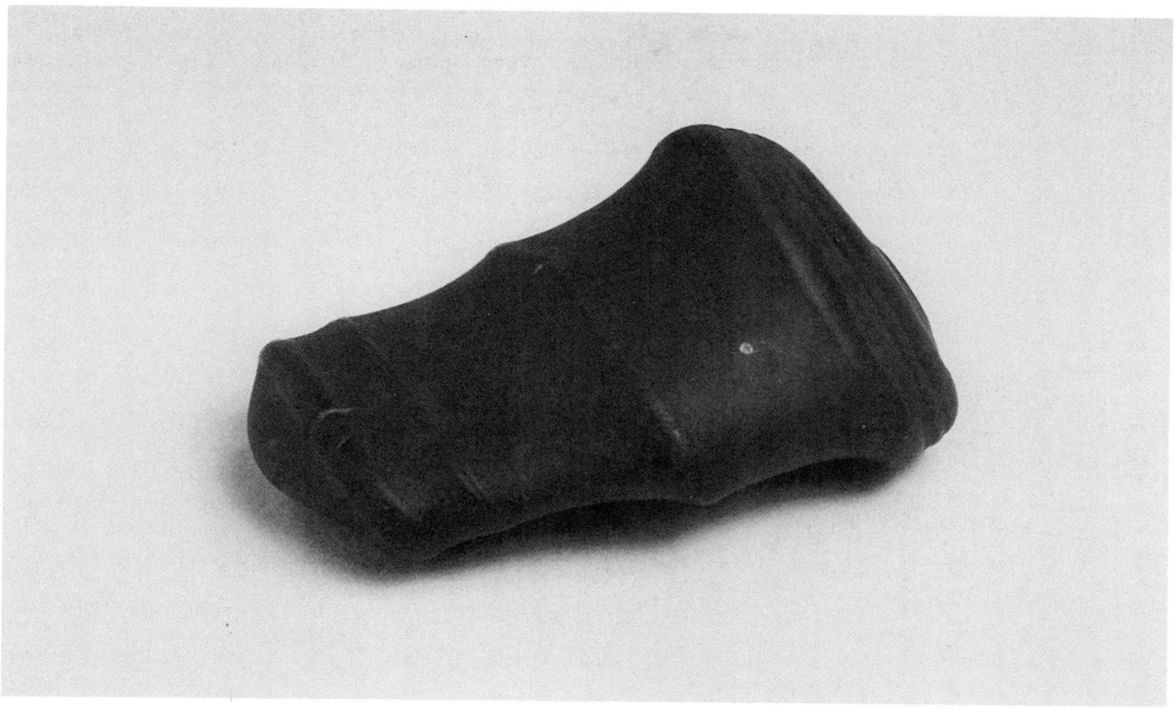

229

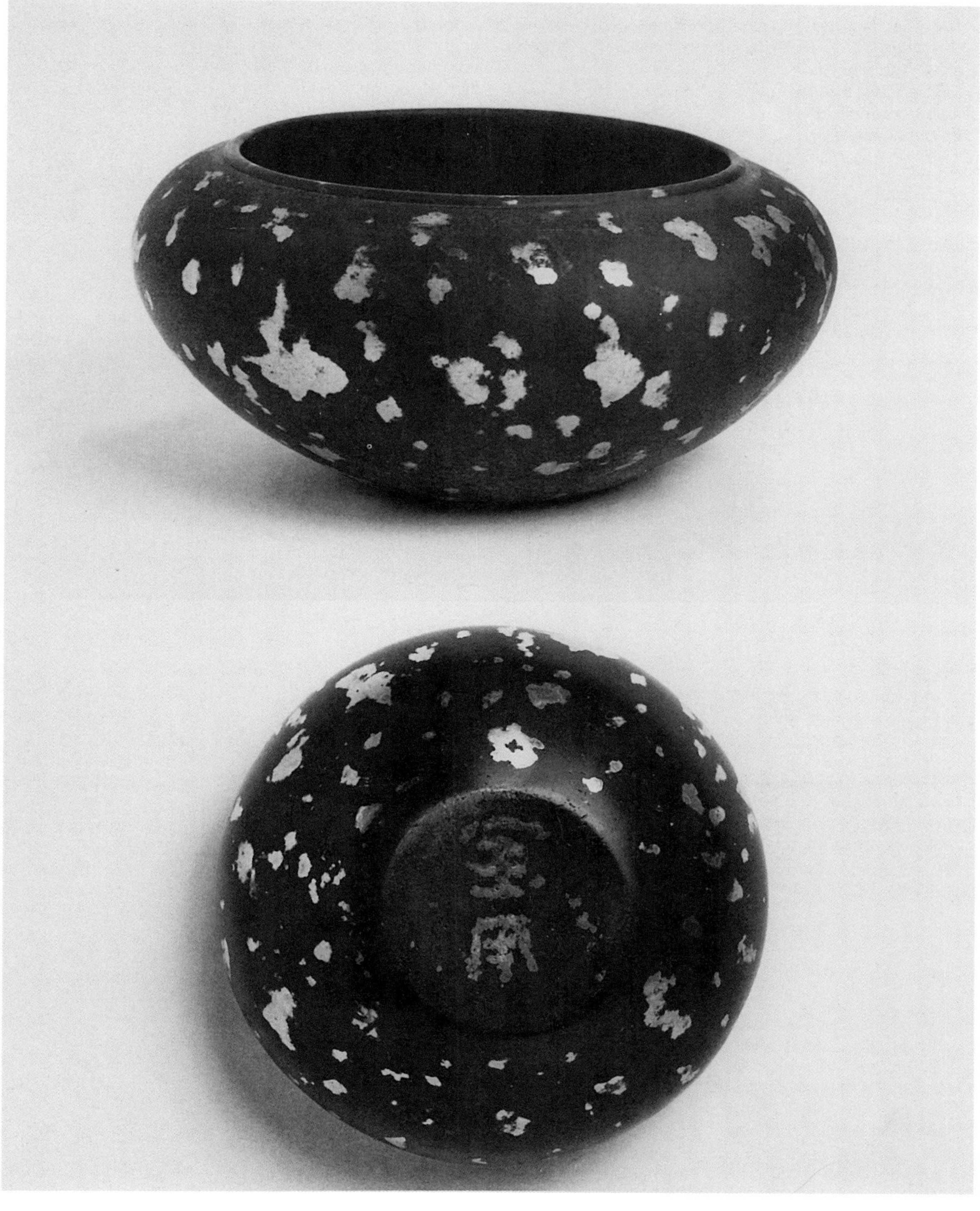

230

Incense Tool Vase

Hu Wenming

Bronze, inlaid with silver and partly gilt; an incense tool vase, decorated with a broad, continuous formalized floral scroll below a neck band of highly formalized floral scroll, all set against a ring-punched ground. The upper neck with a band of inlaid silver, continuous *leiwen;* the raised detail, plain separating bands, lip and foot rims all gilt; the inset copper base inscribed *Hu Wenming zuo* ('made by Hu Wenming') in seal script.
Yunjian, *circa* 1560-*circa* 1620.
Height: 11.5 cm.
Formerly in the Dr. Ip Yee collection.
Published: *Chinese Metalwork of the Hu Wenming Group,* p.52, no. 24.

鎏金纏枝番蓮青銅筋瓶•胡文明製
明代(約1560-1620),高11.5厘米

The incense tool vase, incense burner and incense powder box were the 'three friends of incense' (see no. 229 and Fig. 1 for a drawing taken from a painting of a typical set standing on an incense stand). Although genre paintings will sometimes show a scholar seated in a rustic retreat, or even in the wilderness, with just an incense burner in front of him, he is, as a rule, accompanied by the set of three. Indeed, they appear so often in illustrations of all sorts that when they are absent one feels they are simply on a side table out of sight. The incense tool vase is nearly always shown containing a pair of metal chopsticks and a spade (see no. 229 for their usage).

One of the mysteries of the incense cult from the modern collector's point of view is the whereabouts of all the old tools. There are in existence vast quantities of old incense burners of all kinds, and reasonable numbers of early incense tool vases and powder boxes, but early tools are practically non-existent. We have managed to locate none for the exhibition, and have never seen any by Hu Wenming, who was noted in his day for their manufacture. In Wen Zhenheng's *Changwu Ji* ('Notes on Superfluous Objects') in a section on incense tools the following appears: "Purple bronze is good. Yunjian Hu Wenming and white bronze from Nanjing are also good for use. One should avoid gold, silver or long, large inlaid tools."[1]

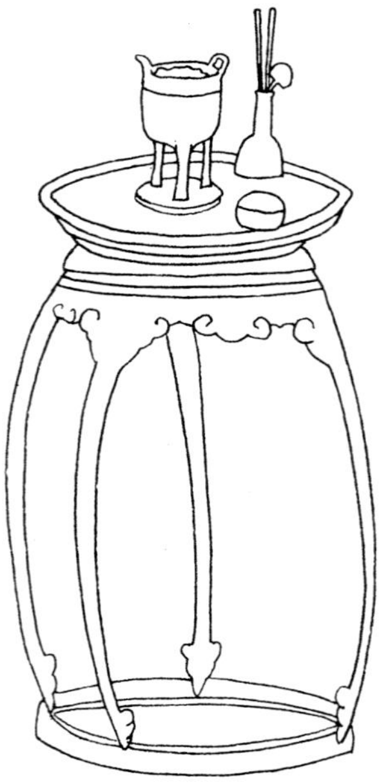

Fig. 1

Incense tool vases are designed to be heavy and sturdy to offset the top-heavy set of tools they contain. Hu Wenming was in the habit of making his in bronze, but in common with many of his bronze forms with a cylindrical base, he then made the base inside the foot rim of copper. Genre paintings show a very wide variety of shapes, sizes and materials serving as incense tool vases. Wen Zhenheng in a section entitled 'Chopstick vases' writes: "*Guan, ge* and *ding* wares, even though they were good, are not suitable for everyday use. In the central Wu area (around Suzhou) there have recently been products made with short necks and a small hole, where you place the chopsticks. They are heavy and won't fall over." He then continues with one of his characteristically dismissive statements, consigning all bronze incense tool vases to aesthetic oblivion: "Bronze ones are beneath discussion."[2]

The design on this vase is typical of Hu Wenming's non-archaistic themes and is contemporary in the same way as was the decoration on 16th century ceramics — that is to say they were based on earlier themes but stylistically evolved in a specifically 16th century manner.

1. *Juan* 7, section 4.
2. Ibid. *juan* 7, section 5.

231

Incense Powder Box and Cover

Hu Wenming

Bronze, partly gilt; an incense powder box and cover; decorated on the lid with a flowering crab-apple tree growing from a rocky ground; the base with various blossoming plants and trees including lotus and prunus; all set against a double-Y diaper ground; relief detail, lip and foot rims all gilt; the base inscribed *Hu Wenming zhi* ('made by Hu Wenming') in seal script in a rectangular, gilt cartouche.
Yunjian, *circa* 1560-*circa* 1620.
Height: 3.3 cm. Diameter: 7.25 cm.
Published: *Chinese Metalwork of the Hu Wenming Group,* p.50, no. 19.

鎏金花果青銅香盒•胡文明製
明代(約1560-1620),高3.3厘米,直徑7.25厘米

The incense powder box, one of the 'three friends of incense', is designed to hold powdered incense for lighting the sandalwood chips which provide fragrant smoke (see no. 229 for usage). They are usually small and heavy, and those by Hu Wenming all have an incurving inner rim on the lower section to protect the powder from gusts of wind while the lid is off. However, many other forms were used as is demonstrated by illustrations showing matched and unmatched sets of 'friends' of many different shapes and sizes. Carved lacquer was apparently particularly favoured.

232

Incense Burner

Bronze, gilt; an incense burner in the form of a mythical beast, the head removable, the animal with a scaled chest, paws, shaggy tail, mane, and eyebrows, and flames rising from its legs; the exterior gilt.
Probably late Ming dynasty.
Height: 10.9 cm.

鎏金異獸青銅香爐
可能晚明,高10.9厘米

There is a group of bronzes which appear to be gilded in a quite different manner from the normal mercury gilding process applied to gilt bronzes (which results in a reasonably thick layer of evenly applied gold). With this group the gold appears to have been applied in thin layers of gold leaf, some overlapping, which are then melted onto the surface of the bronze. Being much thinner and layered where they overlap, as the gold wears through handling, the impression is given much more of a texture of gold blending with the surface of the bronze than of a distinctly separate layer. It is a distinctive and pleasing effect, more evident perhaps on no. 51, which is also gilded in this manner but is considerably more worn. This method may provide clues to provenance and dating, or it may be simply an alternative method of gilding used over a long period of time in various different places. At the feet of this vessel, where there is even wear as a result of constant contact with a flat surface, the gold appears to be superimposed on a layer of copper, as if the whole thing has been flashed with a thin layer of copper prior to gilding — perhaps to improve its colour.

It is not known when the mythical beast incense burner with removable or sometimes hinged head was first developed. A larger example, dated to the second year of Tianqi (1622), is in the Shuisongshi Shanfang collection, and a similar beast is found in a woodblock illustration published in 1645, at which time it was already in a collection and probably considered an antique.[1] Several others are known which may be reasonably dated to the late Ming or early Qing period. However, examples also exist in celadon glazed ceramics of the *longquan* group, from earlier in the Ming dynasty, and it is likely that it was a type popular in later Ming based upon an earlier prototype.

The idea behind this type of incense burner is that once the incense is lit the smoke emerges from the beast's mouth, giving the impression of a living creature breathing smoke.

1. *Shizhu Zhai Zhencang* ('Precious Collection of the Ten Bamboos Studio'), illustrated in *Chinese Bamboo Carving,* Part I, p.179, Fig. 15.

230

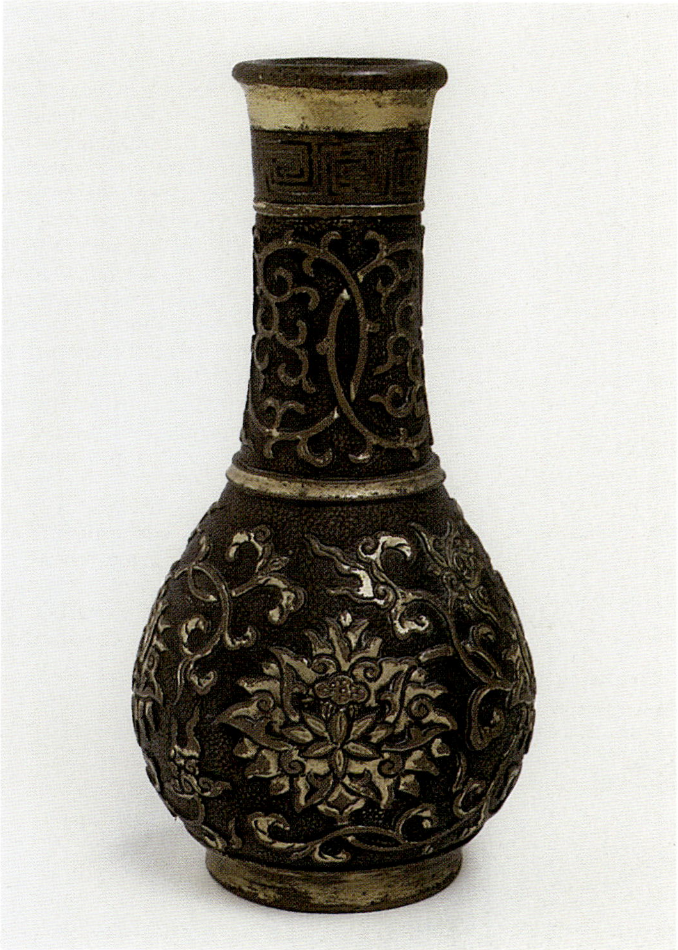

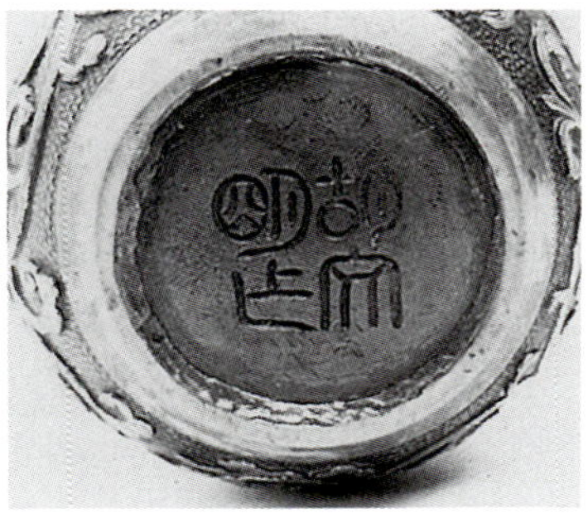

232

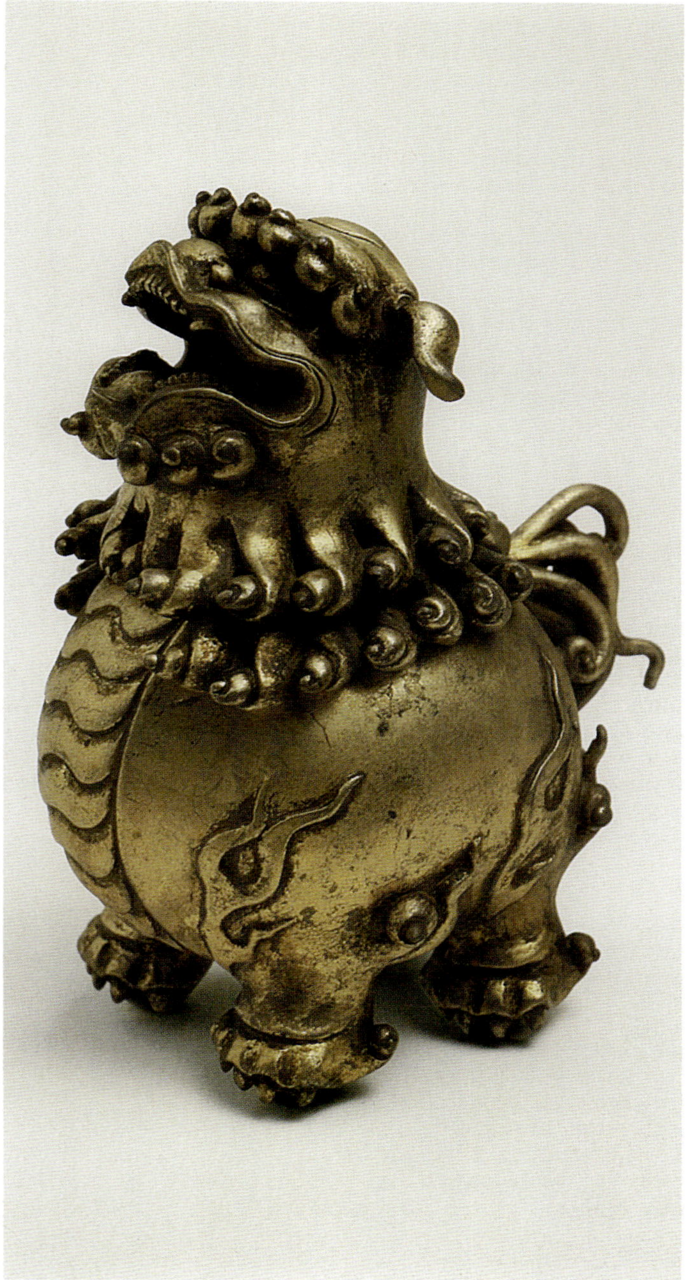

231

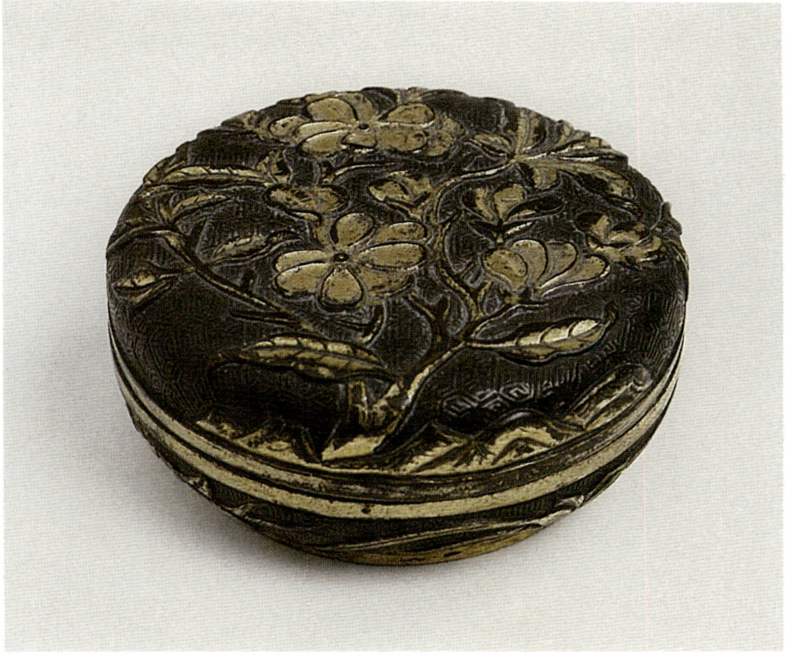

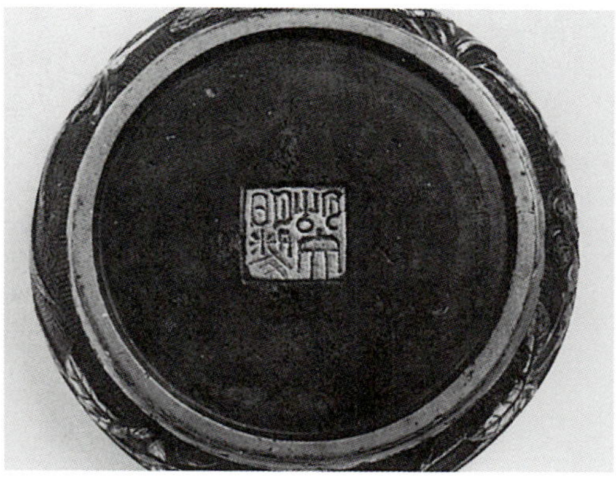

233

Incense Cylinder

Gu Jue

Bamboo, of rich golden brown colour; an incense cylinder, carved with a continuous, pierced scene of a scholar seated playing a *qin* at a natural root table, which grows from the bases of nearby ancient trees, a pine and a *wutong;* an attendant and two ladies stand listening nearby; incised with the signature *Zongyu.*
Jiading, late 17th or early 18th century.
Missing its original top and bottom fittings and now fixed to a wood stand and fitted with a copper liner.
Height including fixed wood stand and liner: 21.9 cm.
Formerly in the Dr. Ip Yee collection.
Published: *Chinese Bamboo Carving,* Part II, p.265, no. 78.

竹雕高士撫琴圖香筒•顧珏製
十七世紀末或十八世紀初，總高21.9厘米

These pierced cylindrical containers, which usually have wood or horn end fittings with matching plugs (see Fig. 1 for a diagram, and *Chinese Bamboo Carving,* Part I, p.307, no. 86 and p.317, no. 91 for examples) are nowadays generally referred to as perfume holders although other suggestions have been put forward for their use. They appear to have been, however, for the burning of incense sticks. They are mentioned by Wen Zhenheng[1] under the heading of 'incense cylinders': "In earlier times there were those made by Li Wenfu (Li Yao). They were decorated with carved flowers and birds, bamboo and rocks; those that are archaic, simple and elegant, are to be treasured.

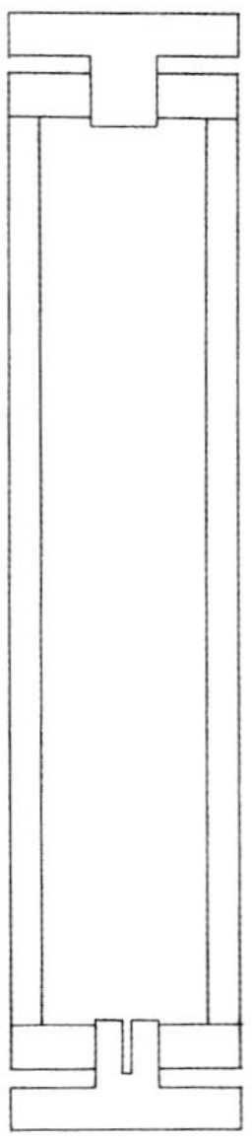

Fig. 1

If they are overdecorated, resembling more those used by ladies, or carved with figures or stories then they are vulgar and should not be placed about one's body or in the sleeve." Apparently incense sticks were stuck into one of the removable end plugs and the smoke would drift out through the piercing. The reference to them being placed about the body or in the sleeve must refer to their use in giving clothing a pleasant aroma, possibly their principal function.

One of these cylinders was excavated from the tomb of Zhu Shoucheng, at Baoshan in Jiangsu province, datable to the Wanli reign[2] and they seem to have been popular throughout the late Ming and Qing period.

Gu Jue (*zi:* Zongyu) was a native of Jiading, Jiangsu province; he is thought to have been active in the Kangxi period. He was reputed to be one of the best carvers of his day, and to have taken one or even two years to finish each piece. Given the exquisite carving on this example it is not difficult to understand how he acquired such a reputation, even if the time taken to complete works was an exaggeration.[3]

1. *Changwu Ji, juan* 7, section 8.
2. *Bamboo Carvings of China,* p.21.
3. Ibid., nos. 28 and 29 for two further examples.

234

Incense Tool Vase

Wood, *zitan,* of dark blackish-brown colour; an incense tool vase of formalized foliate form, the five-petalled cross-section creating a fluted exterior, set on five small feet; the base plugged with a separate piece of wood.
Probably late Ming dynasty.
Height: 10.9 cm.

紫檀五瓣形筯瓶
可能晚明，高10.9厘米

This is the wooden equivalent of the ivory vessel of no. 114. We believe that they were probably made for incense tools, although an alternative use is a container for the peacock feather tassle on a court official's hat when not in use.[1] As one of the 'three friends of incense' the incense tool vase appears frequently in genre paintings, although it is often difficult to judge the materials involved from paintings.

Wen Zhenheng's comments on chopstick vases have been discussed elsewhere. It is interesting that Wen mentions them only as chopstick vases, while most paintings show them also holding a small spade. It is possible that the set of three (the pair of chopsticks and the spade) was only kept together like this in some instances and that sometimes the chopsticks were kept in the vase alone, and the spoon or spade for shaping the ash was kept elsewhere. This might be sensible, as the spoon would be covered in ash and incense dust and might be better kept with the other, messier incense cult accoutrements. It is also possible that Wen merely used the chopsticks as a designation to stand for the whole set.

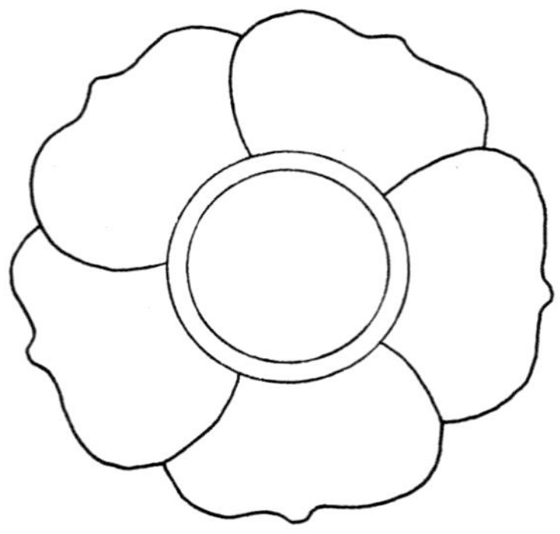

Fig. 1

The design of this vessel (a cross-section of which is illustrated in Fig. 1) was also found on late Ming brush pots. Wen singles them out to be specially avoided if one is to rise to the heights of good taste.[2]

This rather noble vessel, somewhat weathered and a little damaged, might well be a late Ming example. The inset base of a separate piece of wood would also tie in well with late Ming practice in making this type of vessel in other materials (see no. 230). Whenever it was made, it is certainly a serviceable vessel, well able to hold its own against the top-heaviness of a set of incense tools and with the capacity to hold all three, rather than just the chopsticks, as seems to be the case with no. 114.

It is tempting to associate this vessel with Wen Zhenheng's description of incense tool vases made during the late Ming in Zuzhou "made with short necks and a small hole" (see no. 230).

1. A suggestion put forward by Robert H. Ellsworth based upon what he was told by a lady who had lived for many years at the Court and remembers seeing them so used, which does not necessarily, of course, exclude the possibility of them having been originally designed for incense tools.
2. Grudgingly acknowledging that one may use *zitan,* blackwood and *huali* brush pots on occasions, he goes on to state "...but one should avoid octagonal, petal-shaped ones" (*juan* 7, section 12).

233

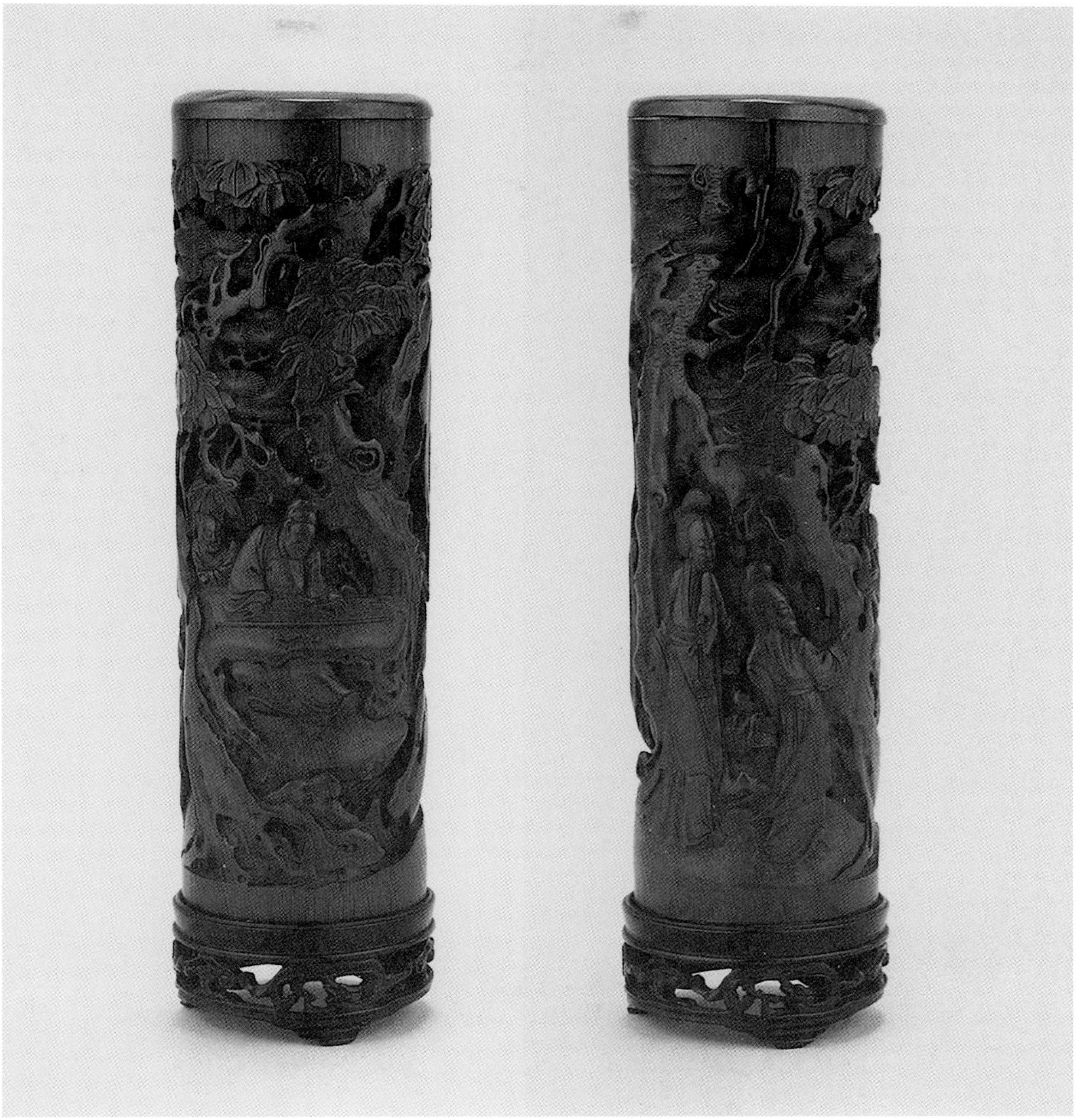

234

235

Flower Vase

Crystal; the flawless material carved as a small vase, decorated with five horizontal, raised ribs, one of which forms the lip; the base inscribed *Qianlong nianzhi* ('made in the Qianlong period') in raised regular script in a recessed square with a roughly stippled ground.
Probably Beijing palace workshops, Qianlong period.
Height: 8.6 cm.

水晶五弦紋花瓶•乾隆年製銘
清乾隆(1736-1795), 高8.6厘米

This vase is currently boxed in a set with no. 130, to which it is related and where the group is discussed. Its use would have been to hold a single, elegant floral spray to place on the scholar's desk to induce the right atmosphere for reflection and creativity. As a rule this sort of vessel would be unlikely to have had a tall stand originally, as this would have made it rather unstable. In genre paintings the usual stand for flower vases seems to have been a large, enclosing stand into which the vase sat to a level well above its foot (see Fig. 1, no. 209).

The early Ming book on connoisseurship *Gegu Yaolun* mentions that the best pieces of crystal are lustrous and flawless, and that undecorated vessels are preferred; carving is used only to cover up flaws. It mentions that the best crystal was imported from Japan, and records imports from other countries as far away as Ceylon, as well as indigenous sources.[1]

1. *Chinese Connoisseurship.*

236

Miniature Vessels

Bronze; two miniature vases; a small, squat jar, with a decorative collar of *ruyi* heads and two *taotie* mask and ring handles, both gilt; joined to a taller gold-splashed vessel decorated with five gilt bats flying amidst clouds, the shoulders with a formalized *ruyi*-head border, the neck and flared foot with various decorative borders, the elongated cylindrical neck with two tubular handles; the base of the taller vessel incised with the mark *Qianlong nianzhi* ('made in the Qianlong period') in regular script.
Attributed to the Beijing palace workshops, Qianlong period.
Height: 6.5 cm.

鎏金五蝠雙連青銅小瓶•乾隆年製銘
清乾隆(1736-1795), 高6.5厘米

There is a class of objects beloved of the literati, which have a high artistic content, various levels of symbolic meaning, and are ideal decoration for the studio, particularly for collectors' cabinets (cabinets which stand in the studio, usually constructed with a number of different levels of small shelves in an intricate pattern, and often in pairs). They are small, precious objects which can be appreciated visually, picked up and played with, or discussed for their meaning. The French word 'bibelot' perhaps comes closest to describing them in a European language. They are essentially meaningful, decorative playthings, which might also be put to some use or other, but whose main function exists finally in the mind of the connoisseur. We know that such collectors' cabinets were popular throughout the Ming and Qing by the large numbers of genre paintings in which they appear, and we may be reasonably sure that although evidence of their existence becomes rarer in the Song and earlier periods, they were also popular before the beginning of the Ming dynasty.

As the objects for these display cabinets evolved from primarily functional roles to primarily aesthetic ones, the trend towards miniaturization developed. The original size of a bronze vessel was not an important factor once it became a primarily aesthetic object. This trend towards miniaturization may be seen in the Ming dynasty, but reached its zenith under the Qing, and particularly in the reigns of the Qianlong and subsequent rulers.

The Taiwan Palace Museum has a large collection of miniature collectors' cabinets (known as 'multi-tiered treasure boxes'), of all sorts of materials and forms ranging from miniaturized cabinets of the traditional form, to boxes of different shapes (some even of Japanese lacquer presumably imported for the purpose) with their interiors fitted out to contain a host of small objects.[1] The Qianlong Emperor was particularly fond of these miniature art forms and was largely responsible for the Qing imperial vogue for them. While many contain small jade carvings and other treasures from earlier periods, they also contain a good many pieces made in the palace workshops (enamels, glass, ivory, and so on).

Wen Zhenheng describes the late Ming vogue for collector's cabinets and is informative about the wide variety of objects that might legitimately be considered 'scholars' objects'. In a section headed "Container for literary objects" he writes: "Cupboards in which literary objects may be kept are fashionable nowadays. However, excellent ones can be found among those made by ancient famous craftsmen. Those cupboards made of *nanmu* (cedar), *yingmu* (knar — probably intended to mean what is today called *huamu or* burl) and *shuiluomu* (red horse-chestnut) are very elegant. Those made of *zitan* (purple sandalwood) or *huali* (presumably *huanghuali* and *laohuali)* are vulgar. These cupboards have three shelves and a drawer. Within the drawer one places a small inkstone from Duanxi (Guangdong province), a dish for brush testing, a book, a small brush rest in the form of mountain peaks, a Xuande ink-stick and a Japanese lacquered box for an inkstone. On the top shelf one places a jade wrist rest, a paper weight made of archaic jade or bronze, a large and a small archaic knife made of fine iron, a coir brush with archaic jade handle, a boat-shaped brush container, and two Korean brushes. On the second shelf, one places an archaic bronze water basin, a glue container, a sealing wax container, an archaic bronze ladle and a small gilded, green bronze brush washer. The lowest shelf should have more vertical space. One places there a small Xuande bronze incense burner, a Song carved red lacquer box, a Japanese lacquer box with carrying handle, a white *ding* and a five-coloured *ding* porcelain small box, a Japanese floral decorated wine cup or a small wine cup, a box for books within which one keeps an archaic jade seal vermilion container, an archaic jade seal, several pieces of excellent gilt bronze seals, a small Japanese lacquer comb box within which one keeps a small tortoise-shell comb, an old jade water vessel (*kouyi*), and two small rhinoceros horn/jade cups. Other exquisite and elegant items of curios can be placed therein for appreciation."[2] It is interesting to note how often imports from Japan figure in Wen's works.

This little double vessel was probably made for a miniature treasure cabinet. The decorative allusions, apart from those of the bats, are to ancient forms and decoration, and in the case of the larger vase with its two cylindrical handles, to the ancient game of throwing arrows into a vase (see no. 264). The bats, in a more contemporary style, add a little auspicious symbolism for good measure.

There is a group of bronze vessels and other objects (see no. 156 for a brush rest), generally on a miniature scale, which are of high quality, often gold-splashed and characteristically bear four-character Qianlong reign marks for which a palace attribution seems reasonable if still not certain. Subject-matter on several of these vessels may be associated with other output from or for the palace. The four-character marks are typical (see discussion of no. 130) and the miniature forms are characteristic of part of the palace output. If not made in the palace, we may be sure that they were made for it.[3]

1. One of these is illustrated complete with its objects — in this instance all small jade carvings — in *Masterpieces of Chinese Miniature Crafts in the National Palace Museum,* 1970, no. 7.
2. *Changwu Ji, juan* 7, section 56.
3. A 'hero's' vase of this group is illustrated in *Chinese Art,* Vol II, no. 50, which bears a similar four-character reign mark to this example. There is another unusually large example (height 17 cm), ibid. no. 67, which we believe to have a Qianlong mark, although none is mentioned in the text.

235

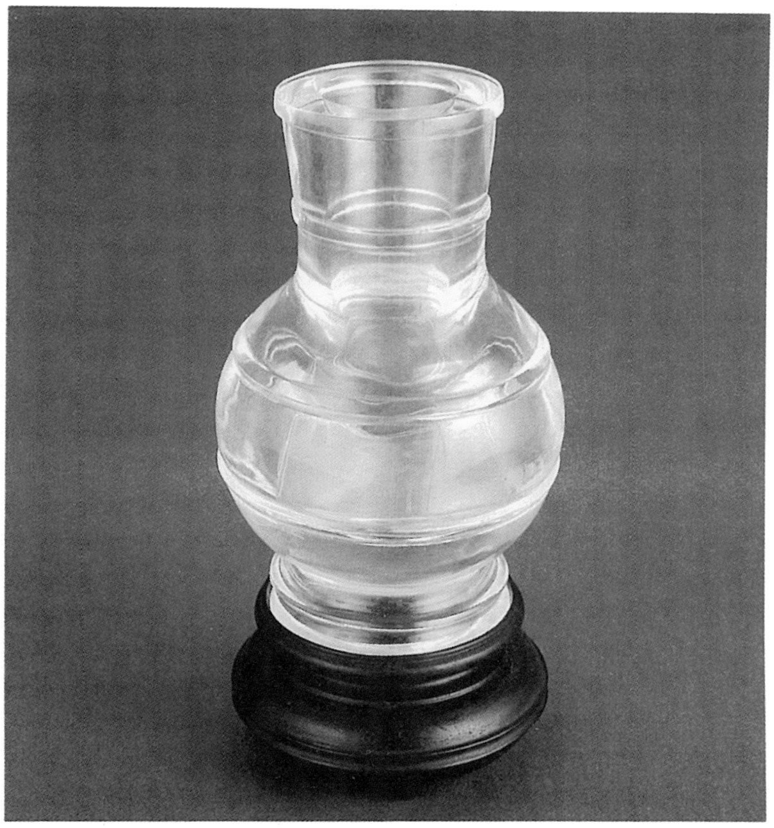

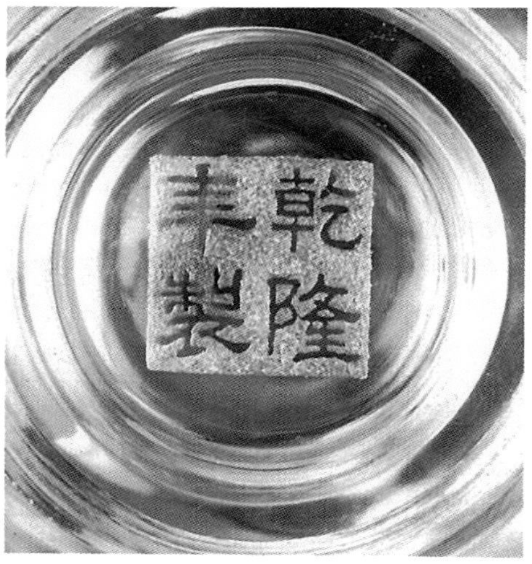

236

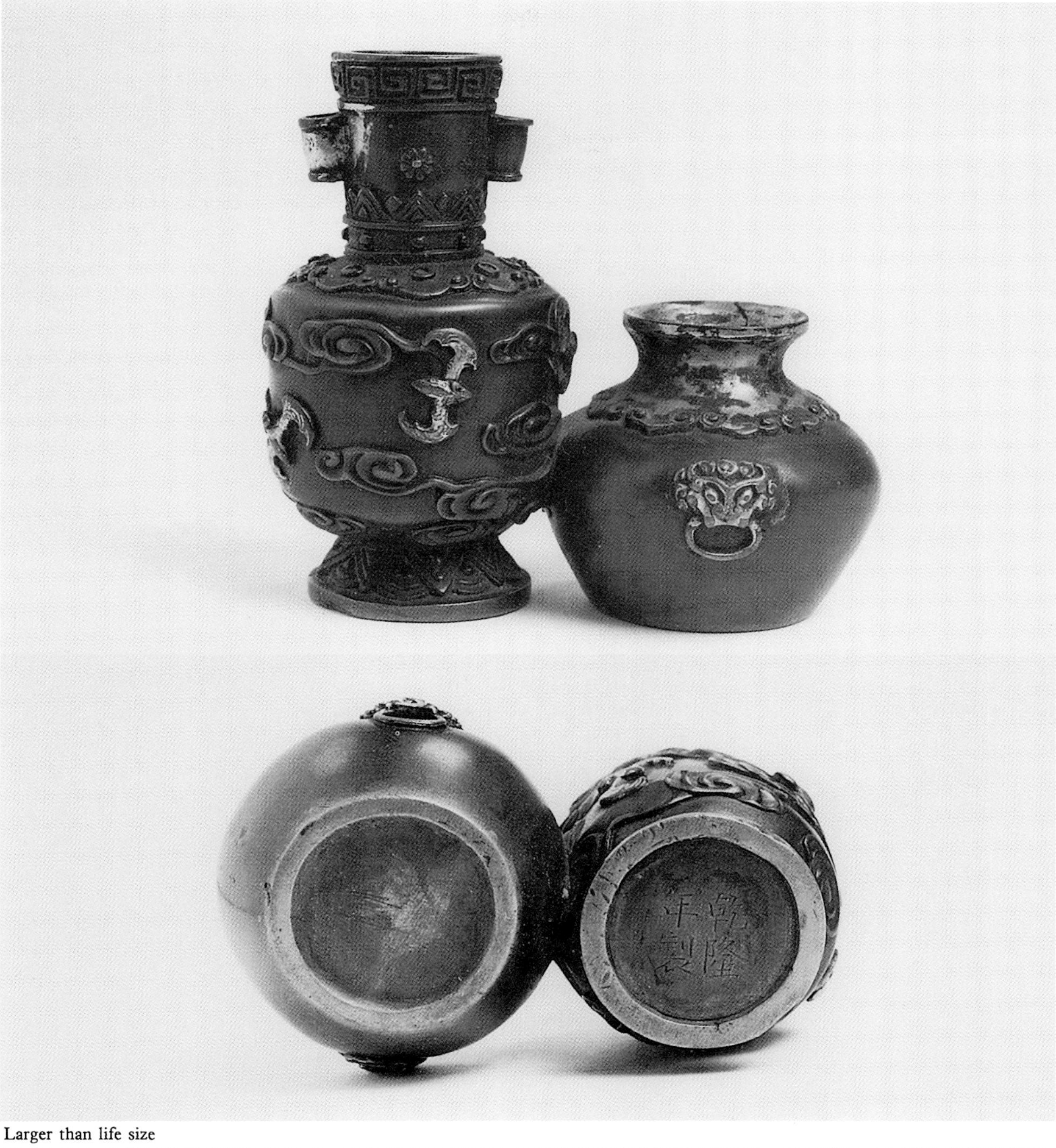

Larger than life size

237

Vase

Hu Wenming

Bronze, partly gilt; a vase in the form of a *gu*, decorated on the central section with a *taotie* mask repeated on each side, above four cicada-shaped lappets and below a lower neck band of *kui* dragons, above which are four extended cicada-shaped lappets each decorated with a highly stylized *taotie* mask below a cicada motif, all set against a double-Y-punched ground; the lip rim and four raised flanges separating the central section of the body have continuous *leiwen* design; relief detail, plain separating bands, lip and outer foot rim and flanges all gilt; the deeply recessed base inscribed *Hu Wenming zhi* ('made by Hu Wenming').
Yunjian, *circa* 1560-*circa* 1620.
Height: 21.4 cm.
Published: *Chinese Metalwork of the Hu Wenming Group*, p.54, no. 29.

鎏金饕餮紋觚•胡文明製
明代(約1560-1620), 高21.4厘米

This example is based loosely on a late Shang prototype of a *gu* ritual wine vessel. Existing primarily as works of art, such vessels were pressed into service as flower vases (to which function this particular vessel has quite clearly been devoted for some time) to hold the elegant and often symbolic spray of flowers so often seen in literati genre scenes, or to hold such other trappings as a branch of coral, peacock feathers, an inspiringly shaped piece of wood, or anything the scholar might chose to put into it. It might also have served on occasions as an incense tool holder. In a painting of Ni Zan, inscribed by Wen Peng in 1542, the artist has beside him a side table displaying various scholar's objects, including a *gu* used to contain peacock feathers (see Fig. 1).

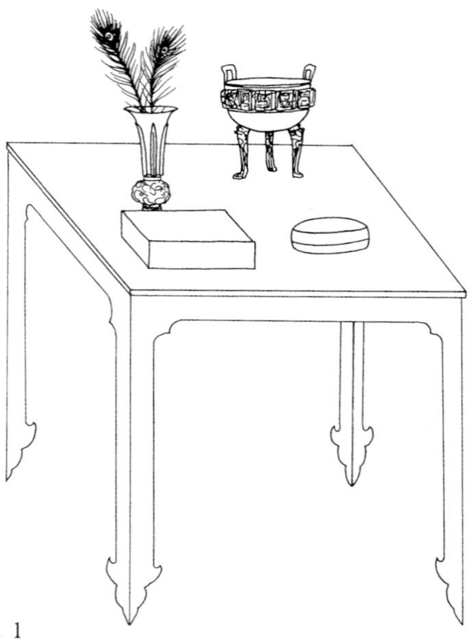

Fig. 1

A proper appreciation of archaism has been hindered by a tendency to look upon its decoration as inadequate, misunderstood, or corrupt versions of original archaic pieces, leading us to see them as second-rate 'copies' of fine originals, and therefore worthy of little attention or appreciation. The type of decoration on this vessel, where the elements of a *taotie* mask (in the upper lappets, for instance) have been so formalized and abstracted that they are barely recognizable, is an example in point. To look upon this, however, as an indication of inadequacy in artist or audience is incorrect. One might as well dismiss the best of Chinese poetry for failing to express itself in a manner which might better avoid ambiguity of meaning. As E.E. Kellett and Achilles Fang have pointed out, "...the finest flower of Chinese education is that which, steeped in the Chinese classics, can convey in three pages of allusive writing, to the right readers, what would otherwise take thirty." To the highly sophisticated minds of the patrons of archaism these barest of allusions to the *taotie* and other classic archaic motifs add an extra level of subtlety, making them not poor copies but an independent form of high artistic communication. The fact that today we may need a rash of footnotes to explain them is hardly a failing in the work of art.

238

Cricket Cage

Chen Jintang

Gourd of yellowish-brown colour, grown into a plain, shaped mould to form a cricket cage, the neck mounted in ivory, the ivory lid with an inset coconut shell domed panel pierced with a repeating, overlapping cash design; the gourd carved in low relief with various scholarly trappings including old vessels with flowers, one growing around a rock sculpture; another rock; a basket of flowers; a scroll; a *ruyi* sceptre; two wine cups; two volumes of books; a fluted brush pot with two brushes, a branch from which hangs an elaborately corded double gourd and what might be a rolled sheet of paper; a teapot with a flower in it and various fruits; a relief inscription around the neck reading: "made by Jintang in the ninth month of autumn in the *dingmao* year (1867)", with seal *Chen*.
Probably 1867.
Height: 13.8 cm.
Published: *Chinese Decorated Gourds*, p.72, no. 32.

葫蘆刻文玩蟋蟀筒•陳錦堂製
清代丁卯(可能1867), 高13.8厘米

The influential minority became involved in a number of hobbies and pastimes, many of which were transformed by their involvement into art forms with highly artistic related paraphernalia. Among these were the keeping of singing birds, snuff taking, tea drinking and incense burning. They also delighted in the keeping of crickets, valued for their chirping song and their fighting ability. The keeping of crickets required a certain amount of specialized equipment, and that which seems to have created the greatest interest artistically was the cricket gourd — a hollowed out gourd which acted as a cage for the insect.

The earliest known cricket gourds are those from the Kangxi Emperor's Beijing palace workshops.[1] They continued to be made in the palace until the Daoguang period in the 19th century, and were predominantly manufactured using the primary wood mould system (see no. 91). However, at some time around 1800 the popularity of keeping crickets in these small gourd cages seems to have spread widely outside the Court. At about the same time a method was evolved using a wood master mould[2] to produce large numbers of clay secondary moulds, which greatly increased potential for production. This secondary mould system was capable of moulding surface decoration as well as form, or simply form (as was the case here) for later decoration by either carving or decorating with a heated metal point. The clay moulds taken from the wood master were tied around the growing gourd, impressing upon it both form and surface decoration which remained in the mature fruit. The upper bulb of the fruit was then cut through, the interior cleaned out, a neck of a different material, usually ivory, fixed to it, and into this an elaborate pierced cover was fitted.

Chen Jintang is one of the very few known gourd carvers. He probably worked during the late 19th century. A number of pieces are recorded[3] all bearing cyclical dates ranging over a period of six years. The reason for attributing his active period to the years 1862-1868 are given elsewhere.[4]

1. *Chinese Decorated Gourds*, nos. 21-23.
2. Ibid. no. 13.
3. Ibid. nos. 30-37, and *Emperor, Scholar, Artisan, Monk: The Creative Personality in Chinese Art*, no. 112.
4. Ibid. pp.75-76.

237

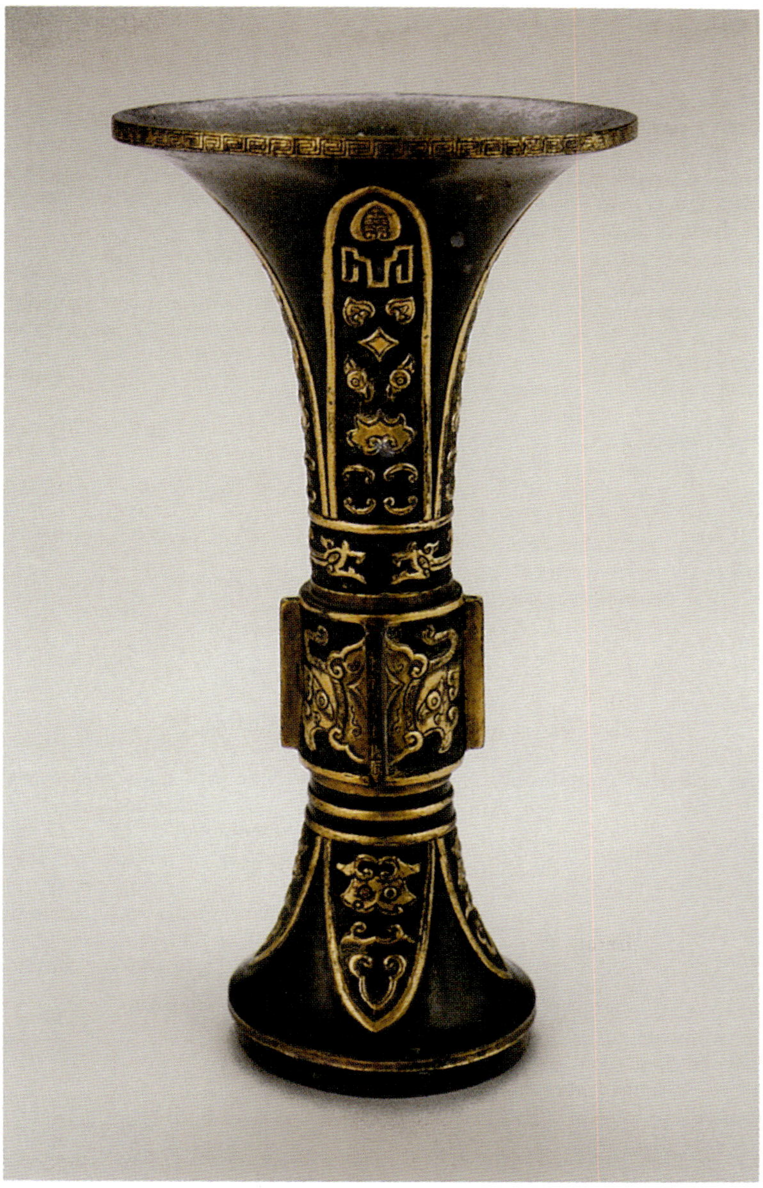

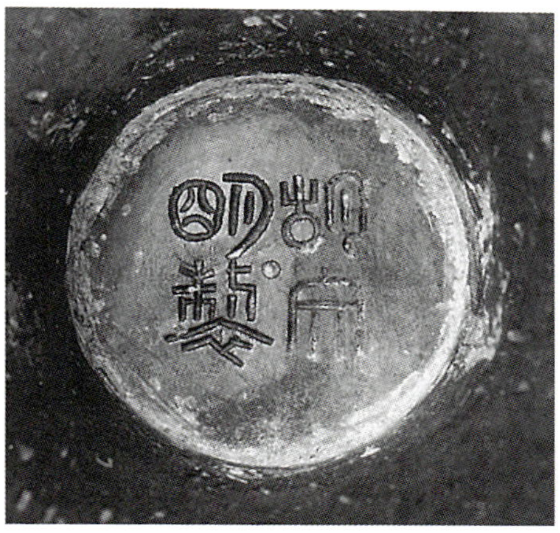

238

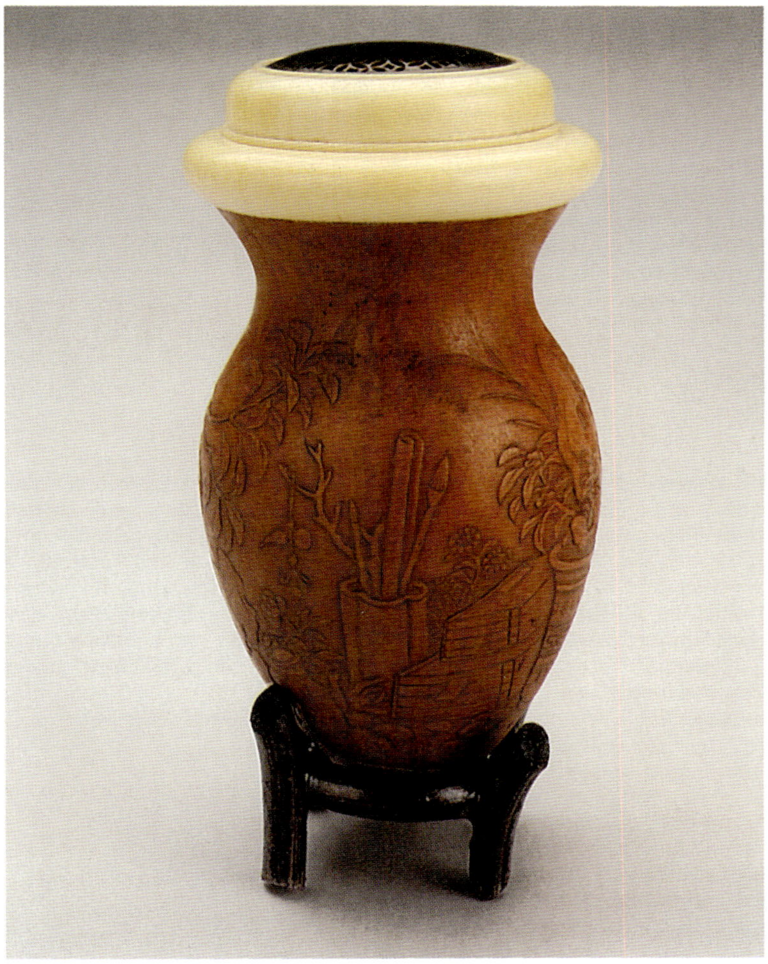

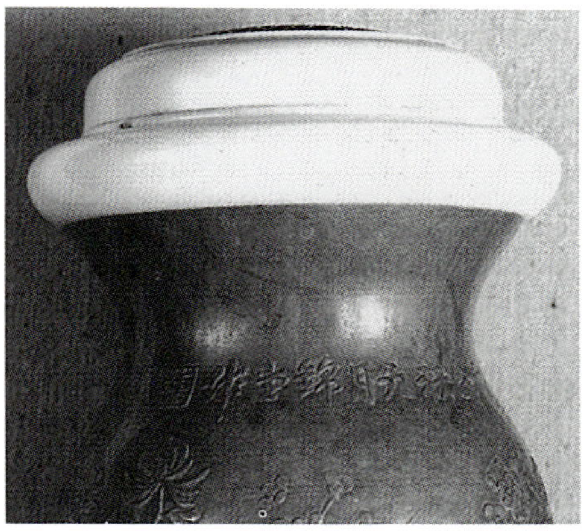

239

Table

Wood, *huanghuali*, of well-figured yellowish-brown colour; a *qin* table of rectangular form, the top of standard mitre, mortise and tenon frame construction with exposed tenons in the shorter members of the frame; the tongue-and-grooved floating panel with four dovetailed, transverse stretchers which are mortised and tenoned into the mitred frame; all four tenons are exposed; the outside edge of the frame tapering inwards and ending in a beaded edge; a recessed panel and a curved, beaded-edged curvilinear apron are just below the mitred frame; the apron mitred, half-lapped, mortised and tenoned into the legs; the beaded edge of the apron continuing down the inside of the square legs and following the contour of the strong, hoof feet; below the apron is a beaded-edged 'humpback' stretcher, mitred, mortised and tenoned into the leg.
Late Ming dynasty, probably 16th century.
87.6 cm × 139.8 cm × 59 cm.

黃花梨有束腰羅鍋棖琴桌
晚明，可能十六世紀，87.6×139.8×59厘米

Scholars are shown playing the *qin* in many paintings, seated on the ground with the instrument in their lap or at a number of different tables. A suitable table adds considerable resonance to the gentle sound of the *qin* and was preferred when indoors. Although from time to time certain tables were designated as *qin* tables, any number of tables were suitable, and *qin* tables probably differed little, if at all, from other forms. Wen Zhenheng repeats advice given in the early Ming *Gegu Yaolun* in advocating the use of large hollow bricks from antiquity (a number of very large hollow grey pottery bricks are known from Han times which would have been suitable). When played on these resonating bricks, the *qin* makes a sound which Wen describes as clear and lovely. He also states that tables about one foot longer than the instrument itself and of width sufficient for three instruments are elegant. On the other hand he dismisses as vulgar those with *zitan* frames, with a metal basin and a crystal top, wherein fish and water weeds are placed. He continues by recommending the use of a folding chair while playing to allow a little more height and freedom than the usual chair.[1]

Although this table fits perfectly Wen's description of a *qin* table, it might equally have been used for a number of other purposes. A square table which seems a companion to this example, of very similar construction and perhaps from the same workshop, is in the Philadelphia Museum of Art.[2]

1. *Changwu Ji, juan* 7, section 49.
2. *Chinese Furniture: Hardwood Examples of the Ming and Early Ch'ing Dynasties,* pl. 75.

240

Brush Handle

Ivory, of creamy yellow colour, with rich brown patination on one side; carved as a brush handle in the form of Liu Hai, in loosely fitting robes, standing on the back of his familiar three-legged toad; the creature looking up at him and reaching with its mouth for the tassle of a large cash held by Liu Hai; the bristle bed in the form of formalized scrolling clouds; one bracelet of the figure carved free of the wrist so that it hangs loosely.
Late Ming or early Qing dynasty.
Length: 6.6 cm.

象牙雕劉海引蟾筆把
晚明或清初，長6.6厘米

The purpose of these little brushes is a mystery and is discussed in relation to an early bronze example (no. 126). That they existed in so similar a form and size for such a long time would seem to indicate a rather specific use. If they were indeed connected with the influential minority it may have been as general brushes for the studio. In this regard they may have been associated with the mysterious "coir brush with archaic jade handle" mentioned by Wen Zhenheng in relation to scholars' cabinets (see no. 236).

Apart from the Warring States example mentioned above, the majority are very close in size and form to this one, and made mostly of ivory from the late Ming or Qing dynasties.

241

Brush

Wood, *zitan;* a brush handle carved as a miniature *ruyi* of *lingzhi* fungus form, set with horsehair bristles.
Qing dynasty.
Maximum length including bristles: 22.5 cm.

紫檀雕靈芝如意掃筆
清代，長連毫22.5厘米

Stiff brushes of this type might have served a number of functions in a scholar's studio. Among these were brushing off charcoal after sketching, brushing away spilled incense powder (almost inevitable in the incense cult), removing dust from the lower rollers of hanging scrolls before rolling them up, brushing dust away from the less accessible areas of the *qin* (beneath the strings at the bridge, for instance) and dusting difficult areas of gnarled wood pieces. This brush has proved ideal, in its present home, for all these purposes.

The size of this example makes it very unusual, the standard being represented by no. 240.

242

Drinking Tray

Ivory, of mottled and patinated creamy yellow and brown tones; carved as a small tray in the form of a gnarled section of peach tree, with fruiting and blossoming branches curling in from the bark-like rim of the tray to form the relief decoration of the surface; also carved with two bats in relief facing the central, plain area; the reverse plain except for the edges which are carved as bark.
Probably first half of the Qing dynasty.
1.3 cm × 18.5 cm × 10.4 cm.

象牙雕壽桃雙蝠小盤
可能清代上半期，1.3×18.5×10.4厘米

There is a series of small trays of this type, most in ivory, and mostly made during the Qing period. They appear to have been used as a standard type of tray in a poetic drinking game. In a work by Zhang Zhao (died after 1698) in which he advises an ailing friend on various remedies for curing his malaise, the following appears: "And when the dinner is finished, start drinking again with ivory trays. The wine games shall be refined and the punishments not too severe, while the friends shall be simple and tireless. Such is the joy of drinking."[1] The form of the reference suggests that ivory trays are standard to the game. The game in question is called *hangjiuling* ('running wine order'), where participants compose poetic lines based upon prescribed rhyming schemes: an opening character is given to them and they must compose in a certain time. Failure to do so results in a punishment of a cup of wine. The rhyming schemes might be carved or written on small plaques, which are drawn by the participants. We suggest that these ivory trays, with the elegant carving leaving just enough room for one cup of wine, were used to pass the punishment cup to the failed poet.

1. Quoted in *The Importance of Understanding,* p.96.

239

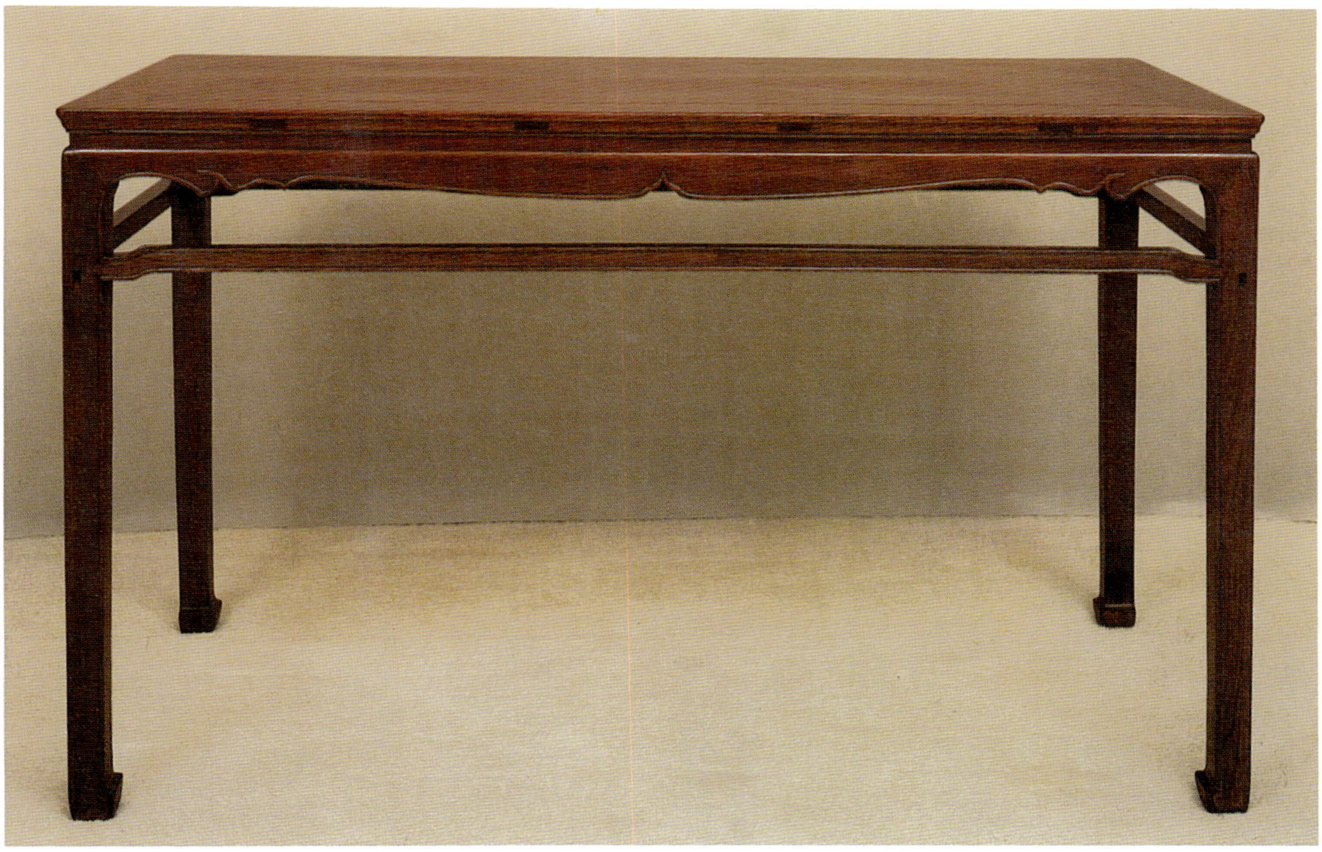

240

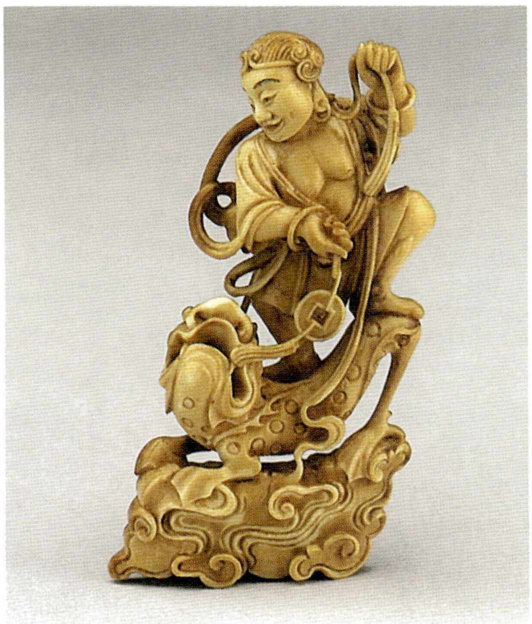

241

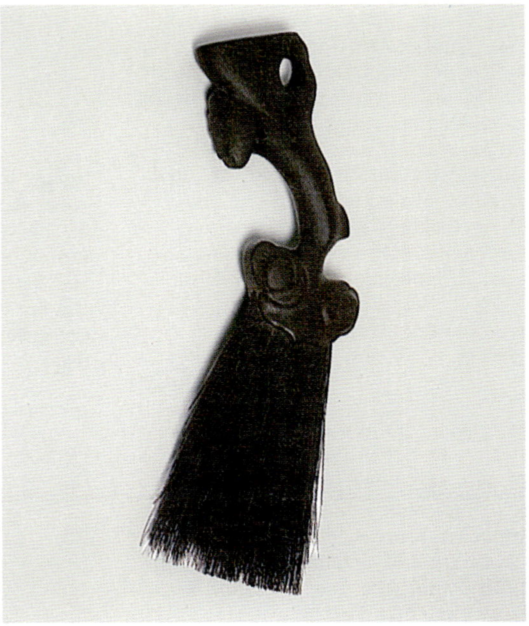

242

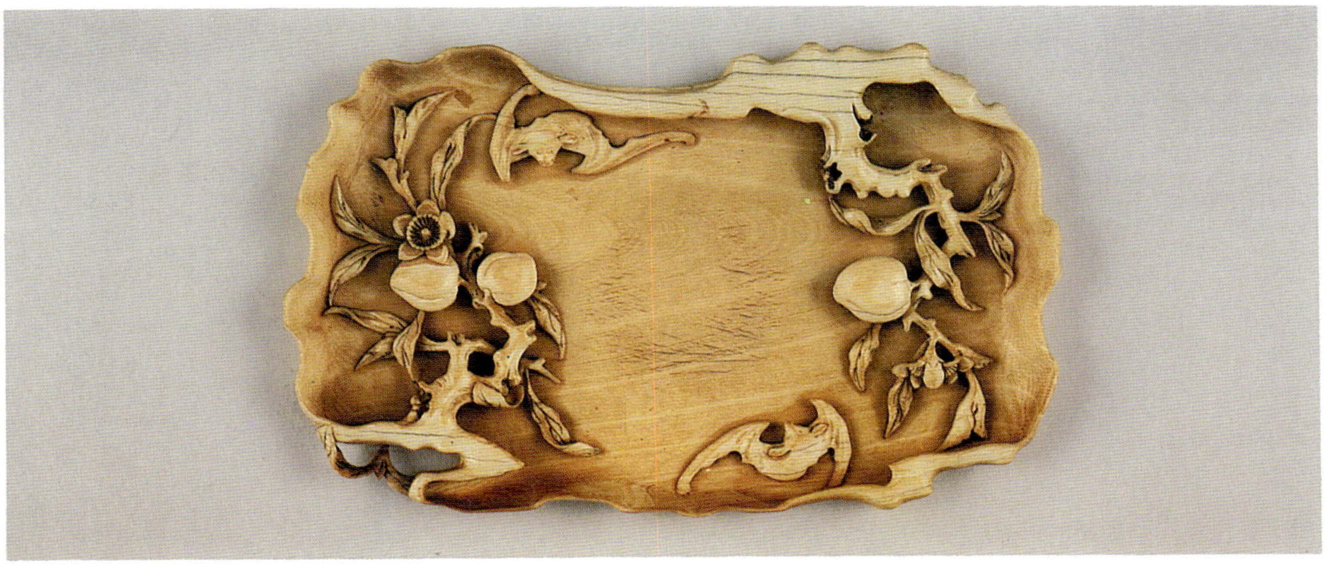

243

Stationery Tray

Wood, *zitan,* of richly figured dark purplish-brown colour; a stationery tray of two irregularly sized sections of wood, surrounded by elaborate sides of interlinked, elongated 'H' motifs between plain borders of square section, set on four small feet.
Mid to late Qing dynasty.
5 cm × 46.1 cm × 32.5 cm.

紫檀文具盤
清代中至晚期, 5×46.1×32.5厘米

Stationery trays were used to keep a variety of scholars' utensils on, partly so that they could be easily moved together, and partly for purposes of display. One appears in a painting of the Elegant Gathering in the Western Garden, a Northern Song event (see no. 27), which is attributed to a Song artist and from which we reproduce the utensils that appear on one table-top (Fig. 1).[1] It shows a tray, with high sides and set on four small feet, containing a brush rest, holding two brushes and a stick of ink; a small water vessel in the form of a miniature *ding* tripod with a ladle; and an inkstone in use. The other utensils are a sheet of blank paper, two scroll or paper weights, and an incense burner. In the original, Su Shi holds a brush and is about to write on the paper, while three friends look on.

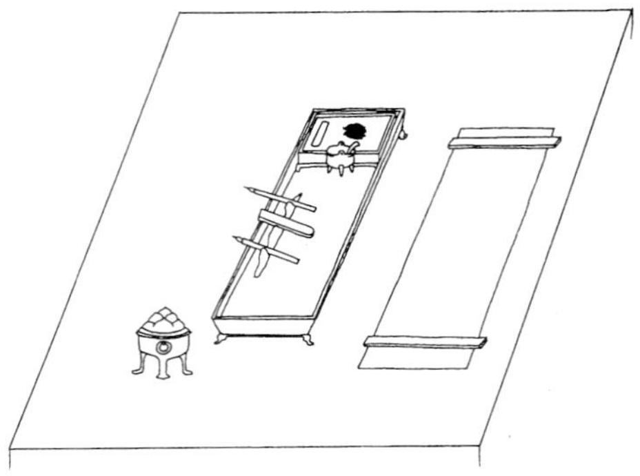

Fig. 1

1. *Gugong Zhoukan,* Beijing, 1936, no. 251, p.482.

244

Picnic Box

Wood, *zitan,* of rich, dark reddish-brown colour with orange filling in the grain; a two-tiered picnic box, the side members of the top and the sections below joined by dovetail joints, their bases tongued and grooved into the four side members, the top of the lid glued; the upper tier with an interior tray supported on a lipped rim, also with dovetailed side members and tongued and grooved base; the tiers separate from a carrying frame, the handle of which is mitred, mortised and tenoned into the frame base and has four shaped spandrels in the form of highly stylized *chi* dragons joining the handle and the base by a mortise and tenon join; a brass pin (a replacement) passes through the handle and an interior wooden tunnel attached to the underside of the lid to emerge at the opposide end for locking; the handle corners and base joint bound with brass surface mounted strips, the lower ones with visible brass pins.
Qing dynasty, probably 18th century.
22.9 cm × 32 cm × 19 cm.

紫檀雙層提盒
清代, 可能十八世紀, 22.9×32×19厘米

The picnic box appears frequently in woodbock illustrations and from them, augmented by other sources, we are able to build up an accurate and detailed picture of its use. The *Sancai Tuhui* (the encyclopaedia of 1607) illustrates one (Fig. 1) where it is described as a travelling box for wandering the mountains, and its contents are various dishes, the bottom section being for chopsticks, wine cups, etc. In his *Youju Jian* ('Notes on Travelling Accountrements') the late Ming scholar Tu Long describes them as 'carrying boxes' (*tihe*). He states that the bottom layer is for the storing of six wine cups, one wine pot, six pairs of chopsticks, and two punishing wine cups (for a popular drinking game — see no. 242). In the spaces above are kep six dishes with fruit, and more wine cups; plus four larger dishes with fish and vegetables. He goes into some detail about precise measurements for each of the segments, and how many there should be, which seem to accord with the illustration in the *Sancai Tuhui,* although he does not mention the air vents that version obviously has. Both of these versions have six trays above a deeper base tray.

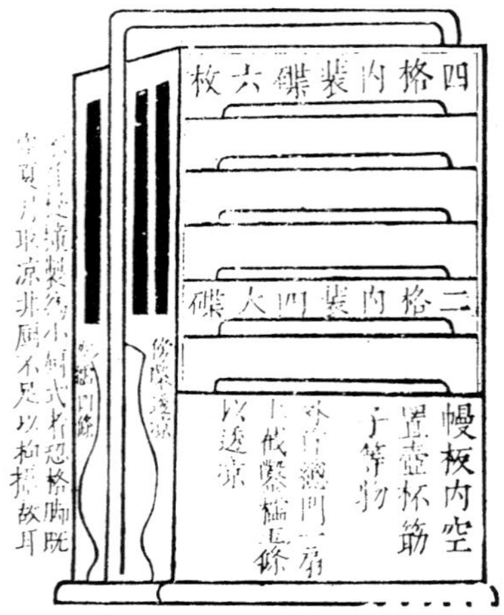

Fig. 1

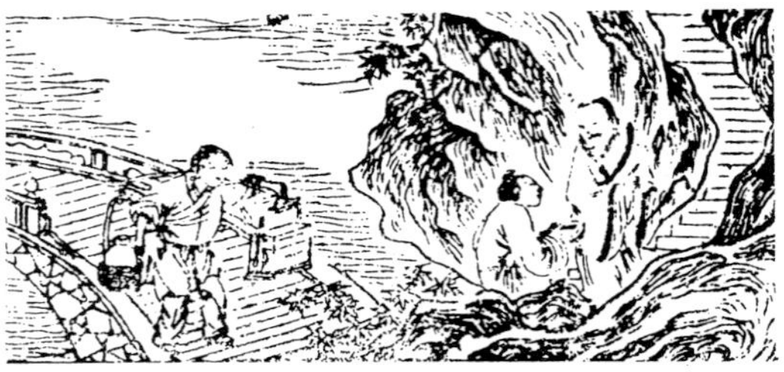

Fig. 2

The more usual form to have survived has fewer divisions, and there were clearly various sizes. In the *Liuyan Tangshi Huapu,* a woodblock edition of the Wanli/Tianqi period (late Ming), a servant carries a picnic box for two scholars on a day's outing to a mountain temple. It balances a large wine jar held at the other end of the servant's carrying stick (Fig. 2).

In the same work another is shown, similarly carried together with a *qin,* a sword and a bag of other necessities for the travelling scholar (Fig. 3). Fig. 4 shows a similar group of travelling necessities set on the ground, while two servants await their master outside a waterside house. It is from the Wanli woodblock edition of *Xiyou Ji.*

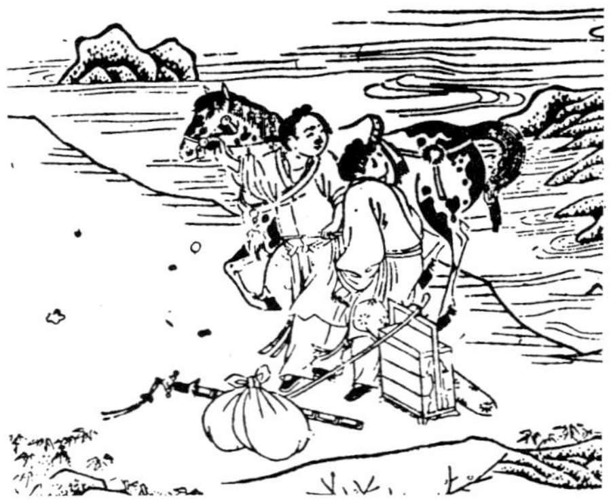

Fig. 3

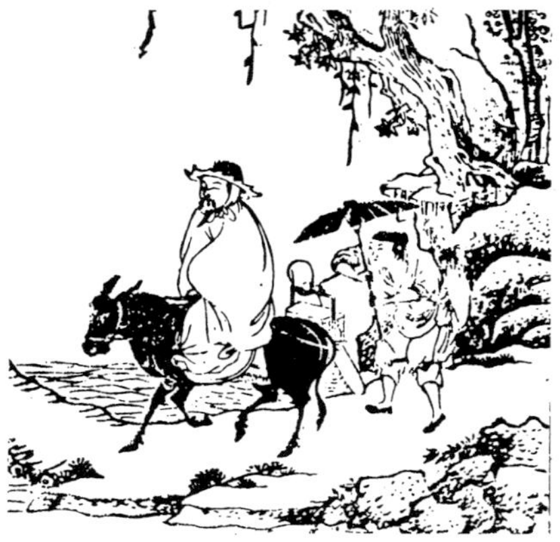

Fig. 4

243

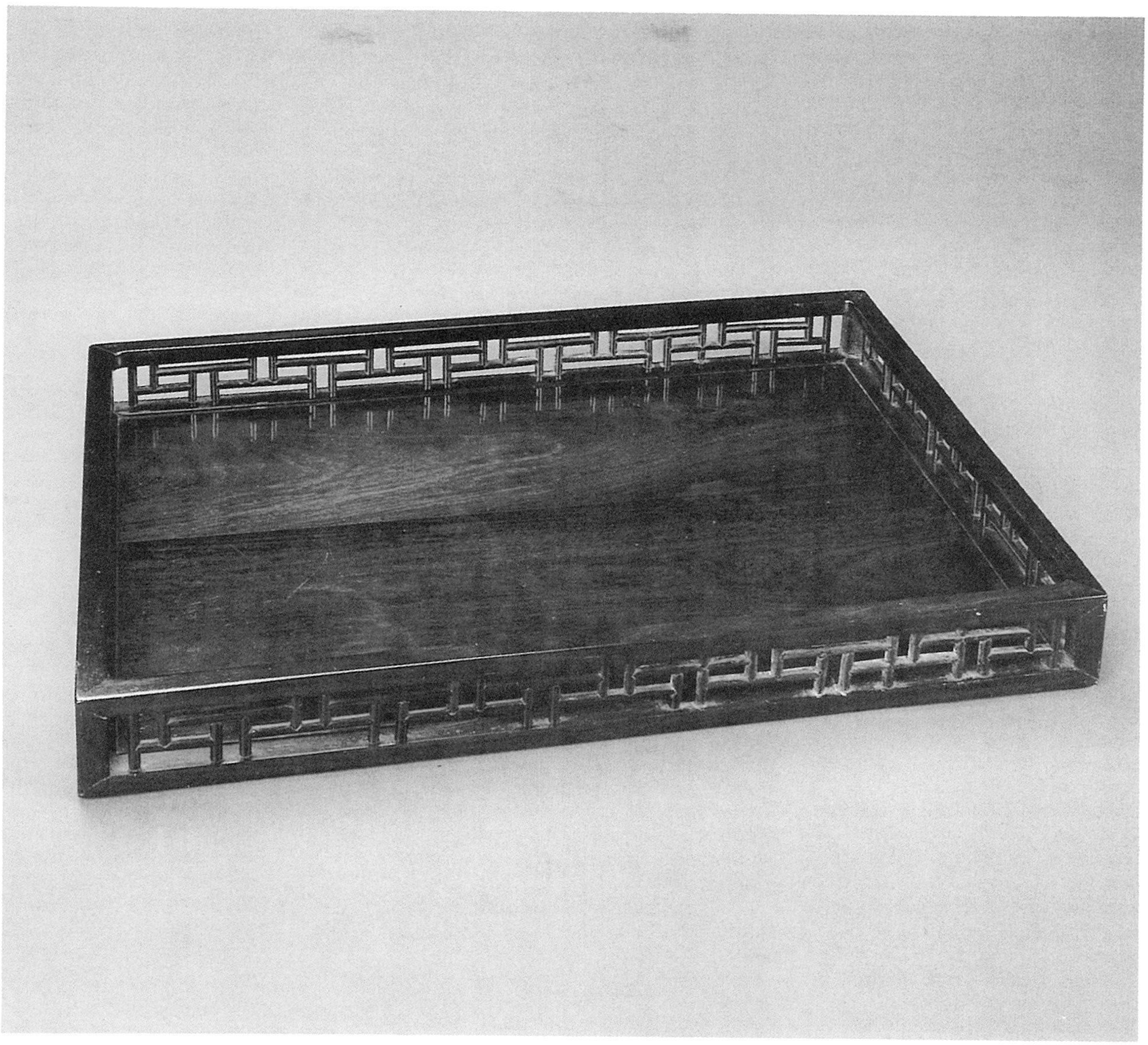

244

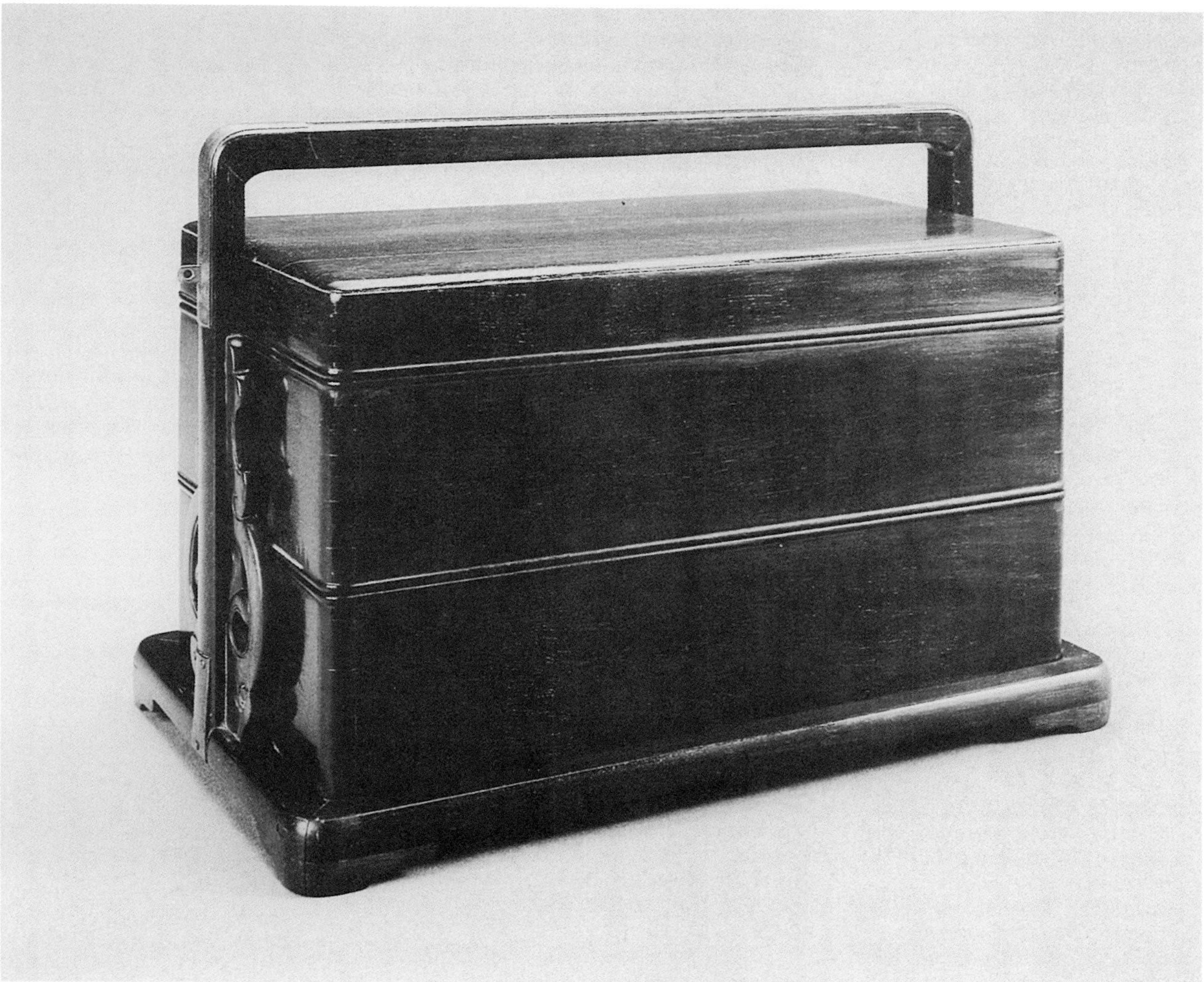

245

Hu

Ivory, of richly patinated tones of golden-brown and creamy-yellow; a *hu* (ceremonial mnemonic device).
Ming dynasty or earlier.
Length: 58.2 cm.

象牙素笏
明或較早, 長58.2厘米

The *hu* seems to have served originally as a mnemonic device for audience with figures of authority. It appears to have been a tablet, originally of bamboo or wood, upon which notes were written to help remember what was to be said to the ruler, or perhaps for writing down his instructions. Probably quite soon after its practical introduction, the tablet itself became a symbol of one who was in a position to be summoned before the King or, later, Emperor. Quite early in the archaic period its functional role seems to have given way to a mainly symbolic one. By Tang to Song times, when the evidence of large numbers of paintings (particularly Buddhist works) comes to our aid, it was evidently primarily a symbol of respect and courtly position. A painting after the Tang artist Wu Daozi (born *circa* 680) shows human sinners before the judge of the dead in which an official stands beside the judge, brush poised to inscribe his *hu* while a female attendant stands nearby grinding ink on an inkstone ready for his use (see Fig. 1).[1]

In later times ivory seems to have been the most common material for the *hu* and extant examples are mostly in this material. They did not apparently form any part of Qing ceremony so presumably all are earlier than Qing, unless made as copies. The large quantities we have seen over the years are nearly all of ivory, and are extremely well-patinated and worn. Archaeological ivories exist from the Shang dynasty, although in much decomposed condition, so it is not unreasonable to expect early ivory *hu* to have survived from the Tang.

The *hu* is reasonably constant in length, varying betwen 50 and 60 cm long, but may differ in width quite markedly. This example is unusually wide, with a maximum width of 7.7 cm, but others less than 4 cm wide are known. This *hu* is as beautifully marked and patinated as any we know, with areas of surface decomposition coinciding with the position in which it would have been most frequently held.

1. Illustrated in *Chinese Painting,* by Peter Swann, p.48.

246

Hand Warmer

Hu Wenming

Copper, patinated to an almost black colour, beaten into the form of a hand warmer and cover, with separate lugs riveted to the body to hold a split, semi-circular wing handle; decorated with a design of one hundred children (seventy on the body and thirty on the lid) playing among pavilions, waterways, rocks, trees and balustrades, all set against a 'Y'-punched ground; the pierced lid with a decorative outer border of precious symbols set against clouds; the separately made handle mounts in the form of tiger masks, their foreheads inscribed with the character *wang* ('king'); the handles decorated with various precious emblems set against a ring-punched ground; the base inscribed *Yunjian Hu Wenming zhi* ('made by Hu Wenming of Yunjian') within a rectangular cartouche.
Yunjian, *circa* 1560-*circa* 1620.
Height with handles down: 16.7 cm.
Diameter: 29.5 cm.
Published: *Chinese Metalwork of the Hu Wenming Group,* p.57, no. 32.

透雕百子圖溫手提爐•胡文明製
明(約1560-1620), 高16.7厘米, 直徑29.5厘米

The hand warmer was filled with hot coals, the heat from which would rise through the pierced lid to warm the hands. The Chinese have always concentrated on warding off the cold on an individual basis rather than by heating entire rooms or houses. Extra clothing, a hand warmer (which was probably also used on occasions to warm the feet) or a charcoal brazier were the usual defences against the often bitter cold. For the scholar in need of digital flexibility for painting and writing, the hand warmer was an essential piece of winter paraphernalia.

Apart from symbolism of abundance represented by a large number of children (one hundred is simply a nominal number representing plenty) this design is geared to entertain the scholar. Here we see children involved not only in the usual games that children play but in the pursuits of the literati. They are reading books, playing and listening to the *guqin* and other musical instruments, matching crickets, playing *weiqi,* seated at conversation over tea, playing with a branch of cassia (*kui* flower; a symbol of success in the examination system) and examining a calligraphic scroll. On the cover is a delightful scene of a group of children pretending to be a scholar and his retinue returning successfully from the imperial examinations in Beijing. One child rides a hobby-horse, attended by others, while ahead of them others pick cassia sprays to present to him.

It appears that all of Hu Wenming's output was of either cast or chased bronze or beaten copper, depending on the function of the item as much as cost or quality. Hand warmers, which needed to be light, were always made of copper, while incense tool vases and *gu* vases were nearly always either of bronze or of copper apparently cast or spun on a lathe to give much greater thickness and weight. Incense boxes were usually of bronze, and burners of either material, as the weight of ash would compensate for the lack of inherent weight in beaten copper sheet and give the broad-footed vessel a practical sturdiness. Hu Wenming made a number of hand warmers, although only two are recorded of this large size.[1]

1. The other was offered by Sotheby's (Hong Kong) Ltd. as Lot 519, in their sale of 20th November 1984 (illustrated in colour).

247

Clip

Zhu Zhizheng

Bamboo, of rich golden brown colour set in wood, probably *zitan;* a clip, the bamboo section carved as a sage beneath a pine tree set on pivots in an wood mount carved to simulate a gnarled, rocky grotto; signed in draft script at the back of the grotto *Sansong.*
First half of the 17th century.
Height: 9.8 cm.
Published: *Chinese Bamboo Carving,* Part II, p.233, no. 41 (where the height is incorrectly printed).

竹雕松下老人夾子•朱稚征製
晚明十七世紀上半葉, 高9.8厘米

A series of these clips is known, all of which share certain characteristics[1]. They are of a similar size, of broadly 'C' or inverted 'C' shape, with the pivoted central section overlapping the central gap. They are generally early (late Ming or early Qing dynasty) and were obviously made to be used flat (some, like this example, will also stand but the degree of wear at the back demonstrate that they were used flat). They have been variously described as wrist rests and clips, but the reason for their specific shape remains a mystery.

Zhu Zhizheng (*hao:* Sansong) was a native of Jiading, Jiangsu province, and the second son of the famous Ming bamboo carver Zhu Ying. He was active during the reigns of the Tianqi and Chongzheng Emperors of the Ming dynasty (1621-1627 and 1628-1644 respectively). It was said of him, "He excels in painting distant mountains and pale rocks, bamboo groves and weathered trees, and is especially fond of drawing mules. He does not lightly apply his knife, but waits until inspiration moves him, often taking months and years to complete an object."[2] He was reputed to have carved mainly for his own enjoyment. He was the third generation of a family of distinguished carvers, whose reputation even in his day was widespread. He was not considered a primarily commercial carver, and apparently would not work even for large sums of money, unless inspired to do so. In using his knife as a brush his works were considered to be simple, rustic and rich with interest, easily capturing the spirit.[3]

Zhu's signature, usually in the form of *Sansong* or *Zhu Sansong,* has been used by many later carvers, and recently added to unsigned pieces. However a widely accepted example of superb quality was in the imperial collection, now in the National Palace Museum, Taipei.[4] It is a brush pot carved with ladies. Another brush pot attributed to him is in the collection of the Hong Kong Museum of Art.[5]

The signature on this example is confidently and finely inscribed and well worn, indicating that it has been there if not since the original carving at least for a long time. The taste and quality of the carving are commensurate with his style and period, and we see no reason to doubt its authenticity.

1. *Chinese Bamboo Carving,* Part II, p.230, no. 40, and p. 232, no. 42; *Chinese Bamboo Carving,* Part I, p.170, no. 22, and p.172, no. 23; *Bamboo Carving of China,* p.100, no. 38 and p.66, no. 4.
2. *Zhuren Lu* ('Record of Bamboo Carvers'), by Lu Tingcan.
3. Ibid.
4. *Masterpieces of Chinese Writing Materials in the National Palace Museum,* no. 22.
5. *Chinese Bamboo Carving,* Part I, p.206, no. 37.

245

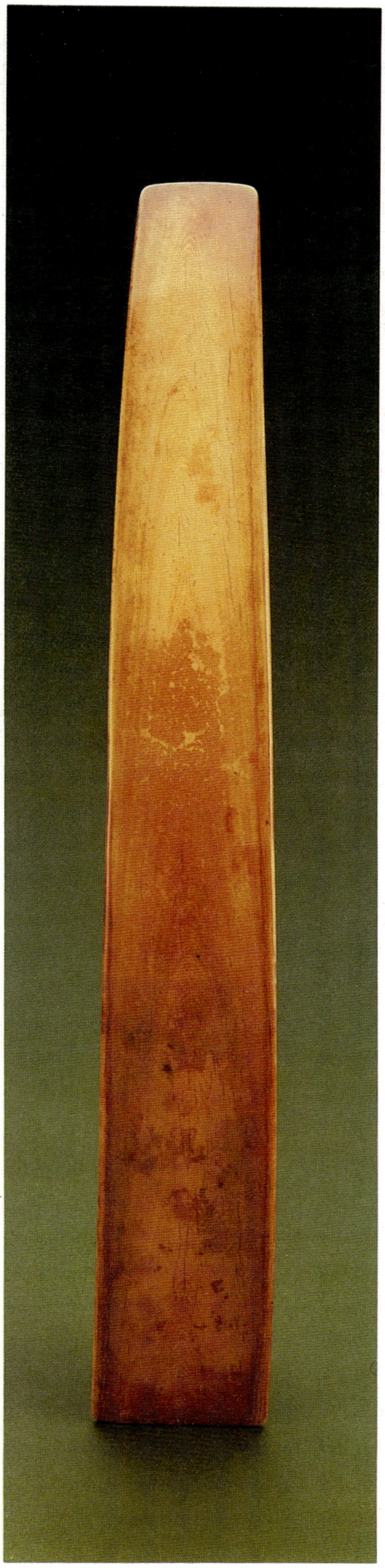

246

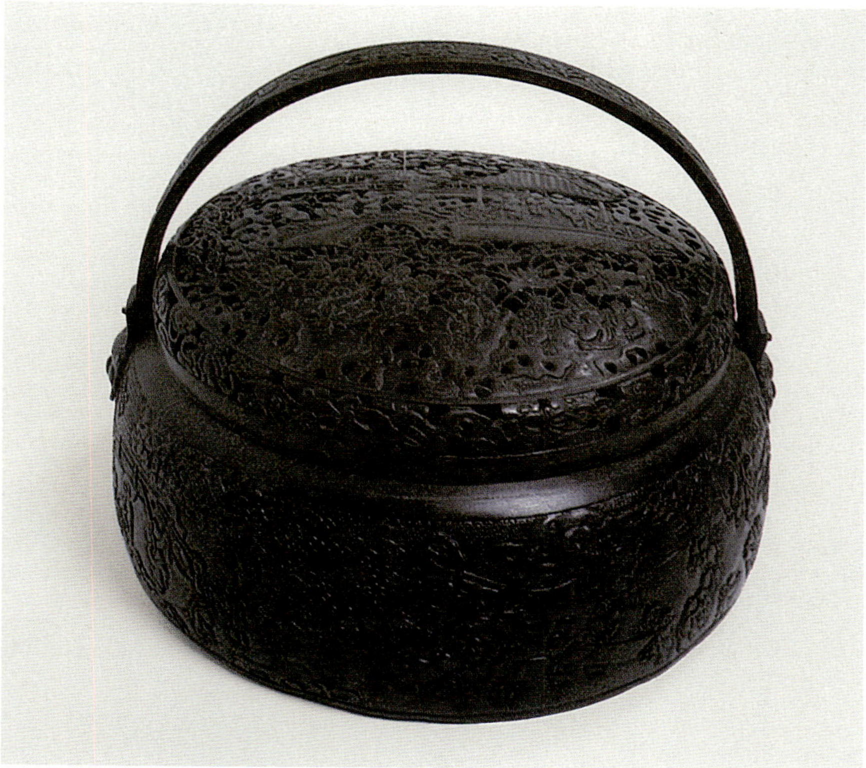

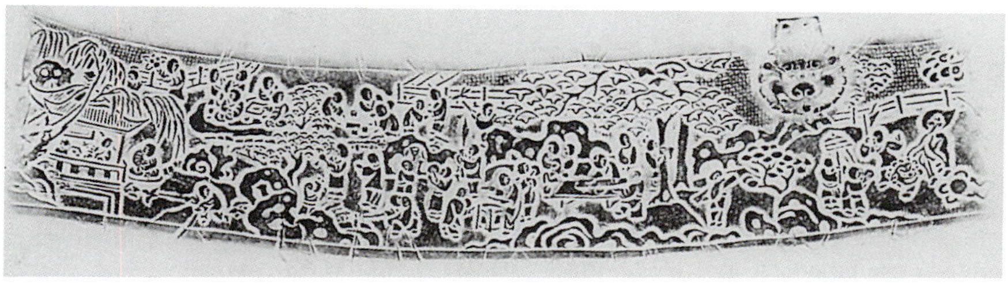

247

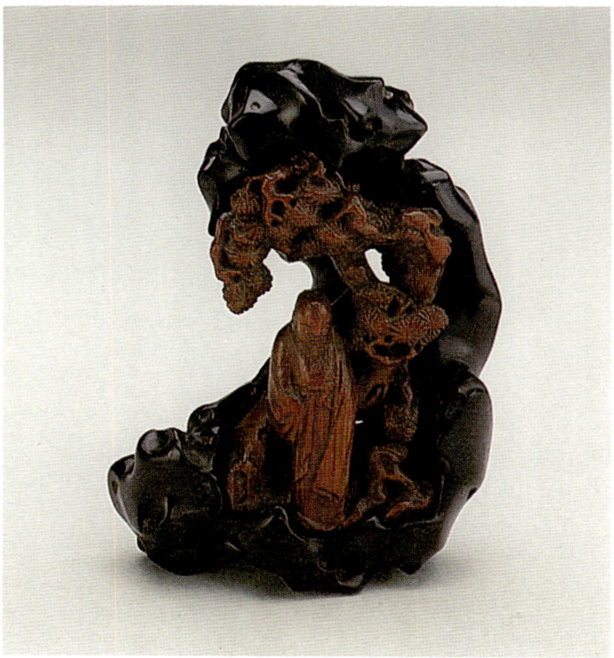

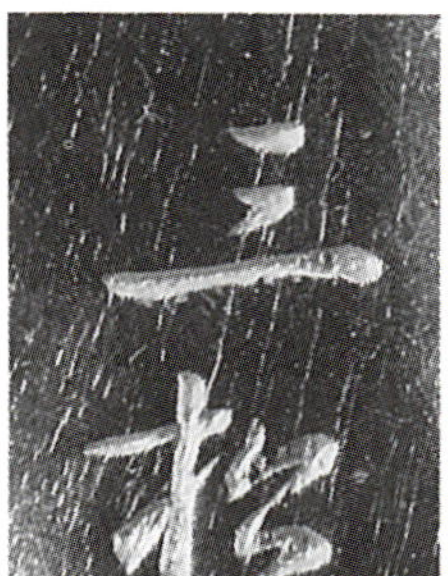

248

Display Stand

Wood, *qiu* (catalpa), of golden-brown colour; a two-level display stand, each square display surface set on supports based on archaic *kui* dragon motifs, the taller segment with naturalistically carved auspicious flora (bamboo, chrysanthemum, and what is probably intended to be prunus and orchid) decorating the spaces between the galleried legs.
Qing dynasty.
9.7 cm (lower level 6.8 cm) × 39.7 cm × 17.8 cm.

楸木雕花卉相連器座
清代，高9.7(低6.8)×39.7×17.8厘米

Display stands of all sorts were widely used by the literati. They range from tall rectangular or circular stands, which might be as much as two-thirds the height of an adult on which incense burners were frequently placed (often together with the other two 'friends of incense' — see no. 230 — but also with vases of flowers or other visually pleasing objects), to miniature tables, *kangs,* drums, or whatever else might make a suitable stand for precious objects, vases of flowers, etc. They exist in a wide variety of materials, including stone, lacquer, *lac-burgauté,* and various metals, but are most common in various woods, including root formations.

Works of art were not only considered individually, but in the broader context of life as a work of art. In the scholar's studio, or elsewhere where he entertained himself and his friends, additional layers of meaning were added to individual works of art by their meaningful juxtaposition. Strangely shaped rocks, incense burners, root sculptures, jade carvings and the like placed elegantly on suitable stands in just the right setting became, like all art, so much more than the simple sum of their parts. With the holistic concept of art and the understanding of the importance of the audience in the whole process, the extension of the work of art to its display was inevitable, as was the artistic development of the paraphernalia of display. This also applied to connoisseurship where a study of usage and display became as serious a business as that of the works of art themselves. Wen Zhenheng devotes entire sections of his book on connoisseurship to the correct use and display of various scholarly trappings, from garden stones and potted plants, to furniture, to minute details about the placing of specific items in a collector's cabinet (see no. 236).

The holistic attitude of the literati to their arts is directly related to their attitude to the development of the inner self in education. The education system for the influential minority was aimed not at producing a number of specialists to perform this or that function, but at producing self-aware and self-possessed, sage-like beings with a pure heart. The belief was that once the self was assured, it could turn with equal success to any endeavour. Every aspect of their lives, including the arts, then became the manifestations of their inner spirit in the ordinary world and assumed great importance in communication, allowing the placing of a group of objects on a side table to carry the same weight, to those who understood the languages of communication involved, as a painting or piece of poetry.

249

Display Stand

Wood, *huanghuali* of well-figured, deep reddish-brown colour; a display stand in the form of a miniature altar table; the top made of one piece of wood with flared flanges mortised and tenoned into it at either end, the tenons exposed, the side of the top tapering inwards; set on two supports the width of the table-top and fitted to it by what appear to be shoulder inserted joints, each carved from a single piece of wood, and with a pierced *ruyi*-shaped central motif; with plain aprons and end pieces.
Probably late Ming or early Qing dynasty.
15.5 cm × 41.7 cm × 18 cm.

黄花梨翹頭案形器座
可能晚明或清初，15.5×41.7×18厘米

The range of small stands for displaying works of art was immense, but many were miniature versions of larger pieces of furniture. Here we have a rather unusual miniature altar table. The altar table was used in the home for ancestor worship or for Buddhist worship. It would support a number of devotional objects, but always including an incense burner. Such a stand as this might be ideally suitable for an incense burner, but it is also an elegant stand for a number of other vessels or objects.

It is solidly constructed (lacking the usual floating panels between the legs of a conventional sized example) and might also have served conveniently as an occasional arm rest. The scholar frequently reclined on couches of various descriptions or on mats, and genre paintings show a variety of reclining supports in use.

248

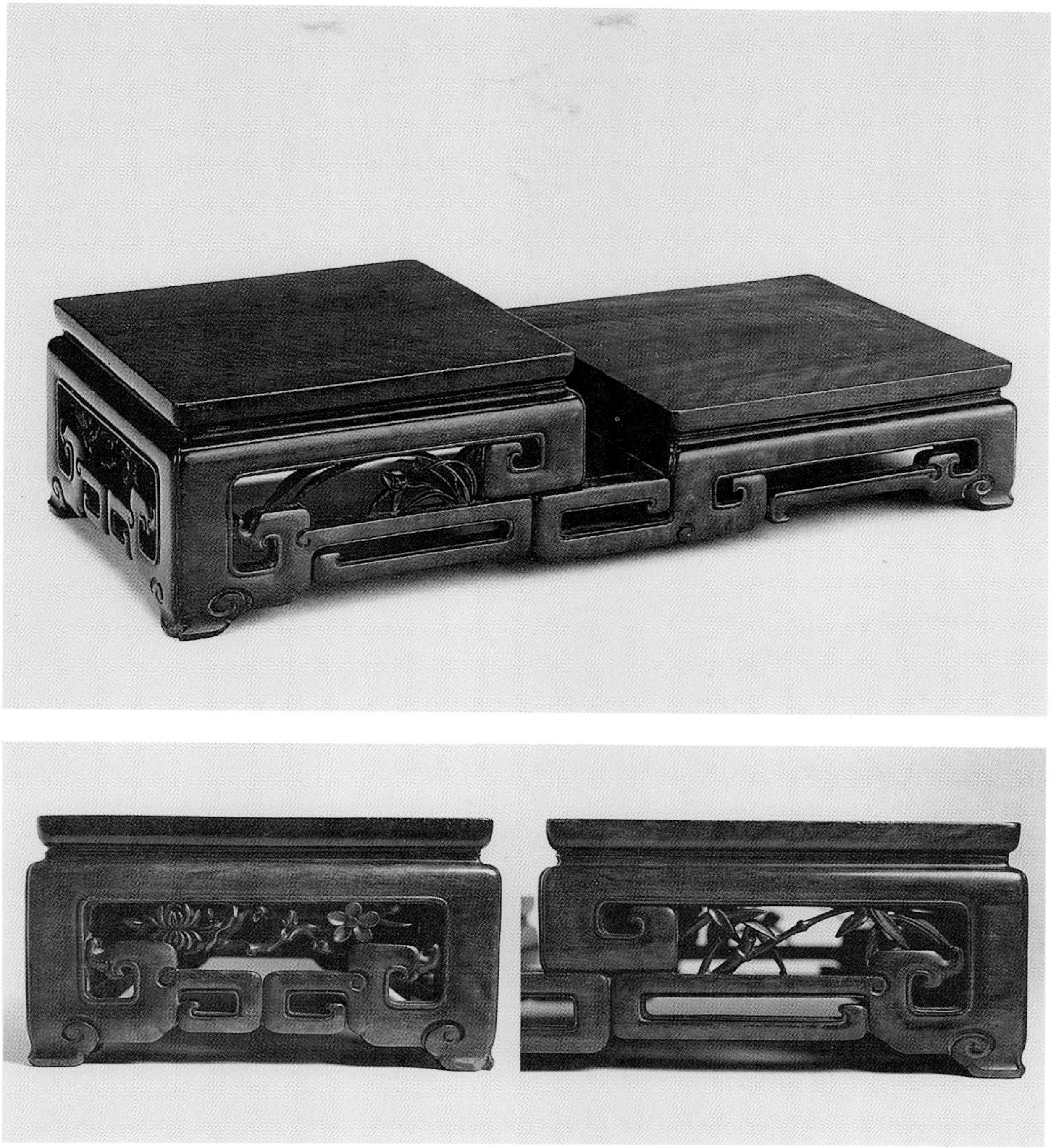

249

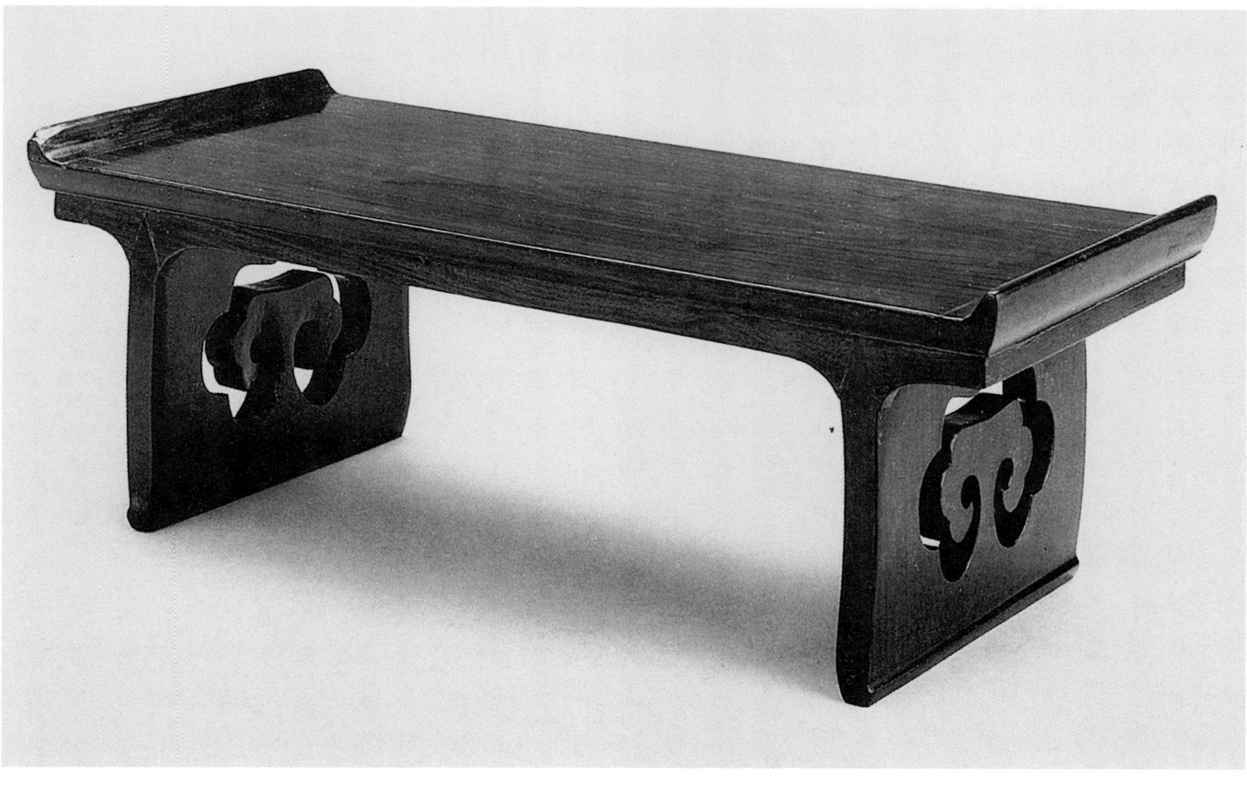

250

Hua Tianyi's Rustic Drinking Vessel

Wood, probably *nanmu* (cedar), with red and black lacquer; a rustic drinking vessel, the exterior and lip largely formed of a natural section, the base and probably the interior carved; the lip with a flying bat painted in red lacquer; the interior lined with partly marbled black and red lacquer in a swirling, smoke-like pattern; the irregularly shaped, recessed base edged with similarly marbled lacquer and inscribed in lacquer "For the elegant appreciation of Hua Tianyi".
Qing dynasty.
Height: 3.5 cm. Length: 10.3 cm.

楠木髹紅蝠漆杯·華田簃銘
清代, 高3.5厘米, 長10.3厘米

Although this small container might have served any number of functions, the lacquered interior suggests the possibility of its being designed originally to contain a liquid. We have designated it as a rustic drinking cup not because we are convinced it was (it may equally have been an artist's water vessel) but because it represents a type that was widely used for drinking. A similar vessel in the Shuisongshi Shanfang collection, of irregular root formation, is inscribed as a drinking cup, and genre paintings frequently show scholars drinking out of strangely shaped vessels of this type (see no. 210 for one particularly bizarre-looking example). The rusticity of the material and workmanship would have brought to wine or water an added dimension, concentrating the attention on the pleasure of drinking as an act in itself rather than just quenching thirst or getting drunk.

In the absence of positive identification of Hua Tianyi it is not possible to accurately date this vessel.

251

Box and Cover

Wood, *huanghuali;* box and cover of rectangular form, the well-figured wood of top and bottom separated by beaded lips; set with two plain, elongated exterior hinges, the front set with a cloud-shaped clasp on a circular, split base-plate, also with beaded lips; the ends with continuous swing handles, set in chrysanthemum-shaped fittings, and falling onto a similar knocking plate, all in white brass.
Probably late Ming or early Qing dynasty.
15.8 cm × 37.1 cm × 20.3 cm.

Published: *Wood From the Scholar's Table*, p.90, no. 50.

黄花梨長方小箱
可能晚明或清初, 15.8×37.1×20.3厘米

It is extremely difficult to identify the exact functions of the wide range of boxes and containers used by the scholar. Containers such as this might have held documents, handscrolls, writing utensils, or any number of other precious belongings. Its size suggests that it would have been suitable for handscrolls and it might have been used to store scrolls at some time during its career, but to call it a 'scroll box' would be unnecessarily limiting of a multi-functional container.

The elegance of undecorated wood, particularly the range of hardwoods most favoured by the Chinese, is demonstrated here. The beautifully grained wood with its richly variegated orange and brown colouring has an independent level of fascination, with its swirling markings and evocative patterns.

252

Seal or Cosmetic Chest

Wood, *huanghuali* of well-figured golden brown colour; a seal or cosmetic chest, the classic cuboid form with a deep hinged top, and two hinged doors, opening to reveal an upper tray and seven drawers of varying sizes; the top, sides and base constructed with hidden dovetailed joints; the doors mitred, mortised and tenoned with floating centre panels; the shaped stand attached to the chest; edge and corner protectors, floral-shaped centre lock plate, door and drawer pulls, and hinges all in white brass and surface mounted, those on the top corners decorated with cloud patterns, the lock plate and door pulls also decorated with swastika design.
Probably early Qing dynasty.
34.2 cm × 33 cm × 24.1 cm.

黄花梨官皮箱
可能清初, 34.2×33×24.1厘米

Chests of this type, which are standard and were obviously made in fairly large quantities throughout the late Ming and Qing periods, have usually been referred to as seal chests in the West, but in a recent publication on Chinese furniture by Wang Shixiang[1] they were called cosmetic boxes. This description was backed up by the evidence of a chest with two drawers and a cover, inside which was a retractable mirror stand, excavated from a Song tomb at Changzhou. However these two forms are not necessarily related. There is a whole group of such cosmetic boxes, still made in the present century, which have retractable mirror stands, sometimes with mirrors attached. The group represented by this chest are characterized by their deep domed lids which do not usually have internal fittings for mirrors, and their twin doors hiding the drawers. They represent two apparently different types.

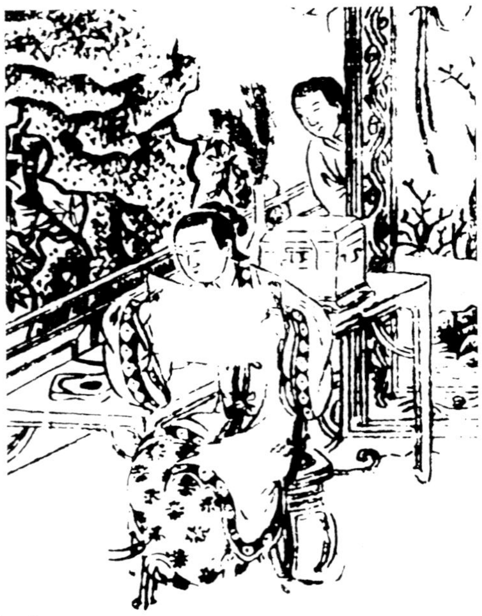

Fig. 1

These chests, however, were possibly also used for cosmetics. There is an illustration in the woodblock edition *Xixiang Ji,* of the Wanli period, of a lady seated at a table, reading a letter. On the table are an inkstone and a chest of this type. An episode entitled 'Reading a letter at the cosmetic table' (see Fig. 1) is depicted. The original novel is of the Yuan dynasty, so the Wanli illustrator would presumably have placed on the cosmetic table something to identify it as such, implying that the chest was for cosmetics.

This form is certainly ideally suited to function as a seal chest. Scholars frequently had many seals, particularly in the Ming and post-Ming developments in seal carving, and these chests would conveniently hold a number of them together with the other trappings necessary for making seal impressions. Perhaps they were used for both purposes.

1. *Mingshi Jiaju Zhenshang;* English edition, *Classic Chinese Furniture.*

250

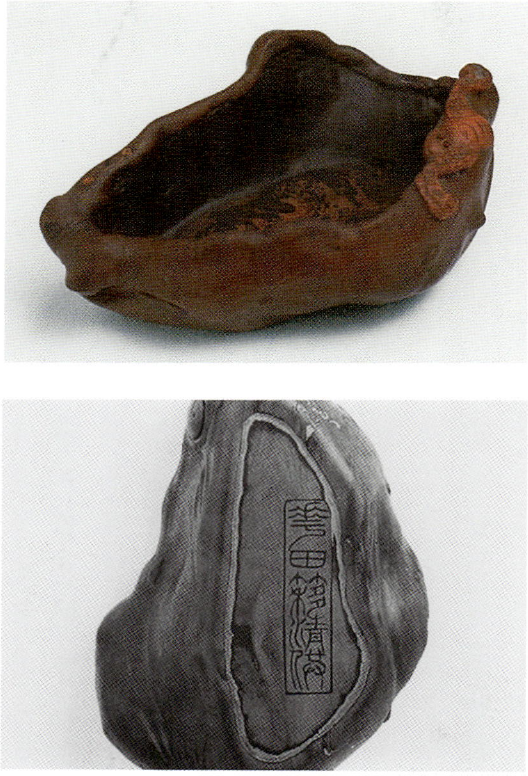

251

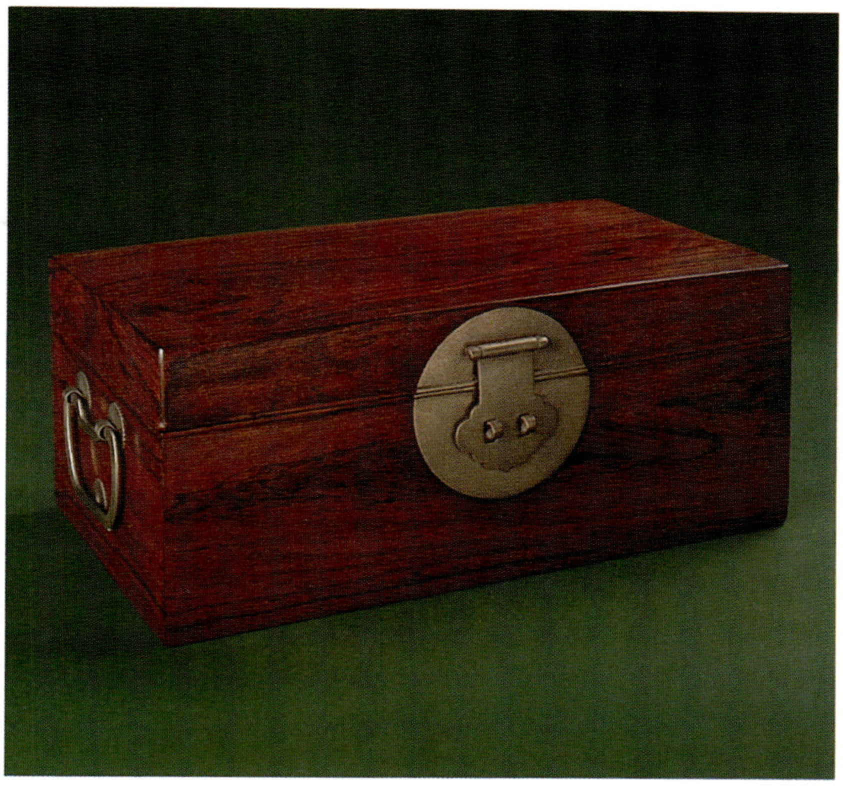

252

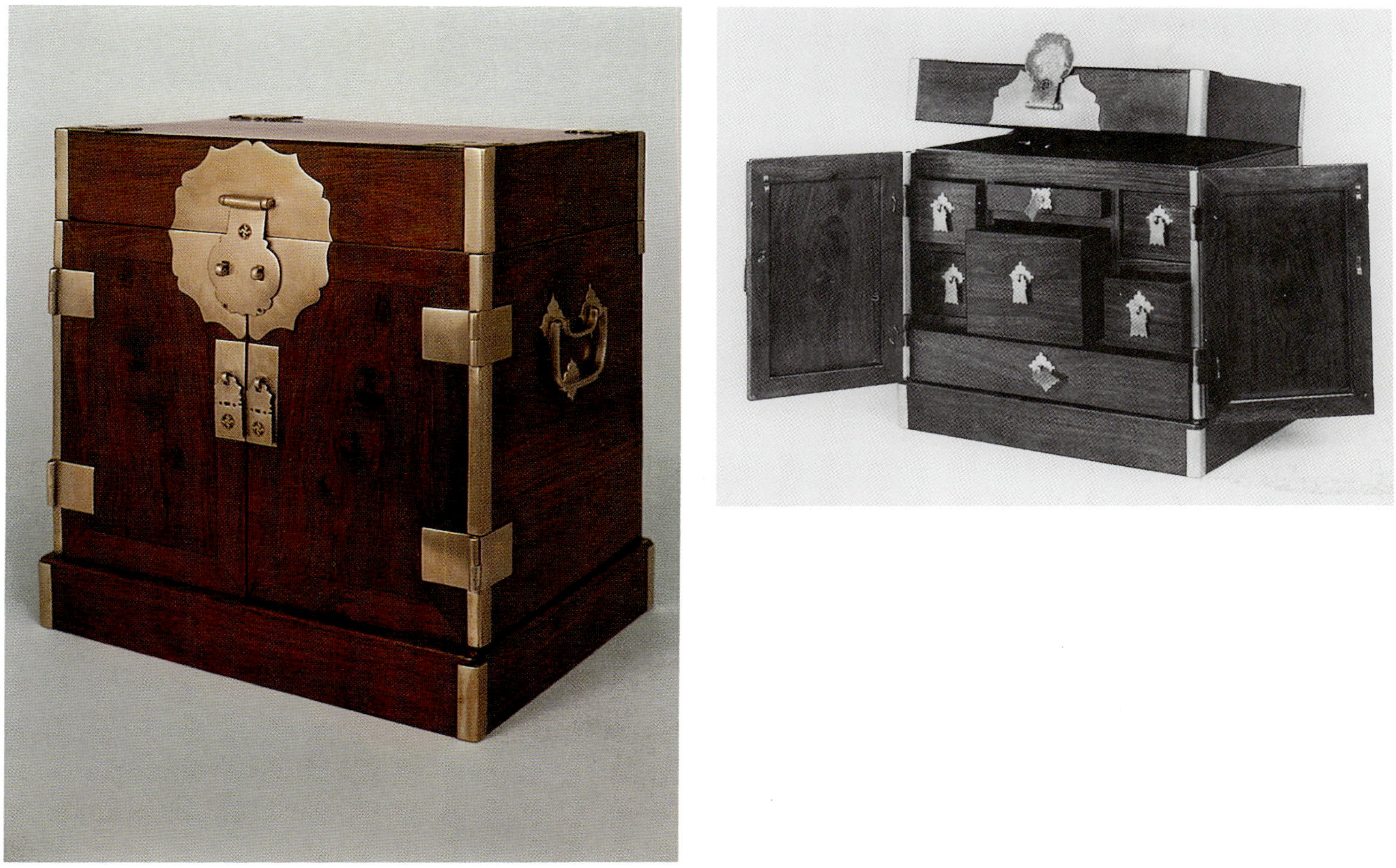

253

Seal or Cosmetic Box

Wood, *huamu* (burl), of brilliant orange-brown colour; the rectangular, domed form set with a shallow interior tray which sits on the inside lip of the box; set on simple feet at each corner. Probably late Qing.
11.7 cm × 14 cm × 11.4 cm.

樺木連盤奩盒
可能晚清，11.7×14×11.4厘米

These boxes with a small shallow tray sitting on the inner lip, dividing the interior into deep lower and shallow upper sections (see Fig. 1) are widely called 'seal boxes'.

Presumably the seals were kept in the lower section while the upper tray was for the other accoutrements such as a seal-paste container, a seal position regulator (like a small set-square so that the seal may be lined up with the edge of the paper accurately), small pieces of flimsy paper for covering seals until they dry, etc. Boxes of this type and size are not uncommon, and others exist of larger, rectangular shape also with interior trays.

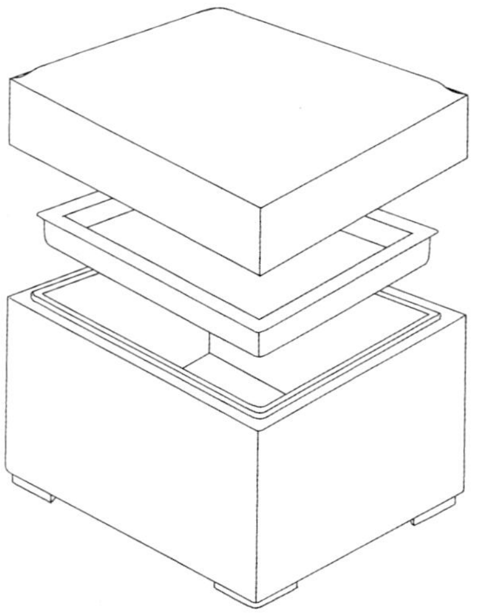

Fig. 1

However, we believe that they were more likely to have been made as cosmetic boxes, whatever their extended later use. A recent excavation of a Jin dynasty tomb (1115-1234) in Datong in Shanxi province yielded a *guri* lacquer box of this shape with a similar interior tray which contained a wooden comb, a lacquer bowl, a small undecorated gourd, a bone rouge box, a red lacquered wooden ladle, two red lacquered wood powder boxes, and traces of bronze patination suggesting the existence at one time of a bronze mirror.[1]

1. *Wenwu* 1985, no. 12 pp.79-81.

254

Fitted Collector's Box

Wood, *zitan, zong* (palm) and *huangyangmu* (boxwood); a box and cover to contain precious objects; the box made in the form of a portfolio of books, their ends simulated in palm wood, enclosed in a *zitan* folio case carved to simulate brocade, with a title panel inlaid in boxwood; the interior (now stripped) originally padded with material and specially fitted for (probably) five separate objects.
Probably mid- to late Qing dynasty.
8.7 cm × 30.5 cm × 18.6 cm.

紫檀木雕書函形蓋盒
可能清中至晚期，8.7×30.5×18.6厘米

Precious objects for the studio were frequently boxed in such a manner that the container itself began to take on significance as a work of art in its own right. The brush box, no. 213, seems to be such a case, and it was common for the finest of inksticks to be contained in fitted cases made in wood or lacquer.[1]

That this container held five objects is suggested by the marks left in the silk lining of the base of the box, where quite clearly five separate rigid and shaped brocade 'stands' have been removed. (After separating the objects for disposal it was a natural impulse to remove the fittings, as the box is more valuable as a box in its own right than as an empty fitted case.) It may have contained a set of seals, inks (although it is rather deep for the usual shapes of ink), or even a group of objects related only in the eye of the owner.

This object also fits into a category of scholar's furniture which is related to the treasure boxes of the Qianlong Emperor (see no. 236). They consist of imitations in other materials of books, piles of scrolls, rolls of brocade, etc., which are used as containers, sometimes in conjunction with, or even as an integral part of miniature display cabinets. In them may be kept a variety of precious objects for appreciation or use.

1. See *Masterpieces of Chinese Writing Materials in the National Palace Museum* where a box of brushes is displayed, no. 4; a box of inks, no. 9, and two *lac-burgauté* boxes of coloured inks, no. 13. None is illustrated with its cover, but they all have them, and in the case of the latter, inlaid in various iridescent shells, remarkably fine ones.

255

Box and Cover

Wood, *huangyangmu* (boxwood), of golden brown colour; carved as a box and cover in the form of a 'Buddha's hand' fruit divided horizontally to form an irregularly shaped container, the surface convincingly carved as a gnarled, mature fruit; a groove around the upper part of the fruit giving the appearance of it having been confined in growth by a cord and providing a channel around which a cord may be fixed to hold the box closed; set on an elaborately carved, probably original, blackwood stand carved as a complex growth of interlocking roots on a simple plinth of a lighter coloured wood, set on five small feet.
Late Ming or early Qing dynasty.
Height including stand: 10.2 cm.
Length: 19.6 cm.

黄楊木雕佛手形蓋盒
晚明或清初，高10.2厘米，長19.6厘米

The 'Buddha's hand' fruit was featured frequently in groups of scholarly trappings. The original fruit may have been popularly tied with a cord (somewhat like the idea of a gourd moulding on a simpler scale) to allow for a ribbon to be tied around it for presentation. On this box it performs a similar function, providing a groove around one end of the box where a ribbon may be tied, thus appearing like the original fruit and at the same time keeping whatever was in the box at presentation safely contained. Since this box was likely to have acted as an auspicious container for a suitable gift, it might have contained any number of things such as rare herbs, medicines or health aids, Daoist longevity potions, or a precious or symbolic gift. It is quite likely that a number of the small boxes associated with the scholar originally functioned as part of an elaborate presentation.

The intricately carved wood stand which is fitted so carefully to this piece is probably the original. It is of equal quality of carving and would appear to be of similar age. The history of stands for works of art is a particularly difficult one to resolve. Many scholars probably employed their own craftsmen and it would not be unusual for the large staff of a wealthy official to include a craftsman skilled in making stands, repairing and making furniture, etc. Any precious object acquired might be fitted for a stand at any time. Equally there would have been in every major craft centre (and most minor ones) independent shops and workshops capable of providing the same service. To what extent objects were made with original stands rather than being fitted up later is not clear. However, with this piece, the fact that it does not stand independently suggests that it must have had a stand of some sort originally, and the present one seems a likely candidate. Stands for objects and vessels were obviously considered as part of the overall work of art from at least the Tang dynasty onwards, as the vast majority of objects in genre paintings have stands of various types.

253

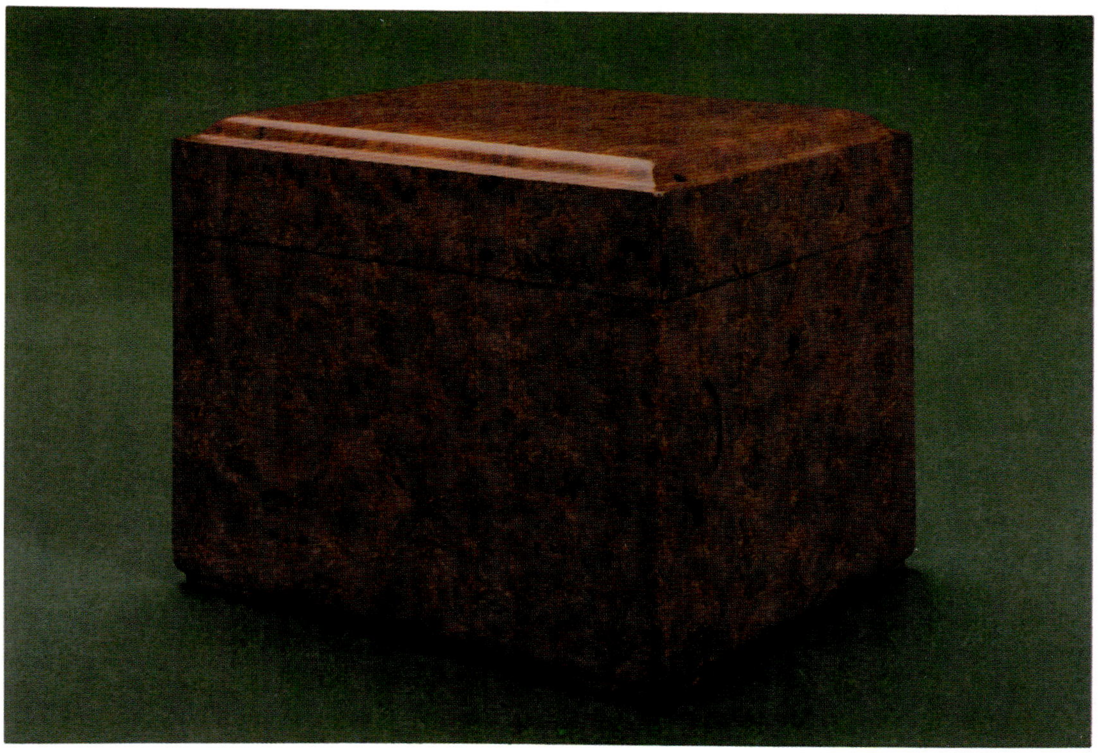

254

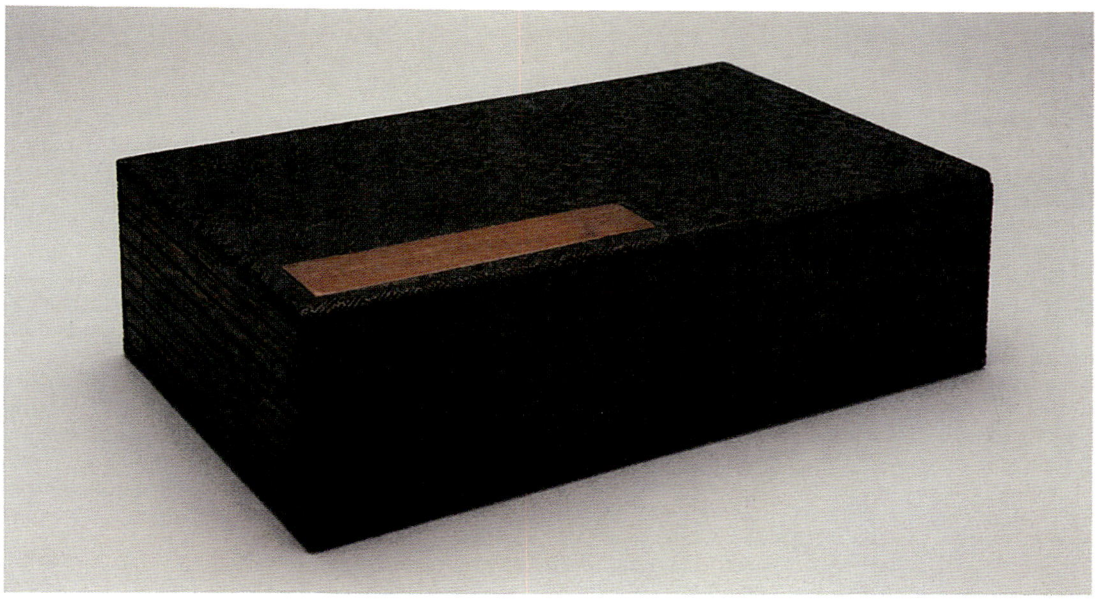

255

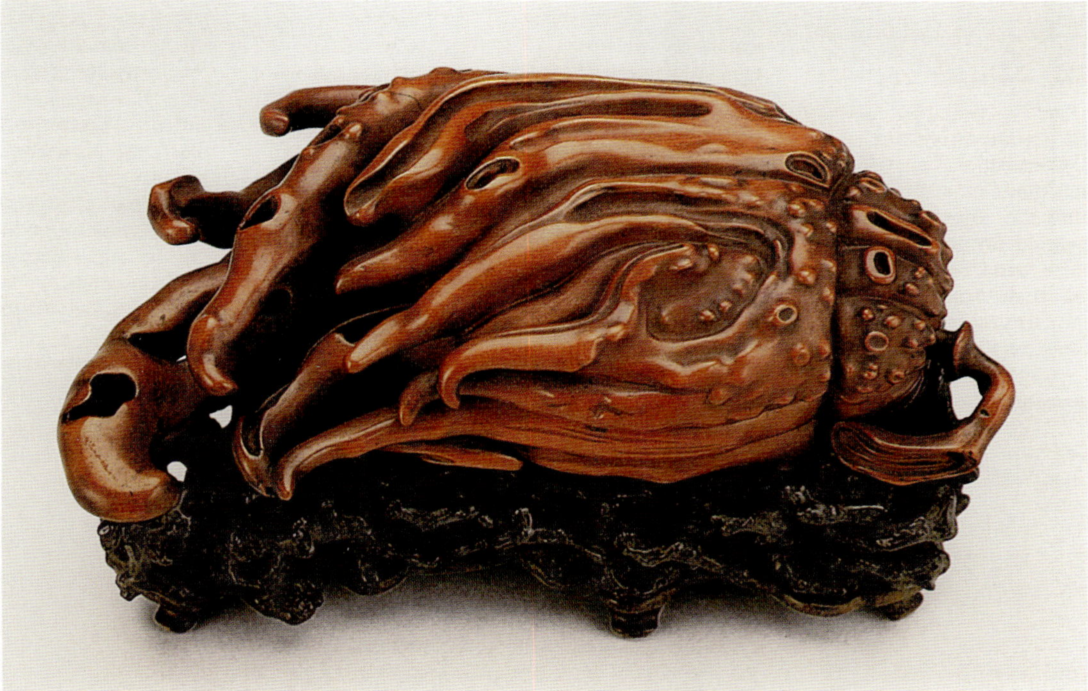

256

Wine Cup

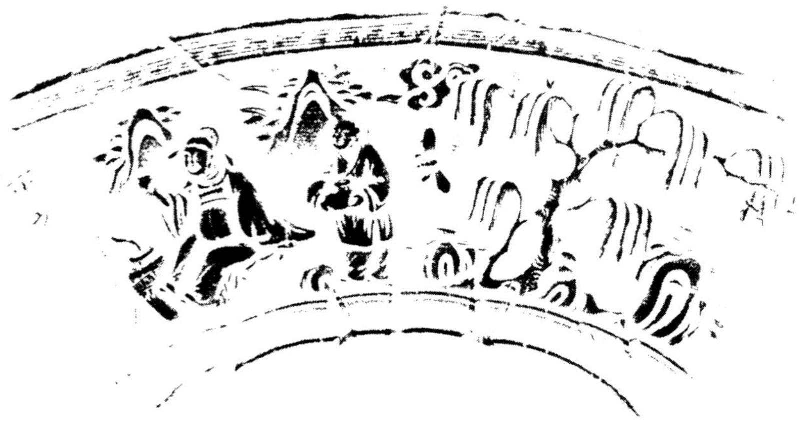

Coconut shell (*yezi*) of speckled, dark purplish-brown colour; a wine cup lined with silver-plated copper, the exterior carved in relief with a pastoral scene of a scholar, seated on a low table, beside a large wine jar, raising his cup of wine as if toasting the delights of spring; behind him an attendant stands dutifully holding a box probably containing food, while a butterfly joins with distant mountains, wafting clouds and willow trees in setting the idyllic spring mood; a poem in rather elegant relief draft script fills the rest of the surface; a narrow band at the lip filled with continuous *leiwen* pattern, the foot with plain, raised borders.
Probably 16th or 17th century.
Height: 5.2 cm. Diameter of mouth: 7.35 cm.

椰殼雕春宴圖酒杯
可能十六或十七世紀，高5.2厘米，
口徑7.35厘米

Alcohol was never treated with the same moralistic fervour in China as it has been in the West. Quite the opposite: its potential as an aid to spiritual release has been recognized and valued, and over the centuries poets and musicians, calligraphers and painters have frequently given of their very finest while far from steady on their feet. The single most influential piece of calligraphy known (the *Lanting Preface*) was written while Wang Xizhi was inebriated, and any amount of subsequent effort to recreate its magic while sober failed (see no. 28); and the arts of China are redolent with references, explicit and otherwise, to the creative potential of a little, or in many cases a lot of wine. In the charming scene depicted on the side of this wine cup we are left in no doubt as to literati preference while enjoying the delights of spring; the scholar's wine jar, of which he appears to be the sole beneficiary, is enormous, while his only other trappings (a low table of a type on which it is interesting to see a scholar sitting, as they are usually called footstools; and a box and cover held by the attendant) are minimal.

With such a positive attitude to wine (the Chinese drank mostly rice wines until quite recently) the literati had what we might be forgiven for calling a consuming need for wine vessels. These included large storage jars, such as depicted here; serving vessels in the form of ewers, sometimes in association with deep bowls in which they rested surrounded by hot water so that wines drunk warm could be kept within the correct temperature range; and wine cups. The *jue* (see no. 161) was an early form of elaborate wine drinking vessel, which seems to have continued in use as a drinking vessel, and frequently appears in later genre paintings and illustrated books. Animal horns were obvious drinking vessels, and the wide range of rhinoceros horn vessels — a large number of which might otherwise be considered pouring vessels were used as drinking cups. Stem cups of vessels — were used as drinking cups. Stem cups of various kinds were a popular Tang and post-Tang form from which wine could be taken, and a variety of other vessels in endless materials including jade and other hard stones, bronze, silver and gold, lacquer, wood, gourd and ceramics were all used over the centuries.

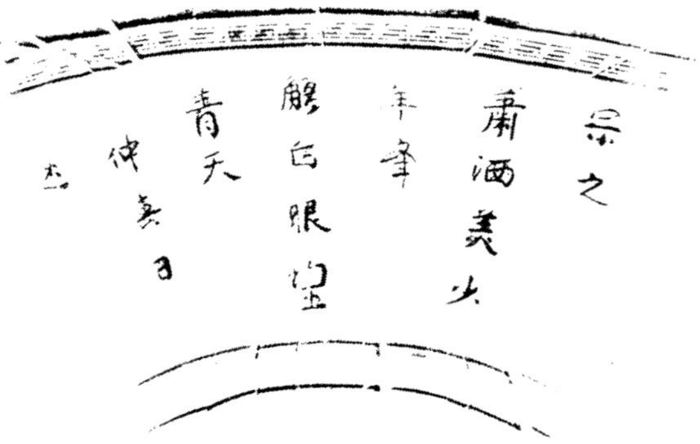

At what stage the southern material coconut shell began to be used is uncertain. It was such an obvious container in its natural form that it must have been used in the south by the earliest settlers. It was noted by the early Ming connoisseur Cao Zhao in his *Gegu Yaolun* where, in a section on coconut cups, he mentions them as a product of Annam (present-day Vietnam), Guangdong and Guangxi provinces. He describes the shell as being cut with a saw and "then either painted or set in silver to make wine cups, wine pots, individual plates, wine ewers and water ladles". In a later edition (1462) the following information is added: "The small ones are the most expensive and hard to come by."[1] Clearly small wine cups of this type, lined with silver (or silvered copper — a Chinese connoisseur would be unlikely to make a distinction between the two) were standard throughout the Ming dynasty, and probably continued to be made during the Qing (we know from a reasonable number of 19th century snuff bottles in coconut shell that the material itself continued to be popular, and Lu Dong, the famous Yangzhou lacquerer — see no. 63 — used it as an inlay material on his embellished works in the first half of the 19th century).

Many of these small cups are known, nearly always with subject-matter suited to literati taste, and although they are usually considered to be 19th century, we believe this might be another case where a re-examination of a large group would be likely to reveal that some are very much earlier. It is highly unlikely that a type which was popular in the 15th century should suddenly spring up again in the 19th with no significant production in between.

1. *Chinese Connoisseurship*, p.156.

257

Wine Cup and Stand

Grey stoneware, covered with a variegated lavender glaze, opaque where thick, but running to a transparent, greyish colour where thinner; a small wine cup and stand; the cup of elegantly curved, very slightly inverted form, standing on a small, unglazed foot; the stand with a central, hollow section of similar shape to the cup, surrounded by a wide, upcurving integral saucer, the whole standing on an unglazed footrim.
Jun ware, Henan province, Northern Song dynasty.
Height of cup: 3.7 cm. Height of cup in stand: 5.95 cm. Diameter of cup: 7.05 cm.
Diameter of stand: 8.5 cm.

鈞窯酒杯連托子
北宋，總高5.95厘米，杯直徑7.05厘米，
托直徑8.5厘米

The cup stand was considered in Song times to be an invention of the Tang dynasty as a practical contribution to tea drinking. A Song expert on tea wrote: "The bowl stand first appeared in the Tang dynasty and was not to be seen prior to that. When the daughter of Cui Ning drank tea, she was often disgusted by the hot teabowl which scorched her fingers. She took a plate and melted wax in it in a shape that fitted the ringed foot of the teabowl. When the teabowl is fitted into this wax mould, it was discovered that the device also prevented spilling. Lacquer workmen were ordered to reproduce the device. The invention was much favoured by Cui Ning and he named it *tuo*."[1] Song Boyin is of the opinion that it in fact developed earlier[2] and it is not unusual for a story of this sort to evolve in retrospect. However, the Tang was probably the time when it was first popularly used.

When tea was drunk in powdered form (see no. 104) the teabowl and stand were standard. But this vessel would appear to be too small for tea in Song times, and as a rule flared bowls were preferred for tea as opposed to those with incurving rims, suggesting that this is a wine cup. It is also clear from early references that the colour of the ceramic ware was valued for its ability to enhance the colour of the tea, an important criterion in the early tea cult. It is likely that the colour of *jun* ware and tea were not considered compatible.

Jun ware was made at a number of kiln sites in Henan province and was best known for its range of glazes of lavender blue and purple colours, sometimes using the two in a combination of abstract splashes. This bowl is of a typically *jun* shape, although smaller than usual, and is extremely rare in having an original stand. A larger stand is known in the far rarer, but related *ru* ware.[3]

1. Quoted from *Yanfanlu* ('Elaboration on Luxuriant Dew') by Cheng Dachang, in 'Tea Drinking, Tea Ware and Purple Clay Ware', by Song Boyin, in *K.S. Lo Collection in the Flagstaff House Museum of Tea Ware*, Part II, p.15.
2. Op. cit. p.16.
3. See *Song Ceramics* by Mary Tregear, p.127, no. 151.

256

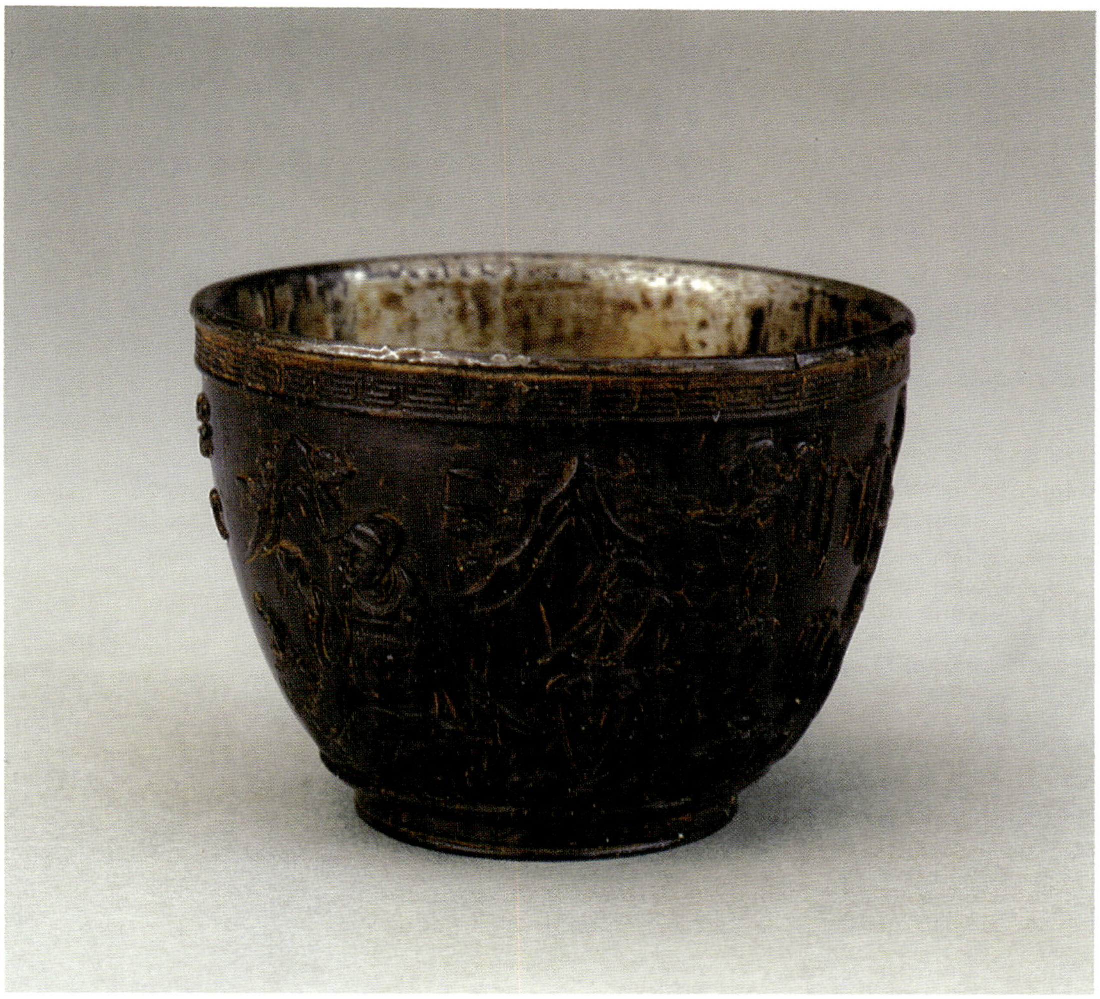

Larger than life size

257

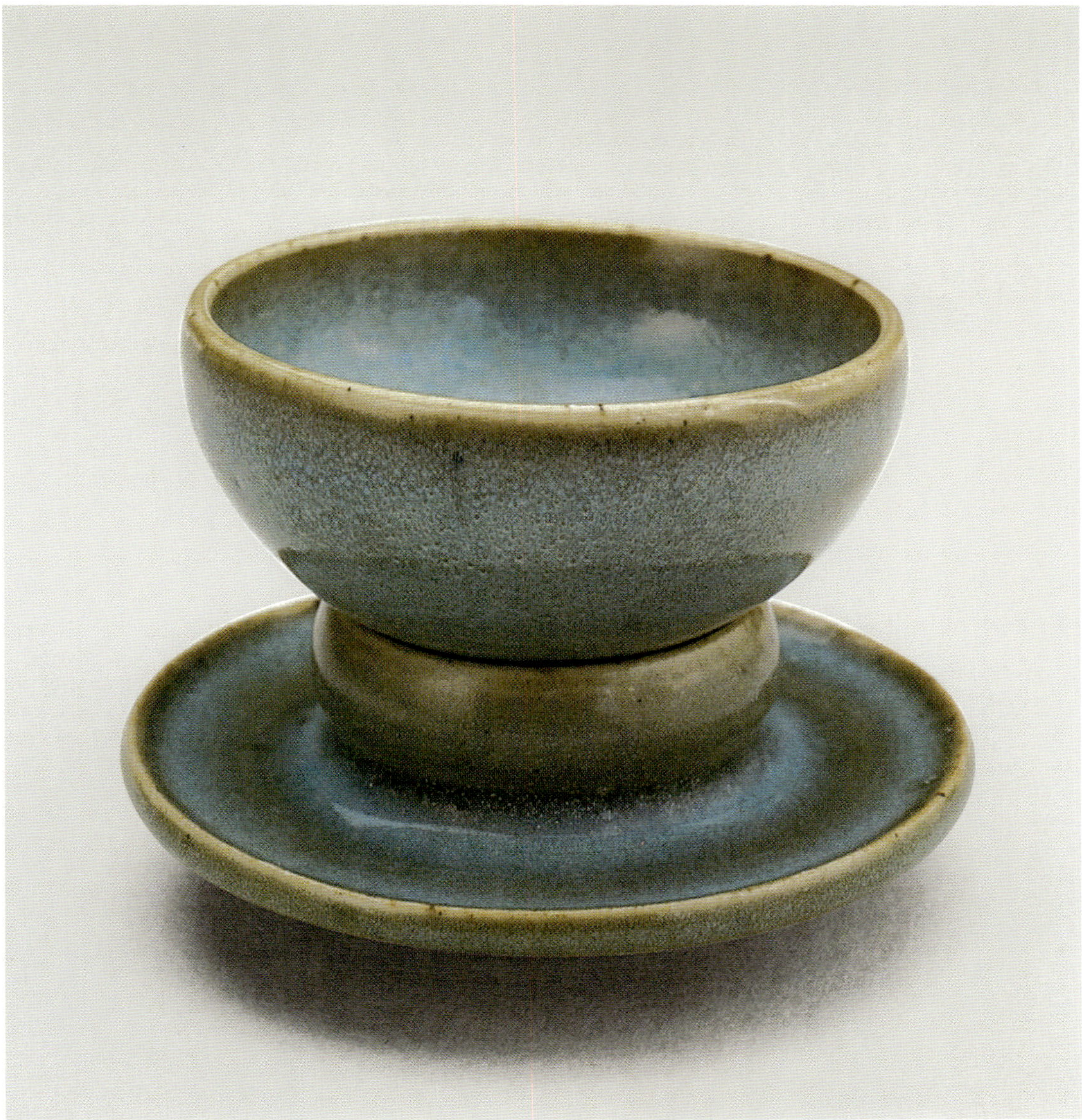

Larger than life size

258

Drinking Vessel

Rhinoceros horn, of variegated rich, golden brown and dark brown colour; a drinking vessel carved in the form of a small *yi* pouring jug of asymmetrical shape, standing on a flared, oval foot; the handle in the form of a *chi* dragon, pulling itself over the rim of the vessel; a central band of decoration consisting of eight whorl motifs set against a multiple *leiwen* ground; the base inscribed with the two characters *Zhizheng* (the reign title adopted from 1341-1368 by the last ruler of the Yuan dynasty).
Possibly Yuan dynasty, 1341-1368.
3.5 cm × 7.7 cm × 5.7 cm.

犀角雕螭杯•至正銘
可能元至正(1341-1368), 3.5×7.7×5.7厘米

Despite their often eccentric shapes, rhinoceros horn vessels were apparently used as drinking cups. There is a popular tale that the horn was capable of detecting certain poisons which might have marginally encouraged their use, but we may assume that generations of the influential minority in China did not live their lives in the daily expectation of being poisoned. In Han dynasty Tomb No. 1 at Mawangdui a wooden substitute for a rhinoceros horn cup was excavated, of elongated, horn shape.[1] By the Tang dynasty these elongated horns were supplemented by smaller natural horn shapes, or by worked horns of simple designs.[2] A long horn, which may or may not be of the rhinoceros but which demonstrates usage, appears on the plectrum guard of a seven-stringed musical instrument, also in the *Shoso-in* (see sketch of relevant detail, Fig. 1).

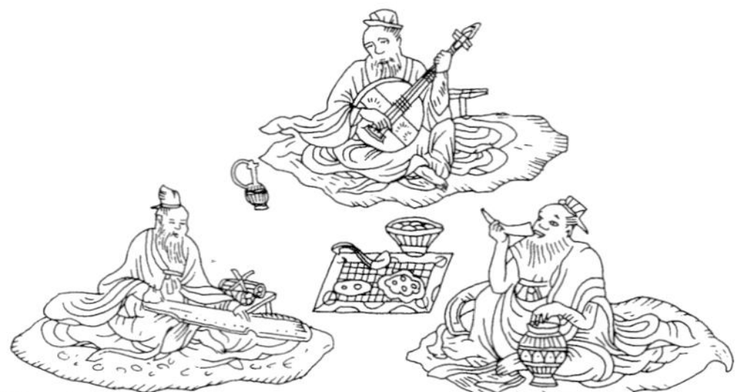
Fig. 1

It seems difficult to imagine that it took the Chinese a thousand years to decide to decorate the surfaces of their rhinoceros horn drinking cups, but from what little evidence there is that would seem to be the case. By the Yuan or early Ming dynasty decorated cups had become the standard form, frequently standing on a distinct foot or flattened surface. A typical later cup appears to be held in the hands of Nalan Xingde in a portrait by Yu Zhiding (1647-1716), the Yangzhou painter.[3] The fact that it is of pale colour is perhaps due to the darkness of the robe against which it is held — it may even be a porcelain copy of a rhinoceros horn cup, but it still demonstrates its use. See Fig. 2 for a drawing.

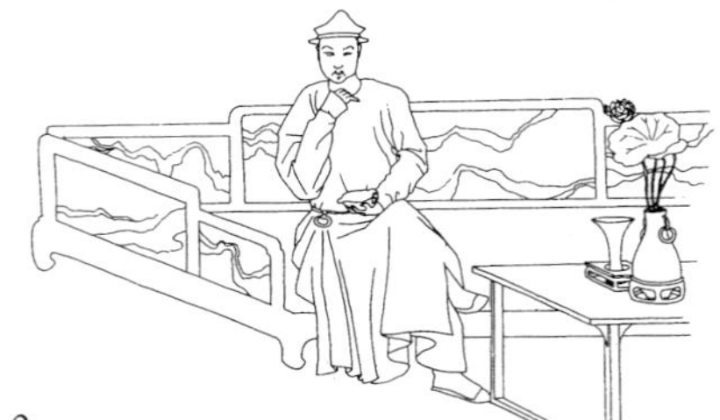
Fig. 2

Although many later rhinoceros horn cups may appear to be pouring vessels these were standard drinking cups in China. The *jue,* a ritual wine vessel from antiquity which would seem to be a pouring vessel, was also used for drinking well into the Qing dynasty, as is proven by a number of genre paintings and illustrated books.

According to the *Liji* (*Book of Rites*) a rhinoceros horn cup was used in the game of throwing arrows into a vase (see no. 264) in antiquity, and this practice may have continued. This was a favourite game of the later literati and they would all have been familiar with the contents of the *Liji.* It is possible that the large number of later rhinoceros horn cups were made in response to their correct usage as outlined in this work, which would account for these cups remaining an art form centred around the literati for so long.

This unusual small vessel bears a reign mark of the last years of the Yuan dynasty, the authenticity of which is not beyond question. However, it certainly fits in with the type of horn one would expect of the period, as described in the *Gegu Yaolun* (see no. 159). It is decoratively quite acceptable for the period, and we believe it should be given serious consideration.

1. *'Guwenwu Zhongsuojianzhi Xiniu',* by Sun Ji, in *Wenwu,* 1982, no. 8, pp.80-84.
2. For Tang cups in the *Shoso-in* collection in Japan, see *Chinese Art,* Vol 4, p.204, p.123, a and b.
3. *Paintings by Yangzhou Artists of the Qing Dynasty from the Palace Museum,* p.124.

259

Hand Exercisers

Walnuts, of rich orange brown colour; a pair of hand exercisers, the shells of the nuts carved, retaining the original form, with panels of decoration exploiting the irregularity of the surfaces; each of the four panels carved with five symbolic creatures, the titles for each, 'Five Poisonous Creatures' (toad, lizard, scorpion, snake and centipede), 'Five Rats', 'Five Lions' and 'Five Birds', inscribed in a small panel at the upper edge where the two sides of the shells meet; the various creatures described shown amidst a number of different plants and trees.
Mid- to late Qing dynasty.
Height: 4.7 cm. each.
Published: *Wood From the Scholar's Table,* p.166, no. 112.

雕鳥獸蛇蟲核桃一對
清中至晚期, 高各4.7厘米

To keep the hands supple and dexterous (a useful aid in calligraphy) exercisers were frequently used. These consisted of two small objects, pebbles, balls, or walnuts such as these, which were passed around one hand, manipulating the fingers, the idea being that they should not touch each other in the process. This was a practice by no means limited to the literati, but like so much in Chinese art their involvement tended to encourage the introduction of aesthetic flights of fancy and arcane symbolism which manifested itself in a simple, practical tool evolving as an art form. These small exercisers abound from the Qing dynasty, although we know of none which could be confidently dated to an earlier period, and the walnut was a popular material for them.

The Qing saw a vogue for 'clever' carving, perhaps inspired by the often extraordinary excesses of the Qianlong Emperor's palace workshops output (see no. 96), although it is just as likely that Qing production generally was responding to a general shift in taste towards technical cleverness for its own sake. During the mid- to late Qing there was a vogue for minutely detailed carving on peach stones, walnuts and various other fruit seeds, which aimed at ever more unlikely demonstrations of technical ability. The culmination came with the late 19th century art of incising on ivory, where carvers were capable of writing the Diamond Sutra on so tiny a scale that a high-powered lens was needed to read it (see no. 27). In this artistic technocracy tasteless exhibitionism was inevitable; that the Chinese managed frequently to rise above it and imbue the most unlikely arts with a degree of artistic integrity is perhaps a measure of the deep influence the literati, with their grasp of the nature of art, exercised over the country's artistic production at all levels.

The carving of peach stones, walnuts, etc., as miniature crafts is the subject of an article, illustrating a walnut shell carving by Chen Ziyun, in the *National Palace Museum Monthly of Chinese Art,* no. 14, 1985, pp.108-110.

260

Folding-Fan Cases

Embroidered silk; two fan cases; one decorated with a poetic inscription and four seals, beneath formalized *ruyi* heads, the cord with pink glass beads; the other simulating a partially wrapped *qin,* complete with its tassles; the wrapping decorated with lilies, *lingzhi* fungus, and two further tassles, the cord with elaborate knots as beads.
Late Qing dynasty.
Length: 32.2 cm and 30.5 cm respectively.

織錦摺扇袋二件
晚清, 長32.2厘米及30.5厘米

The fan was a standard Chinese accoutrement, used by the highest and lowest in the land. From a simple leaf to the elaborate productions of the palace workshops, in either fixed or folding forms, the fan was standard for centuries. In later times the folding fan became the favourite of the scholar class, not only as a functional form, but as a vehicle for their painting and calligraphy. Folding fans are said to have been invented as early as the 7th century in Japan, but were apparently not introduced to China until the 11th century.[1] They became extremely popular in Ming times and continued throughout the Qing as the favoured form.

These cases, with their literati allusions to the *qin,* poetry and fanciful seals are typical of very large numbers made during the Qing period. They enabled the folding fan to be suspended conveniently from the belt along with various other portable accoutrements.

The first of the seals on one of the fan cases may be translated as "The hills are bright, the sky beyond distant." The other seals are also of the fanciful variety: "Wandering clouds and flowing waters"; "A fine time on the third day of the third moon" (a reference to a well-known Tang poem) and "Facing the wine you should sing" (meaning that opportunities for happiness should be eagerly embraced).

1. *Ming and Ch'ing Exotica: A Reflection of Literary Taste,* by Chuang Shen, in *Journal of Oriental Studies,* Centre of Asian Studies, Hong Kong University Press, Vol. IX, No. 1. 1971, p.126.

258

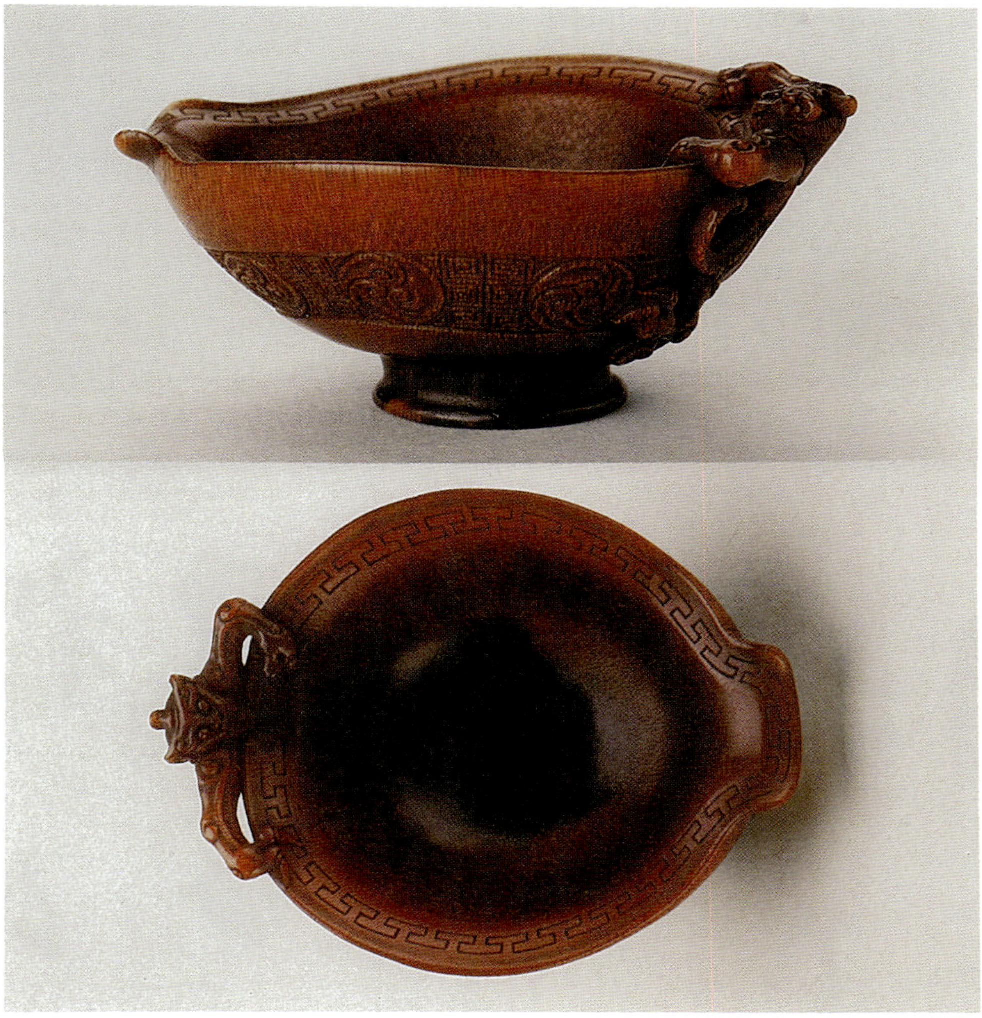

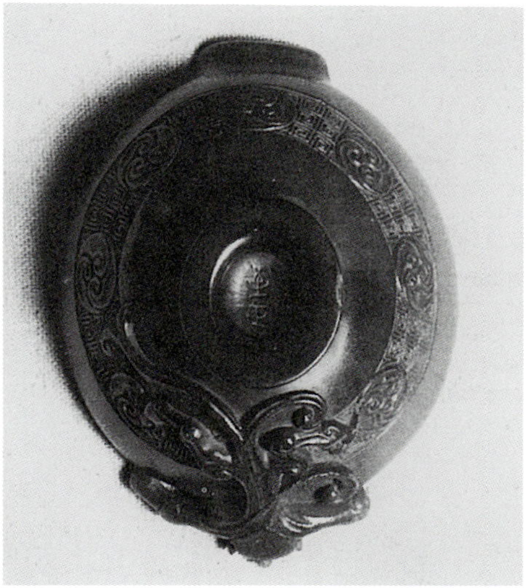

259

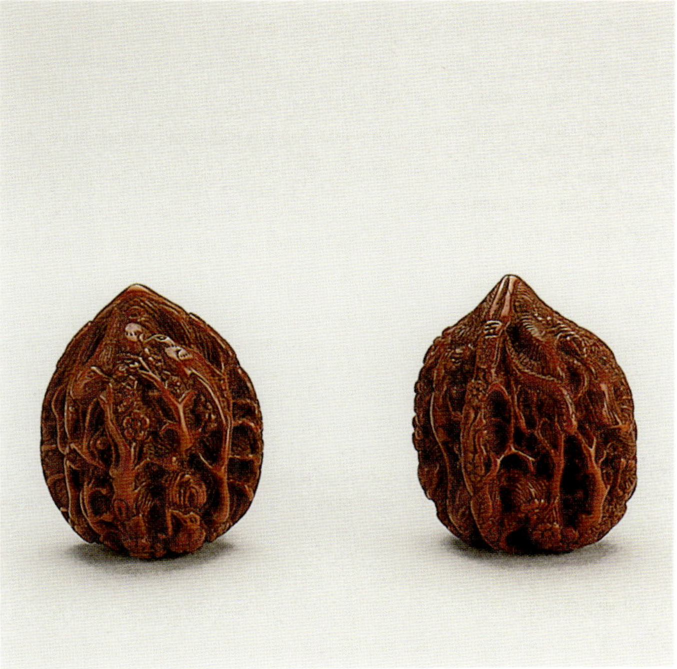

260

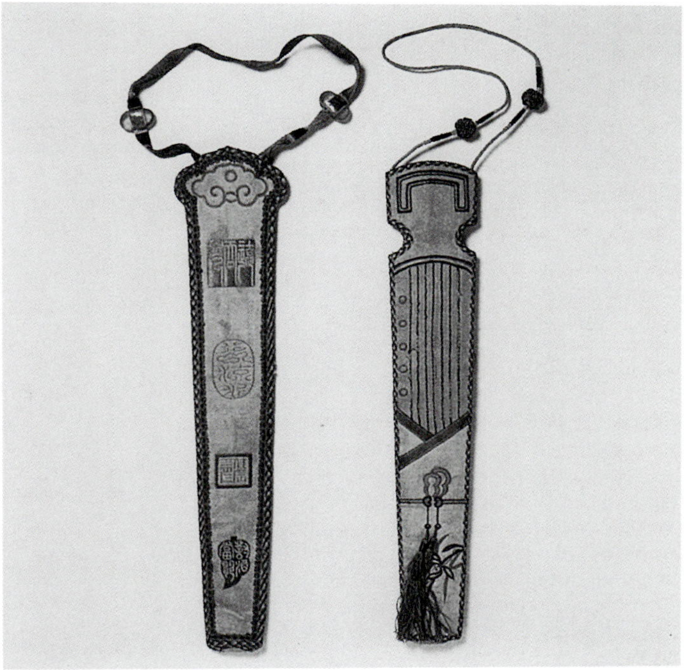

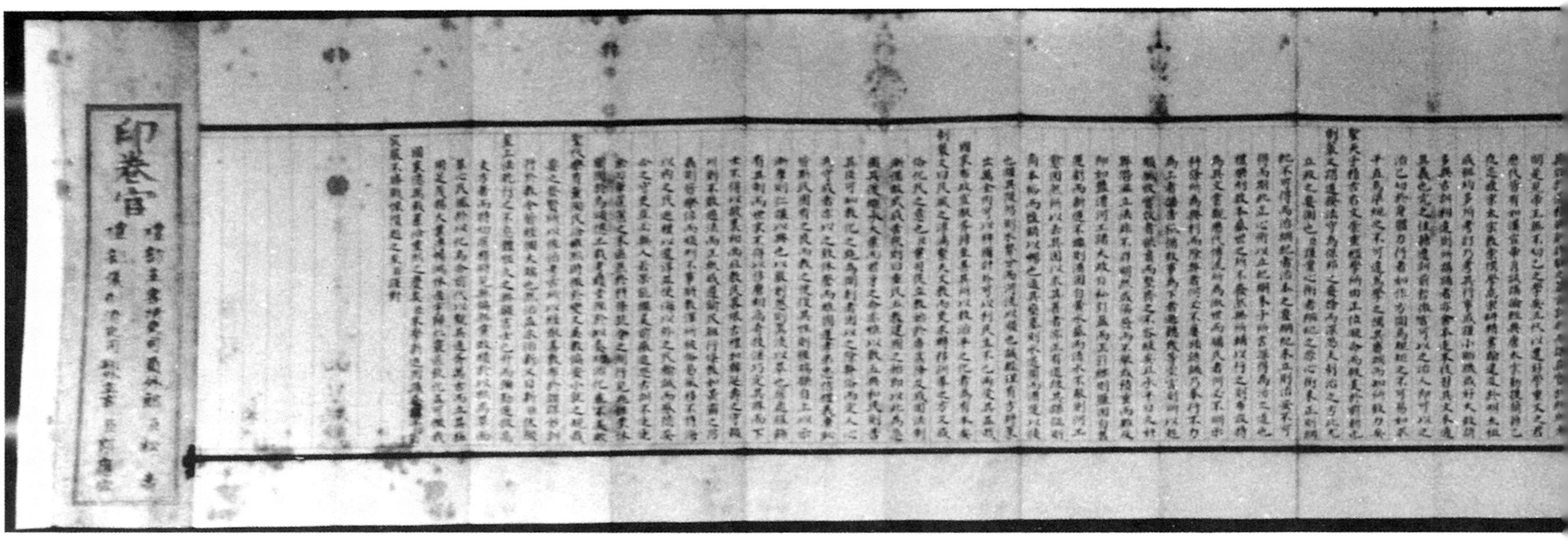

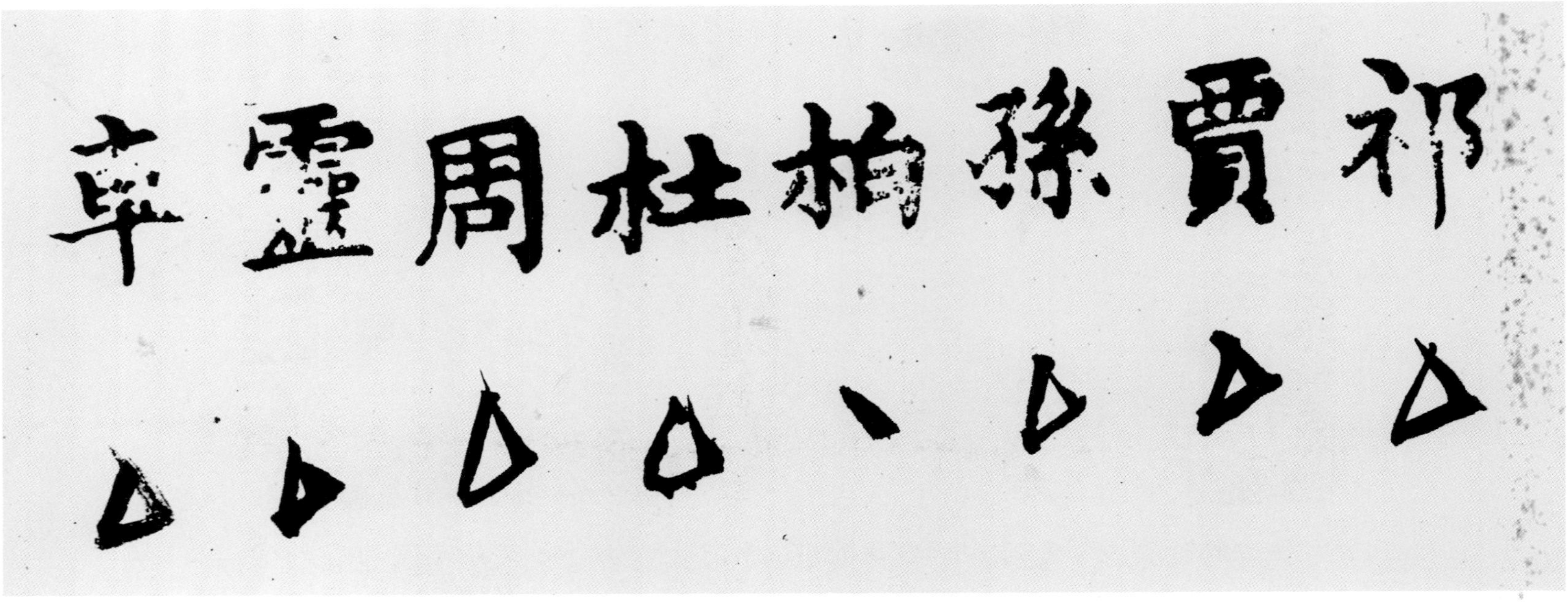

261

Imperial Examination Paper

Xu Yinggui

Ink on pre-printed, thick paper, the paper printed with double upper and lower margins and verticle red lines; it is folded into 22 pages; an imperial examination paper.
Front cover: inscribed by the candidate "Taking the imperial examination is your loyal servant Xu Yinggui, a *juren*." With official seal of the Ministry of Rites. The final position in the examination marked in red ink: "The fifth position in the third class of honours".
Page one: Inscription by the candidate: "Your servant, *juren* Xu Yinggui, aged eighteen, a native of Panyu district, Guangzhou *fu*, Guangdong. I took the district examination as a graduate student (from a government school) and passed in the twenty-ninth year of Daoguang (1849). I took the provincial capital examination and passed as a *juren* in the thirtieth year of Daoguang (1850). Now I take the imperial examination and I list the background of my ancestors: great-grandfather, Yongming; grandfather, Gengyang; father Liguang."
Page two: blank.
Page three: half an official seal and serial number (remains of a system for ensuring confidentiality of papers).
Page four: the remains of a flimsy sealing paper.
Pages five to 19: The examination essay written in the *bagu* ('eight heads') format in which the theme was treated under eight headings.
Page 20: blank.
Back cover: bearing the name and title of the official of the Ministry of Rites responsible for printing the examination paper.

At the back of page three are the remains of the thin sealing paper which was attached to the front of page four, with two seals of the Sealing Official. When this flimsy was in place, the beginning of the examination paper was sealed, keeping confidential the details of the candidate, but leaving the essay itself accessible, ensuring that those who mark the papers are not influenced by knowing the examinee's identity. There is also a yellow paper glued to this page stating the result: "The fifth position in the third class of honours".
At the back of page 20 there appears the pre-stamped surnames of eight examiners, their markings given in code (A=a circle; B=a triangle; C=a dot; D=a vertical stroke and E=a cross). The candidate received seven B's and one C.
1850.
44 cm × 11.4 cm (when folded, ie. each folded sheet is 11.4 cm wide).

殿試試卷•許應騤書
清道光三十年(1850),總大44×11.4厘米

During the Ming and Qing dynasties the examination system for scholars became standardized. Whoever passed the examination at the district level became a *xiucai;* at the provincial level (held at the provincial capital) a *juren* and at the national level (held at the national capital) a *jinshi.* The examinations for *xiucai* were held annually; for *juren,* triennially, and for *jinshi* occasionally (in the Ming dynasty they were held 88 times, and in the Qing 111 times, including special examinations for various reasons, which the Emperor might decide upon). The eight-headed essay became a fixed form in the early Ming dynasty and was not abandoned until 1901.

Xu Yinggui (*zi:* Yunan — 1832-1903) was appointed a minister of the Ministry of Works in 1896 and in the next year was transferred as a minister to the Ministry of Rites. For one year in 1898 he was the Commissioner of Fujian and Zhejiang provinces. Although his marks were not extraordinary in obtaining his *jinshi* degree, he was only 18 years old at the time, and many scholars were still attempting this degree late in their lives. It should also be noted that he took his *jinshi* degree in the same year as having become a *juren.* His essay is written in a strict, regular script without a single careless stroke or error.

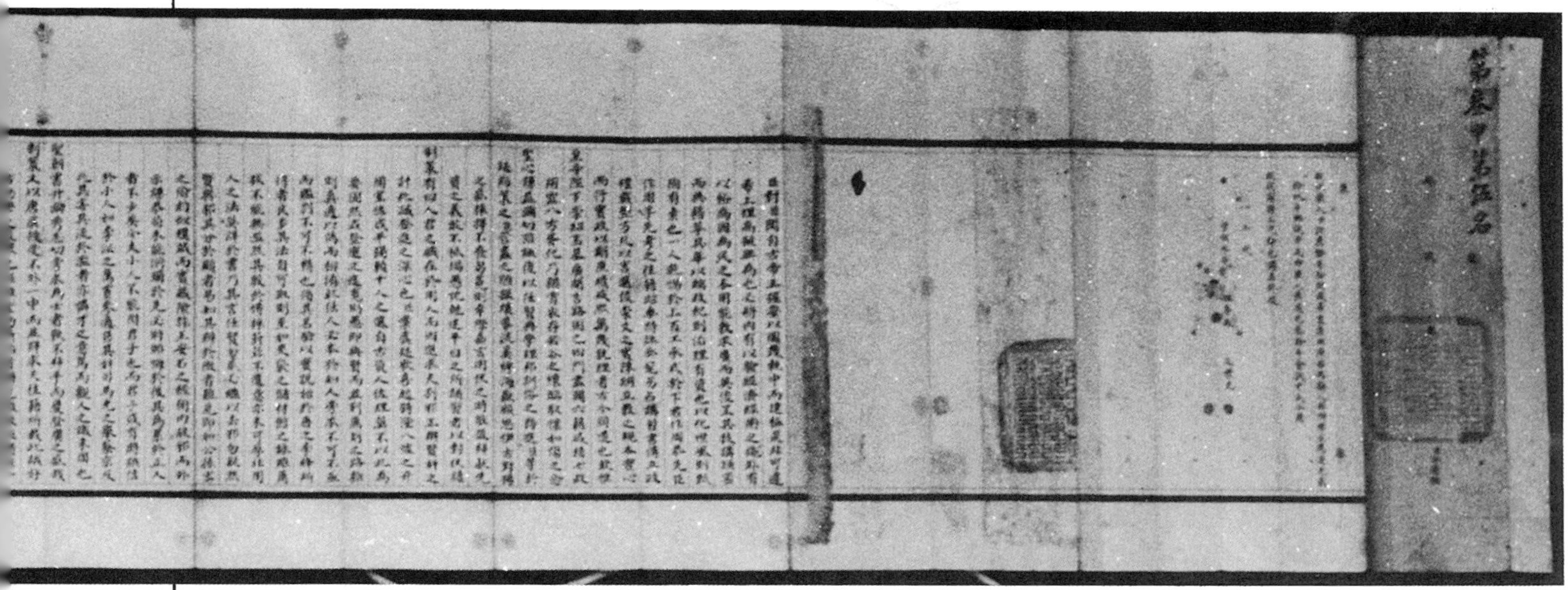

261

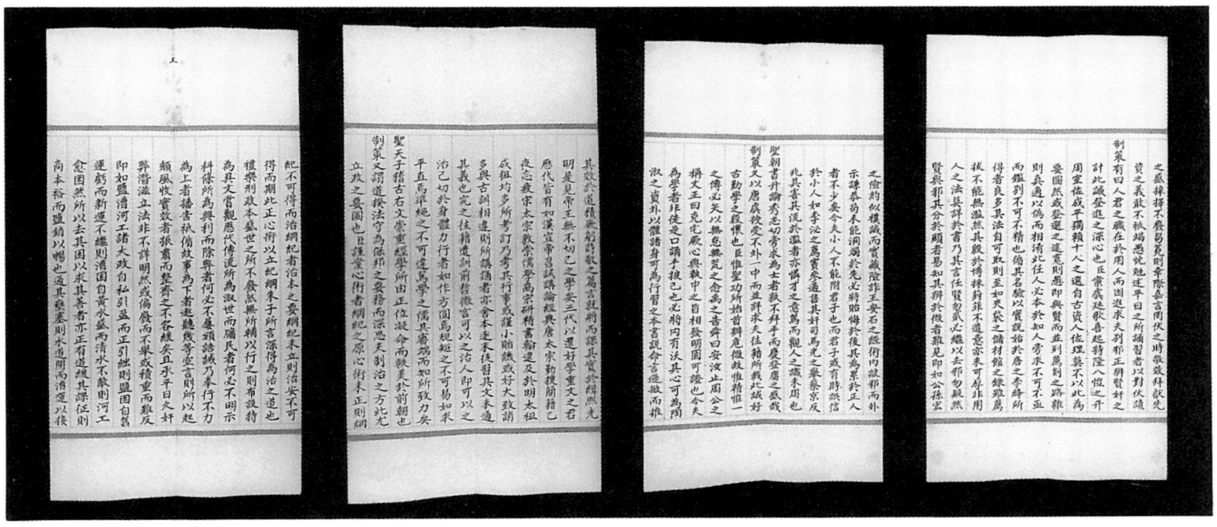

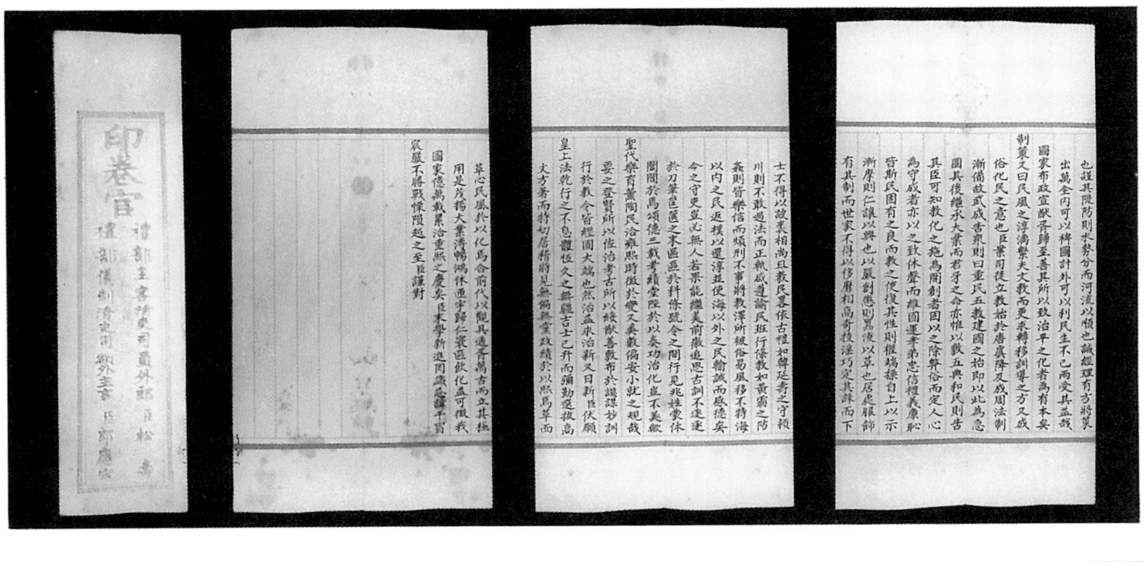

262

Cheat's Handkerchief

Silk, inscribed in ink; a handkerchief, both sides covered in minute calligraphy with selections from the Classics.
Probably late Qing dynasty.
41.2 cm × 41.2 cm.

小楷應試作弊手帕
可能晚清，41.2×41.2厘米

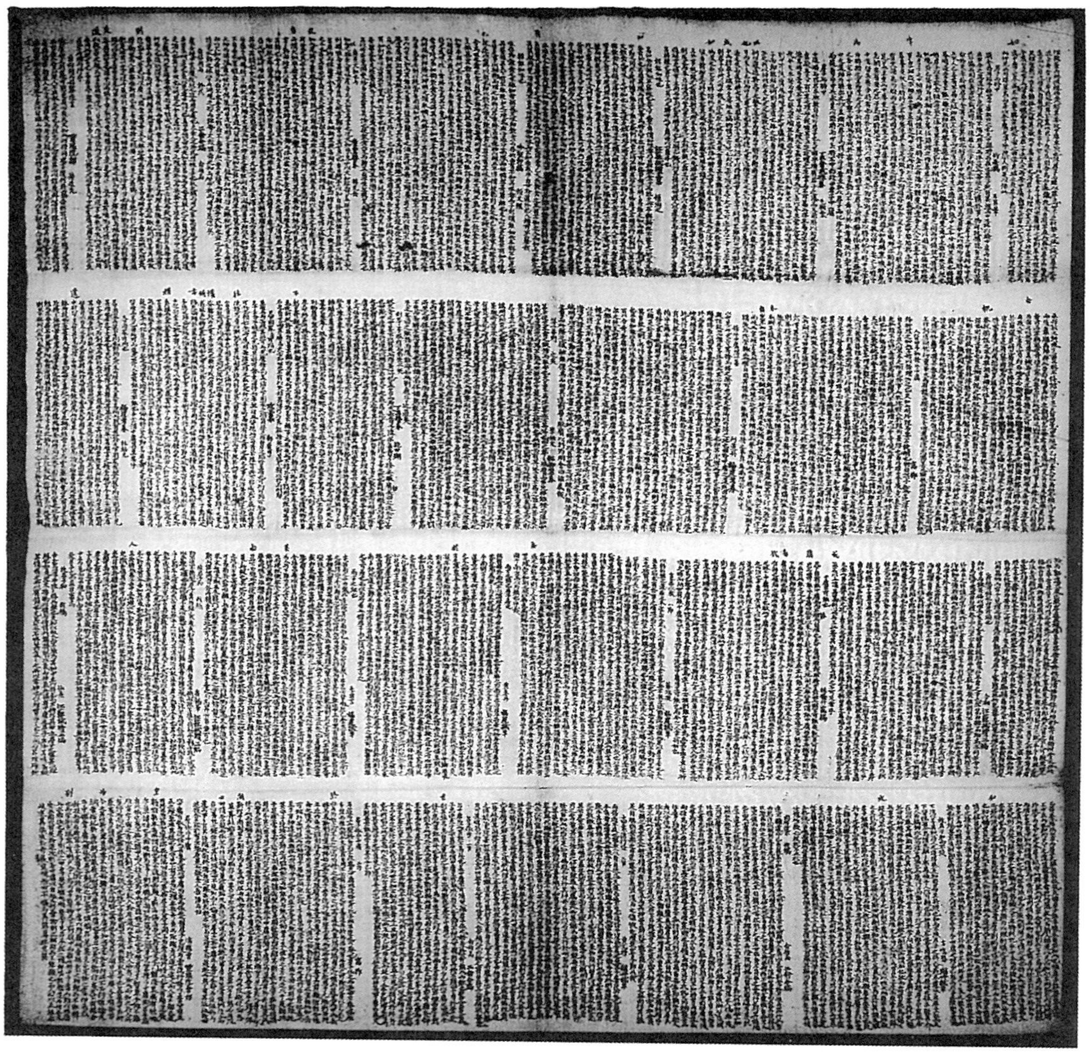

The imperial examinations took place under rigidly enforced conditions to prevent entrants from cheating. Each entrant was assigned to an individual cell and allowed to carry in with him only the basic essentials of ink, inkstone, brush etc. and throughout the lengthy examination process no communciation was permitted. Human nature being what it is, people constantly found methods of cheating, either by corrupting the examiners or attendants, or by tricking them in some manner. The basis for the imperial examinations was a knowledge of the Classics; the frequent quotations from them, supposedly from memory, were supposed to be exact, demonstrating complete familiarity. Frequently large sections of them were transcribed carefully onto various parts of the entrant's clothing, despite the disgrace and punishments for cheating, which were severe. Here a candidate has managed to cover both sides of his handkerchief with a minute transcription.

A brief insight into the examination system may be found in *A Scholar in Imperial China* by T.C. Lai, together with various examination papers and their translations.

263

Pair of *Weiqi* Boxes

Wood, *hongmu* ('redwood') of well-figured, rich reddish-brown colour; a pair of compressed globular boxes and covers to contain *weiqi* pieces; the bodies with plain central bands enclosed by continuous bands of formalized lappets, the covers with similar decoration enclosing central motifs based loosely upon the shape of Chinese cash. Containing *weiqi* pieces of black and greenish-white glass.
Qing dynasty.
Height: 7.9 cm. Diameter of body: 13.4 cm.

紅木棋子蓋盒
清代，高7.9厘米，身直徑13.4厘米

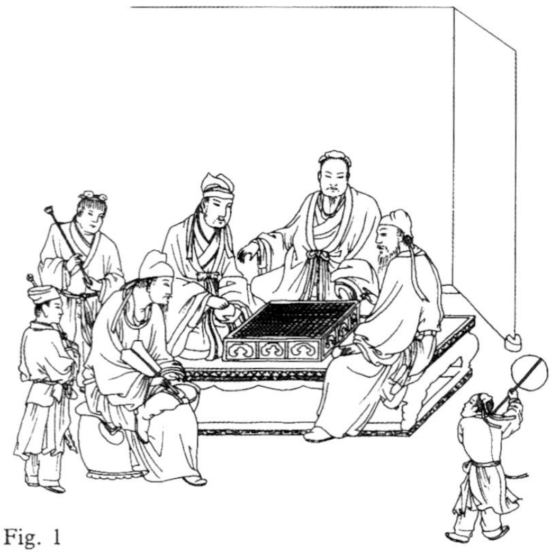

Fig. 1

Weiqi was a game beloved of well-educated Chinese for centuries. It is recorded as early as the 7th century BC in Chinese writings[1] and continued to intrigue the literati into modern times. It appears to be a fairly simple game, but is really very difficult, its mastery requiring a high degree of mental sophistication. It was considered to be the noblest of all games. The object of the game is to occupy as much territory on the board as possible by alternately placing a piece on a point; areas which are then surrounded by one player's piece count as his territory, including empty spaces so enclosed. Enemy pieces may be captured by enclosing them, thus acquiring all their previously occupied territory as well. It is a game of subtle strategy.

Like the game of *taohu* (throwing arrows into an arrow vase) winning is only a minor part of the matter. The nuances of how the game is played are of considerable importance, as are the analogies of life in the complex strategy involved, played out at many levels.

Weiqi pieces have traditionally been kept in boxes such as these, with curved interior surfaces, allowing pieces to be easily scooped out one by one. Fig. 1 shows a game of *weiqi* in progress from an anonymous Song painting, one of a set showing various scholars at different pursuits;[2] the player on the left is about to select a piece from a box similar in form to these examples. The board shown is the traditional one, which occurs so frequently in genre paintings that it is disappointing that we were unable to find one for this exhibition.

1. See *Encyclopaedia Sinica.*
2. See *l'Eunuque aux Trois Joyaux: Collectonneurs et Esthetes Chinois,* p.79, no. 49.

262

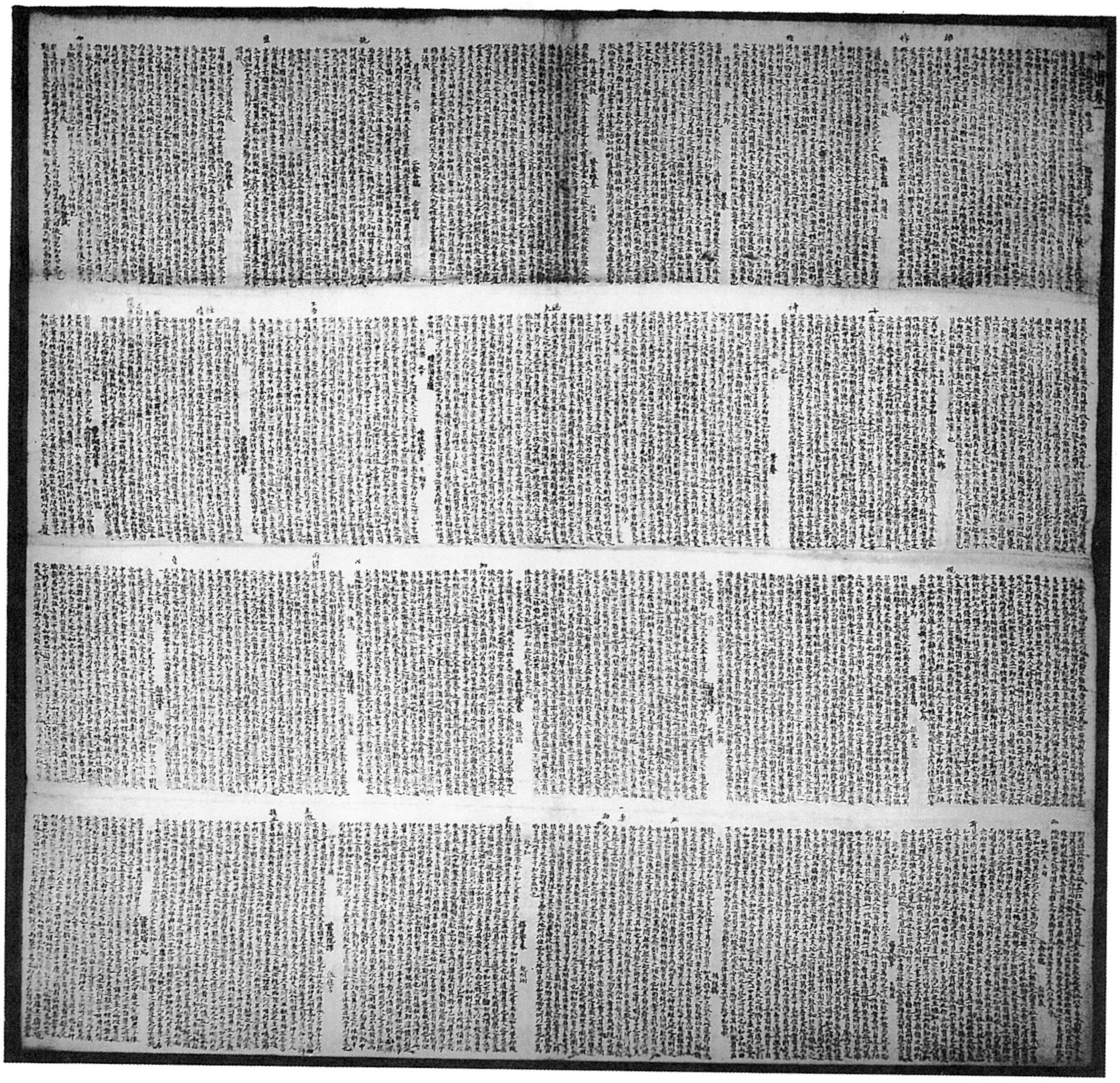

263

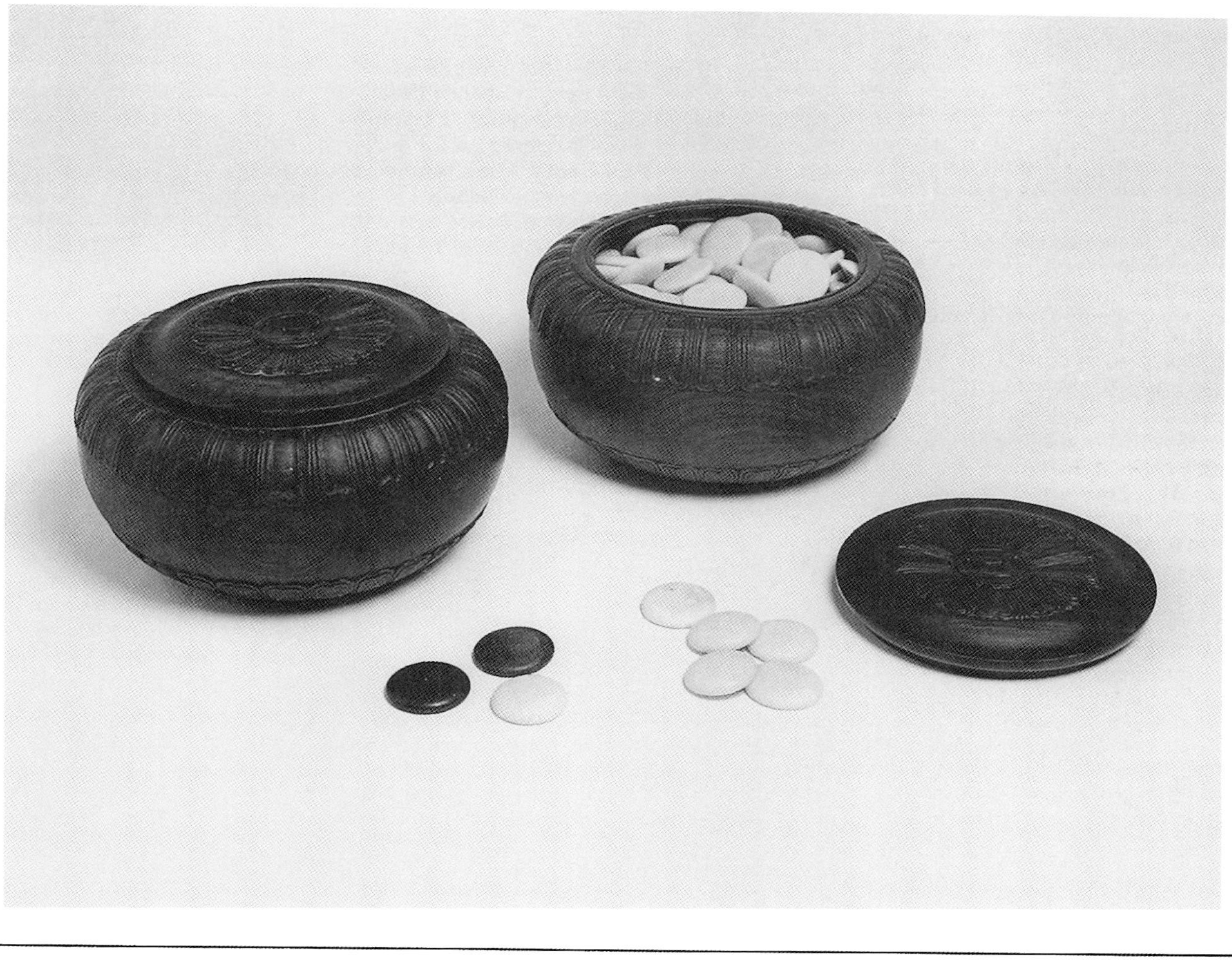

264

Arrow Vase

Bronze, partly gilt; an arrow vase for the game of *taohu;* the globular body with four vertical flanges separating panels of design of a dragon chasing a flaming pearl above waves, alternating with Buddhist lions playing with brocaded balls, with various precious symbols amidst clouds; the shoulders with a continuous band of scrolling Indian lotus leading to a flanged joint from which an elongated neck arises, which is decorated with two formalized, patterned grounds, the lower of interlocking swastikas, the upper of square floral motifs, a *chi* dragon in relief curling around the upper section, the lip with two attached cylinders echoing the form of the mouth, the three areas decorated with *taotie* mask motifs; the body set on a deep, flared foot, with a straight flange decorated with a continuous design of scrolling *lingzhi* fungus; various details and certain areas all gilt.
16th century.
Height: 50 cm.

鎏金龍戲珠紋貫耳壺
十六世紀, 高50厘米

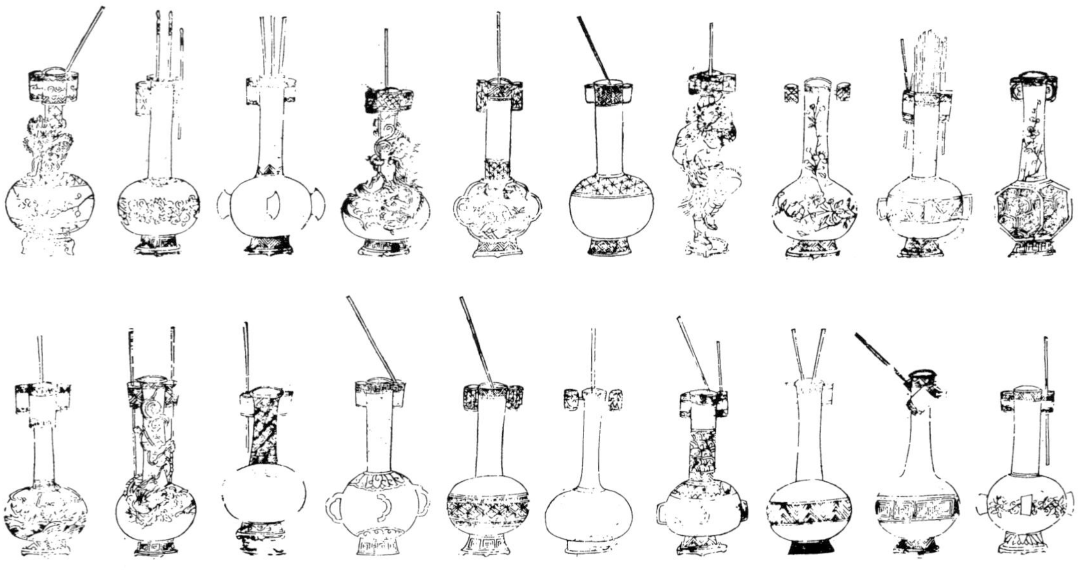

Fig. 1

The arrow vase was for the game of *taohu,* where arrows are thrown by hand into the three necks of the vase — although the number of necks can vary. This is an ancient game arising out of the time when archery was one of the six arts of the accomplished gentleman (see p.23). The *Liji* (*Book of Rites*), one of the Classics, goes into considerable detail about the game and it is clear that even at that remote time it was a game of considerable complexity, not so much in the fairly simple task of throwing the arrows into the various position of the neck, nor even in the different possible combinations of scoring, but in the complications of etiquette involved — hence the lengthy section in the *Liji.* Like all pastimes adopted by the literati the game became not so much a game to be won or lost, but a vehicle for complex ritual. It is beyond the scope of this work to go into the details of the game, but it is worth exploring a little just to indicate its intricacies.

If play is between two people, they each have a number of arrows. The senior person playing places his on the ground, something the younger player should not do, out of deference. They are thrown one by one, and the process repeated for the allotted number of games until a winner is declared. If the winner is the senior his attendant will pour a drink, which the loser will kneel and consume. However, if the junior wins, he would not dare ask his senior to kneel, expecting him only to raise his loser's cup. It becomes more complicated if the host is the junior, and so forth. If the senior drinks it will be from a rhinoceros horn cup, which the junior will not dare to emulate, using a *jue* instead. With more than one player there are more rules allowing for certain low scorers to be incorporated as the game progresses with the higher scorers, thus allowing them to be taken over by those with higher marks, unless of course it is a senior who has the lower score, in which case the rules change, and so on. The game is more concerned with accuracy of ritual and etiquette than with accuracy of eye and arrow, and has survived for so long intact because it is ultimately, like Zen archery, a game aimed directly at self-cultivation through ritual.

Fig. 1 shows a series of arrow vases from the *Sancai Tuhui* of 1607, where the game is explained at length, and indicates the types of archaistic vessels existing by the early 17th century, including one that looks somewhat like this example, and the possible permutations of arrow placing.

265

Duster

Wood, lacquer and horsehair; a duster, the handle covered with a thick coating of deep red lacquer; set with horsehair decoratively mounted with a succession of elaborate knots and bindings, also of horsehair.
Probably Qing dynasty.
Maximum length, including hairs: 60.5 cm.

紅漆木柄馬尾塵拂
可能清代, 總長60.5厘米

The duster, or flywhisk as they are sometimes called, has already been discussed (see no. 117). They were not used in the conventional sense of dusting; the term refers more to idly flicking than to housework. Although they served a practical purpose as flywhisks, they were also elegant extensions of the wrist for the influential minority, used to add emphasis to movements and to statements — a gestural aid. Such dusters or whisks were also used as symbols of authority in master-disciple situations, where the teaching master would hold the duster as an indication that he was going to do the talking.[1]

Their role is perhaps best summed up by one of the charming illustrations to the *Sancai Tuhui,* showing the pursuits of the elegant mind. One shows a sage with a whisk, and the title is simply 'Dusting' — meaning idling in the wilderness, pondering weighty matters while lightly flicking the duster (for other illustrations see Figs. 1-10, pp.27-28). Also from the same encyclopaedia we illustrate an elaborate duster (Fig. 1 — along with a *ruyi* sceptre). They are frequently seen in genre paintings, and Fig. 2 shows a drawing taken from a Ming painting of a scholar seated among a host of literati playthings, holding the type of duster where the hairs are contained in a separate holder linked to the handle by a chain.[2]

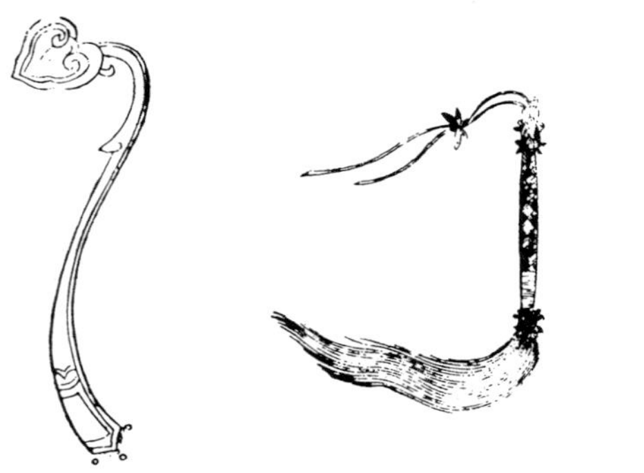

Fig. 1

A principle appeal of these simple gnarled wood and horsehair dusters is in the complex knotting techniques which both decorate and strengthen the join between horsehair and wood. This example is made up of two layers of interlinked knots enclosing a central large knot, the horsehair being divided into tufts which are retained by cylindrical bindings, attaching to the root handle by way of the various knots. The whole structure, while being extremely decorative and intriguing in its complexity, provides a very stable bond.

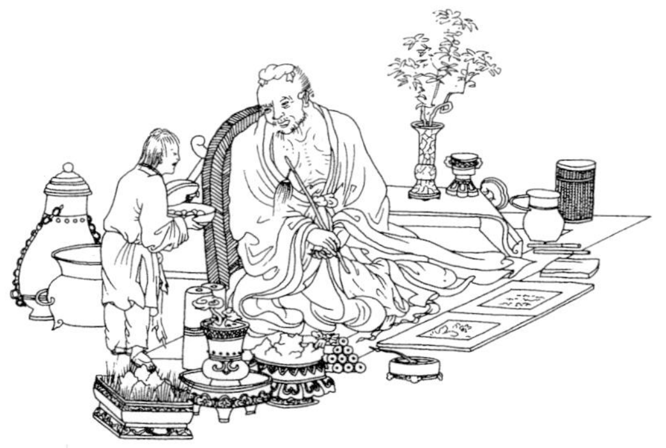

Fig. 2

1. In a contemporary biography of the artist Zhu Da (see no. 32) by Shao Changheng, we are told of Zhu's entry into a Buddhist monastery where "After only a few years he held the whisk in his hand and was honoured as a teacher." *(Chinese Masters of the Seventeenth Century).*
2. Taken from *Gugong Zhoukan (Palace Museum Bulletin),* Beijing, 1936, pp.401-425.

264

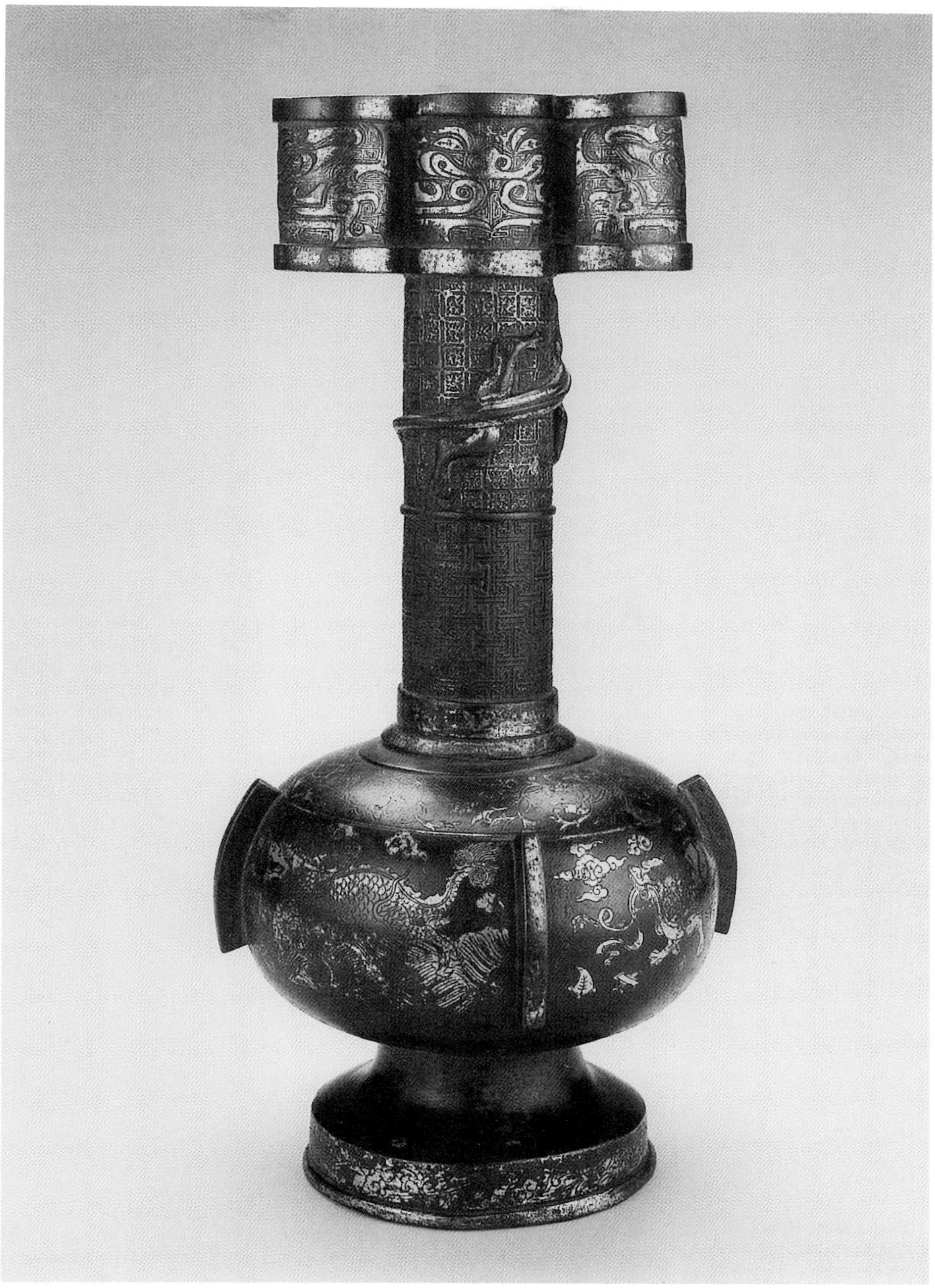

265

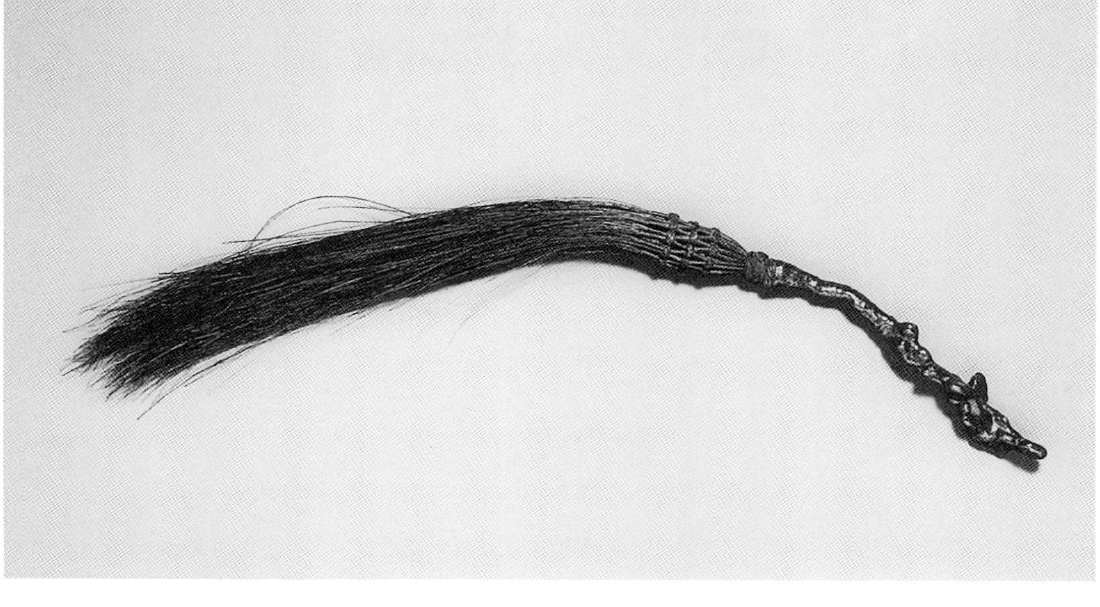

266

'Companion to the Inkstone' Rock Sculpture

Stone, of sandy-beige colour and elongated shape; inscribed in a smoothed panel low on one side: "Lone peak standing upright by the side of the inkstone"; set in a wood stand, the upper section of which is carved to represent gnarled wood.
Probably Qing dynasty.
Height, including stand: 37.5 cm.

石雕孤峰
可能清代，高連座37.5厘米

The title on this rock sculpture describes part of its function as envisaged by the inscriber of the stone, who may have been different from whoever first isolated it as a work of art. Here the rock is intended to be a companion to the inkstone, a sculpture to stand on the desk for the elegant enjoyment of the scholar while he grinds his ink, writes or paints.

The sources of sculptural stones were potentially limitless. Some were found ready for use as works of art without further ado: river pebbles or rocks or a strangely shaped specimen simply lying on the ground, for instance. Others needed no more than a little polishing or 'editing', while at the other end of the scale were those which had to be quarried, cut away from unsuitable matrix materials, or artificially formed into eccentric shapes. The Chinese connoisseur, at least of the 12th century, seemed not to put any special premium on naturalness. Schafer tells us that in the *Stone Catalogue of Cloudy Forest* there are frequent references to the 'artistry' *(qiao)* of specimens needing to be enhanced by human hands and metal tools. Indeed, on larger stones for garden use monoliths were constructed of a number of different pieces of stone, as they still are today in Chinese gardens.

However, what was clearly required of such additional manipulation by man was that it ended up looking natural. The stones of Lake Tai (Grand Lake) were frequently cut and shaped and then re-immersed in the flowing waters of the lake to be naturally smoothed. Popular legend has it that sometimes such stones would be left for generations so that the contrived holes and grottoes in them became as naturally smoothed as those which were dug out of the lake with such natural configurations.

267

Landscape
Wang Zhu

Soapstone, of mottled dark brown and beige colour probably of the variety known simply as Shoushan stone; carved as a miniature landscape, with a village nestling amid tree-clad peaks, a stream tumbling down from the heights to form a river on which, on the other side of the mountain, a boat is moored. Signed *Wang Zhu.*
Probably late Ming dynasty.
Height: 7.6 cm. Length: 13.2 cm.

壽山石雕山水座•汪洙製
可能晚明，高7.6厘米，長13.2厘米

Although this piece was clearly meant to function as a brush rest (it even has the five peaked format of the traditional mountain brush rest — see no. 211), it also serves as a miniature landscape, allowing the scholar to wander in an idealized rustic setting without leaving his studio. The microcosmic landscape figured prominently in Chinese aesthetics, in strange stones, miniature trees (which in Japan were developed into *bonsai*), gardens laid out to represent the whole of nature, and miniature gardens and landscapes in trays, to be enjoyed around the house. These microcosmic landscapes were essentially retreats from the dusty world into which the scholar could project himself — some even gained a reputation for doing so physically. There are stories of magicians such as Xuan Jie, who lived in the Tang court and was supposed to have been able to disappear into a miniature landscape whenever he chose.[1]

This is one of only three pieces known which are signed by Wang Zhu (see no. 48), an unrecorded soapstone carver.

1. 'The Earthly Paradise: Religious Elements in Chinese Landscape Art', by Lothar Ledderose, in *Theories of the Arts in China,* p.175.

268

Mythical Animal

Turquoise, of well-patinated yellowish-green colour, with some brown patches, carved as a scholar's plaything, the beast curled up, looking back over its shoulders, the haunches with stylized flames, the bushy tail curled under the hind legs, the base fully carved.
Probably Ming or early Qing dynasty.
Height: 2.95 cm. Length: 3.8 cm.

綠松石雕異獸
可能明或清初，高2.95厘米，長3.8厘米

This miniature carving falls into the category of objects whose main role is simply as a scholar's trinket, a precious little item to have around, play with, carry about and, if occasion demands, press into service from time to time (although its small size makes its value as a paper weight doubtful).

Turquoise has been known to the Chinese since the Shang dynasty, when it was most often used as an inlay in bronze. In later times it appears to have been more often used in this manner, or as beads or inlaid precious stones (particularly in Buddhist sculptures of the post-archaic period). Early objects and sculpture are rare, although there has been a flood of carved turquoise from the modern period where an export demand has developed for Chinese carvings in obviously valuable and pretty materials.

It is a porous stone, which absorbs grease from the hand and turns from a bright turquoise colour to a pleasing variegated yellowish green, blue-green or sometimes brown colour through use, a characteristic of all early pieces made to be used. However excavated inlaid pieces may retain their original brightness of colour.

266

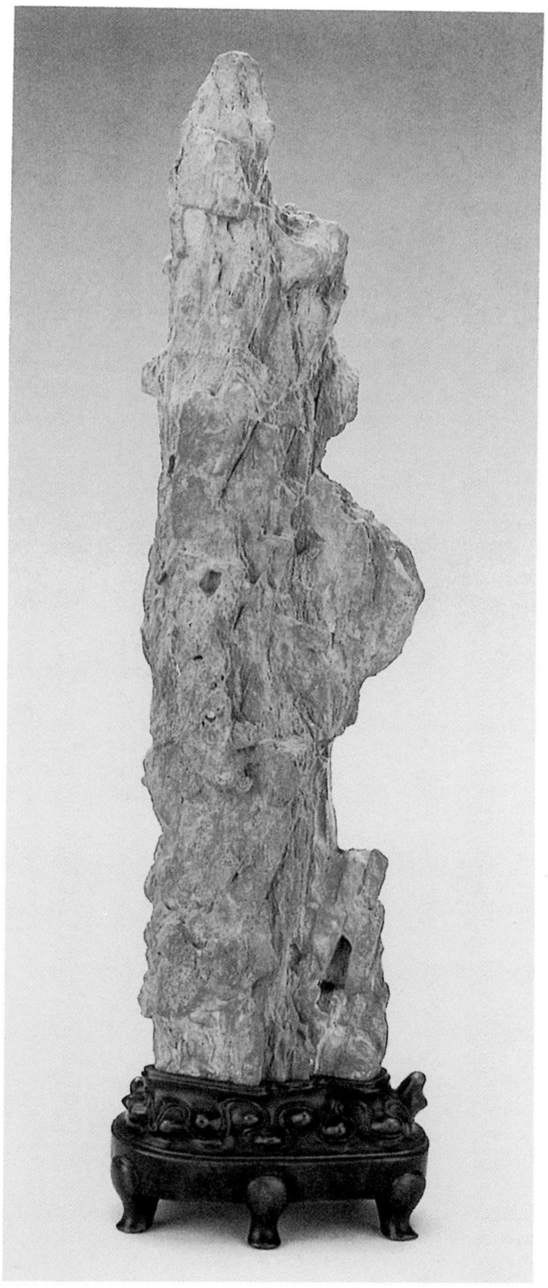

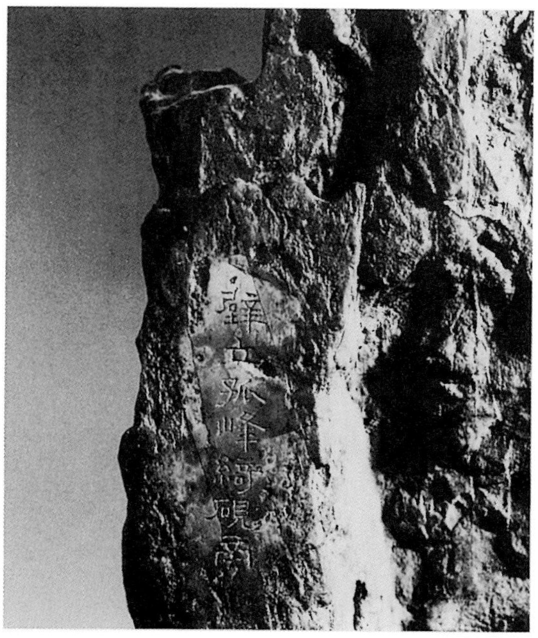

267

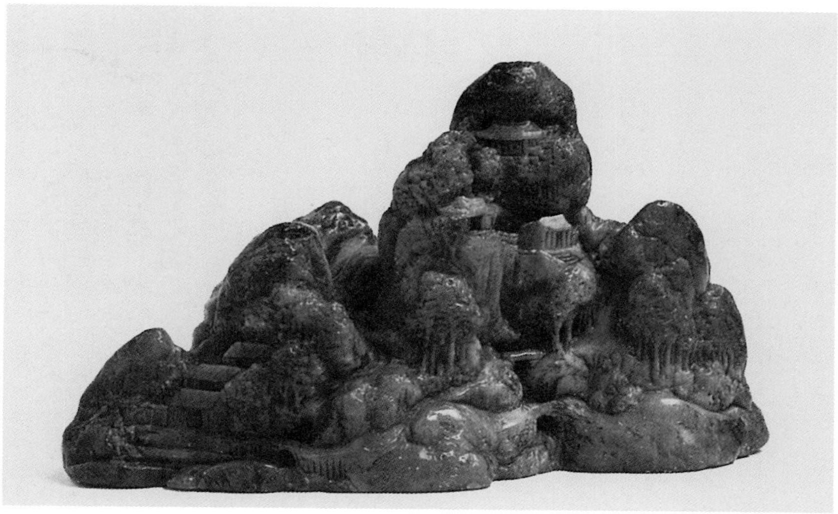

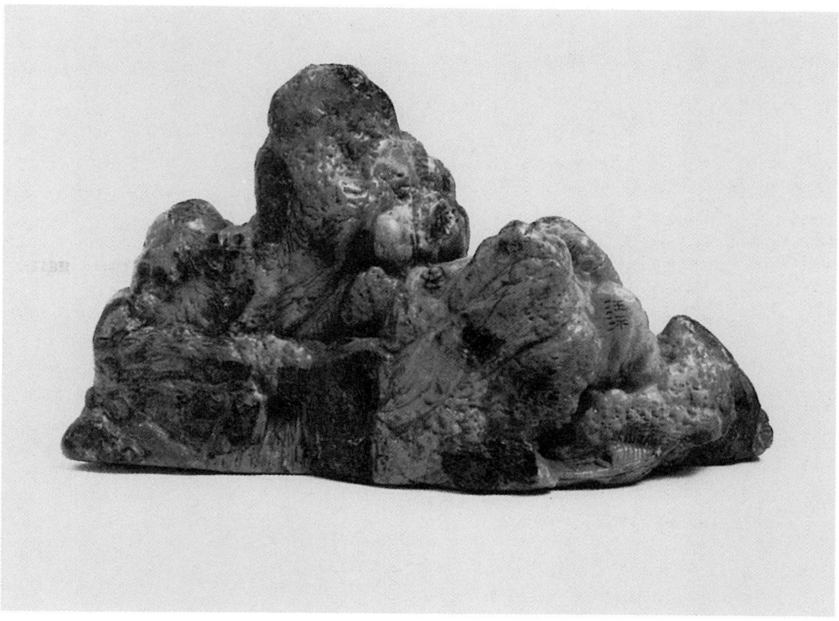

268

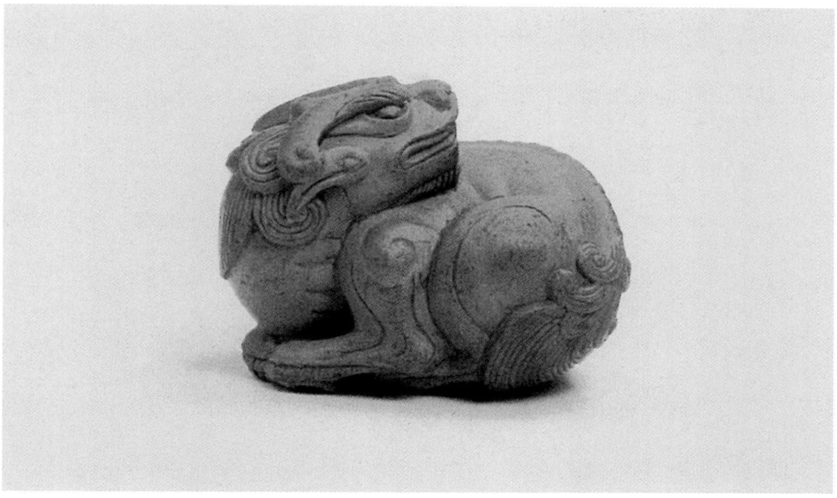

269

Scholar's Plaything

Gourd, of well patinated dark brown colour; of natural 'double-gourd' form, carved overall in low relief with a design of fruiting gourd vines; the neck with a single band of *leiwen* design; the base carved with the mark *Kangxi baowan* ('treasured plaything of the Kangxi Emperor') in regular script, enclosed within a series of squares.
Beijing palace, Kangxi period.
Height: 14.8 cm.

葫蘆刻果文玩·康熙寶玩銘
清康熙(1662-1722), 高14.8厘米

The surface of the gourd has been carved, an early alternative to moulding. The dried rind of the gourd presents a surface to the carver's blade not unlike soft wood, but with the advantage of having no grain to interfere with the direction of the cutting edge. Carving remained popular throughout the Qing florescence of gourd decorating, but always played a secondary role to moulding.

270

'Ten Thousand Years of Whatever You Wish' *Ruyi* Sceptre

Wood, *zitan;* carved in the form of a *ruyi* sceptre simulating a natural *lingzhi* fungus, the upper stalk inscribed *Wannian ruyi* ('Ten thousand years of whatever you wish'); the end of the stalk pierced to receive a cord.
Probably Qing dynasty.
Length: 36.4 cm.

紫檀雕靈芝如意
可能清代, 長36.4厘米

The origin of the *ruyi* sceptre is obscure and various writers have, over the centuries, incorporated different original functions into the later relatively standard form of the *ruyi* based upon a *lingzhi* fungus. However, its designation in English as a sceptre is misleading and covers only a minor part of its development. A sceptre-like object carried in the hand has been known in China for centuries and probably developed its latter-day form as a *ruyi* gradually. According to the *Encyclopaedia Sinica,* the 13th century writer Zhao Xigu believed that it was originally made of iron and was used to point the way and for self defence — a polite sword that could be carried unobtrusively but also, presumably, serve as a weapon. Others have said it derives from an Indian tradition where it originally served as a backscratcher.

Over the centuries the *ruyi* sceptre became associated in China with the *lingzhi* fungus and its Daoist longevity symbolism, thus making it an ideal gift, particularly for birthdays. In recent centuries this is its most common form. A *ruyi* might be carried around as an elegant and auspicious plaything, and would certainly have taken on some of the functional aspects of the duster or flywhisk, as an elegant extension of the body for posing and gesturing. It thereby may have assumed a certain symbolism of authority. Depending upon who was holding it, it would mean different things; with a Confucian scholar, it would imply that he held a certain place in the hierarchy of things and thus be a symbol of authority, while to the Daoist it would represent detachment from mundane affairs. It was, in short, a multifunctional symbol. In Fig. 1 from a woodblock illustration, we see a *ruyi* carried by a man of authority; in Fig. 2 (taken from a portrait of the Qianlong Emperor) it is used as a symbol of worldly detachment to demonstrate that the Emperor is being portrayed in a private environment — out of uniform, so to speak; and in Fig. 3 (taken from an auspicious painting of the Qing dynasty) it is used amusingly, linked into the top of a root as a hook from which to suspend a musical chime.

The *ruyi* was also kept on side tables (sometimes in very fancy glazed, fitted boxes) as an auspicious symbol; in brush pots as a decorative fancy; and on desks where it was sometimes used as a paper weight. It is perhaps the most common form of such playthings for the scholar, found in an amazing variety of materials. It was used widely in China, transcending social class, and certainly by the entire influential minority, from Emperor to monk. As their popularity as birthday gifts developed, so did their application to all levels of society; and as the *ruyi* or *lingzhi* form is one of the most popular elements of decoration and design in later Chinese art at all levels, so the sceptre and its symbolism became meaningful to all.

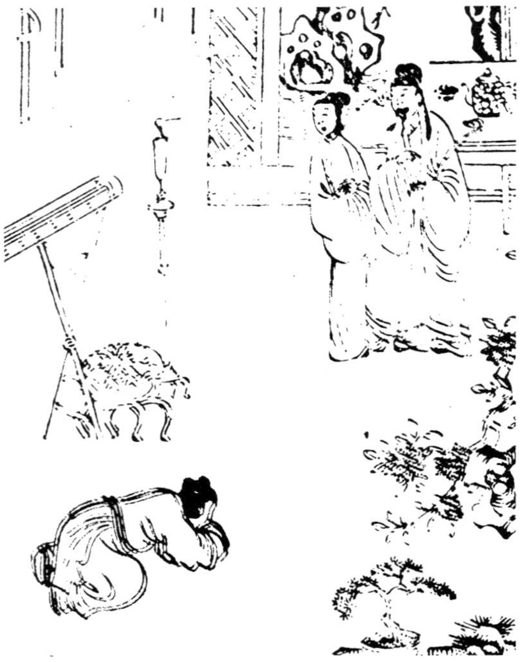

Fig. 1

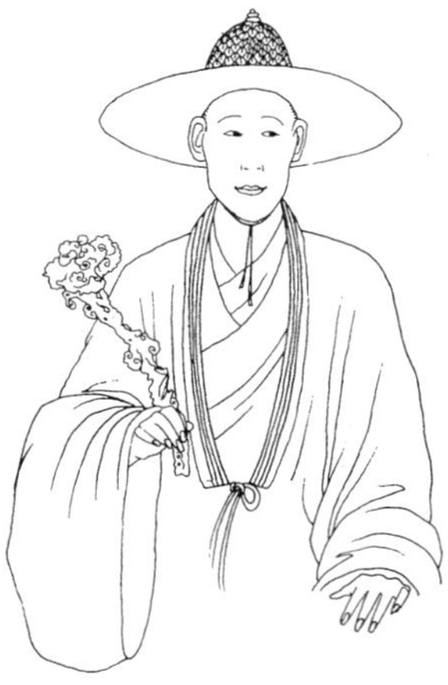

Fig. 2

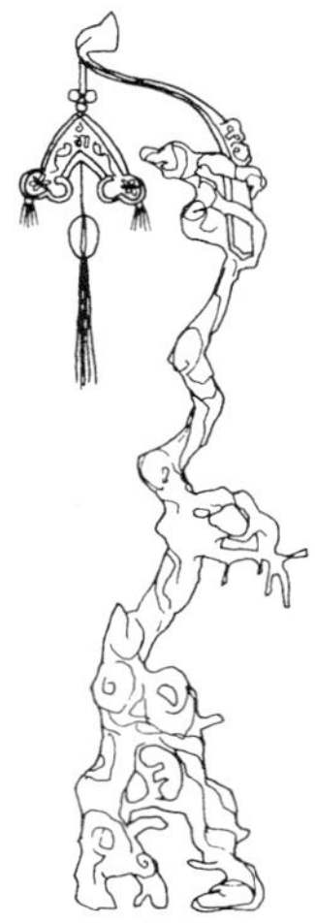

Fig. 3

269

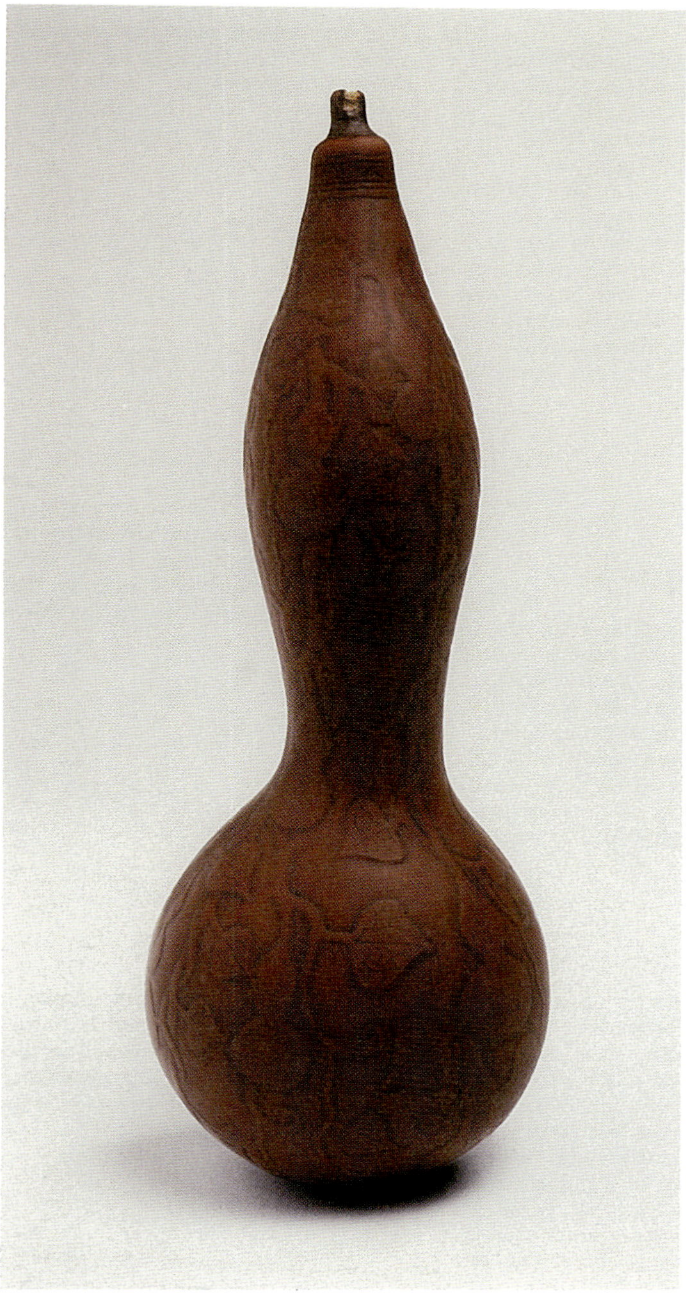

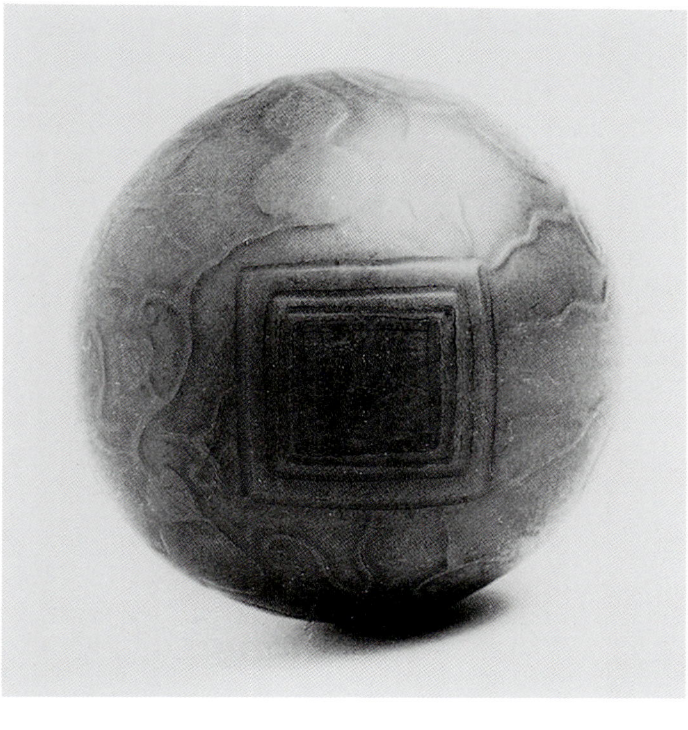

270

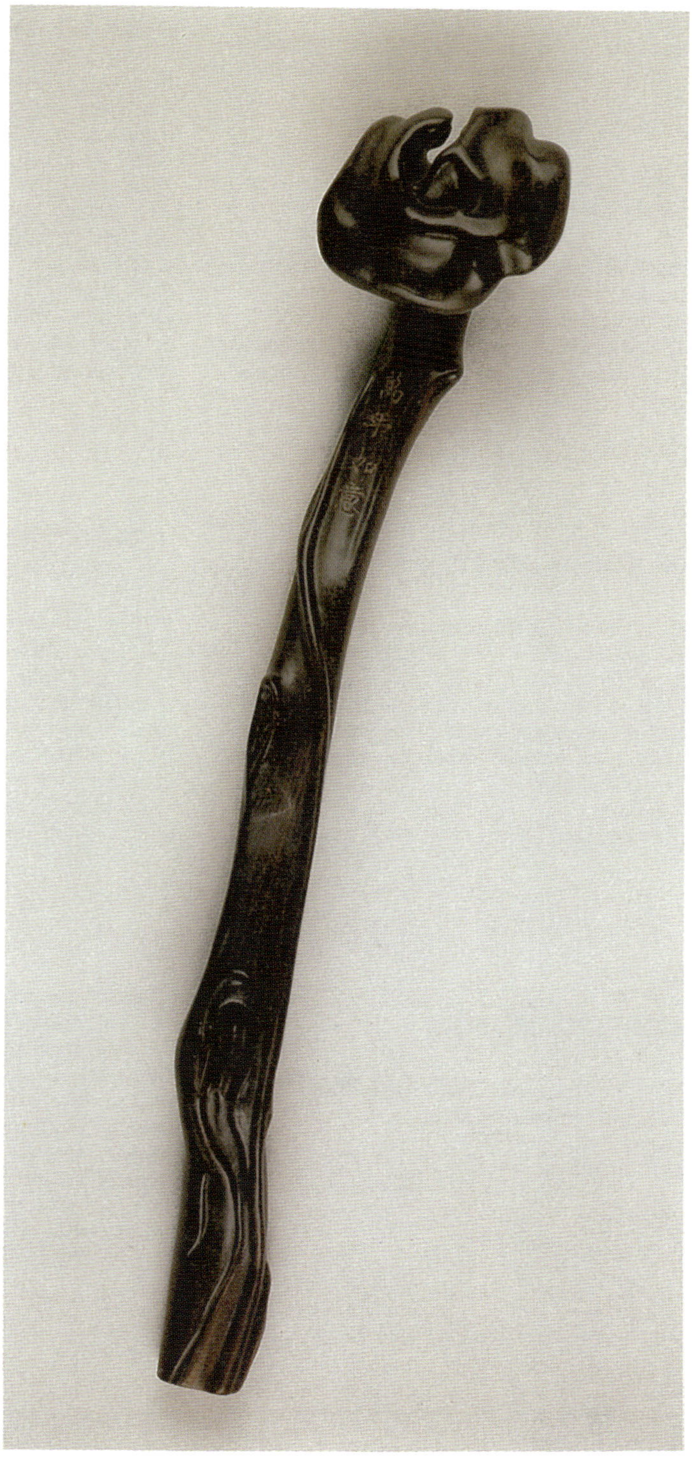

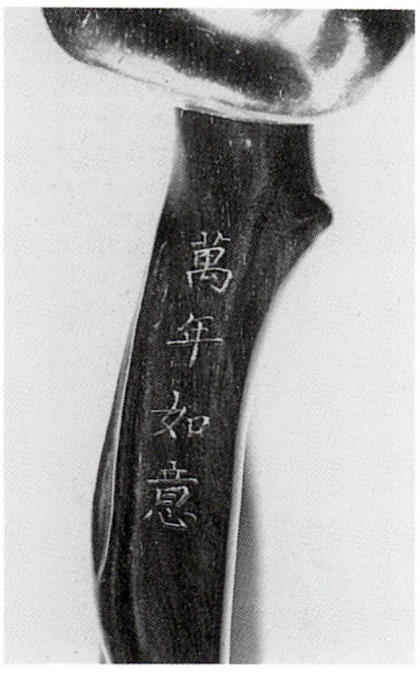

271

Luohan and Rock

Wood; carved to utilize a considerable section of natural burl as a *luohan* seated either in voluminous robes or at a rock 'table', his naked toes peeping out from underneath, his wizened face, under a bald head, set in concentration.
Probably Qing dynasty.
Height: 8.3 cm.

木雕羅漢坐像
可能清代, 高8.3厘米

A range of small figure carvings, Buddhist, Daoist, historical and legendary, served to inspire by representing a particular figure or belief, and (most notably from the Ming dynasty onwards) they represent some of China's major sculpture, albeit often on a small scale. They were used about the studio in the same way as so many other scholars' playthings, but as a sage in real life has a palpable presence, an aura of wisdom and understanding, so power is invested in many of these small figures by the subject-matter they represent.

The *luohan* (Sanskrit *arhat* or *arhan*) are Buddhist figures who have travelled the eight-fold path and reached enlightenment, thus transcending the cycle of birth and rebirth. They are essentially connected with the Hinayana phase of Buddhism, but the Chinese have always been quite happy to adopt any number of religious deities without feeling overly bound to accept their specific dogma as well. The *luohan* is an ascetic, who is free from all fetters, whether of this world or beyond — a completely emancipated individual, and therefore to the Chinese mind a sage. He is also thought to have acquired transcendent powers over nature, matter, time and space. He can reach any place and assume any shape and has knowledge of all things, recollection of all previous existences. In short, he is perfectly wise. It is a metaphor for enlightenment.

The popular numerical groupings of these *luohan* can vary from time to time and from country to country, ranging from as few as four to as many as 5,000. In China, however, the usual number is 18, or more rarely 16.

272

Box and Cover

Wood, stained and patinated to a rich, deep reddish-brown colour; the natural gnarling enhanced by hand to form a box and cover in the form of two lychees growing from a leafy sprig; the irregularly shaped foot rim surrounding a recessed base; the interior covered with black lacquer.
Qing dynasty.
Height: 4.45 cm. Width: 9.8 cm.

木雕荔枝形蓋盒
清代, 高4.45厘米, 寬9.8厘米

This is another of those works of art that are really little more than an excuse for another 'plaything' around the studio. With its well-lined lacquer interior it might have served to hold pigments, paste or other damp material, but it would hardly have been ideally suitable. It might also have served as a box for another work of art, but the evenness of the slope into the irregular interior suggests that it has not been specially fitted to something. It was probably no more than a small container that remained as empty of content as it was full of meaning as a playful symbol of man's relationship with nature.

273

Eccentric Bottle

Gourd; a bottle, grown into an eccentric form by being tied during growth.
Qing dynasty.
Length: 15.2 cm.

葫蘆鵝形壺
清代, 長15.2厘米

Plain undecorated gourds were often used as containers for water or wine while journeying in the countryside, and appear frequently in genre paintings. They were also valued for their pleasant shapes and patination, and for their symbolism; it was not at all unusual to have a few about the studio or home, hanging from a stick, a piece of furniture, or a *ruyi*, set on a stand, or just lying on a table or in a bowl or dish. This example, which from a certain angle resembles a young goose, has been restrained during growth by a series of cords to achieve a delightfully eccentric form. A cord (newly attached) is tied around its waist so that it may be suspended, either from the belt for practical (or symbolic) use or elsewhere.

274

Lotus Leaf

Wood; the natural form with additional carving to form a lotus leaf.
Qing dynasty.
Length: 25.2 cm.

木雕荷葉
清代, 長25.2厘米

This leaf falls into a class of objects which, although used occasionally as brush rests or paper weights, was designed largely as decoration for vases and brush pots. An archaic or archaistic bronze *gu* beaker, an ancient porcelain vessel or perhaps a root vase was frequently filled with flowers, leafy branches, feathers, sprigs of coral or any other pleasing objects. In this context it was a natural development to make the floral aspects of these decorative elements in wood or root. Occasionally one finds complete sets of carved wooden flowers (flowering lotus with a number of large leaves, for instance), sometimes gilded, which have developed from this idea; however these probably represent a reflection of literati taste rather than its epitome, in the same way that other elements of the host of scholarly trappings became absorbed into popular decoration.

271

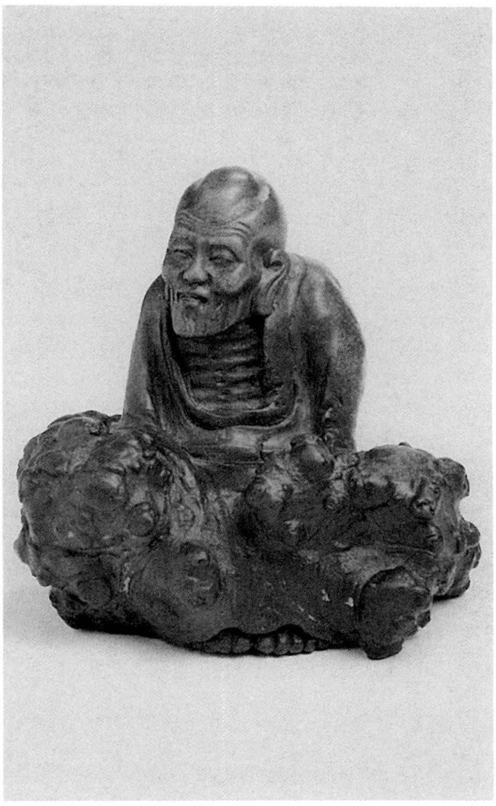

273

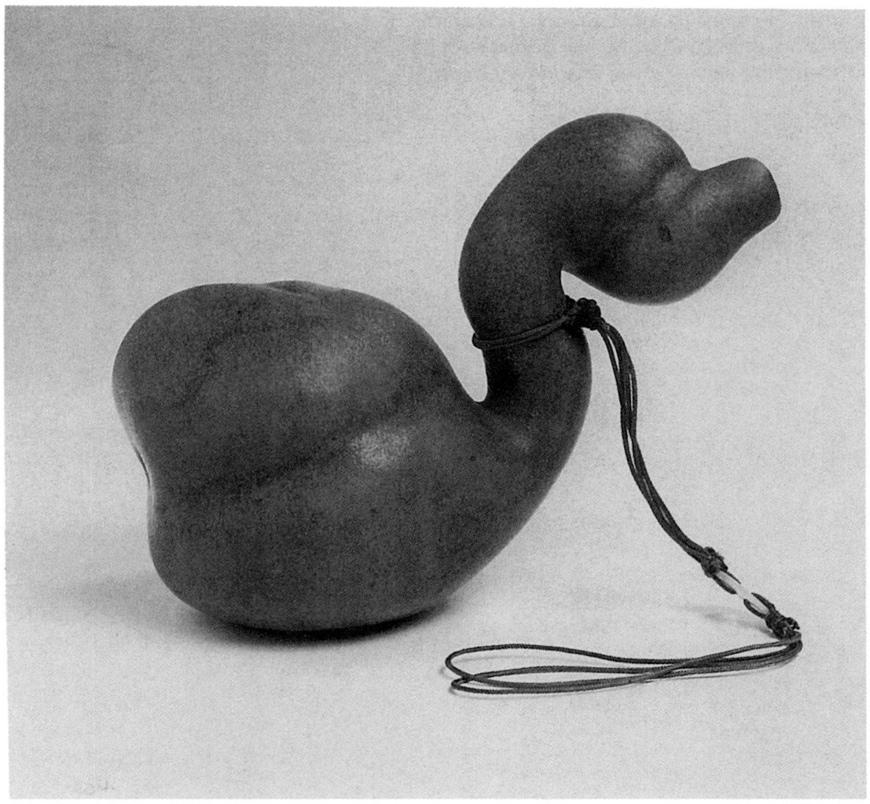

272

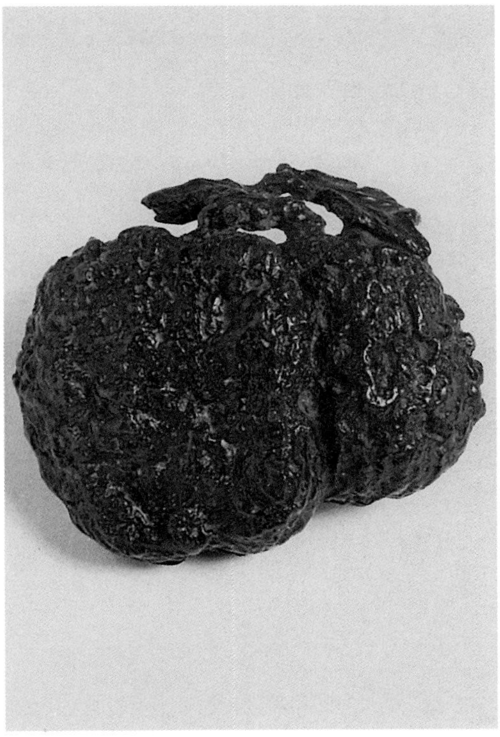

274

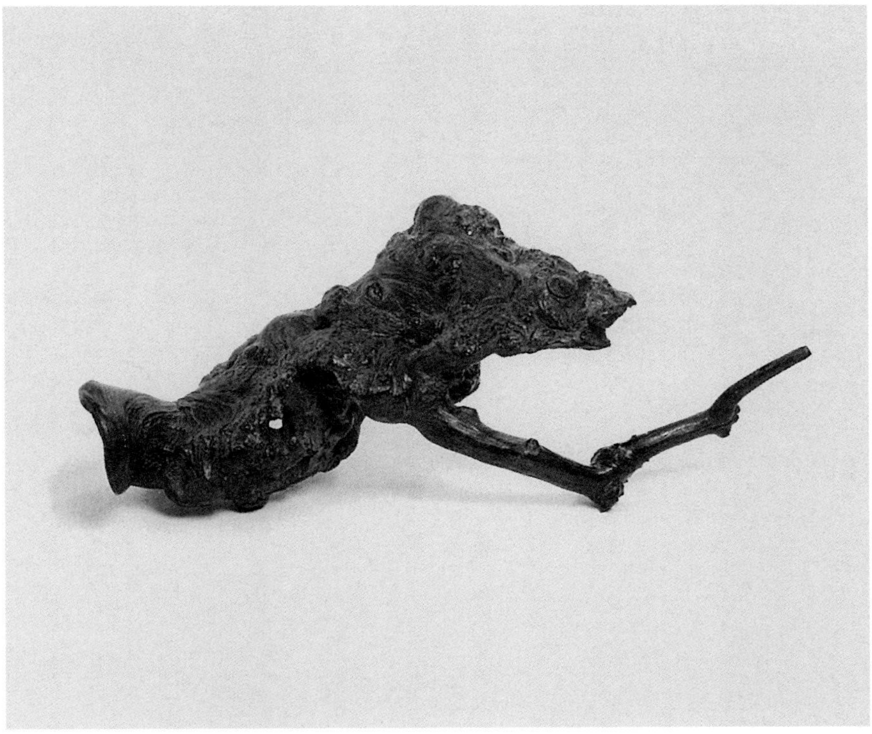

275

Scholar in the Wilderness

Wood, *huangyangmu* (boxwood), of golden brown colour; carved as a miniature landscape, with a scholar, followed by his attendant carrying his *qin* wrapped in a brocade case, as they stroll beneath an overhanging rock amidst trees; the reverse continuing the scene with a stream running beneath the layered strata of the rock.
Probably early Qing dynasty.
Height: 4.5 cm.

黄楊木雕携琴遊山座
可能清初，高4.5厘米

This tiny sculpture acts as a three-dimensional painting, allowing the scholar seated in his studio to project himself into the idealized situation depicted. There are very many extant miniature landscapes, mostly in jade (usually referred to as 'boulder carvings'), but also in bamboo, wood and other materials, from the late Ming and Qing dynasties. They range from pieces of this size to jade examples which are larger than a man. As a rule, however, they are in the region of 10 to 20 cm high. There is no doubt that the idea stems from the microcosmic landscapes enjoyed by the scholar in his table rocks, miniature gardens in bowls, etc. (see no. 267). In this development of the idea, however, more specific stories are told. The abstract form becomes host to an actual scholar roaming the landscape, or to more specific meaning in the form of deities, legendary figures, and illustrations of popular tales. The largest known, in the Beijing Palace Museum[1] is even self-referential — it is an enormous mountain, crawling with men engaged in quarrying what we may assume to be jade.

1. *Selected Handicrafts from the Collection of the Palace Museum,* Wen Wu Press, Beijing, 1974 (Chinese text with separate English translation) — see dust-jacket only, no caption or details given.

276

Linked Rings

Wood, *huangyangmu* (boxwood); carved as two linked rings *(lianhuan).*
Mid- to late Qing dynasty.
Diameter of each ring: 10.4 cm.

黄楊木製連環
清中至晚期，直徑各10.4厘米

Linked rings probably served as handling pieces, but their main function was symbolic. Zhuang Zi in his *Tianxia Pian* ('Essay on the World') stated: "Linked rings are unlockable." The rings appear to be incapable of being separated; however, they cannot last forever, and there must come a time when they are broken, and therefore unlocked. The very existence of the linked rings, therefore, demonstrates that they are separable, because their manufacture sets up the conditions necessary for their eventual separation. They thus form a symbol of the changeability of all things, the impermanence of all phenomena. Playing with them, the scholar is reminded of Zhuang Zi and his philosophy, and of the essential nature of the universe.

277

Dress Hook

Bronze, inlaid with gold and silver; a dress hook, the elongated, curved, tapering form with three fluted facets and terminating in a dragon-head; the flat back set with a stud for attachment to the garment; the front inlaid in gold sheet and thick silver lines with three formalized *chi* dragons, two adorsed on the main, bulging section, and one facing them on the upper, tapered section, its tail towards the hooked end, the dragon's head with forehead and eyes inlaid in gold; the sides with inlaid silver formalized floral scrolls; the back with the stud inlaid with a formalized flourish, and with a single, patterned motif at the broad end.
Huai style, 4th-3rd century BC.
The hook has been broken off at some stage and repaired, at which time a gold circular *yinyang* symbol was set at the front and a silver one at the back, perhaps to cover a holding pin.
Length: 18.3 cm.

嵌金銀螭龍帶鈎
淮式，公元前四至三世紀，長18.3厘米

Apart from their considerable appeal to later connoisseurs as archaic works of art, belt and garment hooks of this kind were also put to use by later scholars. Wen Zhenheng in his *Changwu Ji* ('Notes on Superfluous Objects')[1] is uncharacteristically forgiving of belt hooks, managing a whole section without disparaging remarks: "One finds antique bronze belt hooks inlaid with gold, silver or turquoise, although they may also be made entirely of gold and silver; some are in the form of animals. These are all from the Xia, Shang and Zhou dynasties. Some have ram's-head hooks and others are in the form of a preying mantis catching a cicada. Those with gold are all of the Qin or Han dynasties. One should have several of these about the studio, so that they will be ready when one needs to hang paintings, 'dusters' and feather fans — all most elegant. They may measure from as small as an inch to over one foot in length."[2]

The interior beam and rafter structure of Chinese architecture provided large numbers of possible hanging points. A belt hook would be very easily suspended on a cord from any of these to provide a hook at a convenient height for hanging.

As we have seen with the use of ancient bronze vessels for water pots, brush pots, flower vases, etc.; ancient jades as wrist rests and paper weights; and belt and dress hooks as hanging hooks, the works of antiquity were frequently pressed into service by later scholars. A wide range of other earlier objects may also, from time to time, have gained popularity in a specific function for which they were never originally intended.

The repair on this hook may have been carried out a long time ago. It is likely that a modern repairer would have tried to match invisibly the original design, whereas here no attempt has been made to do so. Indeed, the *yinyang* symbol does not appear on Warring States works of art.

For a pair of dress hooks of similar style, also inlaid with gold and silver dragon motifs and with identical stud design, see *Ancient Chinese Bronzes from the Stoclet and Wessen Collections,* Eskenazi, 1975, p.46, no. 8.

1. *Juan* 7, section 29.
2. These are Chinese feet and inches, which varied from time to time. In the Zhou dynasty a foot was 21 cm; in the Han it was 23.3 cm; in the Song it was 28.4 cm and the Qianlong foot was 31.5 cm. Each foot was then subdivided into 10 inches.

275

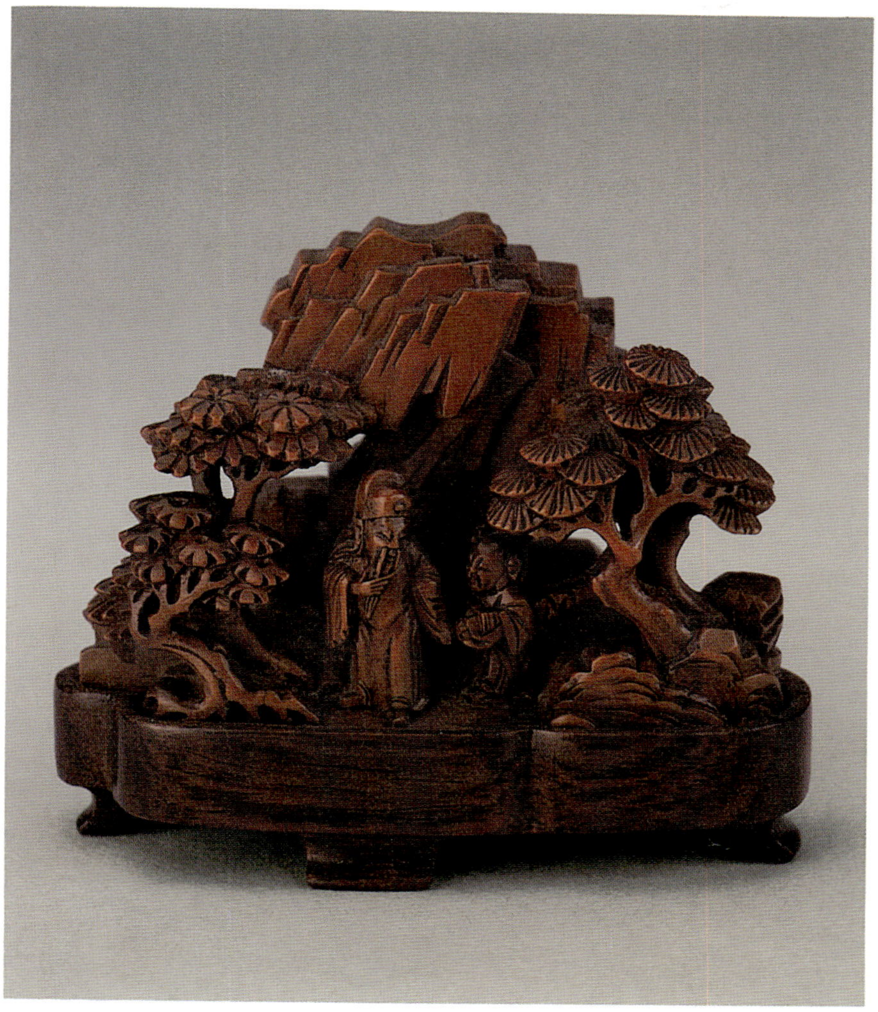

277

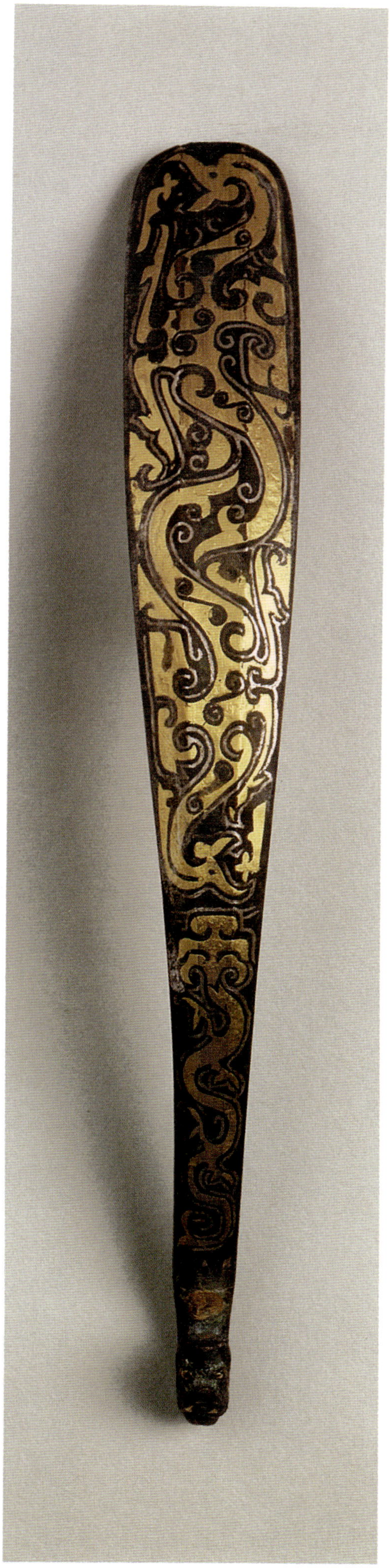

276

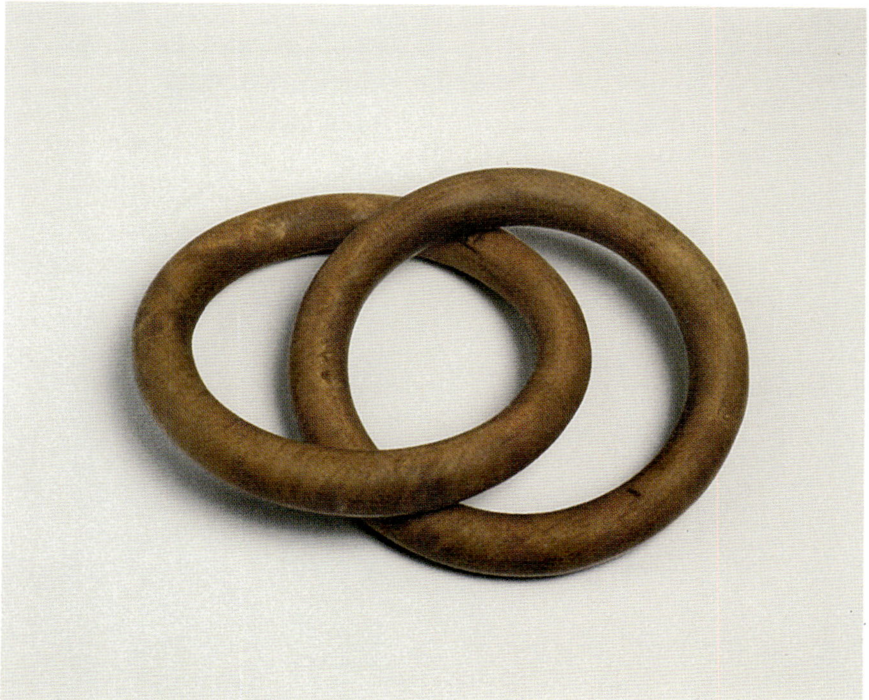

Chronology

PALEOLITHIC PERIOD	*c.* 600,000-*c.* 7000 BC	
NEOLITHIC PERIOD	*c.* 7000-*c.* 1600 BC	
BRONZE AGE*	*c.* 1600-*c.* 1027 BC	SHANG DYNASTY
	c. 1027-771 BC	WESTERN ZHOU DYNASTY
	771-256 BC	EASTERN ZHOU DYNASTY "Spring and Autumn Annals" period 722-481 BC "Warring States" period 403-221 BC
THE FIRST EMPIRES	221-206 BC	QIN DYNASTY
	206 BC-AD 220	HAN DYNASTY Former Han dynasty 206 BC-AD 8 Wang Ming interregnum AD 8-23 Later Han dynasty 25-220
PERIOD OF DISUNION known as THREE KINGDOMS- SIX DYNASTIES	220-589	THREE KINGDOMS 220-80
	220-80	SHU HAN 221-63 / WEI 220-66 / WU** 222-80
		WESTERN JIN DYNASTY

north China		south China
SIXTEEN KINGDOMS 304-439 ("barbarian" invasions)		EASTERN JIN DYNASTY** 317-420
NORTHERN WEI (TOBA) DYNASTY 386-535		LIU SONG DYNASTY** 420-79
WESTERN WEI (TOBA) DYNASTY 535-57	EASTERN WEI (TOBA) DYNASTY 534-50	SOUTHERN QI DYNASTY** 479-502 LIANG DYNASTY** 502-57
NORTHERN ZHOU DYNASTY 557-81	NORTHERN QI DYNASTY 550-77	CHEN DYNASTY** 557-89

SUI DYNASTY		
TANG DYNASTY	618-907	
PERIOD OF DISUNION known as FIVE DYNASTIES- TEN KINGDOMS or FIVE DYNASTIES PERIOD	907-60	FIVE DYNASTIES — TEN KINGDOMS

north China	south China
LATER LIANG 907-22	WU 902-37
LATER TANG 922-36	SOUTHERN TANG 937-75
LATER JIN 936-48	JINGNAN 907-63
LATER HAN 946-50	CHU 927-51
LATER ZHOU 951-60	EARLIER SHU 907-25
	LATER SHU 934-65
	WU-YUE 907-78
	MIN 909-44
	SOUTHERN HAN 907-71
	in Shanxi NORTHERN HAN 951-79

LIAO DYNASTY	947-1125	("barbarian" rulers of northeast China)			
SONG DYNASTY	960-1279	Northern Song Dynasty 960-1126 Southern Song Dynasty 1127-1279			
JIN DYNASTY	1115-1234	("barbarian" rulers of north China)			
YUAN DYNASTY	1279-1368	(Mongol rulers of all China)			
MING DYNASTY	1368-1644	Honwu 1368-1398	Yongle 1403-1424	Xuande 1426-1435	Jingtai 1450-1456
		Tianshun 1457-1464	Chenghua 1465-1487	Hongzhi 1488-1505	Zhengde 1506-1521
		Jiajing 1522-1566	Longqing 1567-1572	Wanli 1573-1619	Tianqi 1621-1627
		Chongzhen 1628-1643			
QING DYNASTY	1644-1912	(Manchu rulers of all China)			
		Shunzhi 1644-1662	Kangxi 1662-1722	Yongzheng 1723-1735	Qianlong 1736-1795
		Jiaqing 1796-1820	Daoguang 1821-1850	Xianfeng 1851-1861	Tongzhi 1862-1874
		Guangxu 1875-1908	Xuantong 1909-1911		
REPUBLIC OF CHINA***	1912-1949	REPUBLIC OF CHINA 1949 (Taiwan)	PEOPLE'S REPUBLIC OF CHINA 1949 (Mainland)		

*The traditional dates for the Shang dynasty are 1766-1122 BC. Revision of the lower date on the evidence of the original of the *Bamboo Annals* brings it to 1027 BC, leaving the higher date to be estimated as 1600 BC 1027 BC is a conservatively low estimate. Some scholars prefer other modern calculations, which yield a final date for Shang toward the middle of the eleventh century BC. Thus far, radiological dating has not allowed these dates to be more accurately fixed.

**The Six Dynasties, so called because each had its capital at Nanjing.

***In 1916 Yuan Shikai tried but failed to establish a new dynasty, taking Hongxian as his reign title. The above chronological chart is taken from *Art of Dynastic China* by William Watson, to which have been added the reign titles of Ming and Qing Emperors.

Cyclical Dating System

Since the Han dynasty a system of dating has been commonly used which identifies the years within a sixty-year cycle. It uses a series of ten characters as 'stems' which repeat six times, and twelve as 'branches' which repeat five times, giving sixty different combinations. Every sixty years the whole cycle begins again. These are frequently used in conjunction with reign titles, allowing a precise date to be fixed. However, even where no further indication of general period is given, they are frequently very useful as it is often possible to establish a likely period for a piece which will help to identify a particular cycle and therefore the date within it.

The cycle is set out below, with the years added for the period from 1744 to 1983. To arrive at earlier dates one simply subtracts in multiples of sixty (i.e. 1744 is also 1684, 1624, 1564, etc.)

甲申	1744	1804	1864	1924
乙酉	1745	1805	1865	1925
丙戌	1746	1806	1866	1926
丁亥	1747	1807	1867	1927
戊子	1748	1808	1868	1928
己丑	1749	1809	1869	1929
庚寅	1750	1810	1870	1930
辛卯	1751	1811	1871	1931
壬辰	1752	1812	1872	1932
癸巳	1753	1813	1873	1933
甲午	1754	1814	1874	1934
乙未	1755	1815	1875	1935
丙申	1756	1816	1876	1936
丁酉	1757	1817	1877	1937
戊戌	1758	1818	1878	1938
己亥	1759	1819	1879	1939
庚子	1760	1820	1880	1940
辛丑	1761	1821	1881	1941
壬寅	1762	1822	1882	1942
癸卯	1763	1823	1883	1943
甲子	1764	1824	1884	1944
乙丑	1765	1825	1885	1945
丙寅	1766	1826	1886	1946
丁卯	1767	1827	1887	1947
戊辰	1768	1828	1888	1948
己巳	1769	1829	1889	1949
庚午	1770	1830	1890	1950
辛未	1771	1831	1891	1951
壬申	1772	1832	1892	1952
癸酉	1773	1833	1893	1953
甲戌	1774	1834	1894	1954
乙亥	1775	1835	1895	1955
丙子	1776	1836	1896	1956
丁丑	1777	1837	1897	1957
戊寅	1778	1838	1898	1958
己卯	1779	1839	1899	1959
庚辰	1780	1840	1900	1960
辛巳	1781	1841	1901	1961
壬午	1782	1842	1902	1962
癸未	1783	1843	1903	1963
甲辰	1784	1844	1904	1964
乙巳	1785	1845	1905	1965
丙午	1786	1846	1906	1966
丁未	1787	1847	1907	1967
戊申	1788	1848	1908	1968
己酉	1789	1849	1909	1969
庚戌	1790	1850	1910	1970
辛亥	1791	1851	1911	1971
壬子	1792	1852	1912	1972
癸丑	1793	1853	1913	1973
甲寅	1794	1854	1914	1974
乙卯	1795	1855	1915	1975
丙辰	1796	1856	1916	1976
丁巳	1797	1857	1917	1977
戊午	1798	1858	1918	1978
己未	1799	1859	1919	1979
庚申	1800	1860	1920	1980
辛酉	1801	1861	1921	1981
壬戌	1802	1862	1922	1982
癸亥	1803	1863	1923	1983

Bibliography

Anthology of Chinese Art: Min Chiu Society Silver Jubilee Exhibition, Hong Kong Museum of Art, Hong Kong, 1985.
(The) Arts of the Ch'ing Dynasty in *Transactions of the Oriental Ceramic Society* , Vol. 35, London, 1963-1964.
(The) Arts of the Ming Dynasty in *Transactions of the Oriental Ceramic Society* , Vol. 30, London, 1955-1957.
(The) Arts of the Sung Dynasty in *Transactions of the Oriental Ceramic Society,* Vol. 32, London, 1960.

Bartholomew, Terese Tse, *I-Hsing Ware,* China Institute in America, New York, 1977.
Beurdeley, Michel, *The Chinese Collector Through the Centuries* (translated by Diana Imber), Office du Livre, S.A., Fribourg, Switzerland, 1966.
Beurdeley, Michel, *Chinese Furniture* (translated by Katherine Watson), Office du Livre, S.A., Kodansha International, Tokyo and New York, 1979.
Beurdeley, Michel and Marie Therese Lambert-Brouillet, *L'Eunuque aux Trois Joyaux,* Office du Livre, S.A., Fribourg, Switzerland, 1984.
Bickford, Maggie *et al., Bones of Jade, Soul of Ice: The Flowering Plum in Chinese Art,* Yale University Art Gallery, 1985.
Bimozhiyan Tulu (Brush, Ink, Paper and Inkstone Pictorial), Shanghai Museum, 1981.
Birch, Cyril (ed.), *Anthology of Chinese Literature,* Grove Press Inc., New York, 1965.
Bunjinga Suihen (A Miscellany of Literati Painting), 10 vols, Tokyo, 1975-1979.
Bush, Susan, *The Chinese Literati on Painting: Su Shi (1037-1101) to Tung Ch'i-chang (1555-1636),* Harvard University Press, 1971.
Bush, Susan and Christian Murck (eds.), *Theories of the Arts in China,* Princeton University Press, 1983.
Bushell, Stephen W., *Chinese Art,* London, 1924.

Cahill, James, *The Art of Southern Sung China,* Asia House Gallery, 1961.
Cahill, James, *Chinese Painting,* Editions d'Art Albert Skira, Geneva, 1960.
Cahill, James, *The Compelling Image,* Harvard University Press, London, 1982.
Cahill, James, *The Distant Mountains,* John Weatherhill Inc., New York, 1982.
Cahill, James, *Hills Beyond a River,* John Weatherhill Inc., New York, 1976.
Cahill, James, *Parting at the Shore,* John Weatherhill Inc., New York, 1978.
Cahill, James, *The Restless Landscape,* University Art Museum, Berkeley, 1971.
Cahill, James (ed.), *Shadows of Mt. Huang,* University Art Museum, Berkeley, 1981.
Capra, Fritjof, *The Tao of Physics,* Shambhala Publications Inc., distributed by Random House Inc., Boulder, Colorado, 1975.
Carter, Thomas Francis, *The Invention of Printing in China and its Spread Westward* (revised by L. Carrington Goodrich), The Ronald Press, New York, 1955.
Caswell, James O., *The Single Brushstroke: 600 Years of Chinese Painting from the Ching Yuan Chai Collection,* Vancouver Art Gallery, 1985.
Chapman, Jan, *The Chester Beatty Collection of Chinese Carved Rhinoceros Horn Cups,* in *Arts of Asia,* May-June 1982.
Chiang Yee, *Chinese Calligraphy: An Introduction to its Aesthetic and Technique,* Methuen, London, 1938.
Chinese Blue and White Porcelain, OCS Hong Kong exhibition catalogue, 1975.
Chinese Decorative Arts, Bluett and Sons Ltd., London, 1974.
Chinese Exhibition at Burlington House in 1935-36, Faber and Faber, London, 1936.
Chinese Jades: Archaic and Modern from The Minneapolis Institute of Art, Lund Humphries Publishers Ltd., London, 1977.
Chinese Jades Throughout the Ages, Arts Council of Great Britain and the Oriental Ceramic Society, London, 1975.
Chinese Jades Throughout the Ages, a definitive catalogue in *Transactions of the Oriental Ceramic Society,* Vol. 41, 1976.
Ching, Julia, *To Acquire Wisdom: The Way of Wang Yang-ming,* Columbia University Press, New York and London, 1976.
Contag, Victoria, *Chinese Masters of the Seventeenth Century,* Lund Humphries Publishers Ltd., London, 1969.
Contag, Victoria and Wang Chi-ch'ien, *Seals of Chinese Painters and Collectors of the Ming and Ch'ing Periods,* Hong Kong, 1966.
Couling, Samuel, *Encyclopaedia Sinica,* Oxford University Press, Hong Kong, 1984.

d'Argencé, R-Y.L. (ed.), *Treasures from the Shanghai Museum: 6,000 Years of Chinese Art,* Shanghai Museum and the Asian Art Museum of San Francisco, 1983.
David Foundation of Chinese Art, London, 1973.
David, Sir Percival, *Chinese Connoisseurship: The Ko Ku Yao Lun — The Essential Criteria of Antiquities,* Praeger Publishers, Inc., New York, 1971.

Ecke, Gustav, *Chinese Painting in Hawaii*, Honolulu, 1965.
Ecke, Gustav and Tseng Yu-ho, *Chinese Calligraphy*, Philadelphia Museum of Art, 1971.
Ecke, Gustav and Tseng Yu-ho, *Poetry on the Wind*, Honolulu Academy of Arts, 1981.
Edgren, Soren (ed.), *Chinese Rare Books in American Collections*, China Institute in America, New York, 1984.
Edmunds, Will H., *Pointers and Clues to The Subjects of Chinese and Japanese Art*, Sampson Low, Marston and Co. Ltd., London, 1934.
Edwards, Richard, *The Art of Wen Cheng-ming*, Ann Arbour, 1976.
Edwards, Richard, *The Field of Stones: A Study of the Art of Shen Chou*, Washington, D.C., 1962.
Ellsworth, Robert Hatfeld, *Chinese Furniture: Hardwood Examples of the Ming and Early Ch'ing Dynasties*, Random House Inc., New York, 1970.
Ellsworth, Robert Hatfield and Howard Link, *Chinese Hardwood Furniture in Hawaiian Collections*, Honolulu Academy of Arts, 1982.
Eskenazi: Twenty-five Years catalogue, Eskenazi Ltd., London, 1985.

Fang Zonggui, *Shoushanshi zhi* (Records of Shoushan Stone), Fujian, 1982.
Fong Wen (ed.), *The Great Bronze Age of China*, Thames and Hudson, London, 1980.
Fong Wen *et al.*, *Images of the Mind*, Princeton University Press, 1984.
Franke, Herbert (ed.), *Song Biographies*, Franz Sterner Verlag GMBH, Wiesbaden, 1976.
Fu, Marilyn, *Studies in Connoisseurship*, Princeton University Press, 1973.
Fu Shen *et al.*, *Traces of the Brush*, Yale University Art Gallery, 1977.
Fung Yu-lan, *A History of Chinese Philosophy*, translated by Derk Bodde, Vol. 1, Henri Vetch, Beijing and George Allen and Unwin Ltd., London, 1937; Vol. 2, E.J. Brill, Leiden, 1953.

Garner, Sir Harry M., *Chinese and Japanese Cloisonné Enamels*, Faber and Faber, London, 1962.
Garner, Sir Harry M., *Chinese Lacquer*, Faber and Faber, 1979.
Giles, Herbert A., *A Chinese Biographical Dictionary*, Literature House, Taipei, 1962.
Goodrich, L. Carrington and Chaoying Fang (eds.), *Dictionary of Ming Biography*, Columbia, 1976.
Gure, D., 'Selected Examples from the Jade Exhibition at Stockholm, 1963: A Comparative Study', *B.M.F.E.A.*, Vol. 36, Stockhom, 1964.

Hansford, S. Howard, *Chinese Carved Jades*, Faber and Faber, London, 1968.
Hansford, S. Howard, *Chinese Jade Carving*, Lund Humphries Publishers Ltd., London, 1950.
Hansford, S. Howard, *A Glossary of Chinese Art and Archaeology*, The China Society, London, 1954.
Hay, John, *Kernels of Energy, Bones of Earth: The Rock in Chinese Art*, China Institute in America, 1985.
Herrigel, Eugen, *Zen in the Art of Archery*, translated by R.F.C. Hull, Arkana, London, 1953.
Ho Wai-kam *et al.*, *Eight Dynasties of Chinese Painting*, Cleveland, 1980.
Hummel, Arthur W. (ed.), *Eminent Chinese of the Ch'ing Period*, Government Printing Office, Washington, 1943-1944.
Hyland, Alice R.M., *The Literati Vision: Sixteenth Century Wu School Painting and Calligraphy*, Memphis Brooks Museum of Art, 1984.

(The) I Ching or Book of Changes, translation by Richard Wilhelm, Routledge and Kegan Paul, London, 1951.
Illustrated Catalogue of Ancient Jade Artefacts in the National Palace Museum, Taipei, 1982.
Ip Yee, *Chinese Jade Carving*, Hong Kong Museum of Art, 1983.
Ip Yee, *Notes on a Collection of Chinese Rhinoceros Horn Carvings*, in *International Asian Antiques Fair Catalogue*, Andamans East International Ltd., Hong Kong, 1982.
Ip Yee and Laurence C.S. Tam, *Chinese Bamboo Carving*, Hong Kong Museum of Art, Vol. 1, 1978; Vol. 2, 1982.

Jenyns, Soame, *Chinese Art: The Minor Arts II*, Vol. IV, Oldbourne Press, London, 1965.
Jenyns, Soame, *Later Chinese Porcelain*, Faber and Faber, 1971.
Jenyns, Soame and William Watson, *Chinese Art: The Minor Arts*, Vol. II, Oldbourne Press, London, 1963.
Jingdezhen Wares, OCS Hong Kong exhibition catalogue, University of Hong Kong, 1984.

Kao Mayching (ed.), *Paintings by Yangzhou Artists of the Qing Dynasty from the Palace Museum*, Chinese University of Hong Kong, Hong Kong, 1985.
Kerr, Rose, *The Evolution of Bronze Style in the Jin, Yuan and Early Ming Dynasty*, in *Oriental Art*, XXVIII, No.2, Summer 1982.
Keswick, Maggie, *The Chinese Garden*, Academy Editions, London, 1978.
Komeigen (Famous Old Inkstones), 5 vols, Tokyo, 1976.

Lady David, *Illustrated Catalogue of Ch'ing Enamelled Ware in the Percival David Foundation of Chinese Art*, London, 1973.
Lai, T.C., *Chinese Couplets*, University Book Store, Hong Kong, 1969.
Lai, T.C., *A Scholar in Imperial China*, Kelly and Walsh, Hong Kong, 1970.
Lai, T.C., *Treasures of a Chinese Studio (Ink, Brush, Inkstone, Paper)*, Swindon Book Company, Hong Kong, 1976.
Ledderose, Lothar *et al.*, *Palastmuseum Peking: Schatze aus der Verbotenen Stadt*, Berlin, 1985.

Ledderose, Lothar, *Mi Fu and the Classical Tradition of Chinese Calligraphy*, Princeton University Press, Princeton, 1979.
Lee, Sherman and Wai-kam Ho, *Chinese Art under the Mongols: The Yuan Dynasty (1279-1368)*, Cleveland, 1968.
Lee Yu-kuan, *Oriental Lacquer Art*, John Weatherhill Inc., New York, 1972.
Levenson, Joseph R., *Confucian China and Its Modern Fate*, Routledge and Kegan Paul, London, 1965.
Li Chu-tsing, *A Thousand Peaks and Myriad Ravines*, 2 vols, Ascona, 1974.
Lin Yutang, *The Gay Genius: The Life and Times of Su Tungpo*, The John Day Company, New York, 1974.
Lin Yutang, *The Importance of Understanding*, William Heinemann Ltd., London, 1962.
Lippe, Aschwin, 'Two Archaistic Bronzes of the Ming Dynasty', *Archives of the Chinese Art Society of America*, XI, 1957.
Lion-Goldsmidt, Daisy and Jean-Claude Moreau-Gobard, *Chinese Art*, Studio Books, London, 1960.
Loehr, Max, *Ancient Chinese Jades from the Greville L. Winthrop Collection in the Fogg Art Museum*, Harvard University, 1975.
Loo, C.T., *Chinese Archaic Jade*, New York, 1950.
Lui Wingfong, *Chinese Traditional Rubbing Techniques* (translated by Gerard Tsang), Hong Kong Museum of History, 1986.

Masterpieces of Chinese Inkstones in the National Palace Museum, Taipei, 1974.
Masterpieces of Chinese Miniature Crafts in the National Palace Museum, Taipei, 1971.
Masterpieces of Chinese Seals in the National Palace Museum, Taipei, 1974.
Masterpieces of Chinese Writing Materials in the National Palace Museum, Taipei, 1971.
Medley, Margaret, *The Chinese Potter: A Practical History of Chinese Ceramics*, Phaidon Press Ltd., Oxford, 1976.
Medley, Margaret, *A Handbook of Chinese Art*, G. Bell and Sons Ltd., London, 1964.
Ming Qing Zhuanke Liupai Yinpu (Ming and Qing Seal Carvers and Schools), Shanghai, 1980.
(The) Minor Arts of China, exhibition catalogue, Spink & Son Ltd., London, 1983.
Miyagawa, Torao, *A History of the Art of China: Chinese Painting*, John Weatherhill Inc., New York, 1983.
Morgan, Brian, *Dr. Newton's Zoo*, Bluett and Sons Ltd., London, 1981.
Moss, Hugh, *By Imperial Command: An Introduction to Ch'ing Imperial Painted Enamels*, Hibiya Ltd., Hong Kong, 1976.
Moss, Hugh, *The Experience of Art: Twentieth Century Chinese Paintings from the Shuisongshi Shanfang Collection*, Umbrella Ltd., Hong Kong, 1983.
Moss, Hugh, *The Four Seasons Handscroll,* supplement to *The Experience of Art*, Umbrella Ltd., Hong Kong, 1985.
Moss, Paul, *Documentary Chinese Works of Art in Scholars' Taste*, Sydney L. Moss Ltd., London, 1983.
Moss, Paul, *Emperor, Scholar, Artisan, Monk: The Creative Personality in Chinese Works of Art*, Sydney L. Moss Ltd., London, 1984.
Moss, Paul, *The Literati Mode: Chinese Scholar Paintings, Calligraphy and Desk Objects*, Sydney L. Moss Ltd., London, 1986.

Na Chih-liang, *Yu-Ch'i Tzu-Dien* (Dictionary of Chinese Jade), Taipei, 1982.
Na Chih-liang, *Selection of Masterworks in the Collection of the National Palace Museum*, Taipei, 1972.
Needham, Joseph, *Science and Civilization in China*, 5 vols, Cambridge University Press, 1954-1983.

Okada, Y. and S. Aoyama, *Bunku Mandara*, Mainichi Shimbun, Tokyo, 1980.

Peng Zeyi, *Zhongguo Jindai Shougongyeshi Ziliao* (Research Information on the History of Chinese Handicrafts), Beijing, 1984.
Piccus, Robert P. (ed.), *Wood From the Scholar's Table*, Gulliver Books, Altfield Gallery, Hong Kong, 1984.
Poole, Cecil, *Mysticism — the Ultimate Experience*, Supreme Grand Lodge of Amorc, 1982.
Proceedings of the International Symposium on Chinese Paintings, Taipei, 1972.

Rawson, Philip and Laszlo Legeza, *Tao: The Chinese Philosophy of Time and Change*, Thames and Hudson, London, 1973.
Riddell, Sheila, *Dated Chinese Antiquities: 600-1650*, Faber and Faber, 1979.

Salmony, Alfred, *Archaic Chinese Jades From the Edward and Louise B. Sonnenschein Collection*, The Art Institute of Chicago, 1952.
Salmony, Alfred, *Carved Jade of Ancient China*, Han-Shan Tang, London, 1982.
Salmony, Alfred, *Chinese Jade through the Wei Dynasty*, The Ronald Press, New York, 1963.
Schafer, Edward H., *Tu Wan's Stone Catalogue of Cloudy Forest*, University of California Press, 1961.
Selected Handicrafts, Gugong Museum, Beijing, Wenwu Press, 1974.
Shodo Zensu, Vol. 4, Tokyo, 1960.
Sickman, Laurence (ed.), *Chinese Calligraphy and Painting in the Collection of John M. Crawford, Jr.*, New York, 1962.
Siren, Osvald, *Chinese Painting: Leading Masters and Principles*, 7 vols, Hacker Art Books, New York, 1973.
Siren, Osvald, *A History of Later Chinese Painting*, Hacker Art Books, New York, 1978.

Soper, Alexander Coburn (translated and annotated by), *Kuo Jo-Hsu's Experiences in Painting*, American Council of Learned Societies, Washington, D.C., 1951.
Speiser, Werner *et al.*, *Chinese Art*, Vol. 3, Oldbourne Press, London, 1964.
Spence, Jonathan D., *Emperor of China: Self-Portrait of K'ang-hsi*, Alfred A. Knopf, New York, 1974.
Stevens, Bob, *The Collector's Book of Snuff Bottles*, John Weatherhill Inc., New York, 1976.
Style Transformed: A Special Exhibition of Works by Five Late Ming Artists, National Palace Museum, Taiwan, 1977.
Sullivan, Michael, *The Meeting of Eastern and Western Art*, Thames and Hudson, London, 1973.
Sullivan, Michael, *Symbols of Eternity: The Art of Landscape Painting in China*, Clarendon Press, Oxford, 1979.
Suzuki, Daisetz T., *Zen and Japanese Culture*, Princeton University Press, 1973.
Suzuki, Kei, *Comprehensive Illustrated Catalog of Chinese Paintings*, 5 vols, Tokyo, 1983.
Swann, Peter, *Chinese Painting*, Universe Books, New York, 1967.

Togari, Soshin-an, *To-boku Wa-boku Zusetsu* (The Book of Chinese and Japanese Inksticks), Tokyo, 1964.
Tregear, Mary, *Song Ceramics*, Thames and Hudson, 1982.
Treasures from the Metropolitan Museum of Art, China Institute In America, 1979.
Tsang, Gerard and Hugh Moss, *Chinese Decorated Gourds*, in *International Asian Antiques Fair Catalogue*, Andamans East International Ltd., Hong Kong, 1983.
Tsang, Gerard and Hugh Moss, *Chinese Metalwork of the Hu Wenming Group*, in *International Asian Antiques Fair Catalogue*, Andamans East International Ltd., Hong Kong, 1984.
Tsang, Gerard and Hugh Moss, *Snuff Bottles of the Ch'ing Dynasty*, Hong Kong Museum of Art, 1978.
Twitchett, Denis, *The Birth of the Chinese Meritocracy: Bureaucrats and Examinations in T'ang China*, Bendles Ltd., Torquay, 1974.

Van Gulik, R.H., *Chinese Pictorial Art as viewed by the Connoisseur*, Rome, 1958.
Van Gulik, R.H., *The Lore of the Chinese Lute*, Tokyo, 1969.
Van Gulik, R.H., *Mi Fu on Ink-stones*, Henri Vetch, Beijing, 1938.

Waley, Arthur, *The Book of Songs*, George Allen and Unwin, London, 1937.
Waley, Arthur, *The Way and Its Power: A Study of the Tao Te Ching and its Place in Chinese Thought*, Houghton Mifflin, Boston and New York, 1935.
Waley, Arthur, *Three Ways of Thought in Ancient China*, George Allen and Unwin, London, 1939.
Wang Shixiang, *Mingshi Jiaju Zhenshang* (Appreciation of Ming Furniture), Hong Kong, 1985.
Wang Shixiang and Wan-go Weng, *Bamboo Carvings of China*, China Institute in America, 1983.
Watson, William, *Art of Dynastic China*, Thames and Hudson, London 1981.
Watson, William, *The Genius of China*, Royal Academy, London, 1973.
Watson, William, *On Some Categories of Archaism in Chinese Bronzes*, in *Arts Orientalis*, 1973.
Watt, James C.Y., *Chinese Jades from Han to Ch'ing*, The Asia Society, New York, 1980.
Watt, James C.Y., *The Qin and the Chinese Literati*, in *Orientations Magazine*, November 1981.
Watts, Alan, *The Meaning of Happiness: The Quest for Freedom of the Spirit in Modern Psychology and the Wisdom of the East*, Hutchinson Publishing Group, London, 1978.
Watts, Alan, *The Supreme Identity: An Essay on Oriental Metaphysic and the Christian Religion*, Random House, New York, 1972.
Wen Zhenheng, *Changwu Ji* (Notes on Superfluous Objects), a late Ming work contained in *Meishu Congshu*, Vol. 3, Section 9, Taiwan, 1975.
Weng Wan-go, *Chinese Painting and Calligraphy: A Pictorial Survey*, New York, 1978.
Weng Wan-go, *Gardens in Chinese Art*, New York, 1968.
Weng Wan-go and Yang Boda, *The Palace Museum Peking: Treasures from the Forbidden City*, Orbis Publishing, London, 1982.
Werner, E.T.C., *A Dictionary of Chinese Mythology*, The Julian Press, New York, 1961.
Whitfield, Roderick, *In Pursuit of Antiquity*, The Art Museum, Princeton, 1969.
Williams, C.A.S., *Outlines of Chinese Symbolism and Art Motives*, Kelly and Walsh, Shanghai, 1941.
Wills, G., *Jade of the East*, John Weatherhill Inc., New York, 1972.
Wilson, Marc and Kwan S. Wong, *Friends of Wen Cheng-ming: A View from the Crawford Collection*, New York, 1974.

Yangxian Shaqi Jingpin Tupu (Pictorial of Selected Yixing Pottery), Taipei, 1985.
Yixing Pottery, Hong Kong Museum of Art, Hong Kong, 1981.
Zhao Ruzhen, *Guwan zhinan* (Handbook of Chinese Antiquity) and supplement, Chung Mei Bookstore, Hong Kong, 2nd edition, 1970.
Zhongguo Lidai Shuhua Zhuanke Jia Zihao Suoyin (Index of Assumed Names of Chinese Artists of Past Generations), 2 vols, Chinese Calligraphy and Painting Institute, Hong Kong, 1968.
Zhongguo Meishujia Renming Cidian (A Dictionary of Famous Chinese Artists), Shanghai Peoples' Press, 1980.
Zhongguo Meishujia Zhenglue, Taipei, 1968.
Zhongguo Niyin Yuanliu (Chinese Seal Carvers), Hong Kong, 1974.
Zhongguo Renming Daicidian (Encyclopaedia of Chinese Biographies), Commercial Press Ltd., Taiwan, 2nd edition, 1974.
Zhongguo Yishujia Zhenglue (Collected Summary of Chinese Artists) compiled by Li Juanya, published by Li Kehuan, Taiwan (undated).

Index to Exhibits

All numbers refer to exhibit numbers. Indexed are forms, materials, reign and other imperial marks, selected primary subject matter and the personal, studio, hall, and retreat names of all those people directly associated with the works of art as artist, inscriber or past collector. Other aspects are extensively cross-referenced in the captions and exhibits are broadly grouped into four categories: nos. 1-82 where questions of aesthetics, art and artists are the primary concern of the captions; nos. 83-119 where the primary concern is with patronage; nos. 120-199 where questions of collecting and connoisseurship are dealth with; and nos. 200-277 which deal primarily with function.